A CATALOGUE OF FRENCH PORCELAIN IN THE BRITISH MUSEUM

AILEEN DAWSON

Published for The Trustees of
The British Museum by
BRITISH MUSEUM PRESS

First published in 1994 by British Museum Press
A division of The British Museum Company Ltd
46 Bloomsbury Street, London WC1B 3QQ

Revised paperback edition first published 2000

A catalogue record for this book is available from the British Library

ISBN 0-7141-2801-5

Designed by John Hawkins
Maps and line drawings by Jim Farrant
Typeset by BAS Printers Limited, Over Wallop, Hampshire
Printed in Slovenia by Korotan

Contents

Hard-Paste Factories in Paris

Preface

The history of the British Museum's collection of French porcelain goes back more than one hundred years. As with so many areas of the collections A.W. Franks laid its foundations over a long period. He finally published his collection of European porcelain in 1896, when he lent it to the Bethnal Green Branch Museum, and in the following year it came to the Museum on his death. His intention had been to chronicle the European history of the material (he had also collected and catalogued Oriental porcelains, another of his gifts to the Museum). To this end, he concentrated on signed and dated examples. Indeed, the objective of the Museum's collection has never changed, in spite of its growth through purchases, gifts and bequests. Its publication is long overdue. At various times the collection has been under the care of such ceramic historians as R.L. Hobson, William King, and Hugh Tait, but the French porcelain has remained largely unpublished, with the exception of some pieces of Vincennes and Sèvres published by William King, and a few rare items from these and other factories which have found their way into standard reference works, many of a general nature.

This catalogue represents the fruit of sustained study of pieces from over forty French factories, dating from the early 18th to the early 20th centuries, and attempts to paint as complete a picture as possible of the objects, their function and their *raison d'être.* The author has drawn heavily on the documents of the French formerly royal, now state factory of Vincennes/Sèvres, for precise details of the production process, and has analysed as many surviving documents as possible to shed light on pieces from elsewhere. Wherever possible, sources of forms or decoration have been discussed and illustrated. Prices and provenance are given when they have been discovered, and every attempt has been made to follow the entire history of each item. Thus, the catalogue sheds light on technological, artistic, historical and economic developments during the period, as well as on the history of collecting itself.

The J. Paul Getty Museum, Malibu, enabled Aileen Dawson to devote a three-month period as a Getty Scholar to concluding the writing of the catalogue. The Ceramica Stiftung, Zürich, has generously helped to fund the illustrations, and the British Antique Dealers' Association has also provided sponsorship. In addition, a number of collectors and dealers have helped to make this book possible by supporting it financially. The Museum is grateful to these benefactors for their commitment to object-based scholarship.

Neil Stratford
Keeper of the Department of
Medieval and Later Antiquities

Preface
to the paperback edition

Since the publication of the catalogue in 1994 much new information about French porcelain has come to light and new fields of enquiry have opened up. We now know much more about the histories of the Saint-Cloud and Chantilly factories and the Limoges porcelain industry has been the subject of a major exhibition at the Musée du Luxembourg, Paris. Stages in the development of colours and of hard-paste porcelain at Vincennes and Sèvres have been studied in detail. Much new light has been shed on the art of dining at the French court during the eighteenth-century, which was the subject of an exhibition at the château of Versailles, with the consequence that the use of Sèvres dinner- and dessert-services is now much better understood. Catalogues of several important collections have been published, each of which has added significantly to our knowledge of French porcelain production, in particular of nineteenth-century productions.

Because of constraints on space, it has only been possible to make minor alterations and corrections to the text of this catalogue. However, new acquisitions made since 1994 have been incorporated in an appendix at the end of the book. The original bibliography could not be extended, but further reading has been added to some of the factory histories, and a brief list of recent publications is given below:

Bibliography

Chevallier, Bernard, *Les Sèvres de Fontainebleau, Porcelaines, Terres Vernissées, Emaux, Vitraux (pièces entrées de 1804 à 1904)*, Paris, 1996.

D'Albis, Antoine, 'Les debuts des pourpres en France, de Chantilly à Vincennes: Salomon Taunay et son fils Pierre Henri Antoine', in *Sèvres, Revue de la Société des Amis du Musée national de Ceramique*, no. 3, 1994, pp. 34–9.

D'Albis, Antoine, 'Sèvres, 1756–1783. La conquête de la porcelaine dure, histoire inédite de la manufacture au XVIII', *Dossier de l'Art*, 1999, no. 54, January–February 1999.

Ducrot, Brigitte, *Musée National du Château de Compiègne. Porcelaines et Terres de Sèvres*, Paris, 1993.

Guillebon, Régine de Plinval de, *Faïence et Porcelaine de Paris XVIIIe–XIXe siècles*, Paris, 1995.

Lahaussois, Christine, *Porcelaine de Saint-Cloud. La collection du Musée des Arts Décoratifs*, Paris, 1997.

Le Duc, Geneviève, *Porcelaine tendre de Chantilly au XVIIIe siècle. Héritages et influences*, Paris, 1996.

Le Duc, Geneviève, 'Rodolphe Lemaire et la manufacture de porcelaine de Meissen: style extrême-oriental ou goût français', *Revue de l'Art*, no. 116, 1997, pp. 54–60.

Ostergard, Derek E. (ed.), *The Sèvres Porcelain Manufactory. Alexandre Brongniart and the Triumph of Art and Industry, 1800–1847*, New Haven and London, 1997.

Peters, David, *Decorator and Date Marks on Eighteenth-Century Vincennes and Sèvres Porcelain*, privately printed, 1997.

Rondot, Bernard (ed.), *Discovering the Secrets of Soft-Paste Porcelain at the Saint-Cloud Manufactory, ca 1690–1766*, New Haven and London, 1999.

In addition many useful articles have appeared in *Sèvres, Revue de la Société des Amis du Musée national de la Céramique*, in the yearly publication of the French Porcelain Society, London and in *Mélanges en souvenir d'Elisalex d'Albis (1939–1998)*, privately printed (Paris).

Exhibition Catalogues

Versailles et les tables royales en Europe XVIIème–XIXème siècles, Musée national des Châteaux de Versailles et de Trianon, November 1993–February 1994.

Meslin-Perrier, Chantal, *Chefs d'oeuvre de la porcelaine de Limoges*, Musée du Luxembourg, Paris, 30 January–28 April 1996.

De Juvigny, Sophie, *Il y a 300 ans . . . La porcelaine de Saint-Cloud, une entreprise pionnière sur les bords de la Seine*, Musée de Saint-Cloud, 30 September–30 November 1997 (contains a list of personnel in Soudée-Lacombe, Chantal, 'Les porcelainiers de Saint-Cloud d'après les archives', pp. 18–22).

Boone, MaryLou, *Terre et Feu. Four Centuries of French Ceramics from the Boone Collection*, Clark Humanities Museum, Scripps College, 26 January–27 March 1998.

Dal Carlo, Elisabetta, *Le Porcellane dell'ambasciatore*, Museo Querini Stampalia, Venice, December 1998–May 1999.

Miller, Markus and Dobler, Andreas, *Königliches Porzellan aus Frankreich, Sammlerstücke und Service der Manufaktur Vincennes/Sèvres aus dem Besitz der Hessischen Hausstiftung Museum Schloss Fasanerie*, Museum Schloss Fasanerie, Eichenzell and Kunstgewerbemuseum der Stadt Bielefeld, Bielefeld, June 1999–January 2000.

Chevallier, Bernard, 'Sèvres et l'Egypte', in *Napoleone Bonaparte in Egitto. Una spedizione tra conquista e conoscenza 1798–1801*, Rome, Museo Napoleonico, May–June 2000.

Acknowledgements

The author owes a special debt of thanks to the following who have given her particular help: Antoine d'Albis, Bernard Dragesco, Elisabeth Fontan, Clare Le Corbeiller, Geneviève Le Duc, Régine de Plinval de Guillebon, John Mallet, Tamara Préaud, Rosalind Savill, Tony Stevenson, John Whitehead, Gillian Wilson.

This catalogue is the fruit of a considerable period of work and could never have been undertaken without the support of the Trustees, the former Director, Sir David Wilson, and especially the Keeper of my Department, Neil Stratford. Hugh Tait offered encouragement and advice, particularly in the early stages. I owe a particular debt of gratitude to members of other Departments: in Prints and Drawings: Frances Dunkels, Hilary Williams; in Greek and Roman Antiquities, Ian Jenkins; in Coins and Medals, Mark Jones (now National Museums of Scotland); in Central Archive, Janet Wallace and her staff; in the Typing Pool, Carole Cosgrove and her staff, as well as the late Valerie Springett and Pamela Goss of Medieval and Later Antiquities who also bore the burden of typing the various drafts; in Photographic, Ivor Kerslake and his staff; in Conservation, the late Nigel Williams and his staff.

In other Museums many curators have allowed me to examine and discuss collections, and have provided photographs and information, notably, in Britain: Sir Geoffrey de Bellaigue, Charles Truman, Anna Somers Cocks, Jennifer Opie, Robin Hildyard, Hilary Young, Fiona Hirst, Hilary Bracegirdle, Ann Eatwell, Rosalind Savill, Susan Newall, John McKee, Richard Beresford, Ian Lowe, Lavinia Wellicome, David Legg-Willis, Julia Poole, Emmeline Leary, Sally Macdonald, Peter Saunders, Joan Jones, the late David Garlick, Sarah Medlam, Howard Coutts, Virginia Glenn, Dale Idiens.

In France the following Museum, Library and archive personnel have been especially helpful: Daniel Alcouffe, Pierre Ennès, Gérard Mabille, Maxime Préaud, Antoinette Faÿ-Hallé, Jean Saliou, Isabelle Laurin, Chantal Meslin-Perrier, Daniel Ludmann, Claire Aptel, Michel Coudreau, Danielle Heckenbenner, Pantxika Beguerie, Dr Michel Hachet, Monique Jacob, Maurice Noël, Matthieu Pinette, Jacqueline Du Pasquier.

In the United States much support has been given by the following Museum personnel, who have shown me pieces in their care and discussed them with me: Edgar Munhall, Jeffrey Munger, Bonnie Lilienfeld, Ann Odom, William Johnston, Henry Hawley, Laura Camins, Charissa Bremer-David, the late David Cohen, Adrian Sassoon, Shelley Bennett.

In Russia Natasha Kasakevitch has given me assistance over a long period of time, including a period of study spent at the State Hermitage Museum, St. Petersburg. In the Netherlands, A.L. den Blaauwen and Reinier Baarsen gave me access to the Rijksmuseum collections and Jan van Dam kindly responded to a series of enquiries.

I have received valuable help from dealers and auctioneers, particularly Robert Williams, Kate Foster, Armin Allen, Brian Haughton, Anton Kristensen, Errol Manners, Peter Arney, Roger McIlroy, Anton Gabscewicz, Louise Newman, and from collectors who have kindly allowed me to study their pieces: T.H. Clarke, Simon Goldblatt, Mr and Mrs Levine, David Peters, Lady Cynthia Postan, Mr and Mrs Galliers Prat, and Mrs Wendy Russell in the U.K.; Letitia Roberts in the USA; Michel Vandermeersch, Didier Cramoisan, Jacques Bastian in France.

During the compilation of the catalogue Sarah Keeling, Justine Wright, and Janet McKee have helped with research, checking and proof-reading. Ruth Nelson has also assisted in the checking process and I am grateful to them all for their support.

My particular thanks go to Peter Stringer for his painstaking attention to the photography for this catalogue in its final phase, to Jim Farrant for drawing the maps and various almost invisible incised marks, to Judy Rudoe for constant support and help throughout, and to Carolyn Jones of British Museum Press for her patience and hard work.

Acknowledgements
to the paperback edition

The author would like to thank Madame Tamara Préaud, archivist of the Sèvres factory, for her unstinting support and Madame Antoinette Hallé and her staff at the Musée National de Sèvres for their kind assistance. John Mallet generously gave valuable help with the new text and Christie's provided information on the *service des arts industriels* (see cat. 306) and other matters. Hilary Young kindly allowed me to examine pieces in the Victoria and Albert Museum. Saul Peckham has cheerfully undertaken new photography and my editor, Carolyn Jones, has once again made it all fit together. The author is grateful to both, and to Emma Way, British Museum Press, for undertaking the new edition.

Trustees Acknowledgement

The Trustees of the British Museum gratefully acknowledge the generous assistance towards the production of this book from:

Ceramica Stiftung der Schweiz
British Antique Dealers' Association

*

Armin B. Allen
Errol Manners
The Lord Rockley
John Shearer

and other benefactors who wish to remain anonymous.

Introduction

The nucleus of the French porcelain collection in the British Museum was the creation of Sir Augustus Wollaston Franks (1824–97). By his bequest the Museum became the repository not of a great group of Sèvres porcelains (John Jones' collection could already be seen at South Kensington), but of a range of both soft- and hard-paste French porcelains from the eighteenth and nineteenth centuries. The pieces had already been exhibited in a loan exhibition at the Bethnal Green Museum in 1896 and had been published by Franks himself on that occasion. His catalogue has remained, to this day, the only printed record of the Museum's holdings of French porcelain, even though it rapidly ceased to be complete. Additional pieces from the Franks estate, considered perhaps by him of lesser importance, soon joined the collection (where they are still known by the prefix FB), to be followed in 1899 by more French porcelain, this time from the bequest of C.D.E. Fortnum, who was another great connoisseur and also a Museum Trustee. In the following years the collection grew slowly, as can be seen from the catalogue, which records details of the acquisition of each piece. However in 1948 the generous bequest of Sir Bernard Eckstein finally brought into the Museum what it had always lacked, some splendid pieces of Sèvres porcelain. These include a flower vase bearing the arms of Choiseul (cat. 108), a plate from the famous service ordered by the Empress Catherine the Great of Russia in 1778 (cat. 121) and a water jug and basin formerly in the Hertford Collection (cat. 124). The majority of acquisitions since then have been mostly purchases, for modest sums; these have included a small number of pieces of eighteenth-century Sèvres. Some additions to the holdings of nineteenth-century Sèvres have been made. The small Vincennes collection, long acknowledged as one of the finest in the world, was augmented in 1989 by a cup and saucer (cat. 77), the first addition from that factory for fifty years. One factory not represented in the Franks Collection, probably because of the rarity of its surviving pieces, is the Brancas-Lauraguais factory; the Museum now has one example of this porcelain (cat. 221). Generous gifts of individual pieces (cats 7, 40, 249) show that the public continues to support the Museum's collecting in this field.

The collection preserves the character of its founder: it is in some ways idiosyncratic and atypical of other British collections of French porcelain, whether public or private. It is not noted for outstandingly beautiful tablewares, or splendid ornamental vases, and indeed represents unevenly the range of any one factory's production. It is, however, noted for its signed/dated pieces, as are the rest of the British and Continental post-medieval ceramic collections. From the outset it has been built up with one view in mind: to chronicle the development of porcelain in France. The same objective has governed the writing of this catalogue. For several decades after the appearance in 1906 of that indispensable work of reference, *L'Histoire des manufactures françaises de porcelaine*, by the comte de Chavagnac and the marquis de Grollier, based on the study of surviving documents allied to a deep knowledge of the porcelains themselves, little work was published. Since the Second World War a spate of books and articles has shed a great deal of light on the royal factory of Vincennes/Sèvres, but other factories in production in France during the eighteenth century have received much less attention. This lacuna in our knowledge has been, to some extent, filled in the last two decades, but so far not one full-scale work has been devoted to any one of these so-called 'minor' factories. It is true that some detailed studies have been written by pupils of the Ecole du Louvre, but these remain unpublished and the valuable information they contain virtually inaccessible. Somewhat more readily available are unpublished theses of the Faculty of Arts of the University of Nancy, on which I have drawn heavily. I have also tried to incorporate as much information as possible from contemporary documents, especially the records surviving in the archive of the former royal factory at Sèvres. The publications of the French Porcelain Society of London have been invaluable.

Limoges, France's centre of porcelain production in the nineteenth century, as today, still remains almost unstudied, in notable contrast with Stoke-on-Trent, Staffordshire, where many of the factories have been the subject of encyclopaedic works and numerous exhibitions.

Very little archaeological excavation has been carried out on porcelain factory sites in France. Rouen is almost the only exception to this, because of the overriding interest in France in the tin-glazed earthenware industry. There is a general failure to link this industry with the development of porcelain, which often in the eighteenth century shared the same site, as for instance at Saint-Cloud. Evidence of wasters and kilns would add a great deal to our knowledge of the chronology, technology, and product range of the porcelain factories.

Many aspects of porcelain production in France will in the future be a fertile field of research for scholars and enthusiasts: the origin of the raw materials, techniques such as mould- and block-making, the preparation of colours, the development of gilding, kiln design, the involvement of sculptors, painters and other specialised craftsmen, the capitalisation of enterprises and patterns of trade. I hope that this catalogue, offered as a record of the collection, will serve as a useful starting-point for future study.

Finally, I have received endless help from colleagues in France and in many other countries, not all of whom can be individually acknowledged; all errors and omissions are of course my own.

Santa Monica, October 1990

Scientific Analysis

No complete programme of analysis has been carried out on the French porcelain in the British Museum. However, a considerable number of individual analyses have been done on a variety of pieces, principally to determine the composition of the body and/or the glaze. Both X-ray diffraction and X-ray fluorescence have been used. The first is, in theory, destructive since it involves sampling, but only a minute particle of porcelain is required, normally only removed from an already-damaged object using dental tools. Reference numbers of all tests are quoted in the catalogue text, and precise results may be requested from the British Museum Department of Scientific Research by scientific personnel in other institutions, as they have not been given in full by the author.

In several instances, such as a Chantilly cup of the late eighteenth or early nineteenth century, the analysis has added a new dimension to our study of French porcelain (cat. 48). Sometimes, indeed, the laboratory results have raised more questions than they have answered, but this is the nature of the game.

The writer wishes to acknowledge her gratitude to the staff of the Research Laboratory, and in particular to Mavis Bimson, whose enthusiasm and wide knowledge of ceramics have contributed greatly towards the preparation of this catalogue.

Bibliography

M. Bimson, 'The examination of ceramics by X-ray powder diffraction', *Studies in Conservation*, 14, 1969, pp. 83–9

W.D. Kingery and P. Vandiver, 'The Development of European Soft-Paste (Frit) Porcelain', *Ceramics and Civilisation, Ancient Technology to Modern Science*, Vol. I, Columbus, Ohio, 1985, proceedings of the 86th annual meeting of the American Ceramic Society, 1984, Pittsburgh, Pennsylvania, pp. 273–92

W.D. Kingery and P. Vandiver, 'A Boucher Soft-Paste Bisque Sculpture – La Danseuse', in *Ceramic Masterpieces, Art, Structure and Technology*, New York and London, 1986

F. Treppoz and A. d'Albis, 'Identification de différents types de porcelaines anciennes à l'aide de l'analyse par diffraction X', *Faenza*, Ann. LXXIII, n. 1–3, 1987, pp. 40–63

French Porcelain: A Technical Discussion

FRENCH SOFT-PASTE PORCELAIN

Soft-paste or artificial porcelain is a term used for the porcelains developed at various places in Europe in the search for hard-paste or true porcelain. It is translucent in transmitted light, its surface can be scratched and it may shatter if exposed to boiling liquids. In France it was perfected in the late seventeenth century, perhaps by Edmé Poterat who took out a patent in 1673 to include the making of porcelain. However, there is little evidence that porcelain was made commercially at his tin-glazed earthenware pottery in Rouen. It was almost certainly in production at the Saint-Cloud factory outside Paris (see pp. 3–29) before the end of the seventeenth century.

The soft-paste porcelain made at Sèvres consists of silica-sand, alum, gypsum, soda, niter and sea-salt heated together to make a 'frit'.[1] Calcination and grinding of the alum and gypsum was usually carried out before the mixing, because of their high water content. The frit was ground and washed before being made into the body or paste, with the admixture of clay and chalk for plasticity. The composition was ground up and filtered and left to 'rot' for some time (from a period of several months to several years) before use.

The first, or biscuit, firing (the term means twice-fired in French and was used because the frit had already been fired) transforms the paste into porcelain when it matures at a temperature of about 1150–1200°C. During this firing the paste softens and shrinks by a factor of about one-sixth and the pieces must therefore be supported in the kiln to prevent distortion. Most kiln losses occur at this stage. In the eighteenth century (and indeed until the later part of the nineteenth century) there was no scientific measurement of temperature, which was done by rule-of-thumb methods.

Unless left in the unglazed or 'biscuit' state, as might be the case for figures, groups, plaques and medallions, the surface was coated with a glaze. This rendered vessels impervious to liquids. French soft-pastes are usually covered with a shiny glaze containing lead. Sometimes tin was added to glazes, as during the early years at the Chantilly factory, to disguise a body which was not considered white enough. Temperatures during the glaze firing reached about 1000–1100°C. As the paste had matured in the first firing, the porcelain is stable at this stage.

Decoration was usually the last process, as most metal oxides from which colours are derived will not withstand the glazing temperatures. Only cobalt, which can be fired at high temperatures, could be used under the glaze. Other colours were painted over the glaze and fired at around 850°C. Gilding was fired last at an even lower temperature of 800°C.

Until the 1750s only soft-paste porcelain was made on French soil. From the 1770s hard-paste porcelain was in commercial production both at Sèvres and at numerous other factories, principally in Paris.

For a detailed account of manufacturing techniques at Vincennes, see Préaud and d'Albis, 1991, pp. 103–20. These methods, broadly speaking, were in use at other French soft-paste factories, but these await further study.

French soft-paste porcelains will be found on analysis to contain wollastonite and tridymite or cristobalite.

1. Brongniart, 1844, II, p. 460.

FRENCH HARD-PASTE PORCELAIN

Made of china clay and china stone (predominantly kaolinite and a felspar), chalk, silica-sand and occasionally ground-up porcelain, hard-paste porcelain is translucent and much more durable than soft-paste. Its surface is not easily scratched and it will withstand boiling liquids. It is generally a rather cold white in tone, although some Paris hard-pastes of the early 1770s, such as those made by Locré, can have a deceptively glassy look. When chipped or broken, the fracture is conchoidal in appearance, rather than granular as in soft-paste. Unglazed figures, for which a slightly different proportion of raw materials was used, are rougher to the touch than the silky soft-paste biscuit porcelains.

The discovery of china clay on French soil was apparently made by the chemist Guettard in 1751, probably in the region of Alençon. But this was a poor clay, firing to a greyish colour, and mass-production did not begin until finer raw materials were found at Saint-Yrieix-la-Perche south of Limoges in the late 1760s. These were quickly exploited both by the royal factory and the various Paris concerns, which obtained their clay from specialist suppliers exploiting the claypits. The composition of a typical French hard-paste porcelain is described by the Sèvres factory director Alexandre Brongniart in his *Traité de la Céramique*, published in 1844,[1] but no details are given of the formulae used at the eighteenth-century French factories, apart from Sèvres.

The firing process differs from that used for soft-paste porcelain. Hard-paste porcelain is fired at higher temperatures and the body and glaze mature together in the second firing. The first or biscuit firing (now known in France as the *dégourdi* firing) takes place at around 950–1000°C; the ware does not shrink appreciably, and the paste is not yet impervious to liquids. During the glaze firing the temperature reaches a maximum of around 1400°C, and because of the formation of a glassy phase the paste contracts and may be subject to distortion. Another difference between hard- and soft-pastes is that feldspathic glazes do not soften at the temperatures used for enamel colours, and the colours do not therefore fuse into the glaze as on the soft-pastes.

Towards the end of the nineteenth century new compositions were devised at Sèvres, which by this time had become a school and ceramic laboratory. These new bodies, such as *porcelaine nouvelle* (see cat. 191) could be fired at lower temperatures and were therefore more economical and allowed different types of decoration.[2]

Hard-paste porcelain will be found on analysis to contain mullite, an aluminium silicate. Occasionally quartz (silica) is also present, as in the porcelain made by the comte de Lauraguais (see cat. 221) or, when the composition is underfired, anorthite, a calcium aluminium silicate.

1. Brongniart, 1844, II, pp. 257–66.
2. C. Lauth, *La manufacture nationale de Sèvres et la porcelaine nouvelle*, conférence faite le 28 Octobre 1884 au Palais de l'Industrie, Paris, 1884; C. Lauth and G. Vogt, *Notes techniques sur la fabrication de la porcelaine nouvelle*, Paris, 1885.

Donors

1897	Sir A.W. Franks
1899	C.D.E. Fortnum DCL, FSA
1901	J.H. Fitzhenry
1909	Mr and Mrs Isaac Falcke
1913	Rev. A.H.S. Barwell
1923	The Rt. Hon. Viscount Dillon, in memory of his son
1924	Major H.M. Gallatly
	W.W. Winkworth MC
1926	Mrs M.A. Francis
1928	The Misses M.S. and A. Bloxam and W.R. Bloxam
1934	R. Fenouil
	Mrs Willoughby Hodgson
1935	C.B.O. Clarke
1936	F. Howard Paget
1937	William King
	Gilbert Lévy
	Adolphe Lion
1938	S.G. Davies
	William King
	Adolphe Lion
1940	Arthur Hurst
	William King
1948	Sir B. Eckstein
1957	A.D. Passmore
1971	D.A. MacAlister
1977	Dr Douglas Barrett
1981	D.A. King
	Miss C.M. Woodward
1986	D.A. King
1987	Mrs Wendy Russell and family in memory of Richard Russell
	Dr Henry Ginsburg
	Mrs L.M. Slot in memory of L.M. Slot
1988	E. Manners
	Armin B. Allen

Explanation of the Catalogue

The catalogue is arranged as far as possible chronologically in three main sections; soft-paste factories including Vincennes/Sèvres which runs through to the twentieth century and includes hard-paste pieces, with the sculptural items such as figures and groups, medallions and plaques grouped separately; hard-paste factories; Paris hard-paste factories. Brief histories of each factory precede the catalogue entries.

The entries include the contemporary French name of the piece, if known, its date of manufacture (several 19th century pieces were thrown or cast many years before their decoration was completed so a wide date range is given), its dimensions, marks and signature and registration number followed by a description. Measurements are given in centimetres except for objects in North American collections where they are in inches. Marks are reproduced photographically within the catalogue entry. In a few instances where the incised marks are indistinct they have been reproduced from drawings. Notes on provenance and comparable examples are given before the detailed discussion. In some entries the author is aware that the piece is far from unique, but has not been able to discover other examples; here the words 'none noted' indicate the probability that there are comparable pieces. Footnotes complete the entries.

In general, figures are treated after undecorated or painted tablewares and pieces intended for the boudoir. Those attributed to the factory in the absence of a factory mark are to be found at the end of the sequence, and items of doubtful authenticity are at the end of each section. Pieces catalogued by A.W. Franks in 1896 as French but now reattributed are in an addendum at the end of the catalogue. The bibliography is arranged alphabetically by author, with exhibition catalogues listed separately and indicated in the text by the prefix *exh.*

In general, eighteenth- and nineteenth-century French spellings have been preserved.

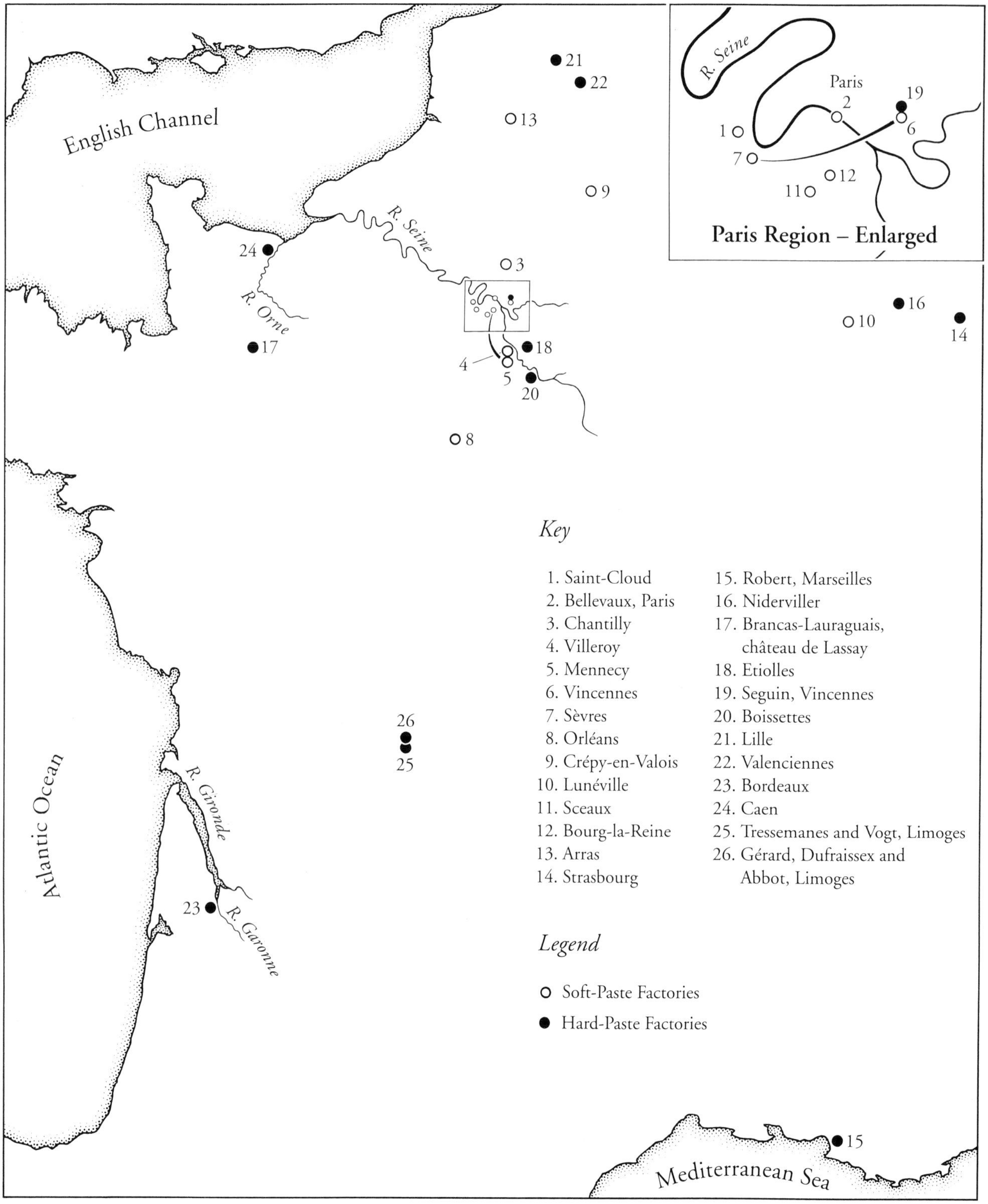
English Channel
R. Seine
R. Orne
Atlantic Ocean
R. Gironde
R. Garonne
Mediterranean Sea
Paris Region – Enlarged
Paris
Key
1. Saint-Cloud
2. Bellevaux, Paris
3. Chantilly
4. Villeroy
5. Mennecy
6. Vincennes
7. Sèvres
8. Orléans
9. Crépy-en-Valois
10. Lunéville
11. Sceaux
12. Bourg-la-Reine
13. Arras
14. Strasbourg
15. Robert, Marseilles
16. Niderviller
17. Brancas-Lauraguais, château de Lassay
18. Etiolles
19. Seguin, Vincennes
20. Boissettes
21. Lille
22. Valenciennes
23. Bordeaux
24. Caen
25. Tressemanes and Vogt, Limoges
26. Gérard, Dufraissex and Abbot, Limoges
Legend
Soft-Paste Factories
Hard-Paste Factories

THE CATALOGUE

SOFT-PASTE FACTORIES

Saint-Cloud[1]

This factory, situated beside the river Seine at Saint-Cloud,[2] began making porcelain in the early 1690s, perhaps as an indirect result of patronage extended by the King's brother, Philippe, duc d'Orléans (1640–1701) to Henri Trou (b. about 1650, m. 1678, d. 1700), although no evidence of this has yet been discovered. The factory had originally been established by Claude Révérend in 1666 to make tin-glazed earthenwares, which continued in production on the site throughout the eighteenth century.[3] Trou was the second husband of Barbe Coudray, or Coudret, whose first husband Pierre Chicaneau, a faïence-painter, had carried out various experiments to produce porcelain and before his death in about 1678 had passed on his secrets to his wife. Trou *père*, referred to in several *mémoires* as 'huissier de l'antichambre du duc d'Orléans', and in legal documents of 1688 as 'Officier de S.A.R. Monsieur', was an organiser and entrepreneur rather than a potter, although he was a *maître faïencier*. Later documents of 1741 show that Barbe Coudray's children enjoyed the sole right to the 'secrets' or formulae of the porcelain body and its preparation. From a study of the letters patent granted by the King on 16 May 1702 (see below), it is clear that the privilege of making porcelain everywhere in France except at Rouen was given to Pierre Chicaneau's wife and children, and that the porcelain factory was established in about 1690–3, around fourteen years after her second marriage. It has been suggested, although no proof of this assertion has been discovered, that the chemist and naturalist François Morin, who is known to have succeeded in making porcelain experimentally, may perhaps have played a role in the experimental work carried out before full production was established.[4]

An account of the factory at the end of the seventeenth century is given by the English physician Dr Martin Lister in his *Journey to Paris in the Year 1698*.[5] As Geoffrey Wills noted in his discussion of early French porcelain, Lister's description of the Saint-Cloud factory covers nearly three pages of the *Journey* as printed. Lister emphasised the whiteness and perfection of the glaze, the careful preparation of the clay, the great number of firings (he mentions that some pieces had more than three and up to eleven) and the expense of the finished pieces. 'Ordinary' chocolate cups were 'Crowns a-piece'.

By the turn of the century the factory was flourishing, as is shown by an account of a visit by the duchesse de Bourgogne in October 1700 published in the *Mercure*:[6]

> Madame la duchesse de Bourgogne ayant passé par Saint Cloud et tourné le long de la rivière pour aller à Puteaux chez Madame la duchesse de Guiche, fit arrêter son carrosse à la porte de la maison ou MM. Chicannaux ont établi depuis quelques années une manufacture de porcelaines fines, qui, sans contredit n'a point de semblable dans toute l'Europe. Cette princesse prit plaisir à voir faire sur le tour des pièces d'un très beau profil; elle en vit peindre quelques autres sur des desseins plus réguliers et mieux executés que ceux des porcelaines des Indes. Elle alla ensuite voir travailler aux fayences qui se fabriquent dans la même manufacture; après quoi MM. Chicanaux la conduisirent dans leur cabinet, où elle vit quantité de fines et belles porcelaines dans leur perfection, dont elle fut si contente qu'elle leur promit d'y revenir. Elle ne sortit de chez eux qu'après avoir marqué sa satisfaction par les liberalités qu'elle fit aux ouvriers.
>
> LL.AA.RR. Monsieur et Madame font souvent l'honneur à MM. Chicanaux d'aller voir leur manufacture. Ils reçoivent aussi de fréquentes visites de princes, de seigneurs, d'ambassadeurs et de toutes sortes

de curieux qui viennent chaque jour admirer la beauté des ouvrages qui s'y fabriquent, et dont il se fait un grand débit pour les pays étrangers. Ils ont établi leurs magasins pour la vente de leurs porcelaines à Paris, au coin de la rue Coquillière et de la rue Petits-Champs, proche la place des Victoires.

After passing through Saint-Cloud, the Duchess of Burgundy followed the river towards Puteaux to see the Duchess of Guiche, and stopped her coach at the door of the house where a few years ago Messieurs Chicannaux [*sic*] established a factory to make fine porcelain, the like of which does not exist in all Europe. This princess took pleasure in seeing pieces of very beautiful outline being thrown on the wheel; she watched several others being painted with designs which were more regular and better executed than those on Far Eastern porcelain. Next she went to see tin-glazed earthenwares being made in the same factory. After this Messieurs Chicanaux took her to their private room where she saw a quantity of fine and beautiful porcelains in all their perfection, with which she was so pleased that she promised to return to the factory. She did not leave before showing her satisfaction by liberally rewarding the workmen.

Their Royal Highnesses Monsieur and Madame often pay Messieurs Chicanaux the honour of going to see their factory. They are also visited by princes, noblemen, ambassadors, and all sorts of cognoscenti who come every day to admire the beauty of the pieces made there, and which are sold in such quantity to foreign lands. They have opened a shop in Paris for the sale of their porcelain at the corner of the rue Coquillière and the rue Petits-Champs, near the place des Victoires.

The shop was run by Jean-Baptiste Chicaneau (1665–1734, son of Pierre I Chicaneau and Barbe Coudray), who left Saint-Cloud in 1696. At present nothing is known of the export of Saint-Cloud products.[7]

Another contemporary who commented on Saint-Cloud porcelain at the beginning of the eighteenth century was the German chemist Ehrenfried Walther von Tschirnhausen (1651–1708), whose experiments with various clays led to the development of the first European hard-paste porcelain. In 1701 he paid his fourth visit to Paris and wrote:[8]

Zu Saint Cloud in der Porcelain Manufaktur kauffte ich mir unterschiedene Stücke, die mir aber hernach von selbst zersprangen, denn in der Composition viel Salia gebrauchet werden. Sie geben sie sehr theuer und viel hoher als guten Porcelain. Wesswegen der Abgang sehr schlecht ist. Der Ofen und die Machinen zum Zeiben der Materialen war das beste, wiewohl noch nicht volkommen, wie es seyn sollte; das andere war mir alles bekannt. Die blaue Farbe, so er brauchet, ist viel zu tunckel schwarz.

At the porcelain factory at Saint Cloud I bought myself various pieces, which later broke of themselves, because of the large quantity of salts contained in the composition. These pieces are sold very dear and cost more than good porcelain [i.e. hard-paste porcelain]. For this reason sales are very poor. The kiln and the machines for preparing the [raw] materials were the best, although not yet as good as they should be; the rest was all familiar to me. The blue colour they use is far too dark black.

In 1702 letters patent[9] were granted to 'Barbe Coudray, veuve de Pierre Chicanneau, Jean, Jean-Baptiste, Pierre et Geneviève Coudray, frère et soeur, enfants de ladite Coudray et dudit Pierre Chicanneau [*sic*]' to make porcelain in 'un ou plusieurs établissements de la manufacture de porcelaine fine de toutes couleurs, façons et grandeurs'. This has been taken to show that the factory was capable of painting in enamel colours at this early date. Chavagnac and Grollier draw attention to an earlier request from all those named above except Barbe Coudray for a privilege for 'Henri Trou leur beau père, pour la composition de la porcelaine dont chaque pièce sera marquée d'une fleur de lis et un soleil'. This document is said to be dated 1696 in pencil in the margin;[10] this writer knows of no official confirmation of the grant of privilege, but the mark is usually thought to have been used in tribute to the Sun King, Louis XIV, between the end of the seventeenth century and 1715, the year of the King's death.

On 3 January 1708 an *arrêt*,[11] or decree, mentions the subject of wood used in the kilns at Saint-Cloud. The letters patent were renewed in 1713, 1722 and again in 1742. Barbe Coudray's son Pierre II Chicaneau ran the factory until late 1709 when he is last recorded at Saint-Cloud. It has been suggested that he was replaced by his nephew Dominique-François Chicaneau (1686–1743?), referred to in contemporary documents between 1707 and 1723 as 'inspecteur de la porcelaine'.[12] However, it is known that Pierre II Chicaneau's half-brother, Henri II Trou (1680–1746), was director of the factory from 1710 until his death. Pierre II's brother Jean (d. 1742) is first documented in 1690 when he was registered as a 'maistre esmailleur marchand vitrier fayancier' in Paris. Until 1705 he was apparently resident at Saint-

Cloud. In 1706 he was living in the rue Ville l'Evêque and the following year he moved to the rue de Charonne, faubourg St. Antoine, where he stayed until 1717. Between 1717 and 1723 Jean Chicaneau resided in the rue de Charonne and later in the rue de Charenton, moving in 1723 to the rue Aulmaix. Evidence exists to show that he almost certainly made small articles, such as knife-handles. Barbe Coudray died in 1717 at the age of 77.[13] Henri II and Gabriel Trou, her sons by her second marriage, renewed the patent in their own names, together with those of the Chicaneau heirs, Jean, Jean-Baptiste and the widow Moreau, after their mother's death. The mark *STC* (in several variations) is known to have been used between 1726 and at least 1755 on the basis of two dated pieces: (a) a long-necked bottle decorated with underglaze-blue lambrequins dated 1726;[14] (b) a saucer moulded in relief and painted in blue bearing the arms of Madame de Pompadour dated 1755.[15] This mark may well have been in use from 1722, when Trou became owner of the factory after the death of his mother.

In 1737 the factory at Saint-Cloud was partly destroyed by fire, but was rebuilt.[16] Three years later the 'secrets' of making Saint-Cloud porcelain, which originally had been vested in Barbe Coudray and her offspring from her first marriage, were passed on by a judgement of 14 September 1741, following a legal battle, to Marie Moreau (widow of Pierre II Chicaneau), Jean-Baptiste Chicaneau, Nicolas Chicaneau, Thérèse Chicaneau *femme* Briguet, Pierre Chicaneau, Marie-Anne Chicaneau *femme* Hébert, Marie-Elisabeth Chicaneau *femme* Claude Gayot, Michelle Barbe Chicaneau *femme* Denis Jaquemart and Henri II Trou.

Marie Moreau died shortly afterwards on 11 March 1743, leaving Henri II Trou in complete control. He in turn died on 14 April 1746, but not before bringing his son, Henri-François, into the firm in 1745.

The discovery by Charles Truman[17] of four manuscript sheets dated between 13 November 1747 and 28 July 1749 listing various items of porcelain which can reasonably be assumed to be of Saint-Cloud manufacture, with their prices, has cast light on a small area of the firm's production.[18] The 'pots à pommade à Relief' or 'Bleux' (costing 40 or 50 sous and 30 sous respectively), 'petits pots pourris à feuillages sur terrasses' at 12 *livres* each, teapots, sugar bowls, cups and saucers with relief decoration, tobacco pots and artichoke pots are all typical of the factory. Many surviving examples are known, and it is likely that the sheets, discovered inside a *nécessaire* belonging to the Victoria and Albert Museum, where they were used to form the compartments and stiffen the cushion in the lid, were part of a daybook of a *marchand-mercier*. There were many of these middlemen, who had a thriving trade in selling all kinds of travelling sets (together with a variety of other objects), which included mounted porcelains. Most of the pieces were modestly priced, at least by comparison with Sèvres porcelains, although they were sold only to the wealthy. The most expensive items are two tobacco pots described as 'feuillages guirlandes' sold in May 1749 at 24 *livres* each. The majority of pieces were undecorated but some were 'en couleur', including 'un moyen pot à paste' which cost 10 *livres*, and a handled cup with saucer at 8 *livres*. Even the illustrious Madame de Pompadour purchased 'huit gobelets & soucoupes de Saint-Cloud & six coquetiers pour la laiterie' on 9 July 1755 from the leading *marchand-mercier* Lazare-Duvaux, and the goods were charged at the high price of 58 *livres*.[19]

In 1764, in a desperate attempt to raise capital, Henri-François Trou went into partnership with Edmé Choudard des Forges. An undated document in the Sèvres factory archives reveals his distress. He petitioned the King to let him succeed Boileau as the director of the royal factory.[20] However, on 29 September 1766 he was forced to close the Saint-Cloud factory because of its numerous debts, and the stock was sold off. An inventory taken at the time of the liquidation of the stock[21] shows what was being manufactured. It included ornamental pieces as well as tablewares, figures and groups, and 'fayence' (valued at only 466 *livres*). There were two shops ('magasins'), one at Saint-Cloud, the other 'près la porte de Paris rue Saint-Denis'.

Little is known of the organisation and personnel of this factory, the longest-lived of all eighteenth-century concerns with the exception of the royal factory. A list of workers at the factory between 1692 (i.e. around the time when porcelain began to be made) and 1766, based on the Saint-Cloud parish registers, comprises a total of over 90 males, of whom quite a large number are without any precise occupation.[22] Names of around 24 painters have been traced, including several who moved on to the Sèvres factory (Henry Bolvry, Louis-Pierre Massüe, Henri-Martin Prévost). Fifteen throwers are named by Chavagnac and Grollier between 1695 and 1766, including Henri-

Etienne Leguay who went to be a *peintre en bleu* at Vincennes in January 1747. Some of these throwers may have worked on tin-glazed earthenwares. Only one sculptor, Louis-Jacques Goujon, appears in the records, being mentioned between 1736 and 1741. The *charretier* (carter) Gerbois (1698), the *enfourneur* (kiln-master) Pierre Beaudoin (1710) and the *volatiseur de four* (fireman) Jean-Leonard Vallet (1713) were amongst the rest of the workforce.

The chronology of Saint-Cloud remains difficult to establish in the virtual absence of dated and signed examples, and is usually based on stylistic criteria. Even the date of the introduction of overglaze enamel colours remains uncertain.[23] It may well have begun around 1700 but the writer knows of only one piece, a beaker decorated in iron-red,[24] which can be from this period. Another beaker[25] painted in colours was conceivably made around 1710–15, and a sauceboat[26] painted with lambrequins in colours is also likely to have been made around this time. Judging from the style of the motifs on some *chinoiserie*-decorated pieces, it seems likely that colours were in common use by the late 1720s. Brownish-purple (from manganese), blue, emerald green (from copper), iron red, brownish-black, yellow and pink are used, often in conjunction with gilding. Yellow and lime green were probably first used as ground colours in the 1740s.

An advertisement was issued in 1731 and was still current in 1741.[27] Although the factory used the title 'La Manufacture Royale des Porcelaines de Saint-Cloud', it had not been formally granted this title by the King. It gave its address as 'Ruë de la Madeleine, Faubourg S. Honoré à Paris'. Dominique-François Chicaneau announced that he made and sold, both wholesale and retail, 'toutes sortes de belles Porcelaines, bleües, blanches, en relief à feuillages & en toutes sortes de couleurs', the following: casseroles and their stands (*pots à oeüil et leurs plats*), barbers' bowls, *pots-pourris*, soup tureens (*pots à boüillon*) and stands, chandeliers, water jugs with matching basins, covered bowls and stands (*écuelles couvertes & leurs souscoupes*), large wine- and liqueur-coolers, white plates with relief decoration, sauceboats, pepperpots, salt-cellars, mustard-pots, inkstands, sets of covered or uncovered cups (*gobelets*), cups and saucers, teapots, sugar boxes decorated in relief in the Japanese manner, all sorts of grotesque figures and tree-trunks for candlesticks (*girandoles*), all sorts of knife-handles with relief, blue or coloured decorations, spoons, forks, variously-shaped tobacco-boxes, mounted or unmounted, and various sorts of cane-handles. All these could be sent to the provinces or exported. He also sold faïence, mirrors and glass.

No information has yet come to light about the source of the raw materials. A *mémoire* read by Guettard to the Académie des Sciences on 13 November 1765 declares that the paste contained 'terre de Garches', sand and potassium.[28]

1. This account is based on Chavagnac and Grollier, 1906, pp. 9–34 and on G. Le Duc and R. de Plinval de Guillebon, 'Contribution à l'étude de la manufacture de faïence et de porcelaine de Saint-Cloud pendant ses cinquante premières années', *Keramik-Freunde der Schweiz Mitteilungsblatt Nr. 105*, March 1991, pp. 3–53. This publication gives extensive details of factory personnel. Additional biographical details of Jean and Pierre II Chicaneau were kindly provided in personal correspondence by Le Duc in December 1991. For subsequent research see Rondot (ed.), 1999 (full reference on page vii).
2. A map of Saint-Cloud by the Abbé Delagrive inscribed 'M. Fourreau scripsit' and 'M. Marÿe sculp', dated 1744 and sold by Longuet (whose trade card is attached to both the map and its marbled cover) gives the location of the glass works, the *fayancerie* on the river bank below the Pont de Saint-Cloud (on the outskirts of the estate) and of the *four à chaux* or lime kiln; it does not name the porcelain factory, which shared the same site as the pottery (MNS, Archives de Sèvres, M 37). For further details see Le Duc and Guillebon, 1991, pp. 9–12. This site was known in the early 1970s and some buildings still survived until the *autoroute* N13 was built and they were demolished. No rescue archaeology was carried out.
3. For the history of the faïence factory, see 'Faïences françaises XVIe–XVIIIe siècles', exh. Paris, Grand Palais, June–August 1980, pp. 236–8, and the fuller account given by Le Duc and Guillebon, 1991, *passim*. Some pieces, attributed to Saint-Cloud, but according to Geneviève Le Duc quite possibly from one of the various other faïence factories in the Paris region, made for royal *châteaux* are illustrated in *Musée de L'Ile de France, Catalogue Raisonné des Collections*, compiled by G. Poisson, M. Aries, C. Henry, F. Flot, 1985, nos 858–62; for others see exh. cat. cited above, pp. 238–40 and Le Duc and Guillebon, 1991, figs 1–7.
4. Le Duc and Guillebon, 1991, p. 15.
5. Wills, 1958, pp. 74–6, quoted Chavagnac and Grollier, 1906, p. 13.
6. Chavagnac and Grollier, 1906, p.13. A transcript in the hand of Riocreux is kept at the Sèvres factory archive, Y35 *bis, dossier* 52 (Saint Cloud). It is said to have been taken from the October 1700 edition of the *Mercure*, pp. 96–9, but Le Duc and Guillebon, 1991, p. 16, f.n. 22 give December 1700.
7. However, the Reverend William Cole (1714–82) noted in his Journal on 11 May 1766, 'Jem brought me a letter from the Post Office from Mr Walpole inviting me to fetch from Strawberry Hill the porcelain of St. Cloud & Pastilles which he had brought from Paris', quoted by N. Stretton, 'The Blecheley Diary of the Reverend William Cole, M.A., F.S.A., 1765–67', *Proceedings of the Wedgwood Society*, No. 13, 1990, p. 25. The author is grateful to John Mallet for bringing this reference to her attention.
8. See F. Hofmann, *Porzellan der Europaïschen Manufakturen im*

XVIII. *Jahrhundert*, Berlin, 1932, p. 53. Hofmann does not give the whereabouts of Tschirnhausen's account.
9. Partly reproduced in Chavagnac and Grollier, 1906, pp. 9–10.
10. Geneviève Le Duc has kindly pointed out in correspondence with the writer in February 1992 that Henri Trou's name is mentioned in the first request for the privilege since he was supporting the Chicaneau children. Although no document pertaining to the privilege is officially dated, one, A.N. 67 429, is addressed to Monsieur de Pontchartrain, Contrôleur Général des Finances 1689–99.
11. Chavagnac and Grollier, 1906, pp. 14–15.
12. Le Duc and Guillebon, 1991, p. 37.
13. *Ibid.*, p. 39.
14. In a private collection (not seen by this writer), illus. exh. Saint-Cloud, 1980, no. 19.
15. USA, Saint Louis Art Museum, inv. 57:1938, not seen by this writer, who is indebted to Bernard Dragesco for bringing this piece to her attention. John Mallet has suggested in conversation with the writer that the saucer may have been part of Lazare Duvaux' delivery to Madame de Pompadour in July 1755, see note 16.
16. Chavagnac and Grollier, 1906, p. 16, information said to be from Archives de la Seine, D. I. Geneviève Le Duc has searched unsuccessfully over a long period for this document, which may well no longer survive. She has pointed out in correspondence with the author that the fire may have affected the main kiln rather than the factory buildings.
17. C. Truman, 'A St. Cloud *Nécessaire de Voyage* circa 1750', *Connoisseur*, Vol. 203, no. 818, April 1980, pp. 253–5.
18. The range of the factory's products is well represented in the exhibition catalogue referred to in note 14.
19. Courajod, 1873, Vol. II, 9 July 1755.
20. MNS, Archives de Sèvres, D 2, *liasse* 2.
21. Chavagnac and Grollier, 1906, pp. 18–19, the Archives de la Seine, *Bilans* no. 18.
22. Chavagnac and Grollier, 1906, pp. 27–9. Further archival work, notably in the *registres paroissiaux de la mairie de Saint-Cloud*, which are more complete than those used in 1906, finished in 1989 by Chantal Soudée-Lacombe, is published by Le Duc and Guillebon, 1991, pp. 30–53. The later publication fills lacunae existing in 1906.
23. For a discussion of the introduction of polychrome decoration on Saint-Cloud in which no firm conclusion as to dating is expressed, see Fourest, 1960, pp. 172–83; the subject is discussed further by Le Duc and Guillebon, 1991, pp. 16–17. Geneviève Le Duc has pointed out in correspondence with the author that Tafel 12, fig. 22, should be captioned 1715.
24. Inv. MNCS 22846, ill. Fourest, 1960, p. 181.
25. Le Duc and Guillebon, 1991, fig. 21.
26. Frégnac, 1964, p. 62.
27. Chavagnac and Grollier, 1906, p. 32.
28. See Treppoz and d'Albis, 1987, pp. 44–5. These ingredients were the basis for the frit, to which chalk and calcareous clay would have been added to produce soft-paste porcelain. No evidence is known to this author that tin-opacified glaze was used initially at the Saint-Cloud factory, as stated by W.D. Kingery and P.B. Vandiver, *Ceramic Masterpieces, Art, Structure and Technology*, New York and London, 1986, p. 17.

---

1 Cup, *c.* 1700–10

See colour plate 1

H.	8.3 cm
D.	7.6 cm
Marks:	none
Reg. No.	1940,4–1,7

Soft-paste porcelain, thinly potted, highly translucent and with a shiny glaze. Of flared form, the rim slightly out-turned, deep foot. Interior of foot rim only partly glazed. Painted in dark underglaze-blue with a zigzag motif around the foot, two groups of acanthus scrolls enclosing a covered vase on three feet with scroll handles, surmounted by another containing three flowers. A lambrequin, scroll and vase motif is painted below the rim, around the inner part of which is a simplified zigzag motif.

Provenance: Bequeathed by Arthur Hurst, Esq., 1940

Literature: Unpublished

Comparable Examples: London, Victoria and Albert Museum, cup, inv. C. 497–1909, Fitzhenry Collection, illus. G. Wills, 'Dr Martin Lister and Early French Porcelain', *Connoisseur*, Vol. CXLI, no. 568, March 1958, p. 75, fig. 3

Scotland, Private Collection, cup

Paris, Musée des arts décoratifs, cup and saucer, inv. 32405, illus. H. Landais, *French Porcelain*, London, 1961, fig. 9

Paris, Musée des arts décoratifs, cup, inv. unknown[1]

This cup is remarkably finely potted and in this respect is unlike other pieces made at the Saint-Cloud factory. It has evidently been turned on the lathe, like its counterpart in the Victoria and Albert Museum, in order to achieve the crisp shape. The decoration can be related in general terms to that found on Saint-Cloud examples, but here it is organised and executed

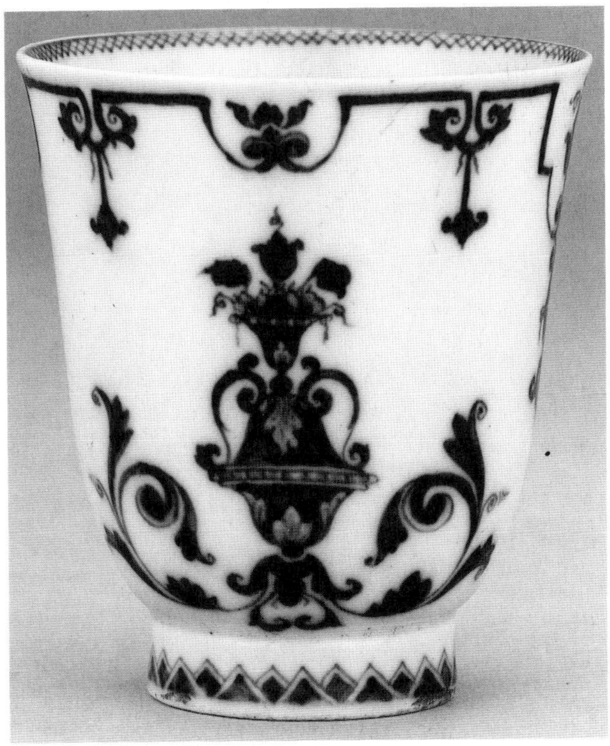

1

with noticeable care. The discoloured foot rim is diagnostic of Saint-Cloud.

Although in the past it has been classified as one of the products of the Rouen factory, it does not correspond with the small group of pieces which could be attributed to Rouen on the grounds of their similarity to the mustard-pot and cover painted in underglaze-blue with the arms of the Rouen politician Asselin de Villequier.[2] All of these exhibit a distinctly bluish glaze, whereas the glaze on the cup is clear and exceptionally shiny in appearance.

1. The author is grateful to Bernard Dragesco for bringing this piece to her attention. The writer has handled neither of the Paris examples, but in November 1991 she re-examined them in the Museum gallery and is now of the opinion that they are different from the London pieces. The paste is less white, they are more clumsily potted and the underglaze-blue decoration is less assured.
2. Musée national de Céramique, Sèvres, inv. 4006 illus. in colour by Frégnac, 1964, p. 39.

2 Vase, *c.* 1700–10

See colour plate 1

H. 15 cm
Marks: none
Reg. No. FB 26 (AF 3193)

Soft-paste porcelain, globular with six moulded 'ribs' on the body, flared foot rim, unevenly glazed. Decorated in underglaze-blue with scrolls and stylised leaves on the body, a zigzag pattern on the foot and a trellis pattern with dots on the neck. Thick colourless glaze is visible at the top of the ribs; the glaze on the foot is opaque. Chip to rim.

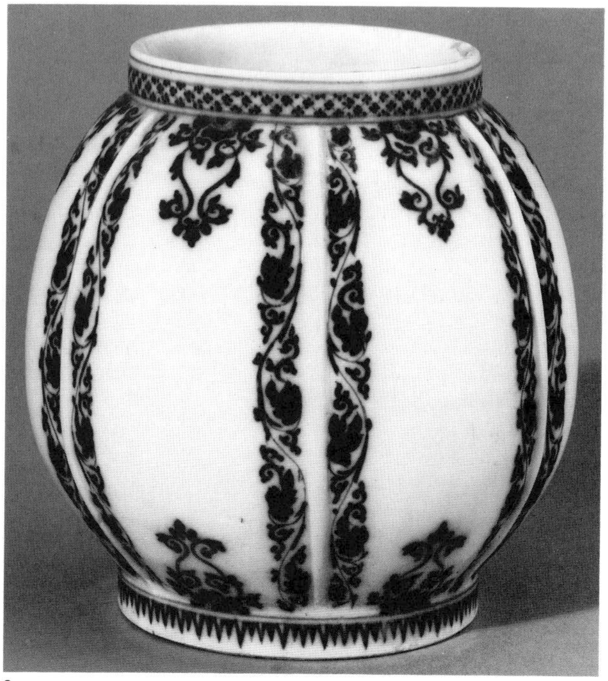

2

Provenance: Bequeathed by Sir A.W. Franks, 1897

Literature: Savage, 1960, pl. 2b; 1970 edition, colour illus. on jacket

Comparable Examples: Comte X. de Chavagnac Collection, sold, Paris, Hôtel Drouot, 19 June 1911, Lot 64, sold to 'de Chavagnac' for 405 francs

The form of this vase, which may once have had a cover, is reminiscent of a marked Saint-Cloud *pot-pourri* in the Musée des arts décoratifs, Paris,[1] although it has no 'ribs' in relief. A vase with 'ribs' from a French private collection, apparently unmarked, was exhibited at the Musée historique du Parc de Saint-Cloud in May–June 1980.[2] A vase from the Chavagnac Collection, measuring 16 cm in height and extremely similar in appearance to the Museum example, was attributed without hesitation by its owner to the Saint-Cloud factory.[3]

The colour of the body and glaze of this piece (with the exception of the blue-toned glaze on the foot) can be usefully compared with that of the salt-cellar Franks 330.

The decoration suggests an early eighteenth-century date.

1. Illus. Frégnac, 1964, p. 57.
2. Exh. Saint-Cloud, 1980, no. 16, p. 5, illus.
3. See comparable examples.

3 Salt-cellar, *c.* 1700–10

D. *of base:* 8.8 cm
Marks: sun face painted in underglaze-blue
Reg. No: Franks 329

Soft-paste porcelain with a lead glaze; of waisted form with a flared foot moulded with a ribbed pattern near the base and on the projecting rim. Painted in underglaze-blue with a stylised flower and scroll pattern, and in the central well with a *style rayonnant* device. The motifs are enclosed by a blue line, and both foot and rim are defined by a rather unevenly painted blue line. Rim restored.

Provenance: Bequeathed by Sir A.W. Franks, 1897

Literature: Franks, 1896, no. 329

Savage, 1960, colour illus. on jacket

Comparable Examples: Numerous (see cat. 4)

The form doubtless derives from a metalwork prototype. The crazed matt appearance of the glaze on the upper surface suggests over-firing.

Even more elaborate radiating motifs can be found on tin-glazed earthenware from Rouen.

Several different forms of salt-cellar were made at Saint-Cloud, notably a rectangular model.[1] An octagonal form with relief decoration was sold unpainted.[2]

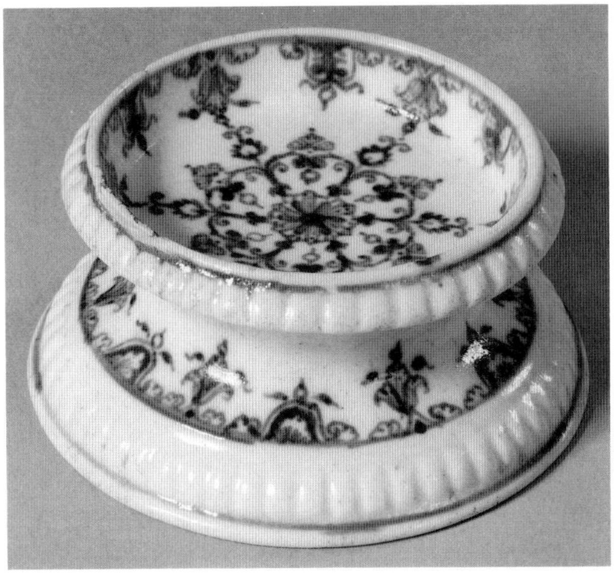

3

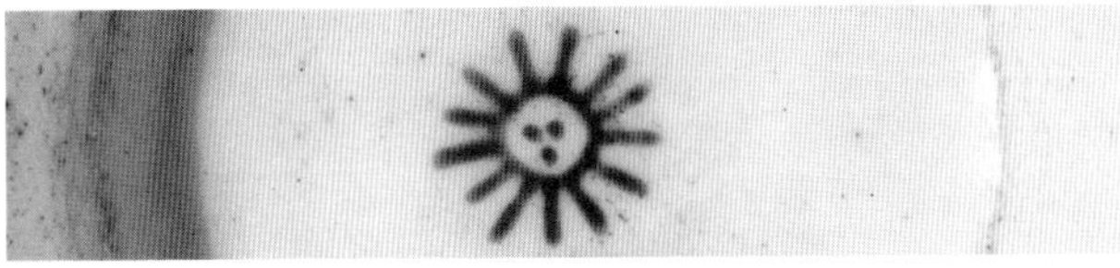

3 *mark*

1. Malgras (ed.), 1983, p. 75, collection and dimensions unrecorded. A similar salt-cellar was on the London market in 1989.
2. Parke-Bernet, New York, 16 May 1959, Lot 227, L. $3\frac{1}{8}$ in. and $3\frac{7}{8}$ in., Thelma Chrysler Foy Collection.

4 **Salt-cellar,** *c.* 1700–10

See colour plate I

D. *of base:*	8.5 cm
Marks:	sun face painted in underglaze-blue
Reg. No:	Franks 330

Soft-paste porcelain with a lead glaze; of waisted form with a flared foot moulded with ribbed pattern near the base on the projecting rim. Painted in underglaze-blue with a stylised flower and scroll pattern enclosed on the inner rim only with a blue line, and in the central well with a *style rayonnant* pattern. Painted blue line on outer surface of rim and foot. Rim chipped.

Provenance: Bequeathed by Sir A.W. Franks, 1897

Literature: Franks, 1896, no. 330

Comparable Examples: Paris, Musée des arts décoratifs, inv. D 33199, similar pattern, sun face mark, D. 8.2 cm

Private Collection, illus. Dallot-Naudin and Jacob, 'Saint-Cloud I', 1983, p. 77

This piece is comparable with cat. 3 although it differs slightly in both its dimensions and decoration, which is slightly less elaborate. Further variations on the decorative theme can be found on a salt-cellar in the Victoria and Albert Museum[1] and on another in the

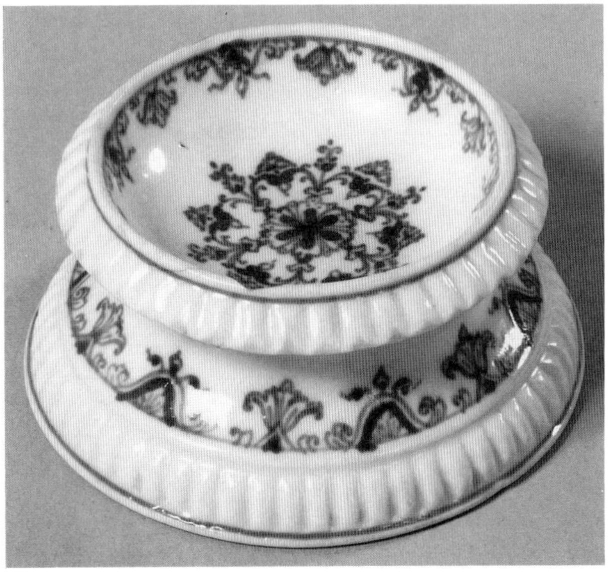

4

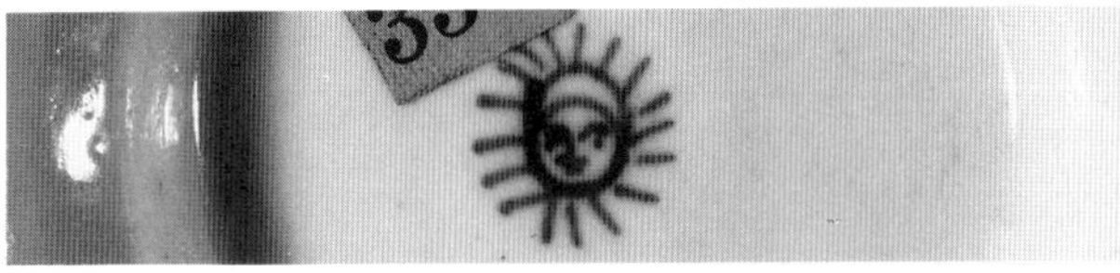

4 *mark*

collection belonging to Simon Goldblatt, Esq., which was sold at Sotheby's in 1956.[2]

1. Illus. Honey, 1950, pl. 6a.
2. Sotheby's, 1 May 1956, Lot 85, bearing the mark of a cottage.

5 ***Trembleuse* Cup and Saucer,** *c.* 1700–10

See colour plate I

D. *of saucer:*	12.5 cm
H. *of cup:*	7.5 cm
Marks:	sun face painted in underglaze-blue on both
Reg. No.	Franks 331

Soft-paste porcelain, the handleless cup highly translucent. Ribbed moulding on body of bell-shaped cup, which has a shallow foot, and on the deep saucer, except near the rim. The saucer has a gallery in the centre, and a shallow foot. Both are painted in underglaze-blue with stylised flowers alternating with bushes on shaped pedestals near the rim and a zigzag pattern on the foot of the cup, the outside of the gallery and the outer surface of the saucer. Two blue lines are rather unevenly painted on the inside of the cup and around the outer edge of the foot rim. Two small chips to the gallery.

Provenance: Bequeathed by Sir A.W. Franks, 1897

Literature: Franks, 1896, no. 331

Savage, 1960, colour illus. on jacket

Comparable Examples: Paris, Musée des arts décoratifs, inv. D959, sun face mark

Limoges, Musée national Adrien-Dubouché, inv. 2865, unmarked, acquired in 1873

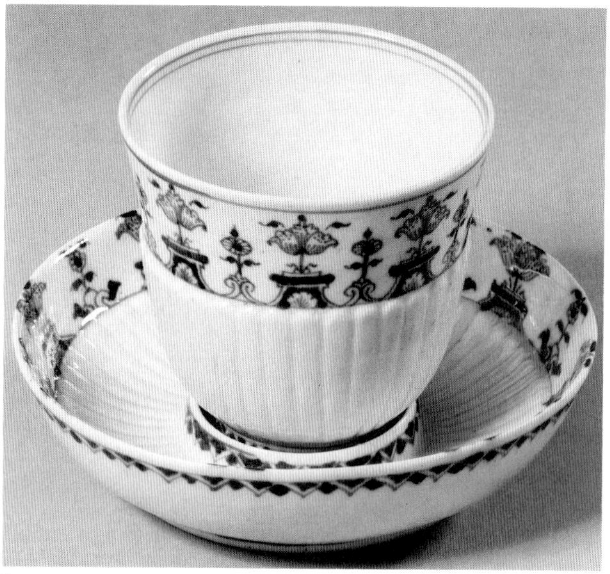

5

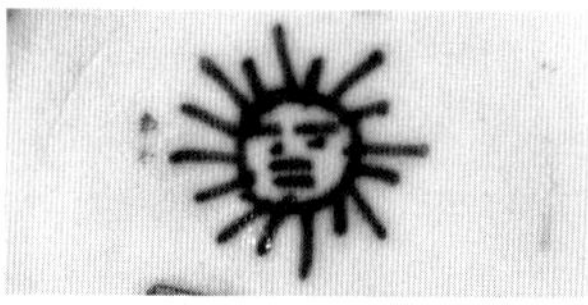

5 *mark (cup)*

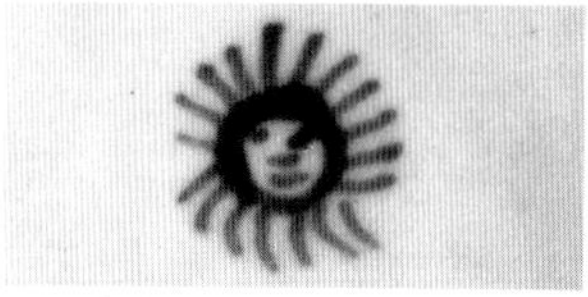

5 *mark (saucer)*

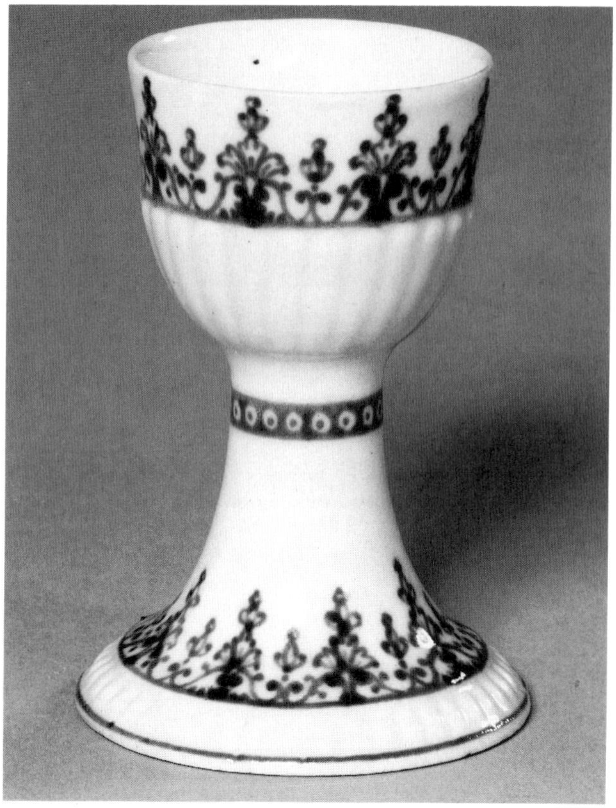

6

In the Musée national Adrien-Dubouché, Limoges, there is a waster of a collapsed cup with similar decoration, which was acquired from the Gasnault Collection in 1881, regrettably without any provenance. The British Museum example, despite rather uneven glaze and poor moulding on the cup, is of good quality, and is surprisingly different in both paste and potting from Franks 336 (cat. 24).

6 **Egg Cup**, *c.* 1700–10
See colour plate 2

H.	8 cm
Marks:	none
Reg. No.	Franks 332

Soft-paste porcelain, ribbed moulding near foot and on lower part of bowl. Convex base. Decorated in underglaze-blue with a regularly-painted stylised shell and scroll pattern, and a band of blue with white circles containing dots. Chip to rim.

Provenance: Bequeathed by Sir A.W. Franks, 1897

Literature: Franks, 1896, no. 332

Comparable Examples: None

The rather greyish tone of the blue suggests overfiring, confirmed by slight blisters near the foot. Although of different dimensions and with a differently formed foot, the decoration on this egg cup is similar to that of Franks 354 which bears the mark of the Mennecy factory.

Egg cups were made in at least one other form at the Saint-Cloud factory, including one with a different stem.[1]

1. For an example in the Musée des arts décoratifs, Paris, with a different foot and more elaborate stem, see Dupont, 1987, p. 20, fig. 2; an example in the Bowes Museum, Barnard Castle, County Durham, inv. Cer. 1988.349, with the sun face mark, of another differing form, is illustrated by P. Klaber, 'The Enid Goldblatt Collection', *Antique Collector*, October 1987, p. 86, fig. 5.

7 **Mug** (*chope*), *c.* 1715–20
See colour plate 1

H.	9.1 cm
Max. D.	8.1 cm
Marks:	none
Reg. No.	1987,12-6,1

Soft-paste porcelain, heavily potted, cylindrical, divided into eight compartments by eight groups of two vertically incised lines. The scroll-form strap handle is out-turned at both ends; shallow foot rim and glazed foot. The decoration consists of complex interlocking scrolls and a flower-like motif near rim and foot with wide panels alternating with similar stylised bell flowers enclosing a daisy head in the narrow panels, all in underglaze-blue.

Provenance: Presented by his family in loving memory of Richard Russell, 1987

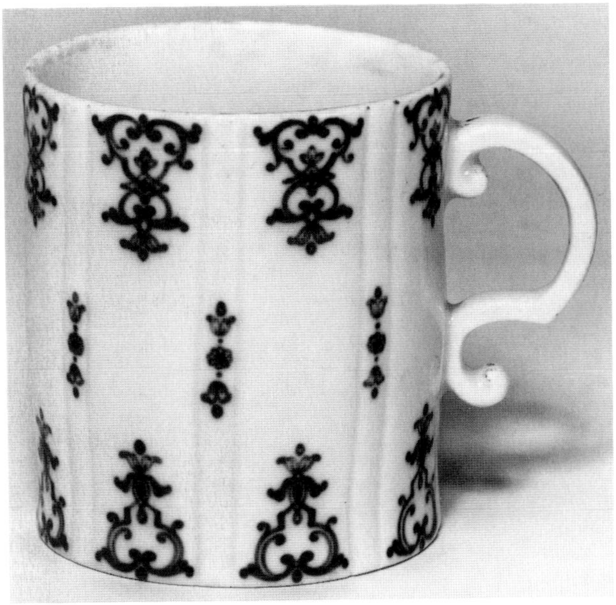

7

Literature: A. Dawson *et al.*, 'Recent acquisitions of post-medieval ceramics and glass in the British Museum's Department of Medieval and Later Antiquities', *Burlington Magazine*, Vol. CXXX, no. 1022, May 1988, p. 400, fig. 79

Comparable Examples: USA, California, Gillian Wilson Collection, H. 7.5 cm, unmarked, with turned and underglaze-blue decoration

The mug was apparently fired on its rim, where there are traces of bedding material.

The baroque handle, the simple shape of the mug and its *Régence*-style decoration all indicate an early date of production. However, the quality of the underglaze-blue and the precision of the painting are remarkable and show considerable technical accomplishment.

Few mugs seem to have been produced at French porcelain factories, perhaps because wine rather than beer was the usual drink, although covered mugs of much the same size were made at Vincennes,[1] and a Chantilly example without a cover measuring 13 cm in height and painted in the *chinoiserie* style is recorded.[2] Tournay manufactured mugs later in the eighteenth century.[3] Another Saint-Cloud mug with a cover and metal mount painted in the Kakiemon style[4] testifies to the long-lasting appeal of the mug at this factory.

An umarked pot and cover decorated with similar motifs to those on the Museum mug and whose domed cover is also divided into sections by incised lines is in the Musée des arts décoratifs, Paris.[5] Incised decoration seems to be characteristic of Saint-Cloud porcelain made in the first half of the eighteenth century and of its white glazed productions. The arrangement of the underglaze-blue motifs reached great heights of sophistication, as in the scroll, strapwork and stylised floral designs found on a water jug and cover and its matching basin in the Musée national de Céramique, Sèvres.[6]

1. See exh. Vincennes, 1977–8, p. 125, no. 369; a slightly smaller example is illus. in 'Eighteenth-Century French Porcelain', exh. Williams, 1978, no. 13, and a larger covered example, *ibid.*, no. 4. Another covered example, and one without a cover, were sold at Christie's, New York, The Elizabeth Parke Firestone Collection, Part I: Important French Porcelain, 21–22 March 1991, Lots 178, 179.
2. Malgras (ed.), 1983, p. 34. Another painted with a dragon was sold at Christie's, New York, The Elizabeth Parke Firestone Collection, Part I: Important French Porcelain, 21–22 March 1991, Lot 54, and a comparable piece in the Victoria and Albert Museum, London, is referred to in the catalogue, illus. Savage, 1960, pl. 18b.
3. C. Deroubaix, *Les porcelaines de Tournai du Musée de Mariemont*, Mariemont, 1958, pl. 41, no. 875. The decoration of this piece may indicate an early-nineteenth century date; see also pl. 45, no. 939.
4. Illustrated in an advertisement in *Apollo*, Vol. XCIX, no. 148, June 1974, p. 119, for exh. Williams, 1974.
5. Inv. MAD 8334, H. without cover about 10.8 cm.
6. Illus. F. Labayle, *La porcelaine de Saint-Cloud*, Rennes, 1982, pp. 19–21.

8 **Triple Spice Box** (*boîte à épices*), or triple salt-cellar, *c.*1715–20

See colour plate I

H.	8.1 cm
Marks:	none
Reg. No.	Franks 333

Soft-paste porcelain, in two parts. The lower consists of three shaped receptacles each resting on a paw foot with a central well into which the drum-shaped centre of the upper part fits. The upper part consists of three similarly-shaped covers, articulated by means of a metal fitting. There is a moulded chrysanthemum around the base of the cauliflower knop. Cover and sides decorated in underglaze-blue with a stylised pattern of flowers and leaves, rim of upper part painted blue interrupted by a pattern of white horn-like motifs. Base glazed except for an oblong area in the centre around the metal fitment. Knop restuck, one cover repaired.

Provenance: Bequeathed by Sir A.W. Franks, 1897

Literature: Franks, 1896, no. 333

Comparable Examples: London, Victoria and Albert Museum, illus. Honey, 1950, pl. 5B

Saumur, Château de Saumur, Musée des arts decoratifs, illus. H. Landais, *French Porcelain*, London, 1961, fig. 13, and *The Castle of Saumur and the Museum of Applied Arts* guidebook compiled by Monique Jacob, 1980, pl. LXVI

Sèvres, Musée national de Cèramique, illus. Frégnac, 1964, pp. 58–9

Exh. Saint-Cloud, 1980, no. 27

Northamptonshire, Althorp, Earl Spencer Collection, see R.J. Charleston, 'Sèvres and Other French Porcelain in Earl Spencer's

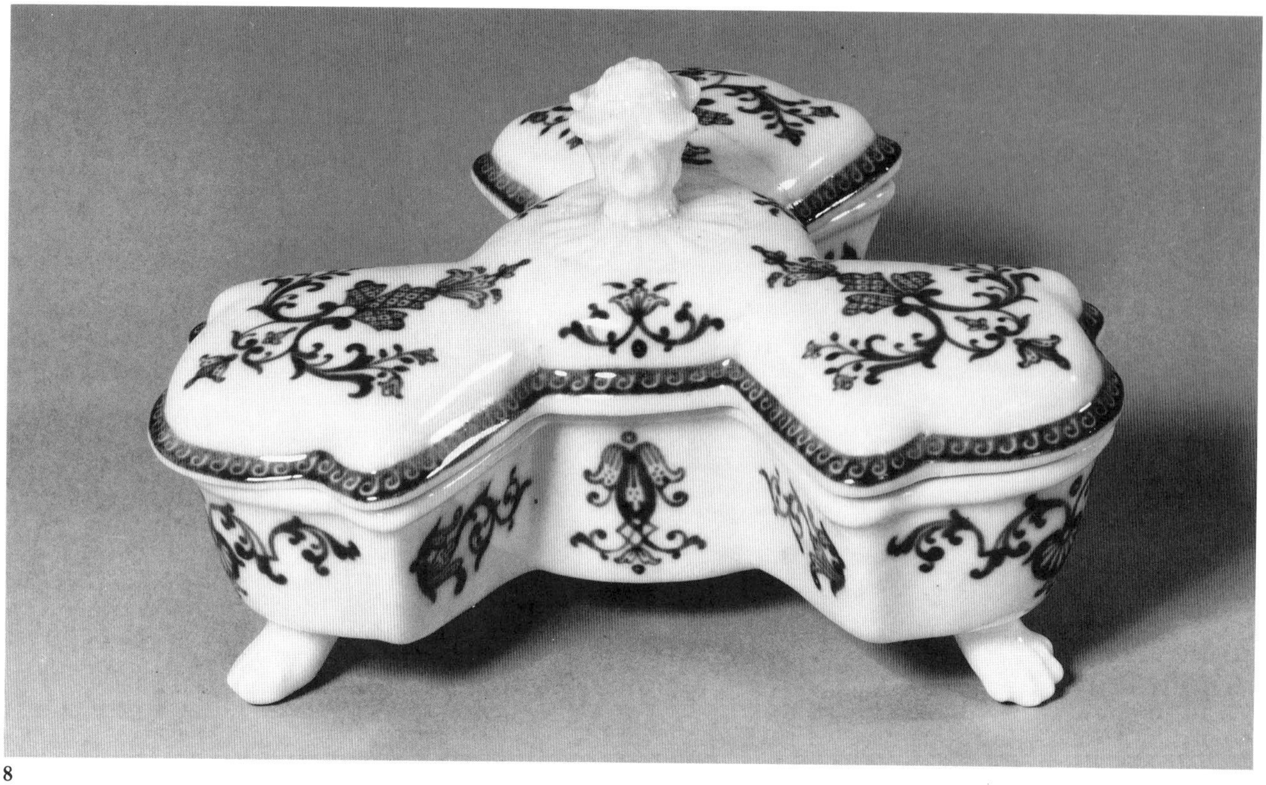

8

Collection at Althorp', *Connoisseur*, Vol. CLXXIII, No. 696, February 1970, p. 77, fig. 1

Christie's, 30 June 1975, Lot 86; 26 March 1984, Lot 155

The shape appears to be peculiar to the Saint-Cloud factory in French porcelain[1] although it is known in tin-glazed earthenware from Rouen,[2] and the knop is found on tureens made at the Saint-Cloud factory.[3] Double spice boxes mounted in silver are also recorded.[4]

Meissen triple spice boxes appear in the factory records as 'Creutzformigte Dosen' from 1725. In July 1737 the modeller Eberlein is documented as making a new model of this form, perhaps a revision of the original one.[5]

1. Honey, 1950, p. 10.
2. See Faïences françaises, 1980, no. 331, Paris, Musée des arts décoratifs, inv. 23 243.
3. As on an example painted with *chinoiseries* in the Musée des arts décoratifs, Paris, illus. Malgras (ed.), 1983, p. 108, and on another in the same museum, undecorated, with reliefs of exotic birds and flowers, p. 98.
4. Malgras (ed.), 1983, p. 75, of tomb form, collection unrecorded; p. 77, oval, private collection.
5. The author is indebted to Dr R. Rückert of the Bayerisches Nationalmuseum, Munich, for this information.

9 **Cane-handle**, first quarter of 18th century

See colour plate 2

H. 5.4 cm
Marks: none
Reg. No. Franks 334

Soft-paste porcelain, hollow, moulded with ribs which are continued on the pommel except for the centre. Painted in underglaze-blue with a zigzag and circle pattern at the lower end, a Bérainesque motif, and on the pommel a stylised flower.

Provenance: Bequeathed by Sir A.W. Franks, 1897

Literature: Franks, 1896, no. 334

Comparable Examples: Paris, Musée des arts décoratifs, inv. D30348, H. 5 cm, painted with similar motifs

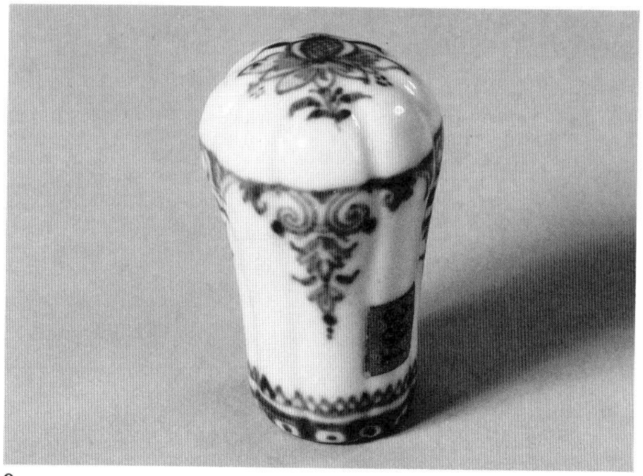

9

Cane-handles were made during the early part of the factory's existence and this example, on the evidence of its decoration, can be probably dated to the beginning of the eighteenth century. Ribbed moulded handles such as this survive in much smaller quantity than simpler pommel forms, which are known in several sizes.[1]

For a study of cane-handles, see Dike and Bezzaz.[2]

1. Some can be found in the Musée des arts décoratifs, Paris, and see Malgras (ed.), 1983, p. 77, private collection, and p. 85, private collection.
2. C. Dike and G. Bezzaz, *La canne, objet d'art*, Paris, 1988.

10 **Knife and Fork with Porcelain Handles**, second quarter of 18th century

L. *of handle:*	7.5 cm (knife); 6.3 cm (fork)
Total L. *of knife:*	21 cm
Total L. *of fork:*	16.9 cm
Marks:	none
Reg. No:	FB 30 (AF 3230)

Soft-paste porcelain, each moulded with two panels of strapwork, scrolls and a flower. Silver ferrules and steel blade and tines.

Provenance: Bequeathed by Sir A.W. Franks, 1897

Literature: Unpublished

Comparable Examples: Paris, Musée des arts décoratifs, illus. G. Benker, *Alte Bestecke*, Munich, 1978, pl. 251

Manchester, City Art Gallery, inv. 1947. 811, Macdonald, 1986, no. 79

Ruth Parke Firestone Collection, illustrated R. Berges, 'Mennecy Porcelains from the Ruth Parke Firestone Collection', *Connoisseur*, Vol. 170, no.686, April 1969, p. 248, fig. 2, two fork handles

E & H Manners, London, exhibited International Ceramics Fair and Seminar Ltd., London, June 1990

It has been suggested by Anthony North of the Victoria and Albert Museum that the form of the handle is related to earlier ivory knife handles.

By analysis[1] the porcelain was found to be non-phosphatic. Its origin has been the subject of some discussion but the author is inclined to attribute it to the Saint-Cloud factory. As Sally MacDonald remarked,[2] the body of the Manchester knife and fork is characteristically yellow in tone like other Saint-Cloud pieces.

On the basis of the style of the ornament, a date of manufacture during the second quarter of the eighteenth century is suggested. An advertisement published by Chavagnac and Grollier in 1906,[3] issued on behalf of the 'La Manufacture Royale Des Porcelaines de Saint-Cloud, Ruë de la Madeleine, Faubourg S. Honoré, à Paris' by Dominique-François Chicaneau, announced all the different items which he

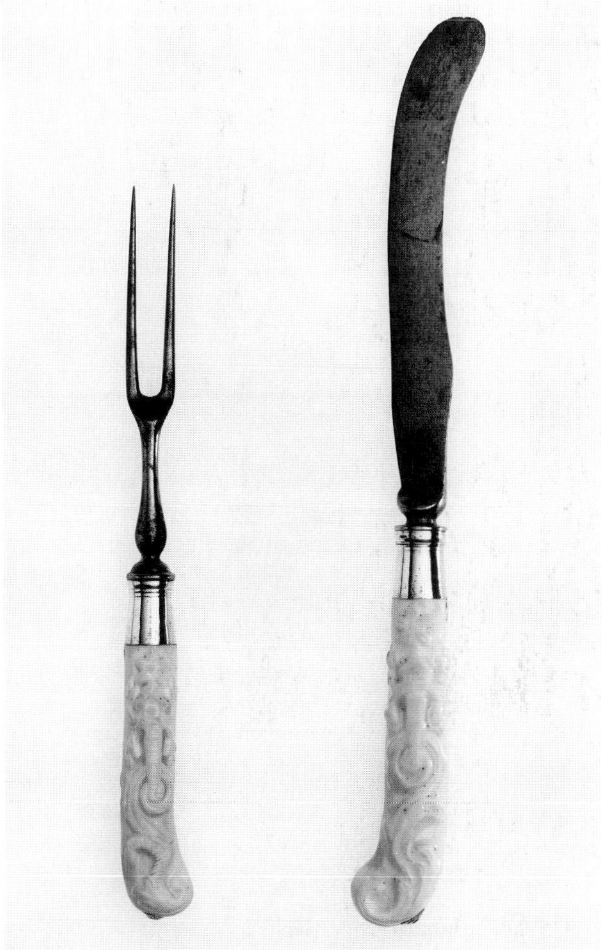

10

made and sold both wholesale and retail. It includes 'toutes sortes de Manches en relief, en couleurs & en bleu pour couteaux, Cuillières & Fourchettes'. The advertisement, printed in 1741, concludes 'Le tout sans sursaire. 1731.', so that we may conclude that the factory had been manufacturing handles well before that date.

The knife blade is of English workmanship. From bills preserved in the Department of Prints and Drawings from the razor-maker James Bernadeau,[4] it is clear that shagreen cases were fitted out to contain sets of knives and forks. A case of this kind containing similar but not identical knives and forks was exhibited by Winifred Williams, London, in July 1978.[5]

1. British Museum Research Laboratory, Weimer, 21 March 1962.
2. 'Porcelain from Europe', compiled by S. MacDonald, Manchester City Art Galleries, 1986, no. 79.
3. Chavagnac and Grollier, 1906, p. 32.
4. See cat. 41.
5. Exh. Williams, 1978, no. 60.

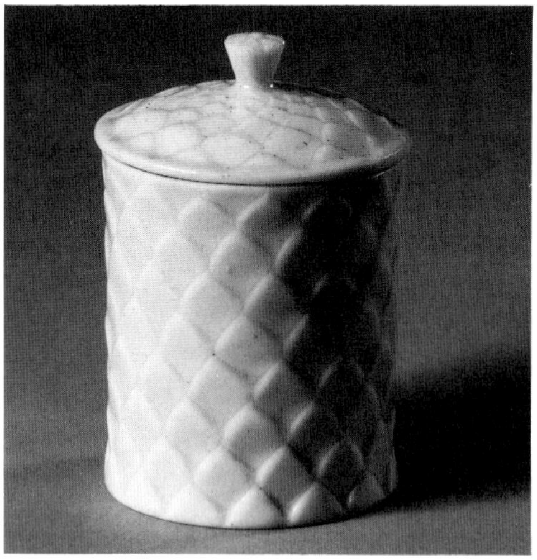

11

11 Toilet Pot and Cover, *c.* 1730–40

H. 7.3 cm
Marks: none
Reg. No. Franks 342

Soft-paste porcelain, highly translucent, straight sides with pointed-leaf moulding, small out-turned foot. The cover is slightly domed; it has the same moulding, continued on the flattened triangular knop. Glaze on knop contains numerous black specks and inner rim of lid still has sand, or other bedding material, adhering to it.

Provenance: Bequeathed by Sir A.W. Franks, 1897

Literature: Franks, 1896, no. 342

Comparable Examples: None noted[1]

The moulding is characteristic of Saint-Cloud and exists in a closely related version. The large number of small black specks visible in the colourless glaze on the cover suggests that this piece may have been second quality. Both the inner rim of the cover and part of the foot of the pot have a brownish stain, possibly from bedding material used to prevent pieces sticking to each other, or to their saggars, or containers.

1. Frégnac, 1964, pp. 64–5, shows teawares and toilet pots with a variation of the moulding used on this toilet pot.

12 Wine-cooler (*seau à rafraîchir*), *c.* 1730–40

D. 12.5 cm
Marks: t/S.C/T incised
Reg. No. Franks 340

Soft-paste porcelain with a lead glaze, moulded with a gadroon pattern on the out-turned foot, the lower part of the body and on the flange below the rim; two moulded rudimentary handles formed as grotesque heads, with pierced circular holes of differing sizes denoting the ears, eyes and mouth. The cooler is also decorated with a panel of moulded floral ornaments, including a chrysanthemum, on each side. Stepped foot.

Provenance: Bequeathed by Sir A.W. Franks, 1897

Literature: Franks, 1896, no. 340

Comparable Examples: Paris, Musée des arts décoratifs, inv. A6067, slightly smaller (D. 8.1 cm), minor variation in pattern, mark *S4C* and D32936A, *STCT* mark

Sotheby's, 23 November 1965, Lot 79, similar pattern with slight variation

USA, New York, Christie's, 3 December 1977, Lot 157 (illus. *Apollo*, Vol. CVI, no. 189, November 1977, p. 93, one of a pair)

The *seau* has several firing defects: it is warped, has a considerable number of inclusions in the porcelain body where the glaze does not 'fit', especially inside the vessel, and has an unintentional speck of blue on one of the flower stems, showing that it was probably made alongside decorated items, or perhaps even fired in close proximity to them. The moulding is noticeably faulty below one of the handles, and the glaze is a poor fit on the base. Such defects appear to be characteristic of pieces bearing the *STC* mark and its variations.

The gadroon moulding derives from contemporary metalwork. There was clearly a large market for these

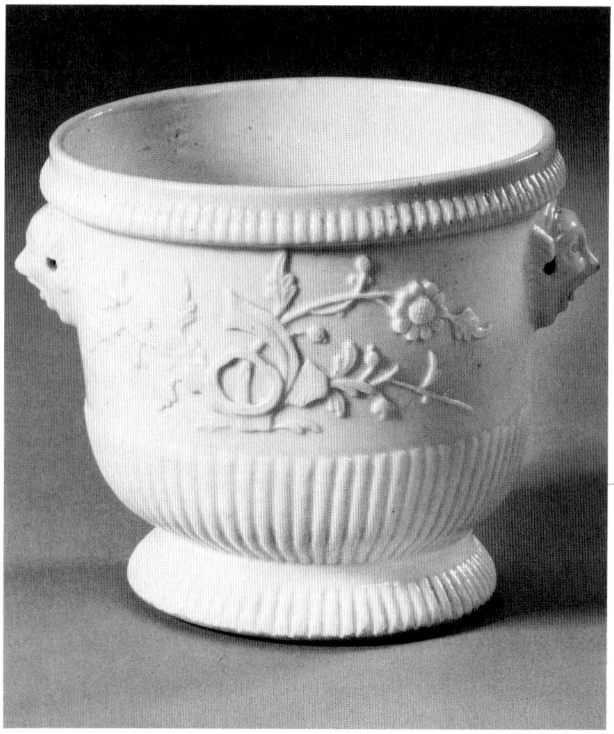

12

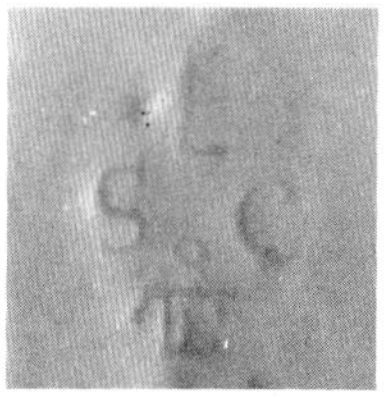

12 *mark*

wine-coolers, as many differing examples have been noted.[1] Madame de Pompadour owned around 60 Saint-Cloud wine-coolers at the time of her death in 1764. They were in use at Versailles, Compiègne and Fontainebleau.[2]

Two white *seaux* apparently of the same form as this piece, one with the neck of a green glass wine-bottle protruding from it, are shown in Nicolas Lancret's *Le Déjeuner de Jambon* painted in 1735 and now in the Museum of Fine Arts, Boston, USA.[3] This work is a study for a large painting made for the *petits appartements* at Versailles and now in the Musée Condé, Chantilly.

1. Malgras (ed.), 1983, pp. 92–7. A smaller and slightly differently-moulded example is in the Seattle Art Museum, USA, inv. Unit II 65.135, D. 12.4 cm.
2. J. Cordey, *Inventaire des Biens de Madame de Pompadour rédigé après son décès*, Paris, 1939, p. 63, no. 702, 'Trois sceaux [*sic*] à bouteilles, de Saint-Cloud; prisés neuf livres' (Versailles); p. 131, No. 1714, 'Vingt-huit sceaux [*sic*] blanc à relief, dont deux fêlés; quatre autres à liqueurs, dont un fêlé; quarante-deux autres à verres, dont un fêlé, prisés cent quatre-vingt-douze livres' (Compiègne); p. 134, no. 1758, 'Vingt-six sceaux [*sic*] blancs à bouteille, en relief, de Saint-Cloud, dont cinq mutilés, prisés cent livres' (Fontainebleau).
3. Illus. P.T. Rathbone, *The Forsyth Wickes Collection, Museum of Fine Arts, Boston*, Greenwich, Conn., 1968, col. pl. opp. p. 18 and Munger *et al.*, 1992, no. 15.

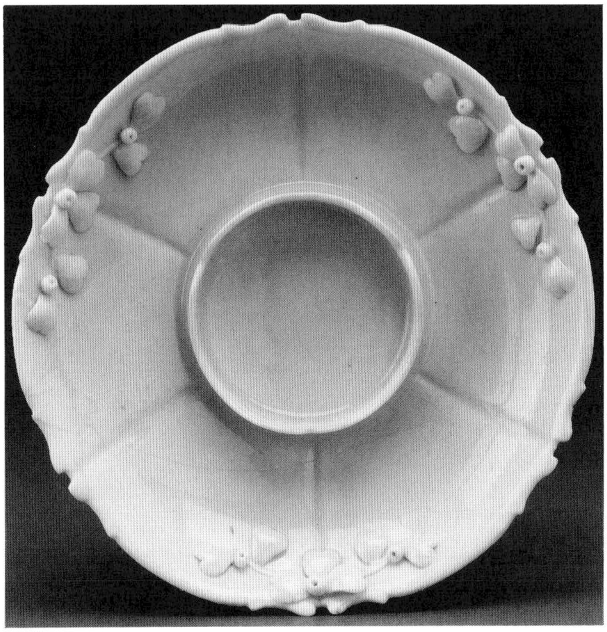

13

corded) is evidence that the moulded and relief pattern was used on several types of ware.[2]

1. Exh. Nord-Pas-de-Calais 1986–7, no. 35, attributed to Mennecy, although unmarked, dated to around 1750.
2. Malgras (ed.), 1983, p. 90, private collection; see also p. 102 for a sugar bowl and cover (whereabouts unrecorded) of similar pattern.

13 *Trembleuse* Saucer, *c.* 1730–40

D. 12.8 cm
Marks: none
Reg. No. Franks 343

Creamy-coloured soft-paste porcelain, heavily potted, moulded, the surface divided into six zones by five radiating depressions and with hexafoil rim of rococo outline; lobed gallery. Near the rim are three groups of applied flowering branches. Repaired.

Provenance: Bequeathed by Sir A.W.Franks, 1897

Literature: Franks, 1896, no. 343

Comparable Examples: Musée de Boulogne, inv. L 402, cup and saucer, D. of saucer, 13.2 cm[1]

Sotheby's, 5 December 1989, Lot 63 (part, cup and saucer).

Pieces such as these, with their characteristic incised lines and flowering branch ornament, are traditionally attributed to the Saint-Cloud factory despite the lack of factory mark. This may be explained by their origin in one of the branches of the factory, or alternatively as the work of imitators capitalising on the popularity of Saint-Cloud wares. It is also possible that such unmarked pieces may merely have been second-quality pieces made at Saint-Cloud.

A covered pot with a silver mount (marks unre-

14 Pair of Toilet Pots, *c.* 1730–35

H. 7.2 cm
Marks: none on porcelain; chancellor's mace *décharge* mark on silver-gilt mounts, used by the *sous-fermier* Jacques Cottin between September 1727 and December 1732 (Nocq, IV, p. 232)
Reg. No. Franks 344, 344A

Soft-paste porcelain with a lead glaze, cylindrical with slightly domed cover and flattened tapering knop. Silver-gilt mount. The ornamentation consists of gold in relief, partly enamelled green. On the cover of both pots are three female medallion heads in classical style within a strapwork frame, alternating with a small shell-like motif. The lower part of one (344) is ornamented with an exotic dancer in a tunic with a tambourine, Cupid and Psyche, two dancers and a musician as above, a leaping stag near a tree. The other pot (344A) is decorated as follows: three Indian or African warriors in short tunics, one playing a pipe (left), one dancing with an arrow (damaged, centre), the third dancing with a bow (right); on either side are trees with birds above; two lovers between trees; Cupid and Psyche near trees. Losses of gold and enamel.

Provenance: Bequeathed by Sir A.W. Franks, 1897

Literature: Franks, 1896, no. 344

Chavagnac and Grollier, 1906, p. 22

A. Dawson, 'Gold foil decoration on enamel, glass and porcelain: a new look', *Burlington Magazine*, Vol. CXXXII, no. 1046, May 1990, pp. 340–41, figs 49, 50

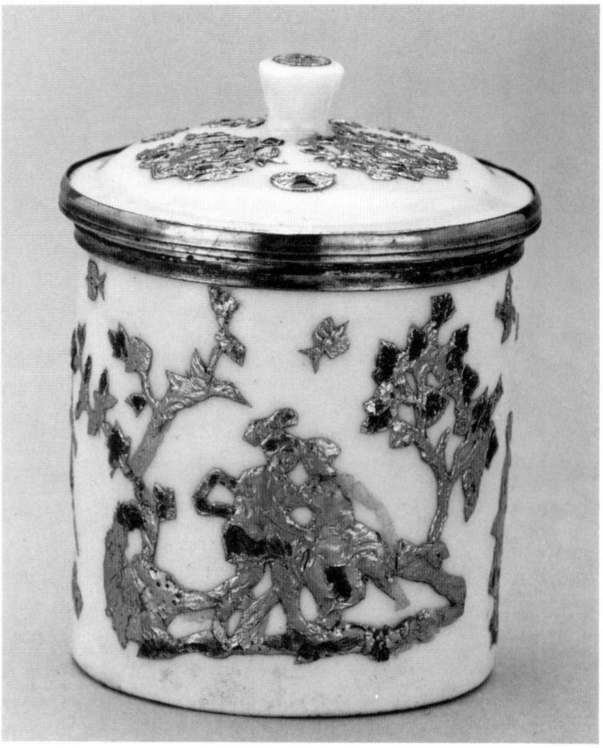

14 *Franks 344*

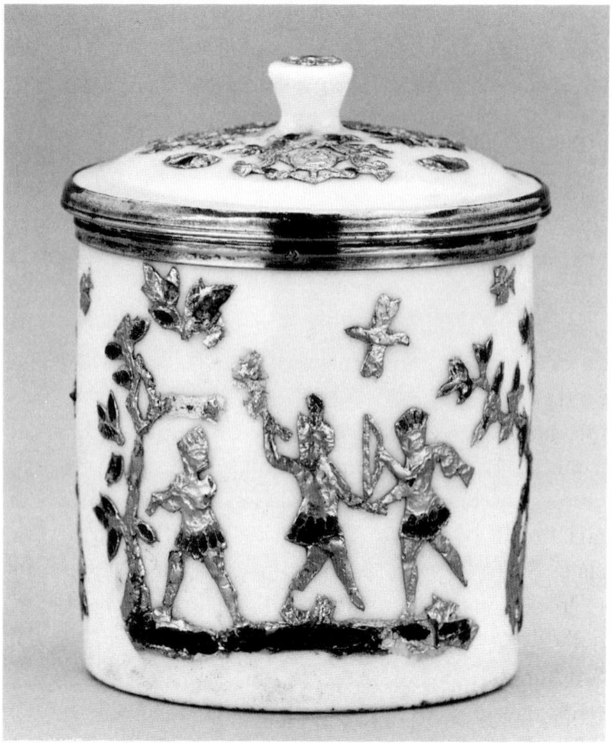

14 *Franks 344*

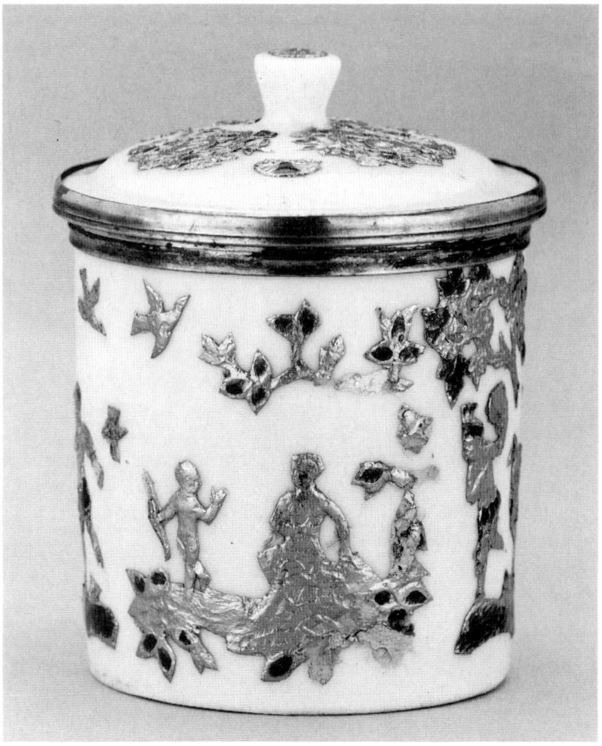

14 *Franks 344A*

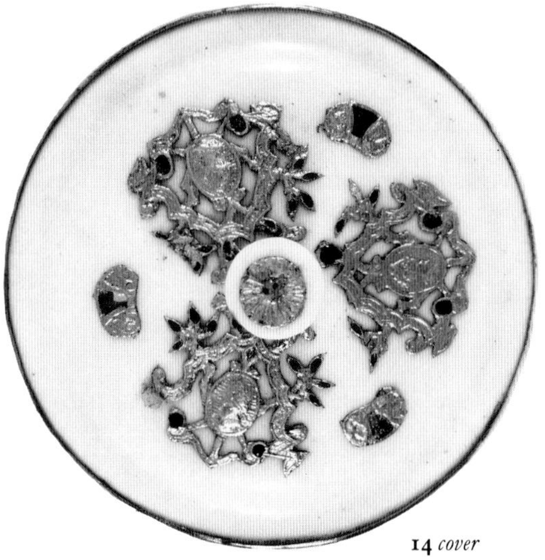

14 *cover*

Comparable Examples: Paris, Louvre, inv. OA 2371, cane-handle decorated with figure of flute-player similar to that on BM toilet pot, see R. de Plinval de Guillebon, *Musée du Louvre, département des objets d'art, Catalogue des Porcelaines françaises* I, Paris, 1992, no. 1

Paris, Musée des arts décoratifs, inv. D33302, cane-handle

Sèvres, Musée national de Céramique, inv. MNCS 8989, cane-handle[1]

England, private collection, hunting scene in extended form, and exotic figures with bow and arrow and playing a flute (this scene occurs on a snuff- or bonbon-box and cover enamelled green, reg. no. 1929,4–18,1)[2] with the addition of a stork, a pagoda on a rock and a tree, enamelled red and green

Russia, St Petersburg, State Hermitage Museum, sugar bowl and cover, Indian figure with tambourine running towards Cupid and Psyche on body and medallion heads in strapwork on cover

USA, New York, Metropolitan Museum, toilet pot and cover, inv. 47.117.1.A; sugar bowl and cover, inv. 64.101.358b

On stylistic grounds these pots can be dated to around 1730–35. In the absence of any factory marks they are tentatively attributed to the Saint-Cloud factory, but they may well have been made elsewhere, perhaps in one of the small Paris concerns operating at this period, about which we know very little. The decoration, for which the source has not been discovered, was done outside the factory, and has nothing to do with porcelain manufacture.[3] This is proved by the presence of similar scenes in the same technique on an enamel mustard-pot in a private collection in England,[4] and dancers – one with a bow, the other with an arrow – on the cover of a rectangular enamel box.[5] The making and application of these gold reliefs is likely to have been the work of a member of the Paris guild of *paillonneurs*, but as yet no information has come to light about this aspect of production.

Profile heads in the classical style within circular medallions have been noted in an engraving by Jean Bérain.[6]

1. Illus. Frégnac, 1964, p. 76.
2. Illus. Dawson, 1990, p. 341, figs. 51, 52.
3. This has been demonstrated in the case of Sèvres some 50 years later (see cat. 125); Le Guay and Parpette were taken on by the royal factory on a contract basis to assist in producing 'jewelled' pieces.
4. See Dawson, 1990, cited in cat. 15, n.2.
5. In a private collection, San Francisco, USA, decorated with gold reliefs and coloured enamels. The mounts appear to be later and are not date-marked.
6. J. de La Gorce, *Bérain, dessinateur du Roi Soleil*, Paris, 1986, p. 31.

15 **Snuffbox and Cover,** mount dated 1733

L. 8.7 cm

Marks: none on porcelain; silver-gilt mount marked as follows:
1) *a* crowned (charge mark for silver, Nocq IV, p. 232–3)
2) date-letter *R* for 1733 (Nocq IV, p. 215)
3) dog's head, (*décharge* mark for the *sous-fermier*, H. Louvet, Dec. 1732 – Oct. 1738 (Nocq, IV, p. 233)
4) maker's mark *CJC* below two *grains* and a fleur-de-lys crowned for C.-J.-B. Clérin, *maître* 18 July 1732 (Nocq, IV, p. 275)
5) another mark, twice

Reg. No. Franks 345

Soft-paste porcelain with a lead glaze, the lower part of *bombé* form, flat cover, silver-gilt mount with thumbpiece. The ornamentation consists of gold in relief, partly enamelled in emerald green. On the cover is a scene of a Chinese figure seated on a rock holding a bird opposite a tree in which a fox is perched; at the right is a pagoda; either side of the scene is a rosette and below an ornamental motif of X form. The lower part is decorated with three groups of a medallion head within a strapwork surround (as on the covers of cat. 14) separated by single rosettes and fleur-de-lys, a shell-and-branch motif, and at the corners by two further motifs, the lower one repeating the X motif on the cover. Where the gold is missing, a clear glaze-like substance is visible, on to which the gold, in the form of foil, appears to have been pressed. The green enamel is held in depressions or cages of differing outline. Both gold and enamel have been attached to the porcelain by means of a low-temperature firing. The surface of the gold is finely worked to depict contours and details of dress, leaves etc. Slight losses of gold and green enamel.

Provenance: Bequeathed by Sir A.W.Franks, 1897

Literature: Franks, 1986, no. 345

Chavagnac and Grollier, 1906, p. 22

Tait, 1962, pl. XVII; revised ed. 1972, pl. 27

Comparable Examples: USA, New York, Parke-Bernet, 3 April 1948, Lot 237, Mrs H. Dupuy Collection (previously Gilbert Lévy, Paris)

The medallion heads are related to those in the frontispiece of the first volume of *Parodies du Nouveau Théâtre Italien*, 1738,[1] the engraving signed 'Mathey fecit'. The source of the orientalising ornament is unknown. In style the decoration is midway between the stiff, formalised Régence and rococo fantasy. The shape of the box betrays its rococo inspiration.

Technically the decoration is peculiar to a small

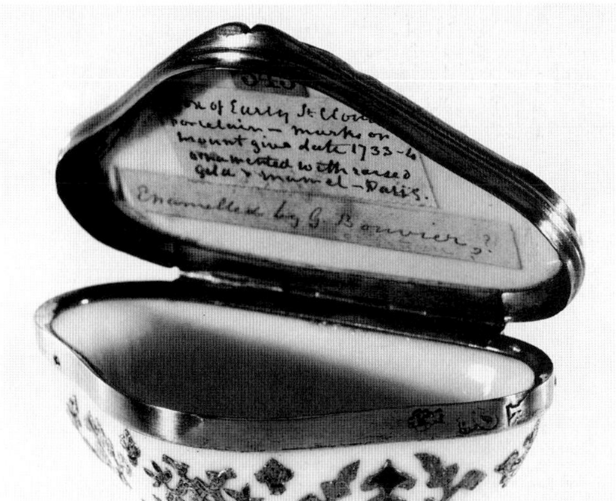

15

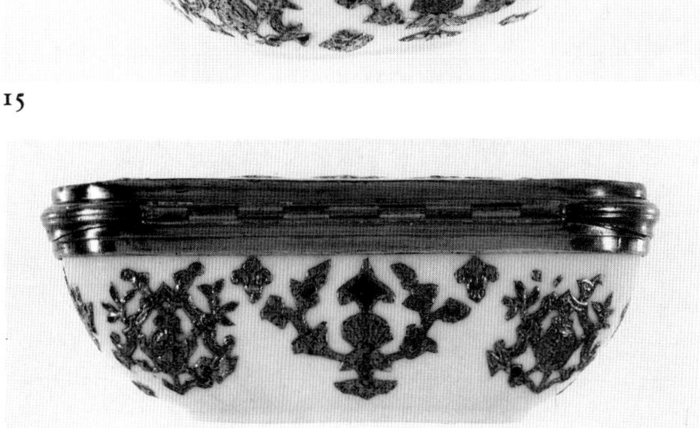

15 *back of box*

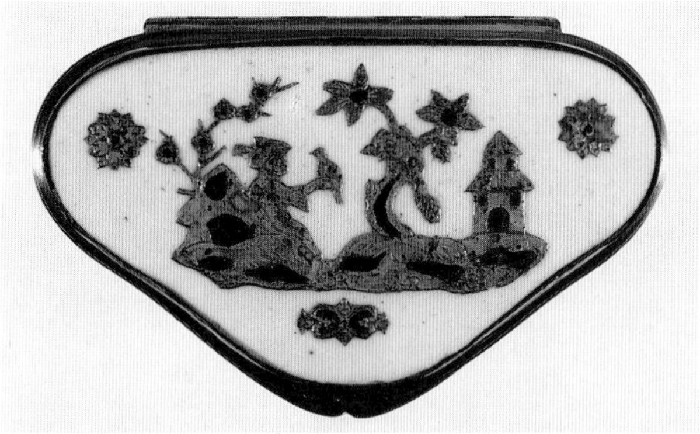

15 *lid*

group of pieces including the toilet pots (cat. 14) which are attributed to the Saint-Cloud factory. The decoration may well have been done outside the factory by a member of the guild of *paillonneurs*, but this has not yet been securely established.[2] In the present state of knowledge, even the origin of the porcelain, invariably unmarked, is not entirely certain.

1. There is a copy of this in the Bibliothèque de l'Arsenal, Paris.
2. For a survey of gold relief decoration on various materials, see A. Dawson, 'Gold foil decoration on enamel, glass and porcelain: a new look', *Burlington Magazine*, Vol. CXXXII, no. 1046, May 1990, pp. 336–42

16 **Cat**, *c.* 1735–45

H. 4.6 cm
L. 6.8 cm
Marks: none
Reg. No. 1923,3–14,135

Soft-paste porcelain with a lead glaze, hollow, moulded in one piece, painted in yellow, green, blue and orange enamels with flowers, insects, a building and figures, in the oriental style. The cat's mouth and eyebrows are painted in orange and the eyes are green.

Provenance: Presented by the Rt. Hon. Viscount Dillon, FSA, in memory of his son, 1923

Literature: Tait, 1962, pl. XVII; revised ed. 1972, pl. 17

Comparable Examples: Limoges, Musée national Adrien-Dubouché, inv. 1065, mounted, illus. H.-P. Fourest, *La Céramique française*, Milan, 1982, pl. 208, and Beaucamp-Markowsky, 1985, pp. 426, 448.

London, Victoria and Albert Museum, inv. C.1311–1919, with silver mounts bearing Paris discharge mark 1738–44

Private collection, illus. in R. Steiskal-Paur, 'Kostbarkeiten aus Porzellan', *Weltkunst*, 15 October 1982, fig. 14, p. 2901

USA, New York, Christie's, Christner Collection, Vol. III, 9 June 1979, Lot 133 (called Chantilly *c.* 1745), silver mounts

Phillips, 8 June 1988, Lot 193, silver mounts

Sussex, Sotheby's, 22 May 1991, Lot 873, modern mounts

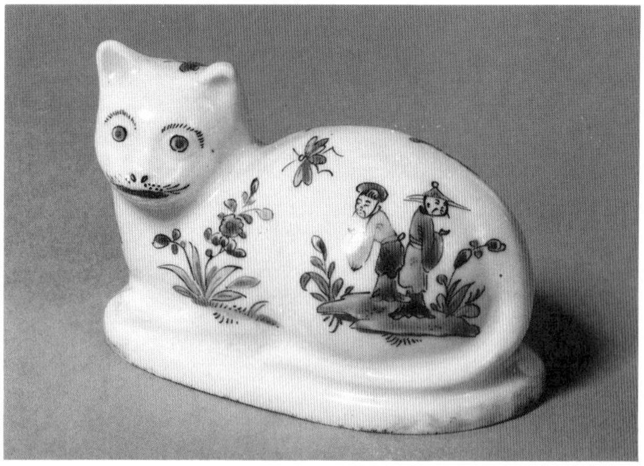

16

The piece was evidently intended to be mounted as a box. A dog mounted in silver is in the Musée des arts décoratifs, Paris,[1] with same type of decoration and gilding. A rather different cat in the same collection is mounted in silver-gilt, the mount stamped with the *décharge* mark used in Paris between 1738 and 1744.[2] Other animals, such as a lamb, a hare and a spaniel, were clearly part of the same series and are similarly decorated.[3]

1. Inv. MAD 32 707, dog's head discharge mark for the *sous-fermier* H. Louvet, Dec. 1732–Oct. 1738. The author is grateful to Gérard Mabille for providing information about this piece.
2. Jarry, 1981, p. 113, fig. 116.
3. Beaucamp-Markowsky, 1985, pp. 448–9.

17 **Snuffbox Top, or Base**, 1730–45

D. 7.3 cm
Marks: none
Reg. No. 1934,7–22,12

Soft-paste porcelain, edge unglazed, decorated on both sides in opposite directions in green, yellow, blue, orange and gold with *chinoiserie* scenes of figures, a pagoda in front of a hill and a tree, and a plant, all outlined in orange. Slight chip to rim.

Provenance: Presented by Mrs Willoughby Hodgson, 1934

Literature: Tait, 1962, pl. XVII; revised ed. 1972, pl. 17

Comparable Examples: None

Traces of wear around the rim on both sides suggest that this plaque was once mounted in silver or silver-gilt as the base or cover of a box. Examples of that form decorated in the same palette with similar scenes have been seen in the trade.[1] The mounts on such boxes frequently bear the Paris *décharge* mark of a griffin's head used by the *sous-fermier* Hubert Louvet between 1732 and 1738 or the mark of a dog's head

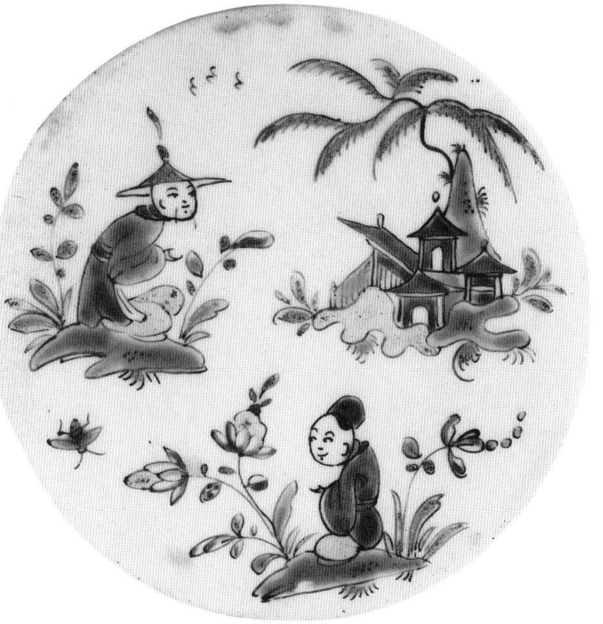

17

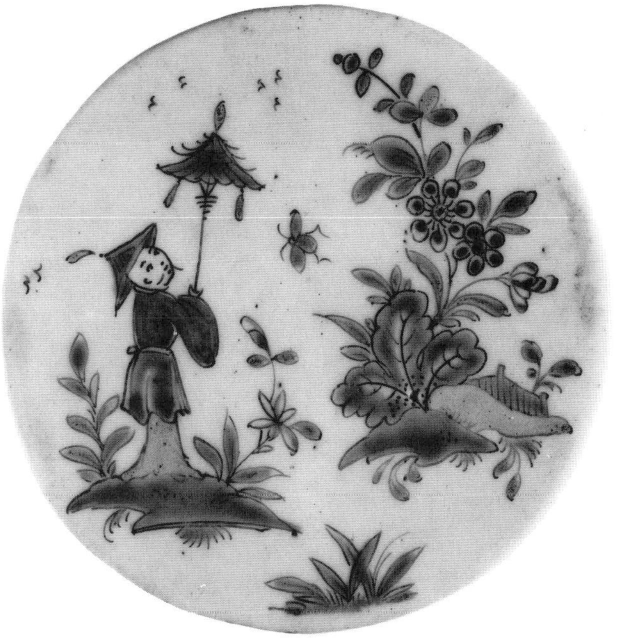

used by the *fermier* Louis Robin from 1 October 1738 until September 1744.

1. For example with Vandermeersch, Paris, exh. International Ceramics Fair and Seminar Ltd., London, June 1988; an example in the Musée des arts décoratifs, Paris, is illus. in Jarry, 1981, p. 109, fig. 111.

18 *Trembleuse* Teabowl and saucer, *c.* 1740

D. *of saucer:* 12.5 cm
H. *of cup:* 7 cm
Marks: none; printed label *Lot 362* on saucer
Reg. No. FB 8 (AF 3211)

Creamy-coloured soft-paste porcelain, heavily potted, moulded, the upper surface divided into panels by depressions, lobed rims. The saucer, similarly moulded, has a lobed gallery. Decorated in blue, green, yellow, red-brown and dark brown enamels with stylised flowers and a banded hedge in the Kakiemon style. Green trefoil leaf outlined in brown painted in centre.

Provenance: Bequeathed by Sir A.W. Franks, 1897

Literature: Unpublished

Comparable Examples: None noted

There are tiny gritty inclusions visible inside the cup, which is unevenly glazed near the foot, and several small blackened firecracks on the base of the saucer. The base of the teabowl fits very tightly into the saucer so that it is unstable, and it seems unlikely that the two originally belonged together.

Although the pattern is the same as on cat. 19, the colours on the saucer are much paler. The painting on the cup is rather poorly executed with specks of red-brown on the white areas. The blue enamel on the cup is overfired.

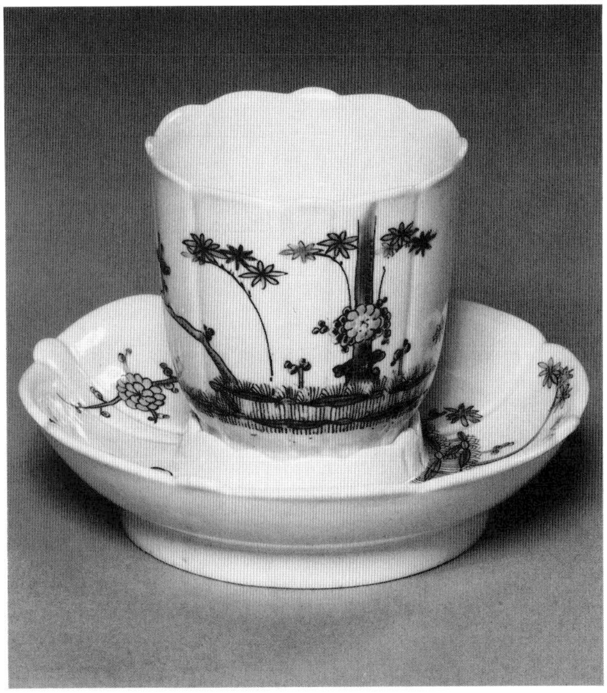

18

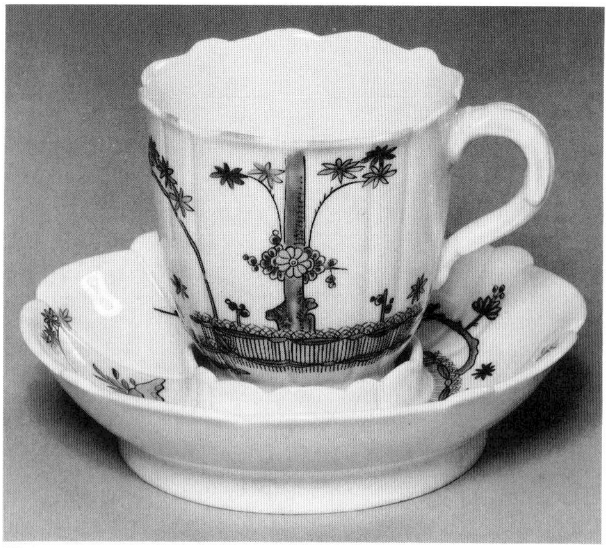

19

19 *Trembleuse* Cup and saucer, *c.* 1740

See colour plate 3

D. *of saucer:*	12.6 cm
H. *of cup:*	7.1 cm
Marks:	none
Reg. No.	Franks 338

Creamy-coloured soft-paste porcelain, heavily potted, moulded, the upper surface divided into panels by depressions, lobed rims and twig handle, the saucer with a similar moulding and lobed gallery around the well. Decorated in green, yellow, blue, red-brown and dark brown enamels with stylised flowers and a banded hedge pattern in the Kakiemon style. Red-brown trefoil leaf painted in centre. Small hairline crack to cup.

Provenance: Bequeathed by Sir A.W. Franks, 1897

Literature: Franks, 1896, no. 338

Exhibited: 'Porcelain for Palaces, The Fashion for Japan in Europe 1650–1750', British Museum, July–November 1990, cat. compiled by J. Ayers, O. Impey, J.V.G. Mallet, no. 313

Comparable Examples: Paris, Musée des arts décoratifs, inv. D32940 A + B, illus. Frégnac, 1964, p. 72

Denmark, Copenhagen, The David Collection, inv. 17/1972, illus. Eriksen, 1980, no. 8

The rim of the cup is incompletely glazed, each lobe being unglazed at its highest point. The blue enamel is overfired and the glaze shows signs of overfiring in the same area.

The banded hedge pattern, ultimately based on the decoration of Japanese Arita porcelains reaching Europe in the early eighteenth century, was one of the most popular motifs on early Western porcelains, especially at Meissen in the 1720s and 1730s, at Saint-Cloud in the 1730s and 1740s, at Chantilly from around 1730–5 and at Chelsea in the next decade.[1]

The model was apparently also produced in a smaller size.[2]

1. Exh. British Museum, 1990, *passim.*
2. Christie's 3 July 1978, Lot 155, no measurements given but illustrated with cup resting on saucer, Parke-Bernet, New York, 3 April 1948, Lot 260, and see Frégnac, 1964, p. 72, where another in the Musée des arts décoratifs, Paris, is illustrated with an example similar to the BM piece.

20 Knife and Fork with Porcelain Handles, *c.* 1740–50

See colour plate 1

L. *of handle:*	8.8 cm (knife); 8 cm (fork)
Total L. *of knife:*	27.8 cm
Total L. *of fork:*	20.8 cm
Marks:	none
Reg. No.	FB 28 (AF 3228)

Soft-paste porcelain, decorated with an underglaze-blue painted pattern of shell-like motifs near the silver ferrule and scroll ornament at the end of the handle. Knife-handle pitted in firing. The blade and tines are of steel.

Provenance: Bequeathed by Sir A.W. Franks, 1897

Literature: Unpublished

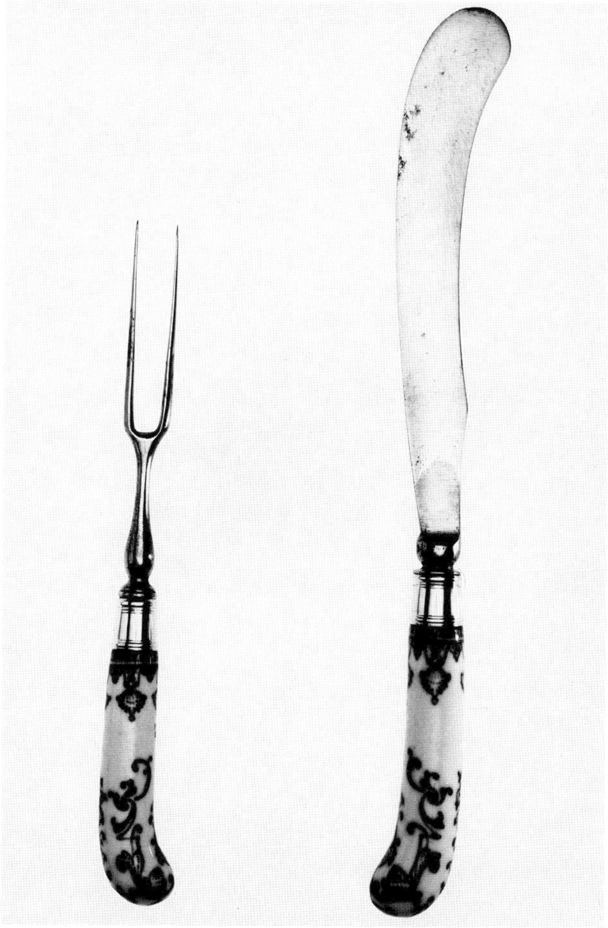

20

Comparable Examples: Sceaux, château de Sceaux, Musée de l'Ile de France, see G. Poisson *et al.*, *Catalogue raisonné des collections*, Hauts-de-Seine, 1985, nos. 855, 856

Manchester City Art Gallery, inv. 1966.620

By analysis the porcelain was found to be non-phosphatic.[1] Similar decorative motifs are found on English porcelain knife-handles, such as those from the Bow factory.[2]

The dating of underglaze-blue decorated handles such as these remains problematical, since no securely datable examples are known. They were probably made with more tightly-conceived decoration from the beginning of the eighteenth century and were produced in several different shapes and sizes.[3] A spoon-handle in the David Collection, Copenhagen, which is decorated with a rather similar underglaze-blue pattern, is fitted with a silver sleeve bearing the Paris discharge mark for 1714–17 and a partly-obliterated maker's mark, thought to be that of J.-B. Loir, *maître* 1689 and active up to 1718.[4] Six of tapering form survive with a tooled leather container, which may be contemporary, and was doubtless supplied by a *marchand-mercier* who arranged for the mounting of the porcelain handles.[5]

The blade and tines may be of English workmanship and a knife and fork of similar shape are shown on Henry Patton's trade card.[6]

1. British Museum Research Laboratory, Weimer, 21 March 1962, BMRL 1414.
2. A. Gabszewicz and G. Freeman, *Bow Porcelain, The Collection formed by Geoffrey Freeman*, London, 1982, nos. 90–2, p. 68.
3. Twelve handles of differing form with more tightly conceived painted patterns were sold at Christie's, 2 July 1990, Lot 1, cutler's mark I.
4. Eriksen, 1980, no. 1a.
5. J. Terrasson, *Madame de Pompadour et la création de la 'Porcelaine de France'*, Paris, 1969, pl. VII, whereabouts unknown.
6. Illus. A. Heal, *London Tradesman's Cards of the XVIII Century*, London, 1925, pl. LXXX.

21 **Sugar Bowl and Cover** (*sucrier et son couvercle*), *c.* 1740–50

H. 10 cm
Marks: none
Reg. No. Franks 341

Soft-paste porcelain, with three groups of applied prunus sprays on pot and cover; cover slightly domed, with triangular knop and well-fitting lid. Rim of bowl chipped.

Provenance: Bequeathed by Sir A.W. Franks, 1897

Literature: Franks, 1896, no. 341

Comparable Examples: Exh. Allen, 1989, no. 54

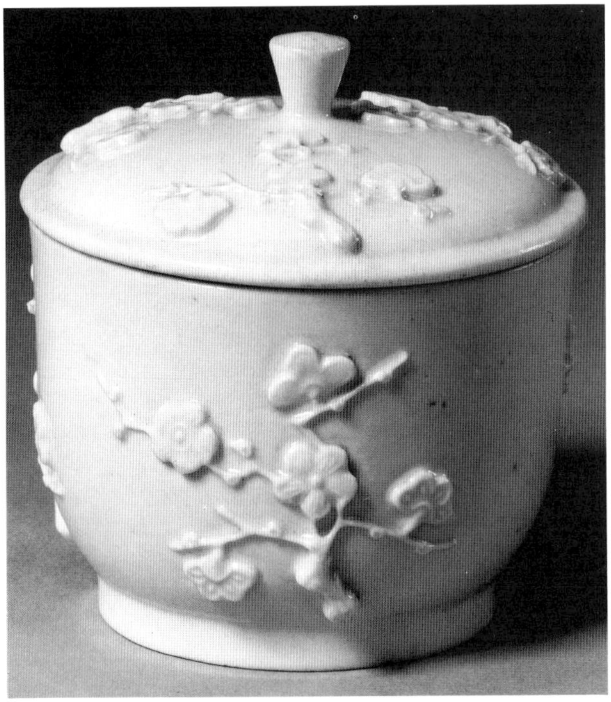

21

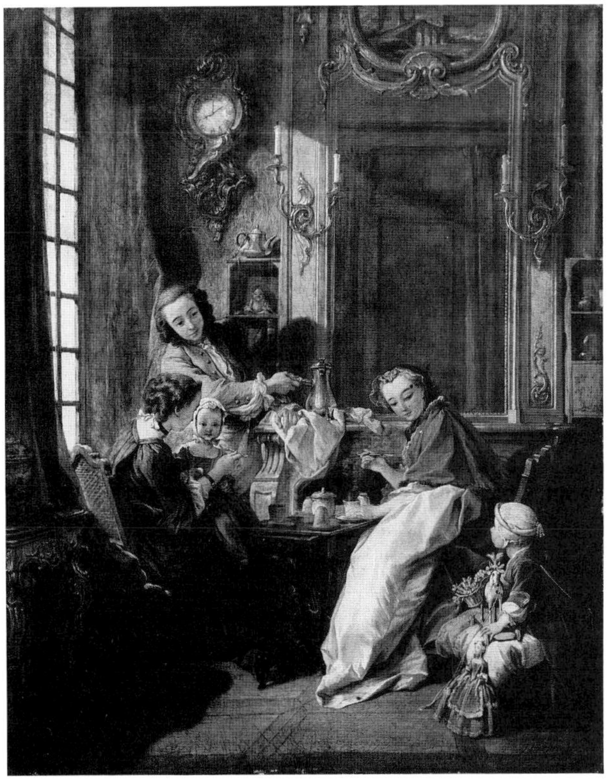

Fig 21a

The prunus moulding was probably copied from Meissen and ultimately derives from *blanc de Chine* porcelain.

The surface of the bowl has numerous pinholes and

small firecracks and the cover has a greyish appearance resulting from the large number of black specks in the paste. The piece may have been made at the Saint-Cloud factory as a second-quality item, or perhaps produced at a branch of the factory, or even made by an imitator.

A sugar bowl which resembles cat. 21 and several cups and saucers can be seen in François Boucher's painting *Le Déjeuner*, dated 1739 in the Louvre Museum, Paris (fig. 21a).

22 **Tobacco Pot**, *c.* 1740–50

H. 12.6 cm
Marks: incised 4/S.C/T; paper label inscribed *Saint-Cloud* and *B CH*
Reg. No. 1931,10–19,7

Soft-paste porcelain, cylindrical, slightly flared at foot, deep foot rim. Moulded with two chrysanthemum sprays. Chip to foot rim.

Provenance: Transferred from Salisbury and South Wiltshire and Blackmore Museum, 1931

Literature: Unpublished

Comparable Examples: Paris, Musée des arts décoratifs, glazed dish on foot with similar relief and including an insect in the centre, inv. D33298

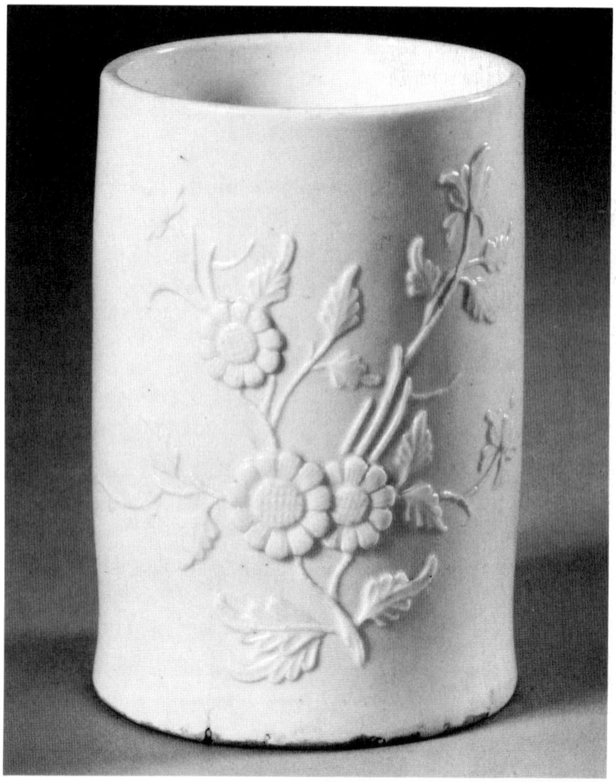

22

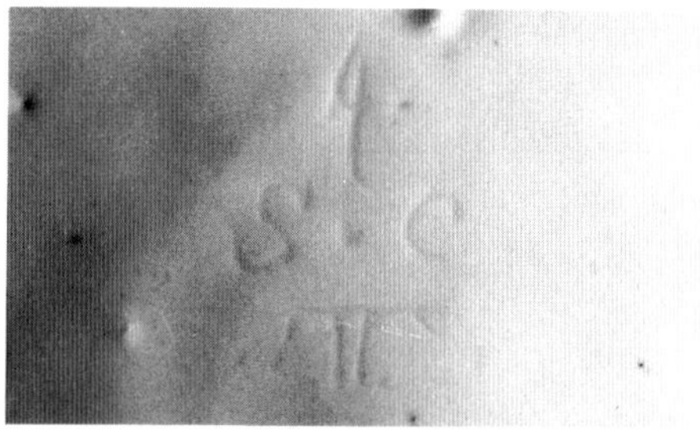

22 *mark*

The form derives from a Chinese brush pot, and the appearance consciously imitates *blanc de Chine* porcelain made in Fukien Province, China, and imported to Europe in the early eighteenth century. However, the chrysanthemums have been interpreted in purely Western fashion. An ill-fitting glaze and a small chip which has been glazed over indicate some problems of production.

Although no exactly comparable covered examples are known, this pot was almost certainly provided with a lid and may once have had a travelling box. Undecorated pots of unmarked soft-paste porcelain of the Saint-Cloud type, some mounted in silver as tobacco pots, have survived.[1]

1. See D. Gage and M. Marsh, *Tobacco Containers & Accessories, Their Place in European Social History*, London, 1988, pp. 87–91.

23 **Toilet Pot and Cover**, *c.* 1740–50

H. 8.4 cm
Marks: t/SC/T incised
Reg. No. 1931,10–19,8

Creamy-coloured, lead-glazed soft-paste porcelain, moulded as an artichoke, with a scalloped moulded rim and a moulded slightly convex cover with gallery. The cover, which has a grooved bulbous knop, does not fit properly, although it appears to belong with the pot. Lid and foot rim chipped.

Provenance: Transferred from Salisbury and South Wiltshire and Blackmore Museum, 1931

Literature: Unpublished

Comparable Examples: See F. Labayle, *La porcelaine de Saint-Cloud*, Rennes, 1982, p. 8, slightly differing form (location incorrect)

Sotheby's, René Fribourg sale, Part 2, 15 October 1963, Lot 392, with matching *trembleuse* stand

Belgium, Kortrijk, Museum voor Oudheidkunde en Sierkunst, *Keramiek*, cat. compiled by A.G. Pauwels and E.J. van Hoonacker, 1981, no. 736, H. 8 cm, unmarked, inv. 4385

Pieces of this form without the moulding made at the Vincennes factory were used at table for holding gravy or cream,[1] but on the evidence of *La Marchande des Modes*,[2] a painting by François Boucher dated 1746 which shows a similar waisted artichoke-moulded pot on a dressing-table, it seems likely that this is a toilet

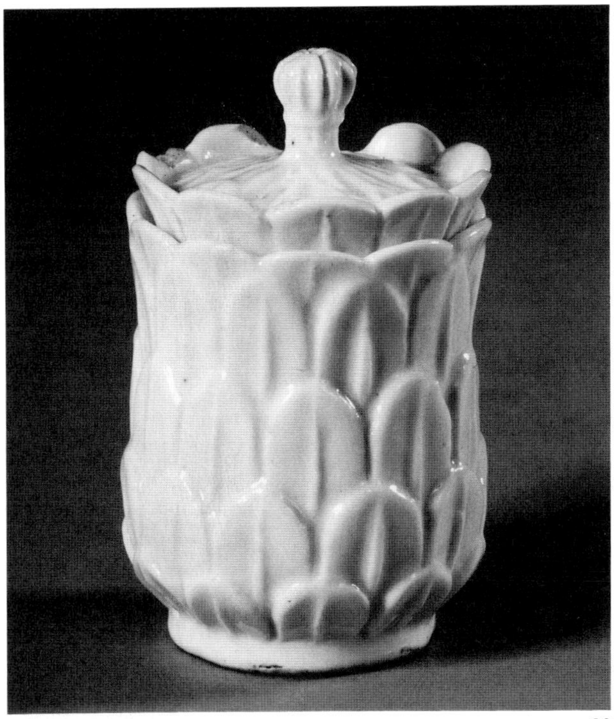

23

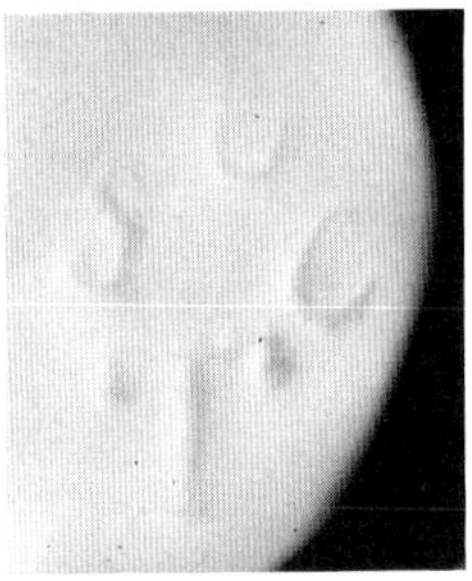

23 *mark*

pot. Many variations in the forms, mouldings and knops show that there was a considerable market in these pots.[3] The recent discovery of documents listing porcelain which is probably from the Saint-Cloud factory, used as stiffeners and compartments in a box containing a *nécessaire de voyage*,[4] has shown that on 27 September 1748 a *moyen pot en artichaud à relief* cost 4 *livres*.

Despite its relatively late date, the foot is crudely formed and the glaze does not 'fit'. Poor technique appears to be a feature of many pieces bearing this or a similar mark, and cannot be explained in the present state of knowledge.

A white glazed artichoke-moulded 'tureen' and cover with a pecking bird finial was made at the Chelsea porcelain factory around 1755.[5]

Artichoke-moulded 'custard cups' with covers, not dissimilar in shape to the Saint-Cloud pots, were made in pearlware around 1785–90 at the Wedgwood factory.[6]

1. Exh. Vincennes, 1978, p. 76.
2. In the Nationalmuseum, Stockholm. A reduced version is in the Wallace Collection, London, illus. P. Verlet, *La Maison du XVIII Siècle en France*, Paris, 1960, pl. 98.
3. One of a pair of pots shaped and moulded like artichokes, H. 8 cm incl. cover, is illustrated by Eriksen, 1980, pl. 6b. For three more globular pots in two different sizes, H. 8 cm and 11 cm, see Phillips, 6 June 1990, Lot 118, and H.-P. Fourest, *Masterpieces of Western and Near Eastern Ceramics, Vol. VI French Ceramics*, Tokyo, 1979, fig. 53, H. 8 cm, D. 6.8 cm, marks *ASCT*, Musée national Adrien-Dubouché, Limoges, inv. ADL 2.196.
4. C. Truman, 'A St.-Cloud Nécessaire de Voyage circa 1750', *Connoisseur*, Vol. 203, no. 818, April 1980, pp. 253–5.
5. See S. Spero, 'English Porcelain Rarities', *Antique Dealer and Collectors' Guide*, Vol. 43, no. 3, October 1989, p. 40, no dimensions given.
6. Reilly, 1989, I, p. 321, fig. 403.

24 **Cup and *Trembleuse* Saucer**, second quarter of 18th century

H. *of cup:*	6.8 cm
D. *of saucer:*	11.9 cm
Marks:	*S.* painted in underglaze-blue on cup; $\underset{\text{T}}{\text{S}^{4}\text{C}}$ painted in underglaze-blue on saucer
Reg. No.	Franks 336

Handleless cup of soft-paste porcelain with ribbed moulding on body. Decorated in underglaze-blue near the rim with a stylised scroll pattern, and with an arcaded pattern on the foot. The saucer has a ribbed moulding and a gallery; painted in a pattern similar to that on the cup.

Provenance: Bequeathed by Sir A.W. Franks, 1897

Literature: Franks, 1896, no. 336

Comparable Examples: See cat. 25

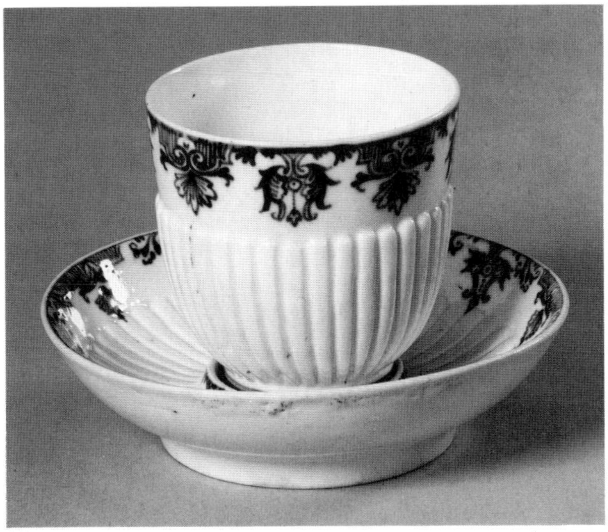

24

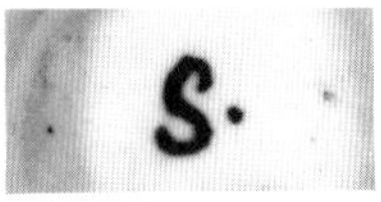

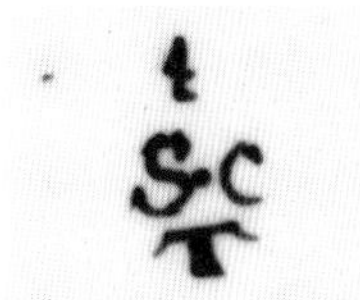

24 *marks*

The glaze does not 'fit' on part of the ribbing, the base and in one area on the rim of the cup.

The cup shape was probably in use at the earliest period of the factory's activity, as an example stamped [*imprimée en creux*] with the fleur-de-lys mark, mentioned in a document of around 1696 addressed to Monsieur de Pontchartrain by the heirs of Pierre I Chicaneau (see p. 4), can be found in the Musée national de Céramique, Sèvres.[1] However, the decoration suggests a date near the middle of the eighteenth century. The significance of the mark 'S' is unknown.

1. Frégnac, 1964, p. 56. The writer has not examined this piece.

25 Cup and *Trembleuse* Saucer, second quarter of 18th century

D. *of saucer:*	12.2 cm
H. *of cup:*	6.2 cm
Marks:	t/S.C/T painted in underglaze-blue on saucer; t/SC/T/D painted in underglaze-blue on cup
Reg. No.	OA 10450

Soft-paste porcelain, thickly potted; ribbed moulding on body of cup, which has a grooved loop handle and an exceptionally deep foot. The moulding is continued on the deep saucer except near the rim. The saucer has a curved gallery in four parts in the centre. Both are painted in underglaze-blue with stylised flowers alternating with bushes on mounds near the rim. A single blue line is painted near the rim of each; around the foot of the cup are two unevenly painted blue lines with a zigzag pattern depending from the lower one. The zigzag pattern is crudely repeated on the outside of the gallery. Cup cracked and rim chipped in two places, rim of saucer chipped.

Provenance: Residue of the bequest of the late D.A. MacAlister Esq., given in 1971 to complement the MacAlister gift, 1959

Literature: Unpublished

Comparable Examples: Sèvres, Musée national de Céramique, inv. 13404, (mark includes *H*)), 13400 868 (mark includes *F*), 22428

The glaze on the foot of the saucer is wrinkled and does not 'fit', the foot rim on both pieces is discoloured, and the paste contains numerous impurities. Around the handle terminals are the remains of a yellowish substance which may be bedding material. The quality of this piece is markedly inferior to that of cat. 24.

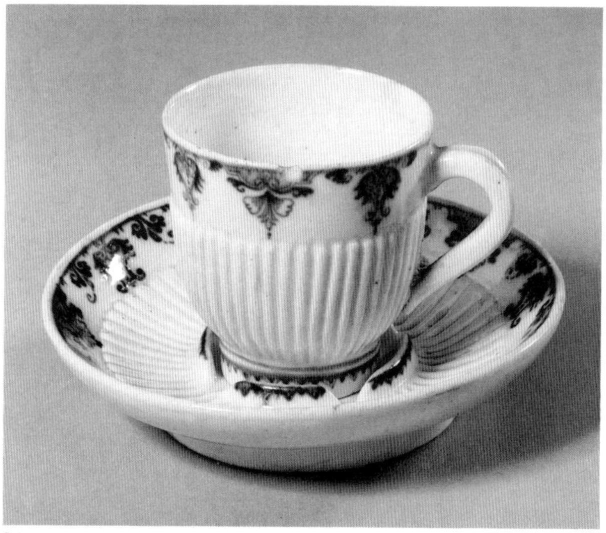

25

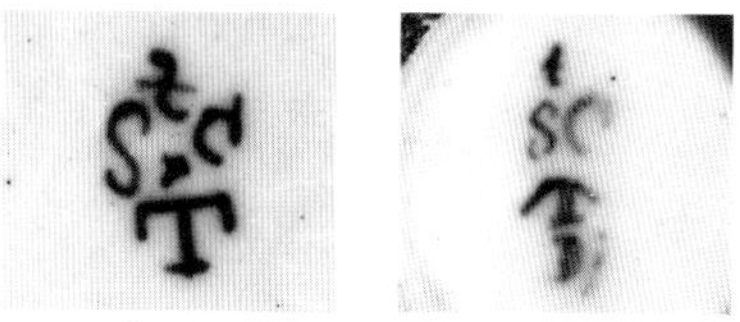

25 *marks*

26 *Trembleuse* Saucer, second quarter of 18th century

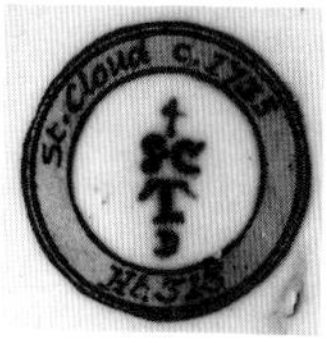

26 *mark*

D.	12 cm
Marks:	s t c / T / D painted in underglaze-blue
Reg. No.	1981,1–1,106

Soft-paste porcelain with a lead glaze; ribbed moulding near well which is enclosed by a gallery consisting of four separate curved walls; deep foot. Decorated on the rim with a pattern stylised floral motifs alternating with a bush on a mound in underglaze-blue and with a zigzag motif on the outer surface of the gallery. Small chip to rim.

Provenance: Bequeathed by Miss C.M. Woodward, 1981

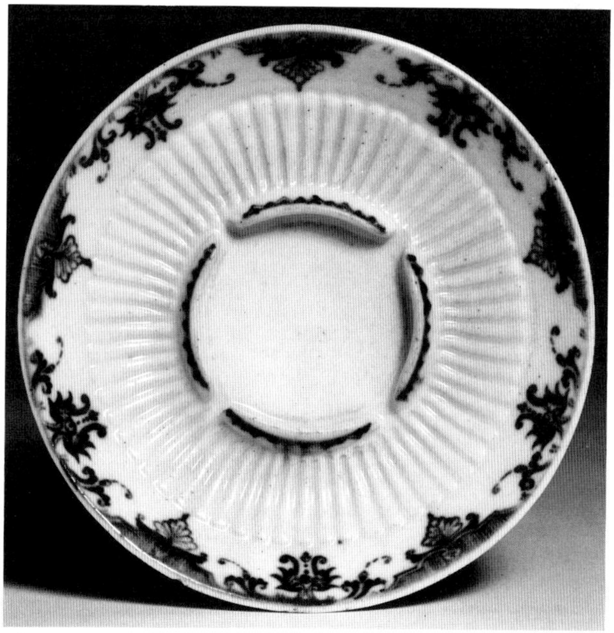

26

Literature: Unpublished

Comparable Examples: See cat. 25

Firing defects, inclusions in the porcelain body and specks of underglaze-blue on the reverse are typical of the production problems characteristic of pieces bearing the *STC* mark. On one part of the gallery the blue has flowed downwards.

The significance of the numeral and the letter 'D' has not been determined.

27 **Toilet Pot and Cover**, second quarter of 18th century

See colour plate 2

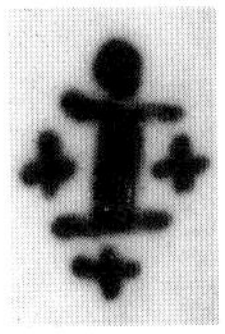

27 *mark*

H. *incl. cover:* 7.9 cm
D. *of base:* 8.2 cm
Marks: +i+ painted in underglaze-blue
Reg. No. Franks 335

Soft-paste porcelain, straight sides slightly out-turned at base. Shallow concave foot. Domed cover with flattened button knop. Painted in underglaze-blue with a shell, flower vase and trellis motif alternating with stylised vases of flowers and scrolls near the rim and on the cover; at the foot is a zigzag and dot motif. The button has a star device.

Provenance: Bequeathed by Sir A.W. Franks, 1897

Literature: Franks, 1896, no. 335

Comparable Examples: Limoges, Musée national Adrien-Dubouché, inv. 1205, H. 9 cm, D. of base 8.4 cm, mark *R* painted in blue

There are signs of overfiring near the base, which is unevenly glazed.

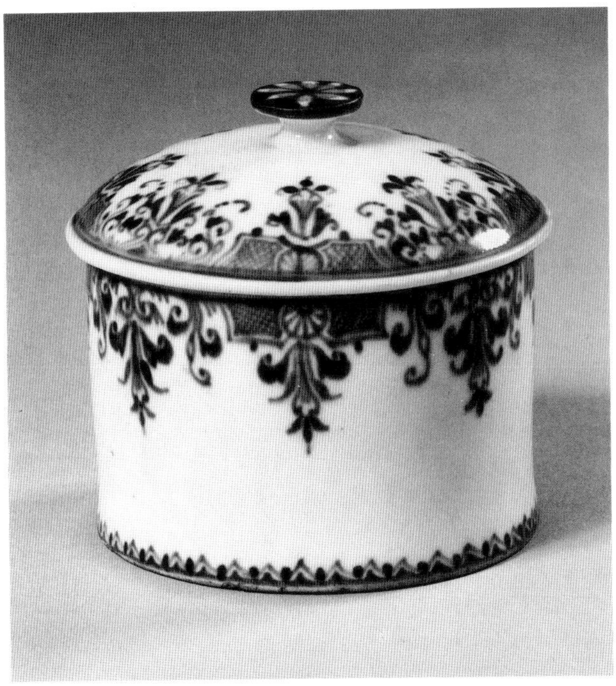

27

The significance of the mark, which was listed by Chavagnac and Grollier,[1] is unknown.

The pot probably held powder for the face.

1. Chavagnac and Grollier, 1906, p. 26.

28 **Toilet Pot,** second quarter of 18th century

See colour plate 2

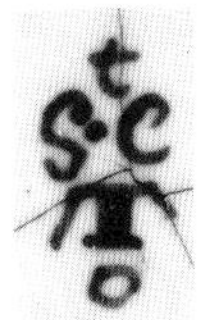

28 *mark*

H. 5.9 cm
Marks: t/SC/T/o painted in underglaze-blue
Reg. No. OA 10719

Soft-paste porcelain, highly translucent, cylindrical. Painted in underglaze-blue with stylised floral motifs near the rim and with a zigzag pattern around the foot. Base cracked, crack running up the side of the pot.

Provenance: Residue of the bequest of the late D.A. MacAlister Esq., given in 1971 to complement the MacAlister gift, 1959

Literature: Unpublished

Comparable Examples: None noted

The surface of the pot is pinholed, the foot rim is discoloured and the glaze on the foot uneven. In addition there are blue specks inside the base of the piece, which seems abnormally thin. It must once have had a cover and was probably intended to hold face-cream.

The significance of the painted marks is unclear, and the dating of the pot difficult. It may well have been made towards the end of the 'Trou period' since the decoration is cursory.

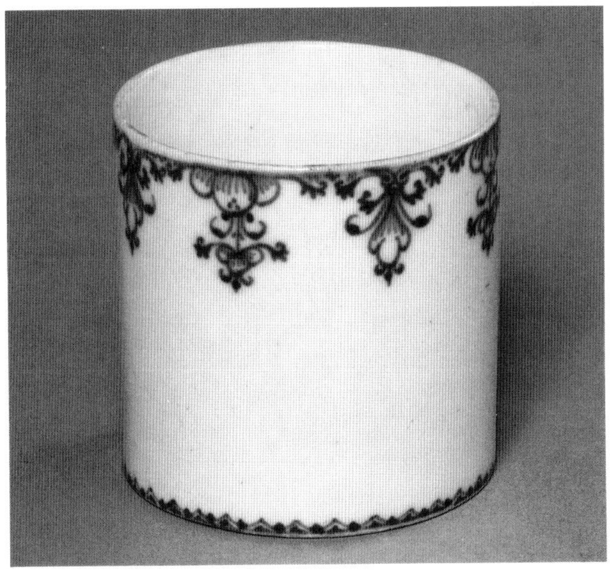

28

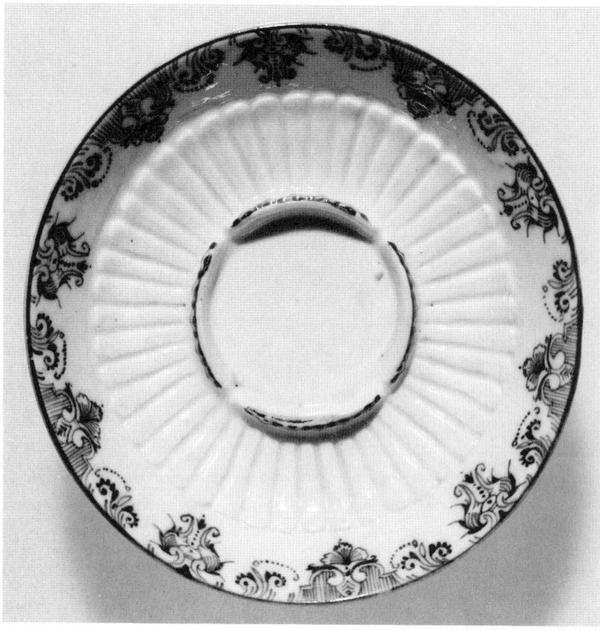

29

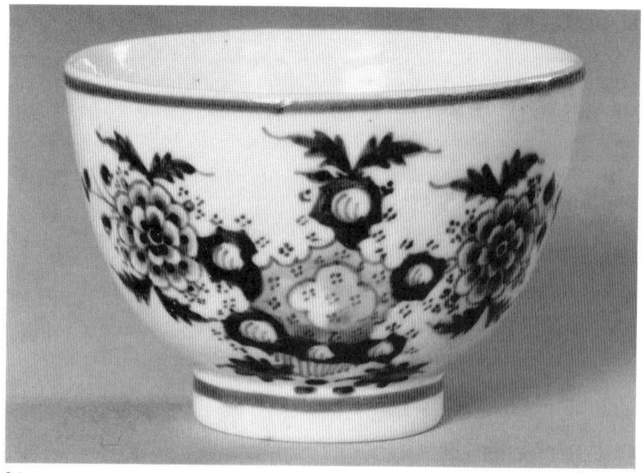

30

29 *Trembleuse* Saucer, second quarter of 18th century

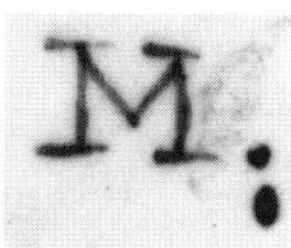

29 *mark*

D. 12.6 cm
Marks: *M:* painted in underglaze-blue
Reg. No. FB 9 (AF 3212)

Soft-paste porcelain, thickly potted and with numerous inclusions in the paste, glazed base and partly discoloured foot rim. Ribbed moulding in well of saucer, gallery composed of four curved parts. Decorated in underglaze-blue with a stylised scroll and flower pattern on the rim, and with a zigzag motif on the outer edge of the gallery. One part of gallery chipped.

Provenance: Bequeathed by Sir A.W. Franks, 1897

Literature: Unpublished

Comparable Examples: Limoges, Musée national Adrien-Dubouché, inv. 1213, D. 12.5 cm, acquired from the Gasnault Collections, 1881

This mark on this piece is not dissimilar to an initial *M* with dots shown by Chavagnac and Grollier[1] and its form and decoration are close to other examples of marked Saint-Cloud porcelain. It is possible that this mark was used by Marie Moreau, widow of Pierre II Chicaneau, between 1718 and her death on 11 March 1743, when she was working at the sister factory (*succursale*) to Saint-Cloud in the rue ville l'Evêque, faubourg Saint-Honoré, an independent operation.[2]

1. Chavagnac and Grollier, 1906, p. 26.
2. Le Duc and Guillebon, 1991, pp. 22–3.

30 Teabowl, mid-18th century

See colour plate 2

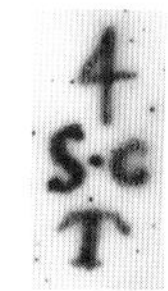

30 *mark*

D. 8.3 cm
Marks: 4/S.C/T painted in underglaze-blue
Reg. No. Franks 337

Soft-paste porcelain, with an extremely glassy glaze, which does not 'fit' very well; painted in underglaze-blue with two groups of stylised chrysanthemums and rocks on one side and stylised peonies and rocks on the other, and with a butterfly inside the cup at the base; blue line near rim and on foot.

Provenance: Bequeathed by Sir A.W. Franks, 1897

Literature: Franks, 1896, no. 337

Comparable Examples: Paris, Musée des arts décoratifs, inv. A 13616, D. 8.5 cm, butterfly inside cup, same mark

The bowl is warped and was probably overfired, causing bubbling of the glaze. Pinholes and small firecracks, as well as many inclusions, are visible. A Chantilly teabowl with comparable decoration, probably dating from no earlier than the mid-1760s (size unknown), is in the Musée des arts décoratifs, château de Saumur, France,[1] and a larger bowl, painted with a similar motif, can be seen in an undated still life, *Le Buffet*, by Pierre-Nicolas Huilliot (1654–1751).[2]

1. Illus. H. Landais, *French Porcelain*, London, 1961, p. 30, fig. 17, probably the same as shown in M. Jacob, *The Castle of Saumur and the Museum of Applied Arts*, Saumur, 1980, pl. LXVIII (saucer next to it does not match).
2. Helft Collection, Paris, illus. M. and F. Faré, *La vie silencieuse en France, La Nature Morte au XVIIIe siècle*, Fribourg, 1976, p. 30, fig. 27.

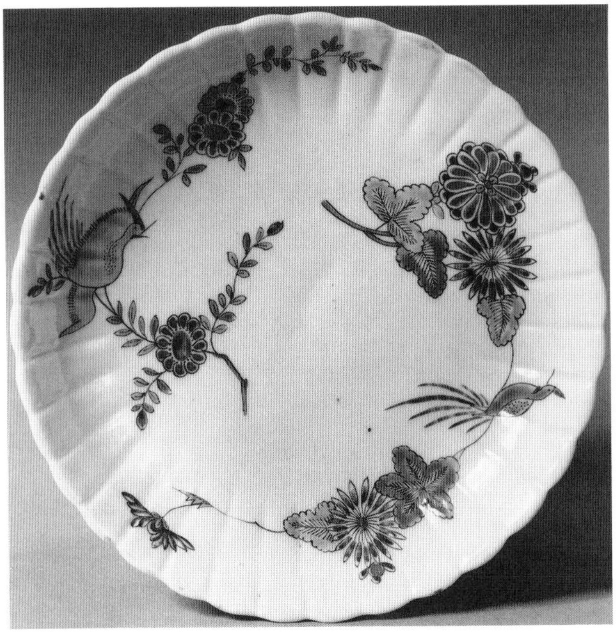

31

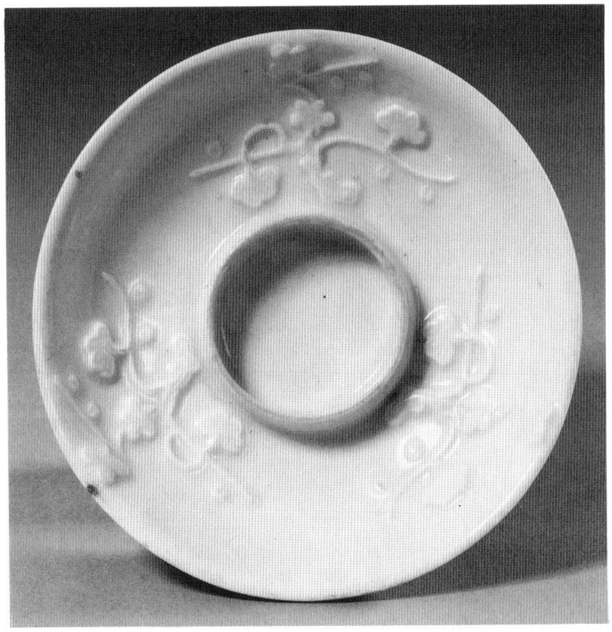

32

31 **Saucer,** *c.* 1735–45

See colour plate 4

D. 13.5 cm
Marks: none
Reg. No. Franks 339

Soft-paste porcelain, heavily potted, ribbed moulding around scalloped rim. Decorated in orange-red, blue, turquoise and brown enamels with birds and flowers in the Kakiemon style, embellished with gilding. Small chip to foot rim. Firecrack on base.

Provenance: Bequeathed by Sir A.W. Franks, 1897

Literature: Franks, 1896, no. 339

Comparable Examples: None noted

The thickness of the potting, the creamy colour of the paste and the style of decoration suggest an attribution to Saint-Cloud.

The use of gilding suggests that this piece was completed before 1745 when the Vincennes factory was granted a privilege to 'faire et fabriquer pendant vingt années consecutives . . . la porcelaine façon de Saxe peinte et dorée à la figure humaine' and all other factories were prohibited from gilding their productions.

A slightly larger fluted dish painted in a similar style and palette was made at the Chelsea porcelain factory around 1753–5.[1]

1. Victoria and Albert Museum, inv. C. 375–1918, exh. 'Porcelain for Palaces, the Fashion for Japan in Europe 1650–1750', British Museum, July–November 1990, No. 194.

32 ***Trembleuse* Saucer,** probably Saint-Cloud, date uncertain, perhaps *c.* 1740

D. 12.6 cm
Marks: none
Reg. No. 1931,10–19,9

Soft-paste porcelain, thickly potted, moulded in relief with three prunus sprays; central gallery of circular form. Chip to rim.

Provenance: Transferred from Salisbury and South Wiltshire and Blackmore Museum, 1931

Literature: T. Harrison Tidswell, 'The Influence of Oriental Porcelain on Western Ceramics', *Apollo*, Vol. CX, no. 211, September 1979, fig. 7

Comparable Examples: Paris, Musée des arts décoratifs, inv. A9019, D. 13.2 cm, unmarked, firecracked

Paris, with G. Lefebvre, *trembleuse* saucer and cup and cover mounted in silver, which is not contemporary

USA, Birmingham (Ala.), cup and saucer, illus. *Porcelain from the Frances Oliver Collection*, Birmingham, 1980, p. 40

The moulding is of a different type from that found on cat. 21 and the porcelain was fired at a higher temperature.

Although not as white as some Meissen hard-paste, the saucer is considerably less creamy in tone than much Saint-Cloud porcelain. It may possibly have been made at another French factory.

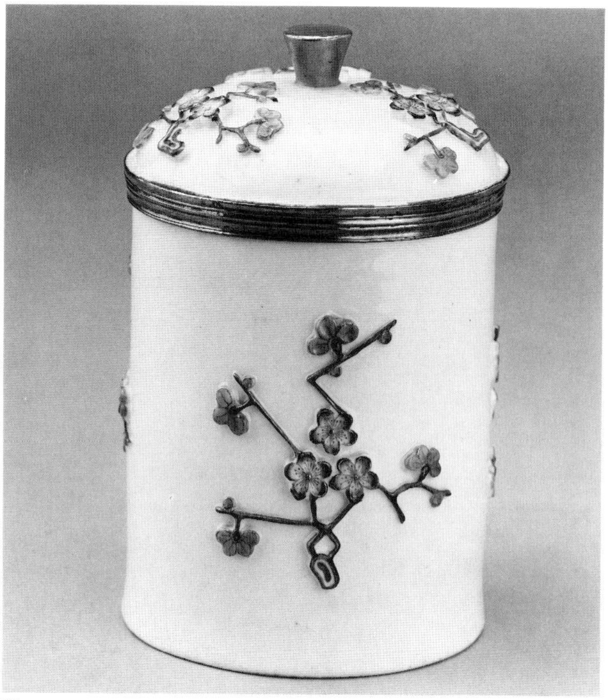

33

33 **Tobacco Jar and Cover** (*pot à tabac*), made 1740–50, decorated later

H. *incl. cover:*	13.8 cm
Marks:	none on porcelain; salmon's head discharge mark on silver-gilt mount to cover, for the *sous-fermier* Antoine Leschaudel between October 1744 and October 1750 (see Nocq, IV, p. 234)
Reg. No.	1913,12–20,134

Soft-paste porcelain, highly translucent. Of cylindrical form with domed cover surmounted by a flattened conical knop. The rim of the cover has been ground off. Both cover and pot are moulded with three groups of prunus branches painted in pink, two colours of green and pale brown, heightened with gilding. Knop gilt.

Provenance: Bequeathed by the Reverend A.H.S. Barwell, 1913

Literature: Unpublished

Comparable Examples: Paris, Baroness von Seidlitz Collection

USA, New York, Parke-Bernet, 16 May 1959, Lot 239, Thelma Chrysler Foy Collection, pair sold for $1300

USA, New York, Sotheby Parke-Bernet, 17 May 1980, Lot 171, Bernice Chrysler Garbisch Collection, Volume Two

USA, Washington, Smithsonian Institution, National Museum of American History, on loan from the Estate of Dr H. Syz, October 1991, inv. 1386

The jar and cover, although unmarked, are typical of the pieces usually left undecorated which are attributed to the Saint-Cloud factory. The shape of the knop and the disposition of the ornament is similar to cat. 21 but the prunus sprays differ and the paste of the tobacco jar is much whiter.

Prunus branches in relief on pots of this kind were left uncoloured, and many examples survive.[1] The colour scheme used here is unparalleled on eighteenth-century pieces, although the two colours of green and the pale brown may have been copied from Chantilly overglaze colours.

The gilding of the knop and the grinding away of the rim of the lid to accommodate the genuine eighteenth-century mount are additional evidence of the later embellishment of this rather undistinguished jar.

1. See exh. Williams, 1975, cat. 9.

34 **Three Toilet Pots and Covers,** 19th or 20th century, probably Samson, Paris

H. *incl. cover:*	11.2 cm; 9.5 cm; 8 cm
Marks:	t/S.C/T (largest); t/S.C/xT
Reg. No.	1988,10–10,1 to 3

High-fired opaque earthenware body, moulded, each pot and cover divided into four compartments by a depression, and ornamented with an applied flower. On the pot there is an applied leaf at either side of the flower near the rim, the inside of which is unglazed and discoloured. Firecracks to two covers, black specks, inclusions and pinholes in glaze.

Provenance: Purchased, 1988

Literature: Unpublished

Comparable Examples: Sotheby's 'Black Museum', pair exhibited 1983, no. 42 in handlist kept on file[1]

USA, Boston, Museum of Fine Arts, inv. R.62.12, L. 9.7 cm

The body, which is not in fact porcelain, and shape of these pots bear a superficial resemblance to the products of the Saint-Cloud factory[2] but the body is white rather than creamy, and the glaze is dull in appearance. The marks are not dissimilar to those on cat. 23, but are more crudely incised.

These pieces almost certainly correspond to the two original factory models from the showroom of Etablissement Edmé Samson, sold at Christie's, 24 September 1979, Lot 34, which measured 9.5 cm and 7.5 cm in height.

A rather similar mark, including the *X*, all in dots, has been noted on a glass cooler decorated with gold foil and with red and green enamels.[3] Both the body and the foot rim are unlike Saint-Cloud products.

1. The author is grateful to Gordon Lang of Sotheby's for this information.
2. See, for example, a covered pot illus. Malgras (ed.), 1983, p. 102, whereabouts unknown, no measurements given.
3. Metropolitan Museum, New York, inv. 50.211.135.

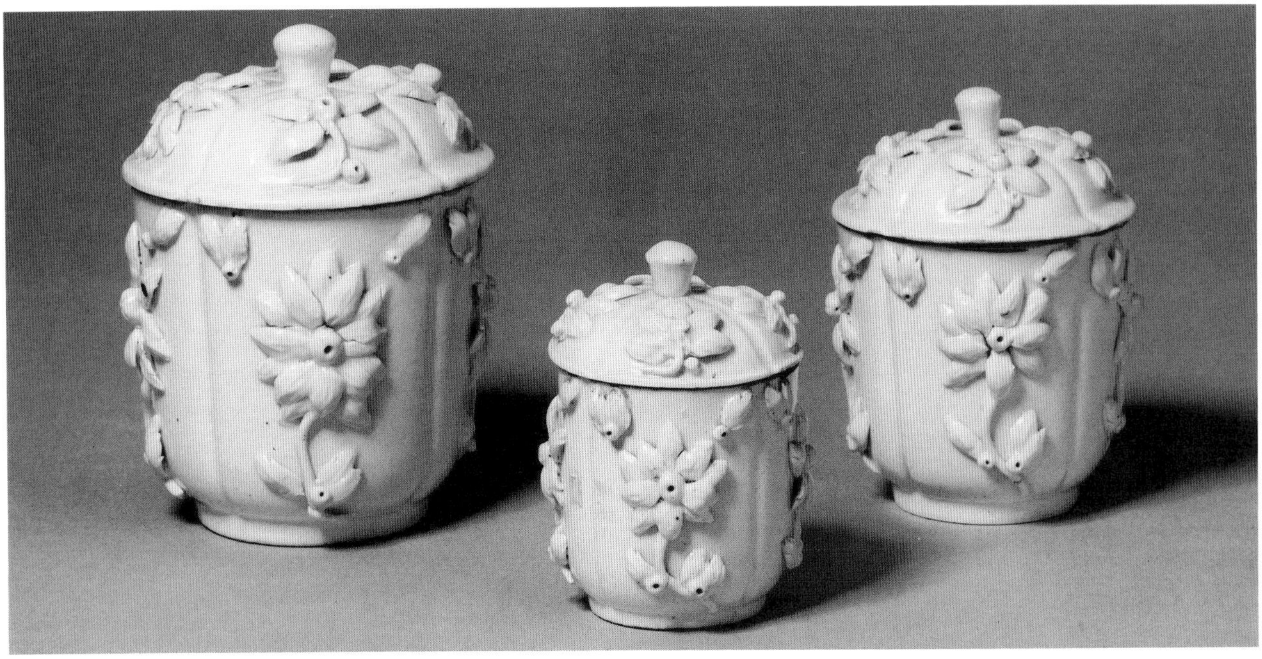

34 *Left 1988, 10–10, 3, centre 1988, 10–10, 1, right 1988, 10–10, 2*

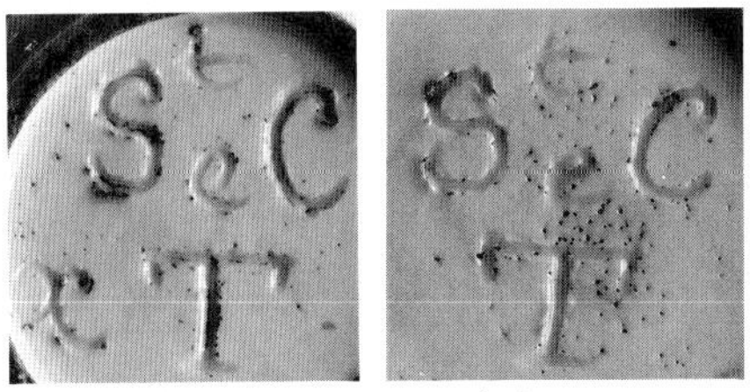

34 *marks (on 1988, 10–10, 1 and 3)*

Paris, Jean-Baptiste Bellevaux's factory[1]

Little is known about Jean-Baptiste Bellevaux or the short-lived porcelain factory he operated in Paris around 1715. His dates of birth and death have not yet been discovered. He was apparently the nephew of Henri I Trou and first cousin (*cousin germain*) of Gabriel Trou, whose guardian or *tuteur* he was between 1700 and 1707. He had close links with Saint-Cloud, where he is first recorded in 1685 when his marriage to Marie Germain appears in the parish records. His eldest child died there in the same year. Bellevaux witnessed the death certificate of Trou senior at Saint-Cloud on 30 March 1700, in company with Trou's two sons, his sons-in-law and the three sons of his wife Barbe Coudray by her first husband (Jean, Jean-Baptiste and Pierre II Chicaneau).

Bellevaux is documented as a *maître verrier faïencier* in Paris betwen 1701 and 1706, but his family continues to be recorded at Saint-Cloud. The death of his second child appears in the parish records in 1706. In February 1708 his son Jean Henri was baptised. The child's godfather was Henri II Trou, his godmother Pierre II Chicaneau's wife, Marie Moreau. In the same year Bellevaux was godfather to Jean Baptiste Henry Bolvry, son of Nicolas Bolvry and Jeanne Prévost, appearing in the parish register as 'faïencier à Paris'. Clearly he was employed in some capacity at the Saint-Cloud porcelain factory before he left for Paris, but his precise role remains unclear.

The most damning evidence of his porcelain-making activities in Paris, which contravened the monopoly status granted to the Saint-Cloud factory, is the seizure carried out by the Paris authorities on 11 July 1715 at his premises in rue Saint-Jacques par Saint-Benoît. It was made at the request of Dames Coudret, Moreau and the Trou and Chicaneau heirs. In the document, the following appears beside Bellevaux' name: 'transfuge de St Cloud, a volé des secrets'.

It was a year before Bellevaux could make an official protest about the seizure, in which cups, salt-cellars, mustard-pots, ointment pots, inkstands, knife-handles and spoons were confiscated. These must have been made on site, since moulds, raw materials for porcelain manufacture and unfired knife-handles were also recovered. On 15 June 1716 Bellevaux, together with another faïence maker, Antoine Pavie, who operated from premises in the rue de Charonne, enlisted the support of officers in their *communauté* (or corporation) to obtain the nullification of the seizure. On the decision of the monarch himself, the conseil du Roi proclaimed in favour of Saint-Cloud on 3 May 1717. It is not clear what happened between Bellevaux and Pavie and the Saint-Cloud factory subsequently, but relations between the parties must at some point have been patched up, since in 1726 Bellevaux acted as godfather to one of Henri II Trou's sons.

As the items taken from Bellevaux' premises were small, it seems likely that he had only one kiln, and probably very few workers. He is not recorded as having registered a factory mark, and cat. 35 can be only tentatively attributed to him at this stage. For other pieces bearing the monogram *JBB*, see p. 31.

1. The author wishes to acknowledge that information on Bellevaux has been extracted from Le Duc and Guillebon, 1991, *passim.*; she has been unable to analyse the document pertaining to the seizure, A.N. Y 15148.

35 **Toilet Pot and Cover,** probably *c.* 1715

See colour plate 2

H. 5.4 cm

Marks: *JB* in monogram painted in underglaze-blue; printed label of comte de Chavagnac; label printed *294* of *Exposition Natle de Céramique, 1897*, inscribed *431*

Reg. No. 1938, 7–13, 1

Soft-paste porcelain with a lead glaze; cylindrical, the almost flat base showing traces of glaze, slightly domed cover surmounted by a button knop. Decorated in underglaze-blue with three panels of stylised flowers within rectangular reserves alternating with stylised flowers behind fences enclosed between blue lines. The cover has blue stylised scroll and flower ornament and the knop, encircled by two lines, is painted with a stylised flower. Cover chipped.

Provenance: Comte de Chavagnac collection, Lot 294 with another (possibly now in New York, French Institute), Paris, Hôtel Drouot, 19–21 June 1911.

Presented by Monsieur Adolphe Lion, 1938

Exhibited: Paris, Exposition nationale de Céramique, 1897, no. 431

Literature: Chavagnac and Grollier, 1906, p. 46

Comparable Examples: See below

The monogram on this cosmetic pot, which once had a companion (see above) was attributed by Chavagnac and Grollier to François and Barthélemy Dorez of Lille.[1] They were the sons of Barthélemy Dorez, who was authorised to establish a porcelain factory in Lille in April 1711 and who produced examples of his wares in November 1712, and were in charge of the factory from 1720 until around 1730. The style of decoration of this piece suggests a date of manufacture early in the eighteenth century. As well as the two toilet pots, three *trembleuse* saucers and a salt-cellar, each bearing a similar mark, were recorded by Chavagnac and Grollier.[2] The salt-cellar, which is now in the Musée national de Céramique, Sèvres, was illustrated with its mark by H.P. Fourest.[3] One *trembleuse* saucer formerly in the Gasnault Collection is now in the Musée national Adrien-Dubouché, Limoges,[4] and another saucer is in the Musée national de Céramique, Sèvres.[5] A heavily-potted salt-cellar decorated in underglaze-blue bearing the same mark is in the Bowes Museum, Barnard Castle, County Durham (formerly Goldblatt Collection, London).[6] The mark on a glazed white figure of a girl in *sabots* formerly in the Grollier Collection[7] may be compared with the marks on the pieces mentioned above.

However, Chavagnac and Grollier admitted that the marks were difficult to interpret with any certainty. They discounted a previous attribution to François Boussemart since they found no documents to prove that he ever made porcelain at Lille, and established a porcelain factory at Arras (q.v.) only in the 1770s. They also ruled out a faïence manufacturer named Jean Bossu. Their reading of the monogram on this pot, once accepted by this writer as plausible, has now been revised to *JB*, the earliest and the most evident reading. It has been suggested[8] that the maker was Jean-Baptiste Bellevaux, operating in Paris in around 1715, when he was prosecuted for making porcelain. (For the few biographical details we have on Bellevaux, see p. 30.)

1. Chavagnac and Grollier, 1906, p. 44.
2. *Ibid.*, p. 46.
3. H-P. Fourest, 'Origines de la porcelaine tendre en France au XVIIIe Siècle', *Cahiers*, no. 16, 1959, p. 243, fig. 20.
4. Inv. 1179.
5. Inv. 8344.
6. P. Klaber, 'The Enid Goldblatt Collection of Continental Porcelain' (Part 2), *The Antique Dealer and Collectors' Guide*, August 1984, p. 30., fig. 1b, inv. Cer. 1988.191.
7. Chavagnac and Grollier, 1906, p. 47, in Musée national de Céramique, inv. MNCS 13364.
8. By Bernard Dragesco, to whom the writer is indebted.

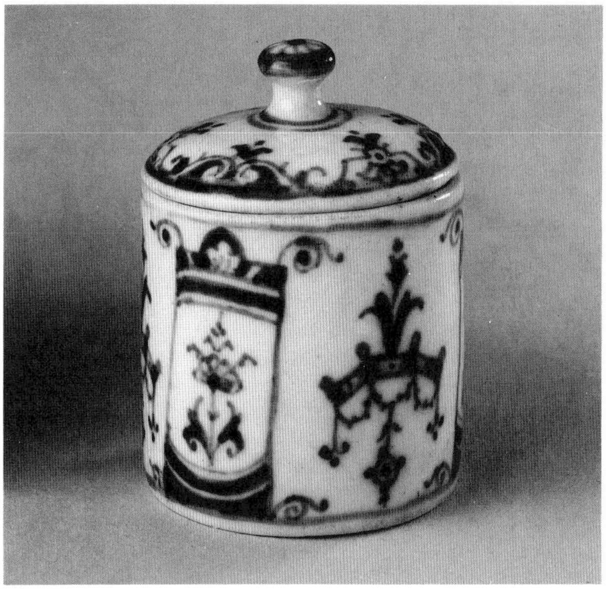

35

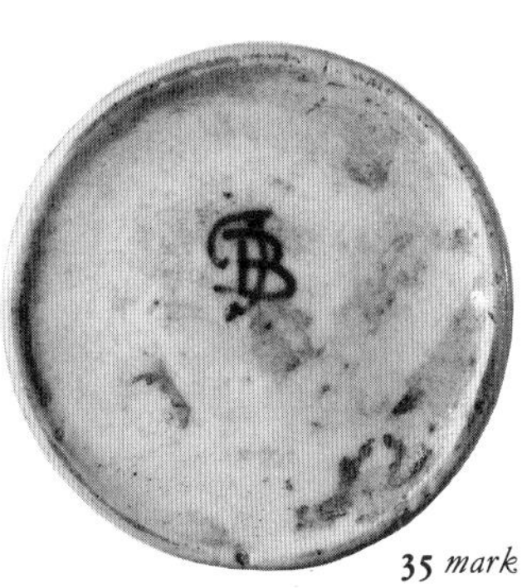

35 *mark*

Chantilly[1]

This factory was establised through the influence, and possibly partly with the capital, of Louis-Henri, duc de Bourbon, prince de Condé (1692–1740), known as 'Monsieur le Duc'.[2] Exiled to his château at Chantilly in 1726, the prince de Condé purchased land and buildings for the factory in 1730.[3] These were in Petit Chantilly, abutting on the rue du Marais which led to the Pavillon du Manse. In the letters patent granted on 5 October 1735 to Ciquaire Cirou (1700–55)[4] neither its precise location nor the exact date of its foundation are mentioned. It is possible that the first porcelain was made in the château itself, in a room near the place now occupied by the library.[5]

Cirou's early life remains obscure,[6] although he is said in the patent to have been making porcelain 'like that made in Japan' for more than ten years. This porcelain was supposed to be superior to Meissen, and to be in great demand in England,[7] Holland[8] and Germany. However, requests from French porcelain factories for royal protection tend to exaggerate the quality of the product as well as the length of time over which it had been made. There is no direct evidence that porcelain was made at Chantilly as early as 1725, although two workmen were apparently traced there in that year.[9] Cirou can be traced in the Saint-Cloud parish records from October 1722 until January 1729, but is noted in September 1726 as resident in Paris, where he was a porcelain painter in the parish of la Madeleine.[10]

The letters patent of 1735 authorised Cirou to make 'porcelaine fine de toutes couleurs, espèces, façens et grandeurs à l'imitation de la porcelaine de Japon' for a period of twenty years. The notebooks of Claude Humbert Gérin (who lived in Chantilly during his first marriage and was the brother-in-law of Michel Gabin, recorded as a thrower at the factory in 1750 and 1752), give the composition of the Chantilly body. The frit was made up of 75% white sand, 25% soda, the paste of 67% frit and 33% marl.[11] Initially at least the body was not white enough, and ashes of tin were used as an opacifier in the glaze to improve the colour of the surface. The restricted range of high-temperature overglaze colours included iron-red, violet-brown (from manganese), and pale yellow, two shades of blue and two shades of green. During the first period, colours were applied 'flat' with no shading, and outlines sometimes painted in manganese-brown or red. Gilding was not used on the earliest pieces, and probably not until after 1752 (see p.33). The effect was carefully calculated to achieve an oriental look for the decorative subjects chosen. These included pagodas, playing boys, chrysanthemums and other standard Kakiemon patterns, such as the 'banded hedge' and 'squirrel'. It is highly likely that this repertoire was developed shortly before or after the publication in December 1735 of the *Livre de Desseins Chinois*, a collection of engravings by Sieur Fraisse,[12] painter to the prince de Condé from 1732, which is dedicated to the Prince. The source of the painter's inspiration is elegantly acknowledged in the dedication: 'Mais quel lieu dans le monde pouvoit me fournir une plus belle collection de ce qui est sorti de plus précieux de la Chine & des Indes, que le Château de Chantilly?'

The dedication reveals the wide interests of the Prince, who kept a menagerie 'remplie des Animaux les plus rares', had a cabinet of natural history and a marvellous collection of oriental works of art, including textiles, lacquer and porcelains. The existence of the porcelain factory is confirmed in the same preface.

Little evidence survives of the scale and scope of the factory's production in its earliest years, apart from the considerable number of pieces in public and private collections.[13] From names traced in the parish registers[14] the factory appears to have grown rapidly in the 1730s. Gilles Dubois, younger brother of Robert, was taken on, apparently as an apprentice, in 1731.[15] Three years later Antoine Grémy (born at Delft in 1705), a painter, Pierre Lannoy, Antoine Fauchet, a moulder, and Marguerite Douillet were all employed at the factory, although it is not certain when they were first engaged. In 1736 Louis Goujon (b. 1711), a master sculptor originally from Rouen, is recorded as working for Cirou, although by 1737 he was living at Saint-Cloud.[16] No less than thirteen names of workers have been traced for 1737. One of these was Henry Bulidon (later of Vincennes, like so many Chantilly personnel). Few names occur in the parish records during the 1740s, probably because of the death of the Prince in 1740. The estate paid a final 2772 *livres*, a considerable sum, to 'Cirou, marchand de porcelaines à Chantilly, pour ses fournitures en 1737, 1738 et 1739'.

As the new prince, Louis-Joseph de Bourbon (1736–1818) was only four years old when he inherited the title, he was under the guardianship of his uncle, the comte de Charolais. This seems effectively to have meant retrenchment at the factory. No new employees appear in local records until 1745, when Jean Robin and two demoiselles Duclos, all painters, are recorded as working at the factory. Another painter, Edmond Robin, is recorded there three years later. A thrower, Michel Gabin, is known to have been there in 1750, the year before Cirou's death.

It is clear that in 1752 the factory received a new injection of capital and underwent reorganisation and consequent expansion of its administrative personnel. The new head of the factory was a certain de Roussière, in association with Jean-Baptiste-Suzanne Buquet de Montvallier. The latter, 'intéressé dans les affaires du Roy', was in sole charge from 1754. In this period two directors, Charles-Joseph Le Bouteiller de Bordage and Jacques Briet succeeded each other in 1752 and 1754. Nicolas-Claude Guenel was appointed inspector in 1754.

The workforce also grew in the early 1750s. In 1752 the painter Charles Buteux (at Sèvres from 1756)[17] and the sculptor Louis Fournier (at Vincennes in 1746–9, went to Copenhagen in 1759 to establish his own factory)[18] were recorded at Chantilly, and around twenty-five employees have been traced between 1752 and 1756. It is probable that improvements were made in the porcelain body around this time so that tin was not necessarily added to the glaze. Pieces such as cat. 44, although decorated with *chinoiserie* motifs (which remained popular in the early 1750s and were used at Vincennes), can be dated to around 1750 on the basis of their rococo form, but are covered with a colourless lead glaze. Gilding too may have been introduced in the 1750s. Jean-Mathias Caillat[19] was imprisoned in 1753 as punishment for selling the secret of his colours and gold to Chantilly.[20] Ground colours, including yellow, yellow-green, mid-blue and green and black trellis or marbling, were also probably put into production at this period, in parallel with the royal factory. Rococo forms, some highly exaggerated, and naturalistic flower and bird decoration appear in the middle period.[21]

In 1760 the régime of Buquet de Montvallier was replaced. Pierre Peyrard, principal concierge of the château of Chantilly and treasurer to the prince de Condé, who had now reached the age of majority, became the director (*maître de la manufacture*), probably acting on behalf of the Prince. Sieurs Nicolet and Lenoir, residing at the château, are respectively described as *conducteur* (works foreman) and *commis* (secretarial administrator) of the factory. Only two new workmen, Jean-François Drand[22] and Jacques Mathieu, both painters, are recorded in the 1760s, although no less than twelve new names appear in local records for 1774 – only two years before Peyrard sold out to Louis-François Gravant, whose father had worked at Vincennes.[23] Gravant's tenure was brief. In 1779, soon after reaching her majority, his wife Madeleine-Caroline-Gasparine Adam bought the factory from him, selling it in turn in July 1781 to André-Joseph Antheaume de Surval and his wife. Financial control was again evidently in the hands of the Prince, since Antheaume, *avocat au Parlement*, was *procureur fiscal* for the *Châtellanie et grurie* of Chantilly, and was married to the daughter of Jean-François Bourgeois, principal concierge of the château.

From documents recording these changes of ownership it is known that in 1781 the factory site was in the quartier des Fontaines and had extensive outbuildings. There were two biscuit kilns, four glaze kilns, workshops, a *magasin*, gardens and stores occupying 521 *toises* of ground.[24] The watermill for preparing the clays occupied a further twenty-six *toises* in the park.

The Chantilly factory ended the century under the ownership of an Englishman, Christophe(r) Potter, who purchased it in 1792 for a total of 64,142 *livres*. He made hard-paste porcelain. He also owned a factory in the rue de Crussol, Paris, acquired in 1789[25] (see p. 379). Potter sold the Chantilly concern in 1805 to S.G. Brecht. Hard-paste porcelain and creamware was made in Chantilly in the nineteenth and even in the twentieth centuries.[26] It is not represented in the Museum collections, with the exception of nos. 48, 49.

At the outset, oriental forms as well as decorative motifs were used (see cat. 38 and 39). However, it was not long before wine-coolers with rudimentary grotesque handles, bowls, jugs, salt-cellars and spice boxes (see cat. 40) came into production, to rival the Saint-Cloud tableware in the 1730s. As at Saint-Cloud, many forms were moulded rather than thrown. Figures of Chinese personages were probably made in the 1730s, but figure production clearly increased in the 1750s when elaborately painted examples serving as candelabra or *pot-pourri* supports or even incorporated into clock surrounds were mounted in ormolu and embellished with porcelain flowers. Meissen provided inspiration for some rather fine animal figures. Surviving examples show that boxes for snuff, bonbons or patches, and cane- and knife-handles were also produced in quantity.

Although never registered, a red hunting horn painted overglaze was probably used from the outset as the factory mark. It appears in blue or even pink enamel after about 1760, and is sometimes incised. Various signatures have been recorded,[27] but dated pieces are unknown. Pieces bearing the hunting horn mark and *P* are thought to date from after 1760 when Peyrard took over. This mark is often seen in underglaze-blue on service pieces with flower decoration in that colour. As some services, such as the one made for Louis-Philippe, duc d'Orléans, at Villers-Cotterets, have armorials, they were presumably made to order. Basketwork-moulded borders are particularly characteristic of plates and other service items made in the 1760s, and blue flowers are the most popular décor.

A surviving list of pieces supplied to the prince de Condé between 1781 and 1788, totalling 6602 *livres*[28] shows that a wide range of tablewares was in production. Gravy pots, mustard-pots and spoons, cheese dishes, *compotiers*, sugar bowls and boxes, salt-cellars, wine bottle- and glass-coolers all appear on this list. Most were inexpensive in comparison with Sèvres, although their decoration was of course much simpler than on most pieces sold from the royal factory. The dearest items were *seaux à bouteilles* priced at 72 *livres*. Fluted and gilt juice or gravy-pots cost 6 *livres*, perhaps not so much less than the equivalent piece sold by Sèvres in the 1780s.

Horace Walpole purchased a 'sceau for liqueurs' for 18 *livres* in 1765–6, a mug and small basin for 36 *livres*, two plates for 6 *livres*, and in 1767, two butter pots and two plates for which no price is given in his *Journals*.[29] The porcelain ceded to Potter in February 1792 by Sieur et dame Antheaume[30] included a variety of shapes: 'compotiers gros osier' and 'forme de Sève', 'plats ronds, ovales, carrés', 'seaux à verres', 'à liqueurs' and 'crennelés', 'coquetiers à pied' and 'à pied plat', 'salières à triangle' and 'doubles'. The most common decoration was 'oeillet', or pink, probably painted in underglaze-blue.

1. This account is largely based on Chavagnac and Grollier, 1906, pp. 59–90. For recent research see Le Duc, 1996 (full reference on page vii).
2. For a portrait of Mr le Duc, see Frégnac, 1964, p. 84. It must be said that no evidence has come to light to confirm the hypothesis that Condé backed the factory.
3. According to Frégnac, 1964, p. 85, no source given. Tony Stevenson has kindly drawn the writer's attention to information given in the Frédéric Halinbourg sale catalogue, Paris, Hôtel Drouot, 22, 23 May 1913, p. vii, quoting Archives de Condé, *quittance* dated 15 November 1730.
4. Chavagnac and Grollier, 1906, pp. 59–60.
5. According to Ballu, 1958, p. 105.
6. Several spellings of his name are known including Sicaire Sirou. See F. Chapard, 'Cicaire Cirou, premier maître porcelainier de la manufacture de Chantilly', *Le Musée Condé*, No. 1, October 1971, pp. 9–12. Ciroux' [*sic*] signature is shown on a parish register illus. p. 12.
7. Porcelain was not made in England until the mid-1740s.
8. The Weesp factory was the first to make porcelain in Holland from 1757.
9. Chavagnac and Grollier, 1906, pp. 70–1, Robert Dubois, thrower, and Jacques Poisson, later a moulder.
10. Le Duc and Guillebon, 1991, pp. 38–9.
11. See A. d'Albis, 'Les premières années de la manufacture de porcelaine de Vincennes', *Faenza*, Vol. LXX (1984), nos. 5–6, p. 486, extracted from the notebooks of Hellot, MNS, Archives de Sèvres, Y 51 *bis*. Chavagnac and Grollier, 1906, p. 74, n.1 quote Académie des Sciences, *mémoire* dated 13 November 1765, p. 92, 'La porcelaine de Chantilly se compose de marne de Luzarches citronnée de sable blanc de la butte d'Aumont et de potasse'.
12. For two illustrations from this work see Frégnac, 1964, p. 86.
13. The most notable are the Victoria and Albert Museum, London, the Musée des arts décoratifs, Paris, the Musée national de Céramique, Sèvres, and the Musée national Adrien-Dubouché, Limoges. Several remarkable pieces, including an elaborate cartel clock-case, are in the Metropolitan Museum, New York, see Linsky Collection catalogue 1984, no. 147, p. 238.

14. These names were published by Chavagnac and Grollier, 1906, pp. 70–3; signatures of modellers or moulders discovered by these authors on surviving pieces are listed pp. 73–4.
15. For some deatails of the peregrinations of the Dubois brothers see N. Ballu, 'La Carrière des Dubois', *Cahiers*, 10 (1958), pp. 92–3.
16. Le Duc and Guillebon, 1991, p. 41.
17. An outline of his career is given in Savill, 1988, III, pp. 1007–9.
18. See B. Grandjean, 'Louis Antoine Fournier', *Kunstindustrimuseum Virksomhed*, Copenhagen, 1969, pp. 79–128.
19. Caillat was a painter at Vincennes who was also employed to prepare colours, working period 1745–51. He had been imprisoned in early 1751 for trying to emigrate to England. Biographical details are given in Préaud and d'Albis, 1991, p. 203.
20. N. Ballu, *op cit.*, p. 92. According to documents kept at the Sèvres factory, he sold the secret to 'Manvallier' for 5632 *livres*, MNS, Archives de Sèvres, A2, *liasse* 4.
21. Some elaborate forms are illustrated by N. Ballu-Loureiro in 'Chantilly porcelain in the last half of the 18th century', *Antiques*, January 1961, pp. 88–91, and see Honey, 1950, pls. 18–33.
22. François Drand is recorded at Sèvres as a painter from May 1764 and was still there in 1779.
23. Louis-François Gravant was originally a maker of faïence at 'Vaureal proche de l'Isle Adam'; he is first recorded at Vincennes in 1741 and supplied paste and glaze until his death aged 49 on 4 March 1765, see A. d'Albis, 'Procédés de fabrication de la porcelaine tendre de Vincennes d'après les livres de Hellot', *Faenza*, no. 3–4, 1983, p. 202, f.n. 3. The son followed in his footsteps at Sèvres, but was dismissed in 1774.
24. A *toise* varied from district to district.
25. For a letter of 16 January 1793 addressed to William Duesbury, owner of the Derby porcelain factory, referring to 'Mr Potter' and his 'manufactory', see J.V.G. Mallet, 'Johnson and Porcelain Manufacture', *Journal of the Royal Society of Arts*, August 1985, p. 627.
26. A. Jacob, 'Chantilly XIXe au XXe. De la porcelaine dure à la faïence fine', *ABC Decor*, no. 217, February 1983, pp. 25–38.
27. See Chavagnac and Grollier, 1906, pp. 80–90. Marks are drawn in a supplement to N. Ballu, 'L'Influence de l'Extrême-Orient sur le style de Chantilly au XVIIIe siècle, *Cahiers*, 11, 1958, between p. 112 and p. 113, but unfortunately the pieces bearing signatures are not described or illustrated. The signature *Bonnefoy* together with a blue hunting horn above *A* has recently been seen by the writer on a *seau à verre* from the Villers-Cotterets Service, in the Museum of Fine Arts, Boston, inv. 65.1944.
28. Chavagnac and Grollier, 1906, p. 78.
29. F.J.B. Watson, 'Walpole and the Taste for French Porcelain', in W.H. Smith (ed.) *Horace Walpole, Writer, Politician and Connoisseur, Essays on the 250th Anniversary of Walpole's Birth*, New Haven and London, 1967, Appendix I, 'Walpole's Purchases of Porcelain', pp. 328, 331, 333, 335. A list of Chantilly porcelain belonging to the Duchess of Richmond in London on 25 June 1739 is published by Zelleke, 1991, p. 3.
30. Chavagnac and Grollier, 1906, pp. 79–80.

36 **Jug**, *c.* 1735–45

H.	5 cm
L. (*without handle*):	7.5 cm
Marks:	none
Reg. No.	OA 10454

Soft-paste porcelain, glazed, moulded with an acanthus leaf pattern, the hollow handle (now missing) forming a stalk, wavy rim with lip opposite handle. The cup stands on four rudimentary feet (one missing) formed of small rolls of clay luted to the cup with slip, of which traces remain around the missing foot. Sandy adhesions on base, and some discoloration in the glaze.

Provenance: Residue of the bequest of the late D.A. MacAlister Esq., given in 1971 to complement the MacAlister gift, 1959.

Literature: Unpublished

Comparable Examples: Besançon, Musée des Beaux-Arts et d'Archéologie, inv. 897.602, 1 & 2, with stand, marked, Kakiemon decoration

USA, Seattle, Seattle Art Museum, inv. 87.142.13, with stand, L. of stand incl. handle 13.7 cm, H. to top of cup handle 9.6 cm[1]

The porcelain has been analysed and the glaze found to contain a small amount of tin,[2] which is visible to the naked eye. It is not at present possible to distinguish analytically between French soft-paste types and those made at the English porcelain factories.

The jug is similar to Chelsea leaf-moulded tea-coffee- and chocolate-wares of the so-called Triangle Period (1745–9)[3] but the shape cannot be paralleled. Although the feet on the Museum example are separately modelled by hand, those on the Besançon jug are integrally moulded, as was done at the Chelsea factory, rather than luted to the piece. The existence of a marked Chantilly example of similar shape and dimensions published by John Mallet suggests that the Museum example was made at the same factory, although detailed physical comparisons have not been made, and this writer has not seen the Besançon pieces.

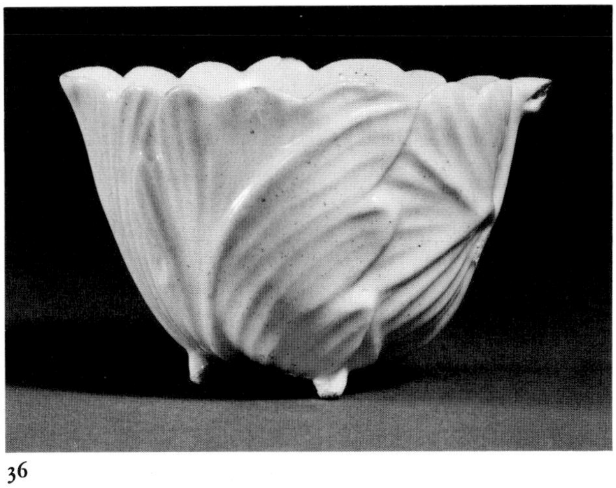

36

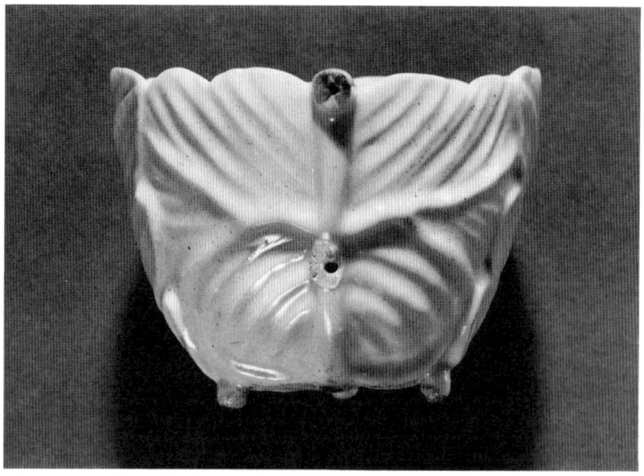

36 *remains of handle (broken)*

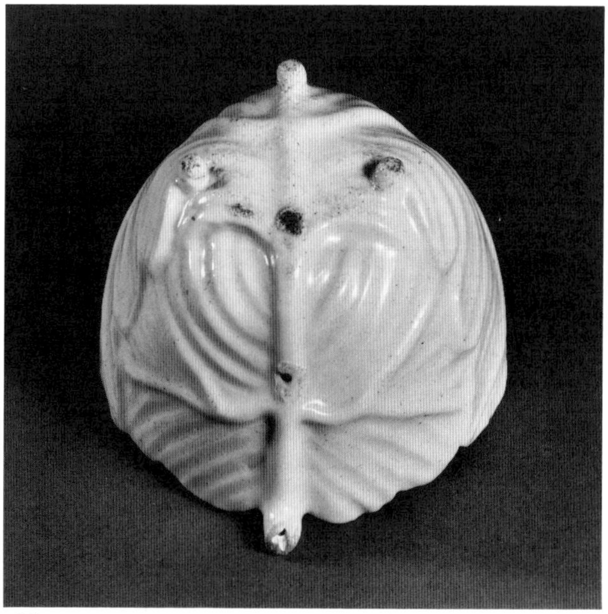

36 *base*

T.H. Clarke has drawn attention to the close relationship between raised and red anchor marked (1750–2 and 1752–8 respectively) Chelsea scolopendrium pattern wares and Chantilly pieces.[4]

1. J.V.G. Mallet, 'A Chelsea Talk'. *ECC Trans*, Vol. 6, Part 1, 1965, pl. 24b and p. 16. The author is grateful to John Mallet for this reference, and to him and Robert Williams and Julie Emerson for discussing these pieces with her. For the Seattle example see Emerson, 1990, p. 5, illus.
2. BMRL 34826Q; X-ray diffraction analysis shows this is a high calcium glassy paste. The author is grateful to Miss Mavis Bimson for her assistance in analysing this piece.
3. See J.C. Austin, *Chelsea Porcelain at Williamsburg*, Williamsburg, Virginia (USA), 1977, p. 41 and F.S. Mackenna, *Chelsea Porcelain, The Triangle and Raised Anchor Wares*, Leigh-on-Sea, 1948, pl. 2, no. 4. Mr Austin kindly informed the writer in correspondence of July 1990 that he now believes the piece to be French. Similar jugs marked with the incised triangle used at Chelsea were sold at Sotheby's, 23 January 1968, Lots 320, 321. Examination of the Williamsburg piece by the writer in October 1990 inclined her to believe that it was English (i.e. Chelsea), and its attribution must still remain unresolved.
4. T.H. Clarke, 'French Influences at Chelsea', *ECC Trans.*, Vol. 4, Part 5, 1959, pp. 50–5.

37 Teabowl, *c.* 1730–40

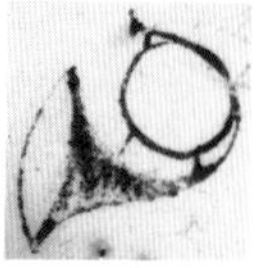

37 *mark*

D.	8.1 cm
H.	4.5 cm
Marks:	hunting horn painted in red
Reg. No.	Franks 347

Soft-paste porcelain with a tin glaze, flared sides and out-turned rim, shallow foot. The decoration consists on one side of a fan-shaped panel bounded by two red lines enclosing flowers and a rock in the Kakiemon style, painted in blue, green, yellow, red and brown; and on the other side of two plants painted in green, red and brown and blue, red and brown respectively, above green dots enclosed in brown (*Paulownia imperialis*). Inside the cup are two insects painted in green and brown disguising firecracks and around the base of the body is a red line which is repeated twice around the foot. Two chips to rim.

Provenance: Bequeathed by Sir A.W. Franks, 1897

Literature: Franks, 1896, no. 347

Comparable Examples: Limoges, Musée national Adrien-Dubouché, inv. 1270, slightly different size, Gasnault Collection, acquired 1881

Paris, Dragesco and Cramoisan, 1989, pair of cups with curved sides, and shallow saucers, similarly decorated

The uneven surface of the glaze, especially near the foot and rim and the inclusions in the paste suggest an early date of manufacture.

It is known that the oriental porcelain collection of more than two thousand pieces belonging to Monsieur le Duc, Louis-Henri de Bourbon Condé (1692–1740), provided inspiration for the Chantilly potters but no direct source for this cup has been found.[1] However, the fan-shaped panel was used on other cups and saucers made at Chantilly.[2]

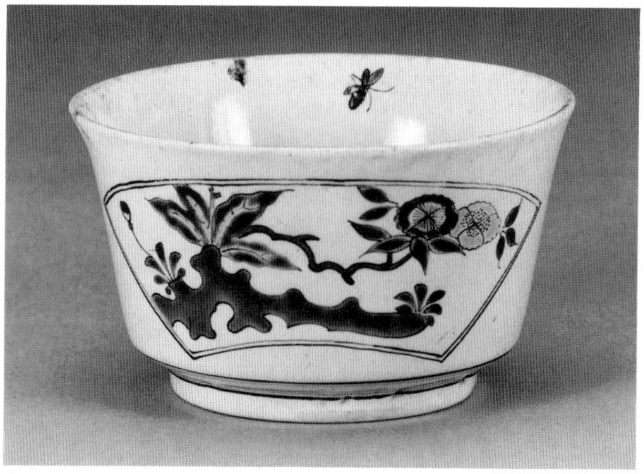

37

1. The author is grateful to John Ayers for his helpful comments.
2. See, for example, a handled cup of flared shape and saucer both painted with similar panels containing Kakiemon flowers sold at Sotheby's, 22 February 1966, Lot 7. The form (no dimensions given) differs slightly from the small Kakiemon-decorated flared beakers made at Meissen around 1725–30 from a private collection in Portugal illus. M. Shono, *Japanisches Aritaporzellan im sogenannten 'Kakiemonstil' als Vorbild für die Meissener Porzellanmanufaktur*, Munich, 1973, fig. 99, D. 7.9 cm, H. 6.7 cm.

38 **Fluted Dish,** second quarter of 18th century

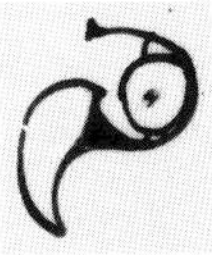

38 *mark*

L. 21.5 cm
Marks: hunting horn painted overglaze in red
Reg. No. FB 7 (AF 3192)

Soft-paste porcelain with a tin glaze, ribbed moulded body. Painted on both inner and outer surface in brown, blue, green, yellow and red-brown enamel colours with flowers and insects in the Kakiemon style. Two chips on rim.

Provenance: Bequeathed by Sir A.W. Franks, 1897

Literature: Honey, 1950, pl. 21B

T. Harrison Tidswell, 'The Influence of Oriental Porcelain on Western Ceramics', *Apollo*, Vol. CX, no. 211, September 1979, fig. 18, p. 218

Comparable Examples: None

This sparingly decorated dish is of an unusual form based on an oriental prototype or possibly on contemporary metalwork. There is a Kakiemon mould which is close to this form.[1] The decoration was probably adapted rather than copied from Kakiemon porcelain. The function of this dish is uncertain – it may perhaps have been part of a table service, but whether for dinner or dessert is unclear. A fluted bowl in the Metropolitan Museum, New York, is similarly decorated.[2] Other fluted forms, such as a bowl, are known at Chantilly.[3]

1. 'The World of Kakiemon', exh. cat., eight venues in Japan, March–July 1982, compiled by Y. Nagatake, Y. Yabe, H. Minamoto, publ. Asahi News Western Department, no. 138, a modern water bowl, possibly for the tea ceremony. The author is grateful to Victor Harris of the Department of Japanese Antiquities, British Museum, for help in translating parts of this catalogue.
2. Inv. 50.211.116; D. $5\frac{3}{8}$ in; H. $2\frac{3}{8}$ in.
3. Chantilly, Musée Condé, illus. Dallot-Naudin, 'Chantilly', 1983, p. 26, H. 5 cm.

39 **Saucer-dish (*compotier*),** second quarter of 18th century

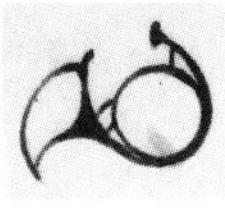

39 *mark*

D. 18.8 cm
Marks: hunting horn painted in red
Reg. No. 1931,10–19,13

Soft-paste porcelain with a tin glaze. Deep dish with lobed rim. Painted in blue, two colours of green, yellow, orange, purple and brown with stylised flowering branches and insects in the Kakiemon style. Rim painted in brown.

Provenance: Transferred from the Salisbury and South Wiltshire and Blackmore Museum, 1931

Literature: Unpublished

Comparable Examples: Co. Durham, Barnard Castle, Bowes Museum, inv. X1332

Christie's, 29 October 1973, Lot 113 (minor variation in size, pattern different)

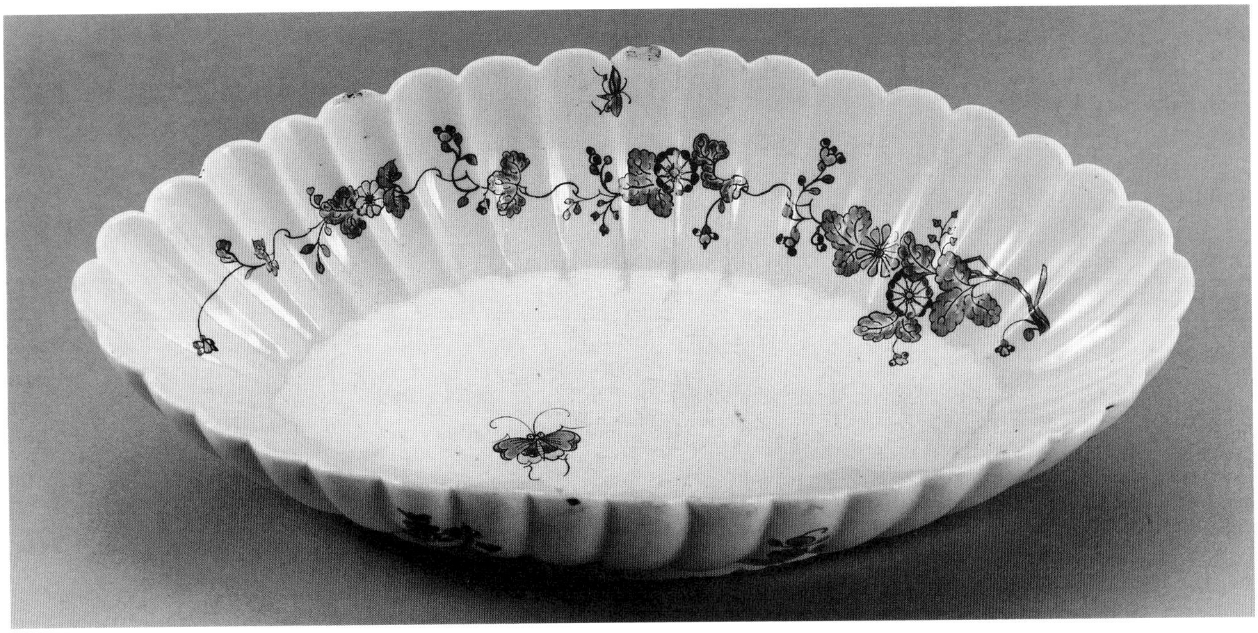

38

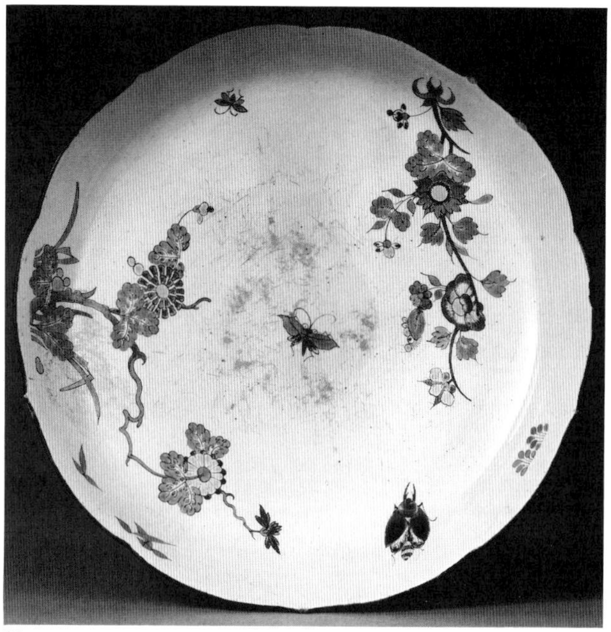

39

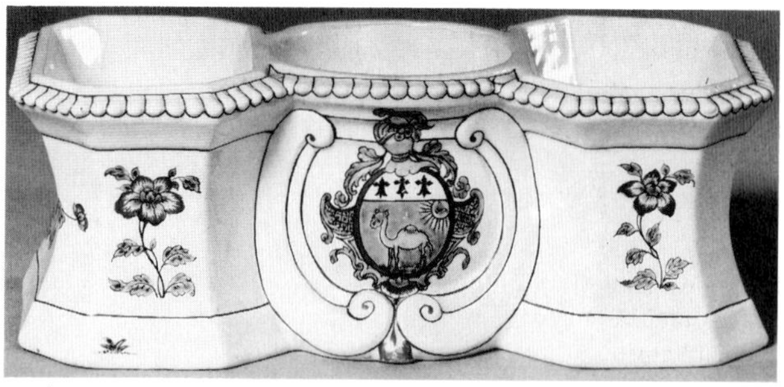

40 *front*

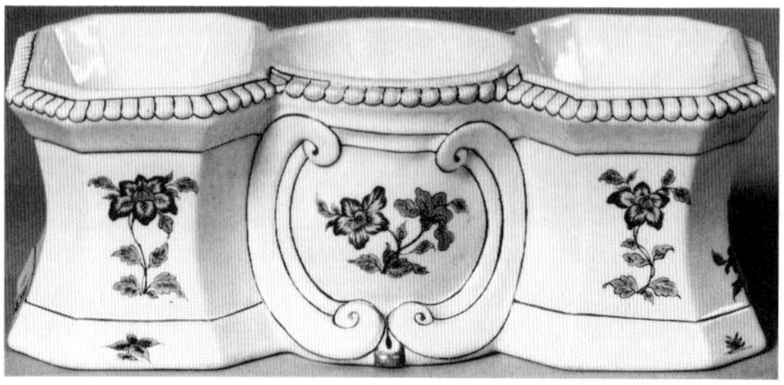

40 *back*

A firecrack in the centre of the dish and another on the outside of the rim show that the factory experienced difficulty in firing this exceptionally large piece. The brown rim and the decorative scheme are likely to have been copied from oriental porcelains in the collection of the duc de Bourbon.[1]

The purpose of this dish is uncertain. It may have been intended for fruit compôte. A rather similar form was manufactured at Chantilly some decades later.[2]

1. See a Japanese dish with a slightly simpler moulded rim made around 1700, D. 23 cm in the Museum für Angewandte Kunst, Vienna, illus. Shono, 1973, fig. 26.
2. Chantilly, Musée Condé, painted with scattered blue flowers, D. 24.5 cm; illus. Dallot-Naudin, 'Chantilly', 1983, p. 59; a fluted variation on the shape of the Museum example, with a similar decorative scheme, D. 14.5 cm, in the Musée Condé, Chantilly, is illus., *ibid.*, p. 46.

40 **Spice Box,** *c.* 1760

H.	5.7 cm
L.	15.8 cm
Marks:	hunting horn painted in red
Reg. No.	1987,1–7,1

Soft-paste porcelain with a tin glaze, hollow, moulded, the lower part made separately from the upper and luted to it. The ends are of waisted form, the central panel is slightly bulbous and is framed by moulded rococo scrolls. The three compartments, the flanking ones of octagonal shape, the central one oval, are bordered by a ribbed moulding. The decoration consists of flowers painted in the Kakiemon style in black, green, yellow, blue and orange enamels. In the front central panel in the same palette is a (fanciful) coat of arms; *on an oval escutcheon amidst scrolling mantling surmounted by a helm set sideways or the visor closed, azure a*

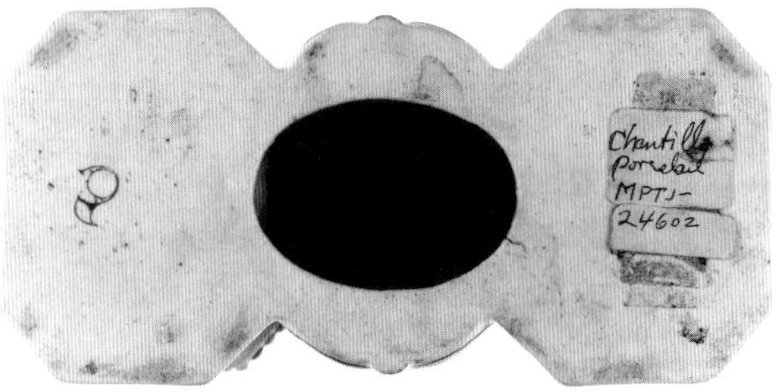

40 *base*

camel statant or, in sinister chief the sun with a human face; a chief argent. The moulding is picked out in orange. The base is unglazed and has an oval hole. The edge of the back of the central compartment has been restored: it once had a porcelain attachment to allow for the fitting of a lid, now missing.

Provenance: Presented by Dr Henry Ginsburg, 1987; perhaps from the Dupuy Collection

Literature: Unpublished

Comparable Examples: Paris, with Bernard Dragesco and D. Cramoisan, 1986 (cover missing)

Sotheby's, 4 July 1967, Lot 26; pair with arms identified as those of Poterat/Condé, with porcelain cover.

USA, New York, Parke-Bernet Galleries, Estate of the Late Pauline Riggs Noyes (Karrick Riggs Collection), 7–8 February 1947, Lot 50

Examples without armorials:

France, Comtesse de Cristenoy de Lyonne (illus. *Cahiers*, no. 11, 1958, p. 107, fig. 10

Sotheby's, 2 March 1982, Lot 129, painted with two birds in front panel, silver-gilt mount by Bointaburet, Paris, about 1900

London, Armin B. Allen, The Henry C. and Martha L. Isaacson Collection, June 1989, cat. 73, two, covers missing, decorated with birds and flowers (further examples listed)

London, E. & H. Manners, exhibited International Ceramics Fair and Seminar Ltd., June 1990, cover missing

USA, New York, Parke-Bernet Galleries, Estate of the Late Pauline Riggs Noyes (Karrick Riggs Collection) 7–8 February 1947, Lot 49

USA, New York, Parke-Bernet Galleries, Dupuy Collection, 2 April 1948, Lot 101

USA, Mr and Mrs William Brown Meloney Collection (illus. *Connoisseur*, Vol. CXLIII, no. 577, April 1959, p. 138, fig. 7, two, one with cover)

Spice boxes with two compartments of this shape were made in Paris in silver as early as 1713–14.[1] The number of surviving Chantilly porcelain examples with three compartments indicate that they were produced in some quantity. On most examples it is clear that the central compartment had a shell-moulded porcelain cover, attached by means of a porcelain 'hinge', missing on this example.[2] The central compartment was clearly intended for a substance which needed to be kept covered, possibly mustard.

The rather free style of flower painting and the palette used relate closely to the decoration of the sugar bowl and cover (cat. 44), and the marks are similar.

A rather similar Meissen spice box with central shell-moulded cover painted in the Kakiemon style and dating from about 1735–40 is in the Rijksmuseum, Amsterdam.[3]

1. Faith Dennis, 'Three Centuries of French Domestic Silver: its makers and its marks', exh., Metropolitan Museum of Art, New York, 1938, fig. 326 and p. 218–19.
2. A covered example was sold at Sotheby's, 4 July 1967, Lot 26, illus.
3. Shono, 1973, fig. 72, inv. RBK 17357, overall L. 19.2 cm.

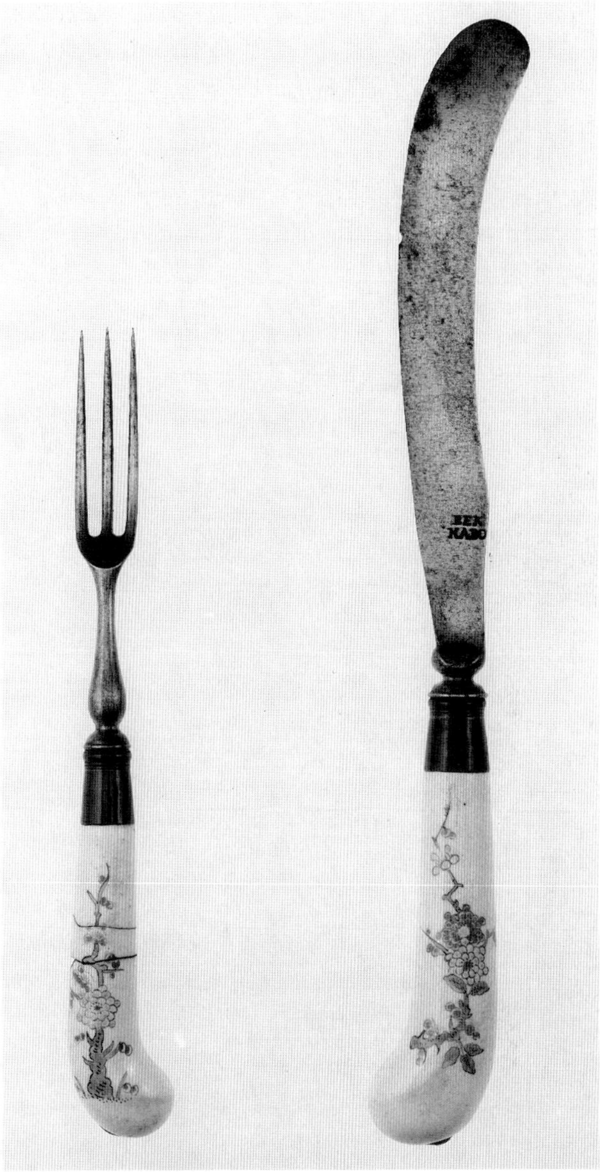

41

41 **Knife and Fork with Porcelain Handles**, second quarter of the 18th century

L. *of handle:*	7.9 cm (knife); 6.5 cm (fork)
Total L. *of knife:*	23.6 cm
Total L. *of fork:*	17 cm
Marks:	porcelain unmarked: knife blade stamped BER/NADO
Reg. No.	Franks 351

Soft-paste porcelain with a tin glaze, painted in blue, green, yellow, orange and black enamels with flowers in the Kakiemon style. At the end of each handle is a metal button. Both handles have signs of wear; around the fork handle are two cracks, on one of which is a chip. The ferrules are silver, the blade and tines of steel.

Provenance: Bequeathed by Sir A.W. Franks, 1897

Literature: Franks, 1896, no. 351

Comparable Examples: England, private collection, fork illus. *Collins Encyclopaedia of Antiques*, London and Glasgow, 1973, p. 204

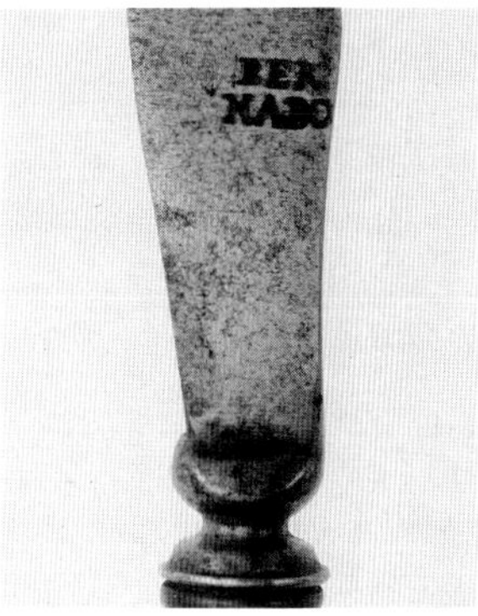

41 *mark on blade*

USA, Seattle, Seattle Art Museum, inv. 87.142.8[1]

USA, Washington D.C., Smithsonian Institution, National Museum of American History, two fork-handles of pistol form with steel tines, inv. 529A, B

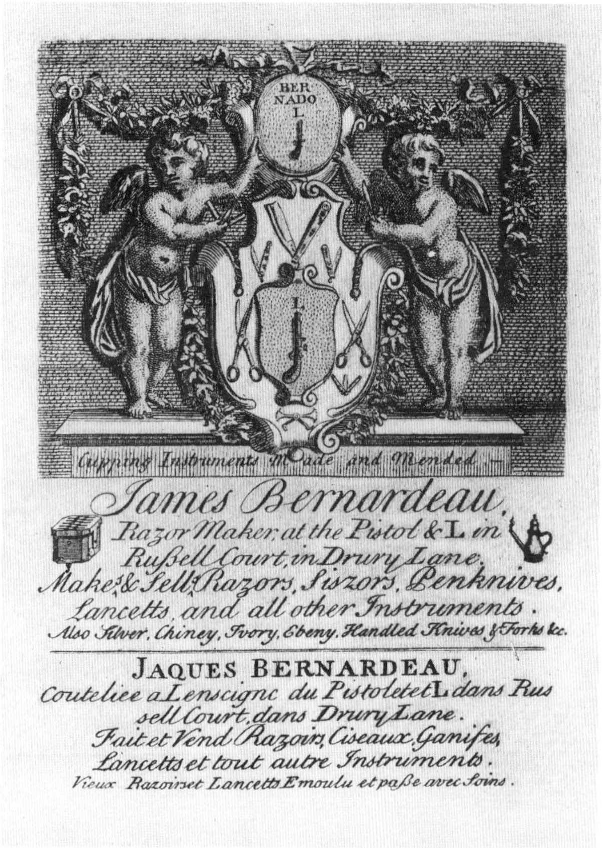

Fig 41a Trade card

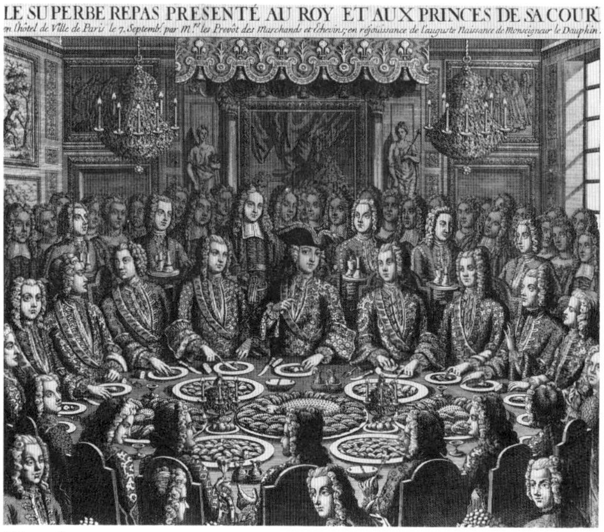

Fig 41b

The knife blade is English and bears the mark of the razor maker James Bernadeau 'at the Pistol and L in Russell Court in Drury Lane'.[2] He is recorded there as early as 1726 when he took out a policy with the Sun Insurance Company, but by 1770 he had died and had been succeeded by his nephew Stephen Gagnon.[3] His wife is mentioned in John Bowcocke's *Memorandum Book* under the date 24 July 1756: 'The knife handles: how many sold of Dresden flowers? and to have a double dozn. mounted. Has Mrs Bernadeau had what she ordered of the wheatsheaf?'[4]

Forks with three tines can be seen in use in an engraving of the 'Superbe Repas presenté au roy . . . en réjoüissance de l'auguste Naissance de Monseigneur le Dauphin' on 7 September, 1729 (see fig. 41b).[5]

1. Emerson, 1990, p. 8.
2. Bernadeau's trade card was published by Heal, 1925, pl. LXXXI (see fig. 41a).
3. Two bill heads from the Heal Collection from James Bernadeau to Sir Richard Hoare, dated 8 January 1746/7, and to Mr Bennett, dated 22 December 1753, also show this cutler's mark. They are annotated with Bernadeau's Policy No. 40910, and information about his nephew (British Museum, Department of Prints and Drawings, Heal Collection, 52.8, 52.9).
4. Quoted E. Adams and D. Redstone, *Bow Porcelain*, London, 1981, Appendix IV, p. 211.
5. Bibliothèque Nationale, Paris, Département des Estampes.

42 **Box and Cover,** *c.* 1740–50

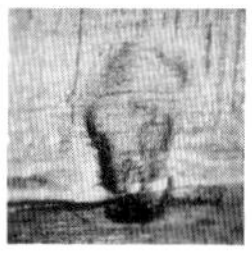

42 *mark on mount*

D.	5.2 cm
H.	3.5 cm
Marks:	indecipherable mark on silver-gilt mount(?)
Reg. No.	Franks 349

Soft-paste porcelain with a tin glaze, thrown; of waisted form, with slightly domed cover, mounted in silver with slight traces of gilding. The decoration on the cover consists of a stylised oriental flowering tree on a mound and a flying insect painted in yellow, green, blue, orange-red and brown; on the exterior and inside the cover are leaves and flowers similarly painted and on the base two insects in orange-red, blue and manganese.

Provenance: Bequeathed by Sir A.W. Franks, 1897

Literature: Franks, 1896, no. 349

Comparable Examples: None noted

In view of its size, the box may perhaps have been intended for bonbons or face patches, rather than for snuff.

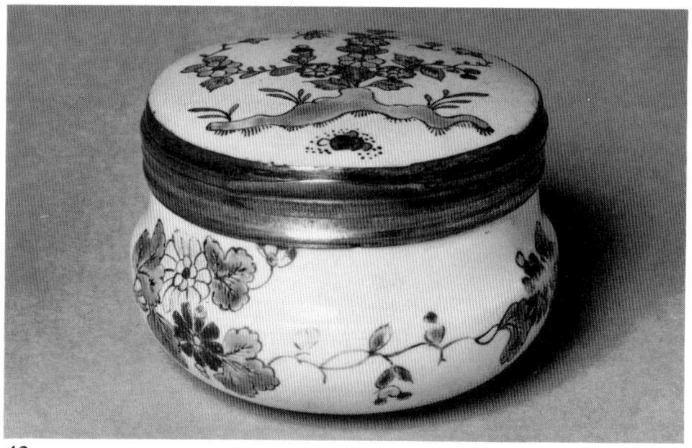

42

This jar once contained *refrigerans Galeni Ceratum*, a 'cerate compounded from oil of roses (or oil of sweet almonds), white wax and chilled water'[1] apparently used for inflammations and as an emollient.[2]

1. Drey, 1978, p. 226.
2. *Ibid.*

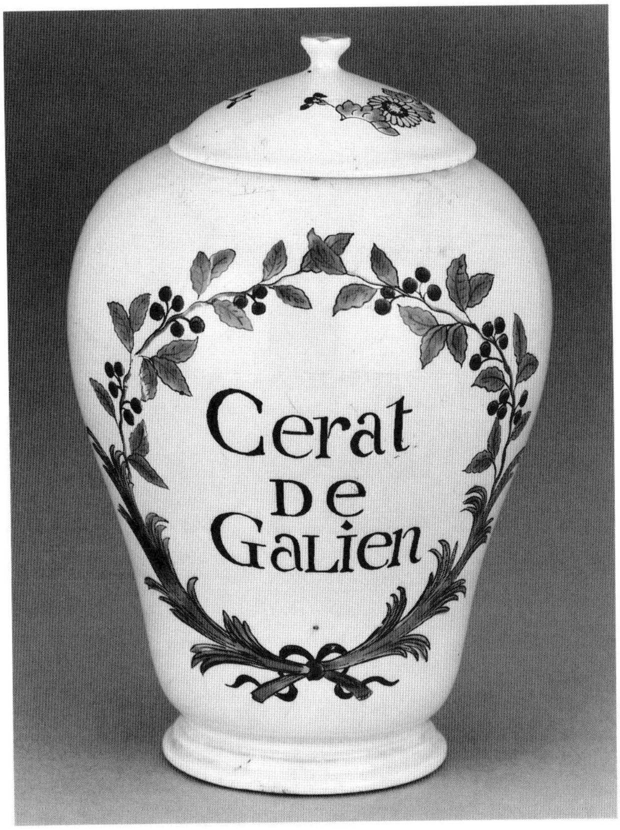

43

43 **Drug Jar and Cover,** *c.* 1750

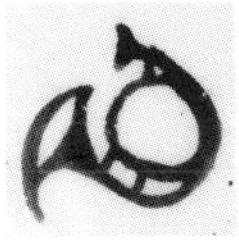

43 *mark*

H. *incl. cover:*	15.5 cm
Marks:	hunting horn painted overglaze in red
Reg. No.	1901,12–16,1

Soft-paste porcelain with a tin glaze. Of undulating, high-shouldered form with domed cover and flattened knop of conical section. Decorated on the reverse with flowers painted in blue, green, yellow, brown, and red-brown enamels in the Kakiemon style, repeated on the cover. On the front is an inscription in black *Cerat De Galien* within a leaf and berry and reed wreath tied with a ribbon. Foot and knop chipped.

Provenance: Presented by J.H. Fitzhenry, Esq., 1901

Literature: R.E.A. Drey, 'Une série de vases de pharmacie en porcelaine tendre de Chantilly', *Revue d'Histoire de la Pharmacie*, Vol. XX, no. 210, September 1971, pp. 475–8, pl. LXXXI

R.E.A. Drey, *Apothecary Jars*, London, 1984, p. 84, pl. 57A

R.E.A. Drey, *Apothekengefässe*, Munich, 1980, p. 184, fig. 215

R.E.A. Drey, *Pots de Pharmacie du Monde Entier*, Paris, 1978, fig. 226

Comparable Examples: A series of drug jars of this type are listed by Drey (1971). Examples have appeared on the market, e.g. Christie's, 28 November 1977, Lot 8, no inscription (lacked cover)

The existence of drug jars painted with the leaf and berry wreath but with no inscription suggests that the jars may have been supplied to order, or that the legend was painted on after the jar had left the factory.

44 **Sugar Bowl and Cover,** *c.* 1750

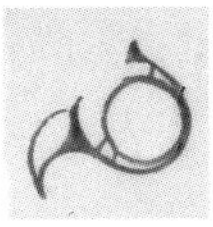

44 *mark*

H. *incl. cover:*	10.8 cm
Marks:	hunting horn painted overglaze in red
Reg. No.	1977,11–2,1

Soft-paste porcelain, finely potted, with a lead glaze. Of undulating form, with domed cover surmounted by three large applied bell-shaped flowers. Decorated in two shades of green, blue, yellow, brown, purple and orange enamels with flowering branches and insects in the Kakiemon style. The flowers on the cover are partly painted in yellow, blue and orange respectively, two with an orange stamen, the orange flower with a yellow stamen.

Provenance: Presented by Dr Douglas Barrett, 1977, former Keeper of Oriental Antiquities, to whom it had been given by his friends to mark his retirement, 1977

Literature: Probably the one shown in *Apollo*, Vol. XCIV, no. 148, June 1974, p. 54 (Supplement, Fine Art & Antiques Festival), fig. 20 'European Porcelain Decorated in the Kakiemon Style' as being exhibited by Winifred Williams Antiques

Comparable Examples: Christie's, 29 October 1973, Lot 136

Christie's 20 October 1975, Lot 29

Exh. Allen, 1989, cat. no. 79 (cover missing)

The decoration resembles that found on the spice box (cat. 40). A teapot and cover with matching decoration and finial is in the Musée national Adrien-Dubouché, Limoges.[1]

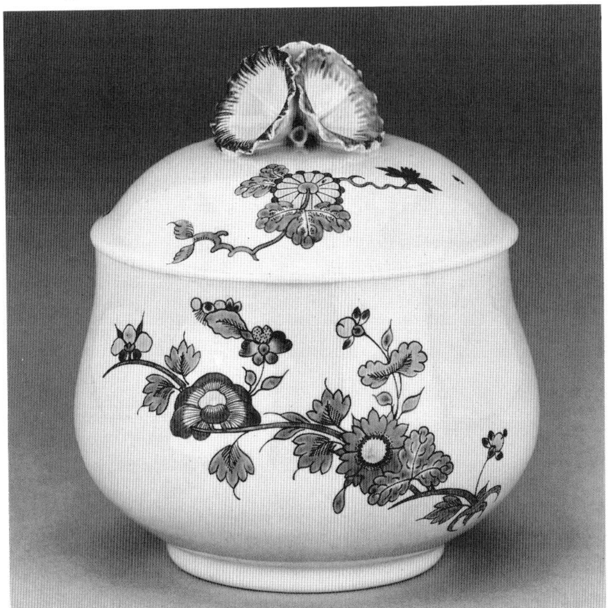

44

The same type of flower finial favoured at Chantilly can be seen on cream-coloured earthenwares made at the Pont-aux-Choux factory, Paris.[2]

1. H.-P. Fourest, *Masterpieces of Western and Near Eastern Ceramics, Vol. VI. French Ceramics*, Tokyo, 1979, no. 74, inv. ADL 106.
2. Dr. Chompret, J. Bloch, J. Guérin and P. Alfassa, *Répertoire de la Faïence Française publié à l'occasion de 'L'Exposition rétrospective de la Faïence Française' au musée des arts décoratifs*, Vol. III, Paris, 1933, pl. 5, C, D; pl. 8, B, C.

45 **Plate**, *c.* 1760

See colour plate 5

D. 24.5 cm
Marks: hunting horn above *B* painted in overglaze in blue; *B* incised
Reg. No. 1931,10-19,12

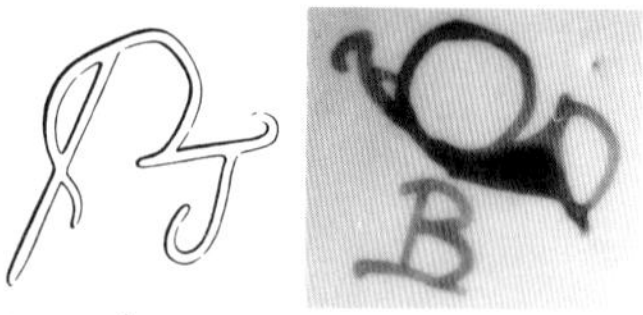

45 *marks*

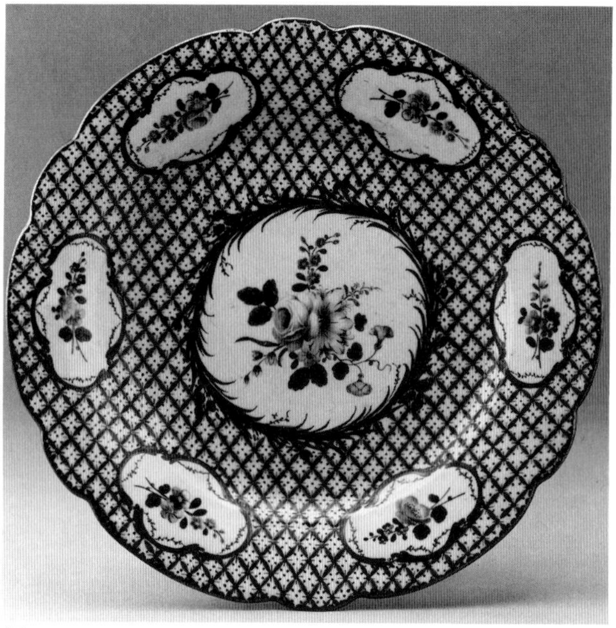

45

Soft-paste porcelain with a lead glaze, moulded with six lobes alternating with six smaller lobes. The decoration consists of six quatrefoil-shaped reserves near the rim painted with flowers in pink, purple, blue, green, yellow, orange and black on a white ground outlined with gilt scrolls and a central panel of flowers outlined with gilt fronds on a blue diaper-pattern ground enriched with blue and gilt dots. Gilt dentil pattern on rim.

Provenance: Transferred from the Salisbury and South Wiltshire and Blackmore Museum, 1931

Literature: Unpublished

Comparable Examples: Paris, Musée des arts décoratifs, illus. Frégnac, 1964, p. 110 (dish)

Limoges, Musée national Adrien-Dubouché

Saumur, château de Saumur, illus. Jacob, 1980, pl. LXVIII

Christie's, 2 October 1989, Lot 202, painted hunting horn mark and *R*, incised hunting horn

Former Mrs H. Dupuy Collection, sold New York, Parke-Bernet, 2 April 1948, Lot 183 (from the Yanville sale, Paris, Hôtel Drouot, 20-22 February 1907, Lot 165; from the Halinbourg sale, Paris, 22-23 May 1913, Lot 78)

A. Chevet Collection, sold Paris, Hôtel Drouot, 5-6 November 1951, Lot 60

René Fribourg Collection, sold Sotheby's, The René Fribourg Collection V French Faïence and European Porcelain Part 2, 15 October 1963, Lot 396, oval dish, L. 24.7 cm (with further references)

Sisted Hall, Lionel Faudel-Phillips Collection, 1926, illus. *Burlington Magazine*, Vol. XLIX, no. CCLXXX, July 1926, p. 24, pl. III, fig. D, oval dish (probably a *plateau* or stand)

A *compotier rond* from the richly decorated service is in the Musée des arts décoratifs, Paris,[1] and another is in the Museo Duca di Martina, Naples.[2] An oval *compotier* is in the Rijksmuseum, Amsterdam.[3] A *seau à bouteille* can be found in the Musée Condé, Chantilly.[4] The same diapered blue ground was also used in combination with bird, hunting or fable decoration in reserves[5] and as a border pattern.[6] It appears to be peculiar to the Chantilly factory, although both the royal factory and Mennecy used quadrilobe patterns. It was even used as an all-over pattern, as on a cup and saucer in the Cleveland Museum of Art.[7]

It is just possible that the pattern may have been the one described as 'à mosaïque' in the list of porcelain delivered to the prince de Condé by Monsieur de Surval, the owner of the Chantilly factory, between 1781 and 1789. Wine-coolers (supplied in 1787) were priced at the relatively high sum of 72 *livres*, plates at 24 *livres*, *seaux à demi-bouteilles* at 72 *livres* and a *seau à mosaïque pour mettre des fleurs* at 60 *livres*.[8] However, this seems a remarkably late date for this type of pattern, unless the pieces were intended as replacements.

A large number of marks which include painted and incised initials together with the hunting horn are listed by Chavagnac and Grollier,[9] but their significance has not so far been explained. Until more information has been discovered concerning the functions of the workmen at the factory, the marks on this dish must remain anonymous.

1. Dupont, 1987, p. 57
2. M.L. Casanova, *Le Porcellane Francesi nei Musei di Napoli*, Naples, 1974, p. 110, no. 42.
3. Inv. R.B.K. 1966-108, see *Bulletin of the Rijksmuseum*, no. 14, 1966, p. 90-1, fig. 11.
4. P. Kjellberg, 'Peu d'obstacles pour reconnaître les porcelaines de Chantilly', *Connaissance des Arts*, Vol. 146, April 1964, p. 82; two wine-coolers decorated with flowers were in the Yanville sale, Paris, Hôtel Drouot, 20-22 February 1907, Lot 164.

5. Kjellberg, *op. cit.*, fig. 25, painted with the *Fable of the Stork and the Fox*, private collection, and another fable piece (with a second fable-decorated plate both D. 24.2 cm) were sold from the René Fribourg Collection, Sotheby's, The René Fribourg Collection v French Faïence and European Porcelain Part 2, 15 October 1963, Lot 395. An unusual plate, its reserves painted with hunting subjects, including a stag at bay in the central reserve, was sold from the Mrs H. Dupuy Collection, New York, Parke-Bernet, 2 April 1948, Lot 180. A plate with the same subject in the centre and its six border reserves left undecorated was in the Yanville sale, Paris, Hôtel Drouot, 20–22 February 1907, Lot 166. Another with a boar hunt in the centre and undecorated border reserves is in the Victoria and Albert Museum, London, inv. 329–1905, and a stag hunt is shown on a tray in the Forsyth Wickes Collection, Museum of Fine Arts, Boston, see Munger *et al.*, 1992, no. 176. A plate with birds in each reserve was sold from the A. Chevet Collection, Paris, Hôtel Drouot, 5–6 November 1951, Lot 61; another was in the Chavagnac Collection, see Chavagnac and Grollier, 1906, p. 86, no. 54.
6. Honey, 1950, pl. 30A, Victoria and Albert Museum, London.
7. Inv. 62.345,a, D. of saucer $2\frac{5}{16}$ in; H. of cup $2\frac{3}{8}$ in; hunting horn mark and *R* in blue, *D* incised.
8. Chavagnac and Grollier, 1906, p. 78.
9. *Ibid.*, pp. 80–90.

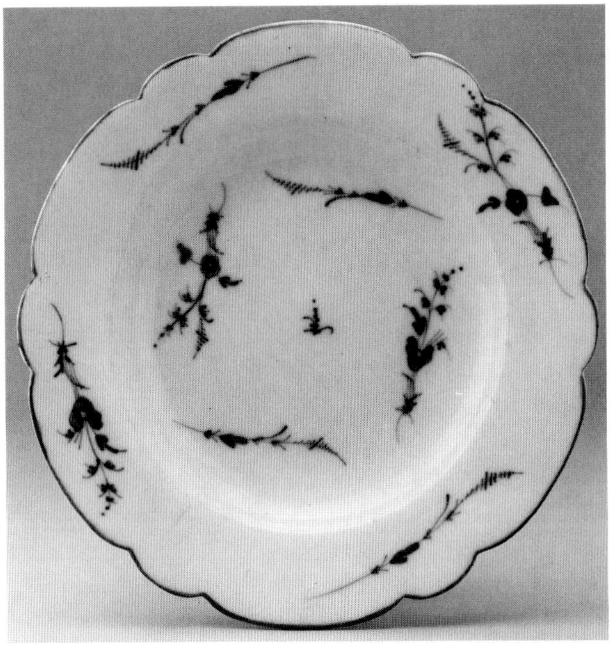

46

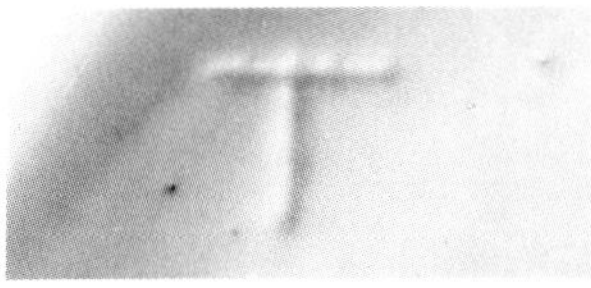

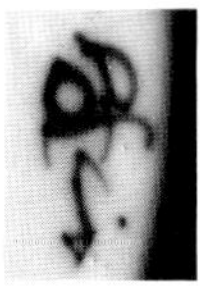

46 *marks*

46 **Soup Plate**, third quarter of 18th century

D. 24.1 cm
Marks: hunting horn above *L.* painted in underglaze-blue; incised *T*
Reg. No. 1924,2–11,1

Soft-paste porcelain with a lead glaze. Deep plate with wide border moulded with six wide lobes alternating with a smaller one. Painted in underglaze-blue with scattered leaf and flower sprays; border outlined in blue.

Provenance: Presented by W.W. Winkworth, Esq., MC, Assistant in the Department of Ceramics and Ethnography, 1922–6, British Museum, 1924

Literature: Unpublished

Comparable Examples: Denmark, National Museum, illus. K. Ortengren, *Klassiska porslinsdekorer*, Århus, 1973, no. 9
USA, New York, Christie's, 30 January 1988, Lot 143

The style of the plate is characteristic of the late eighteenth century and the painted motifs can be compared with the spare underglaze-blue decoration found in Arras[1] and Tournay[2] porcelains, as well as with Caughley porcelains produced contemporaneously in Shropshire, England.[3] A rather similar motif was used at the Locré factory, La Courtille, Paris.[4]

For other similarly decorated Chantilly domestic wares, see Frégnac[5] and d'Albis *et al.*[6]

The significance of the marks is unknown. Either of two workmen listed by Chavagnac,[7] Lay and Jean Ledoux, both there in 1774, might perhaps have been responsible for the painting.

1. See for example a plate in the Musée d'Arras, inv. prov. 371, exh. Nord-Pas-de-Calais, 1986–7, no. 6., see also A. Notter, Porcelaine d'Arras, collection du Musée d'Arras, exh. Musée des Beaux-Arts, Arras, February 1992, pp. 63–73.
2. M. Jottrand, 'Cent Ans de Porcelaines de Tournai, le legs André Belley', exh. Musée royal de Mariemont, Belgium, March–August 1984, no. 89, D. 25.8 cm.
3. B. Watney, *English Blue and White Porcelain of the 18th Century*, London, 1979 (repr. 2nd ed.), pl. 89B, wine-cooler, Victoria and Albert Museum, London. For the influence of Chantilly on Caughley, see pp. 118–19.
4. Bloit, 1988, p. 22, *compotier carré*, erroneously called a 'cake tray'.
5. Frégnac, 1964, p. 114.
6. D'Albis *et al.*, 1989, pp. 108–9.
7. Chavagnac and Grollier, 1906, p. 73. The list of artists and workmen employed at Chantilly was compiled from the archives of the château de Chantilly, parish registers and archives of the Sèvres factory.

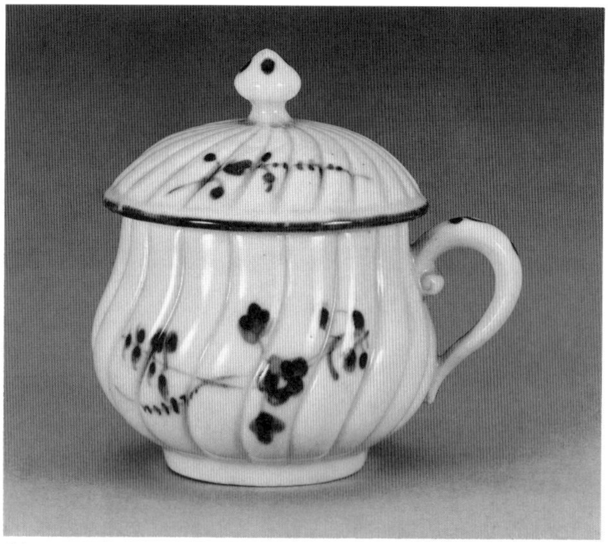

47

47 Gravy-pot and Cover (*pot à jus*), probably *c.* 1775–80

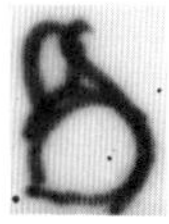

47 *mark*

H. *incl. cover*: 7.4 cm
Marks: hunting horn painted in underglaze-blue
Reg. No: Franks 348

Creamy soft-paste porcelain with a lead glaze; the cup of bulbous form, its ear-shaped handle terminating at the upper end in a scroll, the domed cover with knop of conical section. Both moulded with a differing spirally-fluted ribbed pattern. Decorated in underglaze-blue with two stylised flower sprays, four dots on knop and a line and dot motif on the handle. Rim of cover painted in blue. Firecrack inside cup.

Provenance: Bequeathed by Sir A.W. Franks, 1897

Literature: Franks, 1896, no. 348

Comparable Examples: USA, Washington D.C., Smithsonian Institution, National Museum of American History, blue horn mark and *B*, incised *PB*, inv. 480A; blue horn mark and *Y*, incised *8*, inv. 480B, both about 8 cm in height

Sotheby's, 11 April 1972, Lot 101, mark as above, incised *D* and *Aba* (also see Chavagnac, p. 86, no. 55, incised *D. Abbany*)

In about 1750 the factory began to use a lead glaze. This pattern, or variants of it usually called 'à la brindille' or 'Chantilly sprig', was popular in the later part of the century and was in production elsewhere, for example at Arras.[1] An unusual cup and saucer at present attributed to the Orléans factory is similarly decorated.[2]

1. A closely related pattern described as 'décor de M. de Calonne' is found on a plate in the Musée d'Arras, inv. prov. 371, illus. exh. Nord-Pas-de-Calais, 1986–7, no. 6.
2. Washington, D.C., Smithsonian Institution, National Museum of American History, inv. 1437 a and b, deep saucer and conical cup, tapering handle, both marked with label and *C*, cup incised *P11*, soft-paste porcelain. There is some controversy about the origin of pieces bearing this mark, as it is close to the one registered by Seguin at Vincennes (see p. 299).

48 Cup and Saucer (*tasse et soucoupe de limonadier*), late 18th or early 19th century

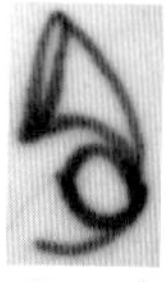

48 *mark*

D. *of saucer*: 12.3 cm
H. *of cup*: 5.1 cm
Marks: crudely drawn hunting horn painted in underglaze-blue on each
Reg. No. 1937,6–14,1

'Hard-paste' porcelain,[1] the saucer with curved sides, the thickly potted cup having an exceptionally deep foot rim. Both pieces painted in underglaze-blue with a debased *chinoiserie* design. Inclusion on underside of saucer, both crazed, rim of cup chipped.

Provenance: Presented by Monsieur Adolphe Lion, 1937

Literature: Unpublished

Comparable Examples: Limoges, Musée national Adrien-Dubouché, inv. 1923, incised *g*, Dubouché Gift, 1869

Chantilly, Musée Condé, illus. Dallot-Naudin, 'Chantilly', 1983, p. 58, apparently a larger size

Sèvres, Musée national de Céramique, inv. 13313, Grollier gift, probably Chavagnac and Grollier, 1906, p. 88, no. 73, inv. 13319, and inv. 6300 marked *Chantilly*, acquired 1835

Paris, Louvre excavations, illus. N. Lacoudre, *Electricité et Archéologie*, Paris, 1988, pp. 50, 52–3

A drawing of a *tasse à café* or coffee cup, *en usage à Paris*, dated March 1809, is preserved in the archives of the Manufacture nationale de Sèvres. The drawing bears the caption 'Limonadier no. 5'.[2] However, the form was probably in use in the 1760s since *tasses à limonade* are mentioned in the inventory made at the time of the liquidation of the Saint-Cloud porcelain factory in 1766.[3] An example bearing the factory mark 'h' and decorated in underglaze-blue in the Chinese style, made at Hannong's factory in the rue du faubourg Saint-Denis, Paris, dates from the early 1770s,[4] as does an example from the Locré factory.[5] Chantilly also seems to have manufactured the cup and saucer in a larger size (see comparable examples). In a printed list of prices issued by Pouyat brothers of rue Fontaine-au-Roi, faubourg de Temple, Paris, and Tours, département of Nièvre,[6] is a section entitled *Objets de limonadier*. It includes cups and saucers in three sizes and three qualities, a *bol à pied détaché à drageoir* (comfit dish), a *génieu épais et soucoupe* (according to Régine de Guillebon 'le "génieux" est une grande tasse cylindrique qui n'est jamais accompagnée d'une soucoupe et dont on peut trouver l'équivalent en Grande-Bretagne sous le nom de "mug"')[7], a chocolate cup and saucer and a teapot in three sizes. Each was supplied in several sizes and in a variety of decoration, with gold lines or cornflowers (*barbeaux*, abbreviated to *barbx.* in the list).

The crudely drawn hunting horn mark is said to

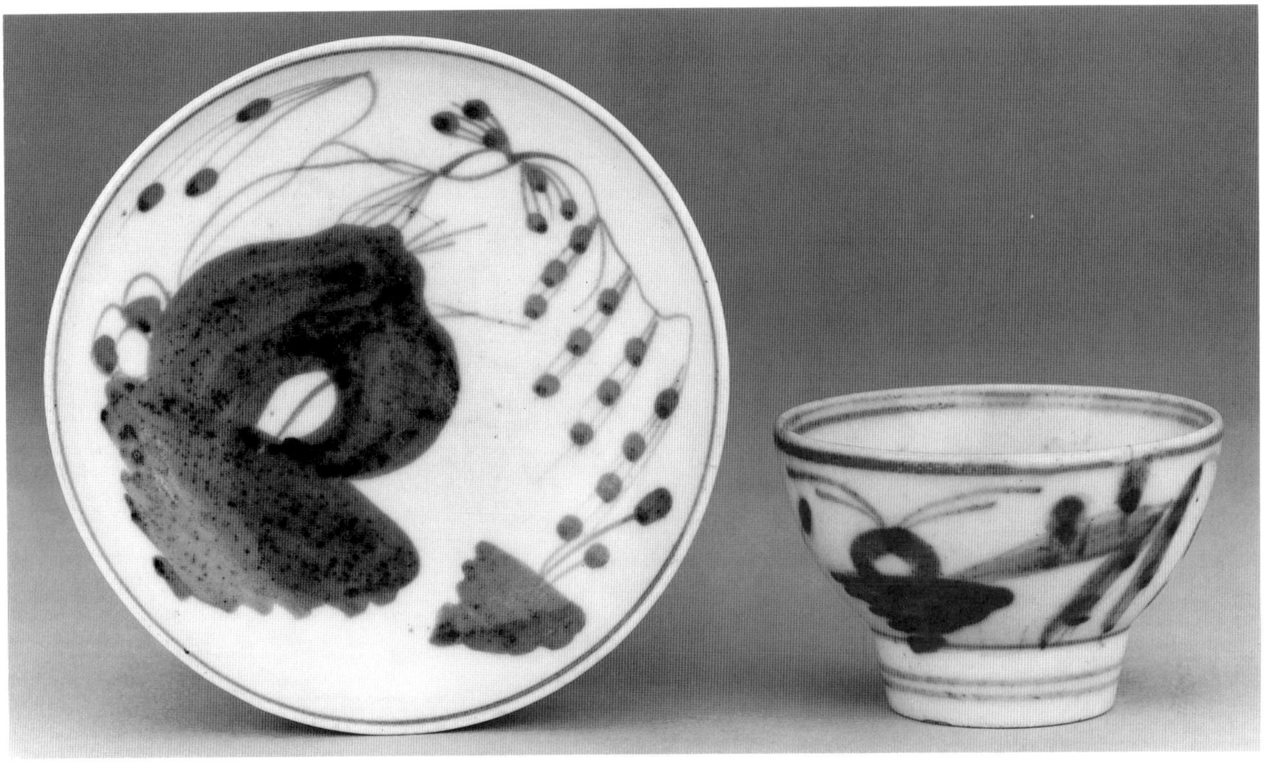

48

have been used by Pierre Peyrard, who bought the Chantilly factory from Antheaume de Surval in 1760 and sold it to Louis-François Gravant in 1764.[8] But the dating of this piece is problematical. In view of the unusual nature of the composition of the body (see note 1), it may have been manufactured after the acquisition of the factory by Christopher Potter, who made hard-paste, in 1792.

1. The British Museum Research Laboratory has analysed the porcelain body (File 5819) to find that a poorly-developed mullite phase may be present, which would indicate hard-paste, but the crystalline phase is chiefly made up of coarse quartz particles. The author is grateful to Mavis Bimson for this information.
2. MNS, Archives de Sèvres, *tiroir* BI (*tasses diverses*); illus. Guillebon, 1985, pl. XII, fig. 20. Shown below in fig. 21 is an example decorated in underglaze-blue in a pseudo-Chinese style by Pouyat.
3. Chavagnac and Grollier, 1906, p. 19.
4. Sèvres, Musée national de Céramique, illus. R. de Plinval de Guillebon, 'Premières porcelaines dures de Paris', *Antologia di Belle Arte*, Nuova serie, nos. 29–30, 1986, p. 30, fig. 1.
5. Bloit, 1988, p.22.
6. MNS, Archives de Sèvres, U19, *liasse* II, *dossier* I. The list is dated 1820 in ink. The author is grateful to Tamara Préaud for drawing these documents to her attention.
7. Régine de Plinval de Guillebon, *Musée du Louvre, département des objets d'art. Catalogue des Porcelaines françaises I*, Paris, 1992, p. 193. However, it seems that sometimes these 'mugs' did have saucers.
8. Chavagnac and Grollier, *op. cit.*, pp. 68–9, citing Archives de la Seine, Bilans no. 18, a reference which is believed to be no longer correct because of reorganisation of the archives.

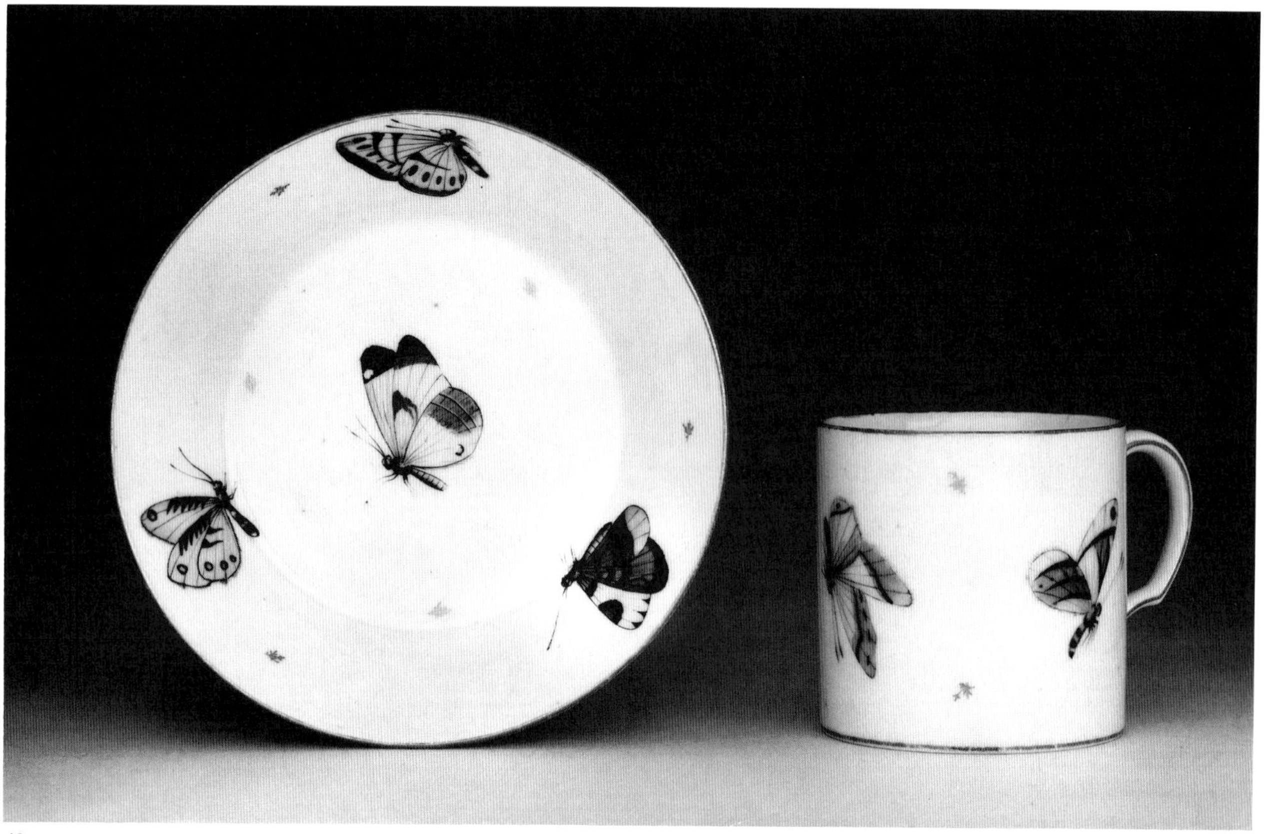

49

49 **Coffee cup and Saucer (*tasse à café*)**, early 19th century

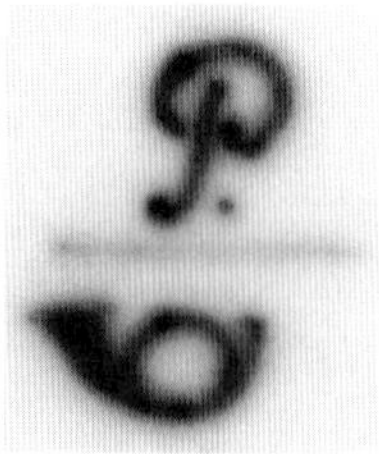

49 *mark*

H. *of cup:*	6.2 cm
D. *of saucer:*	12.4 cm
Marks:	*P.* and blue hunting horn below a line painted in underglaze-blue on both
Reg. No.	1931,10-19,11

Hard-paste porcelain; straight-sided cup with shaped handle, its lower terminal out-turned; saucer with flared sides, both decorated with butterflies painted in black, yellow, brown, green, red-brown and purple and small scattered gilt leaves. Rims and edges of handle gilt, gilt dot-and-leaf motif on handle. Handle and rim of cup repaired.

Provenance: Transferred from the Salisbury, South Wiltshire and Blackmore Museum, 1931; formerly in the W.D. Wilkes Collection (no. 110), bequeathed by him (through his widow), 1917

Literature: Reports of Salisbury, South Wiltshire and Blackmore Museum, 1902-3, 1903-4, 1916-17, 1917-18, 1919-1920, 1921-2, 1929-30, 1930-31, 1931-2 (on W.D. Wilkes Collection)

Comparable Examples: Sèvres, Musée national de Céramique, *seau à bouteille*, inv. MNC 13.816

Butterflies were an extremely popular decorative motif in the early years of the nineteenth century, and were often depicted with great accuracy.

50 **Dish**, probably made late 18th century, factory uncertain, decoration 19th century

D.	31 cm
Marks:	hunting horn above cursive *P* and dot, all in gold; incised [?] *4*, drilled hole in foot rim
Reg. No.	Franks 350

Hard-paste porcelain with shaped rim and deep border. Painted in underglaze-blue with a hawking scene within a square reserve outlined with gilt flowers and with a stag, a dog, a hare and a chamois[?] in shaped reserves outlined by gilding, all on a yellow ground. Gilt flower sprays and gilding around central reserve laid over underglaze-blue decoration of flower sprigs. Gilt rim.

Provenance: Bequeathed by Sir A.W. Franks, 1897

Literature: Franks, 1896, no. 350

Chaffers, 1926, Vol. II, p. 335, fig. 287

E. Hannover and B. Rackham, *Pottery and Porcelain, A Handbook for Collectors* III. *European Porcelain*, London, 1925, p. 25, fig. 26

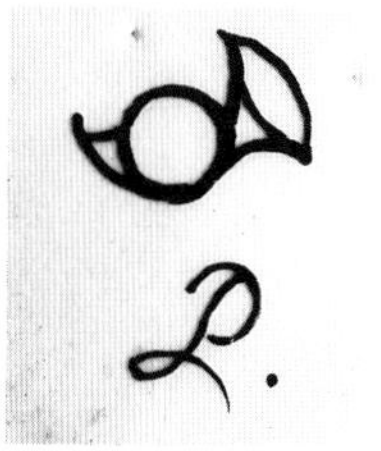

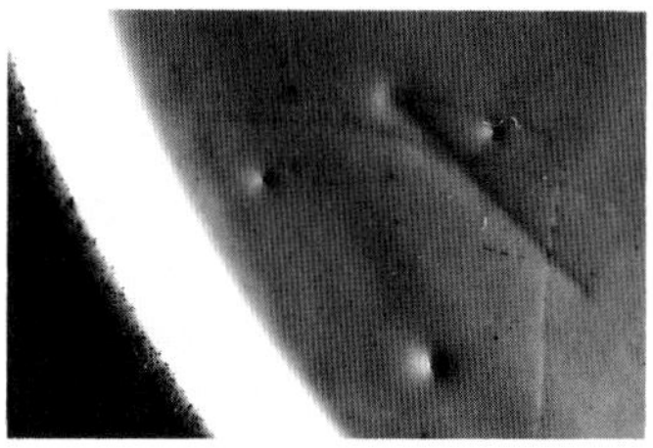

50 *marks*

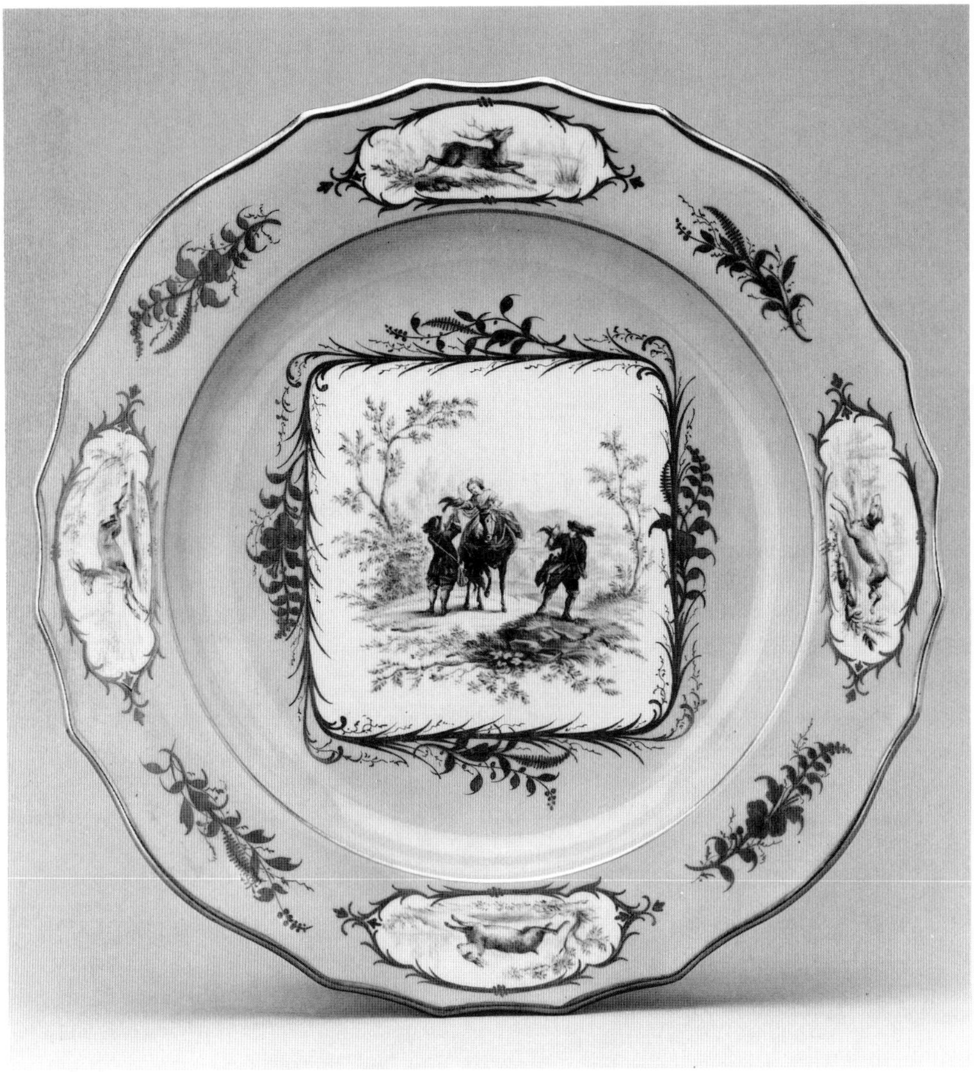

50

F.H. Hofmann, *Das Porzellan der Europaïschen Manufakturen im XVIII Jahrhundert*, Berlin, 1932, pl. 522

Comparable Examples: London, Wilfred J. Sainsbury Collection, yellow-ground plate with square reserve containing gilt birds and gilt floral and bird decoration, blue hunting horn mark. The shape differs from the museum piece and it has a suspension hole at the back. Attributed to Brussels about 1830, illus. W.J. Sainsbury, 'A Rogue's Gallery of Continental Soft-Paste Porcelain', *Apollo*, Vol. LIII, no. 311, January 1951, p. 11, fig. 1.

The body and decoration of this piece do not accord with any known product of the Chantilly factory. The plate is likely to have been made in the late eighteenth or early nineteenth century on the evidence of the flower sprigs below the yellow ground which was added later. The gilding is also a later addition. Its place of manufacture has not yet been determined; Mireille Jottrand has suggested that the dish was made at the Bettignies factory, Saint-Amand-les Eaux (Nord), in the early nineteenth century, but as yet no parallel has been discovered.[1] Some details of this factory's productions, often in the Sèvres manner, are given by Chavagnac and Grollier.[2]

1. Mireille Jottrand has kindly drawn to the author's notice a Tournai dish measuring 24.2 cm and decorated in underglaze-blue with 'Chantilly sprigs', illus. *Cent Ans de Porcelaines de Tournai, le legs André Belley*, exh. March–August 1984, Musée royal de Mariemont, Belgium, no. 89.
2. Chavagnac and Grollier, 1906, pp. 508–11.

Villeroy

The early history of the Villeroy-Mennecy factory remains unclear.[1] Both faïence and porcelain manufacture were apparently carried out by François Barbin from about 1737 (if not earlier) at the hamlet of Villeroy in the parish of Mennecy, in the grounds of the château owned by François-Louis-Anne de Neufville (1695–1766), who became fourth duc de Villeroy in 1734.[2] Barbin was born about 1689–90,[3] probably in Paris, the son of a carpenter and *maître-tourneur* of the same name and died in Mennecy aged 74. In a complaint to the police about his neighbours in the rue de Charonne, Paris, Barbin described himself in November 1733 as 'Manufacturier de Faïence et de Porcelaine'.[4] Porcelain fragments of cane- and knife-handles, one markd *DV* in blue, were found at the end of the nineteenth century by Aymé Darblay[5] in the ruins of the château and in its grounds, together with (?) kiln bricks and crucibles. The concern existed for twelve years and, as a total of only fifteen employees appear in local parish records, it is clear that production was on a small scale. It closed soon after November 1748.

Only one item, a tin-glazed earthenware jug in the Musée national de Céramique, Sèvres,[6] can with certainty be ascribed to the Villeroy enterprise. It bears the mark *DV*, is dated 1738 and is decorated with the arms of Villeroy. On stylistic grounds, pieces bearing the painted mark *DV* (sometimes with as many as three dots between the initials) are currently attributed to Villeroy, whilst those with the mark incised are thought by Geneviève Le Duc to have been produced at Mennecy (see below). A feeder in the form of a fish with sharp teeth (perhaps for fish broth), painted with Chinese figures, flowers, birds and a running dog, is inscribed with an anchor above *DV* and *Pierre/Bon/*[*?*]*Ducet* and dated 1745.[7] This feeder is the only dated piece known to this writer.

During the period of activity of the Villeroy concern, Barbin is recorded between 1734 and 1748 as a 'marchant fayancier porselainier' at a house in the rue de Charonne, faubourg Saint-Antoine, Paris, which he purchased in 1734 and subsequently enlarged.[8] In May 1748 he is recorded as having lived there fourteen years when his porcelain was seized by the authorities and sold, forcing him to work under the protection of the duc de Villeroy. In a *procès verbal* of that month he sought permission to build a furnace or enamelling kiln at rue de Charonne, but no evidence exists to show either that this was to replace an earlier one, or that it was ever built and used. Indeed in a decree of the Council of State of 6 August 1748 he was expressly forbidden to set up any new establishment to make porcelain, which would infringe the monopoly status granted to the Vincennes factory.[9] A study of his house suggests that lacking any suitable doorway (*porte-cochère*), to bring in raw materials, it could not have been used for porcelain manufacture; it may perhaps have been the premises of a decorating workshop, or simply no more than a warehouse for porcelain.

During the twelve or so years it was in production, only three men worked continuously at Barbin's factory. They were Nicolas Meunier, a painter, Joseph Huet, a sculptor, and Jean-Baptiste Biesse, a *compagnon-fayancier*. A total of approximately fifteen employees seem to have been attached at one time or another to the factory, excluding Barbin's two sons, who assisted him. It has been estimated that there were two sculptors, or figure-makers, five painters, one kiln-master (*enfourneur*) and seven workmen (*ouvriers*). Only one of these was local. No employees have been traced after leaving Villeroy.[10]

The exact range of pieces made at Villeroy has not yet been securely established. It is possible that porcelain production included not only the modest knife-handles and other domestic articles decorated in underglaze-blue, but also some coloured figures in the oriental style marked with a painted *DV*, as well as grotesques and figures of the Cries of Paris. The pieces were sold in Paris by Barbin's wife, Marie-Marguerite Bertrand (d. 1753, aged 64) from their house at 33, rue de Charonne. Some decorating may conceivably have been done there. The scale of production is uncertain, but an inventory of 1762 mentions '1 millier de pièces ou environ tant en faïence en biscuit anciennement faites à Villeroy lors que ladite manufacture y était établie que pièces de porcelaines, manches de couteau, pommes de cannes, tabatières, gobelets, soucoupes et autres la plupart défectueuses cassées ou brisées' (about one thousand pieces of undecorated tin-glazed earthenware made at the former factory at Villeroy when the said factory was located there and porcelain knife-handles, cane-handles, snuffboxes, cups, saucers and others mostly defective or broken).[11]

The last we hear of the factory on this site is in a notarial act of November 1748.[12]

1. The most recent account, based on archival research and reproducing a number of important documents, is by Duchon, 1988. A shorter study by G. Le Duc, *La porcelaine de Villeroy*, privately published in typescript by the French Porcelain Society, London, 1987, is also valuable. Both should be read in conjunction with Chavagnac and Grollier, 1906. pp. 96–105, the only other account based on the surviving documentation.
2. A detail of an engraving representing the Duke is illus. Frégnac, 1964, p. 118. It has been suggested that an unmarked white glazed porcelain bust formerly in the Chavagnac Collection and sold at the Hôtel Drouot, Paris, 18–21 June 1911, Lot 20 (as Saint-Cloud), now in a private collection in Great Britain, may perhaps represent the Duke, but if so he is shown without orders of any kind, even though he was a Marshal of France.
3. Le Duc, 1987, pp. 5–6; Duchon, 1988, p. 7.
4. Duchon, *op. cit.*, pp. 10–11.
5. Darblay, 1901, p. 75 and pl. XXVII.
6. Inv. MNC 6.415, illus. and described in exh. Faïences françaises, 1980, no. 128, p. 112.
7. Metropolitan Museum, New York, inv. 54.147.8.
8. Le Duc, *op. cit.*, p. 8.
9. The *arrêt* is quoted by N. Duchon, *op. cit.*, pp. 28–9.
10. Le Duc, *op. cit.*, p. 23.
11. The inventory is transcribed by Duchon, *op. cit.*, pp. 145–7.
12. Le Duc, *op. cit.*, p. 29, no archival reference cited.

51 **Egg Cup,**
perhaps Villeroy 1737–48

See colour plate 2

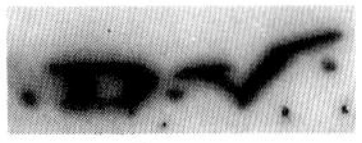

51 *mark*

H.	9.6 cm
Marks:	*D. V.* painted in underglaze blue
Reg. No.	Franks 354

Soft-paste porcelain, heavily potted, with a slightly milky lead glaze;[1] lower part of the cup and foot moulded with a ribbed pattern, underneath of foot turned; decorated with a delicately painted scroll and stylised flower pattern on the foot and near rim, and with a cell pattern at upper end of stem.

Provenance: Bequeathed by Sir A.W. Franks, 1897

Literature: Franks, 1896, no. 354

Comparable Examples: C.W. Reynolds Collection, 1863, see W. Chaffers, *Marks and Monograms on Pottery and Porcelain*, London, 1863, p. 203.

Underglaze-blue painted decoration on Villeroy-Mennecy porcelain, with the exception of knife-handles, is rare.[2] The heaviness of the piece, its moulding, style of decoration and unusual mark suggest an early date of manufacture. A silver egg cup by Aymé Joubert with Paris hallmarks for 1725–6, which has a gadrooned foot, is in the Metropolitan Museum, New York.[3]

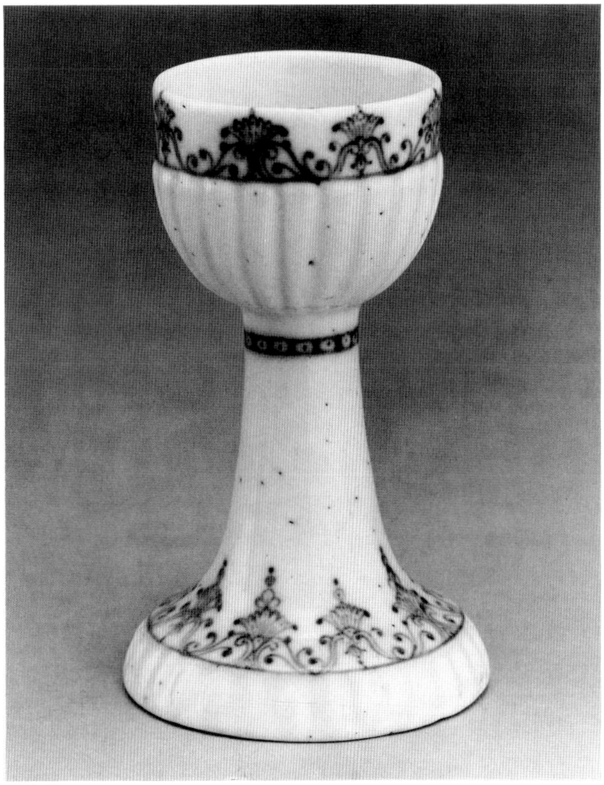

51

1. By analysis it has been established that the glaze of this egg cup contains around 2% tin, BMRL 31602X. Two grotesque figures marked *.D. V.* also have a milky look to the glaze; these have not been analysed, Boston, Museum of Fine Arts, Rita and Frits Markus Collection, inv. 1982, 778, 779. Hawes and Corsiglia, 1984, pl. XII, no. 55.
2. A teapot and two small pots and covers painted in underglaze-blue from the Musée des arts decoratifs, château de Saumur are illustrated by Duchon, 1988, p. 27, who presumably attributes them to Villeroy-Mennecy even in the absence of a factory mark. A tobacco jar and cover marked *D, V*, its silver-gilt mount bearing the discharge mark for Louis Robin, 1735–8, carefully painted in underglaze-blue with scrolls and stylised flowers, and two blue bands near the foot, is illustrated by D. Gage and M. Marsh, *Tobacco Containers and Accessories*, London, 1988, pp. 102–3.
3. A. Grüber, *L'Argenterie de Maison du XVIe au XIXe siècle*, Fribourg, 1982, fig. 212, p. 156.

Mennecy[1]

In 1749 François Barbin and his wife bought a house in Mennecy, in the rue Milly.[2] In the following year they established in the rue du Puits-Massé a factory 'ditte de Villeroy établie au village de Mennecy' with their son Jean-Baptiste Barbin (1720–65).[3] In 1753 both men were referred to as 'l'un des entrepreneurs de la manufacture de porcelaine'.[4]

Jean-Baptiste Barbin is next mentioned in a document of 1756 concerning the exchange with the duc de Villeroy of a parcel of land in the rue du Puits-Massé in Mennecy for another on ruelle du cul luy faut. Barbin senior, who was almost illiterate, was forcibly retired in 1762 and the business taken over by his son. He died aged 74 on 27 August 1765. His son died, deeply in debt, only a few weeks afterwards. From March 1766 Joseph Jullien and Symphorien Jacques, both of Sceaux, rented the factory from the Widow Barbin.[5] In 1769 the men are referred to in parish registers as 'maîtres des manufactures de Villeroy et de Sceaux'.[6] A report dated 19 August 1774[7] to the head of the Paris police, Sartine, by Buchot, one of his *inspecteurs*, refers to Villeroy under the name of 'Le S. Jacques', as follows: 'Cette manufacture L'une des plus anciennes a eu quelques succès. L'éloignement de Paris a déterminé Le S. Jacques à La quitter à l'Expiration de son Bail prochain. Elle peint de toutes Couleurs Et dore'. The dating is inaccurate, as the lease in fact expired in 1773, although rent was paid by the two men to the widow Barbin up to March 1775.[8]

The earliest description of the constituents of the Mennecy porcelain body is probably to be found in the notebooks compiled by Jean-Mathias Caillat, a painter at Vincennes who also prepared colours for use there, and transcribed by Jean Hellot in 1751 when he compiled his report for the minister of finance, Machault d'Arnouville. The formula of the frit, which contained 59% sand, has been published by Antoine d'Albis,[9] together with that for the body, made up of 80% frit and 20% *marne* (marl) 'from Monsieur Menard's quarry'. An anonymous note sent perhaps some ten years later to the duc d'Orléans contains details of various porcelains.[10] Villeroy porcelain (which was still referred to by this title in the 1770s, as we have seen) was said to be made of Fontainebleau sand, tripoli[11] and potassium.

The varied products of the Mennecy factory included: snuff- and patch-boxes, many with moulded basketwork decoration, or covers moulded as figures of shepherdesses or animals, especially dogs; toilet pots painted with flowers; knife- and fork-handles decorated over the glaze in colours with figures in the Chinese style; cane-handles with *commedia dell'arte* characters, and inscribed with gallant verses; cups and saucers, teapots, sugar bowls, salt-cellars, plates, jugs and basins, glass-coolers, vases of various shapes and even a wall-fountain (a *fontaine en rocaille en biscuit cassé* is listed in the inventory of 2 August 1762).[12] Figures were sold unglazed, glazed and glazed and painted. Many, such as those of orientals, musicians, figures of the 'Cris de Paris', and even animals, were small in scale and were intended as table-decoration.[13] Impressive sculptural works and large biscuit portrait medallions were also part of the factory's considerable output.[14] Horace Walpole owned 'a Villeroy ewer', probably purchased after 1767 on one of his trips to Paris.[15]

The palette included a characteristic pink, extensively used in depicting flowers, together with green, yellow, brown and blue. Lime-green grounds were produced, sometimes pebbled, or *caillouté*, in black.

Names of some of the workers at the factory have been extracted from the parish records of Mennecy, Bourg-la-Reine, Sceaux and Montereau-fault-Yonne.[16] The total number of workers exceeded one hundred and twenty. Several of the eight sculptors documented between 1753 and 1764 had been at, or passed on to, other porcelain factories: Christophe Mô came from Sceaux (listed there in 1766 and at Mennecy in August 1767) and went to Locré's factory at Paris, rue Fountaine-au-Roy; Jean-Baptiste Mô[17] went to Bourg-la-Reine after the closure of Mennecy; Bernard Huet, at Mennecy in May 1764, was at Orléans in 1767 and had lived in Paris in the faubourg Saint-Laurent before going south. Of the six throwers, one, Jean-Edmé Pinard, was at Sceaux in 1781 and another, Antoine Tamise, who was at Mennecy before 1756, went to Sèvres in that year. Seventeen painters are documented between 1737 and 1766 and, of these, Etienne-Nicolas Boucher, a flower-painter recorded in 1753, went to Sèvres the following year. One gilder (*maître-doreur*) and one kiln-master (*enfourneur*) and a number of workers without any precise occupation are also to be found in these records. The presumed signature ('Gauron 1754') of the modeller Nicolas-François Gauron is incised on the base of a white glazed porcelain figure of a river god which forms part of the base of the ormolu clock in the Louvre Museum. Gauron was employed at Mennecy around 1753–4.[18]

The factory probably continued in production until the end of 1773 when it was transferred by Jullien and Jacques to Bourg-la-Reine. Marks for both Mennecy (*D.V.*) and Bourg-la-Reine (*B.R.*) were registered with the lieutenant general of police on 23 July 1773 and were very occasionally found on the same piece.[19]

1. The factory has been most recently studied by Duchon, 1988.
2. Duchon, *op. cit.*, p. 40, quoting Etude de Villeroy, 9 March 1749.
3. The partnership agreement is dated 11 November 1750, Archives nationales, Minutier central XI–573, Le Duc, 1987, p. 29; bibliography, p. 7.
4. Chavagnac and Grollier, 1906, p. 100.
5. Duchon, *op. cit.*, p. 81; this author points out that there were links between the Mennecy and Sceaux enterprises several years before 1766.
6. Chavagnac and Grollier, 1906, p. 101.
7. MNS. Archives de Sèvres, A2, *liasse* 7.
8. Duchon, *op. cit.*, p. 84.
9. A. d'Albis and F. Treppoz, 'Identification de différents types de porcelaines anciennes à l'aide de l'analyse par diffraction X', *Faenza*, Ann. LXXIII, nos. 1–3, 1987, pp. 49–50. Some notes on comparative analyses of Saint-Cloud, Villeroy and Sèvres bodies are given in Darblay, 1901, pp. 83–5, together with a resumé of Brongniart's recipe for soft-paste and its method of preparation, taken from the *Traité des Arts Céramiques*, Paris, 1844, Vol. II, pp. 459–63.
10. See d'Albis and Treppoz, *op. cit.*, p. 50, note 19.
11. 'Tripoli', according to d'Albis and Treppoz, *op. cit.*, p. 50, was an old name for diatomite 'qui est une formation sédimentaire due à l'accumulation de carapaces siliceuses de diatomées'.
12. See Duchon, 1988, p. 147, quoting Archives départementales des Yvelines, B. Villeroy Pièces du greffe, 1762.
13. For a selection of the various types of figures, see Dallot-Naudin, 'Mennecy', 1983, pp. 113–30, many examples illustrated are in the Musée des art décoratifs, Paris.
14. A framed example of Henri IV measuring 8¼ in, described as 'bust-length profile to the left of the bearded monarch with bare head and military attire' sold Parke-Bernet, New York, 7 February 1947, Lot 106, Karrick Riggs Collection; another of Louis XV to right, framed, H. 8 in, was Lot 335. A fine biscuit bust of Louis XV on a waisted pedestal with palm fronds in relief at each corner is in the Musée des arts décoratifs, Paris, inv. 28621.
15. F.J.B. Watson, Walpole and the Taste for French porcelain', *Horace Walpole, Writer, Politician and Connoisseur, Essays on the 250th Anniversary of Walpole's Birth*, New Haven and London, 1967, Appendix I, 'Walpole's Purchases of Porcelain', p. 335, no. 41. In his sale in 1842 the ewer was part of Lot 59 on the 16th day and sold for £1. 1s. 0d.
16. Duchon, 1988, pp. 99–118. See also Chavagnac and Grollier, 1906, pp. 114–19.
17. A biscuit group of a gallant couple and two other young men (probably theatrical), incised on the base *J. MO DV* and dated 1771, is in the Smithsonian Institution, National Museum of American History, Washington, DC, inv. 73.8.
18. T. Clifford, 'Nicholas Gauron – A Virtuoso Modeller at Tournai and Chelsea', in *The Rococo in England, a Symposium*, ed. C. Hind, Victoria and Albert Museum, London 1986, pp. 161–74.
19. As on an inkstand supported by a figure of a river god in the Victoria and Albert Museum, London, inv. C. 352–1909, incised *D.V.* and bearing the marks *D.V.* and *B.R.* painted in blue enamel.

52 **Knife with Porcelain Handle,** *c.* 1740

L. *of handle incl. button:*	8 cm
Total L:	21.6 cm
Marks:	*D.V.* painted overglaze in red-brown; knife blade stamped with a [?] fleur-de-lys
Reg. No.	1942,4–8,2 (purchased)

Soft-paste porcelain painted in red-brown, blue, green and yellow, with a Chinese-style scene of flowers, a pagoda and a Chinese boy flying a kite. At the end of the handle is a metal button. Signs of wear and extensive cracks. The ferrule, which is slightly damaged, is silver, the blade steel.

Provenance: Mrs E. Guy Ridpath sale, Sotheby's, 19 February 1942, Lot 168, from a set of seven similar knives. Purchased, 1942

Literature: Unpublished

Comparable Examples: France, Albert Jacquemart Collection (late 19th century), reproduced Dallot-Naudin, 'Mennecy', 1983, p. 134, *chinoiserie* decoration, mark *.D.V* on part normally covered by ferrule[1]

London, private collection, ex Ridpath Collection

Small pieces such as this are rarely marked, although there is a similarly decorated marked cane-handle in the David Collection, Copenhagen.[2] Both these pieces are remarkably close in appearance to unmarked porcelains traditionally attributed to the Saint-Cloud factory,[3] such as the cane-handles, cat. 53, 54. The inventory of the factory's outlet in Paris on the rue Saint-Honoré, taken between 26–29 July 1754,[4] lists no fewer than '814 douzaines de manches de couteau de différentes façons, unis ou en relief, blancs ou bleus ou en bleu et blanc, ou en couleurs, peints ou en couleurs (dont 110 douzaines de rebut blancs ou couleurs) prisées entre 2 livres et 7 livres la douzaine'. It is clear from this that knife-handle production was on a considerable scale.

The blade, which is of French type, is contemporary with the handle, but the cutler's mark has not been identified.

Other pieces with a comparable mark are known.[5]

1. Chavagnac and Grollier, 1906, p. 106, where mark is noted as *.D.V.*
2. Eriksen, 1980, no. 9a.
3. See a group of twelve knife-handles of tapering shape, the blades bearing a fleur-de-lys stamp, and another group of eleven handles in two different sizes sold at Christie's, Monaco, 7 December 1987, Lots 147, 148.
4. Duchon, 1988, p. 137; Archives nationales, Minutier central XI-586.
5. Chavagnac and Grollier, 1906, pp. 105–7.

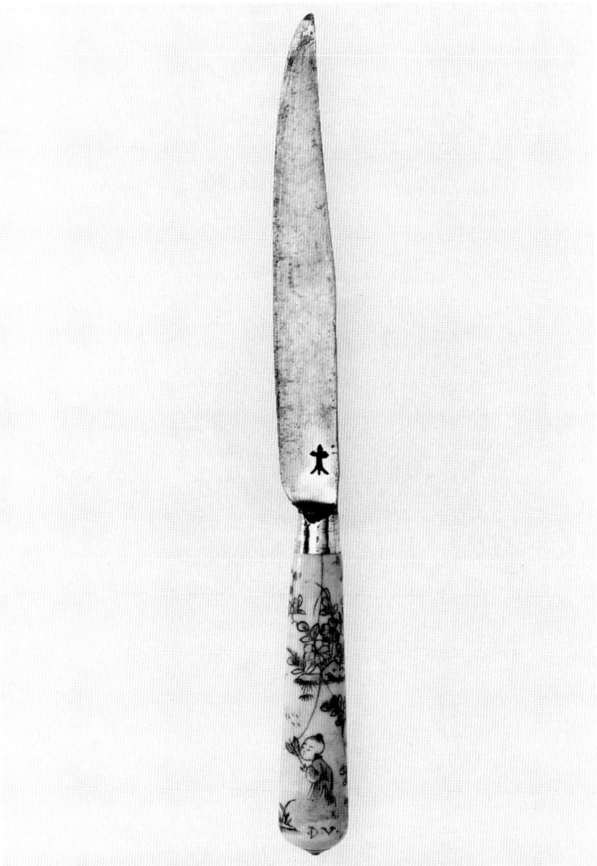

52

53 **Cane-handle,** *c.* 1740

H.	6.1 cm
Marks:	none
Reg. No.	Franks 352

Soft-paste porcelain, partly hollow. Decorated on the upper surface in blue, green, yellow, red and brown enamels with flowers in the Kakiemon style and in orange and brown with a standing figure of a man in a fanciful oriental costume, holding a bird. Inscribed in black *Il a trouve|la pie au nie.*

Provenance: Bequeathed by Sir A.W. Franks, 1897

Literature: Franks, 1896, no. 352

Comparable Examples: Paris, Musée des arts décoratifs, inv. D33276, painted in red with figure playing a *cornemuse*, and inscribed *Tu adore* [sic] *ce quy te brulle* ('You adore that which burns you'), Frégnac, 1964, illus. p. 78

Italy, Naples, Museo Duca di Martina, inv. 1609, mounted in gold, painted with a cock and inscribed *Quand ce Coq|Chantera, mon| Amour finira* ('When this cock crows my love will end'), illus. M.L. Casanova, *Le porcellane francesi nei Musei di Napoli*, Naples, 1974, no. 14

See cat. 54

The porcelain and the style and colouring of the painted decoration are closely related to the marked knife-handle (cat. 52), permitting an attribution to the Mennecy factory.

The inscription can be translated 'He found the bird on the nest'. Like that on cat. 54 and other examples, it has an erotic significance.

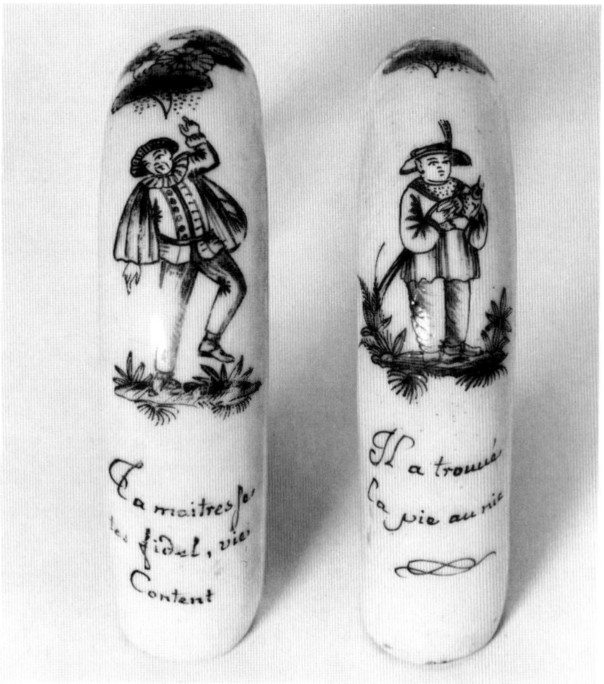

53 *(right) and* 54 *(left)*

Cane-handles were made in many forms and sizes by Saint-Cloud, Mennecy and Vincennes, and by other factories operating in the Paris region. 'Pômes de Cannes, Marteaux, Becs de Corbins, pour toutes sortes de Cannes', were for sale from the Saint-Cloud succursale on the rue de la Madeleine, faubourg St Honoré, Paris, between 1731 and 1741,[1] and doubtless before and after this date.

At least two marked Mennecy cane-handles are known. One, probably the kind called a 'crow's beak', is marked *D.V.* in brown,[2] the other could be a *marteau*, or hammer, and is marked *D.V.* in black.[3]

1. See the advertisement reproduced by Chavagnac and Grollier, 1906, p. 32.
2. Copenhagen, David Collection, inv. FK 230, illus. Eriksen, 1980, no. 9a.
3. New York, Christie's, 8–9 June 1979, Lot 130, Mrs John W. Christner Collection. Vol. III.

54 **Cane-handle,** *c.* 1740

L.	6.1 cm
Marks:	none
Reg. No.	Franks 353

Soft-paste porcelain, partly hollow. Decorated on the upper surface in blue, green, yellow, red and brown enamels with flowers in the Kakiemon style and, in red with a dancing figure in Watteauesque costume. Inscribed in black *Ta maitresse/tes fidel, vie/Content.*

Provenance: Bequeathed by Sir A.W. Franks, 1897

Literature: Franks, 1896, no. 353

Comparable Examples: Sceaux, Musée de l'Ile de France, with same inscription, inv. 86.6.24

Christie's, 28 October 1963, Lot 72, property of a nobleman, inscribed *L'on a beaucoup destine pour toy*

See cat. 53

The figure of Pierrot is of theatrical derivation. The inscription can be translated 'Your mistress is faithful to you, live happily'.

55 **Tobacco Pot and Cover,** 1750–60

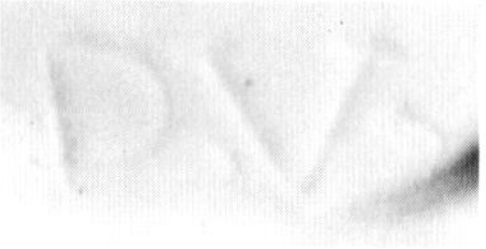

55 *mark*

H. *incl. cover:*	13.6 cm
Marks:	*D, V*, incised
Reg. No.	Franks 358

Soft-paste porcelain with a lead glaze; cylindrical with domed cover surmounted by an applied rose and leaf finial. Painted in pink, purple, green, yellow, blue, dark brown, and purple enamels with naturalistic flower sprays. Rims painted pink. Pot repaired.

Provenance: Bequeathed by Sir A.W. Franks, 1897

Literature: Franks, 1896, no. 358

Comparable Examples: USA, New York, Parke-Bernet, 2–3 April 1948, Lot 309, Mrs H. Dupuy Collection

USA, New York, Sotheby Parke-Bernet, 11 April 1980, Lot 235, Nelson A. Rockefeller Collection

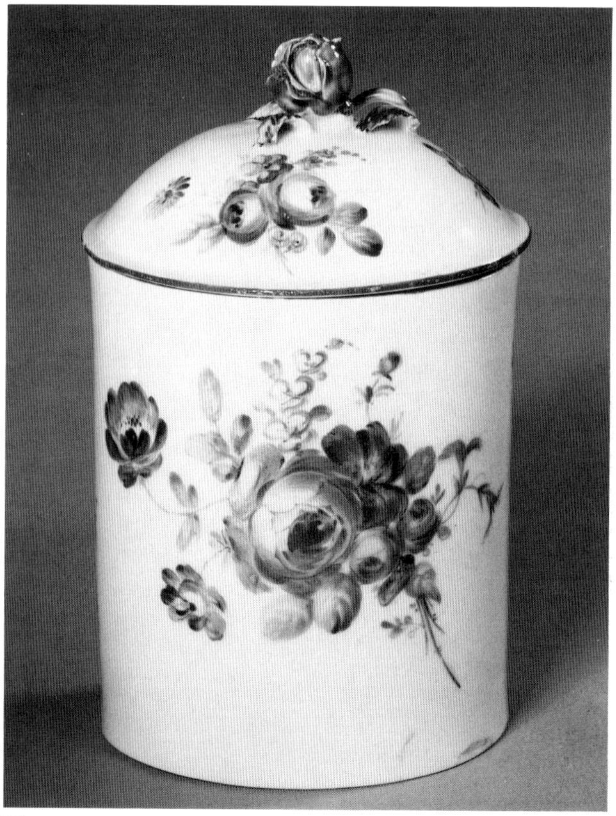

55

Pots such as this were sometimes part of toilet sets provided with their own boxes. There is a set with a box by Lacroix in a private collection.[1] They appear to have been made in more than one size.[2] The inventory of the rue Saint-Honoré, Paris, shop made between 26–29 July 1754[3] includes '120 pots à tabac de différentes grandeurs en blanc et en couleurs prisés entre 3 et 7 livres pièce'.

The finial appears to be typical of the Mennecy factory, and the painting of the rims takes the place of gilding which could only be used at Vincennes/Sèvres from 1749.

1. Frégnac, 1964, p. 148, illus., see also D. Gage and M. Marsh, *Tobacco Containers and Accessories*, publ. Gage, Bluett and Company, London, 1988, pp. 100–101.
2. An example incised *D, V*, measuring 18.5 cm in height including the cover is illustrated in Gage and Marsh, *op. cit.*, pp. 98–9, and a pair, each measuring 15.9 cm, both incised *DV*, are shown with a marquetry travelling-case attributed to Lieutaud, pp. 100–101.
3. Quoted Duchon, 1988, p. 141; Archives nationales, Minutier central XI–586.

56 **Cup and Saucer,** *c.* 1750–60

56 *mark*

H. *of cup:*	6.9 cm
Max. D. *of saucer:*	13.5 cm
Marks:	*D, V,* incised on both
Reg. No.	1957,12–1,52

Soft-paste porcelain with a lead-glaze, thrown, thickly potted. The curved sides of the saucer have warped in the firing and the cup, which has a tapering loop handle, is also slightly distorted. Both cup and saucer are painted in pink, blue, yellow, grey-brown and two colours of green with scattered flower sprays, which include pink and yellow full-blown roses, and yellow and blue daisy-like flowers on a white ground. The handle is painted with pink dots and stylised leaves.

Provenance: Presented by A.D. Passmore, Esq., 1957

Literature: Unpublished, but see H. Tait, 'The Passmore Gift', *BMQ*, Vol. XXV, no. 1–2, 1962, pp. 41–4

Comparable Examples: None noted

On both cup and saucer the glaze has shrunk away from the foot rim and there are discolorations and pinholes in the glaze. Traces of blackening on the rim of the cup suggest that it may have rested on its rim in the kiln.

The flowers are probably based on prints and are competently executed.

This cup and saucer, which lack the pink[1] or blue[2] rims so often found on Mennecy flower- or bird-decorated pieces in place of gilding (which could only be used by the royal factory), form part of the second- or third-quality range of domestic production at Mennecy.

Like the royal factory, Mennecy made several different cup shapes, including a flared form with loop[3] or angled[4] handle with a deep straight-sided saucer, a bowl-form cup with baroque handle[5] and a cup of undulating form with a twisted-rope handle.[6] A rather similar handle is found on a bucket-shaped cup with accompanying socketed saucer.[7] It has not yet been

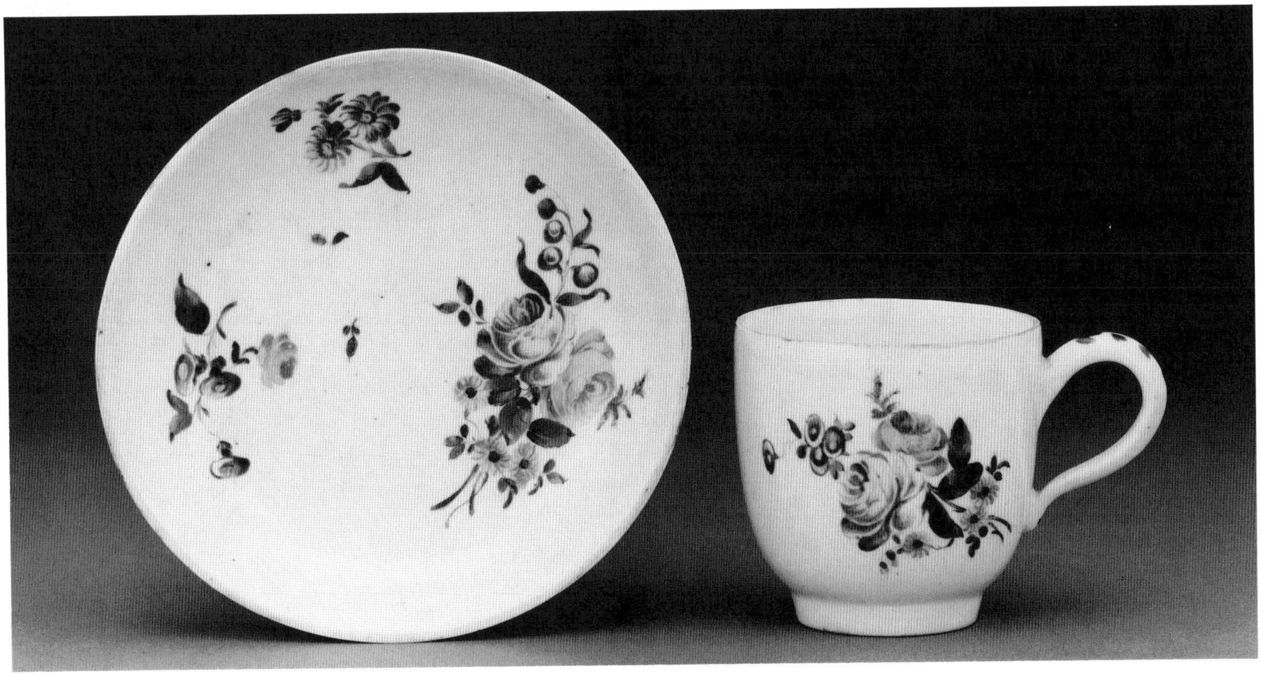

56

possible to ascertain whether these forms evolved chronologically, or were all in production at the same time.

1. A cup and saucer of similar form and dimensions which also has an undecorated rim but is painted with birds is in the Louvre Museum; see Musée du Louvre, 1985, no. 71, p. 126, with leather travelling-case.
2. For a flower-painted cup and saucer of differing form with blue rims, see Malgras (ed.), 1983, p. 147.
3. Exh. Nord-Pas-de-Calais, 1986–7, no. 40.
4. Malgras (ed.), 1983, p. 147.
5. Darblay, 1901, pl. XL.
6. *Ibid.*, 1987, pl. XLI.
7. *Ibid.*, pl. XLV.

57 **Salt-cellar**, *c.* 1750

H. 8 cm
Marks: incised *DV* below *2*
Reg. No. Franks 355

Soft-paste porcelain with a lead glaze, formed as a shell on a base simulating rocks. Hollow base with three small holes, partly glazed. Decorated in green, purple, pink, blue, yellow and brown enamels with flower sprays on inside of well and on the outer surface at the back; rim of shell painted pink and rockwork green and purple. Crack and chip. Firing defects at the back and on the scroll.

Provenance: Bequeathed by Sir A.W. Franks, 1897

Literature: Franks, 1896, no. 355

E. Hannover and B. Rackham, *Pottery and Porcelain, A Handbook for Collectors, III European Porcelain*, London, 1925, p. 30, fig. 39

Comparable Examples: London, Victoria and Albert Museum, inv. C. 1324–1919, enamelled, with boy figure, see Honey, 1950, pl. 47A

New York, Christie's, The Elizabeth Parke Firestone Collection, Part I: Important French Porcelain, 21–22 March 1991, Lot 96 (with variations)

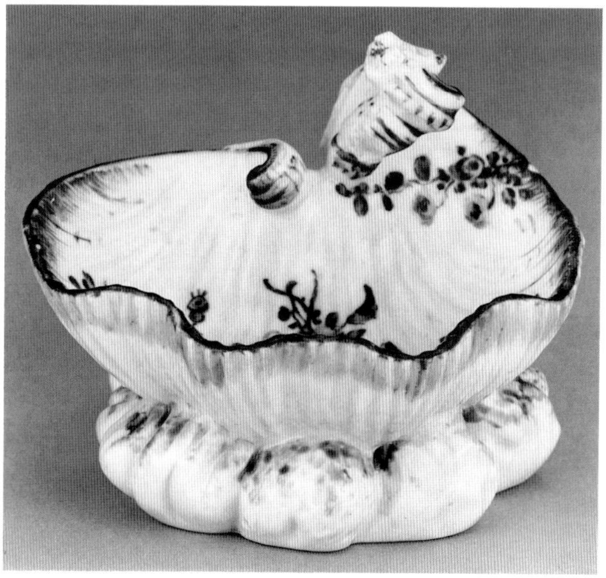

57

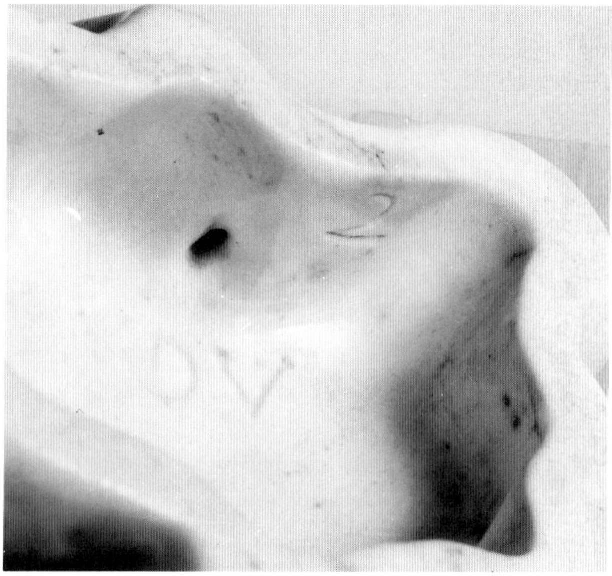

57 *base*

USA, Hartford, Connecticut, Wadsworth Atheneum, inv. 17.929, 17.930 pair of unmarked salt-cellars, enamelled, one with a boy, the other with girl figure straddling the scroll at the back

It is suggested that a figure of a child was once attached to this salt-cellar, but was lost during the firing process, leaving scars on the porcelain.

Amongst the many different forms mentioned in the inventories published in part by N. Duchon,[1] none can be identified with this salt-cellar.

A silver salt of shell form held by a mermaid seated on a rocky base was made by Paul de Lamerie in London in 1739.[2] This piece bears a stylistic relationship to the Mennecy porcelain salt.

1. Duchon, 1988, pp. 137–49.
2. Carl Hernmarck, *The Art of the European Silversmith 1430–1830*, London, 1977, Vol. II, pl. 452.

58 **Pair of Small Vases on Pedestals**, *c.* 1750–55

H. 9 cm and 9.5 cm
Marks: *D. V.* and indecipherable mark incised on both
Reg. No. Franks 357

Soft-paste porcelain with a lead glaze, the vase moulded with six alternating ribs and depressions, everted six-lobed rim, spirally fluted foot fixed with glue to moulded hollow waisted socle pierced inside by a circular hole. Decorated on the panels of the pedestals and body of the vases with flower sprays in red-brown, blue, pink, yellow, green and brown enamels, with blue marbling on base of pedestals; rims of vases and upper edge of pedestals outlined in pink.

Provenance: Bequeathed by Sir A.W. Franks, 1897

Literature: Franks, 1896, no. 357

Chavagnac and Grollier, 1906, p. 102

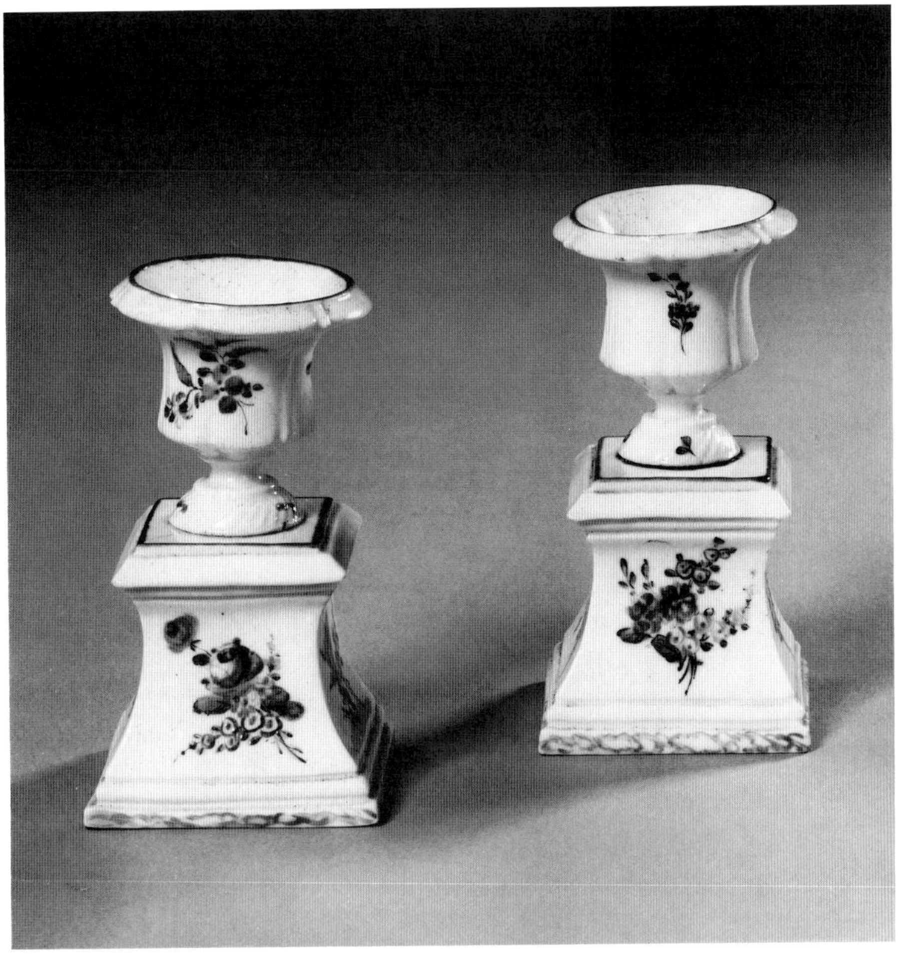

58

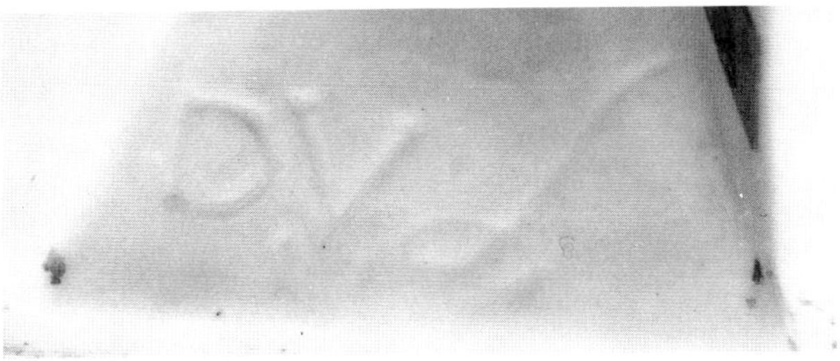

58 *mark*

Comparable Examples: USA, private collection, mounted with bouquets of flowers on metal stems and fixed to quadrangular pedestals, illus. R. Berges, 'Mennecy Porcelains from the Elizabeth Parke Firestone Collection', *American Connoisseur* Vol. 170, no. 686, April 1969, p. 249, fig. 3, and see Christie's, New York, The Elizabeth Parke Firestone Collection, Part I, 21 March 1991, Lot 73

Denmark, Copenhagen, David Collection, inv. 12a–b, illus. Eriksen, 1980, pl. 9b, impressed *D. V.*, lower edge of plinth undecorated.

There are numerous black specks on the surface of both pieces.

The vase shape, which derives from the Medici vase, is only distantly related to the Vincennes model known as the *Vase Parseval*, first noted in the factory inventory in 1752,[1] and seems to be unique to the Mennecy factory. Vases on pedestals, intended as table ornaments and sometimes provided with naturalistically painted porcelain flowers,[2] were produced in many different sizes[3] and versions including one with a leaf moulded at each corner of the pedestal.[4] Unpainted versions in several sizes are also recorded.[5]

It is just possible that this shape is the 'vase à l'antique' of which fifty were inventoried at Mennecy on 3 October 1765.[6]

1. Exh. *Vincennes*, 1977–8, pp. 145–6.
2. A pair with the original flowers but without pedestals are in the Musée national de Céramique, Sèvres, illus. Frégnac, 1964, p. 147.
3. Jacob, 1980, pl. LXIX.
4. H. Landais, *French Porcelain*, London, 1961, pl. XIII, Saumur, Museum of Applied Arts.
5. New York, Parke-Bernet, 15, 16 May 1959, Lots 228–31 Thelma Chrysler Foy Collection, no pedestals, probably two sizes.
6. Duchon, 1988, p. 147; Archives départementales des Yvelines B Villeroy Pièces du greffe 1765.

59 **Pot-pourri Vase and Cover,** *c.* 1755–60, with some decoration added later

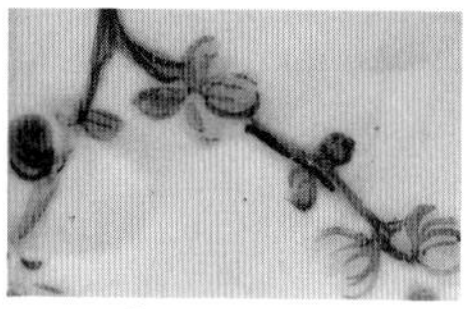

59 *mark*

H. *incl. cover:*	16.1 cm
Marks:	*D, V* incised
Reg. No.	Franks 356

Soft-paste porcelain with a lead glaze. Of undulating outline moulded with eight lobes separated by an alternating depression and a 'rib', the moulding repeated on the cover. Neck of vase and cover pierced with four flower motifs; leaf and flower knop. Painted in pink, green, yellow, orange, blue and brown enamels with sprays of naturalistic flowers and insects, and on one side in a similar palette with a scene of two putti in clouds within a gilt rococo-style cartouche embellished with flower garlands; gilt dentil at base, pierced motifs outlined in gold, scroll and dot pattern on neck, rim of cover gilt. Firecrack on base disguised with two forget-me-not sprigs painted in green, blue and brown. Rim cracked.

Provenance: Bequeathed by Sir A.W. Franks, 1897

Literature: Franks, 1896, no. 356

Hannover and Rackham, 1925, p. 30, fig. 40

Comparable Examples: None

Pot-pourri vases of various kinds were on sale in the Paris shop located on the rue Saint-Honoré, as an inventory made between 26–9 July 1754 reveals. It lists '32 pots-pourris blancs, avec ou sans terrasse, ou blancs à feuillages, prisés entre 10 et 30 livres pièce' as well as '25 pots-pourris de différentes couleurs à 7 livres pièce'.[1]

The figure decoration and the gilding were added during the nineteenth century. It is just possible that a moulded tobacco jar decorated with floral scrolls and putti in the Museo Duca di Martina, Naples, measuring 16 cm in height and marred by firecracks, is the work of the same painter.[2] This piece is unmarked, and may not be Mennecy porcelain.

1. Duchon, 1988, p.140; Archives nationales, Minutier central XI–586.
2. M.L. Casanova, *Le Porcellane Francesi nei Musei di Napoli*, Naples, 1974, no. 58.

60 **Jug and Cover (*pot à lait et son couvercle*),** with metal mount, *c.* 1760

See colour plate 6

H.	16.9 cm
Marks:	*D, V, A* and *f* incised
Reg. No.	1931,10–19,10

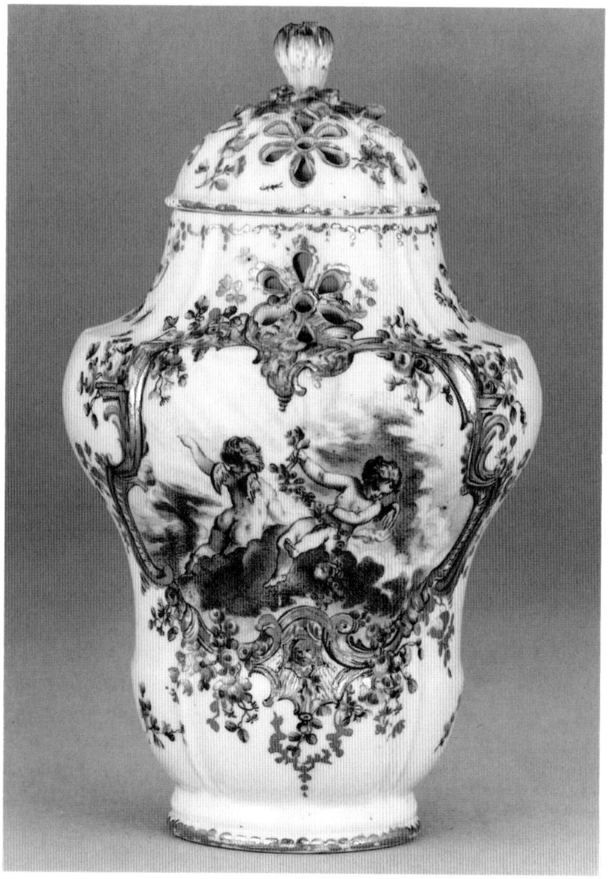

59

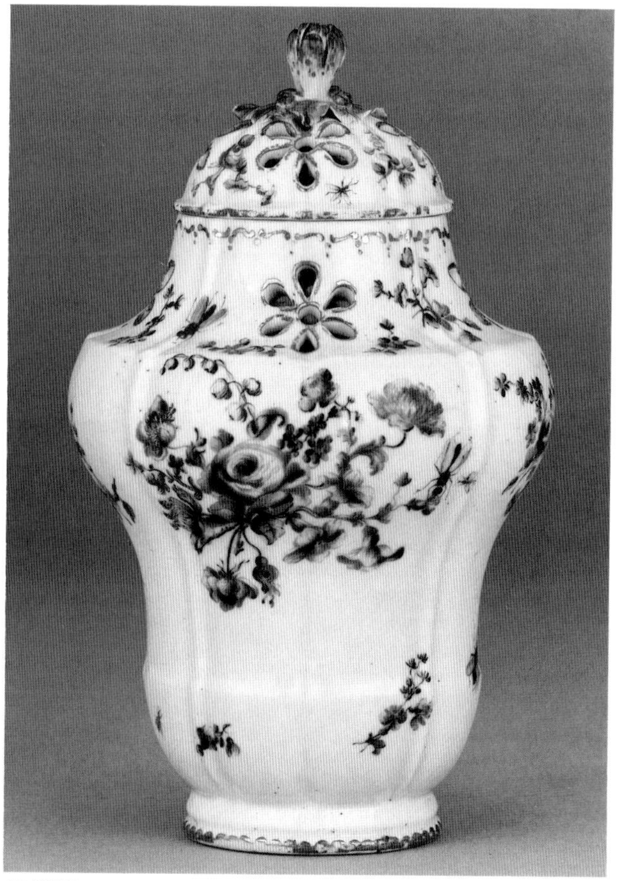

59 *reverse*

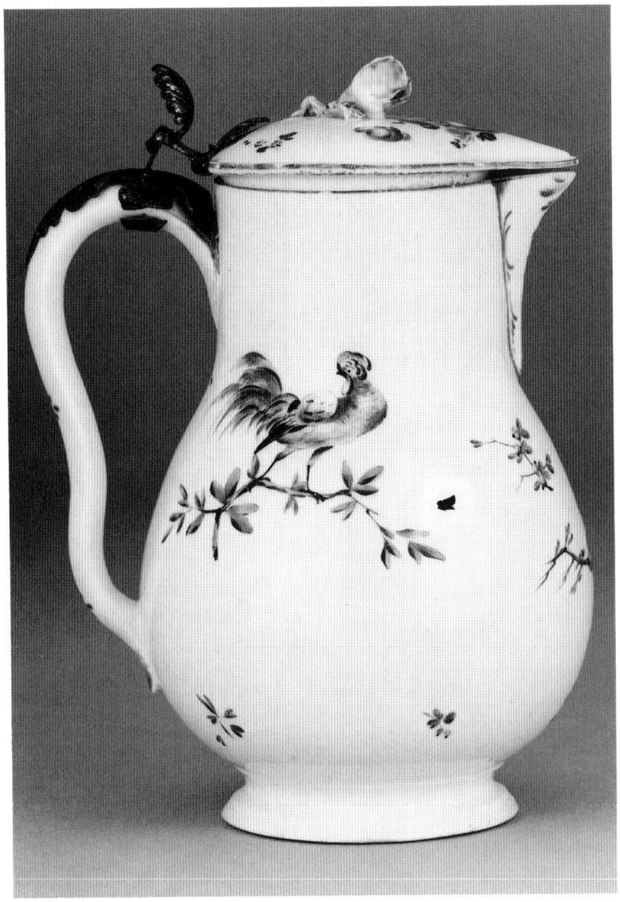

60

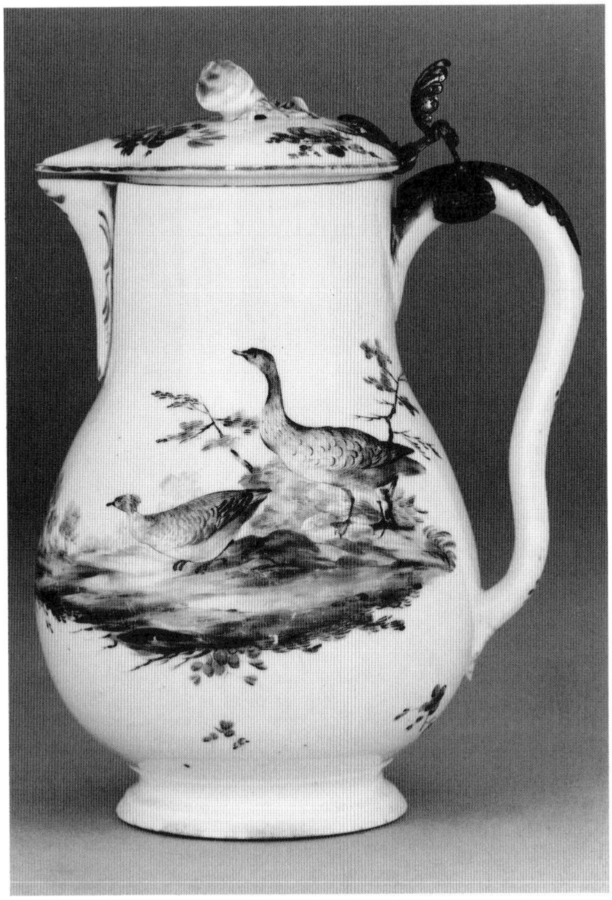

60

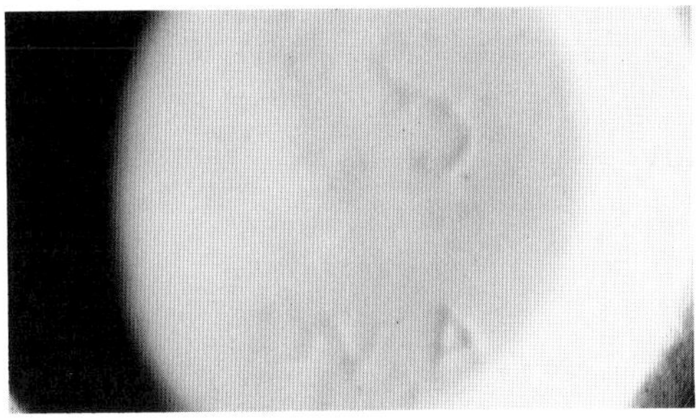

60 *marks*

Soft-paste porcelain, thickly potted, with a lead glaze, pear-shaped with a long neck, turned foot, slightly domed lid, applied rose-and-leaf finial. Decorated in green, purple, pink, red-brown, and blue enamels with two waterfowl in a landscape, a bird with a long tail on a branch and scattered flowers on jug, and with naturalistic flowers on cover; star motifs in purple and blue scrolls on lip. Rims and each end of handle painted pink. Imperfections in paste inside jug behind upper handle terminal. Handle repaired, rim of cover and foot chipped.

Provenance: Transferred from Salisbury and South Wiltshire and Blackmore Museum, 1931

Literature: Unpublished

Comparable Examples: Paris, Musée des arts décoratifs, similar piece with different handle, illus. Landais, 1961, fig. 29; another unmounted, Sèvres, Musée national de Céramique, inv. 23255, illus. H.-P. Fourest, 1982, pl. 212

The same type of handle can be seen on a Mennecy teapot painted with figures in a landscape in a private collection.[1]

Although the draughtsmanship is unremarkable, the colours used in the landscape scene with birds are extremely subtle. Bird subjects were popular at Mennecy and Sceaux.

The significance of the *f* incised in unknown.[2] The following related marks have been recorded:

a) pair of vases decorated with birds incised *A. D. V*; cylindrical cup and saucer painted with polychrome flowers, and another decorated with polychrome birds, same mark;[3] *vase à oignons* in the collection of Mme Alfred André;[4]

b) biscuit bust of Louis XV incised *D. V. F.*[5] (see cat. 61); octagonal double salt-cellar, formerly in the Gasnault Collection incised *D V F*;[6]

c) milk jug and cover painted with polychrome birds incised *D. V. fx.*;[7]

d) two plates of differing design each decorated with two figures in a *paysage maritime*[8] incised *D. V.g.*

The mount, which is attached to the cover by means of a screw and metal washer, is a poor fit and may not be contemporary with the jug, especially since it covers painted decoration. There is a similar mount on a Mennecy jug and cover in the Victoria and Albert Museum, London.[9]

On the evidence of an inventory dated 26, 28, 29 July 1754 of the merchandise in the shop in the rue Saint-Honoré, this jug (probably used for milk rather than water, see cat. 87) should have had a matching basin.[10]

1. Frégnac, 1964, pp. 140–41.
2. Eight workmen whose names begin with F have been listed by Duchon, 1988, pp. 106–7. Only one, Pierre-Louise Feuilleret, a *racheveur* between 1765–9, is a possible candidate for the maker of this jug. Other unusual marks are illustrated by Duchon, *passim*.
3. Exh. *La porcelaine française* 1929, nos. 404, 429, 430.
4. Chavagnac and Grollier, 1906, p. 109.
5. Exh. *La porcelaine française*, 1929, Miss Margaret Gould Collection no. 461.
6. Chavagnac and Grollier, *loc cit.*
7. Paris, Chavagnac sale, Hôtel Drouot, 19–21 June 1911, Lot 160.
8. Darblay, 1901, pls. XLIII, XLIV.
9. Honey, 1950, frontispiece.
10. Archives nationales, Minutier central, XI–586, quoted *in extenso*, Duchon, 1988, see p. 140. A matching jug and basin with a green ground are illustrated by G. Hood, 'French Porcelain from the J.P. Morgan Collection at the Wadsworth Atheneum', *Connoisseur*, Vol. 158, no. 636, February 1965, p. 134, fig. 8.

61 Group of Child Musicians: Girl Playing Pipe and Drum, Boy Playing the Viol, *c.* 1760

H. 17.4 cm
Marks: *D, V f* incised inside base
Reg. No. Franks 361

Creamy-toned soft-paste porcelain with a glassy lead glaze; hollow, press-moulded. Traces of four pad marks on the unglazed base but no apparent signs of kiln supports on the figures themselves. The girl sits on a rock, beating a drum with her right hand and playing a pipe with her left. The boy sits below her playing the viol. Firecracks; chip to girl's skirt, boy's bow missing; neck of boy's instrument and his thumb repaired.

Provenance: Bequeathed by Sir A.W. Franks, 1897

Literature: Franks, 1896, no. 361

Comparable Examples: Paris, Chavagnac sale, Hôtel Drouot, 19–21 June 1911, Lot 147, unmarked

Spain, Valencia, Señor Marqués de Montortal Collection, illus. M. Olivar Daydí, *La Porcelana en Europa*, Vol. II, Barcelona, 1953, fig. 15, p. 141, H. 24 cm, incised *DV*

C.M. and G.R. Scott, *Antique Porcelain Digest*, Newport, 1961, p. 121, pl. 421, H. 6¾ in., incised *DV*, coll. unknown.

London, Victoria and Albert Museum, inv. C. 320–1909, coloured version, illus. Honey, 1950, pl. 47B, incised *DV*, (bow and pipe missing)

Sotheby's, 3 May 1946, Lot 65, from the Hillingdon Collection

USA, New York, Parke-Bernet, 7, 8 February 1947, Lot 74, pair with same model as cat. 62, coloured, mounted, Karrick Riggs Collection

Sotheby's, 22 June 1957, Lot 19

Paris, Hôtel Drouot, Gilbert Lévy Collection, sold 23 November 1967, Lot 50, with companion piece as cat. 62

Christie's South Kensington, 6 December 1990, Lot 121

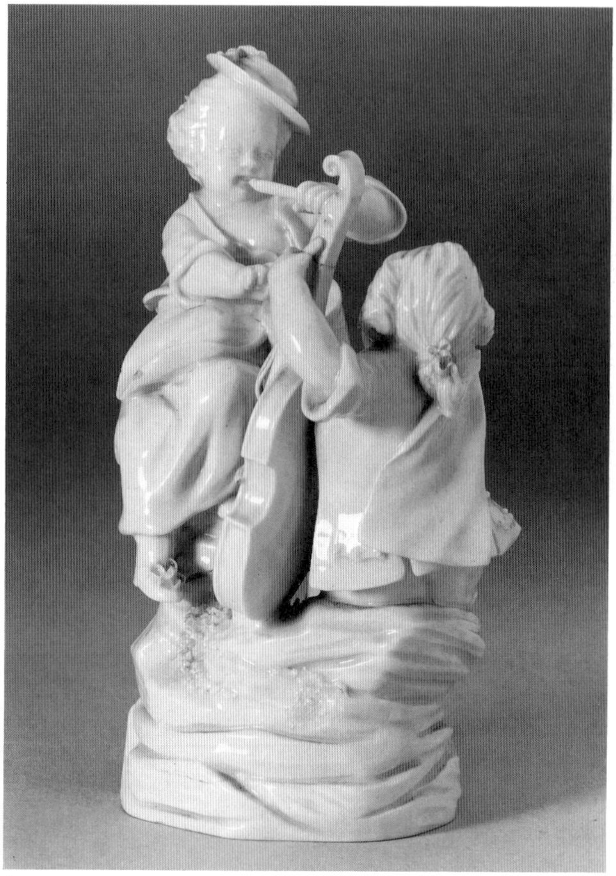

61

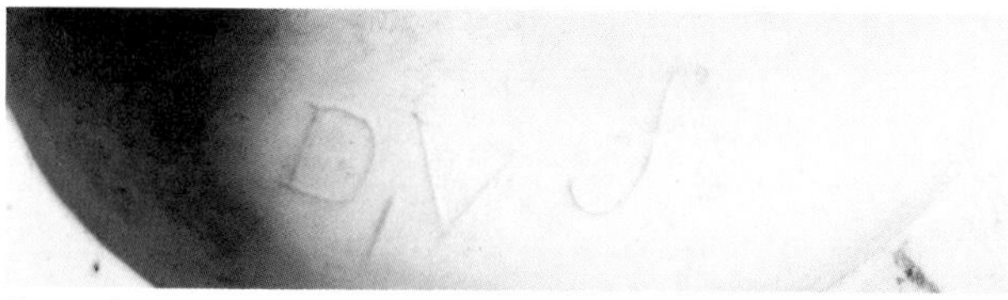

61 *marks*

Like cat. 62, this group is the work of an accomplished modeller, despite the rather chubby faces and attenuated necks. Both are designed to be viewed 'in the round'. A group with a boy and girl together playing the tambourine and another of a boy holding a flute and a girl seated on a pile of books holding an open score are recorded in the René Fribourg Collection;[1]

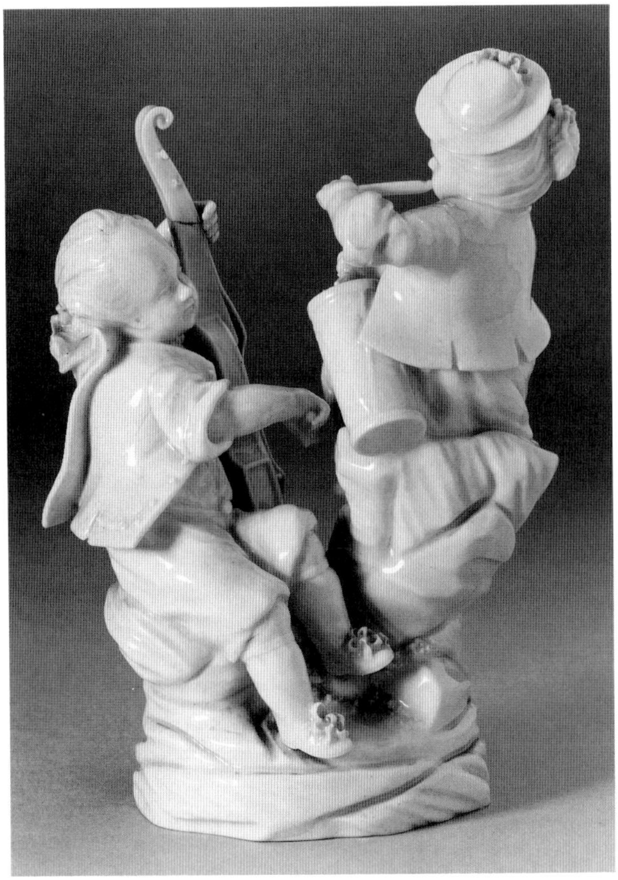

61

and another of a boy playing the pipes and a girl singing was sold on the London market in 1951.[2]

The significance of the incised initial *f* is unknown; a biscuit bust of Louis xv incised *D. V. F.* was in the collection of Miss Margaret Gould in 1929,[3] and a cup painted with birds incised *D. V. f* belonged to Darblay in 1901.[4] A further group of two child musicians incised *D. V. S.* is recorded.[5] This example is painted in colours.

Listed amongst the glazed white groups in the Paris shop of Charles Hennique on 14 November 1765 were '2 groupes de musiciens'; three coloured groups of musicians have also been noted in this inventory, but not in those taken in 1754 and 1762 at the rue Saint-Honoré premises, and at the factory.[6] The inventories of the mid-1750s mention animals, birds, small figures and figures without any description. For the present we may conclude that musical groups date from the early 1760s.

1. René Fribourg Collection: I European Porcelain Part I, Sotheby's, 25 June 1963, Lot 36, notes examples sold 22 June 1951, Lot 19 and 13 November 1951, Lot 127, and Darblay, 1901, pl. xxx; the second group corresponds with cat. 62.
2. Sotheby's, 13 November 1951, Lot 127 (coloured).
3. Exh. *La porcelaine française*, 1929, no. 461.
4. Darblay, 1901, pl. XXVIII.
5. Exh. *La porcelaine française*, 1929, no. 459. No dimensions given.
6. Duchon, 1988, p. 149; Archives départementales des Yvelines B Villeroy Pièces du greffe 1765; Duchon, it should be noted, quotes only extracts from the documents.

62 Group of Seated Child Musicians: Girl with *Musette* and Boy with Recorder, *c.* 1760

H. 18.2 cm
Marks: none
Reg. No. Franks 361

Creamy-toned soft-paste porcelain with glassy lead glaze; hollow, press-moulded. The girl is seated on a pile of books and holds a book in her hand; underneath her right arm is a *musette*, or bagpipes, and behind her a tambourine. The boy sits on a rock, his legs dangling, holding a flute. There are three brownish pad marks on the base, which has traces of glaze, but no apparent signs of kiln supports on the figures themselves. Firecracks, chip to boy's sleeve and back of jacket, girl's finger broken. The girl's hat has been broken and restuck before the glaze firing and it seems likely that the boy's hat was also damaged before the final firing.

Provenance: Bequeathed by Sir A.W. Franks, 1897

Literature: Franks, 1896, no. 361

Comparable Examples: White glazed version illus. C.M. and G.R. Scott, *Antique Porcelain Digest*, Newport, 1961, p. 121, pls 420, incised *DV*, H. $6\frac{3}{4}$ in.

Sotheby's, 3 May 1946, Lot 65, coloured version

France, Darblay Collection, illus. Darblay, 1901, pl. xxx, coloured version

Sotheby's, René Fribourg Sale I, 25 June 1963, Lot 36, coloured version

Paris, Hôtel Drouot, Gilbert Lévy Collection, sold 23 November 1967, Lot 50, with companion piece as cat. 61

Christie's, 3 June 1974, Lot 5, coloured version

USA, New York, Christie's, The Christner Collection, Volume III, Important French Porcelain, 9 June 1979, Lot 173, incised *DV* and *3*

Exh. Williams, 1978, no. 78, coloured version

This group is companion to cat. 61 and is the work of the same modeller. There appears to have been a third figure in the same series (see cat. 61).

The piling up of the books and a tambourine under the girl and the carefully balanced pose of the boy, both of whose feet hang over his rocky support into space, are even more daringly conceived than the disposition of the previous example. The identity of the modeller remains unknown. He was probably also resposible for the coloured group of three children on a rock in the Victoria and Albert Museum, London.[1]

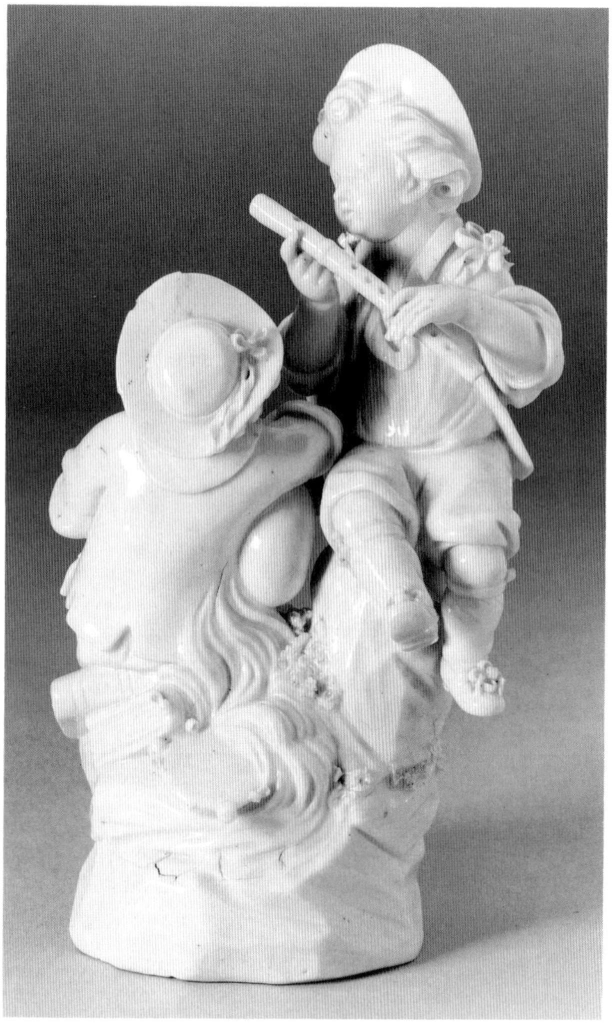

62

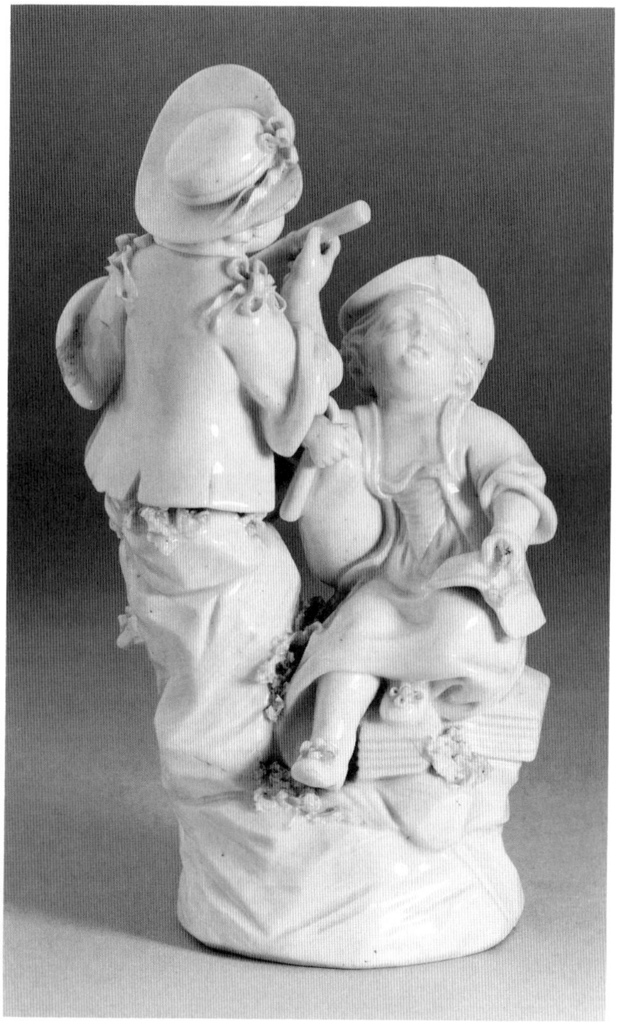

62

The same model was manufactured at the Derby factory in an enamelled version.[2]

1. Honey, 1950, pl. 46.
2. P. Bradshaw, *Derby Porcelain Figures*, London and Boston, 1990, p. 276, no. 140; fig. 225, incised *No. 140*. There may well have been a companion group as W. Bemrose, in *Bow, Chelsea and Derby Porcelain*, London, 1898, nos. 139 and 140, records 'Two groups boy and girl, two in each'. Another musical group with two figures beside a leafy tree is related to a further Mennecy group of a girl with a tambourine and a boy playing a horn with a score on his lap, see Bradshaw, 1990, pp. 274–5, no. 139.

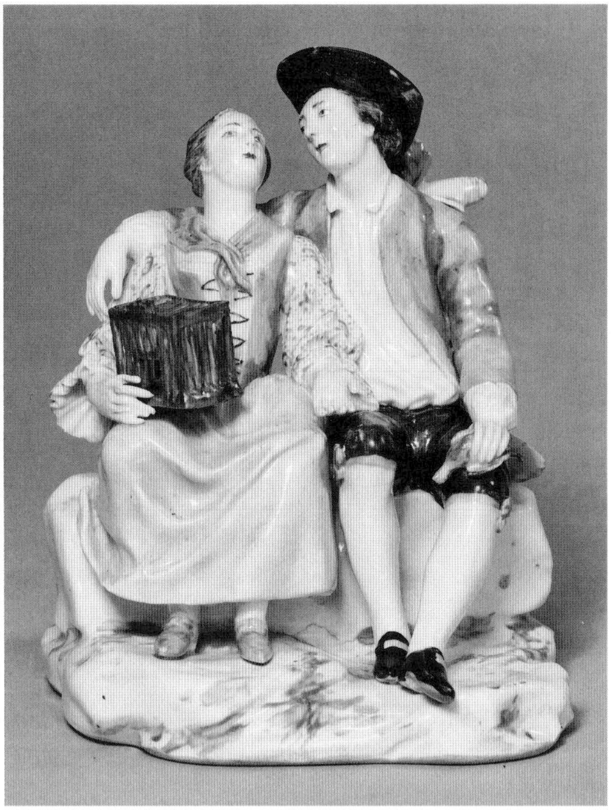

63

63 **Group of Seated Lovers,** *c.* 1760

H. 15.2 cm
Marks: none
Reg. No. 1987,1–6,1

Soft-paste porcelain with a lead glaze, press-moulded. A young man seated on a rock, wearing a black hat trimmed in blue, a pink jacket lined with yellow over a loose white shirt, brown breeches trimmed with blue and black shoes with yellow bows, holds a bird in his left hand, which rests on his knee. His right arm rests on the shoulder of the girl seated next to him. She wears a yellow skirt with pink bodice, its voluminous sleeves painted with a blue pattern, and has a blue scarf round her neck. Her pink shoes have blue bows. In her right hand she holds an empty cage painted purplish-brown which rests on her knee. At the back is a tree painted purplish-brown, yellow and green. The rocky base in partly painted green. Base of tree-trunk firecracked. Man's jacket chipped, woman's hands restored, base cracked.

Provenance: Karrick Riggs Collection, sold Parke-Bernet, New York, 7 February 1974, Lot 75.
René Fribourg Collection: I European Porcelain Part I, sold Sotheby's, 25 June 1963, Lot 35 for £500.
Sold Sotheby's, 26 November 1968, Lot 9 (property of a gentleman).

Presented by Mrs L.M. Slot in memory of her husband L.M. Slot, 1987

Literature: Unpublished

Comparable Examples: Oxford, Ashmolean Museum, inv. 1968.251, incised *B* in reverse, girl on right with right arm resting on basket of grapes perched on a rock. Sotheby's, 1 May 1956, Lot 69, incised *B*, Simon Goldblatt Collection, illus. Rueff, see f.n. 3.

The painting on the woman's sleeves is reminiscent of the 'marbling' on the base of the pedestals, cat. 58. However, although the range of colours is comparable to those found on Mennecy figures and groups, some doubts remain about the origin of groups like this one because of the static quality of the modelling.

Like many mid-eighteenth-century French figure groups, the subject of this one has an erotic significance, the empty cage symbolising the young girl's loss of virginity. The subject was treated by Nicolas Lancret in one of four paintings of the Seasons commissioned by Leriget de La Faye, *Le Printemps*, engraved by Tardieu before July 1730. The paintings, inventoried in 1731 after the death of La Faye, were sold in Paris in 1753, and were on the market again in August 1773 in the sale of the architect Vigny.[1]

A variant in which a youth holds a cage containing a bird which is being offered a leafy branch by the girl at his side is known at Bow, and was the work of the so-called 'Muses modeller'.[2] Another version in which the youth holds a dead bird on his knee is attributed to the Tournai factory.[3] A group of lovers with a bird cage in which the bird is being removed by the youth was modelled by H. Reichart for the Wegely factory, Berlin.[4] A tin-glazed earthenware group of a seated couple, the youth at the left holding a nest filled with chicks, the girl resting her left arm on a bird cage, was made at the Niderviller factory.[5]

1. G. Wildenstein, *Lancret*, Paris, 1924, pp. 70–1, and fig. 8; in the State Hermitage Museum, St. Petersburg.
2. A. Lane, *English Porcelain Figures of the Eighteenth Century*, London, 1961, pl. 38, Victoria and Albert Museum, London; a white version was bequeathed to the British Museum by Wallace Elliot from the Caldwell Collection, reg. no. 1938, 3–14, 78.
3. E. Soil de Moriamé and L. Delplace de Formanoir, *La Manufacture Impériale et Royale de Porcelaine de Tournay*, Tournai, 1937, no. 680, and K. Rueff, 'La Porcelaine de Tournai', *Connaissance des Arts*, August 1954, no. 30, p. 9.
4. S. Ducret, *The Colour Treasury of Eighteenth-Century Porcelain*, Oxford, 1976, fig. 38.
5. Frégnac, 1976, p. 244, fig. 364, Musée des arts décoratifs, Strasbourg.

Vincennes[1]

Recent research has shown that this factory was founded in 1740 by Claude-Humbert Gérin (1705–50), in association with the brothers Robert (1709–59) and Gilles (1713–after 1752) Dubois.[2] While working for Ciquaire Cirou, Gilles Dubois had stolen the secret of the Chantilly paste from him, but this formula differs distinctly from the white body characteristic of Vincennes from its earliest years. Gérin himself claimed to have carried out experimental work on porcelain for a period of twelve years at Chantilly, Pont Sainte-Maxence[3] and Saint-Germain-en-Laye.

The first establishment at Vincennes occupied the Tour du Diable at the château for eighteen months with the permission of the governor, the marquis du Châtelet. It was soon controlled by Jean-Louis Orry de Fulvy (1703–51) *intendant des finances*, director of the French East India Company and half-brother to the Minister of Finance, Orry de Vignory. Orry de Fulvy provided the raw materials and tools. He allowed François Gravant (died March 1764, aged about forty-nine), a former herbalist (*épicier*) from Chantilly who had also made faïence at Vauréal (Oise), to assume the title 'inventeur des porcelaines de France', since he had stolen from Gérin the secret of the white paste, which contained calcined alum. Gérin left some time after March 1742 to make creamware (*terre anglaise*) at Pont-aux-Choux,[4] where he remained for two years, having obtained a royal privilege for creamware manufacture in July 1743. In July 1746, at Gravant's request, he returned to Vincennes as head of the workshop specialising in handles and spouts. Accounts were kept by the factory from May 1741, one month after Fulvy had purchased the secret of a gilding process from a certain comte d'Egmont; this did not, however, mean that the factory could yet produce gilded porcelain, apart from perhaps a few experimental pieces. Gilding was not regularly used until after October 1748 when the secret of the preparation of gold, its mordant (or fixative) and the method of application were purchased from the Benedictine monk Hippolyte Le Faure.

In July 1745 a privilege for 'the manufacture of porcelain in the Saxon manner', that is, 'peinte et dorée à figure humaine', was granted by the King to the shareholders of the factory, which was known as the Charles Adam company, Adam being Orry de Fulvy's *valet de chambre*, presumably acting on behalf of his master. Experimental work with colours was by then in progress although they were probably used only for porcelain flowers. These were made in a workshop directed by Madame Gravant and were the mainstay of the factory in its earliest years. The bouquet of porcelain flowers presented in January 1749 by the Dauphine to her father, Augustus III of Saxony,[5] is evidence of the skill achieved in this branch of the factory. Between 1746 and 1748 sales figures rose from 1,173 *livres* to 43,342 *livres*,[6] but subsequently dropped slightly. These figures did not, however, mean that the investors made a profit, for the costs of establishing the factory were enormous.

From 1746, technical development was rapid. Two sculptors, Laurent and Depierreux, were paid for models in that year, indicating that figures were now going into production. 'Enfants Boucher' were in the kiln in 1748. Initially the figures were hand-modelled. Biscuit, or unglazed, porcelain was in use for figures from 1752, when they began to be made in moulds. As the artist François Boucher had become formally associated with the factory in the previous year,[7] many models based on his work were put into production from this date. In addition bird, animal, allegorical, *chinoiserie* and Fable subjects after Oudry formed part of Vincennes production.[8]

In August 1745 the factory employed six painters, three throwers, three moulders, one sculptor and two kiln-masters (*enfourneurs*), as well as six unskilled journeymen. They had probably all been on the payroll since 1741,[9] and many had come from Chantilly following the death of the duc de Condé in 1740. In July 1749 the entire workforce numbered sixty-three, excluding those employed in making porcelain flowers. More painters and gilders were taken on in 1750, signalling the progress that had been made in the development of colours. In 1747 the formula for a pink colour was purchased from Pierre-Antoine-Henri Taunay and that of a 'chartreuse' from Jean-Mathias Caillat. Sixteen colours were listed in surviving documents dating from April 1747. Two palettes used by factory painters are known. The earlier dates from August 1748 and is signed by Taunay *fils*.[10] The other is dated 9 July 1749 and signed by Armand *l'ainé*.[11] In 1748 a tunnel kiln devised by Gérin for continuous firing of enamel colours was installed,[12] and by the following year a palette of about sixty colours had been developed. Before Orry de Fulvy's death, decoration was heavily influenced by Meissen,[13] as well as by oriental motifs. A view of the château of Vincennes was painted on a bowl now in the Musée national de Céramique, Sèvres. Some pieces were painted with delicate flowers, probably based on engravings (see cat. 67), on white ground; stylised birds either in gold or in pale colours against an underglaze-blue ground and Boucher subjects are also typical of this phase of production.

In January 1751 Jean-Jacques Bachelier (1724–1806) was made responsible for the creation of decorative schemes, under the artistic direction of Hendrik van Hulst of the Académie des Beaux-Arts. Forms of vases and service pieces were designed by Jean-Claude Duplessis (*c*. 1690–1774) who, in his capacity as a goldsmith, assisted in designing the mounts for bouquets such as the one given by the Dauphine to her father in 1749.

After the death of Orry de Fulvy in May 1751, Jacques-René Boileau, formerly the factory inspector, became its director. A shareholder in the company, Jean-François de Verdun, who had links with the King's mistress, Madame de Pompadour, sent a report on the factory's situation to the minister of finance, Machault d'Arnouville (1701–94), requesting state support. The Crown effectively assumed control in 1751, in return for the secrets of manufacture which were written down by Jean Hellot, an eminent chemist and director of the Académie des Sciences. Several coloured grounds, such as underglaze-blue, yellow, green and a pale mauve (called *gris de lin*) were noted in the inventory drawn up of Orry de Fulvy's effects. After his death the Meissen style was soon abandoned and the influence of Boucher became highly important. The factory began a new phase in October 1752 when a new company under the name of Eloy Brichard, in which Louis XV owned a quarter of the shares, replaced the original company. It was at this point that the factory became officially known as the 'manufacture du roi' and was given the right to mark its products with the royal cipher, a practice which had begun some years previously. However, it was not until November 1759 that the King took over complete financial responsibility for the factory, and the Eloi Brichard factory formally ceased to exist.

An exhibition held in 1978[14] revealed the wide range of domestic and ornamental wares and figures and groups made during the sixteen years of the factory's existence. A list of more than 170 workers whose names have been traced in the factory records has recently been published.[15] Sales from the factory were recorded from 1746. They were initially to the shareholders and later to the royal family and high-ranking artistocrats, for prices were out of reach of all but the wealthiest. From 1748 onwards, merchants such as Lazare Duvaux purchased exceptional pieces which they then sold on to clients, including Madame de Pompadour.[16]

1. This account is based on A. d'Albis, 'Les premières années de la manufacture de porcelaines de Vincennes', *Faenza*, Vol. LXX (1984), nos. 5–6, pp. 479–93; A. d'Albis, 'The early years of the porcelain manufactory of Vincennes', International Ceramics Fair and Seminar, London, *Handbook*, June 1986, pp. 10–23; A. d'Albis and T. Préaud, *Les éléments de datation des porcelaines de Vincennes avant 1753*, publications of the French Porcelain Society, II, London, 1986; A. d'Albis, 'Gravant's secret or the first royal privilege of Vincennes', International Ceramics Fair and Seminar, London, *Handbook*, June 1987, pp. 10–19 and T. Préaud and A. d'Albis, 1991, *passim*. A great deal of information can be found in A. Sergène's unpublished thesis *La Manufacture de Sèvres sous l'ancien régime*, 3 vols, Nancy, 1972–4. See also Eriksen and Bellaigue, 1987.
2. For details of the Dubois brothers, see N. Ballu, 'La carrière des Dubois', *Cahiers*, 10 (1958), pp. 92–3, and Préaud and d'Albis, 1991, p. 205.
3. These two places were close to each other in the département de l'Oise. Further details of Gérin's career can be found in Préaud and d'Albis, 1991, pp. 206–7.
4. M. Hosotte-Reynaud, 'La manufacture de Pont-aux-Choux (1743–1788)', *Mémoire de la Fédération des Sociétés Historiques*

et Archéologiques de Paris et de l'Ile-de-France, XVI–XVII, 1967, pp. 271–96.
5. Brunet and Préaud, 1978, pl. I, p. 29.
6. Préaud and d'Albis, 1991, p. 25.
7. R. Savill, 'François Boucher and the porcelains of Vincennes and Sèvres, *Apollo*, Vol. CXV, no. 241, March 1982, pp. 162–70.
8. A number of these are illus. in exh. *Vincennes*, 1977–8, pp. 149–84.
9. Préaud and d'Albis, 1991, p. 16 state that the account book lists five painters, seven sculptors, a thrower, a kiln-loader (*enfourneur*) and a workman (*manoeuvre*) in September 1741.
10. Eriksen and Bellaigue, 1987, pl. A, opp. p. 48.
11. See A. d'Albis, 'A documentary Vincennes *inventaire*', *Sotheby's Art at Auction 1987–1988*, London, 1988, pp. 366–71.
12. This kiln, in use until 1802, is described in detail and illustrated by A. Brongniart, *Traité des Arts Céramiques*, Tome II, 1844, p. 663, and Atlas pl. LIX.
13. For some Meissen-style pieces bearing the mark *OFL* see A. d'Albis and T.H. Clarke, 'Vincennes Porcelain for Orry de Fulvy', *Apollo*, Vol. CXXIX, no. 328, June 1989, pp. 379–83 and 444–5.
14. See exh. *Vincennes*, 1977–8.
15. D'Albis and Préaud, 1986, notes 4–7, and see Préaud and d'Albis, 1991, pp. 200–15.
16. Extracts from Lazare Duvaux' day books were published by Chavagnac and Grollier, 1906, pp. 261–4.

64 **Sauceboat**, 1745–8

See colour plate 7

L.	17.3 cm
H.	6.6 cm
Marks:	TAUNAY painted in pale iron-red over the glaze
Reg. No.	Franks 372

Glazed white soft-paste porcelain moulded at one end with shell forms, their tightly-coiled contours becoming less pronounced towards the lip. Decorated with two pink peonies on a green stem on one side and with a larger similar flower and three bluebells on the other, also on a green leafy stem. The bubbling of the pink indicates overfiring. Two scars reveal that the vessel was intended to have a handle opposite the lip. There is a rough unglazed oval band on the base. It may indicate that, like the handle, the foot broke during firing, probably, but not necessarily, during the firing of the decoration, or alternatively it may be a mark left by kiln furniture used to support the piece in the oven.

Provenance: Bequeathed by Sir A.W. Franks, 1897

Literature: Franks, 1896, no. 372

King, 1930, pp. 280–4, fig. V

King, 1939, pp. 194–7, fig. 5

Brunet and Préaud, 1978, p. 124, nos. 3, 3 *bis*

Exhibited: 1977–8, 'Porcelaines de Vincennes, les origines de Sèvres', Paris, Grand Palais, Oct. 1977–Jan. 1978, no. 243

Comparable Examples: None

The shape is unusual, despite the popularity of shell forms at many porcelain factories, both Continental and English. As Vibeke Woldbye points out,[1] François Boucher, who was associated with the Vincennes factory from an early date, was responsible for the frontispiece of E.-F. Gersaint's *Catalogue raisonné des coquilles et d'autres curiosités naturelles*, 1736. He owned an enormous collection of shells which were sold after his death.[2] He may have influenced the choice of the form, although it is more likely that it was based on Chantilly examples. This is one of the earliest pieces made at Vincennes and has been found by analysis[3] to be covered with a tin glaze. Documents published by Antoine d'Albis[4] show that the factory undoubtedly carried out experiments with glazes containing tin.

William King described this piece as a *bourdalou*,[5] or travelling chamberpot, but as it has a lip it was clearly intended as a pouring vessel. Even contemporaries sometimes found it difficult to distinguish between a chamberpot and a sauceboat, as a letter from Madame du Deffand shows:[6]

> 'On m'apporta sur mon lit un grand sac de votre part. Je me hâte de l'ouvrir, j'y trouve des petits pois, les premiers que j'eusse vus, et puis un vase. Quel peut-il être? Je le tire bien vite: c'est un pot de chambre, mais d'une beauté, d'une magnificence telles que mes gens tout d'une voix disent qu'il en fallait faire une saucière . . .'

Antoine-Salomon Taunay, a master-jeweller originally from Alençon, developed colours including a green, the formula for which he confided to the Vincennes factory chemist, Hellot.[7] In August 1744 he was paid 162 *livres* for two *mémoires* already received by the factory. He also received 150 *livres* 'pour des émaux' and on 14 September 1745 he was paid 96 *livres* for '½ oz violet foncé' and '½ oz pourpre Numero 1'. 'Pour peinture de fleurs' he was paid 74 *livres* 8 *sols* on 22 March 1746, and in August of the same year 'Tonnay' received 450 *livres* for colours. In 1747, 1748, 1751 and 1752 he received the following large sums: 1,305 *livres*, 3,240 *livres*, 3,060 *livres* and 1,200 *livres*.[8]

It is not always easy to distinguish between payments made to Taunay *père*, who may also have been a painter,[9] and those to his son Pierre-Antoine-Henri Taunay, when no indications are given in the documents preserved at the factory. It is possible that the payment made on 19 June 1754 for the secret of

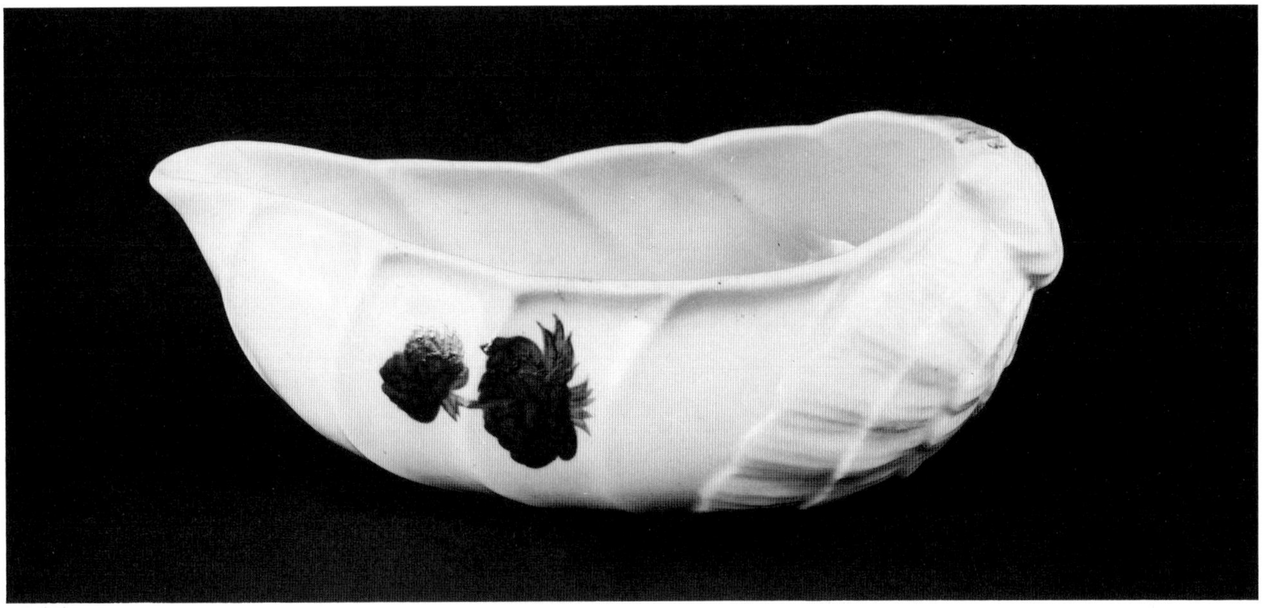

64

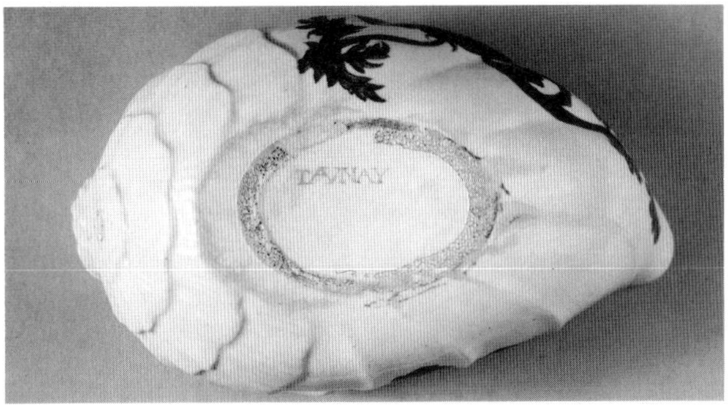

64 *base*

colours was made to the younger Taunay, described as a 'bourgeois de Paris', living in the parish of Saint Germain l'Auxerrois on the quai de la Megisserie.[10] What is now certain is that the only other signed piece by Taunay, a small cup in the Musée national de Céramique, Sèvres,[11] is the work of P.-A.-H. Taunay. Its inscription has now been correctly deciphered as *Inventaire. Fait ce 29 Aout 1748 a Vincennes. Taunay fils.*[12] The cup is painted in monochrome purple, pink, red, violet, blue, brown and black. The colours apparently correspond to those on the sauceboat, but the two pieces have not been compared side by side.

An unmarked teapot and cover of Chantilly type in the Musée des arts décoratifs, Paris, is painted in a similar palette and manner.[13]

No other sauceboat of this kind is known, and some controversy surrounds this piece on account of its shape, tin glaze and unusual painting. It has been suggested[14] that it may possibly be a product of the Chantilly factory.

1. V. Woldbye, 'Shells and the Decorative Arts', *Apollo*, Vol. CXX, no. 271, September 1984, pp. 156–61.
2. The author is grateful to Rosalind Savill for this information.
3. BM Research Laboratory 24911P, XRF analysis.
4. A. d'Albis, 'Procédés de fabrication de la porcelaine tendre de Vincennes, d'après les livres de Hellot', *Faenza*, Vol. LXIX, 1983, Nos. 3–4, p. 211, f.n. 25; d'Albis has now seen further pieces with a tin glaze, including a figure known as *La Dormeuse* and a *bleu céleste* vase both in the Louvre Museum (correspondence with the writer of August 1990).
5. King, 1930, p. 282, fig. v.
6. Quoted Nicolas Peyret, 'Les bourdaloues, des vases de nuit au grand jour', *L'Estampille*, Mars 1970, p. 53.
7. M. Brunet, *The Frick Collection, An Illustrated Catalogue, Vol. VII, Porcelains Oriental and French*, New York, 1974, p. 191.
8. MNS, Archives de Sèvres, F 1, *liasse* 1, *Etat de la dépense depuis le mois de may 1741, jusques et compris le dernier avril 1745.*
9. Taunay (no first name given) was paid as a flower painter between March–August 1746, January 1749–June 1751 and October 1751–May 1752, receiving 80 *livres* a month from July 1749. The author is grateful to Tamara Préaud for assisting in tracing all these payments.
10. Archives de Sèvres, *liasse* C1, notary's act authorising payment by the King for the secret of preparing carmine, purple and violet, dated 19 June 1754.
11. Inv. MNCS 6638.
12. Exh. *Vincennes*, 1977–8, p. 21, no. 381. The correct interpretation of this inscription, the last two words of which were once thought to read 'Taunay *fecit*' was first proposed by Tamara Préaud in a joint lecture with Antoine d'Albis given to the French Porcelain Society, London, in June 1986. For another similar piece, signed by Armand *l'aîné*, see A. d'Albis, 'A documentary Vincennes *inventaire*', *Sothebys Art at Auction 1987–88*, London, 1988, pp. 336–71, and Préaud and d'Albis, 1991, p. 136.
13. Inv. D25584.
14. In discussions between the writer and, amongst others, Préaud and d'Albis, who did not include it in their work on the Vincennes factory. For a recent account see d'Albis, 1994 (full reference on page vii).

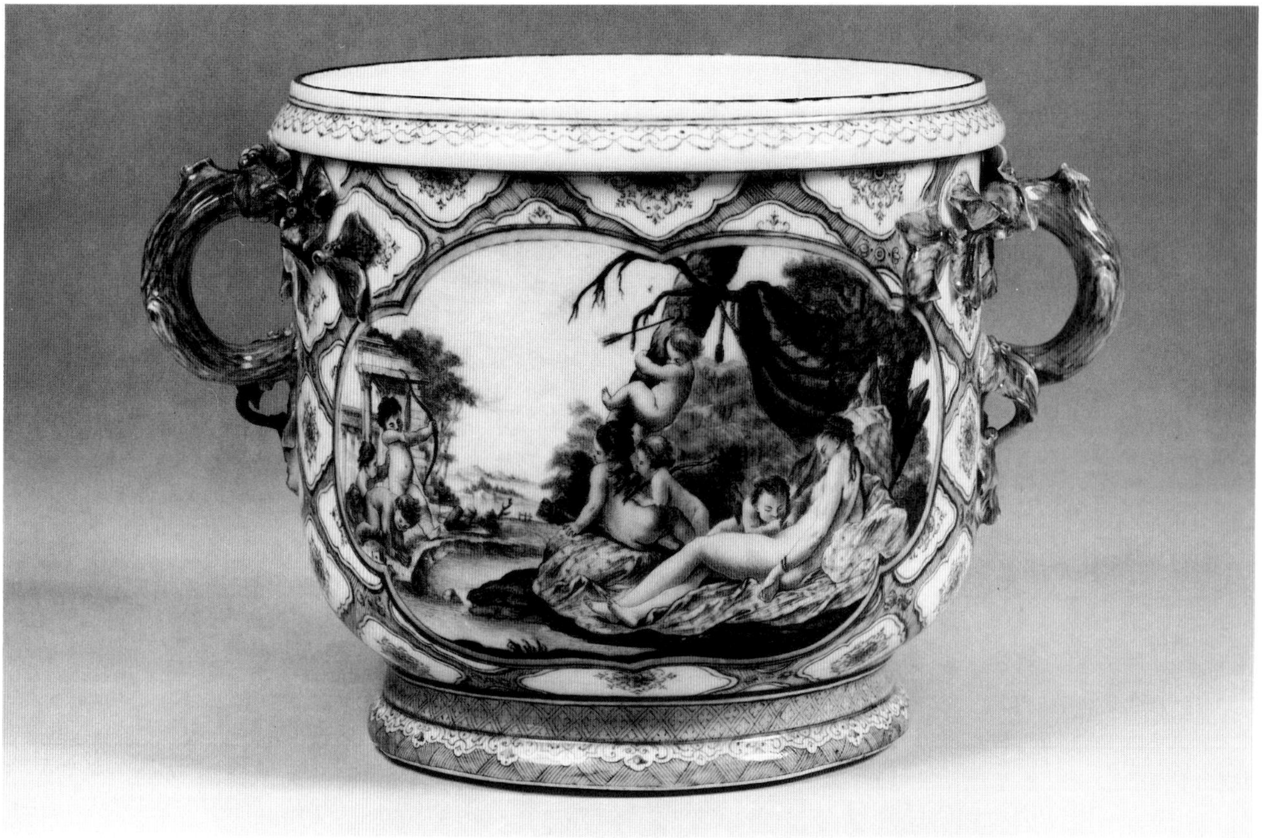

65

65 **Wine-cooler (*seau à demi-bouteille*),** *c.* 1748

See colour plate 9

D.	18.6 cm excl. handles
H.	16.8 cm
Marks:	none
Reg. No.	Franks 506

Thickly potted soft-paste porcelain, double foot and flange near rim, twig handles terminating in apple blossom and leaves, the ground decorated in purple with a mosaic pattern enclosing stylised flowers within a lozenge. The same colour is used at the neck for an ornamental design and at the foot for similar motifs in conjunction with two other designs. In a shaped reserve on each side are polychrome scenes: (a) Perseus and Andromeda; (b) Venus reclining and seven cupids in a landscape. Rim painted pink.

Provenance: Bequeathed by Sir A.W. Franks, 1897

Literature: Franks, 1896, no. 506

King, 1939, p. 196

Savage, 1960, pl. 41

Savage, 1961 ed., pl. 42

Brunet and Préaud, 1978, no. 40

Savill, 1988, III, pp. 971–2

J. Ingamells, *The Wallace Collection, Catalogue of Pictures III*, London, 1989, p. 250

Préaud and d'Albis, 1991, p. 142, no. 87

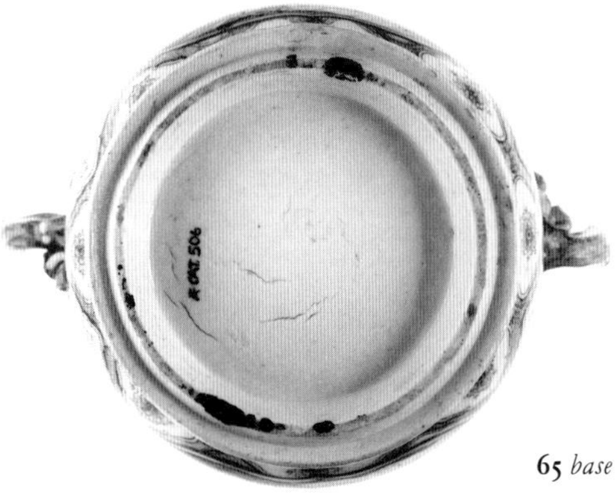

65 *base*

Exhibited: 1977, 'Porcelaines de Vincennes, les origines de Sèvres', Paris, Grand Palais, Oct. 1977–Jan. 1978, no. 249

Comparable Examples: None

The scene of Andromeda being rescued by Perseus is after a painting by F. Lemoyne (1688–1737) dated 1723, now in the Wallace Collection.[1] An engraving by Laurent Cars was announced in the *Mercure*, April 1728 and the subject, in reverse as in the engraving, was painted on a plate in the Louis XVI service.[2] The right-hand part of the scene of Venus and cupids in a landscape is probably after *Le Repos de Vénus* by F. Boucher, engraved by Michel Aubert and announced in the *Mercure*, April 1735 and June 1737.[3]

Several features such as the firecracks on the base (concealed on the inside of the vessel by five painted green leaves), the unevenly formed foot and the thick glaze pooled and bubbled in places at the foot strongly suggest an early date of production. Some scholars, such as William King who did not include it in his articles on the Vincennes porcelain in the British Museum,[4] have been hesitant to attribute the piece to the Vincennes factory. No design exists in the factory for this shape. However, although there is no other *seau à bouteille ordinaire* or *seau à verre* known to have been made at the factory which has such elaborate decoration, there are a number of pieces from the factory with figure scenes and pieces decorated in a similar palette, such as a milk jug on three feet in the Musée national de Céramique, Sèvres.[5] The use of red or purple on the rims was not confined to Vincennes; it was also used elsewhere, notably at the Chelsea porcelain factory. The absence of gilding on such an otherwise splendidly-decorated piece indicates a date of production before the end of 1748.

It is just possible that this piece may be the one described as having a 'mignature' and sold for 108 *livres* on 20 August 1753, as it was noted as having come from one of the earliest firings,[6] but the writer is inclined to believe that it was perhaps produced as a special order during the earliest period of the factory's existence.

1. J. Ingamells, *The Wallace Collection, Catalogue of Pictures III*, London, 1989, pp. 248–50. This writer has noted the same composition on the Meissen porcelain cover of a gold box (see Christie's, Geneva, 16 November 1992, Lot 354) and in a Fürstenberg porcelain group. The picture was in the possession of a *fermier général* named Bouret in the mid-eighteenth century. There were two brothers Bouret, Etienne-Michel (1710–77) and François Bouret d'Erigny (1713–79), both tax-farmers and shareholders in the Eloi Brichard Company established in 1753. According to Savill, 1988, Vol. III, p. 970, it was Etienne-Michel who owned the picture and, perhaps, allowed it to be copied. The painting on the wine-cooler is not reversed, as might be expected if the engraving had been used as the source by the porcelain painter. The author is grateful to Tamara Préaud for drawing her attention to *Mémoires de Dufort de Cheverny–la Cour de Louis XV*, notes by Jean-Paul Guicciardi, Paris, 1990, note 74, p. 498 where Bouret d'Erigny's dates are given.
2. Bellaigue, 1986, p. 69, no. 2.
3. Jean-Richard, 1978, no. 192.
4. King, 1930, Vol. XII, no. 70, pp. 280–4, Part I; June 1931, Vol. XIII, no. 78, pp. 367–70, Part II.
5. Exh. *Vincennes*, 1977–8, no. 171, inv. MNCS 1838.
6. MNS, Archives de Sèvres, Vy 1, f. 4, 20 August 1753, sale of piece with 'mignature' 108 *livres*.

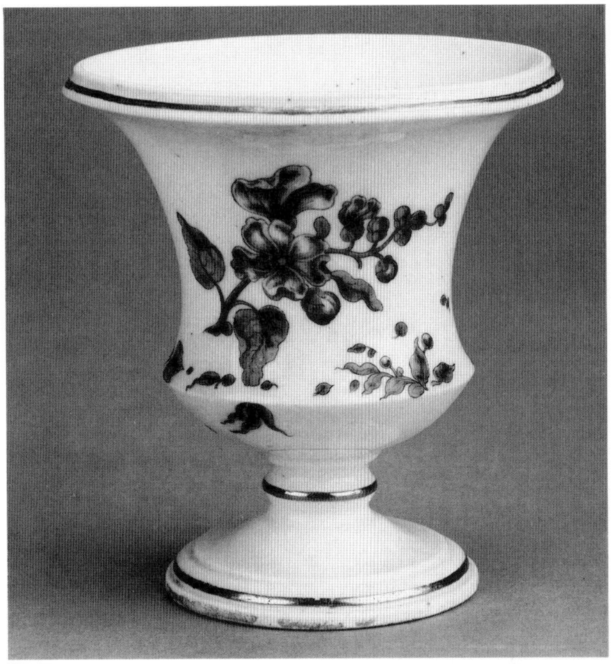

66

66 **Vase (*vase Parseval*)**, 1748–9

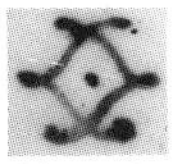

66 *mark*

H. 12 cm
Marks: interlaced LL enclosing a dot painted in blue over the glaze
Reg. No. Franks 376

Glazed white soft-paste porcelain; circular slightly domed turned foot supporting the waisted body with everted turned lip, which is thrown in one piece. Decorated in green, pink, yellow, blue, brown and black enamels with tulips, forget-me-nots, pink flowers and blue berries. There is a gold line on the stepped foot, the stem and the rim.

Provenance: Bequeathed by Sir A.W. Franks, 1897

Literature: Franks, 1896, no. 376

King, 1930, pp. 280–4, fig. IV

King, 1939, pp. 194–6, fig. 4

Honey, 1950, pl. 53A

Comparable Examples: Sèvres, Musée national de Céramique, inv. 23068 1, H. 10.7 cm; inv. 23068 2, H. 10.5 cm; 23068 3

France, Paris, Musée des arts décoratifs, inv. 31133, pair, H. 10 cm and 10.4 cm

Germany, Düsseldorf, Hetjens-Museum, inv. 1941/143, illus. A. Klein, *Kataloge des Kunstmuseums Düsseldorf, Keramik, Band 1, Europaïsches Porzellan im Hetjens-Museum*, Düsseldorf, 1966, no. 247

The vase is named after a shareholder in the Charles Adam Company called Philibert de Parseval. The shape, which is ultimately based on the Medici Vase, was achieved by lathe-turning and was used throughout the eighteenth century for table decoration. It is first noted in the factory inventory in October 1752, but the shape is known from the records of kiln firings to have been in production considerably earlier. On the evidence of the style of the flower painting this may have been one of the earliest made, although as it is gilded it is unlikely to date from before the end of 1748 when the factory purchased the secret of gilding on porcelain. The factory mark of interlaced LL was probably introduced in the late 1740s. Four sizes were produced, of which this example is the first and largest size.

Examples are known painted with landscape-and-figure scenes, either on white[1] or on a *bleu lapis* ground.[2] Perhaps the most striking is an example of the largest size painted with the monogram *MH*, possibly for Louis xv's daughter Marie-Henriette, with a *bleu lapis* ground.[3] Some mounted *vases Parseval* were mounted in gilt bronze, presumably because the foot did not always fire well.[4]

1. Paris, Musée des arts décoratifs, inv. 28689.
2. Christie's, 2 February 1981, Lot 11.
3. Paris, Louvre Museum, inv. OA 10301; the interpretation of the monogram has been put forward by Rosalind Savill. It has been suggested by Tamara Préaud and Antoine d'Albis that this vase has been over-decorated.
4. Paris, Musée des arts décoratifs, inv. 6297 a & b, exh. *Vincennes*, 1977–8, no. 94.

67 **Bowl**, *c.* 1748–50

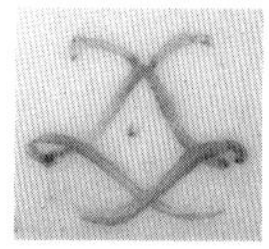

67 *mark*

H. 8.5 cm
Marks: interlaced LL enclosing a dot painted in blue over the glaze
Reg. No. Franks 373

Thickly potted glazed white porcelain bowl with shaped rim, decorated on the outer surface in pink, purple, green, yellow, blue and black with scattered flowers including violets, tulips and a rose and leaves. The rim has a purple stylised ornamental pattern. Rim and foot gilt. Chip to underside of rim. Flaked glaze on underside of rim.

Provenance: Bequeathed by Sir A.W. Franks, 1897

Literature: Franks, 1896, no. 373
King, 1930, p. 281, fig. 11
King, 1939, pp. 194–6, fig. 2
Honey, 1950, pl. 58B
Préaud and d'Albis, 1991, p. 146, no. 100

Comparable Examples: None

Discoloration on the exterior of the foot and the appearance of the interior surface of the foot indicate that this piece was glost fired upright in refractory bedding material.

The form of the bowl suggests that it may once have had a cover which rested on the inner flange, but there are no signs of wear to confirm this supposition. Its function remains a matter of conjecture: it appears to be too large for a sugar bowl,[1] but it is uncertain

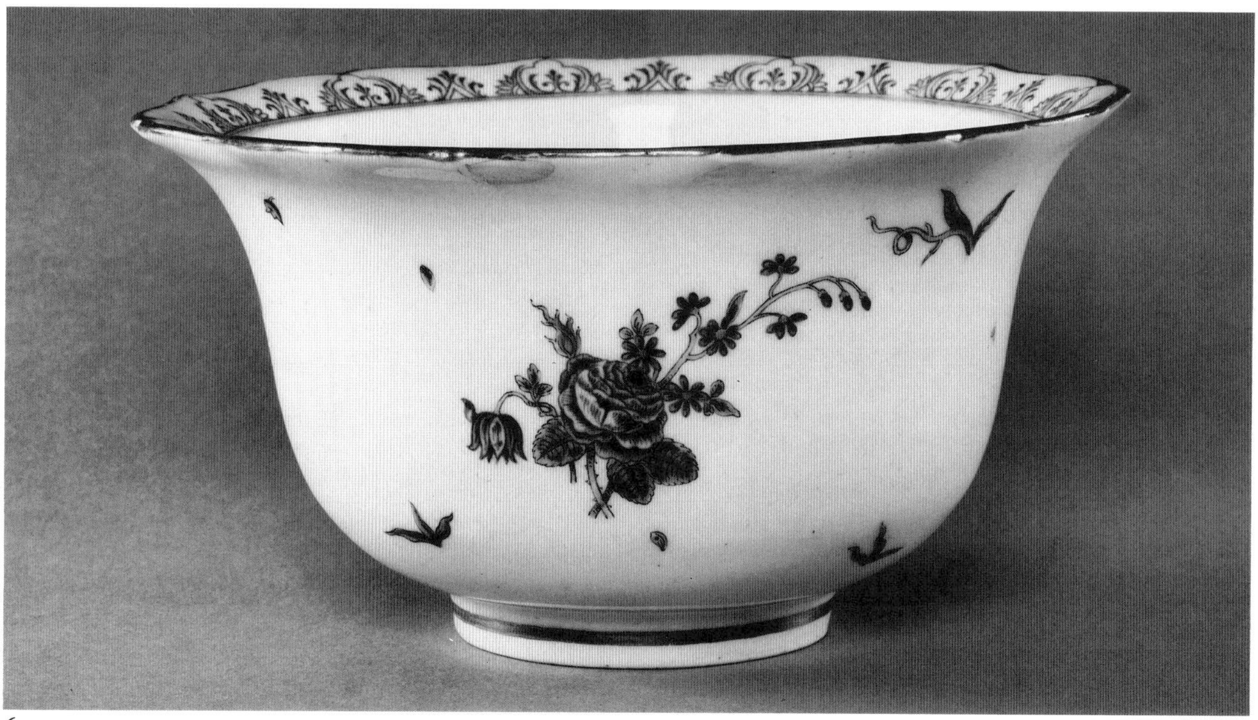

67

whether it could be a salad bowl (*saladier*) or mortar (*mortier*). It is just possible that it was based on a Chantilly bowl with shaped rim, two examples of which appeared on the London market in 1976.[2]

The rose has been adapted from Maria Sybilla Merian, *Histoire des insectes d'Europe*, Amsterdam, 1730, pl. LVI.[3]

1. It has been compared with bowls tentatively classified in 1977 as sugar bowls but the profile and dimensions do not correspond, see exh. *Vincennes*, 1977–8, nos. 209, 210, Préaud and d'Albis, 1991, p. 146, tentatively classify it as an *écuelle* but this author is more inclined to believe that it is a sugar bowl, despite its unusual size.
2. Sotheby's, 13 July 1976, Lot 37, pair decorated with Kakiemon flowers, red hunting horn mark, 11.7 cm (probably the diam.).
3. The author is grateful to Tamara Préaud for kindly providing this information, now published in 'Recherches sur les sources iconographiques utilisées par les décorateurs de porcelaines de Vincennes (1740–1756)', *Bulletin de la Société de L'Histoire de l'Art français*, 1990, pp. 105–15.

68 **Cup and Saucer (*gobelet lizonné et soucoupe*)**, *c.* 1748–50

max. D. *of saucer:*	13.7 cm
H. *of cup:*	7 cm
Marks:	interlaced LL with dot below, in centre and above painted in underglaze blue, incised *6* [?] (saucer); interlaced LL with dot above and below painted in blue over the glaze, incised *C* (cup)
Reg. No.	Franks 374

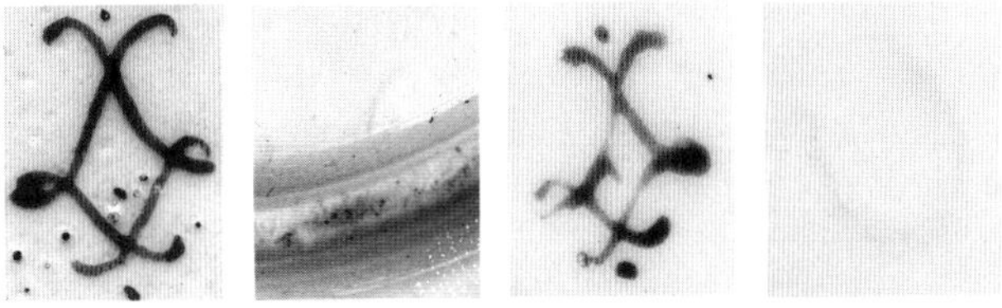

68 *marks*

Glazed white porcelain, moulded octagonal lobed shape, decorated in blue, purple, green, yellow, and black enamels with scattered flowers, including carnations, cornflowers, cherries and an insect on each. Rims painted red-brown. Thin handle with leaf ornament. Chips to rim of saucer.

Provenance: Bequeathed by Sir A.W. Franks, 1897

Literature: Franks, 1896, no. 374

King, 1939, pp. 194–6, fig. 3

W.J. Sainsbury, 'Vincennes Porcelain', *Connoisseur*, Vol. CXXXIII, no. 535, Feb. 1954, pl. IV

Préaud and d'Albis, 1991, p. 11, no. 67, p. 134

Exhibited: 1977, 'Porcelaines de Vincennes, les origines de Sèvres', Paris, Grand Palais, Oct. 1977–Jan. 1978, no. 370

Comparable Examples: Paris, Hôtel Drouot, Gilbert Lévy Collection, sold 23 November 1967, Lot 117

Shropshire, private collection, with gilding on handle and rims

USA, private collection, formerly Professor Plumb Collection, Cambridge

A design for this shape, known as *gobelet lizonné et soucoupe*, is preserved in the factory archives (see fig. 68a). It bears the date 19 fevrÿe mil 1753,[1] but repre-

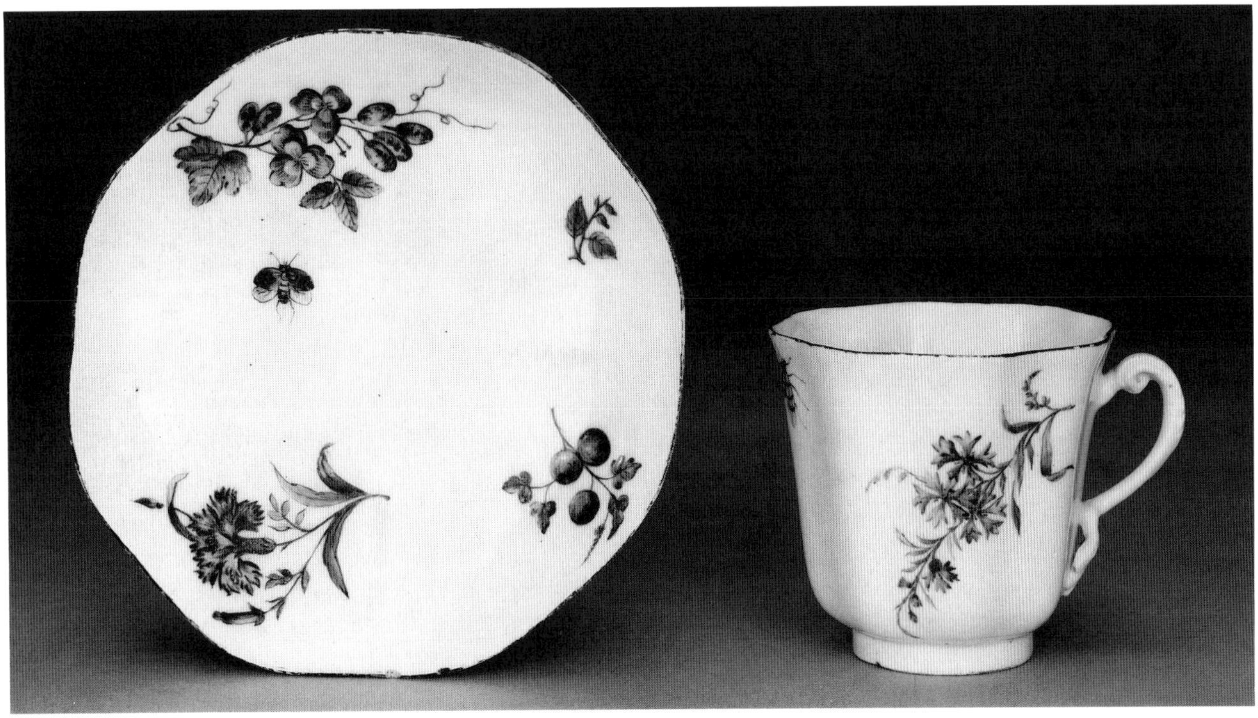

68

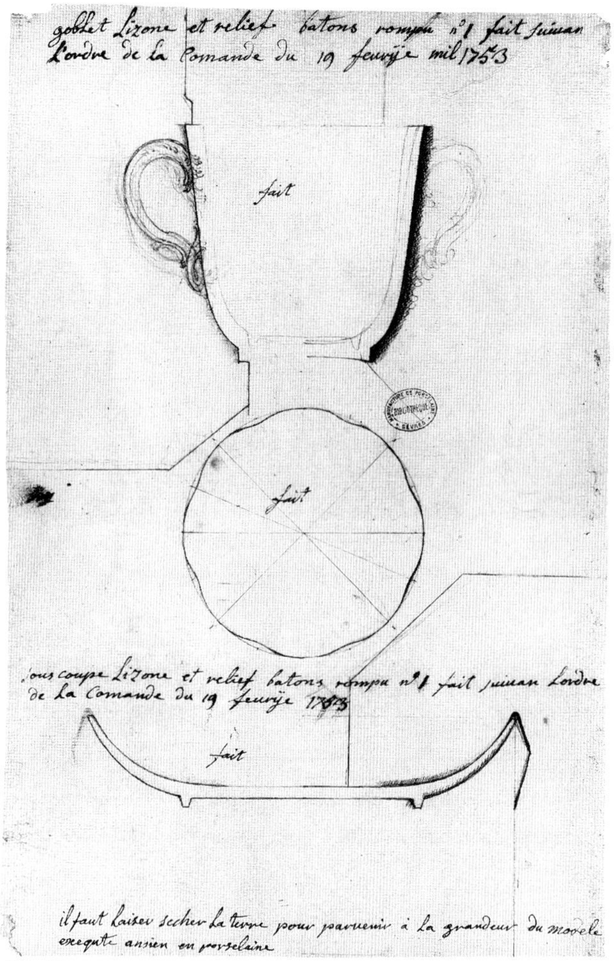

Fig 68a

sents a second version of the shape which was in production before August 1752.[2] The shape was made in three sizes, this example being of the third, or smallest, size. Examples decorated with flowers sold to Monsieur Bailly in December 1753 cost 15, 9 and 6 *livres* respectively.[3]

Savill has noted the incised marks *j* and *C*.[4]

The compilers of the Vincennes exhibition catalogue[5] drew attention to the shallowness of the saucer and the rather unskilled decoration, which derives from Meissen porcelain, as indicative of an early date of manufacture; in addition the handle is rather inexpertly formed. A similar cup and saucer was illustrated by T. H. Clarke[6] next to a Chelsea example marked with the raised anchor, to show the close parallels between the productions of the Vincennes and Chelsea factories at this period.

The cup and saucer were doubtless intended to be part of a *cabaret* with a matching teapot and cover[7] and sugar bowl and cover.[8] It is uncertain whether there was a matching milk jug.

1. Exh. *Vincennes*, 1977–8, p. 125.
2. An example was sold on 26 April 1753 and noted in the sales register as having been in the 55th enamel kiln, probably fired in early 1750, Archives de Sèvres, Vy 1, f. 2v.
3. MNS, Archives de Sèvres, Vy 1, f. 22, f. 26, f. 22v respectively.
4. Savill, 1988, III, pp. 1110, 1092.
5. *Op. cit.*, no. 370.
6. T.H. Clarke, 'French Influences at Chelsea', *ECC Trans.*, Vol. 4, part 5 (1959), plates 21d and e.
7. Exh. *Vincennes*, 1977–8, nos. 395, 396, the latter painted with flowers, handle, spout, rim of cover gilt; the design for this form bears the same date, 19 février 1753.
8. *Ibid.*, nos. 197, 198, 199; first mention of biscuit firing in November 1753.

69 **Cup and Saucer (*gobelet Calabre*)**, 1749

See colour plate 8

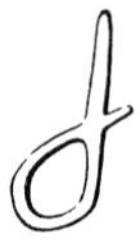

69 *mark*

D. *of saucer:* 13.5 cm
H. *of cup:* 7.5 cm
Marks: interlaced LL enclosing a dot, in blue; saucer incised *d* near foot rim; suspension hole part way through foot rim on saucer
Reg. No. 1926,12–22,1

Glazed white soft-paste porcelain, thickly potted, deep saucer with curved sides, bell-shaped cup with out-turned rim, the handle in the shape of a lizard. Decorated *en camaïeu pourpre* with landscape scenes, the rims and foot of the cup gilded. The lizard handle, painted in the same palette, is enriched with tiny gold dots. Minor chips to rims.

Provenance: Christie's, 30 November 1926, John McDowell sale, Lot 64 (from Departmental Register). Purchased, 1926

Literature: King, 1931, pp. 367–70, figs. IV, V

King, 1939, pp. 194–6, figs. 12, 13

Brunet and Préaud, 1978, p. 125, no. 5

Exhibited: 1977, 'Porcelaines de Vincennes, les origines de Sèvres', Paris, Grand Palais, Oct. 1977–Jan. 1978, no. 335

Comparable Examples: London, private collection, formerly in Florence Gould Collection, sold Sotheby Parke Bernet, Monaco, 27 June 1984, Lot 1531, illus. Préaud and d'Albis, 1991, p. 156, no. 129 and wrappers

Shropshire, private collection

Paris, Jules Archdeacon Collection, exh. *La porcelaine française*, 1929, no. 593

Los Angeles, private collection, sold Sotheby's, Chester, 9 July 1989, Lot 713

The slightly out-turned profile of the cup is the original form, altered to the more usual form (see no. 78)[1] in 1753. It was named in honour of Pierre Calabre, one of the shareholders in the company established in the name of Charles Adam in 1745. The shape was made in two sizes, this example being the first or larger size. It has not been possible to trace this example amongst the many sold decorated with *paysages camaïeux*, and the factory records do not appear to

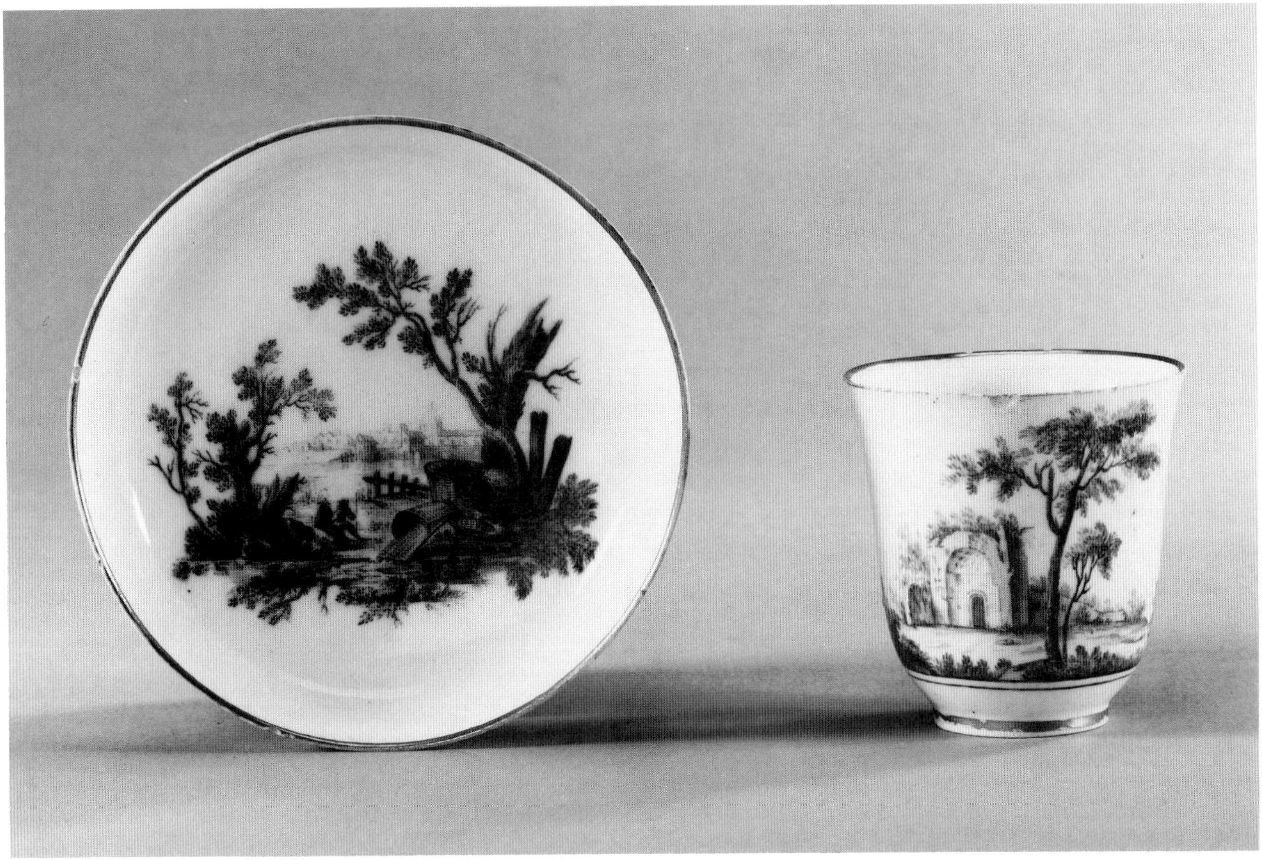

69

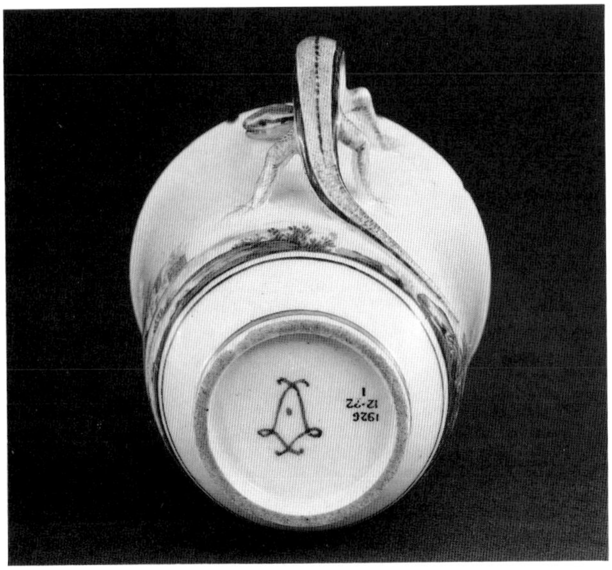

69 *base and handle*

mention any cups with lizard handles. The writer has dated this cup following Préaud and d'Albis, who believe it may have been made as early as 1749.[2]

1. See exh. *Vincennes*, 1977–8, pp. 118–21 for a series of cups and saucers of this form.
2. Préaud and d'Albis, 1991, p. 156, no. 129.

70 Sugar Bowl, Cover and Stand (*boîte à sucre ovale uni et plateau*), 1752–3

See colour plate 10

L. *of stand:*	25.7 cm
L. *of bowl:*	15.4 cm
H. *of bowl and cover:*	11.4 cm (to top of handle)
Marks:	interlaced LL with dot above, at each side and either side of lower intersection painted in underglaze blue; *4* incised; suspension hole in foot rim (stand); elaborate interlaced LL with fleur-de-lys above painted in underglaze blue; *9* or *6* incised, suspension hole in foot rim (bowl); *24* printed in black on label attached to stand
Reg. No.	1923,3–14,162

Glazed white soft-paste porcelain with uneven underglaze-blue ground (*bleu lapis*). The decoration in gold consists of stylised flying birds on a white ground enclosed within scrolled reserves from which spring asymmetrically-disposed pines, palm and oak trees, etc. There are two reserves on each component part. Inside the sugar bowl are three birds painted in gold to disguise firing damage more noticeable on the base where a long crack is covered by an elaborate factory mark. Gilt dentil rims, handle formed of two twisted ropes of clay with leaf terminals. Partly gilt. Foot rim of stand chipped.

Provenance: Presented by the Rt. Hon. Viscount Dillon, FSA, 1923 in memory of his son

Literature: King, 1931, pp. 367–70, fig. 1

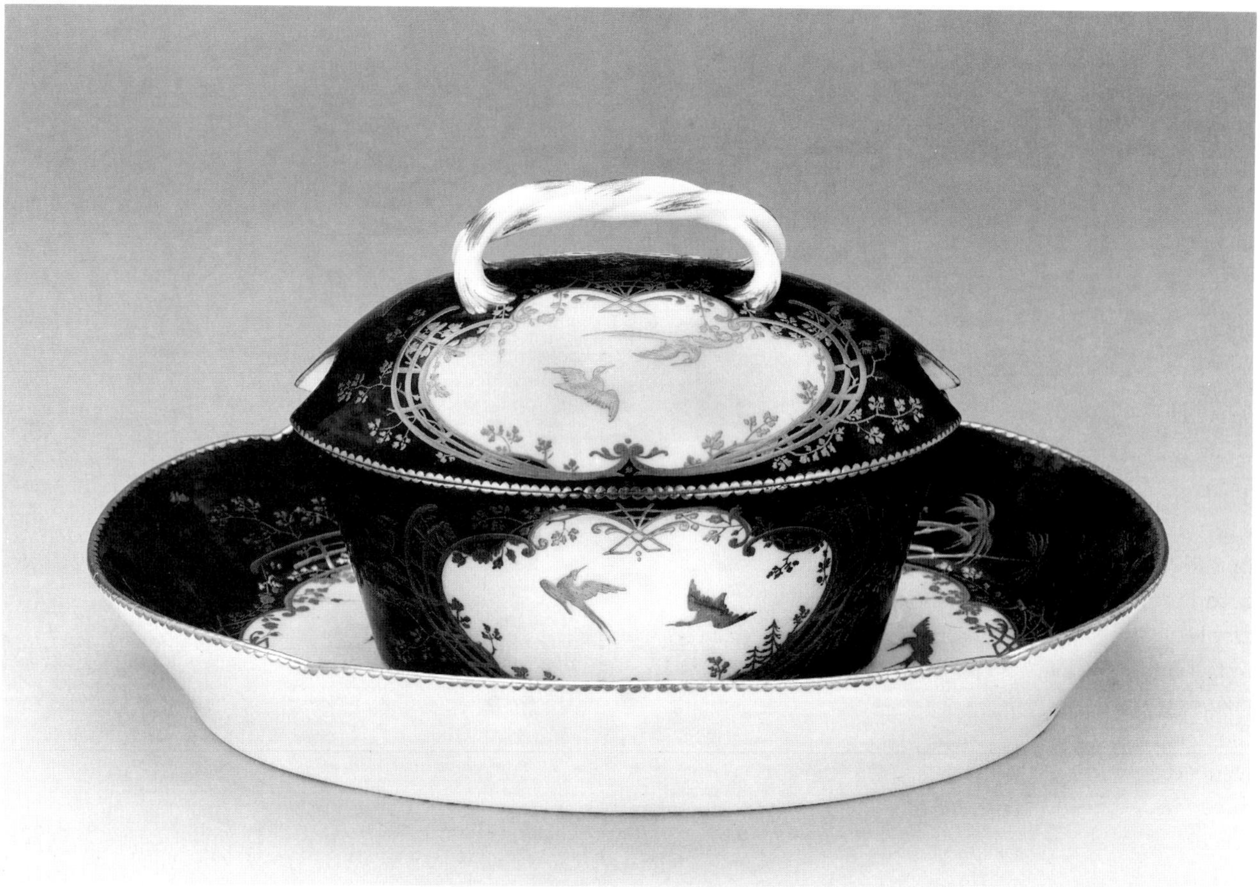

70

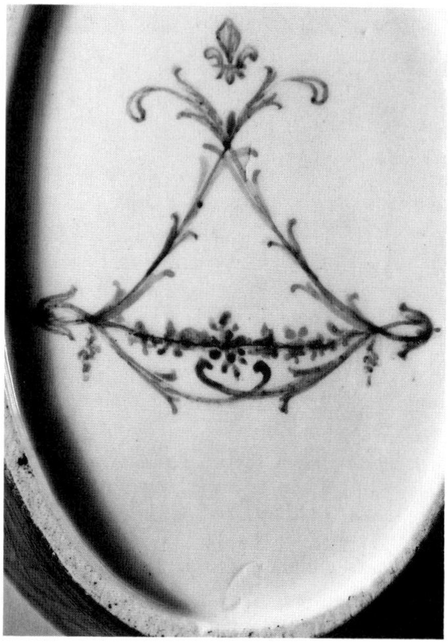

70 *mark (bowl)*

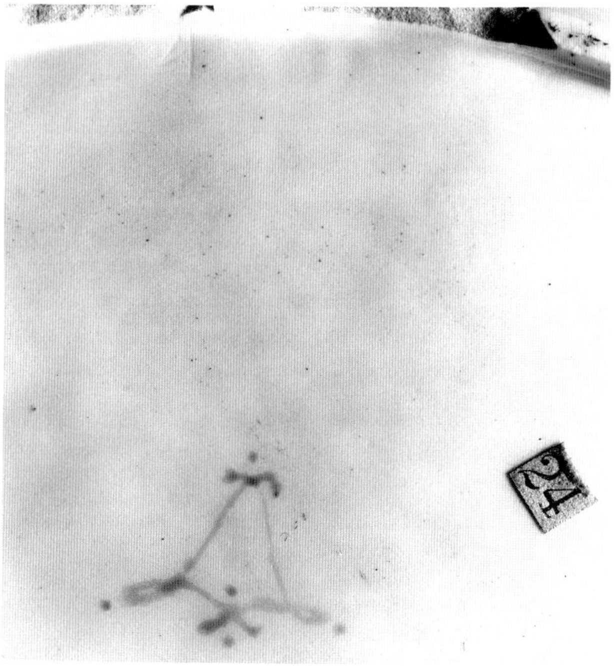

70 *marks (stand)*

King, 1939, pp. 194–6, figs 9, 10

Honey, 1950, pl. 62B

Préaud and d'Albis, 1991, p. 162, no. 144

Exhibited: 1977, 'Porcelaines de Vincennes, Les Origines de Sèvres', Paris, Grand Palais, Oct. 1977–Jan. 1978, no. 202

Comparable Examples: France, Saint Germain-en-Laye, Hôtel des Ventes, 21 February 1988, Lot 108, bowl and cover only, D. 15.5 cm, mark large LL and dots

Paris, Musée des arts décoratifs, inv. 28716, mark LL, flower decoration on a white ground, exh. *Vincennes*, 1977–8, no. 201

Whereabouts unknown, illus. W.J. Sainsbury, 'Vincennes Porcelain', *Connoisseur*, Vol. CXXXIII, no. 535, February 1954, pp. 3–8, fig. XI, date-letter A

Shropshire, private collection

The shape, known as *boîte à sucre ovale uni et plateau* (the '*uni*' was sometimes omitted from the descriptions in the factory sales records), was difficult to fire. A comparable piece in an English private collection displays exactly the same firing fault along the base of the bowl. As the first mention of a *bleu lapis* ground occurs in Fulvy's probate inventory dated May 1751,[1] the technique of suspending pieces on a cruciform stand during the firing of the decoration was introduced in 1752,[2] and date-marking began in 1753, these pieces can be quite closely dated.

The unidentified incised mark *4* has been noted as early as 1753 and *6* or *9* from 1754.[3]

It is tempting to identify this sugar bowl and its stand, which must surely be the larger of the two sizes manufactured,[4] with an example described as 'lapis et or' purchased by Madame de Pompadour on 12 May 1753 for 144 *livres*. It is recorded as having been in the 71st firing of the enamel kiln,[5] which is reckoned to have taken place some time between March and May 1752, by which time the colour was in regular production. Few sugar bowls of this shape and decoration are recorded. Those of the second size sold for 120 *livres*, but this example may owe its relatively low price to the firing fault.

1. Eriksen and Bellaigue, 1987, p. 50.
2. See Savill, 1988, III, p. 1176, from A. d'Albis, 'Procédés de fabrication de porcelaine tendre de Vincennes, d'après les livres de Hellot, *Faenza*, Vol. LXIX, 1983, pp. 202–16.
3. Savill, 1988, III, pp. 1126–7.
4. A bowl and cover of this shape in the Ariana Museum, Geneva, decorated with naturalistic flowers on a white ground inv. AR 1884 measures 14 cm in length; the stand is 23 cm long, inv. 1909.
5. MNS, Archives de Sèvres, Vy 1, f. 7. Antoine d'Albis has suggested a date of 1752–3 on account of the gilt dentil decoration on the rims.

71 Vase and Cover (*vase urne Pompadour*), *c.* 1752

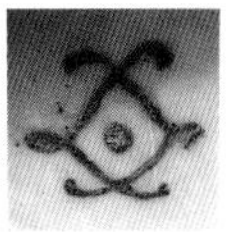

71 *mark*

Total H.	23.4 cm
D. *of base:*	10.1 cm
Marks:	incised LL enclosing dot, in gold
Reg. No.	Franks 377

Soft-paste porcelain, the circular turned domed foot attached (rather roughly, as visible on the inside of the foot) to the ovoid body, which is surmounted by a domed cover with flower finial, decorated in uneven underglaze-blue (*bleu lapis*) with gilded birds in elaborate rococo reserves. On one side are cormorants catching fish in the midst of watery plants, on the other a hen on the nest with a cockerel beside her. These, together with the elaborate scroll, the fantastic birds above and the basket of flowers springing from the central upper part of the cartouche, are all carefully tooled. Two more scrolls, asymmetrically placed on the foot, have similar decoration which is again repeated on the cover. Its finely-formed carnation finial, which actually consists of two flowers, one much smaller than the other, and several leaves, is partly gilded. Gilt dentil rims and foot. The cover has been restored. A few firecracks are visible inside the vase on the flat base.

Provenance: Bequeathed by Sir A.W. Franks, 1897

Literature: Franks, 1896, no. 377

Chaffers, 1926, Vol. II, p. 361, fig. 328

King, 1930, pp. 280–4, fig. VII

King, 1939, pp. 194–6, fig. 7 (cover)

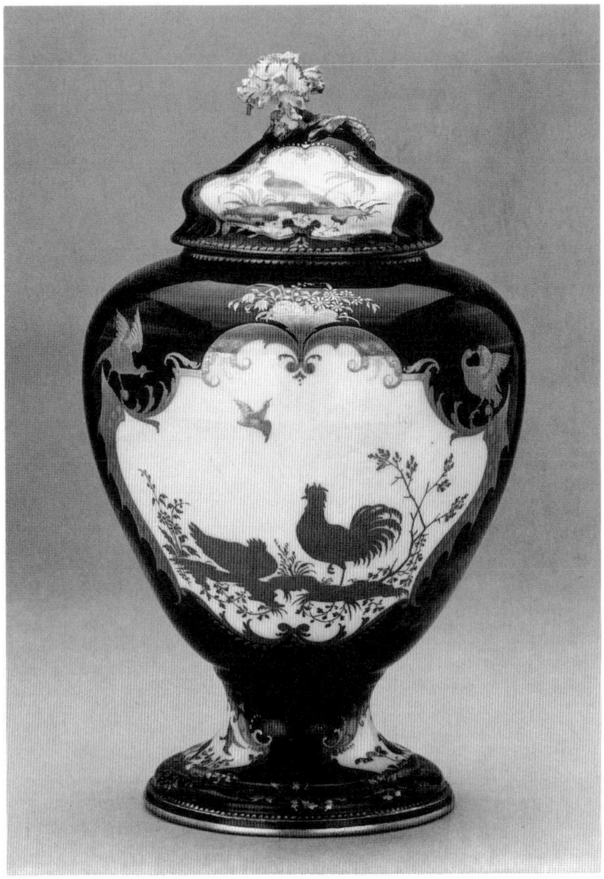

71

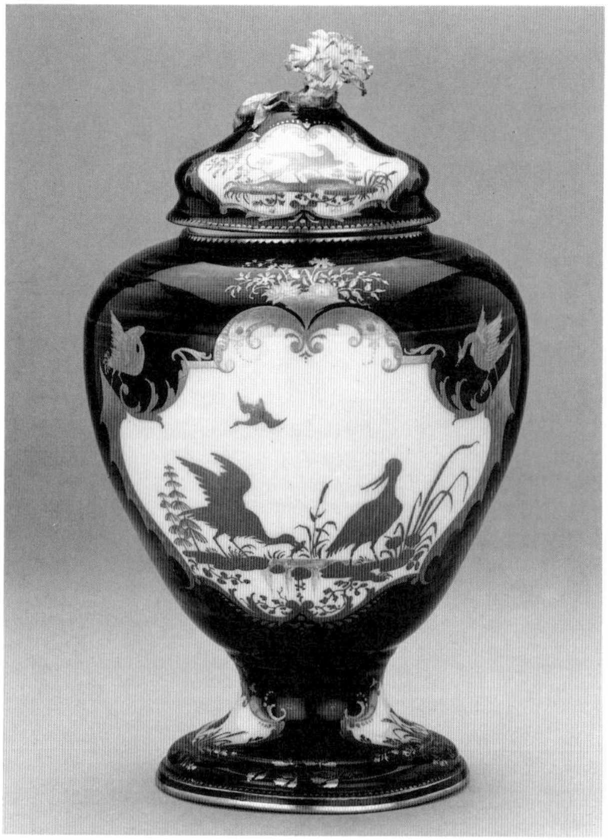

71

Honey, 1950, pl. 62A

Tait, 1962, revised ed. 1972, fig. 19

L.B. Hunt, 'Gold in the Pottery Industry. The History and Technology of Gilding Processes', *Gold Bulletin*, Vol. 12, no. 3, July 1979, p. 120

L.B. Hunt, 'The Gilding of European Porcelain', *Connoisseur*, Vol. 204, no. 820, June 1980, p. 109

Comparable Examples: Christie's, 9–17 May 1895, Lot 478, Mrs Lyne Stephens Collection (bought by Stettiner for £267–15s)

Christie's, 28 October 1963, Lot 147. The unusual cartouche is closely paralleled on an undated circular chamber pot with the same ground-colour in the Musée Jacquemart-André, Paris (Brunet and Préaud, 1978, no. 44)

Germany, Düsseldorf, Hetjens Museum, inv. 1941/101, illus. A. Klein, *Europaïsches Porzellan im Hetjens Museum, Düsseldorf*, 1966, no. 248 (without cover). This example has been examined and is considered to be later decorated

USA, formerly Prof. Plumb Collection, Cambridge (perhaps the example sold at Christie's, 1963)

Although magnificently decorated, the vase shows several defects of manufacture attesting to its early date, such as the presence of firecracks on the base and shoulder inside the vase and roughness inside the foot where it is attached to the body. For the introduction of the *bleu lapis* ground, see p. 75. The vase is likely to have been completed before 1753 when the date-letter system was introduced, but not before October 1752.[1]

Jean-Claude Duplessis (employed at the factory 1748–74), an Italian whose real name was Ciamberlano, who had come to France in about 1740 and is principally known for his bronzes – he was created *orfèvre du Roi* in 1758 – probably designed this shape, achieved by throwing and turning. He is thought to have joined the Vincennes factory in 1748. The shape is more generally found as a *pot-pourri* with pierced holes of rococo design in the shoulder and cover. It is possible that this was an early version of the *pot-pourri* and is purely ornamental. Like many other Vincennes and Sèvres vase shapes, it appears to have no prototype and to be purely original.

The vase is known to have been in production at least as early as late 1751 or early 1752, on the evidence of a vase of the first size sold to Lazare Duvaux in March 1753 and fired in the 68th enamel firing.[2]

It was made in four sizes, the most popular decorative scheme being *bleu lapis* and gold. Prices varied according to the richness of the decor; Monsieur Machard (Machault?) was prepared to pay no less than 180 *livres* each for two examples of the fourth size on 5 May 1753,[3] although they were sold for 120 *livres* at other times during the same year, and even for 84 *livres* at the end of 1754.[4] On the evidence of *pots-pourris* of the same form, this example is probably the fourth size, the first or largest measuring 43 cm in height. It has not been possible to trace the sale of this vase since at least fourteen are recorded between 1753–4.

1. Antoine d'Albis does not believe that the factory was capable of producing decoration of this quality before October 1752 (private correspondence, 1991).
2. MNS, Archives de Sèvres, Vy 1, f. 8.
3. MNS, Archives de Sèvres, Vy 1, f. 11v.
4. *Ibid.*, Vy 1, f. 54v.

72 Two-handled Toilet Pot, Cover and Stand (*tasse à toilette et soucoupe*), 1753–4

D. *of stand:*	12.7 cm
H. *of pot and cover:*	8 cm
Marks:	interlaced LL painted in dark blue under the glaze, *3* incised (both); trace of suspension hole (stand)
Reg. No.	1938,2–16,1

Soft-paste porcelain, deep saucer with central well, cup with straight sides swelling from small foot; uneven dark blue ground (*bleu lapis*) decorated in gold with a flower spray on a white ground enclosed by flowers and reeds in two reserves on each component

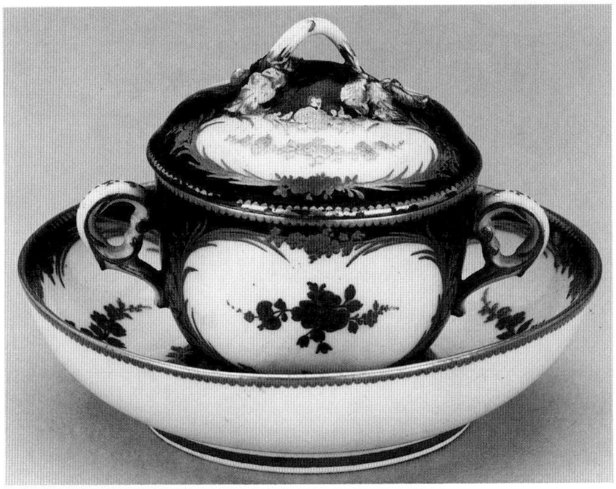

72

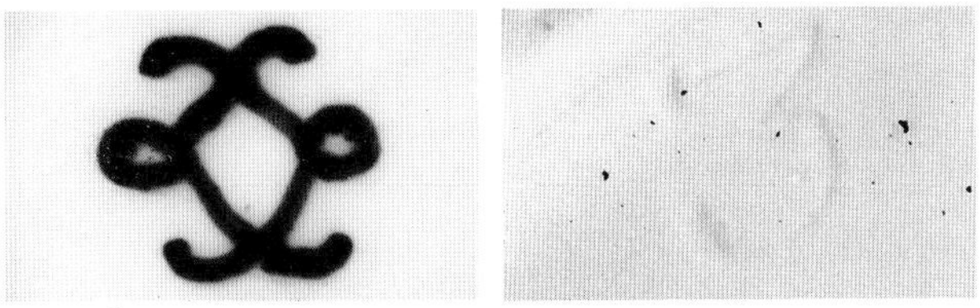

72 *marks*

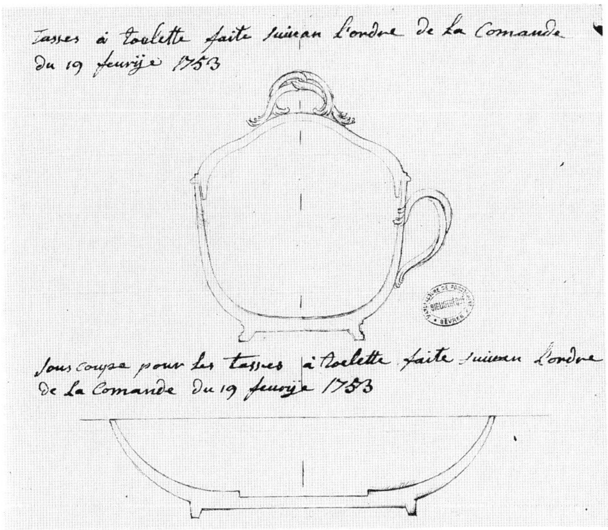

Fig 72a

part. Partly gilded scroll-form handles and twig finial on domed cover terminating in leaves. Gilt dentil rims and foot. Saucer warped in firing.

Provenance: Presented by Monsieur A. Lion, 1938

Literature: King, 1939, p. 196

Comparable Examples: None noted

Marked discoloration of the porcelain of the cover and patchy overfired glaze suggest the possibility that the cover may have been decorated some time after it received the initial biscuit firing.

The shape, known as *tasse à toilette*, is mentioned in the factory inventory of October 1752.[1] Forty-nine glazed examples were listed at 4 *livres* 10 *sols* each. The precise purpose of this form is still uncertain. Its domed cover was probably intended to prevent powder used during the *toilette* from falling into the broth or hot drink held in the cup. Savill, who discussed its function in 1988,[2] has kindly drawn to the author's attention a passage in Diderot's *Encyclopédie*[3] concerning a medicinal potion concocted from orange flowers which might have been drunk from a covered cup like this.

A drawing for this shape dated 19 February 1753 is preserved in the factory archive (see fig. 72a).[4] Only one size was made. These pieces may have been in the sixth enamel firing of the second series between November 1753 and January 1754 sold to Lazare Duvaux for 48 *livres* on 31 December 1753,[5] as the absence of a date-letter does not necessarily indicate a date of production before 1753.

The incised mark *3* is listed by Savill.[6]

1. Exh. *Vincennes*, 1977–8, p. 113, MNS, Archives de Sèvres, E 7.
2. Savill, 1988, II, p. 719.
3. D. Diderot and J. d'Alembert, *Encyclopédie ou Dictionnaire raisonné des Sciences, des Arts et des Métiers*, Paris, 1757–80, Vol. II (1765), p. 558.
4. Exh. *Vincennes*, 1977–8, p. 113. MNS, Archives de Sèvres R1, *dossier* 2, *laisse* 2, f. 1.
5. MNS, Archives de Sèvres, Vy 1, f. 30v, described as '*bleu ancien et or*'.
6. Savill, 1988, III, pp. 1125–6.

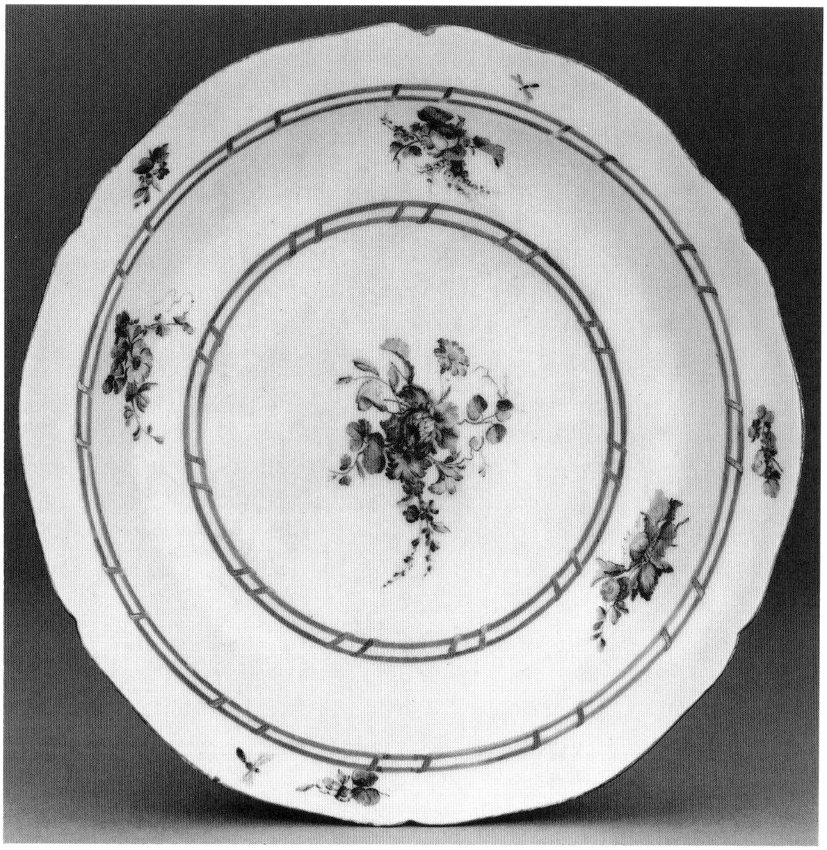

73

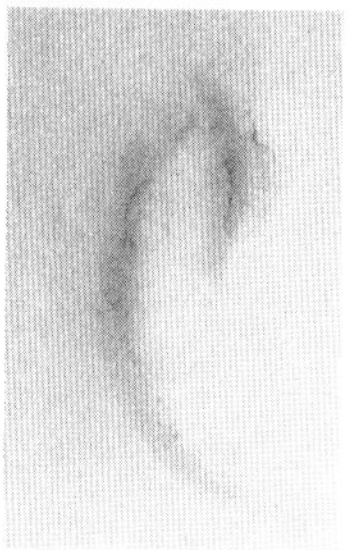

73 *mark*

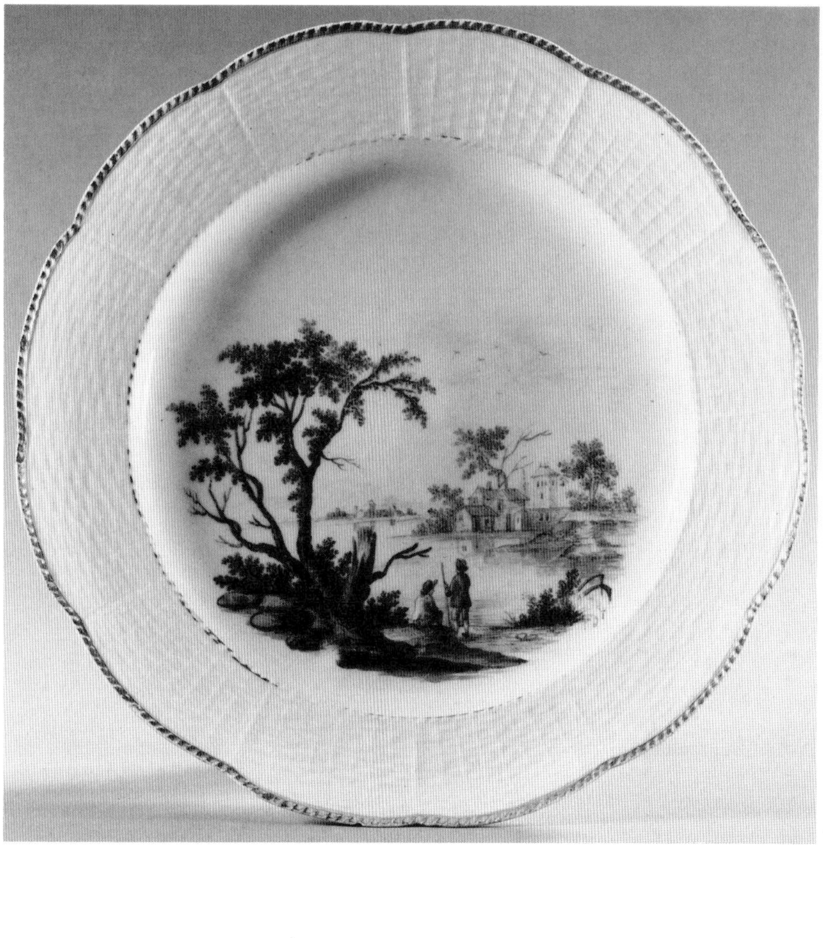

74

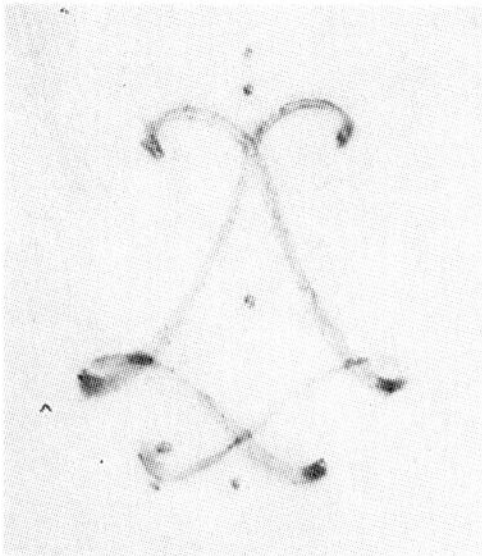

74 *mark*

73 **Round Fruit Dish (*compotier rond*)**, *c.* 1752

D. 19.4 cm
Marks: incised *C* near foot rim, trace of suspension hole
Reg. No. 1928,5–19,1

Glazed white soft-paste porcelain decorated in green, purple, blue, yellow and black with scattered flowers and flower groups, with two series of blue lines with gilt lines crossing them and with insects on the border. Gilded rim. The decoration is worn and there are chips to rim.

Provenance: Purchased, 1928

Literature: King, 1931, pp. 367–70, fig. VI

King, 1939, pp. 194–6, fig. 14

Comparable Examples: None noted

A considerable range of *compotiers* for use in the dessert service was produced at Vincennes. A plaster model for this version is preserved at the factory. In the sales records for the early period of the factory's existence, no mention is made of the various shapes (*à coquille*, *à côtes*, *à feuille de choux*, etc) so that it has not been possible to trace this piece.

The incised letter *C* is listed by Savill.[1]

1. Savill, 1988, III, p. 1092.

74 **Plate (*assiette à osier*)**, *c.* 1752

D. 22.7 cm
Marks: interlaced LL enclosing a dot with two dots above and one below painted in underglaze-blue
Reg. No. Franks 375

Glazed white soft-paste porcelain with moulded rim and edge simulating basketwork, decorated in the centre *en camaïeu pourpre* with a landscape scene of two figures standing by a lake, the rim and edge of the well of the plate gilded. The plate exhibits pinholes and discoloration on the reverse. The rim is chipped in several places.

Provenance: Bequeathed by Sir A.W. Franks, 1897

Literature: Franks, 1896, no. 375

King, 1930, pp. 280–4, fig. I

King, 1939, pp. 194–6, fig. I

Comparable Examples: Paris, Hôtel Drouot, 29 November 1920, Lot 92, Vente Ctsse de B(éarn)

Paris, private collection, illus. exh. *Vincennes*, 1977–8, no. 27

Christie's, 21 June 1976, Lot 115

The factory inventory records moulds (*moules* and *contre-moules*) for basketwork-moulded plates called 'assiettes à ozier' in October 1752.[1] An unglazed soft-paste porcelain model is preserved in the Sèvres factory archive. The form is closely based on the Meissen porcelain *altozier* pattern introduced in 1735.[2]

The Vincennes plate was made in two sizes, this example being the second, smaller, size. Seventy-one defective plates painted with a *paysage camaïeu* were valued at 6 *livres* each in the inventory taken at the factory in 1752.[3]

The Museum plate was probably made around 1752, when the practice of drilling a hole in the foot rim for suspension of the piece in the enamel kiln began.[4] It may have been one of the 36 sold for 12 *livres* each on 20 April 1754 and noted in the margin of the sales records as having been fired in the first series of firings before August 1752.[5]

1. MNS, Archives de Sèvres, *Carton* E7.
2. Exh. Rückert, 1966, no. 284.
3. MNS, Archives de Sèvres, *Carton*, E7.
4. D'Albis and Préaud, 1986, p. 9.
5. MNS, Archives de Sèvres, Vy l, f. 38.

75 **Cup and Saucer (*tasse gauffrée et soucoupe*)**, 1752–3

D. *of saucer* 15.4 cm
H. *of cup:* 7.9 cm
Marks: interlaced LL enclosing dot with short line above painted in pink over the glaze; incised *Tt*, trace of suspension hole (saucer); interlaced LL enclosing dot painted over the glaze in pink, incised *8* or *B* and (probably) *T* (cup)
Reg. No. 1929,10–17,1

Thickly potted soft-paste porcelain. Deep saucer with eight-lobed undulating rim and tall cup moulded with a swirling fluted pattern, and in the well of the saucer with a raised band enclosing a central motif of ovals around a star-shaped flower. The moulding is picked out in pink. Gilt dentil pattern on rims; sides and terminals of simple loop handle and foot of cup gilt. The saucer has a 'bloat' near the centre and a chip to the foot rim is apparently glazed over; inside the cup are two further firing defects.

Provenance: Purchased, 1929

Literature: King, 1931, pp. 367–70, fig. VII

King, 1939, pp. 194–6, fig. 15

Préaud and d'Albis, 1991, p. 156, no. 128

Exhibited: 1977, Porcelaines de Vincennes, les origines de Sèvres', Paris, Grand Palais, Oct. 1977–Jan. 1978, no. 350

Comparable Examples: Paris, Hôtel Drouot, 24 October 1986, Lot 42

The form is known as a *tasse gauffrée*, although it is not mentioned under this name in the eighteenth century in the factory archives. The shape conforms to the *gobelet Calabre, gauffrée* referring only to the moulded decoration. A plaster model, described as a *tasse gauffrée* in the inventory taken in 1814, is preserved at the Sèvres factory. The form continued in use until the mid-1760s or later, and was apparently copied by at least one Paris factory.[1]

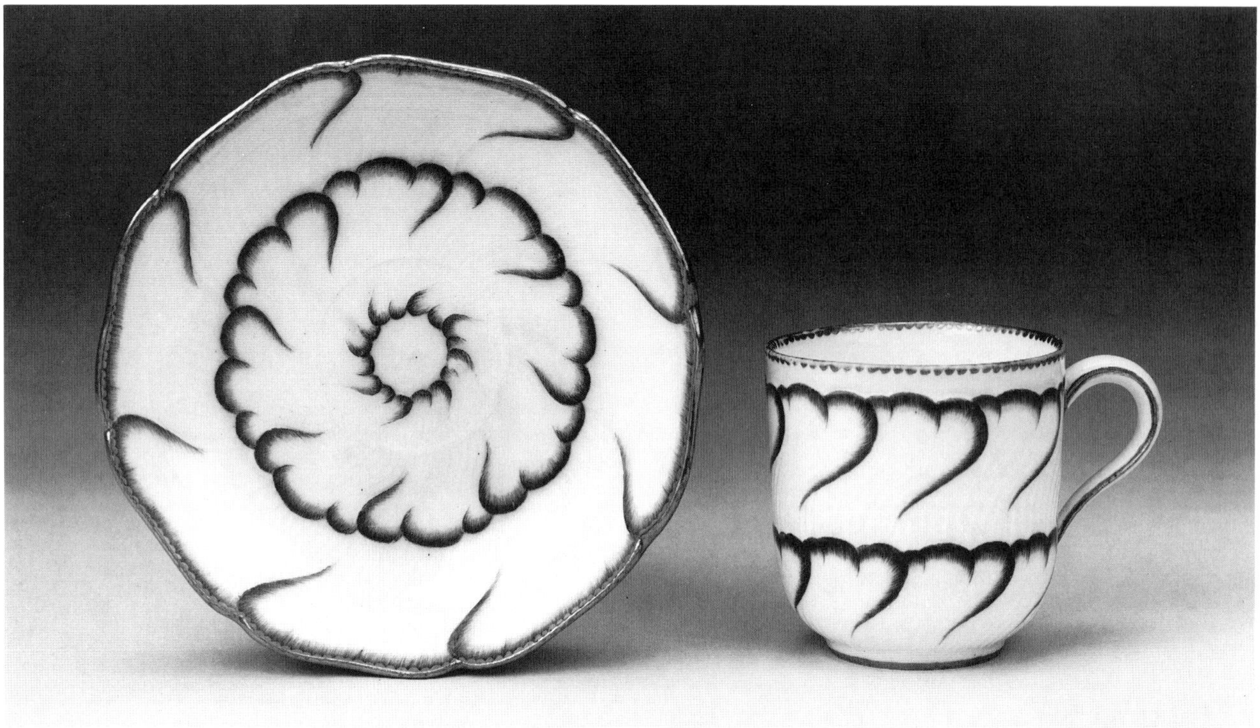

75

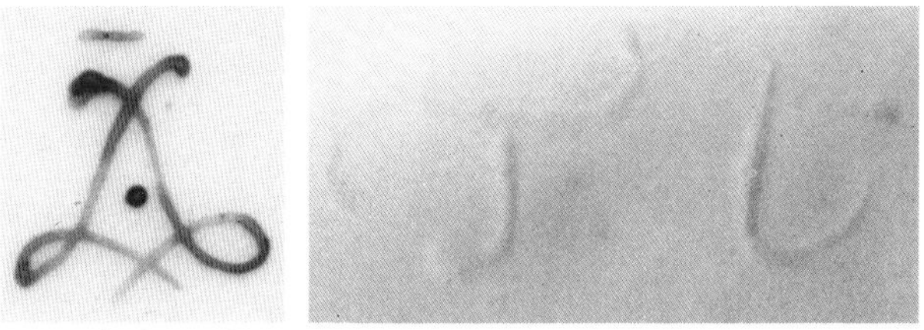

75 *marks (saucer)*

75 *marks (cup)*

The moulded pattern, based on a Chinese original, enjoyed some popularity at Vincennes and was used for plates, *compotiers*, and sugar bowls and covers with stands. Gold, and even *bleu céleste*, were used to decorate these pieces, which might also be left in the white or painted with scattered flower sprays.[2]

Only one size of cup and saucer has so far been noted; if others were made, this example would surely have been the first, or largest, size.

The saucer can be dated to 1752, when the practice of suspending pieces from a metal support in the enamel kiln was adopted.[3] Because of the lack of precision in the records about this form, it has not been possible to trace this cup and saucer since a large number of *gobelets Calabres* were produced.

The incised marks *T* and *8* are listed by Savill.[4]

1. A part-service decorated in blue and dated 1766 was sold at Christie's, 30 June 1980, Lot 59; it included 'two Paris shaped-oval dishes *en suite*'.
2. See exh. *Vincennes*, 1977–8, nos. 35, 65–7, 195.
3. d'Albis and Préaud, 1986, p. 9. For an illustration of the support, see A. d'Albis, 'Les Premières Années de la Manufacture de Porcelaine de Vincennes', *Faenza*, Vol. LXX (1984), nos. 5–6, *tavola* CLXX, and Préaud and d'Albis, 1991, p. 231.
4. Savill, 1988, III, pp. 1109, 1128.

76 Two-handled Cup and Saucer (*tasse à toilette et soucoupe*), *c.* 1752–3

D. *of saucer:* 12 cm;
H. *of cup:* 4.5 cm
Marks: interlaced LL with dot above, below and in centre painted in blue over the glaze on both; incised cursive *e*, *l* or *c* (saucer).
Reg. No. 1930,5–14,1

Glazed white porcelain, the shallow saucer with a central raised well, the two handles on the cup of twig form, terminating at either end in leaves, decorated in gold with *chinoiserie* scenes and insects. The foot of the cup has been turned to form an inner and outer foot rim. Rims and feet gilded. Chip to rim of cup.

Provenance: Purchased, 1930

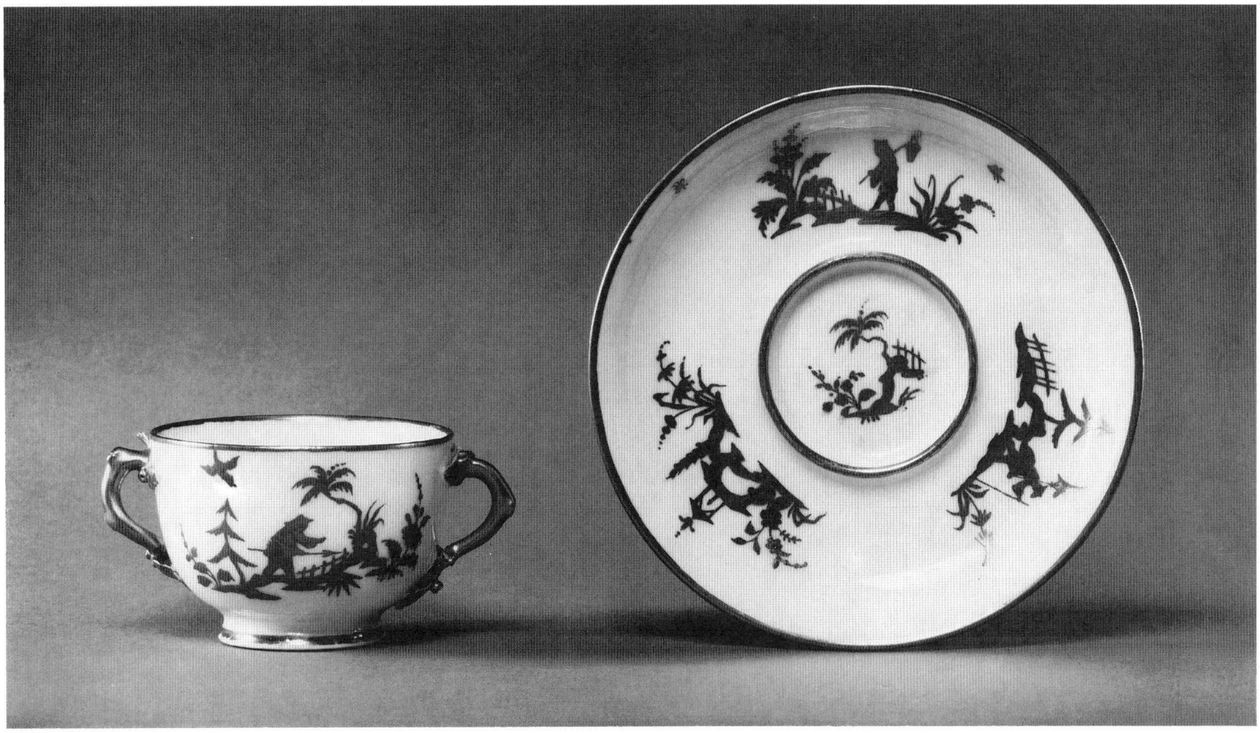

76

Literature: King, 1931, pp. 367–70, fig. VIII

King, 1939, pp. 194–6, fig. 16

Comparable Examples: Paris, Musée des arts décoratifs, inv. 19386 A and B, illus. exh. *Vincennes*, 1977–8, no. 309, decorated with military trophies on the cup and animals on the saucer

Cambridge, Fitzwilliam Museum, inv. MAR. C. 37–1912, ill. Savage, 1970, pl. 40, decorated with animals on the cup and cover and trophies on the saucer

New York, Sotheby's, 17–18 December 1982, Lot 310, decorated with flowers on the cup and cover and animals on the saucer

For a discussion of the form, see cat. 72. Prices of the *tasse à toilette*, which was made in one size only, varied widely according to the decoration. On 21 August 1753 one *tasse à toilette blanc et or* from the second glaze firing of December 1752 was sold for 24 *livres*.[1] Another two from the same firing were sold to Lazare Duvaux on 31 December of the same year for the slightly higher price of 30 *livres*,[2] while on 15 November 1754 Monsieur Bazin purchased a single *tasse à toilette blanc et or* and its saucer from one of the earliest firings for 12 *livres*.[3] It may have been one of nine described as a second quality with this type of decoration listed in the *magasin de vente* in the inventory of October 1752, which were then valued at only 9 *livres*.[4]

The incised marks *e*, *l* and *c* are listed by Savill.[5]

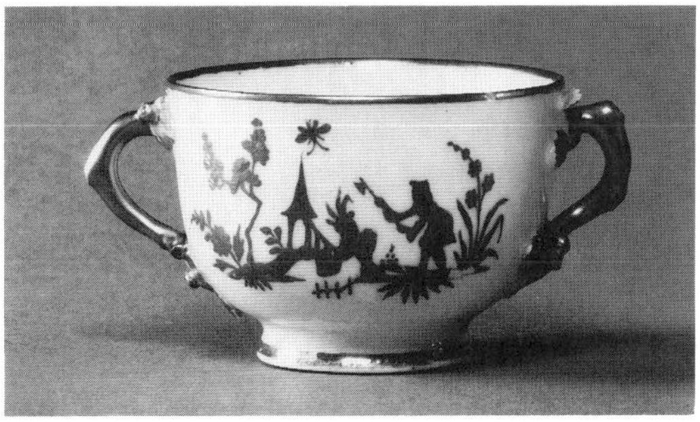

76 *reverse of cup*

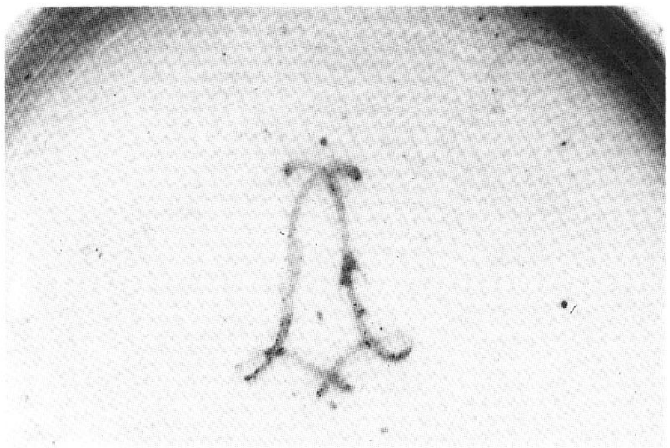

76 *mark (saucer)*

1. MNS, Archives de Sèvres, Vy 1, f. 4.
2. *Ibid.*, f. 26 v.
3. *Ibid.*, f. 53 v.
4. MNS, Archives de Sèvres, *Carton*, I 7.
5. Savill, 1988, Vol. III, pp. 1100, 1111, 1092.

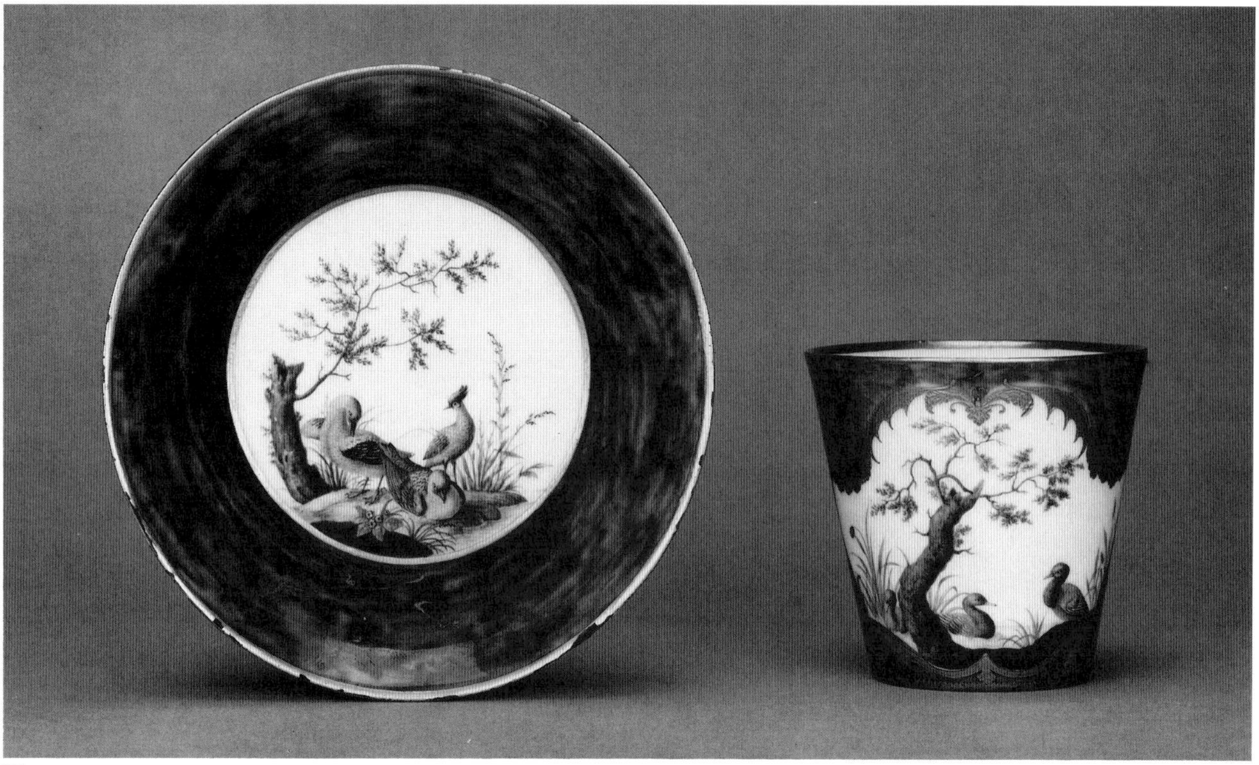

77

77 Cup and Saucer (*gobelet à la Reine*), *c.* 1752–3

See colour plate 11

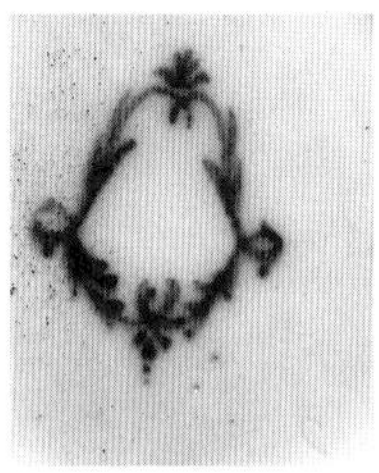

77 *mark (cup)*

D. *of saucer:*	15.6 cm
H. *of cup:*	8.5 cm
Marks:	elaborate interlaced LL painted in underglaze-blue on both; *d* incised on both
Reg. No.	1989,5–6,4

Soft-paste porcelain, moulded. The cup is of conical form; the handle is slender at the lower end and broadens out to become thicker and grooved at its upper end, which curves downward to a quatrefoil terminal. The deep saucer has flared sides. Painted with waterfowl, damaged trees and grasses in green, browns, orange, red, yellow, blue, purple and pink on a white ground in reserve against an uneven underglaze-blue ground. An elaborate gilt cartouche, thickly applied and carefully tooled, encloses the decoration on the cup. Inner and outer rims gilt, handle gilt except on upper side which is ornamented with a gilt floral motif on a white ground; gilt line around well of saucer; gilt lines on blue ground to simulate either Chinese 'cracked ice' patterns or lapis lazuli. Slight loss of gilding on foot of cup, rim of saucer, lower part of handle.

Provenance: Simon Goldblatt Collection, Sotheby's, 1 May 1956, Lot 131. Purchased, 1989

Literature: Dawson *et al.*, 1990, pp. 673–4, no. x

Préaud and d'Albis, 1991, p. 41, no. 137, p. 160

Comparable Examples: London, Victoria and Albert Museum, inv. C. 135–1914, saucer

Northamptonshire, Althorp, Earl Spencer, illus. R.J. Charleston, 'Sèvres and other French porcelain in Earl Spencer's collection at Althorp', *Connoisseur*, Vol. CLXXIII, no. 696, February 1970, fig. 6, D. of saucer 14 cm, H. of cup 6.5 cm

London, private collection

Shropshire, private collection

Christie's, 2 December 1974, Lot 24, a pair, Lot 25 another pair (two cups and a saucer from Lot 25 and a saucer from Lot 24, sold Paris, Hôtel Drouot, 20 October 1975, Lot 111)

London, exh. Allen, 1987, no. 11, from Ambassador Henry Norweb Collection, Cleveland, USA

Paris, private collection, illustrated front cover *ABC Décor*, October 1983, no. 225 and Malgras (ed.), 'Vincennes', 1983, p. 228.

Paris, Musée des arts décoratifs, inv. 36946, illus. exh. *Vincennes*, 1977–8, no. 290, D. of saucer 14 cm, H. of cup 6.5 cm

USA, New York, Metropolitan Museum, undated, painting attributed to Tabary by Clare Corbeiller, illus. Eriksen and Bellaigue, 1987, p. 255

There are several versions of this form with different handles and banded decoration.[1] A drawing inscribed *Gobelet à cuvier servant en uny et à serceaux fait suivan l'ordre de la comande du 19 févriÿe 1753...* for two sizes survives at the factory.[2] It is the same shape as the plaster model for a 'Gobelet à lait à la Reine', mentioned in the inventory of October 1752 and manufactured in two sizes from August 1753.[3] A version with a cover was in production in 1753,[4] as well as one with a cover with two handles (see cat. 97). This example is of the first size.

The most expensive *tasses à la Reine* sold from the factory in the early period are of the first size, with a *bleu lapis* ground and coloured birds. Duvaux purchased one for 48 *livres* on 12 May 1753, whilst 'M. le Grand pour le duc de Duras' paid 60 *livres* for another on 28 May 1753.[5]

Examples of this shape made before the introduction of date-letters were often decorated with gilt stylised birds on a white ground,[6] with coloured stylised birds against a *bleu lapis* ground,[7] or with painted and gilt waterfowl against a *bleu lapis* ground, flecked with gold to imitate lapis lazuli.[8] There seems little doubt that the cups and saucers painted in colours with waterfowl, their plumage carefully 'stippled' in gold, belonged to a specially-made set, since so few are known, all with elaborate marks. There is no parallel for this kind of decoration at Vincennes. The fowl are probably based on engravings; their painter remains unknown.

Various incised *d* marks have been recorded by Dauterman, of which the closest is on an early Vincennes saucer in the Metropolitan Museum, New York.[9]

Waterfowl in a more elaborate setting are painted on two Meissen plaques in the Residenz, Ansbach,[10] thought to date from about 1760. During the early 1760s waterfowl were used on two saucers and a teapot from services painted with birds made at Gotzkowsky's porcelain factory in Berlin.[11] Pieces from a coffee-service made at Fürstenberg and painted by C.G. Albert around 1770 show the continuing popularity of bird decoration. A teabowl and saucer painted with waterfowl may be taken from the same source as the birds on the *gobelet à la Reine*.[12]

1. Exh. *Vincennes*, 1977–8, pp. 108–11.
2. *Op. cit.*, p. 108.
3. An example of the second size with saucer, decorated in blue and gold, was sold for 36 *livres* on 7 September 1753, MNS, Archives de Sèvres, Vy 1, f. 16v.
4. Exh. *Vincennes*, 1977–8, no. 295, Musée des arts décoratifs, Paris, inv. OA. 6241.
5. MNS, Archives de Sèvres, Vy 1, f. 8v.; Vy 1, f. 12.
6. Exh. *Vincennes*, 1977–8, no. 289, London, private collection.
7. Scotland, Blair Castle.
8. Paris, private collection, illus. Malgras (ed.), 1983, p. 228.
9. Dauterman, 1986, pp. 188–9; inv. 50.211.173.
10. Exh. Rückert, 1966, no. 742, inv. P 275.
11. See W. and I. Baer and S. Grosskopf-Knaack, *Von Gotzkowsky zur KPM*, Berlin, 1986, nos. P18, P234, P231.
12. Exh. 'Weisses Gold aus Fürstenberg, Kulturgeschichte im Spiegel des Porzellans 1747–1830', Munster, Westfälisches Landesmuseum für Kunst und Kulturgeschichte, Dec. 1988–Feb. 1989, Brunswick, Herzog Anton Ulrich-Museum, cat. 106–11, esp. no. 110.

78 Cup and Saucer (*gobelets Calabre*), 1753–4

D. *of saucer:*	13.8 cm
H. *of cup:*	7.1 cm
Marks:	interlaced LL painted in dark blue under the glaze, incised *3*, trace of suspensions hole (saucer); interlaced LL enclosing *A* painted in dark blue under the glaze (cup)
Reg. No.	Franks 378

Finely potted highly translucent soft-paste porcelain deep saucer and straight-sided cup, painted under the glaze with deep uneven blue ground (*bleu lapis*) and richly decorated in gold with (on cup) two birds each carrying a branch (on the saucer only one bears a branch) on a white ground within a shaped reserve surrounded by reeds, branches and flowers. Gilt dentil rims, partly gilded handle and foot (on cup). Both slightly warped in firing.

Provenance: Bequeathed by Sir A.W. Franks, 1897

Literature: Franks, 1896, no. 378

Chaffers, 1926, Vol. II, p. 361, fig. 239

King, 1930, pp. 280–4, fig. VIII

King, 1939, pp. 194–6, fig. 8

Comparable Examples: Sotheby's, 5 June 1990, Lot 252, undated

Pierre Calabre was a shareholder in the Charles Adam Company from June 1750. He also had an interest in the succeeding Eloi Brichard Company until at least 1756.[1]

In 1753 six *gobelets Calabres* and saucers of this second size were sold for 36 *livres* to Lazare Duvaux.[2] As they were noted as having been fired in the sixth enamel kiln in November or December 1753 it is possible that this example may have been one of them. This example is particularly sumptuously decorated.

1. A. Sergène, *La Manufacture de Sèvres sous l'Ancien Régime*, Vol. III, unpublished thesis, Nancy, 1974, p. 100 and p. 162.
2. MNS, Archives de Sèvres, Vy 1, f. 29.

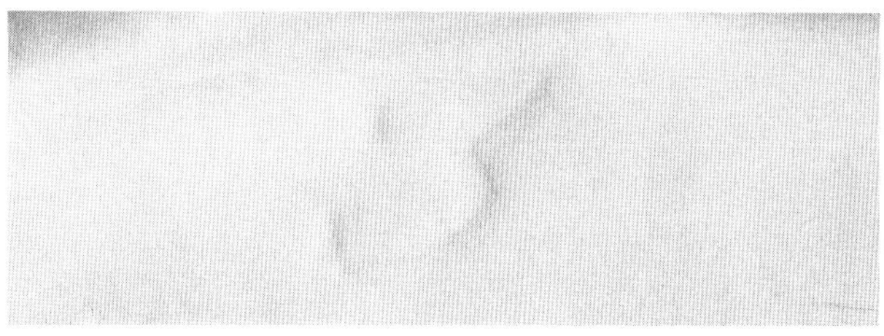

78 *incised mark (saucer)*

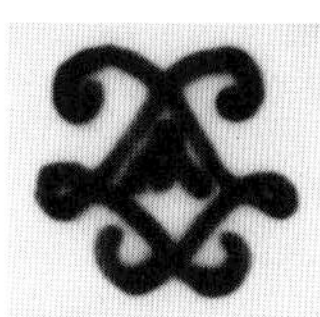

78 *mark (cup)*

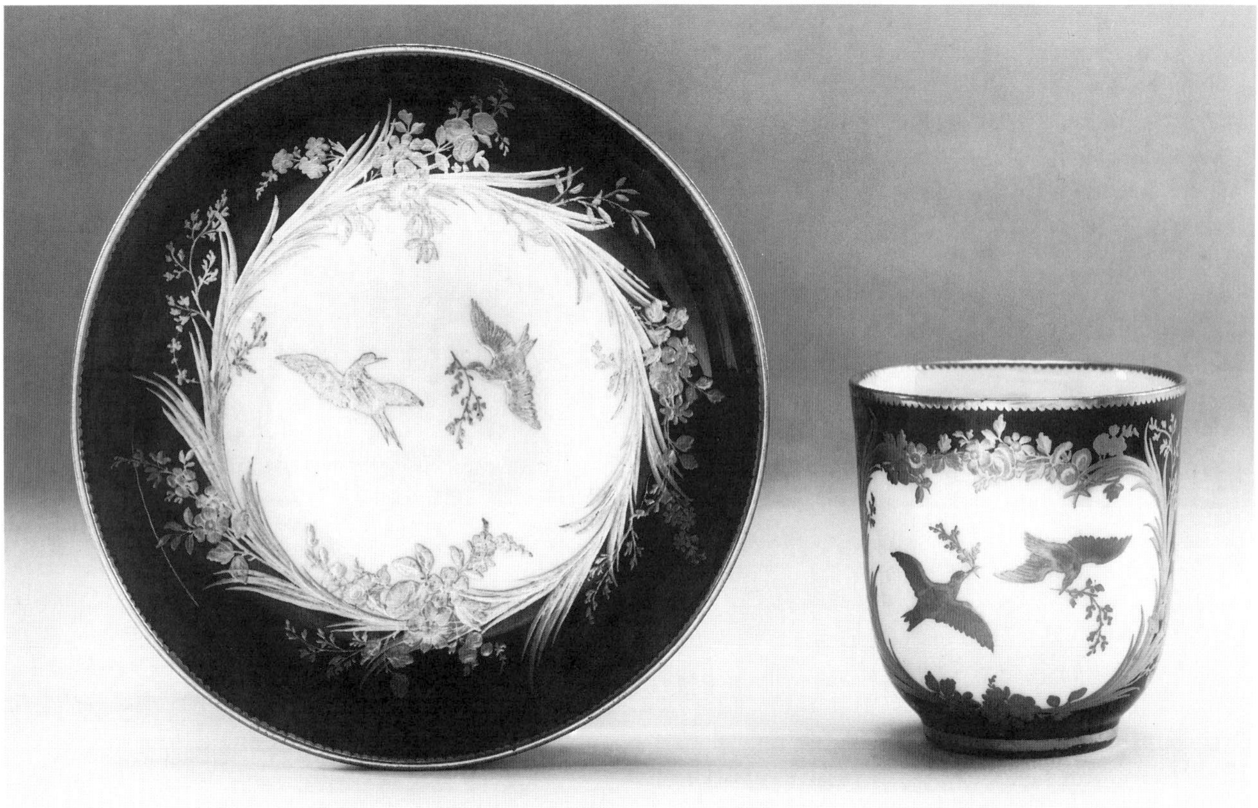

78

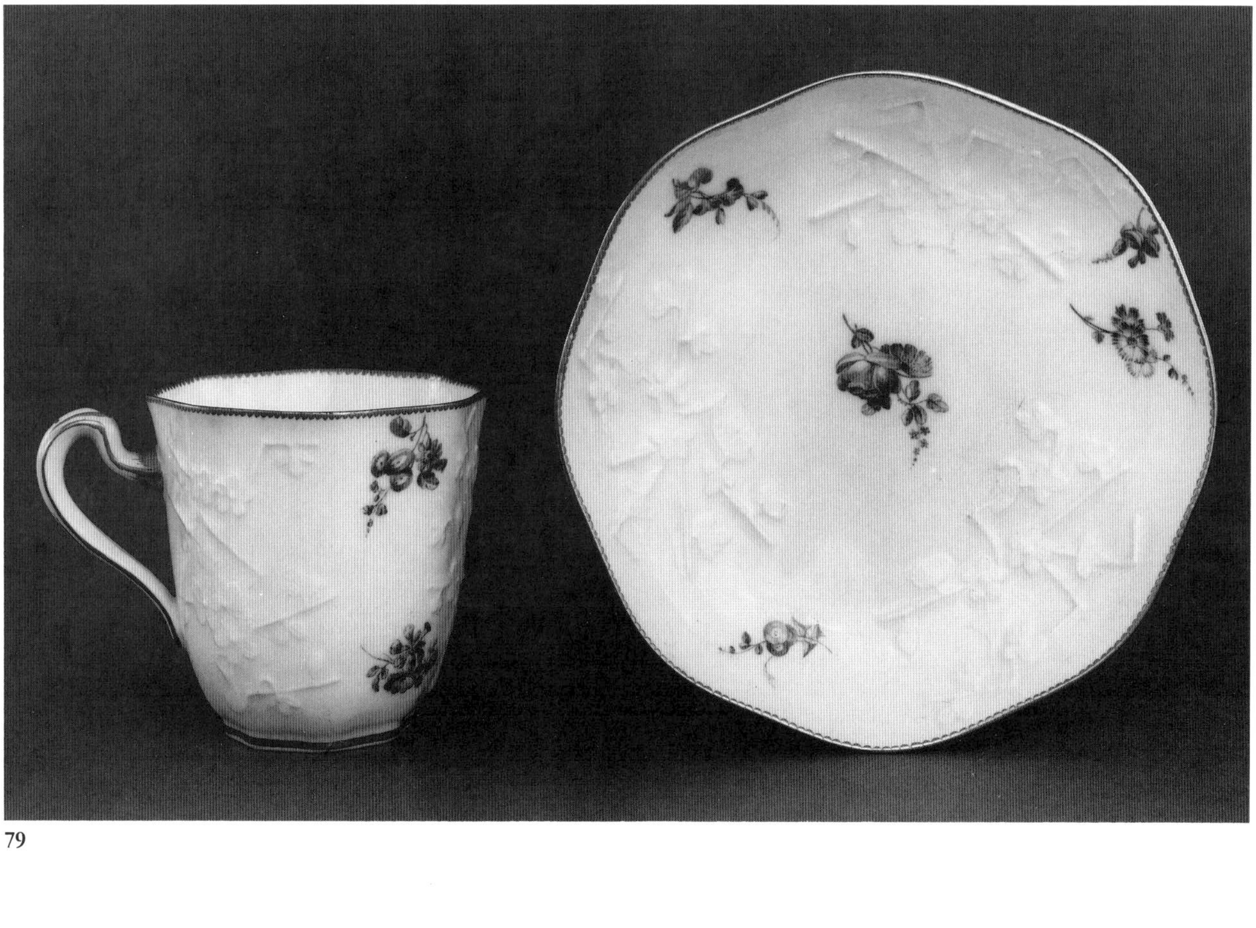

79

79 **Cup and Saucer (*gobelet lizonné à relief et soucoupe*)**, 1753–4

Max. W. *of saucer:* 15.3 cm
H. *of cup:* 7.9 cm
Marks: interlaced LL enclosing *A* above *H* (attributed to the painter Pierre Houry 1725–55, see below), painted overglaze in blue, incised *L* and *JI*, trace of suspension hole (saucer), similar marks on cup without second set of incised marks and suspension hole
Reg. No. Franks 379

Glazed white soft-paste porcelain, which is extremely fine and translucent, of octagonal lobed form moulded in relief with prunus and painted in overglaze cobalt blue (*camaïeu bleu*) with scattered naturalistically painted flower sprays including roses. Partly gilt shaped handle, gilt foot and gilt dentil rims. Three fire-cracks are visible on the underside of the saucer.

Provenance: Bequeathed by Sir A.W. Franks, 1897

Literature: Franks, 1896, no. 379

King, 1930, pp. 280–4, fig. VI

King, 1939, pp. 194–6, fig. 6

Exhibited: 1977, 'Porcelaines de Vincennes, les origines de Sèvres', Paris, Grand Palais, Oct. 1977–Jan. 1978, no. 377

Comparable Examples: Paris, Musée des arts décoratifs, inv. 9305 A & B, see exh. *Vincennes*, 1977–8, no. 376

County Durham, Barnard Castle, Bowes Museum, saucer, reg. no. X 2615, date-letter A, painter's mark *H*, same incised marks as British Museum saucer, W. 15 cm

Cambridge, Lady Cynthia Postan Collection

USA, Washington, D.C., Smithsonian Institution, National Museum of American History, cup with date-letter A, H. 7 cm, inv. 1159a, saucer with date-letter F and painter's mark *H*, incised *d*, max. W. 14 cm, inv. 1159b, on loan from the Estate of Dr. H. Syz, October 1991, illus. Rust, 1973, p. 81.

USA, Baltimore, Walters Art Gallery, illus. C.C. Dauterman, 'Chinoiserie Motifs and Sèvres: Some Fresh Evidence', *Apollo*, Vol. LXXXIV, no. 58, December 1966, fig. 2, date-letter E for 1757 on cup and F on saucer, which bears painter's marks *H* and *Y* for Fauré, W. of saucer 13.7 cm, inv. 48.669A,B

A drawing for the shape, called *gobelet lizonné à relief*, is preserved at the factory.[1] It was made in two sizes, this example probably being the smaller or second size. The prunus decoration is based on Chinese eighteenth-century porcelain from Fukien province and was a popular motif at almost all mid-eighteenth century porcelain factories. It was particularly popular in France. The fineness and whiteness of this cup and saucer distinguish them from the products of the Saint-Cloud factory.

The blue used here was developed by Jean Hellot (1685–1766), President of the Académie des Sciences, before July 1751. It was based on cobalt from the Giston valley, St Jean Mountain in the Pyrenees.[2]

This cup and saucer was almost certainly fired in the fourth kiln of the second kiln series, i.e. sometime in July or August 1753,[3] and was in the *magasin de vente* in September that year. It matches a *théière lizonnée à relief*, dated 1753 and similarly decorated, now in a private collection in the United States.[4] No example of a *sucrier lizonné à relief* with this decor has been traced, but an unpainted example has been recorded.[5] A tea caddy and cover (*boîte à thé des Indes*) with matching decoration and similar marks in a private collection in the United States may have belonged with the Museum cup and saucer.[6]

The painter's mark *H* has traditionally been thought to stand for Pierre Houry, who was born in 1725 and was buried on 30 June 1755.[7] He is first recorded at the factory in December 1746, as a *mouleur* receiving 48 *livres* a month. In 1751 he is listed in the *Etat des frais* as a *répareur* earning 60 *livres*, increased to 66 *livres* in January 1754. By July of that year he had become a flower painter, at the same salary. The

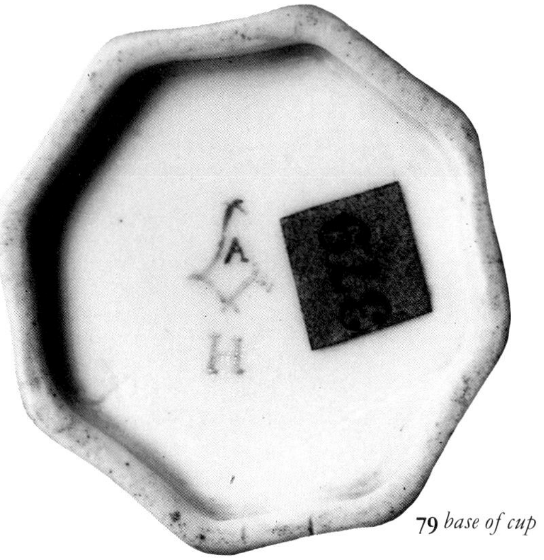

79 *base of cup*

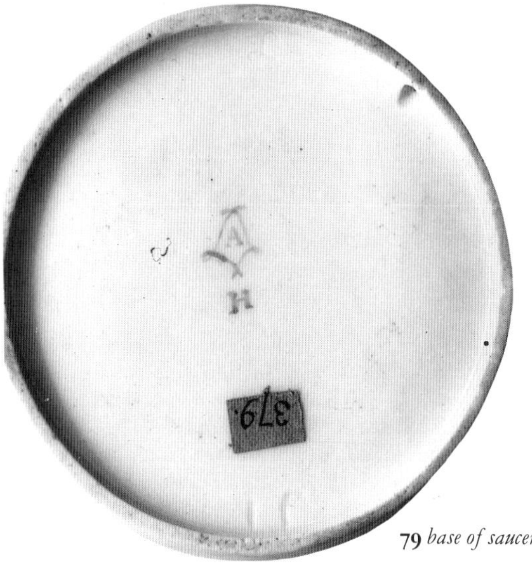

79 *base of saucer*

discrepancy between the date of the cup and saucer and what we know of Houry's career at Vincennes casts doubt on the identification of the mark on these pieces with this painter. A pair of *caisses à fleurs* decorated with flowers on a green ground and dated 1756, in the Wrightsman Collection in the Metropolitan Museum, New York, bear the same painter's mark,[8] as does a tea caddy and stopper of the first size with decoration of prunus in relief and scattered flower sprays painted in blue, seen in the trade in Paris in 1989.

1. MNS, Archives de Sèvres, R.I, *dossier* 2, *liasse* 1, f. 8.
2. D'Albis and Préaud, 1986, p. 7.
3. Institut de France 5626, f. 6.
4. Photograph on file in the Photo Archives of the Getty Center, Santa Monica, California, no. 201933, formerly in the Plumb Collection, Cambridge. An undecorated example is in the Musée des arts décoratifs, Paris, inv. 24190, exh. *Vincennes*, 1977–8, p. 134, no. 397.
5. Paris, Musée des arts décoratifs, inv. 18688, see exh. *Vincennes*, 1977–8, p. 85, no. 200; there is a similar example in the Bowes Museum, Barnard Castle, County Durham.
6. Painter's marks *H* and *Y*, incised *M*, H. 10.7 cm. For the shape, see exh. *Vincennes*, 1977–8, p. 35, no. 44. The name 'des Indes' dates only from the 1780s and may not have been in use in the 1750s.
7. Information in Vincennes Parish Records, Notre Dame, Vol. XVIII, kindly communicated by Tamara Préaud, February 1988, together with details of Houry's career.
8. Dauterman, 1970, no. 79A, B, p. 196.

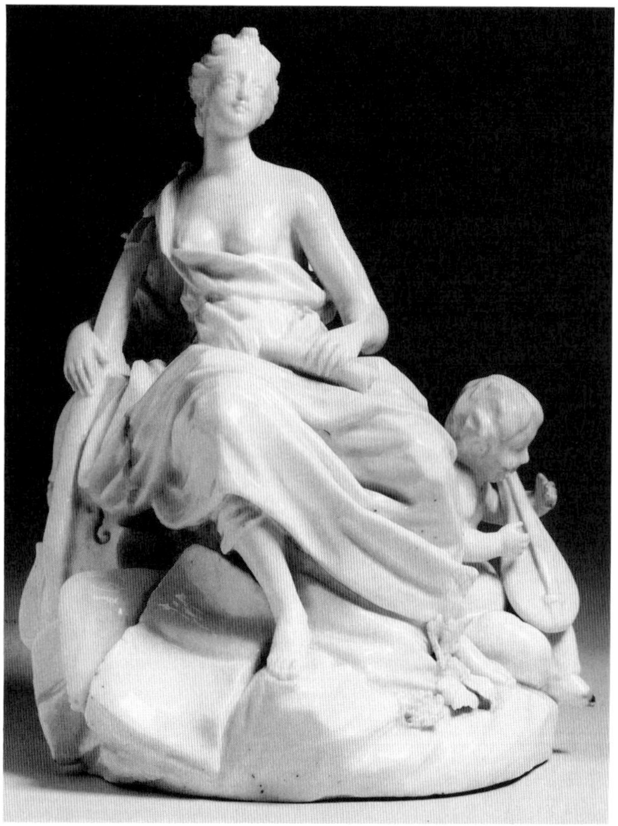
80

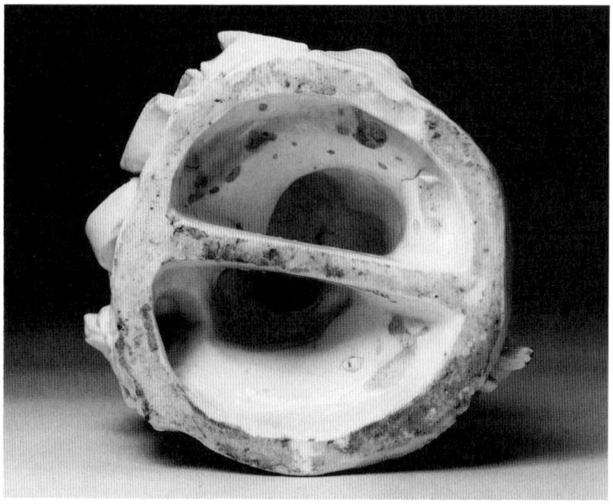
80 *base*

80 **Music**, *c.* 1748

H. 19.8 cm
Marks: none; *No 45* in ink inside base [? collection number]
Reg. No. 1937,11–17,1

Thickly potted white glazed soft-paste porcelain formed by press-moulding.[1] The glaze is faintly blue where it has pooled. A partly draped female figure is seated on a rock. At her right is a musical instrument and by her right foot sheets of music. She holds a scroll in her left hand. To her left is seated putto with another stringed instrument (partly restored). Putto's neck and left hand repaired.

Provenance: Presented by William King (former Deputy Keeper in the Department of Ceramics and Ethnography, British Museum), 1937

Literature: King, 1939, p. 196

Savage, 1960, pl. 69a

Eriksen and Bellaigue, 1987, pl. 3, p. 192

Comparable Examples: A similar group can be seen on the left of the *Bouquet de la Dauphine* presented by Marie-Josephe of Saxony, the Dauphine of France, to her father Augustus III, Elector of Saxony and King of Poland, in January 1749.[2] A comparable group from the Lair Collection is in the Musée des arts décoratifs, Château de Saumur.[3] It is incised *B* on the base at the right.[4] An example was sold on the London market in 1974, and another more recently in 1980.[5] In November 1991 an example incised *B* underneath in a French private collection was exhibited by Dragesco-Cramoisan, Paris.

The base of the piece has the same central partition of clay as Astrology (see cat. 81), although deeper in this case, presumably to strengthen the oval foot. In view of the crudity of the base, the figure was probably intended to be mounted. The modelling of the two allegorical figure groups is closely related.

The group is listed in the factory inventory of 1752 when fifteen examples at 30 *livres* each were on the premises. Only two sales have been noted in the surviving documents, both in 1756, the first on 4 April 1756 '1 figure en Blanc la musique', at 12 *livres*, the other '1 Groupe de la Musique' at 18 *livres*. The latter was sold for cash, the former to M. de Parseval.[6] Only four examples are known to exist; the fate of the other twelve in the *magasin de vente* is still unknown.

It is just possible that the Vincennes group was inspired by Kändler's figure of *Poesie* modelled in June/July 1742[7] but it seems more likely that, like contemporary Bow porcelain figures of the Muses, this group is based on an as yet unidentified French engraving.

1. It has been suggested by Tamara Préaud and Antoine d'Albis in correspondence with the author, Spring 1991, that this group may have been modelled by hand, but the hollow centre suggests otherwise, at least for the body of the female figure.
2. Now in the Zwinger, Dresden, illus. Brunet and Préaud, 1978, pl. 1, p. 28.
3. Inv. 908. An incised *B* was noted in a white glazed figure of *La Dormeuse* sold at the Hôtel des Ventes, Saint-Germain-en-Laye, 21 February 1988, Lot 98, illus. Henry Bulidon (born in 1720 at Chantilly where he worked at the porcelain factory) is listed in the Sèvres factory records as a sculptor who was paid for plaster and terracotta models in 1749, see MNS, Archives de Sèvres, D1, *liasse* 1. A man called Bernard was also listed, but was qualified as an 'apprenti'.
4. Sotheby's, 10 December 1974, Lot 34.
5. Christie's, 1 December 1980, Lot 21.
6. See MNS, Archives de Sèvres, Vy 1, f. 123 and 124 v.
7. L. Schnorr von Carolsfeld, *Porzellansammlung Gustav von Klemperer*, Dresden, 1928, no. 686, Tafel 72.

81 **Astronomy or Astrology**, *c.* 1748

H. 21.7 cm
Marks: none
Reg. No. 1938,2–17,1

Thickly potted white glazed soft-paste porcelain, the main elements formed by press moulding. The glaze has a slightly yellowish-green tone where it has pooled. The seated female, her left breast exposed, holds a sun in her right hand. Behind her is a tree in blossom. At her right knee is a reclining putto drawing on sheets of paper or a book with a pair of dividers. At her left is a globe.

Provenance: Presented by William King (former Deputy Keeper in the Department of Ceramics and Ethnography, British Museum), 1938

Literature: King, 1939, p. 196

Savage, 1960, plate 69b

Eriksen and Bellaigue, 1987, pl. 4, p. 193

Préaud and d'Albis, 1991, p. 143, no. 93

Comparable Examples: Sèvres, Musée national de Céramique, inv. MNC 11095, acquired 1902, illus. exh. *Vincennes*, 1977–8, no. 452

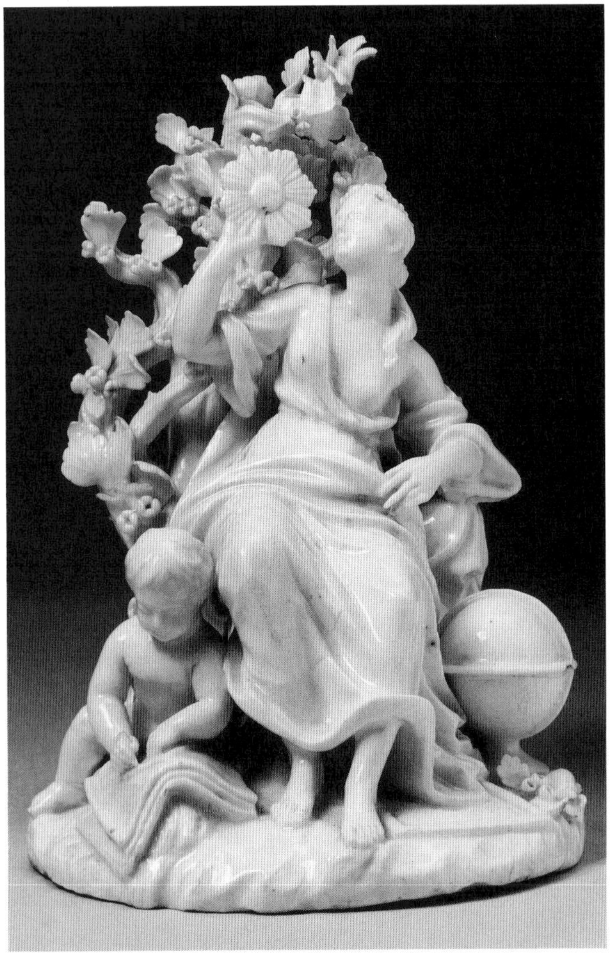

81

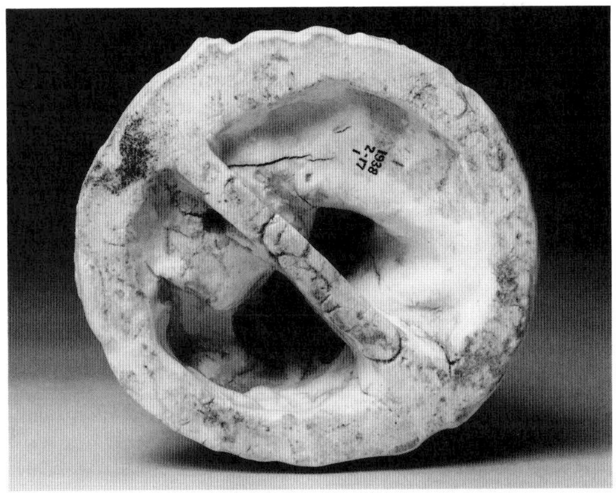

81 *base*

Chaffers, 1872, Vol. II, pl. CXXXVII, no. 273

Chaffers, 1926, Vol. II, p. 330, fig. 282 (formerly in Lady Charlotte Schreiber's collection)

Sotheby's, Simon Goldblatt Sale, 1–2 May, 1956, Lot 129, sold to Acosta for £95; now in a private collection, London

Switzerland, Berne, Schloss Jegenstorf, 1951 exhibition, information kindly communicated by T.H. Clarke, Esq.; this one was probably from the H. Martinet Collection (whereabouts unknown)

USA, New York, Sotheby's, 5 December 1978, Lot 4

Denmark, Copenhagen, David Collection, inv. 2/1977, illus. Eriksen, 1980, pl. 18a, without tree at back, her head differently positioned

The version at the Musée national de Céramique, Sèvres, differs from this one principally in the position of the figure's right hand which is empty. Comparison with the group in a private collection revealed the following significant differences:

a) the child looks ahead, rather than downwards;
b) the book at the front has more pages;
c) the globe is positioned differently;
d) there is a telescope on the map [?] at the front;
e) there are fewer leaves on the tree, which is bent backwards as if it collapsed in the firing.

The source of this figure group remains a matter of conjecture. It has been suggested[1] that it derives from a Meissen model of Thalia by Kändler[2] said to be based on a painting of Uranie by E. Le Sueur made for the Hôtel Lambert and now in the Louvre, Paris.[3] However, the emblem of the sun is generally associated with Truth who is often shown with her foot on a globe as in the statue by Bernini in the Borghese Gallery.[4]

An engraving by François Boucher called *L'Astronomie*[5] includes the attributes of a globe, a book and a telescope and is a possible source of inspiration.

Two titles may have been used for this group. Nineteen examples of *Astrologie* valued at 30 *livres* each were recorded in the *magasin de vente* in the inventory of October 1752.[6] On 20 April 1754 '1 *Astrologie* en blanc' was purchased by M. Bailly for no less than 54 *livres*. It was fired before October 1752.[7] On 30 May he bought '1 *Astrologie*' for the same price from the same kiln.[8] A figure of *Astronomie* valued at 15 *livres* appears in the inventory of 1757 amongst the defective pieces,[9] and two were sold at 24 *livres* in May and November 1761 respectively.[10]

1. Sotheby's, Goldblatt sale, 1–2 May 1956, Lot 129.
2. Thalia, modelled in December 1744, see L. Schnorr von Carolsfeld, *Porzellansammlung Gustav von Klemperer*, Dresden, 1928, no. 687, Tafel 72.
3. E. Mâle, *L'Art Religieux de la fin du XVIe siècle, du XVIIe siècle et du XVIIIe siècle, étude sur l'iconographie après le Concile de Trente*, Paris, 1951, (2nd ed.).
4. *Ibid.*, p. 384, fig. 223.
5. Jean-Richard, 1978, no. 1310.
6. MNS, Archives de Sèvres, I 7.
7. *Ibid.*, Vy 1, f. 38.
8. *Ibid.*, Vy 1, f. 41v.
9. *Ibid.*, I 7
10. *Ibid.*, Vy 3, f. 56 and 62.

82 **Watch Stand**, perhaps Vincennes, possibly *c.* 1750

H. 26.6 cm
Marks: none
Reg. No. 1939,5–4,1

Glazed white soft-paste porcelain, the lower part consisting of asymmetrical scrolls and rockwork formed by press-moulding, with applied flowers and figures. Above the circular opening is perched Cupid holding a flower garland in his left hand and an arrow in his right. The recumbent female figure, her head turned to the right, is partly draped; a basket of flowers rests at her side. The partly-draped male figure, his left foot resting on the rockwork base and his body half turned to the right, holds out his hands stiffly in front of him. The interior is partly glazed. The glaze is greenish where it has pooled. The man's lower right leg is missing.

Provenance: Purchased, 1939

Literature: King, 1939, p. 222

W. King, 'A Vincennes Porcelain Clock-Case', *British Museum Quarterly*, Vol. XIV, no. 3 (1940), pp. 54–6; pl. XXII

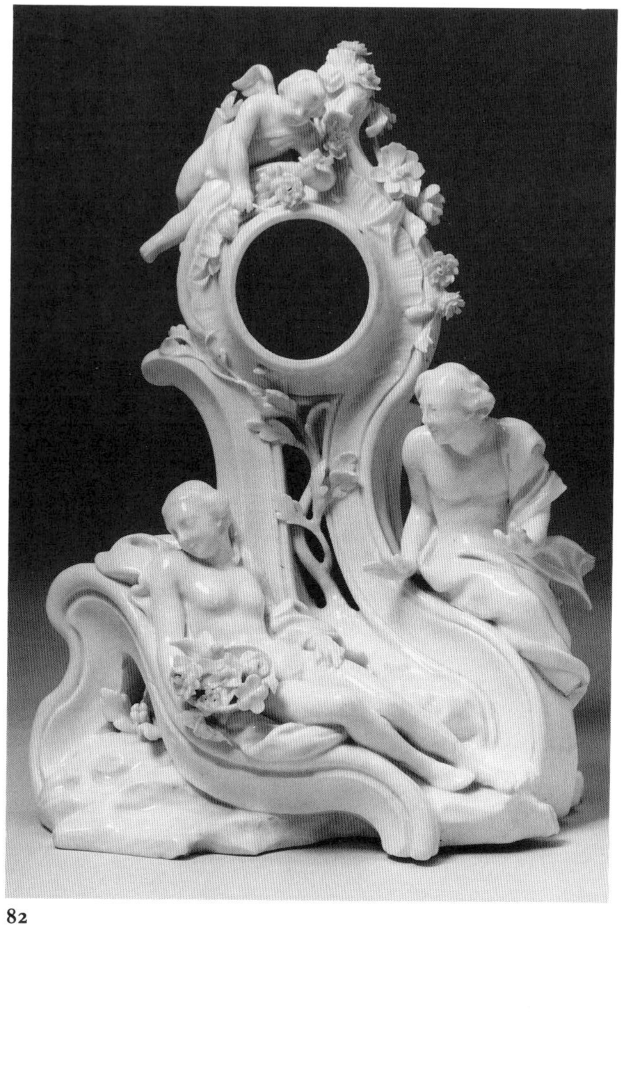

82

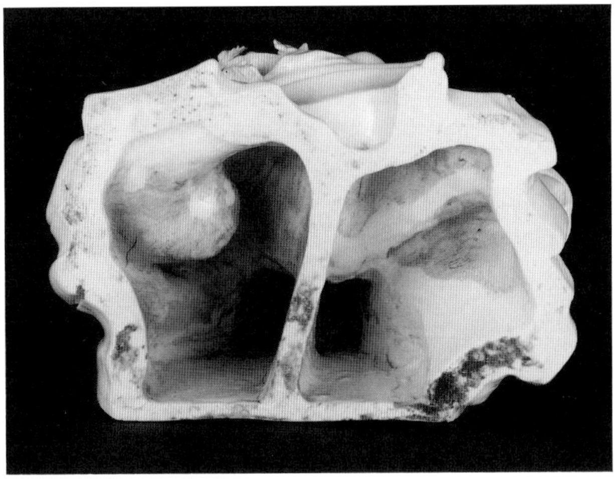

82 *base*

Savage, 1960, pl. 67b

Eriksen and Bellaigue, 1987, pl. 20

Exhibited: 1977, 'Porcelaines de Vincennes, les origines de Sèvres', Paris, Grand Palais, Oct. 1977–Feb. 1978, no. 488

Comparable Examples: A somewhat similar figure group on a rocky base mounted in ormolu is in the Victoria and Albert Museum, London.[1] A coloured clock-case is in the Metropolitan Museum, New York[2] and a more elaborate coloured example was sold on the London market in 1975.[3] This was sold again in New York from the Christner Collection in 1979.[4] A coloured example from the Lair Collection is in the Musée des arts décoratifs, Château de Saumur,[5] one bearing the Chelsea gold anchor mark and probably decorated in the nineteenth century was sold in Rouen in 1986.[6] A version in which the male figure wears a ruff was sold in London in 1971.[7] A coloured example measuring 25 cm was on the London market in September 1991.[8]

This piece is the subject of considerable discussion. The colour of the paste is noticeably creamier than that of the groups symbolising Music and Astronomy, and the style of the group, in particular its scrolled base, has been characterised as English or Germanic,[9] although no suggestion has emerged as to which factory in those countries might have produced it.

It has been analysed by X-ray diffraction and found to be a soft-paste porcelain containing wollastonite and tridymite. No tin has been identified in the glaze.[10]

It is significant that the earliest Vincennes stock list of 1752 contains no reference to clock-cases or watch stands. The white glazed group often known as *L'Heure du Berger*, undoubtedly of Vincennes origin, of which there is an example at the Victoria and Albert Museum, London[11] is composed of a recumbent female figure holding flowers and a seated male figure gesturing towards her. The modelling is more technically accomplished, and the paste whiter.

The rather fussy detail of the watch stand, the appearance of the faces and the profusion of flowers and leaves perhaps suggest a Tournai origin. However, the scrolls are reminiscent of the groups presently attributed to Orléans (see cat. 200).

Watch stands were made at other porcelain factories, including Chelsea,[12] Bow[13] and Derby,[14] as well as in other materials such as gilt-bronze and wood. They apparently made their first appearance in France in the seventeenth century, were highly popular in the eighteenth century, and were still in use in the later part of the nineteenth century.[15]

1. Inv. C.356–1909.
2. Inv. 158 254.
3. Christie's, 30 June 1975, Lot 70.
4. Christie's, New York, 8 June 1979, Christner Collection, Vol. II, Lot 47.
5. Inv. 1152.
6. Rouen, Palais des Congrès, 9 March 1986, Lot 150.
7. Christie's, 4 October 1971, Lot 9. Another with ruff sold at Sotheby's, 19 November 1996, Lot 60.
8. Christie's, 30 September 1991, Lot 103.
9. Exh. *Vincennes*, 1977–8, p. 169.
10. BM Research Laboratory 24351R.
11. See note 1.
12. British Museum, inv. Porc. Cat. II. 32, illus. E. Adams, *Chelsea Porcelain*, London, 1987, pl. XIII.
13. See H. Tait, 'Handel and Bow', *Apollo*, Vol. LXXVI, no. 5, July 1962, pp. 384–90 and A. Gabszewicz, *Bow Porcelain, the collection formed by Geoffrey Freeman*, London, 1982, no. 139.
14. Seattle Art Museum, Seattle, USA, inv. 76.257.
15. See F. Laure, 'Les porte-montre des 18e et 19e siècles', *L'Estampille*, no. 119, March 1980, pp. 28–36, with bibliography.

Sèvres

As there is extensive literature on this factory, only a brief outline of its history will be given.[1] It was the continuation of the factory at Vincennes, which came into the hands of a new shareholding company registered in the name of Eloi Brichard in 1753. This was made up of sixteen eminent financiers,[2] who put up a total of 6,000,000 *livres* to keep the factory afloat. New buildings at Sèvres – close to Bellevue, a property belonging to Louis xv's mistress, Madame de Pompadour – were begun immediately, and in the summer of 1756 the factory moved to its new site. In 1753 a system of date-letters inscribed within the royal monogram of interlaced LL (perhaps used alone from the late 1740s) was instituted to indicate the year of decoration of each piece. The King held a quarter of the factory's stock from 1752, and purchased the entire concern in October 1759. It has remained the property of the French Crown and subsequently of the French Government.

The organisation and staffing of the factory became ever more complex as it grew in size. Detailed written instructions concerning the administration of the various workshops and the daily working hours (from 5 am–9 am, 10 am–2 pm and 3 pm–7 pm in summer, and starting at 6 am to finish at 8 pm in winter) had been drawn up in 1747. These continued in force. Because of the involvement from an early stage of members of the King's staff (the financiers worked in a highly bureaucratic manner), the factory was tightly run along the lines devised for the management of government affairs. Staff numbers increased rapidly: in 1750 there were 100 workers; by 1759 this had risen to 250; in 1772 there were 300 staff, and in its heyday around 1775 the factory had nearly 400 people on the payroll. Ministerial control was assumed by Henry Bertin in 1759 and held by him until 1780, when he was replaced by the comte d'Angiviller. Jean-Jacques Bachelier, a painter, was the artistic director for everything except sculpture from 1751; he was assisted from 1785 by Jean-Jacques Lagrenée *le jeune* who left in 1800, whilst C. van Spaendonck was taken on between 1795 and 1800.

Jean-Claude Duplessis *père* was director of sculpture between 1745 and 1774, assisted by Etienne-Maurice Falconet between 1757 and 1766, when he was replaced by Bachelier who remained until 1773. Louis-Simon Boizot took charge of sculpture between 1773 and 1800. Each of the six workshops (*ateliers*) had its own chief. The work of the painters has been studied in some detail – even their appearance and character is known in many instances[3] – but much remains to be discovered about gilding and sculpture.

The introduction of hard-paste kaolinitic porcelain in the early 1770s brought about the greatest change in the factory's organisation since its establishment. A whole series of new workshops were set up, not only the preparation of the body, but also for colours, since a completely new range of high-temperature colours had to be developed.[4] The impact of this important moment in the factory's history has been little analysed because of collectors' prevailing taste for the early soft-paste productions. However, it had the effect of revitalising the factory, perhaps at too great a financial cost. Most workers began to specialise in either hard- or soft-paste, and the necessary expansion was not covered by receipts. In fact it was at this time that Sèvres experienced its most serious competition from the numerous hard-paste factories springing up in Paris, which the authorities were powerless to control. Because of their relatively small size they had fewer overheads, and could – and did – react quickly to changes in taste. Despite falling revenues, Sèvres made some of its most spectacular services, vases and biscuit sculptures during the late 1770s and 1780s. The sales records show that many foreigners, including kings, princes, dukes and cardinals, were among the factory's customers.[5] The Revolutionary period brought a disastrous drop in sales, but the factory managed against considerable odds to stay in existence. It even produced some quite remarkable pieces, such as the sundial made in 1794, now in the Museum of Fine Arts, Boston, USA.[6]

1. See, for example, Brunet and Préaud, 1978, pp. 27–48 (this book has an extensive bibliography); Eriksen and Bellaigue, 1987, *passim.*; Eriksen, 1968, pp. 13–31. For biographies of the factory shareholders and of sculptors employed by the factory, see Savill, 1988, III, pp. 961–89; this work also contains an extensive bibliography, pp. 936–60.
2. The best study of the establishment of the factory and its administration can be found in A. Sergène, *La Manufacture de Sèvres sous l'Ancien Régime*, 3 vols, Nancy, 1972–4, unpublished thesis.
3. Frégnac (ed.), 1964, p. 21 and Savill, 1988, III, pp. 995–1078.
4. For some new designs and colours for hard-paste, see R. Savill, 'A neglected Sèvres porcelain vase in the Wallace Collection', *Antologia di Belle Arti*, no. 27–8, 1985, pp. 69–72, col. ill. on cover; A. Dawson, 'Sèvres porcelain in the V & A, New light on some eighteenth century hard-paste rarities', *V & A Album 5*, London, 1986, pp. 343–52.
5. For table-services purchased by or presented to emperors and empresses, kings, a duchess and a cardinal, see 'Les Grands Services de Sèvres', exh. Musée national de Céramique, Sèvres, May–July 1951; D.Guillemé-Brulon, 'Le service des Asturies', *L'Estampille*, no. 152, December 1982, pp. 22–33; 'Les grands services de Sèvres: le service de Catherine II', *ibid.*, no. 167, March 1984, pp. 45–56 and 'Le service à rubans verts pour l'impératrice d'Autriche', *ibid.*, no. 179, March, 1985, pp. 22–33.
6. Exh. La Révolution Française, 1989, no. 1037, p. 792.

83 Orange Tub (*caisse carrée*), 1756

H. *to top of finial:*	17.5 cm
Marks:	interlaced LL enclosing date-letter d for 1756 above *B* for an unidentified painter in blue enamel, incised *f*, five circular holes on base
Reg. No.	1948,12–3,9

Soft-paste porcelain, square container on four square feet, each upper corner surmounted by a pine-cone finial. Each side is painted in enamel colours with panels of flowers and fruit, including tulips, roses, gooseberries and blackcurrants, on a white ground within a rococo gilt cartouche of flowers, scrolls and trellis ornament carefully tooled, all against a green ground. The sides, rims, base and top of each finial and outer edges of each foot are gilt. The interior surface has several firecracks, the sides are slightly warped, there are pin-holes on the painted areas and several blisters, one on the base measuring about 8–10 mm across. The underside of each foot has a brownish circular padmark, and there are numerous tiny firecracks at the point of attachment to the base, which is unevenly glazed. Knops to finials restored, chip to rim and side.

Provenance: Bequeathed by Sir B. Eckstein, Bt., 1948

Literature: Unpublished

Comparable Examples: See cat. 84

Although Svend Eriksen noted a drawing for *caisses carrées* in the factory stock lists of 1752,[1] moulds for the form only appear in the factory records in January 1754, so that it must have been devised in 1753. However, moulds for the first and third sizes are not recorded until 1755.[2] This example is of the first size. It is known that trays were made to go underneath the tubs, which were intended for living plants, in 1756[3] but no examples have yet been discovered.[4] *Caisses* were probably originally intended as table decoration,[5] rather than for use on furniture or mantelpieces.

The form was reproduced at the Minton factory, Staffordshire, and was apparently in production as late as the 1920s.[6]

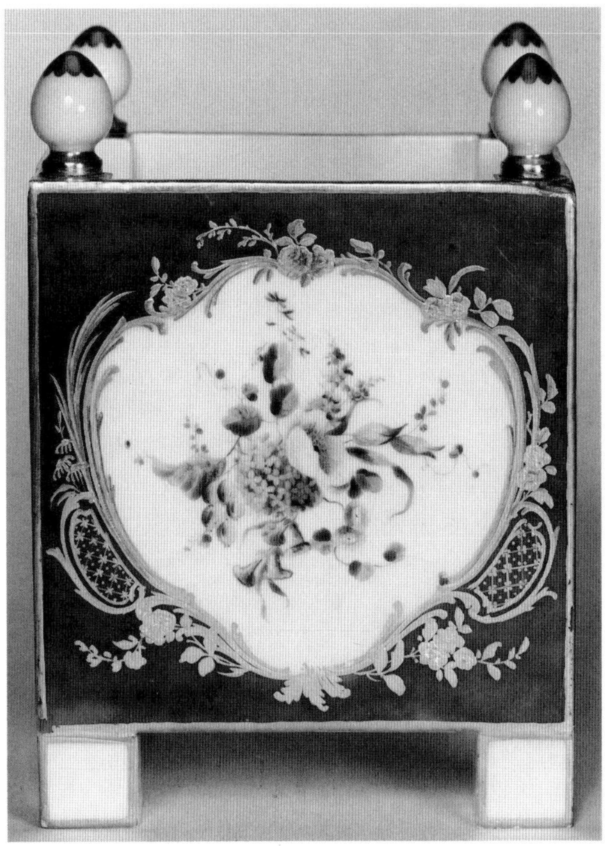

83

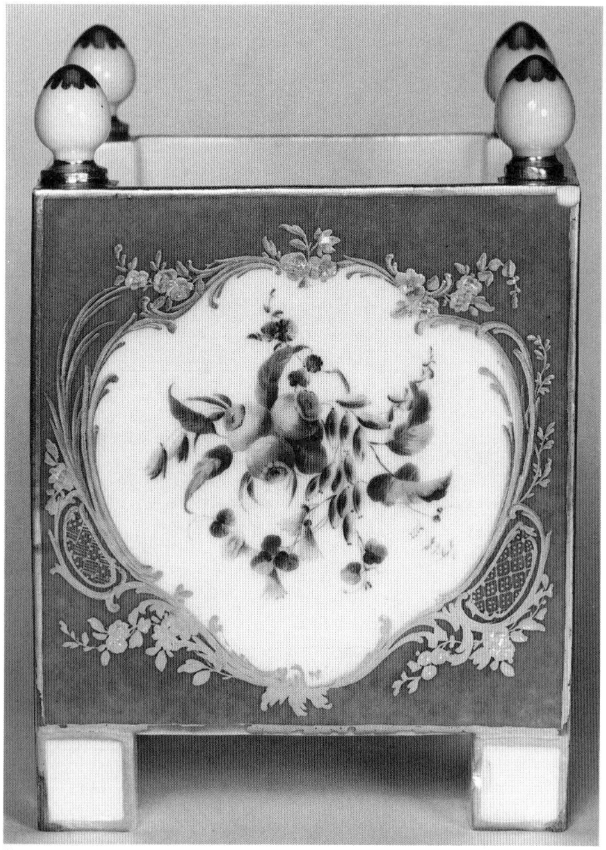

83

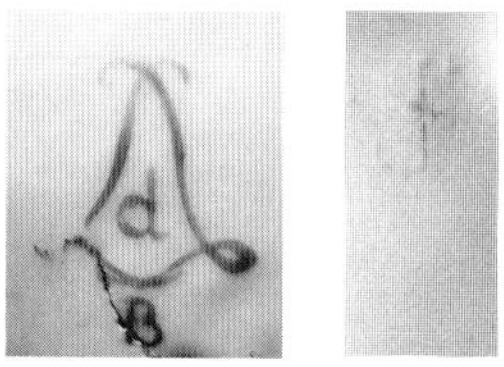

83 *marks*

For the introduction of green as a ground-colour see cat. 85. On this example the colour is noticeably uneven in tone. It is likely that only one layer of colour was applied.

The mark *B* appears in blue enamel on the base of two green-ground glass-coolers dated 1757 painted with flowers at Waddesdon Manor, Buckinghamshire.[7] A pair of undated *bleu céleste caisses carrées* in the Victoria and Albert Museum painted with trophies also bear this mark,[8] as does a jug of 1754 in the Ashmolean Museum, Oxford.[9] It may have been used by Jean-Pierre Boulanger *père* (1722–85) who went to Vincennes as a gilder from Saint-Cloud in 1754, although some pieces dating from 1753 have been recorded with this mark.[10] In view of the elaborate gilding on this orange tub, it is not inconceivable that it bears the mark of a gilder.

The incised mark has not been identified. An undated saucer in the Wallace Collection, probably made around 1753 to judge by its blue and gold decoration, bears the same mark, and Rosalind Savill has given in her catalogue of the collection the range of pieces found with this mark.[11]

1. Eriksen and Bellaigue, 1987, p. 288.
2. Exh. *Vincennes*, 1977–8, p. 37.
3. Eriksen, 1968, no. 4, p. 42.
4. Rosalind Savill has suggested to the author in private correspondence of December 1990 that the *plateau carré* may have been used.
5. Eriksen and Bellaigue, *op. cit.*, p. 288.
6. A pair decorated with birds on a green ground measuring 11.4 cm were sold at Sotheby's Belgravia, London, 18 December 1975, Lot 77.
7. Eriksen, 1968, p. 76, no. 23.
8. Inv. C. 424 and 425–1921.
9. Inv. E 123, *bleu céleste* ground painted with flowers; two further pieces have a *B* below the interlaced LL, and may possibly be by the same painter: a) E 117 1 & 2, a *tasse litron couvert* with *bleu lapis* ground, date-letter A, painted with flying birds; b) 1979.95, a green-ground wine-cooler, date-letter E, painted with flowers.
10. Boulanger's career, and other examples bearing this mark, are discussed in Savill, 1988, III, p. 1005. It should be noted that the date-letter A may have been used in the early part of 1754.
11. Savill, 1988, III, p. 1100.

84 **Orange Tub (*caisse à fleurs carrée*),** *c.* 1756

H. *to top of finial:*	17.5 cm
Marks:	interlaced LL above *G* for an unidentified painter; incised *8*
Reg. No.	1948, 12–3, 10

Soft-paste porcelain, square container on four square feet, each corner surmounted by a pine-cone finial. Each side is painted in enamel colours with panels of flowers and fruit, including roses, a poppy, plums and cherries on a white ground within a rococo gilt cartouche of flowers, scrolls, trellis and *oeil-de-perdrix* ornament. The last two elements have been omitted on one side which is richly gilt with flower sprays. Each cartouche is carefully tooled and the above decoration is all on a green ground. The sides, rims, base and top of each finial and outer edges of each foot are all gilt. In addition there is a gilt star in the centre of each outer edge of the feet. The discoloured interior surface has several firecracks and the sides are slightly warped. The glaze has been wiped away around each of the five holes on the base, and there are firecracks where the feet are attached to the base. Finials restored.

Provenance: Bequeathed by Sir B. Eckstein, Bt., 1948

Literature: Unpublished

Comparable Examples: Christie's, 21 June 1976, Lot 169, pair, first size, dated 1755, *bleu lapis caillouté* and flowers, painter's mark *G*

Sotheby's, Monaco, 26 May 1980, Lot 349, pair, second size, dated 1756, green ground, painted with flowers, painter's mark *H*, one incised *M*, the other *8*

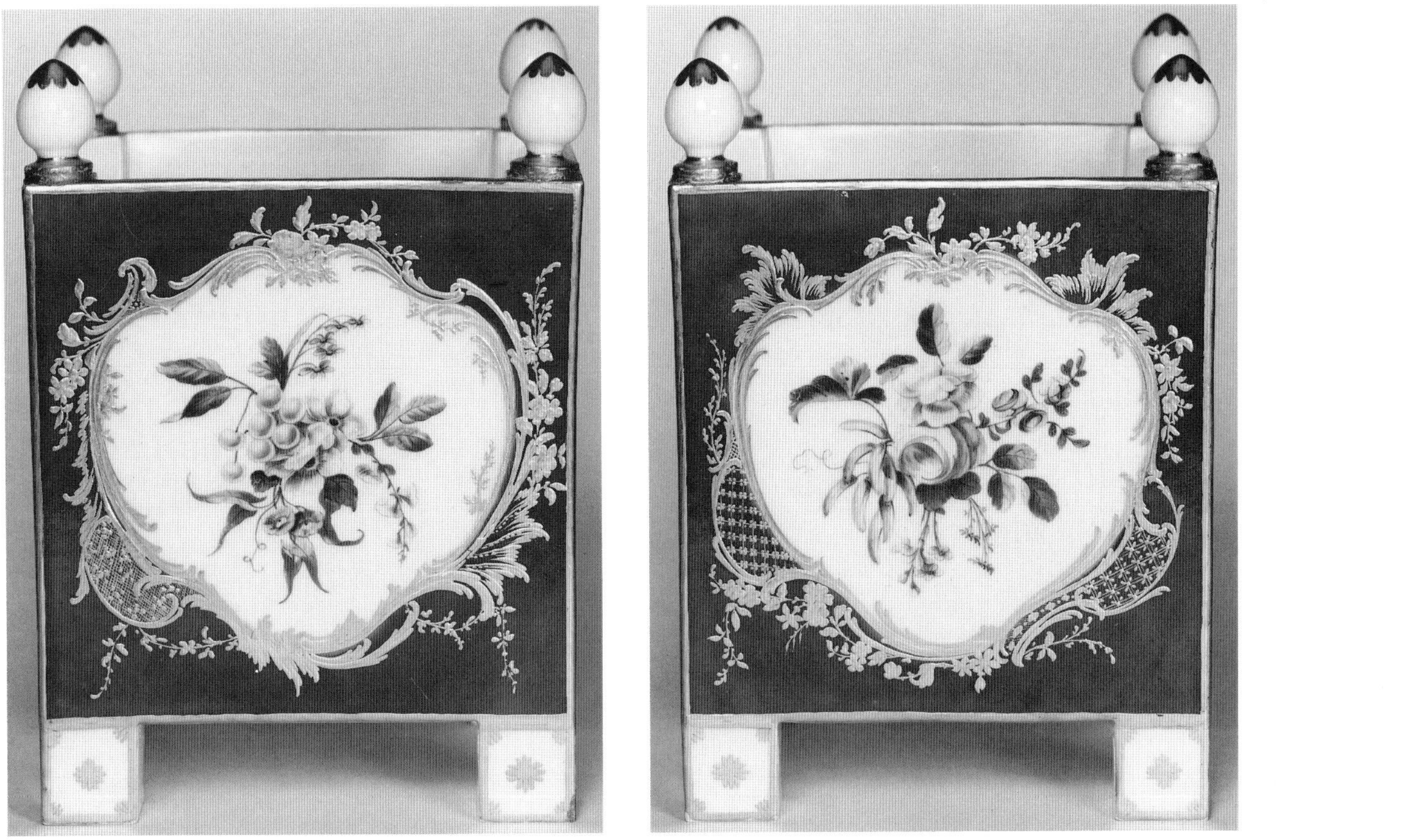

84

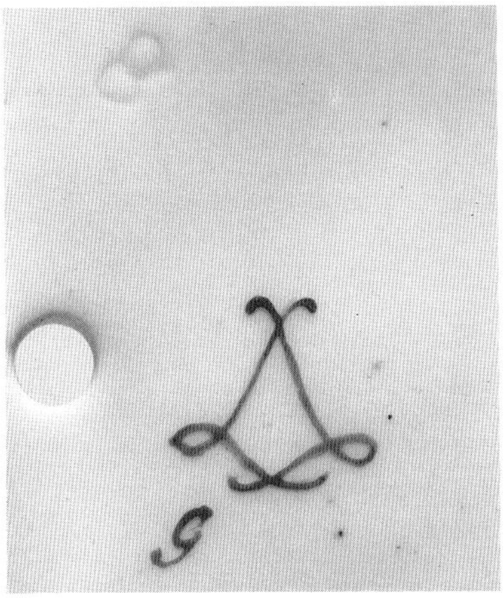

84 *marks*

USA, Seattle, Seattle Art Museum, one of a pair, undated, third size, incised *8*[1]

USA, Boston, Museum of Fine Arts, one of a pair, green ground, painter's mark *G*, inv. 65.1789.90[2]

This example is of higher quality than cat. 83. The ground colour is noticeably more even and may have been applied in two layers, and the gilding is thicker. The painter's mark has not yet been positively identified, but has been traced by Rosalind Savill on a number of pieces painted with flowers between about 1753 and 1770.[3]

The incised mark *8* (or perhaps *B*) appears on four *caisses*, two green and two *bleu céleste*, in the second and third size from the Wrightsman Collection at the Metropolitan Museum, New York, made in 1755 and 1756 and painted with fruit and flowers.[4] It appears again on a *seau crénelé* in the same collection dated 1788. As Rosalind Savill has noted it is frequently found on *caisses à fleurs* of the 1750s.[5]

1. Emerson, 1990, pp. 11–12.
2. Chavagnac, 1910, no. 64, pl. xv and Munger *et al.*, 1992, no. 155.
3. Savill, 1988, iii, p. 1079.
4. Dauterman, 1970, nos 77A, B, 78A, B, 79A, B.
5. Savill, 1988, iii, p. 1128.

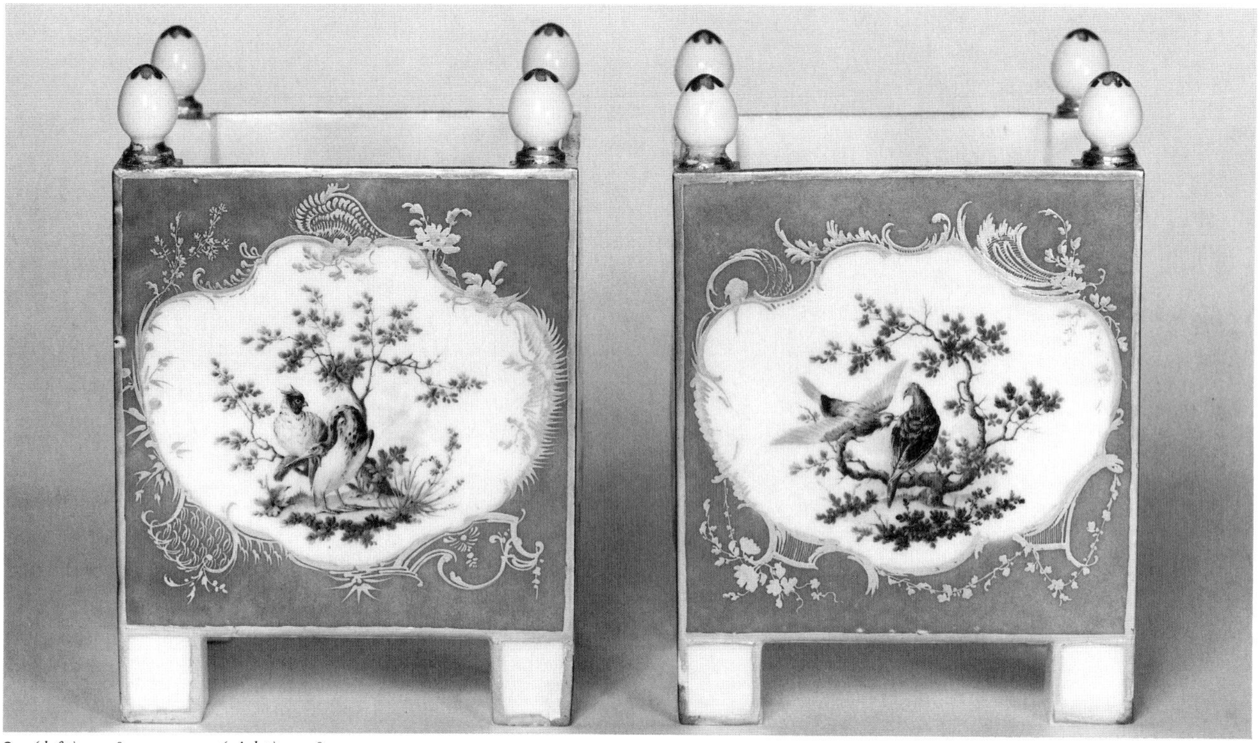

85 *(left) 1948, 12–3, 19; (right) 1948, 12–3, 20*

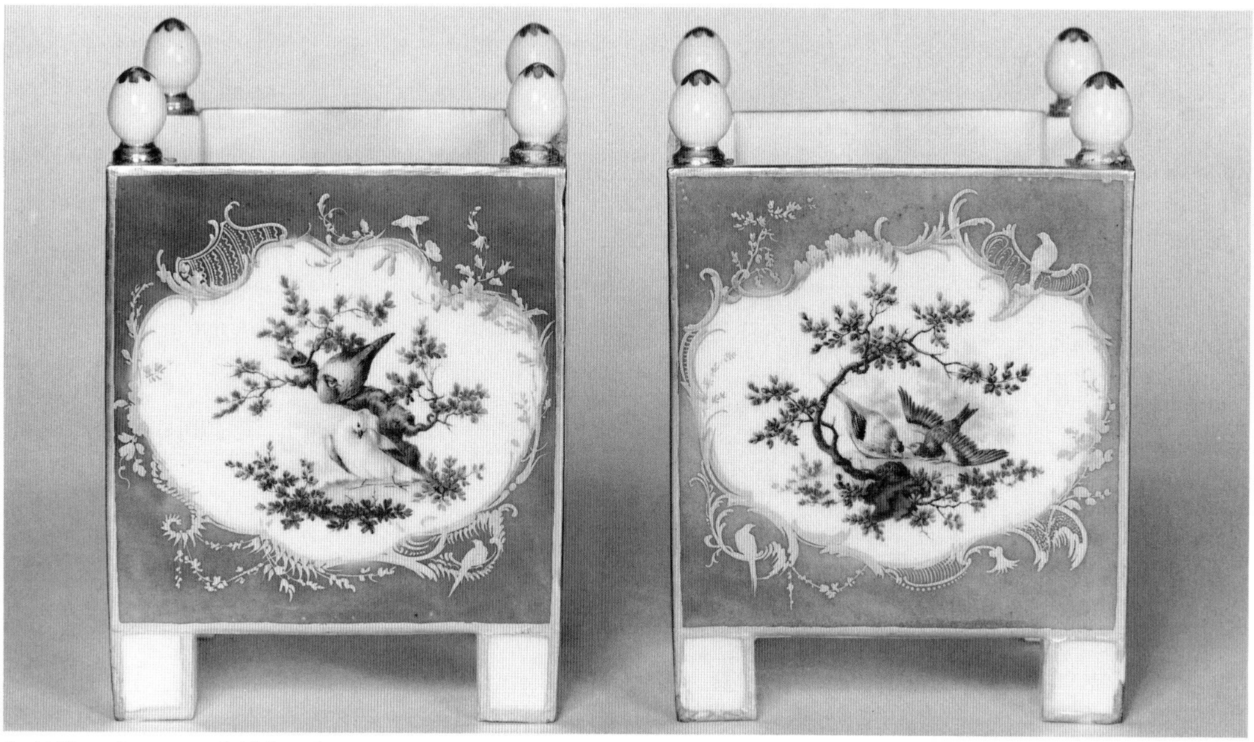

85 *(left) 1948, 12–3, 19; (right) 1948, 12–3, 20*

85 Two Orange Tubs (*caisses à fleurs carrées*), 1756

H. *to top of finial:* 14.3 cm and 14.5 cm
Marks: LL enclosing date-letter D for 1756 below crescent mark attributed to the painter Jean-Pierre Ledoux in blue enamel on both; 1948,12–3,19 incised *M*
Reg. No. 1948,12–3,19 and 20

Soft-paste porcelain, of square form on four square feet, each corner surmounted by a pointed knop, partly gilt. Five circular holes pierced in a cross pattern on each base, now filled with cork. Each is painted in enamel colours with birds on branches in reserve, surrounded by a rococo gilt cartouche with tooled motifs which include birds, flowers and scrolls all on an uneven green ground. The rim, base of each knop, sides, lower edge of the container and the outer edges of each foot are gilt. One knop on each restored. Damage to feet on both.

Provenance: Bequeathed by Sir B. Eckstein, Bt., 1948

Literature: Eriksen, 1968, p. 56, no. 12

Comparable Examples: Christie's, 15 October 1990, Lot 24, second size, 1756, green ground painted with birds, painter's mark of a crescent, incised *8*, now in the Wadsworth Atheneum; the author is grateful to Rosalind Savill for this information

USA, Hartford, Conn., Wadsworth Atheneum, inv. 1917.997, third size, 1756, green ground, painter's mark of a crescent[1]

The form, of which these examples represent the second size, was probably devised in 1753 because four *caisses* are listed in the January 1754 inventory, although moulds for the largest and smallest sizes were not listed until 1755.[2] In the inventory dated 1 January 1755, one *caisse quarrée* of unspecified size valued at 10 *livres* was in the undecorated state in the *dépot de blanc* or in the painters' or gilders' workshop, and must therefore have been produced in 1754.[3] As Eriksen has pointed out, the holes were presumably intended for drainage for living plants, although trays are only listed in the 1756 factory inventory.[4]

Until recently no pieces with a green ground were known with a date-letter earlier than D. The notebooks of Jean Hellot (1685–1766), chemist at the Vincennes factory, show that the formula for green was known from 1747 but, since a mordant to prepare the surface of the once-fired porcelain for colour was not known until 1751, green grounds were not actually put into production until 1753 when green pieces first appear in the sales records.[5] A green-ground bowl (*jatte à lait*) painted with putti, bearing the date-letter A and documented as having been decorated in July/August 1754 has recently come to light.[6]

Eriksen has drawn attention to the other pieces incised with the letter *M* and suggested that it may be the initial of the soft-paste *mouleur* and *tourneur* Pierre Moyé[7] who worked at the factory from 1752–4

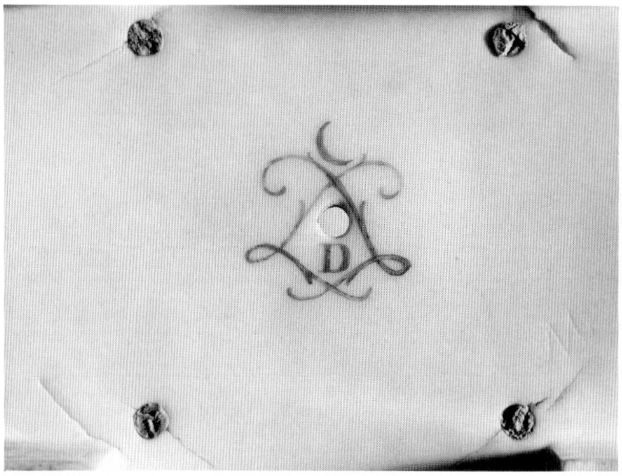

85 *detail of base (1948, 12–3, 19)*

until 1765. For other pieces bearing this mark, see Savill.[8]

Eriksen has also called into question the attribution of the crescent mark to Jean-Pierre Ledoux (1734–5 until probably after 1786), first put forward by Riocreux, as it has not been possible to confirm that he was employed at the factory before 1758.[9] For further pieces decorated by the crescent painter, see Savill.[10]

1. Chavagnac, 1910, no. 85.
2. Exh. *Vincennes*, 1977–8, p. 37.
3. Eriksen, 1968, p. 42.
4. MNS, Archives de Sèvres, I 7
5. D'Albis and Préaud, 1991, p. 233.
6. (Unsigned) '1753: Le premier fond vert', *Connaissance des Arts*, no. 437/438, juillet-août 1988, pp. 82–8.
7. Eriksen, 1968, p. 56.
8. Savill, 1988, III, p. 1114.
9. Eriksen, 1968, p. 329.
10. Savill, 1988, III, pp. 1044–5; additional pieces are a pair of *caisses carrées* in the Victoria and Albert Museum, inv. C. 428 and 429–1921. Several authorities now attribute the crescent mark to the painter Armand *l'aîné*, recorded at the factory between 1745–79. Pieces attributed to him are discussed by Ghenete Zelleke in *From Chantilly to Sèvres: French Porcelain and the Dukes of Richmond*, French Porcelain Society, London, VII, 1991.

86 **Sugar Bowl (*pot à sucre Bouret*)**, *c.* 1756

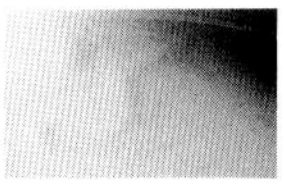

86 *mark*

H. incl. cover: 7.4 cm
Marks: *3* incised
Reg. No. 1923,3–14,168

Soft-paste porcelain with straight sides and domed cover surmounted by a flower knop. The decoration consists of an indifferently painted flower spray on each side on a white ground within a gilt rococo cartouche from which springs a gilt flower spray on the left and a trellis pattern on the right, all against a green ground. The cover, which also has a green ground, is painted with three flower sprays on a white ground in asymmetrical reserves enclosed by a gilt pattern, with further gilt scroll ornament between the panels. Gilt dentil rims, foot gilt, knop partly gilt.

Provenance: Presented by the Rt. Hon. Viscount Dillon, FSA, 1923, in memory of his son

Literature: Unpublished

Comparable Examples: None noted

The form probably takes its name from the *fermier-général* Etienne-Michel Bouret (1710–77), known as Bouret *l'ainé* or *le grand Bouret*, both to distinguish him from his four brothers and on account of his immense wealth.[1] He was indirectly linked by marriage to the marquise de Pompadour, and owed his enormous influence, particularly during the period 1752–5, to her and to Machault d'Arnouville (1701–94), Contrôleur Général des Finances. Bouret was a shareholder in the Eloi Brichard company, as was his less influential brother Bouret d'Erigny.

The sugar bowl is the smallest of three or perhaps four sizes.[2] The first and second sizes, which measure 10.8 to 12.2 cm and 9 to 10 cm respectively, were modelled in early 1753 and Svend Eriksen signalled the existence at the factory of a drawing inscribed *boete a Sucre Bouret no 1 fait Suivan L'ordre de la Comande du 19 fevrÿe 1753*.[3] A turquoise blue example of the second size (9.3 cm) dated 1755 is in the James A. de Rothschild Collection at Waddesdon Manor.[4] The designer of the shape is unknown.

Although this undated sugar bowl bears no factory mark, it is incised with a mark similar to one found on pieces made around 1755.[5] An undated *bleu lapis* example in the Wallace Collection has the same incised mark.[6] The porcelain body, uneven ground colour and decoration of the bowl can be compared with the Museum orange tub (cat. 83). Although the flower painting is not as skilled, it is likely that the bowl dates from the mid-1750s. The cover does not belong, and probably dates from the 1770s. The pattern may be compared with that painted on a pair of mounted

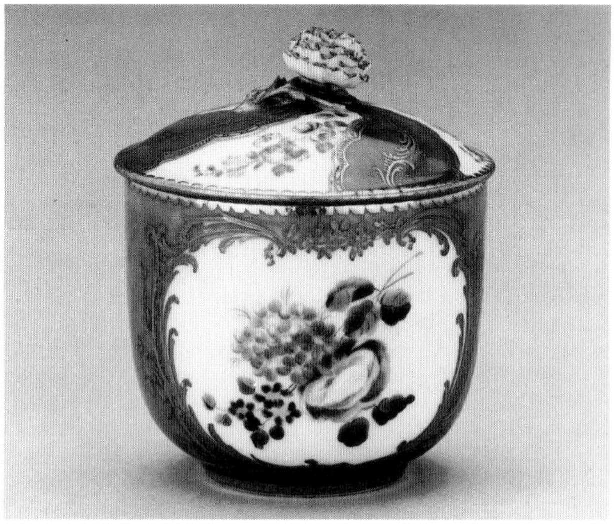

86

candlesticks at Waddesdon Manor[7] decorated with flowers and turquoise (*bleu céleste*) 'ribbons' embellished with gilding.

1. For some fascinating details of Bouret's extravagant way of life – he gave one of his many mistresses a goldfish made of solid gold, as he was unable to get live fish – see Y. Durand, *Les Fermiers Généraux au XVIIIe Siècle*, Paris, 1971, *passim.* Bouret's meteoric career is mentioned and his devotion to Machault is satirised in Diderot's *Neveu de Rameau*, probably written in 1761.
2. Savill, 1988, II, p. 573, lists two examples from the René Fribourg sale, Part II, Sotheby's, 15 October 1963, Lots 414, 416, measuring 7.5 cm and 7.3 cm respectively. These are slightly different in shape from the true third-size examples measuring 8 cm to 8.8 cm in height.
3. Eriksen, 1968, no. 14, p. 62.
4. *Ibid.*
5. On a cup (*gobelet Hébert*) dated 1755 at Waddesdon Manor, *op. cit.*, no. 2, p. 38.
6. Savill, 1988, Vol. II, p. 572.
7. Eriksen, *op. cit.*, no. 102, p. 282.

87 **Bowl (*jatte [de pot] à lait Hébert*)**, 1757

D. 15.3 cm
Marks: interlaced LL enclosing date-letter E for 1757 above a dot; painter's mark for André-Vincent Vielliard (1752–90), cursive *L* incised; suspension hole
Reg. No. 1948,12–3,22

Soft-paste porcelain, thrown, of undulating form. The exterior is painted with an uneven *bleu lapis* ground and with three scenes in enamel colours as follows: a boy seated in a landscape holding a crook tied with a pink ribbon bow; a boy facing right kneeling by a basket of grapes in a landscape; a girl in a landscape seated to left holding a rose in her left hand and a knife in her right. Each scene is enclosed by a richly gilt tooled cartouche from which spring gilt flower garlands. The foot is gilt and there is a gilt dentil

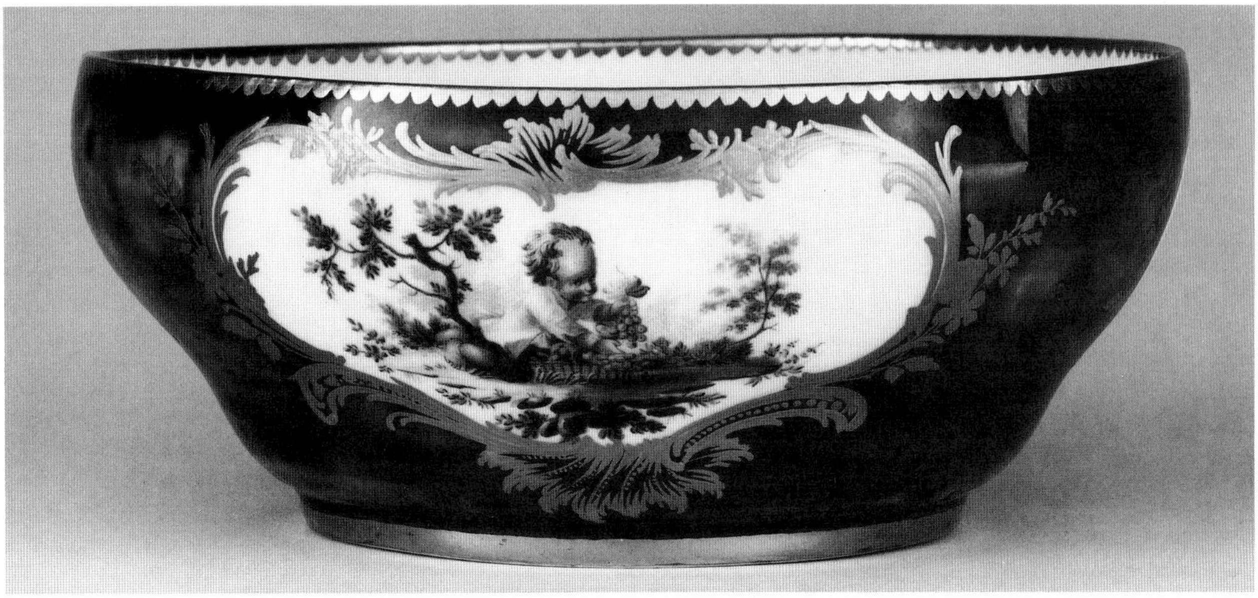

87

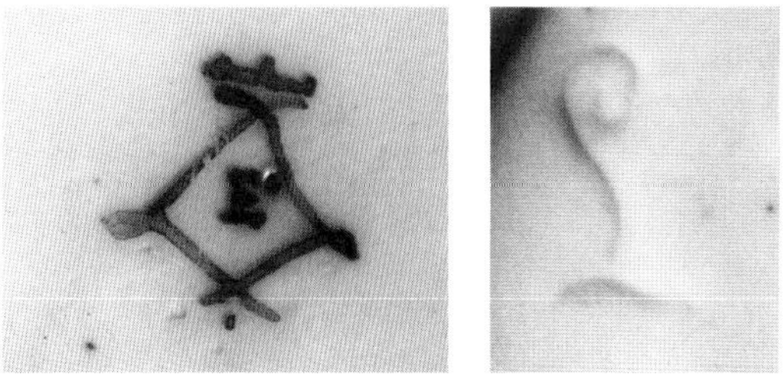

87 *marks*

design on both the interior and exterior of the rim. The bowl is slightly warped and there are some imperfections in the paste, including pin-holes on the base. Inside the foot rim is a blue dot.

Provenance: Bequeathed by Sir B. Eckstein, Bt., 1948

Literature: Unpublished

Comparable Examples: France, Boulogne, Musée des Beaux-Arts et d'Archéologie, 1753, *bleu lapis* ground, panels of birds painted by [?]Evans, D. 16.5 cm, inv. L.424, illus. Brunet and Préaud, 1978, no. 45; exh. *Vincennes*, 1977–8, no. 100

Sotheby's, 8 November 1966, Lot 1, Hon. Jack Mitchelham Collection, dated 1768, pink ground, panels of birds painted by Chappuis *aîné*, D. 16.5 cm

Sotheby's, 1 July 1980, Lot 40, Sir Henry and Lady Tate Collection, dated 1768, blue ground, flower decoration

Italy, Naples, Museo Duca di Martina, inv. 2133, D. 16 cm, decorated with gilt birds, date-letter A, illus. M.L. Casanova, *Le porcellane francesi nei Musei di Napoli*, Naples, 1974, no. 81

USA, Baltimore, Walters Art Gallery, painted with birds and putti by Vielliard, 1754, with matching jug, inv. 48.535, 48.723, D. 16.1 cm[1]

A crayon and ink drawing dated February 1756 (see fig. 87a) is preserved in the factory archive, inscribed *jatte a pot au laict ehiber demande par M. Duveaux en fevrÿe 1756*.[2] It is for a small bowl, whereas this example is almost certainly of the first, or largest, size. It would have had a matching covered *pot à lait Hébert* measuring 13 cm in height. Four moulds for a *jatte* of the first size valued at 1 *livre* each are listed in the inventory of January 1757 under the *travaux*, or new work, carried out during 1756.[3] However the form is known in 1753.[4]

Bowls such as these were used for milk in conjunction with their matching jug. Milk was poured from the jug into the bowl and drunk from it. The form is named either after François Hébert, a *fayancier* and possibly the *marchand* who supplied the factory in 1744[5] or after Thomas-Joachim Hébert, a *marchand-mercier* until 1750 who became *secrétaire du roy*. Sieur Hébert assisted in the preparation of the factory's stock-list of 1 October 1752.[6] Several forms bear this name: the *plateau Hébert*[7] and the *sucrier Hébert* date from 1752,[8] the *pot à lait Hébert* was in production from 1753,[9] and the *pot-pourri Hébert* was probably devised in 1756.[10]

The painted scenes are typical of the work of André-Vincent Vielliard (1717–90) in the style of François Boucher.[11]

For a note on the incised mark *L*, possibly used by the repairers Lauvergnat *aîné* and *jeune*, see Savill.[12]

1. P. Verdier, 'The useful wares of Vincennes and Sèvres', *Antiques*, Vol. LXXV, no. 1, Jan. 1959, p. 101.
2. MNS, Archives de Sèvres, R 1, dossier 2, liasse 6.
3. MNS, Archives de Sèvres, I 7.

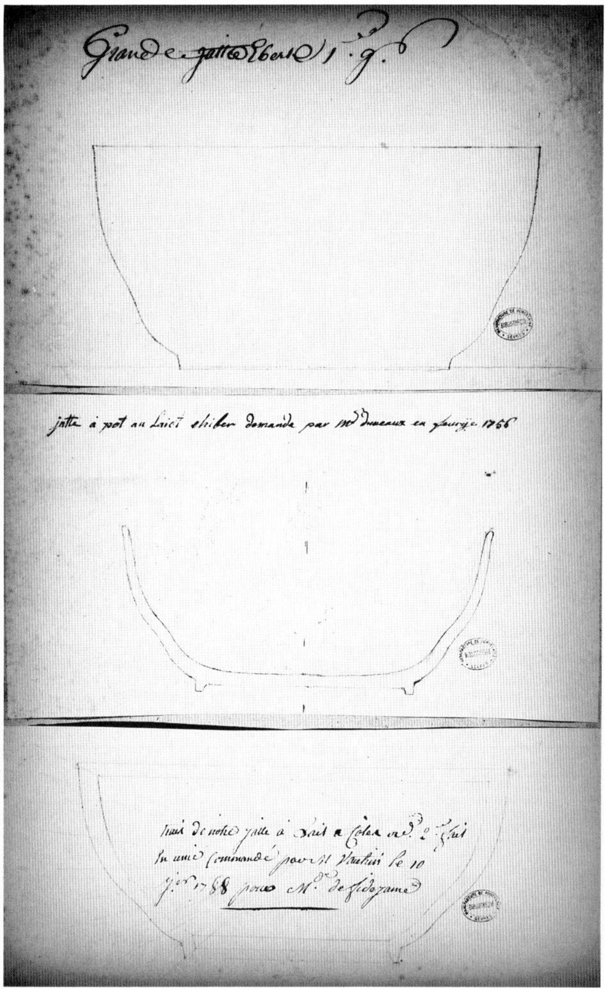

Fig. 87a

4. See n. 9. Préaud and d'Albis, 1991, p. 92, n. 24, list it as in existence even before the inventory of October 1752.
5. MNS, Archives de Sèvres, FI., *Fournitures*, '*9 gros d'or en chaux, des émaux et une molette de verre*' sold by Hébert and paid for on 6 May 1744. Préaud and d'Albis, 1991, p. 236 and p. 81, believe this Hébert was a '*marchand d'émaux*', i.e. a third man with the same surname.
6. Préaud and d'Albis, 1991, p. 44. Thomas-Joachim Hébert was declared bankrupt in 1754.
7. For a *plateau* of 1753 see Eriksen and Bellaigue, 1987, no. 86, pp. 270–1.
8. Brunet and Préaud, 1978, pl. III, yellow-ground *déjeuner Hébert*, including the tray and the sugar bowl, undated, painted by Vielliard, at Wadsworth Atheneum, Hartford, Conn., USA.
9. Brunet and Préaud, *op. cit.*, fig. 50, turquoise ground, 1753, The National Trust, Waddesdon Manor, Buckinghamshire, Eriksen, 1968, no. 3.
10. *Ibid.*, pl. XXVIII, pink ground, 1763, painted by Dodin and Méreaud, The National Trust, Waddesdon Manor, Buckinghamshire, Eriksen, 1968, no. 55.
11. A whole series of pieces with scenes closely based on the work of Boucher are illustrated by R. Savill in 'François Boucher and the Porcelains of Vincennes and Sèvres', *Apollo*, Vol. CXV, no. 241, March 1982, pp. 162–9. A biography of Vielliard, a fan painter and half-brother of the bird-painter Evans, who was employed at Vincennes in 1752 to paint children in landscapes, with gardening and other implements and later figures, and died at Sèvres on 8 June 1790, is given in Savill, 1988, III, pp. 1074–5. For illustrations of Sèvres painted by Vielliard see A.-M. Belfort, 'L'oeuvre de Vielliard d'après Boucher', in *Cahiers*, no. 58, 1976, pp. 6–35.
12. Savill, 1988, III, p. 1111.

88 Cup and Saucer (*soucoupe litron,* possibly *gobelet 'couvert'*), 1757

D. *of saucer:*	12.4 cm
H. *of cup:*	6 cm
Marks:	interlaced LL enclosing date-letter E for 1757 above painter's mark *E* for an unidentified painter in blue enamel; incised *BR* (cup) and a circle containing a cross (both); suspension hole on saucer; printed collection label *Salisbury & South Wilts Museum Loan Collection 1871* inscribed *Wilkes*; remains of painted Wilkes inventory number *117*
Reg. No.	1931,10–19,15

Soft-paste porcelain, thrown, with moulded leaf on upper part of handle, which terminates at either end in leaves. Painted in *camaïeu bleu* with a garlanded putto on clouds (cup), a putto on clouds playing a horn; gilt dentil rims, handle partly gilt. Imperfection in glaze on underside, chip to underside of rim.

Provenance: Transferred from the Salisbury and South Wiltshire Museum, 1931; W.D. Wilkes (d. 1899) Collection, on loan from 1871, acquired 1917[1]

Literature: Unpublished

Comparable Examples: Exh. Allen, 1989, no. 39, dated 1756 and painted in pink with putti by Yvernel.

For a discussion of the shape of this cup and saucer, which are of the second size, and do not appear to be related in shape yet both have similar painted and incised marks, and the decoration matches, see Savill.[2] The putti are loosely based on Boucher but no direct source has been found.[3]

Two pieces bearing the same painter's mark have been noted by Eriksen and Bellaigue:[4] a *pot à lait Hébert* dated 1756 painted with birds against a *bleu lapis* ground[5] and a cup and saucer in the Victoria and Albert Museum, London.[6]

The incised mark of a cross within a circle has been noted by Savill on soft-paste cups, saucers and a sugar bowl between 1756 and 1758 but remains unidentified.[7] It has also been noted in combination with FR [*sic*] on an (?undated) cup.[8]

1. See Annual *Report* of the Salisbury and South Wiltshire and Blackmore Museums, 1917–18, p. 7: 'The outstanding feature of the year has been the Wilkes Bequest, which has now passed into the possesion of the Museum', through Wilkes's widow. The author is grateful to the Curator of the Salisbury and South

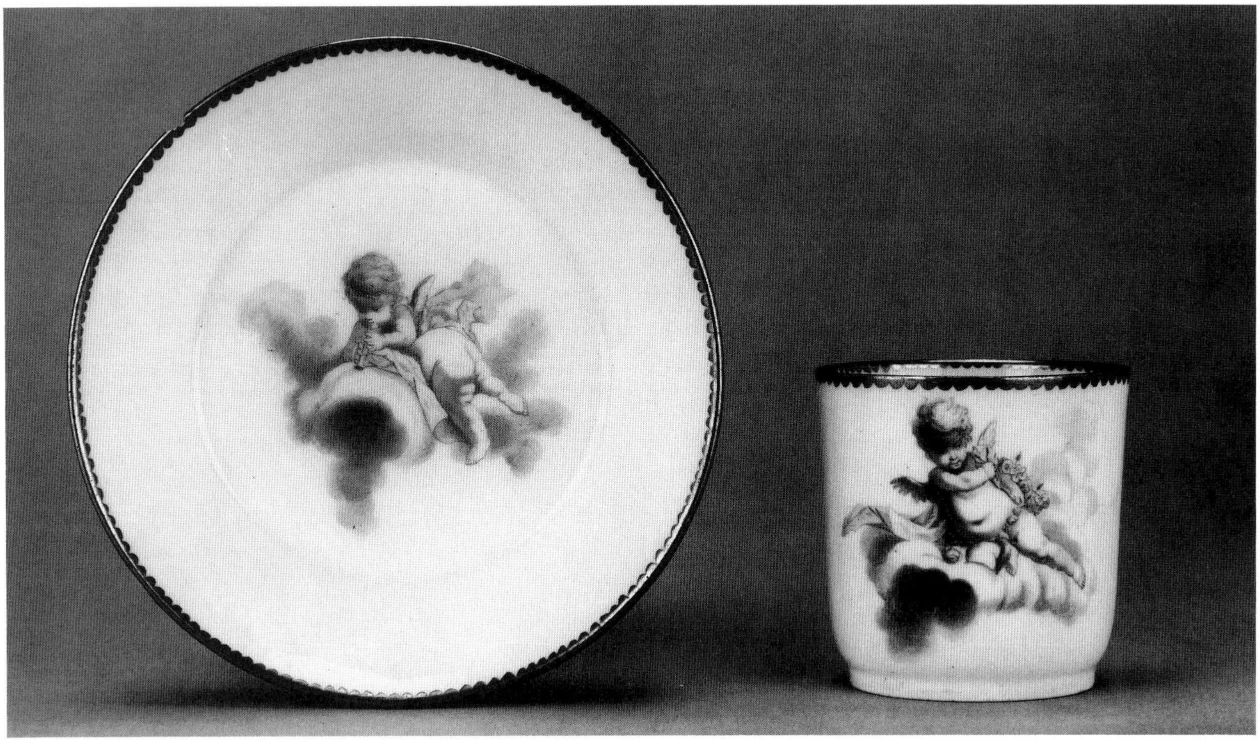

88

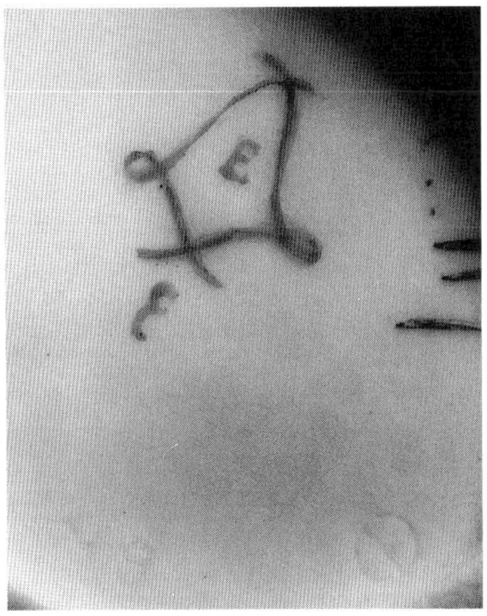

88 *marks*

Wiltshire Museum, Mr. P. Saunders, for kindly allowing her access to the museum papers.

2. Savill, 1988, II, pp. 543–4.
3. But see Ananoff, 1976, p. 1743, no. 244, *La Naissance de Vénus* (cup) and *ibid.*, p. 1733, no. 87, *Vénus Trouvant le Corps d'Adonis* (saucer).
4. Eriksen and Bellaigue, 1987, p. 159, no. 40.
5. Exh. *Vincennes*, 1977–8, no. 165.
6. Inv. C. 1340–1919, a *gobelet Bouillard*, third size, painted with putti in clouds in colours.
7. Savill, 1988, III, p. 1135.
8. *Ibid.*

89 **Cup and Saucer (*gobelet Hébert et soucoupe*)**, 1757

D. *of saucer:*	12.1 cm
H. *of cup:*	6 cm
Marks:	interlaced LL enclosing date-letter E and painter's mark of Charles Buteux (1719–82) almost effaced on cup, painted in blue enamel; saucer incised *3*, suspension hole; cup incised *2*, and *cn*; label printed in blue *Guaranteed Genuine Albert Amor (W. Leslie Perkins)* and collection label of Sir Bernard Eckstein numbered in ink *212* on saucer
Reg. No.	1948,12–3,46

Soft-paste porcelain, thrown. The cup is of undulating outline, its handle of interlaced twig form. Decorated with trophies in blue, grey, pink, orange, green, yellow, mauve and browns within a white reserve outlined by gilt scrolls and flowers against a pink ground. On the saucer the trophies are a lyre, a *musette* or bagpipes, and a crook tied with a ribbon, together with flowers and a spray of laurel; on the cup a bow, a quiver of arrows and a horn. Gilt dentil rims, handle partly gilt, foot on both gilt. Gilding on foot of saucer rubbed.

Provenance: Bequeathed by Sir B. Eckstein, Bt., 1948

Literature: Unpublished

Comparable Examples: None noted

The shape of the cup is known as *gobelet Hébert*, see p. 97. The development of the form, made in three sizes of which this is the third or smallest, is fully discussed by Rosalind Savill.[1]

The introduction of pink as a ground colour is dis-

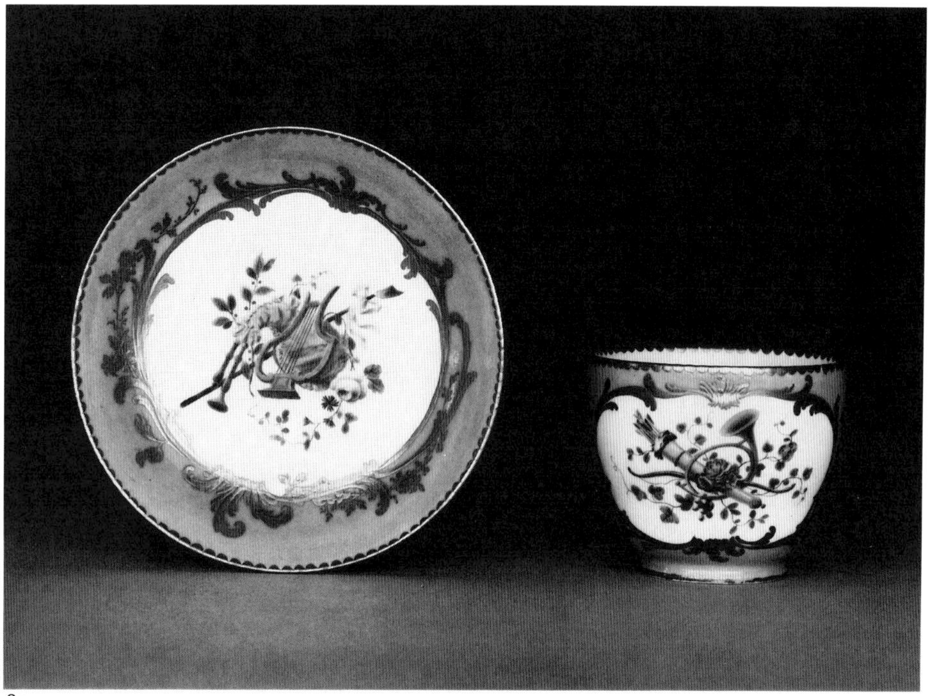

89

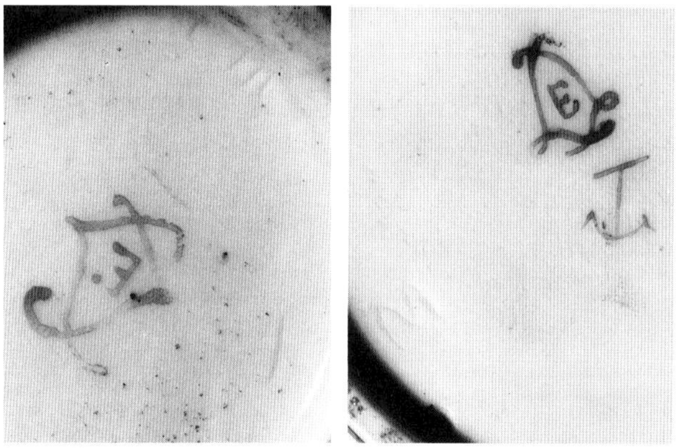

89 *marks*

cussed by Savill.[2] It is first recorded in 1758 but has been found on pieces dated 1756.

As Bellaigue remarked *à propos* two *compotiers ovales* dated 1766 painted with trophies,[3] Buteux specialised in subjects of this kind, probably based on engravings. Buteux worked at the Chantilly factory, joining Sèvres on 4 October 1756 at a monthly wage of 36 *livres*, increasing by 6 *livres* a year.[4] His repertoire included the trophies on this cup and saucer combined in various ways. For instance, the horn and crook are found on a green-ground tray dated 1760.[5]

1. Savill, 1988, II, pp. 496–7.
2. Savill, 1988, III, p. 1175.
3. Exh. Queen's Gallery, 1979–80, no. 51.
4. Savill, 1988, III, pp. 1009–10.
5. IFAR Reports, Vol. 8, no. 2, March/April 1987, tray incised *BLARD 1760*, reported stolen from Leigh-on-Sea, England, 30 January 1987, and H. Bell-Wilson, 'Collecting Sèvres: the fascination of a royal porcelain', *Antique Collector*, December 1973, p. 310, fig. 4.

90 Teapot and Cover (*théière Calabre*), 1757

H. *incl. cover:*	12.3 cm
Marks:	interlaced LL enclosing date-letter E above painter's mark of a quaver for Antoine-Toussaint Cornaille(s) (1755–1800) painted in blue enamel, incised *4* or *h*. Oblong label inscribed in ink *Le Long Collection*; Eckstein Collection label numbered *210*
Reg. No.	1948,12–3,40

Soft-paste porcelain, thrown, ovoid body with ear-shaped handle, interior pierced with five holes leading to spout. The decoration consists of a panel of flowers and fruit on each side on a white ground including a rose, convolvulus, peonies, a tulip, apples and plums, within an asymmetrical gilt cartouche heightened with dark pink all against a pink (*roze*) ground. The spout is painted with a flower trail on white ground. The domed cover has a chrysanthemum knop and is painted with two panels of flowers on a white ground. Gilt dentil rims, and spout, foot gilt, edges of handles and their terminals gilt. Small chip to spout.

Provenance: Madame C. Lelong sale, Paris, Galerie G. Petit, 27 April–1 May 1903, Lots 130–131, also included a sugar bowl and cover, cup and saucer (present whereabouts unknown), 'bt. by Duveen for £300 for W.H. Tuck, subsequently sold by Duveen to Deming James, Christie's, 12 July 1934, Lot 16. Bought by Mallett, sold to Alfred Hill, Sotheby's 15 May 1942, Lot 30, bought by Mallett for £90' (note in BM register)

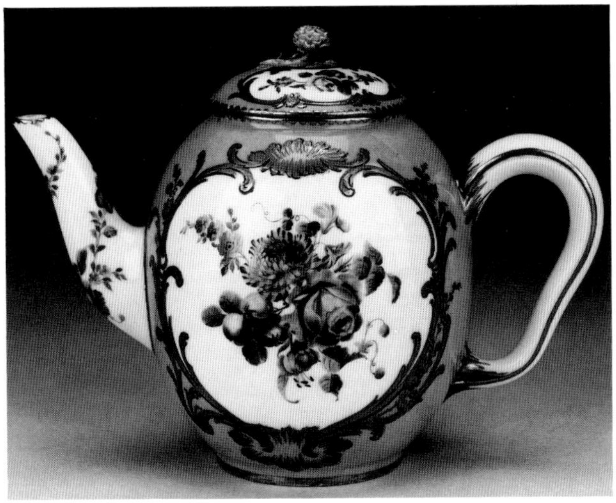

90

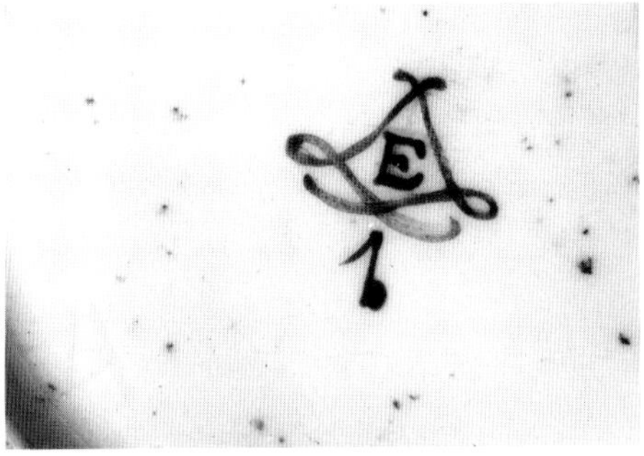

90 *marks*

Bequeathed by Sir B. Eckstein, Bt., 1948

Literature: E. Dacier, 'L'Antiquaire de L'Ile Saint-Louis', *La Revue de l'Art Ancien et Moderne*, Vol. XIII, no. 73, April 1903, pp. 241–54, ill. p. 252

Comparable Examples: Sotheby's, 24 February 1956, Lot 16; 23 May 1967, Lot 90, H. 10.1 cm, date 1757

The *théière Calabre* was in production by December 1752, and existed in two sizes in 1753. It was subsequently manufactured in six or more sizes and was the most commonly made of all Sèvres teapots. Two models and two drawings are preserved at the factory. The form was named for the *conseiller secrétaire du roi, maison couronne de France*, Pierre Calabre, a shareholder in both the Charles Adam and Eloi Brichard Companies. A sugar bowl and *pot à lait* were also named for him, as well as a cup and saucer (see cat. 74).

Rosalind Savill[1] who has reproduced the drawing for this shape, kept at the factory, has divided known examples of the *théière Calabre* into six groups according to size; this piece belongs in group C, the largest group, which probably represents the second size.

The painter Antoine-Toussaint Cornaille[2] is recorded at Chantilly in 1754, moving to Vincennes on 28 April 1755. He specialised in flowers, especially bouquets, garlands and baskets, mainly on tea service and useful wares although in the 1780s he painted monograms, friezes and arabesques.[3] Taken on at a monthly salary of 42 *livres*, he was earning 72 *livres* by 1773. After 45 years' service he was awarded a pension of 300 francs a year in 1800, paid until his death in 1812.

For notes on the incised marks *4* and *h* see Savill.[4]

1. Savill, 1988, II, pp. 577–9. The notes on the development of the shape are based on Savill's work.
2. See Savill, 1988, III, pp. 1026–7.
3. See cat. 111 (green-ground plate, 1765).
4. Savill, 1988, III, pp. 1126–7, 1108.

91 Tray (*plateau 'tiroir' à jours*), 1757

L. 24.2 cm

Marks: LL enclosing date-letter E for 1757 with painter's mark of a caduceus attributed to Edmé Goméry in blue enamel; for incised marks see illus. p. 102, suspension hole

Reg. No. 1948,12–3,39

Soft-paste porcelain, the openwork border of scrolls, tulips and a fleur-de-lys motif decorated in pink and gold. On the exterior surface the scrolls are outlined with gilding but left uncoloured. The ground is decorated with a pink trellis design enclosing a gilt star motif. In the centre, within a shaped cartouche, is a scene painted in blue, brown, green, orange and white of a man with a stick and pack on his back walking through woodland. The foot has a pink ground.

Provenance: Perhaps Lot 52, sale of Madame Dhainaut, Galerie Georges Petit, Paris, 19 May 1924, sold to M. Gradt for 40,000 francs

Bequeathed by Sir B. Eckstein, Bt., 1948

Literature: Eriksen, 1968, p. 102, erroneously referred to as 'square'

Comparable Examples: Cambridge, Fitzwilliam Museum, inv. C. 15–1961, tray dated 1758 with a different pink trellis motif enclosing flowers, and with a bird in a wooded landscape in the central reserve, illus. R. Charles, *Continental Porcelain of the Eighteenth Century*, London, 1964, pl. 53B

This tray, which is the first of four sizes, was made during the first year that 'roze', as it is referred to in the factory's records, was in current production as a ground colour. According to Eriksen,[1] neither square nor oblong openwork trays were made before 1756, although both are known without the piercing from 1754 and 1756 respectively.[2] Savill states that pierced rectangular trays were first made in 1757.[3] They formed part of a *déjeuner* with a cup and saucer and a sugar bowl.

The caduceus painter's mark was discussed by Eriksen[4] in 1968 in connection with dark blue *veilleuse*

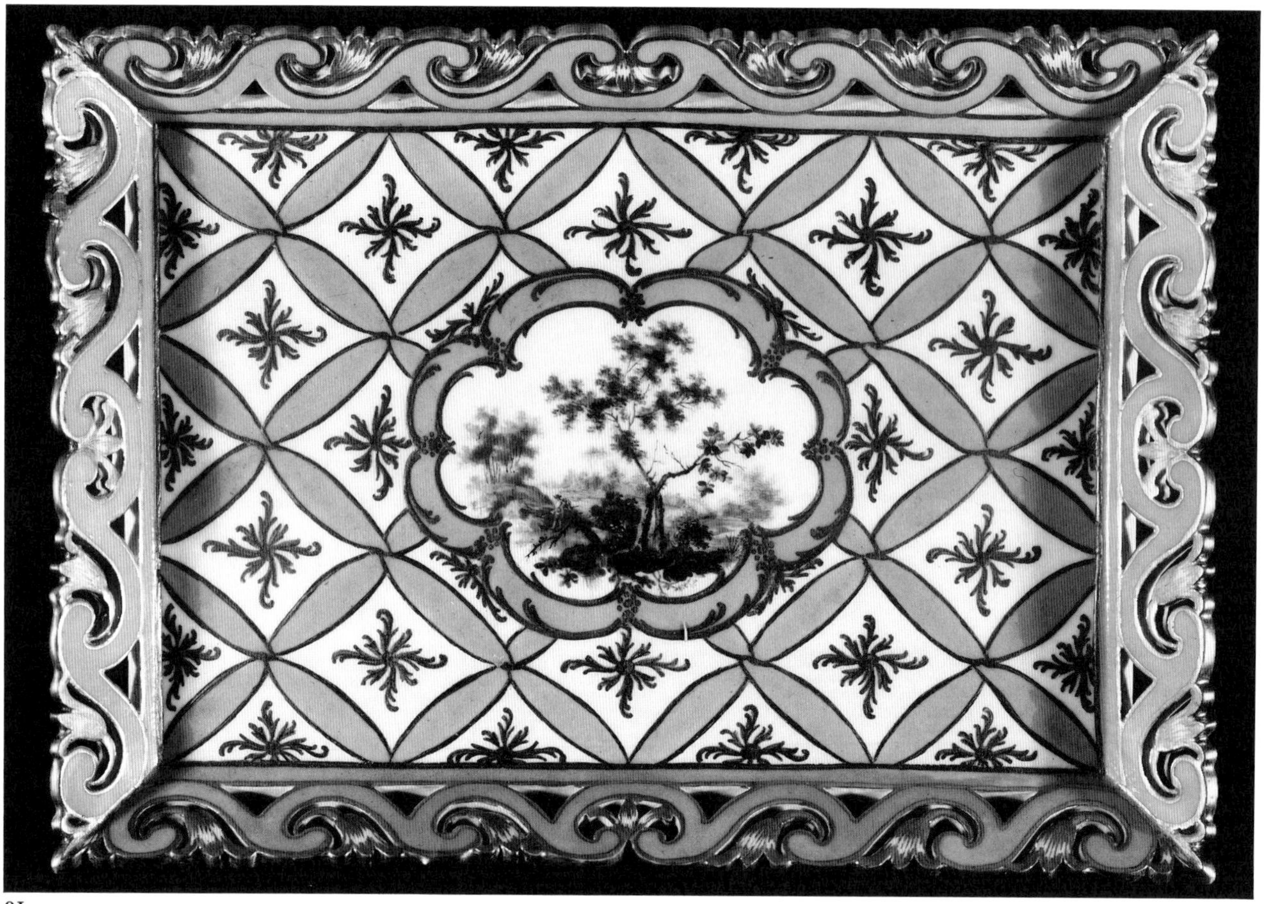

91

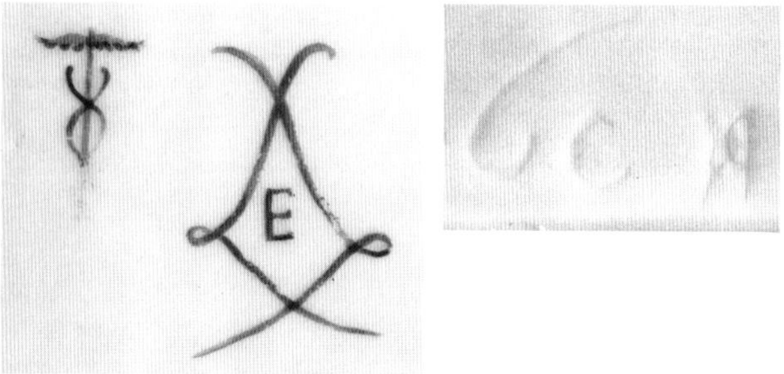

91 *marks*

at Waddesdon dated 1759, painted with landscape scenes. Eriksen apparently revoked his tentative identification of this mark with the painter Edmé Goméry in 1987,[5] believing that the pieces with the caduceus mark 'seem, as far as the decoration is concerned, to be of nineteenth-century manufacture'. However, his co-author Sir Geoffrey de Bellaigue has now (1992) revised his view, and is inclined to accept the pieces as genuine. It is a view shared by this writer, who finds the decoration on the British Museum tray convincingly eighteenth-century in style and execution.

Two pink *caisses carrées* dated 1757, painted with rather similar landscape scenes including diminutive figures, were in the Hodgkins Collection.[6]

A square green tray at Waddesdon dated 1758 is incised with the same mark, also found on other pieces listed by Eriksen.[7]

The incised mark *6cbl* has been convincingly attributed by Savill[8] to Jean-Mathieu Blard, a soft-paste *répareur* employed from 1755–8 and 1763–72, as the mark *Blard* is incised on a *plateau 'tiroir'* of 1758.

1. Eriksen, 1968, p. 102.
2. See exh. *Vincennes*, 1977–8, pp. 66–7. Another rectangular tray with plain sides and four feet was called at the factory 'plateau à tiroir à pieds', and is first recorded in April 1756.
3. Savill, 1988, II, p. 585.
4. Eriksen, 1968, pp. 108–11; for his biography of Goméry, see p. 327.
5. Eriksen and Bellaigue, 1987, p. 174, no. 205, and p. 154.
6. See 'Porcelaines de Sèvres – Collection E.M. Hodgkins', *Les Arts*, no. 89, May 1909, p. 20, supposedly decorated in 1758 by Fouré.
7. Eriksen, 1968, p. 102.
8. Savill, 1988, III, p. 1128.

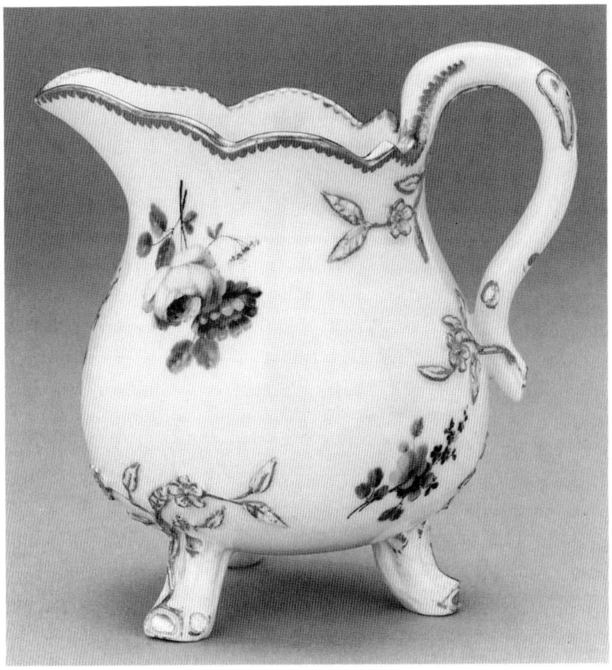

92

1750s, both individually for 12 *livres* and, with four or more matching cups and saucers, to form a tea service.

The identity of the painter using the mark *oe* is unknown.[3] In the *Etat des Employés et Ouvriers* for 1758 no fewer than 68 painters are listed, but Yvernel is perhaps the only one whose name might perhaps be phonetically rendered as 'oe'. However, his mark has been identified as a feathered arrow;[4] he was paid the high sum of 100 *livres* and is thought to have been a landscape and bird painter. The painter using *oe* may well have specialised in flowers since the mark has been noted on a *gobelet à lait chopine* painted with flowers in colours between *bleu lapis* ribbons.[5]

1. Eriksen, 1968, p. 66, no. 18.
2. Savill, 1988, II, pp. 564–5.
3. It does not appear in the total of 211 marks analysed in Eriksen and Bellaigue, 1987, pp. 153–4, based on a compilation of earlier lists of marks and on personal observation.
4. Brunet and Préaud, 1978, p. 383.
5. Exh. Williams, 1978, no. 14.

92 **Milk Jug (*pot à lait à trois pieds*)**, 1758

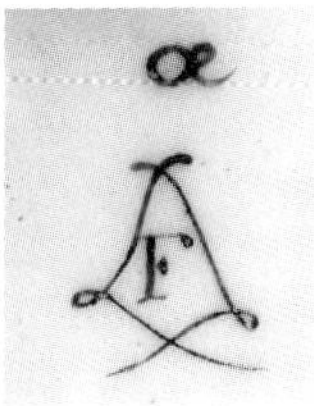

92 *mark*

H. 12.5 cm
Marks: interlaced LL enclosing date-letter F below *oe* painted in blue enamel on base of body
Reg. No. 1931,10–19,16

Soft-paste porcelain of bulbous form, each foot moulded in the form of a tree trunk with flowers and leaves in relief 'growing' from it. The handle is similarly moulded and ornamented at either end with leaves and flowers, partly gilt. Painted in pink, yellow, green, purple, blue, red and grey on a white ground with seven small flower sprays. Gilt dentil rim. Foot repaired, hairline cracks to body.

Provenance: Transferred from Salisbury and South Wiltshire Museum, 1931

Literature: Unpublished

Comparable Examples: Christie's, 3 July 1978, Lot 194, puce date-letter for 1771, first size

Christie's, 2 October 1979, Lots 39, 42, both dated 1786, one marked in puce, first size

The title of this jug, which was introduced in 1752 and produced in three sizes, was identified by Svend Eriksen in 1968.[1] Two sizes were in production by March 1753, the third size appearing in 1756. Rosalind Savill, who reproduces the plaster model kept at the factory, discusses the form in detail.[2]

This example is the largest size. Similar jugs with flowers painted on a white ground were sold in the

93 **Plate (*assiette à guirlandes*)**, 1758

D. 25.1 cm
Marks: interlaced LL enclosing date-letter F below the mark of two semi-quavers used by the painter Louis-Gabriel Chulot painted in blue enamel; incised *T* near suspension hole
Reg. No. 1899,10–6,8

Soft-paste porcelain, the rim with eight lobes alternating with eight smaller ones and moulded with a flower garland. The decoration consists of scattered flower sprays of pink and yellow roses, campanulas, violas and other flowers on a white ground on the well of the plate and a blue bat's wing pattern on the rim. Rim gilt.

Provenance: Bequeathed by C.D.E. Fortnum, Esq., DCL, FSA, 1899 (no. 223)[1]

Literature: Unpublished

Comparable Examples: France, Paris, Musée des arts décoratifs, dated 1759 (see Verlet, *et al*, 1953, pl. 98a)

London, Victoria and Albert Museum, inv. C. 98 & a – 1971, decorated with birds by the 'crescent painter'

The form of this plate was devised in 1753 and examples were first fired in November that year. A plaster model is kept at the factory.[2]

Louis-Gabriel Chulot (1736–1824) worked at Chantilly, where he was born, and at Orléans before coming to Vincennes on 19 October 1755. He was employed at the factory as a painter of flowers, trophies and attributes, as well as other subjects, and also a gilder, ground-painter (of *pointillé*) and burnisher up to 1800, and then between 1805–18. His

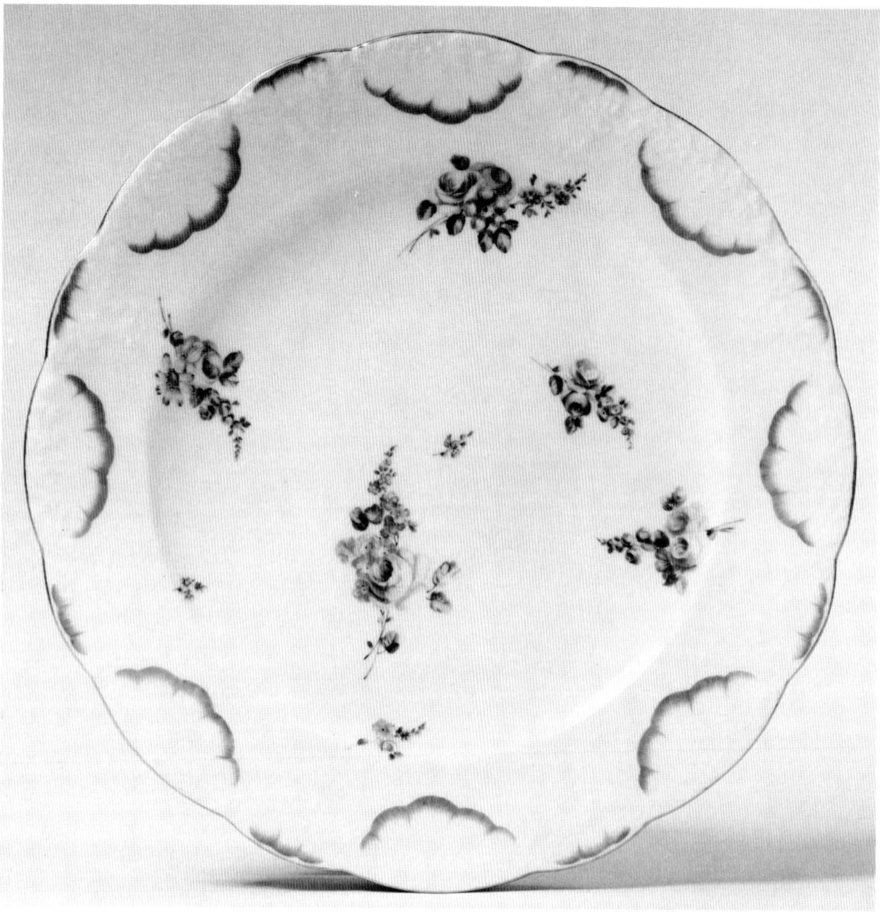

93

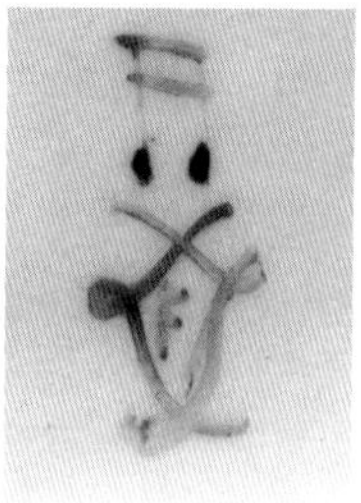

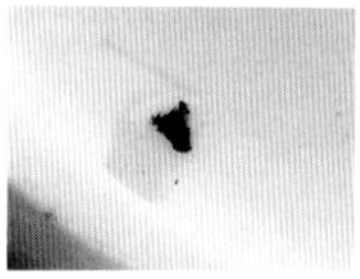

93 *marks*

musical talent (he played the violin) was reflected in his mark.[3]

Of the 87 repairers employed at the factory, several whose names begin with the initial 'T' are listed in the factory records of personnel in 1758: Tamise (paid 36 *livres* a month), Thomassin (33 *livres*), Tristant *l'aîné* and *le jeune* (18 and 9 *livres* respectively).[4] The mark is discussed by Savill but no suggestion as to who used it is made, except for that of Eriksen, who believed it to be the mark of Pierre-Edmond Tristant *l'aîné*.[5]

This plate has a disquieting feature which might cast doubt on the genuineness of the painted decoration. In the well the glaze is noticeably 'scarred'. In addition there are a number of pin-holes in the glaze on the reverse of the foot. The painted mark is also unusually positioned near the foot rim, instead of in the centre of the base, and is particularly small. However, there seems no other reason to believe that the plate was decorated anywhere but at the Sèvres factory.

1. C.D.E. Fortnum (1820–99) was a noted collector and leading authority on bronzes, maiolica and finger rings. He was a Trustee of the British Museum between 1889 and 1899. In 1839, 1840 and 1842 he presented insects, birds, mammals and reptiles to the British Museum (now the British Museum of Natural History). For biographical information, see the DNB. Amongst his publications are: *A Descriptive Catalogue of the Maiolica, Hispano-Moresco, Persian, Damascus, and Rhodian Wares in the South Kensington Museum*, London, 1873; *A Descriptive Catalogue of the Bronzes of European Origin in the South Kensington Museum*, London 1876; *A Descriptive Catalogue of the Maiolica and Enamelled Earthenwares of Italy, the Persian, Damascus, Rhodian, Hispano-Moresque and some French and other Wares in the Ashmolean Museum, Fortnum Collection*, Oxford, 1897. For surveys of aspects of his collections, see C. Lloyd, 'Fox-Strangways and Fortnum: Two Collectors of Italian Art', *Apollo*, Vol. CXVII, no. 254, April 1983, pp. 280–7; J.V.G. Mallet, 'C.D.E. Fortnum and Italian Maiolica of the Renaissance', *Apollo*, Vol. CVIII, no. 202. December 1978, pp. 396–404, illustrating one of two portraits by Charles Alexander, p. 396, fig. 1; D. Scarisbrick, 'Sir John Evans and Charles Drury Fortnum: Two Victorian Ring Connoisseurs' in G. Taylor and D. Scarisbrick, *Finger Rings*, Oxford, 1978, pp. 5–21; J.V.G. Mallet, 'Storico Storicismo, Fortnum, Cantagalli e Castellani', *Faenza*, 1978, 2, pp. 32–47.
2. Exh. *Porcelaines de Vincennes*, 1977, no. 22. The plaster measures 28.5 cm.
3. Savill, 1988, III, pp. 1022–3.
4. MNS, Archives de Sèvres, D1.
5. Savill, 1988, III, pp. 1108–9.

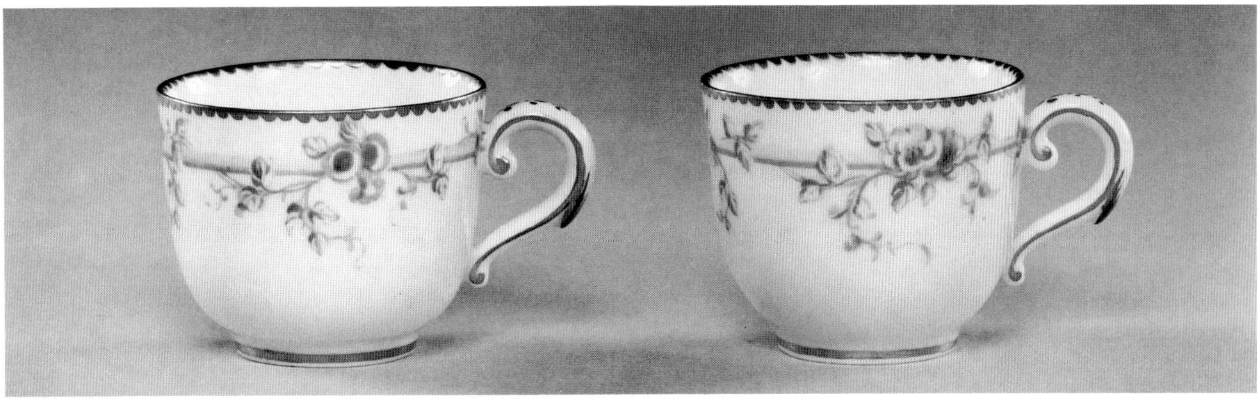

94

94 Two Cups (*gobelets Bouillard*), 1759

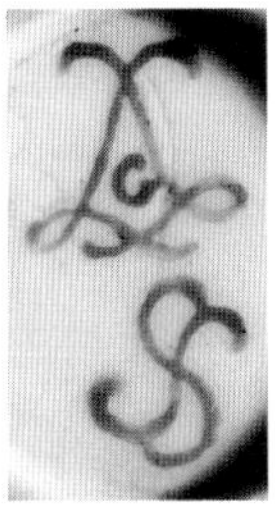

94 *marks*

H.	3.9 cm
D.	4.9 cm
Marks:	interlaced LL enclosing date-letter G for 1759 above painter's mark of interlaced *SS* for Nicolas Catrice; incised *3*, *JB* (or *J8*) and with another indecipherable mark
Reg. No.	Franks 380

Soft-paste porcelain, straight-sided cup swelling from small foot, scroll handle. Both are painted near the rim in blue enamel with a ribbon and flower trail. Gilt dentil rims, handles partly gilt, gilt line around foot.

Provenance: Lady Mary Fox's Collection, formerly in the possession of King William IV (Franks Catalogue)

Bequeathed by Sir A.W. Franks, 1897

Literature: Franks, 1896, no. 380

Comparable Examples: See note 5

These cups are the third size of the *gobelet Bouillard* shape introduced in 1753, when the first and third sizes were in production.[1] The earliest dated example of the second size discovered by Savill was decorated in 1757.[2] The shape was named for the *marchand-mercier* and *fermier-général* Antoine-Augustin Bouillard, a shareholder in both the Charles Adam and Eloi Brichard companies. A milk jug, sugar bowl, teapot, vase, *jatte*, *cabaret*, and *pot à jus* (known only in the form of a plaster) were also named for Bouillard between 1753 and 1781.[3]

Small cups like this were sometimes sold from the factory without saucers, intended for use on trays of various forms. Examples of the third size with their accompanying saucer measuring 9.1 cm or 9.3 cm are in the Victoria and Albert Museum.[4] Six cups without handles on a triangular tray dated 1758 decorated with flowers *en camaïeu bleu* were recently sold as 'mocha cups' on the London and New York markets.[5]

In June 1762 Madame de Pompadour purchased a 'Très petite Tasse et Soucoupe' decorated with 'frizes colorées' for 12 *livres* as well as another painted with birds for 7 *livres* 10 *sols* and four painted with flowers costing 6 *livres* each.[6]

The painted mark is recorded in the eighteenth-century handwritten ledger of painters' and gilders' marks against the name of Catrice.[7] Nicolas Catrice (active 1757–74) was a flower painter. A cup and saucer in the Victoria and Albert Museum dated 1764 is decorated with flowers in monochrome blue.[8] For other pieces incised *3*, and *JB*, see Savill.[9]

The provenance of these cups has not been confirmed.[10] Lady Mary Fox (d. 1864) was the second daughter of William IV (whilst Duke of Clarence) and Mrs Jordan.

1. Savill, 1988, p. 527.
2. *Ibid.*, p. 532, f.n. 30, Victoria and Albert Museum, inv. C. 1364–1919.
3. *Ibid.*, p. 528.
4. *Ibid.*, p. 532, f.n. 3q,w.
5. Christie's, 30 June 1986, Lot 198; Sotheby's, New York, 20 May 1989, Lot 77, estate of Dr Henry A. Chase. The author is grateful to Adrian Sassoon for drawing these pieces to her attention. Five *gobelets Bouillard* on a *plateau Bouret* painted by Catrice with flowers in monochrome pink and bearing the date-letter for 1759 were sold at Christie's, New York, 30 November 1979, Lot 179, Mrs John W. Christner Collection; and a lobed tray dated 1758 painted with flowers in monochrome blue in a private collection in Paris is illus. by Dallot-Naudin and Jacob, 'Vincennes', 1983, p. 194.
6. MNS, Archives de Sèvres, Vy 3, f. 115v.
7. MNS, Archives de Sèvres, Vj' 2.
8. Inv. 3622–1856, see Eriksen and Bellaigue, 1987, p. 170.
9. Savill, 1988, III, pp. 1125–6 and p. 1110.
10. The author is grateful to Sir Geoffrey de Bellaigue, KCVO, Surveyor of the Queen's Works of Art, for checking the records of the Royal Collection.

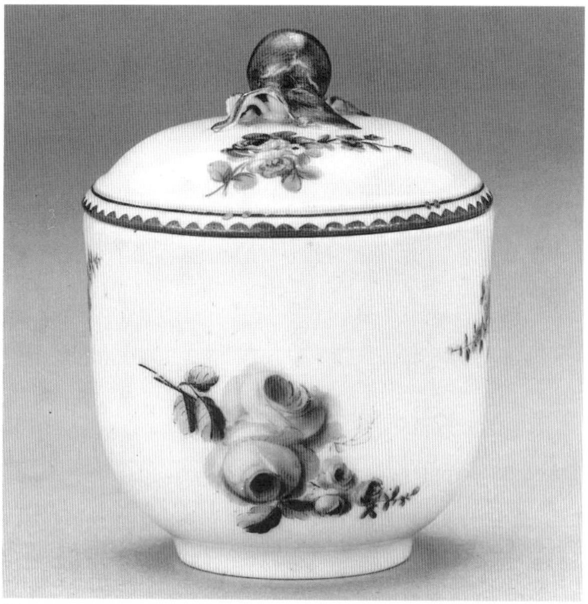

95

95 **Sugar Bowl and Cover (*pot à sucre Calabre*),** perhaps 1759

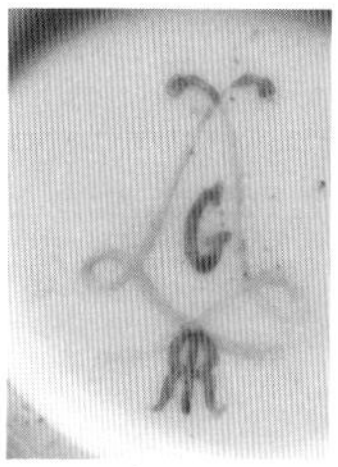

95 *marks*

H. *of pot without cover:*	5 cm
D.	6.1 cm
Marks:	interlaced LL enclosing date-letter G for 1759 above an unidentified painter's mark in blue enamel; incised *2*; printed label of Salisbury and South Wiltshire Museum Loan Collection 187, inscribed in ink *P.W. Read Proprietor*
Reg. No.	1931,10–19,14

Soft-paste porcelain, the domed cover much whiter than the pot, decorated with groups of scattered flowers including roses and peonies in yellow, green, pink, blue, purple and grey, on a white ground. The cherry and leaf knop gilt, blue line interrupted by groups of two gilt dots near rim, gilt dentil on rim.

Provenance: Collection of P.W. Read, loaned to Salisbury and South Wiltshire Museum, date of accession unknown

Transferred from the Salisbury and South Wiltshire Museum, 1931

Literature: Unpublished

Comparable Examples: None

The form, named after Pierre Calabre (see p. 83), was devised in 1752.[1] A pencil drawing inscribed *Sucrÿe calabre no 2ème grandeur rectifié suivan l'ordre de La Comande du 19 fevrÿe 1753* shows that two sizes were in existence by then. An example of the third size measuring 7 cm in height in the James A. de Rothschild Collection, Waddesdon Manor, dated 1754[2] indicates that the third size was almost contemporaneous. It is fitted with a matching cover of flatter profile and with a carnation knop.

This example is of the third or smallest size. Examples of the first size measure between 11 cm and 12.5 cm in height; the second size measures between 9.4 cm and 10 cm and the third size between 5.5 cm and 7.5 cm. The cover of this example does not belong; it does not fit, is much whiter in tone and the gilt cherry and leaf knop suggests a date in the 1770s, although it may be a nineteenth-century confection. Because of its domed shape, it is likely to belong to a *pot à sucre Bouret*.

It is just possible that the painter's mark corresponds with a mark attributed by Riocreux in 1861 to Aubert *aîné*, a flower-painter employed at the factory between 1754–8, whose biographical details are unknown.[3] Although the bowl has been dated 1759, it may have been made the previous year as there are many inconsistencies in the system used.[4] The other possibility, put forward by Savill in view of the absence of gilding on the bowl and upheld by the poor quality of the painting, is that the bowl was decorated in the nineteenth century. The incised mark, the exact significance of which is unknown, has been traced on various ornamental and useful wares from the 1750s to the 1780s.[5]

1. Exh. *Vincennes*, 1977–8, pp. 83–4.
2. Eriksen, 1968, p. 48, illus. p. 49.
3. Eriksen and Bellaigue, 1987, p. 154, no. 208 and p. 175.
4. Savill, 1988, III, 1164–6.
5. Savill, 1988, III, p. 1125.

96 **Pair of Vases (*vases hollandais nouveaux ovales*),** 1759

H.	19.5 cm, 19.7 cm
Marks:	LL enclosing date-letter g for 1759 below *M* and a dot for the painter Jean-Louis Morin; incised *cn* on base of upper and lower parts; *230* painted in red on base of upper part and *8207* below on 1948,12–3,34; similar marks on companion piece, partly effaced
Reg. No.	1948,12–3,34 and 35

Soft-paste porcelain in two parts, the upper fan-shaped part having ten circular holes near the base to draw water up from the lower part. The decoration consists of a camp scene on one side and a group of naturalistically painted flowers on the other in a shaped reserve outlined with gilding on a *bleu céleste* ground on the upper part, and a panel of flowers on each 'end'. Gilt flower sprays on each side. Lower edge of upper part chipped (1948,12–3,34). Feet of lower part restored (both), some restoration to pierced neck of lower part, chip on side panel (1948,12–1,34), foot and piercing restored, overpainting on rim.

Provenance: Bequeathed by Sir B. Eckstein, Bt., 1948

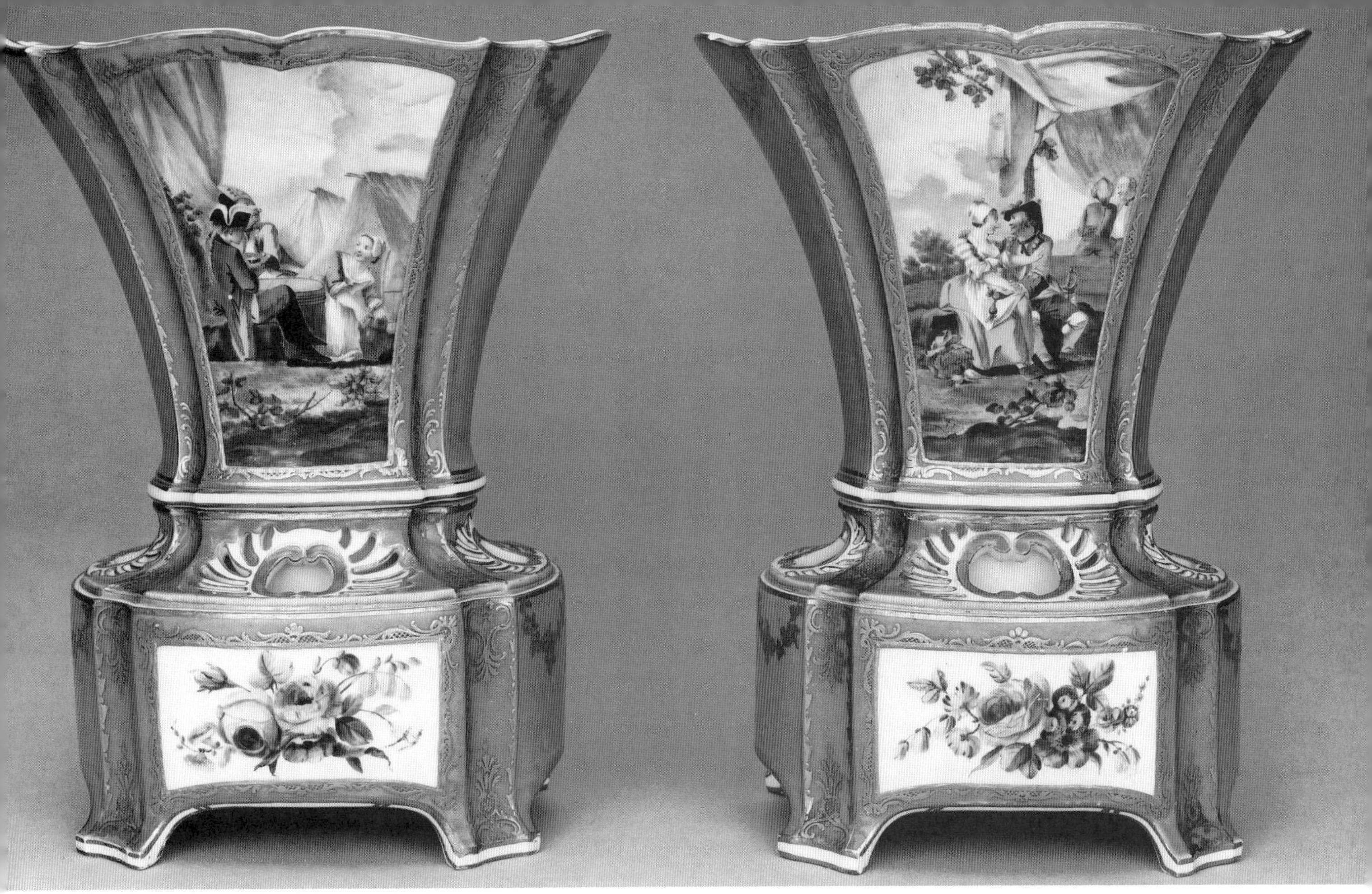

96

96

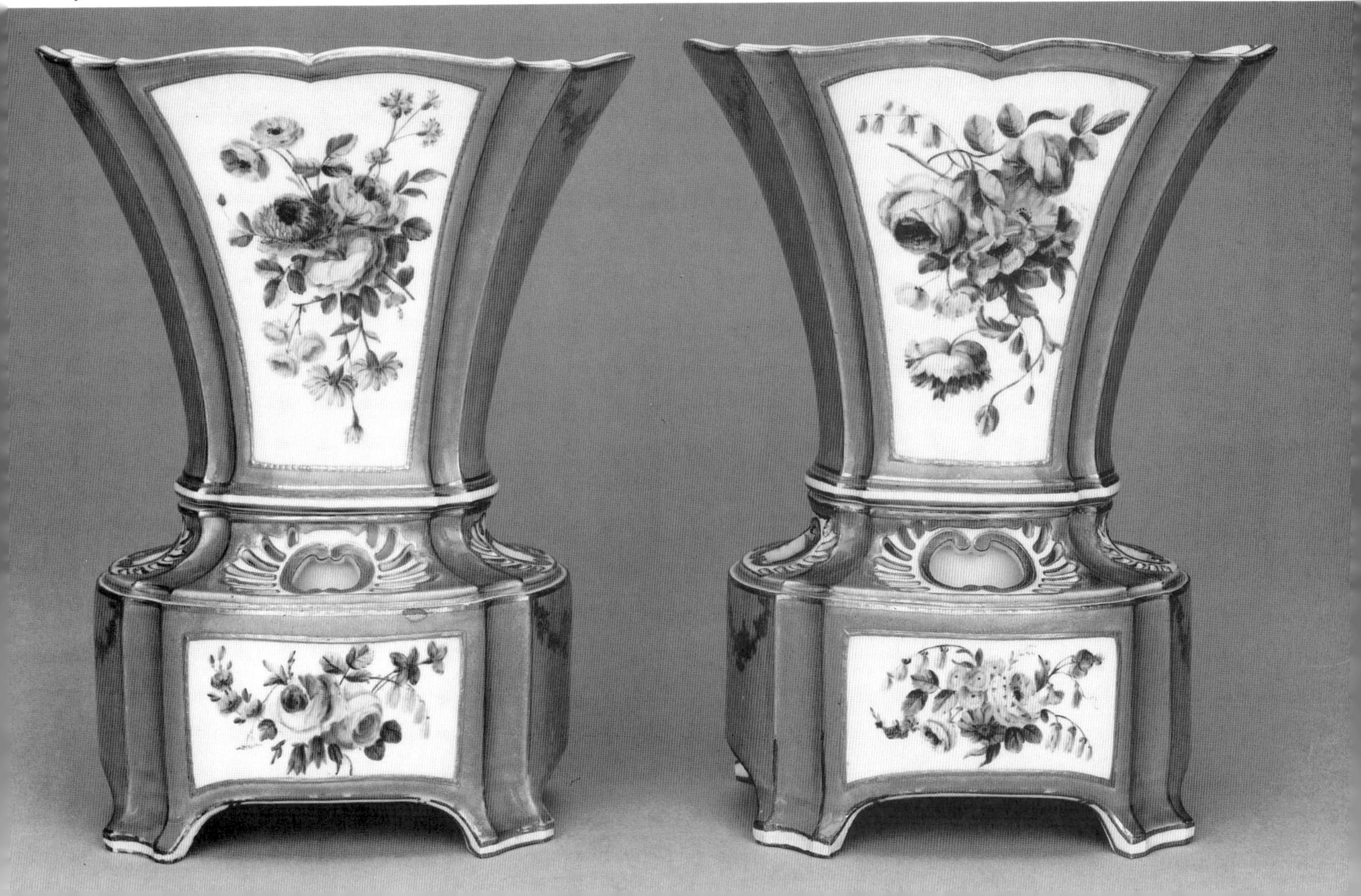

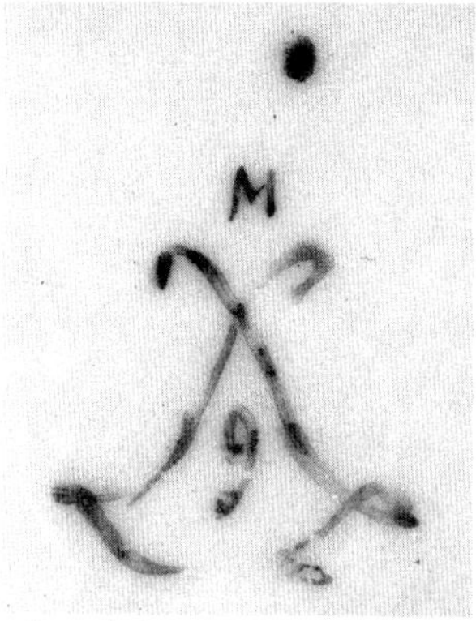

96 *mark (1948, 12–3, 34)*

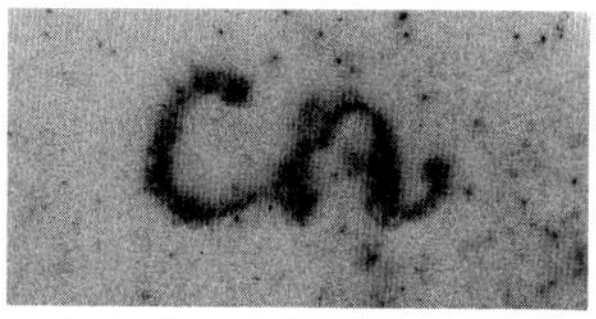

96 *incised mark (1948, 12–3, 34)*

Literature: Unpublished

Comparable Examples: A number are listed by Dauterman, 1970, pp. 211–12. The closest is probably an example in the Musée des arts décoratifs, Paris, inv. 28703, with the same ground colour and panels of flowers, H. 20 cm.[1]

The model was devised in 1758 and five sizes appear in the stock list of models and moulds of January 1759.[2] Despite being early examples, it is likely that these two, which are of the fourth size, received additional gilding after leaving the factory. The sketchy and fussy gilding on one side contrasts unfavourably with the restrained elegance of the 'reverse' and doubtless represents the original appearance of the vases.

The painter Jean-Louis Morin is best known for his camp and port scenes, but was also a competent painter of flowers.[3]

The incised mark *cn* has been attributed to the *répareur* Cejourné employed between 1754 and 1767.[4] It is frequently found on vases of this shape.[5]

A Spode version of this shape measuring 15 cm in height decorated with stylised foliage was on the London market in 1989.[6]

1. Brunet and Préaud, 1978, no. 86, p. 152. The model is fully discussed in Savill, 1988, I, pp. 109–11; the drawing for the fourth and fifth sizes and the plaster model are illustrated.
2. *Ibid.*
3. For a biography of Morin (1732–87, working period from 1754) see Savill, 1988, III, pp. 1051–2.
4. Eriksen, 1968, p. 100.
5. Savill, 1988, I, C232–3, p. 112, pair of the fifth size, 1758, painted with birds.
6. Phillips, 'Good European Ceramics and Glass', 7 June 1989, Lot 486.

97 Milk Cup, Cover and Stand (*gobelet à lait couvert et soucoupe*), 1759

See colour plate 12

H. *of cup and cover:*	15.5 cm
D. *of saucer:*	21.6 cm
Marks:	interlaced LL enclosing date-letter G, above painter's mark *k* for Charles-Nicolas Dodin in blue enamel; *T* incised (cup). LL date letter G and four dots arranged vertically, painted in blue enamel; suspension hole (saucer); suspension hole inside cover; label inscribed in ink *From the collection of the Marquess of Lincolnshire*; another inscribed *62*; printed collection label of Sir Bernard Eckstein *No. C. 25 Oldlands Hall, Fairwarp, Sussex* and label printed *SEVRES* and inscribed *Painted Dodin Date 1759* on cup, saucer has last two only; small paper label printed *86* or *98* inside cover.
Reg. No.	1948,12–3,18

Soft-paste porcelain, thrown, the cup of bucket form with two ear-shaped handles, moulded with a central ridge on both inner and outer surfaces, and terminating at both ends in three stylised leaves; the domed cover is surmounted by a flower knop. The deep saucer has flared sides. Painted within a richly gilt and tooled reserve on either side of the cup are two allegorical scenes:

a) a young woman in a landscape, clothed in a pink classical-style robe which leaves her arms and left upper body uncovered, steps up with her right foot to arrange a flower garland around a full-length statue of Aesculapius; behind her is a bird, perhaps a pelican or other exotic bird;

b) a young girl seated on grassy bank and clothed in a pale blue classical robe which leaves her arms uncovered, caresses a white dog which stands on its hind legs; with her left foot (both are bare) she crushes a human mask, her foot resting on its eyes, beside which is a snake.

On the cover is a French ducal coat of arms and the monogram *PLGFD* beneath a ducal coronet, each within a richly gilt and tooled reserve. The petals of the flower knop are pink, the stalk and leaf yellowish green. The saucer is decorated with three panels of naturalistically painted flowers on the border in reserve. In the centre are allegorical trophies, including a bundle of *fasces*, the scales of Justice, Mercury's thyrsis entwined with two green serpents, and Aesculapius' rod entwined with a green serpent. The gilding around the reserves consists of scrolls and flowers, asymmetrically arranged. Rim of cup and saucer has a gilt dentil pattern on both sides; on cover it is on upper surface only; handles partly gilt, terminals gilt, gilt line near foot of cup. Two tiny chips to inner rim of cover (possibly firing damage), discoloration and severe 'bloating' on inside of cover, well of saucer slightly scratched.

Provenance: Charles Robert, 3rd Baron Carrington (later Marquess of Lincolnshire, 1843–1928), recorded 17 March 1864 at 8, Whitehall, London, *List and Valuation of the Valuable Sevres [sic] Chelsea and Dresden China in the Mansion of the Right Hon. Lord Carrington*, Case 57, p. 18, when it was valued at £250[1]

Marquess of Lincolnshire, GCMG, deceased, sold at Christie's 5 December 1928, Lot 23, £304–10s

Alfred Hill Collection, sold at Sotheby's 15 May 1942, Lot 50 £210

Bequeathed by Sir B. Eckstein, Bt., 1948

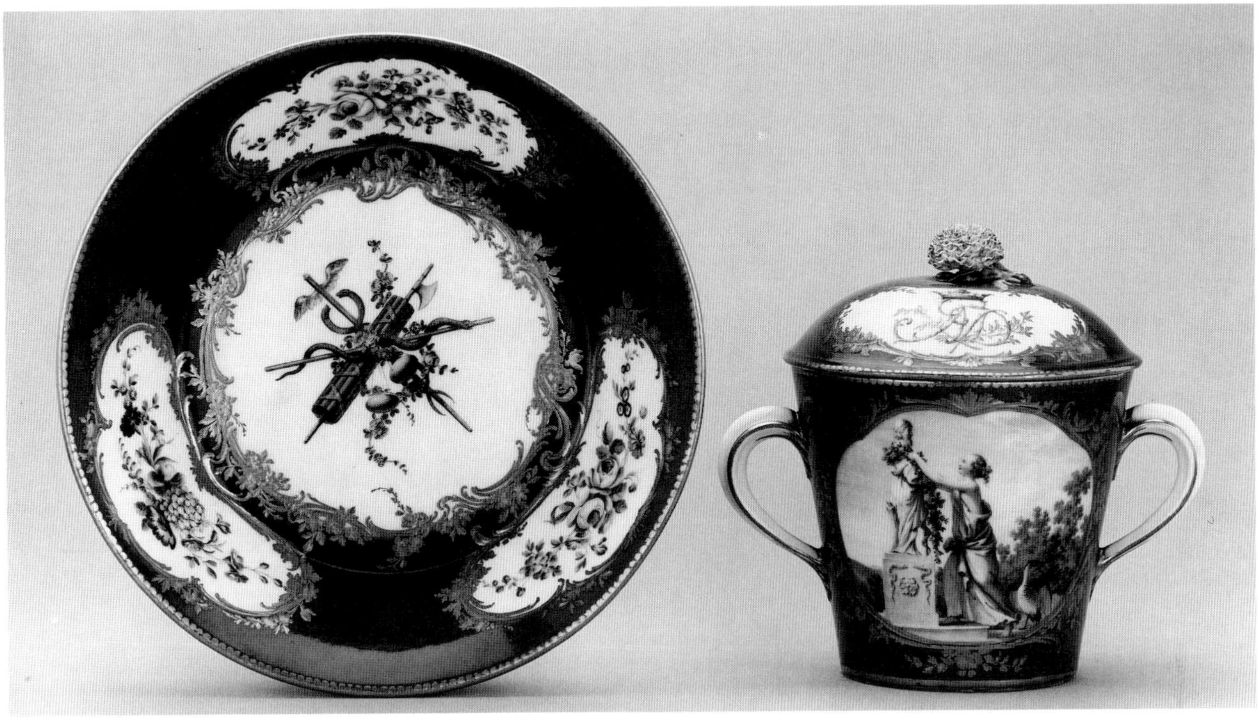

97

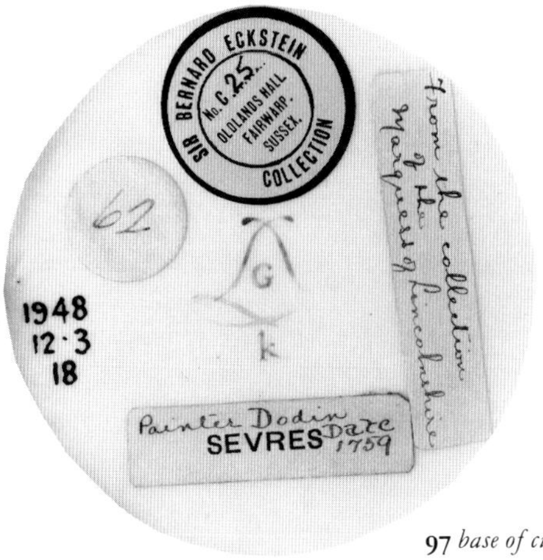

97 *base of cup*

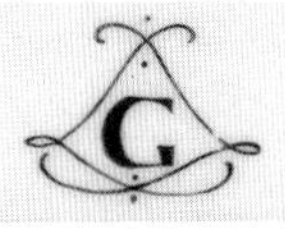

97 *mark (saucer)*

Literature: Savill, 1988, II, p. 673, f.n. 3a

Exhibited: 1985, 'Documentary Continental Ceramics from the British Museum', London, International Ceramics Fair and Seminar, June 1985, no. 46, cat. compiled by A. Dawson

Comparable Examples: Listed by Savill, 1988, II, p. 673, f.n. 3

The form, made in two sizes of which this is the larger, is known at Vincennes in 1752 and was still in production in the 1780s. It is fully discussed by Savill[2] who illustrates two drawings of 1753, and quotes recipes given in the *Encyclopédie* (1772) for milky drinks and diets. The saucer was used for cooling the drink, or for slices of bread.

The decoration on these pieces is exceptional. The significance of the two allegorical scenes on the cup has not been precisely determined, although one is clearly a sacrifice to Aesculapius, perhaps for the health of a child.

The other scene concerns (? the reward of) fidelity, symbolised by the dog, and the defeat of deceit and false appearances represented by the mask and the snake. The trophies on the saucer are almost certainly connected with scenes on the cup.

The key to the iconography rests in the identification of the arms and monogram on the cover. The arms have been traced[3] to a member of the Grollier family, Pierre-Louis, marquis de Grollier et de Trefort, comte de Maisonseule, vicomte de Thil, etc., who was born in Lyon in 1730, married Charlotte-Eugénie-Sophie de Fuligny-Damas (1742–1828) in 1760 and was executed on 26 December 1793. The arms are described and illustrated in W. Poidebard, *Notices généalogiques*.

No trace has yet been found of the cup and saucer in the factory records to confirm that it was made at or near the time of the Grollier/Fuligny-Damas wedding, but it is possible that such special commissions were recorded elsewhere than in the surviving sales registers, especially as no record has been found of cat. 108. Despite the poor quality of the cover, the pieces were certainly decorated at the factory. In later life the marquise de Grollier achieved a considerable reputation as a flower-painter. A pupil of Spaendonck, she was called by Canova the 'Raphael des fleurs'. After the Restoration she opened a studio at Epinay and was once thought to have worked at the Sèvres factory.[4]

Little is known of her early life, so that interpretation of the scenes on the cup must remain incomplete.

For biographical details of Dodin, see Savill.[5] The incised mark *T* is discussed by the same writer.[6]

1. The author is most grateful to Lady Cynthia Postan for assistance in tracing the history of this piece.
2. Savill, 1988, II, pp. 667–9.
3. The arms were identified by Monsieur Philippe Palasi, and the author is indebted to Bernard Dragesco for kindly communicating this information to her.
4. There is no evidence for this. The marquise de Grollier was a member of the Société d'Horticulture. A tribute to her by the General Secretary of the Society, Chevalier Soulange Bodin, was published in *Annales d'Horticulture*, December 1828, *Notice nécrologique sur Madame de Grollier membre de la société d'Horticulture*, pp. 348–54. The author is grateful to the staff of Cambridge University Library for making this number of the periodical available to her.
5. Savill, 1988, III, pp. 1029–32.
6. *Ibid.*, p. 1109, and see cat. 93.

98 **Flower Vase (*cuvette à fleurs Verdun*),** 1760

H. 10.9 cm
Marks: interlaced LL enclosing date-letter H for 1760 above *N* for the painter François-Joseph Aloncle (1758–81) in blue enamel; *K* incised; suspension hole
Reg. No. 1948,12–3,51

Soft-paste porcelain; of oval form with undulating outline and rudimentary scroll handles, moulded. Decorated with a dark blue (*bleu lapis*) ground overlaid with *caillouté* and vermiculated gilding; on the front, in reserve on a white ground, with birds in a landscape and a building in the background painted in blue, yellow, purple, green, grey-green, grey-blue, and brown enamel colours. Small chip on foot rim.

Provenance: Bequeathed by Sir B. Eckstein, Bt., 1948

Literature: Savill, 1988, I, p. 61, f.n. 2 s

Comparable Examples: Paris, Palais Galliéra, 2–3 June 1970, Lot 214, L. 26.5 cm (second size), from the collection of Vicomtesse Vigier, 1760, decoration of rustic scene by Vielliard, dark blue ground with rich *caillouté* and trellis gilding

The shape was devised at Vincennes in 1754 on the order of the *fermier-général* Jean-François Verdun de Montchiroux (dates unknown), chief shareholder in the Charles Adam Company established in 1745, and in 1752 a shareholder in the Eloi Brichard Company.[1]

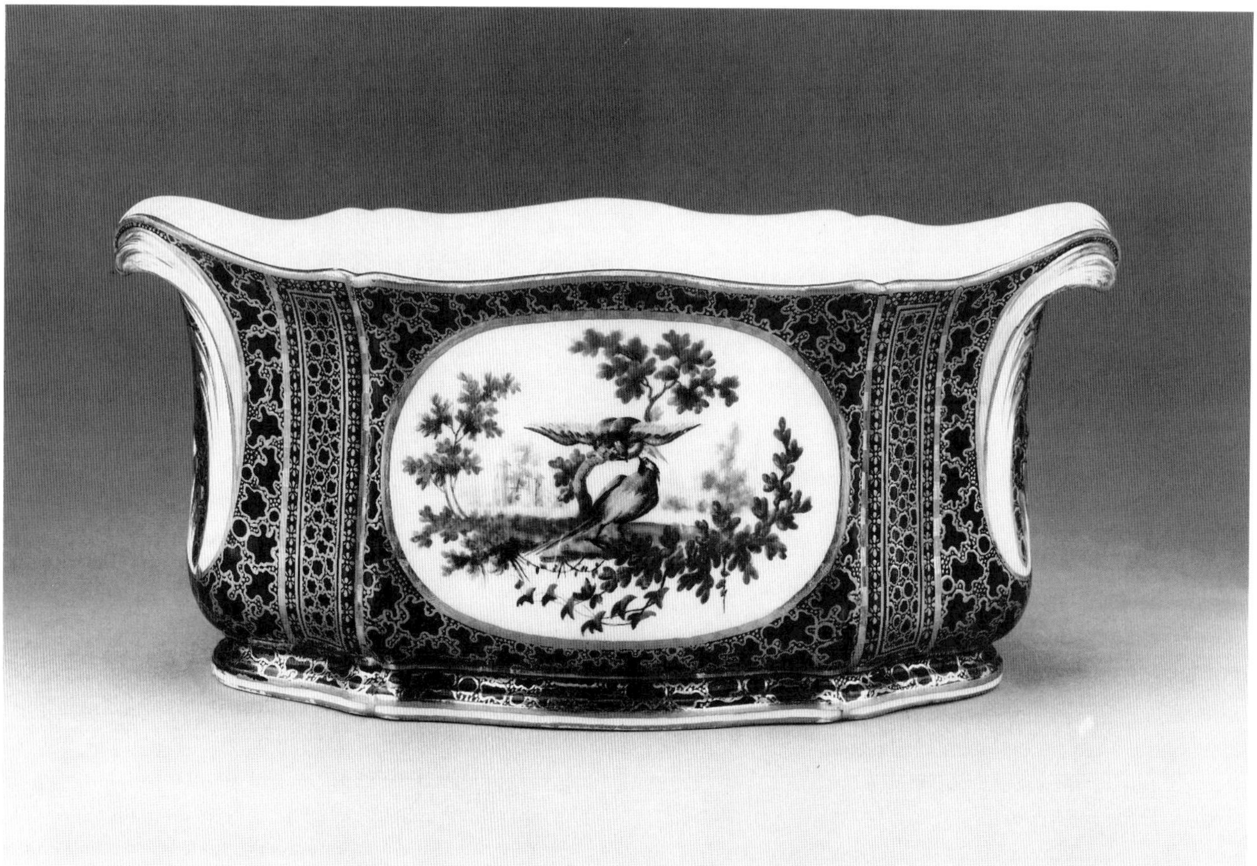

98

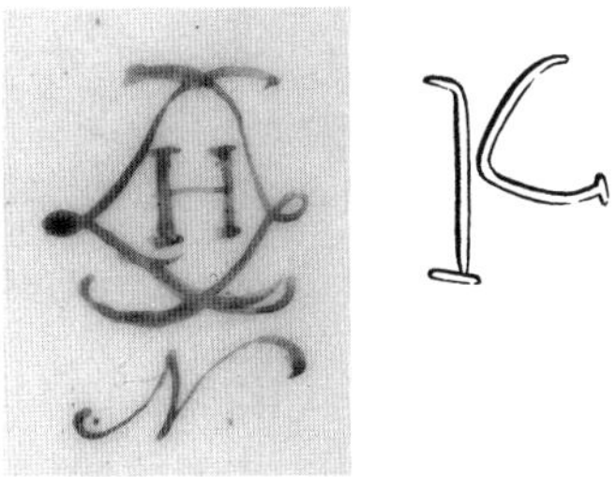

98 *marks*

Other forms named for Verdun included a teapot, sugar bowl, cup, *compotier*, salt-cellar, salad bowl, *pot à jus*, and jampot.[2] The flower vase was introduced in three sizes that year and the first sales were made in late 1755, although only the first size was in production until 1759.[3] It was usually sold singly, occasionally in pairs or as part of a set including a *cuvette Courteille* and a *cuvette à tombeau*.[4]

This example, which is of the third size,[5] is remarkable for its particularly rich gilt decoration of two different types of *caillouté* gilding, a stylised gilt star motif, and the use of two different tooled patterns to enliven gilt lines. Its sale has not been traced in the factory's records.

The painter François-Joseph Aloncle (1734–81) worked at Sèvres between 1758 and 1781, having been employed as a painter in Paris. His wages, initially 36 *livres* a month, rose steadily to reach 78 *livres* in 1774. Known chiefly for his bird paintings, which reached an extremely high standard (as shown on the jug and basin, cat. 124), he also painted animal subjects, attributes and possibly also landscapes, children in landscapes and flowers.[6]

The identity of the repairer using the incised mark *K* is unknown. It is also found on a wine-cooler dated 1757 at Waddesdon Manor, and on other pieces dated between 1754 and 1757.[7]

1. For details of Verdun's shareholdings in and dealings with the Vincennes and Sèvres factories, see Savill, 1988, III, pp. 988–9. Verdun became a *fermier-général* in 1757 through the protection of King Stanislaus of Poland, Duke of Lorraine. His wife was painted by Vigée-Lebrun in 1776.
2. Savill, 1988, I, p. 56, where a drawing inscribed *caisse à fleurs unÿe contourné fait le 7 Mars 1754 par ordre de Mr de Verdun plus en juillet 1759 fait 2ème et 3ème grandeur* is illustrated.
3. Savill, 1988, I, p. 57.
4. *Ibid.*, p. 56.
5. The sizes, from 15 to 16.4 cm in height (first), 12.5 to 13.1 cm (second) and 10 to 11.3 cm (third) are listed, with widths, by Savill, *loc. cit.*
6. A biography of Aloncle is given in Eriksen, 1968, p. 315.
7. *Op. cit.*, no. 22, where other pieces incised *K* are listed.

99 **Cup and Saucer (*gobelet litron et soucoupe*)**, 1760

D. *of saucer:*	12 cm
H. *of cup:*	6.1 cm
Marks:	interlaced LL enclosing date-letter H painted in blue enamel on both; *2* incised on saucer, and *3* incised on cup; suspension hole on saucer; rectangular label printed in black, *ON LOAN FROM* and inscribed in ink *Lord W. d'Eresby May 14 18* (the *18* is printed) *62*; blue printed collection label of Sir Bernard Eckstein and rectangular label inscribed in ink *Collections: Marquis of Lincolnshire/ Lord Willoughby D Eresby* on cup; printed label *SEVRES*, the rectangular label inscribed in ink *Collection/Marquess of Lincolnshire* and *1862* Exhibition label as above on saucer
Reg. No.	1948,12–3,42

Soft-paste porcelain, thrown, straight-sided cup with ear-shaped scroll handle and deep saucer. Decorated with a pink ground and with a painted scene of a diminutive male figure in a red coat and blue breeches (on the cup, on the saucer it is the other way round) and a brown hat walking with a staff in a watery wooded landscape. On the saucer he walks to the left away from an obelisk. On the cup he walks leftwards away from a farm building with a circular tower. The palette is predominantly browns and greens, with yellow, mauve and pale blue. The scene is enclosed by a rococo gilt cartouche. It is outlined in dark red, tooled with a zigzag motif and embellished with tooled flower sprays. At the upper edge is a gilt fan-like motif. Gilt dentil rims, handle partly gilt, gilt line around base of cup and foot of saucer. Rim of saucer restored in two places, gilding rubbed around base of saucer to reveal yellow below.

Provenance: Peter Robert, 21st Baron Willoughby de Eresby (d. 1865)[2]

Charles Robert, 3rd Baron Carrington, later 1st and last Marquess of Lincolnshire (1843–1928),[3] recorded in case 22 at 8, Whitehall, London, on 17 March 1864, *List and Valuation of the Valuable Sèvres Chelsea and Dresden China in the Mansion of the Right Hon. Lord Carrington*, p. 7, when the *déjeuner* of two coffee-cans and saucers, one cream jug, one *sucrier* and cover and a shaped plateau was valued at £200[4]

Marquess of Lincolnshire, K.G., G.C.M.G., deceased, Christie's, 14 December 1934, Lot 149 (*sucrier* and cover, cream-jug and cup and saucer), £300

Bequeathed by Sir B. Eckstein, Bt., 1948

Literature: Unpublished:

Exhibited: London, South Kensington Museum, 1862, *Catalogue of the Special Exhibition of Works of Art of the Medieval, Renaissance and More Recent Periods on loan at the South Kensington Museum*, June 1862, ed. J.C. Robinson, revised edition, London, 1863, no. 1292. ' "Cabaret" of rose Dubarry, with painted medallions of landscapes, richly gilt borders shaded with pink. Date, 1760 (lent by) Lord Willoughby de Eresby'

Comparable Examples: The matching tray (*plateau Hébert*) measuring 28.8 cm in length and 23.3 cm in width was sold at Christie's, 2 October 1989, Lot 214 (see fig. 99a)

See cat. 100 and 101 for matching pieces

The *gobelet litron* was in production by October 1752, and three sizes were in existence in 1753. The fourth

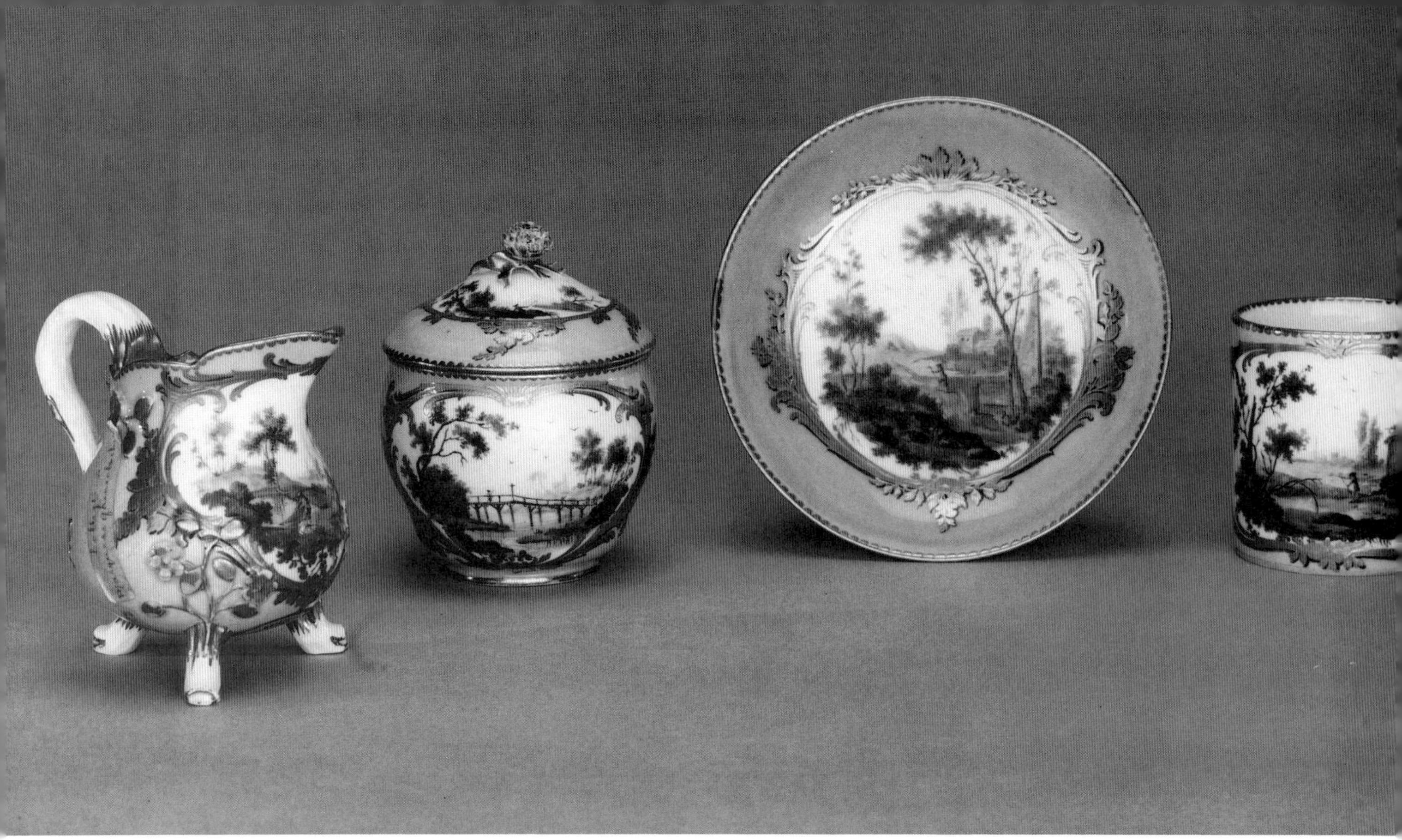

(From left) 101, 100, 99

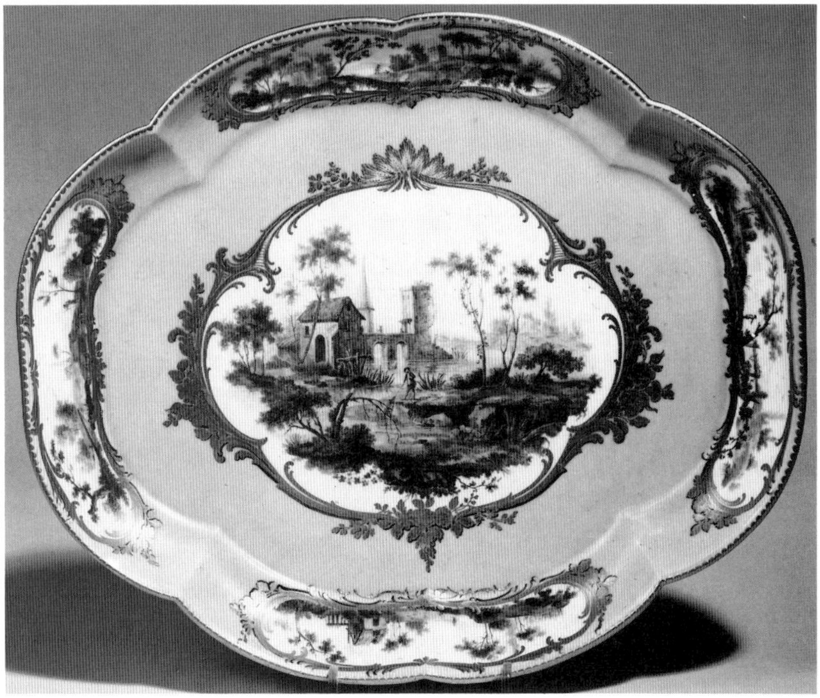

Fig 99a Matching tray (plateau Hébert).

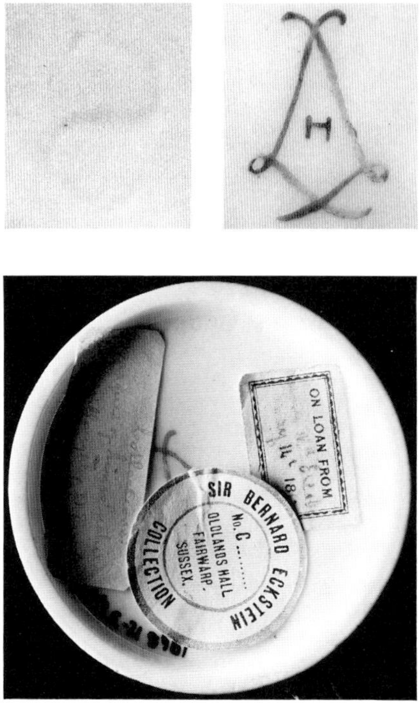

99 *marks*

and fifth sizes followed in 1757. The form is still made today. This example is of the third size, generally used for *déjeuners*.[5]

The identity of the painter is unknown. Scenes like this are found on pieces marked with the caduceus[6] and also on several bearing the painter's mark *y*. These are done in a similar palette.[7]

The painted mark resembles that on a pink-ground *pot à sucre Bouret* dated 1760 decorated in a similar style.[8]

The incised marks *2* (perhaps *S* reversed) and *3* are discussed by Savill.[9]

1. The author is grateful to Tony Stevenson for his help in providing biographical details of the owners.
2. The son of Sir Peter Burrell, Bt., he succeeded his father in 1820 as 2nd Baron Gwydyr, a title assumed by his father in 1796 by virtue of his marriage in 1779 to Priscilla Barbara Elizabeth Ancaster, who was heiress to the title of Baroness Willoughby de Eresby. For details of pieces from the Gwydyr collections, see Savill, 1988, II, p. 900 f.n. 12, 13. In 1838 Lord and Lady Willoughby d'Eresby presented to the British Museum two 'La Tène enamelled bracelets' (reg. no. 1838.7–14,3a, 3b). These, now called 'North British Iron Age', are known as the Pitkelloney armlets, from their find spot in Perthshire, Scotland, and date from 1st–2nd centuries AD; for more details see *Seven Thousand Years of Jewellery*, ed. H. Tait, London, 1986, p. 78, no. 176. In 1851 a bronze sword and dagger (reg. no. 1851,12–30,1 and 2) were presented. The sword is Later Bronze Age, *c.* 900–700 BC, and is illustrated by I. Colquhoun and C.B. Burgess, 'The Swords of Britain', *Prähistorisches Bronzefunde*, Abt. IV, Band 5, Munich, 1988, p. 85, no. 433, pl. 64. The dagger is a Middle Bronze Age dirk, *c.* 1500–1300 BC, illus. C.B. Burgess and S. Gerloff, 'The Dirks and Rapiers of Great Britain and Ireland', *ibid.*, Abt. IV, Band 7, Munich 1981, p. 33, no. 208, pl. 29; both are from Dolwyddlan, Gwynedd, Wales.
3. The Marquess of Lincolnshire was descended from Lord Willoughby de Eresby through his mother Charlotte Augusta Annabella, younger daughter of Peter Robert (q.v.) and sister and co-heir of 22nd Baron Willoughby de Eresby (*Burke's Peerage and Baronetage*).
4. Another catalogue, which on internal evidence appears to have been drawn up by Baron Carrington, records that the 'pink dejeuné' [*sic*] consisting of a tray, two coffee cups and saucers, one sugar basin and a cream ewer, was a present from Lord Willoughby de Eresby in 1862. The author is grateful to Lady Cynthia Postan for assistance in tracing this piece.
5. The shape is fully discussed by Savill, 1988, II, pp. 501–2.
6. Christie's, 15 October 1990, Lot 23, two toilet pots, dated 1757, green ground, and Lot 19, square tray, dated 1758, green and dark blue ground.
7. Christie's, 15 October 1990, Lot 16, miniature tea-set, dated 1754, dark blue ground, and Lot 32, sugar bowl and cover, dated 1754, *bleu céleste* ground.
8. Musée de Boulogne, inv. L 437. Exh. *Nord Pas-de-Calais*, 1986–7, no. 92, and see Christie's, 2 October 1989, Lots 219, 220.
9. Savill, 1988, III, pp. 1125, 1122, 1125–6.

100 **Sugar Bowl and Cover (*pot à sucre Hébert*)**, 1760

H. *incl. cover:*	8.5 cm
Marks:	interlaced LL enclosing H painted in blue enamel (indistinct) incised *T*; oblong black label *ON LOAN FROM*, inscribed in ink *Lord W. d'Eresby May 14 18* (printed) *62*, printed collection label of Sir Bernard Eckstein numbered in ink *213*, and *85* in pencil on oblong label (bowl); 1862 loan exh. label as above, square label printed in black *50* and oblong label printed in black *SEVRES* (cover)
Reg. No.	1948,12–3,43

Soft-paste porcelain, thrown. Of undulating form, the domed cover surmounted by a flower knop. Decorated with a pink ground and in greens, browns, yellow, blue, red, grey and pale mauve with a scene of a figure on a bridge in a wooded landscape and a man near a house in a landscape on the bowl; on the cover with a man emerging from a house and with another scene of a man fishing, each in a wooded landscape. The painted scenes are enclosed by tooled gilt scrolls and flowers, outlined in dark red at their outer side only. The finial is painted pink to imitate a carnation, and the leaves underneath are coloured green. Gilt dentil rims, foot and leaves around finial gilt. The gilding around the foot is rubbed; part of the rim has been overpainted and regilded, probably concealing a small chip.

Provenance: See cat. 99

Bequeathed by Sir B. Eckstein, Bt., 1948

Literature: Unpublished

Exhibited: See cat. 99

Comparable Examples: None

For a discussion of the shape, see cat. 87 and Savill, 1988, II, pp. 575–6. This example is of the third, or smallest, size and matches cats 99 and 101 forming part of a *déjeuner Hébert* complete with tray.

Eriksen has suggested that the incised mark *T* may have been used by the thrower Pierre-Edmond Tristant *l'aîné*, employed at Sèvres between 1758 and 1787/89.[1] The mark is recorded on a green-ground sugar bowl of the second size dated 1758,[2] on a *rose marbré* example of the third size dated 1761[3] and on another of the third size with a *bleu nouveau* ground dated 1763.[4] For a further discussion of this mark, see Savill.[5]

The identity of the painter is unknown. Scenes like this are found on pieces marked with the caduceus[6] and also on several bearing the painted mark *y*. These are done in a very similar palette except that buildings and landscapes in the background are painted in pale blue.[7]

1. Eriksen, 1968, p. 337.
2. Savill, 1988, II, p. 593.
3. *Op. cit.*, p. 594.
4. Eriksen, 1968, no. 58, pp. 166–9.
5. Savill, 1988, III, pp. 1108–9.
6. See cat. 91.
7. Sotheby's, 2 October 1989, Lots 219, 220, *gobelet Bouillard et soucoupe, bleu lapis ground*, 1755; *pot à sucre Calabre*, same decoration; also Lot 218, a teapot with similar painted decoration, the painter's mark indecipherable.

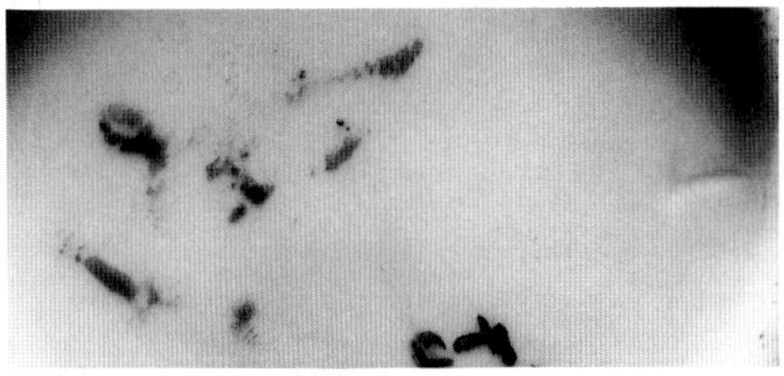

100 *marks*

101 Milk Jug (*pot à lait à trois pieds*), 1760

H. 8.1 cm
Marks: interlaced LL enclosing date-letter H painted in blue enamel on one foot; rectangular label inscribed in ink *Collection/Marquess of Lincolnshire*, printed label *SEVRES* inscribed *Date/1760*, square label printed in black *49*, printed collection label of Sir Bernard Eckstein inscribed *214*
Reg. No. 1948,12–3,44

Soft-paste porcelain, thrown; bulbous body with undulating rim on three branch feet and with crabstock handle. Stylised flower and leaf decoration in relief spring upwards from each foot and from the lower terminal of the handle, and downwards either side of its upper end. Decorated with a pink ground and with a painted scene of a diminutive male figure in a blue jacket, brown breeches and a brown hat casting a net into a lake in a wooded landscape. In the background are buildings. The palette is predominantly browns and greens, with mauve, yellow and pale blue. The scene is enclosed by a rococo gilt cartouche tooled with a zigag motif and outlined in dark pink at its outer edge and embellished with tooled flower sprays. At the upper edge is a gilt fan-like motif. Gilt dentil inner and outer rims, handle and feet partly gilt. Rubbed gilding on parts of relief decoration.

Provenance: See cat. 99

Bequeathed by Sir B. Eckstein, Bt., 1948

Literature: Unpublished

Exhibited: See cat. 99

Comparable Examples: See cat. 99

The form was created in 1752, and the first and second sizes were in existence by March 1753. The third size, of which this is an example, is first known in 1756. A plaster model is illustrated by Savill, who discusses the shape.[1]

The jug, which was part of a *déjeuner* (see cats. 99 and 100), was clearly painted by the artist responsible for the matching pieces. Although there are some black specks behind the handle and elsewhere, and the pink appears uneven, the gilding is of fine quality.

1. Savill, 1988, II, pp. 564–5.

102 Pair of Fan-Shaped Jardinières (*vases hollandais*), *c.* 1760

H. 18.6 cm
Marks: *y* incised on base of upper part; suspension hole on base (1948,12–3,14); *y* incised on base of upper part, three dots in underglaze-blue on side [?], *y* incised on base, suspension hole (1948,12–3,15)
Reg. No. 1948,12–3,14 and 15

Soft-paste porcelain, moulded. Each fan-shaped jardinière is made in two parts, one having ten circular holes near the base of the upper part, the other having eight. Painted in enamel colours with four panels of flowers within reserves outlined in gold above gilt flower sprays. On each side panel and around the upper edge is

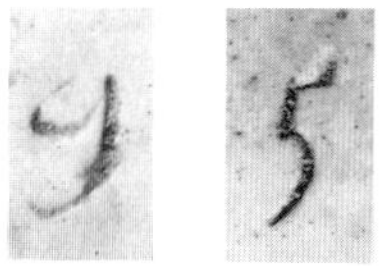

102 *marks*

102

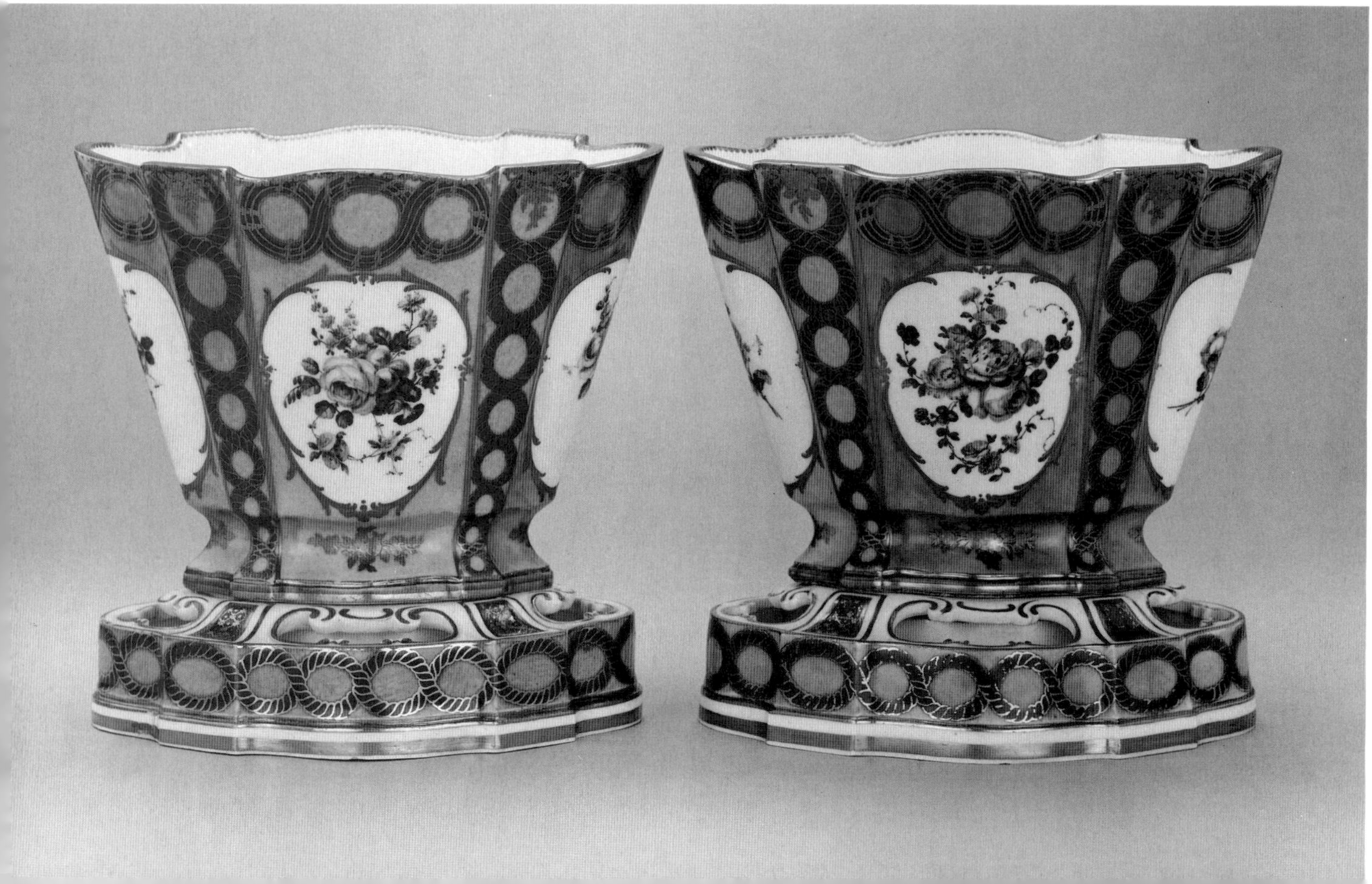

a rope motif in green on a ground of lighter green, also found around the base, which has panels of gilt diaper on a green ground. Gilt dentil rim interrupted by gilt flower sprays. Base of both restored, that of 1948,12–3,14 extensively restuck.

Provenance: Madame de Polès, Paris, sold Galerie Jean Charpentier, Paris, Succession de Madame de Polès, 17 November 1936, Lot 68, pl. XIV

Bequeathed by Sir B. Eckstein, Bt., 1948

Literature: Unpublished

Comparable Examples: None

The form was intended for the display of living plants, which took up water through the holes in the base of the upper part. Introduced in two sizes in December 1754 and in a third size in December 1758, it is fully discussed by Savill,[1] who illustrates both the plaster model and the drawing preserved at the factory.

These undated vases of the second size are decorated in a highly unusual colour scheme of two tones of green which has not been noted elsewhere. It was probably achieved by using two or more layers of green for the darker areas. The closest parallel can be found in a pair of the same colour painted all over, including the inner surface, at Dalmeny House, East Lothian, Scotland, bearing the date-letter E.[2]

A similar incised mark *ʃ* was noted by Eriksen on the base of a *seau à verre* at Waddesdon Manor, Buckinghamshire, and is commonly found, especially on this vase model.[3] It is just possible that the sign may be a 'G', the initial of a repairer, and that it may be repeated on the base of the upper part of 1948,12–3,15, perhaps for Antoine Gambier, a repairer from about 1752 to 1798.[4] It is likely to be the same mark as shown on a pair of pink-ground *vases hollandais* dated 1757 in the Wrightsman Collection at the Metropolitan Museum, New York.[5]

The orginal owner of these vases has not been traced.

1. Savill, 1988, I, pp. 69–72.
2. Rosalind Savill has kindly informed the author that these may belong with a third larger vase in a *garniture* purchased by the Dauphine in 1758.
3. Eriksen, 1968, p. 114, no. 39.
4. Dauterman, 1986, p. 82.
5. Dauterman, 1970, no. 84 A, B.

103 **Pair of Vases (*cuvettes Mahon*)**, 1761

See colour plate 14

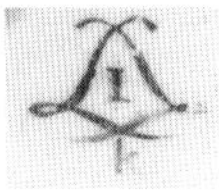

103 *mark*

H.	15.3 cm;
L.	23 cm
Marks:	interlaced LL enclosing date-letter I above the painter's mark *k* for Charles-Nicolas Dodin in blue enamel on one foot on each
Reg. No.	1948,12–3,16 and 17

Soft-paste porcelain, moulded. Each vase has a *bombé* front and back, elaborately moulded grooved 'handles' and four rococo scrolled feet. The ground is pink, painted with a 'cracked ice' pattern in blue with dark pink 'pebbles' and gilt dots. The decoration on the front consists of two Chinese ladies with a boy at a desk (right) and two Chinese boys and two ladies in a landscape painted in lime-green, dark green, emerald green, three shades of blue, pink, yellow, red, brown and black, within a gilt line tooled with a criss-cross pattern. On the reverse in a similar palette which also includes a dark purple and a pale brown are painted stylised oriental flowers on a white ground, enclosed by a gilt line tooled with a simpler pattern. Rims and edges of feet gilt. Perfect.

Provenance: Charles Stein Collection, sold Galerie Georges Petit, Paris, 8–10 June 1899, Lots 286–287[1]

Bequeathed by Sir B. Eckstein, Bt., 1948

Literature: King, 1951, p. 81

A. Lane, 'Sèvres and other porcelains in the collection of Viscount and Viscountess Gage at Firle Place, Sussex', *Connoisseur*, Vol. CXXXV, no. 545, April 1955, p. 162.

Savage, 1960, pl. 48 (front of 1948,12–3,16)

103

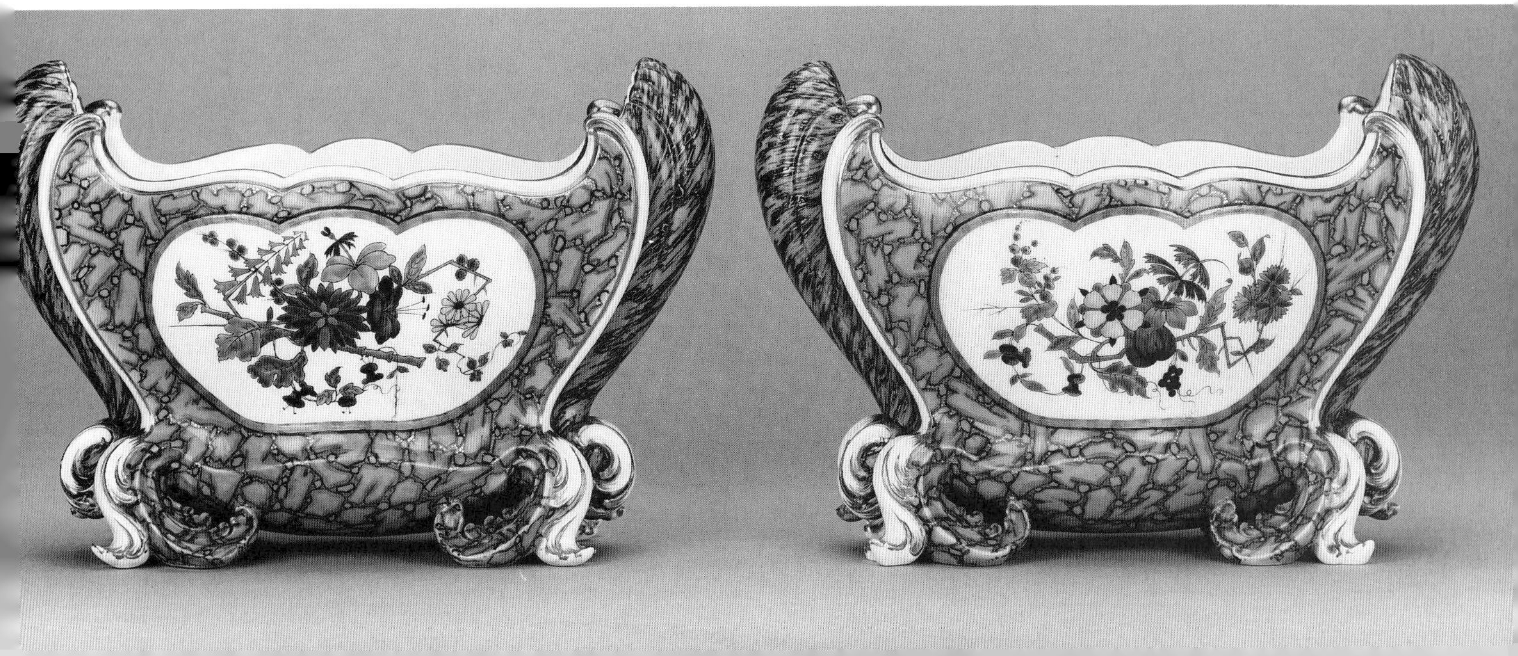

C.C. Dauterman, 'Chinoiserie motifs and Sèvres: some fresh evidence', *Apollo*, Vol. LXXXIV, no. 58, December 1966, p. 479

Eriksen, 1968, p. 88

R. Freyburger, 'Chinese Genre Painting at Sèvres', *American Ceramic Circle Bulletin*, Vol. I, 1970–71, fig. 5, p. 33

B. Shifman, 'Eighteenth-century Sèvres porcelain: two rare *Cuvettes Mahon*', *Apollo*, Vol. CXXI, no. 275, January 1985, figs 1, 2, p. 24

T. Préaud, 'Sèvres, la Chine et les "chinoiseries" au XVIIIe siècle', *The Journal of the Walters Art Gallery*, 47, 1989, note 21

Sassoon, 1991, p. 74

Comparable Examples: None of this form with corresponding decoration

The form, of which this is the third, or smallest size, was devised in 1756. It may have been designed by Jean-Claude Duplessis *père* (*c.* 1690–1774), *orfèvre du Roi* from 1758 and attached to the factory as artistic director perhaps from 1748.[2] Models and moulds are first mentioned in a factory inventory dated 1 January 1757, although those for the second and third size are not recorded until 1 January 1761, when the stock-list reveals that the plasters were made between 1 October 1759 and 31 December 1760.[3] A plaster model and a drawing for the second and third sizes are illustrated by Shifman.[4]

The painted decoration on these vases, which appears to be in a specially-devised palette, is of a type that seems to have been executed only by Charles-Nicolas Dodin[5] on pieces mostly dated 1761.[6] Its source has not been discovered, although both Canton enamels and Chinese export porcelain have been suggested as prototypes. The flowers on the reverse are also found on a porcelain clock-case decorated by Thévenet *père* and dated 1761,[7] and on porcelain plaques mounted on a pair of *meubles d'appui* stamped BVRB, said to have belonged to the finance minister, Machault d'Arnouville. The author has never seen these plaques, which may not be contemporary with the pieces of furniture, even though the factory records contain mention of plaques 'de M. Machault'.[8]

A whole series of pieces painted in this characteristic style were traced by Freyburger and a further group has been listed by Sassoon.[9]

Cuvettes Mahon (named in honour of the capture of Mahon on the island of Minorca in May 1756) are uncommon. Another example of the third size, also dated 1761, is in the Getty Museum.[10] Two other examples of this size, dated 1760 and 1776, have been published by Shifman.[11] Prices ranged from 480 *livres* for a pink example sold to the duc d'Orléans on 30 December 1758, 528 *livres* for a green-ground example painted with children sold to the dealer Poirier in the first quarter of 1760, down to 132 *livres* for an example described as 'mosaïque' sold in the second half of 1760 to the same buyer.[12] The Museum vases have not been traced in the sales records.

A vase of similar form and dimensions was made around 1820 by Flight, Barr & Barr, Worcester.[13]

1. Freyburger, 1970–1, p. 33.
2. For a biography of Duplessis *père*, see Savill, 1988, III, pp. 977–9.
3. Eriksen and Bellaigue, 1987, p. 316.
4. Shifman, 1985, figs. 2, 3.
5. For a biography of Dodin, see Savill, 1988, III, pp. 1029–32.
6. One of a pair of *vases à dauphins* at Firle Place, Sussex, painted in a similar fashion by Dodin, bears the date-letter K for 1764, see D. Gage, 'Masterpieces of Sèvres Porcelain', *Antique Collector*, Vol. 55, no. 6, June 1984, p. 92; the *pots-pourri fontaine ou à dauphins* in the Getty Museum (known as the 'Dudley Vases') date from 1760, see Sassoon, 1991, no. 11, pp. 57–63.
7. Sold Christie's, Monaco, 4 December 1988, Lot 49.
8. Savill, 1988, II, p. 838.
9. Sassoon, 1991, p. 58, no. 11, and p. 63 f.n. 12.
10. Sassoon, 1991, pp. 72–7, no. 14, painted by J.-L. Morin with scenes after Teniers the Younger.
11. Shifman, 1985, pls. V, VI.
12. *Ibid.*, no. 14, f.n. 27, 28, 29, 33.
13. Christie's East, New York City, 6 May 1986, Lot 134.

104 Covered Cup and Saucer (*gobelet couvert et soucoupe Bouillard*), 1761

See colour plate 13

H. *of cup incl. cover:*	9 cm
D. *of saucer:*	13.4 cm
Marks:	interlaced LL enclosing date-letter I for 1761 above painter's mark of a dot within a circle painted overglaze in blue; *pn* incised (saucer), *MC* incised (cup)
Reg. No.	1948,12–3,47

Soft-paste porcelain, straight-sided, indented at the base, ear-shaped handle, domed cover and flower knop; the saucer of curved shape. The painted decoration on the cup consists of a putto on clouds with a lyre emblematic of Music; on the saucer of a putto on clouds with an arrow emblematic of Love, painted overglaze in blue on a white ground enclosed by a tooled gilt line bounded by a pink line. The ground is pink (*roze*) with a trellis motif in blue interrupted by a dark pink star motif with a central gilt dot. Gilt dentil rim; edges and terminals of handle gilt. Flower knop. Cover, knop and saucer repaired.

Provenance: Collection label of Gilbert Lévy, 72 fbg. St. Honoré, Paris, on underside of cover and saucer

Bequeathed by Sir B. Eckstein, Bt., 1948

Literature: Savill, 1988, I, p. 84, p. 90 f.n.75

Comparable Examples: None

For a discussion of the shape, which exists in three sizes and is known between 1753 and about 1780, see Savill.[1] This example is of the first size, and was made for tea or coffee.

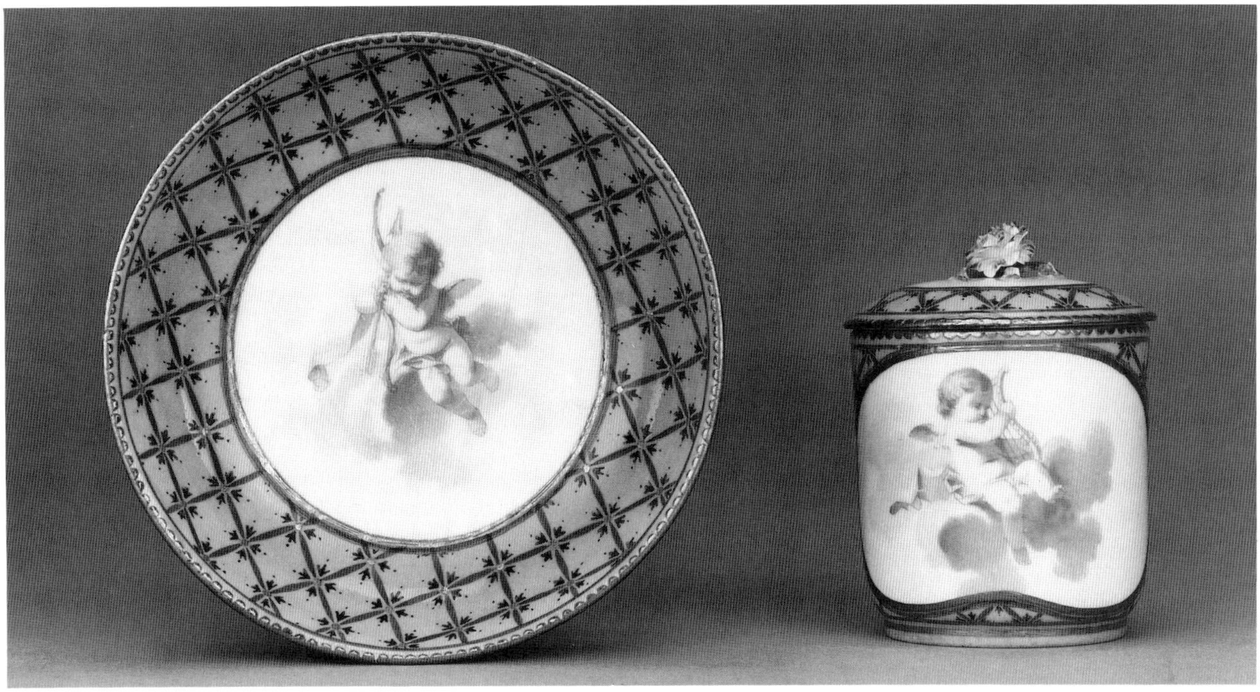

104

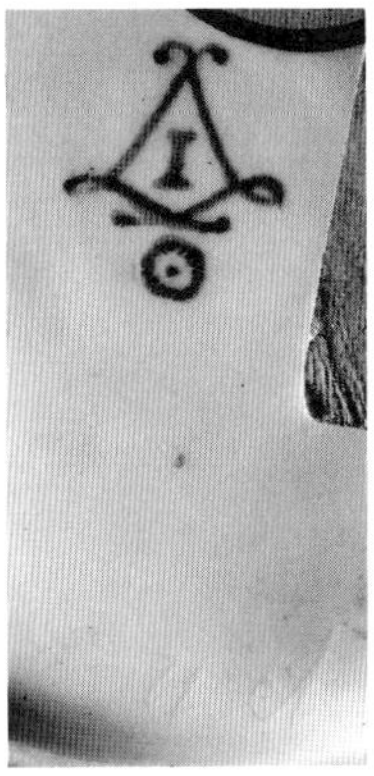

104 *marks (saucer)*

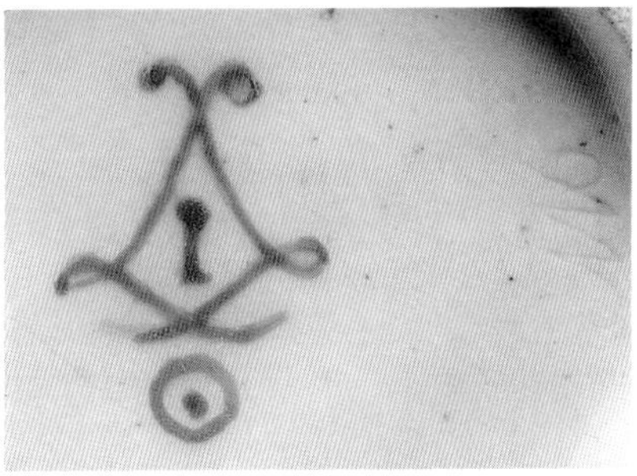

104 *marks (cup)*

The decorative scheme, like that of blue marbling on a pink ground, seems to have been extensively used during 1761 when it presumably enjoyed a vogue. The allegorical putti are loosely based on the work of François Boucher, although no direct source has yet been found. A putto representing Poetry with a lyre and other attributes painted on a *cuvette Verdun* in the Wallace Collection, London,[2] is after Boucher's drawing *La Poésie* engraved by G. Demarteau, but the putto on the Museum cup is somewhat different.

The painter using this mark has not yet been securely identified. The mark has been discussed by Savill,[3] who lists examples with children, cherubs, pastoral and harbour scenes and suggests that it may have been used by a painter named Rousseau. The examples with this mark in the Wallace Collection are a pair of *vases hollandais* of 1763 painted with seascapes, trophies and flowers and a *grand gobelet Saxe et soucoupe* of 1761 painted with children in landscapes after Boucher.[4]

The incised mark *MC* on the cup occurs on a wine-cooler from the du Barry service dated 1771 at Waddesdon Manor, Buckinghamshire.[5] It has been traced by Dauterman[6] on six other pieces and attributed to a repairer named Maublanc, who is not thought to have worked at the factory before 1769. However, Savill has suggested that it was the mark of François-Henry Marcon who was at Sèvres between 1754 and 1773, or Malacria.[7] Dauterman notes the incised mark *pn* on three items, two dated 1761, attributing the mark to Alexis Pépin, a repairer active between 1756 and 1782.[8] However, Savill[9] believes that Pépin used the initials *AP*, and that *pn* may stand for Jean-Christophe Pépin *aîné*, employed at the factory between 1758 and 1769, or possibly for F. Pilon *jeune*. Pilon joined the factory in 1758 or 1759 and was there until 1769. There is no reason why the saucer could not have been made some time before the painted decoration was completed.

1. Savill, 1988, II, pp. 543–4.
2. Savill, 1988, I, p. 58, 60.
3. Savill, 1988, I, pp. 84–5, p. 91, f.n. 76.
4. Savill, 1988, I, *ibid.*, II, pp. 558–60.
5. Eriksen, 1968, no. 92, p. 262.

6. Dauterman, 1986, pp. 220–1, and p. 110.
7. Savill, 1988, III, p. 1115.
8. Dauterman, 1986, pp. 228–9, and p. 118.
9. Savill, 1988, III, p. 1118 and pp. 1086–7.

105 Pair of Fan-Shaped Jardinières (*vases hollandais*), 1761

H. 17.5 cm, 17.7 cm

Marks: LL enclosing date-letter I for 1761 on unglazed bases, both of which have a circular suspension hole; interlaced LL above *X* for the painter Philippe Xhrouet faintly visible on the unglazed base of the upper part of 1948,12–2,26 and the remains of a mark in the same place on 1948,12–2–27; *cn* incised on bases of upper and lower parts

Reg. No. 1948,12–3,26 and 27

Soft-paste porcelain, in two parts. The upper fan-shaped panel is moulded with four curved panels alternating with a flat tapering panel standing slightly proud of the rest of the surface. At the base the vase is waisted before swelling out to form a ledge, below which is the oval base, pierced with eight small circular holes. This fits into the lower shaped stand, the upper surface of which is pierced with four holes of rococo outline. The projecting foot echoes the base of the upper part. The decoration consists of four panels of naturalistically painted flowers on a white ground below scrolls in blue enclosed by delicate gilt leaf trails. Between each panel is a flower in a medallion. On the front of each is a blue and gold mosaic pattern. The lower part is painted with flower sprays on a white ground. At the front the mosaic pattern is painted in two panels above which is a diaper-and-dot pattern painted in blue. Each panel on both the upper and lower parts is outlined in gold and blue, rim and foot gilt. Small chips to rims of upper parts.

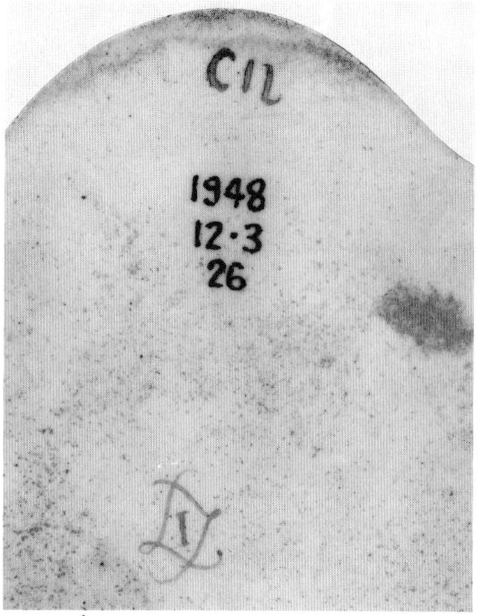

105 *marks*

Provenance: Formerly among the Foley heirlooms, exhibited by Mallett & Son, Exhibition of Art Treasures, 1928, Grafton Galleries, London, cat. 336 and exh. Christie's 1932, cat. 848. [Not identified in cat. of sale at Ruxley Lodge, Claygate, Surrey, by order of the Rt. Hon. Gerald Henry Baron Foley, 14 October 1919.]

Bequeathed by Sir B. Eckstein, Bt., 1948

Comparable Examples: Paris, Musée des arts décoratifs, inv.28 591, pair, presented by Miss Blake Gould, 1933

Christie's, 4 March 1908, Lot 85, C.J. Dickens Collection (oval medallion on front panels), sold to Hodgkins for 1050 guineas

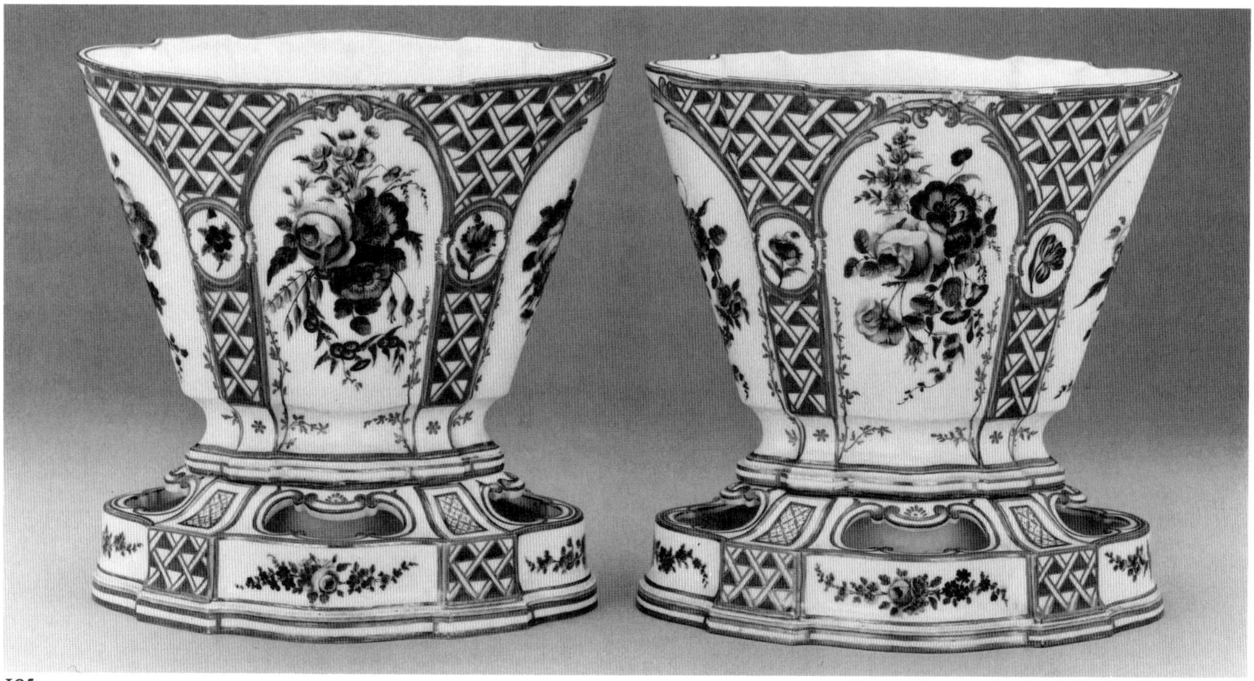

105

The form, introduced in three sizes, of which this is the third or smallest, is fully discussed by Savill (see p. 115). Production of the third size was apparently delayed until 1758, and examples cost between 60 *livres* when painted with flowers, and 240 *livres* with a blue or turquoise blue ground. This pair has not been traced in the sales records.[1]

This type of decoration, called 'mosaïque' in the factory records, is particularly associated with a service presented to the Elector Palatine in 1760 by Louis XV, and now in the Residenzmuseum, Munich.[2] The pattern was in production at the Vincennes factory[3] at least as early as 1752 and is based on a Meissen pattern known as *Altbrandenstein Muster* first introduced in 1738.

In the collection of the Viscountess Harcourt was a *garniture* of a *vase hollandais* and two *vases hollandais nouveaux* of 1760 in which the mosaic pattern was combined with decoration on the upper part of panels of birds in trees on a white ground, said to have been painted by Tandart.[4] A *cuvette Courteille* of 1761, formerly in the Christner Collection, is painted with a mosaic pattern and fruit in the panels.[5] No *vase hollandais nouveau* with decoration similar to the Museum vases has yet been traced. In view of the painted marks on the examples in the Musée des arts décoratifs, Paris, which include a tiny *p* enclosed by interlaced *LL*, dating them to 1768, it seems unlikely that the four *vases hollandais* belonged together.

The incised mark *cn*, which is often found on this shape, is thought to stand for the repairer Cejourné.[6] He is listed in the records for 1760 at a yearly salary of 540 *livres* with the note 'mérite augmentation' scored out and 'ne doit pas être diminué' substituted.[7] The painter Secroix (also written as Xhrouet)[8] was one of the most highly paid in 1760 at a yearly salary of 960 *livres*.[9]

1. Savill, 1988, I, pp. 69–72; the shape was apparently in production in a variant at Meissen in the second half of the nineteenth century on the evidence of a pair of vases sold at Sotheby's, 13 November 1990, Lot 96.
2. Verlet, 1954, pl. 41, p. 207.
3. Préaud and d'Albis, 1991, pp. 70–1, no. 7.
4. Christie's, 22 June 1927, Lot 30.
5. Christie's, 9 June 1979, Vol. III, Lot 212.
6. First suggested by Eriksen, 1968, p. 320. See Savill, 1988, III, p. 1096 for various examples and a discussion.
7. MNS, Archives de Sèvres, D1, *liasse* 1. The records for 1761 are missing.
8. See Savill, 1988, III, pp. 1077–8 for a biography.
9. MNS, Archives de Sèvres, D1, *liasse* 1.

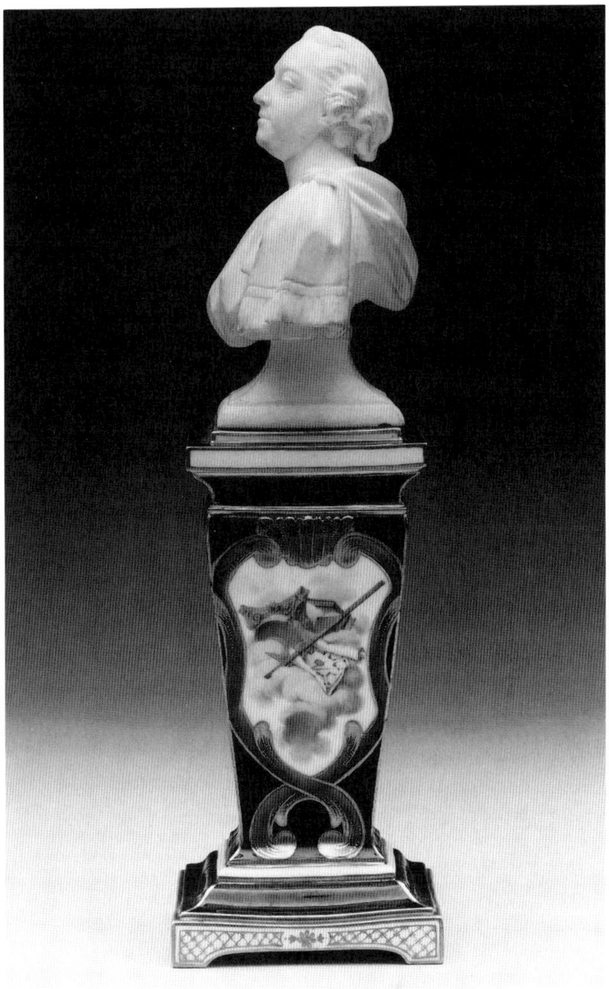

106

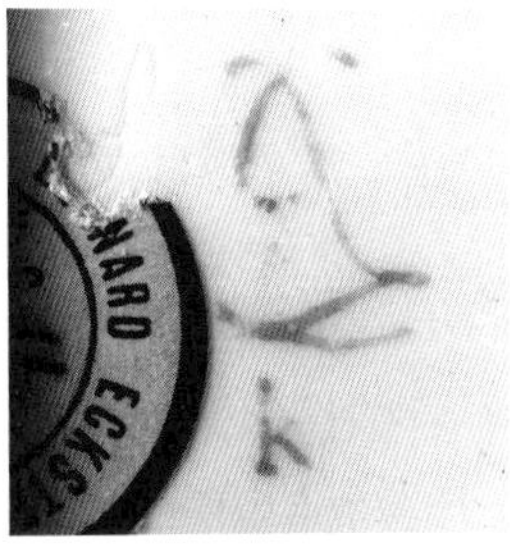

106 *mark*

106 **Biscuit Bust of Louis XV** (reigned 1715–74) **on Painted Pedestal (*piédestal en gaine*)**, probably 1761

See colour plate 16

H.	15.4 cm (pedestal); 11.3 cm (bust); 26.7 cm (total)
Marks:	LL enclosing partly effaced date-letter, perhaps I for 1761, above painter's mark *k* for Charles-Nicolas Dodin (1754–1803); incised *f* (all on base of pedestal)
Reg. No.	1948,12–3,5

Soft-paste porcelain bust of Louis XV, his head slightly turned to left, in classical dress with breastplate, on a square base itself

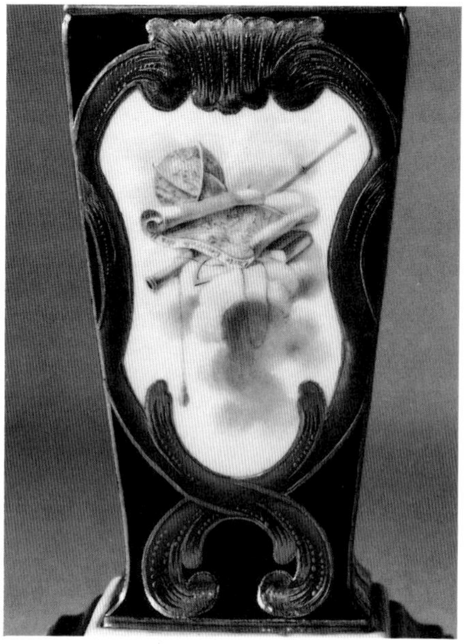

106 *detail of trophies of geography*

fixed to a pedestal of square section. The lower pedestal, although closed off at the base, is probably hollow (it is too light to be solid) and is mould-formed of tapering plaques of clay slightly curved at their upper and lower ends. It is painted with trophies of architecture, sculpture, geography and war and peace in enamel colours within a cartouche formed by green scrolls outlined in gold on a *bleu lapis* ground. The upper and lower parts of the pedestal are decorated in the same colour scheme and the base is decorated with a diaper and flower design.

Provenance: From the collection of the Hon. Mrs John Ashley, 1907, sold Christie's, 29 and 30 May 1907, Lot 93, to C. Wertheimer for £1000.

Charles J. Wertheimer, sold Christie's, 9 May, 1912, Lot 78, to Goldschmidt for £892–10s

Perhaps Walter von Pannwitz Collection, Germany, see O. von Falke, *Die Kunstsammlung von Pannwitz, Band II, Skulturen und Kunstgewerbe*, Munich, 1925, no. 438, 'Biskuitbuste Ludwigs XVI [*sic*], auf vierkantigen Sockel mit königsblauem Grund, vier weisse Felder mit grünem Rand darin gemalt Embleme der Kunst, Wissenschaft, Gerechtigkeit. H. 27 cm'[1]

Bequeathed by Sir B. Eckstein, Bt., 1948

Literature: Savage, 1960, pl. 75A

Charles, 1964, col. pl. H and p. 137, 144

Savill, 1988, I, p. 118 (illus.), p. 125

E. Munhall, 'A recent sculpture acquisition by the Frick Collection: A Sèvres biscuit bust of Louis XV on a gilded pedestal', *Metropolitan Museum Bulletin*, 27, 1992, pp. 123–5, figs. 5, 8, 10.

Comparable Examples: France, Paris, Dragesco-Cramoisan, February 1986, detached glazed hard-paste bust incised *hanon*

London, John Whitehead, exhibited International Ceramics Fair and Seminar, London, June 1990, bust, now in the Frick Collection, New York, with a pedestal sold at Sotheby's, New York, 16 October 1987, Lot 161 (see Munhall, 1992, p. 122, fig. 1)

Russia, St Petersburg, State Hermitage Museum, inv. N 26512, detached bust on circular base with flange, illus., N. Birioukova, *Figurines et groupes en porcelaine des manufactures françaises du XVIII Siècle*, Leningrad, 1962, no. 46, p. 294

USA, Boston, Museum of Fine Arts inv. 1964/53, bust on *bleu lapis* pedestal *en gaine*, with gilt interlaced LL. The companion bust of Marie Leszczynska 1964/54 is the same height, 26.2 cm. See Munger, *et al*, 1992, p.123, fig. 3

The bust has recently been discussed by Edgar Munhall (see above). Nina Birioukova tentatively dated the example in the Hermitage Museum to 1770. However, the subject appears younger than 60, and is more probably around 45–50 years of age. The busts are first mentioned in the records of biscuit kiln firings in September 1759[2] and may have been introduced when the King became the factory's sole proprietor.[3]

The iconography of this bust is the subject of some discussion. It has traditionally been associated with the sculptor Jean-Baptiste Lemoyne (1704–78). Lemoyne exhibited busts of the monarch in the *Salons* of 1745, 1757 and 1763. According to Olga Raggio,[4] Lemoyne worked almost continuously on such busts between 1732 and 1774, and six are mentioned in the inventory of the royal *châteaux*, the *Direction des Bâtiments*; of these only one was known in 1927. The style of the Sèvres bust, and in particular the deeply-cut eyes, has much in common with the marble bust signed by Lemoyne and dated 1757, made for Madame de Pompadour.[5] However, records of any work by Lemoyne for the royal porcelain factory are sketchy in the extreme: in 1768 he was given a bust of Voltaire worth 60 *livres* as a present 'Pour avoir donné un modèle'.[6] There is no corroboration of his authorship of the porcelain bust of Louis XV. Edgar Munhall has pointed out that the lost equestrian monument for the Place Royale, Bordeaux, inaugurated in 1743, is close to the Sèvres bust, as it shows the monarch in a cuirass *à la romaine*. He has suggested that Dupuis' engraving after Cochin's drawing of this sculpture, exhibited at the *Salon* of 1759 may have been used at Sèvres by the unknown sculptor responsible for devising this model, especially since the sitter is of the right age. Also, he has published for the first time a terracotta which corresponds in scale to the Sèvres biscuit bust.

The existence of another example on a similar pedestal (see above) appears to confirm that the British Museum bust has always been associated with its pedestal, even though no archival evidence has been found to show that they were sold together.

The factory sales registers record various busts of the King in several sizes, selling from 24 *livres*, first documented in 1760,[7] to 288 *livres* sold to Madame de Pompadour on 24 December 1761.[8]

The waisted pedestal (*en gaine*) on which the bust

sits is found in one size only and, although not intended as such, it was also used as a bulb vase. Examples are in the Wallace Collection, London,[9] and the Kress Collection at the Metropolitan Museum, New York.[10] An undated *bleu lapis* example decorated with flowers on a white ground supports a *bleu lapis* vase in the neo-classical style draped with a gilt laurel wreath. The vase is doubtless of later date than the pedestal.[11]

It is just possible that the incised mark *f* on the pedestal may have been used by the repairer Fresne who is listed in the records of personnel for 1758 at a monthly salary of 39 *livres*.[12]

The recent appearance of a glazed white hard-paste porcelain bust without pedestal, now in a private collection in France, which corresponds in dimensions and general appearance but which is incised *hanon* underneath poses numerous questions. The inscription probably stands for Paul Antoine Hannong (1700–60) who made hard-paste porcelain in Strasbourg from 1751–4 or perhaps for his son, Pierre-Antoine (1739–*c*.1794). In 1754 Hannong senior transported his factory to Frankenthal since the privileges granted to the Vincennes factory prevented the production of decorated and gilded porcelain anywhere else on French soil. Hannong junior discussed with the Sèvres factory the secrets of hard-paste porcelain manufacture in 1760[13] but whether he obtained a mould or model from the factory for this bust remains a matter of conjecture. The dimensions of the glazed bust corresponds quite closely as it measures 11 cm in height, only slightly smaller than the Museum bust.

Yet more puzzling is a tin-glazed earthenware example on a similar waisted pedestal,[14] decorated in grey for the hair and the chest armour, pink for the drapery, yellow for the shoulder clasp, fringe on left-hand sleeve and upper edge of armour and brown for the pedestal. This bust measures 8 cm in height, the pedestal being 2.7 cm high. It and its companion bust of Marie Leszczynska are both unmarked and are attributed to the Sceaux factory. In view of the size of the faïence example, it was almost certainly moulded from the porcelain version.

The iconography of Louis XV in both pottery and porcelain is complex and awaits detailed study. A Mennecy porcelain bust shows the King looking about the same age as the small Sèvres bust. It has been linked to a marble by J.-F.-J. Saly (1717–76) erected at Valenciennes in 1775.[15] A bust attributed to the Tournai factory shows the King in armour, his head turned to the left; this is said to be based on a Lemoyne prototype.[16] Jacques Chambrette's factory at Lunéville issued a slightly different bust in cream-coloured earthenware (*faïence fine*), its elaborate socle reminiscent of the Mennecy and Chantilly examples.[17]

1. The author is indebted to the late David Cohen for this reference.
2. Biscuit kiln records, 24 September 1759, f. 135/7, '14 bustes du Roy et de la Reyne', quoted Savill 1988, I, p. 125, n.3.
3. Savill, 1988, I, p. 117.
4. O. Raggio, 'Two great portraits by Lemoyne and Pigalle', *Metropolitan Museum Bulletin*, February 1967, pp. 219–29.
5. Now in the Metropolitan Museum, New York, see Raggio, *op. cit.*, figs 1, 3, 4. For a Chantilly porcelain bust dated 1745 attributed to Lemoyne, see J.H. Munger, 'A Chantilly bust of Louis XV in the Museum of Fine Arts, Boston', *International Ceramics Fair and Seminar, London, Handbook*, June 1988, pp. 29–34, and Munger *et al*, 1992, no. 172.
6. MNS, Archives de Sèvres, Vy 4, f. 173; his work on a larger bust of the King which was sold for 240 *livres* is documented in the sales records, Vy 3, f. 46.
7. MNS, Archives de Sèvres, Vy 3, f. 9, '*13 Bustes de Roys et Reynes id.*' (biscuit).
8. *Loc. cit.*, f. 85; Madame de Pompadour's *inventaire après décès* of 1764 lists under 'Porcelaines rapportées de Saint-Ouen', 'Un grand buste du Roy en biscuit, un pied de bois *doré* et cage de verre; prisé [*sic*] *soixante* livres', see Cordey, 1939, p. 96, No. 1316.
9. Savill, 1988, I, pp. 117–26.
10. Dauterman, 1964, nos. 39a–b, figs. 152–3, two with pink and green grounds painted with flowers, one dated 1759.
11. E. Garnier, *The Soft Porcelain of Sèvres*, London, 1892, (reprinted 1988), pl. XLIV, Baron Alphonse de Rothschild Collection.
12. MNS, Archives de Sèvres, D1, *liasse* 1.
13. See R. de Plinval de Guillebon, 'Les fourberies de Pierre Antoine Hannong à Sèvres, Vincennes, Vaux et Paris,' *Bulletin de la Société de l'histoire de Paris et de l'Ile de France*, 113/114e année, 1986–7, pp. 181–2.
14. France, Sceaux, Musée de l'Ile de France, 88–17–2. The author is grateful to Madame M. Aries for supplying information about this piece.
15. J. Paul Getty Museum, Malibu, California, inv. 84DE46, see *J. Paul Getty Museum Journal*, Vol. 13, 1985, p. 179; another Mennecy example is in the Wadsworth Atheneum, Hartford, Conn., USA, inv. 1917–1509, illus. Roth (ed.), 1987, p. 34, fig. 9. An unglazed Mennecy biscuit bust of Louis XV on a biscuit pedestal in the Musée des arts décoratifs, Paris, inv. 28621, shows the King looking rather younger than in the small Sèvres bust.
16. Smithsonian Institution, Washington, D.C., inv. 66.196, see J.J. Miller II, 'A Tournay Portrait Bust', *The Smithsonian Journal of History*, Vol. 2, no. 1, Spring 1967, pp. 67–9; the author notes other examples in the Mariemont Museum, Belgium, and Dunkirk Museum, France.
17. Exh. Nancy and Atlanta, 1990, no. 132, p. 182.

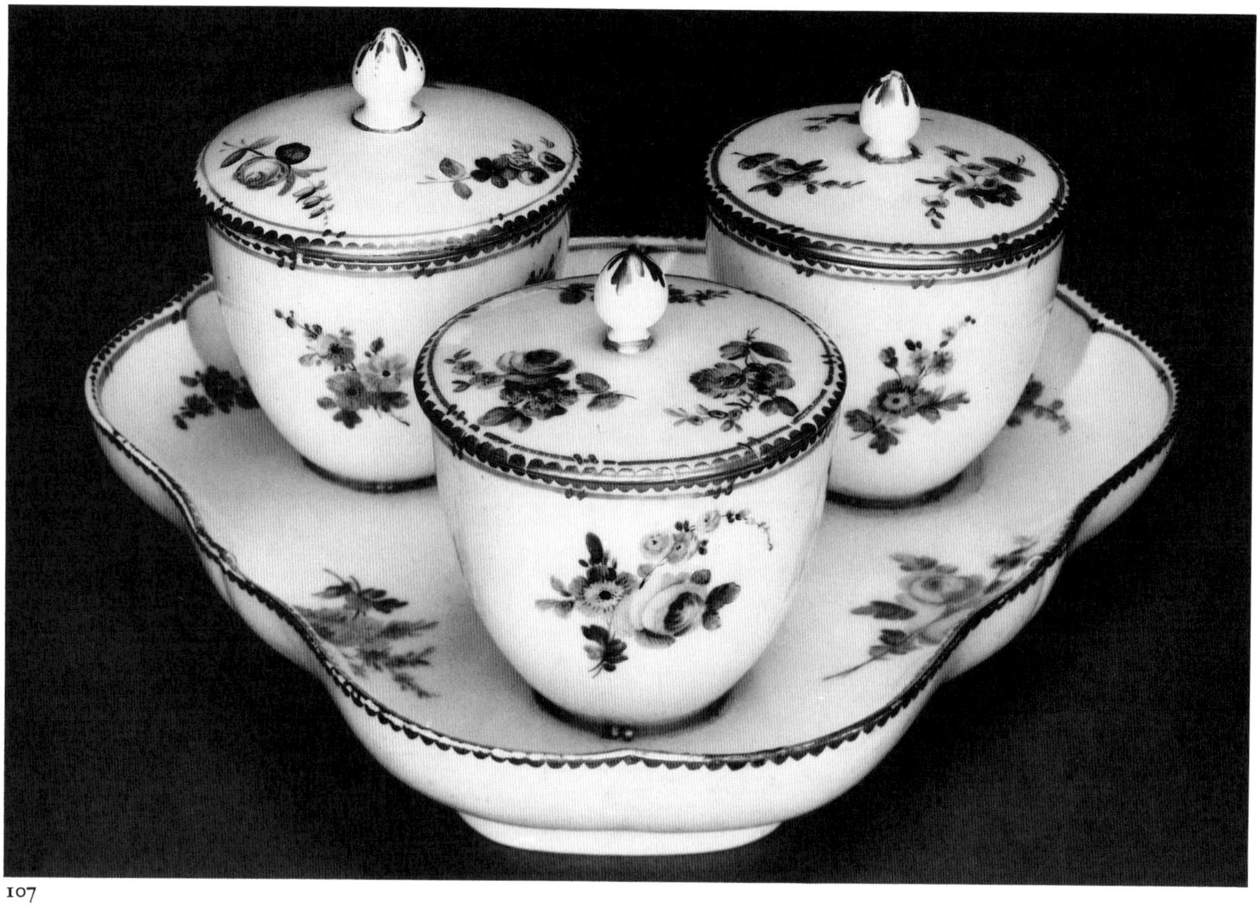

107

107 Tray with Three Jam Pots Attached (*plateau à trois pots de confiture*), 1761

Max. L.	19.8 cm
H. *excl. covers:*	6.6 cm
Marks:	interlaced LL above *L* enclosing date-letter I for 1761; *gp* incised
Reg. No.	OA 10721

Soft-paste porcelain, moulded. The tray is triangular with a lobed rim, and the pots, their flat covers surmounted by a pine-cone finial (the slightly domed one has a more bulbous finial and is a later replacement), are placed at each angle. Painted in pink, yellow, green, purple, orange and dark brown with scattered flower sprays. Gilt dentil rims (on the lids this decoration is on the outer edge only) next to a blue line interrupted by two gilt dashes. Matching decoration is found around the knop of one cover only. Later cover repaired, rim of other covers repaired. Rim of tray repaired in two places, foot rim chipped.

Provenance: Unknown

Literature: Unpublished

Comparable Examples: Sotheby's, Mentmore, III, Porcelain, 24 May 1977, Lot 2020, two with *feuille de choux* borders and scattered flower sprays

This tray with its three pots intended for jam is a model which appeared at Sèvres around 1760. The triangular tray without the pots was in production at Vincennes.[1] It was probably made in one size only, despite slight discrepancies in the measurements of recorded examples.

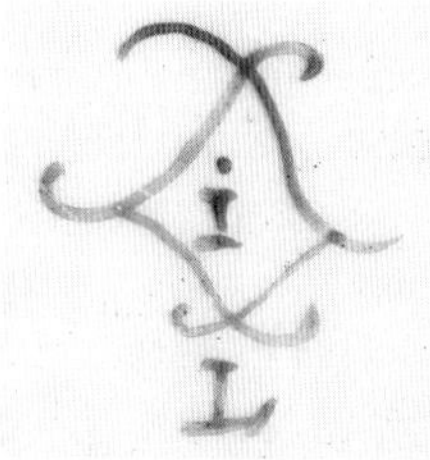

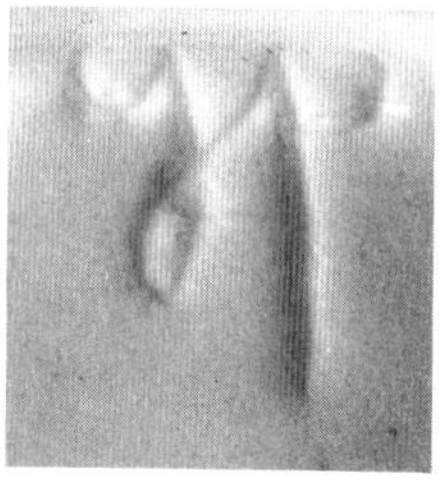

107 *marks*

Although the tray was made at the Sèvres factory, only one cover appears to be original. The pots are not all of the same size. Discoloration on the back of the tray is a possible indication that the indifferent flower decoration was carried out during the nineteenth century.

The incised mark *gp* has been noted by Savill[2] on soft-paste pieces dating between 1757–*c*.90. Of the several suggestions made as to which repairer used the mark, that of Gratien Poulain (active 1758–77) appears convincing.

A rather similar form of tray with three attached jam pots, painted with polychrome and gilt flowers, marked with the *A* of the rue Thiroux, Paris, factory, is in the Musée national de Céramique, Sèvres.[3]

1. Brunet and Préaud, 1978, p. 163, no. 116 and p. 141, no. 55. Moulds for the *plateau triangle* are listed in the factory inventory of October 1752.
2. Savill, 1988, III, p. 1106.
3. R. de Plinval de Guillebon, 'Premières porcelaines dures de Paris, *Antologia di Belle Arti*, nos. 29–30, 1986, p. 34, fig. 9 (the covers do not match).

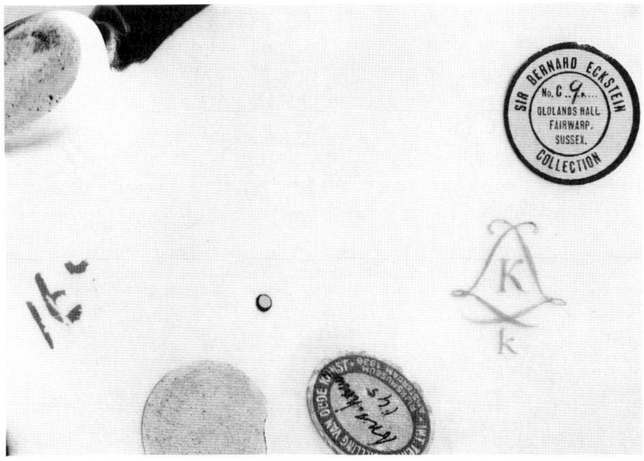

108 *marks*

108 Flower Vase (*cuvette à fleurs 'Courteille'*), 1763

See colour plate 17

L. 29.8 cm
H. 18.7 cm
Marks: interlaced LL enclosing date-letter K, above painter's mark *k* for Charles-Nicolas Dodin (1754–1803) painted in blue enamel; incised *IP* near foot; *16?5* painted in red; faded printed Paris customs label; printed exhibition label of Tentoonstelling van Oude Kunst, Rijksmuseum, Amsterdam, 1936 inscribed in ink *?Ansham 14S*; printed collection label *Sir Bernard Eckstein, Oldlands Hall, Fairwarp, Sussex No. C9*
Reg. No. 1948,12–3,4

Soft-paste porcelain, moulded, of *bombé* form, the two rococo handles in the form of acanthus leaves with a fish-scale moulding in the centre; four scroll feet. The decoration on the front consists of a scene painted in enamel colours of two boys with a dog and a peepshow in a wooded landscape within a tooled gilt reserve on a green ground. In the panels on either side is a flower garland on a blue ribbon suspended from a rosette. On the reverse are painted the arms of Choiseul: *argent a cross or between eighteen billets, five in the upper quarters and four in the lower; ensigned with a ducal coronet*, surrounded by a flower garland. The cartouche containing the armorial is suspended by a mauve ribbon from a rosette and

108

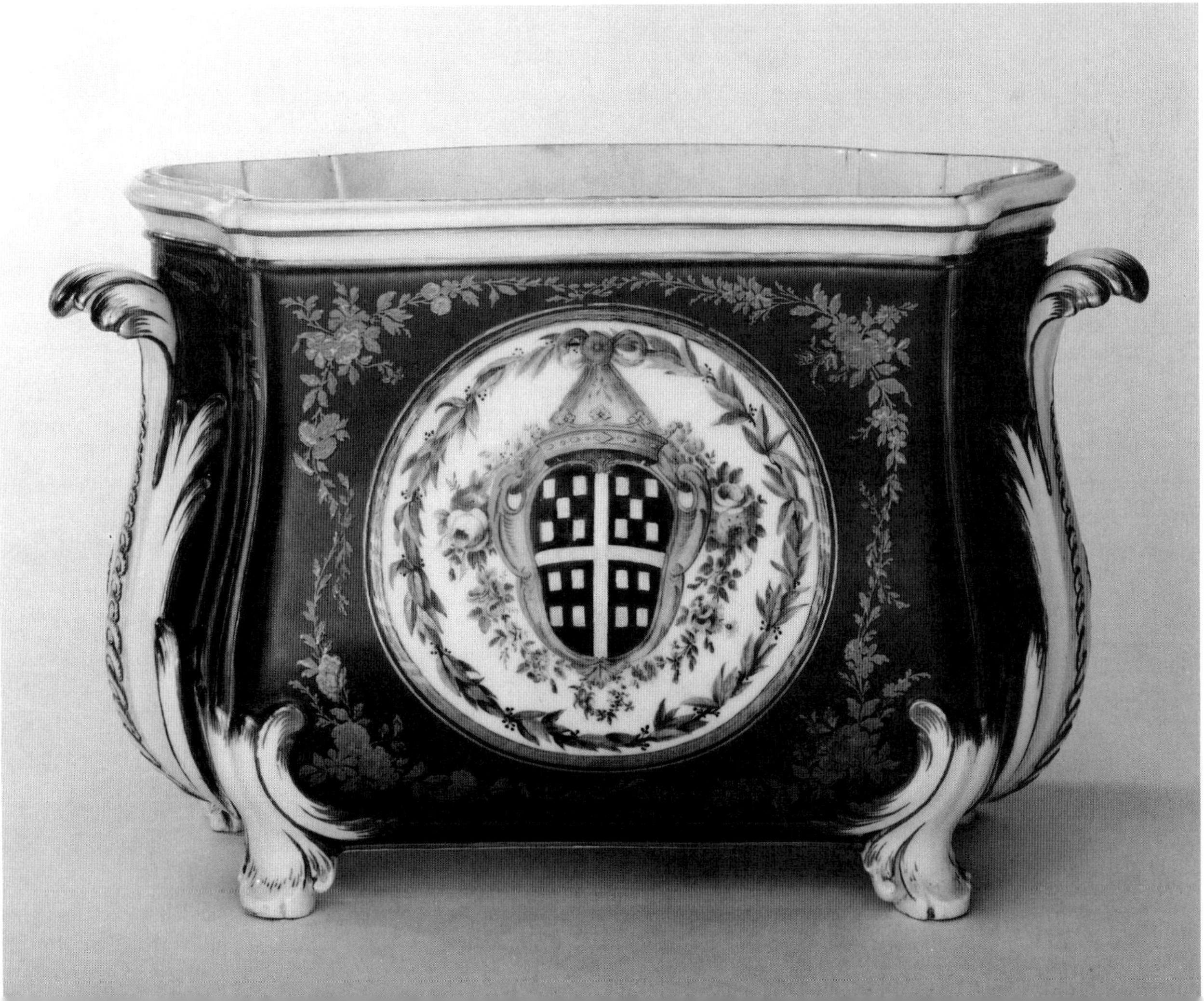

the whole encircled by a laurel leaf and berry wreath, all on a white ground, within two gilt circles. The inner, wider, one is tooled. An irregularly arranged tooled gilt flower trail decorates the green ground on the reverse; leaf, husk, scroll and geometric motifs in gold are found on the front and sides. Gilt lines emphasise the shape of the *cuvette*, the rim is gilt, and the handles and feet partly gilt. There are two small circular holes for drainage in the base (see below). Some rubbing to gilding.

Provenance: Perhaps from the State Hermitage Museum, St Petersburg, Russia, before 1936

Bequeathed by Sir B. Eckstein, Bt., 1948

Literature: King, 1951, p. 81

Savill, 1988, I, p. 45, 52, f.n.2 g

Exhibited: Tentoonstelling van Oude Kunst uit het bezit van den Internationalen Handel, Rijksmuseum, Amsterdam (Exhibition of Ancient Art belonging to the International Trade), 1936, cat. no. 502, p. 112, property of the shop called 'Amsterdam', 'provenant de l'Ermitage'

Comparable Examples: None

The *cuvette Courteille*, probably designed by Jean-Claude Duplessis *père* (employed 1745/8–74),[1] first produced in this (the largest) size in 1753, takes its name from the Intendant des Finances, Jacques Dominique de Barberi, Marquis de Courteille (1696–1767), the King's representative in the factory's finance and administration from 1751–67.[2] The second and third sizes were not devised until July 1759.[3] The presence of three or four minor firecracks attests to the difficulty of firing this piece. The holes in the base appear to have been drilled after the piece was glazed and fired. Surviving examples in the Wallace Collection, London, are fitted with porcelain bulb holders but these may not be original.[4]

The same unidentified incised mark *IP* appears on a vase of the same shape of the second size dated 1772 in the Wallace Collection.[5]

The scene on this example is copied faithfully as to the colours but in reverse from a painting by François-Herbert Drouais (1727–75) entitled *The Comte and Chevalier de Choiseul as Savoyards* signed and dated 1758, now in the Frick Collection, New York.[6] This painting, exhibited in the *Salon* of 1759, was engraved by La Live de Jully, and was initially in the possession of the Choiseul family, although the Frick Collection catalogue does not specify whether it belonged to the duc de Choiseul, Louis XV's foreign minister, or to another member of the family. The two boys depicted are (standing): Marie-Gabriel-Florent-Auguste, comte de Choiseul-Beaupré later Choiseul-Gouffier (1752–1817) and his brother Michel-Felix-Victor, chevalier and later comte de Choiseul-Daillecourt (1754–1815).[7]

The issue of the presumed Russian provenance of this piece, backed up by the half-effaced red number painted on the base which corresponds to inventory numbers on pieces still in the Hermitage Museum and which was the inventory mark of the Chief Chamberlain's Section at the Winter Palace, has not been satisfactorily explained. The piece has not been traced in the records of the State Hermitage Museum,[8] nor has it been noted in any of the catalogues of the sales of pieces from the Hermitage Museum held in Berlin in the late 1920s and early 1930s. However, the elder of the two boys, who took the title of Choiseul-Gouffier on his marriage to Adélaïde de Gouffier d'Ailly in 1777, fled to Russia in 1793. He spent some nine years there before returning to France in 1802. He was appointed by Tsar Paul I (1754–1801) as director of the Russian Academy of Arts, as well as of all the Imperial libraries.[9] It is just possible that it was through him that the *cuvette* came to be in Russia. Choiseul-Gouffier in fact left Russia somewhat suddenly when he fell out of the succeeding Tsar's[10] favour, according to his daughter-in-law. He had a distinguished career as a diplomat and archaeologist. His portrait was painted by Louis-Léopold Boilly (1761–1845) and engraved by Claude-Marie-François Dien (1787–1865).[11] Classical antiquities from his collection have found their way not only into the Louvre Museum but also into the British Museum.[12]

The iconography of the painting on this *cuvette* has been discussed by Edgar Munhall[13] who has identified the equipment as a hurdy-gurdy (on the back of the standing figure), a *boîte à curiosité* or peepshow (to the lens of which the seated figure is pointing), and a box for a marmot or the equipment of a *décrotteur* beneath the seated figure. As Munhall remarks,[14] 'their dog recalls the perennially faithful companion of wandering urchins, and the rough stony background . . . suggests the rigours of a wanderer's life. However, the boys' delicate features and pale complexions contrast with a real Savoyard's 'visage barbouillé de suie', and while the pattern of their clothing is correct, the materials are silk velvets'.

Few pieces of Sèvres porcelain painted with armorials are known (see cats 97 and 181), nor are many porcelains painted as accurately after surviving paintings as this one. Although the scene is in reverse from the painting, it is difficult to imagine that Dodin could have worked entirely from an engraving, but must have seen the painting to achieve such a remarkably close match of the colours.

It has not been possible to discover who was the original owner of the *cuvette*, as it remains unidentified in the factory sales records. The boys' father having died ten years before the piece was made, it is uncertain which member of the extensive Choiseul family might have purchased the piece, which may well have been a special order. As the painters' records for this period have not survived, the *cuvette* cannot be traced by this route.

1. For a biography of Duplessis *père*, see Savill, 1988, III, pp. 977–9.
2. A biography of Courteille is given by Savill, 1988, III, pp. 974–5. Other forms named after him are the *plateau Courteille*, the *compotier Courteille* and the *déjeuner Courteille*.
3. Brunet and Préaud, 1978, no. 111.
4. The shape is fully discussed by Savill, 1988, I, pp. 42–7. Two drawings, one captioned 'caisse a fleurs/fait en juillet 1759 2ᵉᵐᵉ et 3ᵉᵐᵉ grandeur' are reproduced by Savill, 1988, I, p. 43. The plaster is illustrated, *op. cit.*, p. 42.
5. Savill, 1988, I, p. 52. The mark is discussed by the same author, III, p. 1110, and was apparently used by a workman employed between 1757 and 1778.
6. *The Frick Collection, An Illustrated Catalogue, Volume II, Paintings, French, Italian and Spanish*, New York, 1968, pp. 87–90.
7. The boys were the sons of Marie-Gabriel-Florent-Auguste de Choiseul called the comte de Choiseul-Beaupré (1728–53) of the Daillecourt branch of the Choiseul family, and his wife Marie-Françoise Lallemont de Betz, who were married on 10 February 1747.
8. The author is grateful to Madame N. Kasakevich for attempting to find the *cuvette* in the records of the State Hermitage Museum.
9. The author is grateful to Dr R. d'O. Butler for his comments on Choiseul-Gouffier's career. Monsieur J.-D. Augarde kindly provided the information through the present duc de Praslin that a copy of the sale catalogue of the comte de Choiseul-Gouffier at the *hôtel* Marboeuf, Paris, 20 July (or perhaps 17 August as the printed date has been altered in ink) 1818 is kept in the Victoria and Albert Museum Library, London. Choiseul-Gouffier was a noted collector of Egyptian, Greek (he visited Greece in 1776), Roman and Celtic antiquities and, although the catalogue contains only part of his collection, it includes no porcelain except for two large Chinese dishes. Details of his life and work are given in *Nouvelle Biographie Générale*, published by Firmin Didot, Paris, 1856, Vol. x, and Baron Bon Joseph Dacier, 'Notice sur la vie et les ouvrages de M. le comte de Choiseul-Gouffier' in *Mémoire de l'Académie des inscriptions et belles-lettres*, 23 July 1819, published Paris, 1819, and see Duc de Praslin, *Les Choiseul et l'histoire*, Paris, 1988, pp. 153–60. In 1798 Choiseul-Gouffier sent a note to Jacques Necker in which he claimed that he was familiar with porcelain-making, offered to reform the royal factory so that it would no longer need subsidy and act as director without salary, Archives nationales, F12, 1493, quoted Chavagnac and Grollier, 1906, p. 194.
10. Comtesse de Choiseul-Gouffier, *née* Comtesse de Tiesenhausen, *Mémoires historiques sur l'Empereur Alexandre et la Cour de Russie*, Paris, 1829, p. 7.
11. The portrait was exhibited in 'Der Archäologe-Graphische Bildnisse aus dem Portratarchiv Diepenbroick', Westfälisches Landesmuseum Kestner-Museum, Hannover, Antikenmuseum, Berlin, December 1983–August 1984, no. 131.
12. An account concerning a portion of his collection of antiquities now in the Louvre is given by E. Esperandieu, 'Renseignements inédits sur la collection du comte de Choiseul-Gouffier', in *Mémoires de la société nationale des antiquaires de France*, Tome 158, sixième série, Tome VII, 1899, pp. 161–211. A list of his antiquities in the Marseilles museum is appended. A.H. Smith in *A Catalogue of Sculpture in the Department of Greek and Roman Antiquities, British Museum*, Vol. I, London, 1892, no. 309, fig. 9, describes one of the Metopes of the Parthenon which belonged to Choiseul-Gouffier before it came into the possession of Lord Elgin, as well as cat. 209, the earlier so-called 'Choiseul-Gouffier Apollo'.
13. E. Munhall, 'Savoyards in French Eighteenth-Century Art', *Apollo*, Vol. LXXXVII, no. 72, February, 1968, pp. 86–94.
14. *Ibid.*, p. 92.

109 **Pair of Flower Vases (*cuvettes à fleurs à tombeau*)**, 1763

See colour plate 15

Max L. 19.6 cm
H. 14.5 cm
Marks: interlaced LL enclosing date-letter K surmounted by the painter's mark *M* for J.-L. Morin painted in blue enamel, and a branch for the painter Jean-René Dubois(?) near one foot in blue enamel on 1948,12–3,2; Eckstein Collection label numbered *8* on both, paper label faintly inscribed in ink *151*
Reg. No. 1948,12–3,2 and 3

Soft-paste porcelain, moulded in the form of a sarcophagus, the four sides slightly *bombé*, undulating rim and a scroll between each of the four feet, those at front and back being more elaborate. Against the green ground are scenes on the front of a peasant couple drinking outdoors within an oval tooled gilt reserve. On the reverse and on each side is a shaped reserve containing a flower and fruit spray painted in enamel colours on a white ground within a tooled gilt line and another narrower gilt line. The front of each *cuvette* is embellished with gilt motifs including scrolls and flowers, the moulding is picked out in gold, and the rims, feet and scrolls on the base are partly gilt. Slight loss of gilding on both. Base of 1948,12–3,2 repaired, firecrack to base of 1948,12–3,3.

Provenance: Bequeathed by Sir B. Eckstein, Bt., 1948

Literature: Savill, 1988, I, p. 33, 40, f.n. 2 k

Comparable Examples: None of this shape and size with comparable painted decoration

The form has been fully discussed by Savill,[1] who illustrates a drawing kept at the factory inscribed *cuvette a fleurs fait en juillet 1759 2ᵉᵐᵉ et 3ᵉᵐᵉ grandeur* showing the vase in three sizes and a section in two sizes. The plaster model is also illustrated. The first size measures 22.2–23.5 cm in height, the second 17.8–19 cm and the third 14.2–14.6 cm. This example is therefore of the third size.

Surviving examples show that the vase was used for porcelain flowers mounted on metal stems; it was probably also used for cut flowers.

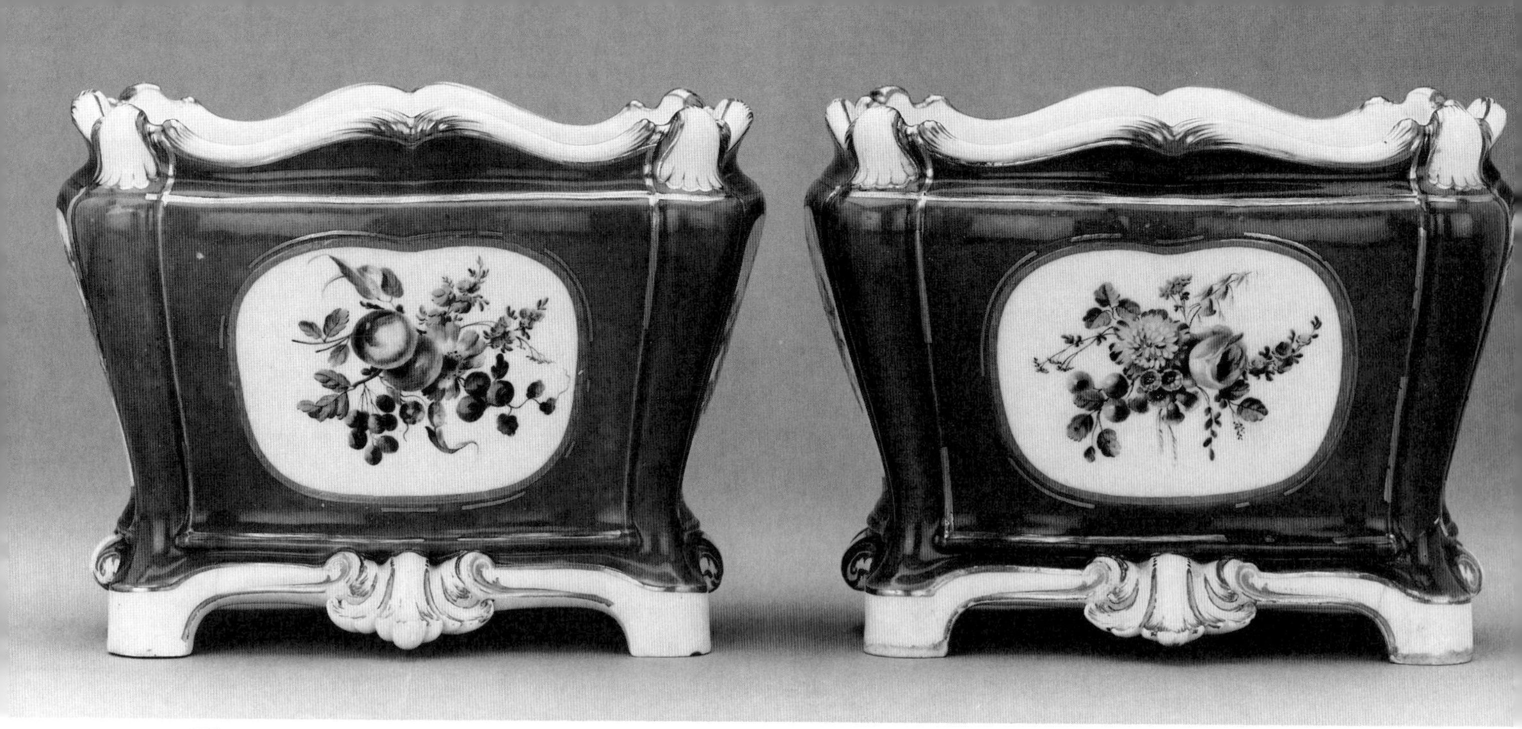

109

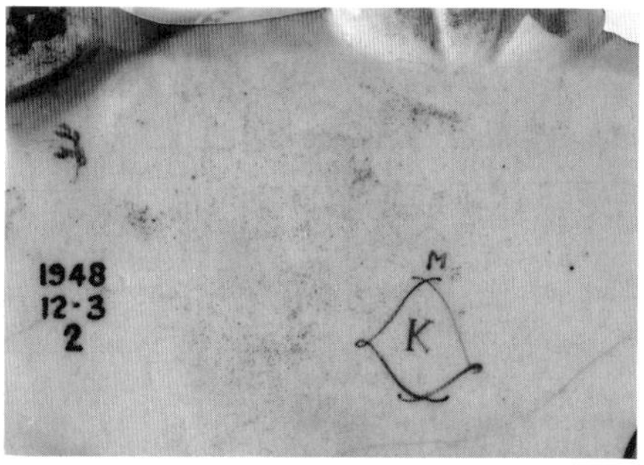

109 *marks*

1. Savill, 1988, I, pp. 32–4.
2. For a biography of Morin, see Savill, 1988, III, pp. 1051–2.
3. BM Department of Prints and Drawings, inv. 50,7–13,74 inscribed 'J.B. Le Bas Graveur du cabinet du roi 1746'.
4. BM Department of Prints and Drawings, inv. 50,7–13,72. An engraving of *La Femme Jalouse* is preserved at the Sèvres factory and bears an inventory number which is perhaps in an 18th-century hand.
5. Savill, 1988, I, pp. 38–9.
6. Eriksen and Bellaigue, 1987, p. 173, no. 189.

The painted scenes are the work of Jean-Louis Morin (1732–87) who worked at the factory between 1754 and 1784,[2] specialising in figure painting, seascapes, military subjects and scenes like these after David Teniers the Younger (1610–90). The scene on the left-hand vase is after *Le Flûteur* engraved by J.B. Le Bas[3] and that on the right-hand vase is after *La Femme Jalouse* also engraved by Le Bas.[4] In both instances the engravings have been adapted by the porcelain painter, principally in the transformation of an interior to an exterior scene. Savill, who believes Morin painted Teniers scenes between 1758–63, discusses these subjects in her commentary on a *garniture* of three turquoise-ground *vases à tombeau* dated 1760 in the Wallace Collection.[5]

The mark of a branch, now thought to have been used by a flower painter named Dubois, is recorded at the factory between 1756–7. It has been traced on pieces from the Maria Theresa service dating from 1756 and 1757, and on Bedford Service pieces dated 1761 and 1763.[6]

110 Cup and Saucer (*tasse litron et soucoupe*), 1764

D. *of saucer:*	13.6 cm
H. *of cup:*	6.9 cm
Marks:	interlaced LL enclosing date-letter L for 1764 below the painter's mark of André-Vincent Vielliard with a dot beneath, painted in blue enamel; cross potent incised on cup; suspension hole on both
Reg. No.	1948,12–3,50

Soft-paste porcelain, painted in enamel colours with a boy in a wooded landscape seated on a mound playing a horn (saucer) and a seated boy with a net (cup), within a tooled gilt reserve on a *bleu Fallot* ground overlaid with *gilt oeil de perdrix* and painted with *incrusté* flowers. Near the rims and near the foot of the cup is a tooled gilt laurel leaf and berry garland. Gilt dentil rim. Large pinhole inside cup.

Provenance: Bequeathed by Sir B. Eckstein, Bt., 1948

Literature: Savill, 1988, I, p. 55, f.n. 48

Comparable Examples: None

The cup and saucer are of the second size, with B form handle, as classified by Savill.[1] The painted decoration in the style of Boucher is typical of Vielliard's work. A *tasse litron* bearing his mark is painted with the same

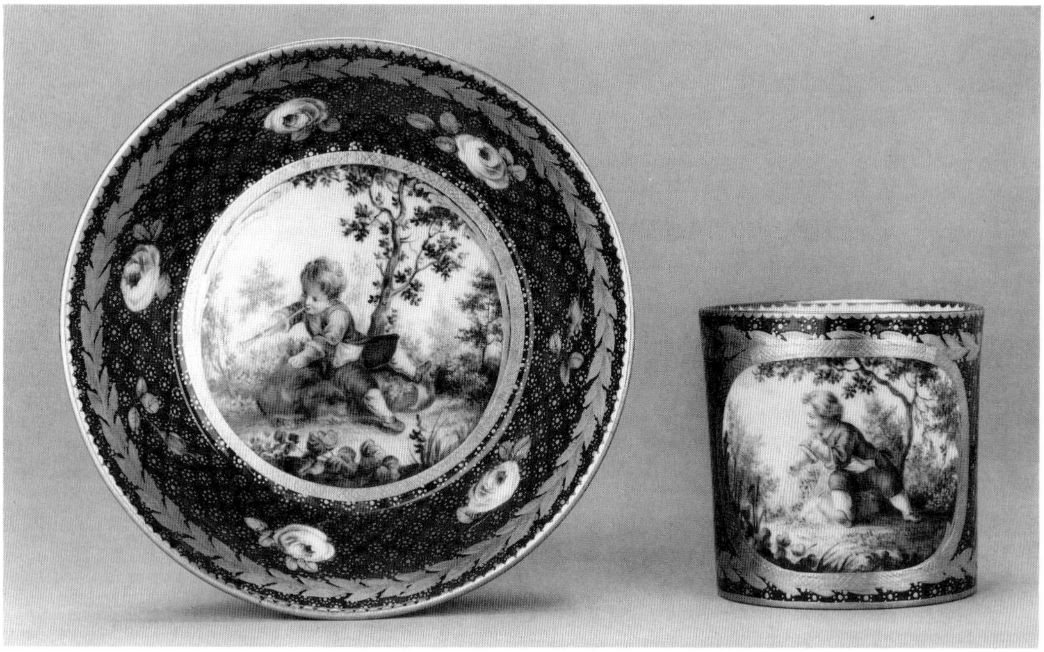

110

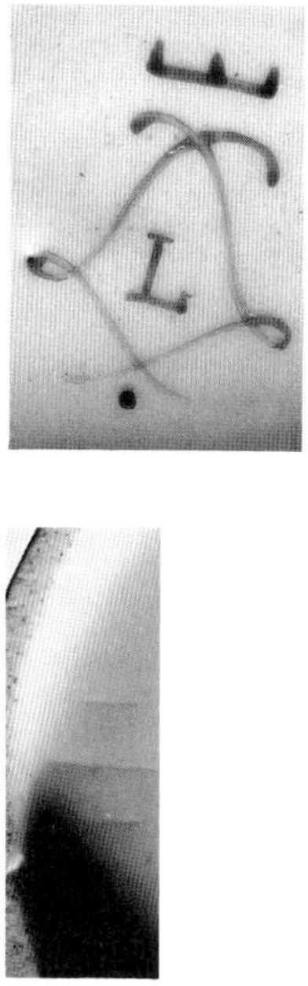

110 *marks*

scene of a boy with a net[2] and a somewhat similar scene of a boy playing a wind instrument can be seen on a *pot à sucre Hébert* of 1758 in the Wallace Collection, London.[3] For a biography of this painter, see Savill.[4]

The so-called *bleu Fallot* ground is known in combination with inlaid painted flowers (*incrusté*) from 1764.[5] It was devised by Fallot (forename unknown) within a year of his arrival at the factory in 1764, when he began work in the *atelier des couleurs*.[6] It is also found on teawares without a miniature,[7] on *compotiers* from a dessert service[8] as well as on vases.[9]

The gilding on these pieces is unusually lavish, especially in the light of the defect inside the cup.

The incised mark of a cross potent, which remains unidentified, has been noted on soft-paste teawares in the 1750s and 1760s.[10]

1. Savill, 1988, II, p. 501.
2. Christie's, 3 July 1978, Lot 228, blue vermiculated ground, dated 1764 with matching saucer painted with a boy playing a horn. A rather similar boy with a wind instrument was painted by Vielliard on a *vase hollandais* of 1758 in the Louvre Museum, inv. OA 9995, H. 17.3 cm.
3. *Op. cit.*, p. 591.
4. *Op. cit.*, 1988, III, pp. 1074–5.
5. Savill, 1988, I, p. 49.
6. For a biographical note on Fallot, see Savill, 1988, III, p. 1033.
7. On a *théière Calabre* dated 1768, inv. 1917.1058, and a cup and saucer (*tasse litron et soucoupe*), the cup dated 1769, inv. 1917.1059 a,b, in the Wadsworth Atheneum, Hartford, Conn., USA. A tray (*plat hors d'oeuvres*) with matching decoration is thought to be spurious. The author is grateful to Mrs Linda Roth for this information.
8. On a *compotier coquille* and a *compotier ovale* in the Metropolitan Museum, New York, inv. 64.174.48.
9. Savill, 1988, I, C210–11, pp. 49–50, pair of *cuvettes à fleurs Courteille*, dated 1768; three *vases consoles*, dated 1769, C311–13, pp. 372–83, including illustrations of examples from Waddesdon Manor, Buckinghamshire, Luton Hoo, Bedfordshire and the Musée Condé, Chantilly.
10. Savill, 1988, III, p. 1135.

111 Plate from a Dessert Service (*assiette à palmes*), 1765

D. 24.9 cm
Marks: LL interlaced enclosing date-letter M above (reversed) crotchet mark for the painter Louis-Jean Thévenet, all painted overglaze in blue; incised *CS* near foot rim; suspension hole; *C. 242* and *CDF* in monogram painted in red, partly effaced
Reg. No. 1899,10–6,9

Soft-paste porcelain, moulded, the rim with six large and six small lobes moulded in relief with palm leaves. Painted in the centre in yellow, green, pink, blue, purple, white, iron-red and grey with flowers and leaves, including roses, and fruit (plums) on a white ground. The border has a green ground interrupted by three reserves painted with flowers and leaves on a white ground. The reserves and the palm leaves are picked out in gold and a garland of gilt flowers connects the scrolls and reserves. Outer and inner edge of rim gilt. Centre of plate worn.

Provenance: Bequeathed by C.D.E. Fortnum, Esq., DCL, FSA, 1899 (no. 242 on Fortnum Register)[1]

Literature: Unpublished

Comparable Examples: Italy, Rome, Palazzo Quirinale, 148 plates, apparently each with different flower decoration, inv. 1097[2]

Italy, Florence, Palazzo Pitti, three cheese dishes, see Eriksen, 1973, no. 35

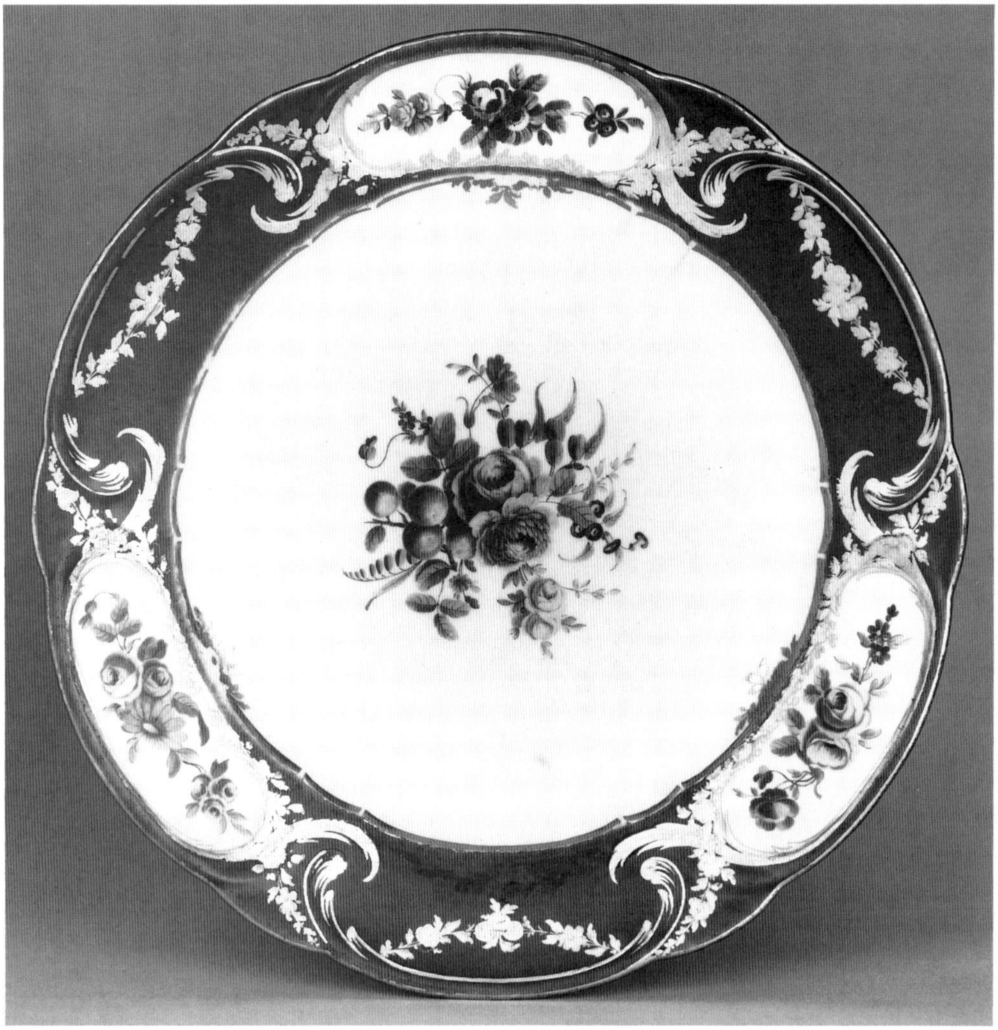

111

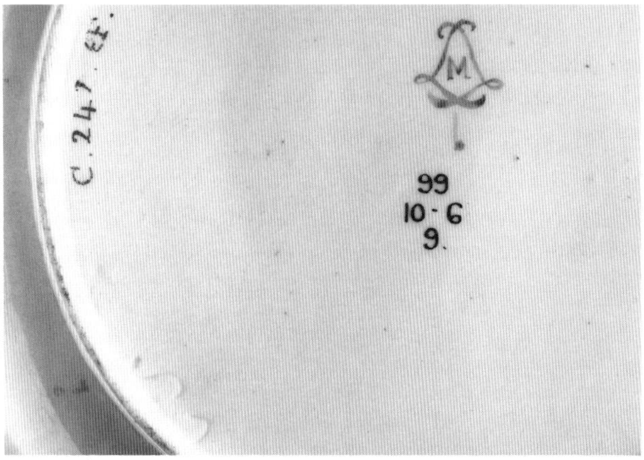

111 *marks*

The shape was in production at Vincennes as early as 19 March 1753,[3] and continued to be popular as an element of the dessert service throughout the eighteenth century.

Louis-Jean Thévenet (Thévenet *père*), who painted flowers and birds, worked at the factory between 1741 and 1777. His mark appears on pieces from the Bedford service.[4]

The incised mark *CS* is also recorded on a turquoise-blue two-handled cup (*tasse de toilette*, cover missing) dated 1756 at Waddesdon Manor, Buckinghamshire, and has been attributed by Eriksen to one or more of the three *répareurs* named Censier who were employed between 1756 and 1775.[5]

On 14 May 1765 a dessert service including 144 plates at 42 *livres* each 'en fond vert' was sold to M. Bonnet, agent for the Court of Parma in Paris.[6] It appears to be the only service matching this plate sold in that year. The service in the Quirinale has not been examined, and it may be that some plates were added to it after 1765. It was previously at the Royal Palace, Milan, and was transferred to Rome in 1893.[7]

1. For a note on C.D.E. Fortnum (1820–99), a Trustee of the Museum, see cat. 93.

2. Mr David Peters, who had not, in February 1989, examined the pieces in the Quirinale, kindly brought them to the author's attention, and Giuseppe Ceccatelli of Sotheby's, Rome, most helpfully provided further information.
3. Exh. *Vincennes*, 1977–8, no. 32, p. 31.
4. See Eriksen and Bellaigue, 1987, pp. 154, 178.
5. Eriksen, 1968, no. 15, p. 62, see also Savill, 1988, III, pp. 1096–7.
6. MNS, Archives de Sèvres, Vy 4, f. 37 and 37v. The total value of the service, which included 32 *enfants Falconet* in two sizes, and 8 *enfants Boucher*, amounted to 22,974 *livres* before the reduction of 9% had been granted. As well as *compotiers*, *plateaux*, *soucoupes à pied*, *tasses à glace*, *sucriers*, *fromagers*, *marronnières*, *saladiers*, *sallières*, *seaux à glace*, *crennelés*, *à bouteilles*, *à 1/2 bouteilles*, *ovales à liqueurs*, the service included *gobelets et soucoupes*, *pots à sucre*, a *theyère* and *pots à lait*. For information on Bonnet see Eriksen, 1973, pp. 11–16 and C. Briganti, 'Documents sur les arts à la Cour de Parme au XVIIIe siècle', *Antologia di Belle Arti*, 1977/4, pp. 380–401.
7. The author is indebted to Giuseppe Ceccatelli of Sotheby's, Rome, for this information. Further historical details are given by A. d'Agliano, 'Alcune considerazioni sulle porcellane di Sèvres delle ex collezioni reali italiane', *Bollettino d'Arte*, n. 35–6, January–April 1986, p. 67.

112 **Sugar Bowl and Cover (*pot à sucre Hébert*)**, 1765

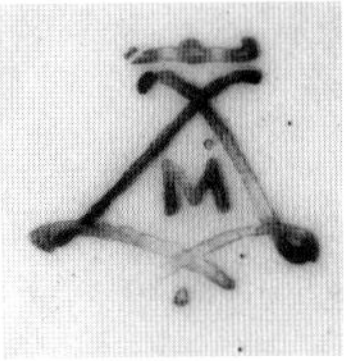

112 *mark*

H. *incl. cover:*	9.3 cm
Marks:	interlaced LL above a dot enclosing date-letter M below the mark of the painter André-Vincent Vielliard (employed 1752–90) painted in blue enamel
Reg. No.	1948,12–3,1

Soft-paste porcelain, thrown, of undulating form with a domed cover surmounted by a rose petal knop (restored). Decorated with scenes in colours on a green ground of a man speaking to two washerwomen by a pond, with buildings inside a wall in the background, and on the other side with a vineyard scene, including a man drinking from a flagon, a lady seated by a basket and at the left a man with a basket on his back walking towards buildings. Each scene is enclosed within a tooled gilt reserve. Gilt decoration near the rim on pot and cover includes a laurel leaf and berry wreath entwined around a gilt line and an *oeil-de-perdrix* motif, rims and foot gilt, gilt dentil inside rim of bowl. Knop gilt. Firecracks on base, interior bubbled and with gritty impurities and a 'bloat'.

Provenance: Bequeathed by Sir B. Eckstein, Bt., 1948

Literature: Eriksen, 1968, p. 188

Comparable Examples: France, Saint-Jean-Cap-Ferrat, Ephrussi-Rothschild Collection, inv. 2467A

Sotheby's, 10 December 1936, Lot 51, sale of Madame Dhainaut of Paris, pair of turquoise-ground toilet pots, 1757, painted with landscape and figure scenes, unmarked, illus.

The poor quality of the porcelain and the unusual form of the marks might perhaps indicate that this piece was decorated during the nineteenth century were it not for the existence of an undated tray at Waddesdon Manor, Buckinghamshire,[1] decorated in a similar fashion, and two green cups and saucers dated 1765 at Longleat, Wiltshire, all with matching gilt decoration. None of these exhibit any signs indicative of later decoration.

For a discussion of the form, see cat. 87.

This example is of the second size, the first measuring 11.4–12 cm and the third 7.5–9 cm in height.[2]

Landscapes with tiny figures are characteristic of the work of the painter André-Vincent Vielliard *père* (1717–90)[3] in the 1760s. It was recognised as early as 1755 that, although prolific, he was a poor painter of figures.

1. Eriksen, 1968, no. 68.
2. Savill, 1988, II, p. 575.
3. See p. 98, n. 11. For a detailed biography see Savill, 1988, III, 1074–5.

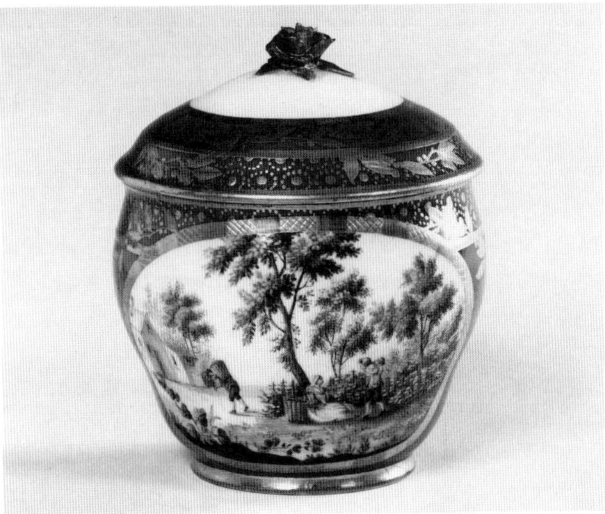

112

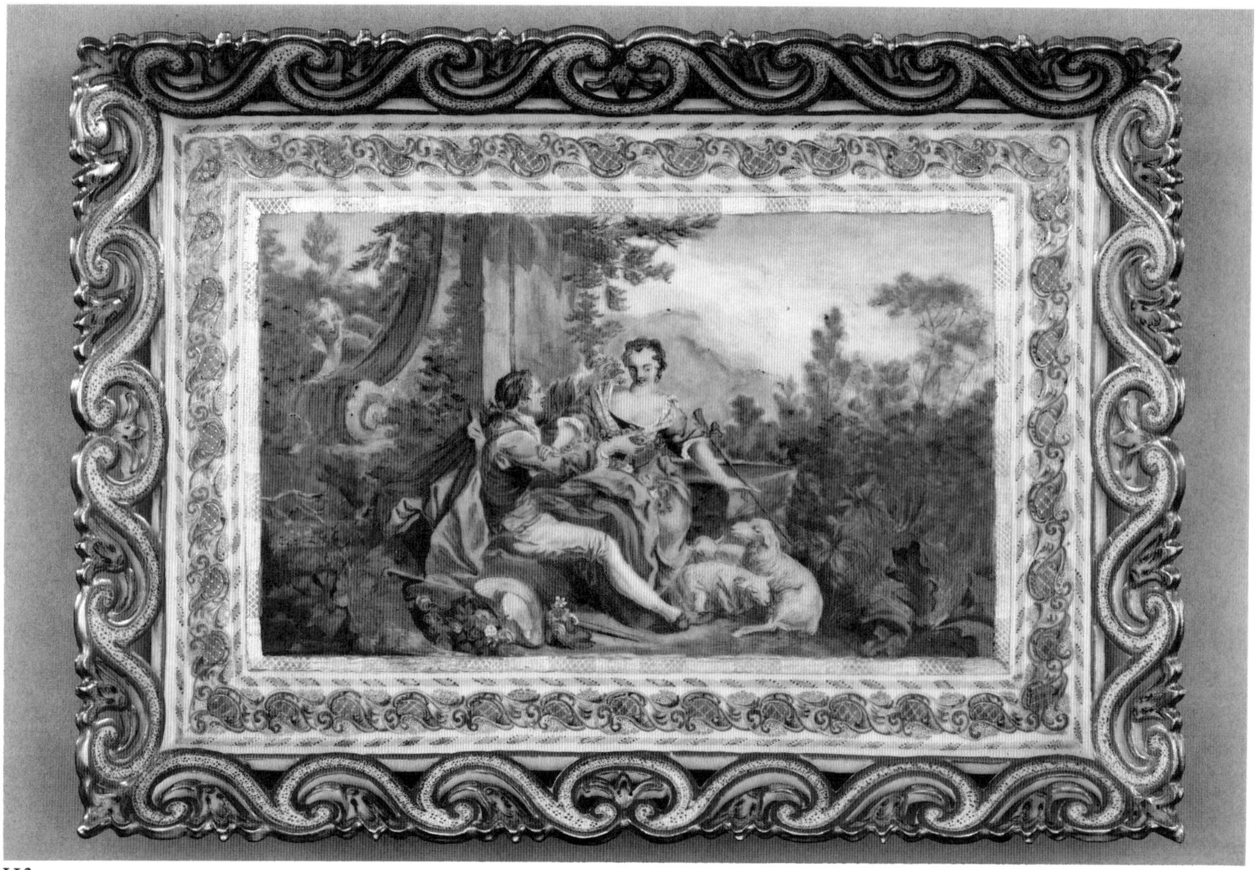

113

113 Tray (*plateau 'tiroir' à jours*), 1766

L.	24.5 cm
Marks:	LL enclosing date-letter N for 1766 above *.ch.* for the painter Etienne-Jean Chabry; *.j.f, fc* incised
Reg. No.	1948,12–3,8

Soft-paste porcelain, the openwork border of scrolls, tulips and leaves painted in pink, green and blue enamels, the scrolls additionally decorated with tiny coloured and gilt dots. On the exterior surface the pierced border has been outlined with gilding but is uncoloured. The edge of the tray is painted with a scroll design in blue, green, pink and gold enclosed between narrow pink bands interrupted by diagonal green lines outlined by blue dots. In the centre is a pastoral scene after Boucher, painted in blue, green, pink, mauve, brown, flesh-colour, white and grey, framed by a gilt line tooled with a criss-cross design.

Provenance: Madame Dhainaut Collection, sold Paris, Galerie Georges Petit, 19 May 1924, Lot 27, sold to Hodgkins for 8,300 francs

E.M. Hodgkins Collection, 1929

Bequeathed by Sir B. Eckstein, Bt., 1948

Literature: Tait, 1962, pl. XLII; revised ed. 1972, pl. 42

T. Burollet, *Porcelaines*, cat. Musée Cognac-Jay, Paris, 1983, no. 25, p. 76

Sassoon, 1991, p. 164

Exhibited: 1929, 'La Porcelaine Française de 1673 à 1914', Paris, Pavillon de Marsan, November–December 1929, no. 747.

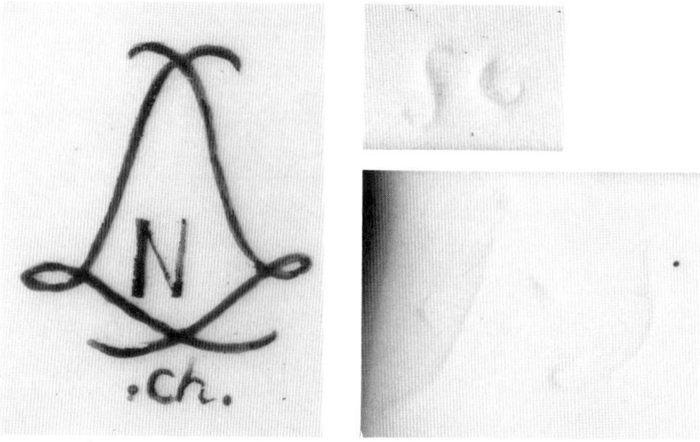

113 *marks*

Comparable Examples: None

The tray is the first or largest of two sizes with this border. For a discussion of the form, see cat. 91.

The painted scene is based on *Le Pasteur galant* by François Boucher engraved by A. Laurent in 1742.[1] An engraving of the subject inscribed in what is probably an eighteenth-century hand is in the Sèvres factory archive.[2] The subject was first used in the Hôtel de Soubise, Paris, and was painted around 1739. It was soon used as the source for a Vincennes group of 1750–2 and subsequently inspired J.J. Kaendler at Meissen.[3] It can be found painted on other pieces made at Sèvres, such as a *rose marbré cuvette Courteille* dated 1761.[4] The decorative scheme found on the openwork border was used as a painted border on a *cuvette Verdun* dated 1764.[5] Its popularity persisted and it can be found on a saucer painted by Chabry dated 1768[6] in the Jones Collection, Victoria and Albert Museum, as an all-over decoration on a *boîte à savonnette* of 1770 in the Louvre Museum[7] and on a water jug and basin dated 1770 at The National Trust, Clandon Park.[8]

For biographical details of Etienne-Jean Chabry *fils* (b. before 1749) a painter, gilder and burnisher at Sèvres from 1764–87, who specialised in pastoral and rustic scenes after Boucher, see Savill.[9]

The incised mark *jf* has been traced on a number of pieces between around 1755 and 1768 but remains unidentified.[10] The incised mark *fc* may perhaps have been used by Farcy, a *mouleur en pâte* employed between 1769 and 1798, although the date of this tray leaves this in doubt.[11]

1. Jean-Richard, 1978, no. 313.
2. Reproduced by Sassoon, 1991, p. 163, who illustrates and discusses a plaque for a tabletop dated 1761 and painted by Dodin in the Getty Museum, Malibu, California, pp. 162–5.
3. See catalogue compiled by T. Burollet, *Porcelaines*, Musée Cognac-Jay, Paris, 1983, no. 25; Victoria and Albert Museum, inv. C. 50–1962.
4. Sold Christie's, 6 October 1986, Lot 257. Sassoon, 1991, pp. 162–3 lists other pieces painted with this scene.
5. Sold Christie's, 28 October 1963, Lot 131.
6. Victoria and Albert Museum, London, *Catalogue of the Jones Collection*, Part II, 1924, compiled by W. King, no. 129.
7. Illus. P. Verlet, *Sèvres*, Paris, 1953, pl. 70a.
8. Illus. J. Cushion, *Continental Porcelain*, London, revised ed., 1982, pl. 50.
9. Savill, 1988, III, pp. 1017–18.
10. Dauterman, 1986, p. 207.
11. *Op. cit.*, p. 194, 78.

114 **Vase and Cover (*vase cassolette Bachelier*),** 1767

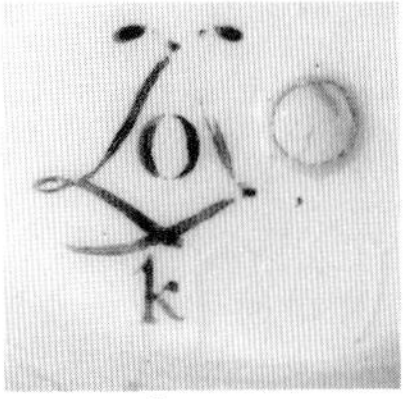

114 *marks*

See colour plate 18

H. *inc. cover:*	19.9 cm
Max. L.	25.6 cm
Marks:	LL enclosing date-letter O for 1767 above *k* for the painter Charles-Nicolas Dodin painted in blue enamel; *CS* incised
Reg. No.	1948,12 3,12

Soft-paste porcelain, the body of hemispherical shape on an oval foot, made separately, the cover domed and surmounted with a pine-cone finial. The sides of the body are moulded with a sunken star-shaped flower between trellis work. The shoulder is similarly moulded, and pierced. A star-shaped flower motif ornaments the outer edge of each handle, through the top of which is 'threaded' a myrtle garland which lies around the neck, and two ribbons which follow the line of the handles, themselves divided at each end to form two scrolls. From the end of each handle hangs a laurel wreath. The decoration consists of a scene of a shepherd and shepherdess in a landscape painted in colours within a tooled gilt reserve on a *bleu nouveau* ground on one side, and on the other of a musical trophy suspended from a ribbon framed by a wreath of myrtle, all in gold, carefully tooled. The applied wreaths near the handles are also decorated with tooled gilding. The handles, the trellis moulding, the rims, knop, neck and foot are all gilt. There is a firecrack underneath the foot. Knop repaired, small chip to rim of cover.

Provenance: Bequeathed by Sir B. Eckstein, Bt., 1948

Literature: Eriksen, 1968, no. 78

Eriksen, 1974, pl. 276 and p. 371

Savill, 1988, I, p. 335, 342, f.n. 3g

Comparable Examples: Buckinghamshire, The National Trust, Waddesdon Manor, companion piece, acquired by Miss Alice de Rothschild (1847–1922) from an unknown source, presumably after her brother's death in 1898 (see Eriksen, 1968, no. 78, where other comparative pieces are listed).

The model, which was designed by Jean-Jacques Bachelier,[1] exists in five alternative forms and this piece is the second size of shape C, as classified by Savill.[2] Biscuit examples of a *vase cassolette* of the first size awaiting glazing are recorded in the factory inventory of January 1765, showing that the form was devised in 1764. They were valued at 48 *livres* each, whilst reject quality biscuit vases of the same size were valued at 10 *livres*.

Models and moulds of the second size were valued at 30 *livres* each in the same inventory.[3] Two years later, moulds and models in the first and second size for a *cassolette Bachelier* were valued at 48 and 36 *livres* respectively.[4] As there is no known example with the festoons and the piercing dated earlier than 1767, it has been suggested that this is the correct name for the vase[5] and not *cassolette à festons* inscribed on the plaster preserved at the factory. Six *cassolettes Bachelier* of the second size in the biscuit state ready for glazing were valued in the inventory of January 1767 at 60 *livres*, whilst a further three glazed and ready for firing are shown at 66 *livres* each.[6] As the sales registers specify only *vases cassolettes*, it has proved impossible to discover either the original owner of this vase or its cost.

For a note on the Censier family, thought to have used the incised mark *CS*, and in particular on the soft-paste repairer Charles Censier (employed 1754–1802), see Savill.[7]

The scene on the front is based on *Les amants surpris*

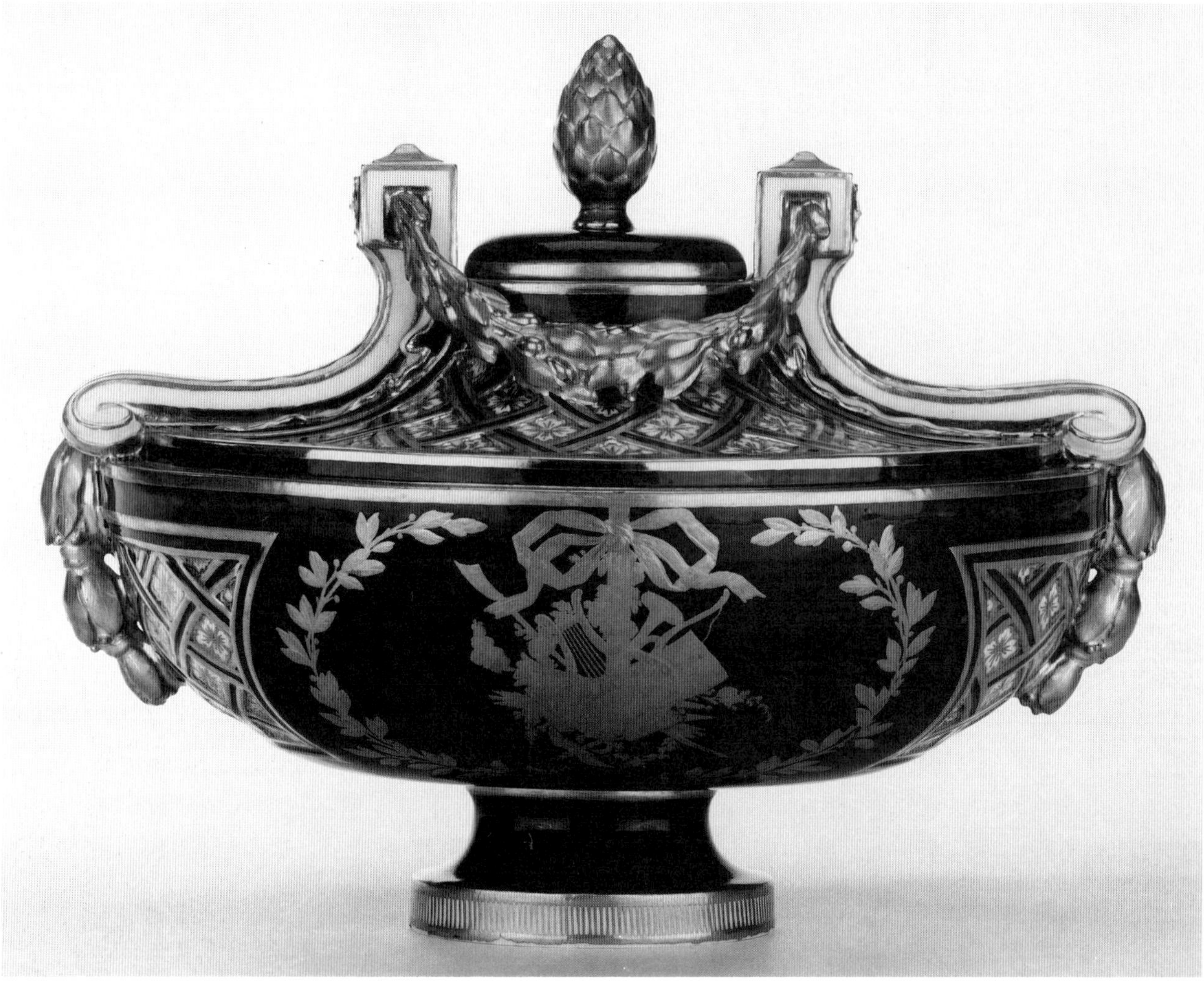

114

by François Boucher, engraved by Gilles Demarteau. A drawing with a slight variant of the scene, signed by Boucher and dated 1764, is in the National Gallery of Art, Washington.[8] For a biography of Charles-Nicolas Dodin (1734–1803) see Savill.[9] The music book on the reverse is tooled with the notation of an imaginary tune.[10]

1. Jean-Jacques Bachelier (1724–1806) was a painter who joined Vincennes in either 1748 or 1751. From 1751 he was an artistic director. In 1765 he began supplying plaster models for vases; replaced as director of sculpture by Falconet in 1757, he succeeded him in 1766. He was dismissed in 1793. A full biography is given in Savill, 1988, III, pp. 961–4.
2. The form and all its variants is fully discussed by Savill, 1988, I, pp. 334–5, who illustrates the plaster. It appeared in A. Troude, *Choix de modèles de la Manufacture Nationale de porcelaines de Sèvres appartenant au Musée Céramique* (1897), pl. 112.
3. MNS, Archives de Sèvres, I 7.
4. *Ibid.*
5. See Eriksen and Bellaigue, 1987, no. 145, pp. 335–6.
6. MNS, Archives de Sèvres, I 8.
7. Savill, 1988, III, pp. 1096–7.
8. Jean-Richard, 1978, no. 633, p. 180.
9. Savill, 1988, III, pp. 1029–32.
10. The author is grateful to Arthur Searle of the Department of Manuscripts, British Library, for his opinion on the music.

115 **Pair of Trays** (probably ***plateaux du Roi***), 1767, with later gilt embellishments

L. 24.7 cm
Marks: interlaced LL containing date-letter O for 1767 above cursive *N* for the painter François-Joseph Aloncle; *97* incised (1948,12–3,30); *9* or *g* incised (1948,12–3,31); suspension hole (both); Eckstein Collection label numbered *201/2*.
Reg. No. 1948,12–3,30 and 31

Soft-paste porcelain, moulded; the glazed base of each discoloured with specks, bubbles and traces of turquoise-ground colour. The decoration, which is on a turquoise (*bleu céleste*) ground, consists of four panels of flowers around the border painted in

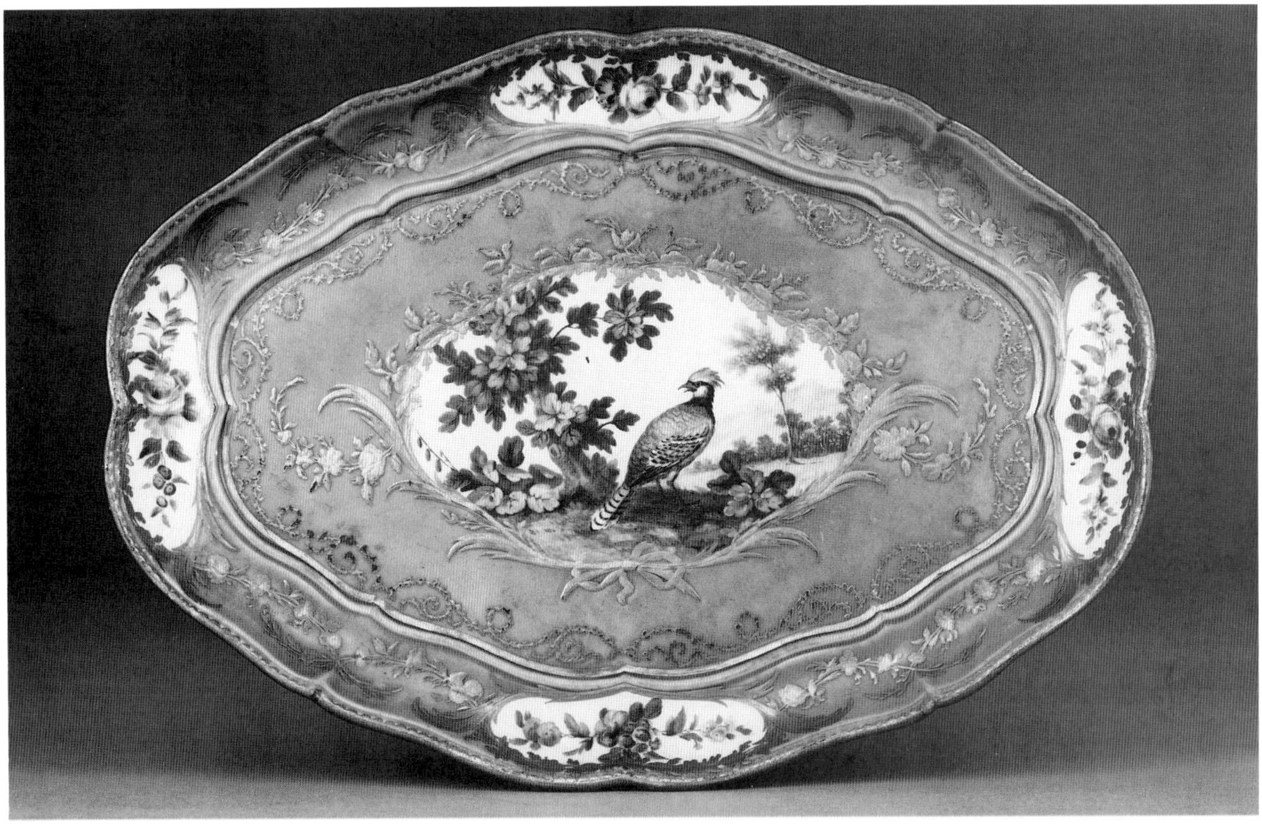

115 *(1948, 12–3, 31)*

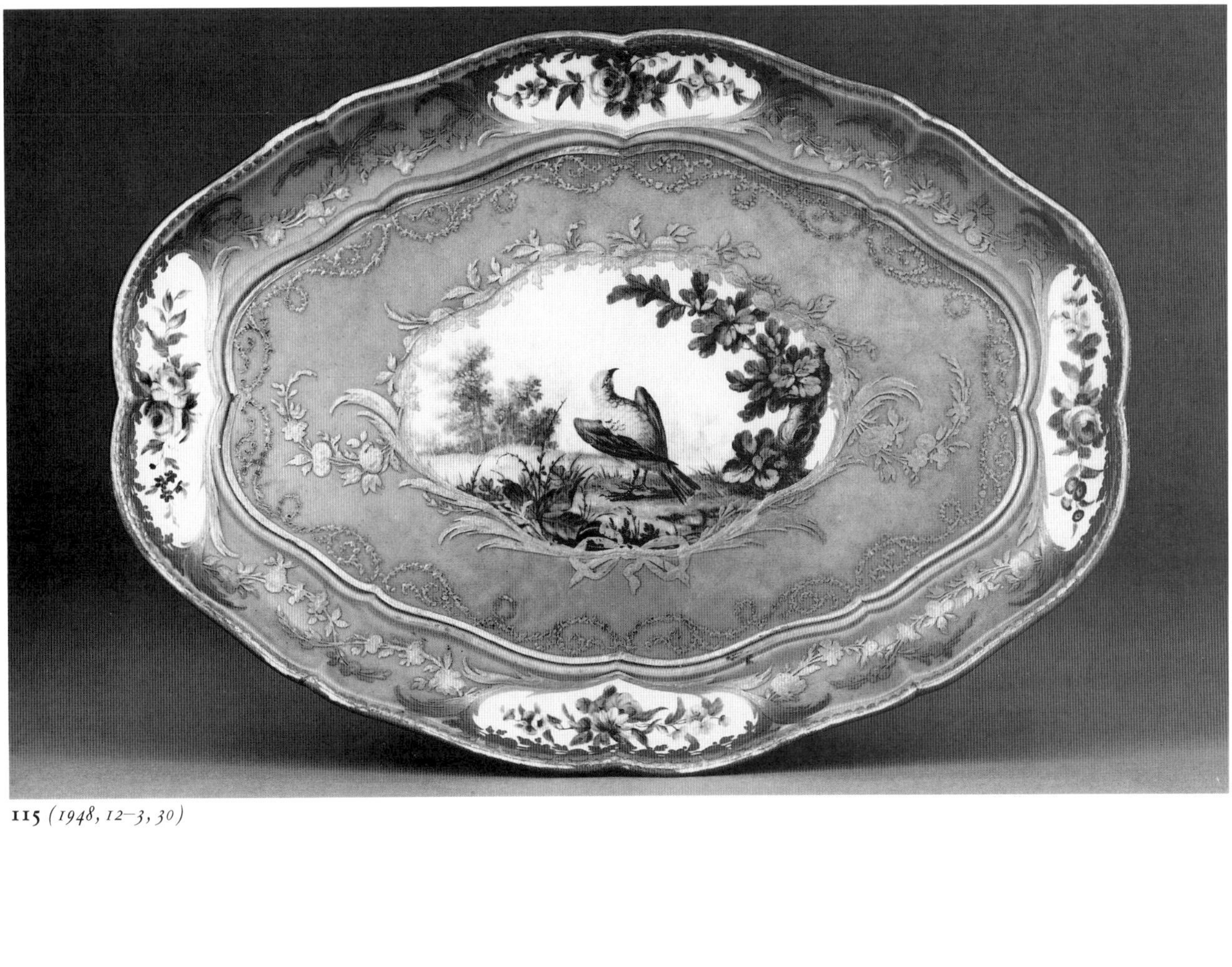

115 *(1948, 12–3, 30)*

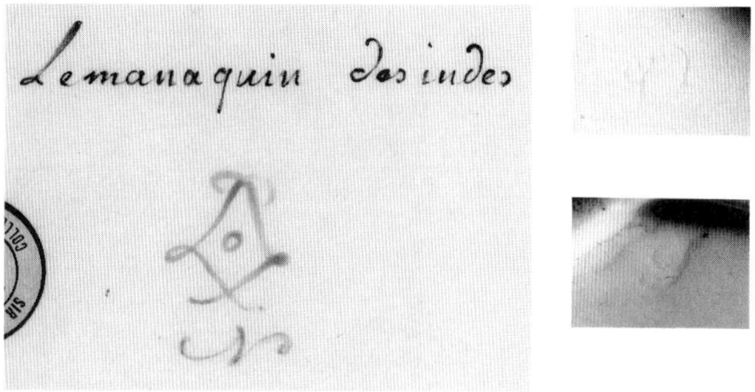

115 *marks*

colours on a white ground within oval reserves outlined by gilt fronds and flowers and linked by gilt flower garlands and, in the centre, of an exotic bird in a landscape with trees. One (1948,12–3,30) is inscribed in black on the reverse *Le manaquin des Indes*, the other *Le geai D'Amerique*. The oval reserve is enclosed by gilt flowers and fronds tied at the lower end with a ribbon bow. Around the inner edge are gilt leaf garlands.

Provenance: Bequeathed by Sir B. Eckstein, Bt., 1948

Literature: Unpublished

Comparable Examples: None

For a discussion of the form, see cat. 118.

These trays were probably originally painted with polychrome birds and flowers only, with simple gilding around the rim. Both the turquoise ground and the over-fussy gilding (which is thick and flaky in places) are likely to have been added later, probably in the mid- to late nineteenth century when turquoise grounds were particularly popular with collectors and were widely faked and imitated.

The style of the bird-painting is consistent with the work of Aloncle,[1] and should be compared with pieces in the Razoumovsky service at Waddesdon Manor, Buckinghamshire.[2] The gilding on this magnificent service, which is dated 1766–7, is much more restrained than on these trays.

The *Manaquin des indes* is painted on a plate in the Razoumovsky service and *Le jai D'amerique* on an ice-cup. In view of the titles and the exotic nature of the birds, it is almost certain that they are not the product of the painter's imagination. However, the source of the bird decoration has not yet been securely identified. Although the 'black and yellow manakyn' is represented in George Edwards' *A Natural History of Uncommon Birds*, London, 1763, part 2, p. 83, this is not the same bird. A bird in the French edition, entitled *Histoire naturelle de divers oiseaux*, Paris, 1751, part III, no. CXX, called 'le grand Martin de l'Amerique' is not dissimilar in colouring to the jay, but the size of the bird, its tail and its eyes are all different, and it is unlikely that the painter would confuse the title of the bird. Further research is needed into other French editions of Edwards before it can be established which source was used at the factory before Buffon began to bring out his many volumes of bird illustrations.

Several different forms of the incised mark *g* have been noted by Dauterman.[3] It is possible that the mark was used by a repairer named Gambier, whose precise identity has not yet been discovered. The repairer using the mark *97* is unidentified.

1. For a biography of Aloncle (active 1758–81), see Savill 1988, III, pp. 995–6.
2. Eriksen, 1968, p. 211 (plate), and p. 226 for a monteith of 1767 not included in the service as delivered.
3. Dauterman, 1986, p. 198, 82.

116 Cup and Saucer (*tasse et soucoupe Calabre*), *c.* 1770

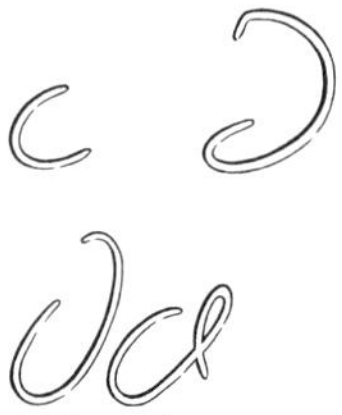

116 *marks*

D. *of saucer:*	15.9 cm
H. *of cup:*	8.2 cm
Marks:	*cd* incised on cup; *da* incised on saucer; suspension hole on both
Reg. No.	Franks 381

Soft-paste porcelain, highly translucent. The decoration on the saucer consists of three medallion heads in the classical style painted *en grisaille* on a red-brown ground within an oval tooled gilt 'frame' and a looped laurel leaf and berry garland tied with a blue ribbon bow in three places near the rim, all on a ground of gold stripes. In the central reserve, contained by a white enamel line and an inner *grisaille* line, is a trophy painted *en grisaille* of a laurel branch, clouds, a sword and a [?]plumed helmet. The cup is similarly decorated with a male and a female cameo head on a gold striped ground. Foot rim of cup and sides of handle gilt. Foot rim of both ground off, damage near suspension hole, central well raised.

Provenance: Bequeathed by Sir A.W. Franks, 1897

Literature: Franks, 1896, no. 381

Comparable Examples: London, Victoria and Albert Museum, *pot à sucre Hébert* (lid missing), H. 5.7 cm, painter's mark in mauve, dated 1769, inv. 1451–1853 (Bandinel Collection)

Although the decoration is superficially of high quality, the trophy in the centre of the saucer is poorly painted, and the blue near the handle is noticeably overfired. Other features such as the convex shape of the centre of the saucer suggesting warping; the grinding off of both foot rims and the consequent damage to the saucer; pinholes and inclusions in the glaze; the gilding-over of a small chip to the exterior of the foot on the cup; and the rather crude tooling over the gold 'frames' around the cameo heads, as well as the exceptionally small size of the suspension holes and their unusual positioning halfway up the foot rim,

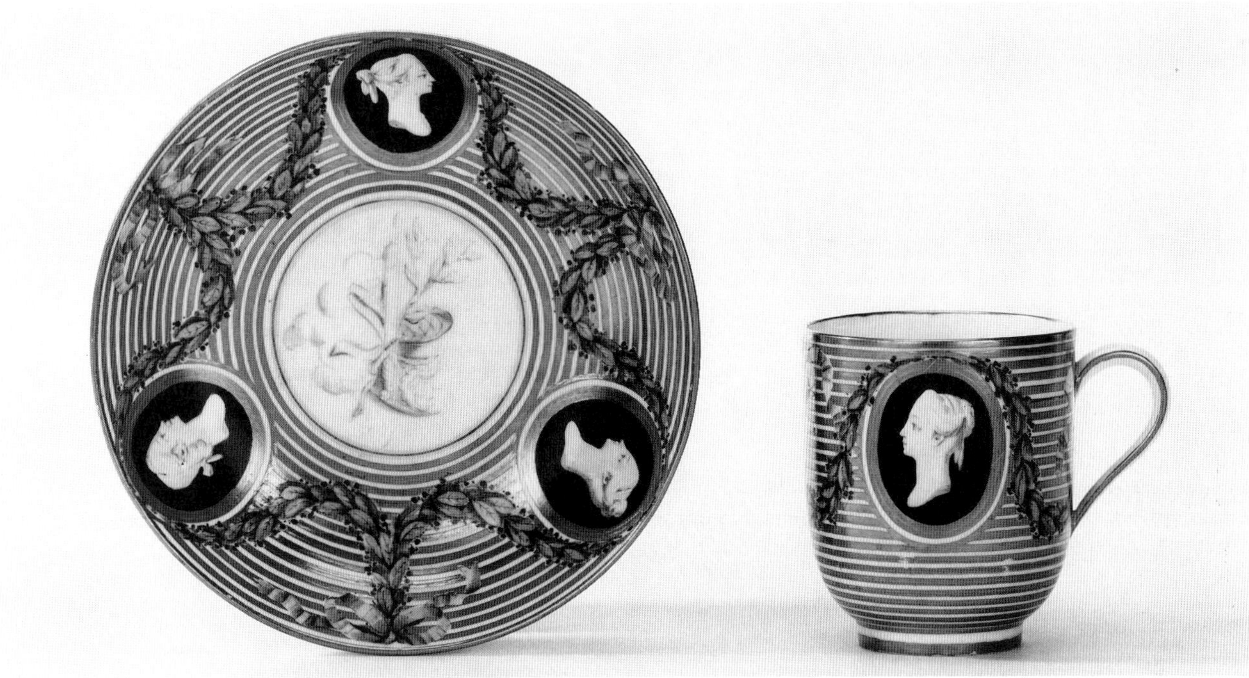

116

might give rise to the suspicion that this cup and saucer may be a nineteenth-century confection. However, the presence of incised marks indicates that the cup and saucer were made at Sèvres. Horizontal gold stripes were occasionally used at Sèvres, as on the garniture of three *vases ferré* in the Wallace Collection, dating from about 1779.[1] A gold striped *gobelet Bouillard* painted with flowers by Tandart and dated 1768 was in the Joicey Collection in 1905 and is now in the Victoria and Albert Museum, London.[2] The factory was also experimenting with gold decoration, producing the design known as *à briques d'or*, found on a *gobelet litron* at Woburn Abbey, Bedfordshire, dated 1770.[3]

Gold striped decoration clearly enjoyed a certain vogue, as it was used at the Derby porcelain factory in the 1770s.[4]

Similar medallion heads in *grisaille* on a red-brown ground in combination with laurel leaf and berry garlands from coloured ribbons may be found on three pieces in the Victoria and Albert Museum.

1. cup and saucer, pale yellow-green and red *pointillé* ground bearing the date-letter q for 1769 within interlaced LL below *m*, same dimensions, inv. 1980–1855, from the Bernal Collection;
2. cup and saucer, green and blue *pointillé* ground, obliterated painted mark on saucer, D. of saucer 13.4 cm; inv. 1981–1855, from the Bernal Collection;
3. covered two-handled cup and saucer, pale blue *pointillé* ground, same painted mark as 1 on both, inv. 2010–b–1855, from the Bernal Collection.

Each exhibits some slight imperfection.

A *gobelet Bouillard et soucoupe* with a pale green and blue *pointillé* ground, dated 1769 and painted by Madame Noualhier, a *gobelet litron et soucoupe* with a blue *pointillé* ground dated 1769 painted by Jacques Fontaine and a *théière Calabre* with a pale blue *pointillé* ground dated 1769 painted by Jacques Fontaine, all in the Wallace Collection, London,[5] are of slightly higher quality, but each piece has some imperfections, and both painting and gilding are not of the highest quality.

No mention has been found of this cup and saucer in the factory records.

The incised mark *cd* is unidentified but has been attributed by Svend Eriksen to Michel-Dorothé Coudray, a soft-paste *mouleur* working at Sèvres between 1756 and 1758 and by Carl Dauterman to Charles Dupré, a soft-paste *répareur* between 1756 and 1773 and a repairer of hard-paste from 1773–8.[6] The incised mark *da* was possibly used by Danet *père* who was a soft-paste *répareur* between 1768 and 1773, and went on to work on hard-paste in different capacities.[7]

1. Savill, 1988, I, C 264–6, pp. 222–33. The author is grateful to Rosalind Savill for drawing these to her attention.
2. Anon, 'Mr J.G. Joicey's Collection of Sèvres Porcelain', *Connoisseur*, Vol. XI, 1905, p. 143; VAM inv. Circ. 631&a–1919, H. of cup 6.1 cm.

3. Eriksen, 1974, p. 373, pl. 282.
4. As on a ewer in the neo-classical style, R.L. Hobson, *Catalogue of English Porcelain in the British Museum*, London, 1905, pl. XIX, no. II 309; and see a teapot and cover with a striped ground and a panel of cupids *en camaïeu*, H.G. Bradley, *Ceramics of Derbyshire 1750–1975*, privately published, London, 1978, no. 235; a sugar bowl and cover painted with putti and trophies is illustrated by J. Twitchett, *Derby Porcelain*, London, 1980, p. 144, fig. 159, a pair of ewers, p. 109, fig. 106, and a pair of vases and covers with biscuit handles, p. 141, fig. 153.
5. Savill, 1988, II, C 359, p. 529, C 347, p. 505, C 381, p. 581.
6. Savill, 1988, III, pp. 1093–4.
7. *Ibid.*, pp. 1097–8. According to Savill, Danet's sons and nephew may also have used this mark.

117 **Cup and Saucer (*tasse litron*)**, 1770

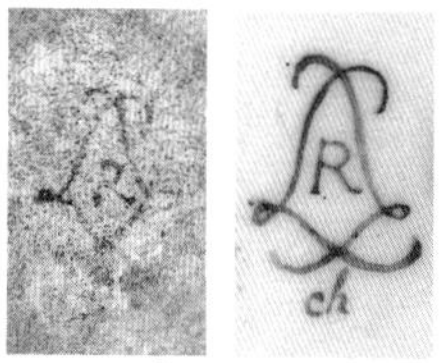

117 *marks*

D. *of saucer*: 12.4 cm
H. *of cup*: 5.8 cm
Marks: interlaced LL enclosing date-letter R for 1770 above the painter's mark for Etienne-Jean Chabry, painted in blue enamel (almost obliterated on cup); suspension hole on saucer
Reg. No. 1948,12–3,49

Soft-paste porcelain. Painted with a scene of a seated boy in an orange-red jacket fishing in a wooded landscape on the cup, and on the saucer with a girl in a striped yellow skirt under a pink overskirt, blue bodice and purple jacket by a tree crying over a basket of broken eggs. The scene on the saucer is enclosed by gilt lines between which is a gilt laurel wreath on a green ground, repeated at the rim. Similar decoration at rim and foot of cup, border of saucer painted with a panel of trophies of gardening (a basket of flowers, a watering can and a sickle) and another containing unidentified trophies, perhaps of the dairy, on a white ground enclosed by gilding and linked by pendent gilt flower garlands. On the cup are similar garlands. Rims gilt, handle partly gilt. Base of saucer discoloured, perhaps overfired.

Provenance: Bequeathed by Sir B. Eckstein, Bt., 1948

Literature: Unpublished

Comparable Examples: None

The cup and saucer are of the third size, the handle of form C as classified by Savill.[1] The scene on the saucer is after François Boucher, *Les Oeufs Cassés*, engraved by G. Demarteau;[2] that on the cup is adapted from the same artist's *Le pêcheur*, or *Le petit pêcheur*, originally a design for a seat-covering,[3] engraved by C. Duflos.[4]

Etienne-Jean Chabry (active 1764–87) specialised in pastoral and rustic scenes after Boucher, often on cups and saucers, particularly in the 1760s and 1770s. For a full biography of this painter, see Savill,[5] where the scene *Les Oeufs Cassés* (which has an erotic symbolism) on a *gobelet et soucoupe 'enfoncé'* of 1769 with a green ground is mentioned.[6]

1. Savill, 1988, II, p. 501.
2. Jean-Richard, 1978, no. 702.

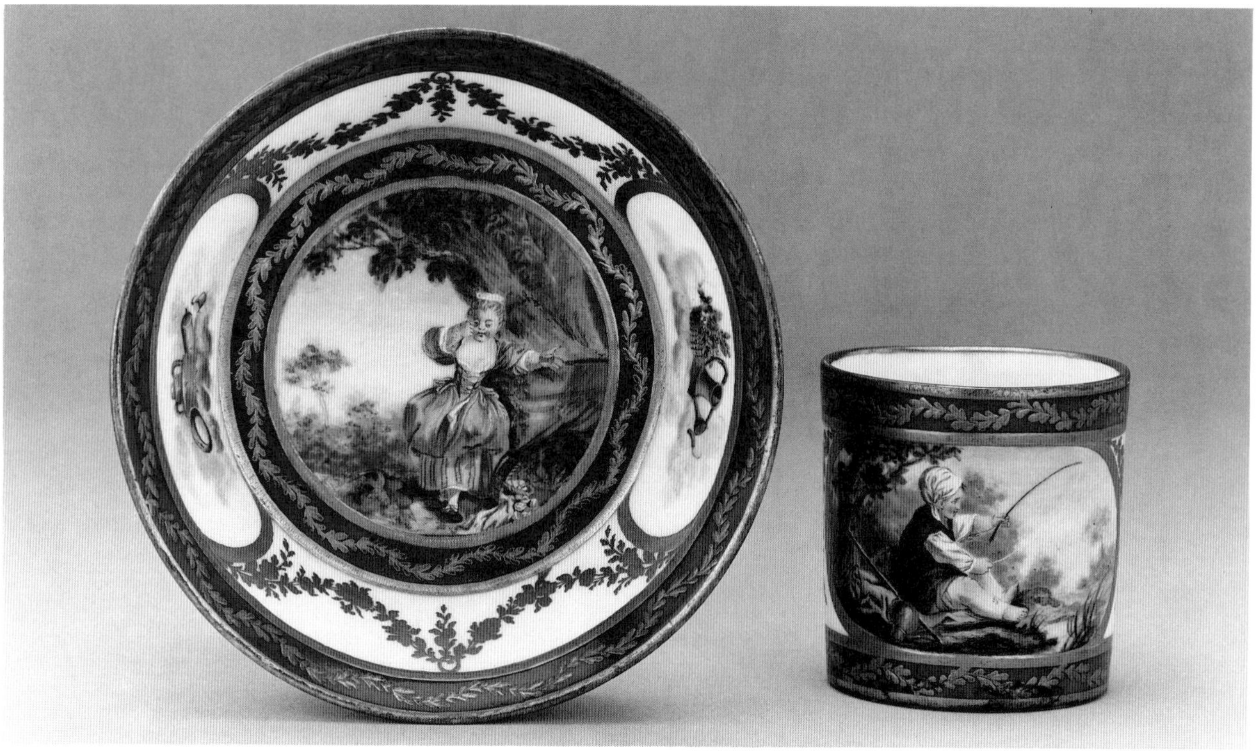

117

3. A. Ananoff, *L'oeuvre dessinée de François Boucher*, Paris, 1976, Vol. II, p. 126, no. 440, fig. 1253.
4. Jean-Richard, 1978, p. 240, no. 935 and Ananoff, *op. cit.*, p. 72, no. 373/3, fig. 1090.
5. Savill, 1988, III, pp. 1017–18.
6. *Op. cit.*, p. 1018, f.n. 3.

118 **Tray (*plateau du déjeuner du Roi*), 1773**

L. 24.7 cm
Marks: interlaced LL enclosing date-letter U above *ch* painted overglaze in mauve, with BD in overglaze blue below; *bj* or *cg* incised; suspension hole.
Reg. No. Franks 382

Soft-paste porcelain, of lobed form, moulded. Painted over the glaze in blue, yellow, pink, green, red-brown and grey with scattered flower sprays. Gilt dentil rim on upper and lower surface.

Provenance: Bequeathed by Sir A.W. Franks, 1897

Literature: Franks, 1897, no. 382

Comparable Examples: None known

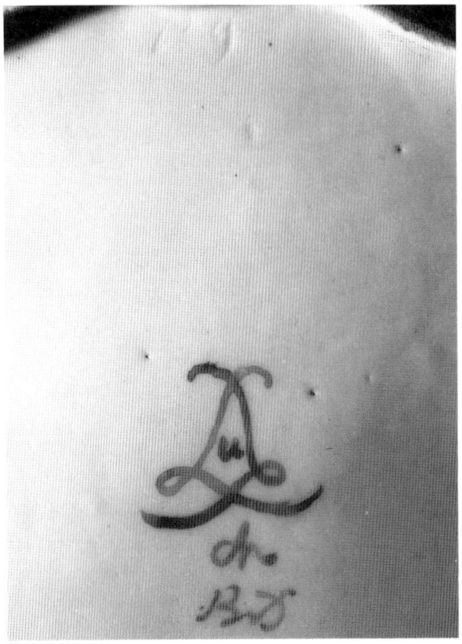

118 *marks*

For a discussion of the form, which was accompanied either by two jam pots or by a *déjeuner* of a cup and saucer and a sugar bowl, or a teapot, or cups without saucers, see Savill.[1] This example is the second of two sizes.

The unusual blue and mauve marks might suggest that this tray was not decorated at the time when it was made. However, the writer considers that the mauve painter's mark *ch* probably stands for Etienne-Jean Chabry (active 1764–87), even though he was principally employed on figure scenes and most of his documented work was almost entirely on teawares

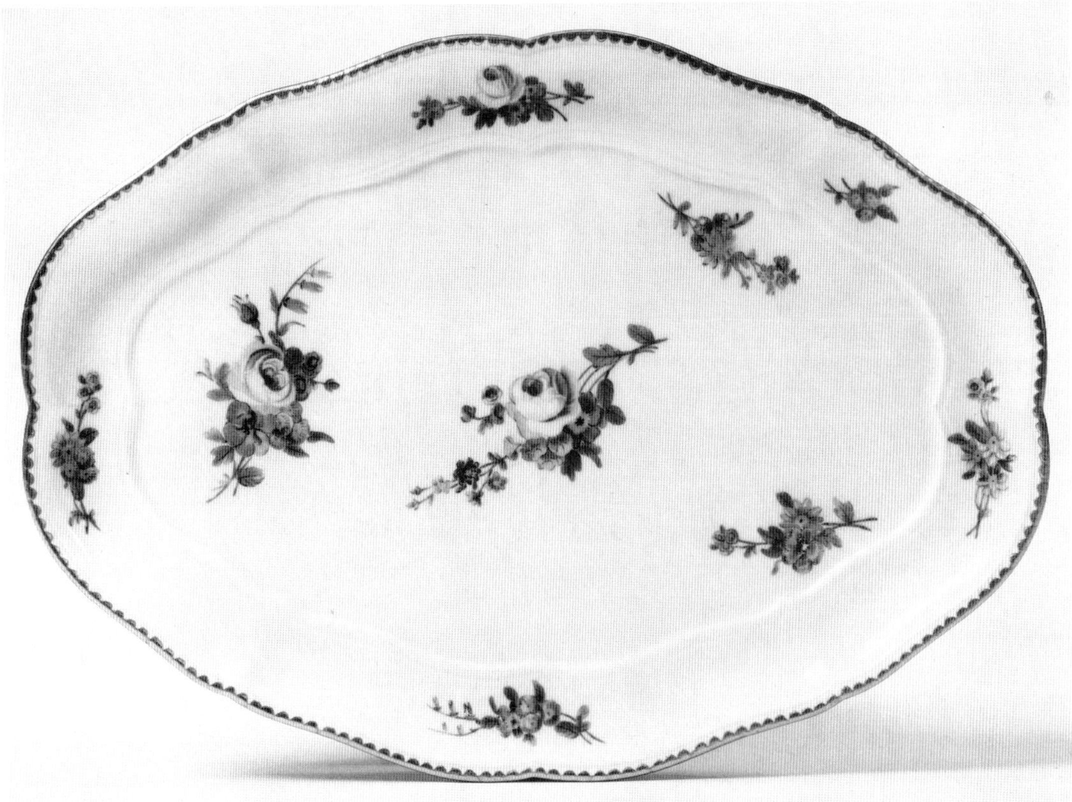

118

and *écuelles* (for a cup and saucer decorated by Chabry see cat. 117).[2] The mark BD was used by François Baudouin *père*, a gilder and occasional painter, employed between 1750 and 1800.[3] As in the case of the pink-ground *compotiers*, which also bear unusual marks which might be considered spurious (cat. 119), the décor is rather old-fashioned, but has every appearance of being genuine.

The repairer whose incised marks appear on this tray has not yet been identified.

1. Savill, 1988, I, pp. 590–3.
2. *Ibid.*, III, pp. 1017–18.
3. Dauterman, 1986, p. 39.

119 **Pair of Oval Fruit Dishes (*compotiers ovales*)**, 1775

L. 27.8 cm (1948,12–3,28) 27.6 cm (1948,12–3,29)
Marks: interlaced LL enclosing date-letter X above painters' and gilders' marks (from left to right) cursive *B.* for the gilder Jean-Pierre Boulanger (employed 1754–81), a dagger for the painter Etienne Evans (employed 1752–1806) and the monogram *vd.* for the painter Jean-Baptiste Emmanuel Vandé (employed 1753–?79) painted in blue enamel (1948,12–3,28); interlaced LL above the monogram *vd.* (1948,12–3,29); suspension hole (repeated on 1948,12–3,29); blue printed label of Sir Bernard Eckstein Collection numbered in ink *177/2*
Reg. No. 1948,12–3,28 and 29

Soft-paste porcelain, moulded, of oval, shaped form. Painted with flowers in colours at either end and a bird in a landscape at either side on a white ground within rococo reserves. The remainder of each dish is decorated with a pink ground embellished with gilt scrolls around the rim and enclosing the reserves, the gilding highlighted by a dark pink line at one edge only; rim gilt. One dish (1948,12–3,28) is noticeably heavier than the other and its underside is unevenly glazed and discoloured in places.

Provenance: Bequeathed by Sir B. Eckstein, Bt., 1948

Literature: Unpublished

Comparable Examples: Christie's, René Fribourg Collection, V, Catalogue of French Faïence and European Porcelain, part II, 15 October 1963, Lot 439, pair of *compotiers ovales* said to be dated 1755 but probably 1775, gilder's mark of Boulanger *père* (not at the factory in 1755) and other indecipherable marks

Northamptonshire, Boughton House, collection of the 9th Duke of Buccleuch, five *assiettes à palmes*

USA, Virginia, private collection, formerly D.M. Currie collection[1]

The model, intended for serving fruit compote, was probably devised in 1754. Models and moulds in two sizes were in existence in that year and finished pieces were fired in the biscuit kiln in May 1754. No model, mould or drawing now survives in the factory archive.[2]

The form, of which this is the first size,[3] is not infrequently found with alternating bird and flower decoration.[4] By 1775 *roze* was no longer an especially fashionable or saleable ground-colour for Sèvres services, and this, taken with the rather unusual number of painters' marks[5] and the strange surface of one *compotier* has caused the author to question their authenticity.

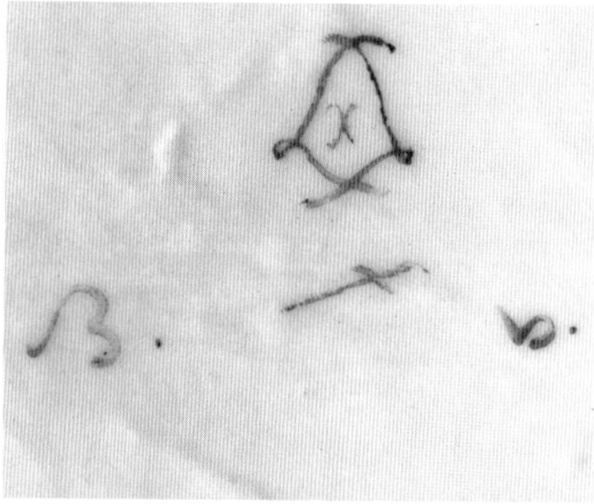
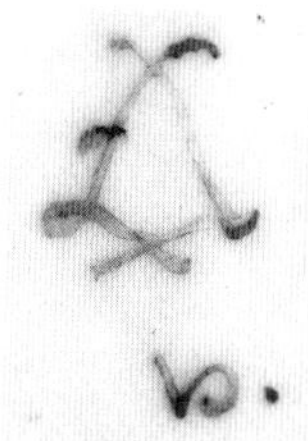

119 *marks*

119

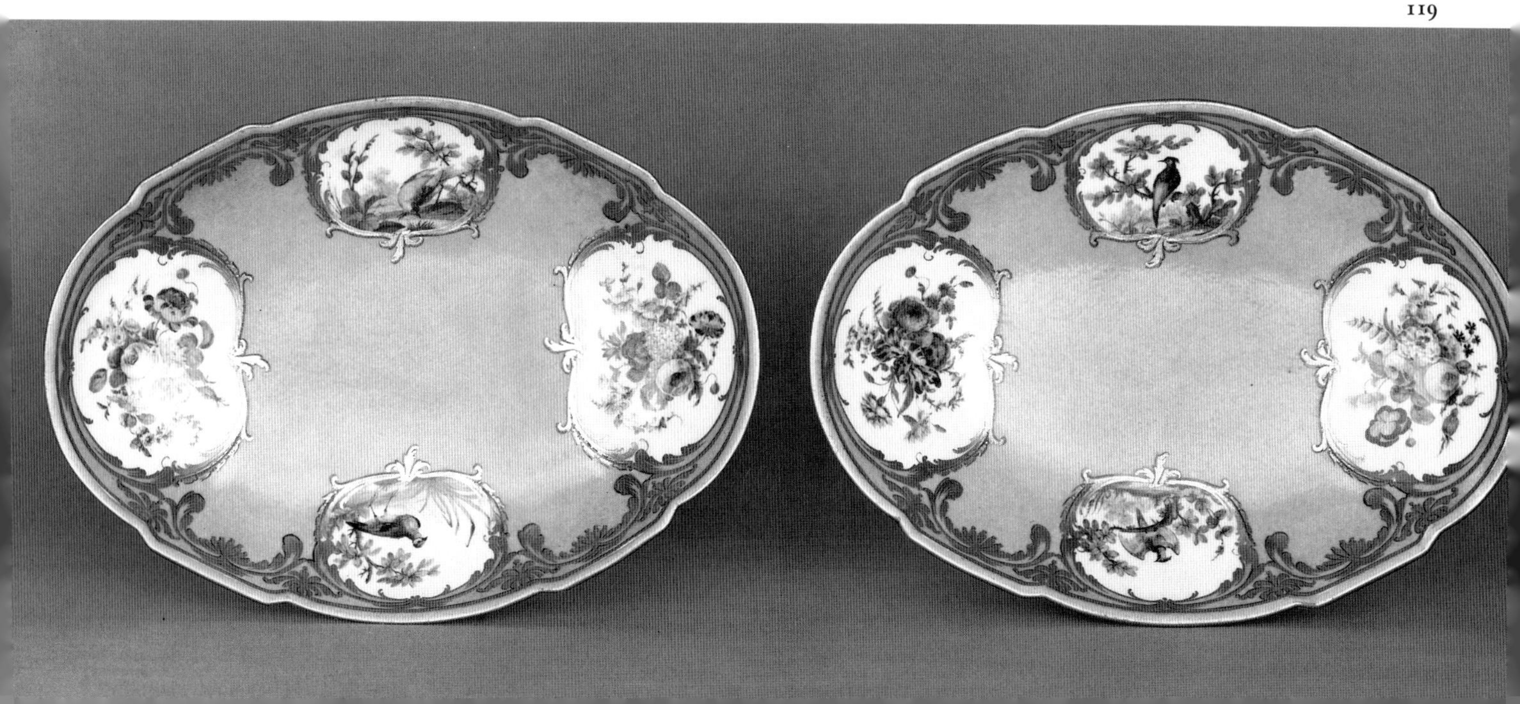

However, the combination of three marks in addition to the factory mark and date-letter as seen on the reverse of one *compotier* is unusual but can be paralleled. It is found, for instance, on an *assiette à palmes*[6] with a pink border interrupted by reserves containing birds, which is painted in the centre with a bouquet of flowers on a white ground. This piece has four marks in addition to the interlaced LL enclosing the date-letter V: a cursive *N* for the bird painter François-Joseph Aloncle, the quaver mark for the flower painter, Antoine-Toussaint Cornaille, *L.G.* for the gilder Etienne-Henry Le Guay and *VD.* in monogram for Jean-Baptiste Emmanuel Vandé, also a gilder. The gilt motif near the border of the plate is similar to that on the Museum *compotiers*, and the technique of highlighting the gold with dark pink is also comparable. The five *assiettes à palmes* in the collection of the Duke of Buccleuch, Northamptonshire, were decorated by Le Guay, Vandé and Aloncle.[7]

Biographical details of Boulanger and Vandé can be found in Savill.[8] For a jug and cover decorated by Evans, see cat. 124 (Comparable Examples); for a plate gilded by Boulanger, see cat. 121.

1. The author is grateful to David Peters for this information.
2. The models and moulds are listed in the inventory dated 1 January 1755, MNS, Archives de Sèvres, I7; the biscuit examples appear in the Bibliothèque de l'Institut, Paris, Mss 5673, f.22. The form may have been revised in 1766 as six plaster models are listed in the inventory of 1 January 1766, *ibid.* The author is grateful to Tamara Préaud for this information.
3. According to David Peters, who has not seen an example of the smaller size.
4. As, for example, on four turquoise-ground *compotiers* in the Razoumovsky service of 1767, illus. Eriksen, 1968, no. 75B, p. 210.
5. David Peters has pointed out that between about 1770 and the mid-1780s service pieces quite often bear the marks of a gilder and more than one painter.
6. This plate has not been examined by the author. It was in the trade in 1988, and the author is grateful to the dealer concerned for providing information about its marks.
7. The author is grateful to John Whitehead for providing this information, and to him and David Peters for their valuable assistance in cataloguing these *compotiers*. In private correspondence of October 1990, David Peters has stated that other pieces, such as four *assiettes à palmes* at the Henry E. Huntington Library and Art Gallery inv. 27.58 and 59.27. 79 and 80 which are painted with flowers and have a different gilded pattern, as well as six ice-cream cups painted with flowers, one of which is dated and bears the marks of Theodore, Buteux (?) and the gilder Chauveaux, are from another service, of which he will give details in a forthcoming publication.
8. Savill, 1988, III, p. 1004, p. 1072.

120 **Tray (*plateau à filet et rubans*)**, 1775

See colour plate 19

L. 41 cm

Marks: interlaced LL enclosing date-letter X for 1775 above painter's mark *k* for Charles-Nicolas Dodin; gilder's mark of Guillaume Noël, incised *Th* twice; suspension hole

Reg. No. 1948,12–3,7

Soft-paste porcelain, quadrilobe shape moulded with a ribbon bow at each end and a crossed loop at either side of the other two lobes. Painted with Venus, Mercury and Cupid in a wooded landscape within a double gilt frame on a green ground. The rim is decorated in gold with a complex design of trellis and dots, scrolls and flower garlands, the last two carefully tooled. The rim is gilt on both sides and below each handle on the underside is a gilt floral spray. Gilding rubbed on ribbon bows.

Provenance: E.M. Hodgkins Collection

Madame Dhainaut Collection, Paris, sold Sotheby's, 10 December 1936, Lot 63, to Mallet for £100

Bequeathed by Sir B. Eckstein, Bt., 1948

Literature: Cte X. de Chavagnac, 'Porcelaines de Sèvres – Collection E.M. Hodgkins', *Les Arts*, May 1909, p. 9
Bellaigue, 1986, p. 182

Comparable Examples: Paris, Musée des arts décoratifs, dated 1754, inv. GR 224, white ground, *bleu céleste* border and floral decoration, with two matching *gobelets Hébert*, a milk jug and sugar bowl as above, painter's mark for Taillandier and Levé, exh. Vincennes, 1977–8, no. 76

Paris, Hôtel Drouot, Vente Arts, 4 April 1960, Lot 79, dated 1774, painted with Chinese subjects with matching jug, two *tasses litrons*, sugar bowl and teapot

Germany, Hamburg, Museum für Kunst und Gewerbe, dated 1775, inv. 1882.295, *bleu nouveau*, painted with flowers and fruit and with matching *pot à lait à trois pieds*, two *tasses litrons*, a *pot à sucre Calabre* and a *théière Calabre*, illustrated H. Jedding, *Europaïsches Porzellan*, Vol. 1, Munich, 1971, fig. 839.

Germany, Düsseldorf, Hetjens Museum, dated 1781, inv. 1941/154 a–e, white ground, floral decoration and with matching pieces as above (only one cup and saucer), unidentified painter's mark and gilder's mark *2000*, illus. Klein, 1966, p. 41, no. 260, length of tray 49 cm

USA, French and Company, once in the possession of Leopoldina, Empress of Brazil, dated 1781, floral medallions and flower garlands on border, scattered flowers on a white ground, with full set of matching pieces as above, painter's marks *FB*, *LF* and gilder's mark *2000* (photograph Getty Photo Archive)

Christie's, Monaco, 7 December 1987, Important Porcelain and Faïence, Lot 240, dated 1780, painted with a *pointillé d'or* border, scattered flowers and cartouches with flower baskets, with matching jug, cup and saucer, sugar bowl and teapot

The tray was made in one size only. There is an oval variant of the shape with ribbons and scrolls on the interior of the body.[1] Another large tray of differing shape measuring 47 cm in length, now at Luton Hoo, Bedfordshire, has been identified by Sir Geoffrey de Bellaigue as part of a *déjeuner Paris*[2] named after Jacques François Paris (active 1746–92), chief repairer at the factory.[3] The *plateau à filet et rubans* is more

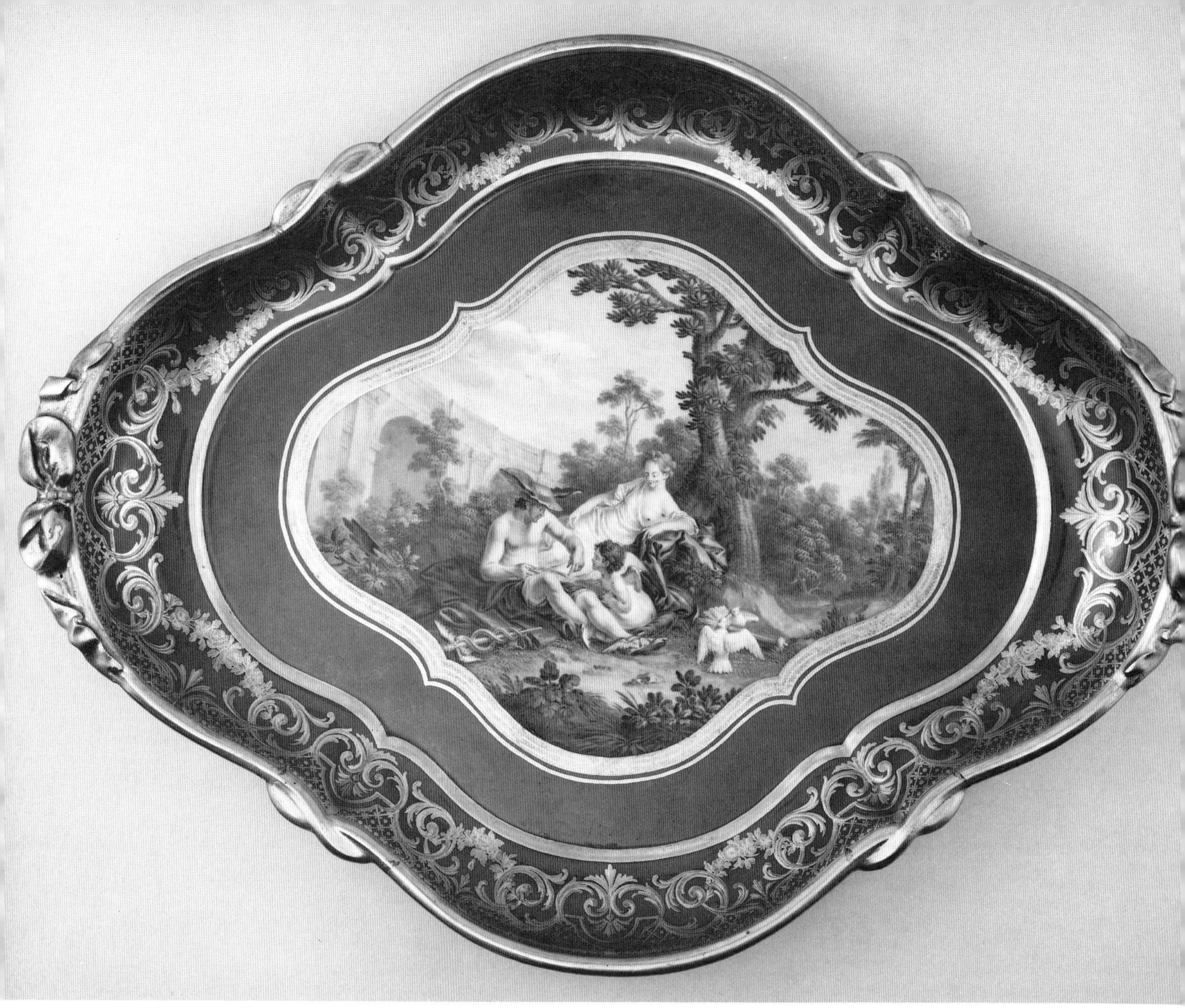

120

likely to be the work of Jean-Claude Duplessis since it appears to have been in production in the early 1750s (see above). On technical grounds, this tray represents one of the most impressive achievements of the factory, since a flat piece of this size is especially prone to distortion in the kiln. This example has a few small firecracks on the reverse, and, unusually, the base has a noticeable inclusion and some pin-holes. The foot is slightly discoloured in places.

The identity of the workman who incised *Th* twice on this tray remains uncertain. The mark has been attributed by Dauterman to the *mouleur* Thiercelin,[4] and Savill has suggested a repairer named Thion.[5] The latter is more likely since he is recorded on 5 November 1773 as working on '1 platteaux [*sic*] filet Rubans' for which he was paid 36 *livres* in January 1774.[6]

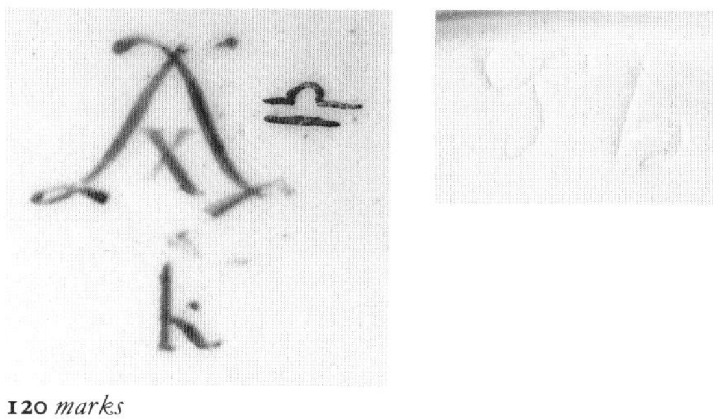

120 *marks*

The matching *tasses litrons*, sugar bowl, teapot and jug have not yet been discovered. In view of its rich decoration, it is not impossible that this tray was part of the *déjeuner ruban* sold to Madame Sophie on 30 August 1775 for 288 *livres*, but since the records of the painters' work in 1775 have been lost, this cannot be confirmed by referring to Dodin's productions during that year; there is no mention of a *déjeuner ruban* in the 1774 overtime records. A *déjeuner fond verd Mignature* presented to the Austrian Emperor and delivered on 3 April 1777 to Vergennes, the Foreign Minister, cost as much as 1,200 *livres*.[7]

The painted scene is based on *L'Amour à l'Ecole* by C. Vanloo,[8] engraved by R. Gaillard in 1744 with the addition of plants in the foreground. An example of the engraving is kept at the Sèvres factory and may perhaps have been there from the eighteenth century. The same subject occurs on a number of pieces of Sèvres, such as a plate from the Louis XVI service painted by Dodin, an undated *vase antique ferré*, a *vase Angora* dated 1772 and painted by Dodin, and an undated *écuelle* painted by E.-H. Le Guay.[9] It may well relate, as Tamara Préaud has suggested,[10] to the group known as *Mercure messager de l'Amour* modelled by Le Riche in 1770.

The gilder Guillaume Noël (b. 1734/5 at Nancy – d. 1804 Sèvres) began working at Vincennes on 22 May 1755 and is recorded as a painter of flowers, fruit, border patterns, friezes and other decorative motifs including textiles and cherubs. He also applied coloured grounds and worked in the gilders' and burnishers' workshops.[11] He was probably responsible for the gilding on this tray, as it is particularly rich, rather than for the ground colour.

A lozenge-shaped tray without ribbons was manufactured at the Frankenthal porcelain factory.[12]

1. Dauterman, 1964, no. 57 a–h, fig. 203, dated 1775. A *déjeuner à rubans* dated 1775 and decorated with flower garlands and a trellis design by Noël is illustrated by F. Masson in 'La Porcelaine de Sèvres, Collection Chappey', *Les Arts*, no. 38, February 1905, p. 2, and is said to have been a present from Louis XVI to Madame Sophie, but see text above. An earlier example of this form, dated 1768, is at Waddesdon Manor, Buckinghamshire, illus. Brunet and Préaud, 1978, no. 156; see also E. Garnier, *La porcelaine tendre de Sèvres*, Paris, n.d. (1889), repr. 1988, sixième livraison, pl. XXVIII, M *** collection, floral decoration; Christie's, 21 June 1976, Lot 78, collection of Lord Hillingdon, *déjeuner*, *bleu céleste*, 1774; Sotheby's, 12 June 1984, Lot 180, Burton-Jones and Gifford-Scott collections, green ground, 1775.
2. Eriksen and Bellaigue, 1987, no. 146, p. 337; for a full discussion of this form and a *déjeuner 'Paris'* see Savill, 1988, II, pp. 621–8.
3. For a biography of Paris, see Savill, 1988, III, p. 985.
4. Dauterman, 1986, p. 238. The mark is recorded by this author on a large tureen stand of 1770 and on another of 1768; see Dauterman, 1970, pp. 236, 262.
5. Savill, 1988, III, pp. 1123–4.
6. MNS, Archives de Sèvres, Va' 1.
7. MNS, Archives de Sèvres, Vy 6, f. 207v.
8. The painting was reproduced in H. Dobler, *Les Ecoles d'architecture et d'art décoratif des XVIIe et XVIIIe siècles à Aix*, Aix, 1910, p. 52, when it was in the Musée d'Aix. At the time it was engraved, it belonged to the Prince Carignan.
9. Bellaigue, 1986, no. 101, 4.
10. In corresondence with the author, Spring 1991; for the model see Bourgeois and Lechevalier-Chevignard, pl. 34, no. 424.
11. Savill, 1988, III, pp. 1053–4.
12. Lepke, Berlin, Sammlung Jean Wurz, Mannheim, 10–11 December 1924, Lots 308, 348.

121 Plate (*assiette de dessert*), 1778

See colour plate 20

D. 26.4 cm

Marks: LL enclosing AA for 1778 above *PH* for the painter François Pascal Philippine *fils aîné*, all in brown; cursive *B* for the gilder Jean-Pierre Boulanger *père* in blue enamel; *33* incised; suspension hole; blue printed label of Sir Bernard Eckstein Collection numbered in ink *21*

Reg. No. 1948,12–3,13

Soft-paste porcelain with shallow central well and large rim. Decorated on the rim with three cameo heads *en grisaille* on a red-brown ground, each within an oval reserve, alternating with three classical subjects in the same manner within larger oval reserves, all interrupting a band of turquoise (*bleu céleste*) embellished with tooled richly-gilt scrolls. This central band is enclosed between flower sprays linked by gold husks. The well of the plate has a turquoise ground. In the centre, enclosed by a tooled gilt band, is the crowned monogram *E11* for the Empress Catherine II 'the Great' of Russia (1729–96) in polychrome flowers and gold within a laurel and myrtle wreath tied by a gilt ribbon bow. Rim gilt with dentil on underside; gilt line around outer edge of foot rim. Foot rim chipped.

Provenance: Bequeathed by Sir B. Eckstein, Bt., 1948

Literature: Bellaigue, 1980, fig. 3, p. 668

Bellaigue, 1986, p. 70, no. 2,2; p. 79, no. 6,5; p. 86, no. 12,4

Comparable Examples: Most of the service from which this piece comes is in the State Hermitage Museum, St Petersburg, Russia, see K. Butler, 'Sèvres for the Imperial Court', *Apollo*, Vol. CI, no. 160, June 1975, pp. 452–7 and 'La France et la Russie au siècle des lumières', Paris, Grand Palais, November 1986–February 1987, cat. 478–486. Other plates no longer in Russia are known, including: Musée national de Céramique, Sèvres, inv. 22 602, illus. Brunet and Préaud, 1978, no. 223; private coll. illus. P. Verlet, *Sèvres*, Paris, 1954, col. pl. opp. p. 68; Victoria and Albert Museum, London, inv. 3644–1856; inv. C.449–1921; Fitzwilliam Museum, Cambridge, illus. C. Winter, 'Louis Clarke as a Collector', *Apollo*, Vol. LXXVII, no. 5, July 1962, p. 381, fig. 13; a plate inv. no. 1896.301 was formerly in the Staatliche Museen zu Berlin, Kunstgewerbemuseum (destroyed), and a photograph is kept on file in Schloss Köpenick, Berlin.

This plate formed part of an extensive dinner- and dessert-service for 60 people, which consisted of 800 pieces.[1] It was ordered by Catherine the Great through Prince Ivan Sergeyvich Bariatinsky (1740–1811 o.s.), the Russian Ambassador at Versailles between 1773 and 1785. The service, which took three years to make, was despatched in June 1779 and

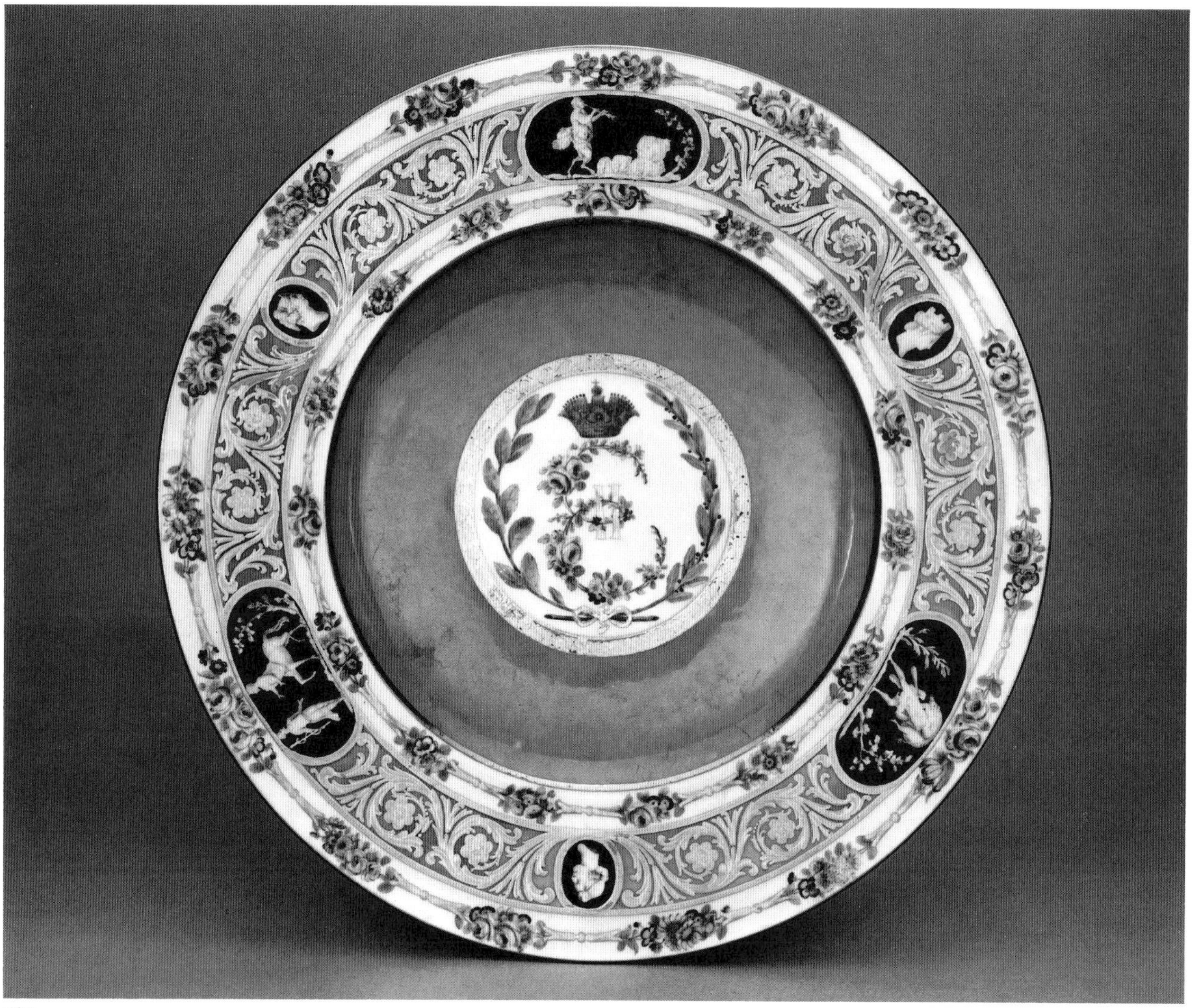

121

arrived in St Petersburg in October of that year, the final instalment of the payment which amounted to a total of 331,317 *livres* being received in 1792.

The forms of the service were specially devised in a strictly classical style. A leather-bound volume tooled in gold bearing a manuscript label inscribed *Dessins et Devis du Service de Porcelaine pour l'Imperatrice de Russie 1778* is preserved in the Bibliothèque Nationale, Paris.[2] The account begins 'Ce Service ne pouvait être executé sur les formes actuellement usitées à la Manufacture de Seves . . .'. The plate shape, to which several subsequent pages of manuscript were devoted in the description of the service,[3] was redesigned eight times before the Empress was satisfied with it.[4]

The mythological scenes on the rim are: *Pan leading his herd of cattle and sheep*; *Aesculapius and a centaur*; and *Hercules with the Erymanthian Boar*. The scene of

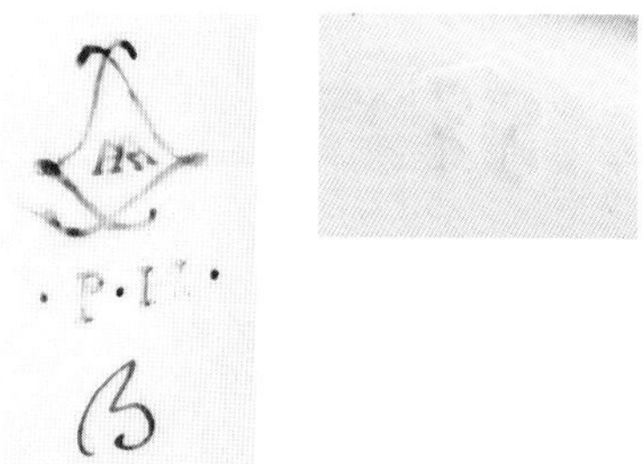

121 *marks*

Aesculapius is repeated in colours on a plate from the service commissioned in 1783 by Louis XVI of France for his own use at Versailles, and now mostly in the Royal Collection,[5] but here the scene is differently treated. The painter J.-B.-E. Genest was responsible for 60 designs (*dessins*) for the service, for which he was paid 180 *livres*.[6]

The cameo heads on the rim which were transfer-printed and filled in with colour by hand represent classical deities. A sheet inscribed in a late eighteenth-century hand *Tetes imprimees avec de la couleur à porcelaine tendre en 1777 au 1778 service* survives in the factory archives[7] but it does not show the heads on this plate, which probably belonged to the seventh batch of a dozen dessert plates identically decorated[8] from a total of 120 in the group painted with mythological subjects.

As indicated in the album of watercolour designs and estimates for every item, the richly-gilt scrolls imitate the decoration of the Theatre of Marcellus in Rome.[9] Two layers of gold were applied so as 'to achieve a sufficiently thick surface for the deep tooling, chasing and polishing'.[10] Jean-Pierre Boulanger, who worked on this plate, was employed as a gilder at the factory between 1754 and 1785.[11]

Each of the 288 plates was sold for 242 *livres*.[12] It was fired eight times and the total production cost was calculated as 221 *livres* each.[13] This example is free of the more obvious firing defects found on some of the plates kept in the Hermitage Museum, Russia, although there is a slight imperfection in the turquoise ground, visible only on close inspection.

The history of the Museum plate has not been traced. In December 1837 about 160 pieces from the service were apparently looted from the Winter Palace which was seriously damaged by fire.[14] Most of these pieces (149 or 150) were acquired by Viscount Lowther in two consignments by July 1842 and Rosalind Savill has argued that most of the service was purchased from Lord Lowther by Lord Hertford in early 1857 and returned through a dealer named Webb to Russia. Other pieces certainly remained in England – some were in Lord Lonsdale's posthumous sale[15] and some in W.J. Goode's sale, where the highest price for a piece from the service was 155 guineas for a plate; others have been sold at various times.[16]

The pieces sold by Goode may well have been the ones copied by Minton in whose archive is a series of photographs of plate borders, although none appears to represent the British Museum plate.[17] The service was copied in bone china by Minton but the general effect achieved was of imitation rather than exact reproduction. Replacement pieces or additional items were apparently supplied to Tsar Nicholas I and Tsar Alexander III by the Imperial Porcelain Factory, St Petersburg.[18] Copeland also produced copies around 1904–6 for which the coloured drawing still exists at the factory.[19]

1. The composition of the services is discussed by Savill, 1988, II, p. 762.
2. B.N., Lf 8 petit folio.
3. The following passage from the account of the service reveals the aspirations of the designer:

'Decoration des Assiettes

'L'Assiette est parfaitement ronde sans aucun chantournement, sa forme est celle d'une Patère antique, tant soit rélevée sur ses bords, destinées d'abord aux Sacrifices, les Etrusques avaient établi l'usage des Patères dans toute l'Italie. On ne s'en servait que dans les Temples, comme on les voit sur les médailles et sur les bas reliefs antiques, ou le Sacrificateur est représenté la Patère à la main, ayant la forme du Disque ou d'une assiette; c'est de là que la forme de notre assiette est tirée.

'Le fond de L'assiette a 6. pouces de diamêtre et ses bords ont 2. pouces de largeur; ce qui forme la Diamêtre du Disque total de 10. pouces.

'La couleur bleue de Turquoise remplit toute l'assiette; mais ce fond est interrompu par des réserves blanches, dans les quelles on a peint différens sujets.

'I°., au milieu de l'assiette; la rèserve blanch a 3. pouces de diamêtre; on y a peint le chiffre de l'Impératrice en fleurs naturelles; deux palmes lui servent de support; l'une de Myrthe et l'autre de Laurier; le tout est surmonté d'une couronne Impériale rehaussée d'or.

'2° sur le bord de l'assiette, il y a encore deux réserves blanches sur un fond bleu: ce Sont deux bandes de largeur d'un petit Ruban de quatre lignes dans lesquelles on a peint des Guirlandes et des festons de fleurs naturelles. Entre ces deux bandes ornées de petites fleurs il reste une Zône bleüe de 15.lignes de largeur, qui est interrompue, à distance égales [*sic*], et alternativement par trois Camées peints en agathe onix, réprésentant des têtes antiques, de la grandeur seulement des pierres dits annulaires parc ce qu'elles sont de la taille de celles qui chez les Anciens, étaient montées en anneau; ces têtes paraissent être enchanînées dans la zône bleue parune sertissure d'or.

'A égale distance des trois têtes et alternativement sont bas-reliefs, en agathe onix, d'après sujets antiques, ils sont d'une forme ovale, et de la grandeur, à peu près, d'une plaque de bracelet; et ces bas-reliefs paraissent également être enchasses dans la zône bleue, par une sertissure d'or.

'L'Intervale entre les camées annullaires et les camées en sujets de plusiers figures des bas-relief; c'est à dire, la partie de la zône bleüe dans la quelle ces Camées sont enchassé est enrichie d'une frise d'or, à fleurons réguliers, interrompus par une rosace d'or; ce dessin est tiré d'une des frizes d'ornements, qui decorent le Théâtre antique de Marcellus, à Rome.

'Dans une quantité de pièces aussi considérables qui celles dont ce service est composé, d'assiettes surtout, qui est de 360, on a diversifié le plus qu'il a été possible les sujets des têtes et des bas-reliefs dont le nombre s'éleve à 2160, pour les assiettes seulement.

'Pour cet effet on a partagé ce nombre de 360 assiettes en divisions. La premiére contient des sujets tirés de la Mythologie; la seconde Division contient des sujets tirés de l'histoire

Grèque; et les sujets de la troisième division sont pris dans l'histoire Romaine.

'Chaque division d'assiettes étant de 10.douz.es ou de 120.assiettes; on les a encore subdivisé de manière qu'il n'y a que 12.assiettes qui portent les mêmes sujets dans l'ordre qui suit.'

4. R. Savill, 'Cameo Fever': six pieces from the Sèvres porcelain dinner service made for Catherine II of Russia,' *Apollo*, Vol. CXVI, no. 249, Nov. 1982, p. 305.
5. Bellaigue, 1980, fig. 4 and p. 668; and Bellaigue, 1986, p. 70. Eriksen, 1968, p. 326.
6. Savill, 1988, II, p. 763 and p. 780, f.n.15.
7. Savill, 1982, p. 307.
8. To avoid repetition of the subjects various different groupings were carefully worked out and these can be seen in the 'Dessins et Devis' referred to in n.2. The subjects for the seventh dozen are detailed on f.8v but 'Bacchus couronné par les Bacchantes' does not appear on the Museum plate. Hercules carrying the Erymanthian boar is in the ninth dozen on f.9.
9. Savill, 1982, p. 306, p. 307, fig. 4.
10. *Ibid.*, p. 306.
11. Jean-Pierre Boulanger *père* (1722–85) worked at Saint-Cloud before joining Vincennes as a gilder in July 1754. He carried out a certain amount of painting from 1768, but never entirely gave up gilding. By 1774 his monthly wage had reached the high sum of 78 *livres*. For further details, see Savill, 1988, III, pp. 1004–5.
12. The sales record is reproduced in full by D. Guillemé-Brulon, 'Les grands services de Sèvres: le service de Catherine II,' *L'Estampille*, no. 167, March 1984, p. 56.
13. *Ibid.*, p. 56.
14. K. Butler, 'Sèvres for the Imperial Court', *Apollo*, Vol. CI, no. 160, June 1975, p. 456.
15. Christie's, 13–18 June 1887, Lots 49–51.
16. Earl of Dudley sale, Christie's, 21 May 1886, Lot 95, sold for 108 guineas.
17. Minton Archive, JJ 161.
18. See D.C., 'Thomas Goode's and the Czar', *The Antique Collector*, October 1987, p. 105.
19. The author is grateful to Mr Robert Copeland for his assistance in photographing this drawing and the plate surviving in the Spode Museum, Stoke-on-Trent.

122 Teapot (*bouillotte*), 1778

See colour plate 21

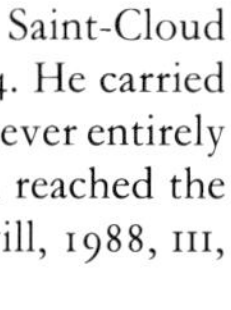

122 *mark*

H. *to top of handle:*	18.3 cm
Marks:	interlaced LL crowned enclosing date-letter AA for 1778 painted in red enamel, surmounted by the mark of the painter Jean-Jacques Dieu (employed at Sèvres 1770–90, 1794–8, 1803–10); the metal mount for the handle bears the crayfish export mark used in France between 10 May 1838 and 30 May 1864[1]
Reg. No.	Franks 385

Hard-paste porcelain; the globular thrown body with grooved moulded spout terminating in a dolphin's head; ebony and silver-gilt handle fixed to the pot at either side by means of a screw and nut attachment. A similar attachment retains the metal finial to which is fixed a gilt chain leading to the handle at one side only. The porcelain is decorated in brown sprinkled with gold and on the body, neck and cover with *chinoiseries* in two colours of gold, carefully tooled, and silver. On one side is a scene of a Chinese lady seated by a bird on a stand and being offered bottles on a tray by a Chinaman; on the other, a Chinese figure kneels by a fountain before two other figures, one seated, one standing; behind them a tree and a pagoda. Spout restored.

Provenance: R. Bernal, M.P. sale, Christie's, 5 March 1855, Lot 468; note in ms in catalogue kept in British Museum 'Bought by Bale at Bernal Sale for £30. "Mr Bernal purchased this remarkable piece of hard paste of Mr Durlacher for eight guineas".'

C.S. Bale sale, Christie's, 23 May 1881, Lot 1332, 10 guineas

C. Beckett-Denison sale, Christie's, 8 June 1885, Lot 183, £6

Bequeathed by Sir A.W. Franks, 1897

Literature: Franks, 1896, no. 385

Dawson, 1985, pp. 14–16, fig. 4

Exhibited: 'Documentary Continental Ceramics from the British Museum', exh., International Ceramics Fair and Seminar Ltd., London, June 1985, no. 47, catalogue compiled by A. Dawson

Comparable Examples: Sèvres, Musée national de Céramique, inv. MNCS 23260, illus. Brunet and Préaud, 1978, p. XLIX, p. 109

Sotheby's, 5 December 1989, Hector Binney sale, Lot 146, gold ground, painted with flowers by Parpette, 1779

Denmark, Copenhagen, David Collection, inv. 24/1978, illus. Eriksen, 1980, no. 62

Switzerland, Geneva, Sotheby's, 14 November 1989, Lot 3, wine-red ground, painted with flowers by Bulidon, 1782

USA, Boston, Museum of Fine Arts, inv. 1975. 658, dated 1779, painted by Castel with an exotic bird in a *chinoiserie* landscape on a white ground[2]

USA, Hartford, Conn., Wadsworth Atheneum, roses in pink on a white ground, date-letter effaced, inv. 1917.1156

N. Ikodinovic & Co., S.C., exh. at International Ceramics Fair and Seminar Ltd., London, June 1990, illus. *Handbook*, p. 65, dated 1779, *chinoiserie* figures in gold and enamels on a salmon-pink ground, no painter's mark, now in a private collection, USA

The brown ground-colour sprinkled with gold corresponds with a ground referred to in a document written in 1781 on the subject of colours for hard-paste porcelain[3] as *avanturine*. Under the heading *Ors en couleur*, the method of achieving the effect is described as follows:

> Avanturine: Pour faire l'avanturine sur des fonds bleus ou bruns, carmins ou violets, on se sert d'une brosse de crin fin, dont on trempe le bout des crins dans de l'or preparé comme pour être employé au pinceau, et en ratissant les crins de cette brosse avec un petit Baton, on en fait jaillir des goutelettes sur la piece [*sic*] qu'on veut aventuriner. (Aventurine: to produce aventurine on blue, brown, pink or violet grounds, a fine brush is used which is dipped in gold prepared as if for use with a paintbrush. By tapping the hairs of the brush with a small stick, droplets are made to fall on the piece which one

wishes to decorate with an aventurine ground.)
X-ray fluorescence analysis has confirmed that the white metal used over the *avanturine* glaze is silver, the yellow gold almost pure gold, and the remaining gold an alloy of silver and gold.[4] A teapot and cover (*théière Bouillard*) measuring around 12 cm in height with similar decoration dated 1781 is in the Metropolitan Museum, New York.[5]

The shape, which was thrown and turned (body) and moulded (spout) is, like most Vincennes/Sèvres teapot shapes, a pleasing one. However, the handle is poorly designed. Its metal parts have a tendency to bend because of the weight of the pot, a feature which is common to the Sèvres, Boston and British Museum examples, all examined by the writer. This may help to explain why the form first introduced in 1774[6] under the name 'bouilloire' or 'bouillotte pour la toilette' (an example was first sold in December 1776)[7] never apparently caught on. It seems to have been made in one size only but also in a gadrooned version.[8]

Dieu, who specialised in *chinoiserie* scenes is recorded in the registers of painters' (overtime) work as having decorated on 9 November 1778 '2 Bouillotes Une brune L'autre Couleur de Bellevue'[9] for which he was paid 42 and 60 *livres* respectively. On 16 November '1 Bouillote fond brun' decorated with 'chinois' by Dieu is recorded in the enamel kiln register,[10] and on 25 November it went for burnishing.[11] Four *bouillottes* were sold for 360 *livres* each in December 1778[12] but the sales records give no details of the decoration, nor of the purchasers. A year later one was sold to the Queen for 360 *livres*[13] and another to the King at 312 *livres*.[14]

The source of the *chinoiserie* decoration, which is the style associated with Pillement, remains unknown.

A silver teapot of related form by the Paris goldsmith Jean-Louis Dieudonné is dated 1785.[15]

122

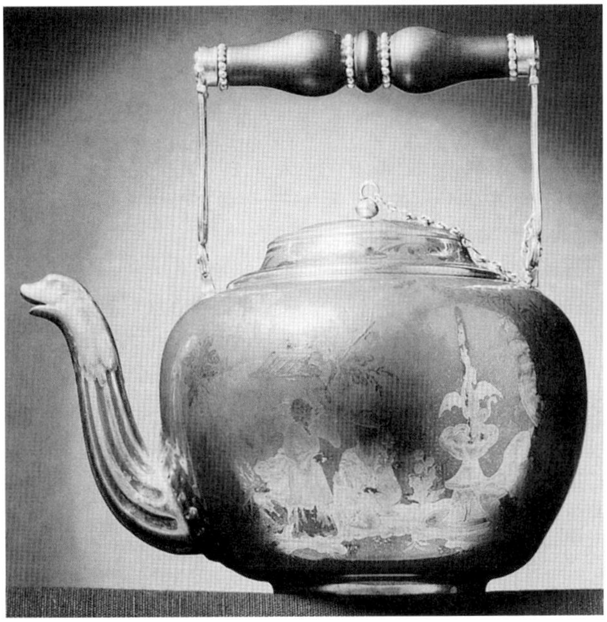

1. Tardy, *International Hallmarks on Silver*, Calne, 1981, p. 206.
2. See J. H. Munger, 'A *Bouillote* in the Museum of Fine Arts, Boston', in *Mélanges en Souvenir d'Elisalex d'Albis 1939–1998*, privately printed, 1999, pp. 103–9.
3. MNS, Archives de Sèvres, C2 *liasse* 2.
4. BM Research Laboratory 23080 X.
5. Inv. 54.147.16A and B, mark in blue crowned, date-letters AA and LG below, incised [?]Rd. The author is grateful to Clare Le Corbeiller for bringing this piece to her attention.
6. First documented in the register of the *travaux des pâtes* – MNS, Archives de Sèvres, Va' 2 under the names of Pépin, Choulet and others. The author is grateful to Tamara Préaud for this information.
7. MNS, Archives de Sèvres, Vy 6, f. 125, sold for 72 *livres* at Versailles on 5 December 1776.
8. A *bouillotte 'à Gaudron'* is mentioned in the factory records in March 1779, MNS, Archives de Sévres, Va 4, Godin, quoted Savill, 1988, II, p. 563, f.n. 7. Only one example has been recorded (whereabouts unknown, seen by David Cohen, 1987, photographs kept at the Archives de Sèvres), which is undated, and bears the mark of the gilder Chauveaux. A drawing for this shape is preserved at the factory.
9. MNS, Archives de Sèvres, Vj'1, fol. 119v°.
10. MNS, Archives de Sèvres, Vl'1, f. 32.
11. MNS, Archives de Sèvres, Vl'1, f. 33v.
12. MNS, Archives de Sèvres, Vj'1, f. 120, f. 125v, 128v, f. 169, 179 on 26 December, on 12 December.
13. MNS, Archives de Sèvres, Vj'1, f. 179.
14. MNS, Archives de Sèvres, Vj'1, f. 178.
15. L. Réau, *L'Art en France au XVIIème Siècle, style Louis XVI 1760–1789*, Paris, 1952, fig. 213, Puiforcat Collection.

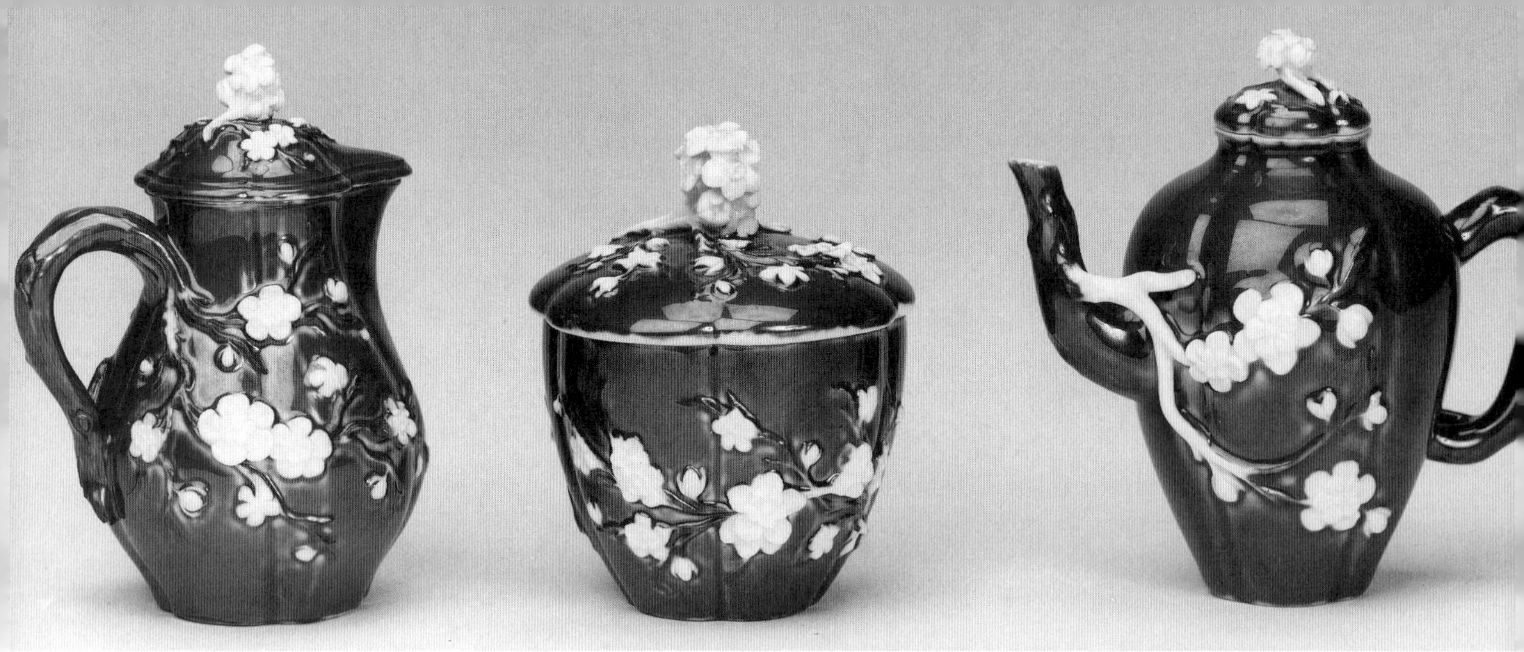

123

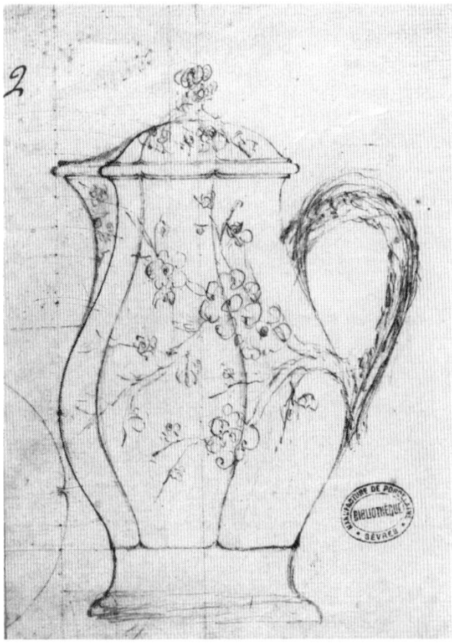

Fig 123a

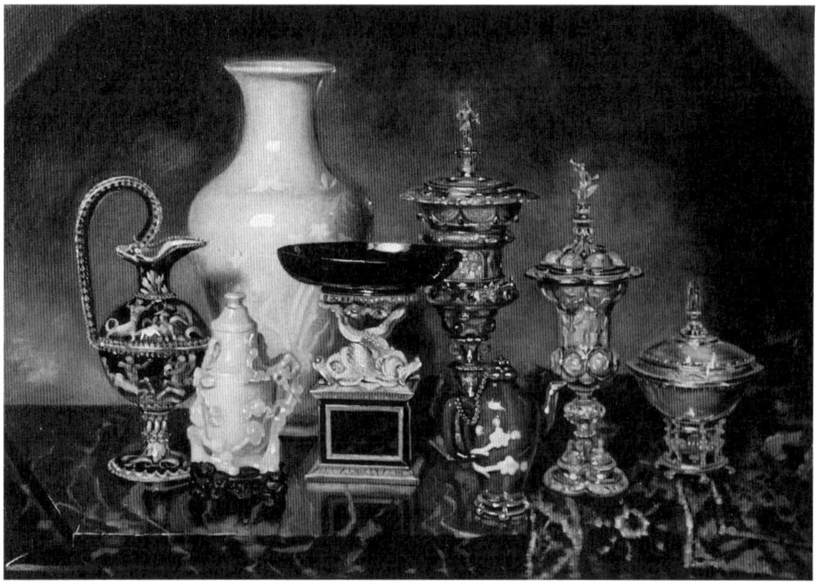

Fig 123b

123 Teapot and Cover, Milk Jug and Cover, Sugar Bowl and Cover (*théière, pot à crème, pot à sucre des Indes*), *c.* 1780

See colour plate 22

H. *incl. cover:*	(teapot) 11.3 cm (milk jug) 11.1 cm (sugar bowl) 9.6 cm
Marks:	none; *78 B* inscribed in black ?ink on base of teapot, *78 B* on base of milk jug, *B* on base of sugar bowl
Reg. No.	Franks 73

Hard-paste porcelain, each of moulded lobed form with two prunus branches in relief. On the milk jug these issue from the lower end of the twig handle on one side and from its upper extremity on the other side. On the teapot, the handle of which is in the form of a twig or branch, the prunus issues from the lower end of the handle on one side and on the other from midway down the branch spout on the other. The covers have elaborate flower knops. The base of each is flat and unglazed. The surface of each, except for the flowers and part of the branches on the teapot and the covers, is covered with a glaze of caramel brown colour. Small chip to teapot spout and inside its cover.

Provenance: Bequeathed by Sir A.W. Franks, 1897

Literature: Franks, 1896, no. 73

Comparable Examples: Sèvres, Musée national de Céramique, inv. 19383, saucer, decor as above, indistinctly marked with LL crowned

Paris, Musée des arts décoratifs; inv. unknown, cup and saucer, tiny gold dots on brown ground, reliefs silvered, gilt decoration, mark in gold of LL crowned enclosing indecipherable letter above *L*

Sotheby's, 5 March 1985, Lot 119, sugar bowl and cover, milk jug, Lot 120 two cups and saucers dated 1781 (now in a London private collection)

Scotland, Isle of Arran, Brodick Castle, The National Trust for Scotland, teapot and cover, mounted in gold

Germany, Berlin, Lepke, 24–26 March 1925 (Darmstaedter Collection), Lot 489 cup and saucer, Lot 490, milk jug and cover, decoration as above, see Tafel 111

USA, Washington, D.C., Smithsonian Institution, National Museum of American History, inv. 1106, unmarked, undecorated

The attribution made by A.W. Franks to the Meissen factory probably owes its origin to the resemblance of the glaze on these pieces to the dead-leaf brown or *Kapuzinerbraun* invented in 1720 by the Meissen arcanist Samuel Stölzel, although the colour is not in fact the same.[1] Pieces of closely comparable type bearing the marks of the Sèvres factory (see above) and the existence of a drawing (see fig. 123a) and plasters in the factory archives[2] are evidence that the Museum pieces were made in France. They may perhaps be experimental, as no others without the silvering have been discovered, with the exception of a mounted teapot and cover which belonged to William Beckford (1759–1844). This piece, now at Brodick Castle, Isle of Arran,[3] was depicted with some of Beckford's other prize pieces in one of three oil paintings (see fig. 123b) by Willes Maddox (1813–53).[4] The date when Beckford acquired this piece is unknown but he may have purchased it on one of his many visits to Paris[5] and had it mounted some long time afterwards between 1815 and 1820.

The date of introduction of this shape, whose prunus ornamentation harks back to fashions of several decades earlier, has not yet been discovered. However, the existence of pieces dated 1781 (see above) suggests an approximate date of manufacture. It is possible that the teawares known in the factory records under the title 'des Indes' were introduced in the late 1770s, as the repairer Liance *fils aîné* was paid for covers for teapots 'des indre' in March 1777.[6] In the following year the firing of five *gobelets*, a *theyere* and a *pot à sucre* described as *relief fond brun* decorated with *fleurs d'argent* by Lécot is recorded on 20 June.[7]

1. For an early example with *chinoiseries* by J.G. Höroldt see exh. 'Documentary Continental Ceramics from the British Museum', International Ceramics Fair and Seminar Ltd., London, June 1985, no. 6, cat. compiled by A. Dawson.
2. MNS, Archives de Sèvres, R. I. *liasse* 2, *dossier* 9, fol. 2 (drawing). A plaster inscribed *pot a sucre des Indes* in a larger size than the Museum sugar bowl and two plasters of a *pot à crème des Indes* are kept at the Sèvres factory.
3. Exh. 'William Beckford Exhibition 1976', cat. C 26; illustrated 'Beckford and Hamilton Silver from Brodick Castle', arranged by the National Trust for Scotland, 1980, Spink and Son Ltd., London, cat. compiled by M. Baker, T. Schroder and E. Laird Clowes, no. B 35.
4. Now at the Beckford Tower Trust, Bath, England, exh. International Silver & Jewellery Fair & Seminar, London, February 1988 with the Beckford Silver.
5. According to M. Snodin and M. Baker in 'William Beckford's Silver I', *Burlington Magazine*, Vol. CXXII, no. 932, November 1980, p. 735, Beckford spent a considerable part of the time between 1788 and 1802 in Paris.
6. MNS, Archives de Sèvres, Va'4 *Travaux de chaque mois fait par les ouvriers qui travaillent la Porcelaine Dure.*
7. MNS, Archives de Sèvres, Vl'1, f. 13.

124 Jug and Basin (*pot à eau ordinaire et cuvette*), 1780

See colour plate 23

H. *of jug:*	21.9 cm
L. *of bowl:*	29.9 cm
Marks:	interlaced LL enclosing date-letters CC for 1780 above *N* for the painter François-Joseph Aloncle and *HP* for the gilder Henry-Martin Prévost painted in blue enamel on both; *3ya* incised on jug, *B16* incised on basin; suspension hole on basin and inside cover; blue printed label of Sir Bernard Eckstein Collection numbered in ink *18.* on both
Reg. No.	1948,12–3,11

Soft-paste porcelain, the pear-shaped jug has a flat cover attached by means of a metal mount pinned through the cover and folded round the upper end of the tapering handle which terminates in an outward kick. Yellowish-green ground, painted with exotic birds within two oval reserves surrounded by a gilt border with a tooled crossed-ribbon motif. The tooled oak and acorn gilding is interrupted by ribbon bows above and below the miniatures. The lip is outlined with gilding (also found near the foot and rim) and ornamented with a gilt flower wreath depending from a ribbon bow. The cover is decorated with a bird carrying an olive branch within a laurel leaf and berry wreath. Gilt flowers and leaves decorate the border of the cover. The basin is similarly decorated, having a panel of birds at each end of the inner surface and at either side of the exterior. The inside of the base has an extensive firecrack. Pin holes in the gilding suggest it was overfired. Silver-gilt mount.

Provenance: 2nd Marchioness of Hertford, 1834, recorded at Hertford House, London, in her Sitting Room on the Principal Floor, Inventory 203, p. 14, valued at £25

3rd Marquess of Hertford, recorded in the inventory of the effects of St Dunstan's Villa made on his death, 1842, and in the inventory made by his executors of the 'China & C removed from the Regent's Park villa to Dorchester House, Park Lane, London'

4th Marquess of Hertford at Hertford House, London, recorded in the inventory made after his death, 1870

An undated *List of Effects removed from Manchester House*, probably drawn up around 1871,[1] lists 'A superb green ewer and font of the rare old Sèvres with six medallions of birds and trees with their names, most beautifully painted and enriched with gold laurel & oak borders' in the 'Marchioness's Private Sitting Room. East Corner'[2]

5th Marquess of Hertford, removed from Ragley Hall, Alcester, Warwickshire, sold Christie's, June 30 1921, Lot 10 for £100 to Mallett

Bequeathed by Sir B. Eckstein, Bt., 1948

Literature: Savage, 1960, pl. 44b

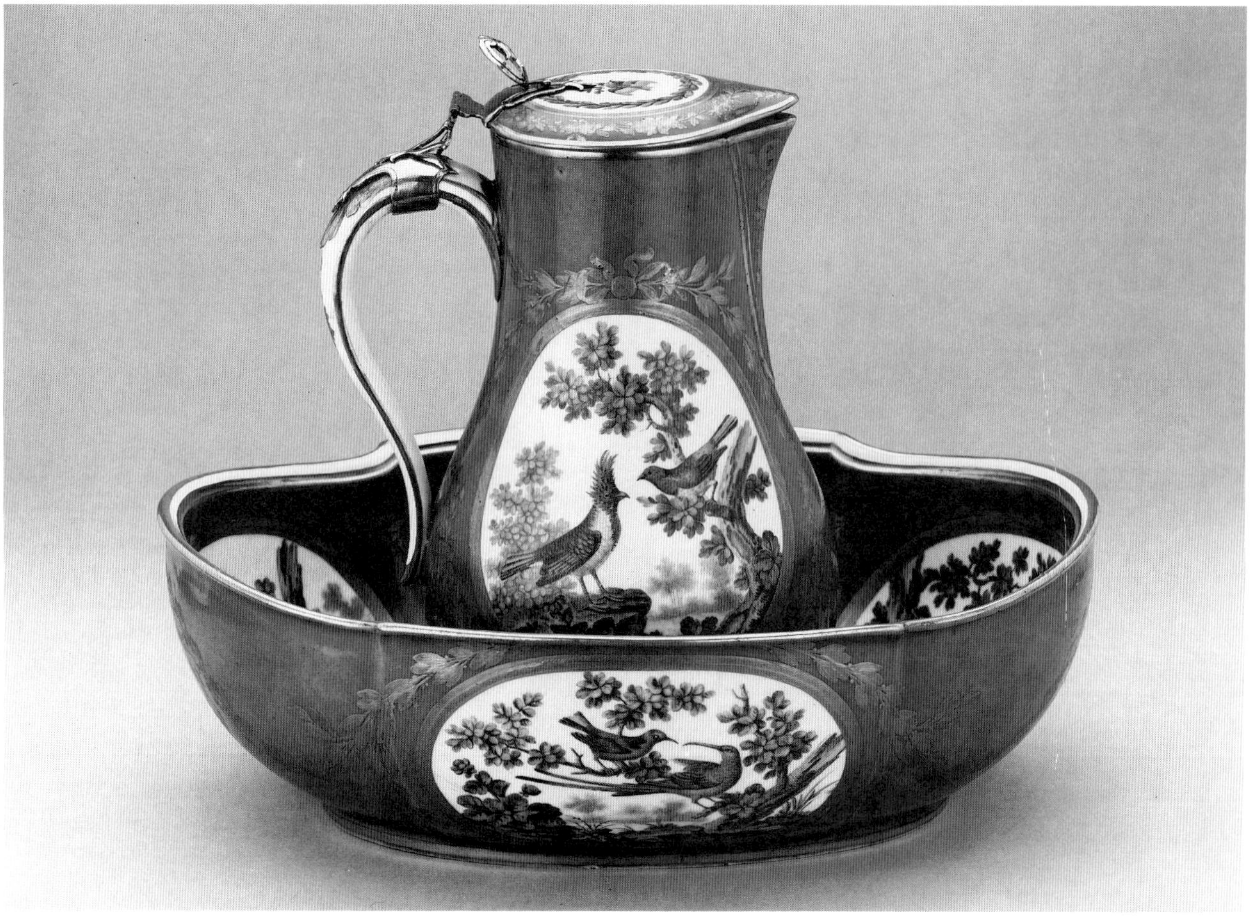

124

Comparable Examples: Paris, Hôtel Drouot, Couturier Nicolay, 15 June 1988, Lot 5, first size, green ground, birds by Evans, *RF* mark, unmounted, formerly Bensimon Collection

USA, New York, see M. Brunet, *The Frick Collection, Vol.* VII, *Porcelains*, 1974, pp. 284–9 turquoise ground, with flowers and fruit, 1776, and pp. 290–4 turquoise ground with marine scenes, 1781

The shape is first recorded in December 1751 when a silver-gilt mount for a Vincennes *pot à eau* was sold to Madame de Pompadour by Lazare Duvaux.[3] The original (undated) drawing and models for three sizes are preserved at the factory,[4] although according to Bellaigue four sizes ranging from 12 cm to 22.5 cm were produced.[5] This example represents the first (i.e. largest) size. Water jugs and basins were used on dressing-tables, and were intended for display, and also for use in the *garde-robe* which in eighteenth-century French royal and aristocratic circles was developing into a proto-bathroom.[6]

The registers of painters' and gilders' work show that Aloncle was paid 36 *livres* on 20 September 1780 for painting birds on '1 Pot à l'eau et Jatte' of the first size with a green ground.[7] Aloncle, who was born

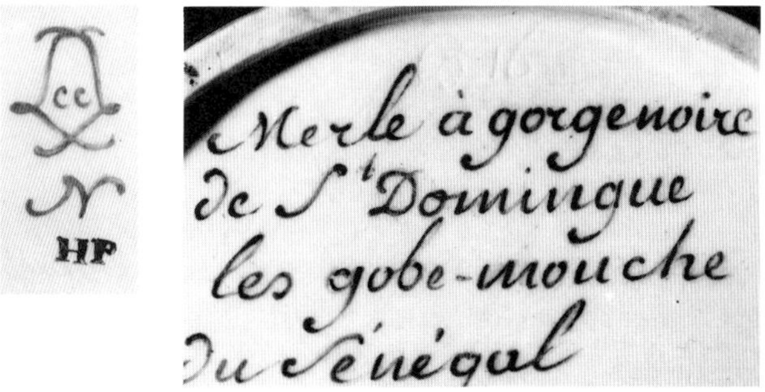

124 *marks*

in Versailles on 15 February 1734, was a painter in Paris before joining Sèvres in May 1758. He died at Sèvres on 25 February 1781, having married Françoise-Felicité Bulidon one week before his death.[8] As early as 1766 he was employed in painting named exotic birds on the Razoumovsky service now at Waddesdon Manor, Buckinghamshire.[9]

The names of the birds are given in blue enamel: on the jug *cardinal de la louisiane et tangara du Brésil* and *lory, des indes-Orientales.* [et] *Martin pecheur de ternate*; on the basin *le couliavan, de la cochinchine gobe Mouche d'amérique et sa femelle; Les Bengali; Merle à gorgenoire de St Domingue et les gobe-mouche du Sénégal; grinpereau du brésil idme et la laongue queue de cap de bonne Espérance.*[10]

The jug dated 1781 in the Frick Collection[11] bears the same incised mark as the British Museum example.[12] Both have metal mounts of similar form. The gilding on the Frick and British Museum pieces is not identical but the quality and arrangement on the New York piece suggest that it is also by Prévost (active 1757–97). The mark incised on the basin has been traced on *plateaux* of around 1779–87/8 and has been tentatively ascribed to the repairer Nicolas Brachard *père*, who worked at the factory from 1754 until 1800/9, but was occupied either with bas-reliefs or sculpture when the basin was made.[13]

The identity of the original owner of this jug and basin has not yet been discovered, as they cannot be traced in the factory's sales records.

1. Warwick County Record Office, CR 114A/720/7.
2. The author is indebted to John McKee, Richard Beresford, Susan Newell and Rosalind Savill of the Wallace Collection, London, for their help in unravelling the provenance of the jug and basin.
3. L. Courajod, *Livre-journal de Lazare-Duvaux, marchand-bijoutier ordinaire du roy 1748–1758, précédé d'une étude sur le goût et le commerce des objets d'art au milieu du XVIIIe Siècle*, 2 vols. Paris, 1878, Vol. II, p. 104, no. 964. The mount (*garniture*) cost 27 *livres*.
4. Brunet and Préaud, 1978, no. 214. The form is discussed in detail by Savill, 1988, II, pp. 692–5, and the drawing reproduced on p. 693.
5. Sir G. de Bellaigue, 'Sèvres' in *J. Pierpont Morgan, Collector, European Decorative Arts from the Wadsworth Atheneum*, ed. L.H. Roth, Hartford, Conn., 1987, no. 71, p. 184.
6. The use of the water jug and basin is extensively discussed by Savill, 1988, II, pp. 691–2.
7. MNS, Archives de Sèvres, Vj' 1, f. 3.
8. A detailed biography is given by Savill, 1988, III, pp. 995–6.
9. Eriksen, 1968, no. 75.
10. Most have been traced in G. Le Clerc, comte de Buffon, *Histoire Naturelle des Oiseaux*, Paris, 1770–86; Vol. V, 1778, p. 33, pl. 127, fig. 2; Vol. VII, 1783, pp. 104–5, pl. 119; Vol. VII, 1783, p. 72, pl. 116; Vol. V, 1778, p. 254, pl. 566, figs. 1, 2; Vol. IV, 1777, pp. 280–2, p. 284, pl. 115, figs. 1, 3; Vol. IV, 1777, p. 102, pl. 559; Vol. V, 1778, p. 29, pl. 567, figs. 1, 3, inaccurate; Vol. VI, 1783, pp. 358–60, pl. 83, fig. 2; *ibid.*, fig. 1. Some of the birds appear in volumes published after 1780, but Buffon himself states in his 'Plan de l'Ouvrage' which prefaces the first volume (1770) that he had issued nearly 500 plates in the preceding five years. A volume recently discovered at the factory entitled *Collection d'Oiseaux Dess. et Gravés par Martinet*, dated 1771 and costing 552 *livres* 'en 8 Cahiers', may have been the source used by the factory painters.
11. M. Brunet, *The Frick Collection, VII, Porcelains*, New York, 1974, p. 290.
12. The mark may correspond to one noted on a cup by Savill, 1988, III, p. 1126 as 37a. It is unidentified.
13. Savill, 1988, III, p. 1088.

125 Pair of Vases (*Vases 'C' de 1780*), 1781

See colour plate 24

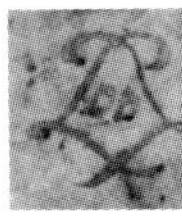

125 *mark*

H. *incl. covers:*	(left-hand vase) 31.6 cm (right-hand vase) 31.8 cm
Marks:	(left-hand vase) interlaced LL enclosing DD painted overglaze in blue on one corner; (right-hand vase) interlaced LL painted overglaze in blue on one corner
Reg. No.	1935,12–18,1 and 2

Soft-paste porcelain, of flattened ovoid form, slightly domed cover with acorn knop. The body is attached to the lower part, which is formed in one piece by means of a screw, nut and paper washer attachment visible on the underside. Its other end can be discerned inside the vase, surrounded by a brown substance. The grooved outer handles curve over at the top to interlock with a series of pierced circles alternating with ovals. The decoration consists of mythological subjects on one side and landscape scenes on the other, within an oval gilt band tooled with a crossed ribbon motif, all on a *bleu nouveau* ground. Around the scenes in reserve, on the neck, foot and cover, is 'jewelling' consisting of 'pearls', rosettes, strawberry leaves and a laurel leaf and berry trail in white, green and orange enamels over embossed gold foils. Some losses of enamel and gold foil.

Provenance: Charles Adeane, Babraham Hall, Cambridge, sold Christie's, 18 May 1916, Lot 64 to Duveen for £1050

Bequeathed by C.B.O. Clarke, Esq., 1935

Literature: W. King, 'Two Sèvres Vases' *British Museum Quarterly*, X, no. 3, March 1936, p. 130, pl. XXXVIII

Honey, 1949, pl. 133

Honey, 1950, pl. 77, p. 39

M. Olivar Daydi, *La Porcelana en Europa*, Barcelona, 1953, Vol. II, p. 171, fig. 53, left-hand vase

Savage, 1960, pl. 54B

Tait, 1962, pl. LII

T. Préaud, 'Sèvres enamelled porcelain: eight dies (and a quarrel) rediscovered', *Burlington Magazine*, Vol. CXXVIII, no. 999, June 1986, appendix 6, p. 397

Eriksen and Bellaigue, 1987, p. 340

Savill, 1988, I, p. 458, p. 461, f.n. 5

Exhibited: 1985, 'Documentary Continental Ceramics from the British Museum', London, International Ceramics Fair and Seminar Ltd., June 1985, no. 48, cat. compiled by A. Dawson.

Comparable Examples: Sèvres, Musée national de Céramique, inv. 22461, pair, second size, dated 1786, *beau bleu* decorated with *singeries* in different colours of gold (covers missing)

Paris, Musée Carnavalet, second size, Revolutionary subject[1]

Chester, Sotheby's, 24/25 April 1990, Lot 1329, H. 45.1 cm, turquoise ground, pastoral scenes, no jewelling, fake

Sotheby's, 13 November, 1990, Lot 176, fake pair

USA, Baltimore, Walters Art Gallery, inv. 48.568 formerly E.M. Hodgkins Collection, first size, jewelled

USA, California, San Marino, Huntington Library, garniture of three *vases Paris nouvelle forme* dated 1781, *rose pointillé* ground, painted with mythological and landscape scenes, jewelled motifs; see R. Wark, *French Decorative Art in the Huntington Collection*, San Marino (Calif.), 3rd ed. 1979, pp. 92–3, fig. 111

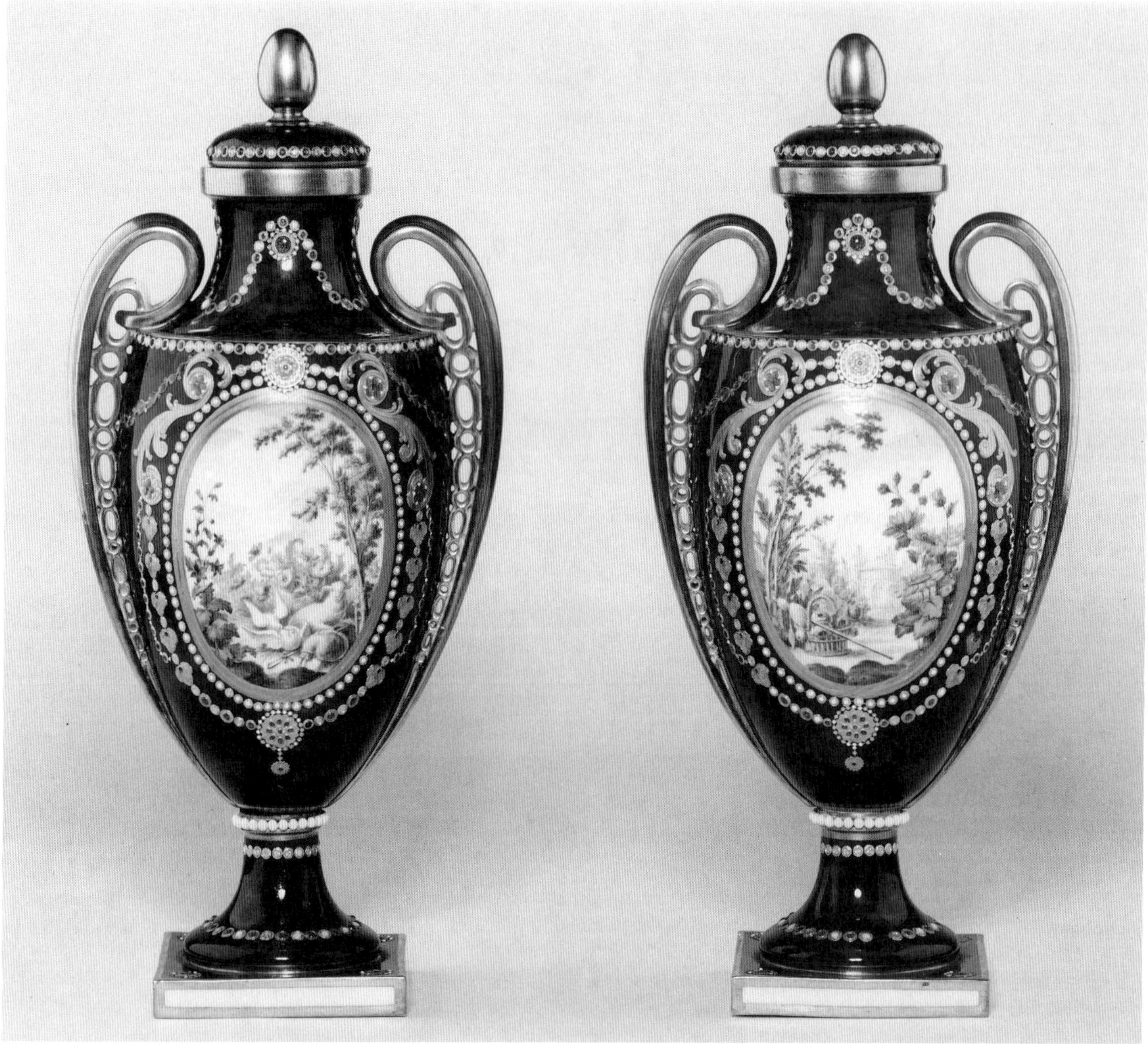

125

In the general inventory drawn up by the Sèvres factory in 1814 this shape was called 'Vase C de 1780'. This title is confirmed by incised marks found on the base of a *garniture* of three jewelled vases with a pink *pointillé* ground in the Huntington Library, San Marino, California. The largest of the three, measuring 16.5 inches in height without its mount and dated 1781, is incised *1780 Vaze C prmr gr.dr 25*; on one side of one of the smaller vases, which is also dated 1781 and measures 13 inches without its mount, is incised *1780 Vaze C 2me grdr* and *18*. On one of those smaller vases *2* is inscribed in ink on one corner.[2] The Museum vase is therefore the second of two sizes.

The shape is also referred to in the factory archive as 'Vase Paris'[3] and its design is attributed[4] to Jacques-François Paris (or Deparis) (1735–97), *chef des répareurs* and head of the soft-paste workshop at Sèvres from 1774.[5] A whole series of *Vases Paris* were introduced in the early 1780s.[6] Two slightly different versions of this vase are known, the other with a more elaborate turned neck, which is perhaps an earlier version.[7] Several different handle forms have been noted.[8] The shape is based on an etching by Marie-Thérèse Reboul Vien (1729–1802) in the *Suite des Vases Composée dans le Goût de l'Antique* after designs by Joseph Marie Vien (1716–1809).[9]

A version of the vase was in production at Sèvres during the nineteenth century.[10] The shape was also produced during the eighteenth century at Chelsea,[11] Chelsea-Derby (in a version with a long neck and goats' head handles as on the etching),[12] by the firm of Wedgwood and Bentley, Etruria,[13] and later by Coalport[14] and Minton directly copying the Sèvres form.[15]

Three drawings, none of which is securely datable, are preserved in the factory archives.[16] A plaster model also survives.[17]

The painted scenes on the front of the vases are (left) *Leucothoé charmée de la beauté d'Apollon, se laisse vaincre sans résistance* after an engraving by J.-B.-B. Simonet (after Charles Monnet) from Bannier's translation of the *Metamorphoses*[18] and (right) Venus and Adonis after C. Eisen from Montesquieu's *Temple de Gnide*, 1772, engraved by N. Le Mire, opposite p. 45. In the absence of any painter's mark it is not possible to establish with certainty who was responsible for these scenes. The scene of Leucothoé and Apollo is also found on a shell-shaped *compotier* in the Louis XVI service, the painting of which has been attributed by Bellaigue to Pithou *le jeune*.[19] The Museum pair and a vase of the first size, now in the Walters Art Gallery, Baltimore, USA, were identified by Bellaigue as the three *vases Paris nouvelle forme* which Pithou *le jeune* received shortly after 28 June 1781 and painted with miniature scenes.[20] Another three of the same form were received by the painter P.-A. Le Guay shortly after 14 July 1781; these are almost certainly the pink-stippled ground vases now in the Huntington Library.[21] In September 1781 three *beau bleu* vases of *nouvelle forme* were painted by Charles-Eloi Asselin, and ornamented with enamels by Philippe Parpette in December of that year.[22]

The flower-painter Edmé-François Bouilliat is known to have painted flowers and garden landscapes on vases.[23] The pink-stippled *vases nouvelle forme* which have decoration on the reverse similar to the Museum vases bear the mark of this painter, whose style is recognisable. Savill attributed a garden landscape on a *vase Paris de milieu* in the Wallace Collection, London, to Bouilliat,[24] mentioning also the name of Pierre-Joseph Rosset as the possible author of garden scenes on the reverse of a *garniture* of three *vases 'E de 1780'*.[25]

The technique of 'jewelling' is particularly associated with Philippe Parpette,[26] a flower-painter who had worked as an enameller before joining the Sèvres factory, and with Joseph Coteau (about 1740–1812), who came to Paris from Geneva and is known as an enameller of clock dials.[27] The process involves beating gold foil into steel matrices[28] and cutting out the scroll, leaf and other shapes. These were then applied and fired on the porcelain, which had already been decorated. A blue substance[29] was used to ensure the adhesion of the metal, which had first been decorated with transparent coloured enamels, fused to the metal by means of a first firing. These enamels, usually emerald green and pale orange, as well as opaque white 'pearls', were placed in 'cells' in the metal, and mostly survive, particularly on these vases.

This pair may be part of a *garniture*, but the only other suitable vase known, now in the Walters Art Gallery, Baltimore, USA (see above), has rather different jewelled motifs and is therefore unlikely to belong with the British Museum vases.

Only two mentions occur in the factory records which could refer to the Museum vases:

1. three vases of *nouvelle forme*, *beau bleu*, with *mignatures* painted by Asselin in September 1781 and ornamented with enamels by Parpette in December of that year;[30]
2. three vases of *nouvelle forme*, *beau bleu* with *mignatures* painted by Pithou *le jeune* and ornamented with enamels by Parpette in December 1781.[31]

1. Illustrated by E. Garnier, *La Porcelaine Tendre de Sèvres*, Paris, s.d. (1889), repr. 1988, première livraison, pl. 2.
2. The author is grateful to Rosalind Savill for passing on this information, kindly communicated by Barbara Roberts of the Huntington Gallery, San Marino. In August 1990, with the kind assistance of Shelley Bennett and her staff, and David Cohen, the writer examined the vases. The transcription of the marks is hers.
3. Eriksen and Bellaigue, 1987, pp. 339–40.
4. Discussed by Savill, 1988, I, p. 451, p. 461, f.n. 5.
5. For a biography of Paris who worked at Vincennes from 1746, see Savill, 1988, III, p. 985. He was described in 1755 as 'bon pour les grandes pièces', see Eriksen, 1968, p. 323.
6. See note 3.
7. The writer has not succeeded in tracing an example of this vase.
8. Brunet and Préaud, 1978, p. 213, fig. 266, pair, undated, first size, *beau bleu*, painted with flowers within a hexagonal reserve, Louvre loan, MNCS, inv. 15491.
9. T.P.P. Clifford, 'Some English Ceramic Vases and their Sources Part I', *ECC Trans.* Vol. 10, part 3 (1978), pl. 82a. The *Suite des Vases* . . . was published at Paris, 1760.
10. See Sotheby's, 13 November 1990, Lot 176, printed marks in blue, green and red.
11. Clifford, *op. cit.*, p. 171.
12. *Ibid.*
13. *Ibid.*, pl. 82b.
14. For an example exhibited at the 1862 exhibition and illustrated in the *Art Journal*, see G. Godden, *Coalport and Coalbrookdale Porcelains*, London, 1970, fig. 231.
15. Known at Minton as 'Vase with perforated chain handle', it was shape no. 4 469. A drawing survives in the Minton Museum, Stoke-on-Trent, Staffs, Estimate Book, 01-01320, undated, H. 15½ inches. The author is grateful to Mrs Joan Jones of that museum for this information. A vase of this shape exhibited in the International Exhibition 1862 is shown

by P. Atterbury and M. Batkin, *The Dictionary of Minton*, Woodbridge, 1990, p. 103. A pair measuring 41.8 cm decorated in Sèvres style with Morinesque harbour scenes on a blue *oeil de perdrix* ground, sold Sotheby's Belgravia (London), 18 December 1975, Lot 81; a pair measuring 37.5 cm in height with a turquoise blue ground painted with 'A Town Dog and a Country Dog at Home' sold Sotheby's, 23 June 1987, Lot 560. Another pair painted with mythological scenes on a dark blue ground measuring 40 cm in height was sold at Christie's, 2 June 1986, Lot 378.

16. Brunet and Préaud, 1978, p. 212, no. 265.
17. A. Troude, *Choix de modèles de la Manufacture Nationale de porcelaines de Sèvres appartenant au Musée céramique*, n.d. (1897), pl. 121.
18. Bellaigue, 1986, no. 17; the engraving, pl. 51 in Publius Ovidius Naso, *Les Métamorphoses d'Ovide, en Latin et en François, de la Traduction de M. L'Abbé Banier*, 3 vols., Paris, 1767–71, is illustrated. An engraving by W. Walker after C. Monnet with an English title published by G. Kearsley, no. 46 Fleet Street, 1 August 1775, is in the Department of Prints and Drawings, British Museum, inv. 1817,10–13,1260. It is in reverse to the scene painted on the vase.
19. *Ibid.* Nicolas-Pierre Pithou *jeune* (1750–1818) worked at the factory between 1759/60–7, 1768–95 and 1814–18. He was responsible for several important painted plaques, portrait and other figure subjects, for designs, an *écuelle* form and watercolours. A detailed biography is given by Savill, 1988, III, pp. 1060–3.
20. Eriksen and Bellaigue, 1987, p. 340, quoting MNS, Archives de Sèvres, Vj'2, f. 220.
21. *Ibid.*, see Wark, *op. cit.* (see Comparable Examples).
22. Savill, 1988, I, p. 462, f.n. 26.
23. Bouilliat *père* (1739/40–1810), a flower-painter, worked at Sèvres from 1758 and was recorded there in 1801. He died at Sèvres. In the 1780s he also painted allegories, attributes, monograms, birds, etc., see Savill, 1988, III, pp. 1002–4.
24. Savill, 1988, I, p. 438.
25. Savill, *op. cit.*, p. 457.
26. For a biography of Parpette see Savill, 1988, III, pp. 1055–7.
27. See Savill, 1988, III, pp. 972–4 for a biography of Coteau; for his signature on a dial dated 1785 and another on a jewelled vase from the comte d'Artois' factory, see Musée du Louvre, 1985, p. 159, figs. 90d, e; for a further signature on the base of a Sèvres jewelled *vase Bachelier* dated 1782 purchased by the comte and comtesse du Nord, now in the State Hermitage Museum, St Petersburg, see P. Ennès, 'The Visit of the Comte and Comtesse du Nord to the Sèvres Manufactory', *Apollo*, March 1989, Vol. CXXIV, no. 325, p. 54, fig. 7.
28. The dies are discussed by T. Préaud in 'Sèvres enamelled porcelain: eight dies (and a quarrel) rediscovered', *Burlington Magazine*, Vol. CXXVIII, no. 999, June 1986, pp. 391–7.
29. This substance has been analysed by Professor W.D. Kingery of the Massachusetts Institute of Technology and found by emission spectrographic and electron microprobe analysis to be a typical lead-alkali-silicate flux to which 5% arsenic has been added as an opacifier and cobalt to produce the blue colour (presumably for aesthetic reasons). The author is grateful to Professor Kingery for allowing her to quote this information.
30. These may well be the three vases in the Wallace Collection, London, discussed by Savill, 1988, I, pp. 451–62.
31. MNS, Archives de Sèvres, Vj' 2, f. 210, and F 23, December 1781.

126 Cup and Saucer (*tasse litron*), 1782

D. *of saucer:*	12 cm
H. *of cup:*	5.9 cm
Marks:	interlaced LL enclosing date-letter EE for 1782 below the gilder's mark *9.* in gold for Charles-Nicolas Buteux on both; incised *43a* on both; suspension hole on saucer
Reg. No.	1939,3–4,1

Soft-paste porcelain. The cup is decorated in gold heightened in grey, on a dark blue ground with a scene of a seated warrior in Roman dress extending his right hand towards a kneeling woman. Behind her are two women chained to a soldier, and at the furthest edge of the scene two kneeling supplicating women. A male figure holding a [?]bundle of rods stands behind the warrior. A band of jewelling consisting of translucent orange 'pearls' enclosing scrolls ornamented with tiny white pearls and translucent green dots runs around the rim on a white ground; it is repeated near the foot on a blue ground with white 'pearls'. In the centre of the saucer is a gilt rosette of laurel leaves and berries and floral motifs, heightened in grey. Martial trophies alternate with vases of flowers on a blue ground on the border, and the rim is ornamented with jewelling.

Provenance: Purchased 1939

Literature: Unpublished

Comparable Examples: None

The cup and saucer are of the third size.

The source of the decoration, which probably represents the Clemency or the Continence of Scipio,[1] is based on an untitled print by Philippe Louis Parizeau (1740–81) dated 1780, the fourth of a series of six, the first of which is titled 'Albinus'. This type of décor, described as 'figures étrusques' against production records of the toilet-set made for the comtesse du Nord, seems to have been first introduced at Sèvres in 1782.

Charles-Nicolas Buteux *fils*, *fils aîné*, or *aîné* (b. 1753 in Chantilly),[2] who joined Sèvres factory staff in November 1763 at the age of nine, painted flowers, border patterns, mongorams, landscapes, and borders or trophies of Republican symbols, as well as applying ground-colours.[3] This may be one of his most ambitious productions. He may well have been a member of the Académie de Saint-Luc in Paris in 1790.[4]

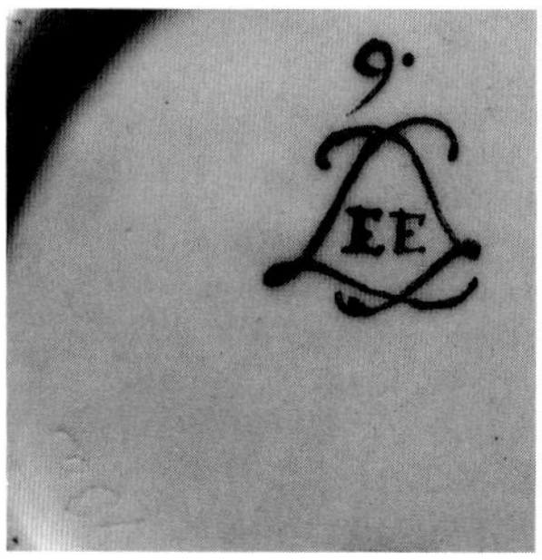

126 *marks*

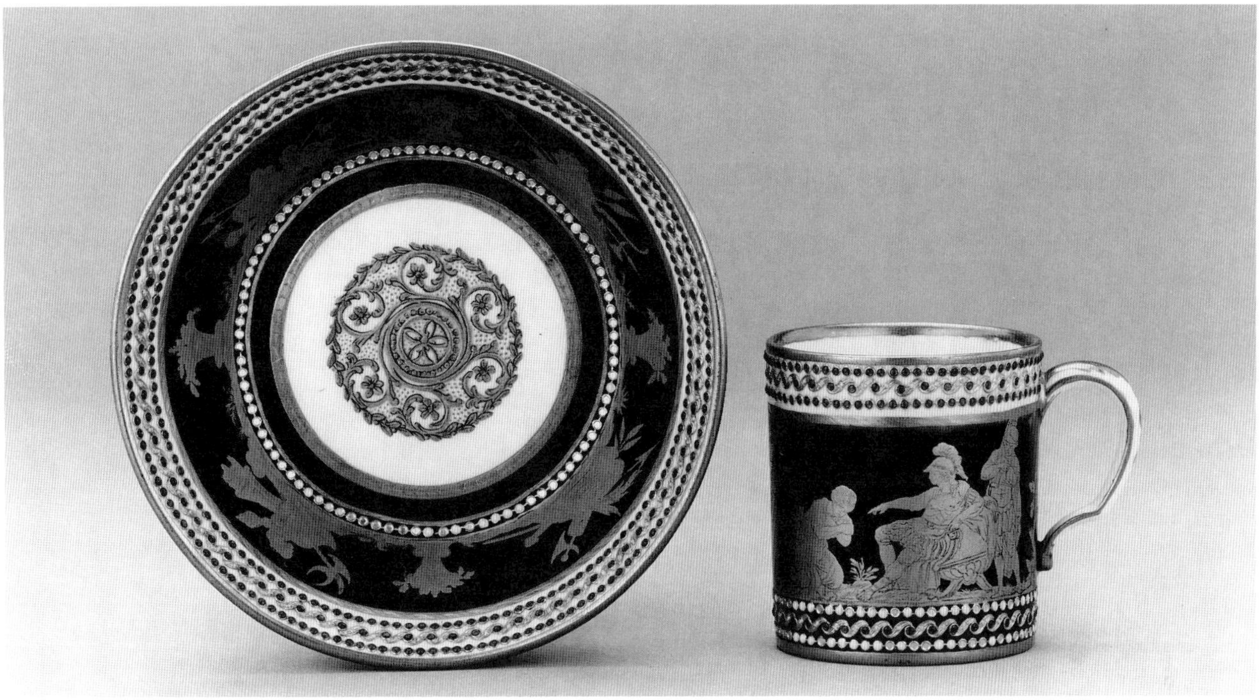

126

The incised mark *43a* has been noted by Savill on soft-paste porcelains between 1765–9 and 1779 and the 1790s.[5]

1. See a scene on a silver-gilt snuffbox by Theodore Dassdorf, sold at Sotheby's, 23 May 1991, Lot 100; Julia Clarke kindly informed the author that the *Continence of Scipio* (showing Scipio returning the slave girl he has been awarded to her betrothed in the presence of her pleading parents) is a likely subject (in correspondence, September 1990). The author thanks Ghenete Zelleke for information about the print source, also used on a tea kettle in the Art Institute of Chicago, which she discovered in the Print Room, Metropolitan Museum of Art, New York.
2. The author is grateful to Tamara Préaud for this information.
3. For full biographical details, see Savill, 1988, III, pp. 1009–10.
4. *Ibid.*, p. 1010.
5. *Ibid.*, p. 1132. Rosalind Savill has cast some doubt on the authenticity of the pieces dating between 1765 and 1769 in private correspondence with the writer in January 1991.

127 Plate (*assiette unie*), 1785

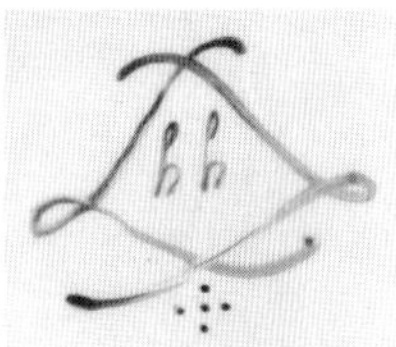

127 *mark*

D. 23.8 cm
Marks: interlaced LL enclosing date-letter hh for 1785 above a dotted cross for the painter Jacques Fontaine or perhaps Mademoiselle Fontaine
Reg. No. 1899,10-6,10

Soft-paste porcelain, moulded, the rim with six lobes; decorated on the border with six medallions containing alternately pink roses within a frame of gilt laurel leaves and cornflowers and a yellow flower within a wreath of green laurel leaves and red berries. Each medallion enclosed within a gilt circular frame. Between the medallions are stylised flowers on a white ground between two blue bands ornamented with gilt dots. The centre of the plate is painted with a spray of pink roses within a gilt band, a blue band and a band of gilt dots. In addition, the well is painted with a stylised flower and arcade design, embellished with gilding. Rim repaired.

Provenance: Bequeathed by C.D.E. Fortnum, Esq., DCL, FSA, 1899[1]

Literature: Unpublished

Comparable Examples: USA, New York, Sotheby Parke Bernet, 16 October 1980, Lots 378 (pair dated 1789), 379 (another pair, 1789), from the collection of the Rt. Hon. the Lord Vernon

Flower patterns in the same idiom as those on this plate were extremely popular at Sèvres in the 1780s and many related designs were put into production, making it difficult to identify the Museum plate in the records. A number of watercolour drawings for designs of this type are preserved in the factory archive,[2] but none corresponds exactly with this example.

The mark is usually attributed to Jacques Fontaine (active 1752–75, 1778–1807),[3] but during the period when this plate was decorated he was occupied in painting *têtes antiques*. It seems more likely that Mademoiselle Fontaine (active 1778–94) was responsible for the painting, since she decorated plates with 'Roses, Barbeaux et Fleurettes' in March and May 1785.[4]

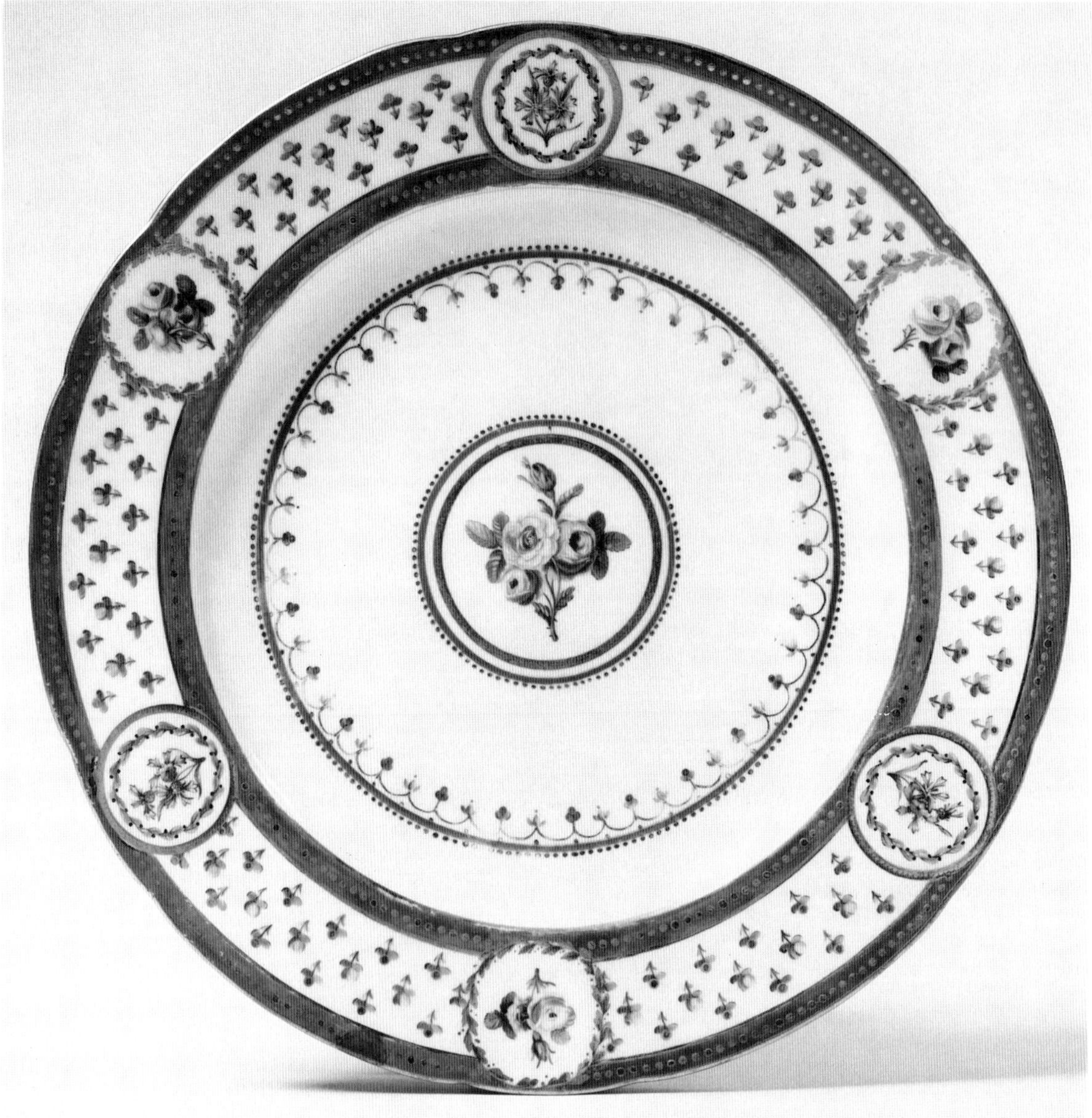

127

Several other pieces with the same decoration have been noted in the trade: a *tasse litron et soucoupe enfoncé*, the cup dated 1785,[5] another dated 1786,[6] an undated *théière Calabre*,[7] and another (possibly the same item) sold a year later.[8] Two glass-coolers dated 1785 are in the Palazzo Pitti, Florence.[9]

1. For a note on C.D.E. Fortnum (1820–99), a Trustee of the Museum, see cat. 93.
2. MNS, Archives de Sèvres, R 182 *bis*.
3. For a biography of Jacques Fontaine, see Savill, 1988, III, pp. 1033–5.
4. MNS, Archives de Sèvres, Vj' 3, f. 264.
5. Sotheby's, New York, 31 May 1978, Lot 228.
6. Christie's, New York, 27 October 1988, Lot 251.
7. Christie's, Monte Carlo, 7 December 1987, Lot 218.
8. Christie's, 3 October 1988, Lot 91.
9. Eriksen, 1973, no. 54.

128 **Miniature Saucer (*soucoupe mignature*)**, 1786

D. 7.8 cm
Marks: *Levé/feu d'or./Teinte faite en Juillet/1786.* painted in grey enamel; *M*[?] incised; suspension hole
Reg. No. Franks 383

Soft-paste porcelain, slightly flared deep sides. Painted *en grisaille* on a white ground with three groups of a bird on branches on the sides, and in the centre with billing doves resting on a quiver of arrows next to a lyre and a rose garland all below a wreath of laurel leaves. Rim gilt. Chip to rim, rubbed gilding.

Provenance: Bequeathed by Sir A.W. Franks, 1897

Literature: Franks, 1896, no. 383

Comparable Examples: None

This small documentary saucer is one of the few pieces of Sèvres acquired by Sir A.W. Franks.

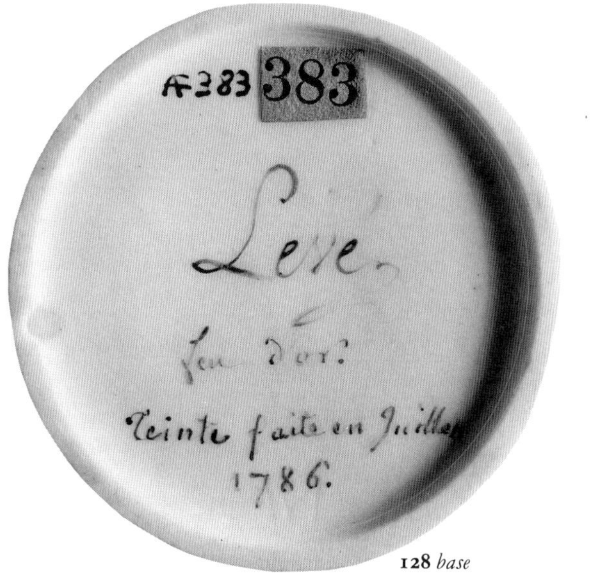

128 *base*

The inscription records that it was fired in the gilding kiln, i.e. at a very low temperature, having been decorated by Denis Levé (1730– after 1806) with a low-firing enamel colour. No record of Levé's work on this piece, or its sale, has been discovered. Denis Levé (working period 1754–1805) was born at Saint-Germain about 1731. He started work at Vincennes at 30 *livres* a month; by 1758 he received 72 *livres* and in 1773 was one of the factory's best-paid workers at 84 *livres*.[1] Two *gobelets Bouillards* possibly dated 1769 at Waddesdon Manor, Buckinghamshire,[2] bearing his usual mark of a capital cursive *L*, are examples of Levé's flower painting.

The type of painting on this saucer is in the manner of Georg Lamprecht[3] (d. 1814) who worked at the Vienna porcelain factory from 1772 and at the Clignancourt porcelain factory, Paris (see p. 325), in 1783, where he was employed as a figure-painter specialising in the *grisaille* technique. He was paid the high salary of 1,200 *livres* at Sèvres between 1785 and 1787. In a letter dated 18 November 1785 from d'Angiviller to Antoine Régnier, he is described as 'un homme de talent tout particulier et auquel la Manufacture tirera très vraysemblement un avantage considerable.'[4] Although Lamprecht had been trained to work on hard-paste porcelain, it is not unlikely that he taught Levé, a painter of flowers and decorative motifs, how to paint in *grisaille* on soft-paste.

The incised mark *M*, which remains unidentified, is discussed by Savill.[5]

1. Eriksen, 1968, p. 330. Levé's son Félix-Clément (b. 1761) was a painter at the factory, but in 1786 had probably not yet acquired the skill to paint this saucer.

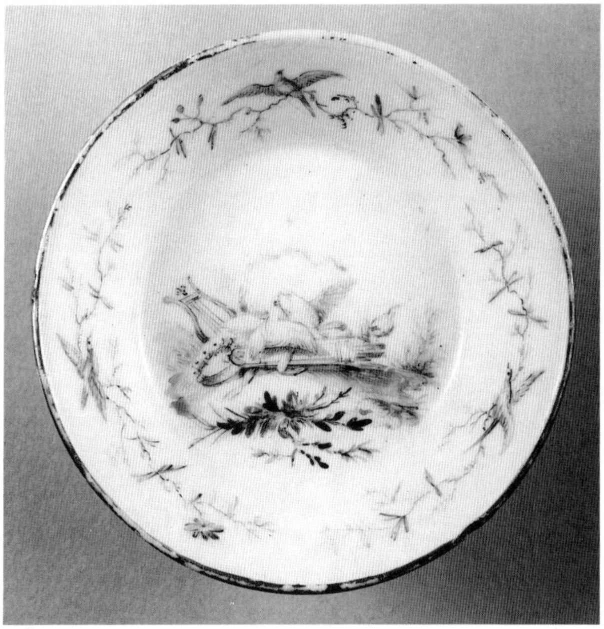

128

2. *Op. cit.*, no. 98, p. 256.
3. For an *écuelle*, cover and stand from Monsieur's factory at Clignancourt signed *Georges Lamprecht pint à Paris 1783*, see Guillebon, 1972, fig. 56.
4. MNS, Archives de Sèvres, *Carton* H3, *liasse* 3.
5. Savill, 1988, III, p. 1114.

129 Sugar Bowl, Cover and Stand (*sucrier de Monsieur le Premier*), 1787

L.	23.3 cm
H.	10.5 cm
Marks:	*KK* to left of interlaced LL, painter's mark *Y* for Edmé-François Bouilliat at the right, painted in blue enamel; *2000* in gold above LL (almost obliterated) for the gilder Henry-François Vincent *le jeune*; incised *2*
Reg. No.	Franks 384

Soft-paste porcelain; moulded lobed stand to which is fixed the moulded oval bowl, which has a domed, shaped cover with oval button knop. Decorated with a border design of turquoise (*bleu céleste*) enclosing sprays of flowers suspended from yellow or purple ribbons (stylised pink roses), growing from the ground (cornflowers) or in blue vases (pink roses or purple flowers). The turquoise border is additionally ornamented with gilt swags and other gilt motifs. Hairline crack and chip to bowl, crack to stand, chips to cover, gilding rubbed.

Provenance: Bequeathed by Sir A.W. Franks, 1897

Literature: Franks, 1896, no. 384

Comparable Examples: Paris, Palais Galliéra, 2 December 1976, Lot 58m, two sugar bowls from the Baron R. de Rothschild Collection, with other items from service

Sotheby's, 17 March 1987, Lot 120, two sugar bowls, with other items from service

Christie's, Monte Carlo, 7 December 1987, Lot 218, teapot (*théière Calabre*), undated

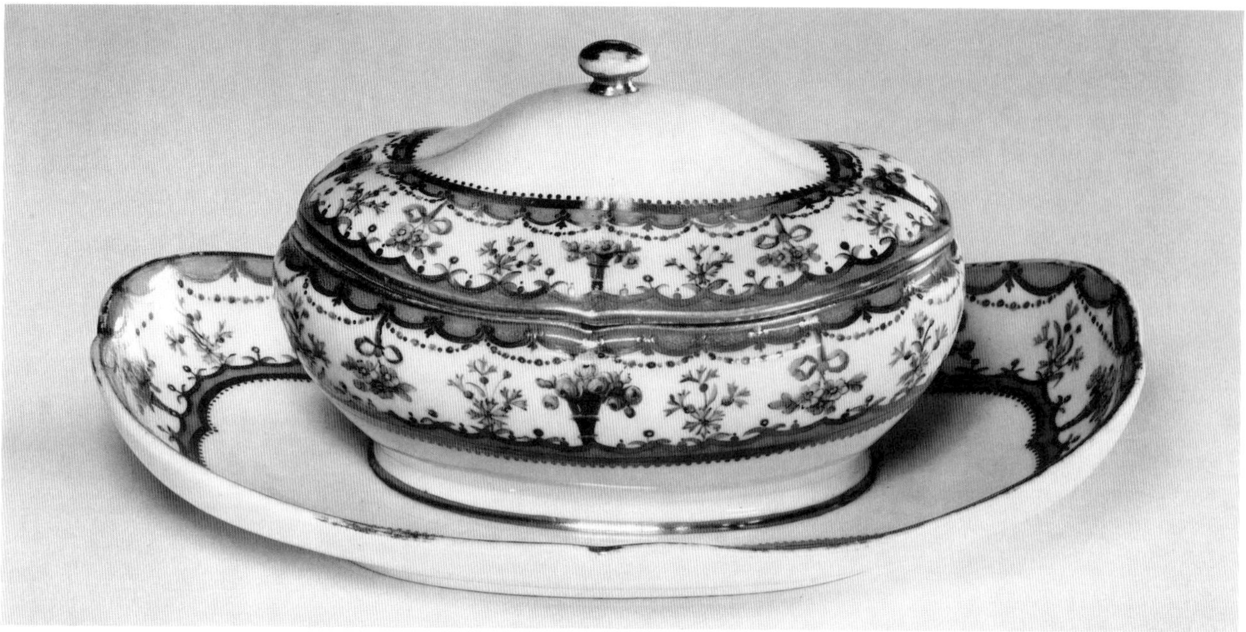

129

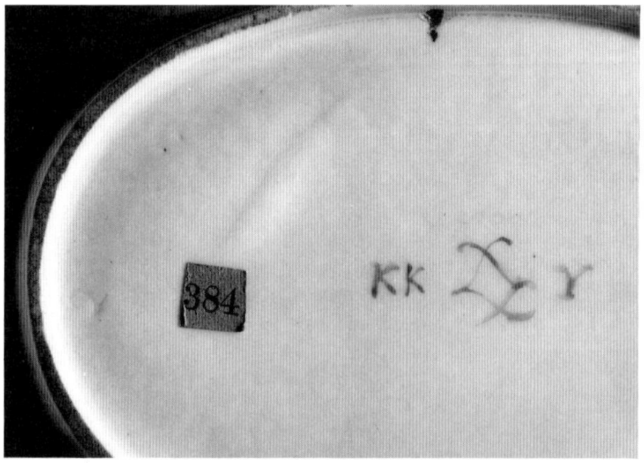

129 *marks*

The porcelain is of poor quality: it contains numerous black specks and several inclusions.

The model was devised in 1758, and plasters for it inventoried in early 1759.[1] It was named for the *Premier Ecuyer*, known as Monsieur le Premier. It is moulded in three parts and was used as part of the dessert service.

The mark *Y* is usually attributed to the painter Edmé-François Bouilliat, called Bouilliat *père*, who specialised in fruit, flowers and butterflies, and was employed at the factory from 1758 until around 1810.[2] Bouilliat *père* is recorded as decorating '14 sucriers de table Service Picaluga' on 1 January 1788,[3] and rather earlier, on 22 July 1786, as decorating two with a 'frize riche'.[4] Neither of these descriptions can, however, be conclusively associated with this sugar bowl. Bouilliat *fils*, sometimes thought to have used this mark,[5] is also recorded as decorating '2 sucriers de table fleurs' on 24 March 1787.[6]

The mark of the gilder Vincent, who worked at Saint-Cloud as a painter before joining Vincennes in February 1753[7] has been traced on pieces from several services, such as the Catherine the Great service, the supplement to the Longleat service made in 1781 and the Louis XVI service on a piece dated 1792.[8]

The incised mark *2* is discussed by Savill.[9]

There appear to have been two dessert services with very similar decoration sold towards the end of the eighteenth century. The first, described as 'Festons, bleu-celeste & C' was sold to the London dealer Enoch Rittener on 4 March 1790. Amongst the items he purchased were '2 sucriers de table' at 132 *livres* each.[10] The porcelain sold to the dealer Empaytas, who was perhaps a government commissioner,[11] between 19 Vendémiaire and 15 Frimaire, l'an III (6 October and 5 December 1794)[12] has been identified by Marcelle Brunet by cross-reference to documents in the Archives Nationales as a 'Service fond bleu céleste, fleurs et fruits'.[13] It therefore seems more likely that Rittener was the purchaser of this sugar bowl, for an unknown client.

A sugar bowl, cover and stand of similar form and dimensions was manufactured at the Mennecy factory[14] and at Boissettes.[15]

1. MNS, Archives de Sèvres, I 7.
2. Eriksen and Bellaigue, 1987, p. 154 and 167. A full biography

of Bouilliat is given by Savill, 1988, III, pp. 1002–4.
3. MNS, Archives de Sèvres, Vj' 5, f. 41v.
4. *Ibid.*, f. 39v.
5. According to Eriksen and Bellaigue, 1987, p. 167, this identification is erroneous.
6. MNS, Archives de Sèvres, Vj' 5, f. 44.
7. A biography of Vincent, who was born at Saint-Cloud on 26 October 1733 and died at Sèvres in 1809(?), is given by Savill, 1988, III, pp. 1076–7. As she points out, his mark *vingt cent* is a pun on his name.
8. Eriksen and Bellaigue, 1987, p. 169, no. 152.
9. Savill, 1988, III, p. 1125.
10. MNS, Archives de Sèvres, Vy 11, f. 15.
11. Chavagnac and Grollier, 1906, pp. 222–3; the sales record kept at the Sèvres factory (see note 10) reads 'par permission de la commission de Commerce et d'approvisionnement de la République et par celle de l'Agriculture, et des Arts'; for a dessert service of 54 pieces reputed to have been sold to Empaytas, see Sotheby's, 17 March 1987, Lot 120; a part dinner service of the same pattern was sold at Christie's, 3 December 1984, Lot 22.
12. *Loc. cit.*, Vy 12, f. 30v.
13. The author is grateful to Tamara Préaud for this reference.
14. A marked example painted with flowers, and with a flower rather than a button knop, was advertised for sale by Winifred Williams, Eastbourne, *Connoisseur*, Vol. CXLII, no. 577, April 1959, p. xlix.
15. Ravel d'Esclapon, 1991, p. 54, Melun Museum.

130 Cup (*tasse à thé*), 1792–3

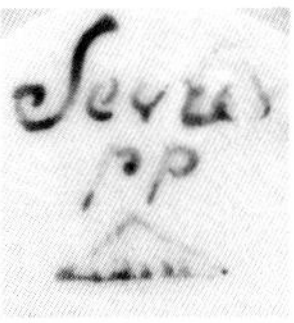

130 *marks*

H.	4.5 cm
D.	8.2 cm
Marks:	*Sèvres* above date-letter PP for 1792 surmounting a triangle for the painter Jean-Jacques Dieu painted in blue enamel; possible indecipherable incised mark below part of the word *Sèvres*
Reg. No.	FB16 (AF 3219)

Hard-paste porcelain, thrown; wide, shallow cup on small foot, shaped handle terminating in a scroll at its upper end. Decorated with two Chinese-style landscapes, each containing two figures in two colours of gold and platinum on a black ground between gilt lines, the lower one around the foot. Near the rim is a band of stylised floral ornament in gold. Handle and inner and outer rim gilt. Hairline crack, lower end of handle chipped, gilding on rims and handle rubbed.

Provenance: Bequeathed by Sir A.W. Franks, 1897

Literature: Unpublished

Comparable Examples: London, Hoff Antiques, exhibited International Ceramics Fair and Seminar Ltd., London, June 1990, date-letter unclear, incised *PT*.

Surviving examples of this shape are uncommon. As Rosalind Savill has noted,[1] *tasses à thé* formed part of a *déjeuner Courteille*, comprising four cups and saucers, a sugar bowl, milk jug, teapot, tea caddy or a coffee-pot and tray. It is possible that the *tasse à thé* was made in more than one size, but all the pieces traced are

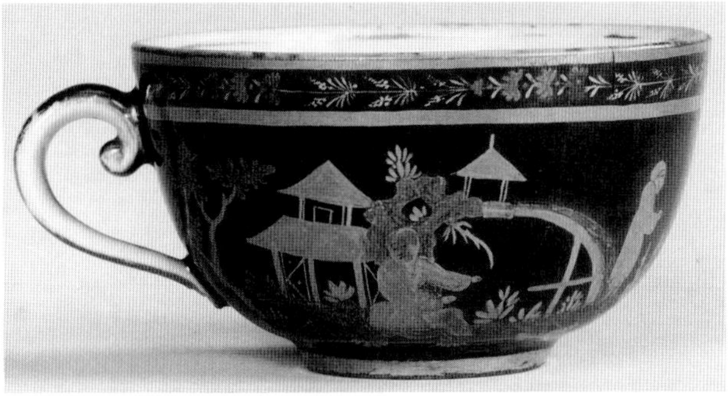

130

the same dimensions as the Museum example. A cup and saucer painted with roses within gilt laurel leaves on a ground of gold dots in the Victoria and Albert Museum, London,[2] is indeed smaller, but it has an out-turned rim, and as it dates from 1768 is probably a quite different form.

Tea-drinking had been popular among the well-to-do classes for several decades. The 1770s was marked by Anglomania, which, despite conflict with England, remained strong in aristocratic and princely circles into the 1780s. In 1777 Ollivier painted his *Thé à l'anglaise* in the house of the prince de Conti,[3] and on 23 November 1772, Bernard-Joseph Saurin's play *L'Anglomane ou l'orpheline léguée* was first performed.[4]

Tasses à thé are the first mentioned in the factory records in 1773 when four decorated with 'frizes d'or pour Mr de Bouflers' were sold to the prince de Conti on 27 May.[5] Four *tasses à thé* in the Victoria and Albert Museum which form part of a *déjeuner Courteille* painted with landscape scenes on a pink ground with the gilt monogram *PN*, have been identified by Rosalind Savill as one of four *déjeuners Courteille* purchased by the prince de Deux Ponts in 1775 for 840 *livres*.[6] The latest known example is painted with a decorative scheme of red, white and blue ribbons, which probably dates it to the early 1790s. It is 5.3 cm in height, and the saucer measures 16.5 cm. The handle form offers yet another variation.[7]

The decoration of the Museum cup is loosely based on Jean Pillement (1728–1808) in a style that enjoyed some popularity for around a decade (see cat. 122). Jean-Jacques Dieu who joined the factory in 1777, leaving in 1791 to return from 1794–8 and who was then employed between 1801 and 1811, was a gilder and painter of flowers and *chinoiseries*, the latter being his particular speciality.

This cup may have been one of six 'tasses à thé fond noir' decorated with 'chinois' fired on 10 December 1792.[8]

Wedgwood produced a cup and saucer of similar form.[9]

1. Savill, 1988, II, p. 616.
2. Inv. C. 1392 & a–1919.
3. Reproduced in Savill, 1988, II, p. 493; for a discussion of tea-drinking, see pp. 492–3.
4. A. Britsch, *La Jeunesse de Philippe-Egalité*, Paris, 1926, Chapter XI *passim.*, esp. p. 393.
5. MNS, Archives de Sèvres, Vy 5, f. 71.
6. Savill, 1988, II, p. 620, f.n. 3h, and private correspondence with the writer.
7. Paris, Musée Carnavalet, inv. C. 2061; photograph Getty Center, photo archive; cup and saucer illustrated in C. Béalu, 'Les porcelaines revolutionnaires', *Art et Curiosité*, April 1989, p. 25, fig. 20. The author is grateful to Roselyne Hurel for kindly providing information about these pieces.
8. MNS, Archives de Sèvres, Vl'3, f. 218v.
9. D. Buten, *18th-Century Wedgwood, A Guide for Collectors and Connoisseurs*, London, 1980, p. 95, fig. 75, dated to around 1800, H. of cup 5.1 cm.

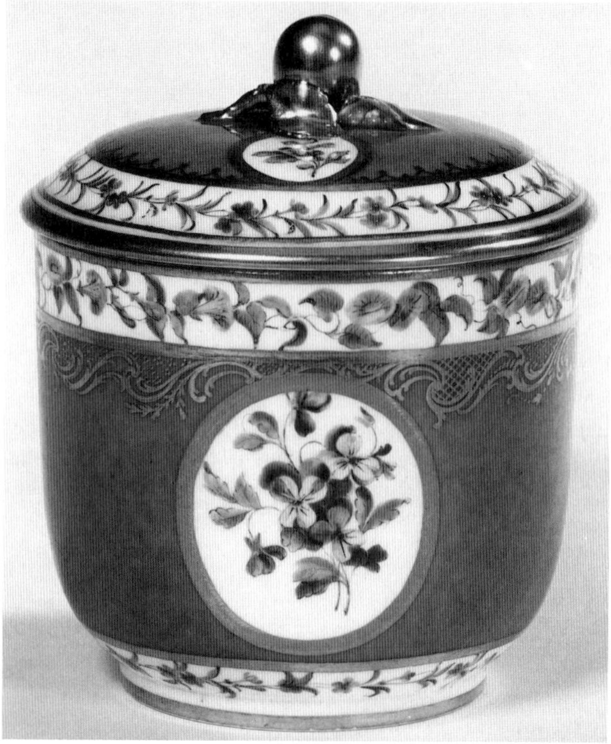

131

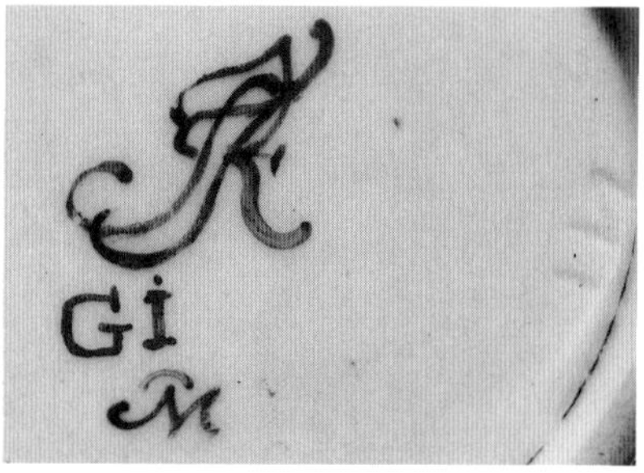

131 *marks*

131 Sugar Bowl and Cover (*pot à sucre Calabre*), *c.* 1794

H. *including knop:*	11.4 cm
Marks:	*RF* in monogram painted in blue enamel above *GI* in gold for Girard *l'aîné*, and *M* for the painter Pierre Massy (1778–1802); *41* incised; suspension hole inside cover
Reg. No.	Franks 386

Soft-paste porcelain, straight-sided with slightly domed cover surmounted by a cherry-and-leaf knop. The decoration on the bowl consists of an oval panel of violas and another of pink roses on a white ground within a tooled gilt frame on a green ground. Near the rim is a band of blue convulvulus on a white ground, and near the foot a band of small pink flowers. The central area is enclosed between gilt lines; depending from the upper one is gilt ornament in the rococo style. The foot and rim are gilt; gilt dentil inside bowl. The cover is painted with violas and roses in smaller panels on a green ground, and with a band of the same small pink flowers near the rim between two gilt lines. Rim and finial gilt.

Provenance: Bequeathed by Sir A.W. Franks, 1897

Literature: Franks, 1896, no. 386

Comparable Examples: None

The *pot à sucre Calabre* is named after Pierre Calabre (see pp. 83, 106). It was in production by December 1752 and a drawing for the second size 'rectifié Suivan l'ordre de La Comande du 19 fevrÿe 1753' is preserved at the factory (see fig. 131a).[1] A plaster model measuring 13 cm in height including the cover is kept at the factory.[2] This example is of the first size.[3]

The flower and bird painter Pierre Massy is recorded at the factory from 1778 and was still there in 1800.[4] On 17 Ventôse, l'an II (6 March 1794) Massy decorated '1 Pot à Sucre $l^{e}g$ fond verd' with

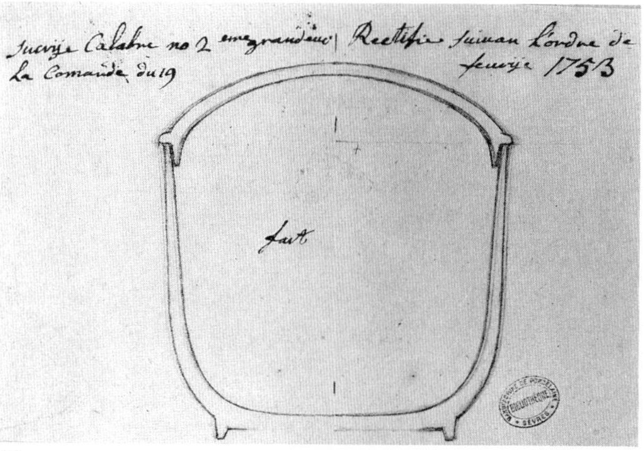

Fig 131a

'Guirlandes et Groupes'.[5] A sugar bowl of the first size, together with a first-size milk jug, both with a green ground, were fired on 25 Ventôse, l'an II.[6] Girard *l'aîné* was taken on at Sèvres as a painter in 1772–3 and became a gilder in 1781, after gilding hard-paste in 1776–7. He worked at Sèvres until 1817. No record of his work on the sugar bowl has been discovered. For a note on the incised mark *41*, which remains unidentified, see Savill.[7]

The sales records at this time are not particularly precise. It is possible that the sugar bowl was part of a service sold to Citizen Lefebure né le Clerq [*sic*] with decoration described as 'pensées et violettes'. On 6 Pluviôse, l'an IV Lefebure paid 5040 *assignats* for two sugar bowls.[8]

1. Exh. *Vincennes*, 1977–8, p. 83.
2. MNS, Archives de Sèvres, *Casier modèle* 782.
3. The first size ranges between 11 cm and 12.5 cm in height, the second is between 9.4 cm and 10 cm and the third between 5.5 cm and 7.5 cm. The form was in production for at least 50 years.
4. Massy, whose date of birth is unknown, was the son of Françoise Griset and Pierre Massy; on 27 March 1789 he married Madeleine-Geneviève-Rose Delatre, the daughter of Pierre Delatre, a thrower, and Marie-Geneviève Moret, a burnisher, at the church of St Romain, Sèvres. A few years previously he appears in parish records of 19 January 1785 as the godfather of Raphael-Aimé Chanou, son of the painter Jean-Baptiste Chanou.
5. MNS, Archives de Sèvres, Vj'5, f. 146.
6. *Ibid.*
7. Savill, 1988, III, p. 1131.
8. *Loc. cit.*, Vy 12, f. 79.

132 Two Saucers (*soucoupes litrons*), 1795

D. 12.3 cm (one showing woman with hair in snood); 12.6 cm

Marks: *RF* in monogram (for République Française), *Sèvres*, *Sis.* for the painter Jacques-Nicolas Sinsson (1795–1845) painted in pink enamel on both; *Lf* for the painter and gilder André-Joseph Foinet called La France (working period 1773–1803, 1813–25) in gold on both; *E.T.* for the painter Jean-Guillaume Etard (working period February 1795–1798, 1803–1804) painted in pink and brown (on one showing woman with hair in snood); *m.c* painted in purplish-grey for the painter and gilder Pierre-Louis Micaud (1794–99, 1801–34) on the other; suspension hole on both

Reg. No. Franks 387

Soft-paste porcelain, deep, flared sides. The border of each is painted with a running trail of full-blown pink roses and leaves on a gold ground. In the well is a female bust portrait to right painted in sepia on a white ground: on one the woman wears a V-necked garment and her hair is piled up on her head behind a bandeau; on the other the woman's classical-style robe leaves her right shoulder bare and her hair is held in a snood behind a bandeau. Each portrait is encircled by a wide gilt band. The remainder of the saucer is painted pale pink and ornamented in

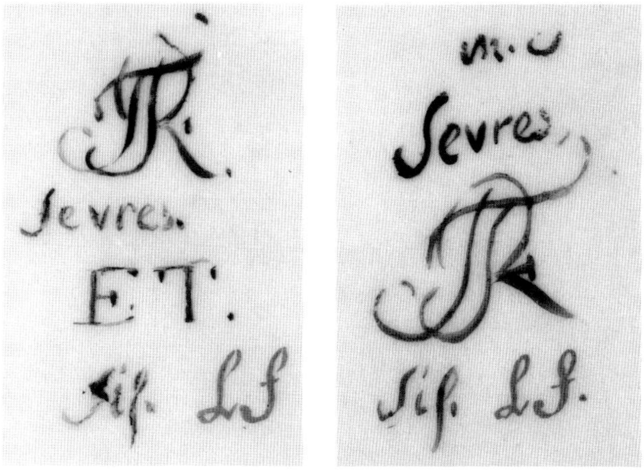

132 *marks*

darker pink with stylised leaves and geometric patterns. Rims gilt. The gilding is rubbed.

Provenance: Bequeathed by Sir A.W. Franks, 1897

Literature: Franks, 1896, no. 387

Chavagnac and Grollier, 1906, pp. 360–1

Verlet, Grandjean and Brunet, *Sèvres*, Vol. II, *Les marques de Sèvres*, 1953, p. 39

Savill, 1988, III, p. 1039

Comparable Examples: None

The saucers are of the third size.[1]

The portraits probably do not represent real people. Although in the style of Angelica Kauffmann (1740–1807), no engraving has yet been discovered with which they correspond.[2] Similar classical-style women are painted three-quarter length in *bistre* on a saucer on the London market in 1990.[3] The head on the saucer showing the woman with her hair in a snood is the work of 'Etard *élève*' (as he is referred to in the factory register), who is recorded as having painted *têtes en bistre* on four cups and saucers of the third size on 29 Germinal, l'an III (18 April 1795), on two similar on 12 Prairial, l'an III (31 May 1795), on two more in Messidor l'an III (between 19 June and 19 July 1795) and on a further four in Vendémiaire l'an IV (between 23 September and 23 October 1795).[4] Little is known about Etard, a figure-painter, except that he entered the Sèvres factory as an *élève* in February 1795 and was paid 36 *livres* 'pour encouragement'. His salary, which remained constant, reveals that he had been trained before joining the factory. During 1794 he seems to have been excused conscription.[5] Pierre-Louis Micaud was the son of Jacques-François Micaud (1732/5–1811), a flower painter who joined the factory in 1757, and his wife Suzanne Tanche. He was apprenticed at Sèvres, becoming a painter in 1794.[6] He was responsible for the head on the other

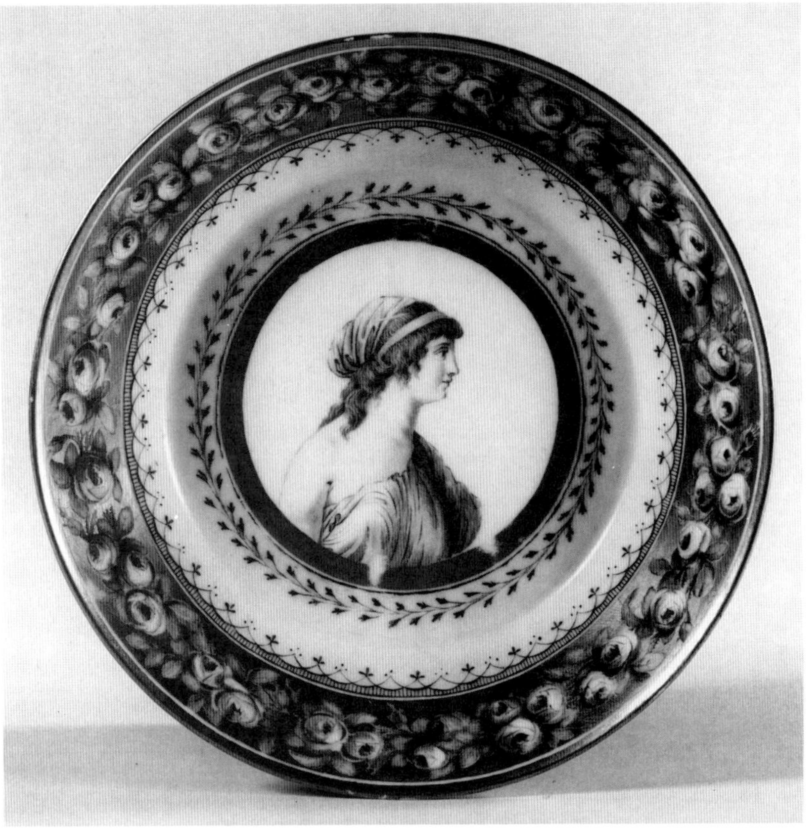

132

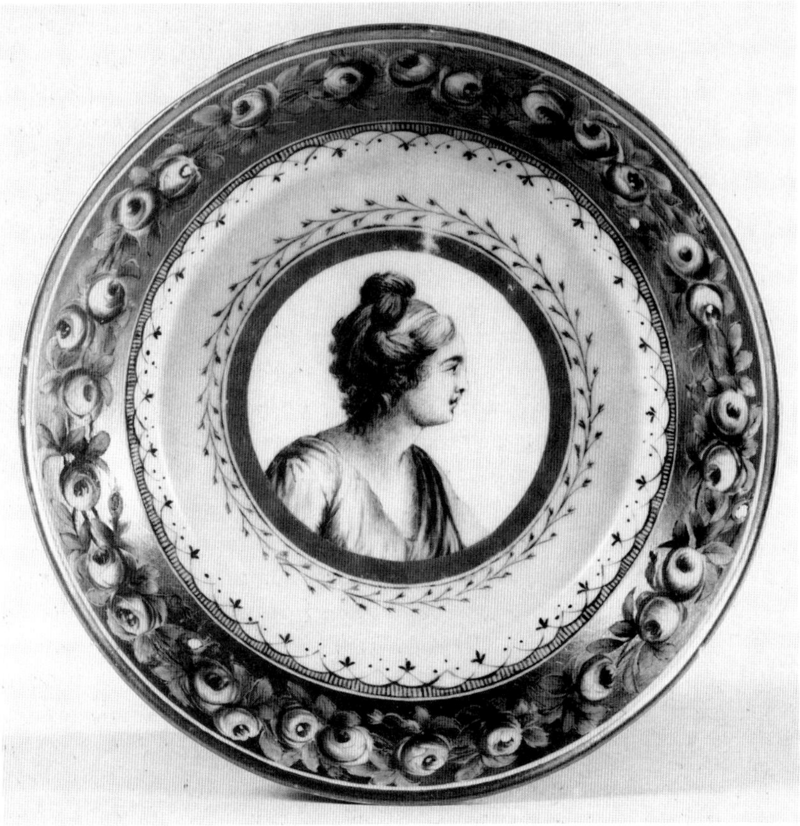

132

saucer, and is recorded as as having painted *têtes en bistre* on four cups and saucers of the third size on 25 Prairial l'an III (13 June 1795), two more in Fructidor l'an III (between 18 August and 22 September 1795) and a further two in Vendémiaire l'an IV (23 September and 23 October 1795).[7]

Jacques-Nicolas Sinsson (also spelt Sisson), son of the painter and gilder Nicolas Sisson, began working in about August 1795 as a painter of flowers, patterns and ground colours. He painted the border decoration on both saucers and is recorded as painting 'Guir(lande) de roses et fond lilas' on two third-size *tasses litrons* on 1 Jour Complémentaire l'an III (17 September 1795) and a further three on 16 Vendémiaire l'an IV (8 October 1795).[8]

The gilding was carried out by André-Joseph Foinet called La France.[9]

Bistre, or sepia,[10] was especially popular at various porcelain factories at the end of the eighteenth century, and notably at Clignancourt. On 24 May 1785 the newly-appointed factory inspector Jean-Jacques Hettlinger invited the comte d'Angiviller, the minister responsible for the factory, to view a *bistre* ground imitating Clignancourt.[11]

1 The shape and sizes are fully discussed by Savill, 1988, II, pp. 501–2.
2. The author is grateful to colleagues in the Department of Prints and Drawings, British Museum, and to Sarah Carthew, Royal Pavilion, Brighton, who is preparing an exhibition on Kauffmann, for assistance with these portraits.
3. Phillips, 5 September 1990, Lot 174, mark *Sèvres* in script and painter's mark *CL*.
4. MNS, Archives de Sèvres, Vj' 6, f. 105 (the register records 'commence à peindre le 21 Ventose an trois'); and Archives nationales, O2 937(2), Overtime/Piecework Lists, Messidor 3 and Vendémiaire 4.
5. MNS, Archives de Sèvres, Vj' 6; M6 *dossier* 1794 contains an undated draft of request that Etard be excused from conscription. His date and place of birth and subsequent career are unknown.
6. See Savill, 1988, III, pp. 1049–51, and Eriksen, 1968, p. 332. Micaud evidently became a painter at Sèvres in 1795, as the entry in MNS, Archives de Sèvres, Vj' 6 against Micaud records: 'Commencé à peindre le 21 Ventoise An trois' (11 March 1795).
7. MNS, Archives de Sèvres, Vj' 6, f. 111; Archives nationales, O2 937(2), Overtime/Piecework Lists, Fructidor An 3 and Vendémiaire An 4.
8. MNS, Archives de Sèvres, Vj' 6, f. 115.
9. A biography of La France (employed 1773–1803) is given in Savill, 1988, III, pp. 1038–9.
10. A. Brongniart, 'Essai sur les couleurs obtenues des oxydes métalliques, et fixées par la fusion sur les différents corps vitreux', *Journal des Mines*, Vol. XII, 1802 (An 10), no. 67, p. 77.
11. Archives nationales, O1 20612, pièce 300, reference kindly supplied by David Peters, to whom the author is indebted for help with the painters and dating of these saucers.

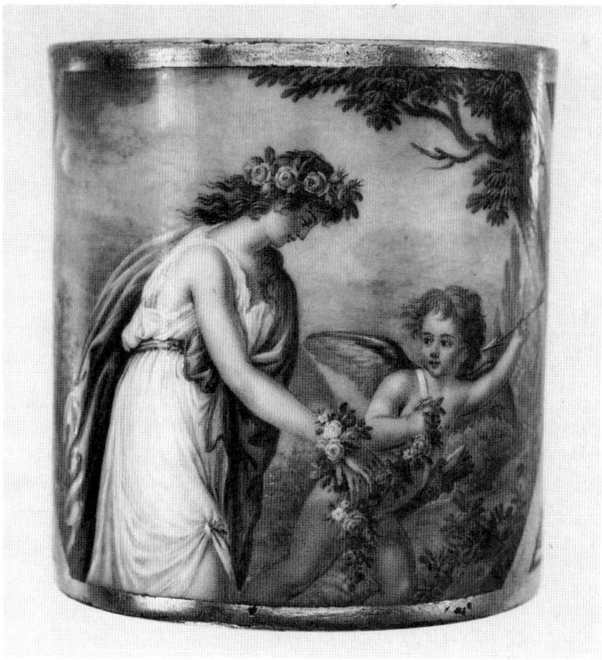

133

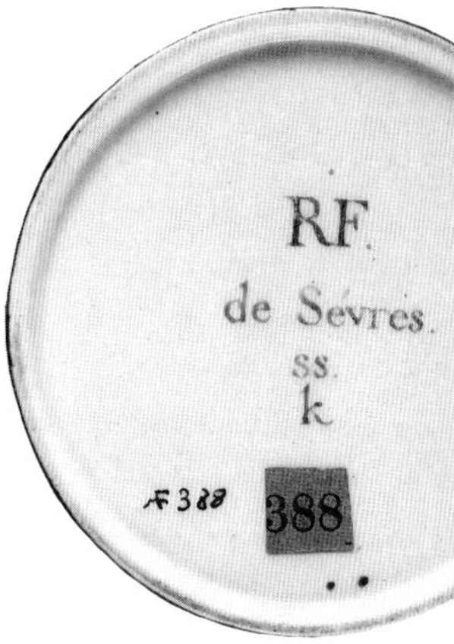

133 *base*

133 Cup (*tasse litron*), 1795

H.	7.4 cm
Marks:	RF. (below a dot)/*de Sevres.* [*sic*] /SS (date-letters for 1795); *k* for the painter Charles-Nicolas Dodin painted in blue enamel; 4 incised
Reg. No.	Franks 388

Soft-paste porcelain, cylindrical, the grooved handle with 'kick' at the lower end. Decorated in enamel colours with a scene of Cupid, an arrow in his raised left hand, and in his right a flower garland which binds Venus' wrists, within a richly gilt reserve on a *bleu nouveau* ground. Venus wears puce drapery highlighted with yellow over a white shift knotted over one knee and fastened at the waist by a blue belt. In her hair is a pink garland. To either side of the handle is a gilt design of acanthus leaves, scrolls and pendent flower garlands. The interior of the cup, handle, and rims gilt. Near the foot is a stylised gilt geometric design. Chip to rim, gilding rubbed on rim and handle.

Provenance: Bequeathed by Sir A.W. Franks, 1897

Literature: Franks, 1896, no. 388

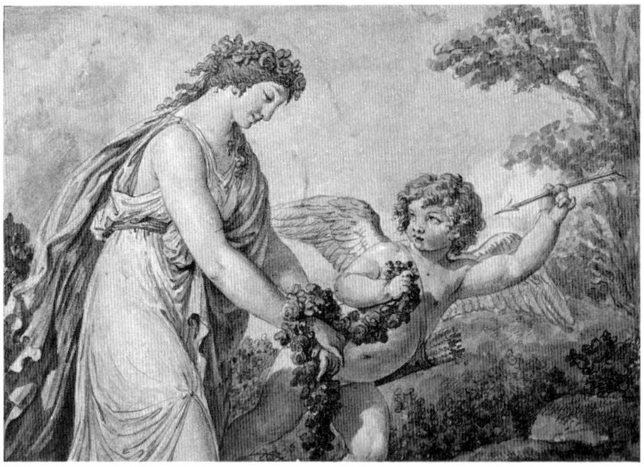

Fig 133a

Comparable Examples: Sotheby's, 13 July 1976, Lot 18, saucer with date-letters qq for 1793 and painter's mark for C.-N. Dodin and gilder's mark for Le Guay *père* and inscribed *l'Amour desarmé*; cup also bears mark *RF/de Sevres*; size unknown

The cup which is of the first size, bears the unusual mark *RF de Sevres*, which makes no sense. A similar mark has been noted on a blue-ground cup painted by C.-N. Dodin, bearing the date-letter qq for 1793, in the Birmingham Museum and Art Gallery.[1]

The painted scene is carefully copied from a watercolour kept at the Sèvres factory, *L' Amour triomphant* (see fig. 133a) by Jean-Jacques Lagrenée called *le jeune* (1739–1821).[2] It is also found on a *vase Leriche, serpents, à bandeau* in the Musée des arts décoratifs, Paris.[3]

Lagrenée, a pupil of his elder brother Louis Lagrenée, had a distinguished career.[4] He received a pension from the King to study in Rome, exhibiting at the Paris Salon from 1771. He became a member of the Académie Royale de Peinture in 1775. By 1781 he was exhibiting as a *professeur* and was mentioned as such by d'Angiviller in a letter of 2 March 1786 to Régnier[5] concerning painting on porcelain. The minister was unhappy about the standard of painting at the factory and proposed attaching a second artist to its service, to act as assistant to Bachelier 'et mon choix s'est arrêté sur M. Lagrenée, le jeune, Professeur de l'Académie Royale de Peinture, dont les Talens et les compositions ingénieuses sont connues [*sic*] de tous les amateurs des beaux arts'. No time was to be wasted: 'Il se rendra lundi prochain à la munuf.e, ou vous voudrez [*sic*] bien le faire reconnoître par les chefs des atteliers de Peinture'. D'Angiviller went on to stress that the role of these eminent artists at the factory was to be strengthened, giving orders that his letter was to be read out to the *chefs d'attelier* to this end.

His orders were evidently carried out for there are many fine examples of painting at Sèvres from the 1780s and even 1790s. The unusually rich decor of this cup lined with gold (*doublée d'or*) hints that it was a special commission but no buyer has yet been traced.

Dodin is recorded as painting two first-size *gobelets* with a *miniature* on a *beau bleu* ground in May 1795. The following June/July he painted a 'miniature après Lagrenée' on a *bleu céleste vase Bachelier*. In January/February 1796 he painted an allegorical figure on a first-size *tasse litron* with a *beau bleu* ground. The Museum cup can perhaps be identified the first of these, or alternatively with the work of early 1796.[6]

The incised mark *4* remains unidentified.[7]

1. Inv. M. 198′ 76. The author is grateful to Miss E. Leary for supplying information about this piece and its companion piece of 1795, both painted with a pastoral scene.
2. MNS, Archives de Sèvres, *Armoire* R2, *dossier Lagrenée*, inventoried in 1814. A companion watercolour of 'L'Amour désarmé' is also kept at the factory, inv. as above. However, M. Sandoz in *Les Lagrenée II – Jean-Jacques Lagrenée (le jeune)*, Paris, 1988, p. 375 states that he believes the attribution is doubtful.
3. Inv. 5349, on loan to the Louvre Museum, illus. Brunet and Préaud, 1978, p. 214, no. 269.
4. For a detailed study of an aspect of his work, see M. Sandoz 'Jean-Jacques Lagrenée peintre d'histoire (1739–1821)', *Bulletin de la société de l'histoire de l'art français*, 1962, pp. 121–33 and for his work for Sèvres, see M. Sandoz, 1988 (see note 2), pp. 112–7. He designed a two-handled cup on a rather solid foot for which a drawing dated 19 June 1786 survives in the Sèvres factory archives, R.1, *dossier* 2, *liasse* 2, f. 21, as well as a whole series of vases bearing his name from late 1785 up to 1813. So far, eight different *vases lagrenée* have been traced. A pair of *vases lagrenée lions* painted by Lagrenée himself were sold at Sotheby's, New York, 9 December 1986, Lot 411, and exhibited by Armin B. Allen, London, 'European Pottery and Porcelain', 8–26 June 1987, no. 15 (now in an American private collection).
5. MNS, Archives de Sèvres, H 3 *liasse* 3.
6. All these references kindly communicated by Rosalind Savill, in MNS, Archives de Sèvres, Vj' 6. It has still not been established when the dating year began at the factory.
7. See Savill, 1988, III, pp. 1126–7.

134 **Broth Bowl, Cover and Stand (*écuelle ronde tournée, plateau ovale uni*)**, porcelain 18th century, decorated later

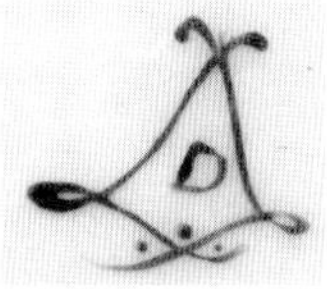

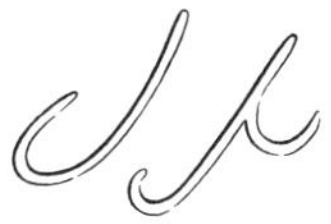

134 *marks*

H. *of bowl and cover:*	10.6 cm
L. *of stand:*	19.8 cm
Marks:	interlaced LL enclosing D, three dots around lower interlace painted in blue enamel on base of bowl and stand and on interior of cover; ?*jp* incised on bowl; suspension hole on stand, smaller one on bowl; printed collection label of Sir Bernard Eckstein, numbered *27* in ink
Reg. No.	1948,12–3,21

Soft-paste porcelain, the moulded shaped oval stand with central depression to hold the round bowl. Bowl with two handles formed of entwined scrolls surmounted by a domed cover with a laurel leaf and berry handle. The decoration consists of landscape scenes including a knife-grinding machine and a peep-show on the bowl, an orchard and a garden scene on the cover, and on the stand an allegory of sculpture and of painting, all on a pink ground. Each reserve is framed by elaborate gilding in patterns not generally found on Sèvres. Foot rim of bowl and stand discoloured; bubbling of gilding and discoloration around well of stand.

Provenance: Bequeathed by Sir B. Eckstein, Bt., 1948

Literature: Unpublished

Exhibited: 1990, 'Fake? The Art of Deception', London, British Museum, March–September 1990, cat. no. 228

Comparable Examples: Sotheby Parke Bernet, Mentmore, Vol. III, 24 May 1977, Lot 2054, pink ground, no date-letter or painter's mark, second size

The shape is discussed by Savill.[1] It was first recorded in Orry de Fulvy's inventory of 1751 and remained popular throughout the century in France for serving broths or soups in the bedroom during a lengthy toilette; the *plateau* was used for bread. Although these bowls and stands were exported to England, they did not sell well, and the shape, unlike many originating at Sèvres, was not taken up by English factories. However, the model was produced at the Locré factory in Paris (see cat. 250).

Pink (called *roze* at the Sèvres factory) was put into production in 1757. The date-letter D is generally held to designate pieces decorated in 1756, and the marks on this piece are evidently spurious.

The painting is distantly related to similar scenes on Sèvres decorated by André-Vincent Vielliard,[2] but the flower sprays and leaf trails underneath the landscape scenes are particularly unconvincing.

It is likely that the pieces, which represent the third of four sizes, were made at the factory, sold as 'seconds' and decorated subsequently, perhaps in England. The incised mark *jp* may have been used by either (Jacques-)François Parpette (d. 1775), a soft-paste repairer between 1757 and 1773 or by Jean-Christophe Pilon, a soft-paste repairer between 1758/9 and 1769.[3] A broth bowl, cover and stand with a marbled ground and Watteau scenes in panels was decorated at Madeley, Shropshire.[4]

1. Savill, 1988, II, pp. 642–4.
2. *Op. cit.*, p. 653, no. C.428–9, illus. p. 655, is a genuine example of Vielliard's painting of children in landscapes against a blue vermiculated ground on an *écuelle* of this type.
3. Savill, 1988, III, p. 1106.
4. W. Turner, 'Madeley Porcelain, Part I' *Connoisseur*, Vol. XXII (1908), no. 11, p. 154.

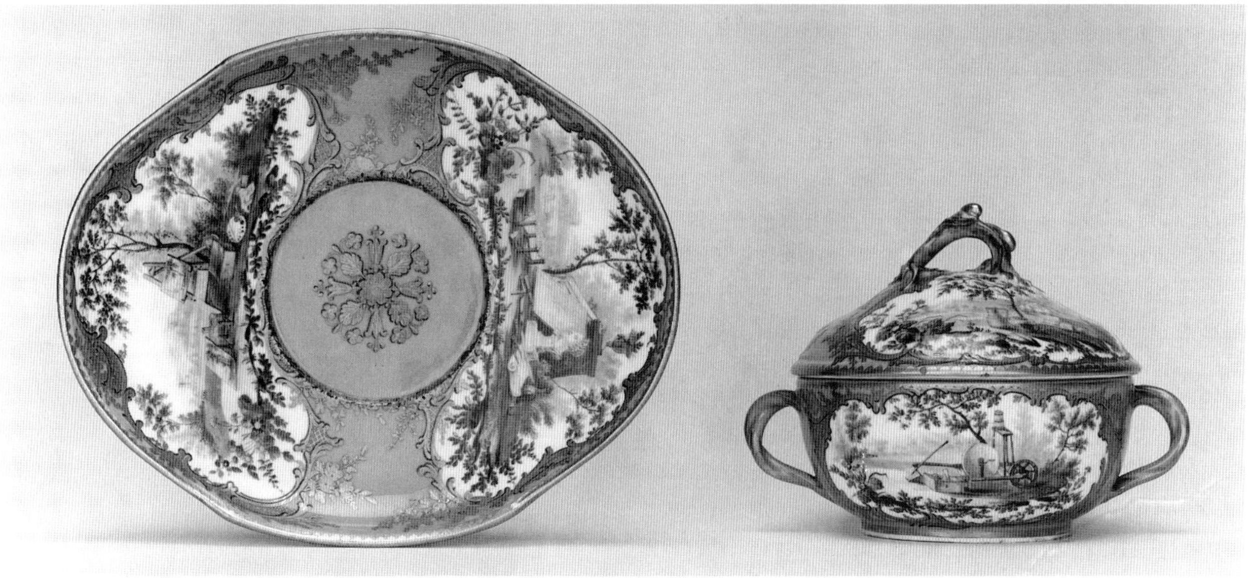

134

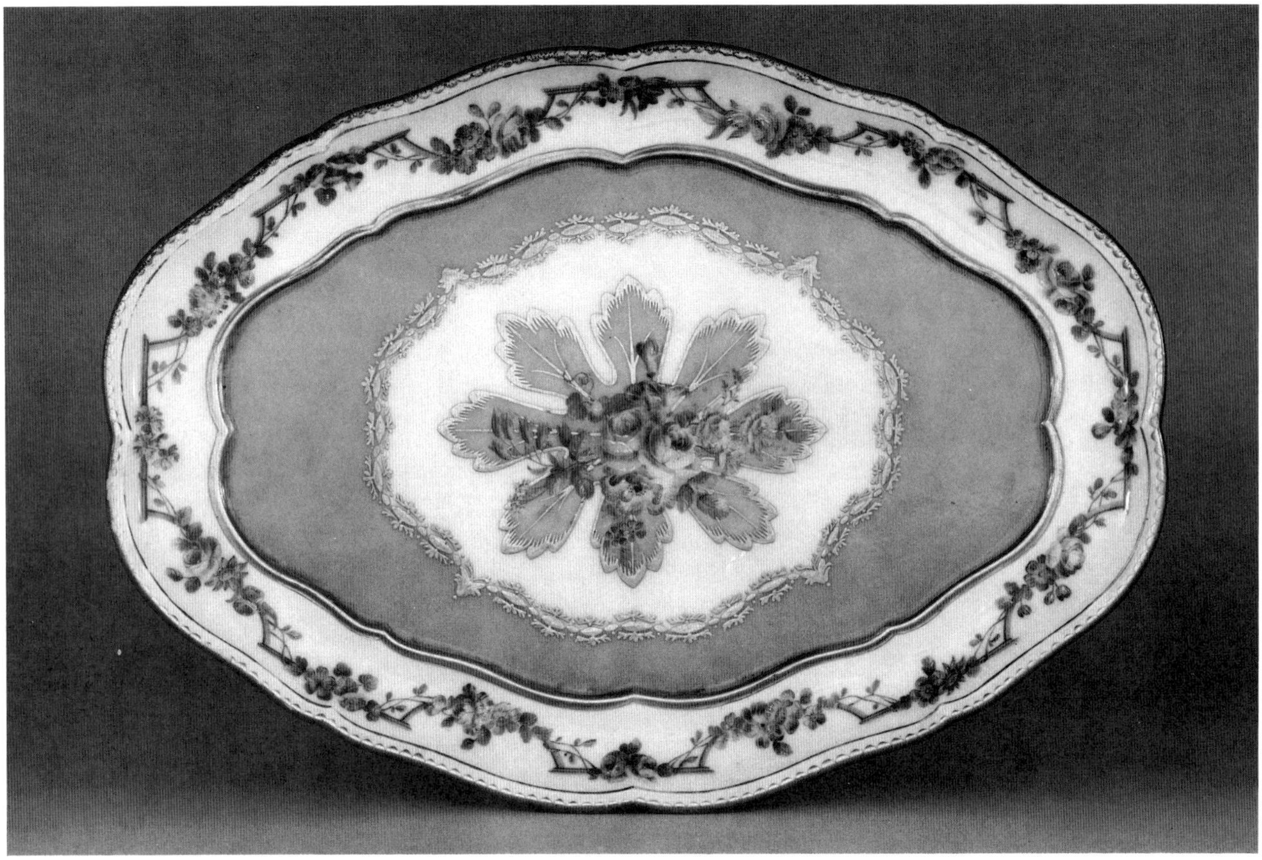

135

135 **Tray (*plateau 'du roi'*)**, porcelain 18th century, probably decorated later

L. 24.6 cm
Marks: LL enclosing date-letter H for 1760; *C Mai* incised; suspension hole; printed collection label of Sir Bernard Eckstein, numbered in ink *200*
Reg. No. 1948,12-3,52

Soft-paste porcelain, shaped rim and slight depression in centre; painted in blue, pink, yellow, white, green and black, with a flower-and-leaf trail winding round a trellis in purple on the border; part of the well of the tray is painted pink; in the centre in reserve on a white ground is a star motif in pink over which a group of flowers are painted in the same palette and manner. They include a yellow and pink full-blown rose, mauve harebells, etc. The edge of the star motif and the veins of the leaves of which it is composed are gilt; the reserve is outlined by a stylised gilt motif, the well is defined by a thick gilt line and the rim has a gilt dentil border. Signs of overfiring on border, black specks on foot rim, and brownish discoloration on underside of border. Foot extensively scratched.

Provenance: Bequeathed by Sir B. Eckstein, Bt., 1948

Literature: Unpublished

Comparable Examples: See discussion

The shape, which is fully discussed by Savill[1] originated at Vincennes and is known from 1753. The tray held a matching cup and saucer and sugar bowl or

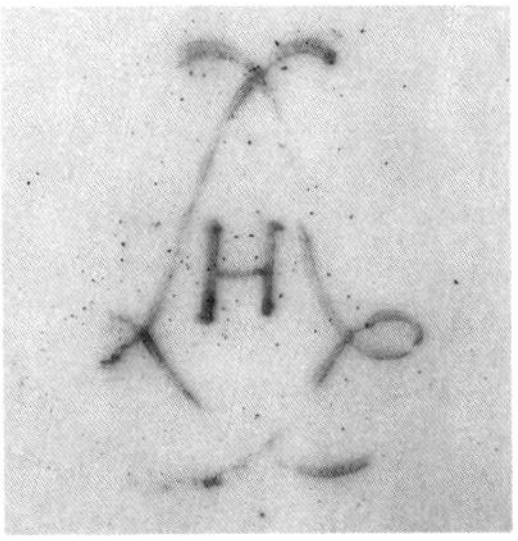

135 *marks*

teapot, or cups without saucers. The title *plateau du déjeuner du roi* appears in the records in 1754. The *plateau* was in production in two sizes in 1755. This example is of the second size, and would have had a cup and saucer and sugar bowl. No matching pieces have been discovered.

The unusual decorative scheme recurs on a square tray intended as a table-top dated 1757 with a pink ground in the Museum of Fine Arts, Boston, USA.[2] It too is decorated in pink and gold with a central rosette similarly overlaid with polychrome flowers. Certain features suggest that part at least of the decoration on the British Museum tray has been added. Brownish discoloration on the reverse, blackening of the gilding in places on the rim and black specks on the edge of the inner border, where pink may have been applied, are not generally found on factory-decorated Sèvres porcelain. The technique of painting flowers on top of a coloured ground is usually restricted to pieces painted in *bleu Fallot*, such as the cup and saucer cat. 110. In addition the pink star in the centre of the tray and the gilt motif around the white reserve do not conform to the factory's decorative practice. However, re-examination of the Boston tray[3] has led the writer to revise her earlier opinion that it had been redecorated. The date of the painting on the British Museum's *plateau du roi* must, therefore, remain to some extent conjectural; it may perhaps be determined by further examples decorated in the same fashion.

The incised mark is highly unusual. A similar mark was noted on a lobed tray (*plateau de tasse à glaces*) decorated *en camaïeu rose* in the trade in 1986.[4] Carl Dauterman discovered the incised mark *mai* on a 'sauceboat/stand' in the Dillon Collection, New York, dated 1760. He attributed the mark to Maillet (also known as Mailly and Mayette) who was employed between 1754–6 on *façonnage*, then became a *répareur* until 1769.[5] Maillet is listed as a repairer at a monthly salary of 48 *livres* in the years 1758, 1759 and 1760.[6]

1. Savill, 1988, II, pp. 590–3.
2. Illus. P.T. Rathbone, *The Forsyth Wickes Collection*, Greenwich, 1968, p. 69, decorator's mark of D. Levé, see also Munger, 1992, no. 166.
3. In October 1991. The author is grateful to Jeffrey Munger for his discussion with her about this piece.
4. Christie's, 3 March 1986, Lot 183.
5. Dauterman, 1986, p. 220.
6. MNS, Archives de Sèvres, D1, *liasse* 1.

136 **Helmet-shaped Jug (*pot à lait*)** decorated in the 19th or 20th century

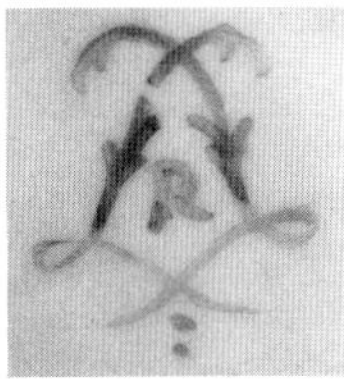

136 *mark*

H. *to top of handle:* 11 cm
Marks: elaborate interlaced LL enclosing R above two dots in blue enamel
Reg. No. 1948,12–3,45

Soft-paste porcelain, moulded on circular foot with loop handle. Decorated with a panel of flowers and fruit on a white ground enclosed by gilt scrolls, flowers and a trellis pattern, all on a pink ground. Handle partly gilt, gilt line around foot, gilt dentil rims. Discoloration to foot.

Provenance: Bequeathed by Sir B. Eckstein, Bt., 1948

Literature: Unpublished

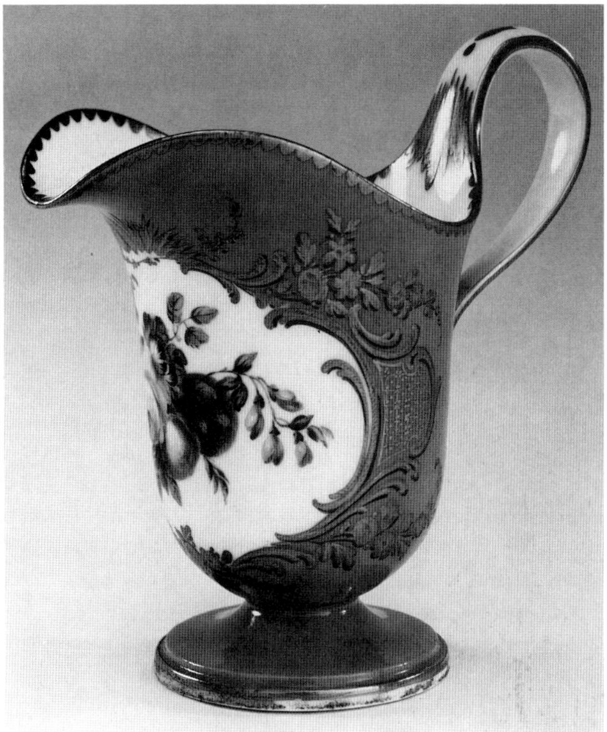

136

Comparable Examples: Manchester, City Art Gallery, inv. 1920.766, turquoise ground, flower decoration, illus. 'Porcelain from Europe', cat. compiled by S. Macdonald, 1986, no. 109.

Christie's, 2 October 1979, Lot 24, H. 11 cm, interlaced LL enclosing date-letter for 1770.

The development of this form, which is neo-classical in style appears to date from the 1780s on the evidence of surviving dated or datable examples which can safely be considered genuine. These are:

London, Victoria and Albert Museum, inv. C.381–1909, marked *RF Sev* (indistinct), gilder's mark *2000*, bright yellow ground, central band of arabesque and other classical ornament in colours on a white ground, H. incl. handle 13.8 cm

USA, Hartford, Conn., Wadsworth Atheneum, inv. 1917.1146, dated 1794, gilder's mark of Vandé II, yellow ground painted with flowers, H. 15.1 cm

Australia, Brisbane, Christie's, collection of Sir Leon and Lady Trout, 6 and 7 June 1989, Lot 453, marked R *F Sevres*, painter's mark of Xhrouet, turquoise ground, central band of roses and triangles on a white ground, H. 14.5 cm

Chappey Collection, illus. *Les Arts*, no. 38, February 1905, pp. 30–1, five examples: green ground with flower decoration; black ground with *chinoiseries* in gold; turquoise ground with a mythological subject; two with dark blue ground and flowers in vases. No marks or measurements given

Paris, Louvre, inv. Th. 1242, illus. Brunet and Préaud, 1978, p. 219, no. 285, dated 1790, painter's mark of Cornailles, dark blue ground painted with flowers in a basket

Sèvres, Musée national de Céramique, illus. C. Dauget and D. Guillemé-Brulon, *La porcelaine française*, Paris, n.d., p. 41, decoration of scrolls in the style of Salembier

Sotheby's, 5 July 1966, Lot 125, H. 4½ in, interlaced LL, pink ground, painted with birds in a landscape in reserve

Christie's, 4 October 1971, Lot 31, H. 11 cm, date-letter for 1782, lime green and blue *oeil-de-perdrix* ground, flowers and fruit on a marble ledge in reserve, painter's mark of Pierre, gilder's mark of Vincent *jeune*

USA, New York, Sotheby Parke Bernet, 4 April 1972, Lot 253, date-letter for 1789, lilac borders, birds, fruit, flowers and body, Harbeson Collection

Christie's, 29 June 1987, Lot 158, H. 14 cm, date-letter for 1759, painter's mark of Aloncle, 'Palatine service' pattern with birds in reserve, not seen by the writer, perhaps spurious [?]

Other examples which apparently date from the 1750s or 1760s on the evidence of their decoration, and which have been examined by the writer, are considered to be spurious.[1]

The style, colour scheme, subject and gilding on this piece do not accord with a date in the 1780s or later. In addition the mark is known to have been used by Randall (see cat. 139). The pink ground is the most widely faked of all Sèvres ground colours.

A rather similar shape of jug was made by Wedgwood around 1780–1800 and produced in several different versions and sizes.[2] A Wedgwood catalogue, never issued but datable to 1790–5, its text in French, illustrates the shape in 'Queen's Ware', or cream-coloured earthenware, as part of a service for tea, coffee or chocolate.[3]

1. Victoria and Albert Museum, London, inv. Circ. 704–1956 decorated with a boy in purple *camaïeu* on a white ground; inv. C. 73–1956 painted with birds in purple *camaïeu* on a white ground; inv. C. 379–1909 painted in *camaïeu bleu* and flesh tones with a girl gardener, dated 1760 and with the mark of the painter Chabry *fils*, who is not listed at the factory before 1765; inv. Circ. 715–1956, pink *oeil de perdrix* ground with flowers in reserve, unmarked. Two further examples have been noted but not examined, and the author is unable to comment on their date of manufacture: Christie's, New York, 30 November 1979, Lot 225, Mrs J.W. Christner Collection, H. 13 cm, *bleu nouveau* ground, landscape scenes, unidentified painter's mark; Scotland, Blair Castle, *bleu céleste* ground, birds.
2. Buten, 1980, p. 131, fig. 119, p. 166, fig. 175; R. Reilly, *Wedgwood*, London, 1989, Vol. 1, p. 439, fig. 624; p. 501, fig. 727.
3. *Ibid.*, p. 340, fig. 439 (no. 71).

137 **Sugar Bowl and Cover (*pot à sucre à la Reine*)**, perhaps made at Sèvres in the 18th century, decorated in the 19th century

H. *incl. cover:*	9.2 cm
D. *of bowl:*	9.4 cm
Marks:	LL and painter's mark possibly imitating that of Chevalier painted in blue enamel; *X* incised; suspension hole inside cover

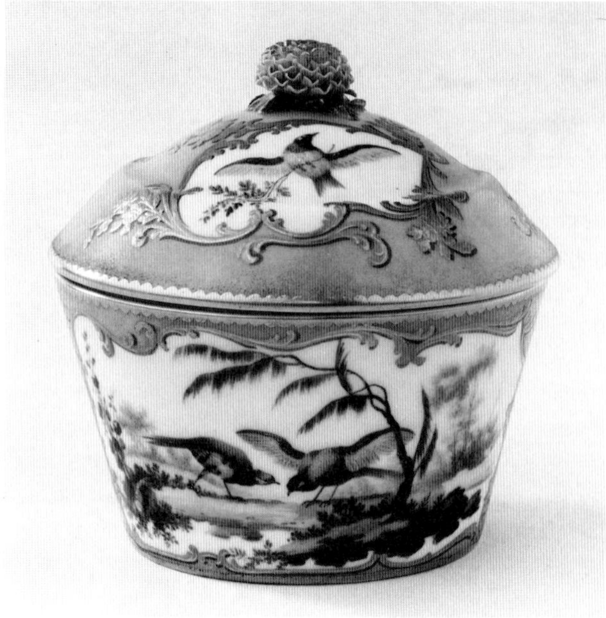

137

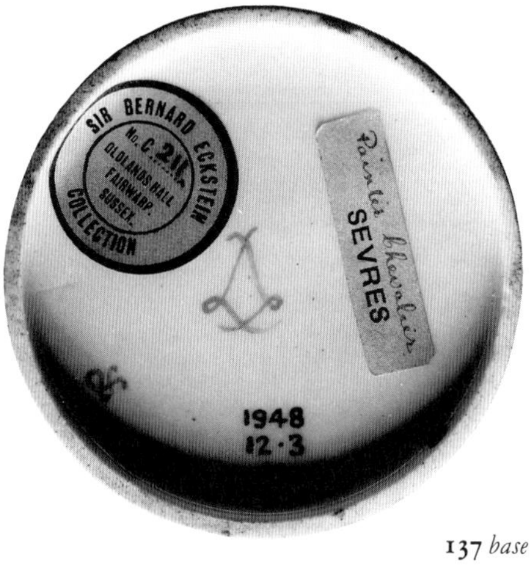

137 *base*

Reg. No. 1948,12–3,41

Soft-paste porcelain, conical with domed cover surmounted by an applied flower finial. Decorated with two panels of exotic birds in landscapes on the bowl and with three reserves each containing a bird on the cover, all on a pink ground. Gilt floral and trellis motifs around reserves, gilt dentil rims and gilt finial.

Provenance: Bequeathed by Sir B. Eckstein, Bt., 1948

Literature: Unpublished

Comparable Examples: None

The form, with an angular handle, originates at Vincennes. A drawing for the second size dated 19 February 1753 is preserved at the Sèvres factory, and moulds for the second size appear in the inventory of 1 January 1756, although examples were fired in the biscuit kiln on 28 March 1753.[1] It is possible that this example represents a revised version of the shape in the second size, with a flower finial or it may be closer to the form called *pot à sucre du Roy*.

The bowl and cover were probably entirely decorated in the nineteenth century. The ground colour is muddy and marred by black specks, especially near the foot and rims, the birds are indifferently painted and the gilding is unconvincing.

Inside the lid is an oblong paper label printed in black *53*.

1. See exh. *Vincennes*, 1977–8, pp. 82–4. An early example measuring 9.3 cm. decorated in *bleu lapis* with gilt flowers and bearing interlaced LL only was sold from the Hector Binney Collection, Sotheby's, 5 December 1989, Lot 77.

138 Cup and Saucer (*tasse litron*) porcelain 18th century, decoration later

D. *of saucer:* 14.4 cm
H. *of cup:* 7.6 cm
Marks: interlaced LL enclosing *L* painted in puce; *S* incised on saucer, incised lines *111* and *1* on cup; suspension hole on saucer; printed collection label of Sir Bernard Eckstein, Oldlands Hall, Fairwarp, Sussex, numbered in ink *218*
Reg. No. 1948,12 3,48

Soft-paste porcelain. Painted on both within a circular gilt reserve with a flower garland in pink, blue, puce, orange, yellow, green and grey; on the cup a garland depends from a ribbon bow and on the saucer there is a flower spray in the centre of the well. Surrounding the reserve is a band of pink, repeated on the rims and around the foot of the cup. The remainder of the surface is painted yellow. Dark red and gilt bead-and-reel motifs pick out these painted areas. Gilt rims, inner rim of cup and outer rim of saucer embellished with a dentil-type pattern. Handle gilt. Underside of rim of saucer chipped. Gilding on rims rubbed.

Provenance: Bequeathed by Sir B. Eckstein, Bt., 1948

Literature: Unpublished

Comparable Examples: None

The cup and saucer correspond with the largest, or first, size made at Sèvres, the handle of form C as classified by Savill.[1] The incised mark and the suspension hole on the saucer point to a Sèvres origin. However, both painted mark and decoration are spurious. Pink and yellow were the Sèvres ground colours most sought after by collectors from the middle of the nineteenth century, particularly in Britain, but they were never used together during the eighteenth century. The gilt patterns and the gilding of the handle are also uncharacteristic of eighteenth century decoration. The suspension hole on the saucer is black, a feature sometimes associated with pieces which have been decorated some time after their manufacture, and probably due to the accumulation of dirt before the enamel firing.

1. Savill, 1988, II, p. 501.

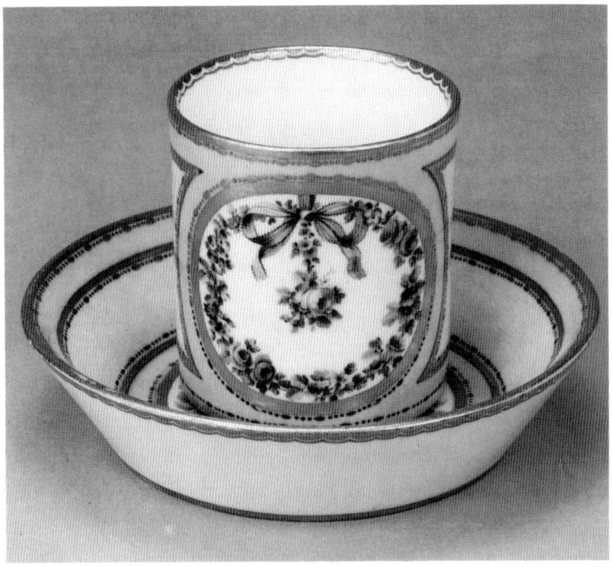

138

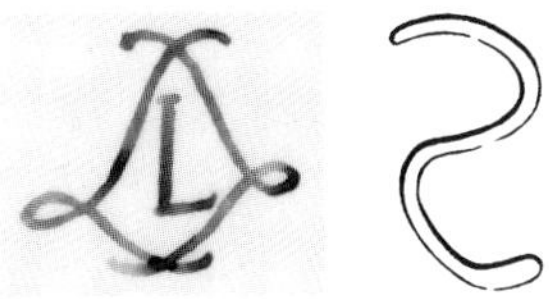

138 *marks*

139 Two Sugar Bowls and Covers, 19th century

H. *to top of finial:* 10.4 cm
D. *of bowl:* 8.6 cm
Marks: interlaced LL (1948,12–3,32), similar mark above *R*, repeated inside cover (on 1948,12–3,33 only); suspension hole inside covers; printed collection label of Sir Bernard Eckstein, Oldland Hall, Fairwarp, Sussex, numbered in ink *202* and *203*
Reg. No. 1948,12–3,32 (flowers on reverse), 33

Soft-paste porcelain, rounded sides tapering to base, domed cover and fruit knop. Painted in enamel colours with a port scene on one side and with flowers on the other on a turquoise ground, with a gilt pattern of scrolls near rim and foot, and pendent gilt flower garlands. Cover painted with two panels of flowers on a white ground, and a similar gilt pattern (1948,12–3,32). The other bowl is painted with two scenes each showing two sailors at work on shore, and on the cover two reserves each containing a single sailor within gilt rococo reserves on a turquoise ground. Gilt dentil pattern on rims, gilt knops.

Provenance: Bequeathed by Sir B. Eckstein, Bt., 1948

Literature: Unpublished

Comparable Examples: None

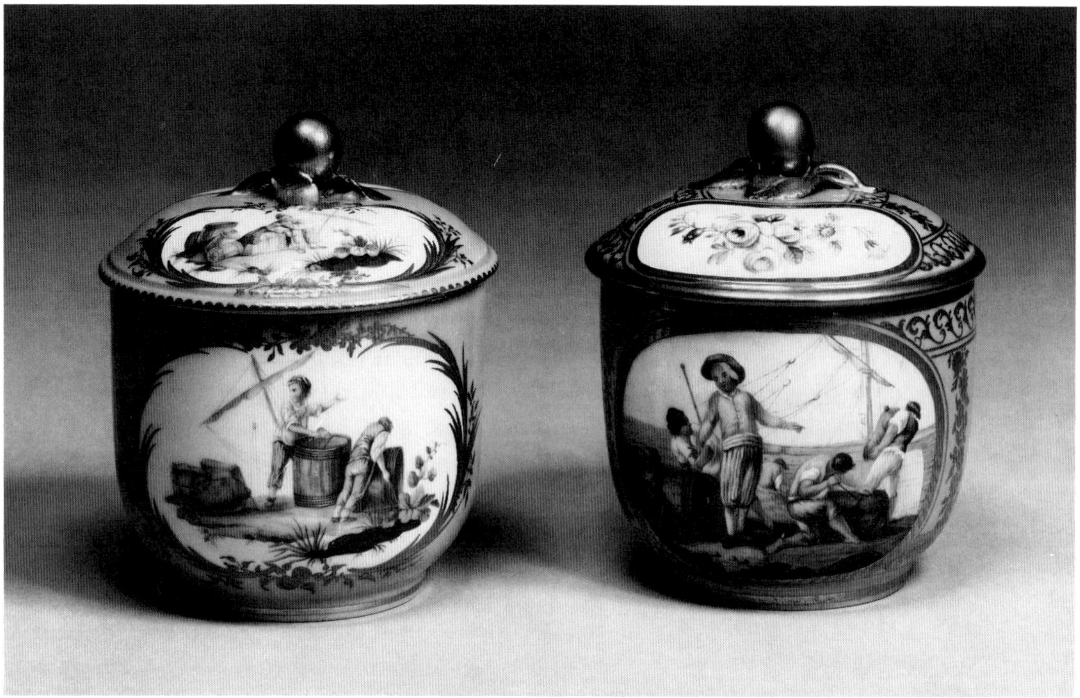

139

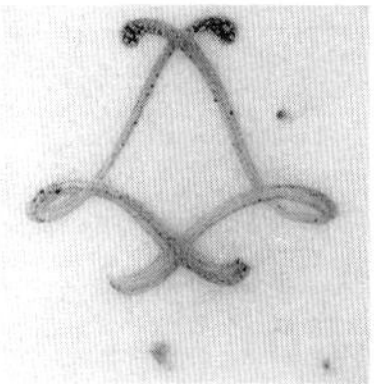

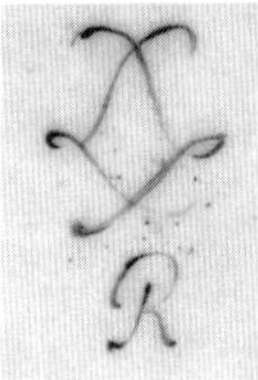

139 *marks (left) 1948, 12–3, 32 and (right) 33*

The shape is similar to the Sèvres *pot à sucre 'Bouret'* but the dimensions differ from the sizes noted by Savill.[1] The painting imitates that of the Sèvres painter Jean-Louis Morin, and even the gilding has been quite closely copied from Sèvres gilt patterns. However, these pieces were made in the nineteenth century, one being marked by Thomas Martin Randall (1786–1859) of Shropshire,[2] and the other presumably also of English manufacture. Its gilt decoration is much more overloaded and it is perhaps of later date. As yet no secure chronology has been established for the manufacture of these Sèvres imitations, which were produced in quantity.

Randall, after running an enamelling business in London between 1813 and 1825, installed himself at Madeley in about 1828 and made soft-paste porcelain which he then decorated. The works were closed in 1840 and Baldock, who had been its chief commissioning dealer, retired in 1843. Randall then set up in Shelton, Staffordshire, where he was succeeded by J. Randall until the works closed in 1856.

1. Savill, 1988, II, pp. 570–2.
2. See Savill, 1988, III, pp. 1167–71 for a brief account of Randall's career.

140 **Milk Jug (*pot à lait à trois pieds*)**, Sèvres, 18th century, decoration later, probably late 19th century

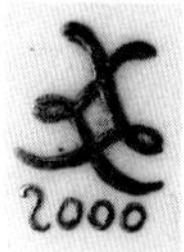

140 *mark*

H. 12.1 cm
Marks: interlaced LL in gold over a similar mark in blue above *2000*
Reg. No. 1938,4–14,1

Soft-paste porcelain, moulded applied handle and feet, decorated with 'jewelled' motifs including a band of green leaves and red dots around the neck and base; a vase decorated in turquoise blue enamel with green festoons and a white finial above a fan and wing motif in turquoise and pink enamel, enclosed by scrolls in green and red below the lip; and a band of scroll and leaf ornament interrupted by a diagonal line around the central area, enclosed by a band of gold scroll and turquoise dot ornament. The handle and feet, moulded to resemble twigs, are partly gilt, relief flower and leaf ornament above each foot gilt, gilt dentil on inner and outer rim. Perfect.

Provenance: Presented by W. King, Esq. (former Deputy Keeper in the British Museum), 1938

Literature: Unpublished

Exhibited: 1990 'Fake? The Art of Deception', London, British Museum, March–September 1990, cat. no. 229

Comparable Examples: Paris, Musée des arts décoratifs, cup and saucer with similar jewelled motifs, illus. Dupont, 1987, p. 112, no. 1

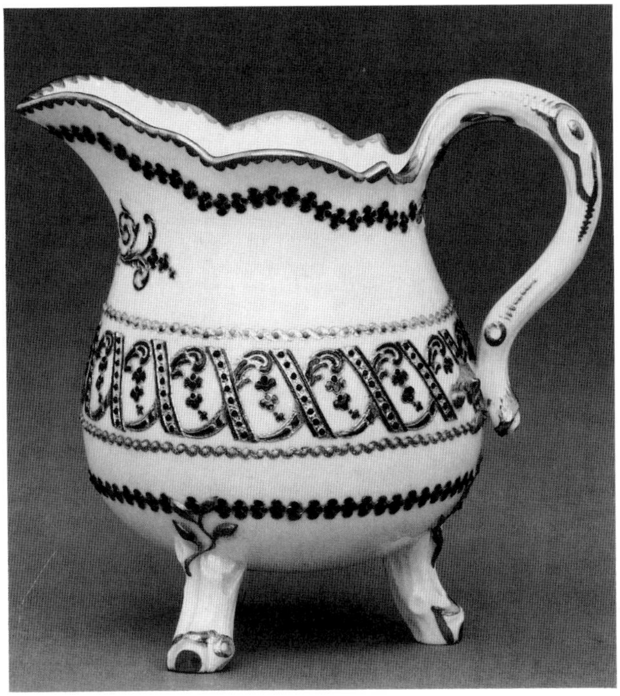

140

Paris, Galerie Georges Petit, 9 March 1911, Lot 44, illus., *déjeuner* from the collection of the late Baron Achille Seillière, including a jug with similar motifs on a blue ground

Paris, Hôtel Drouot, 23 November 1967, Lot 97, a teapot and cover and a bowl sold from the Gilbert Lévy Collection

Paris, Vandermeersch, illustrated as part of a *cabaret* with tray, teapot and cover, cup and saucer, sugar bowl and cover, *L'Estampille*, no. 128, December 1980, p. 83 (not examined)

London, Victoria and Albert Museum, cup and saucer, interlaced LL above *2000* in gold, inv. C. 437 & a–1921; covered cup and saucer C. 436 to b–1921

USA, Baltimore, Walters Art Gallery, two cups and saucers, one with a white, one with a yellow ground, teapot and cover with a white ground, inv. 48.716, A, B; 48.693, A, B; 48.717, A, B

USA, New York, Christie's, The Elizabeth Parke Firestone Collection, Part I, 21–2 March 1990, Lot 286 (teapot)

The jug is the largest of three sizes, in production from November 1752. Although no detailed study of the technique of 'jewelling' or applying coloured enamels on to gold foils attached to the porcelain has yet been carried out, several jewelled vases have been discussed in the literature and the dies used on the larger vases have been recently rediscovered and published by Tamara Préaud.[1] None of the motifs on this piece, which are organised in a noticeably rigid fashion, correspond with those found on vases such as cat. 125. Under high magnification it can be seen that gaps between gold foils have been disguised with gilding, and jewellers' rouge is visible on many of the foils. In addition, there is a 'distressed' effect visible on the glaze close to the 'jewelling'. These features are not found on genuine examples, such as cats 125, 126.

The rather carelessly applied gilder's mark does not conform to the mark used by Vincent, employed as a gilder between 1753 and 1806, and the gold interlaced LL is not normally painted over an existing blue factory mark. For all these reasons the 'jewelling' is thought to be of nineteenth-century date.

Analysis using X-ray fluorescence carried out by the British Museum Research Laboratory[2] revealed that the colourless glassy material used to cause the gold to adhere to the surface of the porcelain contains 15–25% lead oxide whereas analysis of the blue glassy substance beneath the gold foils on the 'jewelled' vase reg. no. 1935,12–18,1 (cat. 125) contains 20–30% oxide. The composition of the gold foil, however, showed no significant difference, that on the jug containing 98.7% gold, 0.9% silver and 0.4% copper, and on the vase 98.3% gold, 1.6% silver and 0.2% copper. It seems, therefore, that the later imitators of the 'jewelling' technique, whilst able to replicate fairly satisfactorily the materials used at Sèvres, could not achieve the quality of craftsmanship characteristic of the royal factory.

1. T. Préaud, 'Sèvres enamelled porcelain: eight dies (and a quarrel) rediscovered', *Burlington Magazine*, Vol. CXXVIII, no. 999, June 1986, pp. 391–7.
2. BMRL 5679, July 1988. The author is grateful to Michael Cowell and Mavis Bimson of the British Museum Research Laboratory for their assistance in establishing the nature of the gold foil decoration.

141 **Vase (*vase 'étrusque'*)**, porcelain 18th century, probably decorated in the 19th century

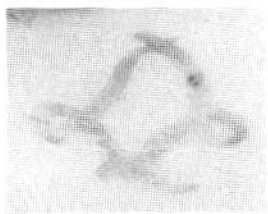

141 *mark*

H. *incl. stand:*	30.2 cm
without stand:	27.7 cm
Marks:	interlaced LL painted in blue enamel
Reg. No.	1948,12–3,6

Soft-paste porcelain, ovoid body on domed stem, the upper part encircled by white glazed porcelain 'pearls', with stepped circular foot. The loop handles are ornamented with white glazed porcelain husks; below their out-turned terminals are three pendent gilt husks. Painted in pastel colours on a turquoise-green ground, within a tooled oval gilt reserve in turn enclosed by gilt floral and scroll ornament, is a gallant landscape scene of a young man in a ruff and striped jacket at the left, holding a sheet of music, teaching a young woman wearing a ruff and low-cut dress to sing. On the reverse is a panel painted with flowers including full-blown roses, a carnation and a peony enclosed by similar gilt decoration. Perfect.

The gilt-bronze mount consists of a plinth with canted corners.

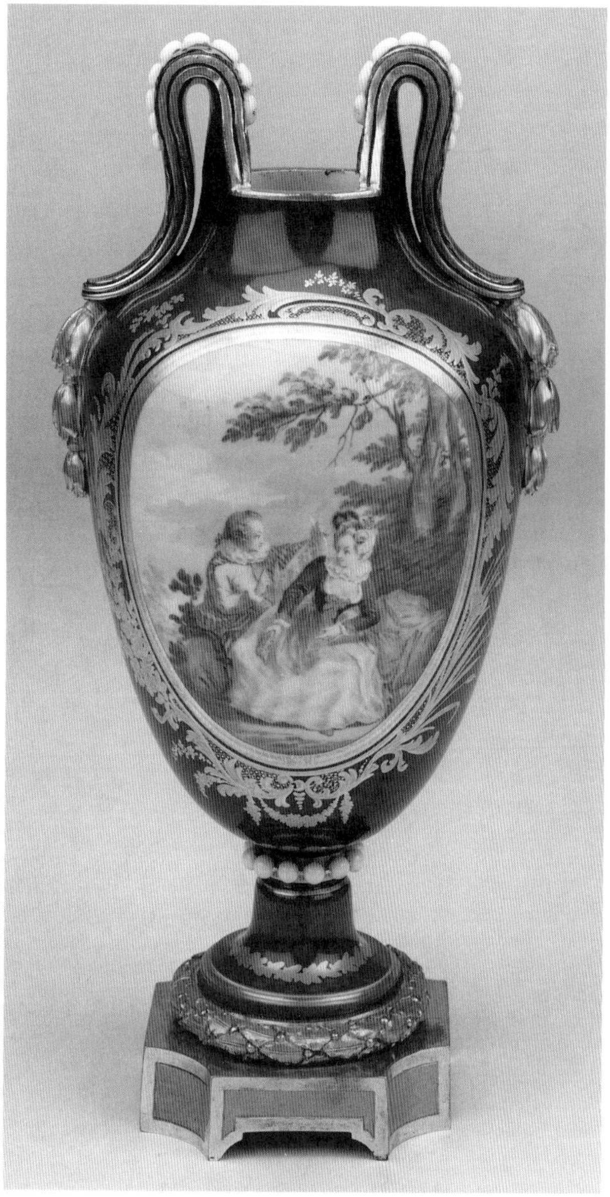

141

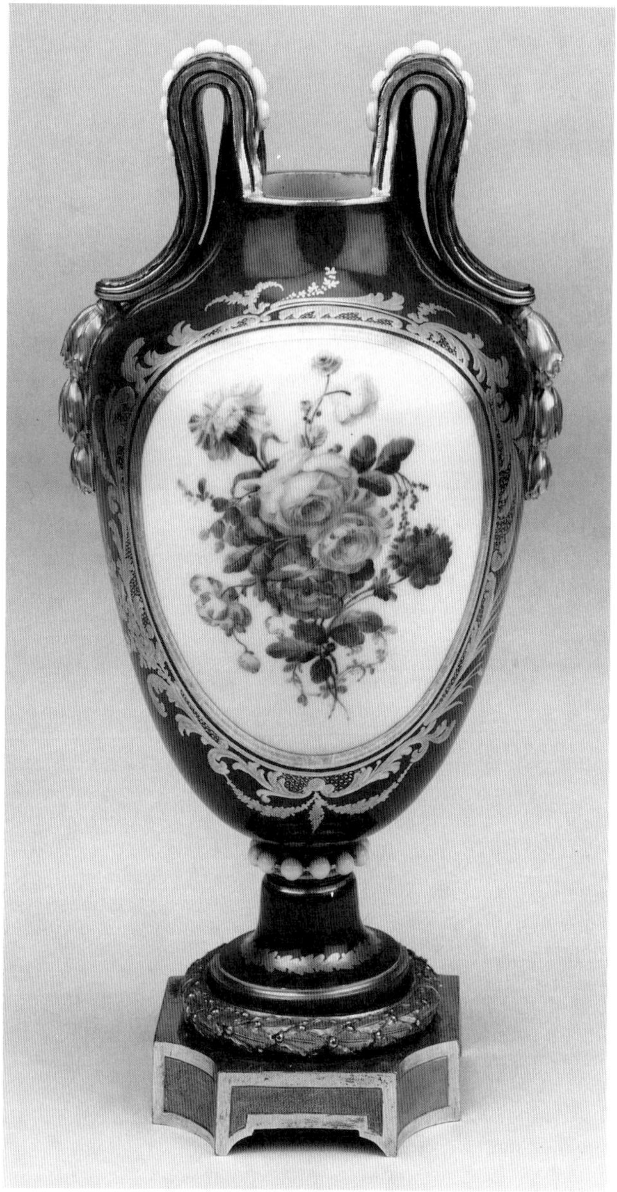

141 *reverse*

The centre of each shaped panel has been roughened with a matting tool; the edges are burnished. A laurel leaf and berry wreath forms the taurus which is attached to the plinth by means of two threaded rods secured by nuts underneath. A metal washer lies between the plinth and the taurus.

Provenance: Bequeathed by Sir B. Eckstein, Bt., 1948

Literature: Savill, 1988, I, p. 238, p. 244 f.n. 38, p. 351, p. 353 f.n. 3e

Comparable Examples: See Savill, 1988, I, pp. 351–2, p. 353 f.n. 3

The form, in production from 1767, has been discussed by Savill, who illustrates a plaster model which is a variant, with moulded decoration of a rope motif, beading, a ribbon bow and branches of foliage around the cartouche on both front and back.[1] This example is the second of two sizes and was not in production until 1768. As Savill points out, the title *vase étrusque* does not appear in the factory sales records during the 1760s and may not have been used to describe this vase.

There are few known surviving examples of this shape, and all are decorated with marine or military scenes.[2] Neither the painting nor the gilding on this example conform with what might be expected on a piece which was manufactured some time after the late 1760s. Floral decoration of this kind on a white ground is not implausible[3] but the theatrical scene in the style of Watteau is much less convincing. No source for it has been traced and it is poorly painted in a sentimental style. As Savill remarks: '"Watteau" scenes are rare on eighteenth-century Sèvres (although they are often found on nineteenth-century imitations).'[4] The gilding is flat and applied in a rococo style in patterns which do conform with factory practice.

It is suggested that the vase was made at the factory and decorated elsewhere, probably during the nineteenth century.

The gilt-bronze mount may date from the second quarter of the nineteenth century; its precise origin is unknown.[5]

1. Savill, 1988, I, pp. 351–2.
2. London, Royal Collection, illus. G. Laking, *Sèvres Porcelain of Buckingham Palace and Windsor Castle*, London, 1907, p. 50, no. 61, blue ground with *caillouté* gilding, H. 43 cm (first size); USA, Baltimore, Walters Art Gallery, illus. *Catalogue of an Important Collection of Old Sèvres Porcelain Louis XV and Louis XVI Period belonging to E.M. Hodgkins, Paris*, privately published, n.d. (*c.* 1928), no. 38, green ground with Turkish harbour scene, dated 1786, H. with stand 46.3 cm; Baron James de Rothschild Collection, sold Paris, Palais Galliéra, 1 December 1966, Lot 60, green ground with Turkish harbour scene dated 1777, H. 43 cm; Paris, Louvre Museum, OA 10256–7, pair, formerly Harewood Collection, blue ground with harbour scenes, illus. Brunet and Préaud, 1978, p. 175, fig. 154; Oscar Dusendschon Collection, pair, sold Sotheby's, 6 December 1960, Lot 68, blue ground with marine scenes dated 1769, H. with stands 30.5 cm (second size).
3. See Savill, 1988, I, C309, pl. opposite p. 363 showing flower decoration on the reverse of a *vase chinois* dated 1773.
4. Savill, 1988, I, p. 238.
5. The author is grateful to Martin Chapman, formerly of the Department of Metalwork, Victoria and Albert Museum, for his help in describing and dating the ormolu mount.

Sèvres Biscuit Porcelain

The production of unglazed figures, groups, plaques and medallions at Vincennes/Sèvres has received little scholarly attention.[1] In a recent work,[2] a succinct account has been given of the preparation of the raw materials: according to the factory chemist Hellot, soda ash, sea salt, potassium nitrate, silica and lime (or gypsum) were milled together and heated for more than thirty hours at the back of the firebox under the hearth of the kiln, forming an opaque white substance. In scientific terms, the process caused the alkali and quartz to react to produce an alkali silicate glass containing residual quartz, which was mostly transformed into crystalline forms of silica, tridymite and cristobalite. From 1740, calcined alum, a hydrated potassium aluminium surface was added to the batch to provide additional potassia and alumina. This was the ingredient that differentiated the extremely white body of Vincennes/Sèvres from the other soft-pastes made in eighteenth-century France. The glass formed in the initial sintering process was then washed with boiling water to remove impurities in the form of soluble alkalis. It was then ground wet, together with 16.5% white limestone and 8.3% washed calcareous marl from Argenteuil, a highly plastic clay, and allowed to settle. After the excess liquid had been drawn off, the body was partly dried out then wedged before being stored for several months in wooden barrels to increase its plasticity. It was then ready for use in moulds, although for throwing and turning the body required the addition of black soap and parchment glue. Because of the 'shortness' of the clay, the final turning of thrown wares had to be done when they were bone dry rather than in the leather-hard state.

To produce a figure, the process was as follows: the original drawings made by, for instance, the painter Boucher, were used by the factory sculptor to create models, usually of terracotta[3] or plaster. A plaster mould was then made from the sculpted clay model. In turn it was then used to make a master piece-mould, from which working moulds (probably discarded after being used at most ten times at Vincennes/Sèvres) were taken. Each figure was made up of a number of separate pieces, from thin slabs of clay pressed into the dampened plaster mould. These were joined together with liquid clay after removal from the moulds and before firing. Whilst some parts of a figure, such as the head and torso, might be left hollow, others, such as arms, were usually solid.[4] The 'repairer' finished the figure whilst it was still in the damp state, removing mould lines, and using an incising tool to increase the sharpness of the modelling. The piece was thoroughly dried out before firing. To prevent distortion during the long firing (it could last up to 90 hours reaching around 1050° centigrade), figures were supported in the kiln by an elaborate structure formed of soft-paste porcelain, separated from the piece itself by finely-ground quartz and gum arabic which could be brushed off afterwards. A sandstone abrasive was used to polish the surface, giving it its characteristic smooth and silky quality.

By 1757, biscuit, which was probably introduced in about 1751,[5] had become a major part of the factory's production. E.-M. Falconet (1716–91)[6] was appointed as director of sculpture in that year. On his departure for Russia in 1766 he was replaced by the painter J.-J. Bachelier (1724–1806).[7] L.-S. Boizot (1743–1809), another sculptor and former pupil of M.-A. Slodtz,[8] took over in 1773 and remained in the post until his death. During this period he was responsible for around 150 figures and groups, principally of historical and mythological subjects.

The earliest productions at Vincennes, chiefly children and subjects after Boucher,[9] were intended as table decoration, instead of the sugar sculpture used during the dessert course. Elaborate centrepieces were known as early as 1753, when one was created for Louis XV.[10] A spectacular biscuit table-arrangement (*surtout*) was produced in 1769–70 for the marriage of the Dauphin, later Louis XVI.[11] Most large services supplied by the factory during the eighteenth century included sculpture. Free-standing sculptural pieces were in production from the 1760s. They were larger than the table sculpture and were often conceived in sets.[12] The 1770s marked the arrival of complex groups consisting of a considerable number of different figures. Usually the maximum number was five, but the centrepiece of the service made in 1778 for the Empress Catherine the Great of Russia consisted of 'some twenty-five figures'.[13] Evidently there was considerable demand for these biscuit porcelain groups, as they were made at rival factories, notably at the Locré factory in Paris,[14] and at Niderviller.[15] Their appearance at Sèvres coincided with the beginning of hard-paste production, which, because it was less subject to distortion in the kiln, was much more suitable for large-scale pieces.

From the portrayal in 1755 of Louis xv's mistress and friend Madame de Pompadour in the guise of *L'Amitié au Coeur*,[16] to the official portrait of Louis xv by Boizot thirty years later,[17] biscuit sculpture at the royal factory played an important role in the strengthening of the image of royalty. The 600 or so biscuit figures and groups created at the factory during the eighteenth century (the total made during the factory's existence now amounts to around 2,600),[18] are a mirror of French cultural life. Subjects drawn from the theatre, opera and ballet were consistently popular. The splendid series of *Grands Hommes*, originally introduced for the monarch himself from 1777, made available to the public in 1782 and augmented right up to 1789, did not, however, prove popular. In 1785 the price, once 30 *livres*, had to be halved.[19] Occupations, mythological, allegorical and religious themes were all treated. Perhaps most typical are the erotic subjects, such as *Le Sabot Cassé* (cat. 145), whose meaning is often lost on the twentieth-century collector unaccustomed to this kind of symbolic language. Some groups – Falconet's *Pygmalion and Galatea* must be amongst them – are works of art in their own right, and move and delight in the same way as marble or bronze.

Sèvres biscuit figures and groups made in the eighteenth century do not bear a factory mark. Some, but not all, are incised with the initial of the head of the sculpture workshop.[20] This is one way of dating them. Another is by touch and appearance. In general, the early soft-paste examples made in the 1750s and 1760s are characterised by a silky feel and glossy appearance, and are highly finished. There is a distinct difference in quality between them and later editions of the same model. Hard-paste groups of the 1770s and 1780s are also carefully 'repaired' or finished. Whilst the names of France's leading sculptors, such as Falconet (cats 142–3, 147–9) and J.-B. Lemoyne (see cat. 106), who worked directly for the factory, and Saly,[21] Pajou,[22] J.-J. Caffiéri (see cat. 151), Clodion,[23] Houdon[24] and Pigalle,[25] whose work was reproduced in porcelain by the factory, are well known, those of the craftsmen actually producing the pieces are much less familiar. Records of their names and salaries have survived, and have been quoted in the catalogue entries wherever possible. The sculpture workshops were important and in 1774 there were no less than 40 repairers, although not all were working on figures and groups.

The prices charged reflected the considerable amount of work and skill required to produce these sculptural pieces. A figure of Louis xv after J.-B. Pigalle cost 72 *livres* in the 1770s and 1780s.[26] In 1780 a figure of Saint Anthony, originally devised in 1765, cost 192 *livres*.[27] In 1783 Louis xvi purchased various figures of *Hommes Illustres* on blue and gold bases priced at 600 *livres* each.[28] A group of children with a dancing dog modelled by Falconet after Boucher, consisting of four children and a dog on a rocky mound with a hat, a plate of cakes and a stool, sold for 300 *livres* in 1758 when it was introduced.[29] The well-known figure of Cupid (*Amour menaçant*) usually sold for 96 *livres*.[30] At the time of her death in 1764, Madame de Pompadour owned Sèvres biscuit porcelain to the value of around 1500 *livres* at Versailles alone.[31]

The production of porcelain medallions began in the 1760s. Since nearly every other European (including English) ceramic factory, as well as some other French porcelain manufacturers, were also making medallions, there was clearly an enormous demand for these cheap substitutes for medals and gems. Sèvres began by making portrait medallions, a few with coloured grounds, and quickly moved on to making plaques of various sizes for mounting in jewellery, box-tops and furniture,[32] although such items were never produced in quantity.

Sèvres biscuit sculpture should not be considered in isolation from what was made contemporaneously elsewhere in France. During the early years of the factory's existence, Saint-Cloud, Chantilly and the mysterious Paris factories did not manufacture biscuit porcelain. The chief rival of Vincennes/Sèvres in this branch was Mennecy-Villeroy, which made figures and portrait plaques. In the 1770s not only Bourg-la-Reine, but also the hard-paste factories, principally Niderviller and the Paris concerns, entered the fray.[33] All could, as far as we know, undercut the prices charged by the Sèvres factory. However, the popularity of portrait sculpture and allegorical subjects seems to have increased in the years just preceding the Revolution, and this aspect of the factory's production continued to play an important official role. Biscuit sculpture, including medallions, remained in production and was particularly favoured by the Emperor Napoleon. Further series of portrait medallions were issued under the restored monarchy, and indeed by later regimes. As the Museum collection does not include examples of figures and groups from the nineteenth and twentieth centuries, these will not be discussed here. For a brief outline of the factory's history during this later period, see pp. 211–13.

1. The principal works are: E. Bourgeois, *Le biscuit de Sèvres au XVIIIe Siècle*, 2 vols., Paris, 1909; E. Bourgeois and G. Lechevallier-Chevignard, *Le biscuit de Sèvres, recueil des modèles de la Manufacture de Sèvres au XVIII Siècle*, Paris, n.d. (1913); G. Lechevallier-Chevignard and M. Savreux, *Le Biscuit de Sèvres. Directoire, Consulat, Empire*, Paris, 1923; N. Birioukova, *Les Biscuits de la Manufacture Nationale de Sèvres, XVIIIe et XIXe Siècles*, Paris, n.d.; C.E. de Ujfalvy-Bourdon, *Les biscuits de porcelaine*, Paris, 1893 should be used with caution; W.J. Sainsbury, 'Sèvres Soft-Paste Biscuit Figures', *Apollo*, Vol. LI, no. 303, May 1950, Part I, pp. 133–6; Vol. LI, no. 304, June 1950, Part II, pp. 168–71; W.J. Sainsbury, 'Les marques sur les biscuits en pâte tendre de Vincennes et Sèvres', *Cahiers*, no. 37, 1966, pp. 14–29; W.J. Sainsbury, 'Large groups and figures in the soft-paste biscuit of Vincennes-Sèvres', *Antiques*, April 1965, pp. 430–3; W.J. Sainsbury, 'Small figures and groups in the soft-paste biscuit of Vincennes-Sèvres', *Antiques*, December 1965, pp. 824–8.
2. W.P. Kingery and P. Vandiver, *Ceramic Masterpieces*, New York and London, 1986, see Chapter 10 'A Boucher Soft-Paste Unglazed Bisque Sculpture: La Danseuse', pp. 179–94; the author has drawn extensively on this work for the technical explanation given in this paragraph.
3. A terracotta of a group known as *L'Alliance* by L.-S. Boizot, celebrating the marriage of the comte d'Artois and Maria-Theresa of Savoy, is illustrated by G. Zick, 'Parva Sed Apta: Boizot in suddeutschem Privatbesitz', *Keramos*, 123, January 1989, pp. 48–9, figs. 3–4; other biscuit terracottas are discussed by J. Draper, 'New Terracottas by Boizot and Julien', *Metropolitan Museum Journal*, 12/1977, pp. 141–9.
4. See Kingery and Vandiver, *op. cit.*, pp. 188–9, for a radiograph and diagram of *La Danseuse* illustrating this. Antoine d'Albis has pointed out that many early figures were directly modelled like sculpture. Between 1746 and 1757 the factory employed thirteen 'sculptors' and only two plaster modellers.
5. Savill, 1988, II, p. 819.
6. For a biography see Savill, 1988, III, pp. 981–2.
7. *Ibid.*, pp. 961–4.
8. *Ibid.*, pp. 967–9.
9. For groups after Boucher, see R. Savill, 'François Boucher and the porcelains of Vincennes and Sèvres', *Apollo*, Vol. CXV, no. 241, March 1982, pp. 163–4.
10. Savill, 1988, II, p. 820.
11. Discussed by P. Ennès, 'Le surtout de mariage en porcelaine de Sèvres, du Dauphin, 1769–1770', *La Revue de l'Art*, no. 76, June 1987, pp. 63–73.
12. Savill, 1988, II, pp. 820–1.
13. Bellaigue, 1986, pp. 18–19, fig. 14.
14. Bloit, 1988, pp. 12, 14, 18, 31, 34–5.
15. See exh. Sarrebourg, 1986.
16. Exh. *Vincennes*, 1977–8, pp. 149–50.
17. Brunet and Préaud, 1978, p. 234, no. 327.
18. J. Mathieu in association with T. Préaud, *La Porcelaine de Sèvres*, Paris, 1982, p. 55. For some figures in production in 1967 from early models, see 'Biscuits de Sèvres', supplement to *Cahiers*, no. 39, 1967.
19. E. Bourgeois, 1909, Vol. 2, p. 176. For a recent discussion of the *Grands Hommes* series, see P. Ennès in Musée du Louvre, 1990, pp. 202–11.
20. Birioukova, 1968, pp. 257–60.
21. The plaster model preserved at the Sèvres factory of the so-called 'Faune de Saly, is illustrated by Ennès, 1987, p. 69, fig. 22.
22. The group *La Naissance du Dauphin*, illustrated by Brunet and Préaud, 1978, no. 324, p. 233, is based on a work by Pajou, as is a bust of Madame du Barry, a biscuit example of which is in the Metropolitan Museum, New York, inv. 43.163.3.
23. Brunet and Préaud, 1978, p. 233, illustrate a terracotta of a figure of Montesquieu 'due a Clodion' in the Musée national de Céramique, Sèvres, inv. 12978; a biscuit example is in the Metropolitan Museum, New York, inv. 05.11. The figure is in fact a reduction of a marble now at the château de Versailles.
24. Houdon was responsible for the figure of the Maréchale de Tourville commissioned for the King through d'Angiviller for the series of *Grands Hommes de la France*.
25. For a figure of Louis XV after a lost statue by J.-B. Pigalle for the Place Royale, Reims, see cat. 152.
26. See note 25.
27. Eriksen and Bellaigue, 1987, p. 325.
28. *Ibid.*, p. 346.
29. *Ibid.*, p. 312.
30. *Ibid.*, p. 313.
31. Cordey, 1939, pp. 60–1.
32. A. Dawson, 'French Biscuit Porcelain in the Style of Wedgwood's Jasperware', *Apollo*, Vol. CXVI, no. 246, August 1982, pp. 94–102, and 'Copiers or Competitors? Wedgwood and the French Porcelain Factories', *Grosvenor House Antiques Fair 1983 Handbook*, pp. 37–9. For a table-top of biscuit porcelain with a blue ground, see Brunet and Préaud, 1978, p. 235, no. 329, and D. Guillemé-Brulon, 'Rare biscuit de Sèvres façon Wedgwood au Palais Royal de Madrid', *Cahiers*, no. 40, 1968, pp. 252–6.
33. See Birioukova, 1962, nos. 86–94, 107–13.

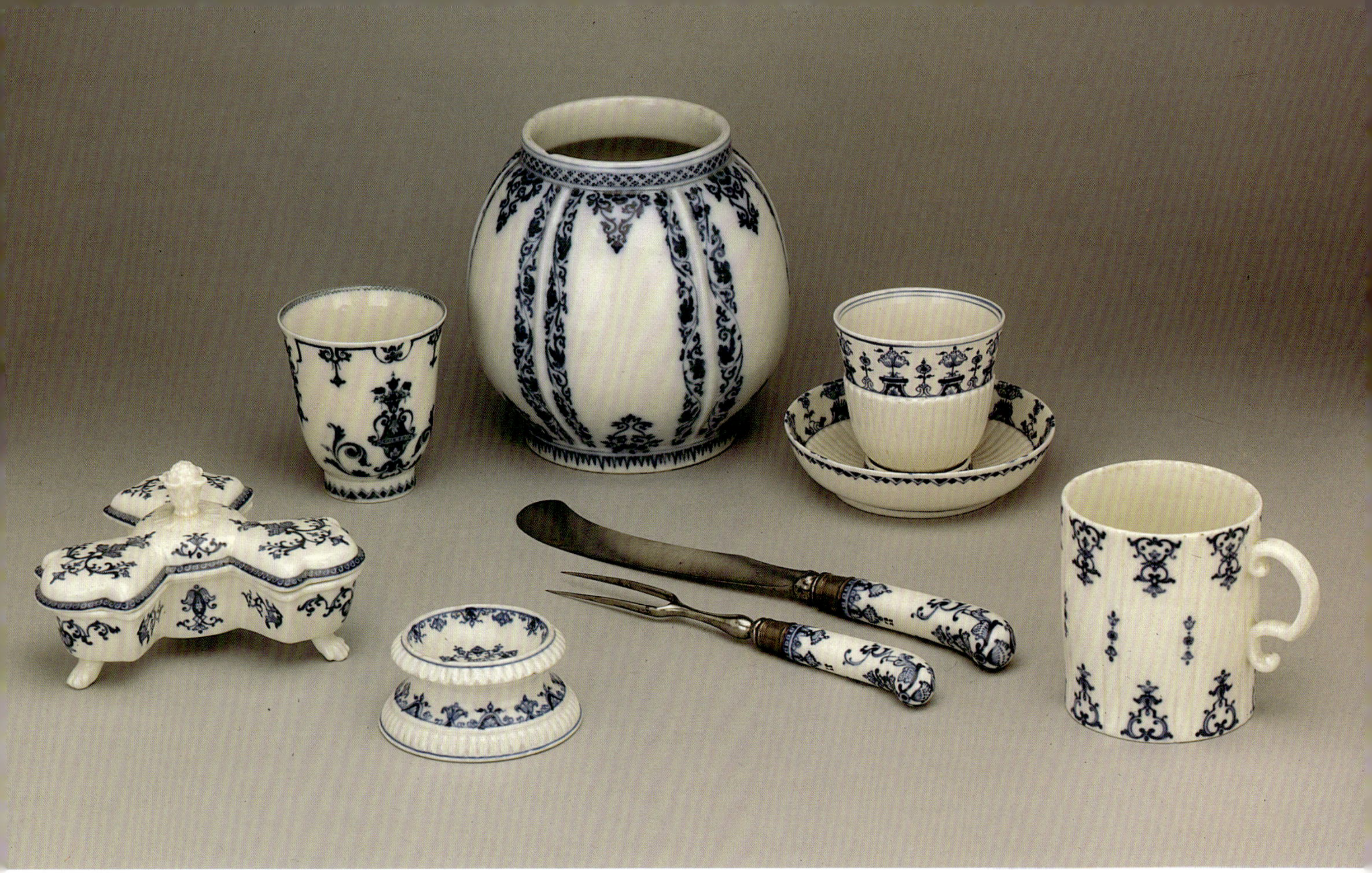

Plate 1 *Saint-Cloud*, clockwise from left: 8, 1, 2, 5, 7, 20, 4. H. of vase 15 cm.

Plate 2 clockwise from left: *Saint-Cloud*, 6, 30, 27, 28; *Villeroy*, 51; *Bellevaux*, 35; *Saint-Cloud*, 9. H. of toilet pot (incl.cover) 7.9 cm.

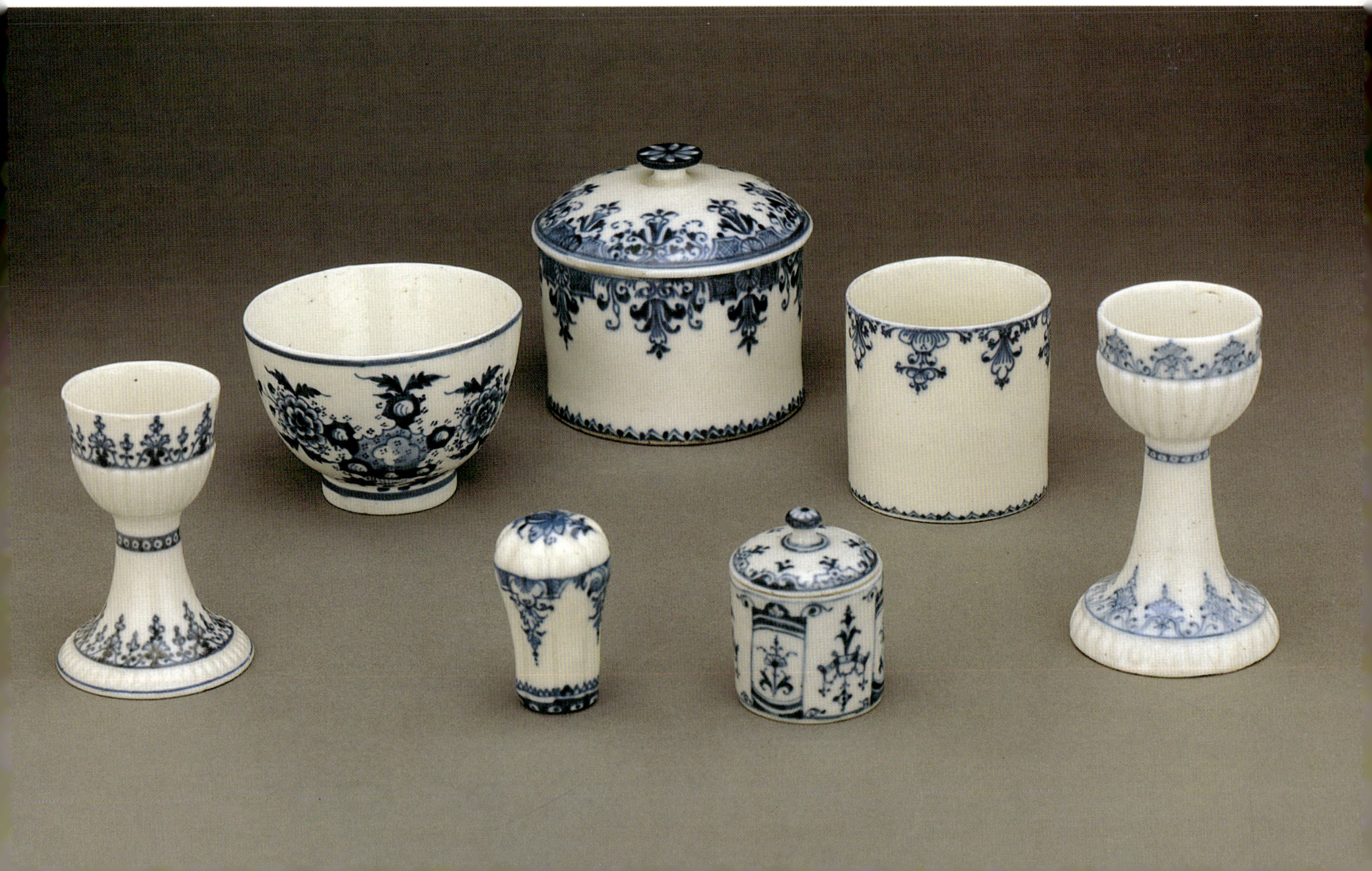

Plate 3 *Saint-Cloud*, 19. D. of saucer 12.6 cm.

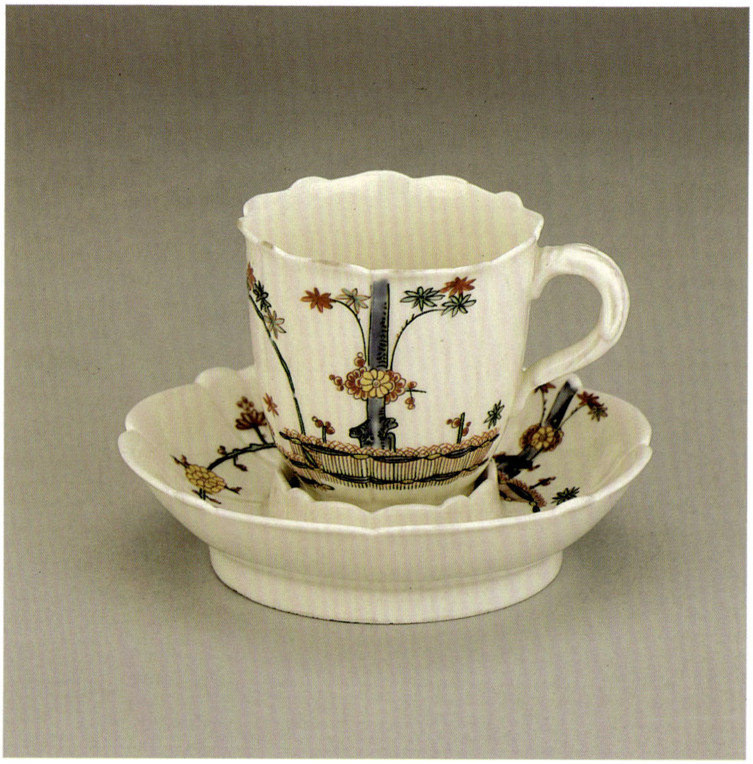

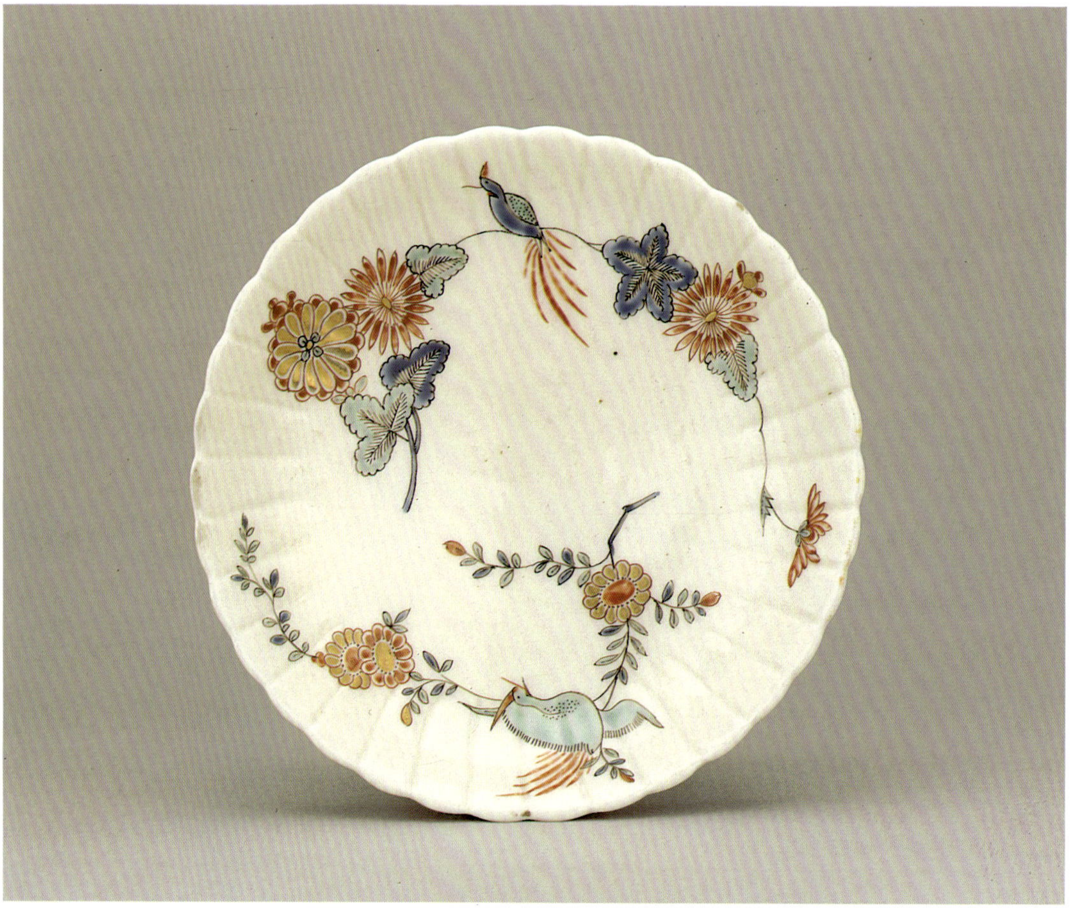

Plate 4 *Saint-Cloud*, 31. D. 13.5 cm.

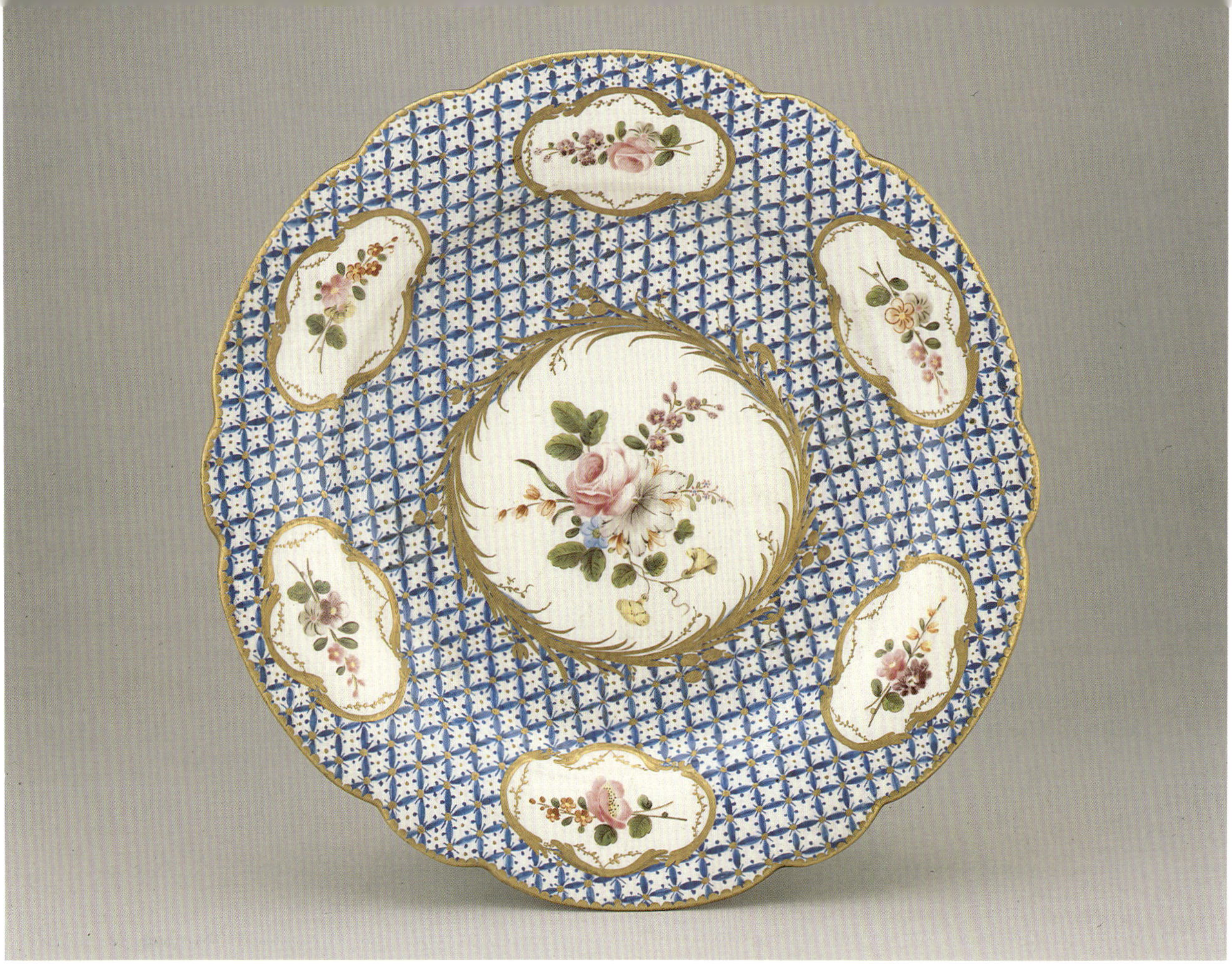

Plate 5 *Chantilly*, 45. D. 24.5 cm.

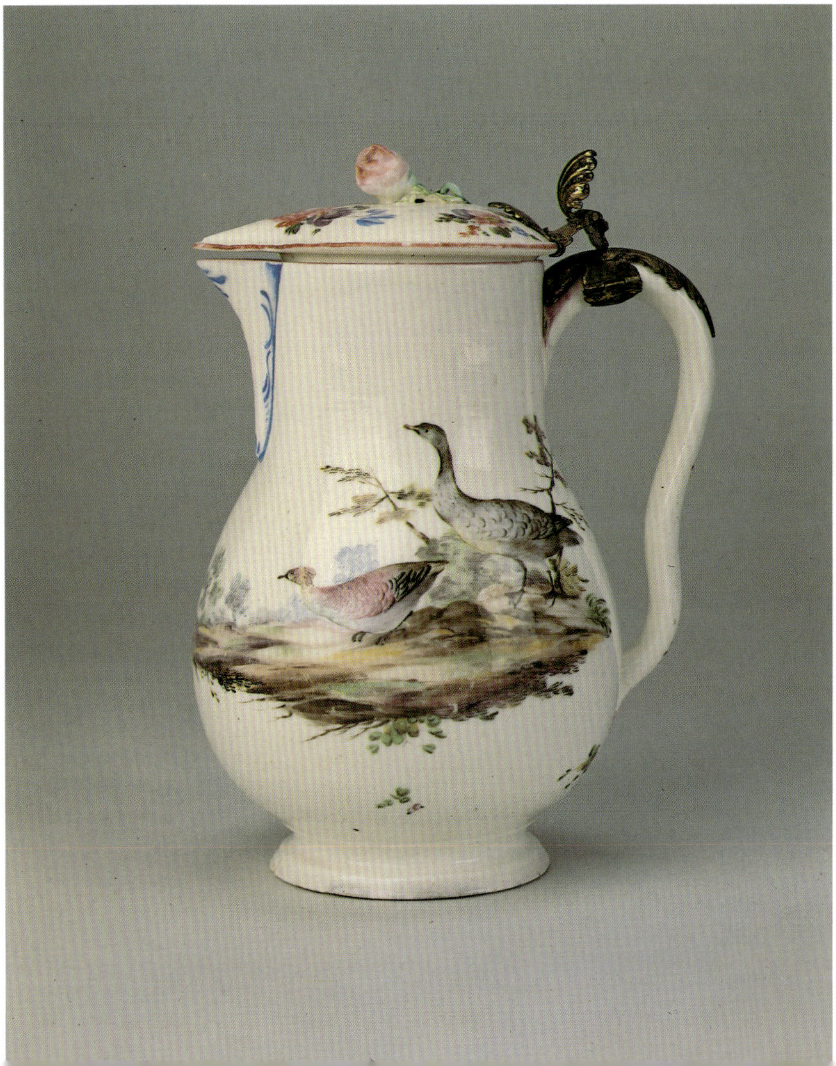

Plate 6 *Mennecy*, 60. H. 16.9 cm.

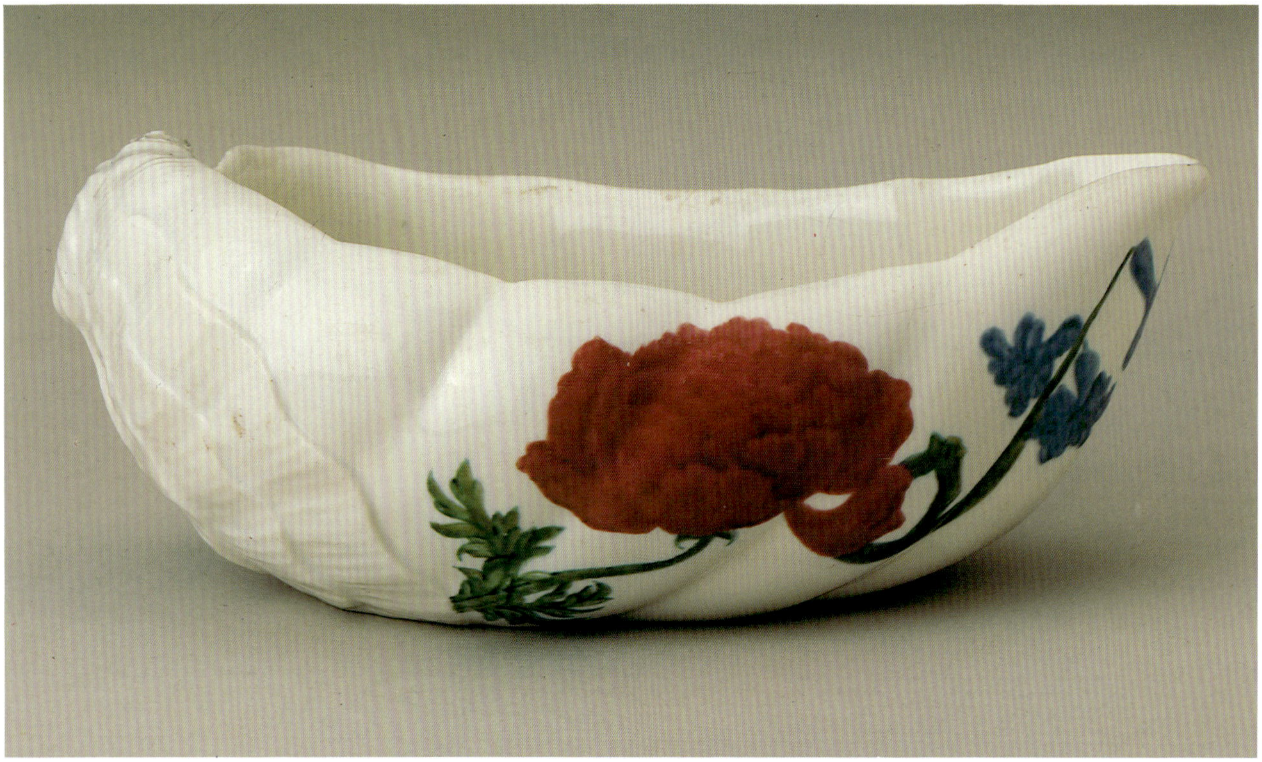

Plate 7 *Vincennes*, 64. L. 17.3 cm.

Plate 8 *Vincennes*, 69. D. of saucer 13.5 cm.

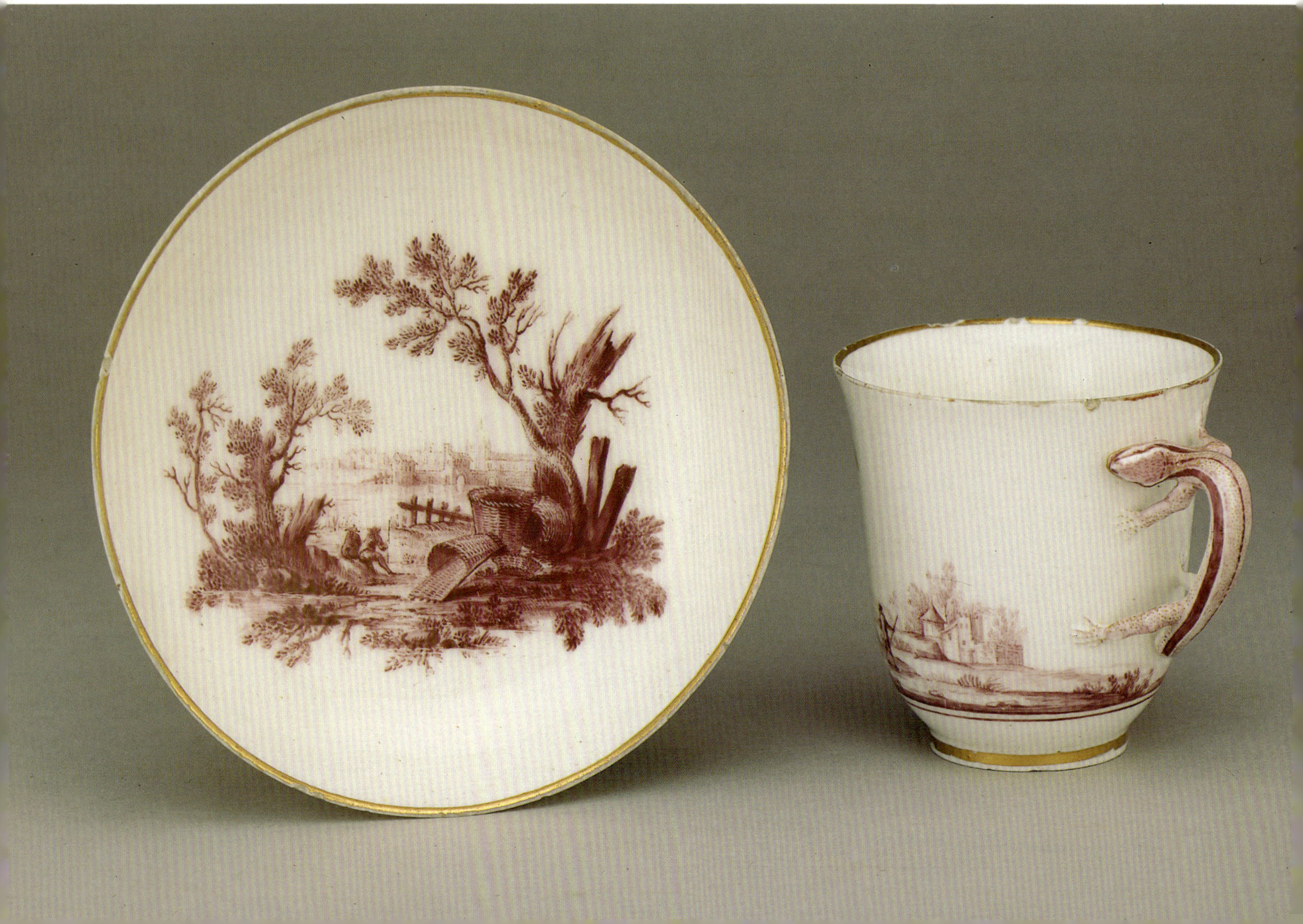

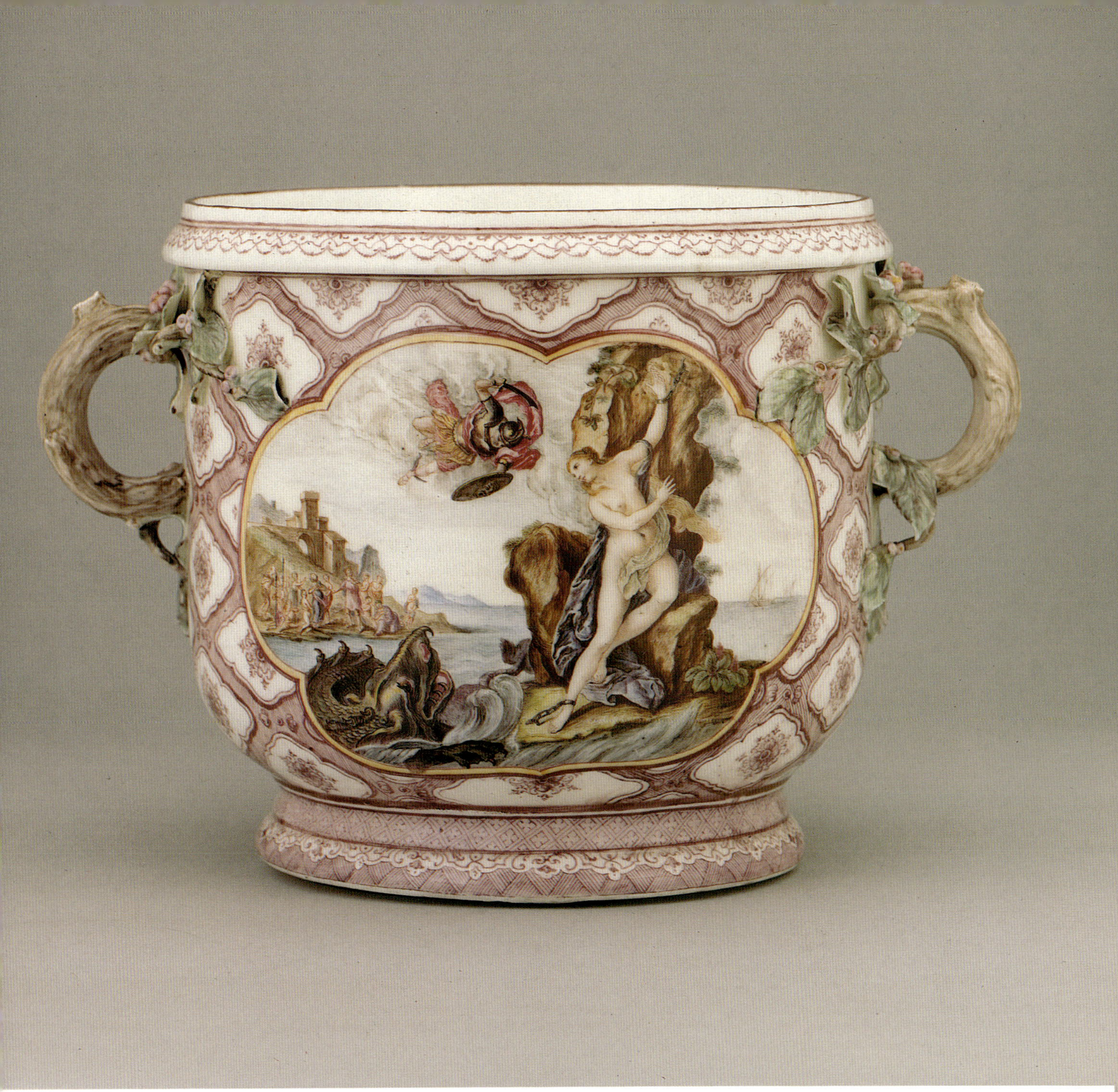

Plate 9 *Vincennes*, 65. H. 16.8 cm.

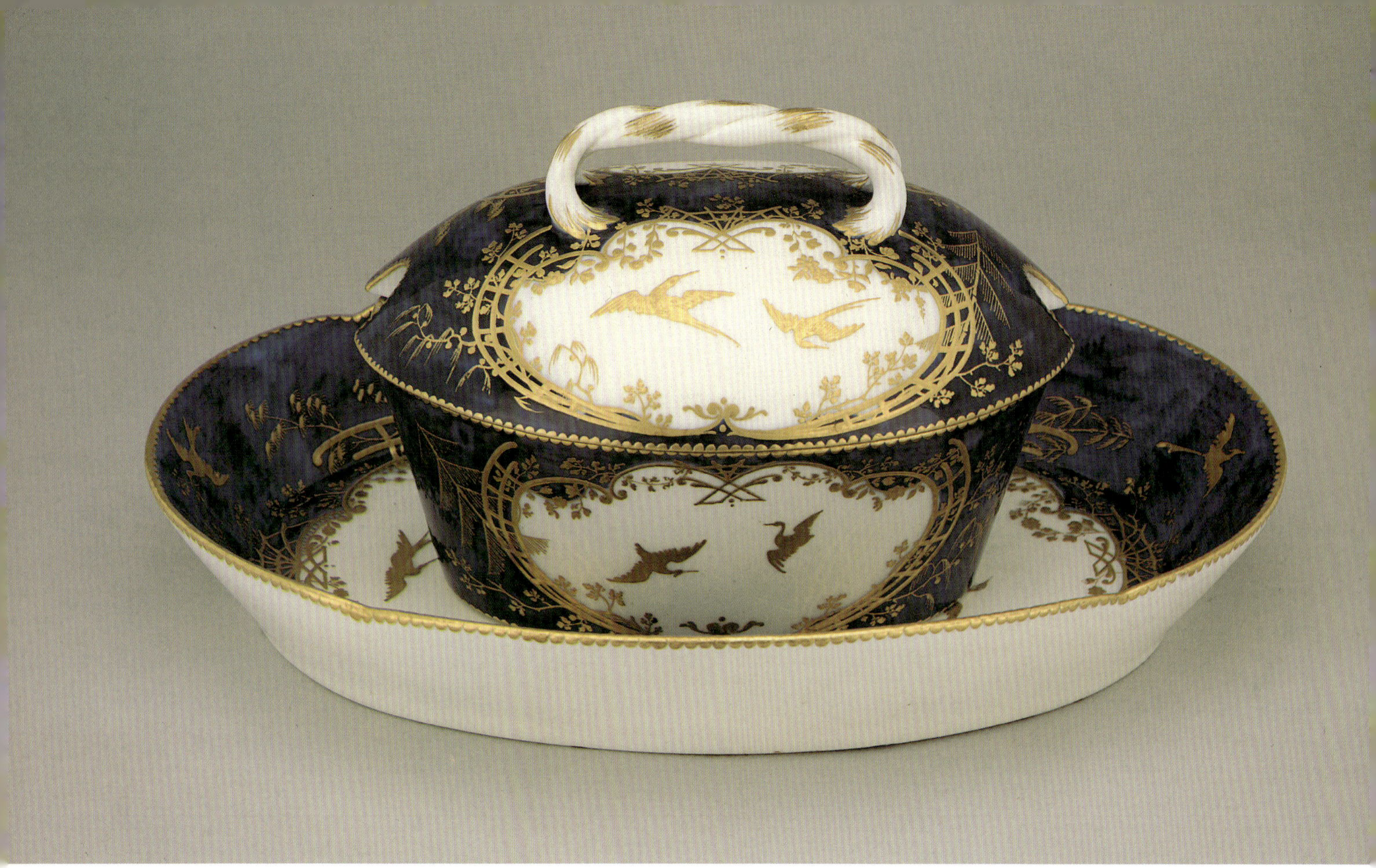

Plate 10 *Vincennes*, 70. L. of stand 25.7 cm.

Plate 11 *Vincennes*, 77. D. of saucer 15.6 cm.

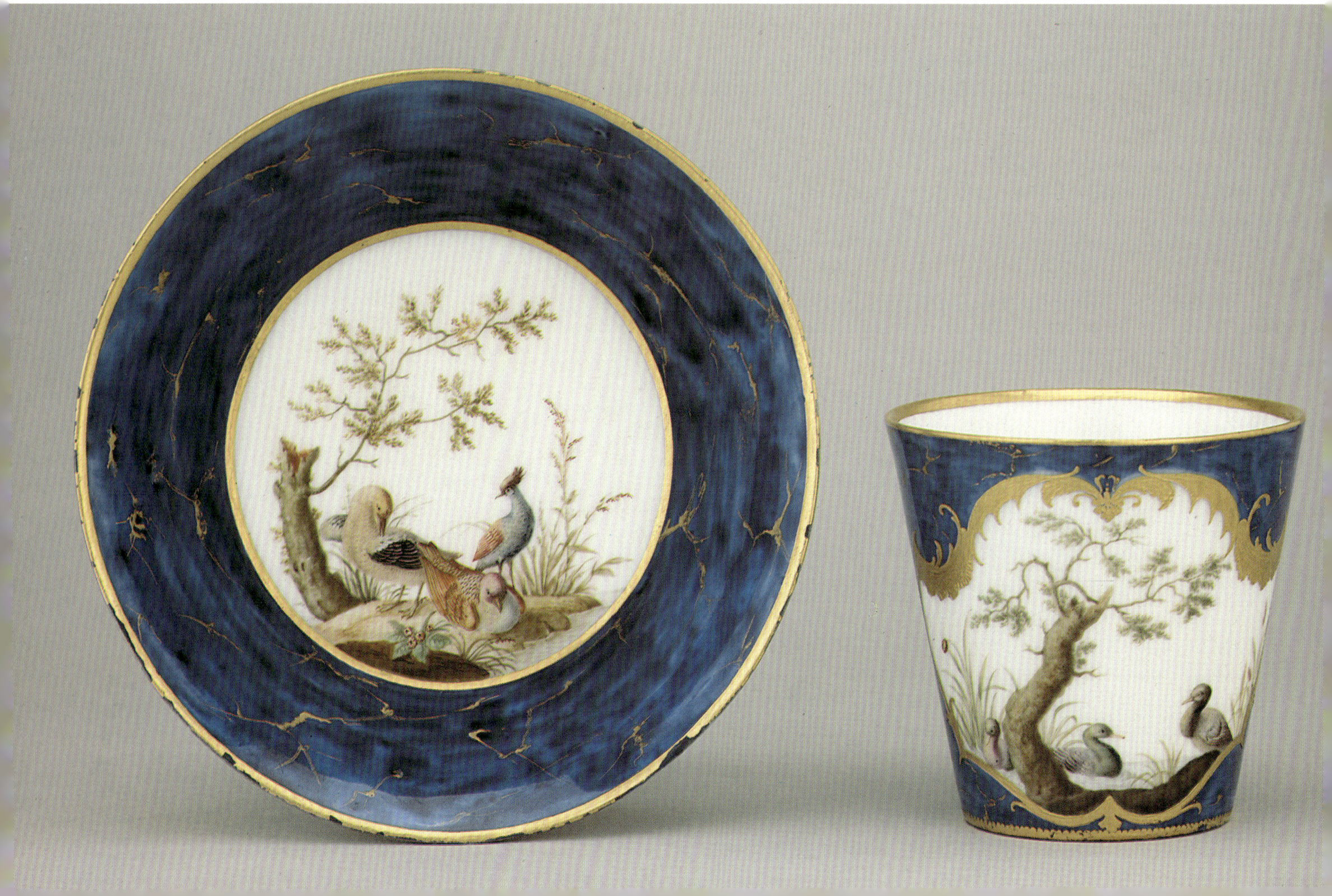

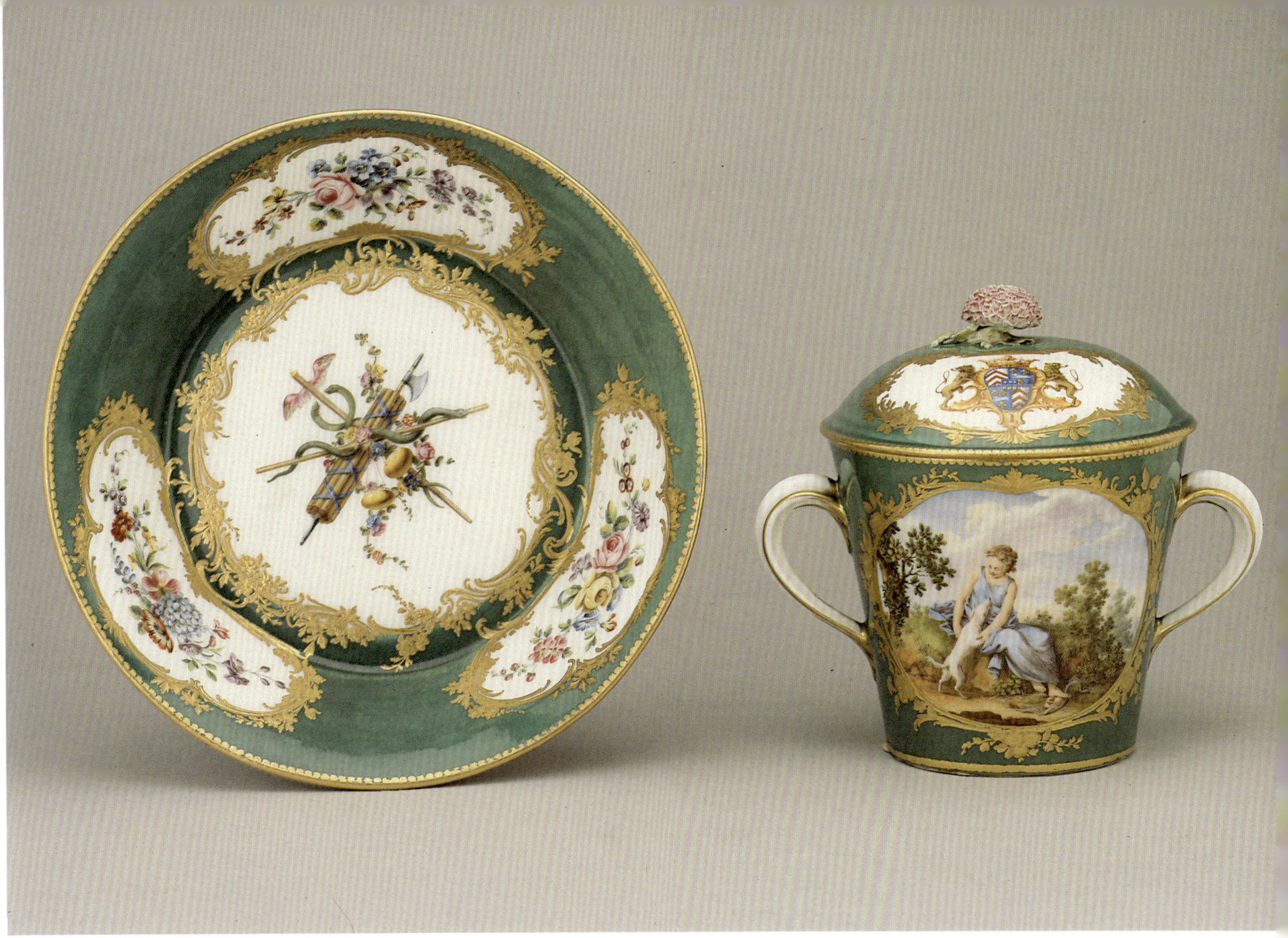

Plate 12 *Sèvres*, 97. D. of saucer 21.6 cm.

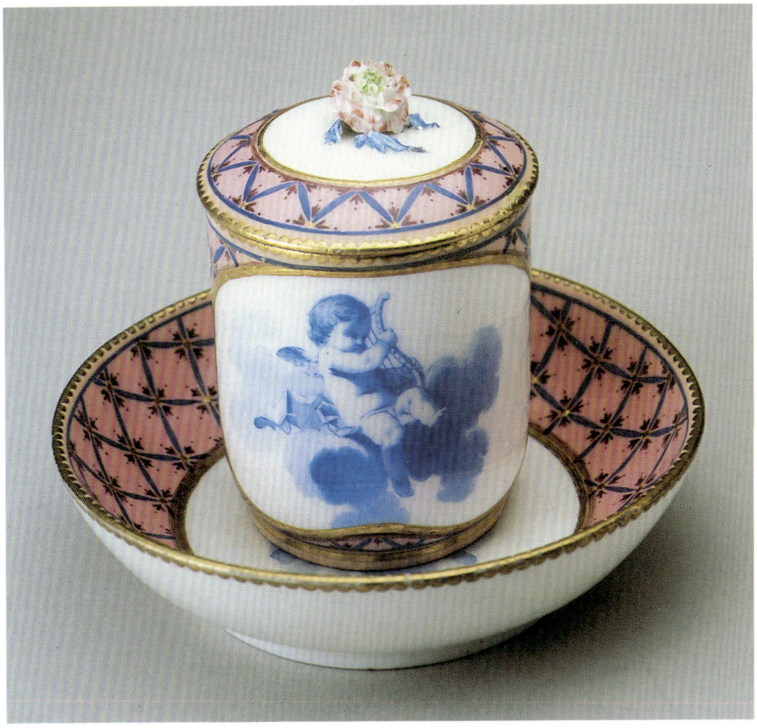

Plate 13 *Sèvres*, 104. D. of saucer 13.4 cm.

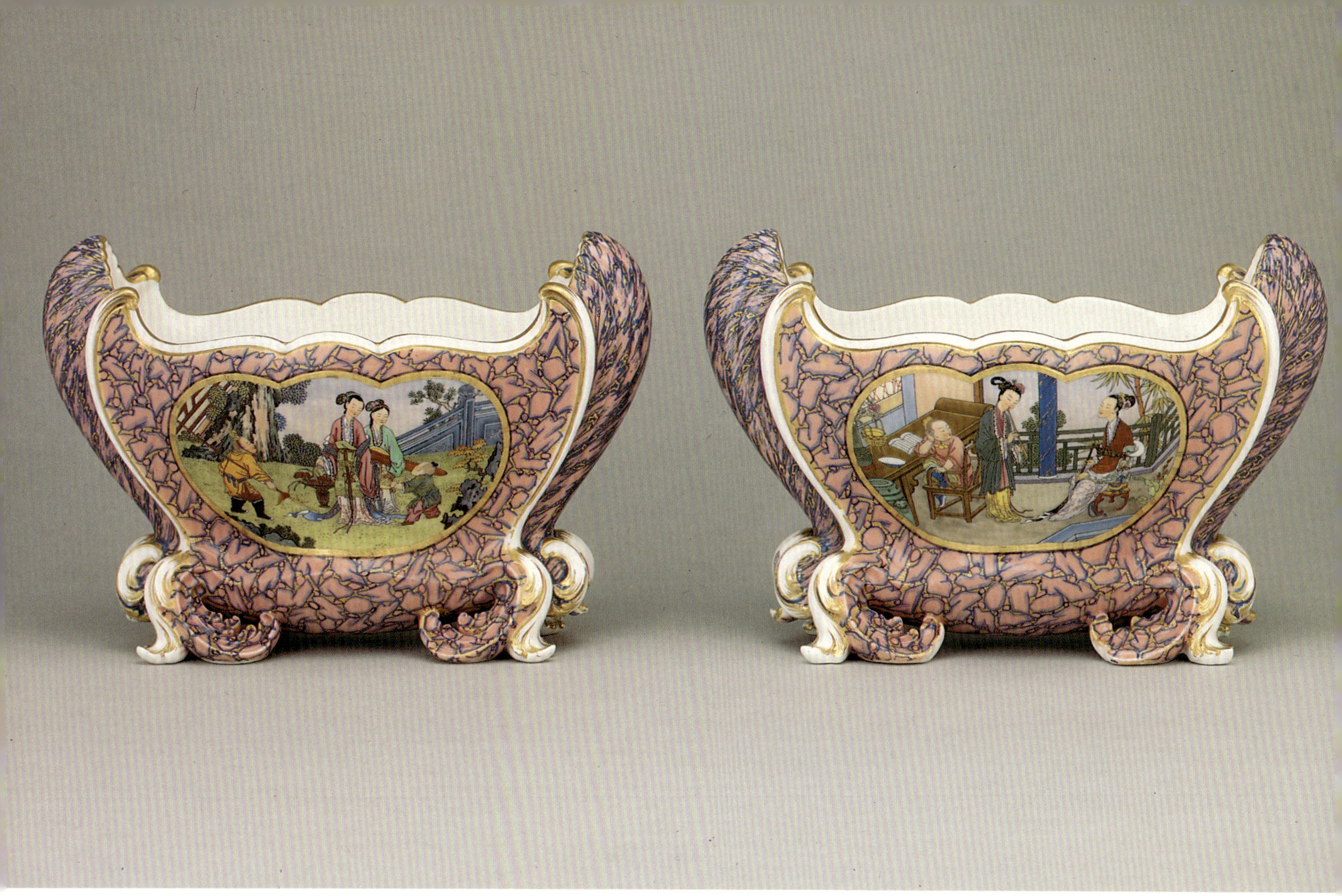

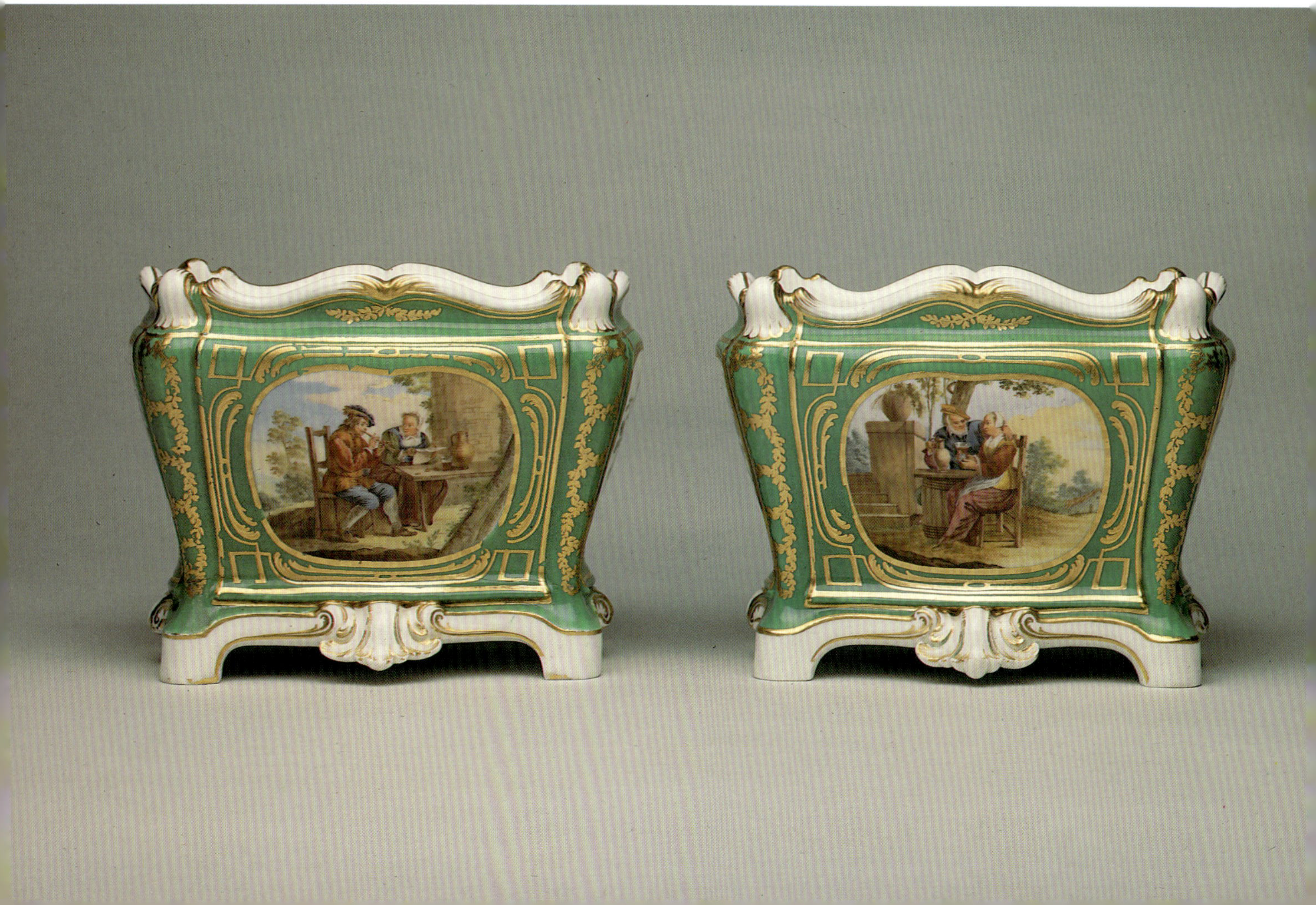

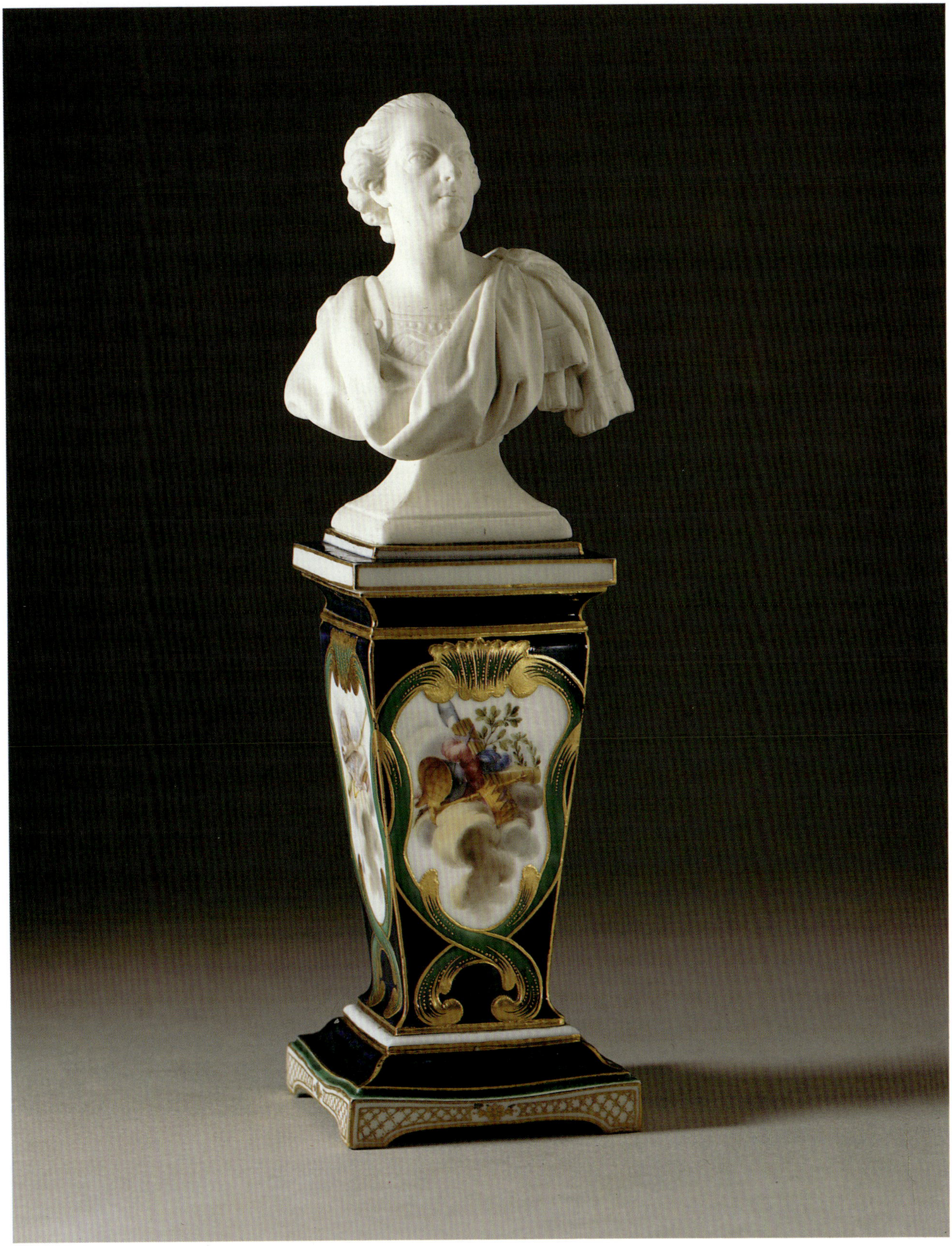

Plate 16 *Sèvres*, 106. H. 26.7 cm.

Plate 14 (opposite above) *Sèvres*, 103. L. 23 cm; H. 15.3 cm.
Plate 15 (opposite below) *Sèvres*, 109. L. 19.6 cm; H. 14.5 cm.

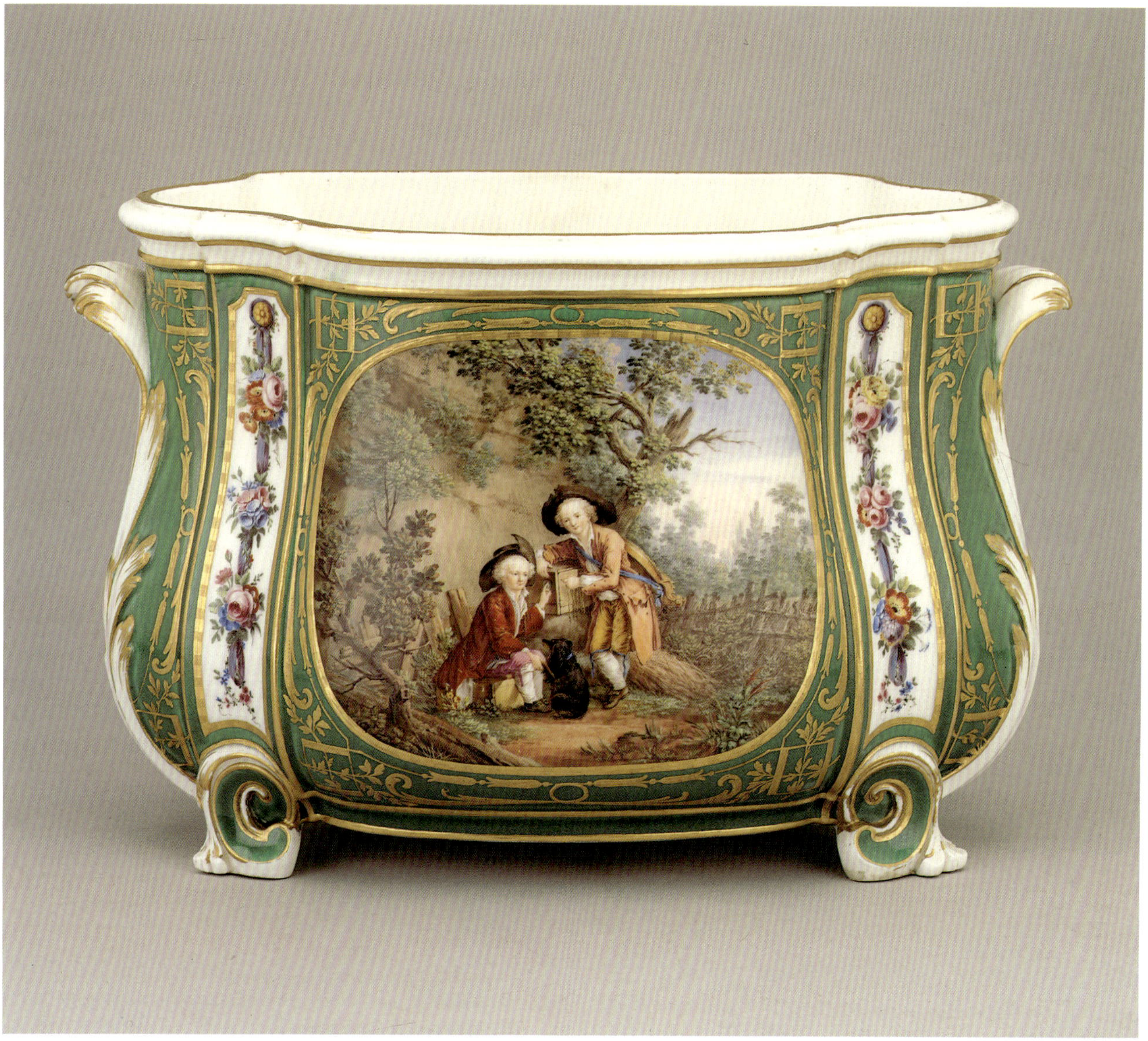

Plate 17 *Sèvres*, 108. L. 29.8 cm; H. 18.7 cm.

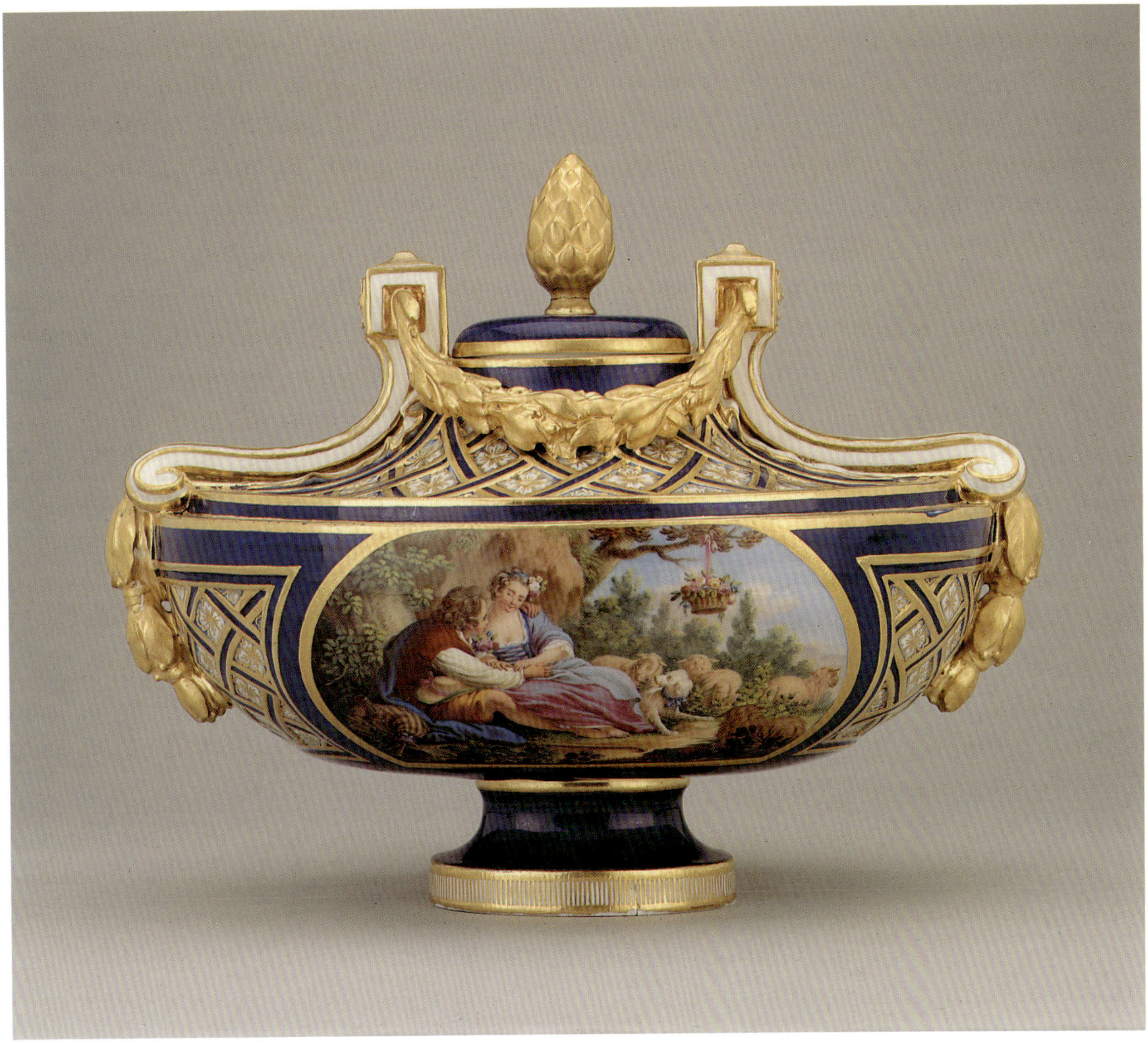

Plate 18 *Sèvres*, 114. L. 25.6 cm; H. (incl. cover) 19.9 cm.

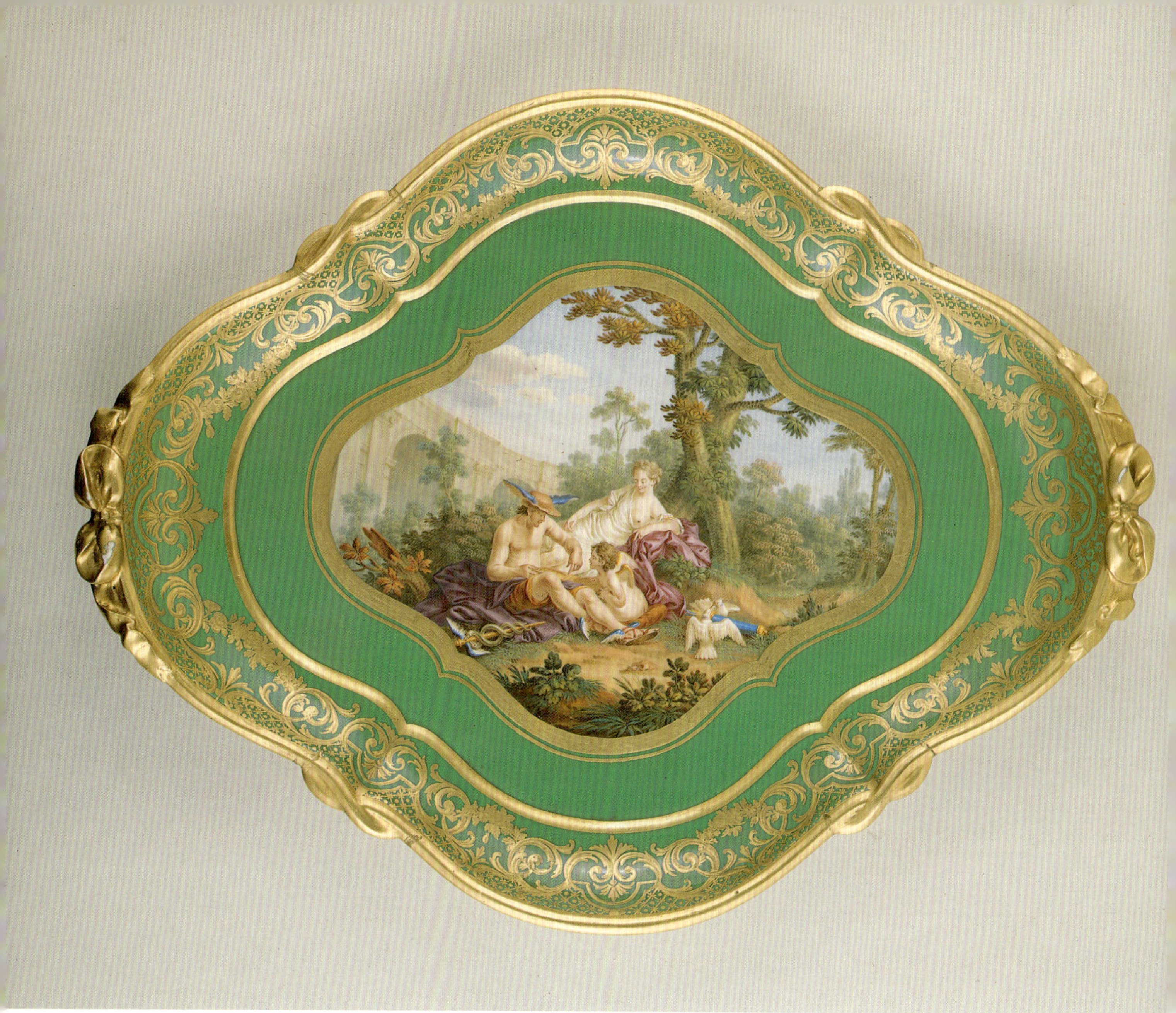

Plate 19 *Sèvres*, 120. L. 41 cm.

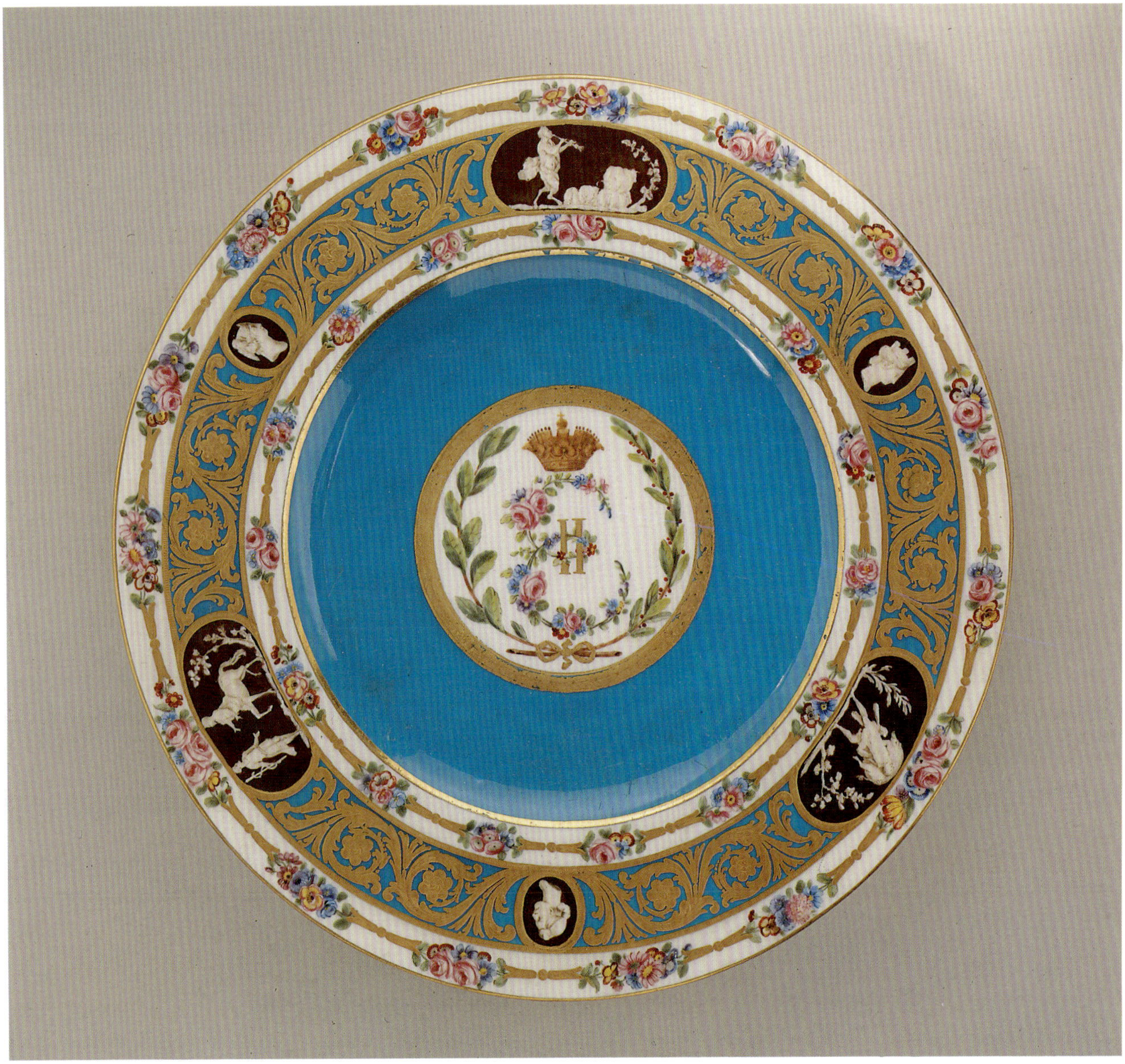

Plate 20 *Sèvres*, 121. D. 26.4 cm.

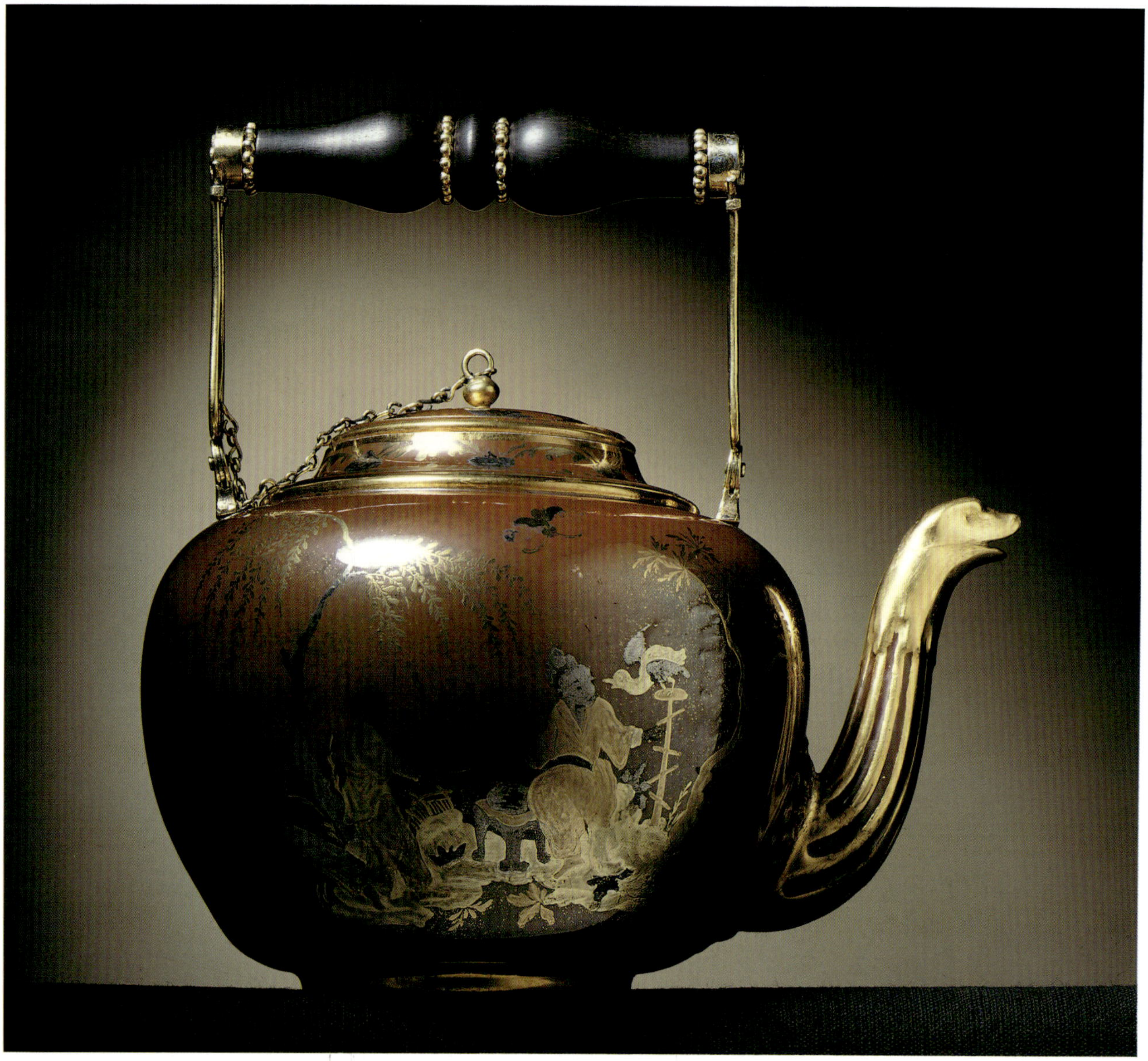

Plate 21 *Sèvres*, 122. H. (to top of handle) 18.3 cm.

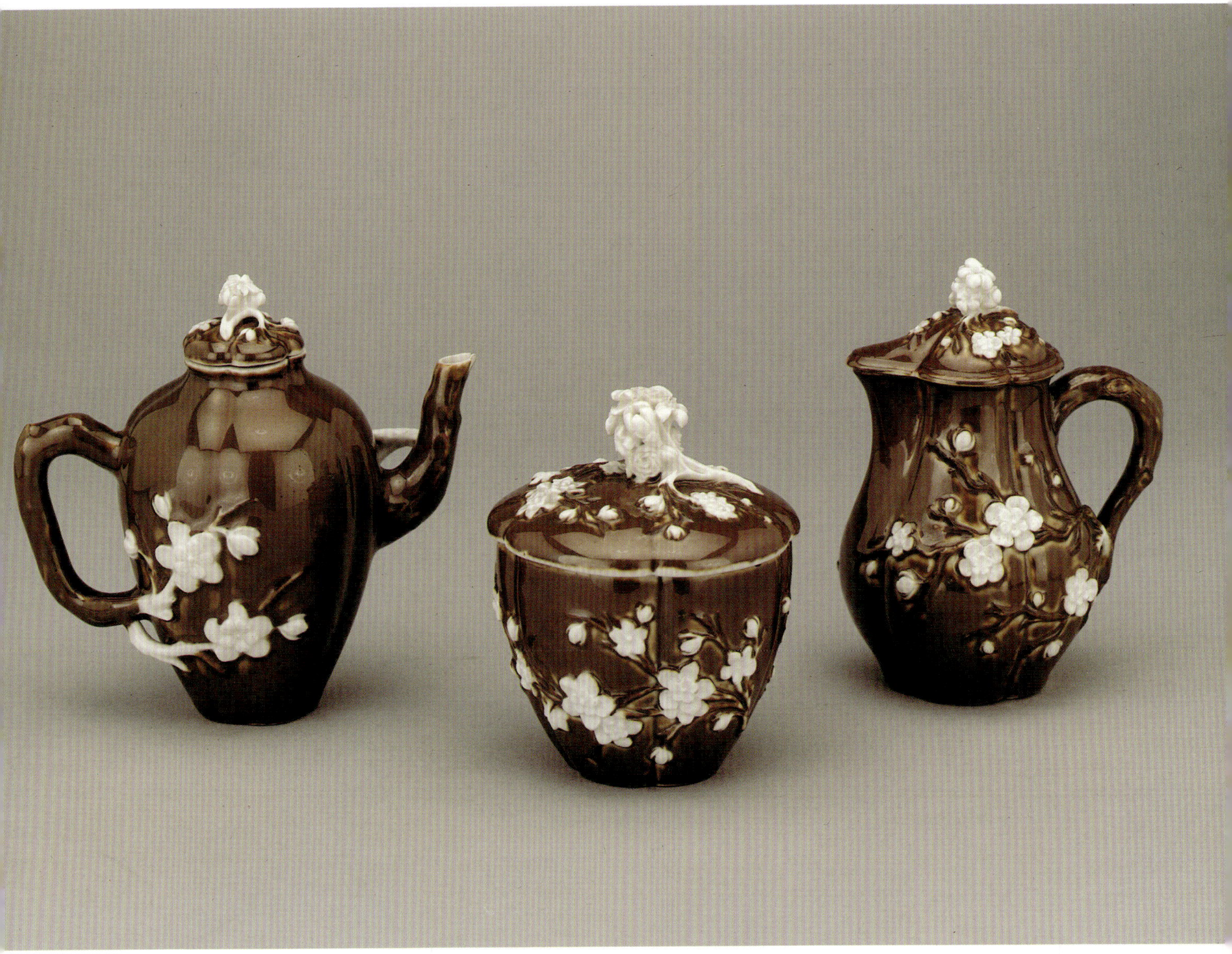

Plate 22 *Sèvres*, 123. H. of teapot (incl. cover) 11.3 cm.

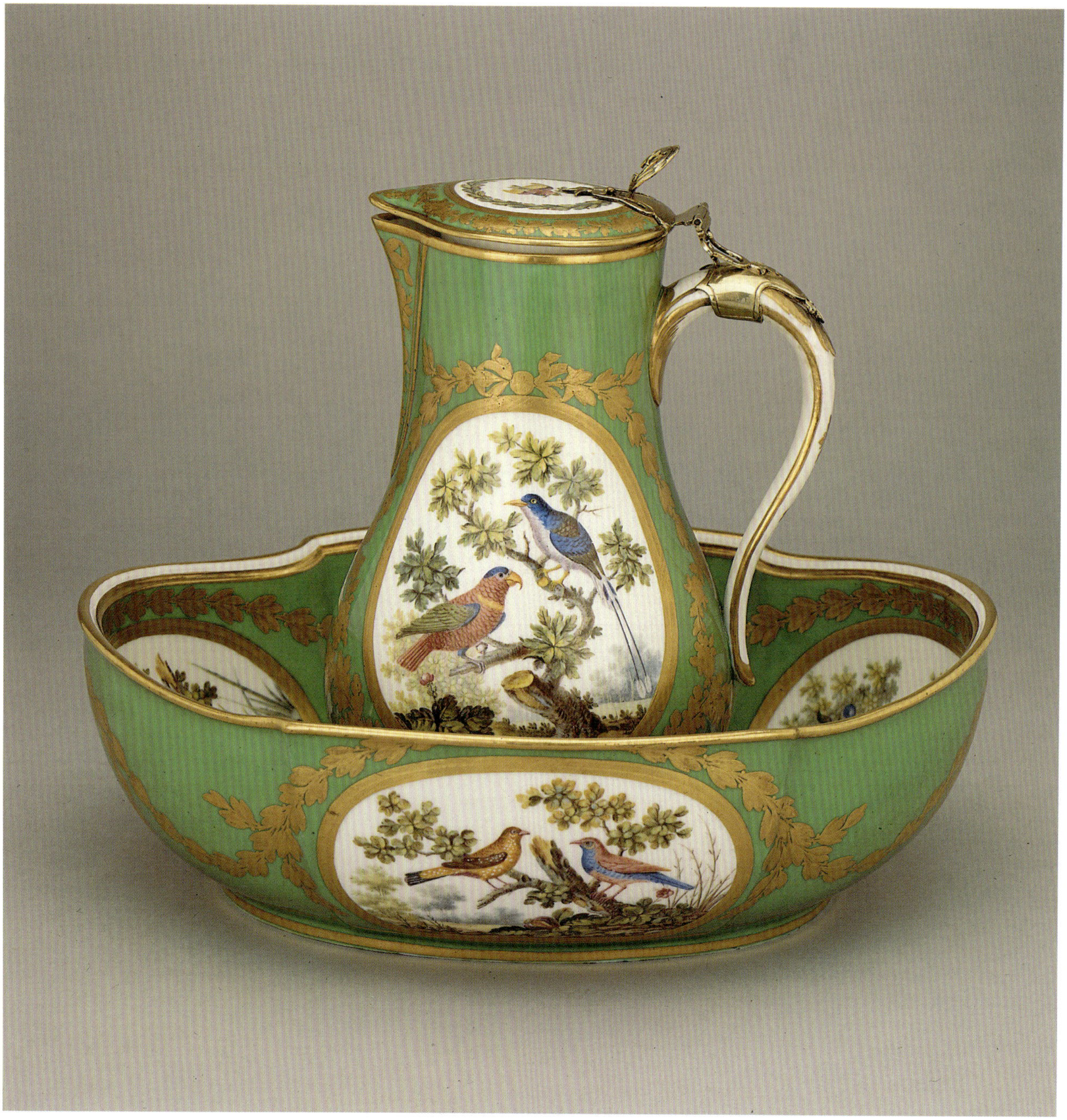

Plate 23 *Sèvres*, 124. L. of bowl 29.9 cm.

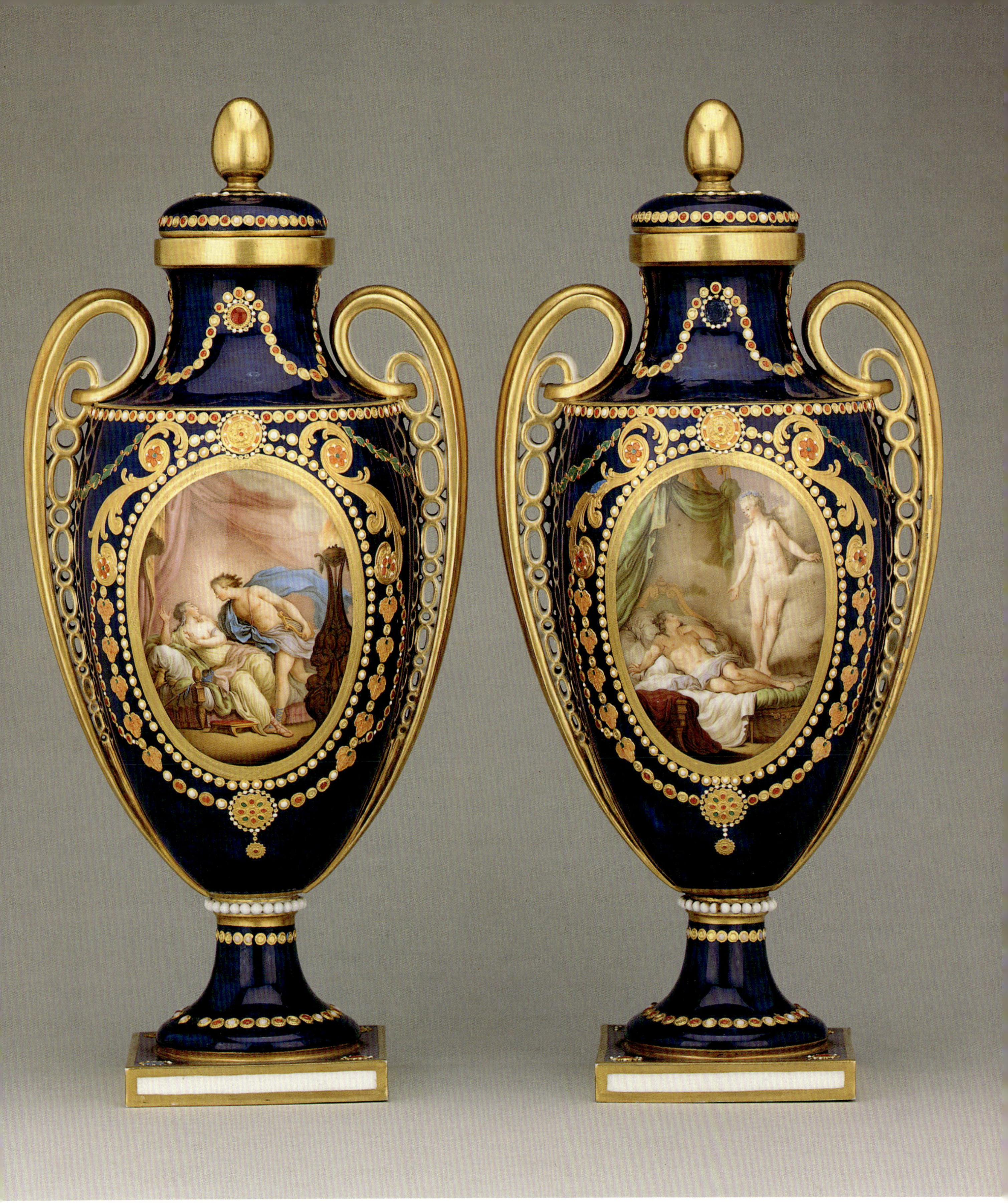

Plate 24 *Sèvres*, 125. H. of vase on right 31.8 cm.

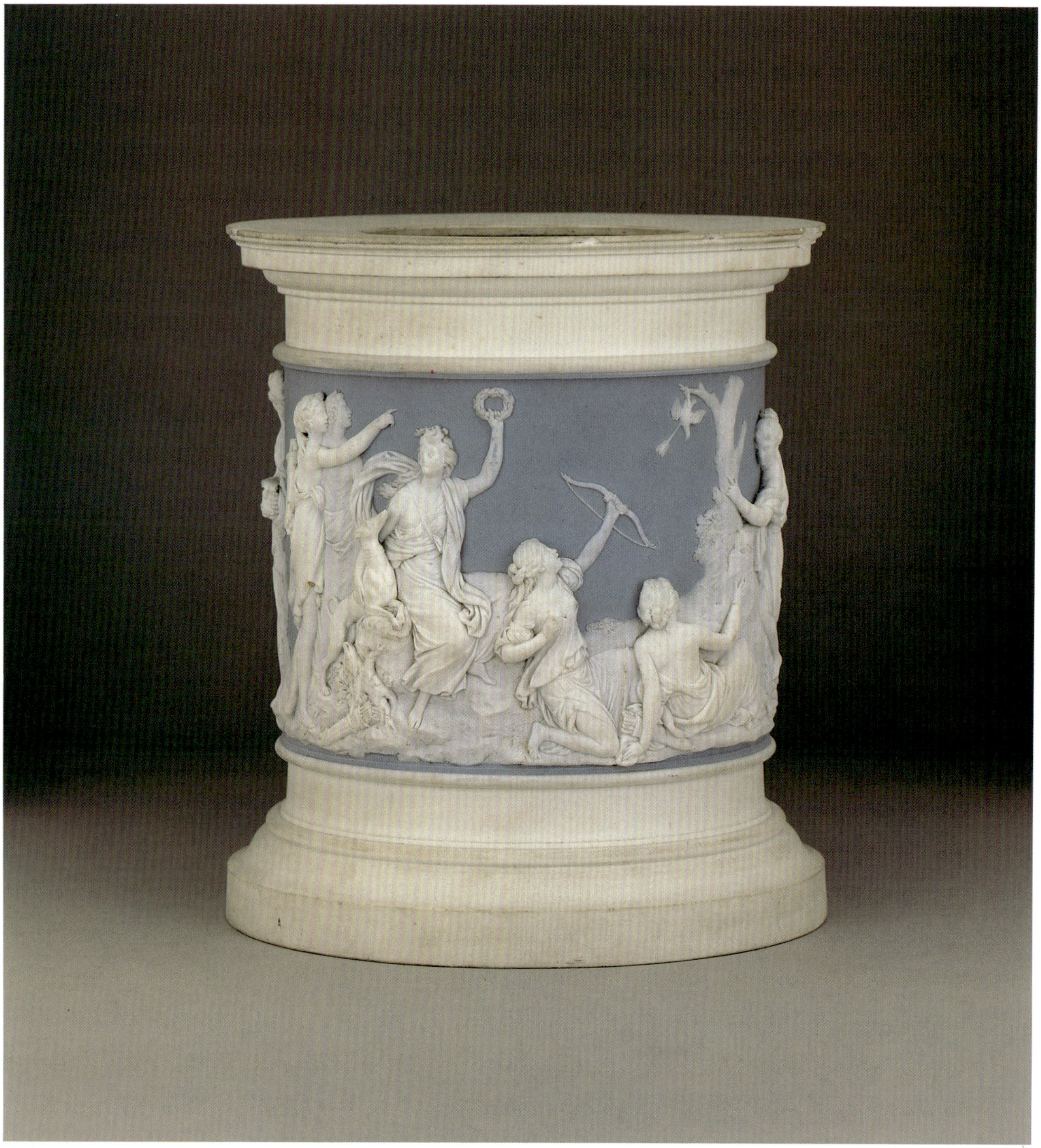

Plate 25 *Sèvres*, 153. H. 24 cm.

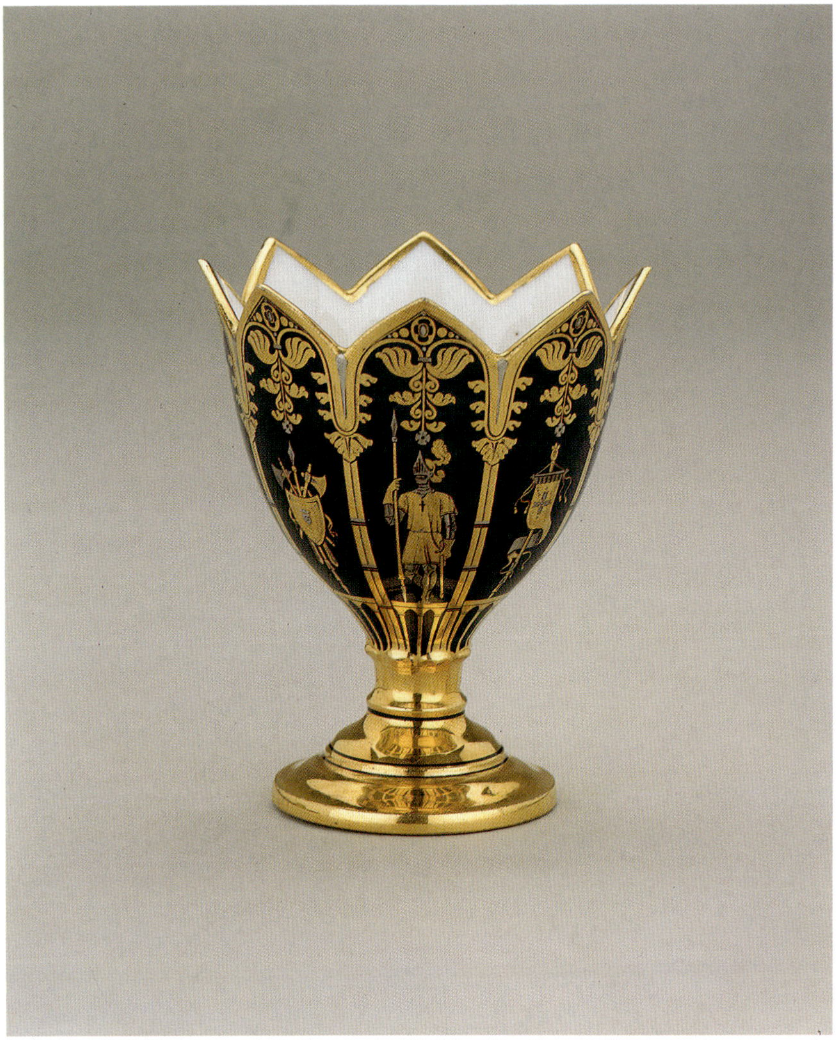

Plate 26 *Sèvres*, 182. H. 9.1 cm.

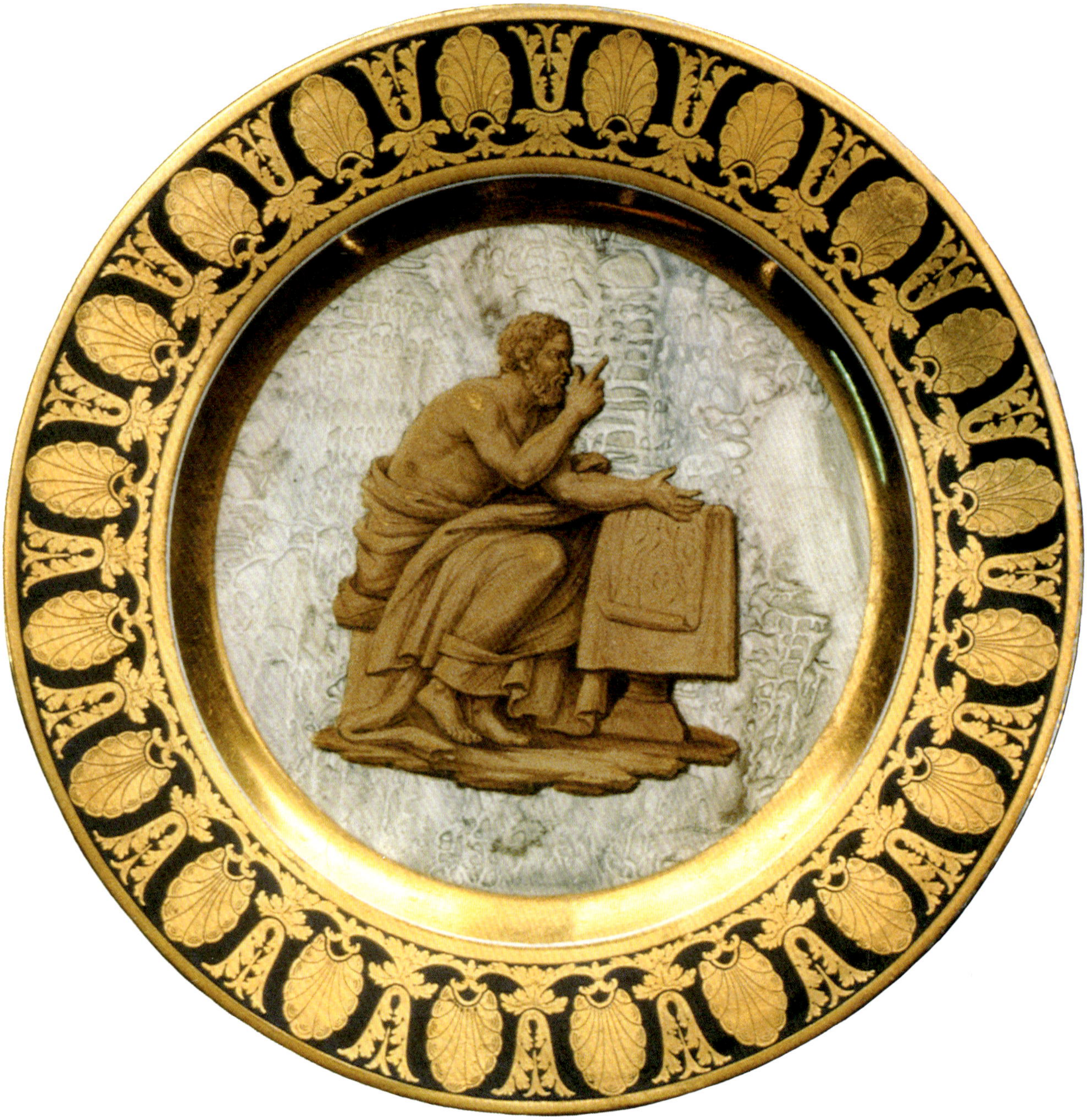

Plate 27 *Sèvres*, 179. D. 23.2 cm.

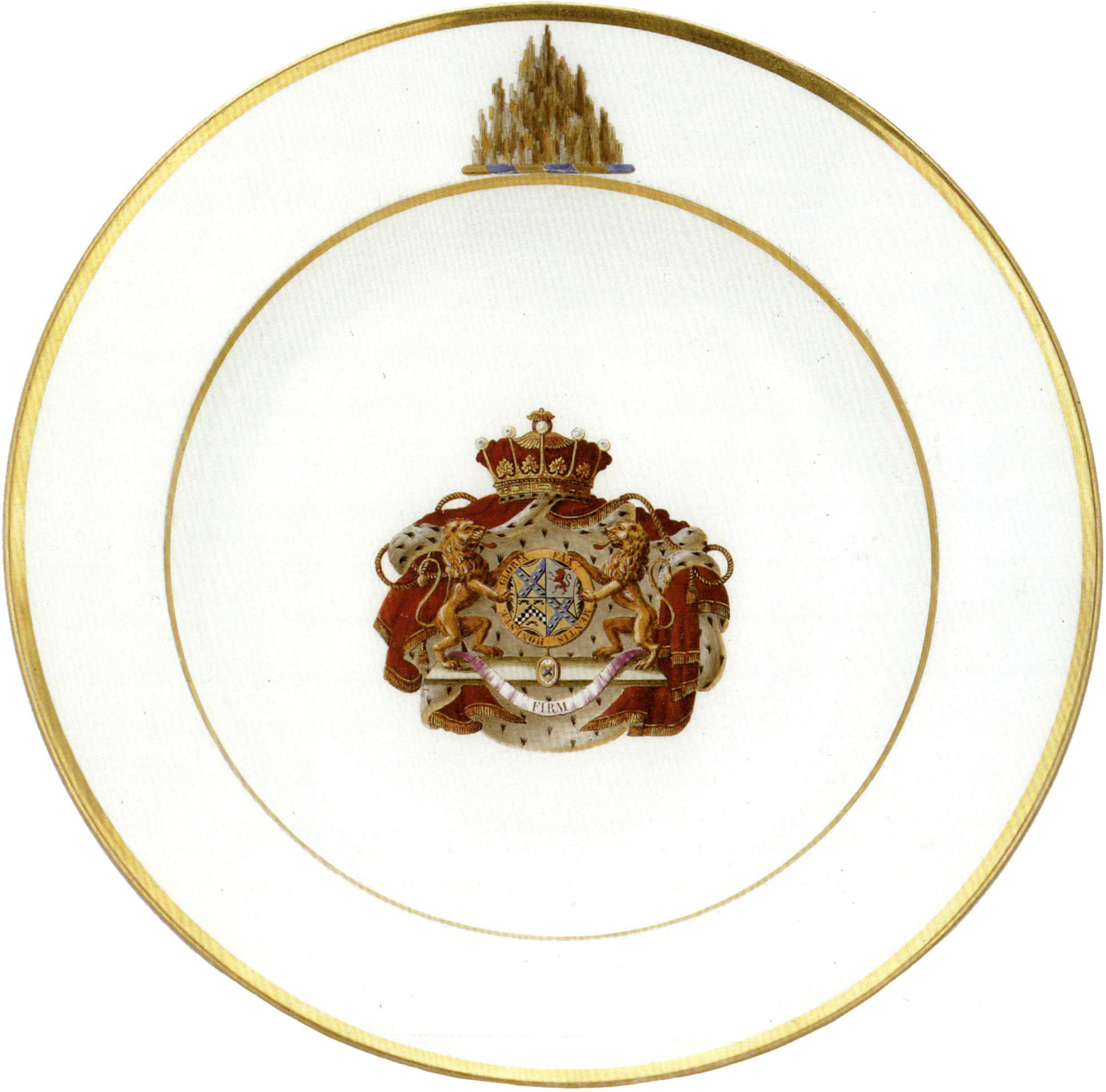

Plate 28 *Sèvres*, 181. D. 23.6 cm.

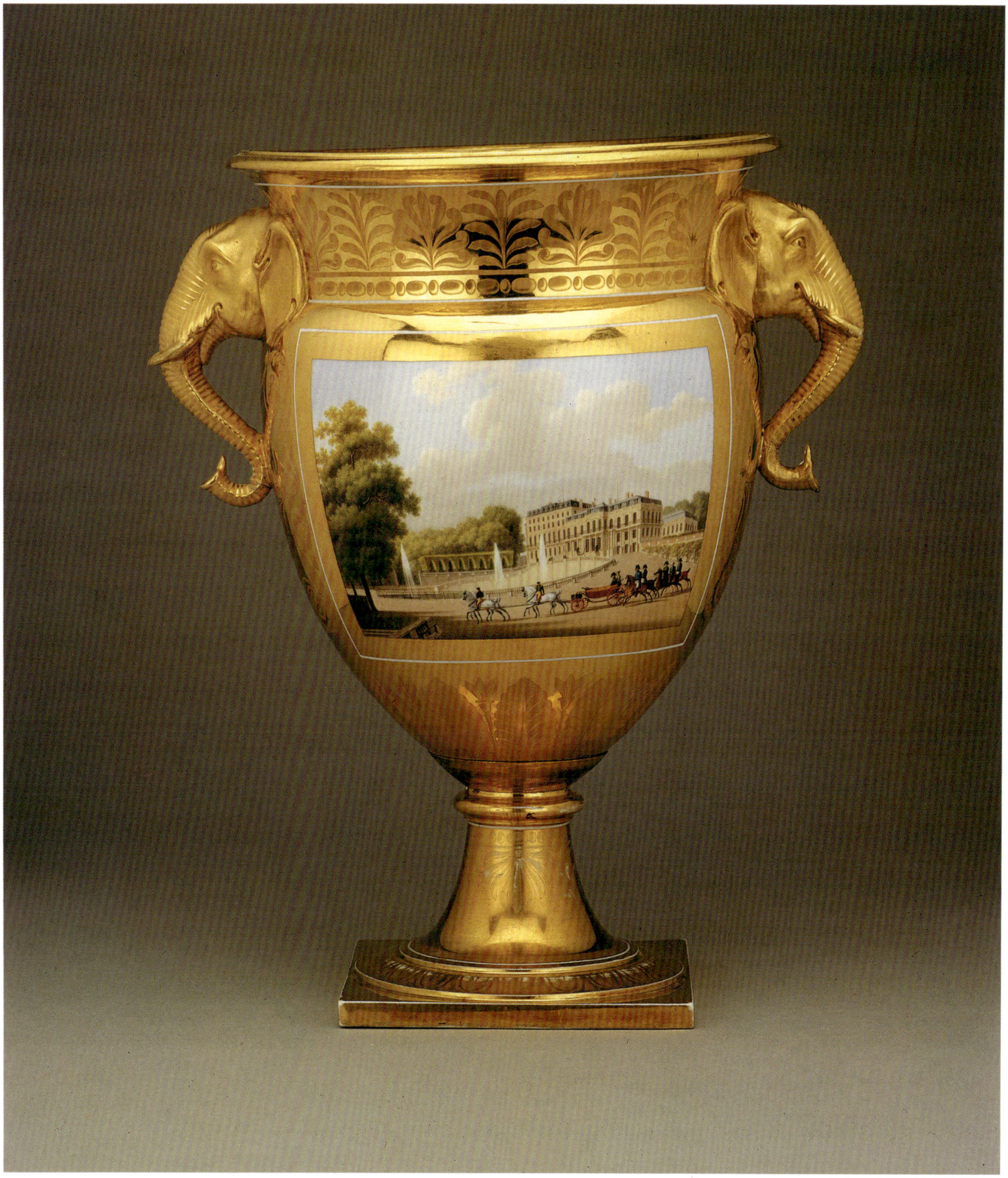

Plate 29 *Sèvres*, 180. H. 34.2 cm.

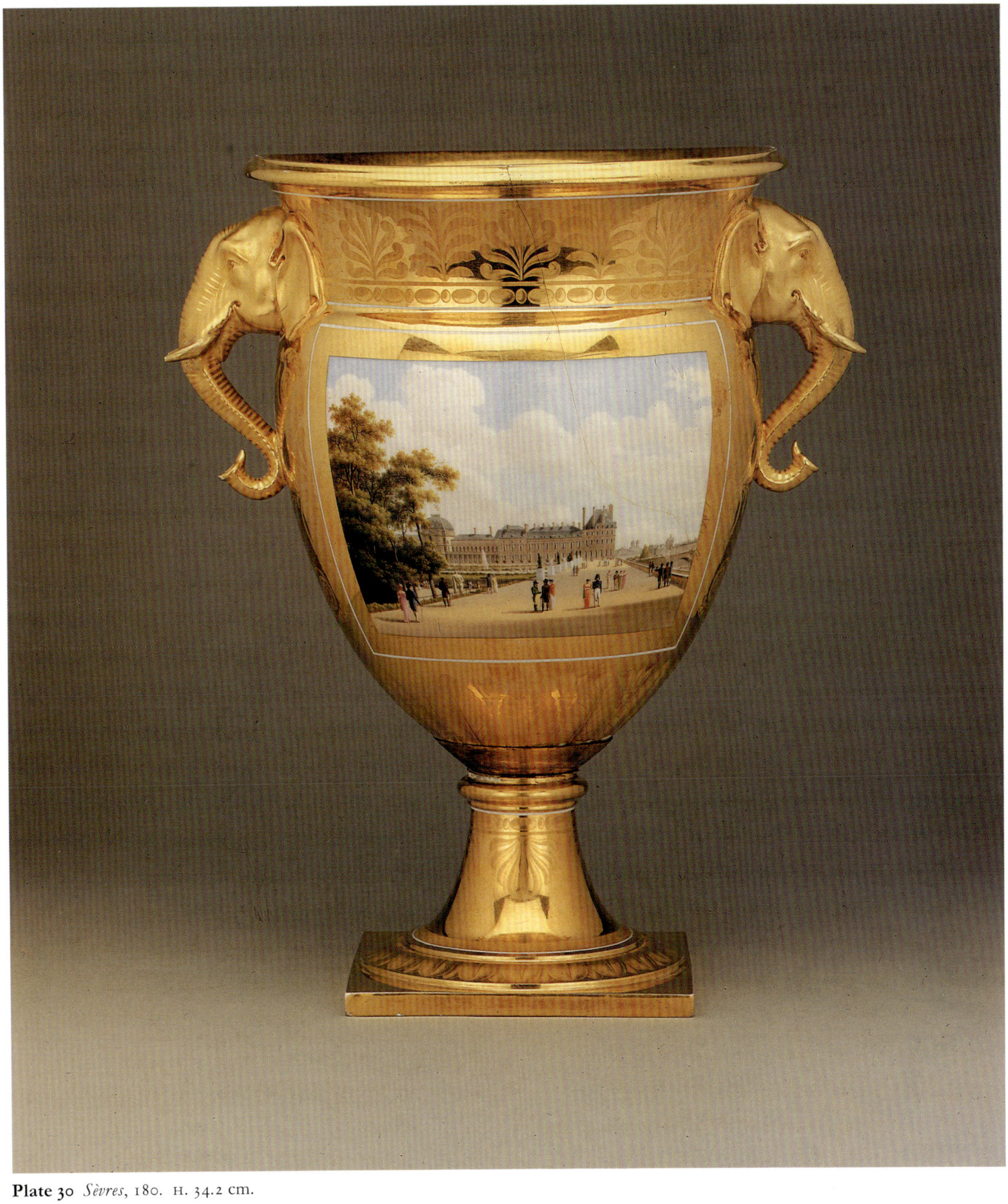

Plate 30 *Sèvres*, 180. H. 34.2 cm.

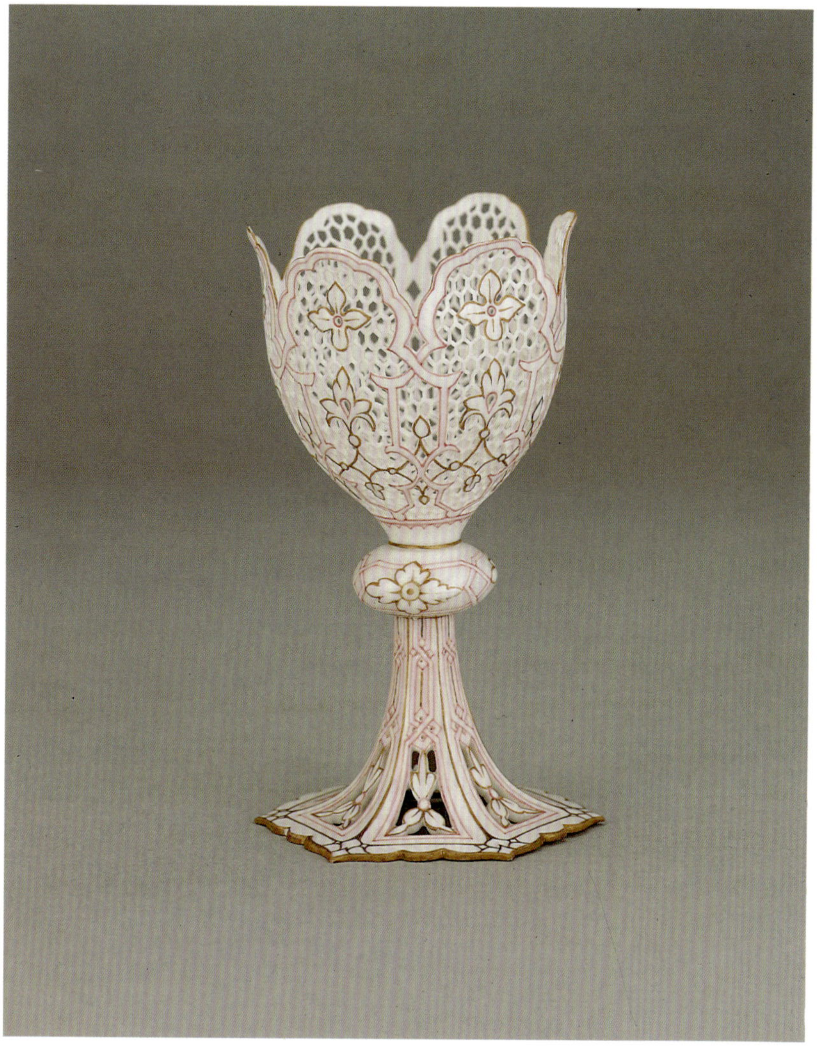

Plate 31 *Sèvres*, 188. H. 10.5 cm.

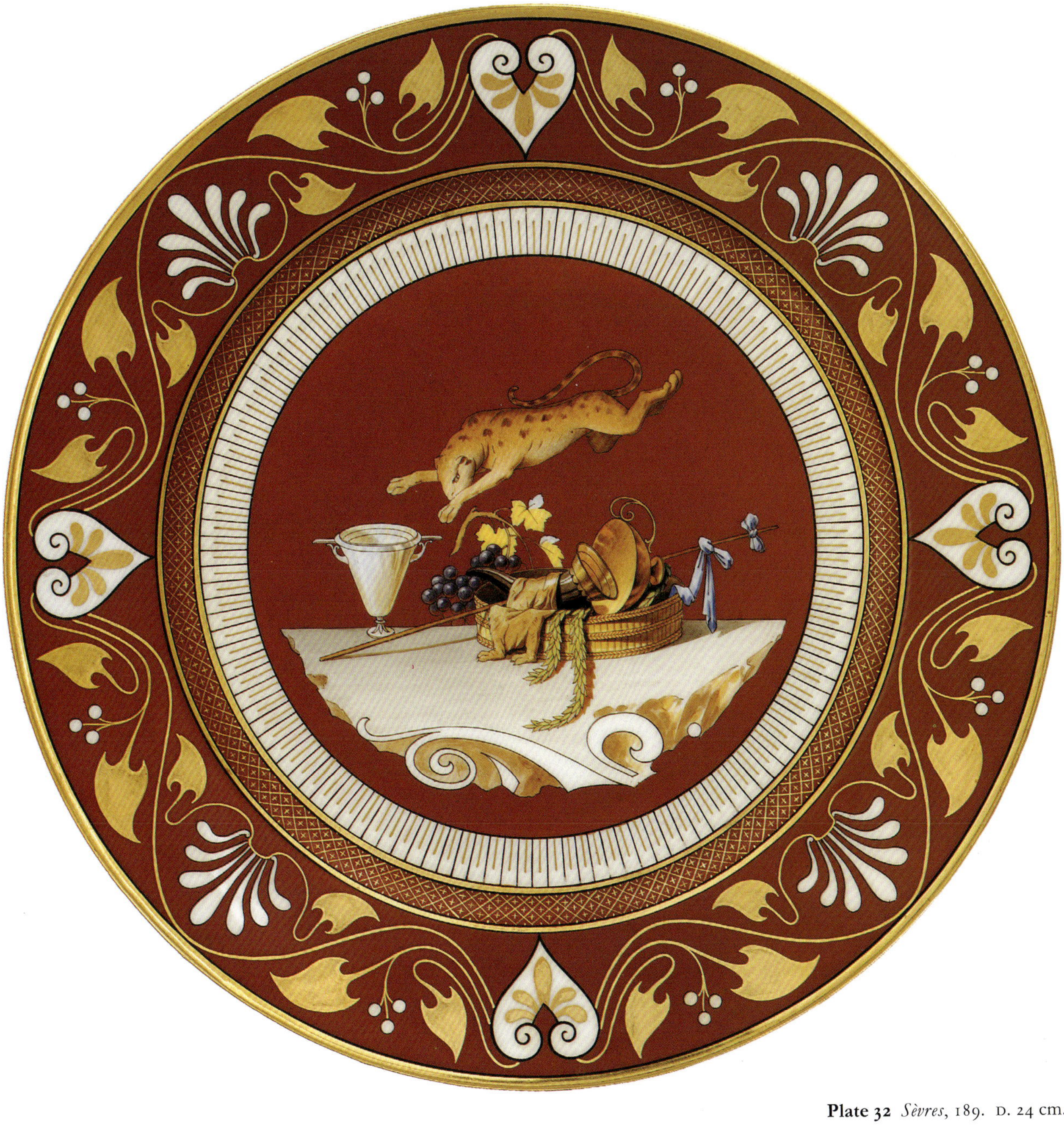

Plate 32 *Sèvres*, 189. D. 24 cm.

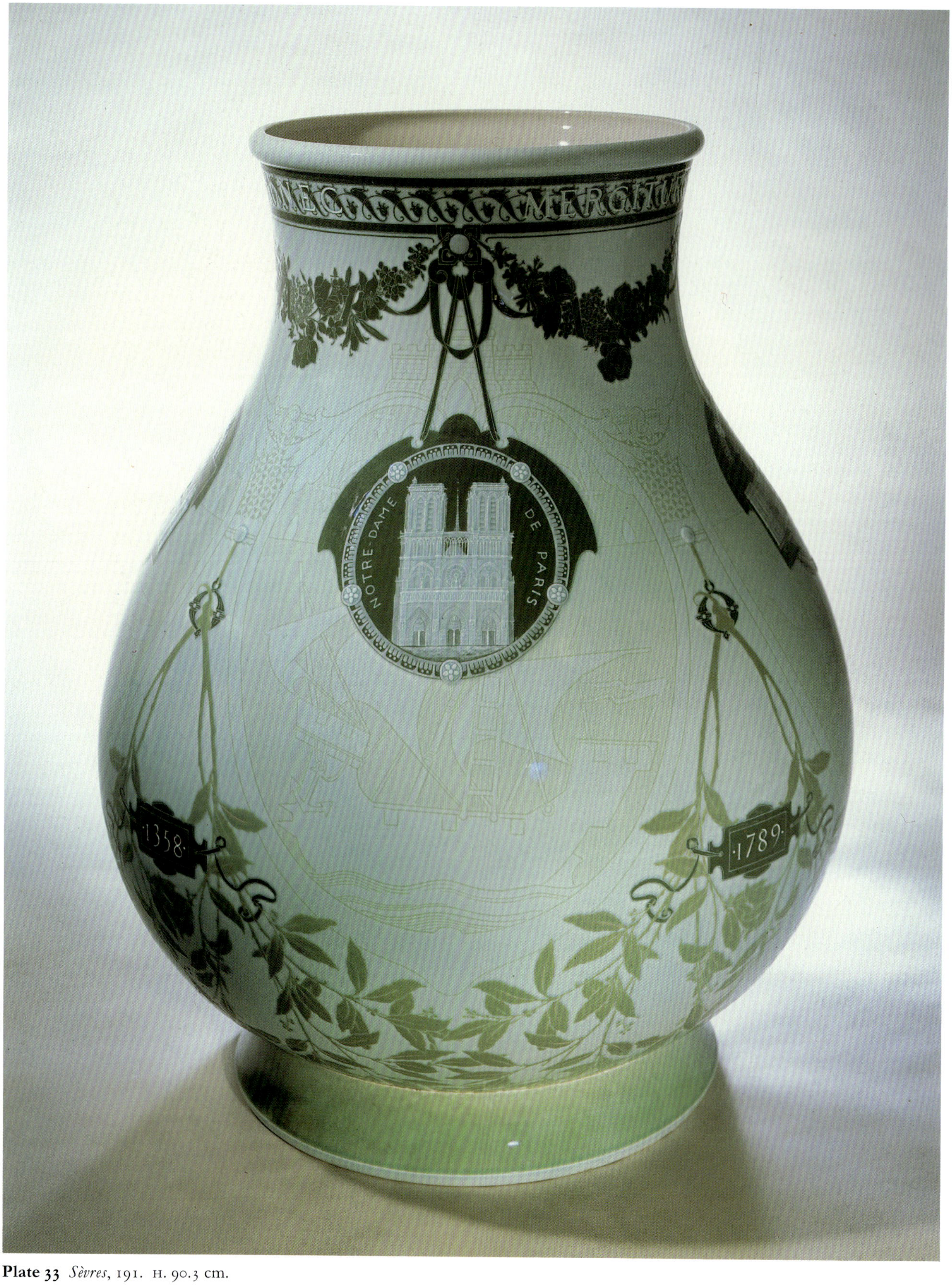

Plate 33 *Sèvres*, 191. H. 90.3 cm.

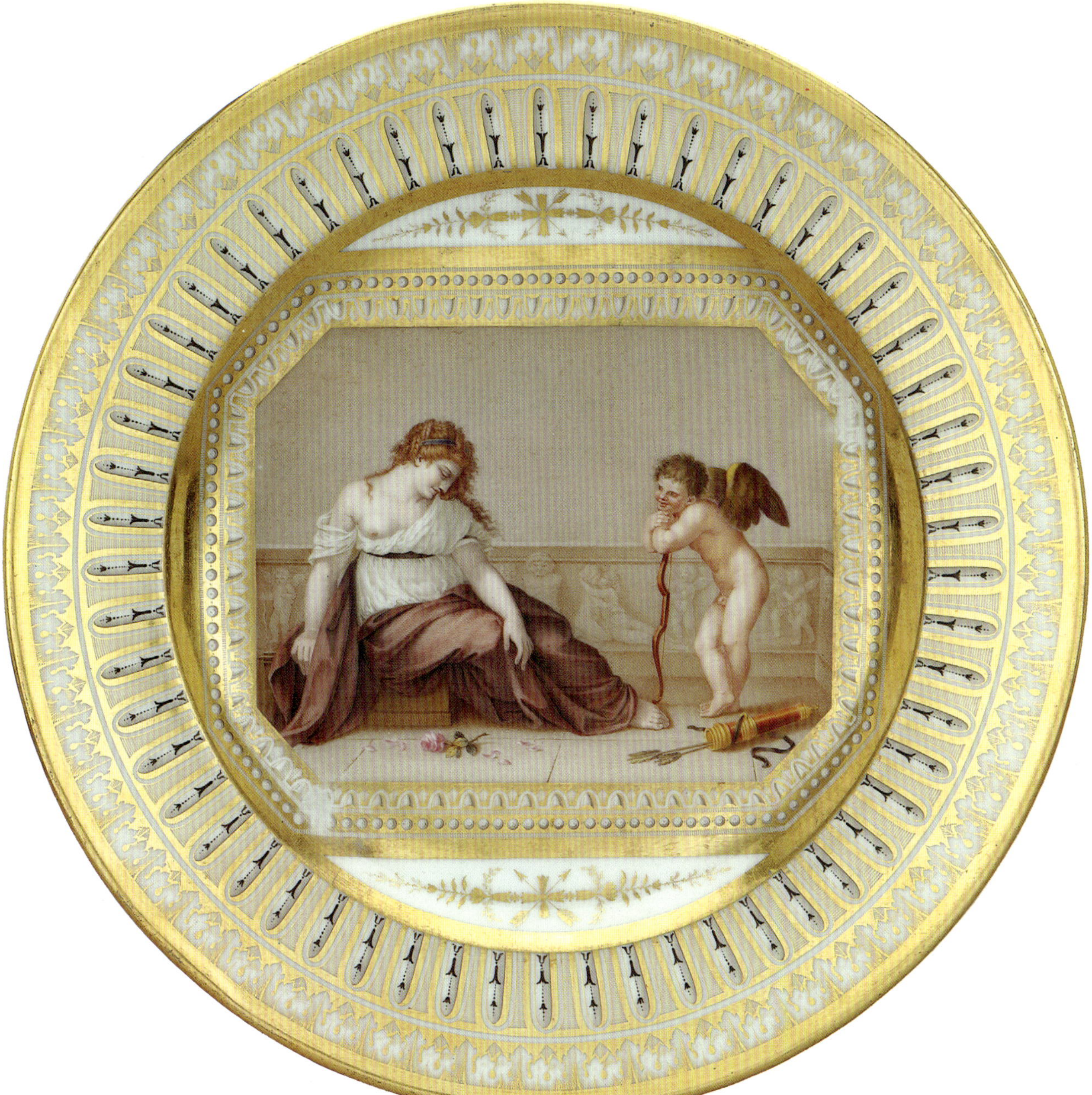

Plate 34 *Paris, Nast*, 273. D. 23.8 cm.

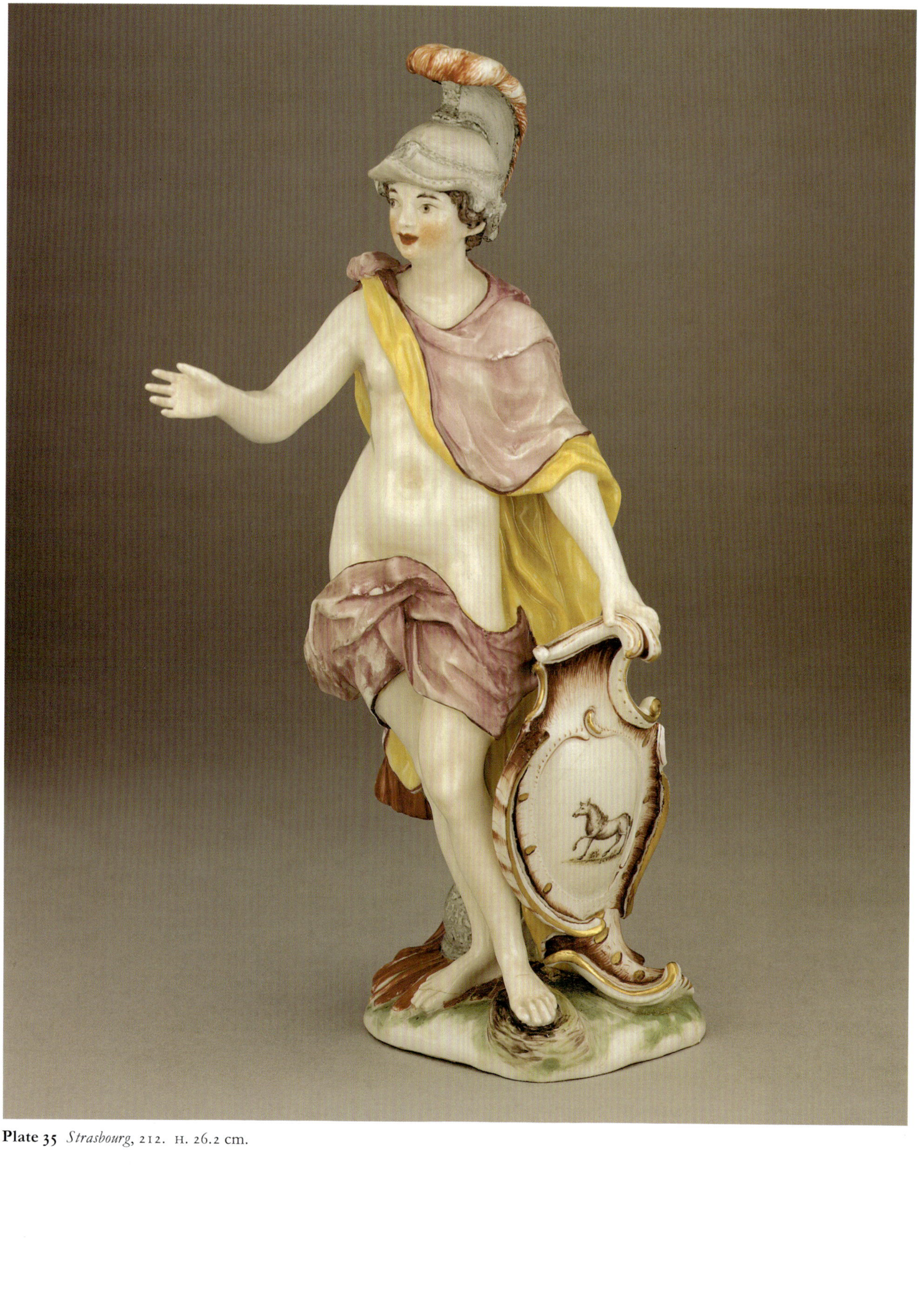

Plate 35 *Strasbourg*, 212. H. 26.2 cm.

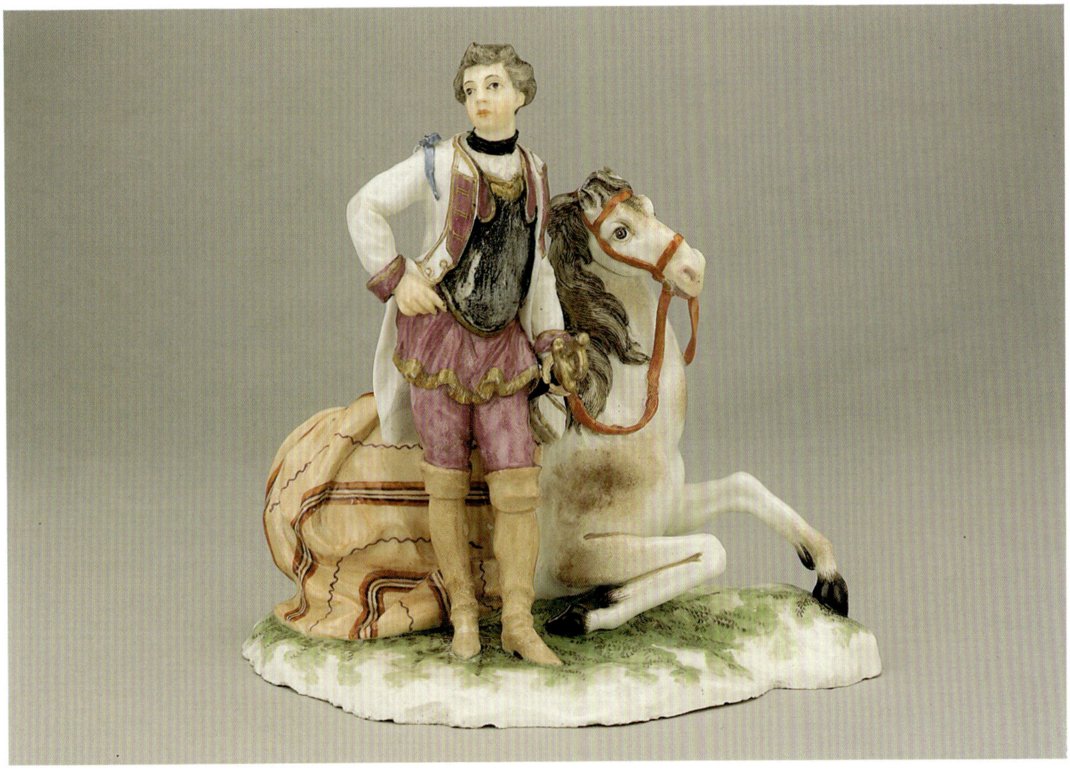

Plate 36 *Niderviller*, 218. H. 13.9 cm.

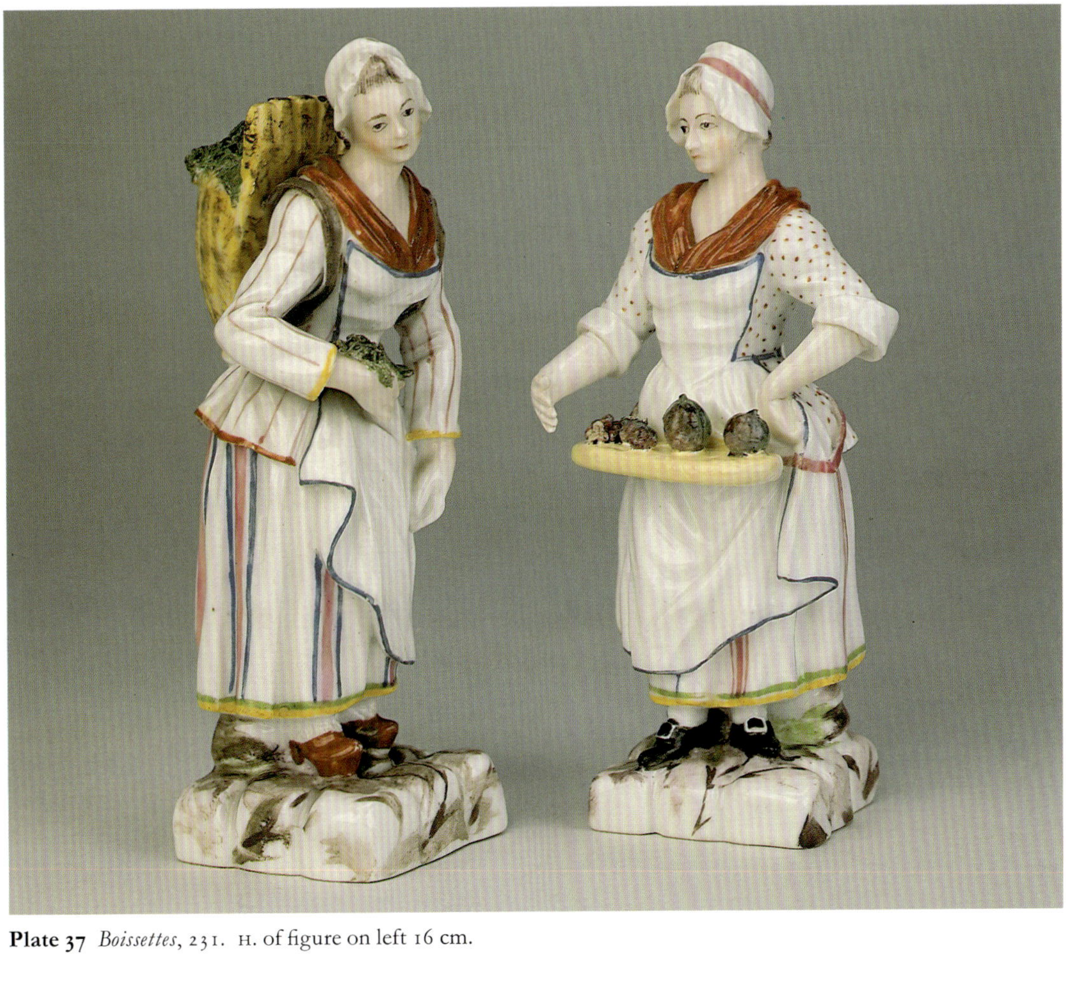

Plate 37 *Boissettes*, 231. H. of figure on left 16 cm.

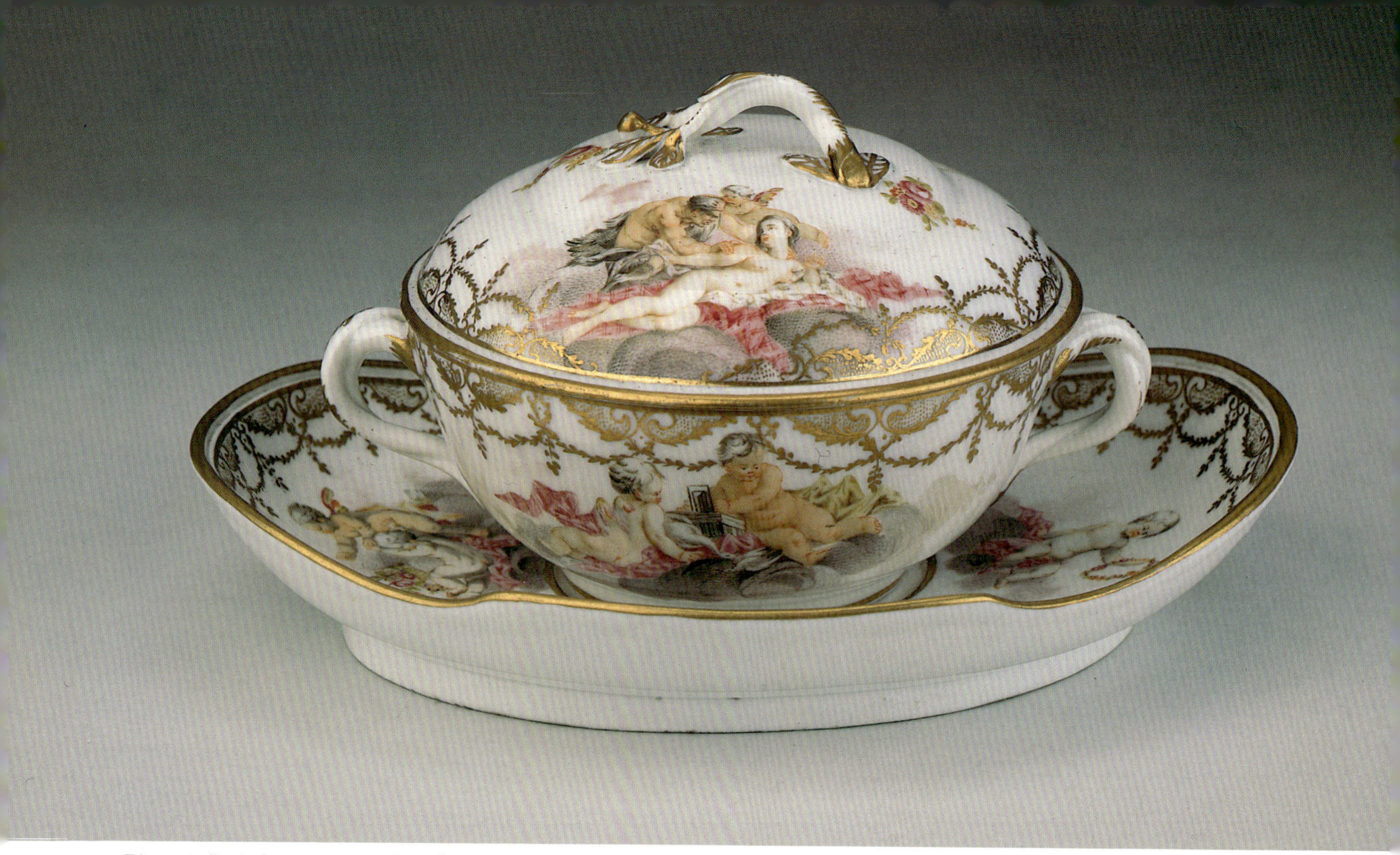

Plate 38 *Paris, Locré*, 250. L. of stand 21.1 cm.

Plate 39 *Paris, comte d'Artois*, 261. D. of saucer 13.3 cm.

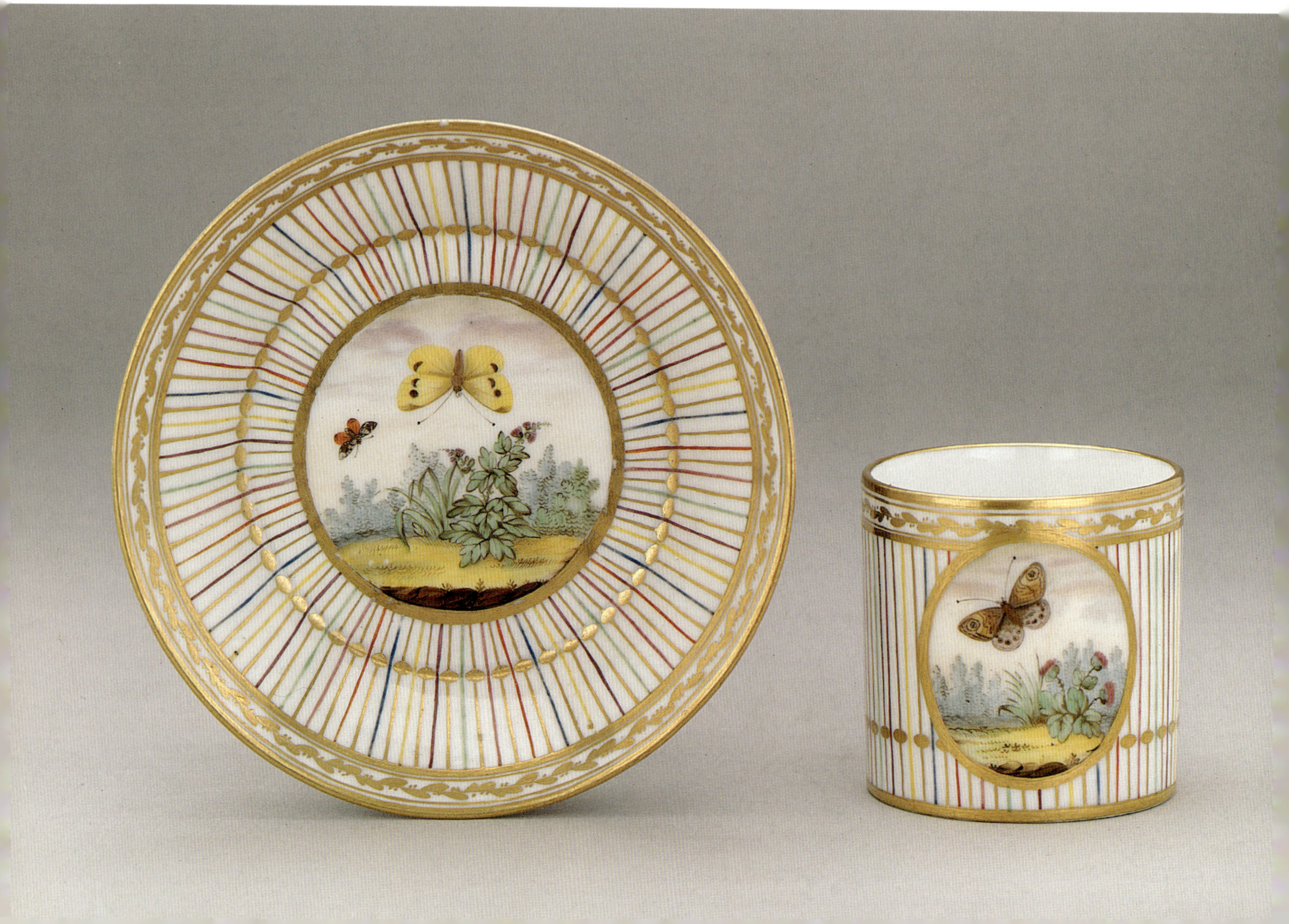

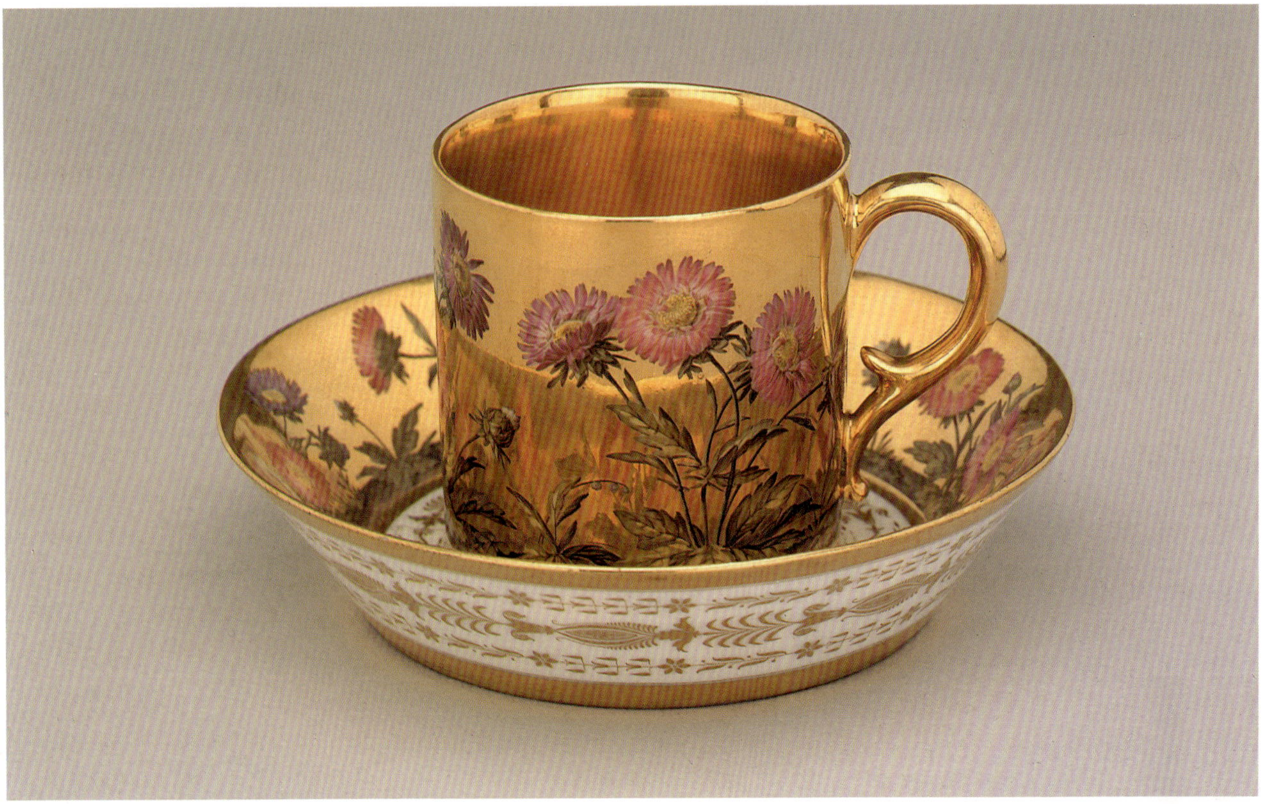

Plate 40 *Paris, Dihl and Guérhard*, 270. D. of saucer 13.1 cm.

Plate 41 *Paris, Chevalier*, 281. L. of tray 24.9 cm.

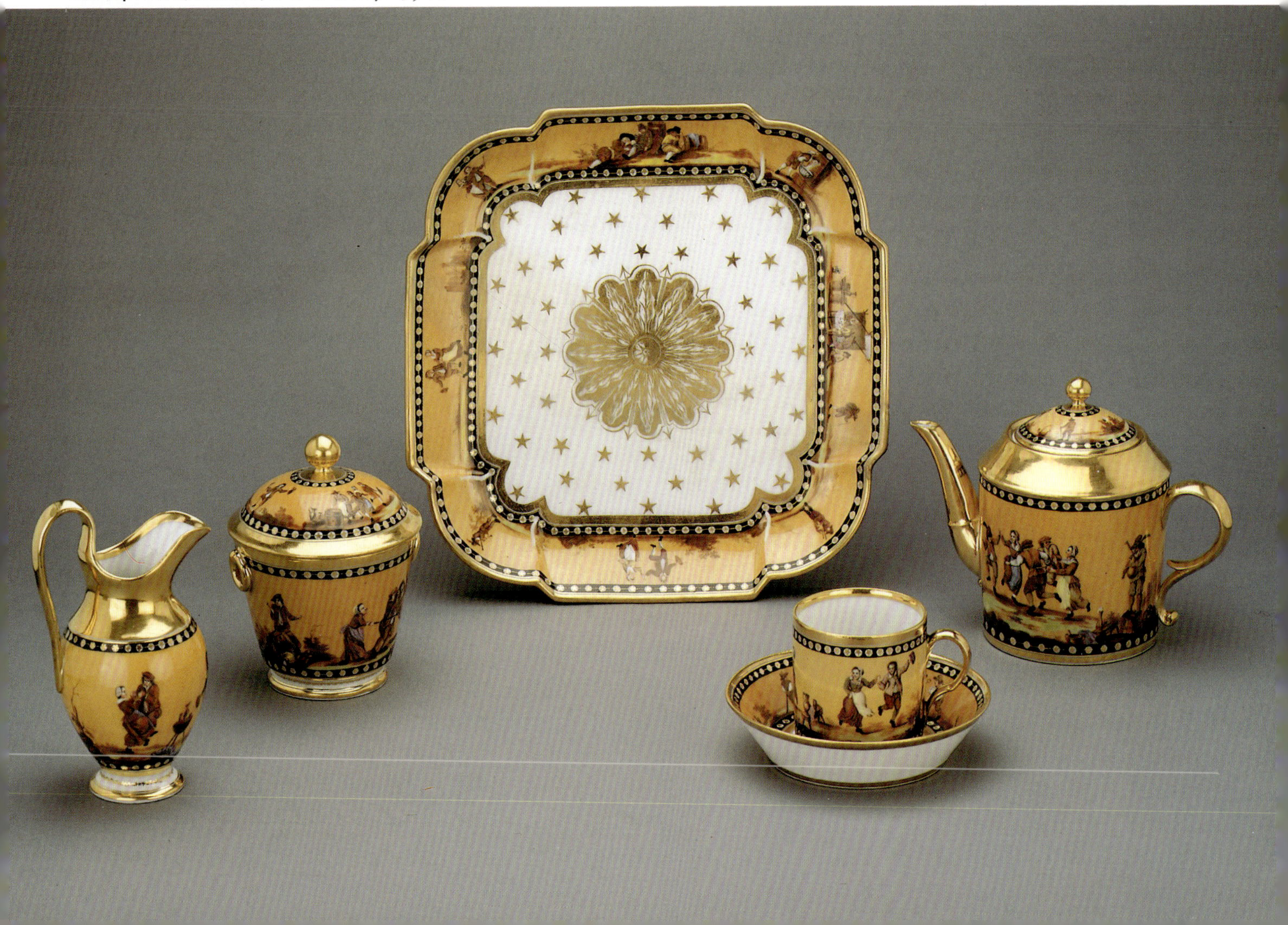

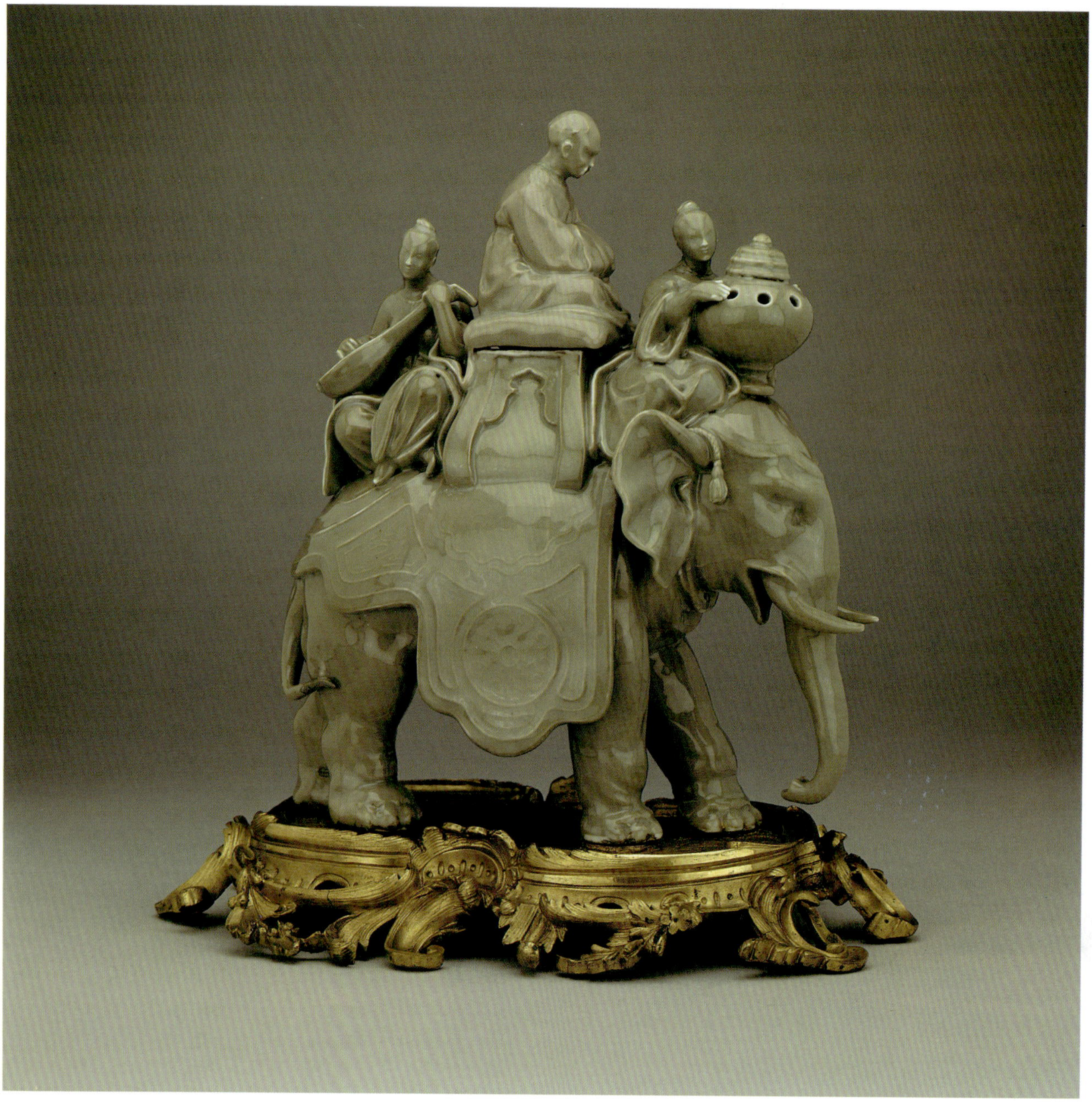

Plate 42 *Paris, unidentified*, 290. Maximum H. with stand 34 cm.

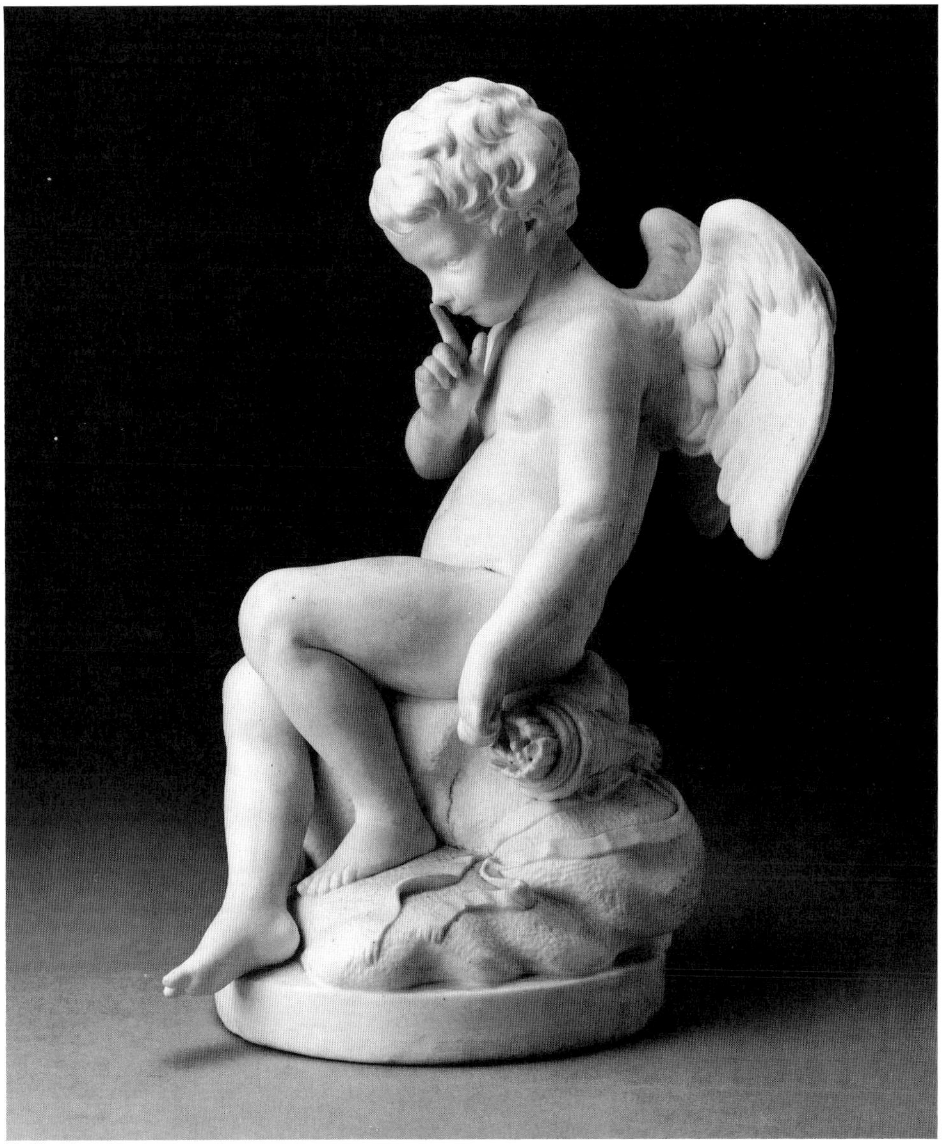

142

142 **L'amour Falconet,** 1758–66

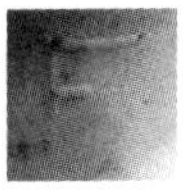

142 *mark*

H.	30.1 cm
Marks:	incised *F* underneath
Reg. No.	1948,12–3,37

Soft-paste porcelain, hollow, press-moulded. Cupid, the fore-finger of his right hand to his lips, is seated on a mound springing from the circular base, over which his right foot projects. Behind him is his quiver, to his right a full-blown rose.

Provenance: Bequeathed by Sir B. Eckstein, Bt., 1948

Literature: King, 1951–2, XVI, no. 3, p. 80

Wilfred J. Sainsbury, 'More about Sèvres Soft Paste Biscuit', *Apollo Miscellany*, 1951, p. 37

Savage, 1960, pl. 71c

Bibliography: Bourgeois and Lechevallier-Chevignard, pl. 9, no. 36

Comparable Examples: London, Wallace Collection, see Savill, 1988, II, p. 823

Probably the most popular figure, with its pendant (see cat. 143), ever made at Sèvres.

Modelled by Etienne-Maurice Falconet[1] in 1758 after a marble group of 1757 now in the Louvre Museum. The sculptor repeated the work for Count A.S. Stroganov in the late 1760s when he was in St Petersburg. This marble example was acquired by the Hermitage in 1931. The Empress Catherine the Great owned an example, kept in the Winter Palace in 1771.[2] The Sèvres model, often known as *L'amour menaçant*, *L'amour silencieux* and *Garde à vous*, was in production until 1801/2 (Revolutionary year x) and was revived in the 1850s.[3] It comprises 15 pieces and is now estimated to require 1830 hours to make. It is still in production.

The figure is fully discussed by Savill.[4] Only one size was made.

The earliest record of a sale of the figure occurs on 28 December 1758 when it cost 144 *livres*;[5] because the overtime records for 1758 and 1759 do not survive, the names of those who first worked on the figure are unknown. Although frequently sold separately, these figures, like so many other examples of biscuit porcelain sculpture from the factory, were usually sold as part of the dessert service and were intended for table decoration. This example dates from between 1758 and 1766 when Etienne-Maurice Falconet was in charge of the sculpture workshop at the Sèvres factory.

A hard-paste porcelain painted version of this model and its companion (cat. 143) made by Joseph Hannong was in a French private collection in 1929.[6]

1. For a biography of Falconet, see Savill, 1988, III, pp. 981–2. The standard reference works on the sculptor's career are L. Réau, *Etienne-Maurice Falconet*, Paris, 1922, and G. Levitine, *The Sculpture of Falconet*, Greenwich (Conn.), 1972.
2. N. Kosareva, 'Masterpieces of Eighteenth-Century French Sculpture', *Apollo*, Vol. CI, no. 160, June 1975, fig. 4, p. 445.
3. The author is grateful to Tamara Préaud for this information.
4. Savill, 1988, II, p. 823.
5. MNS, Archives de Sèvres, Vy 2, f. 57v.
6. Exh. *La porcelaine française*, 1929, no. 981, pl. XI.

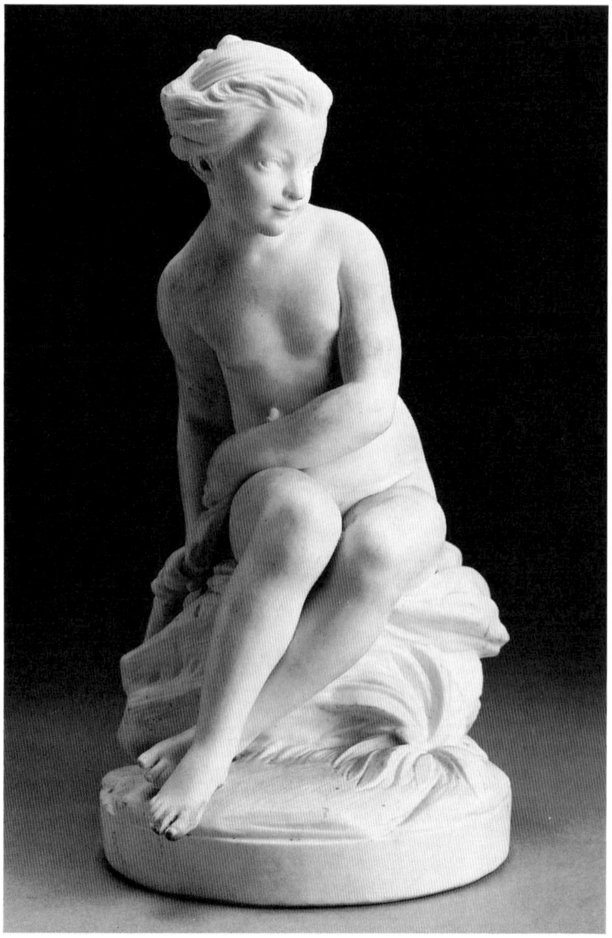

143

143 **Pendant de l'amour Falconet**, after 1761–1801/2

H.	23.3 cm
Marks:	none
Reg. No.	1948,12-3,36

Soft-paste porcelain, hollow, press-moulded. The nymph is seated on a rock resting on a circular base, over the edge of which her right foot projects. She is holding a bow with both hands at her right side. Right foot partly restored.

Provenance: Bequeathed by Sir B. Eckstein, Bt., 1948

Literature: King, 1951–2, XVI, p. 80

Wilfred J. Sainsbury, 'More about Sèvres Soft Paste Biscuit', *Apollo Miscellany*, 1951, p. 37

Savage, 1960, pl. 71b

Dauterman, 1970, no. 119, A, B, p. 293, erroneously described as fitted with a plinth of glazed and decorated Sèvres porcelain

Bibliography: Bourgeois and Lechevallier-Chevignard, pl. 9, no. 467

Comparable Examples: London, Wallace Collection, see Savill, 1988, II, pp. 823–4. Numerous examples exist

Modelled by Etienne-Maurice Falconet in 1761 and created for the factory as a pendant to *Cupid*. According to Dauterman[1] a plaster cast of the subject was listed in the catalogue of the *Salon* of 1761. In a copy of the catalogue kept at the Bibliothèque nationale, Gabriel de Saint-Aubin wrote 'non veue au Sallon mais executée à Sèvre'.

The figure is fully discussed by Savill.[2] Only one size was made. As the *travaux extraordinaires* or records of overtime worked by sculptors and repairers do not survive in the factory archive, the names of those who first worked on the figure are unknown. The first sale recorded shows that one was sold with a matching Cupid to the duc de Choiseul on 24 July 1761 for 96 *livres*, the same price as the Cupid in the 1760s.[3] This example was made between 1761 and 1801/2 (Revolutionary year X) when it went out of production until the 1850s.[4]

1. Dauterman, 1970, p. 293.
2. Savill, 1988, II, pp. 823–4.
3. *Ibid.*, p. 824 for details of prices.
4. The author is grateful to Tamara Préaud for this information.

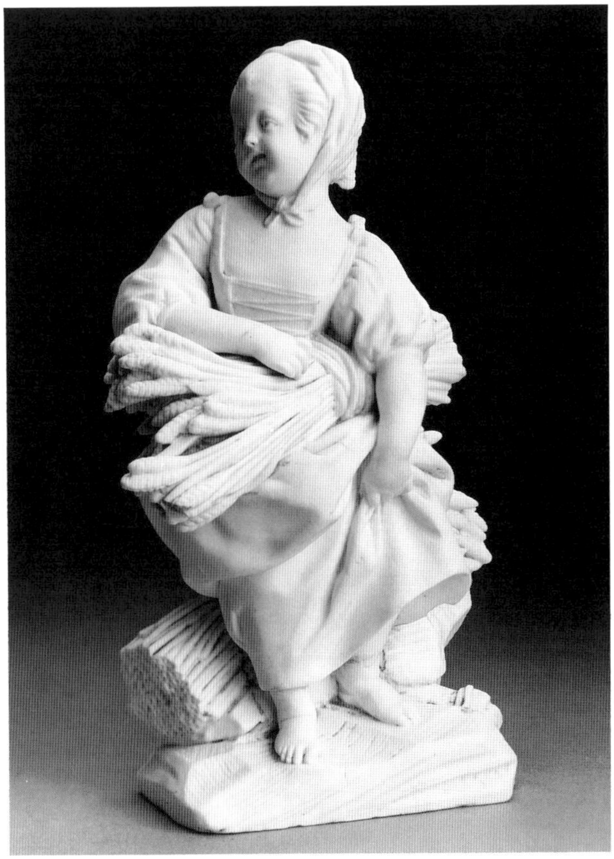

144

144 **La Moissonneuse,** 1780–1800

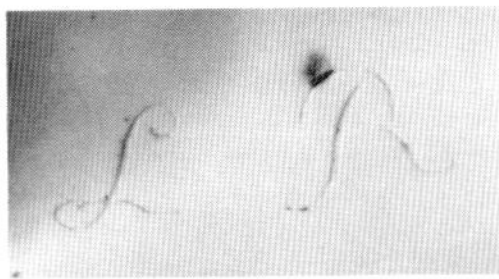

144 *mark*

H.	20 cm
Marks:	cursive *LR* incised underneath hollow base
Reg. No.	FB 36 (AF3236)

Soft-paste porcelain. The young girl, whose hair is partly covered by a kerchief, holds a sheaf of corn across her body, on her skirt which she holds up with her left hand. Her right hands rests on top of the sheaf. At the back is another sheaf of corn on the rocky base. Viewed from the back it is evident that her body bends to the left at the waist.

The edge of the skirt is chipped, and some ears of corn are damaged at the back. There are a number of firecracks, and the porcelain is discoloured in places.

Provenance: Bequeathed by Sir A.W. Franks, 1897

Literature: Unpublished

Bibliography: Bourgeois and Lechevallier-Chevignard, pl. 4, no. 437

Comparable Examples: Exh. *La porcelaine française*, 1929, cat. no. 629, bis, from the Fenaille Collection, incised *F*; sold Paris, Hôtel Drouot, 12 June 1941, Lot 5

Woburn Abbey, Bedfordshire, part of dinner service presented to the 4th Duchess of Bedford by Louis XV of France in 1763, incised *F*, H. 21.6 cm

Sainsbury Collection, sold Sotheby's, 14 March 1967, Lot 35; exh. International Ceramic Fair and Seminar, London, 1985, by Hoff Antiques with companion piece, both incised *F*

USA, New York, Metropolitan Museum, *European Porcelain Special Exhibition*, March–May 1949, cat. no. 159, pl. XXVII, from the French Institute, New York, ex-Chavagnac Collection, sold Paris, Hôtel Drouot, 19–21 June, 1911, glazed white with flesh tints; also illus E. Tilmans, *Porcelaines de France*, Paris, 1953, p. 156; sold Christie's, 28 March 1966, Lot 144 (present whereabouts unknown)

USA, New York, Christie's, 21 April 1982, Lot 128 (with companion male figure)

USA, New York, Christie's, The Elizabeth Parke Firestone Collection, Part I, 21–22 March 1991, Lot 107, incised *L*

USA, California, Filoli, Woodside, inv. FC 86.23.2, incised with cursive capital B^{1}, illus. P. Kite, 'Verdant Mansion, the Splendor of Filoli', *Antiques and Fine Art*, September/October 1990, p. 140

Modelled by Pierre Blondeau after François Boucher in 1752 and inspired by *La Vallée de Montmorency* by Charles-Simeon Favart (1710–92). This play was performed as a pantomime under the title *Les Vendanges de Tempé* in August 1745; in 1752 it took the new title and was transformed into a ballet-pantomime. The figure has a companion piece, *Le Moissonneur*, of the same date. As Rosalind Savill pointed out,[2] Boucher was a designer of costumes and stage-sets from 1737 to 1768 and so came into contact with Favart. As early as 1749 the Sèvres factory owned a Boucher drawing of *Le Petit Jardinier*, also made in biscuit. Boucher executed thirteen drawings of children and '3 groupes de même' listed in the factory's 1752 stock list.

Josse-François-Joseph Le Riche (1738–1812), whose initials are incised under the base of the figure, was born in Mons and baptised on 8 October 1738.[3] Joining the Sèvres factory in 1757, he was employed as a sculptor between 1757 and 1768. Between 1775 and 1779 he was a modeller and from 1780 until his retirement in 1806 was head of the sculpture workshop. In theory, the figure dates from after 1780; however, further research may show it was made earlier, as its appearance would suggest.

The eighteenth-century plaster mould survives at the factory, where there is also a plaster model of the first size. A terracotta model is in the Musée national de Céramique, Sèvres.

The figure was also made at the Chantilly factory; a version was sold from the René Fribourg Collection, Sotheby's, 15 October 1963, Lot 410.

1. The author is grateful to Thomas M. Rogers, Curator of Collections, for providing information about this piece.
2. R. Savill, 'François Boucher and the Porcelains of Vincennes and Sèvres', *Apollo*, March 1982, CXV, no. 241, pp. 162–9.
3. J. Belleudy, 'Joseph Le Riche', in *Bulletin de la Société de l'Histoire de l'art français*, 1924, 1er fascicule, pp. 31–7, and Savill, 1988, III, pp. 384–5.

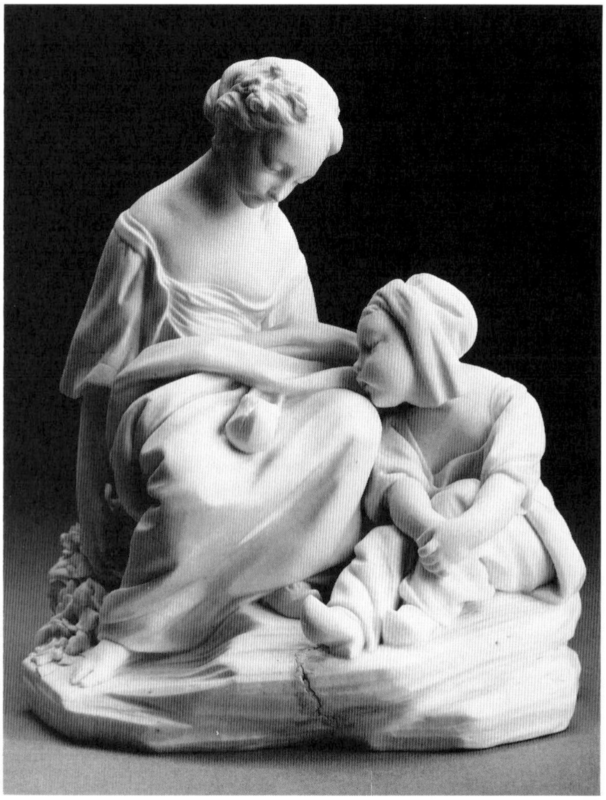

145

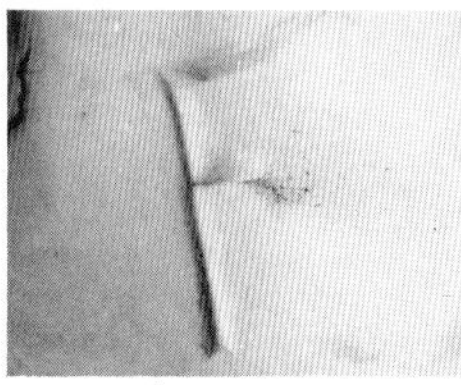

145 *mark*

145 Le Sabot Cassé, 1760–6

H. 17 cm
Marks: *F* incised underneath
Reg. No. Franks 392

Soft-paste porcelain, hollow, formed by press-moulding. A young girl is seated on a rocky mound, wearing a low-cut dress and jacket with half sleeves. On her lap is a *sabot* at which a child seated by her side, wearing a headdress, is staring sadly, his hands crossed over his left knee. Her right hand hangs down to restrain a cascade of flowers falling from a basket.

Provenance: Bequeathed by Sir A.W. Franks, 1897

Literature: Franks, 1896, no. 392

Honey, 1950, pl. 66, p. 36

Savage, 1960, pl. 71a

Wilfred J. Sainsbury, 'Sèvres Soft Paste Biscuit Figures Part I', *Apollo*, Vol. LI, no. 303, May 1950, p. 136

Bibliography: Bourgeois and Lechevallier-Chevignard, pl. 7, no. 543

Comparable Examples: Sèvres, Musée national de Céramique, inv. 22 451, incised *F*; inv. 15 368 Ujfalvy-Bourdon Collection, see C.-E. de Ujfalvy-Bourdon, *Les Biscuits de Porcelaine*, Paris, 1893, p. 9

Exh. *La porcelaine française*, 1929, cat. no. 835 (with *La Feuille à l'envers*) from the Fenaille Collection; sold Paris, Hôtel Drouot, 12 June 1941, Lot 42 and Sotheby's, 5 May 1970, Lot 41

Bedfordshire, Woburn Abbey, unmarked, see Wills, 1956, no. 371, p. 16, fig. v

Sotheby's, 1 July 1980, Lot 54

Sweden, Stockholm, Nationalmuseum, inv. C.XV,1.012, Ivan Traugott loan, see *Bulletin de la Société des Amis de Vincennes*, December 1939, no. 16, p. 221

USA, private collection, see Ruth Berges, *Collectors' Choice of Porcelain and Faïence*, South Brunswick and New York, 1967, no. 256

USA, New York, Smithsonian Institution, Cooper-Hewitt Museum, illus. R. Berges, 'Falconet et Sèvres', *Antique Collector*, April 1988, Vol. 59, no. 4, pp. 74–9, fig. 3

USA, New York, Metropolitan Museum, inv. 52.2.2, incised *F*, see C. Duval *et al.*, 'Figures from Life: Porcelain Sculpture from the Metropolitan Museum of Art, ca. 1740–1780', exh. March 1992–January 1993, Museum of Fine Arts, St Petersburg, Florida; Dixon Gallery and Gardens, Tennessee; George R. Gardiner Museum of Ceramic Art, Toronto, no. 36

USA, New York, Christie's, 6 March 1981, Lot 279 and 1 December 1979, Lot 172 (Mrs J.W. Christner Collection)

USA, New York, Sotheby's, 11 April 1980, Lot 248, formerly Mrs H. Dupuy Collection, sold Parke Bernet, New York, 2 April 1948, Lot 109

USA, New York, Sotheby's, 21 April 1982, Lot 129

USA, New York, Christie's, The Elizabeth Parke Firestone Collection, Part 1, 21–22 March 1991, Lot 134 (with *La Feuille à l'envers*), incised *F*

Modelled by Etienne-Maurice Falconet in 1760 after François Boucher's *Paysanne assise dans un paysage et enfant dormant*, engraved by Demarteau.[1] An engraving by Menil after Falconet *fils* in reverse to this group is kept in the archive at the Sèvres factory, but its date of acquisition is unknown. It is after the biscuit figure. Plaster moulds are preserved in the factory archive, and there is a fired clay model at the Musée national de Céramique, Sèvres. A model and a mould were each valued at 24 *livres* in an inventory dated January 1761 preserved at the factory.

A payment of 27 *livres* to Leclere, a sculptor, is recorded in the *Travaux extraordinaires* or record of overtime work on the group for June 1760,[2] and in the following months a number of other sculptors were paid piecework rates for work on it. There seems little doubt that in this instance the incised *F* stands for Falconet, head of the sculpture workshop from 1757–66. The first sale is noted under the date 18 October 1760, when a group was sold for 48 *livres*.[3] The group was always sold with its companion, *La Feuille à l'envers*. Between 1760 and 1776 each cost 60 *livres*, falling to 54 *livres* between 1777 and 1787 and 48 *livres* from 1787. The inventory made after the death of Madame de Pompadour in 1764 records under 'Porcelaines rapportées de Versailles': 'Un grouppe [*sic*], aussy d'après Mr Boucher: la *Maîtresse d'ecolle* [*sic*]; le *Sabot cassé* et la *Feuille à l'envers*; prisé quatre vingt dix livres'.[4]

Far from being 'a charming specimen of the sentimental *paysannerie* admired by many of the sophisticated nobility of the time' as it was described by Geoffrey Wills,[5] this group like many others made at Sèvres has an erotic significance. The 'broken clog' actually stands for the loss of virginity. The companion group *La Feuille à l'envers* is similarly symbolic.

The subject is painted on an undated *vase cornet* in the Philadelphia Museum of Art, probably made around 1763–8.[6] The same subject was treated at the Sceaux faïence factory, although the figures were juxtaposed. An example was apparently on the market at Versailles on 3 December 1972.[7] This group was in current production at Sèvres in 1967.[8]

1. Jean-Richard, 1978, no. 790; the sabot and the basket are not shown in the engraving.
2. MNS, Archives de Sèvres, F5.
3. MNS, Archives de Sèvres, Vy 3, f. 30.
4. Cordey, 1939, p. 61, no. 668.
5. G. Wills, 'Some French and English Porcelain at Woburn Abbey', *Apollo*, Vol. LXIII, no. 371, January 1956, p. 16.
6. Brunet and Préaud, 1978, no. 132.
7. An example sold at Versailles, 3 December 1973, Lot 22, is recorded by D. Menager, *Catalogue raisonné des biscuits de porcelaine de Vincennes et de Sèvres au XVIIIe siècle dans les collections du Musée national de Céramique, Sèvres*, unpublished *mémoire* for the Ecole du Louvre, April 1985, Vol. II, kept at the Archives de Sèvres.
8. Illustrated *Cahiers*, no. 39, 1967 in a supplement on biscuit porcelains for sale at the factory. It measured 19 cm in height.

146 **Pygmalion and Galatea,** *c.* 1764–73

H. 36.1 cm
Marks: cursive *B* on top of base
Reg. No. 1948,12–3,38

Soft-paste biscuit porcelain, the oval base hollow, showing that the lower part was press-moulded. Pygmalion, in a long robe and with a bandeau around his hair and thonged sandals on his feet, kneels on an oval pedestal, his hands clasped in ecstasy at the sight of the awakening Galatea who stands naked before him on a semi-circular plinth, itself resting on an oblong support. A putto, who kneels on the stone from which she is fashioned, kisses her right hand. A winged cupid holding the remains of a bow is behind her at her left. Beside the hem of Pygmalion's cloak at the left are his tools: a mallet, chisels and a file. Galatea's left hand is restored and the arrow of the cupid behind her is broken.

Provenance: Bequeathed by Sir B. Eckstein, Bt., 1948

Literature: Honey, 1950, pl. 68

King, 1951–2, pp. 80–1

Savage, 1960, pl. 70

Bibliography: Illus. E. Bourgeois and G. Lechevallier-Chevignard, n.d. (1913), pl. 9, no. 529 and mentioned by Ch. E. de Ujfalvy-Bourdon, 1893, p. 83 (model said to be by Duru)

See exh. cat. *Diderot et l'Art de Boucher à David*, Paris, Hôtel de la Monnaie, 5 October 1984–6 January 1985, no. 131

Comparable Examples: Sèvres, Musée national de Céramique, inv. 15 353, hard-paste, first size. H. 75 cm, incised *lo* near a cupid

Paris, Musée des arts décoratifs, inv. unknown

Paris, Musée du Louvre, inv. 10.000, acquired 1960, incised with cursive *B*, soft-paste, rectangular base on rectangular pedestal with inscription

Germany, Berlin, Schlossmuseum, illus. F. Hofmann, *Das Porzellan*, Berlin, 1932, Tafel VI

Russia, St Petersburg, Pavlovsk Palace, inv. 20723, illus, N. Birioukova, 'A propos des marques sur les biscuits de Vincennes et de Sèvres', *Cahiers*, no. 40 (1968) p. 258, illus. p. 259

Russia, St Petersburg, State Hermitage Museum, inv. 24161, see N. Birioukova, 1962, no. 36, fig. 45, hard-paste porcelain, oval pedestal, incised *Bn8A*

Russia, Kuskovo, The State Museum of Ceramics, soft-paste, height 37.5 cm, incised *F*, inv. 11268

USA, New York, Smithsonian Institution, Cooper-Hewitt Museum, illus. R. Berges, 'Falconet at Sèvres', *Antique Collector*, Vol. 59, no. 4, April 1988, fig. 6

USA, Boston, Museum of Fine Arts, illus. P.T. Rathbone, 1968, p. 85 and Munger *et al.*, 1992, no. 144, hard-paste porcelain

USA, New York, Christie's, 27 April 1984, Lot 252, illus.

USA, New York, Christie's, The Elizabeth Parke Firestone Collection, Part I, 21–22 March 1990, Lot 140, incised *F*

USA, New York, private collection, square base, incised *F*, perhaps the example illus. in P. Hunter-Stiebel, 'Louis XV and Madame de Pompadour, a love affair with style', exh. New York, Rosenberg & Stiebel Inc., May–June 1990, cat. 26, p. 77, fig. 56

Private collection, location unknown, on oval base with pedestal bearing inscription, illus. Frégnac 1964, p. 203

This group, widely acknowledged as one of the finest ever produced at Sèvres, is based on a marble by Etienne-Maurice Falconet (1716–91) with the addition of an extra cupid at the back. The marble group, which has a rectangular base, was exhibited at the *Salon* of 1763. There are examples in the Louvre and in the Walters Art Gallery, Baltimore, USA; the Louvre group is dated but the date may have been added later.[1] The subject appears in painted form on an undated green-ground vase without a painter's mark at Waddesdon Manor, Buckinghamshire.[2]

Diderot wrote more about this group in his *Salon* of 1763 than about any other item of sculpture he ever discussed, in terms of unparalleled lyricism: 'O la chose précieuse que ce petit groupe de Falconet! Voilà le morceau que j'aurais dans mon cabinet, si je me piquais d'avoir un cabinet etc'.

The subject is taken from classical mythology and was treated by Ovid in the *Metamorphoses*. Pygmalion, King of Cyprus, fell in love with an ivory figure of a woman which in some versions of the story he is said to have carved himself. At a feast dedicated to Aphrodite he begged the goddess to grant him a

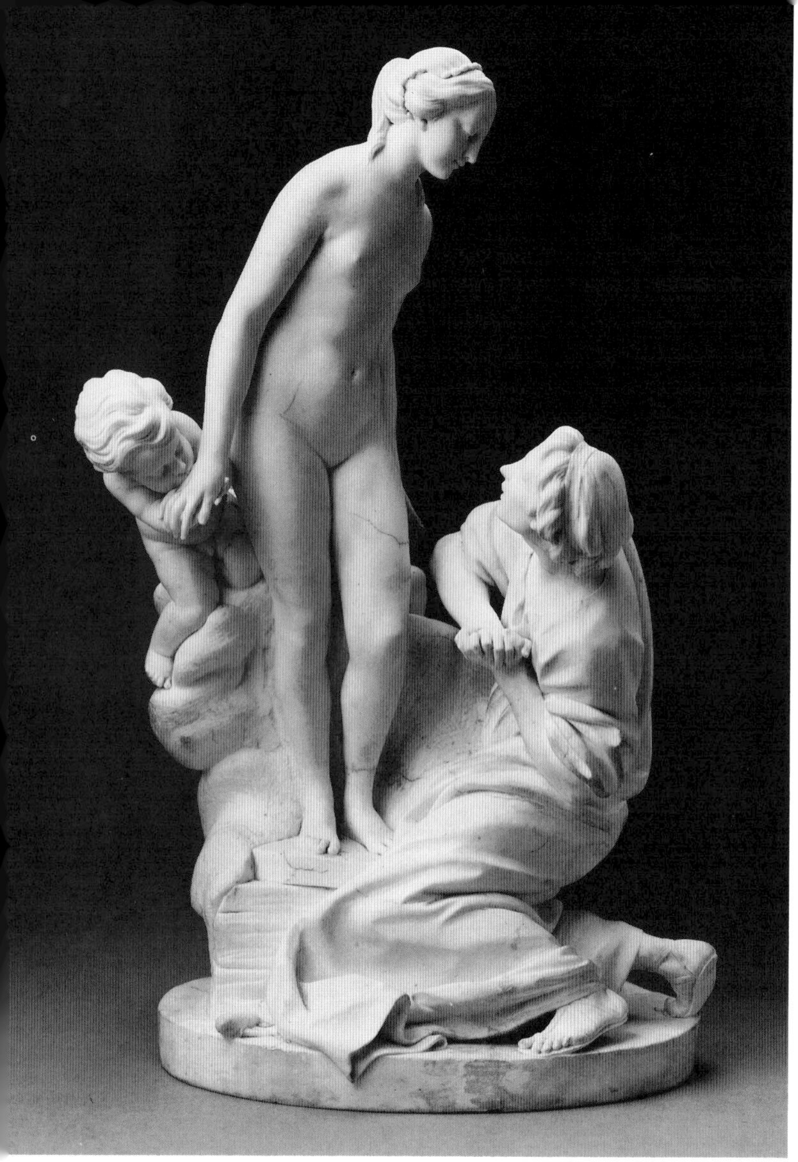 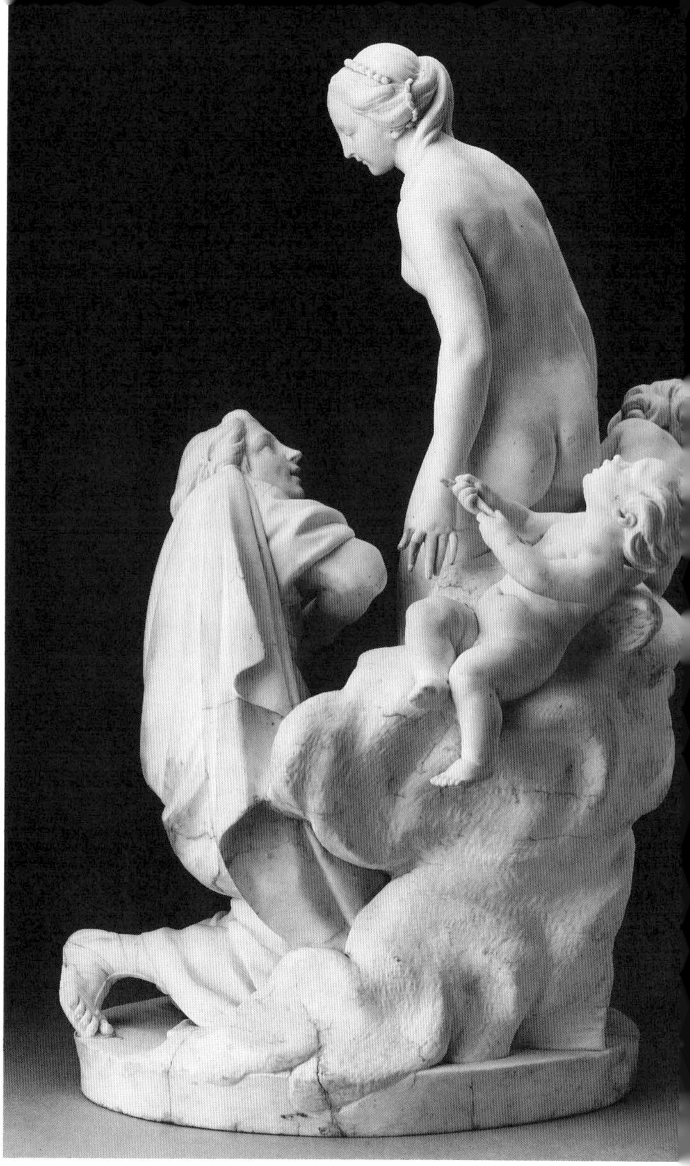

146

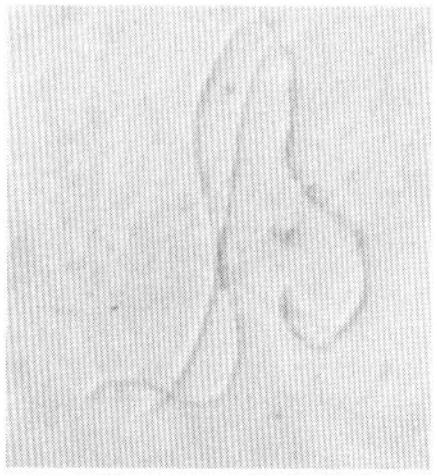

146 *mark*

woman in the image of the figure. On returning home he discovered that the figure had come to life. He married her, the product of their union being a daughter, Paphos.

The story was represented on the stage in several versions. Those of the Italian Comedy in 1734, 1741, 1760 and 1780 have been recorded by M. d'Espinay de Saint-Luc in an unpublished thesis.[3] This author has also traced twelve interpretations given by other theatre companies, including a ballet staged in London in 1734 and the well-known version by J.J. Rousseau given in 1770 at the Hôtel de Ville, Lyon, and at the Théâtre Français in 1775.[4] Falconet's marble, as we have seen from Diderot's commentary, focuses on the instant when the statue comes to life, and symbolises the relationship between the artist and his creation.

D'Espinay de Saint-Luc has rightly drawn attention to the concluding speech given by Pygmalion in Rousseau's drama: 'Oui cher et charmant objet, oui digne chef d'oeuvre de mes mains, de mon coeur et des Dieux . . . C'est toi seule; je t'ai donné tout mon être; je ne veux vivre que par toi.'

The Sèvres version exists in two sizes, of which this example is the smaller. Plaster and clay models are preserved in the Archives de la Manufacture de Sèvres and there is a terracotta in the Musée national de Céramique, Sèvres; the second size was composed of seventeen different parts, the first of thirty-one. In October 1763 Leclere was paid 54 *livres* 'pour remonter la terre' (i.e. for assembling the terracotta model) and 108 *livres* for having 'reparé le plâtre'.[5] His work was carried out before the creation of the moulds for the group. Le Riche and Leclere are recorded as working on the group from November–December 1763 and into 1764. The record of overtime work carried out by the modellers shows that a number of them were involved with this group: Mathias, Chanou *l'oncle*, Gomond, Oreste Chanoux, Levaux, Plocque, Mignan, Furet and Choulair. It is probable that the incised *B* stands for Bachelier who was in charge of the sculpture workshop from 1751–7 and 1766–73, a hypothesis put forward by Madame N. Birioukova.[6]

Both a model and a mould are recorded in an inventory dated January 1764 preserved at the factory.

The group was sold when perfect at the high price of 480 *livres*,[7] and from the yearly inventories it is clear that between 1765 and 1770 only a maximum of ten were ever in stock. They seem to have been sold singly to the *marchands-merciers* such as Poirier, Daguerre, Dulac, Sayde, notably in February 1773.[8] A Pygmalion *doré* at 300 *livres* was in the *magasin de vente* in January 1774 and two 'Pigmalions, Grands et pts' are recorded for sale at 600 *livres* each on 19 February 1785.[9] In 1772 Louis-Joseph de Bourbon, prince de Condé, purchased an example at 480 *livres*, which, however, was listed neither in the inventory made in Paris in 1779, nor in *l'inventaire de l'émigré Condé* made at Chantilly in 1792–3.[10]

The last King of Poland, Stanislas-Augustus Poniatowski owned an example of this Sèvres group.[11]

1. Exh. *Diderot et l'Art de Boucher à David*, Paris, Hôtel de la Monnaie, 5 October 1984–6 January 1985, no. 131.
2. Eriksen, 1968, no. 73. A painting by F. Lemoyne *Pygmalion voyant sa statue animée* dated 1729, which may have belonged to the *fermier-général* Etienne Bouret, one of the shareholders of the Sèvres factory, was exhibited in 'The Age of Louis XV, French Painting 1710–1774', USA, Toledo Museum of Art, 1975–6, cat. 62. Another by F. Boucher entitled *Pygmalion devient amoureux d'une statue qu'il avoit faite, et Vénus la rend animée*, engraved by N. Lemire, was used in 1786 as the subject for a painted scene on a *plateau Bouret* in the Louis XVI service, see Bellaigue, 1986, p. 145, no. 66, fig. 1.
3. 'Contribution à l'Iconologie du XVIIII Siècle, Le Biscuit de Sèvres et le Théâtre italien de 1752 à 1781', unpublished thesis for the University of Nancy, 1968.
4. See J.J. Rousseau, *Oeuvres Complètes*, 1964, Pléiade edition, Vol. 2, pp. 1229–30.
5. MNS, Archives de Sèvres, F7.
6. N. Birioukova, 1968, pp. 257–60.
7. Imperfect groups at 336 or 288 *livres* are documented in the Sèvres factory records in the inventory of the *magasin de vente* on 1 January 1774.
8. MNS, Archives de Sèvres, I 8.
9. *Ibid.*, I, 8.
10. M. Brunet, 'Quelques porcelaines de Sèvres du prince de Condé', *Bulletin de la Société des Amis du Musée de Chantilly*, no. 3, October 1972, p. 4, fig. 3 (illustrates the model).
11. L. Réau, 'Catalogue des oeuvres d'art français de la collection du roi de Pologne Stanislas-Auguste' (extracts only), L'Art français dans les pays du nord et de l'est de l'Europe (XVIIIe–XIXe siècles, *Archives de l'Art français*, nouvelle période, Vol. XVII (1931–2), reprinted 1969, p. 248, no. 44, 'Un groupe de biscuit de Sève de quatre figures représentant *Pygmalion et sa statue*', listed as *Effets de garde-meubles*.

147 **Le Baiser Donné**, 1765–*c.* 1786

H. 18.1 cm
Marks: none
Reg. No. 1948,12–3,23

Soft-paste porcelain, hollow base. The gallant kneels, supporting the kneeling young girl on his left knee and holding her upper back and waist in his arms. His right foot projects slightly over the oblong base which is in the form of a rocky slab. Over his right ankle is a flower garland and behind him her ribbon-trimmed, broad-brimmed hat. He wears breeches tied with a bow at the knee, and a loose shirt tied at the neck under a jacket with two elaborate bows at the side. His hair is tied with a ribbon bow at the back. The young girl wears a dress with a full skirt and low-cut bodice beneath a jacket with half sleeves trimmed with a bow at the elbow. Her hair is elaborately braided at the back. The little finger of her right hand is missing.

Companion to cat. 148.

Provenance: Bequeathed by Sir B. Eckstein, Bt., 1948

Literature: King, 1951–2, p. 80

Honey, 1950, pl. 67

Savage, 1960, pl. 72(a)

Savage, 1963 ed., pl. 47

Bibliography: Bourgeois and Lechevallier-Chevignard, pl. 8, no. 94

Comparable Examples: Exh. *La porcelaine française*, 1929, no. 839, (with *Le Baiser Rendu*) from the Fenaille Collection; sold Paris, Hôtel Drouot, 12 June 1941, Lot 45; sold Sotheby's, 5 May 1970, Lot 37, Wilfred J. Sainsbury Collection, illus. W. Sainsbury 'Large groups and figures in the soft-paste biscuit of Vincennes-Sèvres', *Antiques*, Vol. LXXXVII, no. 4, April 1965, p. 433, fig.9

Sèvres, Musée national de Céramique, inv. 8055 hard-paste porcelain[1]

USA, New York, Christie's, The Elizabeth Parke Firestone Collection, Part I, 21–2 March 1990, Lot 143 (with pendant), formerly Fenaille Collection

Modelled by Etienne-Maurice Falconet in 1765 and based on Taconet's play *Le Baiser Donné et Le Baiser Rendu* performed at the Théâtre des Boulevards in 1765 and on 19 May 1770 at Versailles on the occasion of the marriage of the Dauphin. According to the play, which was printed at Paris, 1771,[2] in Act I, scene 5, Lisette, a young, newly-wed peasant girl, is kissed by the Marquis, the local *seigneur*, who gives her husband, Guillot, some money to buy her 'des rubans et des lacets'. In Act II, scene 6, Guillot asks the

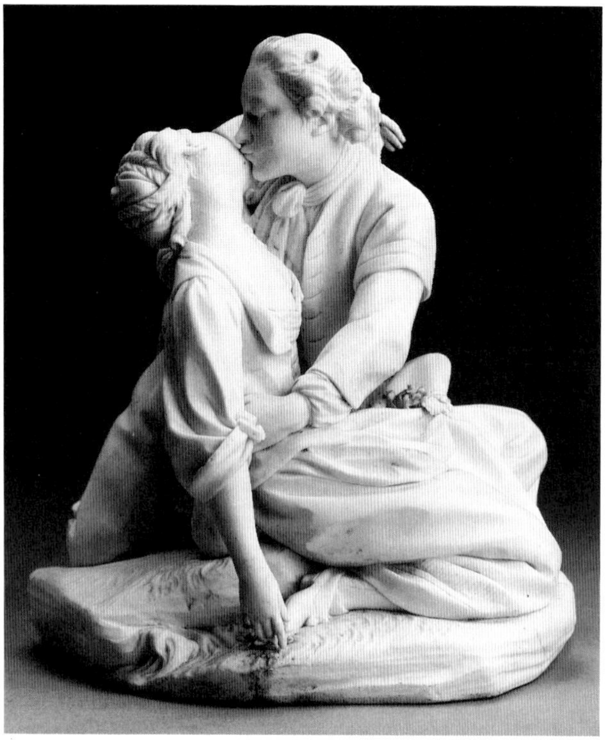

147

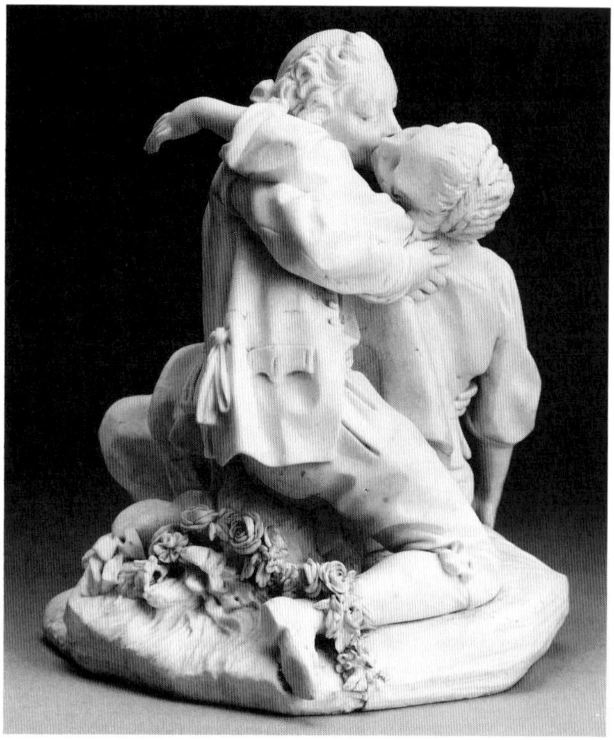

Marquis permission to 'chase on his lands', that is, to kiss the Marquise and repay the debt.

The group, designed to be viewed in the round, again reveals Falconet's skill in positioning figures whose attitudes betray a certain erotic abandon.

The group, which is still in production, but was not reissued after 1786 until late this century,[3] is presently calculated to require 2,160 hours to make. An eighteenth-century plaster mould comprising eleven pieces survives at the factory.[4] The sculptor Perrotin was paid 36 *livres* for work on the group in July 1765,[5] whilst Leclere received 18 *livres* in the following month 'Avoir remonté la terre du Baiser donné' and 'Avoir réparé le plâtre dud.'[6] A plaster model and an eighteenth-century mould are preserved at the factory. Other sculptors, including Mignan, Furet, Levaux and Mathias, worked on the group in 1765, the last mention of 'extra' work on the group occuring in December 1777. The first sale recorded was in December 1765, when a group sold at Versailles cost 144 *livres*.[7] In 1777 it sold at 96 *livres*, and in 1787 the price was lowered to 72 *livres*.

1. Illus. Bourgeois, 1909, Vol. 2, fig. 25, where it is said be be after Boucher. However, no evidence has been found for this statement.
2. There is a copy of the work in the British Library.
3. According to Tamara Préaud in private correspondence with the author in September 1991.
4. The writer is grateful to Tamara Préaud for information about the number of pieces making up this mould.
5. MNS, Archives de Sèvres, F8, *Travaux extraordinaires*.
6. *Ibid.*
7. MNS, Archives de Sèvres, Vy 4, f. 55v.

148 Le Baiser Rendu, 1765–*c.* 1786

H. 18.4 cm
Marks: none
Reg. No. 1948,12–3,24

Soft-paste porcelain, hollow base. The young man is seated, his left leg under his right which projects beyond the oval base. The base is formed as a rocky mound with plants in the fissures at the front. Leaning against him with her body twisted and resting on her left elbow, the young girl plants a kiss on his left chin. Under her elbow is a *musette*, one of the pipes of which she holds suggestively in her left hand. Her right hand supports the young man's head. He wears a broad-brimmed hat trimmed with a wide ribbon, a blouse, jacket and breeches tied at the knee. Her low-cut dress has a full skirt and flowing sleeves. Her heeled shoes are trimmed with bows. Hat and pipe at front chipped; foot restored.

Companion to cat. 147.

Provenance: Bequeathed by Sir B. Eckstein, Bt., 1948

Literature: King, 1951–2, p. 80

Savage, 1960, pl. 72b

Bibliograpy: Bourgeois and Lechevallier-Chevignard, pl. 8, no. 95

Comparable Examples: Exh. *La porcelaine française*, 1929, no. 839, from the Fenaille Collection, sold Paris, Hôtel Drouot, 12 June 1941, Lot 45 (with *Le Baiser Donné*)

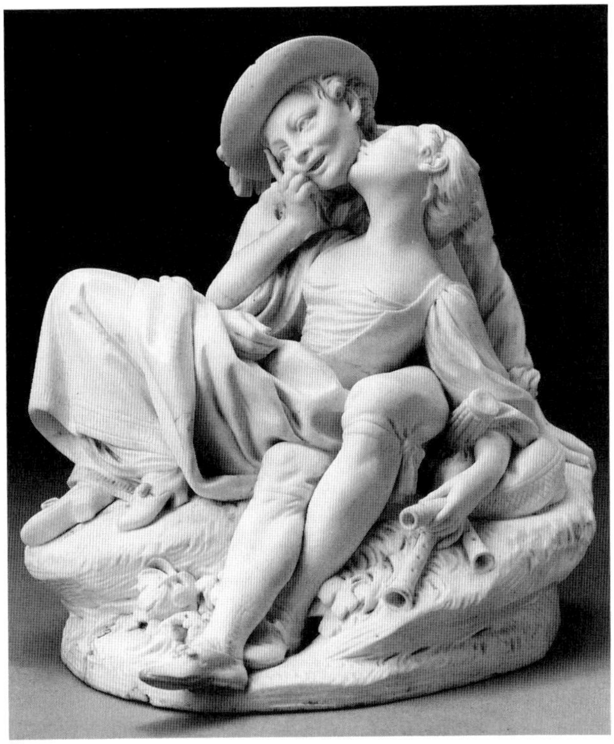

148

Birioukova, 1962, fig. 40, Musée national de Céramique, Sèvres[1]

Christie's, New York, The Elizabeth Parke Firestone Collection, Part I, 21–2 March 1990, Lot 143 (with pendant), formerly Fenaille Collection, incised *F*

Modelled by Etienne-Maurice Falconet in 1765 – see cat. 147.

Although based on the same source as cat. 147, this group can be traced back to a *conte* by J. de La Fontaine published in 1762 and entitled '*Le Baiser Rendu*'.[2] A painting attributed to J.-B.-J. Pater of this subject is in the Musée Cognac-Jay, Paris.[3] An eighteenth-century plaster mould comprising six pieces survives at the factory.[4] A terracotta maquette was in the Derys Collection in 1922.[5] The sculptors Mignan and Levaux were each paid 36 *livres*, the price of work on two and three examples respectively of the group in July 1765. In the following month Leclere received 18 *livres* 'Avoir remonté la terre du Baiser rendu' and 36 *livres* 'Avoir reparé le plâtre dudit'.[6]

The first 'sale' was an example presented to Monsieur Bertin at the end of 1765 and valued at 144 *livres*.[7] The group is still in production, but was not reissued after 1786 until late this century.[8]

The subject was also treated at Höchst, with its companion group, in two different versions,[9] and at Frankenthal.[10]

1. A hard-paste example from this museum is illustrated by Bourgeois, 1909, Vol. 2, fig. 23, where it is said to be after Boucher. However, no evidence has been found for this statement.
2. J. de La Fontaine, *Contes et Nouvelles en Vers*, Amsterdam, 1767 (this is a *contrefaçon* of the Paris, 1762, edition), p. 190.
3. E. Jonas, *Collections léguées à la Ville de Paris par Ernest Cognacq, Catalogue*, Paris, 1930, no. 90.
4. The writer is grateful to Tamara Préaud for information about the number of pieces making up this mould.
5. L. Réau, *Etienne-Maurice Falconet*, Paris, 1922, Tome II, p. 509.
6. MNS, Archives de Sèvres, F8, *Travaux extraordinaires*.
7. MNS, Archives de Sèvres, Vy 4, f. 68v.
8. The writer is grateful to Tamara Préaud for this information.
9. K. Röder, *Das Höchster Porzellan auf der Jahrtausend Ausstellung in Mainz, 1925*, Mainz, 1930, Tafel 25, a–d, nos. 147–50; the date 1755 given for these groups must be inaccurate.
10. E. Heuser, *Porzellan von Strassburg und Frankenthal*, Neustadt an der Haart, 1922, p. 277; 'Der gegebene Kuss, drei Figuren' and 'Der widergegebene Kuss, drei Figuren' are both listed, according to Heuser, in the 1798/99 *Formenverzeichnis* of the Frankenthal factory.

149 **Les Trois Contents**, 1765–73

H. 21.4 cm
Marks: cursive *B* incised on base at front (see cat. 146)
Reg. No. 1948,12–3,25

Soft-paste porcelain, hollow, formed by press-moulding. At the left is a kneeling youth, his left leg extended so that his foot slightly overhangs the oval base. Behind him and under his right arm are clumps of plants. With his right hand he holds to his lips the outstretched right hand of the central seated figure of a young girl. She is looking at the seated figure of a gallant on her left, who is kissing her left hand and holding her left arm with his right hand. The gallant wears a blouse tied at the waist under a jacket with pockets, and breeches tied at the knee. His hair is *en queue*. The girl wears a low-cut long robe under a long overdress with full half-sleeves trimmed with a bow. Her hair is elaborately dressed. The youth wears a broad-brimmed hat with ribbon trimmings, a shirt with full sleeves, jacket and breeches. Man's hat chipped and his right wrist repaired.

Provenance: Bequeathed by Sir B. Eckstein, Bt., 1948

Literature: King, 1951–2, p. 80

Charles, 1964, pl. 54

Wilfred J. Sainsbury, 'Sèvres Soft-Paste Biscuit Porcelain Part II', *Apollo*, Vol. LI, no. 304, June 1950, p. 168

Comparable Examples: Sèvres, Musée national de Céramique, inv. 20 050;15 391

Paris, G. Lefebvre, exh. International Ceramic Fair and Seminar Ltd., London, June 1987, mounted on ormolu base

Exh. *La porcelaine française*, 1929, no. 841

Germany, Munich, Bayerisches Nationalmuseum, illus. R. Schmidt, *Porcelain as an Art and a Mirror of Fashion*, London, 1932, fig. 201, cursive *B* incised, inv. Ker 4016; F.H. Hofmann, *Das Europaïsche Porzellan de Bayer. Nationalmuseums*, Munich, 1908, no. 1126

USA, New York, private collection, mounted on ormolu base, illus, exh. cat. *François Boucher, his Circle and Influence*, New York, Stair Sainty Mathiesen, September–November, 1987, no. 75

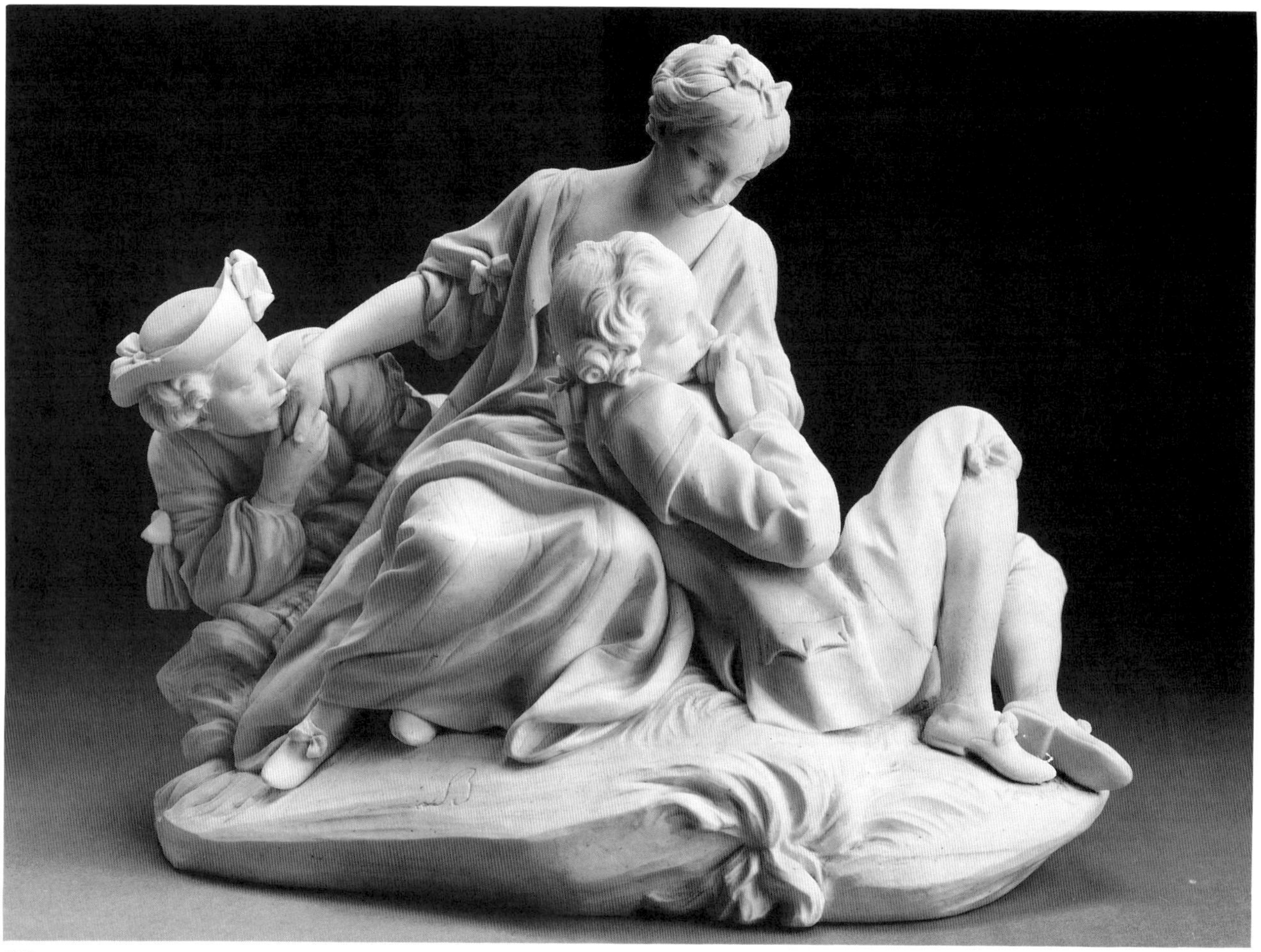

149

Modelled by Etienne-Maurice Falconet in 1765 and probably inspired by La Fontaine's *conte*, *Les deux amis* which was used by the playwright Taconet as the theme for *Les Rivaux heureux ou les Caprices d'Amour*, first performed in 1763. An eighteenth-century plaster mould comprising fourteen pieces is preserved at the factory, where there is also a plaster model.[1]

The sculptor Leclere received 36 *livres* 'avoir remonté la terre du groupe des trois contents' in October 1765[2] and Le Riche completed two groups at 72 *livres* each in the same month. Other sculptors worked on the group, for example, Levaux, Mignon and Mathias in 1765 (and 1767), 1766 and 1767 respectively. An example of the group was sold to the duc de Choiseul in December 1765 for 240 *livres*.[3] The high price reflects the work required, which has been estimated at 4,440 hours for current production. On account of the incised mark, the Museum group is thought to have been made between 1766–73, during the period when Jean-Jacques Bachelier was head of the sculpture workshop.[4]

Although this example was not made under the direct supervision of Falconet, it nonetheless exhibits his technical skill. The placing of the figures in relation to each other to give them balance and symmetry, their liveliness and movement, the particular attention paid to the modelling of the faces and, most of all, the unusual (not to say daring) poses make this group the work of a master. When viewed from the back – it is designed to be seen 'in the round' – the almost outrageous naturalness of the positioning of the limbs is striking.

1. Illustrated by Bourgeois, 1909, Vol. 2, fig. 24, where it is said to be after Boucher. However, no evidence has been found for this statement, and no print or drawing has yet been identified as the source of the porcelain group. The writer is grateful to Tamara Préaud for information about the number of pieces making up this mould.
2. MNS, Archives de Sèvres, F8, *Travaux extraordinaires*.
3. MNS, Archives de Sèvres, Vy 4, f. 57v.
4. For a detailed biography of Jean-Jacques Bachelier (1724–1806), who worked as a painter and then as artistic director at Vincennes and Sèvres from 1748/51 until 1793, see Savill, 1988, III, pp. 961–4; further details of his career as a flower,

fruit and still-life artist, with illustrations of his work, can be found in M. and F. Faré, *La vie silencieuse en France, La Nature Morte au XVIIIe siècle*, Fribourg, 1976, pp. 254–68, and a bust portrait of him by J.-B.-S. Chardin dated 1773 is illus. p. 255, fig. 402. Tamara Préaud informed the writer in correspondence of September 1991 that production of the group appears to have ceased after 1786 until it was reissued late in the twentieth century.

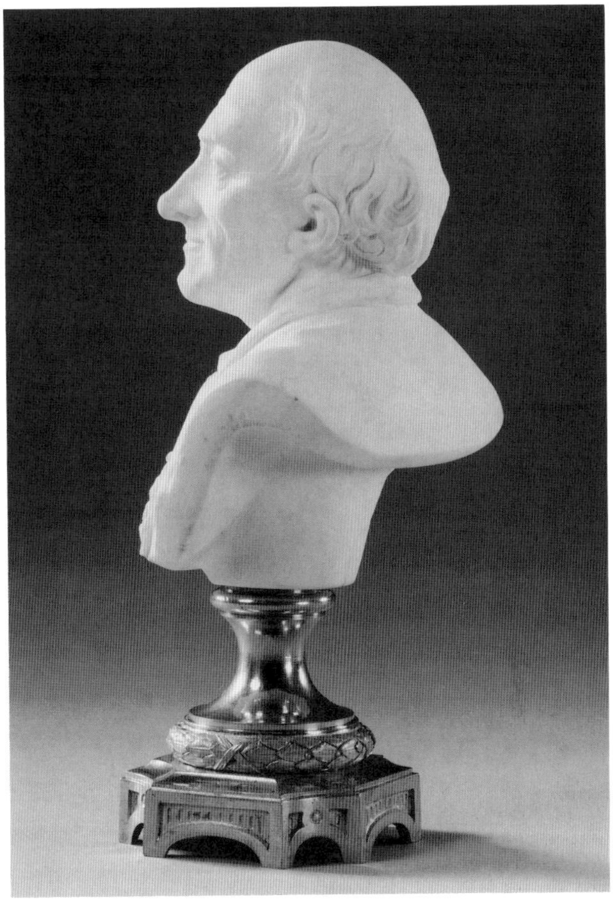

150

150 **Bust of François-Marie Arouet, called Voltaire (1694–1778),** 1767–73

H. *including gilt-bronze socle:*	19.6 cm
Marks:	cursive *B* incised behind left shoulder (see cat. 146)
Reg. No.	1988,7–1,2

Soft-paste biscuit porcelain, moulded. The sitter is shown without wig, his head turned slightly to left, dressed in a shirt with ruff carefully incised to simulate lace, the collar folded over an open jacket with three buttons, their covers incised with a criss-cross pattern. The features are carefully modelled and the eyeballs visible in the eye sockets. Firecracks on right jaw and, near the base at the back, numerous small brown iron stains, middle button poorly formed. Fixed to an ormolu stand in the neo-classical style cast in three sections (plinth, laurel leaf and berry wreath or taurus, socle) and attached by means of a threaded rod secured underneath by a nut.

Provenance: Purchased, 1988

Literature: Dawson *et al.*, 1990, p. 674, no. xi

Comparable Examples: None

The bust was produced as a pendant to Rameau (see cat. 151). At the factory it has become known as *Voltaire à Ferney*, a name not traced in the eighteenth-century records. The model has traditionally been associated with the sculptor Jean-Claude-François Rosset,[1] called Rosset du Pont (1703/6–86), who came to Paris in 1771; he is particularly known for his ivories of Voltaire, some of which were modelled at Ferney in association with his sons Jacques-Joseph and François-Marie. However, no ivory by Rosset corresponding with this porcelain example is known. A plaster or terracotta in the privately-owned Château de Voltaire, Ferney, bears some relationship,[2] but has not been examined by this writer. It is not thought to be by any member of the Rosset family.

The iconography of Voltaire is extremely complex[3] and it has so far proved impossible to trace the source of this bust.[4] The philosopher had a minor stroke in 1767, when he was seventy-three, and appeared to be quite frail. Despite this, he continued working harder than ever from his home at Ferney.[5]

The factory records show that a mould was inventoried in January 1768 and was therefore made in 1767. It was valued at 12 *livres*; no model is listed, and there is no mention of Rosset.[6] A plaster survives at the factory from which a cast was created in 1905.[7] Seven busts of Voltaire priced at 60 *livres* each were in the *magasin du blanc* in January 1768.[8] In January 1769, moulds of a bust of Voltaire and of Rameau were inventoried and valued at 15 *livres* each, the models being the same price.[9] On account of the incised mark, this example is thought to have been made between 1766 and 1773 during the period when Jean-Jacques Bachelier was head of the sculpture workshop.

The bust of Voltaire, like that of the companion piece, sold for 60 *livres*, and thirty busts were listed at that price in the inventory of 1 January 1770.[10] The dealers Poirier and Daguerre, Bachelier, Dulac and Sayde had four, two, three and one on consignment respectively in February 1773.[11] Five were in the *magasin de vente* the following January at 48 *livres*. In January 1778 five of Voltaire, five of Rousseau and four of Rameau in the *magasin de vente* were valued at

48 *livres* each. Eleven of Voltaire and Rameau, still at 48 *livres* each, were there in January 1780. It seems that relatively few were made, and even fewer have survived. Voltaire himself purchased two at 60 *livres* each on 31 April 1773.[12]

1. This is due to confusion created by E. Bourgeois, apparently with a soft-paste porcelain bust measuring 11.5 cm of which there is an example in the Musée national de Céramique, Sèvres, inv. 2033.
2. The author is grateful to Corinne Thépaut for this information.
3. See J. Montagu, 'Some lesser-known busts of Voltaire', *Connoisseur*, Vol. 167, no. 674, April 1968, pp. 225–9. A biscuit bust of Voltaire on a pedestal was modelled by F.E. Meyer for the Königliche Porzellanmanufaktur, Berlin, in 1774, see E. Köllman and M. Jarchow, *Berliner Porzellan*, Munich, 1987, Bildband, no. 170. For illustrations of other ceramic portraits of Voltaire see M. Newman, 'Voltaire and Rousseau', *Antique Dealer and Collectors' Guide*, Vol. 45, no. 3, October 1991, pp. 22–7.
4. The author is grateful to Malcolm Baker, Dr Christian Theuerkauff, the late Sir Francis Watson and Dr Jennifer Montagu all of whom have assisted her in trying to trace the genesis of this image of Voltaire. In August 1992 Bernard Dragesco kindly drew to the author's attention a passage in Bourgeois, 1909, I, pp. 91–2, in which Caffiéri is credited as its author. His lost bust of the poet, once in the collections of the *Académie*, can be seen in an engraving of Voltaire's coronation by the actors of the Comédie Française, 1778.
5. See T. Besterman, *Voltaire*, Oxford, 2nd edn., 1976. The impressions of the traveller and zoologist Thomas Pennant, who saw Voltaire in May 1765, are quoted pp. 501–2, from *Tour on the Continent*, London, 1765, ed. Sir G.R. de Beer, London, 1948.
6. MNS, Archives de Sèvres, I 7.
7. Bourgeois, and Lechevallier-Chevignard, n.d. (1913), pl. 40, no. 617. The cast, belonging to the Musée national de Céramique, Sèvres, was illustrated by S. Taylor, 'Artists and *Philosophes* as mirrored by Sèvres and Wedgwood', *The Artist and the Writer in France, Essays in Honour of Jean Seznec*, ed. F. Haskell, A. Levi, R. Shackleton, Oxford, 1974, fig. 10.
8. MNS, Archives de Sèvres, I 7.
9. *Ibid.*
10. *Ibid.*
11. *Loc. cit.*, I 8.
12. *Loc. cit.*, Vy 5, f. 66.

151 **Bust of Jean-Philippe Rameau (1683–1764)**, 1768–73

H. *including socle:*	20.4 cm
Marks:	cursive *B* incised below left shoulder (see cat. 146)
Reg. no.	1988,7–1,1

Soft-paste biscuit porcelain, moulded. The sitter is shown full-face in wig and wearing a neckcloth. His jacket, which has two incised buttonholes on the left and two buttons on the right carefully incised with a criss-cross pattern, is open to display the ruff of the shirt below. The features are carefully modelled and the eyeballs visible in the eye sockets. Small firecracks under left shoulder and on left side of wig. Fitted to an ormolu stand in the neo-classical style cast in three sections (plinth, laurel leaf and berry wreath or taurus, socle) and attached by means of a threaded rod secured underneath by a nut.

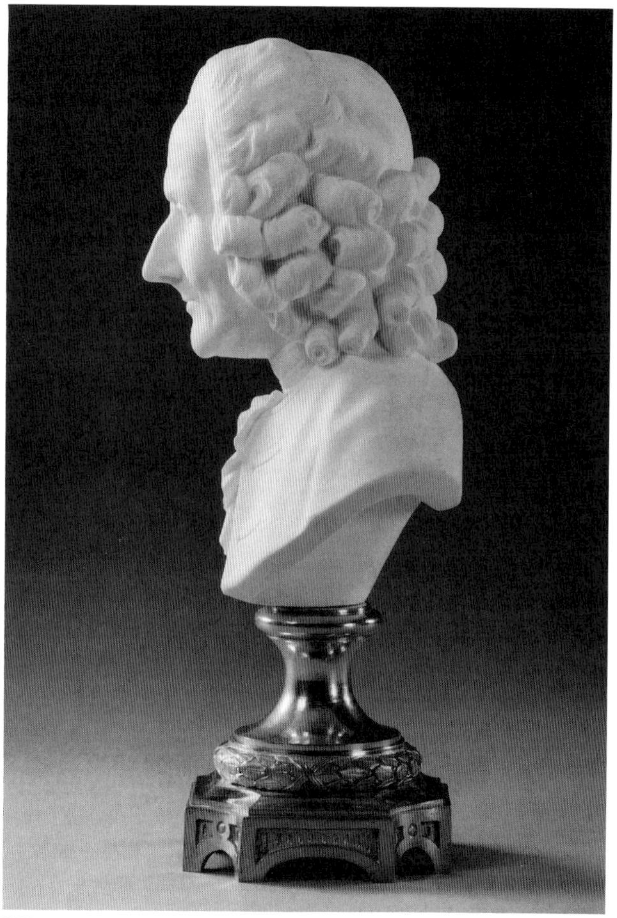

151

Provenance: Purchased, 1988

Literature: See cat. 150

Comparable Examples: None

The bust was produced as a pendant to Voltaire (see cat. 150). It is based on a marble bust (now lost) by Jean-Jacques Caffiéri (1725–92) engraved by A. de Saint-Aubin in 1762.[1] The marble apparently perished in a fire at the 'ancienne salle de L'Opéra' at the Palais-Royal, where it was placed by the King after being exhibited at the *Salon* of 1771. A plaster or terracotta was first shown at the *Salon* of 1761. A plaster presented by Caffiéri himself in 1787–8 was in the Bibliothèque Sainte-Geneviève in 1921;[2] the same plaster was exhibited at the Diderot exhibition in Paris, 1985.[3]

Diderot commented in the *Salon* of 1761, 'Le buste de Rameau est frappant. On l'a fait froid, maigre et sec comme il est; et on a très bien attrapé sa finesse affectée et son sourire précieux'. In 1771 the critic wrote of the marble busts of Quinault, Lully and

Rameau, 'Ces trois bustes ont une vérité admirable et sont d'un ciseau savant; ils rendront Caffieri participant de leur immortalité'.

It is not surprising that the Sèvres factory issued the busts of Voltaire and Rameau as a pair: Chabanon thought Rameau more like a ghost than a man and remarked on his resemblance to Voltaire.[4] An engraving of Rameau and Voltaire by G. de Tersan dated 1765 shows them as thin, stooping old men in conversation.[5] Piron wrote of Rameau, 'Je le voyais venir à l'aide de ma lorgnette. Ce n'était plus qu'un long tuyau d'orgue en l'absence du souffleur'.[6] He was cruelly portrayed by Diderot in *Le Neveu de Rameau*, and Collé, who had known him for several decades, wrote of him in his *Journal* at his death, 'C'était . . . le mortel le plus impoli, le plus grossier et le plus insociable de son temps'.[7] Modern assessments of his keyboard, sacred and dramatic music, and more importantly of his theoretical writings, stress his contributions to the development of harmonic thinking in Western music. D'Alembert rewrote Rameau's *Génération harmonique & Démonstration du principe de l'harmonie* as the *Eléments de musique théorique et pratique selon les principes de M. Rameau* in 1752, but passed from approval to disapproval of Rameau. In 1745 he was created *Compositeur du cabinet du roy*; four months before his death he was ennobled.[8]

The relationship of Caffiéri to the royal porcelain factory was traced by Lechevallier-Chevignard in 1908.[9] According to this writer, the sculptor was responsible for making terracottas of Corneille and Molière for the factory. In 1766 he made a determined effort to replace Falconet as *sculpteur attitré* when the latter went to Russia. A *mémoire* dated 16 January 1767 reads '. . . Le Sieur Caffiéry s'occupe depuis longtemps des ouvrages du genre de la Manuf, et on peut faire voir à Monseigneur des modèles magnifiques d'un service projetté de faire exécuter à la Chine, et dont on a cru devoir empêcher l'envoy. On ne croit pas qu'il y ait rien de plus beau a Seve que ces modèles et dont M peut informer auprès de M. Beaudoin'.

In the hand of Courteille above the *mémoire* is inscribed *Le Roy ne nommera pas encore à cette place.* A renewed attempt in November 1767, with the support of Condé, is marked *La place ne sera pas donnée. C'est Monsieur Bachelier qui continue les fonctions et dirige les sculpteurs.*

No record has been found of Caffiéri's direct involvement with the creation of this bust, the first example of which was sold to the dealer Poirier for 60 *livres* at the end of 1768.[10] It was apparently modelled later than the bust of Voltaire as the mould appears only in the 1769 inventory of the work of 1768 when it was valued at 15 *livres*, with the models at the same price. An eighteenth-century mould and a plaster model measuring 21.5 cm are preserved at the factory. The inventory of biscuit sculpture stock in January 1770 lists thirty 'Bustes de Voltaire, Rameau &c' at 60 *livres* each. On the evidence of both the stock lists and sales records, it is doubtful that more were ever made, and by January 1774 the price seems to have been reduced from 60 to 48 *livres*. The dealers Poirer and Daguerre, Bachelier, Dulac, and Sayde all had examples in 1773, valued at 60 *livres*, but only four, two, three and one (of Voltaire), respectively. On account of the incised mark, this example is thought to have been made between 1768 and 1773 during the period when Jean-Jacques Bachelier was head of the sculpture workshop.

The ormolu plinth is considered to be of early nineteenth-century date.[11]

1. Department of Prints and Drawings, BM, reg. no. 1917,12–8,3910 dated 1762 and 1890,4–15,145. The bust was also engraved by C.-P. Landon for his *Galerie historique des hommes les plus célèbres*, Paris, 1805–9. Another portrait of Rameau by Restout engraved by Benoist in the Cabinet des Estampes, Bibliothèque Nationale, Paris, is similar, see L. de la Laurencie, *Rameau*, Paris, n.d. (1908), opp. p. 9.
2. See A. Boinet, 'Les bustes de Caffiéri de la Bibliothèque Sainte-Geneviève', *Gazette des Beaux Arts*, 5e période, Vol. III (1921), pp. 133–46. The Musée de Versailles has a marble copy of the Sainte-Geneviève bust executed in 1838 by J.-P.-V. Huguenin, see E. Soulié, *Notice des peintures et sculptures composant le Musée Impérial de Versailles*, Versailles, 1854, no. 806. Rameau's inventory after his death lists, besides an oil portrait, two engravings and a plaster bust, presumably the Caffiéri portrait, see L. de la Laurencie, 'Quelques documents sur Jean-Philippe Rameau et sa famille', *Mercure et S.I.M.*, 15 juin 1907, p. 583. Rameau also owned '6 pièces tant de porcelaine que de terre blanche', which were in his wife's room, as was 'un seau de fayance', *ibid.*, pp. 583–4. H. Imbert, 'Un portrait de Rameau', *Jean-Philippe Rameau (1683–1764) Oeuvres Complètes* Tome II, Paris, 1896, repr. New York, 1968, pp. vii–xv, discusses a portrait then thought to be by Chardin; with regard to the Caffiéri bust (see pp. ix–xi) he is now known to be incorrect, he omits this Sèvres bust.
3. Paris, 'Diderot & l'Art de Boucher à David', Paris, Hôtel de la Monnaie, October 1984–January 1985, no. 127.
4. Michel-Paul-Gui de Chabanon (1730–92) a violinist, was the author of *Eloge sur M. Rameau*, published in Paris in 1764. The writer has not seen this work, the quotation is taken from *The New Grove*, Vol. 15, 1980, p.572.
5. La Laurencie, 1908, opp. p. 16.
6. Alexis Piron (1689–1773) was, like Rameau, from Dijon; the quotation is taken from *The New Grove*.
7. The description of his unpleasant personality is quite devastating, see La Laurencie, 1907, pp. 571–2, quoting C. Collé, *Journal et Mémoires*, Vol. II, p. 375; however, C. Girdle-

stone in a modern assessment *Jean-Philippe Rameau: His Life and Work*, London, 1957, rev. ed. 1969, gives a more positive view of Rameau's personality.
8. For biographical information on Rameau, see *The New Grove*, Vol. 15, 1980, pp. 554–73, and P. Berthier, *Réflexions sur l'art et la vie de Jean-Philippe Rameau (1683–1764)*, Paris, 1957.
9. G. Lechevallier-Chevignard, 'Jean-Jacques Caffiéri (1766–1767)', *Archives de l'Art Français*, nouvelle période, Tome II, 1er fascicule, 1908, pp. 129–33.
10. MNS, Archives de Sèvres, Vy 4, f. 166.
11. The author is grateful to Martin Chapman for examining the ormolu.

152 **Figure of Louis XV** (reigned 1715–74) **as a Warrior**, *c.* 1770–73

H. 24.6 cm
Marks: cursive *B* incised on top of base (see cat. 146)
Reg. No. 1992,1–6,1

Soft-paste biscuit porcelain, full-length figure on a circular base wearing a laurel crown, his right arm outstretched, his left hand resting on his sword pommel (restored). He is dressed in a cuirass with pteryges and a long cloak which falls to the ground at the back. His sandals are fastened with leather thongs around the shins. To his left is a truncated fluted column resting on a plinth. The right arm is restored from the original mould at the factory.[1]

Provenance: Purchased, 1991

Literature: Unpublished

Comparable Examples: Paris, Louvre Museum, inv. OA 10976[2]

Sèvres, Musée national de Céramique, inv. MNC 21866[3]

Paris, Hôtel Drouot, Chavagnac Collection sale, 19–21 June 1911, Lot 283 (illus.)

USA, Hartford, Conn., Wadsworth Atheneum, inv. 1917,958[4]

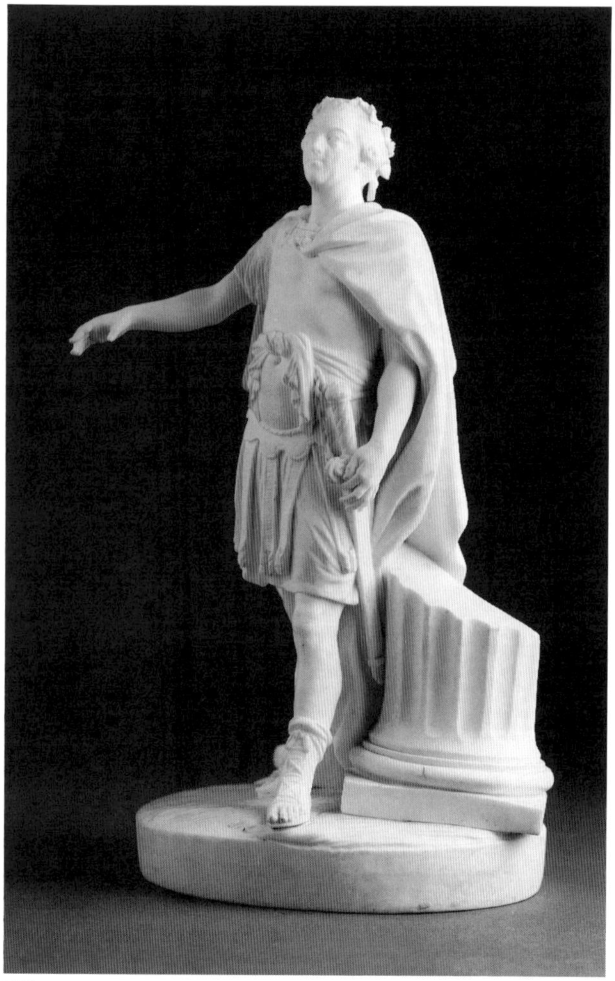

152

The genesis of this figure at Sèvres has been fully discussed by Pierre Ennès.[5] It is a reduction of a bronze statue by Jean-Baptiste Pigalle (1715–85) forming part of a monument in the Place Royale, Reims, which was inaugurated on 26 August 1765.[6] Pigalle was evidently proud of this monument since it appears in the background of a pastel portrait of the sculptor by M.-S. Roslin exhibited in the 1771 *Salon*.[7] A terracotta was supplied to the factory in 1770 by the sculptor who was paid 600 *livres*.[8]

The porcelain figure was destined for an extensive table-centre in biscuit porcelain, specially designed for a dinner given on 16 May 1770 in the Opera House at Versailles to celebrate the marriage of the Dauphin (the future King Louis XVI) and Marie-Antoinette. The table-centre, which has not survived, has been reconstructed by Pierre Ennès. It consisted of a colonnade, figures of children symbolising the Seasons, groups of children beside a column, fountains supported by figures of Atlas (probably based on the fountain by Piranesi in the Villa Albani), several fountains supported by the Three Graces and a series of figures of classical deities. In the centre stood Pigalle's figure of the King. The complete table-decoration cost 11,884 *livres*.[9]

Several sculptors are recorded as having worked on the production of figures of Louis XV, including Perrotin, Mignan, Le Vaux and Mathias.[10] This example was made under the supervision of Jean-Jacques Bachelier (1724–1806), who was head of the sculpture workshop between 1766 and 1773. It is his mark which is found on this piece.

There has been some discussion as to whether more than one size of figure was made.[11] Comparing the measurements of the Wadsworth Atheneum (H. 20.5 cm) and British Museum examples, it does indeed appear that this was so. This would explain the entry in the Stock List of 1 January 1774, discovered by Ennès, which refers to 'one large figure of the King and its base', and the differences in the prices charged. The figure cost 72 *livres* without base in 1770, but in 1778 it was priced at 96 *livres*.[12] Comparison of photographs of the known examples reveals minor differences of detail: the Chavagnac figure has leather fringing under the left arm, for instance, and the sword pommel on the Louvre example differs, possibly because it has been restored.

A somewhat crudely modelled standing figure of Louis xv in the guise of a warrior but without the laurel wreath and the column, standing by a plumed helmet resting on top of a globe adorned with fleurs-de-lys in relief was illustrated by Darblay[13] and has been reproduced by Duchon.[14] Its present whereabouts are unknown, and no others have been discovered. It was presumably made at Mennecy in imitation of the Sèvres model. A glazed and painted Niderviller example is in the Museum of Fine Arts, Boston.[15] An even more rustic Louis xv was made in tin-glazed earthenware at Lunéville.[16]

1. According to the vendors.
2. See Musée du Louvre, 1985, pp. 149–51.
3. See Paris, Hôtel de la Monnaie, 1974, *Louis xv, un moment de perfection de l'art français*, no. 540.
4. Roth (ed.), 1987, no. 70 (entry by G. de Bellaigue) and L. H. Roth and C. Le Corbeiller, *French Eighteenth-Century Porcelain in the Wadsworth Atheneum: the J. Pierpont Morgan Collection*, no. 202. Wadsworth Atheneum, Connecticut, 2000.
5. P. Ennès, 'Le surtout de mariage en porcelaine de Sèvres du Dauphin, 1769–1770', *Revue de l'Art*, 1987, pp. 63–73.
6. The fullest and most-up-to-date study of this sculptor is by J.-R. Gaborit, *Jean-Baptiste Pigalle 1714–1785, Sculptures du Musée du Louvre*, Paris, 1985; for the Reims monument, see pp. 12–14, p. 27.
7. Musée du Louvre, 1985, p. 151, fig. 85b.
8. MNS, Archives de Sèvres, I 8, inventory of 1 January 1771.
9. Roth (ed.), 1987, p. 182.
10. Musée du Louvre, 1985, p. 149.
11. *Ibid.*, pp. 149–50.
12. *Ibid.*, p. 149.
13. Darblay, 1901, pl. xxxvii.
14. Duchon, 1988, p. 73.
15. Munger *et al.*, 1992, no. 188.
16. Exh. Nancy and Atlanta, 1990, no. 126, tin-glazed earthenware painted in colours, h. 28.6 cm.

153 **Pedestal**, *c.* 1788

See colour plate 25

H.	24 cm
D.	21.4 cm
Marks:	[?]small incised *4* on one relief (perhaps a repairer's mark)
Reg. No.	1909,12–1,8

Hard-paste biscuit porcelain, lathe-turned at foot and neck, the central area washed pale blue and decorated with applied reliefs in white biscuit porcelain representing *Diana Hunting* and *Diana and Actaeon*. Chips to rim, damage to one arm and a thumb.

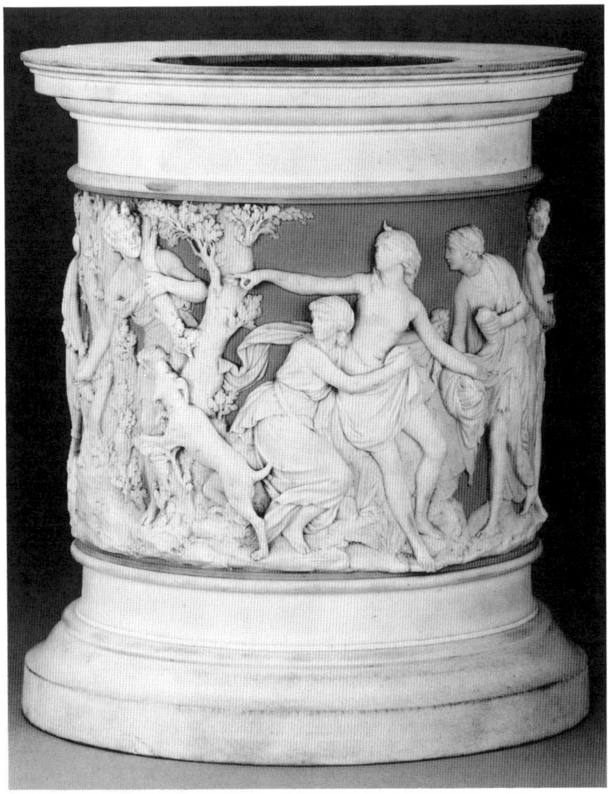

153

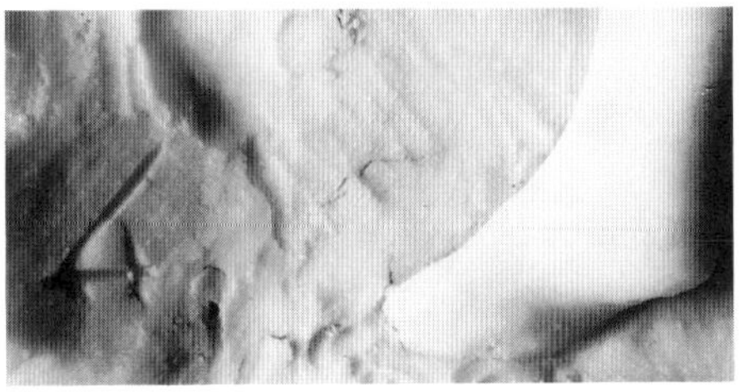

153 *mark*

Provenance: Presented by Mr and Mrs I. Falcke, 1909; formerly in the possession of a Mr Philips, inscribed in pencil on the base *Presented to me by Philips Esqr*

Literature: Dawson, 1982, pp. 94–102, pl. v and fig. 5

Comparable Examples: Germany, G. Hirth, see *Deutsch Tanagra, Porzellan-Figuren des Achzehnten Jahrhunderts*, Munich and Leipzig, 1898, no. 711, illus, supporting biscuit group of Louis XVI's children with dog and hare.

London, Victoria and Albert Museum, inv. 395–74, reliefs of *The Toilet of Venus* and *Diana Bathing*

This may be the 'Piédestal bas relief' sold to an unspecified buyer for 240 *livres* at Versailles on 31 December 1785.[1] Alternatively, it could be the 'socle bas relief' sold for 360 *livres* to the King between 21 December 1787 and 4 January 1788 as a support for the figure of Hebe.[2] Or it may be one of two 'grand [*sic*] pieds d'autel a fond bleu a bas relief' for which the thrower Louis Petion[3] was paid 48 *livres* in 1788.[4] He worked on seven others in the same year, each earning him 24 *livres*. The nature of the *autel* has not yet been determined. Whilst the blue ground is not specified for the pedestal and socle, the factory records show that blue grounds were in production in the 1770s and blue paste in the following decade. A further mention should be made of two 'vases bas relief Pate bleu [*sic*]' which were fired on 8 July 1786.[5]

Coloured grounds were being used for portraits at Sèvres as early as 1773, on the evidence of the factory records[6] and of Thomas Bentley's diary of three years later.[7] Blue grounds were also used for biscuit porcelain plaques which were intended for mounting in furniture, a practice already established in the mid-1780s.[8] The well-known candelabrum by Thomire commemorating American Independence is mounted on the socle with three small curved biscuit blue-ground porcelain plaques with subjects in relief relating to the War of Independence.[9]

A circular table-top with reliefs of 'Telemaque recounting his adventures to Calypso' was shown at Versailles at the end of 1787 to general approbation. On 14 February 1788 it was purchased by the comte de Fernan Nunès, Spanish ambassador to the Court of France, for Charles III, of Spain.[10] Another table with a similar top with the addition of several scenes was a gift to the comte de Livourne, King of Etruria, from the French Minister of the Interior in 1792.[11] A further table mounted with blue-ground biscuit plaques with classical subjects was in the workshop of Thomire on 19 Prairial, l'an XIII (8 June 1805); it is now in the Bayerisches Nationalmuseum, Munich.[12]

A number of blue and white biscuit porcelain figures have been traced, most dating from the second decade of the nineteenth century.[13] A reference in the factory records to a 'Mars pâte bleu et blanche' sold to the Spanish Ambassador for 72 *livres* in early 1788 shows, however, that they were in production in the 1780s.[14] Biscuit groups of *The Toilet of Venus* and *Diana Bathing* are known.[15] As their bases measure 22 cm and 20.6 cm respectively, it is possible that they could have fitted on top of a pedestal of this kind, and their height of 36 cm would have been in proportion. Both groups were modelled by Boizot in 1780.[16]

Classical themes enjoyed great popularity as subjects for reliefs during the 1780s. Curved white biscuit porcelain plaques of *Diana Hunting* and *Diana Bathing* can be found on a pair of monumental Vases Medicis dated 1784, the work of Boizot, Duplessis and Thomire, delivered for the Cabinet Intérieur du Roi at Versailles and now in the Louvre.[17] Another vase with a curved biscuit plaque of *Diana Hunting* from the Palace of Saint-Cloud is datable to a year earlier.[18] In view of the royal origins of the vases mentioned above, there is a possibility that the pedestals too were destined for the King.

The plaques *Diane donnant le Prix* and *Diane Surprise au bain* were also made in flat versions; these originally cost 56 *livres* and were increased by 140 *livres* on 1 November 1787.[19] The source of the relief scenes is unknown, except for the Madrid table, where the Telemaque subject has been ascribed to Jean Raoux.[20]

1. MNS, Archives de Sèvres, Vy 10, f. 8v.
2. MNS, Archives de Sèvres, Vy 10, f. 199.
3. Louis Petion joined the factory in 1770 as a labourer (*manoeuvre*), becoming a repairer two years later. He worked both as a repairer and thrower in the hard-paste *atelier* from 1773 until 1789, leaving the factory in that year. He returned in 1794, becoming chief of the hard-paste kilns. He received a pension in 1818 and died four years later. This information is taken from Dauterman, 1986, p. 119. In 1788 his monthly salary as a thrower of the first class was 75 *livres*.
4. MNS, Archives de Sèvres, Va'11 (4), (5), *Relevé des travaux fait dans l'attelier de porcelaine dure dans le courent* [sic] *de l'année 1788*.
5. MNS, Archives de Sèvres, Vc'3, *Registre de l'enfournement et défournement des pièces en couverte pâte dure*.
6. MNS, Archives de Sèvres, I 8, *Inventaire général des porcelaines trouvées dans la Manufacture de Porcelaine de Roy, au premier janvier 1774*. These pieces must have been made in the previous year.
7. T. Bentley, *Journal of a Visit to Paris 1776*, University of Sussex, 1977, p. 75.
8. For examples see Dawson, 1982, pp. 98–100.
9. Discussed by C. Baulez, 'Notes sur quelques meubles et objets d'art des appartements intérieurs de Louis XVI et de Marie-Antoinette', *La Revue du Louvre*, 5/6, 1978, pp. 359–73, see pp. 360–1, for the candelabrum.
10. D. Guillemé-Brulon, 'Rare Biscuit de Sèvres façon Wedgwood au Palais Royal de Madrid', *Cahiers*, no. 40, 1968, pp. 252–6.
11. D.H. Cohen, 'Four Tables-Guéridons by Sèvres', *Antologia di Belle Arti*, No. 13/14, December 1980, pp. 3–6, figs. 7, 8.
12. *Ibid.*, pp. 2–3, figs 4, 3.
13. See Dawson, 1982, pp. 97–8.
14. MNS, Archives de Sèvres, Vy 10, f. 222 (undated, probably 21 January 1788).
15. Philadelphia Museum of Art, Pennsylvania, inv. 45–49–1 and 45–49–2.
16. Bourgeois and Lechevallier-Chevignard, 1913, pl. 36, nos. 582, 187 (wrongly numbered on plate as 87).
17. Inv. OA 6614–15.
18. Inv. 6627, see C. Dreyfus, *Catalogue sommaire du mobilier et des objets d'art du XVIIe et du XVIIIe siècle*, no. 459, pl. LXI.
19. MNS, Archives de Sèvres, Y 19, f. 52, An example of 'Diana Hunting', measuring 30.1 cm by 15.9 cm, is thought to have been bought by Colonel T.H. Perkins in Paris in 1792, Boston, Museum of Fine Arts, inv. 52.1470.
20. Guillemé-Brulon, *op. cit.*, p. 254.

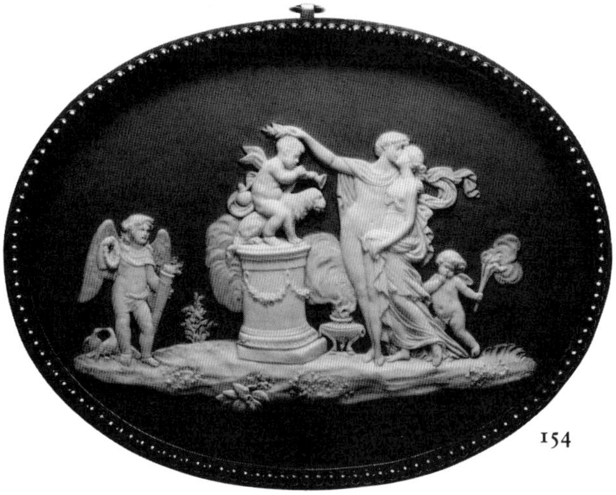

154

154 **Plaque**, probably *c.* 1786

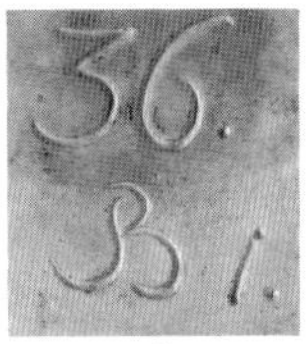

154 *mark*

L. 14.8 cm
Marks: *36. Bi.* incised on reverse
Reg. No. 1909,12–1,218

Hard-paste biscuit porcelain, the ground washed with a pale blue slip. The applied relief in white porcelain represents a couple embracing by a brazier next to an altar on which is a cupid with a dog, accompanied by a cupid on either side, each with an emblem of love; to the left is a pair of billing doves. Mounted in a gilt metal frame.

Provenance: Presented by Mr and Mrs I. Falcke, 1909

Literature: Dawson, 1982, pp. 94–102, fig. 6

Comparable Examples: No unmounted examples are known; for mounted plaques, see discussion

Other plaques showing the same subject, slightly differently interpreted, are incorporated in furniture. There is a rectangular blue-ground biscuit plaque in Marie-Antoinette's jewel cabinet made by J.F. Schwerdfeger in 1787, and a circular version on a *secrétaire* stamped by Weisweiler which was in Bath in 1981 and is closely paralleled by another made for Marie-Antoinette in Schönbrunn Palace, Vienna. A further circular plaque was mounted in a *guéridon* table which belonged to Frank Partridge of London.[1]

The plaque doubtless intended for mounting, is attributed to the Sèvres factory on the grounds of its similarity to the mounted plaques mentioned. Those on furniture made for Marie-Antoinette must have originated at the royal factory. The factory records are lamentably imprecise in describing such plaques.

The sentimental theme corresponds with similar, but not identical, reliefs produced in jasper by Josiah Wedgwood at his Etruria (Staffordshire) factory.

1. Dawson, 1982, p. 100.

155 **Medallion of King Henri IV (1553–1610)**, 1766–*c.* 1782

D. 11 cm
Marks: none
Reg. No. 1992,4–2,1

Soft-paste porcelain, moulded with a bust portrait of Henri IV in armour to right, bearded, his curly hair bound by a laurel wreath. He wears the Order of Saint-Louis suspended from a ribbon around his neck. Around the edge is an inscription in relief *HENRICVS. IIII.D.G.FRANCORVM.ET.NAVARAE. REX* (Henri IV, by the grace of God King of the French and of Navarre). The truncation is incised *1606* and below it is the signature in relief *G.DVPRE.*

Provenance: Unknown, purchased, 1992

Literature: Unpublished

Comparable Examples: None

This medallion is based on a medal by Guillaume Dupré of 1606, of which a seventeenth or eighteenth century aftercast is in the Department of Coins and Medals.[1]

The model was probably first put into production at Sèvres in 1766. No models or moulds survive at the factory. In December a medallion of Henri IV, described as defective, was sold at Versailles for 18 *livres*, together with ten others priced at 24 *livres* each,[2] a rather high price for a medallion of this size, but justified perhaps on the grounds of the quality of the workmanship. The inventory of January 1774 lists 26 valued at 12 *livres* each, as well as a total of 163 classed as 'mauvais rebut' (reject quality) in four sizes. The first size was valued at 7 *livres* 10 *sous*. As examples have not yet been traced, the dimensions of the various sizes are unknown. The Museum example may be the first or (perhaps more likely) second size.

Medallions of Sully (see cat. 156) and Henri IV were nearly always made and sold together. As early as 1768 they are recorded together in the *Etat des pièces de porcelaine que différents Peintres Doreurs et Tourneurs ont travaillés hors de la Manufacture pendant l'année 1768, avec les prix aux quels chaque pièce leur est payée*, when Philippine was paid 8 *sous* each for a total of 60 medallions (size unspecified) of the King and his minister.[3] On 18 July 1773 '2 médaillons d'henry IV et Sully' were sold at 30 *livres* to Messieurs Serrant et Bruneau,[4] presumably dealers, whose identity is awaiting investigation. Single examples of the medallion of Henri IV continued to be sold, however, such as the one which went to an unnamed buyer for cash on 15 July 1773.[5] Another described as 'bon biscuit' was sold for cash on 20 July 1773.[6]

In his article on the visit of the Grand Duke Paul

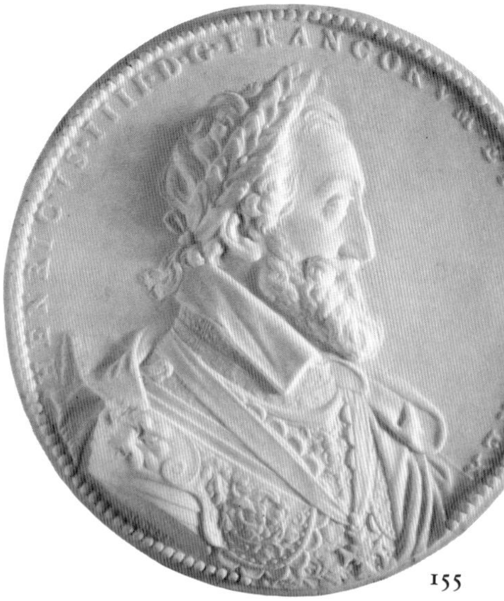

155

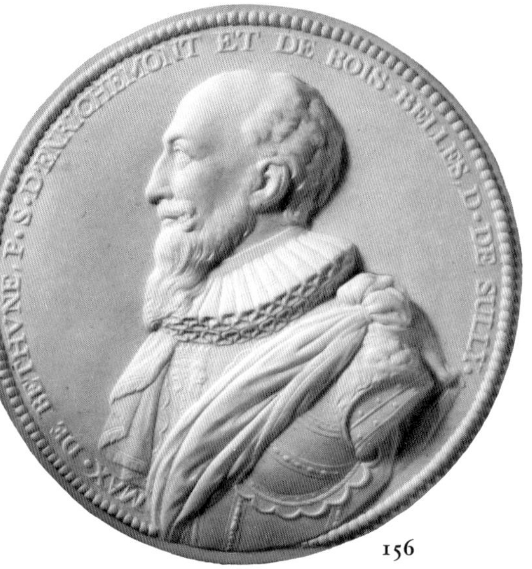

156

of Russia and his wife (who travelled under the names of the comte and comtesse du Nord) to the Sèvres factory in May 1782, Pierre Ennès drew attention to the Grand Duke's admiration for Henri IV and Sully. Along with a magnificent jewelled toilet-service and a pair of jewelled vases which were presented to the royal pair were various medallions of members of the French royal family. These included four large medallions of Henri IV, valued at 12 *livres* each and four small ones at 3 *livres* each. In addition the royal pair were presented with a *creux*, or mould valued at 6 *livres*, perhaps, as Ennès suggests, so that further examples could be made in St Petersburg porcelain.[7]

1. See M. Jones, *A Catalogue of French Medals in the British Museum*, London, 1988, Vol. 2, no. 20
2. MNS, Archives de Sèvres, Vy 4, f. 90. The author is grateful to Tamara Préaud for this and other archival information.
3. The author is indebted to John Whitehead for this information.
4. MNS, Archives de Sèvres, Vy 5, f. 76.
5. *Ibid.*, f. 83.
6. *Ibid.*, f. 84v.
7. P. Ennès, 'The visit of the Comte and Comtesse du Nord to the Sèvres Manufactory', *Apollo*, Vol. CXXIX, no. 325, March 1989, pp. 150–6 and pp. 221–2.

156 **Medallion of Maximilien de Béthune, Duc de Sully (1559–1641),** *c.* 1773–*c.* 1782

D. 10.8 cm
Marks: none
Reg. No. 1989,7–7,1

Soft-paste biscuit porcelain, moulded with a bust portrait of Sully to left with a high domed forehead, mostly bald except for short curly hair at the back, beard and moustache, wearing a ruff and cuirass with drapery tied over his left shoulder. On his chest is a crowned head facing both ways. Around the edge is an inscription in relief *MAX. DE BETHUNE, P.S. D'ENRICHEMONT ET BOIS-BELLES, D.DE SULLY.* (Maximilien de Béthune, Sovereign Prince of Enrichemont and Boisbelles, Duke of Sully). Below the truncation is a trace of a (?) medallist's signature. Enclosing the portrait and inscription is a beaded border. The reverse is flat except for a slight imperfection in the paste. Two small holes for suspension, one at the top on the reverse, one at the top on the edge, have been filled. Perfect.

Provenance: Purchased, 1989

Literature: Unpublished

Comparable Examples: None

Medallions of Sully, who became Secretary of State in 1594, *Surintendant des finances* in 1598, *grand maître de l'artillerie* in 1599, was created a Duke in 1606 and became Marshal of France in 1634, are first recorded at Sèvres in 1773. The first sale was of a reject quality example on 18 July 1773. An unknown buyer paid 30 *livres* for Sully with Henri IV.[1] The two medallions were again listed in conjunction with each other in the inventory of porcelain in the *magasin de vente* dated 1 January 1774.[2] Seventeen medallions of Sully were valued at 12 *livres* each, the same price as twenty-six of Henri IV. A mixed group of 31 medallions of the two men was valued at only 9 *livres* in January 1778, and so may have been of reject quality.[3] Medallions of both the King and his minister were among the gifts of porcelain presented to the Grand Duke of Russia and his wife in May 1782 (see cat. 155). Four 'Grands médaillons de Sully' were on this occasion valued at 48 *livres*.

A plaster model of the medallion measuring 12.5 cm in diameter, inventoried in 1803, exists at the factory.[4]

The medallion may be after a medal but the source

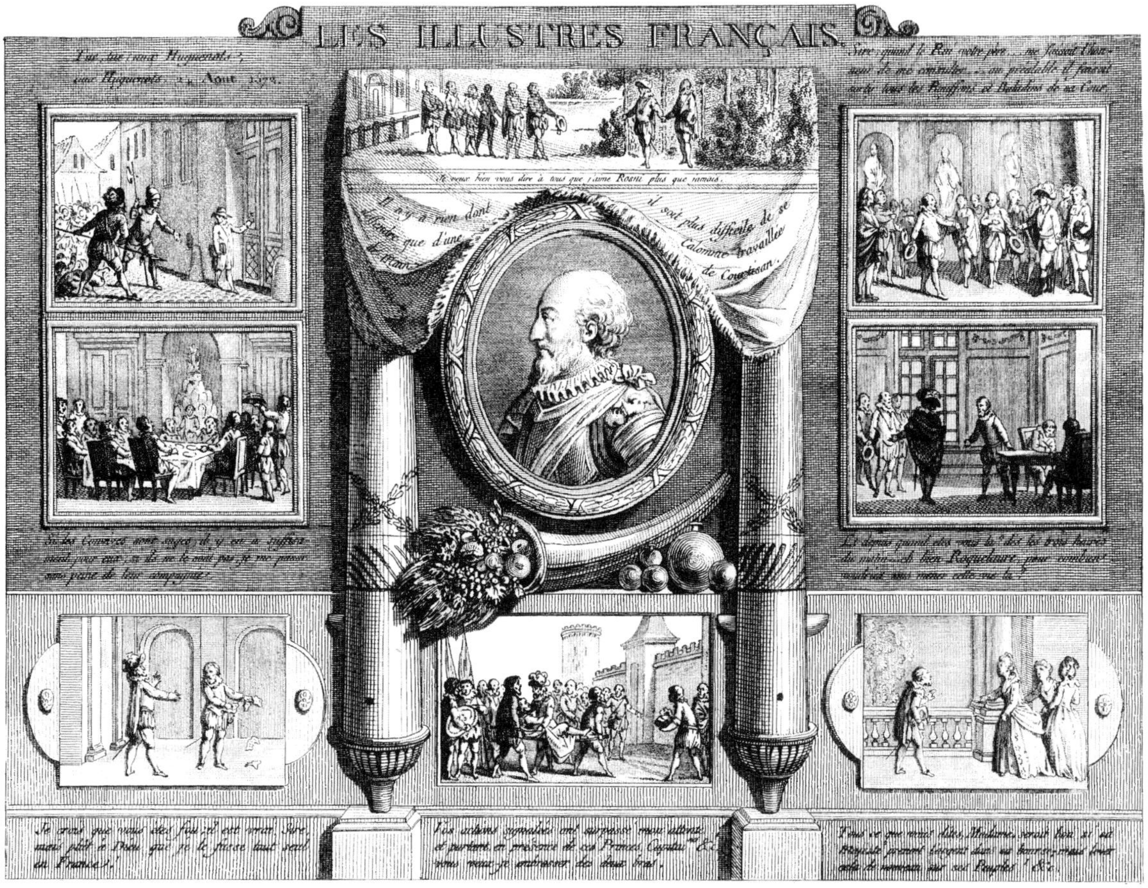

Fig 156a Detail of engraving by N. Ponce

has not yet been identified.[5] An engraving by N. Ponce (1746–1831) after C.P. Marillier (1740–1808) shows a similar but not identical bust portrait in an oval 'medallion' with the legend *A. Paris chez l'auteur, Grav.*^{eur} *de M.*^{gr} *Comte d'Artois, rue S.*^{te} *Hyacinthe N. 19.*[6] (See fig. 156a).

Other images of Sully were manufactured at Sèvres. They include a full-length figure for which Louis-Philippe Mouchy (1734–1801), *sculpteur du roi*, received 1,000 *livres* for a terracotta model on 1 February 1785.[7] Production was on a small scale, as the records of firing reveal, and was mostly confined to the years 1787–9[8] and 1806–11.[9] Although an example was purchased for 480 *livres* by Count d'Orsay on 21 January 1784,[10] few sales were made, and two figures were presented as gifts in 1806 and 1810, on the latter occasion to the King of Bavaria.[11]

Busts of Sully, for which no models, moulds or known porcelain examples survive, were recorded in the kiln in December 1789, February 1790 (these were of the third size) and September 1812.[12]

For a similar but not identical medallion made by Brancas-Lauraguais, see cat. 221.

Portrait medallions of Sully in blue jasper, one very similar to the Sèvres model, were issued by Josiah Wedgwood.[13] A cast glass cameo showing Sully in armour wearing a ruff to the right was seen in the Department of Medieval and Later Antiquities in 1989.[14]

An ivory bust portrait of Sully in armour wearing a ruff to the left, together with one of Henri IV to the right, said to have been made by King Louis XV and now at the Château de Versailles, have been discussed by Christian Baulez.[15]

1. MNS, Archives de Sèvres, Vy 5, f. 76.
2. *Loc. cit.*, I 8.
3. *Loc. cit.*, I 8.
4. Numbered 1803 N° 148 in ink on reverse, *Tiroir* 48S.
5. Mark Jones, formerly of the Department of Coins and Medals, British Museum, has kindly drawn to my attention the unusual form of the inscription which gives Sully's princely possessions before his ducal title and the discrepancy between his dress on this medallion and on contemporary medals.
6. BM, Department of Prints and Drawings, reg. no. 1868–6–12–1061.
7. MNS, Archives de Sèvres, Vf 34, f. 26. A terracotta model and eighteenth-century moulds survive at the Sèvres Museum and factory respectively. The figure is illustrated in Bourgeois

and Lechevallier-Chevignard, 1909, no. 568, pl. 43. A statue of Sully by Mouchy at the Palais de l'Institut, Paris, is mentioned by E. Bénézit in *Dictionnaire des Peintres, Sculpteurs, Dessinateurs et Graveurs*, Paris, 1960, in his list of works by Mouchy.

8. *Loc. cit.*, Vl' 4.
9. *Loc. cit.*, Vl' 6, 7.
10. *Loc. cit.*, Vy 9, f. 86v.
11. *Loc. cit.*, Vy 18, f. 85v; Vy 19, f. 4v.
12. *Loc. cit.*, Vl' 4, 7.
13. Private collection, England. Reilly and Savage, 1973, pp. 316–17. The version shown on p. 316 corresponds to the Sèvres example. There is a Wedgwood jasper version in the Museum collections, reg. no. 1909,12–1,138. Wedgwood listed portrait medallions of Sully in his catalogue issued in 1779. There is no evidence for Reilly and Savage's statement that the portrait of Sully is based on an 'engraving after Rubens'. The author is grateful to Paul Goldman and Martin Royalton Kisch of the Department of Prints and Drawings for investigating this question.
14. Amber-coloured glass relief portrait, attached to opaque-white glass oval plaque, private collection, England; H. of cameo portrait 3.8 cm; cf Reilly and Savage, 1973, p. 317.
15. C. Baulez, 'Notes sur quelques meubles et objets d'art des appartements intérieurs de Louis XVI et de Marie-Antoinette', *Revue du Louvre*, 5/6. 1978, p. 366, fig. 8.

157 **Medallion of Queen Marie-Antoinette (1755–93),** *c.* 1774

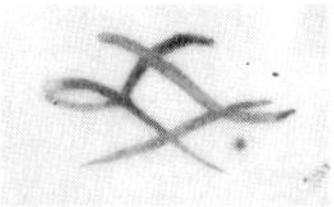

157 *mark*

D.	8.2 cm
Marks:	LL painted in blue
Reg. No.	1986,10–15,1

Hard-paste porcelain,[1] with an unglazed moulded portrait of Queen Marie-Antoinette in profile to left, wearing a coronet, on a green ground. The rim, moulded to simulate a frame, is glazed and decorated with gilt lines (partly rubbed). The unglazed reverse has a hole pierced for suspension which is itself filled with glaze.

Provenance: Purchased, 1986

Literature: Dawson *et al.*, 1988, fig. 85, 402

Musée du Louvre, 1990, p. 196, fig. 94c

Comparable Examples: Sotheby's, 8 November 1966, Lot 43, Wilfred J. Sainsbury Collection

The iconography of Marie-Antoinette is extensive and has been discussed at length during the course of this century.[2] A considerable number of portraits of the Queen were exhibited at Versailles in 1955,[3] but the present example was not included.

Several different medallions of the Queen (always to left) produced at Sèvres in the 1770s have been identified:

A. glazed with moulded frame, hair loose over left shoulder, the portrait enclosed by moulded beads, pierced with two holes for suspension, D. 7.5 cm, Louvre Museum, inv. OA 11162;

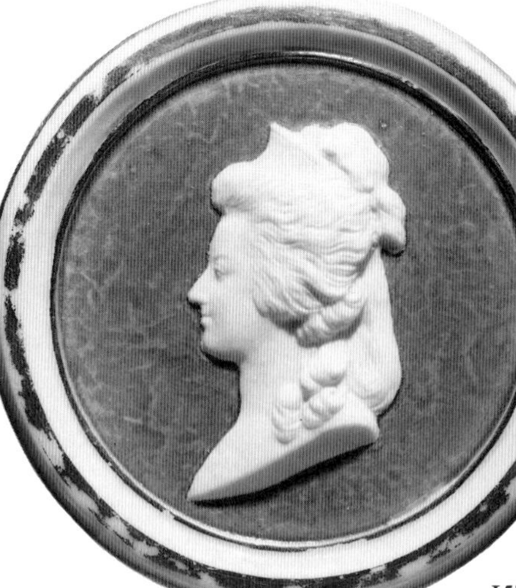

157

B. biscuit [?] in metal frame, same portrait mounted on plaque painted with blue *caillouté* ground, sold Galerie Koller, Zürich, 21–8 November, 1985, no. 1901, with pendant of the young King, present whereabouts unknown; similar one of the Queen sold Sotheby's, 20 March 1956, Lot 122, incised *M*;

C. British Museum example, moulded glazed frame, green ground, hairstyle differs, Queen wears a diadem;

D. biscuit on a blue ground, oval, in metal frame, with diadem, hairstyle differs from British Museum example, D. 5.4 cm, Louvre Museum, inv. OA 11163;

E. biscuit [?] in metal frame, shoulders draped, hair in elaborate formal style, mounted on plaque and enclosed by painted flowers with an inscription below, example illus. Verlet, 1953, pl. 76, from the collection of Arturo Lopez Willshaw, and on plaque in the Museum für Kunsthandwerk, Frankfurt am Main, dated 1774, illus. Jedding, 1971, fig. 854.

Four plasters, of which one is modern and another is a working model from which moulds were taken rather than a 'master model', survive at the Sèvres factory, but none relates to this medallion.

The earliest medallion of the sitter represents her when she was Dauphine, that is before 1774. It shows her to right with a Latin inscription and a beaded border. One example is recorded as having been sold to Madame de Vézelay on 14 October 1773 for 6 *livres*.[4] The British Museum medallion was probably created in late 1773 or in 1774. In 1774 Tristant *le jeune* was paid 4 *sous* apiece for a total of 1,274 'médaillons du Roy et de la Reine', and for the model of the same subjects 'pour Bague', for which he received 72 *livres*.[5] In June 1776 Liancé *fils aîné* was paid a total of 20 *livres* for five medallions of the King.[6]

The earliest sale of blue-ground medallions of the King and Queen took place on 19 February 1774, when Sieur Jouette paid 7 *livres* 10 *sous* for the two.[7] A much more expensive medallion of the queen was sold for 36 *livres* cash on 24 December 1775,[8] but in general a pair of the monarchs cost 12 *livres* during that year. Medallions with a green ground are mentioned in the factory stocklists in January 1774, where six portraits of the King in the largest size '*En fonds vert*' were valued at 12 *livres* each, but no example of this portrait of the Queen has been noted in the factory records. It is likely that this example dates from around 1774 because of its ground colour, and this writer does not consider the sitter looks older than in the portrait incorporated in a plaque at the Carnegie Institute, Pittsburgh, which is datable to 1774.[9]

Sèvres busts of Marie-Antoinette, including an example which entered the Louvre Museum in 1982, have been discussed by Pierre Ennès.[10]

Medallions of the Queen were produced at the Fürstenberg porcelain factory, together with a pendant of Louis XVI, both 6 cm in diameter.[11]

1. The medallion has been analysed and found to contain mullite, BMRL 29473Q.
2. Works on the subject include: E. Bourgeois, 'L'Etat-Civil des Bustes et Médaillons de Marie-Antoinette et de Louis XVI', *La Revue de l'art ancien et moderne*, Vol. XXII, 11e année (10 December 1907), see fig. 1, p. 403 and fig. 2, p. 407; J. Flammeront, 'Les Portraits de Marie-Antoinette', *Gazette des Beaux-Arts*, 49e *année*, 3e *periode*, Tome 18, 19, July, October, 1897, pp. 5–21, 283–303; March, May 1898, pp. 183–95, 379–92; A. Vuaflart and H. Bourin, *Les Portraits de Marie-Antoinette, Étude d'Iconographie critique*, Paris, 2 vols., 1909–10; Lord R. Gower, *Iconographie de la Reine Marie-Antoinette*, Paris, 1883.
3. Exh. Marie-Antoinette, 1955.
4. MNS, Archives de Sèvres, Vy 5, f. 116v. Horace Walpole had in his China Room at Strawberry Hill 'The present queen of France, a large medallion of Seve biscuit; a present from the duchess dowager d'Aiguillon in 1771', *A Description of the Villa of Mr. Horace Walpole . . . at Strawberry Hill near Twickenham, Middlesex*, Strawberry Hill, 1784, p. 11.
5. MNS, Archives de Sèvres, *Travaux extraordinaires*, 1774.
6. *Ibid.*, Va' 2, *registre des travaux des tourneurs, répareurs, mouleurs.*
7. *Ibid.*, Vy 5, f. 167v. The author is grateful to Tamara Préaud for this reference.
8. *Ibid.*, Vy 6, 36v.
9. *Musée du Louvre*, 1990, pp. 195–6.
10. *Musée du Louvre*, 1985, no. 91, p. 163.
11. Exh. 'Weisses Gold aus Fürstenberg', Westfälisches Landesmuseum für Kunst und Kulturgeschichte, Münster, December 1988–February 1989, Herzog Anton Ulrich-Museum, Braunschweig, March–May 1989, no. 368, 367.

158 **Pair of Portrait Medallions of Unknown Sitters**, *c.* 1776

D. 7.5 cm
Marks: none
Reg. No. Franks 394

Soft-paste porcelain, the border moulding partly gilt; the reliefs, which are on a dark blue enamelled ground with gilt enrichments,

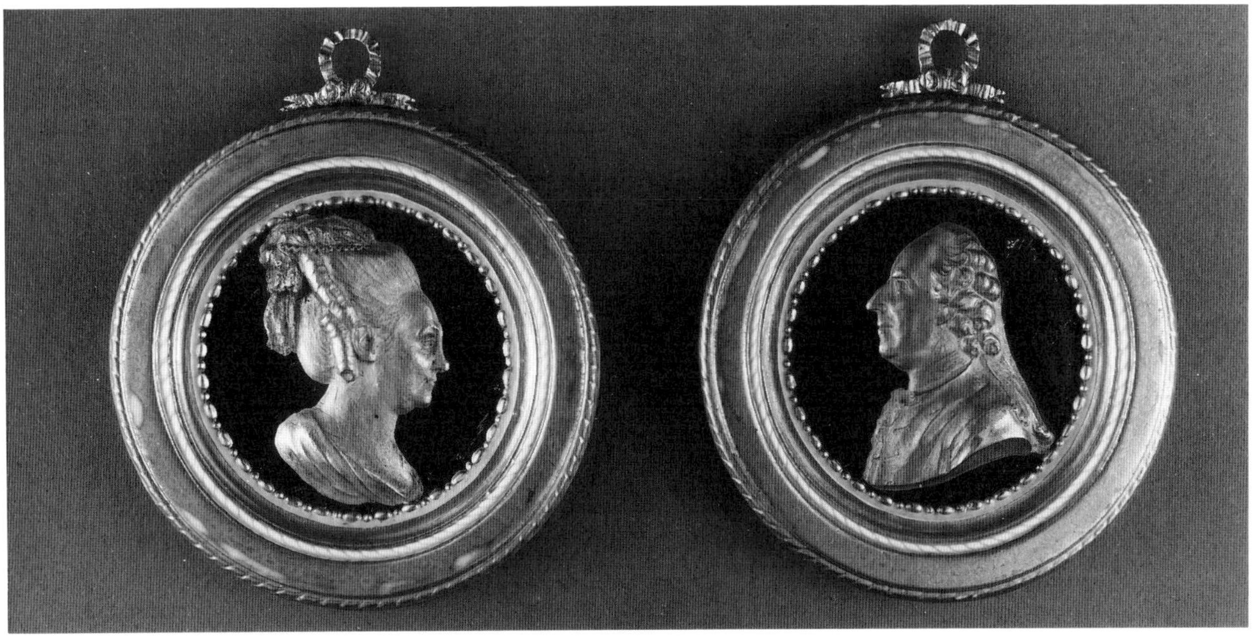

158

are gilded. The metal suspension loops are attached by means of a pin piercing the flat reverse of the medallion. The medallions are undamaged apart from rubbed gilding on the border.

Provenance: Bequeathed by Sir A.W. Franks, 1897; probably formerly in a French collection since there is the remains of a French inscription in ink on the reverse of each.

Literature: Franks, 1896, no. 394

Dawson, 1982, pp. 94–102, pl. VII

Comparable Examples: Paris, Musée des arts décoratifs, white hard-paste biscuit porcelain example with gilt edge of male portrait; mark yellow LL crowned enclosing Y on reverse, inv. unknown

Belgium, Itterbeek, du Bois de Roest Collection, illus. E. Soil de Moriamé and L. Delplace de Formanoir, *La Manufacture Impériale et Royale de Porcelaine de Tournay*, Tournai, 1937, pl. 58, no. 451

The medallions were once thought to represent Charles Frédéric, Maréchal de Luxembourg (1702–64) and his wife, but this identification is not supported by the Sèvres factory records, which do not, however, suggest alternative sitters.

No other examples of portrait medallions with a dark blue enamelled ground are known apart from those mentioned above. As the biscuit medallion in the Musée des arts décoratifs is apparently dated 1776, it is reasonable to assume that the British Museum portraits date from the same period.

159 **Medallion of Prince Henry of Prussia (1726–1802)**, 1784

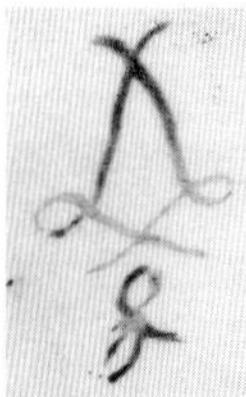

159 *mark*

D. 15.3 cm
Marks: interlaced LL above the mark associated with the gilder Windinger or members of his family painted in blue
Reg. No. 1988,7-2,1

Hard-paste porcelain, circular medallion moulded with a portrait to left in high relief of Prince Henry of Prussia, his hair *en queue*, wearing the Star of the Order of the Black Eagle. The inner rim is moulded with tiny dots and the edge turned and gilt to simulate a frame. Pierced at the top with two small suspension holes. Depression on the reverse corresponding to the shape of the portrait. Gilding rubbed in places.

Provenance: Purchased, 1988

Reputed to have belonged to Monsieur Georges Haumont, former curator of the Musée national de Céramique, Sèvres

Literature: Unpublished

Comparable Examples: Switzerland, Zurich, Schweizerisches Landesmuseum,[1] inv. LM 15119; mark of one of the members of the Weydinger family, who specialised in gilding.

In 1784 Prince Henry of Prussia, brother of Frederick the Great, visited Paris under the name of Count d'Oels. He arrived in August, and was introduced through Baron Grimm to the most distinguished literary, scientific and social circles.[2]

On 22 October 1784 he was presented with a magnificent gift of porcelain consisting of: a green ground dessert service painted with flowers and fruit and accompanied by table sculpture, several vases including three described as *richement émaillés* costing 3,000 *livres*,[3] a bust of the King and one of the Queen. The service was described as follows:

Service fond verd, Groupes de fleurs et fruits

72	Assiettes	36	2592	
16	Compotiers des 4 formes	42	672	
2	Plateaux à 2 pots	120	240	
2	id à 3 pots	144	288	
20	Tasses à Glaces	21	420	
4	plateaux pour les Servir	48	192	
2	Sucriers	126	252	
2	Bateaux	54	108	
2	Seaux à Bouteilles	192	384	
2	id àdemie	144	288	
2	id à Glaces	240	480	
2	id Crennelés	240	480	
4	Pots à oilles et plateaux Service Buffon	800	3200	
	Sculpture			
1	Groupe la Naissance de Bacchus		600	
2	id l'offrande a l'Amour et pend.	288	576	
4	id des Cotes du triomphe de Bacchus	144	576	
2	id les Nimphes a la Corbeille	168	336	
2	id la beauté et la Volupté	132	264	
4	figures	48	192	
8	Vases à tête de Bouc	36	288	
2	Vases à Oreilles	18	36	
2	id	18	36	
14	figures des grands hommes	480	6720	
1	Cabaret riche en Emeaux		1500	
2	Vases fond rouge montés en Bronze		1920	
2	Vases Mediasse beau bleu Paysage		2400	
3	Vases richement Emaillés		3000	
2	Bustes du roi et de la Reine		240	
	Total		28292	
	diminution		2829	12
	Reste à payer		25462	8

The total value of the gift was 25,462 *livres* 8 *sous*.[4] From correspondence between Montucla, the comte d'Angiviller and Régnier at the end of January 1785, it seems that the Prince eventually took delivery of no less than 24 figures of great men, and that the figure of Molière had to be refired, possibly because it had suffered accidental damage.[5]

A tapestry portrait of Louis XVI reproducing a portrait by Duplessis was presented by the King in 1784 to Prince Henry and is now in the Walters Art Gallery, Baltimore.[6]

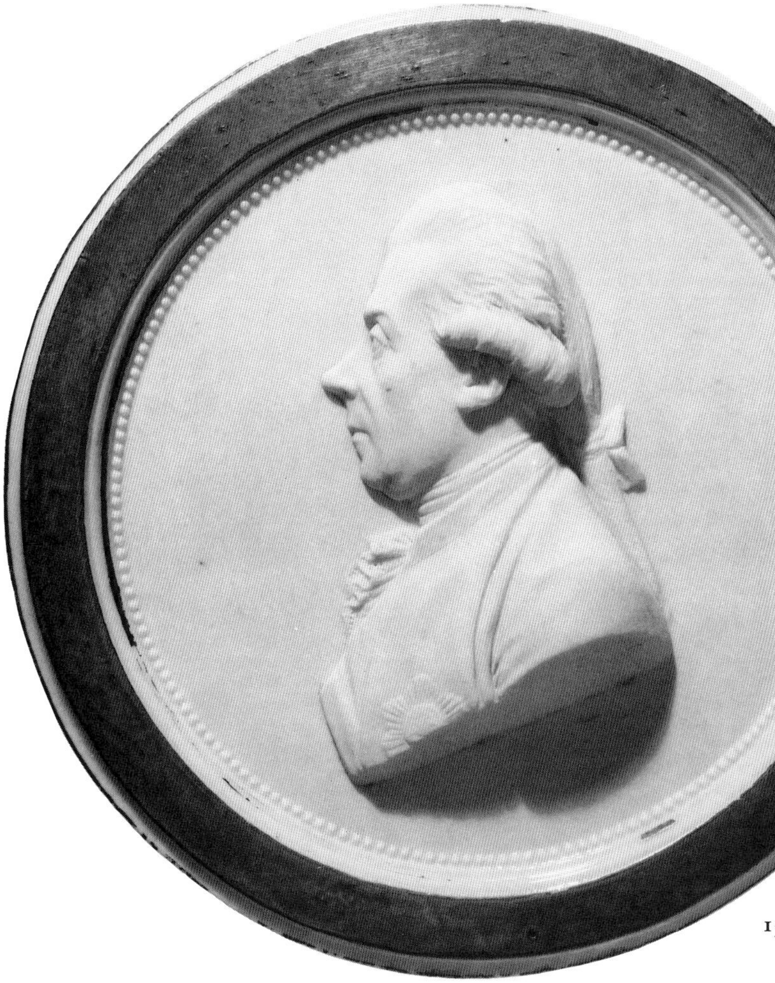

159

The medallion, which is closely related to a bust by Jean-Antoine Houdon, for which a plaster survives in the Weimar Library,[7] was modelled in 1784. In September, November and December of that year there are references in the factory documents to Vindique [*sic*] putting a *filet d'or* on batches of medallions of the Prince,[8] although only a few appear in the sales records at 18 *livres*; this was a rather high price by comparison with that normally charged for medallions (some of which cost as little as 3 or 5 *livres*) but which would be commensurate with this exceptionally large medallion. The first recorded sale was to the duchesse de Polignac in December 1784,[9] while on 5 March 1785 Monsieur Ternesien, described as 'Maître d'hôtel de M Le Marq. de Verac Ambassadeur en Hollande' took delivery of a quantity of biscuit sculpture, small vases for table decoration, a quantity of dice (*dez*) and, in addition, two medallions of Prince Henry.[10] They may have been intended for the Dutch Court.

A medallion in a similar style of Frederick the Great was modelled in 1787 by J.G. Müller for the Königliche Porzellanmanufaktur, Berlin.[11]

1. The author is grateful to Bernard Dragesco for providing this information, and to Dr R. Schnyder for details of the medallion, discussed (and misunderstood) in *Jahresbericht des Schweizerischen Landesmuseums 1919*, Zürich, 1920, p. 21.
2. The visit is mentioned in C.V. Easum, *Prince Henry of Prussia*, Madison, 1942, pp. 315–27, R. Krauel, *Prinz Heinrich von Preussen in Paris Während der Jahre 1784 und 1788 bis 1789*, Berlin, 1901 and C. de Larivière, 'Le Prince Henri de Prusse à Paris en 1784 et en 1788', *Revue Politique et Littéraire*, nos. 11, 13, 4th series, Tome XVI, 1901, pp. 334–40 and 393–8. A. Britsch in *La Jeunesse de Philippe Egalité*, Paris, 1926, p. 438 refers to a visit by Prince Henry to the rue de Provence, Paris residence of the duc d'Orléans, in 1782.
3. These have been identified by Savill, 1988, I, C334–6, p. 458.
4. MNS, Archives de Sèvres, Vy 9, f. 156.
5. *Ibid.*, H3 *liasse* 3, dated 27 January 1785, Montucla to d'Angiviller, 29 January 1785, d'Angiviller to Montucla, includes the sentence 'Il est nécessaire qu'elles [i.e. the figures] soient envoyées au plutot, & c'est-à-dire, mercredi, puisque la circonstance de Molière qui a besoin de repasser au feu exige ce petit retard'. A letter of 1 May 1786 in H3 *liasse* 4 mentions a cup intended for Prince Henry.

6. See P. Verdier, 'Portrait of young Louis XVI', *Bulletin of the Walters Art Gallery*, Vol. 9, no. 5, February 1957, pp. 1–2. The author is grateful to Bill Johnston for this reference.
7. Illus. H.H. Arnason, *Jean-Antoine Houdon, le plus grand sculpteur français du XVIIIe siècle*, Lausanne, 1976, figs. 88 (detail), 145.
8. MNS, Archives de Sèvres, Vl'2, f. 114, 117, 122. The Vindinger, Vindiquer or Weydinger family were responsible for much of the gilding at Sèvres in the late 1770s and 1780s.
9. MNS, Archives de Sèvres, Vy 9, f. 180.
10. *Ibid.*, Vy 9, f. 191.
11. D.J. Ponert, *Berlin Museum, Kunstgewerbe I, Keramik, Hafnerkeramik und Terracotta, Fayence, Porzellan*, Berlin, 1985, no. 36. This example belonged to H.G. (? Lewis) of Malvern Hall, Warwickshire, England. Another from a Berlin private collection is illustrated by E. Köllman and M. Jarchow, *Berliner Porzellan*, Munich, 1987, Bildband, no. 612. An example in the Belvedere-Sammlung, Schloss Charlottenburg, Berlin, inv. B 77/6 is incised '*J.G. Müller, fec. 1787*'. The author is grateful to Dr W. Baer for this information.

160 **Relief Bust of François-Marie Arouet de Voltaire (1694–1778)**, 1788–*c.* 1814

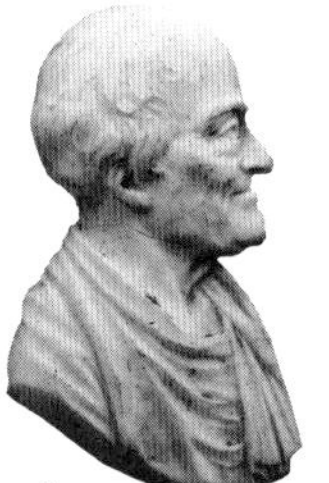
160

H. 3.3 cm
Marks: none
Reg. No. 1931,10–19,20

Hard-paste biscuit porcelain, to right in classical style without wig, the upper part of the body draped in a toga-like garment. Neck repaired.

Provenance: Transferred from the Salisbury and South Wiltshire and Blackmore Museum, 1931; possibly from the Blackmore Collection (note in BM Register); the gift of pottery and porcelain by Dr H.D. Blackmore, Hon. Director of the Museum, was recorded in the 1921–2 *Report* of that museum, p. 8. The Blackmore Museum closed in 1931.

Literature: Unpublished

Comparable Examples: None

Voltaire was a customer of the Sèvres factory in March 1773 when he purchased two biscuit busts of himself at 60 *livres* each.[1] Three busts were in fact produced: the first was modelled in 1768 apparently by Dupont-Rosset (but see cat. 150); the second was modelled by Houdon in the same year after Lemoyne and another is of unknown authorship.[2] Voltaire became closely identified with the Revolution. His body had been refused burial in Paris because of his attacks on conventional religion, but in October 1789 Saint-Just proposed that his remains should be returned to Paris. They were re-interred in the Pantheon in a public ceremony on 11 July 1791.[3] As mentioned under cat. 163, the cults of Brutus and Voltaire were closely entwined. The first mention of *découpé* medallions of Voltaire occurs in the record of a firing on 14 November 1788.[4]

Seven medallions of 'Rousseau, Voltaire etc' were sold for cash on 6 Prairial, l'an VII (25 May 1799). They cost 1 franc each[5] and remained popular at least until 1814 when they were on sale for 1 franc 50 centimes.[6]

Five different plaster models for medallions of Voltaire are preserved at the Sèvres factory, of which one, measuring 4.7 cm in diameter, corresponds to this example.[7]

1. MNS, Archives de Sèvres, Vy 5, f. 66.
2. See Bourgeois and Lechevallier-Chevignard, 1913, pl. 40, no. 617, pl. 50, no. 618, and S. Taylor, 'Artists and *Philosophes* as mirrored by Sèvres and Wedgwood', in *The Artist and the Writer in France, Essays in Honour of Jean Seznec*, ed. F. Haskell, A. Levi, R. Shackleton, Oxford, 1974, pl. 11.
3. See R.L. Herbert, *David, Voltaire, Brutus and the French Revolution: an essay in art and politics*, London, 1972, pp. 68–88.
4. MNS, Archives de Sèvres, Vl' 5.
5. MNS, Archives de Sèvres, Vy 12, f. 164v.
6. MNS, Archives de Sèvres, Vvl, f. 263v.
7. The author is grateful to Tamara Préaud for this information.

161 **Medallion**, 1791–3

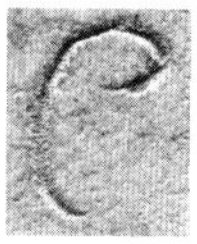
161 *mark*

D. *excl. frame* 3 cm
Marks: *C* incised on reverse
Reg. No. Franks 395

Rather gritty soft-paste porcelain, unglazed, washed blue on the upper surface which is ornamented with an applied relief of a fasces surmounted by a bonnet of Liberty accompanied by three fleurs-de-lys and the legend *VIVRE LIBRE OU MOURIR* within a frame of interlocking circles. There are small areas of discoloration on the blue ground. In metal frame with suspension loop.

Provenance: Bequeathed by Sir A.W. Franks, 1897

Literature: Franks, 1896, no. 395

Dawson, 1982, p. 96

Comparable Examples: USA, New York, Sotheby Parke Bernet, Milton Milestone Collection of Early Wedgwood Pottery, Part II, Lot 288 (wrongly catalogued)

The fasces, one of a series of emblems adopted to symbolise the French Revolution, was defined by the

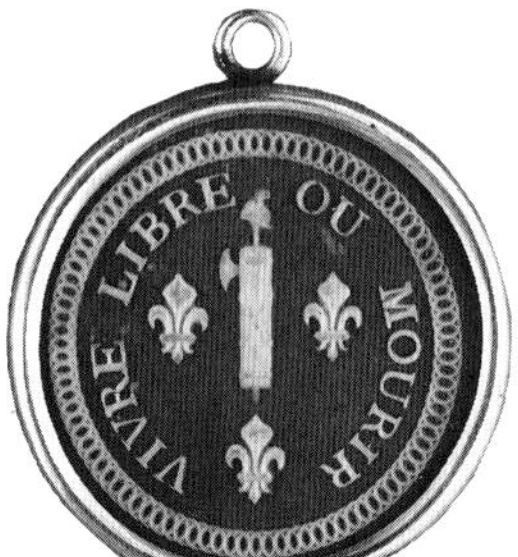

161

French law of 9–15 April 1791 as the emblem of 'unity and armed force'.[1] The presence of the fleurs-de-lys indicates that the medallion was made between 1791 and the execution of King Louis XVI on 21 January 1793.

The repairer using the incised mark *C* has not been identified.

1. M. Jones, *Medals of the French Revolution*, London, 1977, p. 8.

162 **Medallion,** *c.* 1794

D. 5.9 cm
Marks: none
Reg. No. 1909,12–1,367

Hard-paste biscuit porcelain, the upper surface washed dark matt blue with the monogram of *Liberté* applied in relief in white biscuit porcelain.

Provenance: Presented by Mr and Mrs Isaac Falcke, 1909; formerly belonged to E. Joseph, nephew of Isaac Falcke (according to pencil inscription on reverse)

Literature: Dawson, 1982, pp. 94–102, fig. 3

The first sale of a *Médaillon de la Liberté* is recorded in the factory sales records in l'an 2 (1793–4) when an example was sold for 3 *livres*.[1] This medallion was probably intended for mounting in a snuff-box top. No other example is known.

A considerable number of new busts and plaques were issued with Revolutionary subjects from 1792 onwards.[2]

1. MNS, Archives de Sèvres, Vy 11, f. 202v.
2. Bourgeois and Lechevallier-Chevignard, pp. 50–1, 53–5.

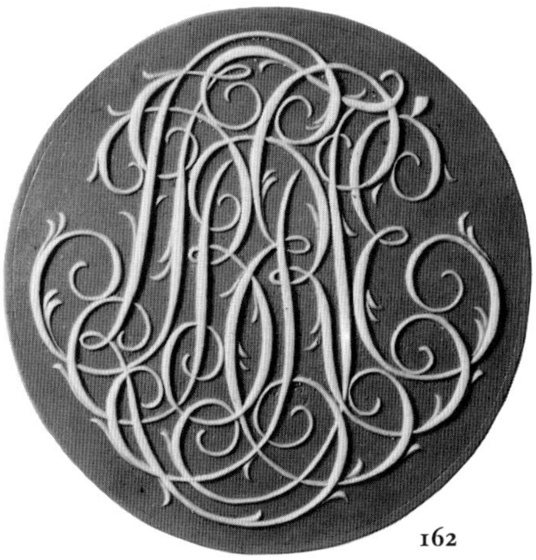

162

163 **Relief Bust of Brutus,** *c.* 1794–1800

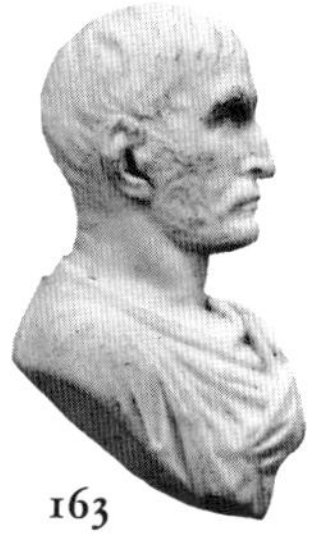

163

H. 3.4 cm
Marks: none
Reg. No. 1931,10–19,19

Hard-paste porcelain, to right, with short hair and beard, the upper part of the body clothed in a toga-like garment.

Provenance: As for cat. no. 160

Literature: Unpublished

Comparable Examples: None

The subject is Lucius Junius Brutus (Brutus the Elder, consul ?509 BC) who killed the last king of Rome, Tarquin, his uncle. Tarquin had put to death most of Brutus' family. Brutus himself escaped only by feigning stupidity and thus earning his name. Following the rape of Lucretia by Tarquin's son and her suicide in the presence of her father, her husband, Publius Valerius and Brutus, he vowed to rid Rome of the Tarquins. In 508 BC the first Roman republic was established, and Brutus was elected a co-consul with Collatinus. When his adolescent sons, Titus and Tiberius, became part of a royalist conspiracy, Brutus ordered and witnessed their execution.

Although he had been celebrated in France from the mid-eighteenth century (Voltaire's play *Brutus* was first performed in 1730), it was in the later years of the century that Brutus' name became associated with the overthrow of monarchy and the establishment of the rule of law. Jacques-Louis David began his *Les Licteurs apportant à Brutus le corps de ses fils* in 1787; it was exhibited in the 1789 *Salon*. Voltaire was successfully rehabilitated by Saint-Just and Charles Villette, and his *Brutus* was revived on 17 November 1790, followed by a second performance two days later, both rapturously received. Excerpts were given on the occasion of the re-interment of the *philosophe*'s remains in the Pantheon on 11 July 1791, and the play continued to be performed through the Revolutionary period. Its last presentation was in 1799. The cult of Brutus has been extensively studied, particularly by the scholar R.L. Herbert in relation to David's painting.[1] The deposition of the King was justified by the Brutus story, and on every public occasion during the Revolutionary years the image of Brutus the Elder was in evidence.

There was also a less important cult of Brutus the Younger (probably 85–42 BC), the murderer of Julius Caesar, who was not, however, depicted in any French painting exhibited in the *Salon* until 1793.[2]

The strength of the cult of the two Brutuses can be gauged by the fact that numerous French towns changed their names (Montfort-l'Amaury became Montfort-le-Brutus), Saint-Pierre-le-Moutiers became Brutus-le-Magnanime) and very many children were named Brutus.[3]

This small bust is close to a marble by F.J. Boiston dated *an 4 de la liberté* (1795–6), a facsimile of a bronze which has been in the Capitoline Museum since 1564.[4] The iconography is unrelated to any known in classical art: men did not wear beards at this period in antiquity.[5] Boiston presented his bust to the Assemblée Nationale on 1 September 1792.[6] Even before this, David had owned a copy of the Capitoline bust, from which he sketched a profile.[7] The bust became an important icon, especially in 1793 and 1794. This Sèvres bust is likely to date from after December 1793 when the Convention encouraged the distribution of the image, sponsoring replicas in plaster, and Sèvres porcelain, as well as engravings.[8] Some tiny engravings were made to be worn pasted on to buttons and badges worn at the Revolutionary festivals,[9] and the small Sèvres busts may have been intended for a similar purpose.

Two plasters are preserved at the Sèvres factory, the smaller of which measures 7 cm in diameter and corresponds with the Museum bust.

It is first noted in the kiln records on 26 Ventose, l'an II (16 March 1794), when three 'médaillons bleu Brutus' were successfully fired.[10] On 16 Thermidor, l'an VII (3 July 1799) no fewer than 336 'médaillons découpés Bonaparte, Rousseau, Voltaire et Brutus' were noted as good from the kiln.[11] Cameo medallions of Brutus were in stock according to an inventory taken on 11 Messidor, l'an IX (30 June 1801).[12] A bust of Brutus was also in production from 5 Messidor, l'an II (23 June 1794)[13] and various purchases in l'an II (September 1794–September 1795) are recorded, including one for a large example bought by *Citoyen* Clin for 5,000 *livres*.[14]

1. R.L. Herbert, *David, Voltaire, Brutus and the French Revolution: an essay in art and politics*, London, 1972.
2. Exh. *La Révolution Française*, 1989, p. xxix.
3. C. Mossé, *L'Antiquité dans la Révolution française*, Paris, 1989, pp. 64, 134–5.
4. *Op. cit.*, cat no. 555. Boiston sold plasters of the bust.
5. The author is grateful to Ian Jenkins of the Department of Greek and Roman Antiquities for this information.
6. Herbert, *op. cit.*, p. 90.
7. *Ibid.*, p. 31, fig. 16; David also sketched Brutus full-face in April 1790, see p. 66, fig. 33.
8. *Ibid.*, p. 105.
9. *Ibid.*, fig. 52.
10. MNS, Archives de Sèvres, VI'4.
11. *Ibid.*
12. MNS, Archives de Sèvres, Y20, f. 8.
13. MNS, Archives de Sèvres, Vy 11, f. 228.
14. MNS, Archives de Sèvres, Vy 12, f. 56.

164 **Medallion**, probably *c.* 1795

D. excl. frame: 3 cm
Marks: none
Reg. No. Franks 395

Soft-paste porcelain washed dark blue on the upper surface, which is ornamented with an applied relief in white biscuit porcelain of a male term supporting a basket of flowers among acanthus scrolls, garlands and lotus flowers. In metal frame with suspension loop.

Provenance: Bequeathed by Sir A.W. Franks, 1897

Literature: Franks, 1896, no. 395

Comparable Examples: None

Medallions like these (see cats 165 and 166) were used to ornament furniture or gilt bronzes.

By analysis[1] the paste of this medallion is of an unusual type containing little calcium; potassium, lead, and possibly sodium and aluminium have been found in the composition. It has been attributed to Sèvres in the absence of any convincing alternative maker.

1. BM Research Laboratory 26692W.

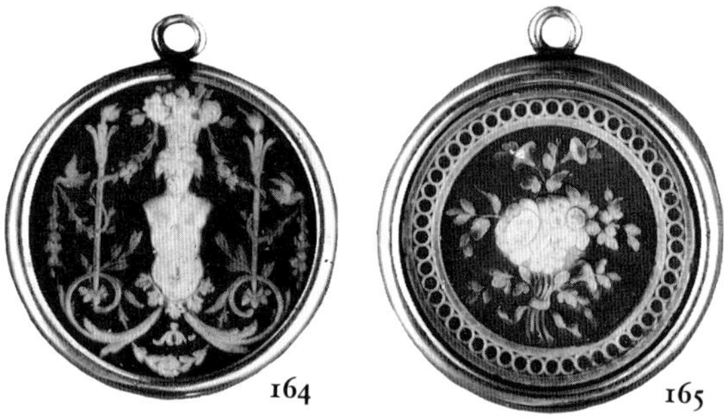

164 165

165 **Medallion**, probably *c.* 1795

D. excl. frame: 3.1 cm
Marks: none
Reg. No. Franks 395

Rather gritty soft-paste porcelain, unglazed, washed blue on upper surface which is ornamented with an applied relief in white biscuit porcelain consisting of a bunch of naturalistic flowers tied with a ribbon within a frame of adjoining circles between two lines. Several firecracks on upper surface and defects to outer relief. In metal frame with suspension loop.

Provenance: Bequeathed by Sir A.W. Franks, 1897

Literature: Franks, 1896, no. 395

Comparable Examples: None

On stylistic and technical grounds, this medallion, probably intended to ornament furniture or gilt-bronze items, can be dated to the late eighteenth century. The poor quality of the body and the presence of firecracks suggest the possibility that it may have been made during the Revolutionary period when production standards may have been difficult to maintain.

166 **Medallion**, probably *c.* 1795

D. *excl. frame:* 3.2 cm
Marks: none
Reg. No. Franks 395

Rather gritty soft-paste porcelain, unglazed, edge bevelled on reverse; upper surface washed dark blue and ornamented with an applied relief in white biscuit porcelain of a vase of flowers festooned with drapery upheld at either side of the vase by an insect. Tiny applied dots encircle the motifs. There are a number of small firecracks on the upper surface. In metal frame with suspension loop.

Provenance: Bequeathed by Sir A.W. Franks, 1897

Literature: Franks, 1896, no. 395

Comparable Examples: None

The poor quality of the porcelain body suggests a date in the 1790s, and it corresponds in appearance with the medallion inscribed *VIVRE LIBRE OU MOURIR* (cat. 161).

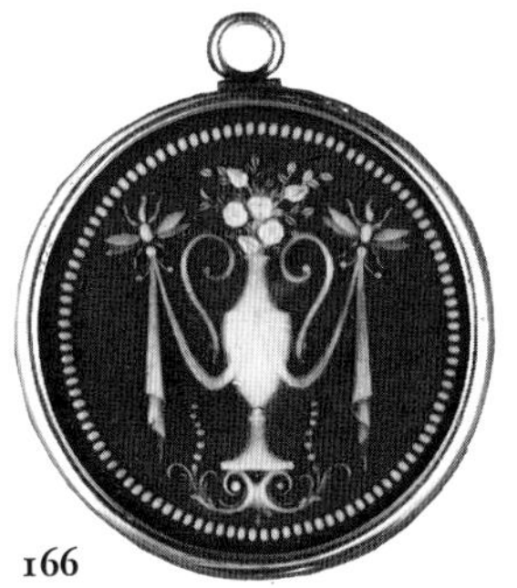

166

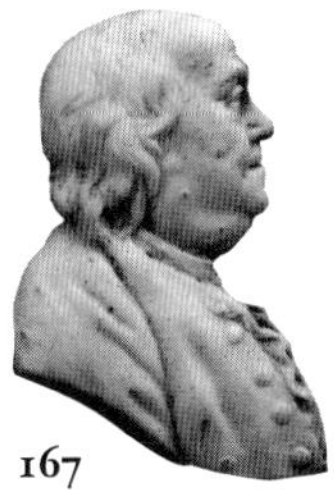

167

167 **Relief Bust of Benjamin Franklin (1706–90)**, 1791–early 19th century

H. 3.3 cm
Marks: none
Reg. No. 1931,10–19,21

Hard-paste biscuit porcelain, to right, short, undressed hair, stock and shirt ruff.

Provenance: As for cat. no. 160

Literature: Unpublished

Comparable Examples: The Netherlands, Amsterdam, Rijksmuseum, inv. BR. 549

This portrait is similar to the one used on an unglazed porcelain medallion with a glazed and partly gilded rim issued by the factory in 1778. Examples were in production by 3 August when they are recorded in the muffle kiln for gilding.[1] However, this detached example is thought to date from rather later. *Découpé* portraits of Franklin first appear in the factory records in December 1791 when 1359 were good from kiln. They were in production during the Revolutionary years, and the subject continued to be a popular one.[2] Small plaster models corresponding with this example, which is also known in a slightly larger size measuring 3.8 cm in height,[3] are preserved at the factory.

A medallion of Franklin was in production in 1967.[4]

Josiah Wedgwood and Thomas Bentley of Etruria, Staffordshire, manufactured a series of jasper portrait medallions of Franklin, including one corresponding with the Sèvres example.[5]

The same portrait, in reverse, was painted in *grisaille* on a Sèvres *tasse litron* with a blue ground.[6]

Richard Champion used the same portrait on a large-size oval biscuit porcelain plaque incrusted with flowers in relief made at his Bristol factory,[7] and James Tassie produced an intaglio glass paste seal.[8] A terracotta version by J.-B. Nini within a circular glass medallion is in the Musée national de Céramique, Sèvres.[9]

Although Jean-Jacques Caffiéri's portrait bust of Franklin was completed in 1777 when the terracotta was exhibited at the *Salon*, it may not have been used as the model for this piece which differs in the details of the sitter's dress.[10]

For the role of Franklin in late-eighteenth century France and his importance during the Revolutionary period, see the essay in the 1989 Council of Europe French Revolution exhibition catalogue.[11]

1. MNS, Archives de Sèvres, Vl'1, *Enfournement et désenfournement de peinture*. The gilder was Prévost. One is illustrated in C.C. Sellers, *Benjamin Franklin in Portraiture*, New Haven and London, 1962, pl. 12, no. 1, pp. 365–7, Henry E. Huntington Library and Art Gallery, San Marino, California. An example of the Sèvres medallion was sold at Christie's, 5 December 1960, Lot 16 and another at Sotheby Parke Bernet, New York, 4 May 1985, Lot 111. An example marked in yellow with crossed LL above a cursive mark, probably that of the gilder Weydinger or a member of his family, is in the Musée des arts décoratifs at the Château de Saumur, inv. Lair Coll. 265. Another bearing the factory mark crowned and the date-letters AA (1778) painted in red was on the Paris market in the late 1980s. This medallion is still in production (1988).
2. MNS, Archives de Sèvres, Vl'4 and 5.
3. Amsterdam, Rijksmuseum, inv. BR 549.

4. See *Biscuits de Sèvres*, supplement issued with *Cahiers*, Vol. 39, 1967.
5. Reilly and Savage, 1973, p. 147(e); BM reg. no. 1909,12–1,151 impressed *WEDGWOOD*, made after 1780.
6. C.C. Sellers, *op. cit.*, pl. 12, no. 3, and p. 368.
7. Hobson, 1905, VIII 7, pl. XXXI; exh. 'Rare and Documentary English Porcelain from the British Museum', International Ceramics Fair and Seminar Ltd., London, June 1987, catalogue compiled by A. Dawson, no. 65.
8. C.C. Sellers, *op. cit.*, pp. 374–5.
9. Jokelson, 1968, fig. 54; MNCS inv. 1310.[3]
10. Sellers, *op. cit.*, pl. 16.
11. Exh. *La Révolution Française*, 1989, pp. 338–40.

168 **Medallion of Alexandre Brachard, called Brachard *fils* (1775–1843)**, 1800

D. 14.2 cm
Marks: *Alexandre Brachard/Né En 1775. le 2 Septembre/Brachard ainé fécit* [sic]*/en Ventose an 8* incised on reverse; *Brachard ainé. f:ct/an 8.* incised on truncation
Reg. No. 1992,2–2,1

Hard-paste porcelain, circular medallion with applied moulded portrait of Alexandre Brachard to left in high relief on a washed blue ground. He wears a double-breasted coat with a high collar and wide lapels underneath which is a waistcoat covering a shirt, the collar partly folded over a white linen stock. His (own) hair is cut short at the front and sides and the long back hair arranged as a club wig (the end of the queue is turned up on itself and

168 *marks*

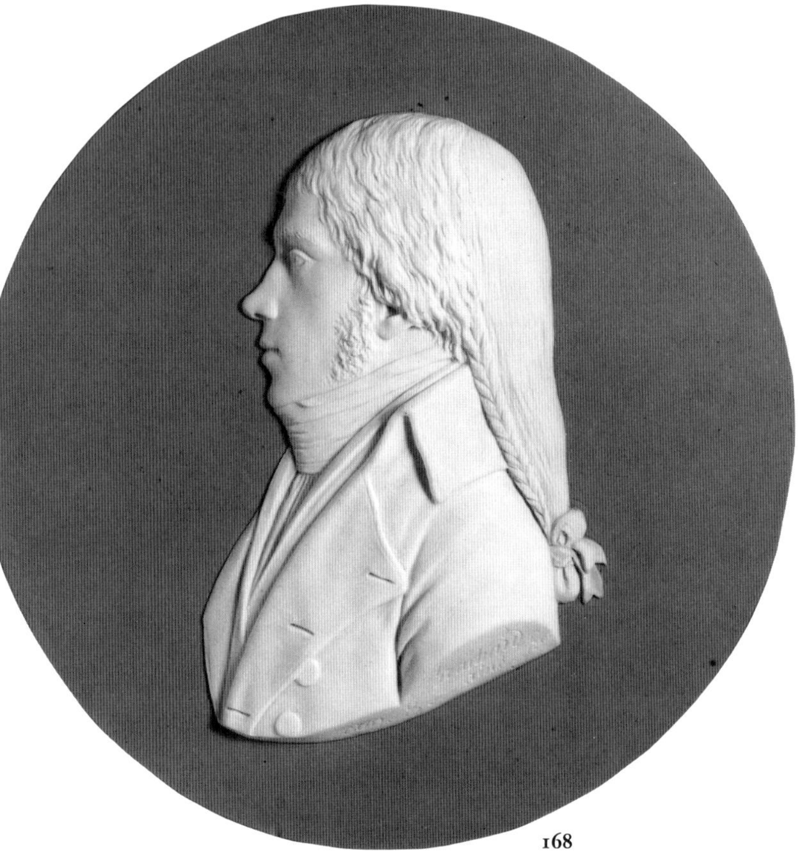

168

tied with a bow) with a plait at the side.[1] He is clean-shaven except for side whiskers. The edge of the medallion is bevelled on the reverse.

Provenance: Unknown, purchased, 1992

Literature: Unpublished

Comparable Examples: None

This medallion was made between 20 February and 21 March 1800. It depicts Brachard *fils* (1775–1843), brother of Jean-Charles-Nicolas Brachard (1766–1846, called Brachard *aîné*). They were the sons of Nicolas Brachard (*c.* 1740/41–1809, called Brachard *père*), who was employed as a repairer from 1754 to 1774. In the same year he moved to the workshop producing bas-reliefs where he was a sculptor-modeller. He retired in 1800 and died in October 1809.

Little is known about the sitter. From 26 July 1784 he was a pupil (*élève*) and has been traced by the author at the factory in the sculptors' workshop under Le Riche in February 1791, when Brachard *fils élève* is listed without payment.[2] The sitter's costume and hairstyle are typical of the last years of the eighteenth century. They do not predate 1785–6 and the hairstyle was no longer fashionable after 1804. The image presented is of a young man of taste poised between two worlds, the short cut of his hair having much in common with styles adopted at the time of the Revolution while the club wig at the back is reminiscent of older styles.

Brachard *aîné* was employed as a sculptor at Sèvres from August 1782. He was in the kiln department in 1787 and became its head in 1789. Between 1791 and l'an III (September 1794–September 1795) he was a painter, after which he continued, with several intermissions, as a sculptor. He is recorded at the factory in this capacity at the date when this medallion was made.[3]

Medallions of workers at the Sèvres factory are otherwise unknown except for a blue-ground example of the factory chemist Hettlinger signed 'Collet' and dated May 1785.[4] Like the sketches of the Sèvres workforce which have survived at the factory,[5] these are of great interest, since most portraits in all media are of members of royalty, of the aristocracy or of foreign monarchs and grandees, or if not their subjects are often anonymous. The portrait is in exceptionally high relief and compares in size and workmanship with cat. 159. It was almost certainly made for the sitter and members of his family. No mention of it has yet been found in documents preserved at the factory.

1. The author is grateful to Dr. Aileen Ribeiro for help in describing the sitter's costume and hair.
2. MNS, Archives de Sèvres, D3, *Etat Nominatif*, February 1791, unnumbered folder, p. 6.
3. The author is grateful to Tamara Préaud for providing information about the Brachard clan, as the author has been unable to carry out archival research on this medallion.
4. With Dragesco-Cramoisan in Spring 1992; another example is in the Musée des Suisses au Service Etranger, Château de Coppet, inv. A 711, see exh. cat. *Grandes Heures de l'Amitié Franco-Suisse*, Château de Coppet, July–October 1967, no. 814, illus. A further example is in the Metropolitan Museum of Art, New York, inv. 45.174.44. The author is grateful to Bernard Dragesco for this reference.
5. Some of these have been published, notably by Savill, 1988, III, Appendix II Notes on painters and gilders.

169 **Portrait Medallion of King Louis XVIII (1755–1824; reigned 1814/15),** *c.* 1814/15–24

D. *excl. frame:*	8.8 cm
Marks:	*og* incised on reverse: *SEVRES* impressed on truncation
Reg. No.	Franks 397

Hard-paste porcelain, unglazed, washed pale blue on upper surface, which is ornamented with an applied portrait bust to left of King Louis XVIII, wearing the Star of the Order of the Saint-Esprit. The reverse has a criss-cross pattern as if the medallion were pressed against a piece of cloth when in the leather-hard state before firing. In gilt metal frame with suspension loop. Repaired.

Provenance: Bequeathed by Sir A.W. Franks, 1897

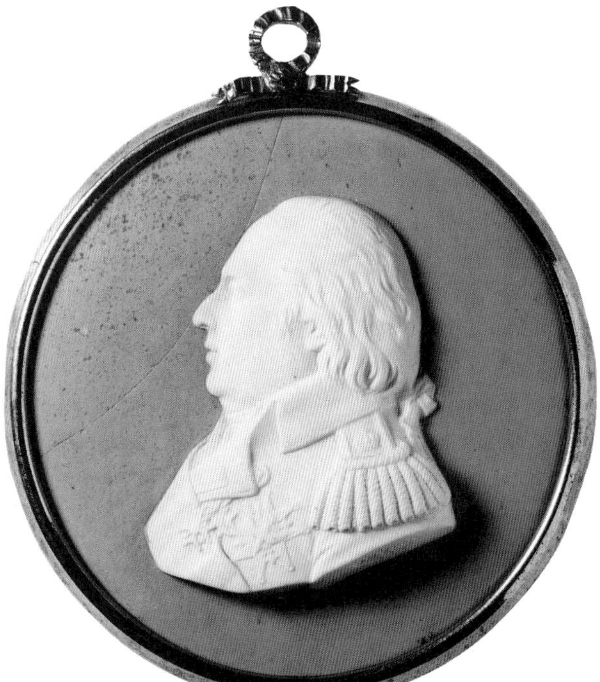

169

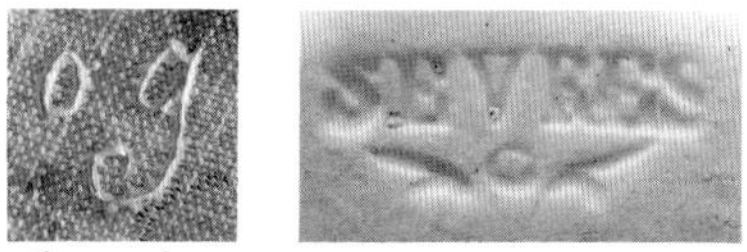

169 *marks*

Literature: Franks, 1896, no. 397

Dawson, 1982, p.96

Comparable Examples: Paris, Musée des arts décoratifs

Jean-Jacques Oger, whose initials are incised on the reverse of the medallion, was employed as a sculptor at the Sèvres factory from 1784–1800 and 1802–21.

Plaster models, inventoried in 1816 and 1817 respectively, are preserved at the Sèvres factory.

Medallions of Louis XVIII are recorded *en magasin* from 10 August 1814.[1] Twenty-four *découpé* medallions were first sold in August 1814 for 2 francs each.[2]

A sulphide portrait of the same subject is in a private collection;[3] another signed *Desprez* belonged to Paul Jokelson.[4] The same portrait was used by Baccarat on a flask[5] and for portrait plaques and a medallion.[6]

1. MNS, Archives de Sèvres, Vzz l, f. l.
2. MNS Archives de Sèvres, Vv l, fol. 264.
3. Illus. P. de Toulgoët-Tréanna, 'Verres et cristaux incrustés dits sulfures', *Cahiers*, no. 40, 1968, p. 239.
4. Jokelson, 1968, figs. 31 and 61.
5. *Ibid.*, fig. 89, Musée des arts décoratifs, Bordeaux, inv. 66, 296.
6. Musée des arts décoratifs, Bordeaux, inv. 66.1303; 55.1.5722; 58.1.5766; 58.1.8714.

170 **Relief Bust of King Henri IV of France (1553–1610),** modelled 1815

H. 6.4 cm

Marks: *Brachard f.* incised on truncation (see cat. 172)

Reg. No. 1931,10–19,17

Hard-paste biscuit porcelain, moulded. The King is shown to the left in a ruff and wearing the Order of the Saint-Esprit.

Provenance. As for cat. no. 160

Literature: Unpublished

Comparable Examples: USA, New York, Metropolitan Museum, inv. 68.186.9

London, Victoria and Albert Museum, inv. C. 459–1928

Scotland, Perthshire, Christie's, Arthurstone, Meigle, 15 and 16 October 1990, Lot 574; Lot 575 on a blue ground

For a discussion of representations of Henri IV see cat. 246.

A medallion of Henri IV, France's most popular king, was issued as early as 1766, when two biscuit medallions of the fourth size costing 12 *livres* each are recorded as having been delivered to Monsieur Bartin

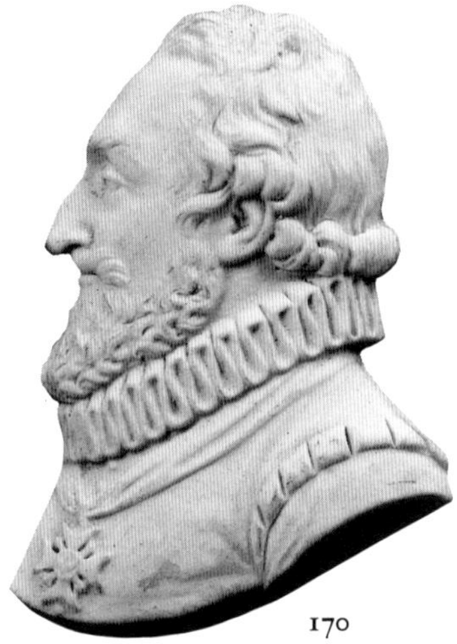

170

[*sic*, for Bertin] Ministre on 31 December 1766.[1] The subject continued in production at least until the early nineteenth century.

Wedgwood and Bentley of Etruria, Staffordshire, listed a portrait medallion in their catalogue issued in 1773. The English firm produced several versions of the subject.[2]

This bust may be based on a print distributed after the King's consecration at Chartres, depicting him as the *Gallic Hercules*.[3] It was modelled by Jean-Charles-Nicolas Brachard (1766–1846) called Brachard *aîné*. A plaster model signed *Brachard f* and incised *août 1815* on the reverse is preserved at the Sèvres factory.

The first sales are recorded in 1815 when cameo medallions cost 8 and 6 francs[4] and *découpé* medallions were 2 francs.[5] They were still in production in 1838 and 100 were sold at 1 franc 50 centimes each.[6]

A sulphide portrait of Henri IV in a slightly different costume and without the Order of the Saint-Esprit was manufactured by Baccarat. An example signed *E. Gatteaux, 1815* was in the collection of Paul Jokelson in 1968.[7]

1. MNS, Archives de Sèvres, Vy 4, f. 104; Dawson, 1982, p. 96 quotes an inventory dated 1 January 1774 where the portrait of Henri IV is paired with that of Sully; the medallions were apparently sold as a pair.
2. Reilly and Savage, 1973, p. 190.
3. Illus. C. Vivanti, 'Henry IV, the Gallic Hercules', *Journal of the Warburg and Courtauld Institutes*, Vol. 30, 1967, pl. 21d.
4. MNS, Archives de Sèvres, Vv 1, f. 267v.
5. *Ibid.*, f. 268.
6. MNS, Archives de Sèvres, Vv 3, f. 121v.
7. Jokelson, 1968, fig. 74.

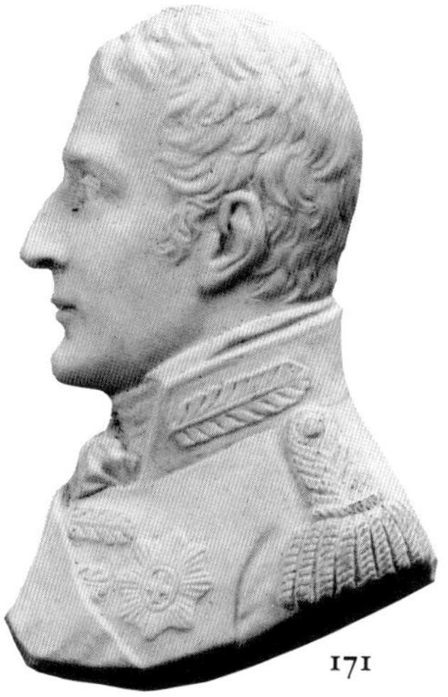

171

171 **Relief Bust of Arthur Wellesley, 1st Duke of Wellington (1769–1852),** *c.* 1815

H. 6.3 cm
Marks: *Brachard* (see cat. 172) and (to left) *1815* incised on truncation
Reg. No. 1931,10–19,18

Hard-paste biscuit porcelain, moulded. The Duke, shown to left, wears the Star of the Order of the Garter which he was awarded on 4 March 1813. Chip to truncation at right.

Provenance: As for cat. 160

Literature: Unpublished

Comparable Examples: Scotland, Perthshire, Christie's, Arthurstone, Meigle, 15 and 16 October 1990, Lot 574; Lot 575, on a blue ground

USA, New York, Metropolitan Museum, inv. 64.186.4, portrait on a blue ground, incised on truncation *1815 Brachard* and on reverse *y*

Plaster models survive at the factory for two versions of the portrait of Wellington, one corresponding with this bust, the other showing him as an older man. This version is probably based on a medal by J. Westwood struck in 1814, known as the Peace at Paris medal.[1]

Examples by Liancé[2] were on sale in 1815 when *decoupé* examples cost 2 francs.[3] In 1819 no less than 73 *médaillons découpés* were sold at 1 franc 50 centimes each.[4]

For details of Wellington's life, see the *Dictionary of National Biography* where he is described as 'five feet nine inches in height, spare and muscular, with aquiline features and penetrating grey eyes'. In February 1814 he was characterised by F.S. Larpent as 'remarkably neat, and most particular in his dress, considering his situation. He is well made, knows it, and is willing to set off to the best that nature has bestowed'.[5] When he arrived in Paris in 1814 he was enthusiastically received, and remained popular at least until the Second Treaty of Paris signed on 20 November 1815 when he succeeded in preventing France losing Alsace and Lorraine. By early 1817 Paris was in a politically unstable state and between then and the Treaty of Aix-la-Chapelle in Autumn 1818, and Wellington's subsequent return to England, his popularity was on the wane. He survived two attempts on his life.

1. L. Brown, *British Historical Medals 1760–1960*, London, 1980, no. 816.
2. MNS, Archives de Sèvres, Vzz 1, f. IV.
3. *Loc. cit.*, Vv 1, f. 268: cameo medallions and framed medallions were also in production at 8 and 12 francs respectively.
4. *Ibid.*, f. 281.
5. Sir G. Larpent (ed.), *The Private Journal of F.S. Larpent, Esq.*, London, 1853, Vol. III, p. 6.

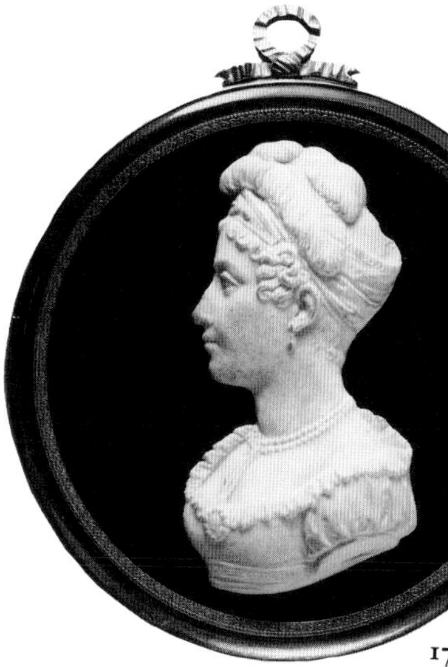

172

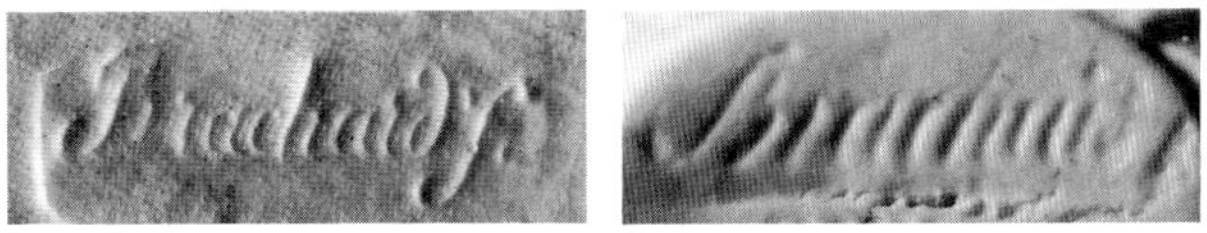

172 *marks*

172 **Portrait Bust of the Duchess of Berry (1798–1870),** *c.* 1820

H. 7.2 cm
Marks: *Brachard f.* incised on reverse, *Brachard* and, to left, *1820* (not shown here) impressed on truncation
Reg. No. Franks 398

Hard-paste porcelain, moulded and mounted on glass. She wears a low-cut dress with pearl choker and pendant, feathers in her hair and a diadem.

Provenance: Bequeathed by Sir A.W. Franks, 1897

Literature: Franks, 1896, no. 398

Dawson, 1982, p. 96

Comparable Examples: Scotland, Perthshire, Christie's, Arthurstone, Meigle, 15 and 16 October 1990, Lot 574, *découpé*

Switzerland, Geneva, Musée Ariana, *découpé*, H. about 6.9 cm, inv. C687

Jean-Charles Nicolas Brachard (1766–1846), called Brachard *aîné*, was employed at the Sèvres factory between 1782 and 1824. A plaster model signed *Brachard aîné ft. 1820* is preserved at the factory and probably represents a second, improved, version of the portrait as it was on sale in cameo and *découpé* form in 1816.[1] The second cost 2 francs each. Production of medallions of the Duchess appears to have ceased on her death.

A sulphide portrait of this subject signed by Acloque *fils* of rue de la Barillerie, Paris, from the Musée des arts décoratifs, Bordeaux, is illustrated by Jokelson.[2]

Marie-Caroline-Ferdinande-Louise de Bourbon, daughter of Francis II, King of the Two Sicilies, married Charles-Ferdinand, Duke of Berry (1778–1820), son of Charles X, in 1816. On 13 February 1820 he was assassinated at the Paris Opera.[3]

The Duchess of Berry was presented with numerous gifts of Sèvres porcelain by Louis XVIII and Charles X. A biscuit bust of her after François-Joseph Bosio was issued by the factory in 1823. A watercolour by Jean-François Garneray (1755–1837) painted between 1823 and 1829 of the drawing-room at the Pavillon de Marsan in the Tuileries Palace, where she lived after her husband's death, shows in the background a large glass-fronted cabinet apparently containing china.[4] A copy of the catalogue of her sale in Paris in December 1830 is kept in the British Library.[5]

1. MNS, Archives de Sèvres, Vv 1, f. 271.
2. Jokelson, 1968, fig. 45; Musée des arts décoratifs, Bordeaux, inv. 58.1.2140.
3. B. Scott, 'The Duchess of Berry as a patron of the Arts', *Apollo*, Vol. CXXIV, no. 296, October 1986, p. 345.
4. *Ibid.*, p. 348, fig. 6.
5. Press number 562 e 74. The sale did not include any porcelain.

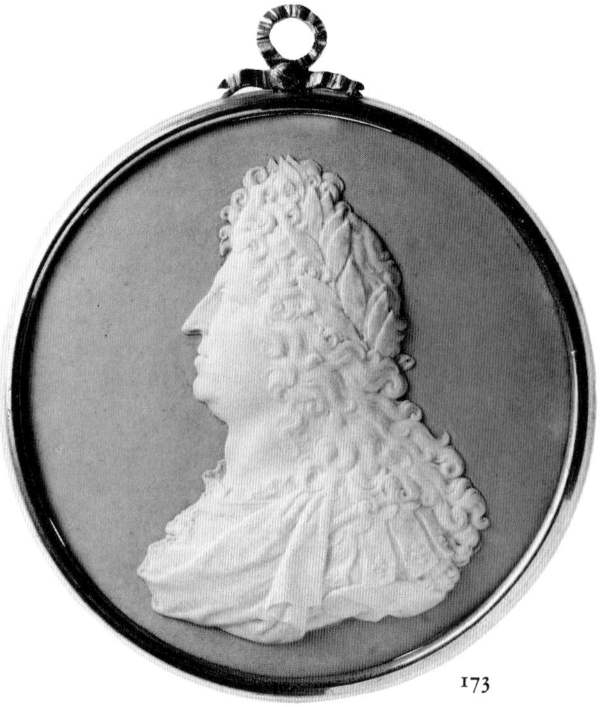

173

173 Portrait Medallion of King Louis XIV (b. 1638, reigned 1643–1715), *c.* 1816–18

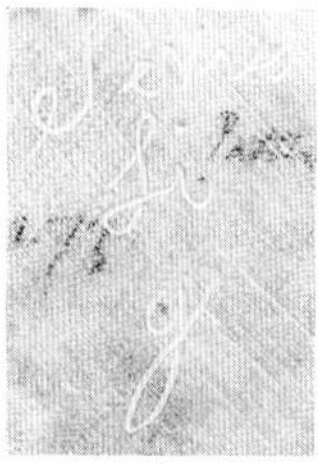

173 *marks*

D. *(excl. frame)*	8.3 cm
Marks:	*Sèvres/Li/g* incised on reverse
Reg. No.	Franks 396

Hard-paste porcelain, unglazed, washed pale blue on upper surface which is ornamented with an applied portrait bust to left of King Louis XIV in relief. He wears a laurel garland and a cuirass with lion mask breastplate and epaulettes. Each epaulette has a moulded relief of a sunburst above fleur-de-lys. The reverse has a criss-cross pattern as if it were pressed against a piece of cloth when in the leather-hard state before firing. The porcelain is discoloured, with greyish specks on the relief, and the ground is lumpy. In gilt metal frame with suspension loop.

Provenance: Bequeathed by Sir A.W. Franks, 1897

Literature: Franks, 1896, no. 396

Dawson, 1982, p. 96

Comparable Examples: Paris, Dragesco and Cramoisan, 1988, incised *M* on reverse

Scotland, Perthshire, Christie's, Arthurstone, Meigle, 15 and 16 October 1990, Lot 575; Lot 574 *découpé*

USA, New York, Metropolitan Museum, inv. 64.186.6, incised with a cursive *M* on reverse

The medallion is after a medallic portrait dating from the early 1670s by Jean Mauger.[1] Several versions of the subject, all dating from the early nineteenth century, can be traced in the Sèvres factory archives. Their proliferation represents the reaffirmation of the idea of monarchy after the Restoration in 1814. This version was modelled by Jean-Nicolas-Alexandre Brachard (1775–1843), referred to in the records of sculptors' work as Alex Brachard. On 29 February 1816 he received 1 franc 25 centimes for each of 24 medallions with a blue ground of Louis XIV.[2] The plaster model inventoried in 1817 is kept at the factory.[3]

In 1816 the medallion was produced in both cameo and *découpé* form, and was sold framed at 12 francs.[4]

This example is quite unusual in bearing the marks of two workmen. The first, Augustin Liancé (1771–1820), was a repairer between 1806 and 1818 and a member of a dynasty working at the factory.[5] The second was probably François-Edmé Godin (b. 1799, employed until 1848), a *répareur garnisseur* of the first class, who worked at Sèvres from 1813. He too came from a family of which many members were attached to the factory.[6]

The portrait was reworked by Jean-Marie-Ferdinand Régnier (1774–1857) in 1822. In March he spent six days 'a retouché Le Camet de Louis XIV' and in August he is recorded as having 'Coulé en soufre les portraits camées de Louis 9, Louis XIV et du duc d'Orléans'.[7]

A sulphide portrait of this subject is in the Agen Museum, France.[8]

Of the jasper portraits of Louis XIV produced by Wedgwood, none corresponds with this version.[9]

1. L. Forrer, *Biographical Dictionary of Medallists*, Vol. III, London, 1907, p. 619.
2. MNS, Archives de Sèvres, Va'21, f. 119.
3. *Loc. cit.*, inv. 1817, no. 174, *Tiroir* 23 (L).
4. *Loc. cit.*, Vv 1, f. 269.
5. For notes on the incised mark *Li* used by Antoine-Mathieu Liancé (1732–77) on earlier soft-paste wares, see Savill, III, 1988, p. 1113.
6. See Chevallier, 1980, pp. 14–15.
7. MNS, Archives de Sèvres, Va'24, f. 135v, 136v.
8. Jokelson, 1968, fig. xi.
9. Reilly and Savage, 1973, pp. 218–20; of these, c and d have probably been wrongly identified, according to T.P.P. Clifford in a review 'Wedgwood at the National Portrait Gallery', *Burlington Magazine*, CXV, no. 849, December 1973, pp. 832–5.

174 **Portrait Medallion of Titian (Tiziano Vecelli, *c.* 1490–1576)**, probably 1800–20

D. 10.8 cm
Marks: *Sèvres* impressed, *titien* incised; printed labels *150*, *359*
Reg. No. 1909,12–1,161

Hard-paste porcelain, the rim moulded to simulate a frame and it and the edge glazed; in the centre on pale blue unglazed ground a moulded and applied bust portrait to the right of Titian bearded, wearing a hat and a coat with a fur collar. The relief is marred by a number of firecracks.

Provenance: Presented by Mr and Mrs I. Falcke, 1909

174 *mark*

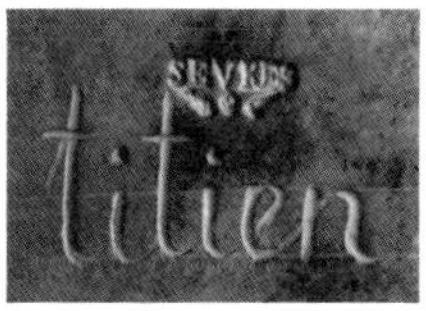

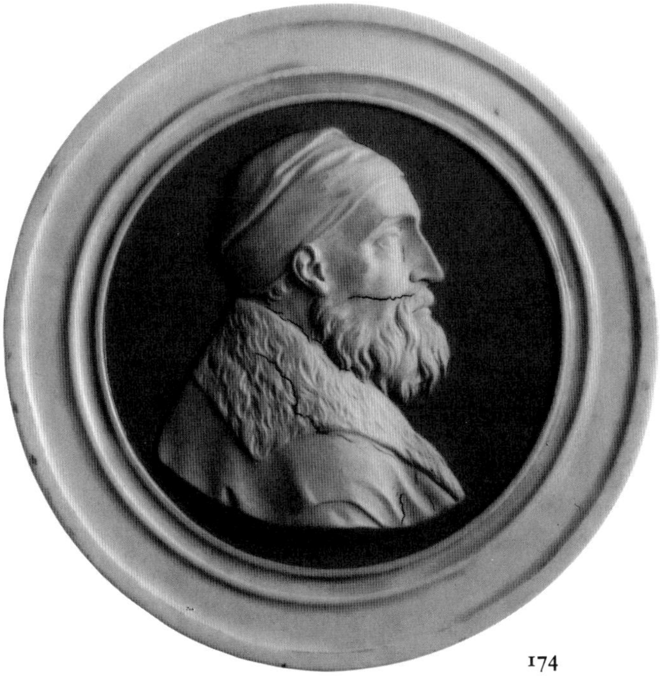

174

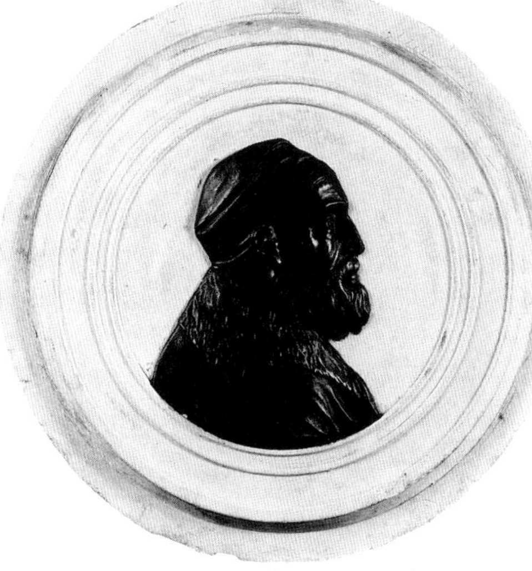

Fig 174a Wax model on plaster support, diam. 14 cm

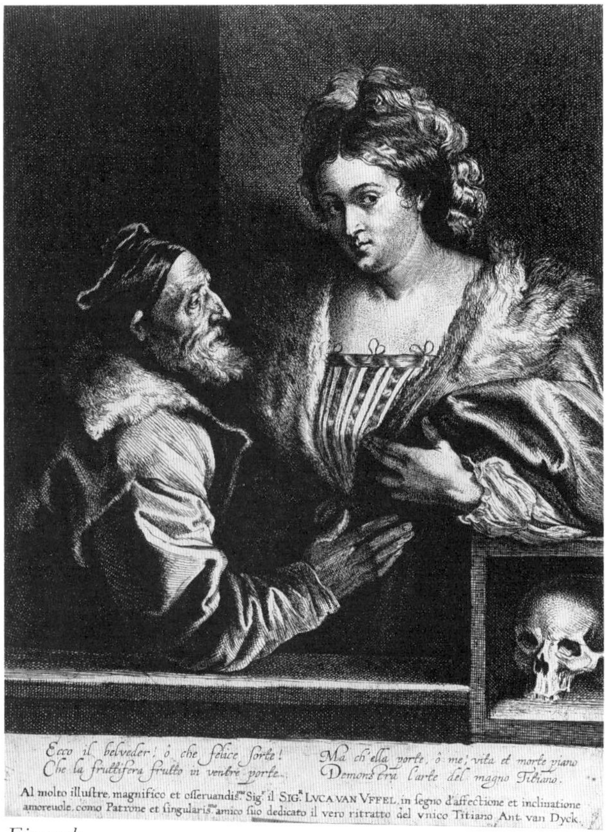

Fig 174b

Literature: A. Dawson, 'Copiers or Competitors? Wedgwood and the French Porcelain Factories', *Grosvenor House Antiques Fair 1983 Handbook*, pp. 37–9, illus.

Comparable Examples: None

This portrait appears to be the same as the one issued by the Etruria, Staffordshire, firm of Josiah Wedgwood and Thomas Bentley and listed in their catalogue of 1773.[1] Both are based on an etching called *Titian and his Mistress* by A. Van Dyck.[2] (See fig. 174b.)

A plaster model of this portrait measuring 11.8 cm in diameter is preserved at the Sèvres factory, together with a smaller one which is 9.5 cm in diameter. A red wax on plaster measuring 13.9 cm in total is in the Musée national de Céramique, Sèvres.[3] (See fig. 174a.)

The impressed mark was used on biscuit porcelain for several decades from the beginning of the nineteenth century. The dating of this medallion is problematical as neither its creation nor its sale have been traced in documents kept at the factory. It was probably made around 1800–20 when other blue-ground pieces are known to have been in production. Like the medallion of Préville, it is a highly finished production.

1. Reilly and Savage, 1973, p. 322.
2. There are four impressions of this print in the Department of Prints and Drawings, British Museum. The one illustrated was catalogued by F. Wibiral, *L'Iconographie d'Antoine van Dyck d'après les recherches de H. Weber*, Leipzig, 1877, p. 69, B III.
3. Inv. MNS 21660.

175 **Portrait Medallion of Pierre-Louis Dubus called Préville (1721–99)**, probably 1800–20

D.	10.5 cm
Marks:	*Sèvres* impressed; *préville* incised; printed label *360*
Reg. No.	1909,12–1,162

Hard-paste porcelain, the rim moulded to simulate a frame; frame and edge of medallion glazed; in the centre on a pale blue unglazed ground is a moulded and applied bust portrait to left of Préville. Rim restored.

Provenance: Presented by Mr and Mrs I. Falcke, 1909

Literature: A. Dawson, 'Copiers or Competitors? Wedgwood and the French Porcelain Factories', *Grosvenor House Antiques Fair 1983 Handbook*, pp. 37–9, illus.

Comparable Examples: None

Préville, one of France's most renowned actors, was born in Paris on 17 September 1721 in the rue des Mauvais-Garçons, faubourg Saint-Antoine, behind the Théâtre Français. His father was *intendant* to the princesse de Bourbon, abbess of Petit Saint-Antoine and the young Dubus was initially clerk to a *procureur* of the Châtelet and then in a notary's office. After a very short time he left this employment and began his acting career in small provincial towns. So successful was his début in Paris at the Théâtre Français in September 1753 that only a month later he became one of the King's comic actors. In 1774 he was made director of a theatre school established by the minister of the King's Household. After a highly successful career he retired in 1786, returning briefly to the stage at the age of seventy. In 1792 he took up residence in Beauvais. He died there on 27 frimaire l'an VIII (18 December 1800). He was also *membre honoraire* of the Institut. Dazincourt[1] was his pupil and read a tribute to him at the Lycée on 19 nivôse l'an VIII (9 January 1800) which was later published.[2]

Diderot wrote of the actor in *Le Neveu de Rameau*,[3] 'C'est un rare corps, que ce Préville. Il faut le voir dans *le Mercure Galant*'. In this play by Boursault he played no fewer than five roles.

No model or mould of the medallion is preserved at the factory; a red wax on plaster measuring 13.8 cm is in the Musée national de Céramique, Sèvres.[4] The dating of the medallion remains problematical as neither its creation nor its sale have so far been traced

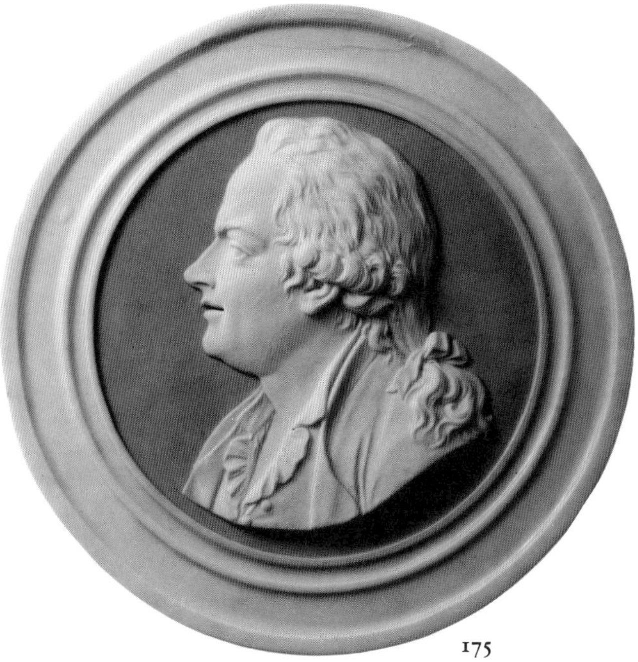

175

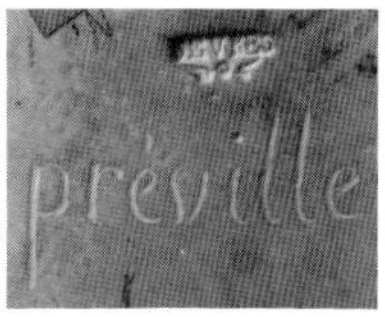

175 *mark*

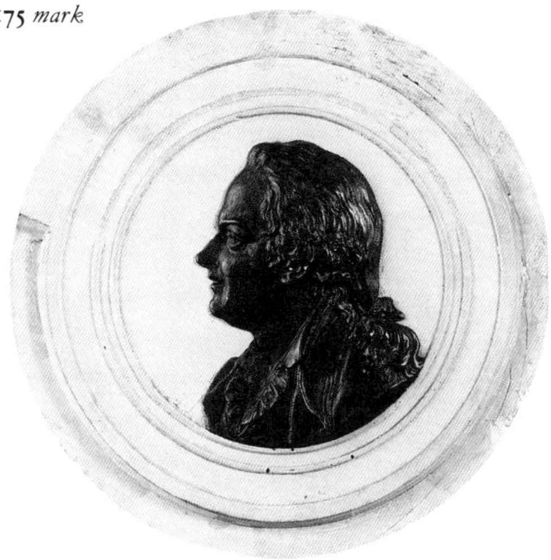

Fig 175a Wax model on plaster support, diam. 13.8 cm

in documents kept at the factory. It was probably made around 1800–20 during the period when other blue-ground biscuit pieces are known to have been in production. It is a particularly highly finished portrait, and may perhaps have been issued shortly after Préville's death. The source is unknown, but it probably shows him at a young age.

A figure of Préville in the role of Figaro modelled by Le Riche was produced at Sèvres in 1775.[5] A biscuit example was sold at Versailles on 23 December 1775 for 72 *livres*[6] and an enamelled example on 20 December 1776 for 144 *livres*.[7] A biscuit bust of Préville is in the Musée des arts décoratifs, Paris.[8] A terracotta bust of Préville in the rôle of Scapin in the Théâtre de Strasbourg recalls the earliest days of the actor's career.[9]

A presumed medallion of Préville is listed in the catalogue issued in 1779 by Josiah Wedgwood and Thomas Bentley of Etruria, Staffordshire. A mould of this portrait is preserved at the Wedgwood factory.[10]

1. Joseph-Jean-Baptiste Albouy, called Dazincourt (1747–1809).
2. J.-J.-B. Albouy, called Dazincourt, *Notice historique sur Préville*, Paris, 1800, copy in the British Library, press number 611.f. 22(11). Details of Préville's life given here are taken from this and from E.T.M. Ourry, *Mémoires de Préville et de Dazincourt*, Paris, 1823.
3. Denis Diderot, *Le Neveu de Rameau*, probably written about 1761 with later insertions, Livre de Poche edition, Paris, 1984, p. 42.
4. Inv. MNCS 21671.
5. Bourgeois and Lechevallier-Chevignard, 1913, pl. 22, no. 515.
6. MNS, Archives de Sèvres, Vy 6, f. 36.
7. MNS, Archives de Sèvres, Vy 6, f. 118.
8. Recorded in the Getty Photo Archive where it is classified as Sèvres, MDA inv. 2626, not examined by the author.
9. Exhibited Musée des arts décoratifs, Strasbourg (not part of the Rohan Collection).
10. Reilly and Savage, 1973, p. 283.

176 **Medallion**, probably *c.* 1885

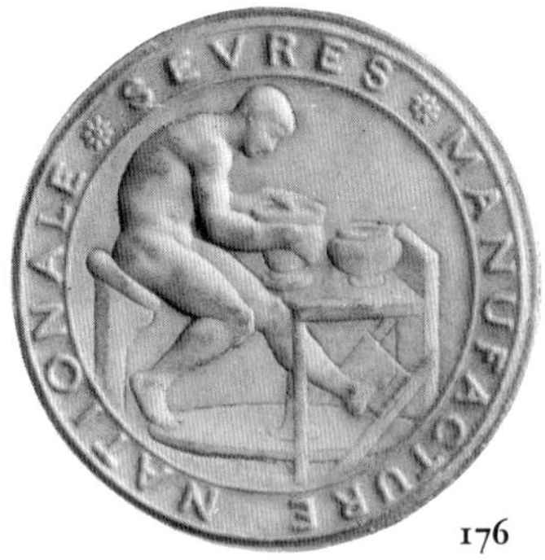
176

D.	4.5 cm
Marks:	none
Reg. No.	1906,11–3,1757

Hard-paste biscuit porcelain moulded with a figure of a nude man seated at the potter's wheel where he is throwing a pot, and inscribed in relief *MANUFACTURE NATIONALE SEVRES.*

Provenance: Presented by F. Parkes Weber, Esq., M.D., 1906

Literature: Unpublished

Comparable Examples: None

There are two models for the medallion at the factory, the smaller 10 cm in diameter bearing the signature of the model maker F. Levillain 1888. However, the medallion appears in a list of *modèles pour la fabrication* thought to date from around 1885. It is not known who was responsible for the design.

There is a rectangular plaque of hard-paste biscuit porcelain measuring 19.2 cm in length and incised on the reverse *RE 74–5* in the State Hermitage Museum (inv. unknown),[1] with a relief of a child throwing a pot; on the bench are potter's tools and above there is a teapot and other vessels. The foot treadle is signed *I Larue 1873*.

The medallion is otherwise unrecorded.

1. The author received a communication from Natasha Kasakevich in July 1992 to the effect that this piece could not be traced, although it was noted by the author in November 1982.

Nineteenth- and Twentieth-Century Sèvres[1]

The history of the factory during this period is complex and its output extremely diverse. Many aspects of its production, and in particular its figures and groups, have yet to be studied, although some authors have given a wide-ranging account of the pieces made,[2] and several exhibitions have focused on one of these centuries or the other.[3] Some of the factory's more adventurous techniques, such as its glaze effects, have been treated in some detail,[4] and interest has been shown in the artists employed there during this period. Outside France, pieces from this period are poorly represented.[5]

During the Revolutionary years production slowed down and the factory's *raison d'être* almost disappeared.[6] However, Bonaparte saw that it could continue to supply diplomatic gifts to heads of state and others, and provide services for his household.[7] His brother, Lucien Bonaparte, Minister of the Interior, appointed Alexandre Brongniart (1770–1847), as administrator of the factory in 1800. Brongniart was an engineer by training, and well-versed in mineralogy, zoology and geology. He quickly reorganised the factory, dismissing half of the 220 people employed, and dividing the *ateliers* into two sections, for fabrication and decoration. He perfected his own hard-paste composition, abandoning soft-paste entirely in 1804.[8] Surplus stocks of undecorated soft-paste were sold off, and much of it found its way to Britain where it was subsequently decorated.[9] The factory was put on the First Consul's Civil List in 1802, and has remained a state concern ever since. Much more rigorous accounting and costing procedures were adopted, as can be seen from the surviving records.[10]

On the technical side, one of Brongniart's most important innovations was the introduction of the two-chamber kiln, which allowed biscuit firing to take place in the upper chamber, whilst high-temperature conditions were achieved in the lower chamber.[11] Other innovations included experimental work on coal-firing (although wood continued to be used), the introduction of engine-turning lathes in 1813 and slip casting (*coulage*) in 1819. A range of new colours was brought into production, to compete with those in use at Paris factories such as Nast (see p. 368).

In the tradition of the factory, a number of artists (mainly painters)[12] and architects such as Charles Percier[13] and Brongniart's father Alexandre-Théodore[14] were taken on, principally to decorate some of the more prestigious vases and services but also to design new forms and decorative schemes.[15] Painters and sculptors were associated with the factory throughout the nineteenth century, and have continued to play an important role. An analysis of the marks used at the factory[16] has revealed the names and functions of some of the workers, although no study of the workforce has been carried out. Copious documentation and other sources of information such as reports and memoranda, together with pamphlets surviving in the factory archive, still await study by historians.[17]

On his death in 1847, Brongniart was succeeded as administrator by Jacques-Joseph Ebelmen, who himself died in 1852. The physicist Victor Regnault then took over until his retirement in 1871. At this point there was great debate about the continuing existence of the factory. Between 1871 and 1879 Louis Robert, who spent his whole working life at the factory, was in charge. In 1876 the factory moved to its present site beyond the Pont de Sèvres on the edge of the Parc de Saint-Cloud. Charles Lauth was its administrator between 1879 and 1887, when he was forced to resign because of his unpopularity with the workforce, whose working practices he had attempted to reform. He was succeeded by the well-known potter Theodore Deck, who was in turn replaced in 1891, this time by an administrator, Emile Baumgart. Several of these men had an important effect on the work of the factory during the second half of the century.

Experimental work, particularly on glazes, was carried out by the chemist Alphonse-Louis Salvetat (employed 1846–80). Two new hard-paste compositions were developed: the *pâte Lauth-Vogt* and the *pâte nouvelle*. Both of these high-quartz bodies allowed the use of a much greater range of colours, the second also permitting the use of crystalline and *flambé* glaze effects, which became wildly fashionable in the 1880s and beyond. The new porcelain was perfected by Georges Vogt, a chemist employed from 1880–91.

The eminent sculptor Albert Carrier-Belleuse (employed 1877–86) was the most important artistic director of the period. It was not until the end of the century that Alexandre Sandier (employed 1897–1916) succeeded in changing the artistic direction to take account of the new movements affecting the whole of French decorative art. At this point, the factory was completely reorganised on several levels in response to severe criticism made in 1891 which had once more called in question the very existence of Sèvres. From this time on until the outbreak of the Second World War, the factory kept up with new trends under the artistic direction of Henri Rapin (1920–34), Jean Mayodon (1934–9) and Emile Decoeur (1939–48).[18]

Throughout the nineteenth century the Sèvres factory participated in exhibitions, both in France (particularly during the early part of the century)[19] and internationally. Its products were always praised for the high quality of their workmanship.

1. This account is based on Lechevallier-Chevignard, 1908, pp. 129–64, 1–94 (this work is divided into two parts); Verlet *et al*, 1953, pp. 54–68; Brunet and Préaud, 1978, pp. 241–334.
2. See A. Faÿ-Hallé and B. Mundt, *Porcelain of the Nineteenth Century*, New York, 1983, pp. 24–36, 114–16, 168–72, 223–33.
3. A comprehensive list of exhibitions up to 1978 is given by Brunet and Préaud, 1978, pp. 351–2: see in particular 'Sèvres Porzellan von 18. Jahrhundert bis zur Gegenwart', Düsseldorf, Hetjens-Museum, October–November 1975, cat. introd. by H.-P. Fourest, compiled by A. Klein, A. Faÿ-Hallé, T. Préaud; 'Porcelaines de Sèvres au XIXe siècle', Musée national de Céramique, Sèvres, May–November 1975, cat. compiled by A. Hallé and T. Préaud; 'Sèvres: de 1850 à nos Jours', Paris, Louvre des Antiquaires, February–April 1983, introd. by T. Préaud; 'Porcelaines de Sèvres au XXe siècle', Musée national de Céramique, Sèvres, April–August 1987, cat. compiled by A. Faÿ-Hallé and V. Guillaume; A. d'Albis *et al.*, *Sèvres, Musée national de Céramique, nouvelles acquisitions (1979–1989)*, Paris, 1989, nos. 248–93.
4. M. Bodelsen, 'Sèvres-Copenhagen, Crystal Glazes and Stoneware at the Turn of the Century', *The Royal Copenhagen Manufactory*, Copenhagen, 1975, pp. 59–88.
5. The Victoria and Albert Museum, London, which acquired pieces at the time they were made, probably has the largest collection, recently re-displayed in Gallery 8; see *Art and Design in Europe and America 1800–1900*, introd. by S. Jervis, London, 1987, for a vase by T. Doat, pp. 122–3. One of the more splendid gifts from the French Government was discussed by A. Dawson, 'Pieces for Presentation', *Ceramics*, February/March 1986, pp. 71–6.
6. Little has been published on the factory during the Revolutionary period, but see E. Garnier, *La Manufacture de Sèvres en l'an VII*, Paris, 1988 and 'La Manufacture de Sèvres pendant la Révolution', *La Nouvelle Revue*, 1891 (extracts bound together and kept at the factory archive); Lechevallier-Chevignard, 1908, Chapter V, pp. 114–28; G. Lechevallier-Chevignard and M. Savreux, *Le Biscuit de Sèvres. Directoire, Consulat, et Premier Empire*, Paris, 1923.
7. For a service presented by Louis XVIII to the Duke of Wellington in 1818, see C. Truman, *The Sèvres Egyptian Service 1810–1812*, London, 1982; a number of Napoleonic productions have been discussed by S. Grandjean in various articles including: 'Le cabaret égyptien de Napoléon', *Musées de France*, April 1950, pp. 62–5; 'Un monument napoléonien en porcelaine', *Bulletin de l'Institut Napoléon*, no. 49, October 1953, pp. 103–5; 'Napoleonic Tables from Sèvres', *Connoisseur*, Vol. CXLIII, no. 577, April 1959, pp. 147–53; 'Un chef d'oeuvre de Sèvres, le Service de l'Empereur', *Art de France*, II, 1962, pp. 170–8; 'Un présent de Napoléon à Pie VII', *Bulletin de l'Institut Napoléon*, no. 106, January 1968, pp. 27–8; 'Deux remarquables souvenirs napoléoniens', *Revue du Louvre*, 1974, IV–V, pp. 323–30; see also C. Samoyault-Verlet and J.-P. Samoyault, *Château de Fontainebleau, Musée Napoléon Ier, Napoléon et la famille impériale 1804–1815*, Paris, 1986, pp. 38–43 and J.-P. Samoyault, 'Les "assiettes de dessert" du Service particulier de l'Empereur en porcelaine de Sèvres', *Le Souvenir napoléonien*, no. 369, February 1990, pp. 3–12. For services see exh. *Grands Services*, 1951, nos. 16–25, and subsequent services for the ensuing period up to 1947; for a detailed study of an exceptionally fine service see G. Barbe, *Le service du roi Louis-Philippe au Château de Fontainebleau*, privately published, Paris, 1989; see also the same author's 'Déjeuners en porcelaine de Sèvres de 1830 à 1848', *L'Estampille*, no. 235, April 1990, pp. 58–69; B. Chevallier has written a useful account of pieces from the later period mostly made for the châteaux of Fontainebleau and Compiègne, 'Sèvres sous le Second Empire', *L'Estampille*, no. 112, August 1979, pp. 28–39.
8. Soft-paste was reintroduced in the second half of the century, according to J. Mathieu *et al.*, *La Porcelaine de Sèvres*, Paris, 1982, p. 28; this work tells the story of the factory in an abbreviated form, giving much useful detail on techniques, and illustrates some of its most impressive productions.
9. This is discussed by Savill, 1988, III, Appendix VII.
10. Some idea of the detailed kind of costings made during Brongniart's time can be seen from his own *Traité des Arts Céramiques ou des Poteries*, Paris, 1844, Vol. II, pp. 340–2, 'Tableau des frais de cuisson de la porcelaine dure de la Manufacture royale de Sèvres en 1843, dans le plus grand four dit A', and 'Tableau des prix de cuisson par les capacités et par les poids'.
11. Brongniart's own account of the factory, *ibid.*, pp. 257–351, includes a section on firing and kilns, pp. 295–301; the kiln is illustrated in the *Atlas*, pls. L, LI. He states that he developed it in mid-1842. Important improvements were made in firing techniques throughout Brongniart's administration, and those he writes about are recent rather than at the beginning of the century.
12. See T. Préaud, 'Un fonds méconnu, la série des paysages conservés à la Bibliothèque de la Manufacture de Sèvres', *Cahiers*, no. 58, 1976, pp. 36–55; further names of artists employed by Brongniart are given in Brunet and Préaud, 1978, pp. 256–8.
13. The so-called 'pendule Percier', a biscuit porcelain clock-case was designed by Percier in 1813, see Brunet and Préaud, 1978, p. 306, fig. 436.

14. Exh. Brongniart 1986, see pp. 239–60. Alexandre-Théodore Brongniart designed the gilt border decoration with a military theme (consisting of a laurel wreath, swords and gold stars) for a plate from the 'service particulier de l'Empereur' of 1810, illustrated by Brunet and Préaud, 1978, pl. LIX, Musée national de Céramique, Sèvres, inv. 6238; for two other plates see J.-P. Samoyault, 'Nouvelles Acquistions pour le futur Musée Napoléon Ier', *La Revue du Louvre*, 5/6, 1985, p. 422, fig. 3.
15. The painter A.-E. Fragonard (employed 1806–39) was responsible for numerous forms and decors, see Brunet and Préaud, 1978, p. 287, fig. 336, p. 290, fig. 352, p. 291, fig. 359, etc.
16. Chevallier, 1980, pp. 5–23.
17. Some references to the printed material can be found in Lechevallier-Chevignard, 1908, pp. 157–60, (2nd part of work).
18. For some outstanding pieces made in the early twentieth century, see A. Sandier and G. Lechevallier-Chevignard, *Formes et Décors Modernes de la Manufacture nationale de Sèvres*, Paris, n.d. (?1914), and G. Lechevallier-Chevignard, *La Décoration Moderne à la Manufacture nationale de Sèvres*, Paris, n.d. (?1929).
19. These are listed in *Porcelaines de Sèvres au XIXe siècle* (see n. 3, p.49); a more complete list for the nineteenth century is given by Lechevallier-Chevignard, 1908, p. 160 (2nd part of work).

177 **Plate (*assiette*)**, 1802

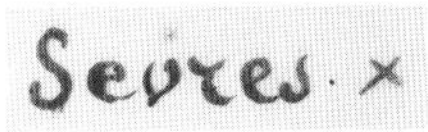

177 *mark*

D. 24.6 cm
Marks: *Sevres. X* painted in iron-red; suspension hole
Reg. No. 1941,4–7,1

Hard-paste porcelain, shallow profile with broad flat rim. Noticeable firing defects, especially on base. Painted in green, blue, purple, yellow and iron-red with a garland of flowers in the oriental taste, outlined and heightened in gold; the rim decorated in gold and platinum on a black ground with three groups of figures, animals and vegetation in the Chinese style. Rim and edge of well of plate gilded. Rim repaired.

Provenance: Presented by William King, Esq. (former Deputy Keeper in the British Museum), 1941

Literature: Tait, revised ed. 1972, fig. 20

Comparable Examples: Paris, Musée des arts décoratifs, inv. 22631, illus. Brunet and Préaud, 1978, no. 300 (plate)

Collection of E. Bernard, 1953, dated 1792, with central floral motif, photograph in Sèvres factory archive

County Durham, Barnard Castle, Bowes Museum, inv. X1291/1–6, with addition of central panel of *chinoiserie* ornament on a black ground, illus. *French Art, the Bowes Museum*, County Museum Service, Durham County Council, n.d., p. 18

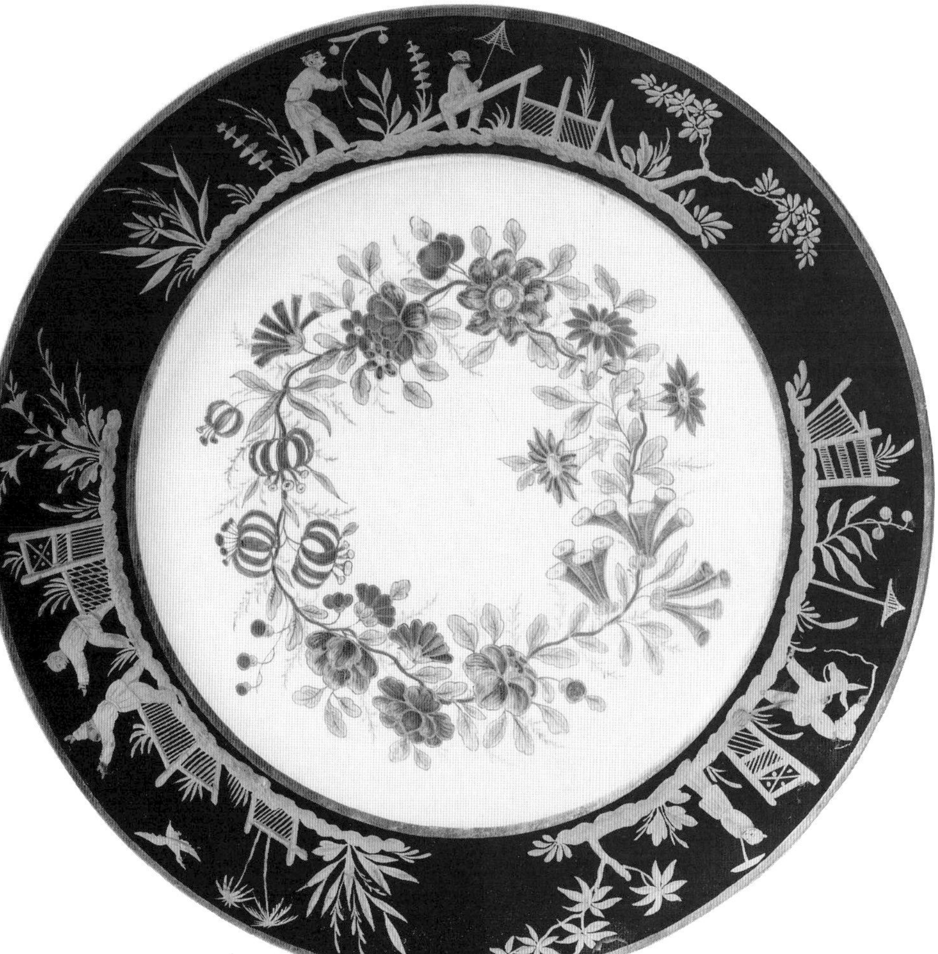

177

Russia, St Petersburg, State Hermitage Museum, two *tasses à glace*, two *seaux à demi-bouteille*, one *glacière*, one *plateau triangle*, one cup and saucer, see K. Butler, 'Sèvres for the Imperial Court', *Apollo*, Vol. CI, no. 160, June 1975, pp. 452–7, fig. 6, showing a *seau*, a *tasse à glace* and the *plateau*, all once in the collection of Prince Nicolay Borisovich Yusupoff (1750–1831)

USA, New York, Metropolitan Museum of Art, inv. 62.165.11 and 12, with the addition of a central floral motif, twelve plates of that pattern, sold, Paris, Ader, Picard, Tajan, 5 December 1979, Lot 21

USA, New York, Sotheby Parke Bernet, 24 February 1978, Lot 47, dish and cover

As Brunet and Préaud pointed out, 'M. de Semonville Ambassadeur' was the first to purchase a service described in the Sèvres factory sales records as 'fond noir Chinois en ors de couleurs et platine, fleurs émaillés', delivered on 6 May 1791.[1]

Chinese-style decoration on a black ground probably based on the designs of Jean Pillement (1728–1808) but in most cases not copied exactly from them,[2] continued to be used for services throughout the Revolutionary, Consulate and Imperial periods, both with and without the addition of enamelled flowers. Even chamberpots with this type of decoration, clearly imitating lacquer, are recorded as having been sold from the factory in Messidor l'an XIII, or 1805, and 1806.[3] Three *seaux à glace coupes*, or ice-cream coolers, dating from 1804–12 in the Metropolitan Museum, New York, are similarly decorated. The technique of outlining in gold oriental flowers painted on a white ground can be seen on a pair of *vases Paris* in the Wallace Collection, London, made around 1779.[4] A recipe for overglaze black is given in documents preserved at the factory.[5] Twenty-seven parts of glaze for hard-paste porcelain, six parts of *terre d'ombre* which had been calcinated in the upper chamber of the hard-paste kiln and three parts of Swedish cobalt were heated until the 'sulphur of arsenic' had been driven off. These ingredients were mixed and 'treated like the blue ground'. The 'bleeding' of dark blue into the white area of the plate, a characteristic noted on other similarly decorated pieces, may be due to the presence of cobalt in the glaze.[6]

1. MNS, Archives de Sèvres, Vy 11, f. 69.
2. For a motif copied from Pillement, *Cahiers de balançoires chinoises* . . . on a plate of this kind in the Metropolitan Museum of Art, New York, see T. Préaud, 'Sèvres, la Chine et les "chinoiseries" au XVIIIe siècle', *Journal of the Walters Art Gallery*, 47 (1989), p. 48, figs. 16, 17.
3. MNS, Archives de Sèvres, Vy 16, f. 30, 7 Messidor l'an XIII (1805), Pour le service du palais de Lacken [*sic*], 1 id. (pot de chambre rond) fond noir et chinois en or, 66 francs; *ibid.*, Vy 17, f. 23v, 6 September 1806, à Madame Toutan, 1 pot de chambre fond noir en or, 60 francs.
4. Savill, 1988, I, pp. 442–6 and R. Savill, 'A Pair of Sèvres Vases: From the Collection of Sir Richard Wallace to the J. Paul Getty Museum', *J. Paul Getty Museum Journal*, Vol. 14/1986, p. 141, fig. 7, and p. 138, where it is stated that Antoine d'Albis has discovered that around 1779 gilding on the hard-paste was applied before the enamel colours, the decoration being first outlined in gilding then coloured subsequently. The author is grateful to the late David Cohen for drawing her attention to this aspect of the decoration of the BM plate.
5. MNS, Archives de Sèvres, C2, *liasse* 5, f. 13.
6. The author is indebted to Rosalind Savill for this suggestion, more plausible than her own original belief that the black was applied over an underglaze-blue ground.

178 Cup and Saucer (*tasse et soucoupe*), 1807

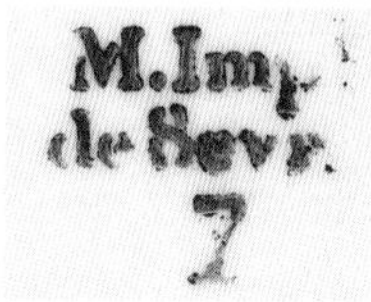

178 *mark*

D. *of saucer:*	13 cm
H. *of cup:*	4.3 cm
Marks:	*M. Imp. le/de Sèvres/7* printed on both, partly effaced; suspension hole on saucer
Reg. No.	Franks 390

Hard-paste porcelain, the shallow saucer with curved sides echoed in the shape of the small wide cup, which has a slightly scrolled handle beginning just below the rim and terminating just before the lower curve of the cup. The decoration consists of a band of gilt stylised floral ornament on a white ground near the rim, bounded by a gilt line enclosing sprinkled gilt decoration on a dark blue ground. Foot rim, handle, and inner and outer rim of cup gilt; rim of saucer gilt.

Provenance: Bequeathed by Sir A.W. Franks, 1897

Literature: Franks, 1896, No. 390

Comparable Examples: None

The name of this shape is unknown. No drawing for it has survived in the factory archives, and it is not shown in the *Tarif avec Formes*, a list drawn up in the 1830s giving prices of various shapes.[1] It was doubtless intended for tea.

Although the porcelain is very white, there are several defects, such as pin holes and black specks in the paste, and the foot rim of the cup has spots of gilding which has clearly been carelessly applied.

The decoration is meant to imitate lapis lazuli, an effect which had been sought at the factory since its early days.[2] It may perhaps be identified with pieces described in contemporary factory records as 'lapissé d'or', or perhaps with a cup and saucer described in factory documents as 'lapis Bleu et or frise Dieu' (the painter Jean-Jacques Dieu worked on this type of decoration). The paste and ground colour cost 2 francs 50 centimes, the *Lapis et frise* 1 franc, the gold 1 franc 60 centimes and the burnishing 40 centimes.[3] By comparing these prices with first and second sizes

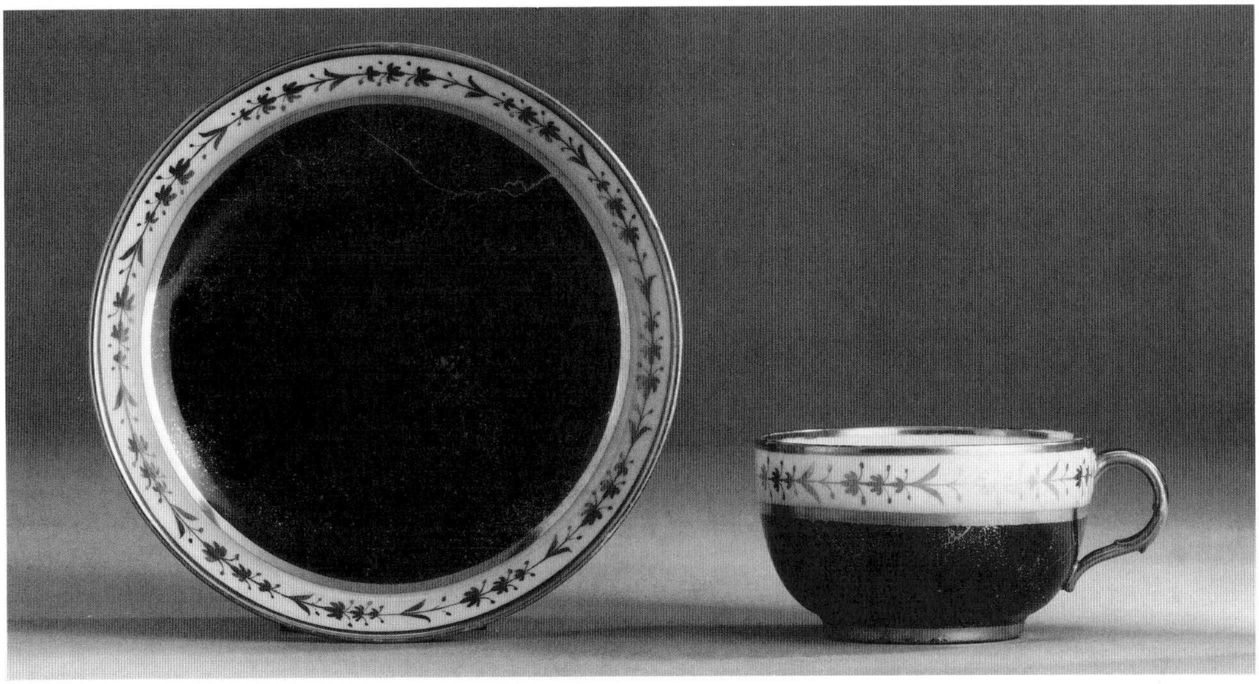

178

of *tasses à thé*, it is evident that the cup and saucer in question were small. On 6 May 1807 a further '6 tasses et Spes a thé forme ancienne a une anse et Blanche Lapis en or et frise dit Dieu' were recorded in the *magasin de vente* at the factory at the same price for the paste and ground colour and 2 francs for the burnishing.[4]

No matching pieces are known to the author. Further research in the nineteenth-century records at the Sèvres factory is needed to establish more precisely the production history of this unusual cup and saucer.

1. MNS, Archives de Sèvres, Y 22.
2. Cat. 77 is an example of this; a later version decorated in 1781 is the pair of vases in the Royal Collection, see Bellaigue, 1979, pp. 36–7.
3. MNS, Archives de Sèvres, Pb 1, *liasse* 11, *Feuilles des Rentrées* 22 April 1807.
4. *Ibid.*, 6 May 1807.

179 **Plate (*assiette de dessert*)**, 1806–8

See colour plate 27

D. 23.2 cm
Marks: *M Imp[le]/de Sevres* painted in red, scratched out; *1161* and *Mun* or *Mon* incised
Reg. No. 1987,7–6,1

Hard-paste porcelain, thrown, with shallow well and broad rim which is almost flat on the upper surface. The decoration consists of a bearded man in the Antique style depicted in profile to right, his feet bare, the lower part of his body covered by a voluminous robe, his left arm outstretched to rest on a scroll supported on a lectern in front of him, his right hand raised to his face with his index finger and thumb outstretched, painted in sepia and dark brown heightened in gold on a grey 'marbled' ground, enclosed by a wide gilt band. The border is decorated with an acanthus and palmette design on a dark blue ground between two gilt bands. The underside of the rim and the exterior of the foot are gilt. The foot rim has been wiped clear of glaze. It has a few apparent chips but each has traces of glaze in the chip itself. Gilding rubbed around the rim in places and restored in one area.

Provenance: Purchased, 1987

Literature: Dawson *et al.*, 'Recent acquisitions of post-medieval ceramics and glass in the British Museum's Department of Medieval and Later Antiquities 1982–88', *Burlington Magazine*, Vol. CXXX, no. 1022, May 1988, p. 402.

Comparable Examples: USA, New York, Metropolitan Museum of Art, inv. 1987.224

USA, Collection of Richard D. Pardue

France, private collection

London, Kate Foster Ltd., 1987

London, Armin B. Allen, 1990

London, Gerald Sattin, 1990

This plate was part of a service (see below) traceable in the factory records as early as 1806 when it was at the decorating stage under the title of 'service Leguay'. The plates were described as 'Marli beau bleu riche frise d'or figures tirées de Fragonard, Landon, etc[a] en bronze rehaussé en or fond caillouté.'[1] The blue border (*marli*) was probably applied first, followed by the 'marbled' ground in the well, which is called 'fond agathe' in the factory records and was

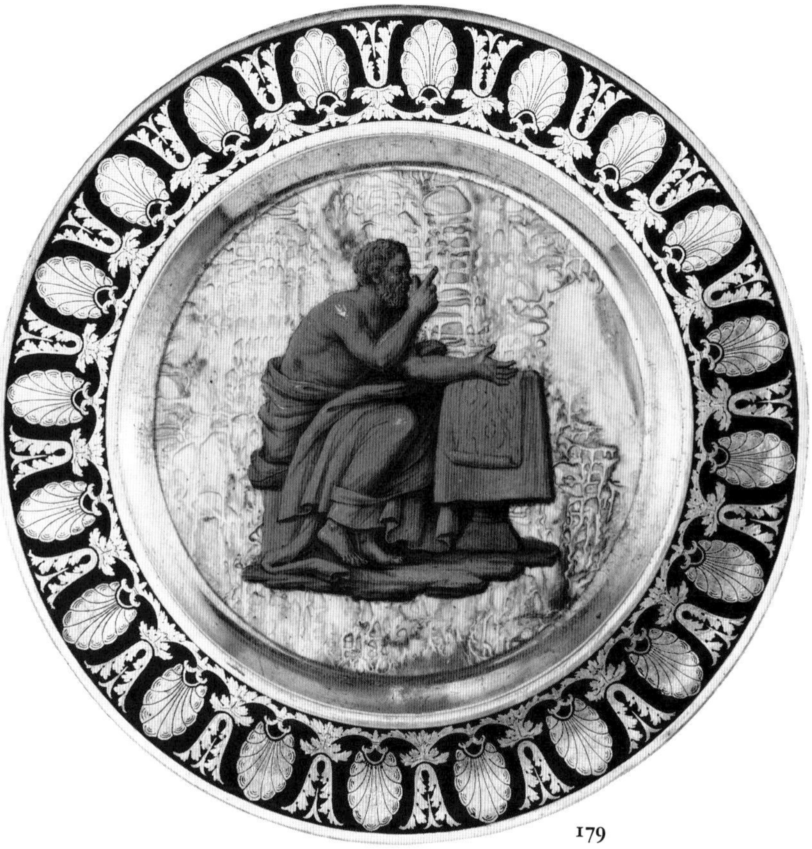

179

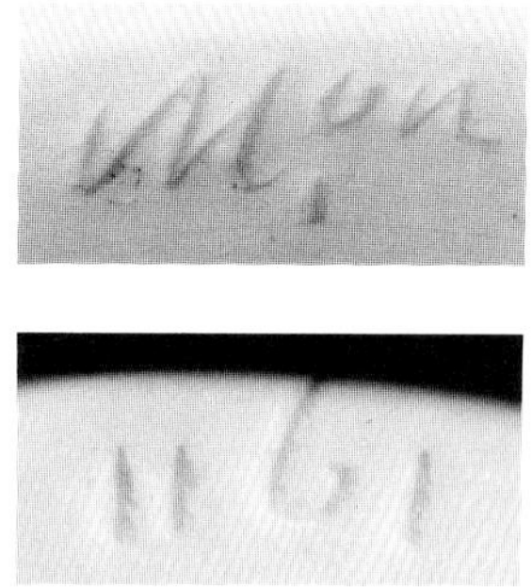

179 *marks*

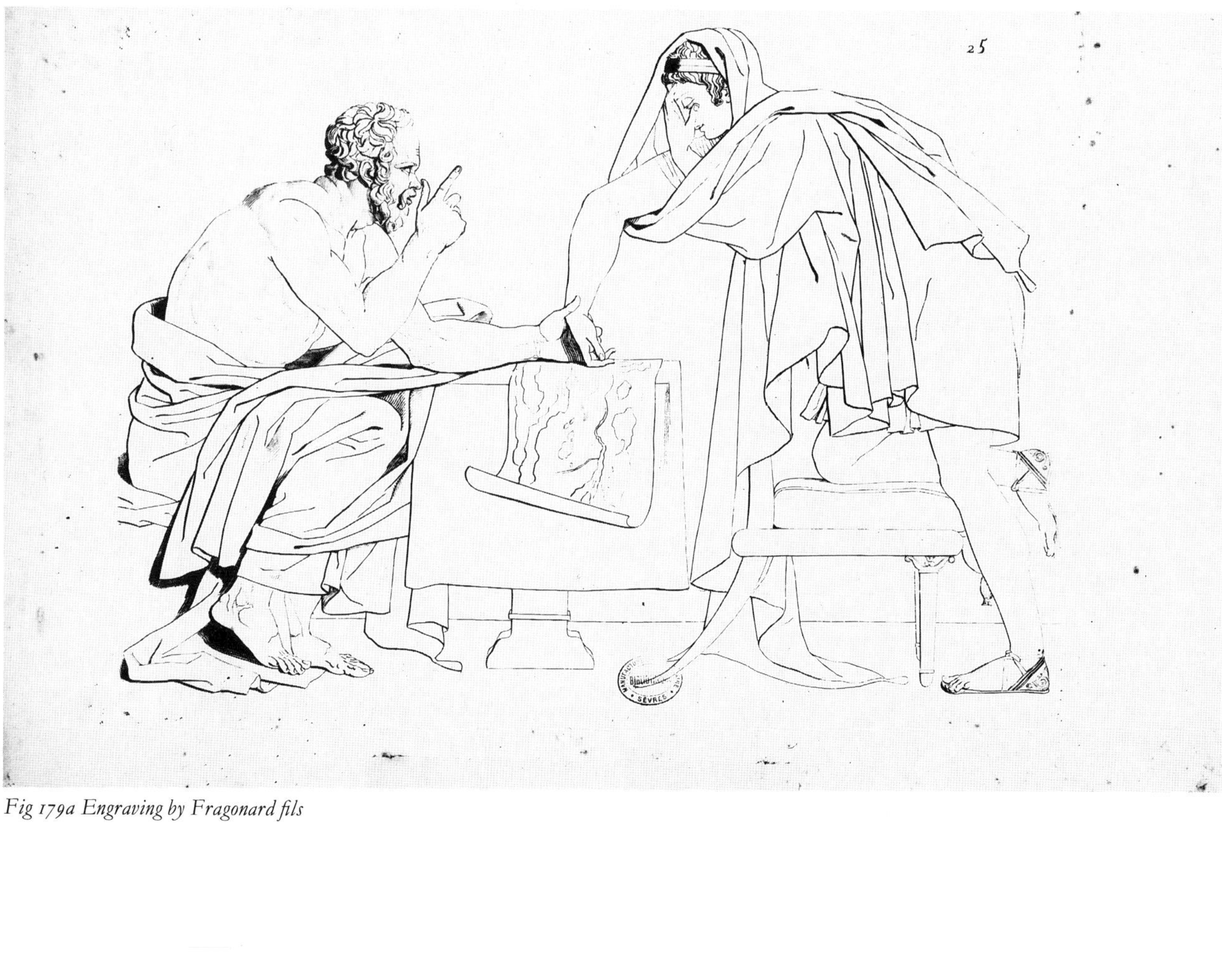

Fig 179a Engraving by Fragonard fils

the work of the ground-layer (*metteur en fonds*) Legros. Two layers of colour were necessary, requiring two separate firings.[2] The figure-painter Le Guay[3] was paid 19 francs 40 centimes for 'figures en brun rehaussés (or 'éclairés') d'or' on six plates from August–September 1806 and work continued until March 1808.[4] The gilder Weydinger and his son both received 12 francs for each *frize d'or* from July 1806; batches of twelve plates were normally noted in the work register.[5]

The gilding on the border is referred to in contemporary factory records as *dorure gratée* because of the incised lines used to render details. More elaborate versions of the technique, a speciality of the burnishers, were known as *bien gratée* or even *très bien gratée*.

Although the cost of burnishing and incising the gilding was minimal, the cost of applying the gilding and of the painting of the centre figure subject alone amounted to at least 27 francs for each plate, accounting for over half the manufacturing costs.

The identity of the workman using the incised mark *Mun* or *Mon* is uncertain, although there were two throwers named Monginot (*oncle* and *neveu*) *c.* 1802. The other incised marks remain unidentified.

On 8 March 1808 the service was received at the factory saleroom and entered in the register as follows:

Service de dessert sur fond beau bleu figures en brun rehaussées en or sur fond caillouté etc[a][6]

	entrée	*vente*
78 Assiettes à	51.65/3.978	40/ 3/120
12 Compotiers	34,00/408	40/480
2 Sucriers	92,00/184	100/200
4 Seaux à bouteilles	120,00/480	125/500
2 Verrières étrusques	125,00/250	140/280
2 Jattes à pied	82,00/164	100/200
2 Glacières for[e] vase	250,00/500	260/520
2 Corbeilles Coupe	100,00/200	120/240
		5.540

The left-hand column of figures was the cost price, the right-hand column the selling price.

The figure has been identified as Socrates, the left-hand figure in an engraving entitled *Morale de Socrate sur le mépris des Richesses* in a *Receuil de 132 sujets; Composés et Gravés par Fragonard Fils* (see fig. 179a). The collection, kept at the factory and inventoried in 1812,[7] is made up of 60 plates of classical subjects sold, according to the title page 'par Cahier de Six Feuilles Prix 6'. Alexandre-Evariste Fragonard (1780–1850) was the son of Jean-Honoré Fragonard and Marie Ann Gerard, and worked at Sèvres from 1812–35, creating both shapes and decors.[8]

No record of the sale of the service nor of its presentation as a gift has yet come to light. The disparity between the sale price of the plates and their manufacturing cost, as shown in the above extract from the factory records, is untypical of the service as a whole. Indeed, a progress report given at the beginning of 1808 makes it clear that only second- and third-quality plates with blue grounds were used. Although the service was described as having *éclat*, the figures 'ayant eté faites par un homme agé et attaché depuis son enfance à la manufacture' were considered to be mediocre. Despite this dismissive note, the plate is a good example of the taste of the period.

1. MNS, Archives de Sèvres, Pb 1, *Traveaux de 2ème trimestre 1806*, no. 12.
2. *Ibid.*, Vj'14, f. 44 *et seq.* (Legros). The first mention occurs in June/July or early August 1806, Vy 13, f. 121v.
3. Pierre-André Le Guay (1743–1819), figure painter of the first class, receiving as much as 100 *livres* a month from 1786 up to the Revolution; for a biography see Bellaigue, 1986, pp. 58–9. In the *Etat Nominatif Pour l'An Dix* (1801–2) it was noted that Le Guay *figuriste* received 125 francs a month, only the head of the workshop of painters and gilders, Asselin, and Dodin receiving more at 167 francs and 145 francs a month respectively. At this time, Micaud, Parpette, Massy and Bouillat earned the same as Leguay, MNS, Archives de Sèvres, MI, *dossier* 8 (service de l'Empereur).
4. MNS, Archives de Sèvres, Vj' 13, f. 50v; Vj' 15, f. 7 (Leguay).
5. MNS, Archives de Sèvres, Vj' 13, f. 112, f. 120 (Weydinger).
6. MNS, Archives de Sèvres, Vu, 1, f. 50.
7. MNS, Archives de Sèvres, N 336.
8. See C. Nordenfalk, *Sèvres et les cinq sens*, Stockholm, 1984, Part III La Coupe dite des Sens. There is no monograph on A.-E. Fragonard, a precocious and prolific artist, pupil of David, holder of the Légion d'Honneur from 1815, but some information can be found in 'Les peintres de la famille de Jean-Honoré Fragonard', exh. cat. compiled by G. Vindry, Grasse, Villa-Musée Fragonard, 16 April–15 May 1988.

180 **Pair of Ice-pails (*glacières à gorge à têtes d'éléphants*)**, 1811

See colour plates 29 and 30

H.	34.2 cm
Max. W.	28.9 cm
Marks:	*M. Imp.[le]/de Sevres/1811.* stencilled in red on both; *31.A.[st]* painted in gold on one with Tuileries/Ecouen; *DC* incised on both for the thrower Louis-Charles Descoins
Reg. No.	1985,12–3,1 and 2

Hard-paste porcelain, the ovoid body with out-turned neck formed in a mould and attached to the trumpet-shaped support which rests on a square plinth, both also moulded, by means of a fitment. The elephants' heads are separately applied. Each pail has a lid with a conical knop resting on a flange inside the neck. The vases are entirely gilt except for a narrow area left white to

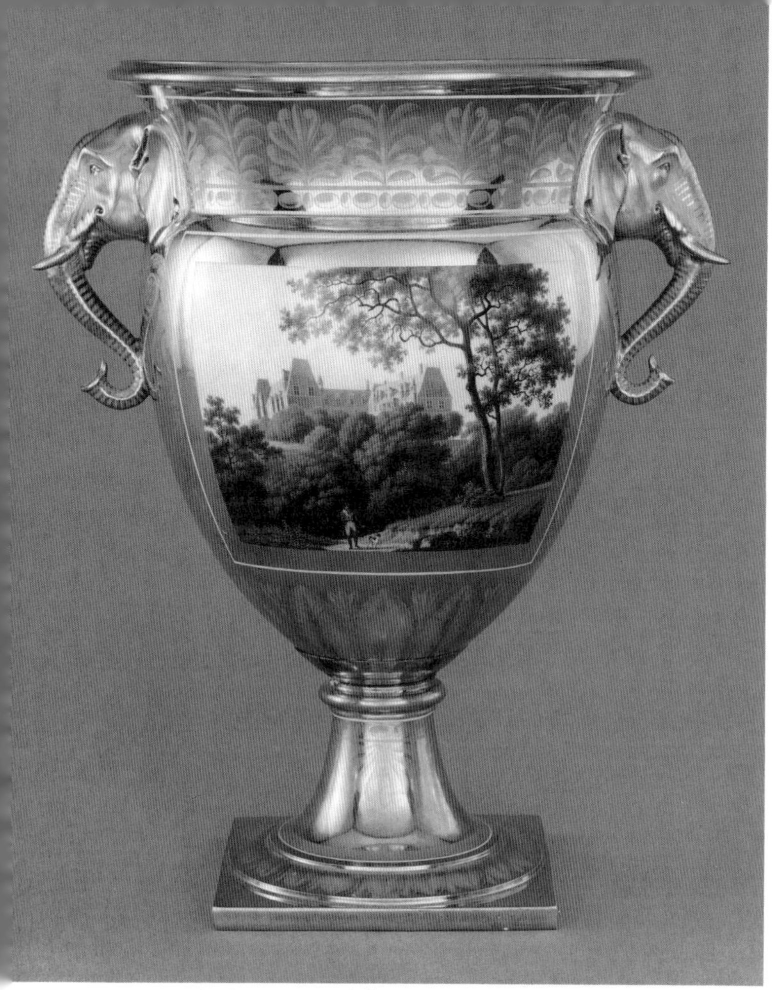

180 *(1985, 12–3, 2) Ecouen*

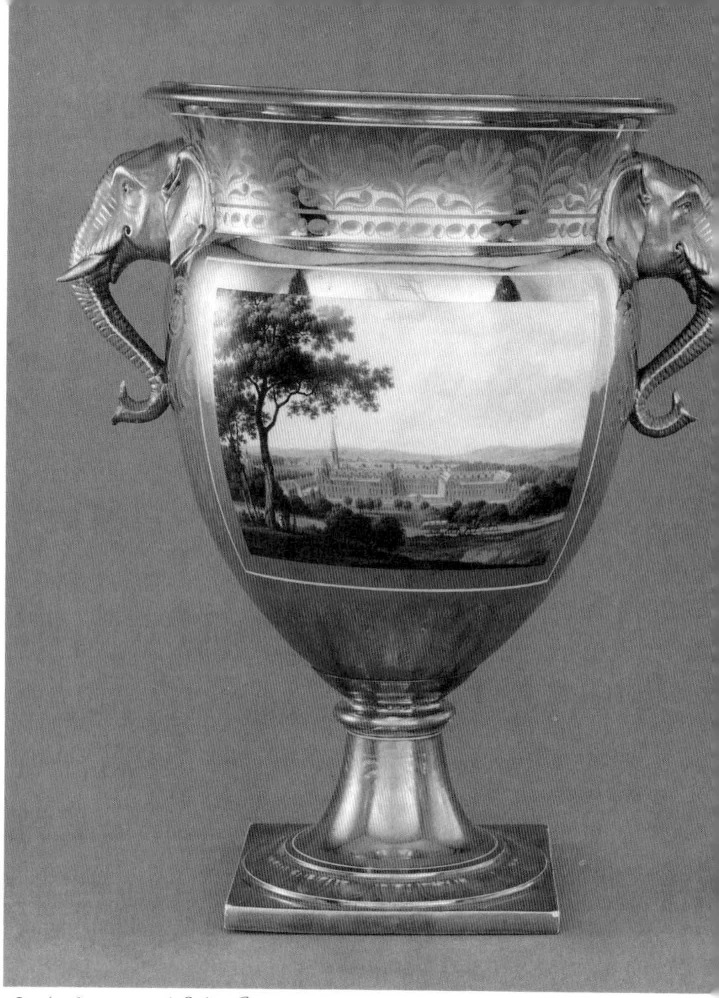

180 *(1985, 12–3, 1) Saint-Cyr*

frame a rectangular panel on each side painted by J.-F. Robert with a scene of a château or other building: on 1985,12–3,1 Saint Cloud and Saint-Cyr (signed Robert); on 1985,12–3,2 the Tuileries and Ecouen (signed Robert). The neck and lower part of the vases are decorated with a burnished palmette and a leaf motif respectively. The elephant trunks and ears are burnished with a striped pattern. Trunks and tusks restored. Crack running through Tuileries scene.

Provenance: Presented to the Emperor Francis II of Austria by Napoleon I, 1812[1]

Purchased; Sotheby's, 22 November 1983, Lot 12 (unsold); from a German aristocratic collection, said to have been in the same family in Riga from about 1830

Literature: A. Dawson, 'Two Napoleonic Sèvres Ice-Pails: A Present for an Emperor, *Apollo*, Vol. CXXIV, no. 296, October 1986, pp. 328–33

A.-M. Nisbet, V.-A. Masséna, N. Blondel, *L'Empire à Table*, Paris, 1988, col. ill. p. 14 (reversed)

Comparable Examples: Wales, Cardiff, National Museum of Wales, inv. NMW A30,050, pair of the same form painted with cameo heads of Julius Caesar and Alexander the Great by J.M. De Gault dated 1812, illustrated by O. Fairclough, 'Two Pieces from the Sèvres "Service Iconographique Grec"' *NACF Review 1990*, p. 151 and 'Recent Acquisitions at the National Museum of Wales', *Burlington Magazine*, Vol. CXXXII, no. 1051, p. 756, XX

Sotheby's, 25 May 1982, Lot 164, pair of same form painted with flowers

Italy, Florence, Pitti Palace, Museo degli Argenti, see S. Eriksen, *French Porcelain in Palazzo Pitti*, Florence, 1973, no. 581, pair of the same form decorated with classical motifs, from the service of the Grand Duchess Elisa, 1809–10

Germany, Berlin, Kunstgewerbemuseum, decorated with a cameo portrait, from the 'Service Iconographique Grec', illus. B. Mundt, 'Ein Empireservice mit Kameenmalerei, zu einer Neuerwerbung des Berliner Kunstgewerbemuseums', *Kunst und Antiquitäten*, November 1990, pp. 20–1, figs. 1, 2

The model was devised by Brachard in 1806.[2] The design survives at the Sèvres factory and shows the position of the metal liner, now missing, which held the ice-cream surrounded by crushed ice.[3] The use of the elephant heads is reminiscent of the famous rococo vase, itself based on a Chinese prototype,[4] but otherwise both shape and decoration are resolutely Empire in style.

The signature of Jean-François Robert (1778–1838) appears on one scene on each pail, i.e. Saint-Cyr and Ecouen, although Robert was responsible for all four, each of which has a Napoleonic connection. Napoleon proclaimed himself First Consul in the Orangerie at Saint-Cloud, which became his summer home in the autumn of 1802 and in April 1810 was the venue for his marriage to Marie Louise of Austria. Damaged by fire in 1870, it was demolished in 1891. This scene is based on an original drawing by J.-F. Robert

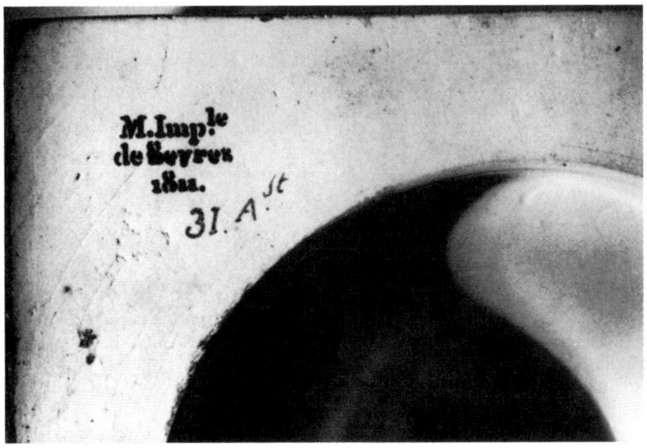

180 *marks*

engraved by J. van Marcke, issued as a lithograph by C. Constans of Paris around 1820.[5] The scene on the ice-pail differs from the print as it shows Napoleon and Marie Louise in a landau, accompanied by General Marquis de Caulaincourt (1772–1827) and Roustam Raza (1782–1845). In 1807 Napoleon established a school at Ecouen (now Museum of the Renaissance) for the daughters of members of the Légion d'Honneur, under the direction of Madame Campan. This view of Ecouen is based on a *Vue du Château d'Ecouen prise du milieu des Bois* published in l'an XIII (1805) by Baltard.[6] In 1802 Napoleon established a preparatory military school, the Prytanée, at Saint-Cyr, and in 1808 moved it so as to house the *école militaire* at Saint-Cyr. A drawing, lacking the hunter and dog, entitled *Vuë du Paÿsage et de la maison royalle de St. Cir* survives in the Sèvres factory archives.[7]

The Tuileries Palace, destroyed in 1871, was Napoleon's residence from 1800 until his exile. A gouache, perhaps by Robert, of the scene on the ice-pail in which the only sculpture is the Farnese Hercules by G. Comino, survives in the Sèvres archives.[8] Four bronze statues can be distinguished in the scene on the ice-pail. They are by Primaticcio after antique originals in the Belvedere and were commissioned by François I for Fontainebleau. Completed at the end of 1543, they were probably moved to the Tuileries between 1797 and 1799, entered the Louvre Museum in 1870 and were returned to Fontainebleau in 1968.[9] The same scene of the Tuileries signed by Robert and dated 1816 is painted on a plaque incorporated into a table formerly on loan to the Getty Museum, Malibu, USA.[10]

The ice-pails were part of a service *marli d'or* (with a gold border) originally consisting of plates with a tooled gold border and painted scenes by the factory's leading artists, made on Brongniart's instructions in between important orders. These two, valued at 1,000 francs each, were part of a gift made on 5 May 1812 to the Emperor Francis II of Austria by his son-in-law Napoleon I, through Prince Schwarzenberg (1771–1820), Austrian ambassador to the French Court.[11] Details of the gift, worth 25,000 francs in all, are recorded in the factory archive[12] but the later history of the ice-pails has not been discovered.

The incised mark *DC* was used by the thrower Louis-Charles Descoins (1767–1828), known as Descoins *fils aîné*, who worked at the factory between 1776 and 1821 (except between 1778 and 1780).[13]

Robert was paid a total of 350 francs for the painting between June and October 1811, the burnishing of the gold being the next most expensive element of production costs, which were detailed as follows:[14]

2 vases a glace a gorge fond d'or 2 cartels de paysages vues de palais imperiaux, ornements en bruni reserve, un

pâte	60
dorure	24
or	60
Peinture des paysages par M. Robert	350
brunissage à l'effet	110
brunissage à plat	25
Total des frais directs	620
faux-frais	155
prix de fabrication	775
prix de vente	1000

The gilding was carried out from July 1811 when an entry appears in the factory work register under Boitel *doreur*: 'Glacière Sve Marly d'or pture du Paysage Par Mr Robert Pour le fond en or'.[15] The first gilding on the other piece was carried out in the next month, as is confirmed by the mark *31.Ast* (31 August) on the pail showing Ecouen and the Tuileries. Dame Noualhier, a burnisher specialising in matt burnishing, received 90 francs on account for the first burnishing of one of the pails[16] and her colleague, Dame Troyon, earned 2 francs in December 1811 for time spent on a 'glacière du Sve Marly, d'or Brunir des aplats de la gorge en dedans et filets'.[17]

1. MNS, Archives de Sèvres, Vy 21, f. 11.
2. As Tamara Préaud has kindly pointed out, the factory records do not specify which particular member of this extensive family was responsible for the design.
3. Illus. Dawson, 1986, p. 328, fig. 1.
4. Eriksen, 1968, no. 43, 51; Savill, 1988, I, pp. 154–6, discusses the shape in detail.
5. See Dawson, *op. cit.*, fig. 5.
6. Louis Pierre Baltard, *Paris et ses Monumens Mesurés Dessinés et Gravés par Baltard, Architecte*, Paris, An XIII (1805), Château d'Ecouen, pl. 8.

7. See Dawson, *op. cit.*, fig. 7. The pen and wash drawing was apparently at the Sèvres factory in 1808.
8. Dawson, *op. cit.*, fig. 6.
9. See S. Pressouyre, 'Les Fontes de Primatice à Fontainebleau', *Bulletin Monumental*, t. 127, III, 1969, pp. 223–39, and G. Bresc-Bautier and A. Pingeot, *Sculptures des jardins du Louvre, du Carrousel et des Tuileries*, Paris, 1986, Vol. 2, nos. 319–23. The author is grateful to M. J.-P. Samoyault for assisting in the identification of these bronzes in Robert's painted scene.
10. See A. Gonzáles-Palacios, *Il Tempio del Gusto*, Milan, 1984, Vol. I, pp. 391–5, col. pl. LXI; Vol. II, p. 280, figs. 643, 644.
11. For a portrait of this Prince by Sir Thomas Lawrence painted in 1819 for King George IV, see O. Millar, *The Later Georgian Pictures in the Collection of Her Majesty the Queen*, London, 1969, 2 vols., no. 912, pl. 200.
12. MNS, Archives de Sèvres, Vy 21, f. 11.
13. See Chevallier, 1980, p. 13.
14. MNS, Archives de Sèvres, *Carton* Pb 2.
15. MNS, Archives de Sèvres, Vj' 18, f. 46v.
16. *Ibid*, f. 88v.
17. *Ibid*, f. 124.

181 Soup Plate (*assiette à potage*), 1824

See colour plate 28

D. 23.6 cm

Marks: LL below a fleur-de-lys enclosing X; *Sevres 24* beneath LL; cursive *MC-* for an unidentified painter in brown; *M 9e* for an unidentified gilder near foot rim in gold, incised *1*, [?] *24–8* (date code for making of plate) and cursive *D4*

Reg. No. Franks 391

Hard-paste porcelain painted with the arms and motto of the Earls of Stair with mantlings in the centre and with the crest of Dalrymple on the rim. The rim and edge of the border are gilt. Two chips on foot rim.

Provenance: Bequeathed by Sir A.W. Franks, 1897

Literature: Franks, 1896, no. 391

Comparable Examples: Sèvres, Musée national de Céramique, MNC 20756, plate acquired in 1944. A soup plate is recorded in the Sèvres Museum files as having been in a private collection at Suresnes in 1944. It has not been possible to discover whether examples are still in the possession of the Dalrymple family.

On 16 December 1824 'Milord Stair' of rue de Clichy N° 42 Chaussée d'Antin ordered 12 soup plates and 60 plates. The decoration was specified as 'deux filets d'or sur le marli armoirie coloriée Au milieu Roche colorié sur un baton rond or et bleu le tout conforme au modèle et aux dessins et instructions données'.[1] The price for the decoration was 9 francs without the rock. The sales registers[2] show that the order was delivered on 4 February 1825, each soup plate costing 11 francs and the model for the plate costing 32 francs. The total cost, which included a 10 per cent discount, amounted to 741 francs 60 centimes.

As the 6th Earl of Stair died in June 1821, the soup plate was presumably ordered by John William Henry

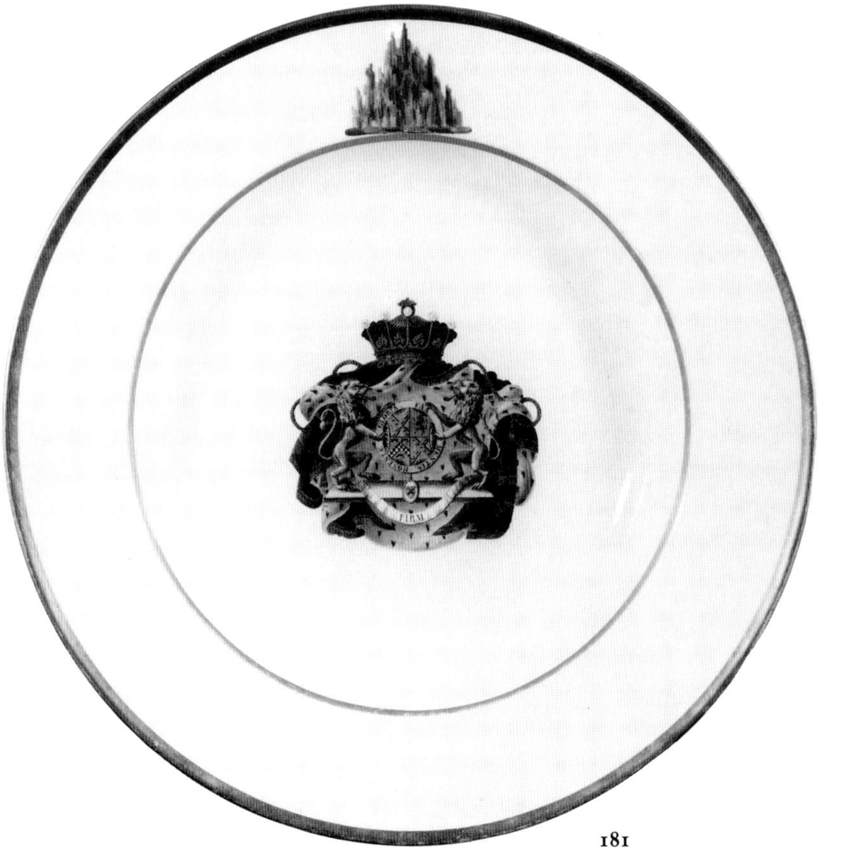

181

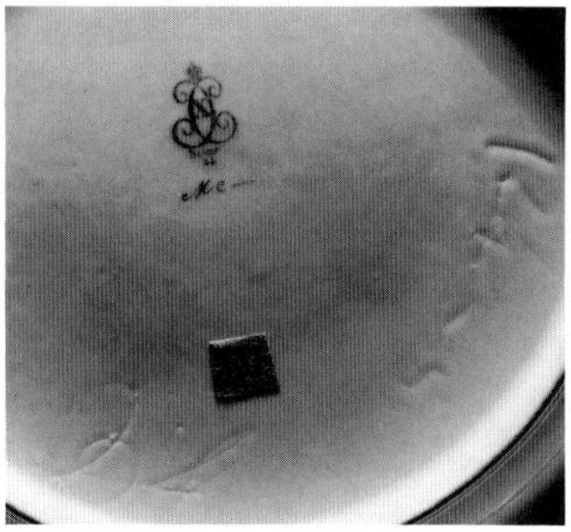

181 *marks*

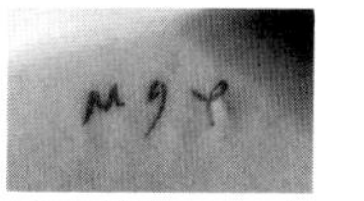

181 *gilder's mark*

Dalrymple, 7th Earl of Stair (1784–1840). The son of General Sir William Dalrymple, he married, in 1808, Laura, youngest daughter of George Manners, Esq. and Louisa, Countess of Dysart. The marriage was dissolved the following year in consequence of his having entered into a marriage contract with Johanna, daughter of Charles Gordon, Esq. of Clunie, Aberdeenshire, Scotland. This marriage was dissolved in June 1820. The earl died at Paris without issue.[3]

A Sèvres plate of 'around 1820' painted with the arms and motto of Baron Combermere and his second wife Caroline Greville was on the London market in 1987.[4]

1. MNS, Archives de Sèvres, Vtt 2, f. 37.
2. MNS, Archives de Sèvres, Vz 4, f. 174v.
3. Biographical information from W. Anderson, *The Scottish Nation*, Vol. III, Edinburgh, 1863, p. 506. Information kindly provided by Tony Stevenson. Sir Hew Hamilton-Dalrymple has kindly drawn to the author's attention another work giving information on this family, H. Hamilton-Dalrymple, *Genealogical Account of the Dalrymples of Stair, Earls of Stair*, privately printed, 1909.
4. Sotheby's, 17 March 1987, Lot 105, present whereabouts unknown.

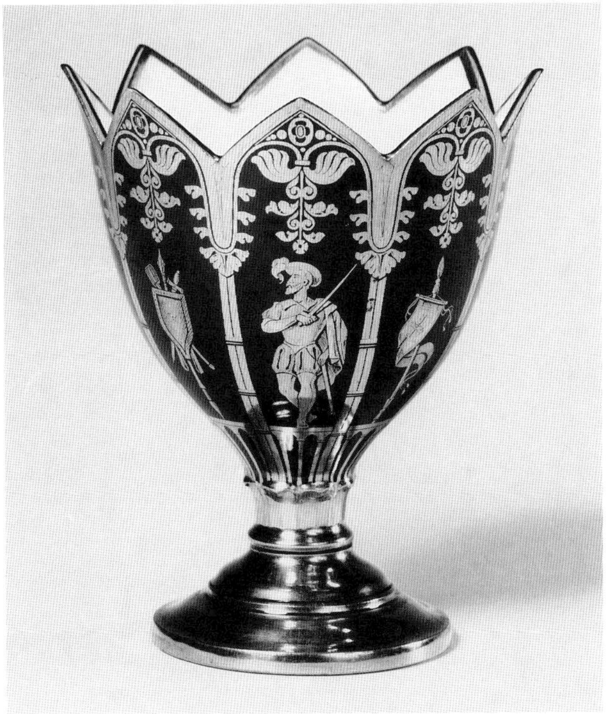

182

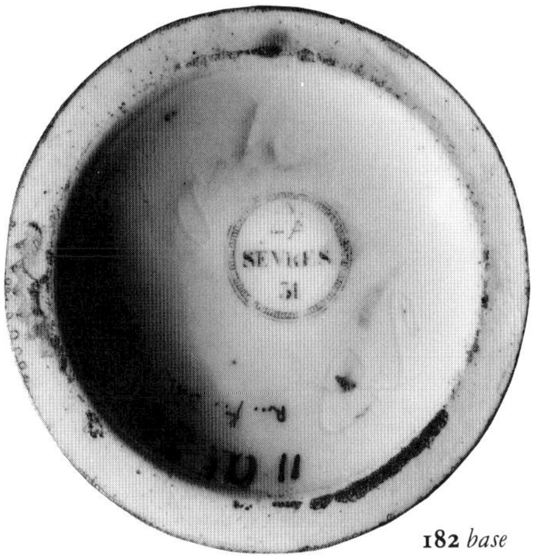

182 *base*

182 **Zarf**, 1830–2

See colour plate 26

H.	9.1 cm
Marks:	*SEVRES 31* within a circle printed in grey; *11a.t 30* painted in green; *R. . .f. .32. .* in gold; *CL* [?] *Dy* [?] incised
Reg. No.	1987,12–1,1

Hard-paste porcelain; cup on circular foot with slightly out-turned arcaded rim, decorated in platinum and gold on a dark blue ground with alternating panels of warriors and courtiers in 'Renaissance' costume and martial trophies.

Provenance: Purchased, 1987

Literature: Unpublished

Comparable Examples: None

The word *zarf* is a transliteration of the Arabic for cup or vessel. In English it is generally used according to the Oxford English Dictionary, to mean 'a cup-shaped holder for a hot coffee-cup, used in the Levant, usually of metal and of ornamental design'. Its first known occurrence (as 'zurf') was in 1836. As this porcelain zarf shows, the form was known in France at least five, or perhaps even ten, years earlier.

A plaster model (see fig. 182a), unfortunately now in a damaged state, survives at the Sèvres factory.[1] It is incised on the base *26–2*, indicating that it was made in February 1826. The incised initials on the base of the plaster, which is made in one piece, appear to correspond with those on this porcelain zarf. A label identifies the plaster as *Zarf ou Support de la Tasse à Thé persanne Enreg.* 1828/1826 *n°5* (i.e. it was registered as the fifth item in 1828, although it originated in 1826). The plaster measures 11.2 cm in height, the diameter of the foot measuring 5.6 cm.

Examples are first recorded in the factory sales registers in 1831–2. A costly example sold to an unknown buyer for 75 francs in October 1832 is simply described as having *riche décor* and cannot therefore be securely identified as this piece, although no others mentioned in the records correspond more closely to it.[2] The model was probably not in current

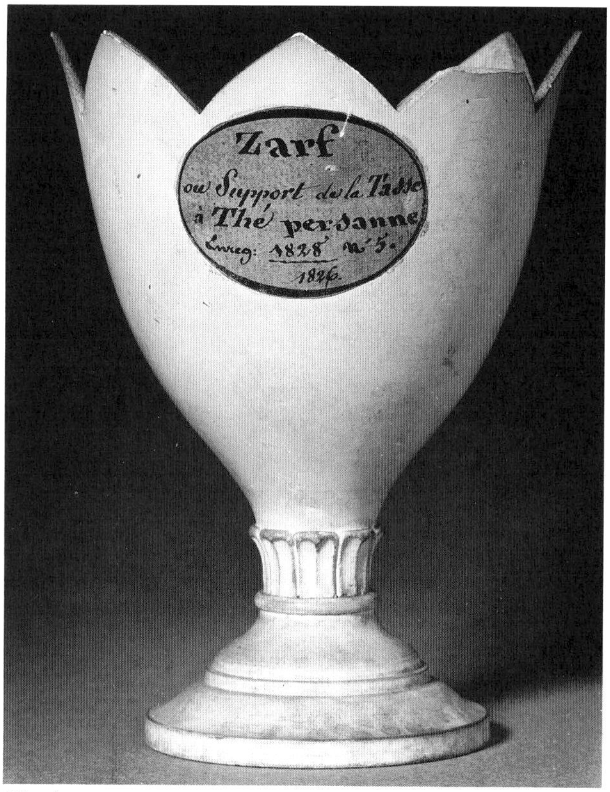

Fig 182a

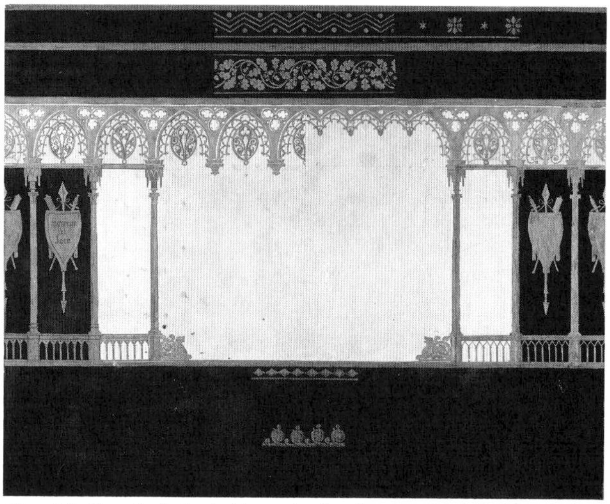

Fig 182b Gouache design in blue and yellow for a service de la Chevalerie

production before September 1833 when the second size which measured 8 cm in height and was 7 cm in diameter was priced. It weighed 40 grams, and was fired twice at a low temperature (*dégourdi*). It cost 3 francs 50 centimes undecorated, if of first quality, 3 francs if a 'second', 4 francs 50 centimes with a blue or green ground and 4 francs in other colours.[3]

Amongst the new ornamental pieces exhibited at the Louvre in 1835 were 'Des Tasses minces formes calices, avec leurs sous-tasses, à la manière orientale dites zarfs'.[4]

A drawing kept at the factory for a *service de la Chevalerie* shows motifs similar to those on this zarf and was inventoried in 1826[5], see fig. 182b.

For a discussion of the 'Troubadour' style at Sèvres, see Préaud.[6]

1. MNS, Archives de Sèvres, *casier* 784.
2. MNS, Archives de Sèvres, Vz 5, f. 86v.
3. MNS, Archives de Sevres, Pb8, *liasse* IV, *feuille* no. 54, *appréciation en conférence*.
4. *Notice sur Quelques-Unes des pièces qui entrent dans l'Exposition des Manufactures Royales . . . de Sèvres, faite au Palais du Louvre 1 Mai 1835*, no. 30. Printed catalogue kept at Sèvres factory.
5. MNS, Archives de Sèvres, R7, *dossier* 6, 1.
6. T. Préaud, 'Le style Renaissance à Sèvres au XIXème siècle', *Revue d'art canadienne*, VI/1, 1979, pp. 28–35.

183 **Bowl for Milk (*jatte à lait hémispherique*) from a service for the Tuileries Palace**, 1829–33

D. 13.5 cm
Marks: a star, *SÈVRES* and *33* below a six-pointed star within a hatched double circle printed in pale blue; *CHATEAU DES TUILERIES* within a double circle enclosed by a seventeen-point sunburst surmounted by a crown between two ribbons printed in red; *M 31 X* painted in gold; *Ly* and *29–4* incised
Reg. No. 1986,10–18,1

Hard-paste porcelain, of hemispherical form, thrown, glazed. Decorated in gold with the printed monogram *LP* crowned enclosed by a wreath composed of an oak leaf and acorn branch on the left and a laurel leaf and berry branch on the right, tied with a ribbon under a rosette at the lower end. The inner and outer rim are gilt, gilt line around the foot.

Provenance: Presented by Mr. D.A. King, 1986

Comparable Examples: See cat. 187

This monogram stands for King Louis Philippe (1773–1850), often known as the 'Citizen King'. He reigned from 1830 until his overthrow in the 1848 Revolution. The royal household was supplied through the royal factory with a large quantity of porcelain for use at the various palaces. Many pieces decorated simply with the printed monogram such as cats 184, 185 were intended for everyday use by the officers attached to the royal household. Many were subsequently redecorated by unscrupulous workmen, especially with turquoise grounds, and sold to unsuspecting collectors (see cat. 195).[1]

The monogram consists of three different transfers and only the pattern for the royal monogram still

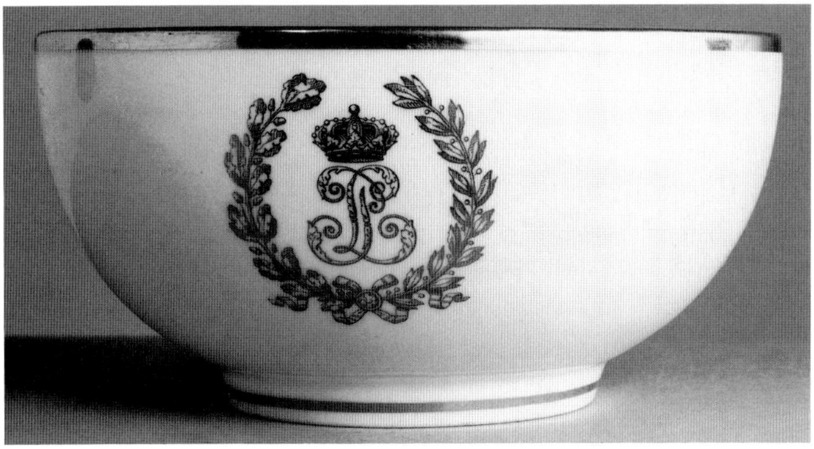

183

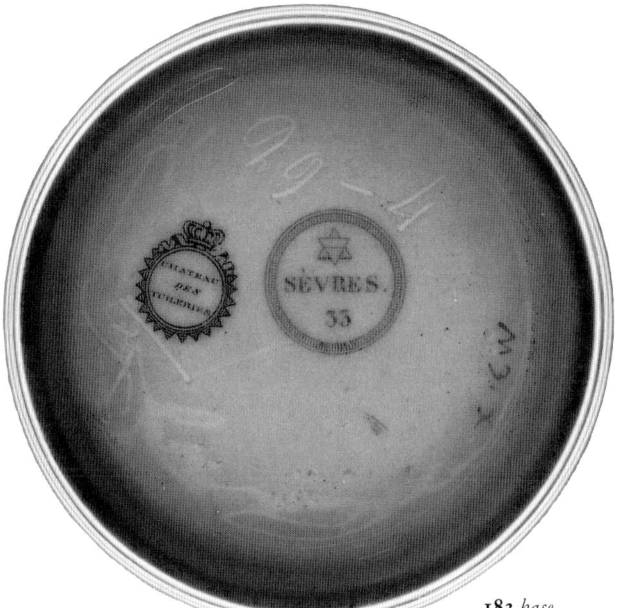

183 *base*

survives at the Sèvres factory.[2] The branches on this example are differently arranged to those on cats. 187 and 190.

Bowls for milk with matching jugs were made at the Vincennes/Sèvres factory from 1756 (see cat. 87). It is not known when the hemispherical form was devised. It usually had an accompanying saucer.

The bowl was made in April 1829. The thrower (*tourneur*) using the incised mark *Ly*, Jean-Michel Leydig (b. 1791), apprenticed at the factory in 1819 and employed between 1823 and 1837[3] is recorded as working on '111 Jattes à lait hémispheriques 1ere' in April 1829. He received a total of 44 francs 40 centimes.[4]

The mark painted in gold is that of an unidentified gilder. On 6 February 1834 17 'Jattes à lait & S' from a service described as 'frise filet & chiffre d'or' were supplied to the Magasin du Matériel aux Tuileries at a cost of 9 francs each.[5]

1. Blue and red monograms were also used for the so-called *services d'office* used by the officials of the royal household, and were subject to the same later redecoration. For a part dinner service decorated only with the gilt *LP* crowned monogram and bearing château de Compiègne marks, see Christie's, 27 September 1990, Lot 35.
2. MNS, Archives de Sèvres, *Ministère de la Maison de l'Empereur et des Beaux-Arts, Manufacture Impériale de Porcelaine de Sèvres, Chiffres et Armoiries*, p. 50.
3. Chevallier, 1980, p. 17.
4. MNS, Archives de Sèvres, Va' 28, f. 76.
5. MNS, Archives de Sèvres, Vy *bis* 10, f. 181.

184 **Milk Jug (*pot à lait grec*)**, 1836–7

H. 14.9 cm
Marks: cursive *LP* in monogram crowned and *SEVRES* 1837 within a double circle printed in blue; *Le* [?]*36* *6* and *Al* incised for the repairer Jean-Baptiste Allard
Reg. No. 1981,6–2,2

Hard-paste porcelain, moulded, glazed; small circular foot, ovoid body, loop handle, long neck and broad lip. Decorated in gold with the printed monogram *LP* crowned. Handle restored.

Provenance: Part of Lot 115, Christie's, 2 March 1981 (unknown owner). Presented by Mr D.A. King, 1981

Literature: Unpublished

Comparable Examples: Switzerland, Geneva, Musée Ariana, similarly decorated, dated 1846 with château de Trianon stamp, H. 24.5 cm (probably first size) inv. AR 1991

For a note on the monogram see cat. 183.

This shape was known as the *pot à lait grec* and occurs in three sizes, of which this may be the third.[1] The form goes back to at least 1785 when a hard-paste example was recorded as having been glazed on 9 July.[2] A plaster is kept at the factory.

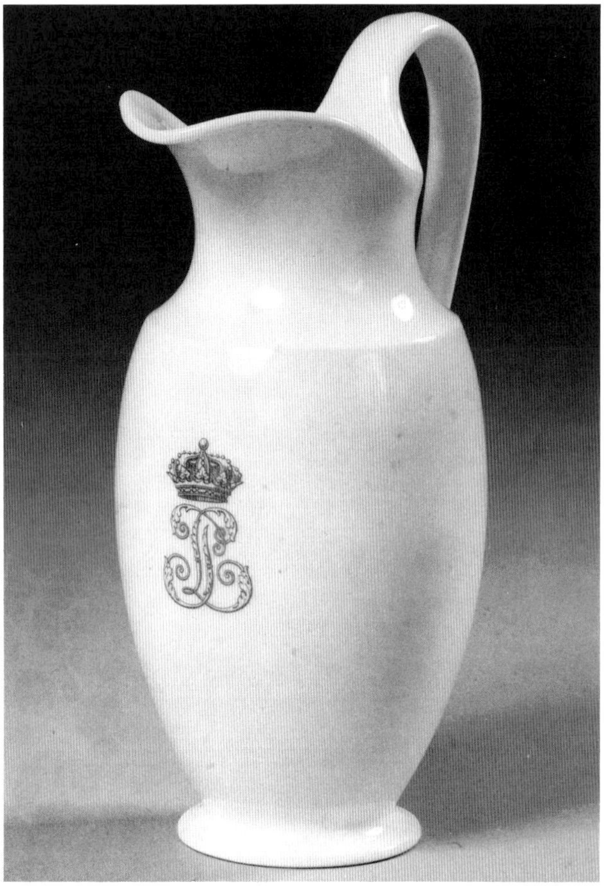

184

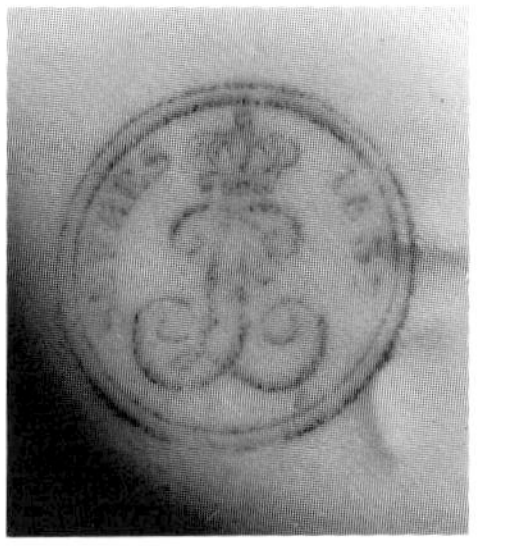

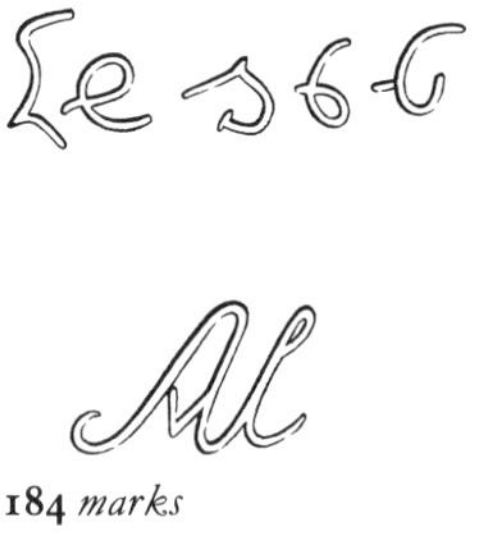

184 *marks*

The jug was made in June 1836 as the incised mark shows, although its decoration was not completed until the following year. The repairer Jean-Baptiste Allard (1803–42) worked at Sèvres from 1832 until 1841.[3]

In 1837 *pots à lait* of unspecified shape in the second size were sold to the Conservation du Matériel, the body responsible for supplying the royal household, for 4 francs 25 centimes each, and in the third size for 3 francs 25 centimes each.[4]

1. MNS, Archives de Sèvres, Y 22, pl. 19, 4.
2. MNS, Archives de Sèvres, VI' 3.
3. Chevallier, 1980, p. 7.
4. MNS, Archives de Sèvres, Vy *bis* 12, f. 64v.

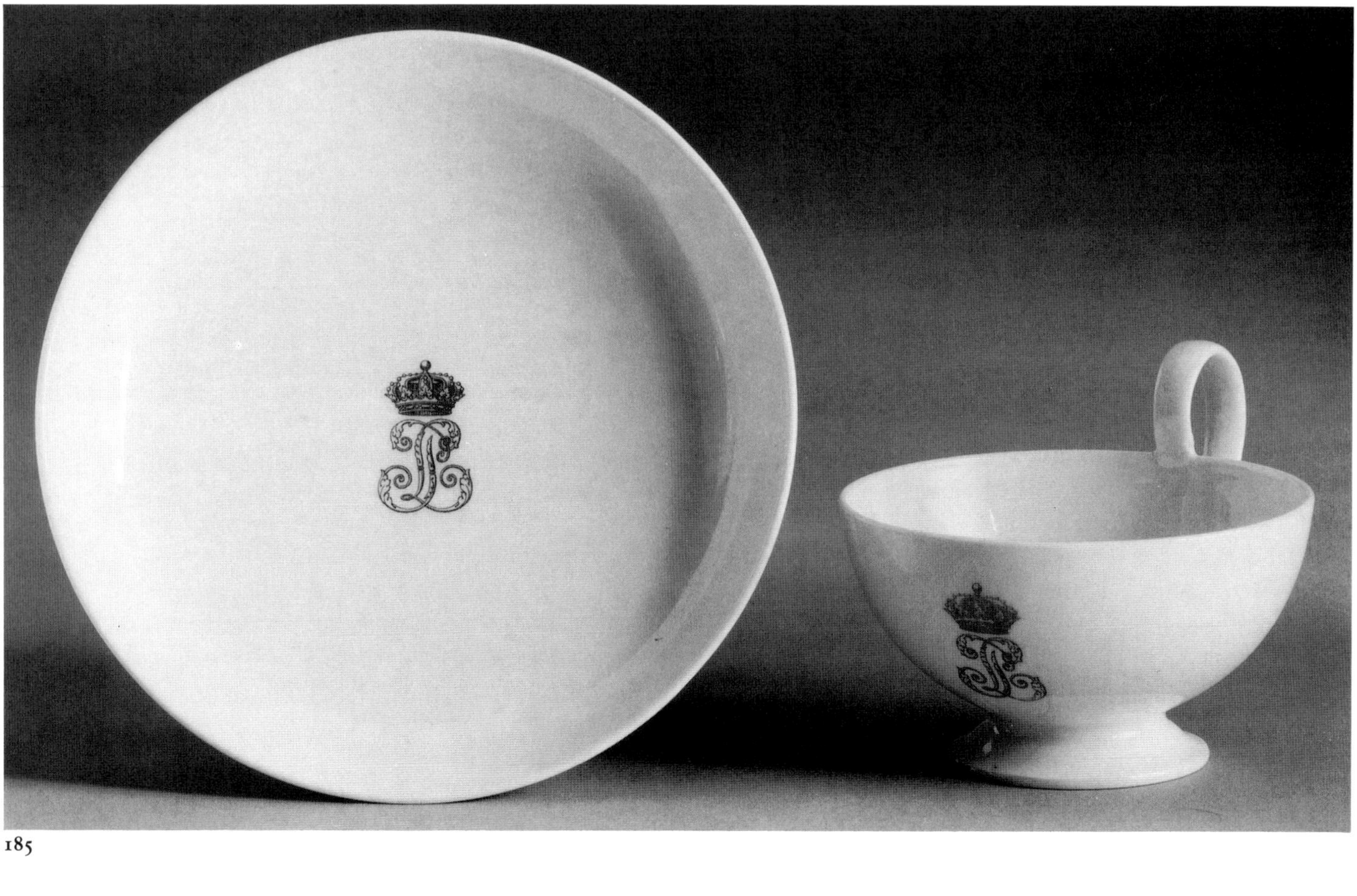

185

185 **Cup and Saucer (*tasse à thé coupe et soucoupe*)**, 1835–7 and 1841

D. *of saucer:*	15.6 cm
H. *of cup:*	5.2 cm
D. *of cup:*	9.6 cm
Marks:	Cursive *LP* in monogram crowned and *SEVRES 1837* within a double circle printed in blue; *Ly* for the thrower Jean-Michel Leydig and *35–10* incised (saucer): similar mark for 1841 printed in blue; cursive *g* incised (cup) for the repairer François-Edmé Godin
Reg. No.	1981,6–2,1

Hard-paste porcelain, thrown, glazed. The saucer has curved sides; the bowl-shaped cup has a small circular foot with flat foot rim, high loop handle joined to the rim with a triform upper terminal, and a flammiform lower terminal. Decorated in gold with the printed monogram *LP* crowned.

Provenance: Part of Lot 115, Christie's, 2 March 1981 (unknown owner). Presented by Mr D.A. King, 1981

Literature: Unpublished

Comparable Examples: Switzerland, Geneva, Musée Ariana, ten cups and saucers similarly decorated bearing marks of the châteaux of Fontainebleau, Trianon, Compiègne and Saint-Cloud, dated between 1835 and 1845, D. of saucer 12 cm, D. of cup 18 cm (first size), inv. AR 1976–AR 1985.

The shape of the cup, used for tea, is called *coupe anse palmette*, and was made in three sizes, of which this is apparently the second. It is shown in the factory pattern book drawn up in the 1830s, called the *Tarif avec Formes*.[1]

The repairer François-Edmé Godin (1799–1867)[2] was probably responsible for finishing the handle of the cup. Jean-Michel Leydig (b. 1791),[3] the thrower whose mark appears on the saucer, is recorded as receiving 125 francs in October 1835 for his work on 500 'soucoupes à thé coupes etc'.[4] the incised mark *35–10* indicates that the saucer was made in October 1835. Fifty 'tasses à thé coupes' of the second size for the 'service des officiers, chiffre d'or' were supplied to the Conservation du Matériel aux Tuileries on 12 February 1841 at a cost of 2 francs 50 centimes each. Twenty-two 'soucoupes pour' cost 2 francs 50 centimes each.[5]

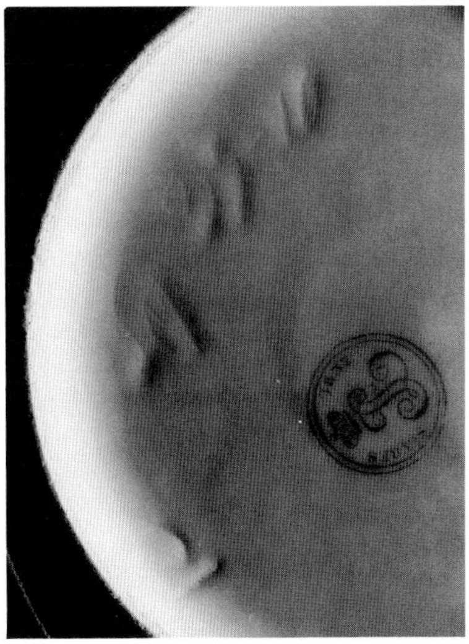

185 *marks*

1. MNS, Archives des Sèvres, Y 22, pl. 29, 1.
2. Chevallier, 1980, p. 15; see cat. 173.
3. *Ibid.*, p. 17.
4. MNS, Archives de Sèvres, Va' 31, f. 72v.
5. MNS, Archives de Sèvres, Vy *bis*, 13, f. 131.

186 **Teapot and Cover and Sugar Bowl (*théière et pot à sucre 'Régnier unis'*)**, 1830–45

H. *of teapot (to top of handle):*	20 cm
Max. W:	17.6 cm
H. *of sugar bowl (to top of handles):*	13.5 cm
Max. W:	12.4 cm
Marks:	*LP* in monogram crowned and *SEVRES 1845* within a double circle printed in blue; *MO* painted in red for the painter Nicolas-Marie Moriot; cursive *T* incised possibly for the repairer Eli-Siméon Thion and *MP* incised for the repairer Pierre Moyé (teapot); similar printed mark and *SEVRES 1841* repeated with *SEVRES 1845*; *M* painted in red for the painter, as above; *CL* incised for the repairer Charles-François-Jules Delehaye and [?]*DM* incised for an unknown repairer; *30–11* incised (sugar bowl)
Reg. No.	1991,10–10,1 and 2

Hard-paste porcelain, moulded. The teapot is of ovoid form with a circular foot, the upper part of its spout moulded in relief with rosettes, scrolls, torches and bay sprigs, and the elaborate handle, its upper end terminating in a feathered mask similarly moulded. Feathered masks form the terminals of the handles on the sugar bowl, which is of corresponding shape. The teapot is painted with 'cameo' portraits within oval shields of Louis de Culant (Marshal of France 1441, d. 1453), and Jean de Poton, Sr de Xaintrailles (marshal of France 1454, d. 1461) and the sugar bowl with Jean Stuart Cte de Buchan (1380–*c.* 1424, Constable of France) and Etienne de Vignolles dit Lahire (imprisoned after failing to rescue Joan of Arc at Rouen, d. 1442). Each portrait is flanked by heraldic emblems surmounted by plumed visors on a white ground embellished with gilt ornament. The upper parts of the spout and the handle on the teapot, as well as other parts of its handle, are all decorated with matte gilding. The handle terminal of the sugar bowl and the rosette within the upper scroll are similarly decorated. The sugar bowl lacks its cover. Finial to cover of teapot and its handle restored.[1]

Provenance: Purchased 1991; purchased from the factory by the Bey of Tunis (1806–55), December 1846,[2] subsequent history unknown

Literature: Unpublished

Comparable Examples: None

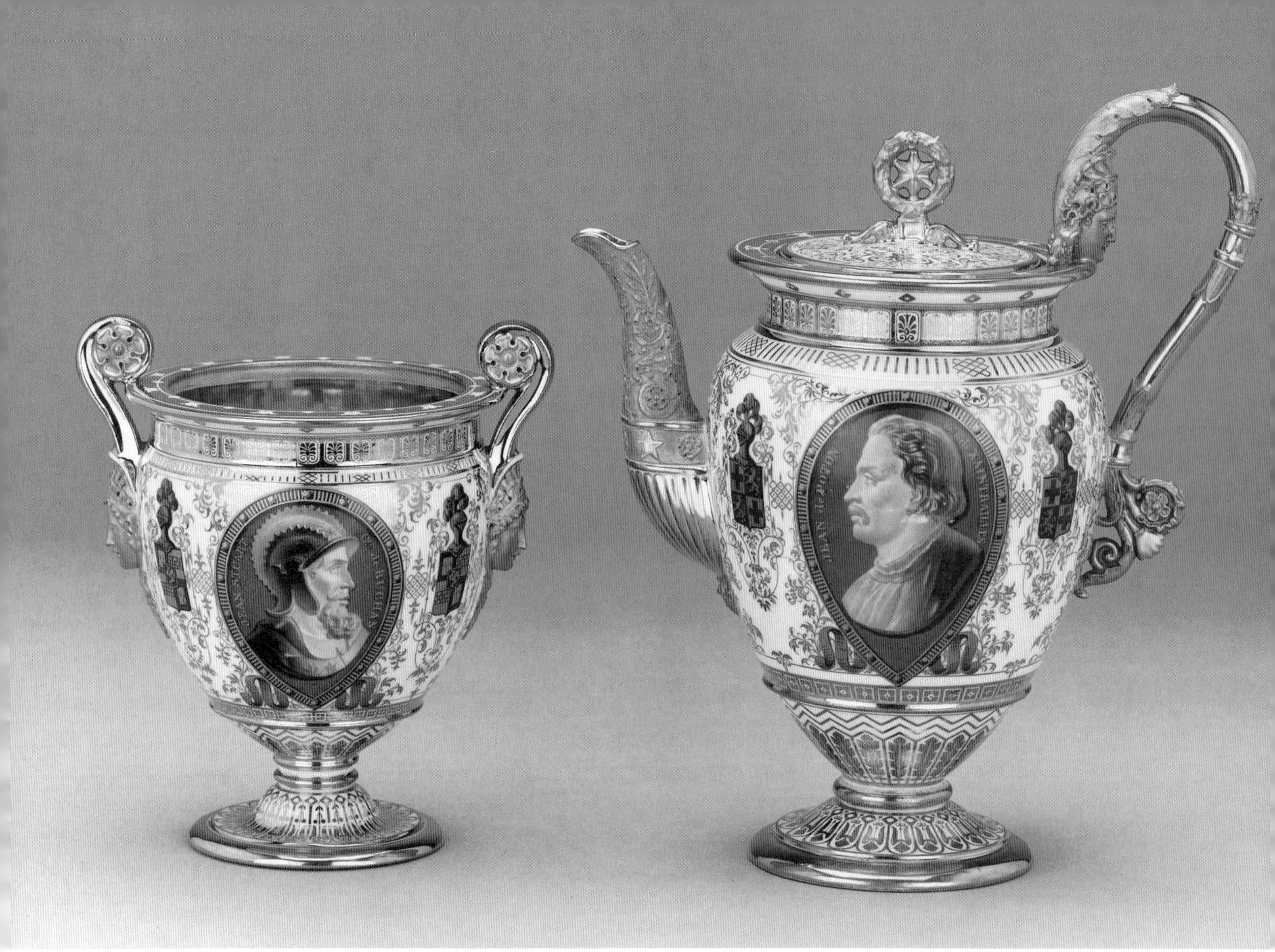

186

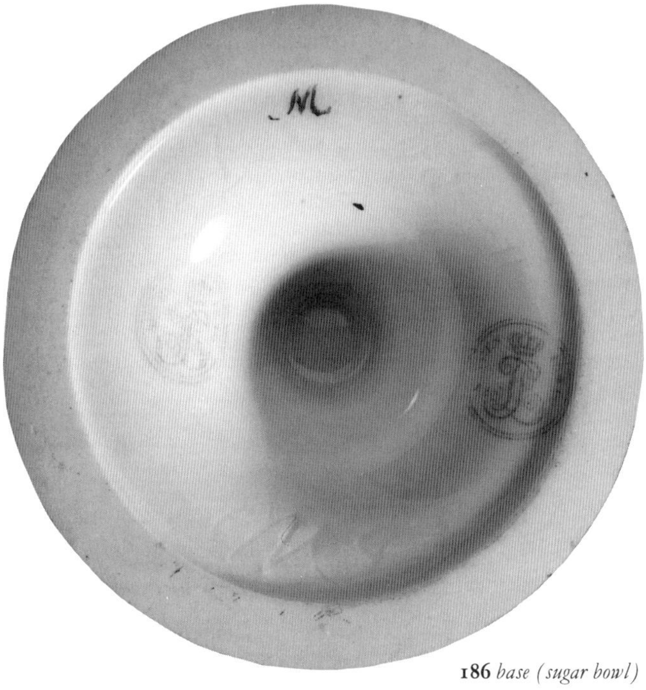

186 *base (sugar bowl)*

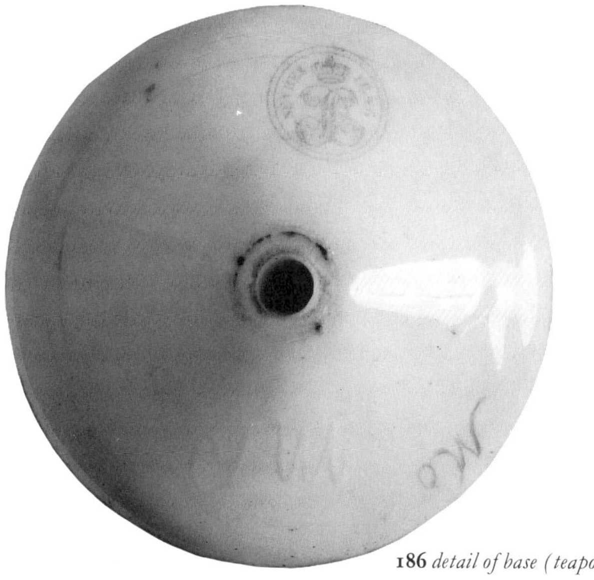

186 *detail of base (teapot)*

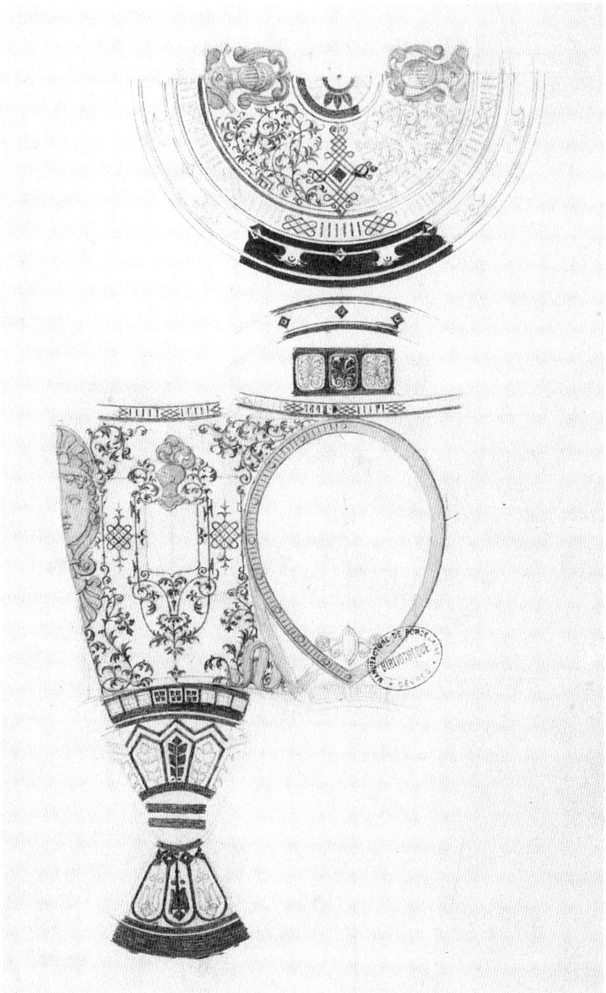

Fig 186a Design for decoration on sugar bowl

The forms were devised by the sculptor-modeller Jean-Marie-Ferdinand Régnier (employed 1812–48) in 1813. Several variations of the design were produced and an example of 1813 is decorated with reliefs.[3] On the *Déjeuner des Femmes Célèbres*[4] the lower part of the teapot spout has not been moulded in relief as on the Museum example. The Museum pieces are part of a *déjeuner* or tea-service known at the Sèvres factory under the title *de Châteaudun*. A matching tray dated 1840 painted by Jean-Baptiste-Gabriel Langlacé with the castle of the Counts of Dunois at Châteaudun (Eure et Loire) and several figures by Charles Develly is in the Musée national de Céramique, Sèvres.[5] The *déjeuner* was exhibited at the Louvre in June 1846.[6] The present whereabouts of the cream-jug and four cups and saucers which completed the *déjeuner* is unknown.

Both teapot and sugar bowl were made long before the *déjeuner* was assembled. The incised date on the sugar bowl indicates that it is probably one of 36 thrown by Collot in November 1830, for which he was paid 3 francs each.[7] In the same month Charles-François-Jules Delehaye is recorded as receiving 3 francs for each of 36 'garnitures de pots à sucre Régnier unis'.[8] The teapot spout and cover may well have been one of the 16 'garnitures de théières Régnier unies' for which the repairer Pierre Moyez received 12 francs each in February 1843.[9]

The production of this *déjeuner* was planned in 1840, according to a document dated 25 May recording the *Travaux des Ateliers*.[10] At this time the tray was already fired but had a fault (*écaille*), which was to be repaired. The decorative scheme on the other pieces was to include nine portraits of the most famous inhabitants of the château. They are listed as Dunois, Joan of Arc, Lahire, Rochefort, Raiz, Boussac, and Xaintraille (two portraits were missing). Another sheet lists Richemont, Buchan and Culant. Some modification clearly took place, and several sources, including the Louvre exhibition catalogue, show that the final scheme was as follows:

Teapot:	Jean de Poton, Seigneur de Xaintrailles
	Louis de Culant
Sugar bowl:	Jean Stuart Comte de Buchan
	Etienne de Vignolles, dit Lahire
Milk jug:	Jeanne d'Arc
Four cups:	Pierre de Rieux, dit de Rochefort
	Artus III de Bretagne
	Jean Dunois
	Gilles de Laval, Seigneur de Rais

The profile portraits on the Museum teapot and sugar bowl are adapted from portraits of admirals, *connétables* and marshals of France in the *Galeries Historiques* at Versailles. These galleries were created by King Louis-Philippe and eight volumes illustrating them and their contents, which were mostly paintings specially commissioned by the King, were published between 1839 and 1846.[11] N.-M. Moriot (painter at the factory between 1828 and 1848) was responsible for painting the cameo portraits on the two Museum pieces between 1842 and 1844.[12] The ornamental designs, for which gouache drawings survive at the factory (see fig. 186a),[13] were devised by Jean Charles François Leloy (active 1816–48) and executed by Joseph Richard (painter 1830–72).[14] He was also responsible for the armorials, but their source is unknown.

Both the production costs and the selling price of the components of the *déjeuner* are recorded.[15] The tray, which was even noted as *écaillant* when it entered the *magasin de vente* on 30 December 1845, cost 1697 francs 50 centimes and sold for 1,800 francs. The four cups and saucers cost 227 francs 10 centimes each and sold for 260 francs. The milk jug cost 178 francs 30 centimes and sold for 200 francs. The sugar bowl cost 268 francs 25 centimes and sold for 325 francs.

As Gérard Barbe has pointed out,[16] only around 120 such *déjeuners* were manufactured between November 1830 and March 1848. They were intended for the luxury market and were usually painted with fashionable décors by the factory's leading artists. Although the forms of the *déjeuner Régnier* were three decades old (and the sugar bowl had been awaiting decoration for over a decade), their neo-classical style, evident in the relief ornament on the spout and in the handle terminals, blends with the medievalising decoration of the cameo heads and armorial shields to result in an eclecticism entirely typical of the 1840s in France. The Bey of Tunis, Ahmed Bey (1806–55),[17] who visited Paris in November–December 1846, also purchased another *déjeuner* decorated more simply with flowers on a white ground consisting of six plates, a *porte-assiette*, a *jatte à laver*, a butter dish, a salt-cellar and an egg cup, in addition to two portraits of the Duke and Duchess of Nemours costing 700 francs each.[18]

1. The teapot handle appears to have been incorrectly restored: see the examples referred to in n. 3, 4 (the latter does not show handle clearly in the illustration).
2. MNS, Archives de Sèvres, Vz 6, f. 247, December 1846, sold for a total of 3,865 francs including a box costing 125 francs.
3. Brunet and Préaud, 1978, pl. LX, inv. MNC 6160.
4. Musée national de Céramique, Sèvres, inv. MNC 23582, exh. *Sèvres XIXe siècle*, 1975, no. 121.
5. Musée national de Céramique, Sèvres, inv. MNC 3576, exh. as above, no. 151.
6. *Notice sur quelques unes des pièces qui entrent dans l'Exposition des Manufactures Royales des porcelaines et émaux de Sèvres . . . Faites au Palais du Louvre au 1er Juin 1846*, no. 34, pp. 28–9. The description of the tray records that the scene showing the valley in which the château of the Counts of Dunois is situated is 'très pittoresque' and was 'pris sur les lieux et peint sur le plateau par M. Langlacé'. The painting used by the Sèvres artist is untraced.
7. MNS, Archives de Sèvres, Va'28, f. 97.
8. *Ibid.*, f. 163v.
9. MNS, Archives de Sèvres, Va'37, f. 80.
10. MNS, Archives de Sèvres, Pb 11, *liasse* 1, *dossier* 1.
11. *Supplément aux Galeries Historiques de Versailles*, lère partie, 4, série IX, pl. 8 (Culant, engraved by Pingeot); pl. 14 (Buchan, bust portrait by Blondel after a portrait in the collection at the château de Beauregard); *Galeries Historiques de Versailles*, 1ère partie, 6, série IX Portraits divers, Section 1, Grands Amiraux, Connétables, pl. 15, no. 1318 (Xaintrailles, painted by Monvoison); pl. 85, no. 1573 (Lahire painted by Dassy).
12. The payments to Moriot are recorded in MNS, Archives de Sèvres, Vj'49–51, and in the *Feuille d'appréciation*, Pb 11, which shows that he received 70 francs for the figures on the teapot and 40 for those on the sugar bowl.
13. MNS, Archives de Sèvres, Section D § 3, 1848, nos. 16–18; D § 4 1848, no. 6.
14. See MNS, Archives de Sèvres, *Feuille d' appréciation*, Pb 11; he received 143 francs for work on the teapot and 146 for the sugar bowl.
15. The most detailed breakdown of costs is given in the *Feuille d'appréciation* dated 30 December 1845, MNS, Archives de Sèvres, Pb 11, no. 95.
16. G. Barbe, 'Déjeuners en porcelaine de Sèvres de 1830 à 1840', *L'Estampille*, April 1990, pp. 58–69.
17. For details of his visit and of a bronze commemorative medal with a portrait on the obverse, see H. Hugon, 'Un document numismatique du voyage d'Ahmed Bey à Paris (1846)', *Revue de l'Histoire des Colonies*, X, 1922, pp. 107–14; further biographical details of this interesting figure (the son of a Christian slave captured in Sardinia and Mustafa Bey) can be found in L.C. Brown, 'Ahmed Bey, un monarque éclairé à l'aube de la Tunisie moderne', C.A. Julien (ed.), *Les Africains*, Vol. IX, Paris, 1977, pp. 17–43.
18. MNS, Archives de Sèvres, Vz 6, f. 247 and 247v.

187 Plate (*assiette*) from a Service for the Tuileries Palace, 1846

D. 24.4 cm
Marks: *LP* in double monogram crowned and *SV.46.* printed in green; cursive *LP* crowned and *SEVRES 1846* within a double circle printed in blue; *CHATEAU DES TUILERIES* within a double circle enclosed by a 17-point sunburst surmounted by a crown between two ribbons, painted in red
Reg. No. 1899,10–6,11

Hard-paste porcelain, moulded, glazed; broad rim; raised lines on reverse near foot rim and in centre, where there is a trace of a stilt mark. Decorated on the border with a gold printed design of ivy leaves and in the centre with the monogram *LP* crowned enclosed by a wreath composed of a laurel leaf and berry branch on the left and an oak leaf and acorn branch on the right tied with a ribbon under a rosette at the lower end. The rim, inner edge of the border and outer edge of the foot rim are all gilt. The foot rim has been wiped clear of glaze and is discoloured.

Provenance: Bequeathed by C.D.E. Fortnum, Esq., FSA, DCL, 1899[1]

Literature: Unpublished

Comparable Examples: Christie's, 2 July 1990, Lot 12, part tea-service, château de Tuileries marks

Paris, Drouot-Richelieu, Christian de Quay, 16th December 1991, lot 150, teawares dated in the 1830s and 1840s, with various château marks.

Switzerland, Geneva, Musée Ariana, six soup plates dated between 1836 and 1841 with château de Saint-Cloud stamp, inv. AR 1960–AR 1965, also one dated 1833 and three dated 1836 without château marks, inv. AR 1966–AR 1969, and other pieces from the same service (tureen, covered jug, sauceboats) with various château marks

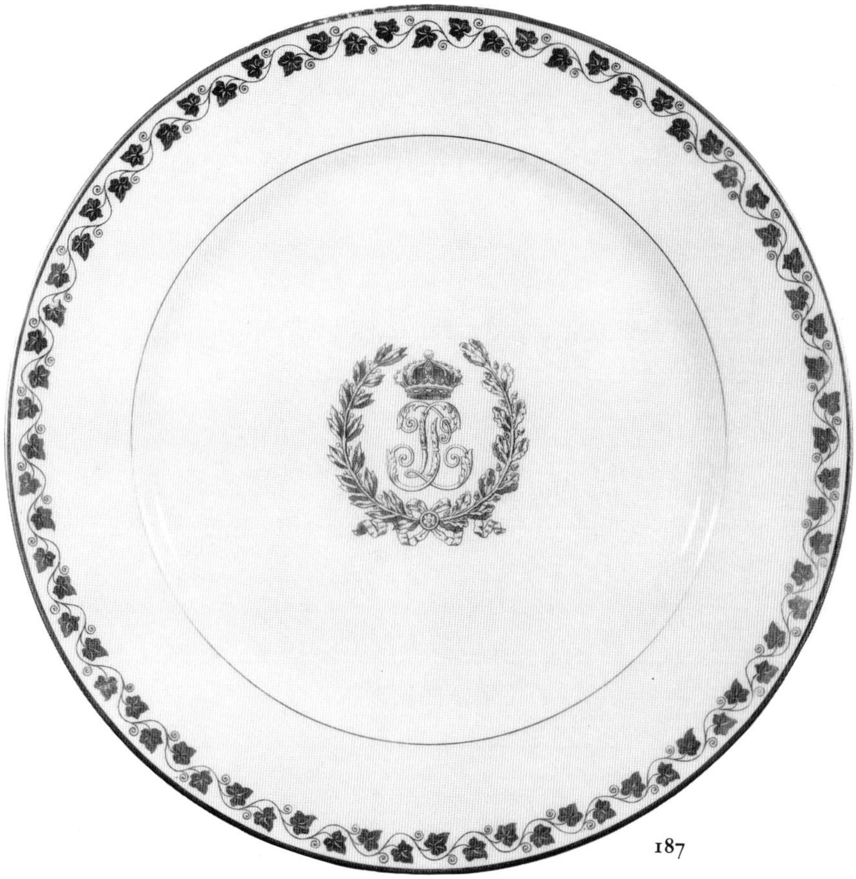

187

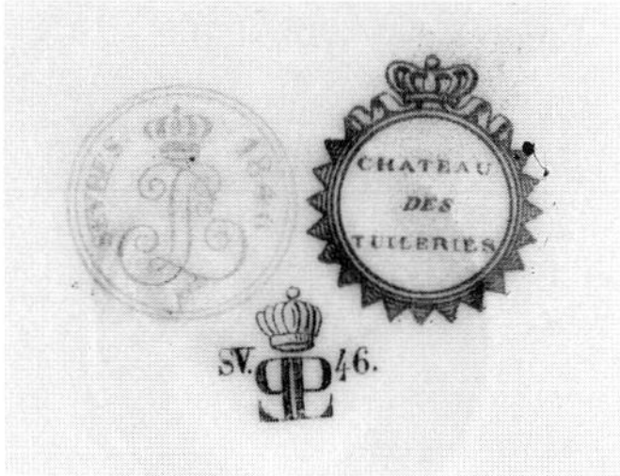

187 *marks*

The plate form, usually known as an *assiette unie*, was devised in the late eighteenth century and has remained in use since that time.

For a note on the monogram see cat. 183. A 'pull' for the *frise lierre* or ivy-leaf frieze, survives in the gilding shop at the Sèvres factory under the number 100, and is said to date from 1834.[2]

Pieces bearing the printed mark of one of the palaces were intended for use there, or might be loaned to other locations for banquets, when the printed legend served as an inventory mark so that they could be returned. Services with this rudimentary printed decoration were intended for everyday use by members of the royal household, in this case the princes.[3] Detailed lists of broken or lost pieces were supplied annually for each of seven properties[4] on printed forms to the director of the Sèvres factory, Alexandre Brongniart, by the Intendance Générale de la liste civile, Direction des dépenses de la Maison du Roi. Four different services are listed[5] for the King, for the Princes, for the Officers (officials), and 'd'Office' (household use), and four types of plates: 'assiettes à couteau', 'à déjeuner', 'à dresser' and 'à potage'. This plate is probably an *assiette à déjeuner*. The services were large. In 1847 there was a total of 3,173 pieces in a *service d'office*.

Several sales are recorded to the authorities at the Tuileries Palace in 1846. On 9 April eight 'assiettes plates' described as 'Service des Princes, frise lierre' were delivered at a cost of 5 francs 50 centimes each.[6]

1. For a note on C.D.E. Fortnum, a Museum Trustree and donor, see cat. 93.
2. The author is grateful to Tamara Préaud for her assistance in tracing the 'pull'.
3. See exh. *Grands Services*, 1951, no. 34, 'service des princes' with gilt ivy-leaf frieze.
4. They included Trianon, Compiègne, Pavillon de Breteuil, Eu, Fontainebleau, Saint-Cloud and Bizy.
5. MNS, Archives de Sèvres, U 2, L 2, D1.
6. MNS, Archives de Sèvres, Vy *bis*, p. 31.

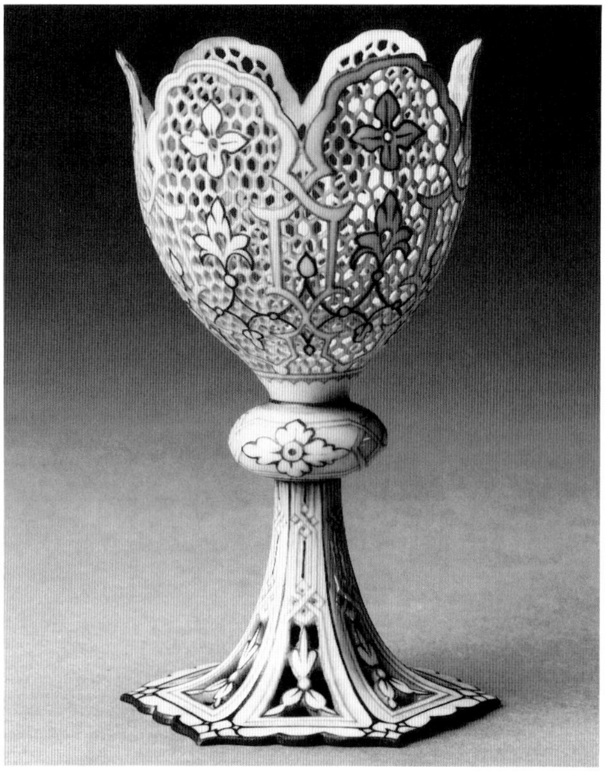

188

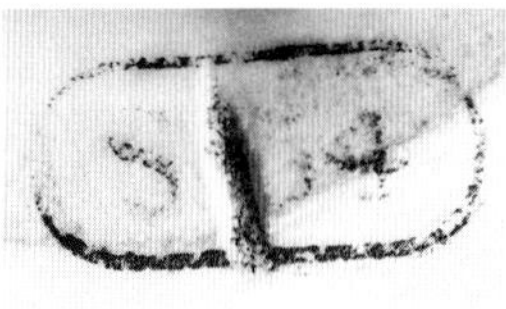

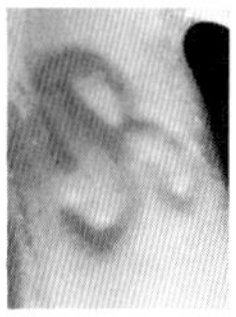

188 *marks*

188 **Pierced Cup or Zarf (*zarph réticulé*), 1854**

See colour plate 31

H. 10.5 cm
Marks: *S54* printed in green within an oval; monogram *FB* incised
Reg. No. 1927,10-13,1

Pierced goblet made in two parts of slip-cast eggshell porcelain with six slightly curved projections of ogival form attached to a flattened circular knop which is in turn joined to a stem flaring out to the pierced hexagonal foot. The zarf, pierced in a network of octagonal cells interrupted by floral ornament and scrolls, is entirely glazed except on the foot rim and inside the bottom of the goblet. It is decorated in pale pink and gold. The central area underneath is gilded.

Provenance: Presented by Mrs J. Spier through the National Art-Collections Fund, 1927

Literature: Unpublished

Comparable Examples: Sèvres, Musée national de Céramique, inv. 7592^{4}, dated 1861, H. 13 cm, illus. Brunet and Préaud, 1978, no. 391

London, Victoria and Albert Museum, inv. no. 135&a-1877

Sotheby's, 5 March 1985, Lot 121

USA, Cleveland, Cleveland Museum of Art, inv. 89.30

For the origin of the form, see cat. 182. This pierced example is a particularly interesting manifestation of nineteenth-century eclecticism.

On the evidence of a plaster kept at the factory and entitled *zarph réticulé 1844*[1] the model seems to date from 1844. A coloured drawing for a pierced zarf dated October 1844 by Hyacinthe Régnier survives at the factory.[2] Régnier worked at Sèvres as a modeller between 1825 and 1863.

Mademoiselle Flaville Brault is recorded in the *Travaux des ateliers de mouleurs répareurs et sculpteurs*[3] as a pupil working at reticulation under the turner Joseph Carré and may have been responsible for the making of this piece.

In March 1854 a 'zarf réticulée fond blanc, décor en or' was sold in the *Exposition de New York* for 95 francs, together with a 'tasse persanne' for 30 francs and a box for both pieces at 15 francs.[4] In May 1854 two 'zarphs réticulés' were sold to M. Jacquet at 30 francs each.[5]

1. MNS, Archives de Sèvres, *Casier* 0.270; another smaller model, and a model for the foot of a zarf are in *Casier* 0.225.
2. MNS, Archives de Sèvres, *Armoire* R III. The drawing is illustrated in *Objets civils domestiques, vocabulaire typologique*, compiled by C. Arminjon and N. Blondel, Paris, 1984, p. 196, fig. 1007 but is wrongly captioned.
3. MNS, Archives de Sèvres, Va'46, f. 94.
4. *Ibid.*, Vz 8, f. 103v.
5. *Ibid.*, Vz 8, f. 188.

189 **Plate (*assiette plate*), 1845–56**

See colour plate 32

D. 24 cm
Marks: N crowned printed in red; S.54 within an oval printed in green; .L.G. for the gilder L. Guyonnet painted in black; *cl* for the repairer Charles-François Jules Delahaye and date code *11-45-5* incised
Reg. No. 1992,7-9,1

Hard-paste porcelain, moulded. The border decoration, which is all on a matt red ground, consists of a pattern of honeysuckle palmettes outlined in black alternating with stylised ivy leaves in matt gold with berries and heart-shaped motifs both outlined in black, their upper end terminating in scrolls, enclosing a gilt palmette. Around the well is a zone of small gilt crosses within a gilt trellis on a red ground within gilt bands bordered by a painted black line and a further inner zone of ornament consisting of painted black lines alternating with shorter gilt lines. The central dionysiac scene is enclosed by a black line. It depicts a leaping panther to left above a marble slab on which rest an oval box containing a gilt-mounted horn, a gilt kylix, a thyrsus tied with two blue ribbons, a laurel wreath and a bunch of black grapes

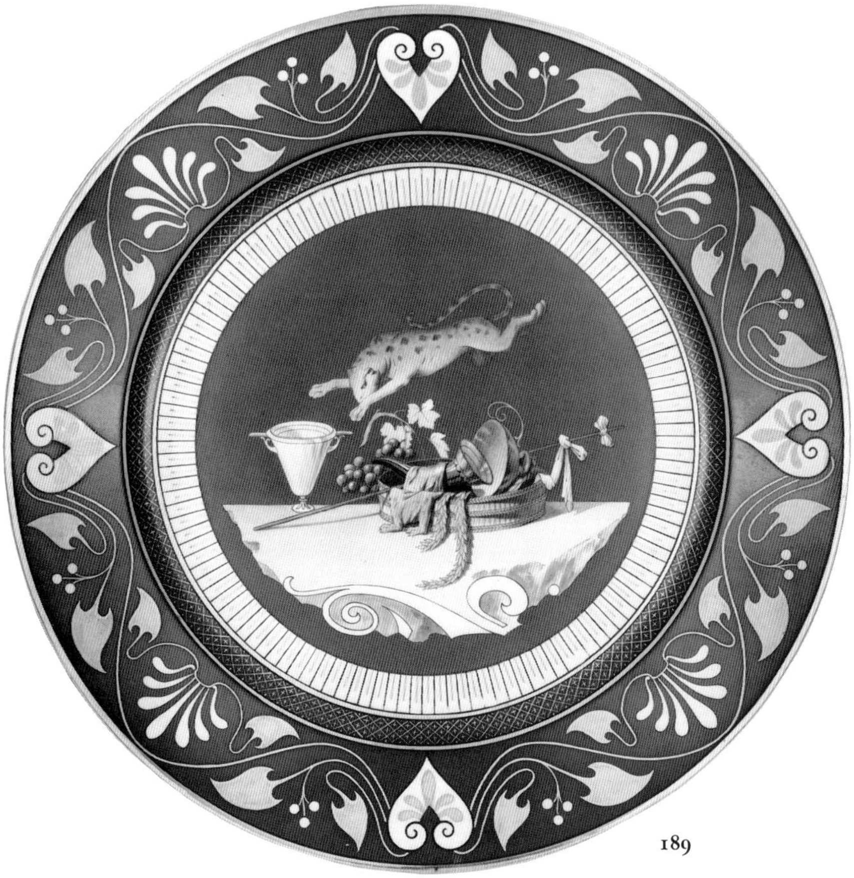

189

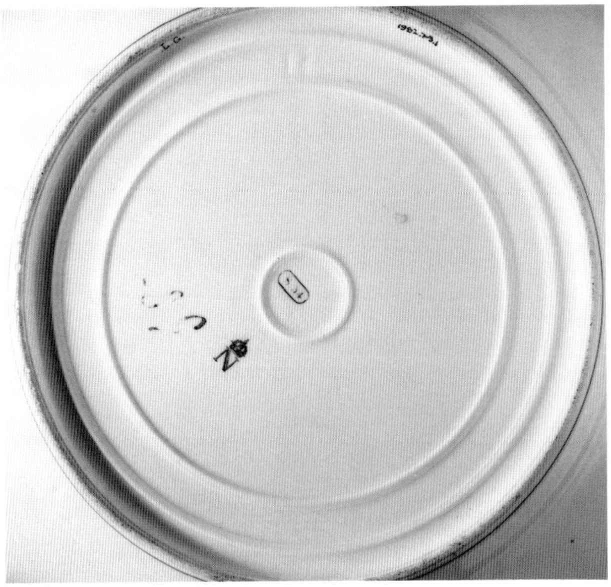

189 *base*

and a kantharos at the left. The rim of the plate is gilt and the foot is encircled by a gilt line.

Provenance: Purchased from the Sèvres factory by Prince Napoleon, March 1856; New York, Sotheby's, 21 May 1992, Lot 28 (part) (Important French and Continental Furniture); purchased, 1992

Comparable Examples: Nine other plates from the same service were sold in five lots in New York (see above), now with Dragesco-Cramoisan, 1992; two further plates from a New York private collection with Dragesco-Cramoisan, Paris, 1992.

This plate is part of a service commissioned on 7 March 1856 by Prince Napoleon[1] (Napoleon-Joseph-Charles-Paul Bonaparte, 1822–91). Models for the service were provided by Dieterle and it was expressly specified that each piece was to be marked with an N crowned. It was to be delivered by 1 October 1856 (although it was not in fact sent until 18 October).[2] The service consisted of twenty-four soup plates decorated with a gilt frieze each costing 9 francs 50 centimes; a hundred and twenty plates (*assiettes plates*) similarly decorated at 9 francs each; six *bateaux à deux anses* at 20 francs each; two melon-dishes (*melonnières à côtes*) at 128 francs each; two chalice-form salad dishes, second size (*saladiers calice 2e*) at 42 francs each; two sauceboats and stands at 40 francs each; twenty-four covered gravy pots at 8 francs each together with four serving dishes for them costing 66 francs. The dessert service is described in the factory records as 'fd. rouge décor étrusque' and consisted of seventy-two *assiettes plates* at a mean price of 76 francs (this part of the service alone totalled 5472 francs), eighteen coffee cups decorated with a gilt frieze at 10 francs 50 centimes each and twenty-four teacups and saucers similarly decorated at 11 francs.[3] This plate, therefore, belongs to the most splendidly decorated part of an exceptional service.

Six painters were responsible for the decoration of the service, including the gilder L. (first name unknown) Guyonnet, who was employed at the factory from 1853–7. Unusually, his signature is in black rather than gold as one might expect. Guyonnet received no payment for the 'trophées du centre', which were executed on the various pieces by Louis-Etienne-Frédéric Blanchard, Frédéric-Alexandre David, Pierre Riton, Joseph Richard and Jean-Charles-Gérard Dérichweiler.[4] The scene in the central well is in reverse to an engraving in *Antichità d'Ercolano*, which does not include the leaping panther or the bunch of grapes.[5]

Charles-François-Jules Delahaye (1806–79) began work as a pupil repairer in December 1818, finally leaving the factory in 1852.[6]

Prince Napoleon probably originally commissioned the service for his mistress, the tragic actress Mademoiselle Rachel (Rachel Félix, 1828–58), who knew him from 1848 until her untimely death (he was at her deathbed on 3 January 1858). She was one of a number of actors and actresses in his circle, such as Madeleine Brohan, Marie Favart and Got. They are shown in Gustave Boulanger's *Rehearsal of 'The Flute Player' in the Atrium of the House of H.I.H. the Prince Napoleon*, now in the Musée national du Château, Versailles.[7] This painting reveals how far the Prince went in creating an architectural fantasy based on a Pompeian dwelling. The painted murals were in the so-called 'Third Style' of excavations at Pompei. The 'Pompeian' house which Prince Napoleon built with the collaboration of several architects (Hittorf, Normand, Rougevin), on the east side of the Avenue Montaigne had a short life: it was sold in 1866 and demolished in 1891.[8]

Rachel worked under the director of the Comédie Française, Arsène Houssaye, who was one of her many admirers and owned a portrait of her by Jean-Léon Gérome (1824–1904).[9] In his *Confessions* he gives a series of pen-portraits of the actress, including several accounts of her supper parties. In one of these which took place in 1853 he mentions her 'salle à manger pompéienne'.[10] In an undated passage referring to the period after 1854[11] he writes about a dinner given one Thursday by Rachel for politicians, diplomats and men of letters when she entertained Morny, Sainte-Beuve and Nieuwerkerke amongst others. There was no political talk, but endless discussions about the Etruscans (*sic*) 'car on sait que la salle à manger de la tragédienne est peinte comme une salle à manger d'Herculaneum; Mlle Rachel a même un service représentant toutes les figures des fresques antiques.' It is on this evidence that this plate is thought to have been made for her.

1. The author is deeply indebted to Tamara Préaud and Bernard Dragesco for supplying archival information and bibliographical references. Any errors or omissions in this late catalogue entry are her own.
2. MNS, Archives de Sèvres, *Registre de Commandes*, Vtt 7, f. 110.
3. The service is briefly described and the prices given in the *Registre des ventes au Comptant*, under the date 23 March 1857, MNS, Archives de Sèvres, V2, 9, f. 58v.
4. Details of the decoration appear in the *Travaux des Peintres*, Vj'62, f. 31, 31v, 33, 43v, 45, 45v, 46, 162, 162v, 180v.
5. *Antichità d'Ercolano*, Naples, Vol. III, 1760, p. 173 (the plate shows only part of the engraving). It is just possible that the Sèvres painter has based the grapes and the panther on other engravings in this volume, e.g. p. 61, 225.
6. Chevallier, 1980, p. 12.
7. Exh. *The Second Empire 1852–1879, Art in France under Napoleon III*, Philadelphia Museum of Art, October-November 1978, Detroit Institute of Arts, January-March 1979, Grand Palais, Paris, April-July 1979, no. VI-12.
8. Some designs for this house are discussed by Marie-Noëlle de Gary in 'Deux dessins pour la Maison Pompéienne du Prince Napoléon', *10 ans de donations, Cahiers de l'Union Centrale des Arts Décoratifs*, February 1978, no. 1, pp. 8–10. For a contemporary account of this 'Rendez-vous de tout Paris', see A. Houssaye, *La Maison Pompéienne*, Paris, 1866. A series of contemporary photographs and engravings were published by M-C. Dejean de La Batie, 'La Maison Pompéienne du Prince Napoléon, Avenue Montaigne', *Gazette des Beaux-Arts*, Vol. LXXXXVII, April 1976, pp. 127–134.
9. See sale of Arsène Houssaye, Hôtel Drouot. 22–23 May 1896, Lot 155.
10. A. Houssaye, *Les Confessions, souvenirs d'un demi-siècle 1830–1880*, Paris, Vol. IV, 1885, p. 243. Rachel's house was the subject of an article in *L'Illustration* published on 3 September 1853, which included engravings of the rooms.
11. *Op. cit.*, p. 333.

190 Plate (*assiette*) from a Service made for Louis Napoleon, 1859–67

D. 24.4 cm
Marks: *SV.59* within an octagonal lozenge printed in dark green; *N* crowned above *67* enclosed by *DORE A* on the left and *SÈVRES* on the right printed in red
Reg. No. 1899,10–6,12

Hard-paste porcelain, moulded, glazed; broad rim; raised lines on reverse near foot rim and in centre, where there are three stilt-marks. Decorated on the border with a gold printed design of

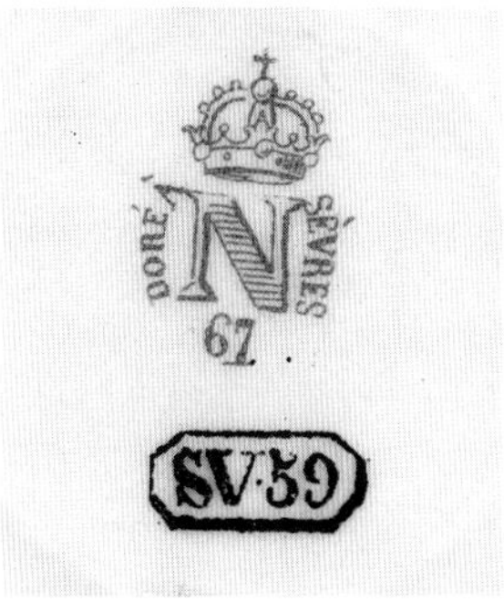

190 *mark*

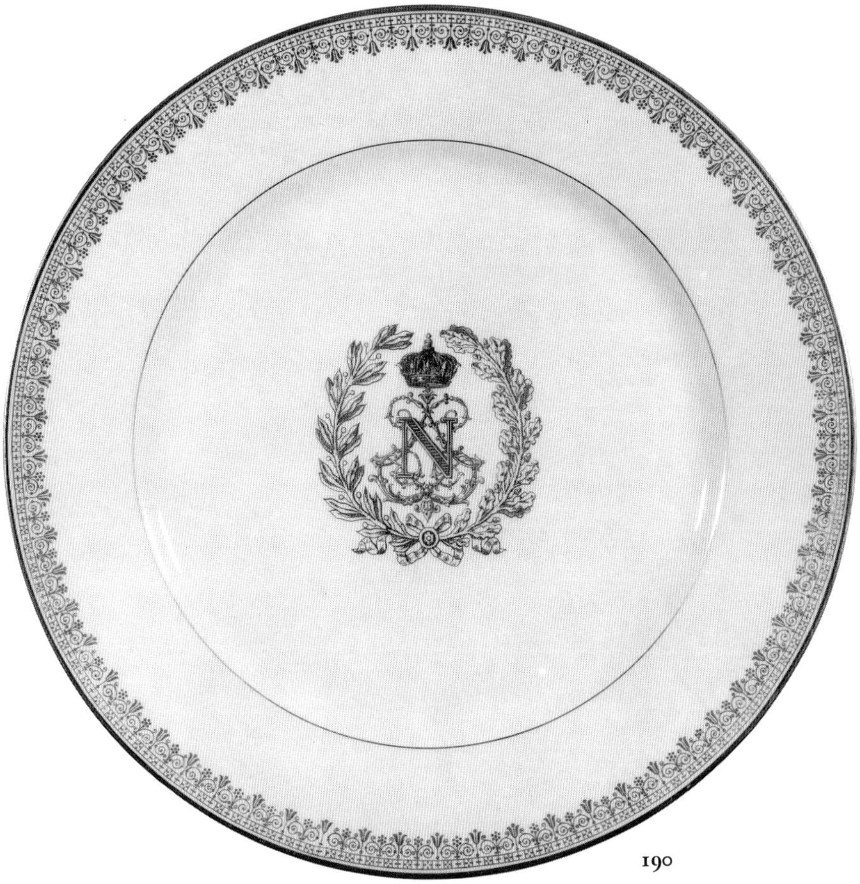

190

stylised flowers, scrolls and geometric motifs and in the centre with an *N* crowned interlaced with cursive *LL* enclosed by a wreath composed of a laurel leaf and berry branch on the left and an oak leaf and acorn branch on the right tied with a ribbon under a rosette at the lower end. The rim, inner edge of the border and outer edge of the foot rim are all gilt. The foot rim has been wiped clear of glaze and is discoloured.

Provenance: Bequeathed by C.D.E. Fortnum, Esq., FSA, DCL, 1899[1]

Literature: Unpublished

Comparable Examples: None noted

Louis Napoleon (1808–73) was elected to the National Assembly in June 1848 and in December of that year was elected President of France. In 1852 he took the title of Emperor Napoleon III, which he lost after his surrender to the Prussian army at Sedan in 1870.

For a note on the shape see cat. 187.

The plate was fired in 1859 but not decorated until several years later, a common occurrence in the nineteenth century at the Sèvres factory.

The border decoration is typical of the period.

1. For a note on C.D.E. Fortnum, a Museum Trustee and donor, see cat. 93.

191 **Vase (*vase d'Entrecolles*)**, 1886–97

See colour plate 33

H. 90.3 cm

Marks: *S97* within oval, printed in green inside neck and *S,96* printed in black on base; *T.Doat 1895* below date *1870–1* on vase (see p. 235); *PN n.3* and *6 86 I* incised inside foot rim

Reg. No. 1901,4–25,1

Hard-paste porcelain (*pâte nouvelle*),[1] cast,[2] bulbous body on flared foot which has been attached by means of a metal fitment, slightly out-turned neck. Celadon ground decorated in *pâte-sur-pâte* in two shades of green and in white with a band of stylised dolphins and an inscription *PARIS FLUCTUAT NEC MERGITUR* below the rim, with naturalistic flower garlands from which are suspended circular medallions containing four views: Hôtel de Ville, Notre-Dame de Paris, Le Louvre, Arc de Triomphe de l'Etoile. Each medallion is enclosed within a larger heart-shaped reserve on which a ship, the emblem of the city of Paris, is depicted. Surmounting each reserve is a bridge. On the lower part of the vase are laurel leaf and berry garlands linked by rectangular 'labels' inscribed with the principal dates in the history of Paris: *56 avant J.C.* (when Caesar's forces were defeated); *1358* (date of the assassination of the provost of the merchants, Etienne Marcel); *1789* (the Revolution); *1871* (the Commune). Foot restored.

Provenance: Presented by the French Government through the Ministre de l'Instruction Publique, 1901[3]

Literature: W.B. (William Burton) on 'Ceramics' in *The Encyclopaedia Britannica*, Cambridge, 1910, Vol. V, p. 758

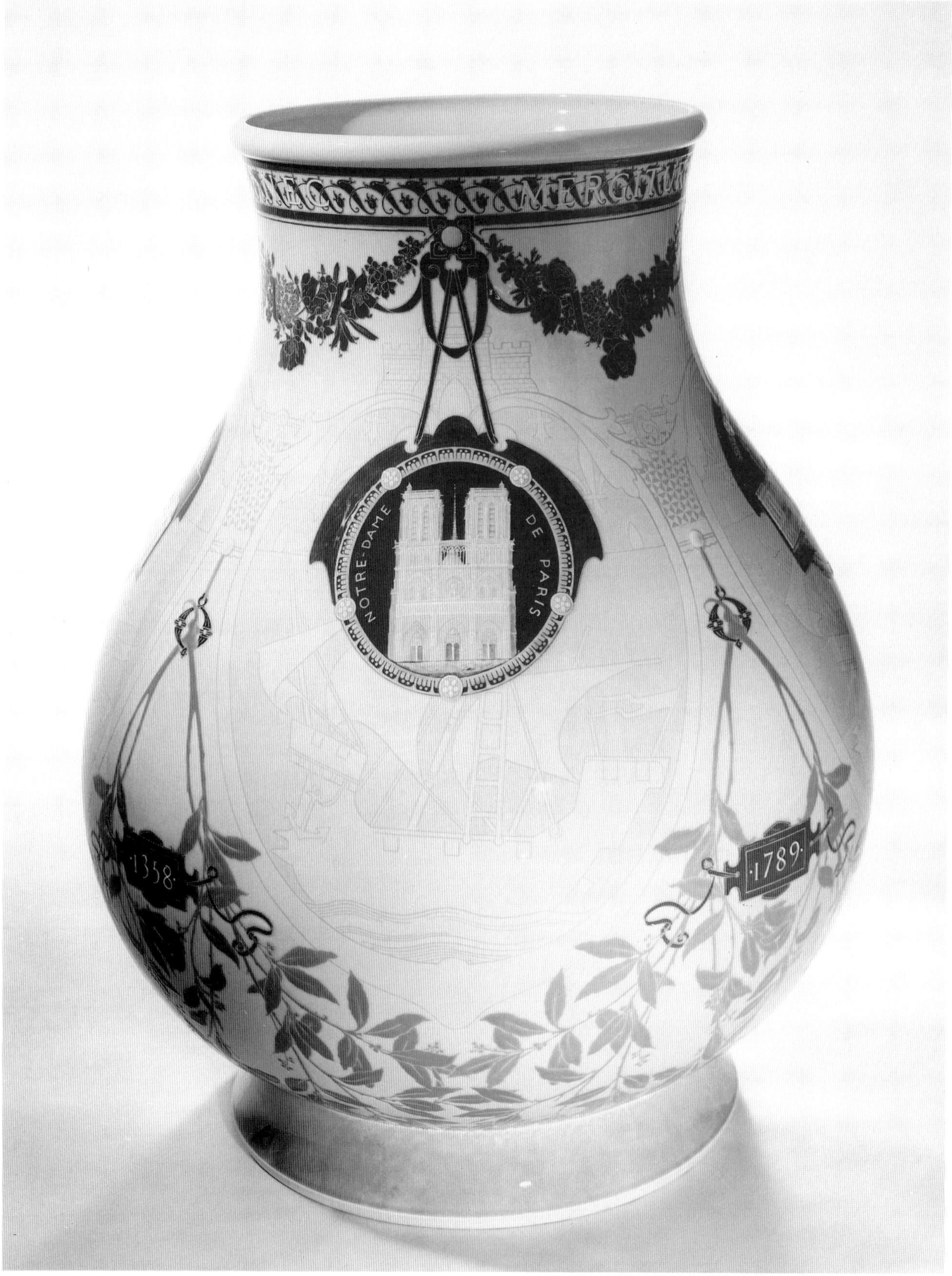

191

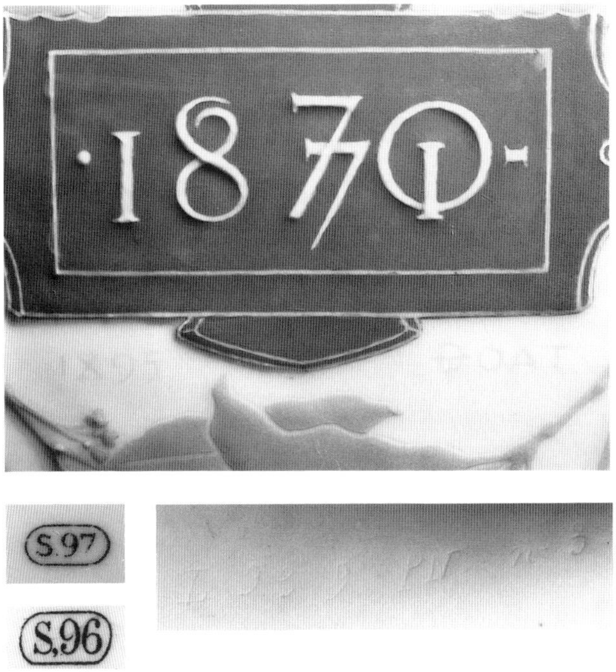

191 *marks*

H. Tait, 'Exciting Pâte-sur-Pâte Find in the British Museum', *Ars Ceramica*, no. 2, 1985, pp. 16–17

A. Dawson, 'Pieces for Presentation', *Ceramics*, February/March 1986, pp. 71–6

J. Rudoe, *Decorative Arts 1850–1950; A Catalogue of the British Museum Collection*, London, 1991, no. 80, pp. 39–40

The shape was devised by an unknown modeller in 1875. It presumably takes its name from François Xavier, Père d'Entrecolles, a Jesuit missionary (1664–1741) who sent letters home describing the manufacture of porcelain in China.[4]

The vase was cast in June 1886 on the evidence of the incised marks. This example was decorated in 1895 by Taxile Maximilien Doat (1851–1939), who joined Sèvres in 1887 as a sculptor, modeller and decorator. He specialised in the *pâte-sur-pâte* technique of building up a raised surface by successive applications of liquid clay (slip) using a brush.

The painters' register[5] records that Doat received the following payments in 1895 for his work on 'un vase d'Entrecolles 1ère gr. [i.e. first, or largest size] (La Ville de Paris)': January, 375 francs; March, 350 francs; April, 375 francs; in November, Lucas, Doat's assistant, received the remainder of the total sum, 1,633 francs 33 centimes, i.e. 522 francs, 33 centimes. Under the name of Lucas are recorded payments of 266 francs 68 centimes (June), 266 francs 66 centimes (July), 266 francs 66 centimes (August), and 566 francs 70 centimes (November). The total cost of decorating the vase was 3,000 francs, Lucas' work amounting in total to 1,366 francs 70 centimes. Further documents in the archives of the factory[6] record that in August 1897 the vase was valued as follows:

Peinture des figures	Doat, Lucas	3000	
Montage en bronze		86	60
Total des frais directs		3086	60
Faux frais		771	65
Valeur de la pièce en fond		1560	
Fonte 7 K^{OS}		28	
Prix de la fabrication par pièce		5446	25
Prix de vente		8000	

The selling price was considerably more than the 7,000 francs at which two vases of the same size decorated with flowers 'en pâte d'application' were valued in June 1895.[7]

In the event, the vase was not sold but was used by the French Government as a presentation piece, a practice dating back to the time of Louis xv. In the Presents Book at the British Museum under Donation 678 is a series of letters commencing July 29 1899 tracing the history of the presentation of the vase to the Museum in return for thirty thousand pamphlets relating to the French Revolution given to the Bibliothèque nationale and the Municipal Library of Paris. Negotiations were carried out by Delcassé, the French Foreign Minister, and the British Foreign Office. It was stipulated that the vase was to be exhibited at the Paris International Exhibition, 1900, but no mention of it has been discovered in any catalogue, nor in the printed list of works exhibited by the state enterprises. Lewis F. Day in 'Modern Pottery at the Paris Exhibition'[8] illustrates some pieces of *pâte-sur-pâte* by Doat, commenting that it has almost gone out of favour but singling out as remarkable 'a beautiful vase with medallions', evidently not the *vase d'Entrecolles*. The vase was delivered in March 1901, and submitted for the Trustees' approval the following month.

The use of a shape devised in 1875 and the rather stiff character of the floral decoration around the neck, together with the use of the by now rather old-fashioned technique of *pâte-sur-pâte* reveals that reforms instituted by the factory administrator E. Baumgart, appointed in 1891, had not yet been completed. Their total acceptance was no doubt delayed until the arrival of a new artistic director, Alex Sandier, in 1897. The decorative scheme was re-used in a variant featuring the attributes of the cities of Bordeaux, Tours and Lille on a *Vase Saigon* decorated by Doat in 1895.[9]

1. For details of this body see cat. 192.
2. A vase of this shape is visible in a photograph of the *atelier de grand coulage* in the new factory i.e. after 1877, illus. T.P. (Tamara Préaud), 'La manufacture de Sèvres au XVIIIe siècle', *Monuments historiques*, no. 128, August–September 1983, p. 48.
3. L. Belot in 'Taxile Doat', *Revue du Département du Tarn*, September 1909, p. 264, states that the vase 'a été apporté à S.M. le Roi Edouard VII par le Président Loubet lors de son voyage en Angleterre'. It was valued at 6,000 francs. The author is grateful to Bernard Bumpus for bringing this reference to her attention.
4. The author is grateful to Rosalind Savill for drawing her attention to the origin of this shape name; see *Biographie Universelle*, Paris, 1852, Vol. x for *d'Entrecolles*.
5. MNS, Archives de Sèvres, Vj'100.
6. MNS, Archives de Sèvres, Vf *Première Série*, f. 213.
7. *Ibid.*, f. 157.
8. See *Art Journal Paris Exhibition 1900*, pp. 91–102.
9. Exhibited London, International Ceramics Fair and Seminar, June 1991 by Galerie Moderne, London. The author is grateful to Martine de Cervens for providing information about this piece and allowing her to examine it.

192 **Vase (*vase Chevilly*),** 1905

192 *mark*

H. 23 cm
Mark: *S 1905* within a triangle printed in grey
Reg. No. 1987,11–2,1

Hard-paste porcelain (*porcelaine nouvelle*); four-sided tapering form, with thin neck springing from rounded shoulders and two handles formed of overlapping vetch leaves. Vase decorated with a yellowish crystalline glaze, handles glazed. Small chip to foot.

Provenance: Purchased, 1987, from the collection of Mr John Scott

Literature: J. Rudoe, *Decorative Arts 1850–1950; A Catalogue of the British Museum Collection*, London, 1991, no. 269, p. 105

Comparable Examples: Sèvres, Musée national de Céramique, inv. 16062.

Limoges, Musée national Adrien Dubouché, inv. ADL 7761, see exh. *Sèvres XIXe siècle*, 1975, no. 557

Saintes, Musée des Beaux-Arts, inv. 08–1–56, illus. *La Collection de Sèvres du Musée des Beaux-Arts de Saintes 1890–1910*, cat. compiled by H. Blanchard and M. Thauré, published by the Museum, 1986, no. 54

Germany, Berlin, Bröhan Collection, see 'Kunst der Jahrhundertwende und der zwanziger Jahre, Sammlung Karl Bröhan', Berlin, 1977, Vol. II, part 2, no. 693.

Germany, Hanover, Kestner Museum, inv. 1970,21, see exh. *Kunsthandwerk in Umbruch, Jugendstil und zwanziger Jahre*, compiled by C. Mosel, no. 125.

The form was designed in 1897 by Alexandre Sandier (art director 1896–1916) and exists in several variants. Henri-Ernst Brécy was responsible for producing the model. Undecorated porcelain examples are first documented in the *Magasin de blanc* in November 1898.[1]

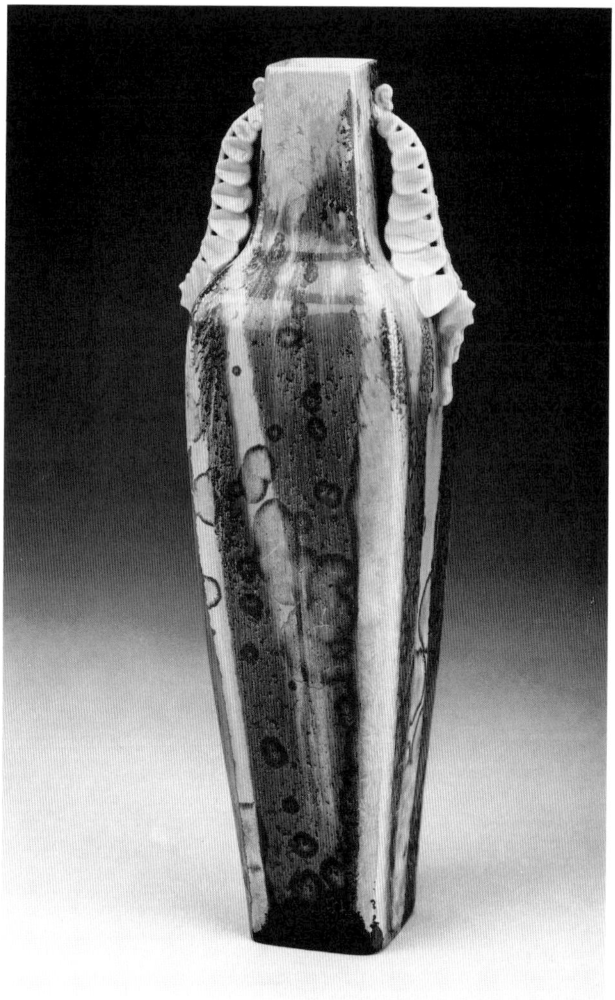

192

Pieces made of the *porcelaine nouvelle*[2] were first publicly exhibited in Paris at the eighth *Exposition des industries d'art* held in 1884 under the auspices of the Union Centrale des Arts Décoratifs. Charles Lauth, the administrator of the Sèvres factory between 1879 and 1887, gave a public lecture in the Palais d'Industrie on 28 October 1884[3] to introduce the new material. The following year he published *Notes techniques sur la fabrication de la porcelaine nouvelle* in collaboration with Georges Vogt, the factory's chief chemist, which was available to French manufacturers on request.[4] The new porcelain contained pegmatite and kaolin from the Limousin region, and is described as being entirely composed of French raw materials and designed for ornamental pieces as opposed to domestic wares. It was developed after analyses of Chinese porcelains made by the earlier generation of Ebelmen and Salvetat had revealed that their composition was entirely different to that of Sèvres hard-paste porcelain which vitrified at the high temperature of 1,600–1,700°C.[5] *Porcelaine nouvelle* was fired at a lower temperature and was therefore suitable for a much wider range of decorative effects.

Crystalline glaze effects were observed by C. Lauth and G. Dutailly in 1888 as a consequence of the use of zinc oxide in glazes, which on cooling formed prismatic crystals which became larger as the cooling period was lengthened. They commented on the 'joli effet' of the crystals which they considered could be made even more attractive were they to be coloured with metal oxides to contrast with the glaze.[6] Despite these comments, it was some years before crystalline glazes were put into regular production, and only at the 1900 Exhibition were they first publicly shown on pieces of several different forms.[7]

1. MNS, Archives de Sèvres, Registre Vr', 3ème série, vol. 8, ff. 13–17. The author is grateful to Tamara Préaud for this information.
2. It consists of 64% silica, 29% alumina, 7% potassium according to a formula given by the present-day factory chemist Antoine d'Albis in F. Treppoz and A. d'Albis, 'Identification de différents types de porcelaines anciennes à l'aide de l'analyse par diffraction X' *Faenza*, Vol. LXXIII, 1987, nos. I–III, p. 61.
3. C. Lauth, *La manufacture nationale de Sèvres et la porcelaine nouvelle*, conférence faite le 28 Octobre 1884 au Palais de l'Industrie, Paris, 1884. A copy of this is preserved at the Library of the Musée des arts décoratifs, Paris.
4. C. Lauth and G. Vogt, *Notes techniques sur la fabrication de la porcelaine nouvelle*, Paris, 1885.
5. Antoine d'Albis, director of the laboratory at the Sèvres factory, has questioned these firing temperatures. In conversation with the author in November 1991 he pointed out that accurate measurement of firing was impossible before the early 20th century in France, and 19th century accounts of firing temperatures are unreliable.
6. C. Lauth, *La manufacture nationale de Sèvres 1879–1887*, Paris, 1889, see section x, C. Lauth and G. Dutailly 'Sur les Couvertes de Porcelaine', originally in *Génie civil*, 21 July, 28 July, 4 August 1888.
7. Lechevallier-Chevignard, 1908, (part two), p. 34.

193 **Cup and Saucer (*tasse litron*),** 19th century

D. *of saucer:* 13.3 cm
H. *of cup:* 6.8 cm
Marks: *27* and [?] *2 Td* incised on cup, suspension hole on saucer
Reg. No. Franks 389

Soft-paste porcelain, saucer warped, both pieces with imperfections in the paste. The cup is painted with a cameo portrait of Charles James Fox (1749–1806) three-quarters to left on a reddish 'marbled' ground within a gilt 'jewelled' 'frame', on a dark blue ground embellished with 'jewelling' and scrolls. Gilt dentil on inside of rim, handle partly gilt. The saucer is inscribed in gold *A patriot's even course he steered/mid faction's wildest storms unmoved/By all who marked his mind revered/By all who knew his heart*

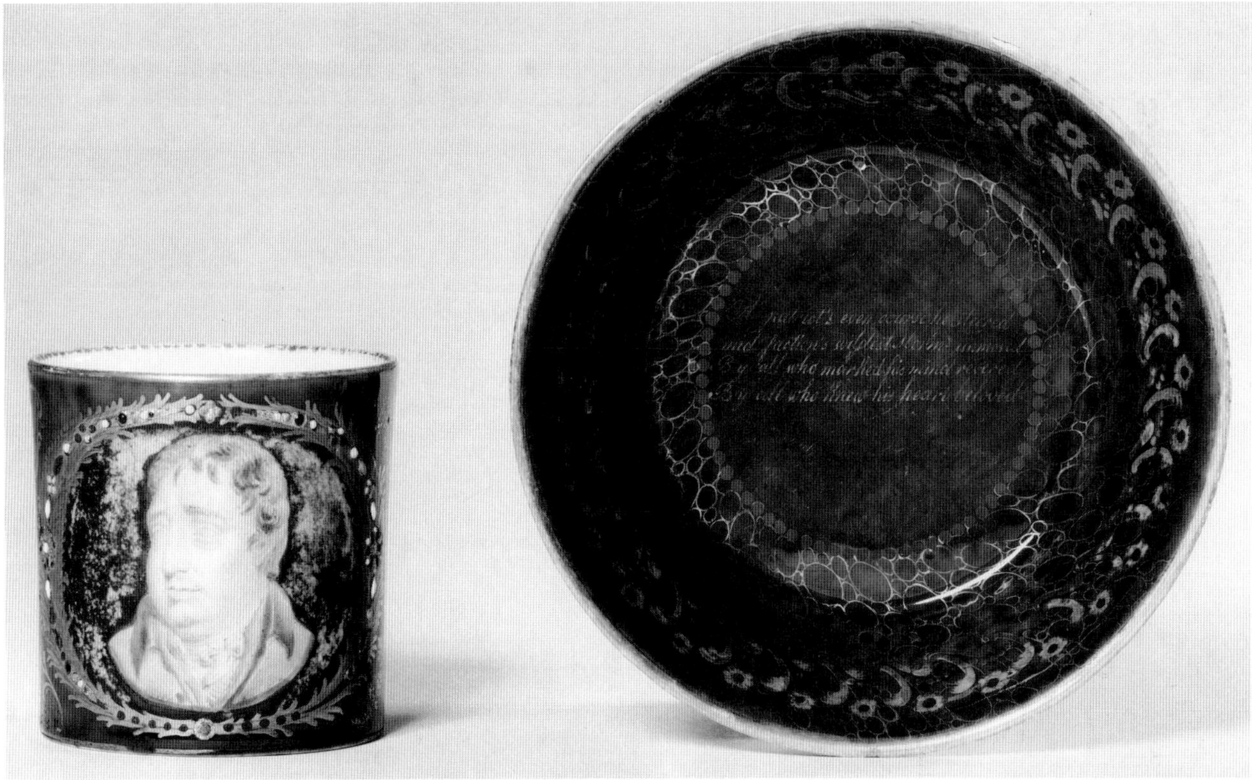

193

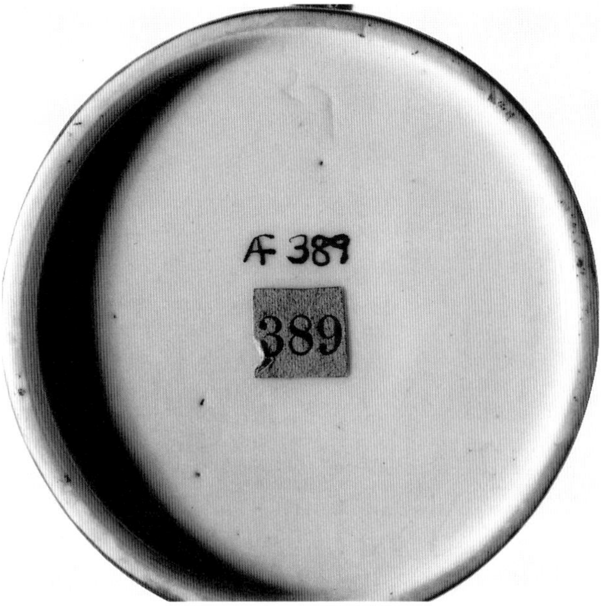

193 *marks*

beloved., on a blue ground partly vermiculated in gold and with a stylised floral pattern. Saucer and handle repaired.

Provenance: Bequeathed by Sir A.W. Franks, 1897

Literature: Franks, 1896, no. 389

Comparable Examples: None

In view of the size and shape of this cup and saucer which correspond to the second size of the *tasse litron* made at Sèvres,[1] and the presence of (unrecorded) incised marks on the cup, it is likely that they were made at the royal factory. They were probably sold off by Brongniart in the early nineteenth century and decorated in England. The style of the gilt scrolls on the cup suggests a date around 1840, but this perhaps antedates the popularity of 'jewelled' Sèvres with collectors. The history of the piece has not been established, but it may have been no more than two or three decades old when it entered the Museum collection. The date of the decoration on the cup and saucer is clearly related to the cult of Fox, and was possibly prompted by the publication of the poet Samuel Rogers' *Table Talk* in 1856, and of Fox's *Correspondence* between 1853 and 1857.[2]

The portrait of Fox is closest to a portrait by John Opie of 1802, which shows him with short hair and sideburns, slightly in profile to left.[3]

The political career of the Whig statesman Charles James Fox was marked by his opposition to King George III, alluded to in the use of the words 'patriot'[4] and 'faction' in the verse inscribed on the saucer. However, he was a close friend of the Prince of Wales, advising him during the Regency Crisis (1788–9) and on the subject of his marriage to Mrs Fitzherbert. Fox was renowned for his gaiety and good nature, for his addiction to gambling and for his political oratory and skill in debate. He was probably the most caricatured figure in eighteenth-century England, if not Europe.

The verse was composed by Fox's most intimate friend Richard Fitzpatrick (1747–1813)[5] and is inscribed on a plaque placed in the chancel of the parish church of St Anne's Hill nr. Chertsey, Surrey, by Fox's widow in 1807.[6]

1. Savill, 1988, II, p. 501.
2. For one assessment of later views of Fox, see L. Reid, *Charles James Fox, A Man for the People*, London and Harlow, 1969, pp. 433–46, and see the bibliography for information on works by and about Fox.
3. Reid, *ibid.*, pl. 4, Elizabethan Club, Yale University.
4. According to I.M. Davis, *The Harlot and the Statesman, the Story of Elizabeth Armistead & Charles James Fox*, London, 1986, p. 36, 'at this period the term "Patriot" almost automatically carried the pejorative significance of, in Dr Johnson's words, "a factious disturber of the government"'.
5. The two men were friends from youth and were related by marriage; for an account of Fitzpatrick's life, see the *Dictionary of National Biography*.
6. Davis, *ibid.*, pp. 176–7. Fox is buried in Westminster Abbey.

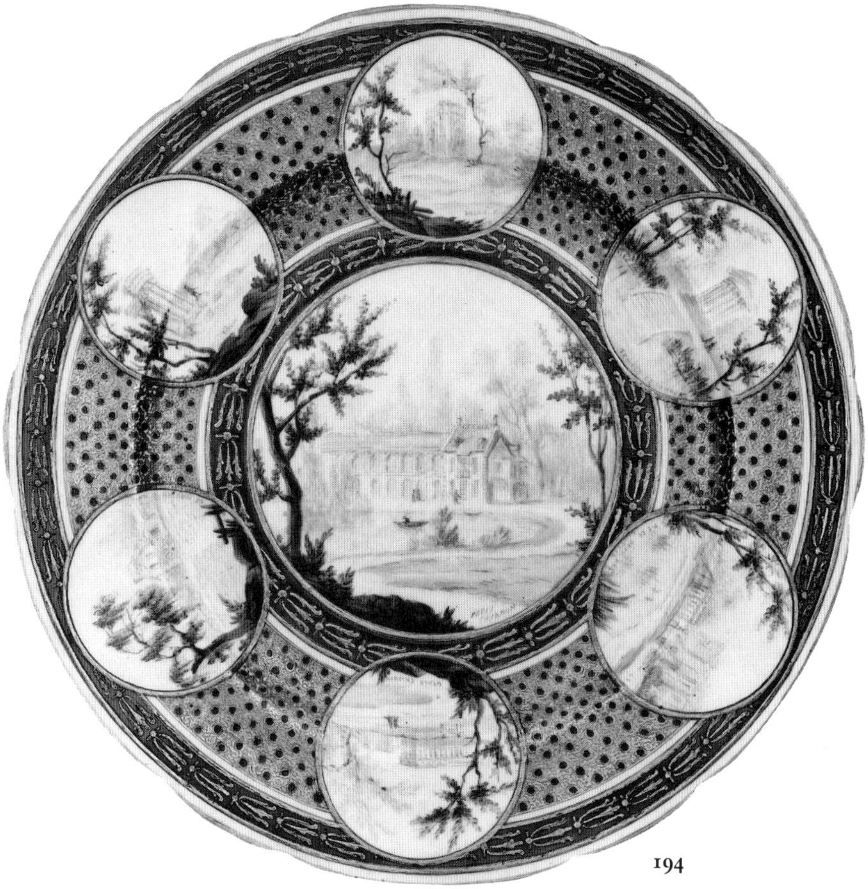

194

194 **Plate**, Sèvres, decorated elsewhere in the 19th or early 20th century

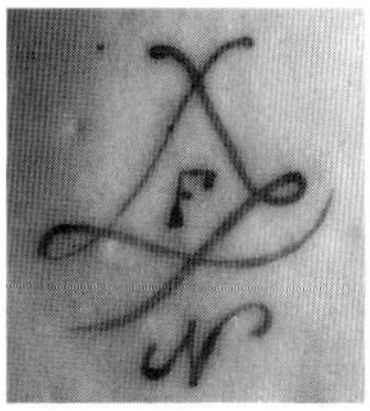

194 *marks*

D.	24.5 cm
Marks:	interlaced LL enclosing *F*, above *N*; suspension hole.
Reg. No.	1913,12–20,133

Soft-paste porcelain, shallow, the rim shaped with six large and six smaller lobes. The decoration consists of six scenes within circular reserves outlined in gold of scenes in the grounds of the Palace of Versailles painted in blue, yellow and green with darker brown, green and yellow for the trees and red and blue for the diminutive figures in three of the scenes. Each is inscribed in grey: *TEMPLE DE L'AMOUR, PIECE D'EAU DES CUISSES, PETIT TRIANON, LE MOULIN, TIVOLI, SALLE DE MUSIQUE.* In the well is a scene with four tiny figures, one in a boat, before a building, inscribed *GRAND TRIANON.* It is enclosed by a gilt line beyond which is a gilt palmette leaf on a royal blue ground bounded by a gilt line. This design is repeated near the rim, which is gilt on both sides. On the border and part of the well is a gilt 'vermiculated' design interrupted by blue dots in gilt circles. The reverse of the plate exhibits numerous pin-holes and is discoloured, notably on the foot rim.

Provenance: Bequeathed by the Reverend A.H.S. Barwell, 1913

Literature: Unpublished

Comparable Examples: National Museums on Merseyside, Liverpool Museum, two *pots à crème* or cream pots, of similar pattern inv. 3788, 3789 acquired by the Walker Art Gallery, 1947, L.R. Warrens Collection

Christie's, 13 March 1989, Lot 8, cup and saucer, mark LL enclosing *H*, saucer has suspension hole, indistinct incised marks

Like the Liverpool pieces, which are also of soft-paste porcelain, this plate was made at the Sèvres factory, and was probably considered to be defective and sold off undecorated. The decoration was done outside the factory at an indeterminate time in the nineteenth or early twentieth century, in a style and palette which is inconsistent with known decoration of genuine eighteenth-century Sèvres porcelains. Careful examination of the gold vermiculated decoration and comparison with other documented pieces shows that the gilding on this piece is rather carelessly executed.

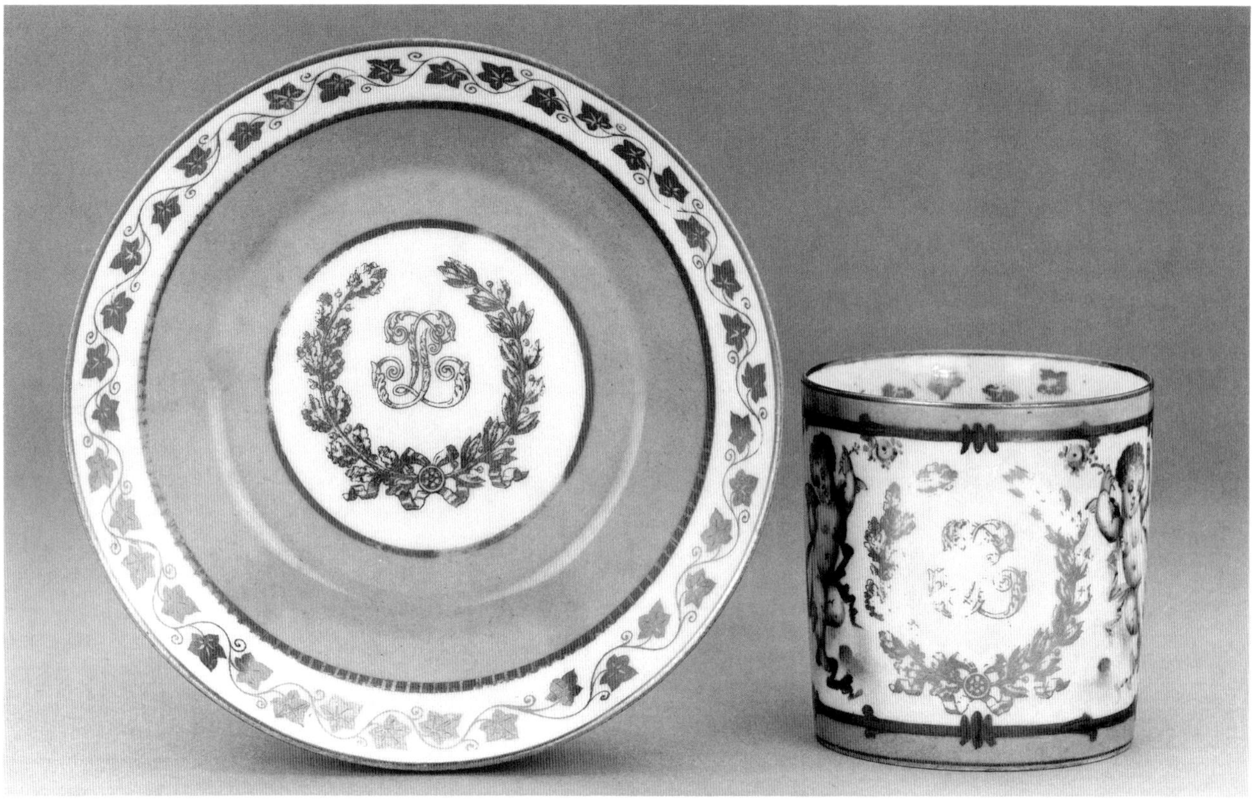

195

195 **Cup and Saucer (*tasse litron*),**
fake Sèvres marks for 1846

D. *of saucer:*	12.6 cm
H. *of cup:*	6.3 cm
Marks:	blue printed mark *SEVRES 1846* and crowned LL within a double circle; grey printed mark *LP* in monogram twice, crowned, between *SV 46*; red printed mark *CHATEAU DES TUILERIES* within a 16-pointed star, crowned; *X* incised on cup, *bln* [?] incised on saucer
Reg. No.	1981,1-1,102

Hard-paste porcelain, finely potted and highly translucent, the saucer with deep flared sides, and the straight-sided cup with simple ear-shaped handle. Printed in gold with the monogram *LP* within an oak leaf and acorn (left) and laurel leaf and berry wreath tied with a ribbon bow on cup and saucer and an ivy-leaf trail printed in gold around the rim of the saucer and inside the cup. The remainder of both is decorated in turquoise-blue, with gilt bands; on the cup two crudely painted *putti* each holding a flower and draped with a pink and orange scarf respectively are shown dancing either side of the monogram. Gilding rubbed.

Provenance: Bequeathed by Miss C.M. Woodward, 1981

Literature: Unpublished

Comparable Examples: Sotheby's, 17 July 1990, Lot 343, six cups and saucers; Lot 359, twelve plates

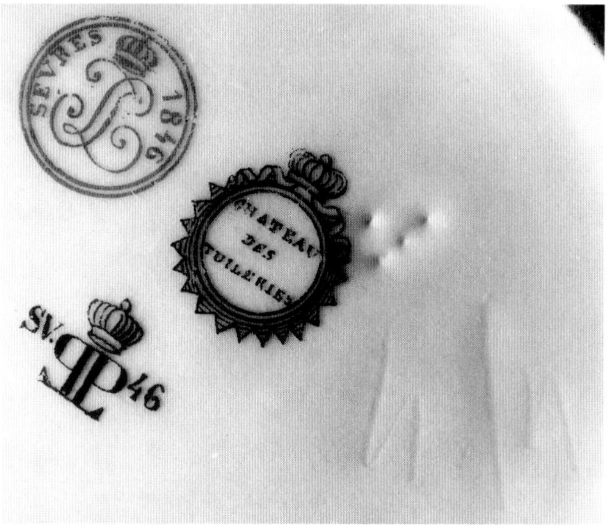

195 *marks*

Italy, Rome, Christie's, 28 November 1990, Lot 230; Lot 231, plate

It is not known exactly when fakes of this kind first went into circulation, but a date in the later part of the nineteenth century is suggested.

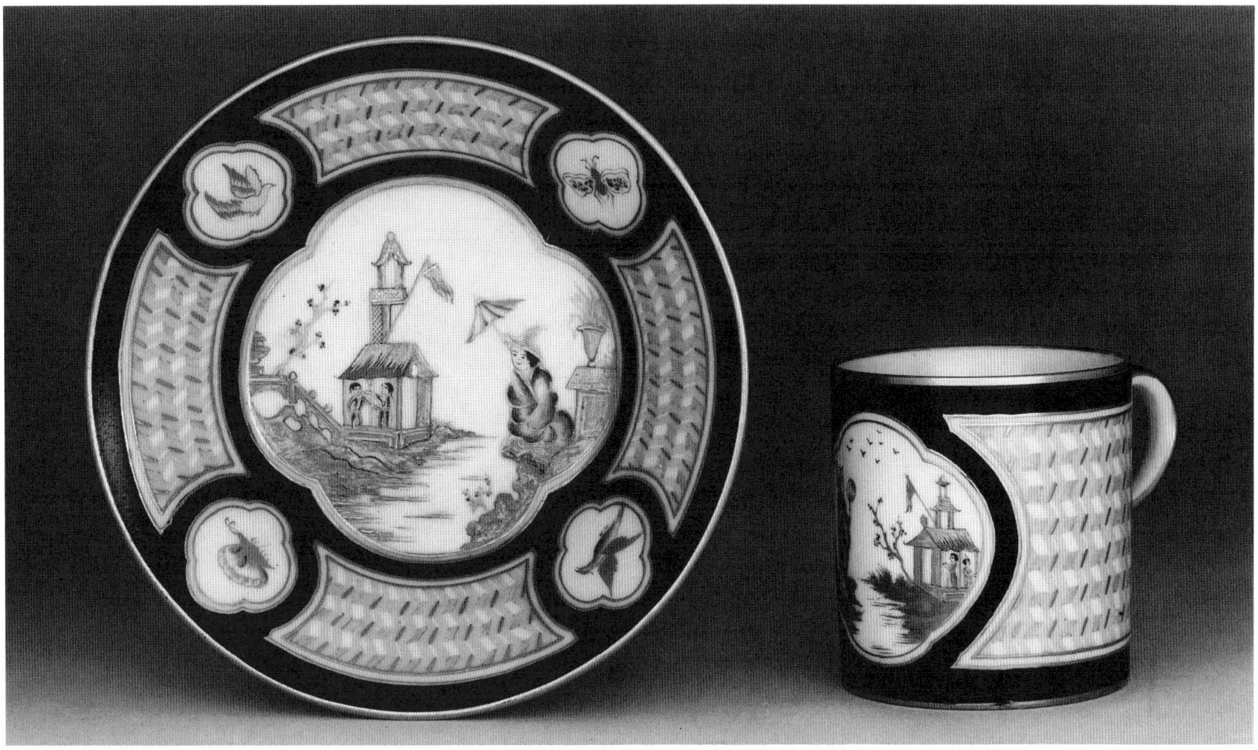

196

196 **Cup and Saucer (*tasse litron*)**, perhaps second half of 20th century

D. of saucer: 12.3 cm
H. of cup: 6 cm
Marks: none; suspension hole on each
Reg. No. OA 10720

Hard-paste porcelain, heavily potted, the saucer with flared slightly curving sides, the straight-sided cup with strap handle scrolling at lower end where it bifurcates. The decoration consists of a mosaic-type pattern in pale purplish-pink, pale turquoise and gold in four panels on the sides of the saucer alternating with quatrefoil lobes each containing a butterfly or a bird in pink, pink and blue or flesh-colour. The well of the saucer is decorated with a quatrefoil panel of a seated oriental figure with a parasol on the right of a river bank on the opposite side of which is a pagoda sheltering two standing oriental figures in pink, blue, orange and gold. On the cup is a rather similar scene in reverse with an oriental standing holding a fan. The borders of each panel are painted in chocolate brown. Rims and handle gilt. Perfect except for scratching on the base of both.

Provenance: Presented as a study item by Armin Allen, 1988

Literature: Unpublished

Comparable Examples: None known

This may be a recent attempt to deceive. It is not from a known class of fakes, shows little signs of wear and imitates *chinoiserie* scenes in the manner of the Sèvres hard-paste painters Denis Levé and Louis-François Lécot, the quality of whose work remained largely unrecognised until the last decade.[1] In 1917 Frederick Litchfield concluded his article on imitations and reproductions of Sèvres as follows:[2] 'In the subjoined chart of Sèvres marks, those of the later hard-paste and Republican periods of the factory are omitted. These are seldom copied in imitations, as Sèvres of these later periods is of small value compared with that of the best time'.

1. For a hard-paste *plateau* and *déjeuner Paris* painted by Lécot, see Savill, 1988, II, C407–13.
2. F. Litchfield, 'Imitations and Reproductions, Part I – Sèvres Porcelain', *Connoisseur*, Vol. XLIX, no. 193, September 1917, pp. 3–14.

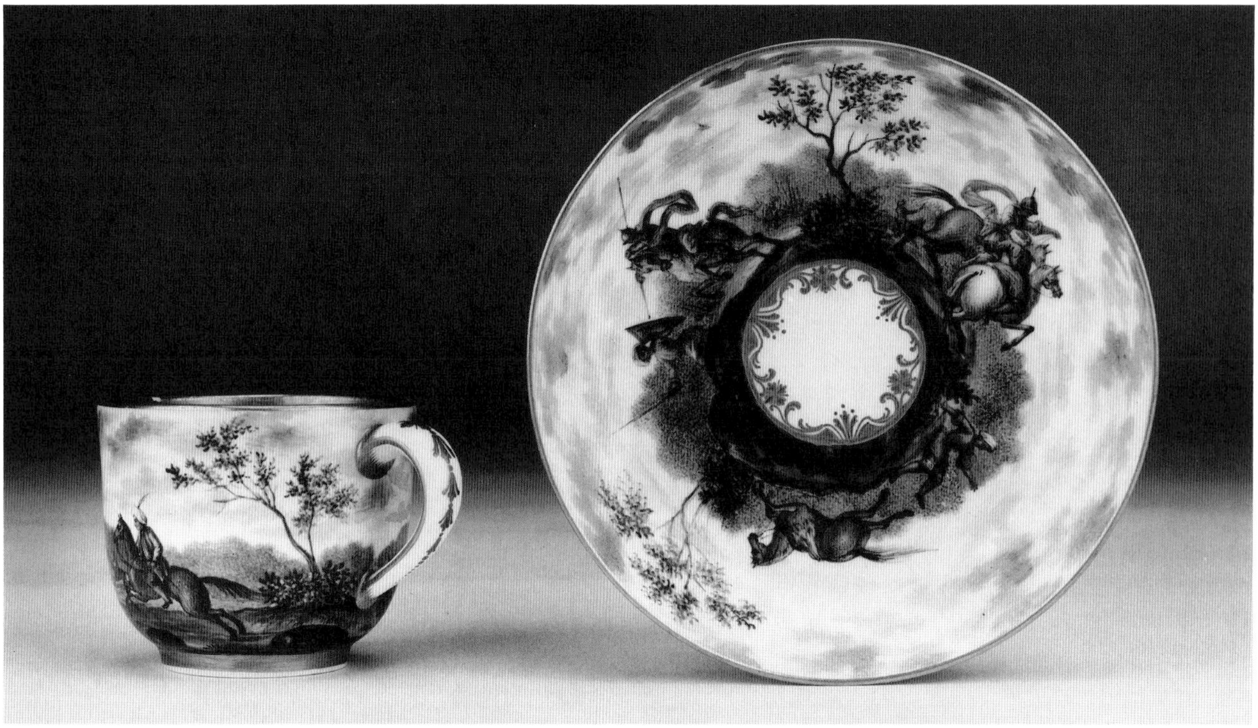

197

197 **Cup and Saucer (*tasse Bouillard et soucoupe*)**, probably decorated in the 19th century in imitation of Capodimonte

D. *of saucer:*	13.5 cm
H. *of cup:*	5.8 cm
Marks:	fleur-de-lys painted in underglaze blue enamel; paper label numbered *62* on both, another with price code in pencil, another inscribed in ink . . ./ *Retiro/6/10/38* on saucer; suspension hole on both
Reg. No.	1940,4–1,21

Soft-paste porcelain, noticeably white in tone, the curved saucer without a well, the cup with curved sides and wide thick loop handle tapering towards the base. Decorated in puce, mauve, orange, yellow, white, green, turquoise, brown and black with horsemen in armour with flowing scarves fighting Turks. Rims gilt, foot of cup gilt, gilt patterns on handle, inside cup and in centre of saucer.

Provenance: Bequeathed by Arthur Hurst, Esq., 1940 (called Buen Retiro, Spain)

Literature: Unpublished

Comparable Examples: Manchester, City Art Galleries, *Porcelain from Europe*, cat. compiled by S. Macdonald, published by the Galleries, 1986, no. 118, saucer is a fake (cup considered genuine Capodimonte) but probably not a Sèvres product

England, private collection[1]

USA, Washington, D.C., Smithsonian Institution, National Museum of American History, on loan from the Estate of Dr H. Syz, October 1991. Group of pieces of which three cups and saucers apparently correspond with the Museum example, inv. 917A a and b, 917B a and b, 917C a and b, also a teapot probably of Sèvres origin, inv. 909a

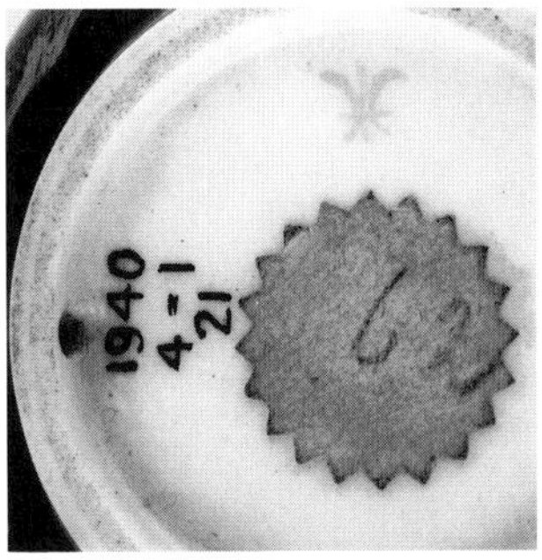

197 *marks (cup)*

The body of this cup and saucer is much whiter than that of Capodimonte porcelain. The shape, dimensions and suspension hole on each suggests that the pieces were made at the Sèvres factory. The underside of the saucer exhibits tears in the paste and other imperfections, so that the pieces may have been sold undecorated as 'seconds'. It is not known when they were decorated.

A plate in the British Museum[2] also bearing a blue fleur-de-lys mark is decorated with a similar battle-scene and gilt pattern. It is evidently redecorated, the surface having numerous black specks. It is fire-cracked on the reverse, and the well is uneven. It too has an exceptionally white body and a hole for suspension in the inside of the foot rim.

1. The author is grateful to Rosalind Savill for this information.
2. Reg. No. MLA 1981,1–1,95, origin undetermined.

Orléans[1]

It is not known exactly when soft-paste porcelain manufacture began in Orléans. A factory in the rue du Bourdon-Blanc, parish of Saint Euverte, was established by an *arrêt* of 13 March 1753 by Jacques-Etienne Dessaux de Romilly.[2] The twenty-year privilege granted to him by the King was for 'une manufacture royale de faïence de terre blanche purifiée'. The material was described as 'dans l'intérieur, comme à la superficie, d'un très beau blanc'. Hellot, member of the Académie des Sciences, had examined experimental pieces made by Dessaux de Romilly. The mark to be used on the products of the factory was an *O* crowned painted in blue under the glaze. It is considered likely that porcelain was made there, if only on a small scale, before the purchase of the concern on 26 February 1757 by Claude-Charles Gérault d'Areaubert (1716/17–1782).[3] The latter was already associated with the factory, along with Louis-François Le Roy, who was its director. Gérault was the proprietor until his death in 1782.

Clays were apparently purchased from as far afield as Beleu in Flanders. Marls from the Paris region were used from 1755, and from 1756 clays were brought from Saint-Mamert near Châteaudun. When taxed with extracting these illegally, Gérault substituted others from Croix Beaulieu, at least until 1763.[4] In a report to the intendant dated 1777 it was claimed that clays from Saint-Yrieix-la-Perche in the Limoges region were used from 1764, but they may well have been used in the making of faïence.[5] Until more information is found concerning the raw materials used, it is impossible to say exactly when soft-paste manufacture began. There is no evidence that Gérault ever made hard-paste, although there was both paste and glaze for the hard body in the Chambre des Pâtes in June 1777. However, the detailed description given in the inventory made after Gérault's death[6] does not show that the factory had two separate *ateliers*, as was the case at the royal factory.

In 1756 and 1757 there was a total workforce of sixty-eight: one modeller (this was Jean Louis, see cat. 198), ten *répareurs-sculpteurs* (repairers), three *estampeurs et mouleurs* (mould-makers), twenty-five flower-makers, six *racheveuses*, four *retoucheurs* (retouchers), two painters, two *enfourneurs* (kiln masters), four *encasteurs* (moulders), six *tourneurs* (throwers), one *garde-magasin* (storekeeper), one porter, one clerk and two millworkers.[7]

Demand for the factory's products fell dramatically during the Seven Years War (1756–63). In 1758 attempts were made to market tablewares and other domestic wares in Blois, Tours, Saumur, Angers, Lyon, Macon, Dijon, Langres, Troyes, Rheims, Soissons, Laon, Amiens and Rouen, but did not prove successful.

New kilns were built and an existing one repaired in 1760, when about forty apprentices for flower-making, repairing, moulding and *stampage* were taken on. Most left after completing their four-year apprenticeship. In 1763 there were only twenty-nine workers:[8] one modeller, one repairer, four throwers (*tourneurs*), two *mouleurs estampeurs et racheveurs*, six flower-makers, one *garnisseuse et racheveuse*, two retouchers (*retoucheuses*), three apprentice flower-makers, six apprentice repairers, one kiln master, one millworker and one storekeeper. Some names of personnel are known from surviving documents recording the disputes between Gérault and his workforce. Models were now provided by artists from outside the factory, including members of the Academy of Sculpture in Paris.

The names of several employees are known from

an altercation between the sculptor Bernard Huet and Gérault in April 1767, and others from surviving bills.[9] Some came from other factories, such as Bernard Huet, who was at Villeroy-Mennecy in 1764, and Louis who had been at Strasbourg and Sceaux. Others, such as the kiln-master (*enfourneur*) Léonard Desroches, wanted to go to Sèvres. Desroches' request was made in 1764.[10] Between about 1757 and 1763 undecorated wares were sold all over France from Paris (through a merchant called Hennique) to Metz, Besançon, Montpellier, Toulouse, Arras, etc., as well as in Spain and Holland.

The range of tablewares made was wide. In the report to the *intendant* of 7 October 1763[11] tureens, dishes, salt-cellars, water jugs, sugar bowls, sauce-boats and 'all sorts of domestic wares' are mentioned, together with figures and groups for the dessert, flowers for wall-lights (*bras de cheminées*). 'Un peu de peinture et dorure' is even mentioned in this report. This would, of course, infringe the privilege granted to the Sèvres factory. Gérault's report to the *intendant* dated 8 June 1777[12] mentions the names of merchants in connection with outlets all over France. In Paris, Bazin in the rue des Fossés-Saint-Germain kept the *magasin de la manufacture*, but Bailly, *veuve* Breaud Grouet, Dubaud, Brillet, Oblede, Robin, Sauveur and Briel also sold Orléans wares (presumably including earthenwares). Becker at Brussels, Durand in Warsaw, Montandre and company in St Petersburg, Ulrich and Van Diest in The Hague and Amsterdam, Pannier in Cadiz and *personnes indirectes* in London handled foreign sales.

A mustard-pot attached to a tray, a *seau à bouteille* and a *pot à crème* all in the rococo style belong to a group of pieces attributed to the factory which are decorated with sprigs of naturalistic flowers in *bleu camaïeu* over the glaze and are marked with a label and *C* in blue.[13] A *caisse à fleurs* in the same style in the Musée des arts décoratifs, Paris[14] and a magnificently painted jug and cover with polychrome flower decoration are marked with an *O* crowned.[15] A tureen and cover in the Seattle Art Museum, USA, bears no factory mark, but is similarly painted to the jug and cover.[16] These pieces seem on stylistic grounds to be earlier than those marked with the label and fleur-de-lys in red, which are neo-classical in style, with angular or ring handles, and are decorated with scattered flowers.[17]

Figures and groups, both glazed and unglazed, of pastoral, historical and fable subjects were in the *magazin* in 1777. As in the case of the rococo soft-paste tablewares, the influence of Sèvres was felt: a group of the *Sabot Cassé* and the *Feuille à l'Envers* were listed in Gérault's *inventaire après décès*, together with the *Le Couronnement de la Bergère*, *Ariane* and *Bacchus*, *Belisarius*,[18] *Henri IV*, *Seneca*, *Voltaire* and *Rousseau*, 'danses allemandes' and busts of women.[19] Presumably the first two were pieces from the earlier production which had not sold, whereas the other subjects were probably mostly introduced in the 1770s.

Flower production was carried out on a large scale. Figures and groups of musicians and gardeners, Bacchic and classical subjects, allegorical and other figures, such as 'Cris de Paris' were also made, and found a market in Paris. A programme of the visit of Louis-Stanislas-Xavier, comte de Provence (1755–1824), Louis XVI's brother, usually known by the title 'Monsieur', on 10 June 1777 provides considerable details of the Orléans factory. There were two kilns (the old and the new), a mill with six sails for bodies (*pâtes*) and two for glazes, a laboratory and 'cabinet de chimie', where gold and silver colours were prepared. In the 'magasine' were no less than 24,000 flowers. The report to the *intendant* of the same year states that these *fleurs de caprices* now cost 18 *sous* a dozen, although before the establishment of the factory (i.e. in the 1740s) they had been 3 *livres*. Creamware in imitation of English pieces was made and sold at fairs within 100 leagues of Orléans.

Production at the factory in the rue du Bourdon-Blanc ceased abruptly on Gérault's death. A Paris merchant bought up the stock and tried to sell some at Orléans before taking the rest to Paris.[20] The moulds, mills, wheels, boards and saggars were sold by Gérault's widow direct from the factory. Some workers probably went to a factory established in the rue du Puits-Saint-Laurent by Bourdon de Saussay. The Museum has no examples from this concern, nor from that of his successors.

Considerable controversy surrounds the identification of the marks used by Gérault at Orléans. A label mark in blue, red-brown or gold, sometimes accompanied by a fleur-de-lys, is thought to have been used by Gérault, although the mark was apparently never registered. Hard-paste porcelains marked in underglaze-blue with a label mark are attributed by this author to Hannong's factory at Vincennes, despite their traditional identification with Orléans, since Hannong registered this mark with the lieutenant of the Paris police (see p. 336).

1. This account is based on Chavagnac and Grollier, 1906, pp. 373–90 and on Dr Garsonnin, 'Manufactures de Porcelaine', in *Mémoires de la Société Archéologique et Historique de l'Orléanais*, Vol. 35 (1920), pp. 305–51. Garsonnin illustrates pieces in the Musée historique, Orléans, and lists others in the Musée national Adrien-Dubouché, Limoges, and the Musée des arts décoratifs, Paris. Both these accounts draw on archival sources, Garsonnin using extensively the Archives départementales du Loiret, C. 66, and E. Piot, 'Etudes Céramiques, la manufacture royale de faïence fine et de porcelaine établie à Orléans en 1753', *Le Cabinet de l'Amateur*, no. 25, Paris, 1863, in which the key documents are quoted.
2. The *arrêt* is published in full in Piot, *op. cit.*, pp. 123–4. Piot states that Dessaux de Romilly was director of the Saint Gobain mirror factory; see E. Frémy, *Histoire de la Manufacture Royale des Glaces de France*, Paris, 1909, p. 180 and C. Pris, *La Manufacture royale des Glaces de Saint-Gobain, une grande entreprise sous l'Ancien Régime*, Vol. I, unpublished thesis, University of Paris IV, 30 June, 1973, pp. 356, 425, 1230. The author is grateful to David Whitehouse, Corning Museum of Glass, for these two references.
3. In 1757 the modeller Jean Louis complained to the *intendant* that although Le Roy had kept to the terms of the agreement drawn up in April 1756 which laid down the modeller's working conditions, Gérault had not done so once he became the sole owner of the factory. Although both the Strasbourg and the Sceaux factories, where Louis had worked previously, manufactured faïence on a considerable scale, it is certainly possible that he was taken on at Orléans to model porcelain forms.
4. Garsonnin, *op. cit.*, pp. 308–9. The raw materials were in use when the comte de Provence visited the factory in June 1777, as can be seen from the plan drawn up for his visit, and from the report presented to the *intendant* dated 8 June 1777, both quoted by Piot, *op. cit.*, pp. 134–5.
5. See J. d'Albis and C. Romanet, *La Porcelaine de Limoges*, Paris, 1980, where attempts to make hard-paste porcelain in the 1760s are described. Experimental work was being carried out by Hellot at this time, and Brancas-Lauraguais (see p. 290) had succeeded in making hard-paste by 1764.
6. Garsonnin, *op. cit.*, quotes the inventory dated 2 or 5 October 1782 in some detail, pp. 335–8. The porcelain, consisting of over 5,000 pieces, was inventoried by three workers (*ouvriers*) at the factory, Jean Pierre Louis Machereau, Pierre Delle and Léonard Desroches. The document was then in the Archives départementales du Loiret B 408.
7. Garsonnin, *op. cit.*, p. 310. Information taken from a report submitted to the *intendant* dated 7 October 1763, quoted *in extenso* by Piot, *op. cit.*, pp. 128–30.
8. Chavagnac and Grollier, 1906, p. 376.
9. *Ibid.*, pp. 384–5, and p. 116 for Bernard Huet, said to have been living in the faubourg Saint-Laurent between 1764 and 1767. Huet's not inconsiderable charges for modelling figures and groups are given in detail in the legal documents pertaining to his claim for 688 *livres* due to him, and Gérault's *mémoire*, together with the witnesses' reports, quoted in full by Piot, *op. cit.*, pp. 131–3.
10. Chavagnac and Grollier, 1906, pp. 384–5.
11. Quoted by Piot, *op. cit.*, p. 129.
12. *Ibid.*, p. 135.
13. Musée historique et archéologique de l'Orléanais, Orléans, inv. A 71667, A 6506, A 7296. I am grateful to Daniel Ojalvo and Françoise Demange of the Musée de l'Orléanais for giving me access to these pieces. The cream-pot is illus. in *La céramique dans la région centre de l'époque gallo-romaine au XXe siècle*, exh. Orléans, October 1980–December 1982, no. 57. Another cream-pot with similar decoration and mark is in the Victoria and Albert Museum, London, inv. C. 511–1909.
14. Dupont, 1987, p. 91.
15. Illus. C. Dauguet and D. Guillemé-Brulon, *La porcelaine française*, Paris, n.d. (*c.* 1988), p. 31.
16. Inv. 64.117; incised *V* with painter's mark *C* or *G*, J. Emerson, *Selections of French Porcelain from the Eighteenth Century European Porcelain Collection of the Seattle Art Museum*, The French Porcelain Society, London, 1990, Vol. VI, p. 5; a tureen with the label and *C* mark said to be soft-paste is illus. in F. Laure, 'La céramique orléanaise', *L'Estampille*, no. 109, May 1979, p. 24.
17. Exh. Orléans, 1980–2 (see n. 13), nos. 58, 59, 61, 62, 63.
18. A terracotta group of Belisarius signed *HAET* on the reverse is in the Musée historique et archéologique de l'Orléanais.
19. See Garsonnin, *op. cit.*, p. 336 for groups.
20. *Ibid.*, pp. 338–9.

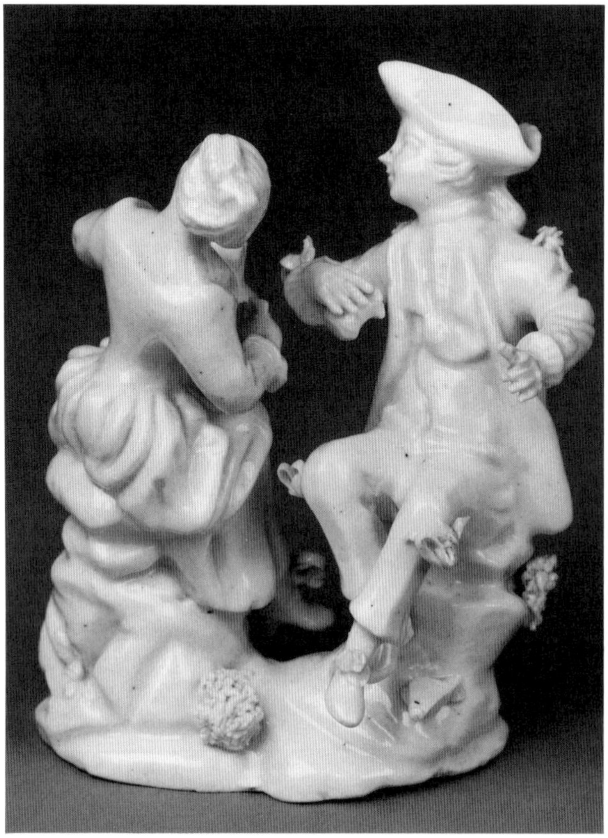

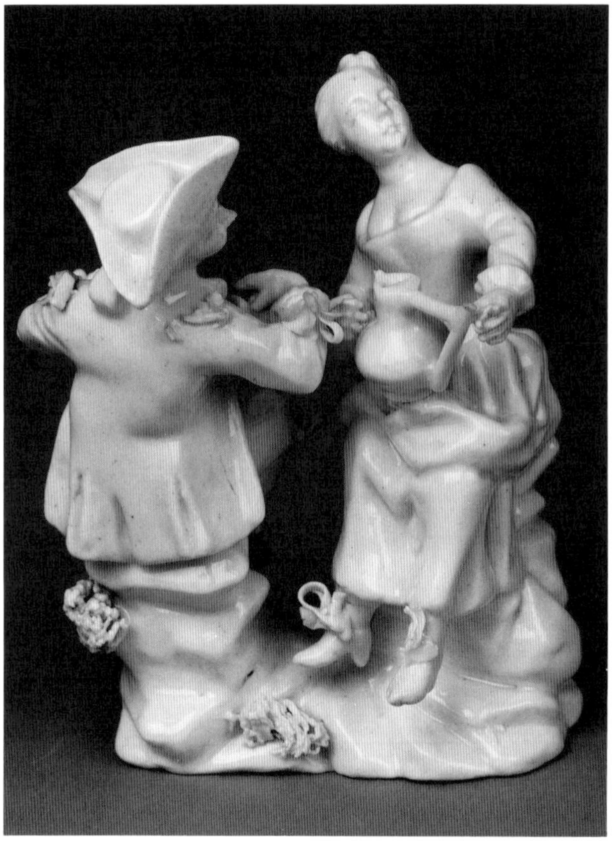

198

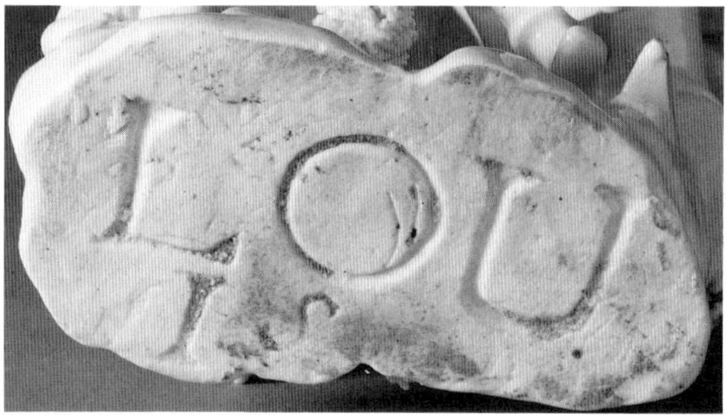

198 *mark*

198 **Group of Seated Toper and Companion,** *c.* 1756–8

H. 13.5 cm
Marks: *LOU* incised
IS
Reg. No. Franks 362

Soft-paste porcelain with a lead glaze, flat unglazed base (there are traces of glaze in the incised letters), perhaps hand modelled. The seated young man, his legs crossed at the ankle, wears a three-cornered hat over his drawn-back hair, a long jacket, the sleeves decorated with bows, a ruffled shirt, and knee-breeches with bows. His front shoe is similarly decorated. In his right hand he holds a small waisted [?] tankard. His left is outstretched and may well have once held something as the index finger is broken and a projecting triangular object near his feet has been damaged. Opposite him, her head with its upswept hair turned to the left away from him, is the figure of a woman in a low-cut dress holding a handled jug on her lap. Her feet, shod in high-heeled shoes with extravagant bows at the front, dangle in space.

Provenance: Bequeathed by Sir A.W. Franks, 1897

Literature: Franks, 1896, no. 362

Chavagnac and Grollier, 1906, p. 112

Comparable Examples: London, Victoria and Albert Museum, C.9–1920, incised *FS*, flat base, also inv. C.41–1920, girl with a jug, unmarked, flat base.

The paste, which is white and obviously lacks plasticity, the clear glaze, and the weight of the figures, which are heavy for their size, are all similar to the group signed by Renault (cat. 199). Both groups exhibit black specks, pin-holes and signs of firecracking.

Bacchic groups consisting of five figures from Orléans were sold by the Paris merchant Hennique in December 1768 for 60 *livres*.[1] Single figures (biscuit or glazed) were sold from the factory itself for as little as 50 *sols* or at most for 1 *écu* if perfect.[2]

A white glazed soft-paste porcelain figure of a seated boy wearing a hat with a broken doll on his lap is incised with a rather similar *L* to that found on the Museum group. It is perhaps also the work of Louis.[3]

Jean Louis, the factory's chief (and in its early days only) modeller, is recorded as living in the rue du Bourdon Blanc, parish of Saint-Euverte, on 7 April 1756 when his conditions of work were legally registered at the Châtelet, Orléans.[4] He was to work on models and 'autres ouvrages de son état qui luy seront demandés' at a salary of 1,248 *livres* a year from the month of May. His hours of work were from seven o'clock in the morning to seven o'clock in the evening, breaking between noon and two o'clock from 15 March to 30 September. During the winter he began work at daybreak. For every day's absence 4 *livres* 10 *sols* would be withheld. He was to train apprentices, and if he gave them drawing lessons outside working hours was to be paid either by the owners of the factory, or by the apprentices' parents. He was forbidden to go and work elsewhere without the express permission of the owners, and they could not dismiss him without granting him this permission. He was to be paid every fortnight (or *quinzaine*).

However, by the end of 1757 Gérault was finding Louis unsatisfactory and was harassing him by depriving him of his own room, docking his pay, and threatening to put him on piece-work. Louis lodged a complaint to this effect with the *intendant*, Barentin.[5] Louis stated[6] that the owner (*entrepreneur*) of the Sceaux factory had summoned him from the Strasbourg factory. The owners (*intéressés*) of the Sceaux concern, who established the factory at Orléans, touched by the ill-treatment of Louis at Strasbourg, rescued him and employed him under proper conditions. Louis complained that although Le Roy had treated him according to the agreement made, Gérault, once he became sole owner of Orléans, tried to economise on wages, and did not abide by the agreement.

In turn Gérault replied at length on 7 December 1757.[7] Louis, he said, was 'long en ses opérations, par des tremblements qui lui sont survenus aux mains, mais encore par sa mauvaise foi à tirer en longueur les ouvrages que Gérault lui commande et à les rendre imparfaits, ce qui oblige à les faire recommencer' ('slow, on account of trembling in his hands as well as through his ill will, drawing out work ordered by Gérault and spoiling it so that it had to be redone'). In addition he stayed away from his studio, working on his own account for certain clients. Some specific complaints about 'oilles simples ou chargées d'ornements', which were too large, 'terrines à godrons trop profondes de 2 ou de 3 doigts, des huilliers en forme de bâteau *vilains*, des écuelles, tant à ornements qu' à reliefs, dont les couvercles était beaucoup trop petits' show that he worked on broth bowls and covers, fluted tureens, boat-shaped oil-casters, covered bowls, sometimes with reliefs, all of which are criticised. His figures were said to be 'lourdes et sans distinction malgré les dessins bien faits et légers qu'on lui avait fournis'. Louis apparently left the factory in 1758.[8]

1. Chavagnac and Grollier, 1906, p. 377.
2. Dr Garsonnin, 'Manufactures de porcelaine,' *Mémoires de la société archéologique et historique de l'Orléanais*, Vol. 35 (1919), p. 316; it must be remembered that regional variations in currency existed in France at this period, and modern approximations are therefore difficult.
3. Musée national de Céramique, Sèvres, inv. 13359, H. 14 cm.
4. Chavagnac and Grollier, 1906, pp. 374–5.
5. Charles-Amable-Honoré Barentin, chevalier de Hardivilliers, les Bellesrueries et autres lieux, Conseiller du Roy en ses conseils (1703–62), *intendant* of Orléans from June/July 1747, named Conseiller d'Etat, 1760, m. 1724 Marie-Catherine Lefèvre d'Ormesson, niece of Chancellor d'Aguesseau. For further details see *Dictionnaire de Biographie Française*, Vol. v, Paris, 1951, p. 434.
6. The 'Supplique de Jean Louis' is quoted in full in E. Piot, 'Etudes Céramiques, la manufacture royale de faïence fine et de porcelaine établie à Orléans en 1753,' *Le Cabinet de l'Amateur*, no. 25, Paris, 1863, p. 127.
7. Piot, *op. cit.*, p. 128 and Chavagnac and Grollier, 1906, p. 375.
8. According to Dr Garsonnin, *op. cit.*, p. 312. No reference is given to substantiate this statement.

199 **Group of Seated Gardener and Companion,** *c.* 1767

H. 15 cm
Marks: *Pierrere/nau* incised
Reg. No. Franks 363

Soft-paste porcelain with a lead glaze, flat unglazed base, perhaps hand-modelled. The seated young man, his legs crossed at the ankle, wears a large hat, a wig *en queue* tied with a ribbon bow, a long jacket, the sleeves decorated with bows, and breeches similarly adorned. His shoes are also decorated with bows. In his left hand he holds a spade; his right is empty. Opposite him but turned in the other direction is the figure of a young woman in a low-cut dress with a jacket, also seated on a rocky mound with clumps of moss attached to it. Her feet, shod in high-heeled shoes with bows at the front, dangle in space. Her right arm is bent at the elbow and her hand empty (it once held something); over her left arm is a bucket of grapes and [?] squash. Minor chips to bows.

Provenance: Bequeathed by Sir A.W. Franks, 1897

Literature: A. Demmin, *Guide de l'Amateur de Faïences et Porcelaines*, Vol. II, Paris, 1873 (4th edn.), p. 685, note 1[1]

Franks, 1896, no. 363

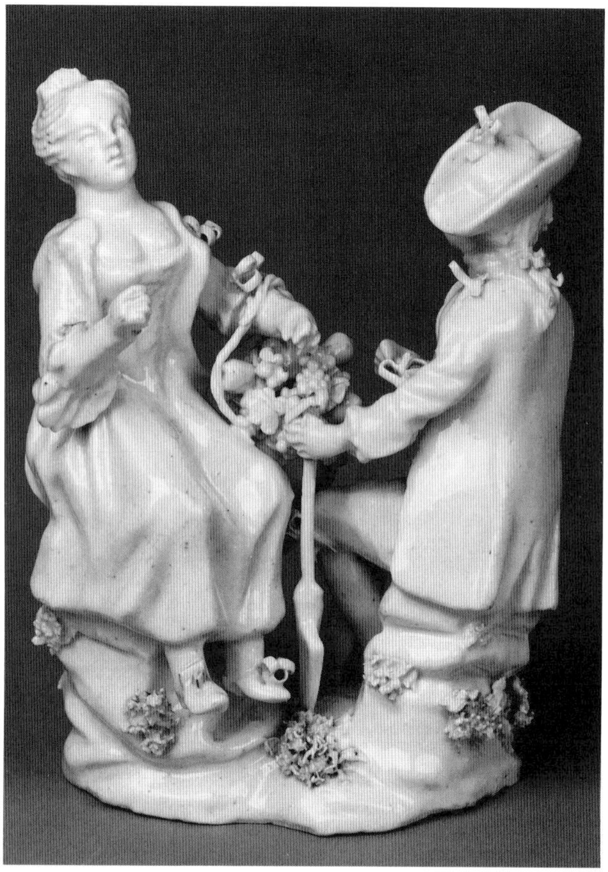

199

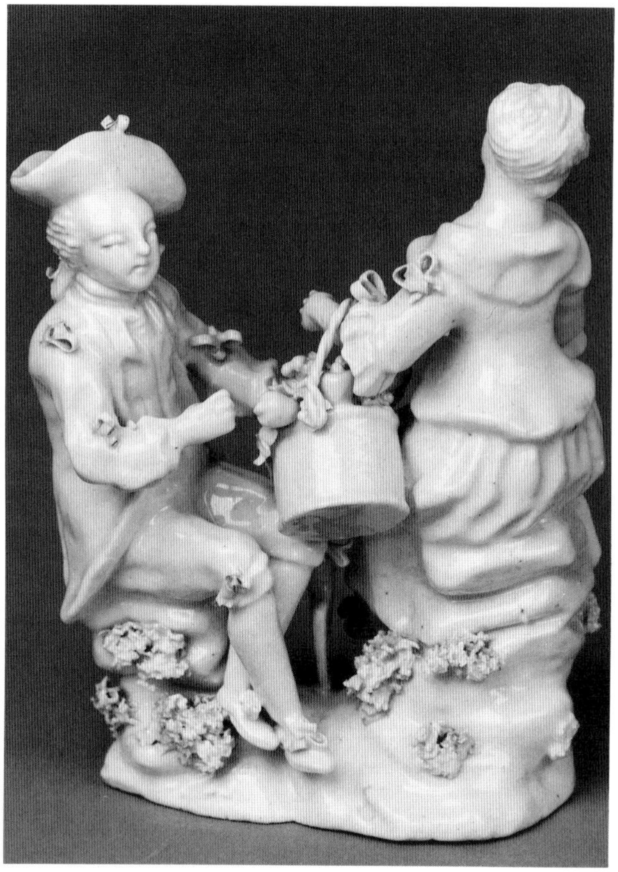

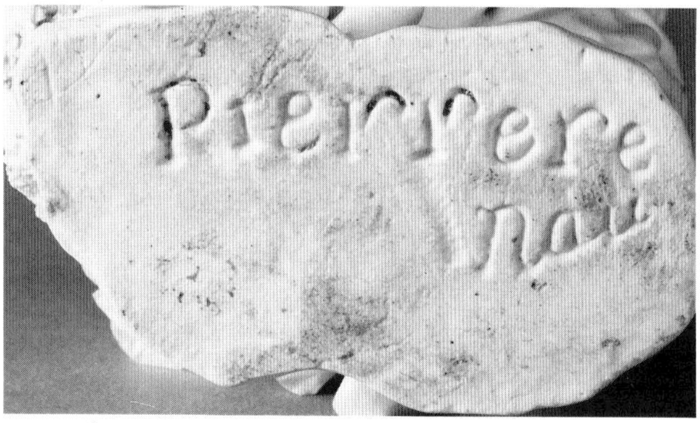

199 *mark*

Chavagnac and Grollier, 1906, p. 112, 385, 838

Comparable Examples: London, Victoria and Albert Museum, inv. C.42–1920, similar undecorated figure of seated female gardener, flat base, incised *RO* probably for Renault Orléans

Pierre Renault was a witness in a dispute between Bernard Huet, a sculptor at the Orléans porcelain factory, and its owner Gérault d'Areaubert in 1767.[2] He was called *sculpteur et répareur figuriste*. Nothing is known about either his earlier or his later career.

A merchant called Hennique is listed by Chavagnac[3] as selling 'Quatre grandes figures assises, de concert et de jardinage' at 28 *livres* on 26 November 1767. Ten years later in preparation for a visit of the King's brother, Monsieur (Louis-Stanislas-Xavier, comte de Provence), a description of Gérault's works was drawn up in which three repairers in the sculpture workshop are mentioned as working on 'figures de jardinages et de vendanges'.[4]

1. '*Pierre Renau* est la signature recueillie sur un groupe en porcelaine à pâte tendre.'
2. The documents relating to the dispute are quoted by E. Piot, 'Etudes Céramiques, la manufacture royale de faïence fine et de porcelaine établie à Orléans en 1753', *Le Cabinet de l'Amateur*, Paris, 1863, pp. 131–3.
3. Chavagnac and Grollier, 1906, p. 377, taken from Archives de la Seine, registres du commerce 1967.
4. *Ibid.*, Archives de la Seine, registres du commerce 1924.

200 **Group of Seated Gallant with a Basket of Flowers and Companion,** probably *c.* 1770

H. 24.3 cm
Marks: none
Reg. No. Franks 364

Soft-paste porcelain with a lead glaze, the female figure press-moulded, hollow base. The young man, his legs half-crossed, and

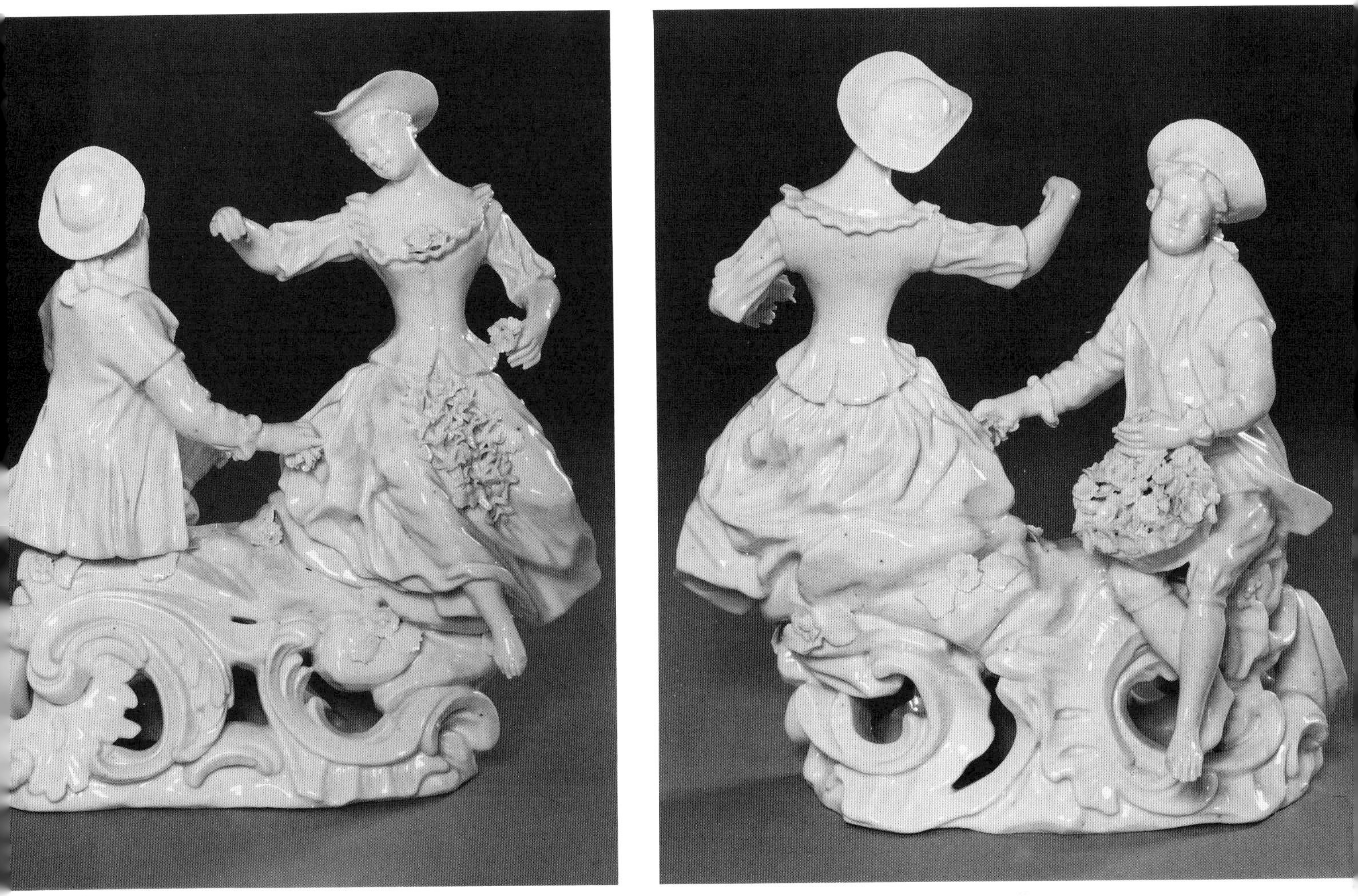

200

barefoot, sits on a scroll base, a basket of flowers held on his knees in his left hand. His right rests on the girl's skirt. He wears a hat, a long jacket with short sleeves over a long-sleeved shirt, and breeches. At his side, but looking the other way and her head held at an angle to her right, sits a young girl in a low-cut long dress with a tight bodice wearing a hat but no shoes. Her right arm is raised, in her left she holds a few flowers; there are more on her lap and some in her corsage. Girl's left leg missing, right foot chipped, right hand restored, chip on back of skirt. Finger of boy's left hand and his left foot chipped.

Provenance: Bequeathed by Sir A.W. Franks, 1897

Literature: Franks, 1896, no. 364

Comparable Examples: Sèvres, Musée national de Céramique, inv. 26234, group of a king carrying off a maiden hung with flower garlands (perhaps Pluto and Proserpine)

USA, New York, Metropolitan Museum of Art, inv. 59.208.10, H. 26.5 cm, group of two figures allegorical of the Four Continents: America and Europe

Christie's, 1 December 1969, Lot 38 (called Buen Retiro porcelain), a gallant couple with a basket of flowers

Phillips, 29 November 1989, Lot 167, group of a gardener with a rake and a pouch on his knee, and female companion holding a watering can (called Tournai)

Private Collection, with another of two figures allegorical of Asia and India

The modelling of this group, with its distinctive scroll base, shares the same characteristic as the seated figure groups signed *LOUIS* and *Pierrerenau* (cat. nos. 198 and 199): the two figures look in opposite directions rather than at each other as one might expect. However the porcelain is quite different; it is much creamier in tone, and is evidently far more plastic. In the absence of any clear evidence of the origin of this group, a tentative attribution to Orléans is suggested.

It is just possible that the watch stand cat. 82 may belong to this class of figures and groups.

Crépy

Little is known about this factory, which has not been studied since 1906.[1] The concern was apparently established at Crépy-en-Valois in October 1762 by Louis-François Gaignepain in association with a Paris *marchand-mercier*, Pierre Bourgeois. It was set up as a faïence factory, perhaps so as not to infringe the monopoly status of Sèvres, but within a short time was making porcelain, particularly snuff-boxes. Louis-François Gaignepain is recorded as a worker (*ouvrier*) at the Mennecy factory on 7 September 1761, when his daughter, Marie-Jeanne-Magdeleine-Félicité, who was born on 4 September, was baptised. His wife's name was given as Marie-Anne Desloges. The godfather of the child was another Mennecy worker, Mathieu Simon.[2] Bourgeois was the second husband of Marguerite Barbin, the daughter of François Barbin (qv) and the widow Evrard. He went bankrupt in January 1768.[3]

In 1767 the factory was experiencing financial difficulties, and additional capital was needed to pay the twenty-two workers and to buy wood for firing the kiln. Gaignepain died in 1770. As his wife became an inn servant, it seems likely that he was destitute. In 1795 she was described at the time of her death as 'veuve de L.F. Gaignepain, entrepreneur de la manufacture de porcelaines à Crépy'. The factory is thought to have shut down shortly after Gaignepain's death.

Preserved in the Archives de Paris is a daybook consisting of 70 folios (140 pages) kept by the dealer Bourgeois between 19 January 1764 and 14 March 1767 for the sale of Crépy porcelains.[4] Only one sale, on 30 October 1766, was made to anyone other than a dealer, or 'outside-decorator', and the document is a rich source for the study of Paris merchants handling porcelain during this decade.[5] In 1764 around 1,500 dozen porcelain flowers were sold, some undecorated, for painting by outworkers such as 'Madame Langlumet, maîtresse peintresse à Paris'. Snuffboxes (*tabatières*) are described in the following enormous variety of forms, not all familiar to connoisseurs of French porcelain: chamberpot, man and woman, wild cat, very small fish, sheep, tomb, suitcase, shuttle, duck, dog, cow, chicken, dog with puppies, hat, 'hunting' boxes, turned (*guillochées*) and undecorated, large or medium-sized. Other pieces sold in this year included small baskets, described as *guillochées*, or turned, small vases, both white and decorated, described as *à côtes*, gravy pots *à colonne torse* (these cost 30 sous, and when painted were 2 *livres*, 15 sous), face-cream pots, cups without handles and saucers, described as *à côtes*. Some pieces were painted in (underglaze-)blue (*unis bleu*, the adjective 'uni' denoting that they were plain rather than gadrooned pieces):[6] eyebaths, small goats, ducks and birds, pedestals (presumably imitating those made at Mennecy), and snuffboxes in the form of small drums, hearts, or women's shoes, suggesting that there was a considerable market for 'toys', such as the scent-bottles made at the Chelsea and 'Girl-in-a-Swing' factories in England,[7] which this factory wished to capture. White glazed groups consisting of two or three figures are described as made in three sizes: large, medium and small. Two flute-players, the Four Parts of the World, male and female dancers, 'trois petits chiens blancs sur leurs pattes' and putti are amongst the pieces sold to M. Randour on 15 January 1765. Teawares were sold to Mlle Legras on 10 July 1765, together with a covered broth-bowl with handles costing 12 *livres*. On 7 September 1765 Mme Bailly purchased, amongst other pieces, a 'sucrier unis [*sic*] blanc, forme de Sèvres', and the following biscuit groups: 'deux grands groupes de deux figures blanches

... sur terrasse', costing 45 *livres* and 'un moyen groupe de deux figures blanches ... de joueur de flute et de vielle, debout sur terrasse' for 21 *livres*. In December 1765 and during the following year coloured pieces begin to appear in much greater quantity. A M. de Lamotte, *écuyer du roi et porte manteau*, purchased a teapot, a sugar bowl, twelve cups and saucers, a milk jug, a mustard-pot with stand and spoon, all decorated with scenes painted *en camaïeu*. He also bought two salt-cellars 'a trois coquilles avec un petit singe pour bouton'.

Not many of the pieces described in the daybook have been identified. Several pieces incised *Crépy* have been noted, including white glazed figures of a gardener and female companion in the Metropolitan Museum, New York.[8] Bernard Dragesco has convincingly identified a pair of tobacco pots in the British Museum (cat. 201) with two entries in the daybook mentioned above, enabling us to ascribe to the Crépy factory pieces bearing the mark *DCO* or *DC,O*, the initials presumably standing for workmen at the factory, in the same way as seems to have been done at Mennecy, or possibly the *O* standing for Orléans. A number of examples marked *DCO* have been noted.[9]

No details of the workforce, nor of the administration of the factory, have yet been discovered.

1. Chavagnac and Grollier, 1906, pp. 391–5. This account is based on Chavagnac and Grollier's work. It is worth noting that the *baillage* (bailiwick) of Crépy, capital of the duchy of Valois, was in the apanage of the House of Orléans (A. Britsch, *La Jeunesse de Philippe-Egalité*, Paris, 1926, p. 61).
2. *Ibid.*, p. 392.
3. The marriage took place in 1755, see Archives nationales, Minutier central, Etude XI, dated 16 March 1755. The bankruptcy is recorded in Archives de la Seine D4 B6, *Carton* 32, *Dossier* 1696 under the date 18 January 1768. The author is grateful to Geneviève Le Duc for this information.
4. The author is indebted to Bernard Dragesco for bringing this inventory to her attention; it is in the Archives de Paris, D5 B6 no. 980.
5. Chavagnac and Grollier, 1906, pp. 393–4; a *maîtresse peintresse* of Paris called Madame Langlumet, a *peintre vernisseur* called M. Detanne and a *marchand ferblantier* called Pirotte, are amongst the merchants recorded.
6. Bernard Dragesco has kindly pointed out that Chavagnac and Grollier's reading *vernis bleu* should read *unis bleu*.
7. G.E. Bryant, *The Chelsea Porcelain Toys: Scent Bottles, Bonbonnieres, Etuis, Seals and Statuettes, made at the Chelsea Factory, 1745–1769, and Derby-Chelsea, 1770–1784*, London, 1925; K. Foster, 'Chelsea Scent-Bottles,: "Girl in a Swing" and another Group', *ECC Trans*, Vol. 6, part 3, 1967, pp. 284–91; E. Adams, *Chelsea Porcelain*, London, 1967, pp. 50–1, figs. 28, 29, 96, 97, 119, pl. III.
8. Inv. 52.70. 1 and 2.
9. Chavagnac and Grollier, 1906, p. 395, recorded a white glazed figure of a child seated on a camel, and another on a crocodile (*caïman*) in the Gérard sale; these figures were presumably symbolic of the Four Parts of the World, and see cat. 201, below.

201 Pair of Tobacco Pots and Covers in a Leather Case, 1762–70

H. 22.4 cm and 22.6 cm
Dimensions of case:
L. 25.5 cm
H. 23.9 cm
W. 17 cm
Marks: *DC, O* incised on both
Reg. No. Franks 359

Soft-paste porcelain, glazed. The pots are each moulded to represent a boar seated upright on its haunches, which are tucked beneath it with the forelegs and trotters held out in front touching the branches of a tree on which each is impaled. The covers form the heads and necks and the ridge of the spine extends from the cover to the cylindrical pots below, terminating in a short curled tail. The fur is realistically rendered, the ears laid back and the tongue protruding through the teeth. Two chips to rim of cover of one, boar's tongue on other broken and small chip to left ear; chip to rim of one pot, the other cracked.

Housed in a tooled morocco leather case simulating volumes whose title *BAIL DES FERMES* is stamped in gold above the volume number of each of nine spines arranged vertically for the base and three more arranged horizontally for the lid. The edges of the 'pages' have been decorated to simulate marbled paper.

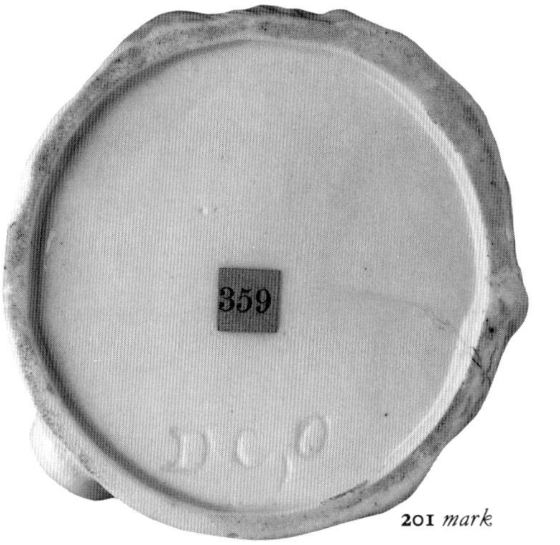

201 *mark*

The case is lined with pale blue silk edged with gold thread. At the front between the tobacco pots is an oval hole edged with gold thread, thought to be for a spoon or grater.

Provenance: Bequeathed by Sir A.W. Franks, 1897

Literature: Franks, 1896, no. 359

E. Hannover, *Pottery and Porcelain, A Handbook for Collectors III*

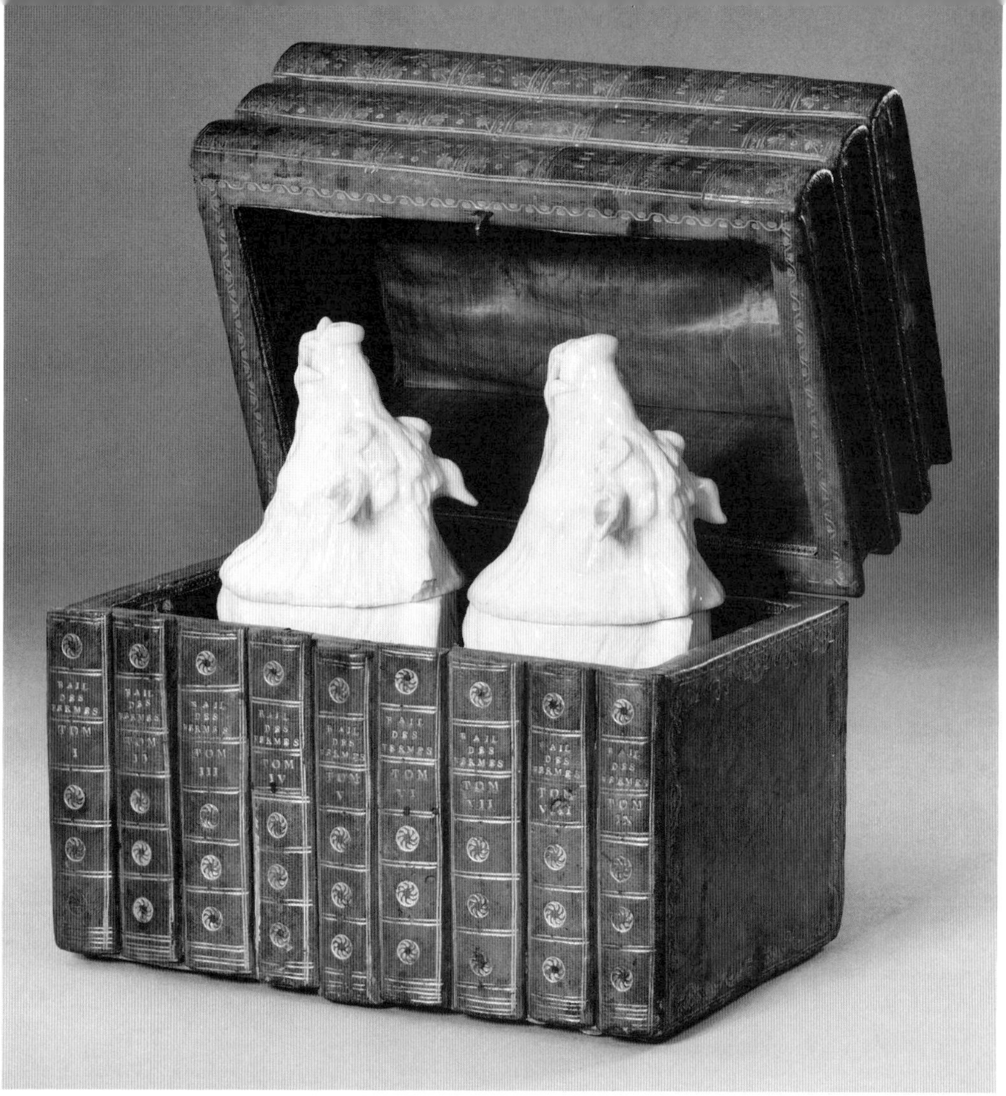

201

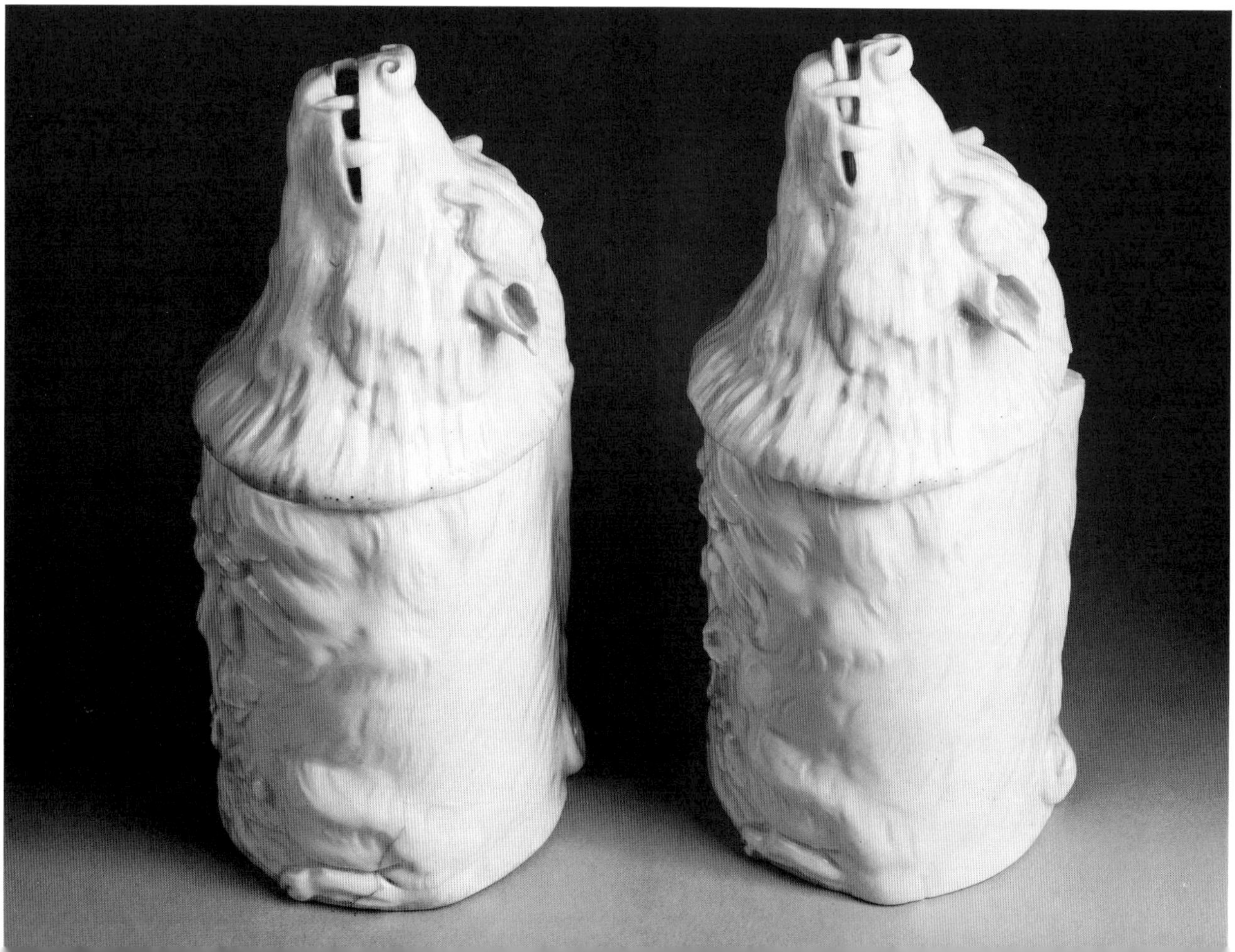

European Porcelain, London, 1925, p. 327

Savage, 1960, pl. 30a

Tait, 1962, pl. xx

D. Gage and M. Marsh, *Tobacco Containers & Accessories, London*, 1988, pp. 94–7

Exhibited: 1985, 'Documentary Continental Ceramics from the British Museum', International Ceramics Fair and Seminar, London Ltd., June 1985, no. 44, cat. compiled by A. Dawson

Comparable Examples: British-American Tobacco Collection, illus. Gage and Marsh, *op. cit.*, no. 13, formerly in the collection of Mr and Mrs William Brown Meloney, New York, illus. *Connoisseur*, Vol. CXLIII, no. 577, April 1959, p. 140, fig. 12

Similar, smaller box containing two Mennecy pots and covers with D. et P. Moufflet, Cannes, 1989[1]

The origin of these tobacco pots, classified by Franks as toilet pots, has long been a matter of debate. Erroneously dated to 1730 when exhibited in 1985 (see literature) they were then cautiously attributed to the Mennecy factory, as they had been by Franks in 1896. D. Gage and M. Marsh have drawn attention to the similarity of the jars to a white glazed Mennecy figure of a boar.[2] However, they are so unlike any other known products of this factory both in body, overall style and factory mark that an alternative origin has been considered. The recent discovery of a document describing tobacco pots of this form indicates that they were made in Crépy. In the *Livre Journal de Vente pur la manufacture de Crépy*[3] are three sales, one of which may relate to the Museum pots. On 23 October 1765 'Huit moyens pot a tabac blanc En hure de Sanglier et de Chien a 12#' were sold for a total of 96 *livres* to 'Madame Veuve Huquier, Négociante a Paris'. Two days later 'Monsieur Scavoy, Marchand-Mercier a Paris' purchased 'Trois moyens pot a tabac en hure de Sanglier Et chien' for 12 *livres*. The low price reflected their reject quality, but in fact the merchant seems to have returned them to the vendor, since the register entry is crossed out and marked 'rendu'. On 6 February 1766 'Monsieur Prévoteaux, Negociant a Paris' bought 'Quatre moyens pot a tabac blanc En hur de Sanglier Et Chien a 8# piece' for 32 *livres*. As they are extremely well made, it seems likely that the Museum pots were of the first quality and sold at 12 *livres* each. Madame Huquier may very well have supplied the luxurious case for the Museum boars, but regrettably the final selling price remains unknown. No similar tobacco pots in the form of dogs have been discovered. It is worth noting that Chavagnac and Grollier recorded a jug decorated with blue sprigs in the style of late Chantilly in the Grollier Collection bearing the underglaze-blue mark associated with Orléans, together with incised marks including *dc*.[4]

A number of other pieces have been noted incised *DCO*: cat. 202, a toilet pot and cover decorated in underglaze-blue in the Metropolitan Museum, New York;[5] a white glazed cylindrical tobacco pot with prunus in relief on the London market in 1985; a [?] sugar bowl, cover and stand, painted in colours with flowers, closely based on a Mennecy original;[6] a white glazed figure of a naked girl in the Museum für Kunst und Gewerbe, Hamburg;[7] a coloured group of two seated child musicians in the Wadsworth Atheneum, attributed to Crépy-en-Valois by Chavagnac;[8] a coloured group of two naked children with bunches of grapes in the Victoria and Albert Museum, London,[9] and a white glazed figure of a pedlar in the National Museums of Scotland, Edinburgh.[10]

On the basis of the tools used to stamp the gilt design on the leather box, it can be dated to between around 1740 and around 1760 and is likely to be of Paris workmanship.[11]

It has been suggested[12] that this case, which was obviously intended to hold these pots, was made for a *fermier-général*. The title stamped repeatedly on the book spines has a direct connection with the system of tax gathering in force before the Revolution, administered by the *fermiers* who obtained the privilege of gathering taxes on their own account within a designated area, or *ferme*, handing over to the King only a predetermined sum and keeping the remaining amount. The only similar volumes traced in a public library can be found in the National Union Catalogue. These are tax-farming leases issued to Maître Jacques in Forceville in September 1738 for six years and to Maître Pierre Carlier in August 1726 for six years. Such leases were issued separately but collections may have been made and bound privately.[13] The *fermiers-généraux* were a rich and powerful group within the *noblesse de robe*.[14] It is just possible that one of their number had a particularly close link with the Crépy porcelain factory.

1. The author is grateful to Bernard Dragesco for drawing this box to her attention. Monsieur Moufflet has kindly sent the dimensions of the box, which contains a pair of tobacco pots and covers painted with flowers and marked *DV*. Made up of two volumes of *BAIL DES FERMES* laid horizontally to form the lid and eleven examples of *LE FINANCIER*, both tooled differently from the Museum examples, it measures 20 cm in height, is 25.5 cm wide and 17 cm deep, and is lined in pale blue [?] silk, without *galons*.
2. Gage and Marsh, *op. cit.*, p. 95; the boars were in the possession of the Antique Porcelain Company, New York, in 1988.

3. Archives de Paris, D5 B6 no. 980. The author is greatly indebted to Bernard Dragesco for communicating this reference.
4. Chavagnac and Grollier, 1906, p. 386.
5. Inv. 55.216.6ab; the author is grateful to Mrs C. Le Corbeiller for providing information about this piece.
6. Sotheby Parke-Bernet, New York, 4 April 1972, The Harbeson Collection of Porcelain, Continental Porcelain – Part 3, Lot 170, length of stand 9½ in.
7. Inv. 1972.39; Dr H. Jedding kindly drew the author's attention to this piece.
8. X. de Chavagnac, *Catalogue de Porcelaines Françaises de M.J. Pierpont Morgan*, London, 1910, no. 35. Mrs Linda Roth kindly allowed the author to examine the group, inv. 17.932.
9. Inv. C.10–1915.
10. Inv. 1956.1208.
11. The author is grateful to Dr M. Foot of Rare Book Collections, British Library, for her assistance in dating this box. Identical tools were found by her on the binding of a copy of La Fontaine's *Fables* printed at Paris, 1755.
12. In conversation with the compiler by Régine de Guillebon, June 1988.
13. The author is deeply grateful to Sheila Rockett of the Humanities and Social Sciences Section of the British Library for this information. The *Bail des fermes* volumes are listed under 'France, Sovereigns, etc., 1715–1774 (Louis xv)', under the reference NF 0316008 and 0316010. No such documents survive in the British Library.
14. For a detailed study of these men see Y. Durand, *Les Fermiers Généraux au* XVIII*e* *Siècle*, Paris, 1971.

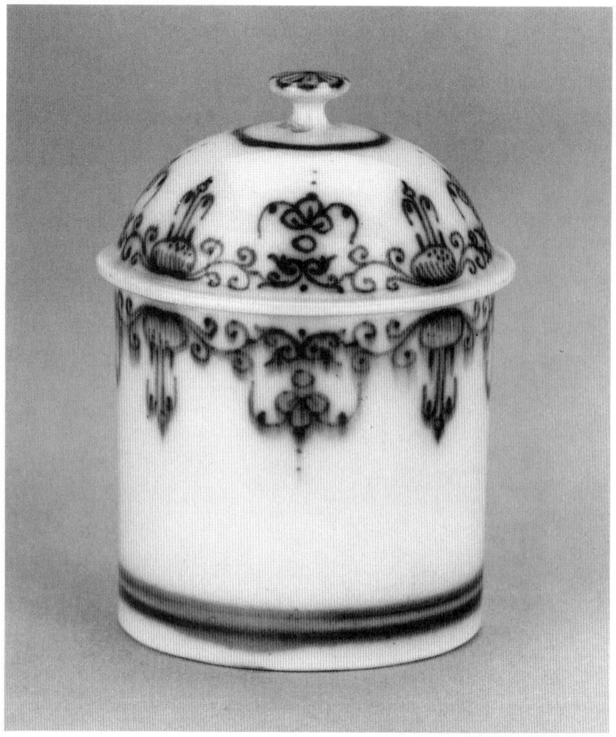

202

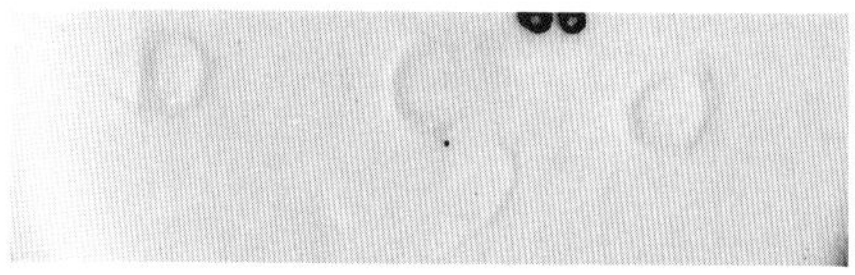

202 *mark*

202 **Toilet Pot and Cover**, 1762–70

H. *incl. cover:* 8.8 cm
Marks: *DC, O* incised across centre of base
Reg. No. 1899,10–6,42

Soft-paste porcelain with a lead glaze, cylindrical with domed cover and flat button knop on stem; decorated in underglaze-blue with scroll ornament near the rims, two blue lines near the foot of the pot and one around the knop, which is painted with a stylised flower. Cover cracked.

Provenance: Bequeathed by C.D.E. Fortnum, FSA, DCL, 1899[1]

Literature: Unpublished

Comparable Examples: New York, Metropolitan Museum of Art, inv. 55.216. 6ab, incised *D*, H. 3⅝ in

France, Paris, Dragesco et Cramoisan, 1986, incised *DCO*

The glaze has a rather 'glittery' appearance and the blue has 'flowed', to produce a rather blurred effect.

There was an enormous demand for pots to hold face cream, which were made by many if not all of the French porcelain factories. They were mostly cylindrical with a domed cover, but did vary in dimensions,[2] and at Bourg-la-Reine were distinctively mould-formed in six panels.[3]

No less than 862 *pots à pommade* of different sizes, undecorated, with relief decoration, or painted in blue or in colours are recorded in an inventory taken of stock at the Mennecy outlet in the rue St Honoré on 26–9 July 1754.[4] They were valued at between 12 *sols* and 1 *livre* each. Three different models of *pot à pommade* (*en bottes de ble*; *en bottes de rave*; *en pelote de neige*) were evidently in production in August 1762 when another inventory was taken.[5] Two sizes were made at Vincennes from 1752. At 96 *livres* when decorated with painted children and flowers and with a turquoise ground,[6] the expensive Vincennes examples represent the other end of the production scale from this rather run-of-the-mill example. As late as February 1792 nine *pots à pommade* were among the porcelain ceded by 'sieur et dame Antheaume' to Potter on his purchase of the Chantilly factory.[7]

No information is available at present about the selling price of pots like these.

1. For a biographical note on C.D.E. Fortnum, see cat. 93.
2. Dallot-Naudin and Jacob, 'Mennecy', 1983, p. 146.
3. *Ibid.*, pp. 156–7, 160.
4. Duchon, 1988, p. 140.
5. *Ibid.*, p. 144.
6. Exh. *Vincennes*, 1977–8, p. 81.
7. Chavagnac and Grollier, 1906, p. 80.

Lunéville[1]

Best-known for its figure production, this factory was established by Paul-Louis Cyfflé (1704–1806) early in 1765, on the evidence of contemporary writers.[2] Letters patent were granted in June 1768.[3] Cyfflé was born in Bruges and had been apprenticed between about 1741–6 to an uncle in Paris who was a goldsmith, before going in about 1746 to Nancy where he worked in the *atelier* of Barthélémy Guibal (1699–1757), sculptor to the Dukes of Lorraine. Early in 1763 Cyfflé became part-owner of the faïence factory of Saint-Clément, 12 km from Lunéville and former sister-factory of Jacques Chambrette's Lunéville faïence factory. Although Cyfflé sold his share within nine months, he seems to have modelled figures there between 1763 and 1765. A letter dated 3 October 1765 to Prince William Henry of Nassau-Saarbrücken from Cyfflé[4] shows that he played a role in the establishment of the Ottweiler porcelain factory, and may have modelled figures there.

In 1768 Cyfflé was authorised to 'faire cuire pendant 15 ans la vaisselle, qui sera supérieure à celle de terre de pipe sans être porcelaine, et qui sera nommé "Terre de Lorraine" comme aussi de la faience commune et ordinaire en employant de la terre de pipe'. Pipe clay was used to make tin-glazed wares at the Lunéville pottery. Few tablewares made by Cyfflé are known, and after continuing experimental work on his (soft-paste) porcelain composition, which he called *pâte de marbre*, he applied for permission to make 'toutes sortes de figures tant pour les desserts que pour la décoration des jardins'. After due consideration and consultation with the Academy of Sculpture and the royal porcelain factory, Bertin gave permission for Cyfflé to go on making figures so long as they still bore the name 'terre cuite', or as Cyfflé called it 'Terre de Lorraine'. The letter of the law of 15 January 1766 preserving the monopoly of Sèvres was observed, and no painted or gilded pieces were sold.

The factory was situated near the rue de Villers, contiguous to the ducal menagerie, in a building on the present-day ruelle de Sainte Anne which still stands.[5] By 1775 there were two rooms for repairers, and probably more than one kiln, doubtless situated in the garden. It is likely that Cyfflé used local clays, since some specimens said to be of the type used by Cyfflé survived into the nineteenth century in the collection of a local amateur geologist.[6]

Three lists of workers at the factory drawn up in 1775, 1778 and 1779 for the lottery for military service show that there were never more than twenty fully trained people employed. In 1775 twenty-seven were listed, but nine of these were pupils. By 1778 the numbers had declined to eleven and in the following year there were only eight. The exact date of the closure of the factory remains unknown, but it was probably barely in production in 1779 and in 1780 was in the process of being shut down. In April 1780 Cyfflé wrote to Lanfrey at Niderviller that he had moulds for sale. Further moulds for figures, groups and vases were offered for sale in the local newspaper in November 1783, together with the horse-drawn mill 'de 6 lanternes' (with six sails), described as nearly new and in good working order ('tout prête à remonter').[7] The buildings were sold in August 1784 for 10,000 *livres*.[8]

The personnel, all male, were described as *répareurs*, *garnisseurs*, and *modeleurs* and were all concerned with figure-making (there were no painters). Several, such as the *premier répareur* Nicolas Remy (1756- ?, at the factory in 1773, gone by 1778), Jean-Nicolas Guillaume (1761– ?), a repairer employed in 1775 but no longer there in 1778, and another, Georges Fayen or Layen (b. 1756), who was at the factory in 1775 and had gone by 1778, were natives of Lunéville. The most important of these was Charles Gabriel Sauvage, called Lemire (1741–1827), the factory's chief modeller. He was from an old Lunéville family, and joined the porcelain factory in 1767, having trained at Niderviller and Saint-Clément. He left Lunéville some time before February 1779, subsequently worked at Niderviller and from 1806 is recorded as a sculptor in Paris.[9]

Other workers came from further afield and most were highly mobile. Jean Bernard Würtzbacker (*c.* 1752–82, found drowned in the mill pond at Niderviller) was born in Würtemberg, Germany, was at Lunéville as a repairer in 1774, is recorded at the Bellevue factory, Toul, in 1778 where he married in the same year and by 1781 had moved to Niderviller.[10] A man named François is reputed to have left to work in one of the Paris factories.

Like the majority of porcelain factories this was a family concern. The second son of P.-L. Cyfflé, Joseph Cyfflé (b. 1752), entered the factory at the age of fourteen and was described as director in 1775. After the closure of the factory he went to Belgium where he worked as a modeller.[11] Cyfflé's fifth child, François (b. 1756), worked for three years as the factory's *commis*, being listed there in 1778, but not in the following year.

The range of figures made was wide and reflects the cultural milieu of aristocratic Lunéville during the Enlightenment in the years following the death of Stanislas Leszczinski who held court there between 1737 and 1766.[12] The *Flute Lesson*, the *Grape Eaters*, the *Broken Eggs* and other subjects are typical of the semi-erotic themes which were treated both here and elsewhere. A bust of Voltaire in a long wig and jacket,[13] various 'Cries of Paris',[14] and classically-inspired groups such as *Venus and Adonis*, *Belisarius*, *Hercules and Omphale* and *Pyramus and Thisbe* (all except the first also had theatrical links) typify the productions of Lunéville. An allegorical group commemorates the marriage of Marie-Antoinette to the Dauphin[15] in 1770, and another shows Louis XVI and Henri IV.[16]

Although little has been discovered about the wages paid, the prices charged for the products and the running of the factory, it is known that there was a wide diffusion of Lunéville figures. The lieutenant of police Nicolas Durival noted 'C'est de là, que sont sortis de très beaux morceaux, entre autres le groupe de Henri IV et Sully, présenté au roi de Danemark à son passage à Lunéville . . .'[17] From the outset Cyfflé advertised in Paris newspapers his 'manufacture de terre de Lorraine d'une blancheur éblouissante avec laquelle il fait . . . des figures historiques et caractérisées ou modelées d'après nature'.[18] An advertisement dated 6 July 1774 by 'Mulnier, Orphèvre-Bijoutier' of the 'Soleil d'Or, sur les Trotoirs [*sic*] à Nancy' states that he 'tient Magasin des Ouvrages de la Manufacture Royale du Sr. Cyfflé, a Lunéville'. A postscript adds 'Les Curieux sont prévenus que ces Figures sont composées d'une pâte nouvelle, d'un plus beau blanc, & qui se lave.[19] This may explain the wide difference in appearance between figures from this factory.

1. This account is based on Noël, 1961. An overview, illustrating some examples of Lunéville figures and groups is given in exh. Nancy and Atlanta, 1990.
2. Noël, 1961, p. 92, quotes N. Durival, *Journal*, Vol. VI, f. 76 *et seq.*, kept at the Bibliothèque municipale de Nancy as evidence for this. Monsieur Noël does not consider the date 1766 given for the establishment of Cyfflé's Luneville factory by E.J. Dardenne in *Essai sur Paul-Louis Cyfflé*, Brussels, 1912, to be correct.
3. Noël, 1961, p. 88, quotes *Registres des insinuations 1764–1772*, Arch. Lunéville, F.F, 21, f. 58 *et seq.*, reprod. E. Gerspach, *Documents sur les anciennes faïenceries françaises et la manufacture de Sèvres*, Paris, 1891, pp. 95–7.
4. Noël, 1961, p. 52, n. 1; Archives d'Etat de Coblenz 22/2804, f. 7, 8, partly produced by K. Lohmeyer, *Die Fürstliche Nassau-Saarbrückische Porzellanmanufaktur Ottweiler*, Leipzig, 1934, p. 7.
5. Noël, 1961, p. 94.
6. Noël, 1961, p. 95, see n. 8 to cat. 203.
7. Noël, 1961, p. 96 quotes *Affiches des Evêchés*, 13 November 1783 announcements, no. 46, p. 361.
8. Noël, 1961, p. 125.
9. Noël, 1961, pp. 111–12.
10. Soudée-Lacombe, 1984, p. 76.
11. A medallion with a bust in relief of a young man signed *J. Cyfflé* illus. E. J. Dardenne, *Essai sur Paul-Louis Cyfflé*, Brussels, 1912, p. 25, fig. 2, said to be dated 1778.
12. See M. Noël, 'Les biscuits de Cyfflé, étude des thèmes', *Annales de l'Est, Mémoire 34 La Lorraine dans l'Europe des Lumières*, Nancy, 1968, pp. 237–52.
13. Victoria and Albert Museum, inv. C.685–1909, illus. S.G. Davis, 'Some English pottery and porcelain figures connected with Alsace and Lorraine', *Burlington Magazine*, Vol. LI, no. CCVI, November 1927, pl. I, fig. C.
14. (Anon) 'Les Terres de Lorraine', *Connaissance des Arts*, no. 20, 15 October 1953, pp. 48–53.
15. This group is discussed by Noël, 1968, pp. 247–8: examples exist in the Louvre Museum, Paris, inv. RF 1618,sc.879 and in the Musée d'Unterlinden, Colmar, signed by Lemire. A bronze of the same subject was sold at Christie's, 8 December 1987, Lot 170, and another, presumably not the same one, exh. *Marie-Antoinette*, 1955, no. 538.
16. Victoria and Albert Museum, inv. C.294–1951.
17. N. Durival, *Description de la Lorraine et du Barrois*, Nancy, 4 vols., 1779–83, Vol. II, p. 78, quoted Noël, 1961, p. 208.
18. *Affiches de Paris*, 1769, p. 6, quoted Noël, 1961, p. 209.
19. An example of this advertisement is exhibited in the Musée historique lorrain, Nancy.

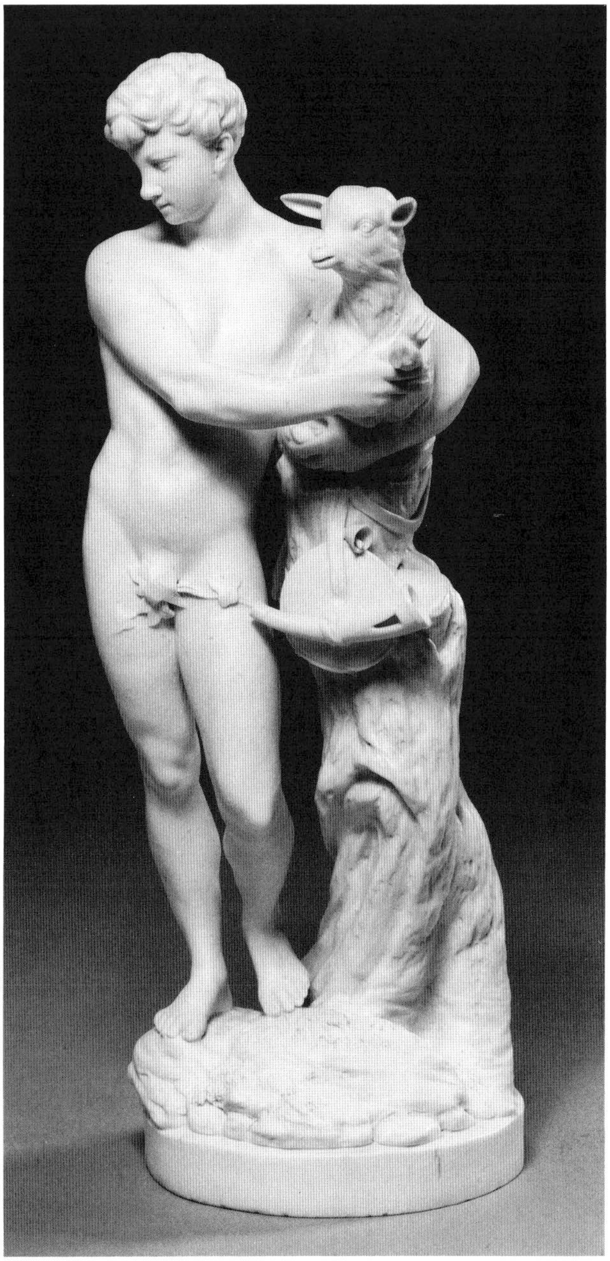

203

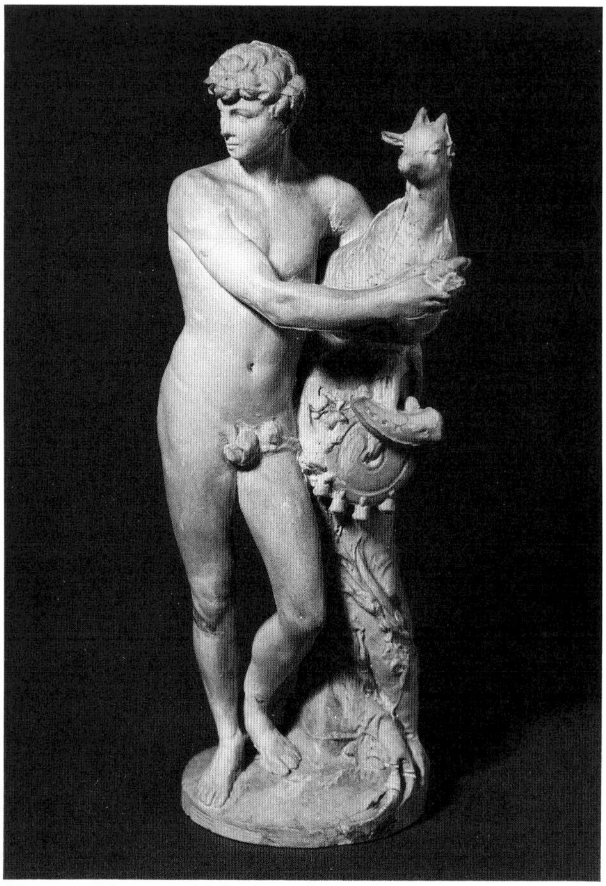

Fig 203a Plaster model for Sèvres biscuit figure of Saly's Faun. H. 22 cm

203 **Figure of a Faun Holding a Kid,** 1765–*c.*1789

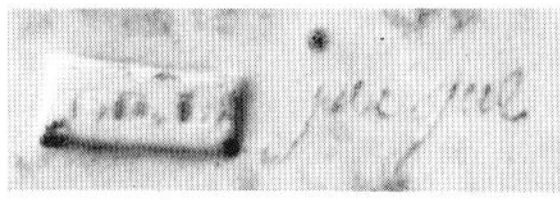

203 *mark*

H. 22.4 cm
Marks: *TDL* impressed within a label on base; *jacque* incised
Reg. No. 1928,7–18,9

Biscuit soft-paste porcelain with slight smear glaze, flat base. The figure is apparently hollow and was possibly slipcast. The young man, naked except for a fig leaf, holds a kid in the crook of his left arm, its crossed forefeet in his right hand. Depending from a thong attached to the tree trunk on which its body is supported, are a bell, a cymbal and a horn. Chip to animal's left ear.

Provenance: Presented by the Misses M.S. and A. Bloxam, and W.R. Bloxam, Esq., from the collection of the late Rev. J.F. Bloxam, M.C., 1928

Literature: RLH (R.L. Hobson): 'Gifts from the Bloxam Collection', *British Museum Quarterly*, Vol. III, no. 2 (1928), pp. 35–8, pl. XX

Honey, 1949, pl. 139B

Honey, 1950, p. 47

M. Olivar Daydi, *La Porcelana en Europa*, Barcelona, 1953, Vol. II, p. 191, fig. 76

Savage, 1960, pl. 84B

Charles, 1964, fig. 56A

Comparable Examples: Paris, Musée des arts décoratifs, inv. 27373 former Dr Chompret Collection, exh. *La porcelaine française*, 1929, no. 1003, illus. P. Dupont, 1987, p. 93, fig. 6

Co. Durham, Barnard Castle, Bowes Museum, inv. no. X1300

The group is closely based on a plaster by Jacques-François-Joseph Saly (1717–76) for whom the incised mark stands. Saly exhibited the plaster at the *Salon du Louvre* of 1750 in Paris. The plaster model was approved by the Académie de France and Saly was requested to execute a marble, on the basis of which he was unanimously received as an Academician on

29 May 1751. The marble was shown at the *Salon du Louvre* in the same year, where it enjoyed great success. It was admired by Count Caylus and Baron Grimm, and La Live de Jully was one of the many collectors who owned an example of the group.[1] The original terracotta was in his sale in May 1770.[2] The marble is now in the Musée Cognacq-Jay, Paris; it was disposed of by the Louvre Museum in 1821.[3] A plaster, presented by Saly himself in 1769 in recognition of his election as an honorary member of the St Petersburg Academy in the previous year, was in the Academy of St Petersburg in 1924.[4]

The initials *TDL* stand for Terre de Lorraine. Paul Louis Cyfflé (1721–1806), who founded the Lunéville factory in 1765,[5] was authorised by Bertin, Minister of the King's household, in 1769 to continue making his composition on the condition that pieces were sold under that name. Cyfflé himself called his porcelain composition *pâte de marbre*, thus anticipating names such as 'statuary porcelain' (Copeland) and 'Carrara' (Wedgwood), given in the mid-nineteenth century by English makers to their soft-paste porcelain most commonly known as Parian, also used to reproduce works of sculpture. Cyffle's composition has been characterised as a pipe clay (*terre de pipe*) to which a considerable amount of 'phosphate de chaux produit par la calcination des os de moutons' was added,[6] but at least one example of *TDL* apparently of hard-paste porcelain (see cat. 213, n. 3) has been discovered. W.B. Honey drew attention to the fine workmanship of this figure of a faun.[7] The clay used probably came from the Lunéville region on the evidence of two rows of samples kept in a drawer by a local man, Dr Gaillardot, documented in his manuscript catalogue.[8]

Biscuit and painted versions of this figure were manufactured at Copenhagen, apparently around 1781.[9]

Nina Birioukova stated that a hard-paste porcelain figure modelled at the Sèvres factory in 1769 was based on the same source, but there are some significant differences. A plaster (see fig. 203a) measuring about 22 cm preserved at the Sèvres factory was illustrated by Pierre Ennès in his discussion of the porcelain table-centre made at the royal factory for the dinner[11] given for the marriage of the Dauphin and Marie-Antoinette in May 1770.

The model in which the faun holds the goat under his arm was also made in earthenware at Toul.[12]

1. Louis Réau in 'Le Faune au Chevreau de Saly', *Bulletin de la société de l'histoire de l'art français*, 1924, pp. 7–8, quotes Caylus' unaccustomed praise in the *Mercure de France*: 'M. Sally [*sic*] a exposé en marbre le petit *Faune*, qu'il a donné à l'Académie pour son morceau de réception. Ce jeune et brillant artiste a été loué avec raison sur le choix de la nature qu'il a saisie et rendue convenable à son sujet: c'est en effet un faune, un pâtre, un homme de la campagne, mais c'est un jeune homme que tous les rapports rendent noble et agréable. Les accompagnements de cette figure ont prouvé que, si l'auteur savait rendre la chair, il savait aussi couper le marbre avec une délicatesse singulière'.
2. La Live de Jully sale, Paris, 5 March 1770, postponed until May 1770 Lot 193, 'Un Faune qui tient un chèvre: c'est le modèle fait à Rome pour le marbre que l'Auteur a executé à l'Académie de France pour son Morceau de réception'. It fetched 37 *livres*. As Réau pointed out (see n. 4), it is not in fact based on the *Faun with Kid*, also known as the *Queen of Sweden's Faun* now in the Prado, Madrid, illus. F. Haskell and N. Penny, *Taste and the Antique, the lure of classical sculpture 1500–1900*, New Haven and London, 1981, pp. 211–12.
3. *Collections Léguées à la Ville de Paris par Ernest Cognacq*, catalogue compiled by E. Jonas, Paris, 1930, no. 249, illus. The marble once belonged to Count Potocki.
4. L. Reau, *op. cit.*, pp. 6–15 and L. Reau, 'L'Hébé de Saly', *ibid.*, 1927, pp. 8–11 where the author claims that the group was 'finalement recueilli dans la collection Cognacq'. Ernest Cognacq died in February 1928.
5. The fullest treatment of Cyffle's career can be found in an unpublished thesis by Noël, 1961, *passim*. A complete bibliography of Cyfflé is included in this work. A brief biography by Nöel can be found in *Dictionnaire de Biographie Française*, Paris, 1961, Vol. IX, fasc. 54, col. 1448s.
6. P. Marot, *Le musée historique lorrain, guide du visiteur*, Nancy, 1948, p. 61. The author is grateful to Claire Aptel for this reference.
7. Honey, 1950, p. 47.
8. Charles Antoine Gaillardot (1774–1833) was a military surgeon. The catalogue, dated 23 August 1878, is preserved in the Bibliothèque de Lunéville, and lists the contents of the two rows on f. 10, no. 10, '16 échantillons de diverses argiles du pays recherches que fit M. Gaillardot sur les terres dont se servit le statuaire Cyfflé, qu'il dénommait: *terre de Lorraine*'. Information from Noël, 1961, p. 95.
9. See S.B. Fredstrup, *Figurer og andre plastike arbejder fra den Konegelige Porcelainsfabrik I perioden 1780–1820*, Copenhagen, 1939, F 13, 14 and G.A. Rust, *Collectors' Guide to Antique Porcelain*, London, 1973, p. 75, Washington D.C., Smithsonian Institution, Museum of American History, inv. 1476.
10. See Birioukova, 1962, pl. 51.
11. P. Ennès, 'Le surtout de mariage en porcelaine de Sèvres, du Dauphin, 1769–1770', *Revue de l'Art*, June 1987, no. 76, pp. 63–73, fig. 22.
12. This model is shown on one of a series of postcards used in the early years of the twentieth century as a factory 'pattern book'. It was called *Le Berger Salise*, measured 22 cm and cost 10 francs. For further details and a price list issued slightly earlier by J. Aubry, director at Toul, in which a 'faune' 25 cm high cost 9 francs, see M. Noël, 'La faïencerie de Toul et les Terres de Lorraine', *Etudes Touloises*, no. 11, 1978, fasc. 1, pp. 13–27.

Sceaux[1]

Louis-François de Bey, architect and *entrepreneur des bâtiments*, owned a faïence factory in the rue des Imbergères, near the château of the duc du Maine, Sceaux, from 1739.[2] On 9 August 1748 he established a concern to manufacture porcelain, of which Jacques Chapelle (1721–73) was co-owner and director.[3] Three other shareholders, Gabriel Bragouze, seigneur d'Alancé, Joseph Mignard and Louis Bellot, seigneur de Châteauneuf, also contributed to the total capital of 30,000 *livres*. Chapelle brought no capital to the enterprise but was to receive a salary of 1,500 *livres*. The factory was originally under the patronage of Louise-Bénédicte de Bourbon-Condé, duchesse du Maine (1676–1753) and then of her son Louis-Charles de Bourbon, comte d'Eu (1712–75), and latterly of Louis Jean-Marie de Bourbon, duc de Penthièvre (1725–93). Nevertheless, Charles Adam soon complained that its products were being sold 'Comme provenent de la Manufacture de Vincennes à ceux qui n'ont pas assez de connaissance pour les distinguer quoy qu'ils soyent d'une qualité bien inférieure'.[4] Louis xv suspended porcelain manufacture at Sceaux as an infringement of the monopoly granted to Vincennes in 1745. However, in 1751 Chapelle was calling himself 'Marchand fayencier à Paris et démonstrateur en chemie de l'Académie royale de Porcelaines et Fayance japonée de Sceaux du Mayne'. In 1751 Charles-François Becquet, a painter who was working at Vincennes in 1749 (and returned to Sèvres in 1765), is recorded at Sceaux.[5] In the next year Taillandier and Vavasseur were amongst the painters employed:[6] both went to Vincennes in 1753. Gilles Dubois and the sculptor Chanou (who also worked at Vincennes) were arrested in 1752 for making porcelain at Sceaux, although they denied the charge.

In 1759 Chapelle became sole owner of the factory on the death of de Bey. Two years later he bought buildings and gardens adjoining the factory. On 12 June 1763 Chapelle returned to Paris, letting the faïence factory for nine years to Joseph Jullien (m.1757–74), a painter, and Charles Symphorien Jacques (*c.*1724–99). Jacques was a sculptor and member of the Académie de Saint-Luc. These two agreed to 'former entr'eux une Société pour la fabrique et le commerce de porcelaines et fayances . . .'. In 1772 Chapelle sold out to Richard Glot (m.1764), *écuyer, fourrier du Logis du Roy*, and related through his wife to the Capitaine Concierge of the château at Sceaux. No marks were apparently used on Sceaux porcelain until Glot registered the mark *S.X.* with the Paris police on 12 July 1773.[7] An anchor, sometimes with the letters *SP*, was used during the period when the factory enjoyed the protection of the Grand Admiral, the duc de Penthièvre (between 1775–93). During the Revolution Glot became mayor and commander of the Garde Nationale, neglecting his business. In 1794 he sold out to Pierre Antoine Cabaret, and retired to Versailles where he died in 1820. It is likely that porcelain manufacture ceased with the Revolution.

The early products of the factory have not been identified. During the Jacques and Jullien period, tablewares painted with putti *en camaïeu rose*, [8] or with birds or landscape scenes,[9] toilet pots painted with flowers in colours,[10] including a characteristic pink, and biscuit porcelain figures[11] were made. The forms were often copied from other factories, including Sèvres, and few large pieces seem to have been made, despite the originality of the faïence being produced at the same factory.[12] Dating remains difficult; marked pieces were probably made only between 1773 and 1793–4 and few if any can be attributed to the factory in its early phase of production purely on the basis of comparison with Sceaux tin-glazed earthenwares.

A considerable number of names of workers at the Sceaux factory have been extracted from parish and *taille* records.[13] More than 100 people were employed during the course of the eighteenth century, but it is not always possible to distinguish those involved in the faïence operation from those making porcelain. Fidelle Duvivier, also known at Tournay and Chelsea, is recorded as a painter at Sceaux in 1775 when he married Elisabeth Thomas. Christophe Mô, a modeller and sculptor, had worked at Chantilly, married Hélène-Françoise Charton in Mennecy in 1768 and is recorded at Sceaux in 1776. His brother, Jean-Baptiste, a workman (*ouvrier*), was at Mennecy in 1768, 1769 and 1771, and at Bourg-la-Reine in 1772. In the following year the death of his wife is recorded at Sceaux. A thrower named Léonard Dumas was at Mennecy in 1764 and 1771 and at Lille in 1772, but is recorded at Sceaux in 1774, 1776, 1779, 1781–3 and 1785.

A record of the seizure of goods made on 20 March 1780[14] gives some idea of the range of wares made by Glot, and of their prices, although the valuations made were probably cost rather than selling prices. The *Magasin au rez de chaussée* contained all sorts of tablewares, including plates at 120 *livres* the dozen, others at 60 *livres* the dozen, but no description of these is given. A considerable number of painted and gilded pieces are listed, such as cups, teapots, sugar bowls and 'quatre petittes Ecuelles à dejeuner à douze Livres'. Vases of various kinds at 3 *livres* and ten groups at 15 *livres* each are also amongst the seized items.

1. This account is based on Dr Thore, *Les anciennes fabriques de faïence et de porcelaine de l'arrondissement de Sceaux*, Paris, 1868, Chavagnac and Grollier, 1906, pp. 365–71, G. Le Duc, 'La manufacture de Bourg-la-Reine, Faïences et Porcelaines Tendres (1772–1804)', *Cahiers*, no. 39, 1967, pp. 162–76 and, exh. Sceaux, 1986.
2. A detail from a map of 1782 made for the duc de Penthièvre shows the position of the factory, see exh. Sceaux, 1986, p. 31.
3. Chapelle was the son of a workman named Bélair, who learned to make sausage under the direction of his stepfather, then became apprenticed in turn to a shoemaker, a locksmith and a marshal. He worked for the faïence-makers Genest and Serrurier, both in the faubourg Saint-Antoine, Paris, went to Montereau to work for a *marchand faïencier* named Mazois, and then returned to Paris. He claimed to have been at Vincennes in 1745 as a *modeleur en porcelaine*, but is actually documented at Strasbourg as a thrower. He died at Paris on 21 October 1773. Tamara Préaud has informed the author in correspondence of Spring 1991 that Jacques Chapelle was paid as a sculptor at Vincennes between August and December 1745, receiving the high sum of 80 *livres* in October. His first name is confirmed by the municipal records which reveal that he married Marie Marguerite Agi on 8 February 1748 when he was described as 'ouvrier en terres d'Angleterre' [cream-coloured earthenwares] au faubourg St Antoine'. He remained in touch with his Vincennes colleagues.
4. Exh. *Sceaux*, 1986, p. 20.
5. *Ibid.*, p. 116.
6. D'Albis and Préaud, 1991, p. 214, 210.
7. Chavagnac and Grollier, 1906, p. 366, quoting Archives nationales O^1, 2060.
8. Musée de l'Ile de France, *Catalogue raisonné de collections, Hauts-de-Seine*, compiled by G. Poisson, M. Aries, C. Henry, F. Flot, 1985, no. 1149, cup and saucer, inv. 79–18–91.
9. C. Dauguet and D. Guillemé-Brulon, *La porcelaine française*, Paris, n.d., p. 30.
10. Poisson *et al.*, *op. cit.*, no. 1148, cosmetic pot, inv. 49–9–1.
11. *Ibid.*, no. 1153, figure of a boy, inv. 51–1–1. This is the only marked figure recorded.
12. See H.-P. Fourest and J. Giacomotti, *L'Oeuvre des faïenciers français du XVIe à la fin du XVIIIe Siècle*, Paris, 1966, pp. 282–95; exh. 'Faïences Françaises' 1980, nos. 368–403; exh *Sceaux*, 1986.
13. Exh. *Sceaux*, 1986, pp. 116–20.
14. MNS, Archives de Sèvres, A4.

---

204 **Gravy-pot and Cover (*pot à jus*)** 1773–1793/4

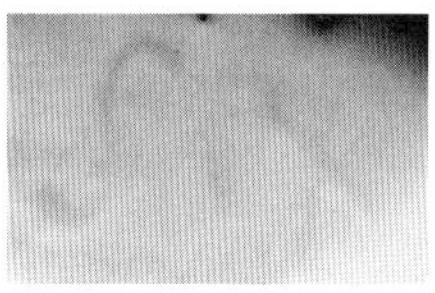

204 *mark*

H. 8.2 cm
Marks: *S.X* incised
Reg. No. Franks 367

Soft-paste porcelain, thrown, with turned foot, the rim everted, thickly potted. Loop handle, domed lid with applied cherry and leaf knop. Decorated in pink, purple, green, yellow, blue and black with flower sprays, consisting of roses, forget-me-nots, honeysuckle and other flowers. Rims and part of handle painted pink. Chips to cover.

Provenance: Bequeathed by Sir A.W. Franks, 1897

Literature: Franks, 1896, no. 367
Comparable Examples: None

Pots like these were used as part of the dinner service. They survive in some quantity and are often almost indistinguishable from those made at Bourg-la-Reine (see cat. 206) without the evidence of the incised factory mark. This example differs in shape from cat. 206. The style of the flower-painting has something in common with flowers on tin-glazed earthenwares, which were also in production at Sceaux.[1]

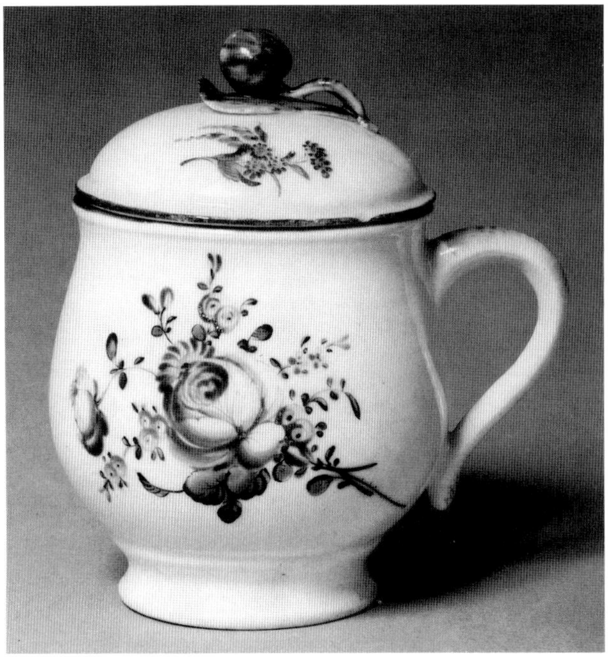

204

A wide range of small pots like these was in production principally at Mennecy, Bourg-la-Reine and Sceaux. Some are spirally moulded.

1. However the standard of flower-painting on Sceaux faïence reached a much higher stage of refinement. For the engraved sources and examples see exh. *Sceaux*, 1986, in particular J. Bastian, 'Les décors floraux', pp. 35–45.

205 Cup and Saucer, 1773–1793/4

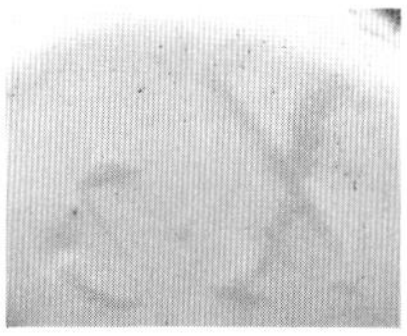

205 *mark*

D. *of saucer:*	12.6 cm
H. *of cup:*	6.8 cm
Marks:	*S.X* incised on cup
Reg. No.	Franks 368

Soft-paste porcelain, thickly potted, glaze unevenly applied and poorly fitting near foot rim. Decorated in blue, green, yellow, pink, brown and black enamels with birds in a landscape. Rims painted pink, loop handle with slight kick painted blue at upper and lower end.

Provenance: Bequeathed by Sir A.W. Franks, 1897

Literature: Franks, 1896, no. 368

Comparable Examples: France, Hélène Fournier Collection, exh. Sceaux, 1986, cat. 191, ill. p. 59, no. 87

Italy, Naples, Museo Duca di Martina, illus. M.L. Casanova, *Le Porcellane Francesi nei Musei di Napoli*, Naples, 1974, no. 205, incised *S.X*, D. 12 cm., inv. 5390. A similar saucer made at Bourg-la-Reine illus. *ibid.*, no. 203.

The quality of both the body, which is marred by a firecrack on the upper surface of the saucer, as well as by a poor glaze, and of the painted decoration, is indifferent.

Bird subjects are also found on faïence made at Sceaux.[1]

1. See exh. *Sceaux*, 1986, pp. 47–61, discussion by C. Béalu of bird decoration, including two series of birds found on porcelain.

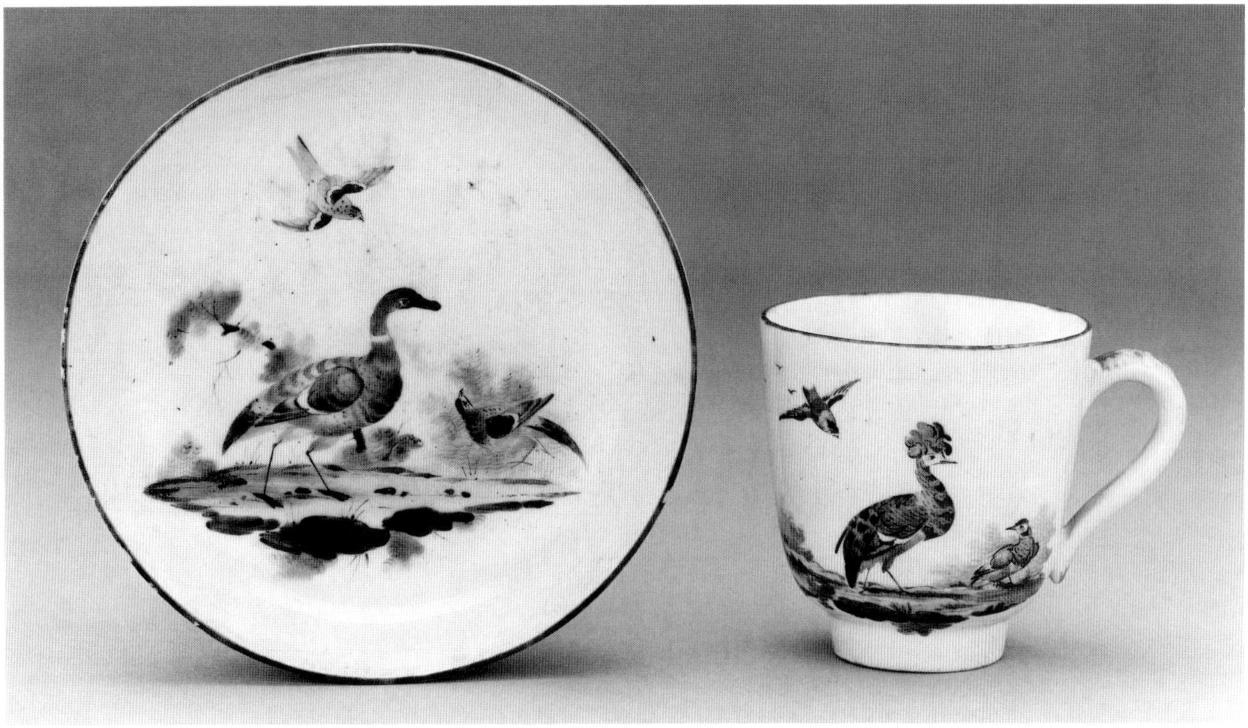

205

Bourg-la-Reine[1]

This concern, which was under the protection of Louis Charles de Bourbon, comte d'Eu (1712–75), is generally considered to be the continuation of the Villeroy-Mennecy factory and had a connection with Sceaux (q.v.) through its owners Charles-Symphorien Jacques (*c.* 1724–1799) and Joseph Jullien (*c.* 1725–74). It was probably in existence by Autumn 1772,[2] or perhaps slightly earlier. In November 1770 Jacques and Jullien acquired a house in the village of Bourg-la-Reine (about 10 miles from the centre of Paris), buying land there in the following year.

Jullien's early death at the age of 49 apparently had little effect on the factory's production since his widow, Marie-Jeanne Leroy, took his place. Their son, Joseph-Léon Jullien, is said to have been employed at the factory from 1773; in April 1778 he is listed in the parish register as a faïence painter, aged 18.

In September 1776 Jacques bought out the widow Jullien for the sum of 68,300 *livres*, and a valuation report dated 17 May 1776[3] gives a precise idea of the size of the factory. It operated two grinding mills and two kilns each for faïence and porcelain. Despite the payment made, Madame Jullien remained a partner until 1 May 1780. Jacques' son worked with him from 1785, but only became a painter in 1790. After Jacques' wife's death in April 1790,[4] he progressively handed over the factory to his son. Jacques *père* died on 15 April 1799 and after lengthy legal proceedings his son assumed full ownership in December 1802. He was declared bankrupt in July 1804, owing 11,620 francs 15 centimes. The factory was sold at auction on 12 October 1805 for 20,000 francs.

The mainstay of the porcelain production at the Bourg-la-Reine factory was tableware of all sorts, except for plates, which seem never to have been made in quantity. Most decorated pieces, whether painted in blue or in colours, with or without gilding, are decorated with flowers, often highly stylised. In many instances, without the evidence of the incised mark *BR* registered on 23 July 1773,[5] it would be difficult to distinguish its products, especially toilet pots, cups and saucers and small *vases Médicis* on pedestals, from their counterparts made at Sceaux or Mennecy, as both the palette and the shapes are closely related. It has been suggested[6] that pieces made at Mennecy were painted at Bourg-la-Reine, but no proof has been found of this assertion.

Although few have survived, the evidence of inventories[7] indicates a large-scale production of figures, medallions and porcelain flowers. In 1774 the subjects included Fame, Louis XV, medallions of Henri IV and Louis XV, and in 1780, mythological, pastoral and anecdotal figures and groups. An ambitious biscuit group of three musicians signed *Mô* (see below) is in the Musée national de Céramique at Sèvres[8] and a group signed *Mo.BR* of Perseus rescuing Andromeda accompanied by putti was formerly in the collection of the sixth Earl of Rosebery.[9]

Around thirty-three workers have been traced at the factory between 1772 and l'an V (1799). Only one sculptor, Jean-Baptiste Mô (baptised 3 August 1749), formerly of Mennecy and Sceaux and whose origins and early training remain unknown, is documented. He appears in the parish records on 3 September 1772. His brother Christophe (baptised 5 November 1739) is documented at Mennecy, but not at Bourg-la-Reine.[10] Five painters, four mould-makers, six throwers, a repairer, and a kiln-master, as well as twelve other workmen (*ouvriers*), all appear in the parish records, showing that the factory was of some size. Their wages are unknown. No evidence concerning the outlets or prices charged for Bourg-la-Reine porcelain is known to the author.

1. The most recent study, on which this account is based, is G. Le Duc, 'La Manufacture de Bourg-la-Reine, Faïences et Porcelaines Tendres (1772–1804)', *Cahiers*, no. 39, 1967, pp. 162–76.
2. Parish registers of September 1772 record the presence of the porcelain painter Nicolas Sisson, formerly of Sceaux, who was to move to Sèvres in 1773, see Le Duc, *op. cit.*, p. 162. For a biography of Sisson, who decorated cat. 131, see Savill, 1988, III, pp. 1066–7.
3. See Le Duc, *op. cit.*, p. 166, quoting Archives nationales, Z2 4207 (not seen by this writer).
4. See *Inventaire après le décès de Dlle honnorée agnès Adam, épouse de M. Charles Symphorien Jacques, Entrepreneur de la Manufacture royale de fayance et porcelaine établie au Bourg-la-Reine 30 avril 1790*, Archives nationales, Minutier central, *Etude* XXVII, *liasse* 499.
5. Chavagnac and Grollier, 1906, p. 101.
6. Duchon, 1988, p. 84. The author is grateful to John Mallet for drawing this point to her attention.
7. *Inventaire après décès* of Jullien, 25 May 1774, Archives nationales, Minutier central, *Etude* XXVII, *liasse* 371.
8. See Le Duc, *op. cit.*, p. 167, figs. 1, 2.
9. Sold Sotheby Parke Bernet, Mentmore, Buckinghamshire, Vol. III, 24 May 1977, Lot 2088.
10. Duchon, 1988, pp. 113–14.

---

206 **Gravy-pot and Cover (*pot à jus*)**, 1773–*c.*1780

H. 8.2 cm
Marks: BR incised
Reg. No. Franks 365

Soft-paste porcelain, thickly potted. Loop handle, domed lid with applied cherry and leaf knop. Unglazed foot rim partly discoloured. Decorated in pink, blue, green, yellow and black enamels with flower sprays. Rims painted purplish-pink, handle decorated with dash design in same colour.

Provenance: Bequeathed by Sir A.W. Franks, 1897

Literature: Franks, 1896, no.365

Chaffers, 1926, Vol. II, p. 340, fig. 293

Comparable Examples: Paris, Drouot Richelieu, 28 October 1991, Lots 114, 116

Pots of this form were made at Chantilly, Meissen and Sceaux as well as at various faïence factories in France, such as Sceaux and Meillonas. Even the Chinese produced a version of the shape decorated in underglaze-blue for export to the West.[1] The Vincennes version, which is similar in shape, was in production by the mid-1750s.[2]

The date of manufacture of this piece is difficult to determine without evidence to indicate how long this kind of flower painting kept its appeal.

1. See Paris, Drouot Richelieu, 28 October 1991, back cover of catalogue.
2. Exh. *Vincennes*, 1977–8, p. 76.

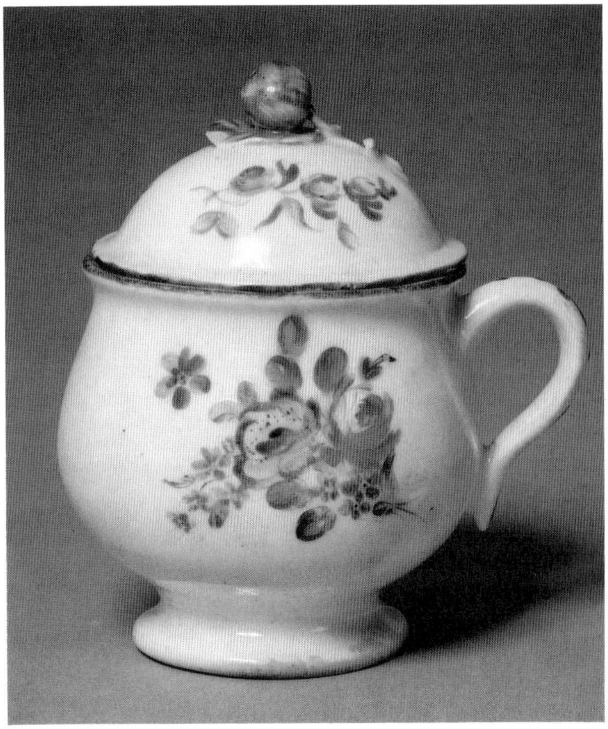

206

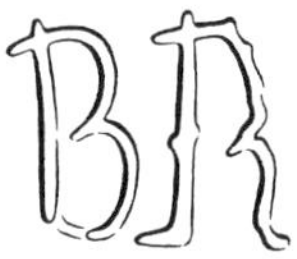

206 *mark*

207 **Toilet Pot and Cover (*pot à fard*),** *c.*1773–1800

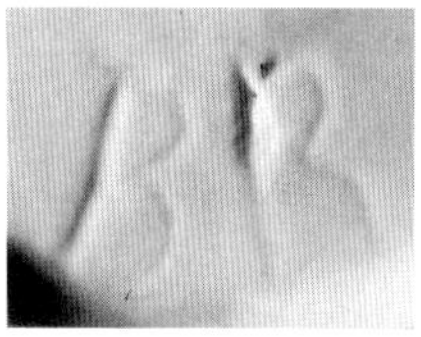

207 *mark*

H.	7.4 cm
Marks:	*BR* incised
Reg. No.	Franks 366

Soft-paste porcelain, the pot cylindrical and the lid domed with flat knop. Decorated with three crudely-painted flowers on cover and pot in underglaze-blue, and with a pattern of dashes on the knop. Knop damaged.

Provenance: Bequeathed by Sir A.W. Franks, 1897

Literature: Franks, 1896, no. 366

Comparable Examples: Sèvres, Musée national de Céramique, illus. G. Le Duc, 'La Manufacture de Bourg-la-Reine, Faïences et Porcelaines Tendres (1772–1804)', *Cahiers*, no. 38 (1967), fig. 3

Chavagnac Collection, mark illus. Chavagnac and Grollier,[1] probably Lot 210, sale of comte X. de Chavagnac, Paris, Hôtel Drouot, 20 June 1911

Although such pieces were presumably made in quantity, few seem to have survived. It is not known how long such pots with flower decoration continued in production.

1. Chavagnac and Grollier, 1906, p. 112.

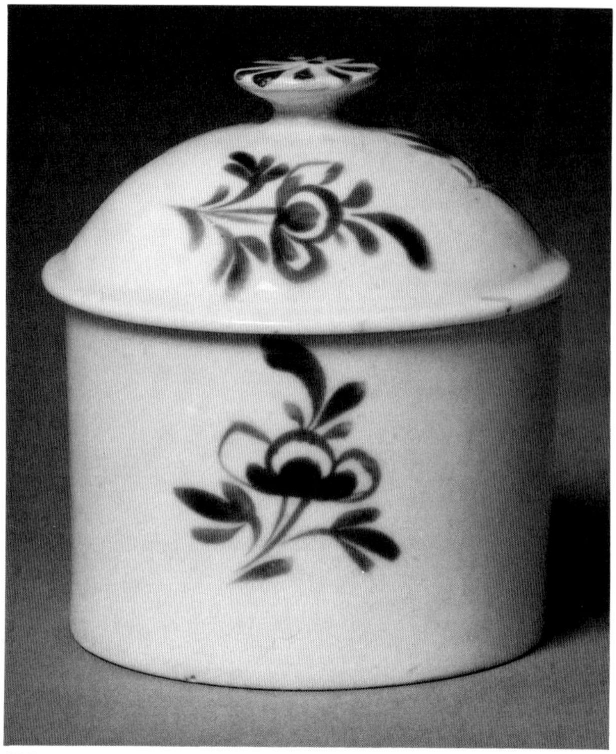

207

Arras

The Arras factory[1] was probably established by J.F. Boussemart in 1770. His associates, Louise, Marguerite, Robertine and Constance Delemer sold faïence and porcelain in the rue Saint-Aubert, Arras, and they seem to have been in charge of the factory from the outset. On 29 October 1771 three deputies of the Etats d'Artois and its lawyer visited the premises in rue de la Comédie at the request of the Delemer sisters.[2] They saw seven kilns: in a cellar were one for calcining lead and tin, a second for preparing the frit ('pour cuire les matières par la réverbération du feu'), a biscuit kiln, a fourth full of fired ware in the Sèvres style ('rempli d'ustensiles cuits, façon de Sève'), a fifth circular kiln with three firemouths ('en rondeur à trois bouches à l'anglaise'); a glost kiln located below the staircase of the cellar 'built like a Chantilly kiln'; on the ground floor ('rez de chaussée') was a seventh reverberatory Meissen-style ('façon de Saxe') kiln for enamel firing and, nearby, muffle-kilns for firing gilding. The firing times were given in the commissioners' report as follows: 48 hours for the frit; 60 hours for both the third and fourth kilns; 18 hours for the kiln with three firemouths; 12 hours for the glost kiln; 15 hours for the enamel kiln and 3 hours for the muffle-kilns.

In 1771 the factory had two throwing wheels located in a workshop upstairs, and a quantity of moulds kept in an adjoining room. At least 1,500 unfired pieces were noted in the first room and a further large number of biscuit pieces in the second, as well as other finished and unfinished pieces in workshops elsewhere. A third wheel was noted in a hayloft on the premises. The wood for firing the kilns and the clay were both kept in the yard. The shop ('magasin') was in a farm by the Ronville gate between two bridges belonging to the King, where some of the best quality clay was also stored. By 1790 there were three *magasins* at the factory itself.[3]

The Delemer sisters were successful in obtaining financial support from the Etats d'Artois in 1771, and in the following year the factory removed to the Refuge of Etrun Abbey, in the rue d'Amiens. The sisters had already been conscious of the lack of space in their original premises, as they had complained in 1771 that they had to store their wood – already cut into lengths for use in firing the kiln – as well as some of their clay, in a farm building situated at one of the gates of the city.

Three years later, in 1775, they obtained permission from the Etats to build a water mill on the bank of the Scarpe river for grinding raw materials used in the preparation of the porcelain body. The source of the clay remains unknown, although some new clay 'qui se trouve sous les pierres et cornüs et que l'on nomme Betun' (*?petuntse*, or clay for hard-paste porcelain) is mentioned in a document of 1771.[4] The water mill was to replace an inadequate horse-driven mill which was capable of grinding only 350 pounds (*livres*) of raw materials a week. The new mill could grind as much in one day as the old one in eight, and was also less expensive to run as only one horse, instead of three, would now be needed to carry materials back to the factory. A site of 20 square feet was requested for the mill together with 10 square feet for a stable where the miller was to sleep, and a room measuring 10 square feet for storing the raw materials. In 1780, as a result of complaints from the users of the waterway, the sisters lost the right to the mill, and were fined for infringing the agreement to use it only on certain days.

In 1775 the Delemer sisters attempted to obtain a reduction of the customs duties payable on their porcelain when it was exported from the region, which was outside the *cinq grosses fermes*.[5] The reduction was to be made on condition that they 'Seront tenus de peindre graver ou imprimer à chaque pièce une marque que nous croyons être AR'. However, competition from Tournai as well as from French factories led to the closure of the Arras concern on 22 July 1790, and the sale of its effects in the following year.

In a report dated 22 December 1790 the architect of the Arras district appointed by *messieurs du Directoire* gave detailed description of the site which he had inspected for the purposes of valuation.[6] Three porcelain kilns were noted in one building and a further small kiln in another building close by. In the yard was a structure housing a horse-drawn mill. A large horse-powered mill is described as in another building in a garden down a passageway. The valuation based on the dilapidated state of the properties 'd'une très ancienne construction hors d'état d'être habités . . . entièrement à démolir'), was 8,500 *livres*. On 20 May 1791 the whole was sold to a gardener named Pollet for 10,000 *livres*.

Wares produced at the factory seem to have been principally service pieces, all of soft-paste porcelain. Moulded borders, underglaze-blue flowers in oriental style, conventional sprigs, and a plain design of a leaf trail are characteristic, and are perhaps conscious copies of some of the patterns used at Tournai, which was its chief rival. Polychrome flowers were also used as decorative motifs. Services painted with armorials, such as those of the *intendant* Lefèvre de Caumartin, were doubtless made to order. Some more elaborate pieces are known, such as a two-handled glass-cooler decorated with landscape scenes on an underglaze-blue ground ornamented with gilt birds,[7] although it is possible that this piece was not painted at the factory. Price lists found in the archives in Arras in the last century have been published[8] and show that basketwork-moulded plates were 18 *livres* a dozen, ordinary plates 15 *livres*. The dearest item is a *plat et soupier rond et long* (tureen and stand) in the largest size at 45 *livres*. The smallest, or fourth, size cost 24 *livres*. A wide variety of domestic wares from service and tea wares to water jugs and basins, barbers' bowls, toilet pots and chamber pots were in production. No names of workers have been discovered. It is known that there were eight artisans and twelve labourers ('manoeuvres') in 1774,[9] suggesting an enterprise of considerable size.

1. This account is largely taken from exh. Nord-Pas-de-Calais, 1986–7, pp. 33–5. The only work devoted to this factory is Baron L. Cavrois, *Le refuge d'Etrun et la manufacture de porcelaines d'Arras*, Arras, 1877, p. 55, also used by the author. As this catalogue went to press, an exhibition held at the Musée des Beaux-Arts, Arras, in February 1992 resulted in a catalogue compiled by Annick Notter, *Porcelaine d'Arras: collection du musée d'Arras*, which publishes much new information including that based on archaeological excavation and unpublished documents. Notter brings to light the establishment by 1775 of a partnership between the Delemer sisters and Claude-François Coquelard of Arras.
2. See *Rapport des commissaires aux industries et manufactures des Etats d'Artois, après une demande d'aide des demoiselles Delemer*, 1771. This document, Archives départementales du Pas-de-Calais, Série C, no. 158, was destroyed in 1915, but had been transcribed. The author is grateful to Annick Notter for this information.
3. See note 6.
4. *Ibid.*
5. Archives d'Arras, Etats d'Artois, 20 September 1775, quoted Cavrois, 1877, p. 55. The 'five large (tax) farms' in the north of France, which represented areas relatively recently subsumed into France, were liable for customs duties on imported and exported goods.
6. Archives départementales du Pas-de-Calais, Série Q, *liasse* 232, 1 Q 58.
7. See Christie's, Brisbane, Australia, 6, 7 June 1989, Sir Leon and Lady Trout Collection, Lot 458.
8. Cavrois, 1877, pp. 57–8 and 60–1. Both lists are undated. It should be remembered that the *livre* in Arras had a different value to the Paris *livre*.
9. Archives départementales du Pas-de-Calais, Série C, no reference, report of 3 December 1774. This document was destroyed in 1915, but there is a transcription in the Souillart ms, according to Annick Notter.

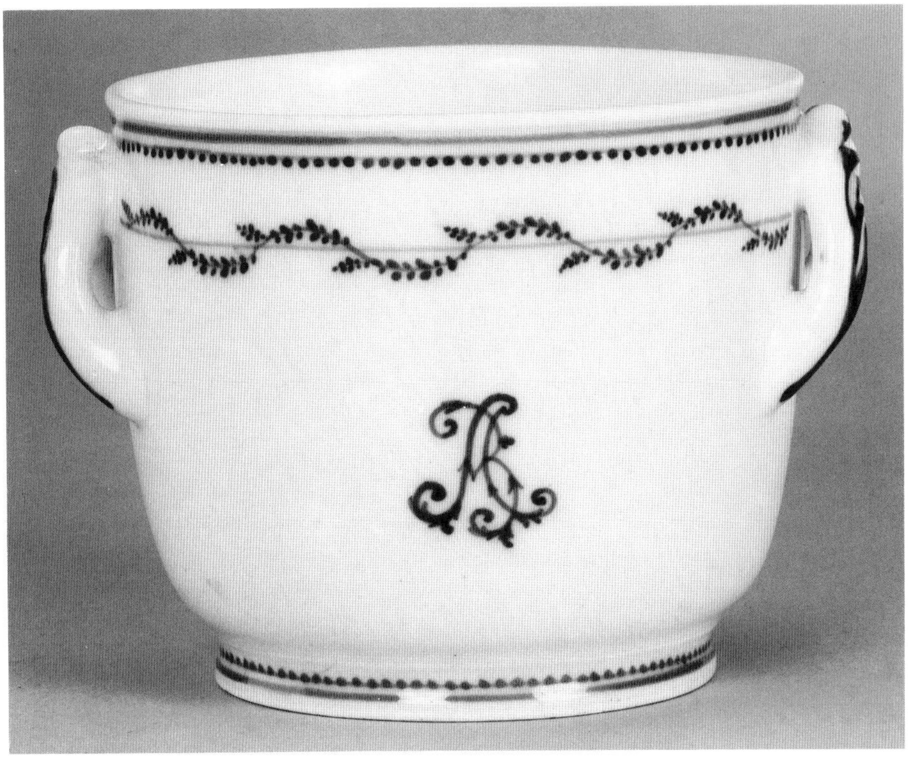

208

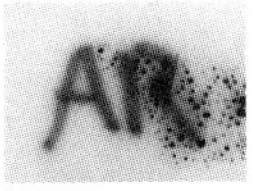

208 *mark*

208 **Glass-cooler (*seau à verre*)**, 1775–90

D. 10.6 cm (excl. handles)
H. 8.8 cm
Marks: *AR* painted in underglaze-blue
Reg. No. Franks 369

Soft-paste porcelain with two leaf-moulded rudimentary handles, each attached at both lower and upper end to the cooler itself. Painted in underglaze-blue with the motif known as the *ronce* pattern[1] and with the monogram *AB* [?] on both sides. Below each handle is painted a single leaf. Foot chipped.

Provenance: Bequeathed by Sir A.W. Franks, 1897

Literature: Franks, 1896, no.369

Comparable Examples: None noted

The same pattern was also used at Tournai[2] but the form of the handles is characteristic of Arras.

According to price lists published by Cavrois,[3] *seaux à verres* sold for 4 *livres*, whilst *seaux à liqueurs* were 6 *livres* and *seaux à bouteilles* 12 *livres*; the latter cost 1 *livre* more if painted with flowers in the so-called 'Dessin de M. de Calonne'.

1. The pattern-name *ronce* is not known in 18th-century documents.
2. C. Deroubaix, *Les Porcelaines de Tournai du Musée de Mariemont*, Mariemont, 1958, no. 1763, pl. 48.
3. Cavrois, 1877, p. 58 and pp. 60–1; the document is undated but it is likely to be before 1778. For a *seau à bouteilles* see exh. Arras, 1992, no. 9, Musée d'Arras, inv. 933.5.437, decorated with the underglaze-blue pattern known as *ronda et cinq bouquets*; a *refraichissoir à verres* (glass-cooler) is illus. in *ibid.*, no. 26, Musée d'Arras, inv. 914.1.301 painted in underglaze-blue with the *brindille* pattern.

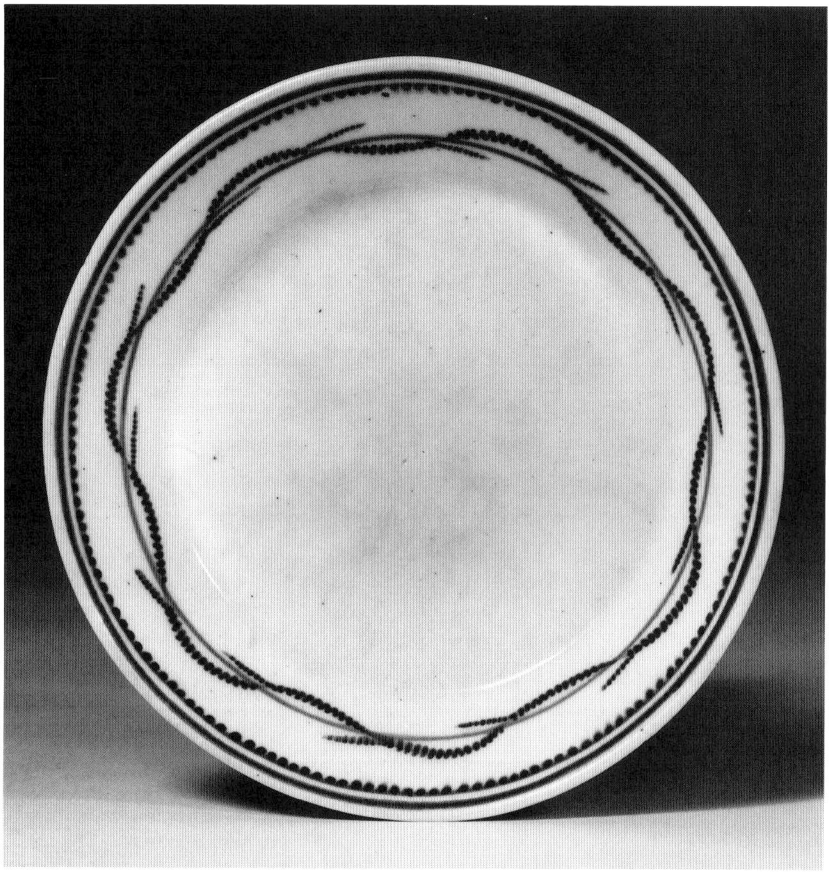

209

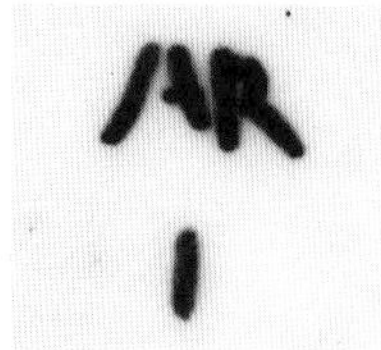

209 *marks*

209 **Saucer,** 1775–90

D. 12.8 cm
Marks: *AR/I* painted in underglaze-blue; ⁄⁄\ incised
Reg. No. Franks 370

Soft-paste porcelain, more creamy in tone than the previous example, marred by several firing defects. Painted in underlgaze-blue near rim of deep border with the motif known as the *ronce* pattern.

Provenance: Bequeathed by Sir A.W. Franks, 1897

Literature: Franks, 1896, no.370

Comparable Examples: France, Musée d'Arras, sugar bowl and cover, teapot and cover, cup and saucer of matching pattern, see exh. Arras, 1992, nos. 51–3, inv. 933.5.537 (1 and 2), 541, 50

The pattern is known as *à la ronce*.[1]

An incised mark ⁄⁄\, which is slightly different to the one on this piece is recorded by Chavagnac and Grollier;[2] however, it appears on a butter dish in the Musée d'Arras.[3] It has not yet been associated with any employee at the factory.

Prices of various tablewares made at Arras as given in a document (apparently undated but before 1778) were published by Cavrois.[4] A *gobelet et soucoupe à manche* cost 1 *livre* 10, a *gobelet à boulion couvert et soucoupe* 4 *livres*. A printed price list compiled after 1778 formerly in the collection of Monsieur Octave Petit lists 'tasses à anse et Soucoupes la douzaine' at 18 *livres* (with a *petit dessin*, probably corresponding to the decoration of this piece).[5]

1. See p. 267, n. 1.
2. Chavagnac and Grollier, 1906, p. 456.
3. Exh. *Arras*, 1992, no. 36, inv. 933.5.517
4. Cavrois, 1877, pp. 57–8
5. *Ibid.*, pp. 60–1.

HARD-PASTE FACTORIES

Strasbourg[1]

The first hard-paste porcelain produced on French soil was made at the Strasbourg factory.[2] Like so many porcelain factories both in France and elsewhere, it developed from a pottery which was already making tin-glazed earthenware.[3] Charles-François Hannong (*c*.1669–1739), a Dutchman born in Maastricht but perhaps of Spanish descent, had come to Strasbourg in 1709 and made clay pipes there from 1715; on 18 August 1721 he went into patnership with Jean-Henri Wackenfeld (1695–1725) to make tin-glazed wares or possibly porcelain. A *Humble Mémoire et supplique . . . au sujet d'un four pour la fabrication de la porcelaine* submitted by Hannong and Wackenfeld was read to the Conseil des XXI on 15 September 1721.[4] It refers to Wackenfeld's repeated attempts to build a kiln, which succeeded only when he had formed an association with Hannong to 'continuer ici la fabrication de la porcelaine dans de meilleurs conditions'. Hannong, according to the *mémoire*, was aware of the necessary raw materials, i.e. refractory high-firing clays, needed to build a kiln and it is probable that he also supplied capital, or had access to it. The association was short-lived, however, as Wackenfeld left Strasbourg the following year.[5] Hannong nevertheless continued in business, establishing a branch in Haguenau in 1724. Good clay was available there, and Hannong obtained exclusive rights to use it not only at Haguenau but also in Strasbourg. Fifteen years later he handed over his business to two of his sons, Paul-Antoine (1700–60) and Balthasar (*c*.1703–53), in return for certain financial arrangements.

During the 1740s Paul-Antoine Hannong, by then in charge of the Strasbourg faïence factory, introduced notable technical advances (which had, in fact, been in use in the Low Countries for several decades). He built a new kiln on the premises in the rue du Foulon (now rue Hannong) and used low-temperature colours and gilding on his wares. Perhaps as early as 1745 he began experimental work on porcelain, probably using clay from Passau in Bavaria. There is some evidence that workers from both the Meissen and Höchst factories assisted him. Among those who brought their skills to Strasbourg in the late 1740s were: the Löwenfinck brothers, Christian Wilhelm (*c*.1720–53), employed from about November 1748, and Adam-Friedrich (1714–54), from May 1749 to some time in 1750, and the latter's wife, the painter Maria Seraphia Susanna Magdalena, *née* Schick, (1728–1805), who had been employed at other hard-paste factories, the brothers both having worked at Meissen, Höchst and elsewhere; Jean-Gottlieb Roth (?d.1753), born in Dresden and formerly employed at Höchst; and Joseph Jacob Ringler (1730–1804), an arcanist who ran away from Meissen and had also worked at Höchst.[6]

The factory's earliest productions in porcelain are thought to date from 1751–4. They are either unmarked or incised or stamped *PH* and painted in underglaze-blue with a lion, the emblem of Strasbourg. Little is known of the tablewares made at this time,[7] but a number of figures have been identified. Some were the work of Jean-Guillaume Lanz, about whom little is at present known. Only one document attests his presence at Strasbourg. It records the baptism of his daughter Marie-Madeleine, born on 8 April 1753 in the Catholic parish of Saint-Pierre-le-Vieux. The child's mother (*née* Moser) had the same forenames. After 1755 Lanz worked at Frankenthal in the Rhine-Palatinate (see below), as head of the modeller's workshop. He was probably responsible for earthenware figures with flowing drapery in the Baroque style, which suggest his early training as a sculptor. Some of these figures were based on garden statuary.[8] Among the known early figures which can be attributed to Lanz are: a figure of Flora,[9] the Four Parts of the World, a naked Saturn with hour-glass and scythe, putti, seated Chinese figures, hunting subjects,[10] Diana asleep with two dogs, two goats on a rock, figures of pug dogs, and two allegories – *Time's Victory over Envy in the presence of History*, and *Time's Victory over Beauty*.[11] Some of the figures made in tin-glazed earthenware, including the Four Parts of the World, had porcelain counterparts.

Certain groups, such as *Le Jeune Suppliant* and *La Moissonneuse* were also produced at Vincennes–Sèvres, and may have been plagiarised by the Strasbourg factory. This may have been the reason why J.-B. Machault, *contrôleur général des finances*, who was deeply involved in the establishment of the royal factory, refused Hannong's request for permission to make and sell porcelain. Hannong claimed 'ce qu'il fait à présent surpasse celle de la Chine et égale celle de la Saxe (. . .). La porcelaine qu'il fabrique se modèle comme une terre fine; elle a le son véritable et elle est à l'épreuve de la braize, on y peut hardiment faire cuire ou bouillir, ce que les autres porcelaines ne souffrent point. Elle est d'ailleurs travaillée si artistiquement que les ouvrages à peintures, jettent un éclat charmant à l'aspect'. ('What he is making at present surpasses the Chinese and equals Meissen (. . .). The porcelain he manufactures can be worked like a fine pottery; it rings like true porcelain and can be exposed to heat; it can be safely used to cook or boil [i.e. foods or liquids], which other porcelains will not stand. In addition it is so artistically fashioned that ornament and painted decoration add a charming touch to its appearance.')[12]

In a second attempt to obtain a licence, examples of Hannong's porcelain were shown to the King by Machault and the duc de Noailles and permission was at last obtained for him to fire, although this only applied to items already made. He then requested the right to make and sell porcelain as before (i.e. commercially) in a new *requête* of 25 April 1754. This document[13] provides evidence that he had help from the Meissen factory, and assistance from Saxon workmen.

After the failure of his *requête*, Paul-Antoine Hannong tried to sell his hard-paste formula to the royal factory at Sèvres.[14] Since kaolin had not yet been discovered on French soil, his attempt proved unsuccessful. Hannong, who had been in Paris, returned to Strasbourg and in 1755 moved the factory to Frankenthal where the Elector Palatine, Charles Theodore, supported the enterprise. In 1759 Hannong went back to Strasbourg once more, and died there the following year.

Pierre-Antoine Hannong (1739–after 1794) was the third son of Paul-Antoine. His co-legatees placed him in charge of the faïence factories of Haguenau and Strasbourg (which continued as before). It quickly became obvious that his dissolute and extravagant character was leading to the ruin of the Strasbourg concern. Jean-Jacques Sorg (1743–1821), an apprentice painter taken on in May 1759, was one of the many workmen who left the factory in early 1761 as the situation worsened. In January 1761 Hannong went to Paris under the auspices of the director of the Sèvres factory, Boileau de Picardie, where he sold his father's secrets to Sèvres for the sum of 6,000 *livres* and an annual pension of 3,000 *livres* which was, however, soon reduced (see n. 14).

The second period of porcelain manufacture at Strasbourg began in 1768 when Joseph-Adam Hannong (1734–*c.*1800) sold up in Frankenthal and took over the Strasbourg factory. Despite large debts, he conducted an enormous series of experiments between 1768 and 1773 and increased production. The abolition of the Sèvres monopoly in 1766 should have meant that he could sell his pieces all over France, but from 1774 onwards the Ferme Générale, responsible for tax collection, imposed a high levy on his products. Hannong's plan to find outlets in France ultimately led to his ruin. He borrowed heavily from the Cardinal Louis-Constantin de Rohan, Prince Bishop of Strasbourg (1756–79), on whom he relied for support in his struggle against the tax-farmers. After the Cardinal's death, Joseph Hannong was imprisoned for debt for more than a year and was only released as a result of a direct appeal to the King on 22 February 1780. Although he restarted the factory on a large scale, he never subsequently freed himself from debt. An *arrêt du Conseil du Roy* of late 1780 decreed that officials should watch over the factory's accounting to see that all profits went to pay off Hannong's creditors. On 2 April 1781 Joseph Hannong presented the Queen with a large vase decorated by his eighteen-year-old daughter Françoise-Adélaïde, and took his entire family to the château de la Muette to beg for the King's aid. Late in 1781 he gave up the struggle, fled abroad and on 24

November, by an *arrêt royal* drawn up on the advice of the *intendant*, was declared bankrupt, his wares to be sold off by auction.

Although some Strasbourg models were made by Pierre-Antoine Hannong at Haguenau with Strasbourg raw materials between 1783 and 1784, the factory effectively closed down in late 1781.

The records of the masons' guild to which potters were obliged to belong, together with those of the *tribu de l'Echasse* which looked after the interests of the painters, have yielded the names of around one hundred workers at the Strasbourg and Haguenau pottery and porcelain factories. Where their origins are documented, it is clear that some came from Saxony and other German-speaking territories, but the majority appear to have been born in Strasbourg itself. Little is known of their conditions of work, nor of the layout of the factory. It had been situated in the rue du Foulon since 1715, gradually expanding, especially in the middle years of the century, and by 1781 it occupied the entire street up to the rue de Jeu d'Enfants. A glaze mill was in operation in the Ziegelwasser from 1722 and another larger one, where the porcelain body was prepared, was established by Paul Hannong in 1745 beside the Pont National at the end of the Grande rue.

In our present state of knowledge, very little can be said about the pricing, distribution and sale of Strasbourg porcelain. In 1772 the *Almanach général des Marchands* listed two outlets for Hannong's Strasbourg factory. One was in the rue de Grenelle-Saint-Honoré opposite the Hôtel des Fermes, in a concern run by the widow Lachenal, the other in Hamburg at the house of Jolliat.[15]

During the first period of activity between 1751 and 1754, the influence of other factories such as Meissen, Chantilly[16] and Vincennes/Sèvres conditioned the style of its limited range of production. The decoration on tablewares was predominantly of flowers or birds. Between 1768 and 1781 Joseph Hannong issued a remarkable number of new shapes, initially in a traditional style which gave way to a strongly neo-classical idiom. Fluted legs on tureens and vegetable dishes, handles in the form of goats', lions' or rams' heads with pendent rings and acanthus-leaf ornament are all characteristic of this period, when Strasbourg produced bold forms. The decorative range included monochrome blue flowers, iron-red landscape scenes, naturalistic flowers, *chinoiseries*, genre scenes in the Teniers style, gallant, pastoral and mythological subjects, La Fontaine fables, and ribbon, garland and flower motifs. Groups and figures, both enamelled and biscuit, measuring between 9 and 30 cm in height and embracing scenes of music, mythology, hunting, animals, children and gardening were made. Some monumental biscuit figures such as *Hercules and Cerberus*[17] and plaques of the *Four Seasons* after Pigalle[18] show that several skilled modellers were employed. A medallion portrait of Henri IV[19] is the sole known example from this factory of the technique of simulating lace by dipping it in porcelain before firing, the fired porcelain then taking on the appearance of the fabric. This became highly popular throughout Europe in the mid- to late nineteenth century, but may well have been first used by Joseph Hannong. It was described by the Professor of Botany at Strasbourg University, Jean Hermann (1738–1800) in a note inscribed in his own copy of Hannong's price list.[20] Hannong's figures and groups, wrote Hermann, were especially magnificent, and he had set aside special rooms for them, and had domes to cover them; he was unwilling to sell anything until the room was complete and the cupboards filled.

> Il avoit imaginé surtout de faire les draperies les plus légères et les plus élégantes en porcelaine et en biscuit. Il fit tremper dans une pâte de porcelaine duement délayée de la mousseline, de la gaze, de la dentelle etc., et les fit appliquer sur les figures, en leur donnant les plis naturels. Cela donne à la draperie une transparence inimitable. J'ai vu pareils morceaux cassés, oû les fils n'etoient pas détruits par la cuisson. J' y ai acheté, à la vente forcée en (1781) une Vénus couchée, drapée de cette manière en biscuit.
>
> (He discovered a way of making the lightest and most elegant drapery in porcelain and in biscuit. This was achieved by dipping muslin, gauze, lace etc. in liquid porcelain, then applying it to the figures, so that it formed folds naturally. This method made the drapery unimaginably fine. I have seen broken pieces of this kind where the threads [of the fabric] had not been destroyed in the firing process. At the [bankruptcy] sale of 1781 I bought a biscuit figure of the seated Venus with drapery of the kind described.)

Both Paul-Antoine Hannong and his son Joseph were inventive porcelain makers. Their factory at Strasbourg awaits detailed study.

1. The fullest account of this factory is by H. Haug, *Les faïences et porcelaines de Strasbourg*, Strasbourg, 1922. See also E. Heuser, *Porzellan von Strassburg und Frankenthal im achtzehnten Jahrhundert*, Neustadt an der Haardt, 1922. For a survey of Strasbourg and its culture see (D. Sutton), 'Eighteenth-Century Strasbourg; a meeting-place of two cultures', *Apollo*, Vol. XCIV, no. 114, August 1971, pp. 86–95.
2. The status of Alsace was that of *province reputée étrangère*; it was considered to be part of France, but had to pay taxes on goods sent into French provinces outside Alsace. The status of Alsace is discussed in an exhibition held in

Strasbourg in September–December 1981, 'Strasbourg, Ville Libre Royale 1681–1792'.

3. The history and products of this factory are described and illustrated by J.-D. Ludmann, in the exhibition catalogue, *Les oeuvres de Hannong: Faïences de Strasbourg et Haguenau*, Palais-Rohan, Strasbourg, January–March 1975. A summary bibliography of Strasbourg faïences is given in this catalogue. For a more recent brief account see J. Bastian, *La faïence et la porcelaine de Strasbourg*, Rennes, 1982.
4. Quoted by J. Terrasson, *Les Hannong et leurs manufactures – Strasbourg, Frankenthal*, Paris, 1971, p. 20.
5. A brief biography of Wackenfeld is given by Haug, 1922, p. 42.
6. According to Ludmann, *op. cit.*, p. 7.
7. A *pot-pourri* and cover from the Musée des arts décoratifs, Strasbourg, rather similar in shape to Vincennes examples and painted with flowers, may well have been produced during this period, illus. Frégnac, 1964, p. 253. A dish moulded in relief with flowers and painted with bouquets from the same collection, illus. p. 252, shows strong Meissen influence. A sugar bowl, cover and stand impressed *PH* twice and stamped *PH* in a label on the bowl in the Metz Museum, inv. 1063, is painted with flowers.
8. H. Haug, 'Les Grandes Statuettes de Strasbourg', *Cahiers*, 9, 1958, pp. 35–40.
9. Frégnac, *op. cit.*, p. 252, Musée des arts décoratifs, Strasbourg.
10. Tin-glazed earthenware figures of hunters attributed to Lanz were sold at Sotheby's, New York, John Dorrance, Jr. Collection, 20, 21 October 1989, Lots 188–91. Some from the Nicolier Collection are illustrated by S. de Plas, *Les faïences de Strasbourg et de l'Est de la France*, Paris, n.d., p. 29.
11. There is an example of *Time's Victory over Envy* in the Musée des arts décoratifs, Strasbourg.
12. Ludmann, 1975, p. 92, source not given.
13. Haug, 1922, p. 11.
14. Savill, 1988, Vol. III, p. 966 and f.n. 15, refers to this episode in her discussion of Boileau de Picardie's career.
15. Chavagnac and Grollier, 1906, p. 52.
16. See H. Haug, 'Strasbourg entre Chantilly et Meissen (1744 à 1749), *Cahiers*, 1, December 1955, pp. 24–38. A faïence sugar bowl, cover and stand from the Nicolier Collection painted in pink *camaïeu* with naturalistic flowers and with gilt decoration on the rims and gallery shows strong Meissen influence, illus. S. de Plas, *op. cit.*, p. 18.
17. Illus. Frégnac, 1964, p. 257, Musée des arts décoratifs, Strasbourg. This museum has the most extensive collection of Strasbourg porcelain known to the writer.
18. *Op. cit.*, p. 256.
19. *Ibid.*
20. Haug, 1922, p. 27, n. 1. In 1922 the book was preserved in the Bibliothèque régionale, Strasbourg.

210 **Cup and Saucer**, 1768–81

D. *of saucer:*	14.1 cm
H. *of cup:*	7 cm
Marks:	*H/C146* in underglaze-blue and incised *A14/C86* on saucer; *C28* in underglaze-blue overpainted in red-brown and incised *A13* on cup
Reg. No.	Franks 401

Hard-paste porcelain, painted in brown, green, orange, blue, black and purple with the Fable of the Wolf and the Lamb within an oval reserve outlined by two gilt lines on the cup and with a goat in a similar panel on the saucer, and with scattered flowers. Inside of cup painted in black with four stylised flowers. Gilt rims, gilt line near foot of saucer and handle partly gilt. Foot rim of saucer chipped. Gilding on rims rubbed.

Provenance: Bequeathed by Sir A.W. Franks, 1897

Literature: Franks, 1896, no. 401
Chaffers, 1926, Vol. II, p. 352, fig. 314

Comparable Examples: Strasbourg, Musée des arts décoratifs, coffee-pot and cover, illus. Frégnac, 1964, p. 258.

USA, Washington, D.C., Smithsonian Institution, National Museum of American History, cup and saucer, inv. 255 and b, *C28* in underglaze-blue on cup (Fable of the Wolf and the Lamb), *H* over *C86* on saucer; cup, inv. 483, *C28* in underglaze-blue overpainted in red (different Fables).

Switzerland, Geneva, Musée Ariana, two cups and saucers, teapot and sugar bowl each on three feet, coffee pot (or water jug), inv. AR 656, 657, 654, 655, 652.

Chavagnac and Grollier[1] mention a milk jug on three feet painted with a sheep from the Grollier Collection on which 'La marque en bleu au grand feu est peu facile à lire a cause d'une autre marque en brun foncé qui est placée dessus (*C541*)' (The underglaze-blue mark is difficult to read on account of another mark in dark brown painted over it (*C541*).) The significance of these complex internal factory marks is unknown.

The scene on the cup depicts the fable of the Wolf and the Lamb and is closely based on the engraving by C.D. Gallimart after J.B. Oudry (1686–1755) in the 1755 Paris edition of *Fables choisies, mises en vers par J. de La Fontaine*, Vol. I, Book I, Fable X (see fig. 210a).[2] The goat painted on the saucer may have been adapted from an illustration in the same work to Fable VI, *La Genisse, La Chèvre et la Brebis, en société avec le Lion.*[3]

Fable scenes were popular on Chelsea porcelain teawares of the Red Anchor period (1752–6) but the painting was far more skilfully executed.

1. Chavagnac and Grollier, 1906, p. 56.
2. BM Dept of Prints and Drawings, c. 161 d. 9 opp. 20 (1869-5-8-13).
3. The author is grateful to Frances Dunkels, formerly of the Department of Prints and Drawings, British Museum, for her help in identifying the sources of decoration.

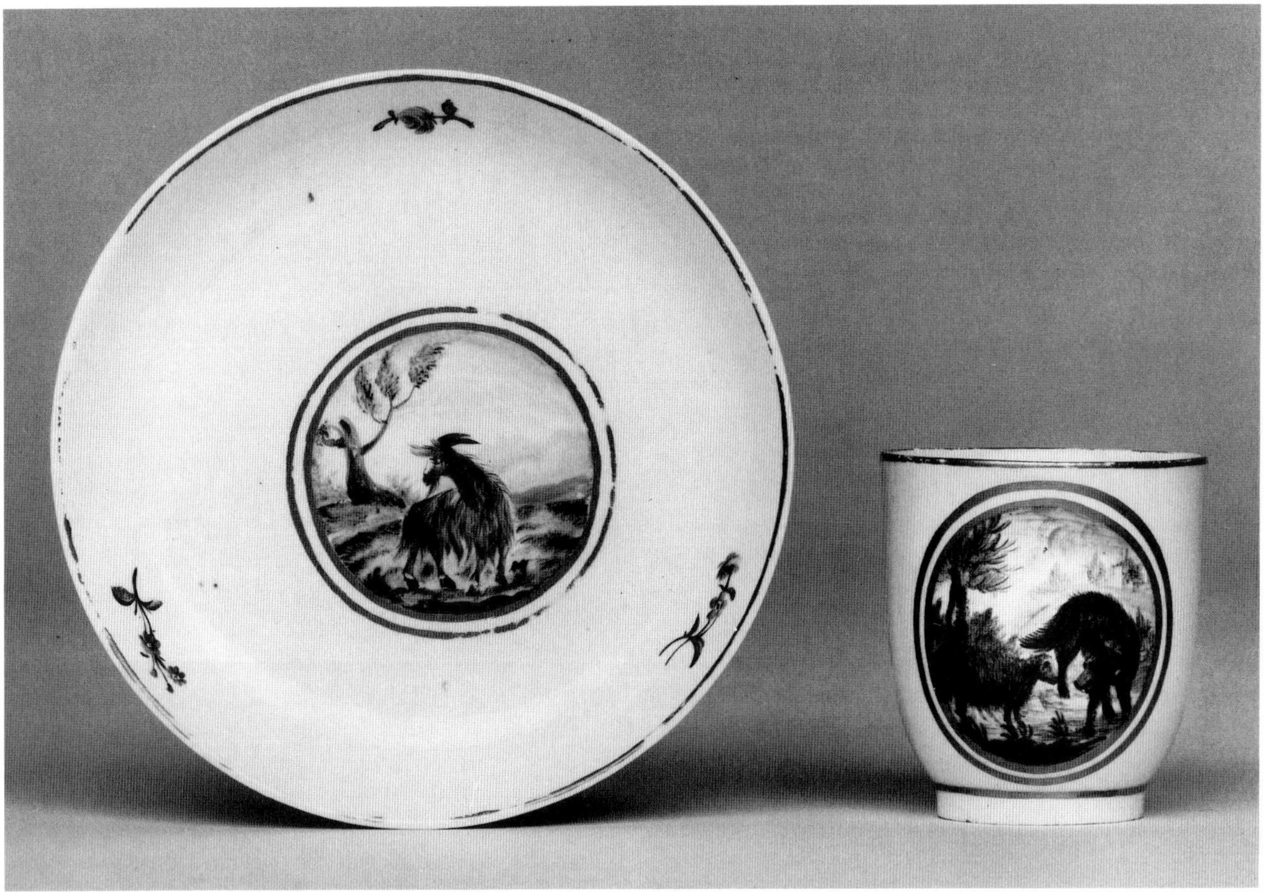

210

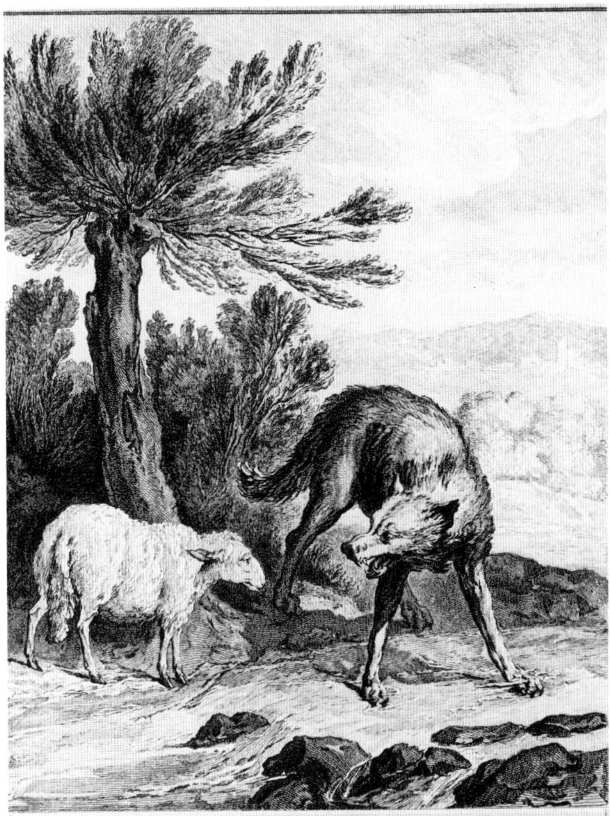

Fig 210a

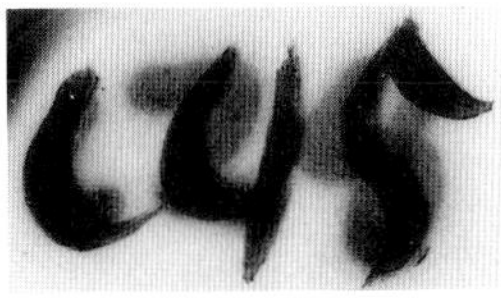

A13

210 *marks (cup)*

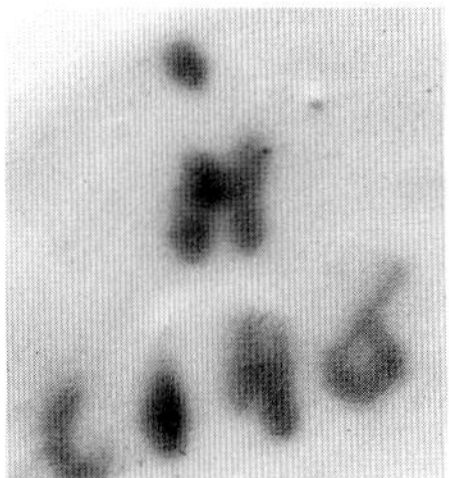

A 14
c 86

210 *marks (saucer)*

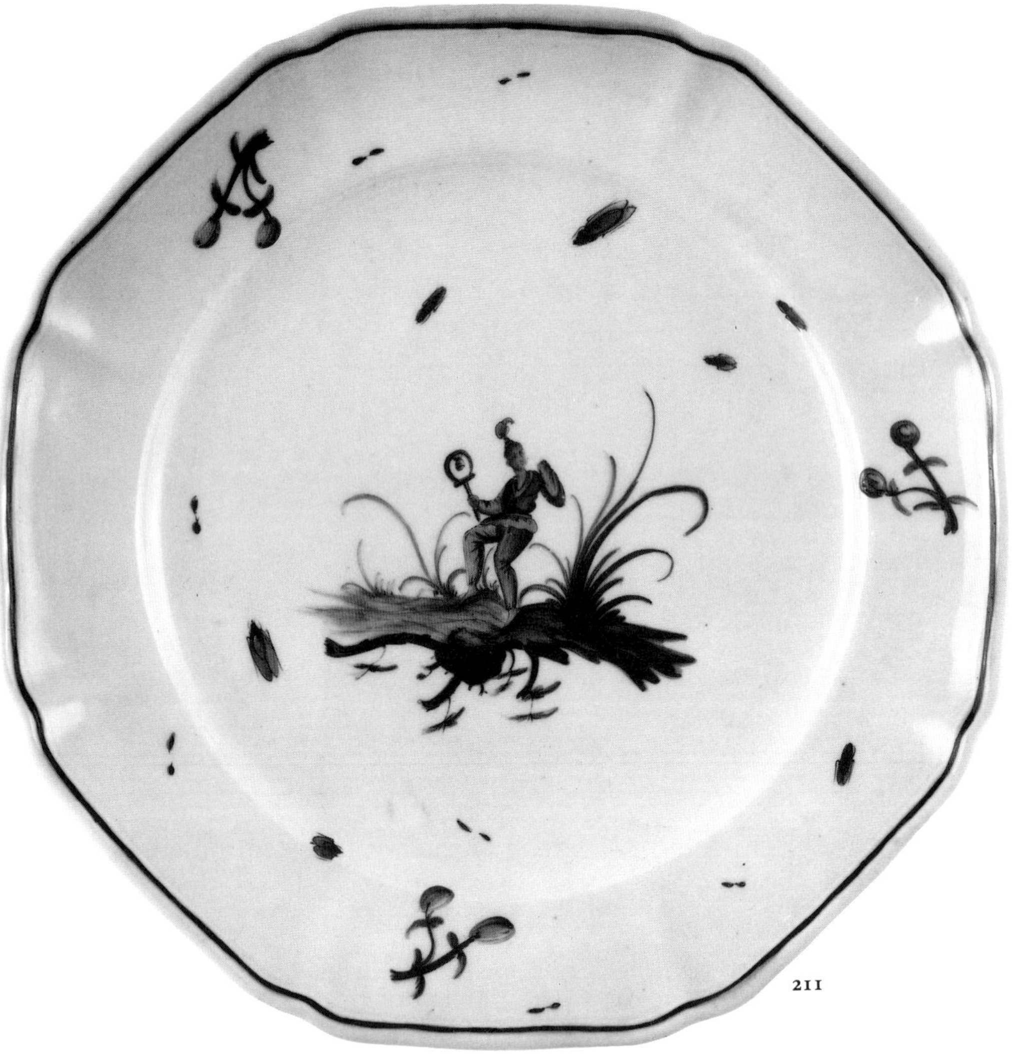

211

211 **Plate**, 1768–81

D. 23.9 cm
Marks: *H* / *VC46* in underglaze-blue; *VC 46* and *A 65 H* incised
Reg. No. Franks 400

Hard-paste porcelain of octagonal slightly lobed form. Decorated in green, pink, yellow, blue, brown and flesh-colour enamels with three stylised flowers on the rim and a dancing Chinese figure among grasses in the centre, and with insects. Purple line near rim. Extremely uneven lumpy glaze in one area on reverse of plate. Perfect.

Provenance: Bequeathed by Sir A.W. Franks, 1897

Literature: Franks, 1896, no. 400

Comparable Examples: Italy, Naples, Museo Duca di Martina, cup and saucer painted with oriental figures, illus. M.L. Casanova, *Le Porcellane Francesi nei Musei di Napoli*, Naples, 1974, pl. 190

USA, Seattle, Seattle Art Museum, inv. 76.139, D. 23.5 cm. Similar incised and painted marks in underglaze-blue, *VG 158* painted over in brown[1]

Chinoiserie decoration of this kind is also found on

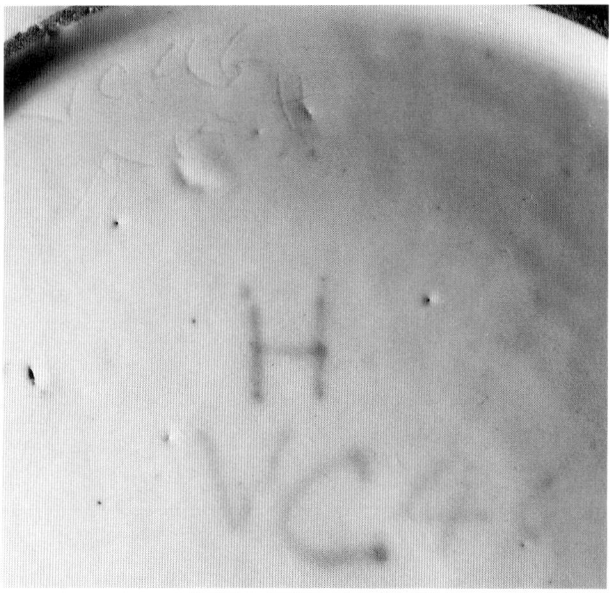

211 *marks*

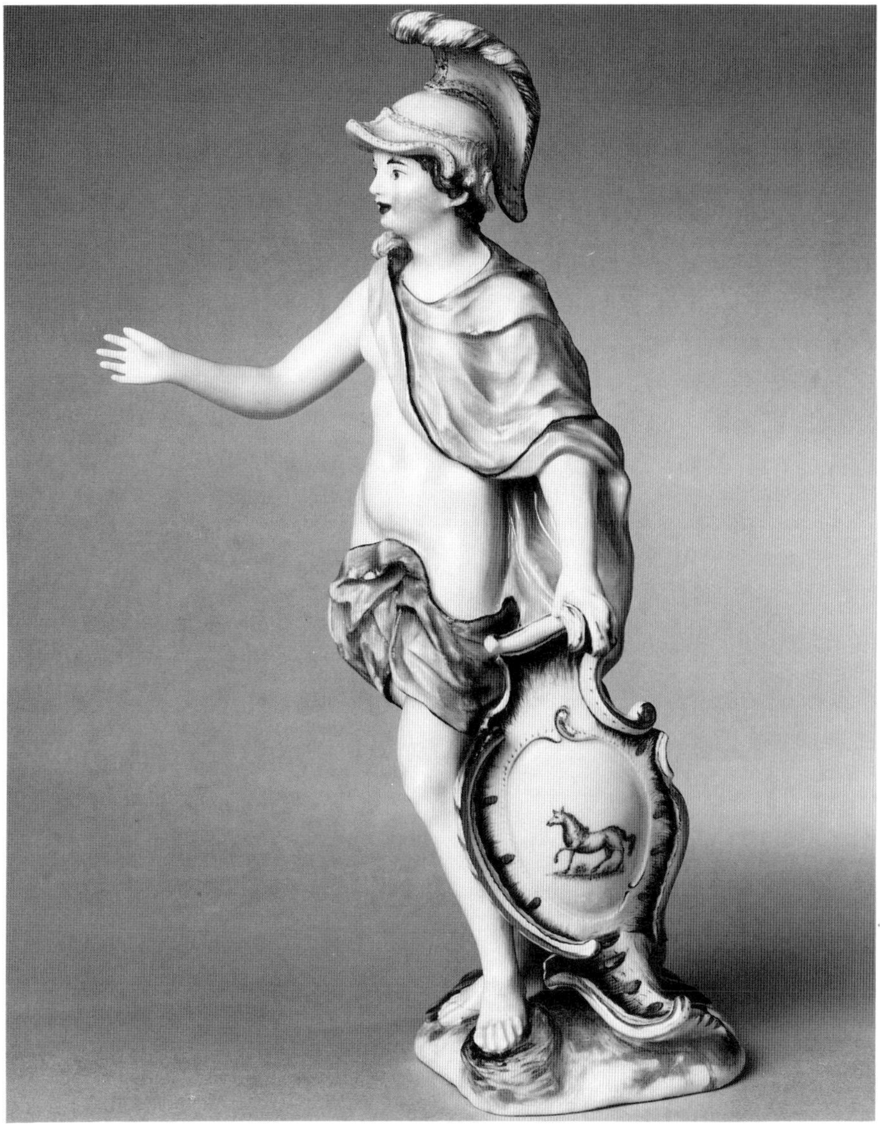

212

Strasbourg faïence. However, although the design sources have been identified for many of the tin-glazed wares, this is not the case for the cruder decoration found on the porcelain,which is of rather later date.[2]

The exact significance of the marks, which are almost certainly internal factory marks, is unknown.

A tureen and cover painted with Chinese figures is illustrated by Dauguet and Guillemé-Brulon.[3]

1. J. Emerson, *Selections of French Porcelain from the Eighteenth Century European Porcelain Collection of the Seattle Art Museum*, privately published by the French Porcelain Society, London, VI, 1990, p. 14.
2. See J. Bastian, 'Essai d'attribution des décors au Chinois dans l'Est de la France', in exh. cat. 'Le Décor "au Chinois" dans les manufactures de céramique de l'Est de la France 1765–1830', Musée de Saint-Dié, October 1981–January 1982, pp. 35–7.
3. C. Dauguet and D. Guillemé-Brulon, *La porcelaine française*, Paris, n.d., p. 49.

212 **Figure of Europe**, *c.*1752–4

See colour plate 35

H. 26.2 cm

Marks: none

Reg. No. 1940,10–2,1

Hard-paste porcelain, moulded. The partly-draped female figure, wearing a pale purple cloak lined with canary yellow, stands with her right arm raised and her left hand resting on a rococo shield on a flat mound base of roughly rectangular form. On her head she wears a grey helmet with an orange plume. Her hair is brown. At the back the cloak rests on a suit of armour painted grey with an orange fringe. On the elaborate shield, painted red-brown and with gilt embellishments on the scrolls, is a galloping horse facing left painted in grey-brown. The base is flat and unglazed. Right hand restored, chips to fringes on armour.

Provenance: Presented by W. King, Esq. (former Deputy Keeper in the British Museum), 1940

Literature: Savage, 1958, pl. 97d

Charles, 1964, fig. 37

A. Dawson, 'Europaïsche Keramik im British Museum', *Weltkunst*, 1 July 1985, p. 1881, fig. 8

Exhibited: 1985, 'Documentary Continental Ceramics from the British Museum', International Ceramics Fair and Seminar, London, June 1985, no. 45, cat. compiled by A. Dawson.

Comparable Examples: Strasbourg, Musée des arts décoratifs, inv. 7194, illus. F. Hofmann, *Frankenthaler Porzellan*, Munich, 1911, Vol. I, Tafel 4, 10, and H. Haug, *La Collection Céramique du Musée des Arts Décoratifs de Strasbourg*, Strasbourg, 1924, fig. 33

Germany, Munich, Residenzmuseum, inv. Res. Mü. R. 76, impressed *PCH* [?]

Germany, Mannheim, Jean Wurz Collection, sold Lepke, Berlin, 10–11 Dec 1924, Lot 105, Tafel 3, lion mark in blue, H. 26 cm
26 cm

The figure is part of a series of Four Parts of the World, attributed to Johann Wilhelm Lanz at Paul-Antoine Hannong's Strasbourg porcelain factory *c.*1752–4. A tin-glazed example of *America* is known in a private collection[1] and a figure of *Europe* is in the Kunstgewerbemuseum, Berlin.[2] Porcelain figures of *Europe*, *Africa* and *Asia* were sold from the Jean Wurz Collection in Berlin in 1924,[3] and an example of *Asia* is in the Musée des arts décoratifs, Strasbourg.[4] A porcelain figure of *America* impressed *PH* four times is in the Seattle Art Museum, USA.[5]

The iconography of the Four Parts of the World was already well established by the middle of the eighteenth century. Its development has been discussed by Petra Krutisch in an essay in the exhibition catalogue 'Europa–ein Erdteil unter anderen'.[6]

The earliest porcelain figure of *Europe* is the one modelled for the Meissen factory by Johann Freidrich Eberlein in 1746 or 1747.[7] A seated female figure of a queen holding an apple surmounted by a cross and sceptre in her left and right hands respectively, her flowered skirt draped over a cartographer's globe, leans on a dappled horse facing right. Europa, who was also represented as a warrior, is a possible confusion with Minerva.

Nothing is known of the career of J.W. Lanz, who was evidently a trained sculptor, apart from his work for Hannong both at Strasbourg and Frankenthal.[8]

1. See exh. *Les oeuvres de Hannong: faïences de Strasbourg et Haguenau*, Musée des arts décoratifs, Palais-Rohan, Strasbourg, 1975, p. 160.
2. Inv. 31, 57, exh. *Die Verführung der Europa*, Staatliche Museen Preussischer Kulturbesitz Kunstgewerbemuseum, Berlin, August–October 1988, p. 271, no. 115.
3. Sold Lepke, Berlin, 10–11 December 1924, Lot 104 (*Africa*) impressed *PH*, 6, H. 24 cm; Lot 106 (*Asia*), impressed *PH*, lion in blue, H. 24 cm. The author is indebted to Kate Foster for bringing these pieces to her attention. Figures of *Africa* and *Asia* were in the trade in Germany in 1996.
4. Illus. Dupont, 1987, p. 99, with *Europe*.
5. J. Emerson, *Selections of French Porcelain from the Eighteenth Century European Porcelain Collection of the Seattle Art Museum*, privately published, French Porcelain Society, London, VI, 1990, p. 14.
6. Petra Krutisch, 'Europa – ein Erdteil unter anderen', in exh. *Die Verführung der Europa*, Staatliche Museen Preussischer Kulturbesitz Kunstgewerbemuseum, Berlin, August–October 1988, pp. 166–80.
7. C. Albiker, *Die Meissner Porzellantiere im 18 Jahrhundert*, Berlin, 1935, no. 310, pl. LXXX.
8. A brief biography of Lanz, who married Marie-Madeleine Moser who bore him a daughter, Marie-Madeleine, baptised in the Catholic parish of Saint-Pierre-le-Vieux, Strasbourg, was published by H. Haug in *Les faïences et porcelaines de Strasbourg*, Strasbourg, 1922, p. 40. The author is indebted to the Director of the Archives Municipales de Strasbourg, M. J.-Y. Mariotte, for the information that Lanz's marriage was registered at the Catholic church of Saint-Pierre-le-Vieux on 26 May 1752. Lanz (called Laütz) is described as a native of Obergladbach in the diocese of Mayence, and was the son of Jean Guillaume Lanz, a tailor. His wife was from Molsheim. Pierre-Antoine Hannong was a witness to the marriage and godfather to the birth of their son Charles-François-Guillaume on 28 July 1754. An outline of Lanz's career, with figures and groups which have been attributed to him together with some of the older literature, not all superseded, is given in Thieme-Becker, *Allgemeine Lexikon der Bildende Künste*, Vol. XXII, Leipzig, 1928, pp. 362–3.

213 **Figure of a Bagpiper**, 1768–81

H. 19.4 cm
Marks: *H* incised
F104
A14
Reg. No. 1937,12–16,1

Hard-paste porcelain, glazed. The boy, who is supported at the back by a tree stump, stands on a square plinth modelled to resemble a rock. At his left on the base is a branch and four [?] boulders. The base is slightly concave and is reinforced with a semi-circular support; a small circular hole is pierced near one end of this support. Traces of pink show through the glaze on the base, tree stump, jacket, hands and elsewhere. Part of bagpipe chanter missing, hat chipped, both feet repaired. Cracked at back where boy's body rests on stump.

Provenance: Presented by M. Gilbert-Lévy, 1937

Literature: Unpublished

Comparable Examples: Whereabouts unknown, enamelled, with *rocaille* socle, incised *JH* and *F104*, illus. J. Terrasson, *Les Hannong et leurs Manufactures, Strasbourg, Frankenthal*, Paris, 1971, p. 89

This model has been attributed (without any evidence) to J.W. Lanz.[1] It seems likely to have been the work of a trained sculptor, but does not share the rather stiff character of other pieces ascribed to Lanz. A biscuit figure of a bagpiper modelled by P.-L. Cyfflé for Lunéville[2] may be related to it; a similar version was manufactured at Niderviller in tin-glazed earthenware and in biscuit porcelain.[3] An engraving by T. Dumont le Rom[ain] dated 1739, in which the piper

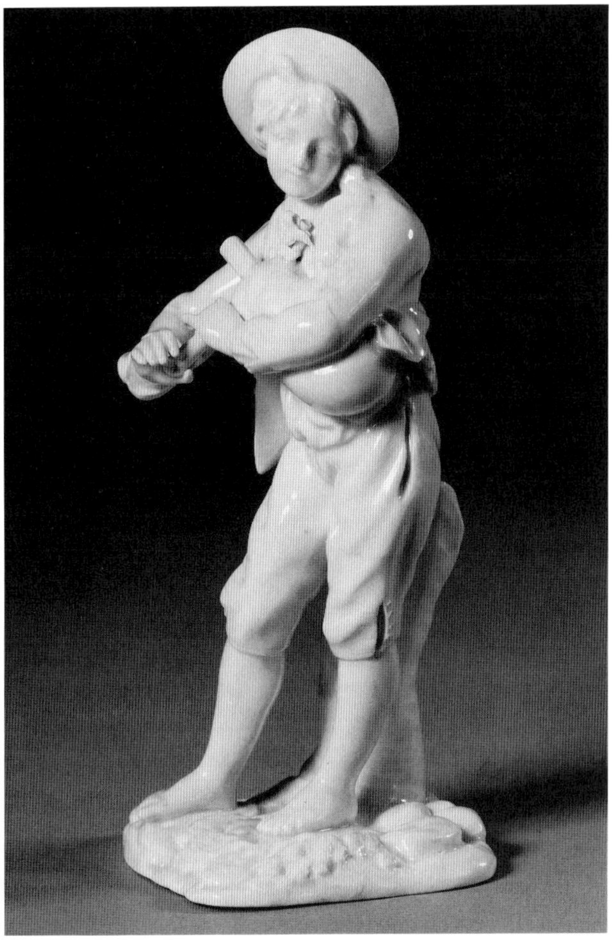

213

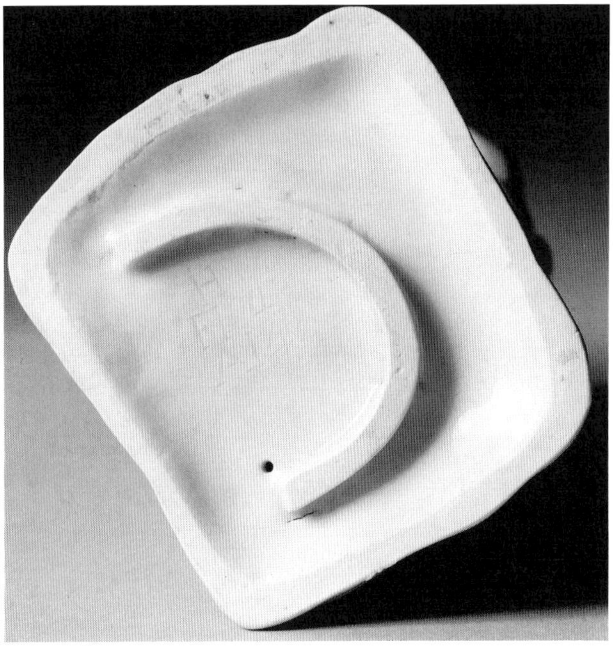

213 *marks*

is working the marionettes with his foot, is a possible source for the model.

It was a popular subject and a different *Joueur de musette* was modelled by Blondeau after François Boucher for production at Vincennes in both biscuit and enamelled versions from 1752.[4]

1. By J. Terrasson, see Comparable Examples.
2. See A.G. Pauwels and J. van Hoonacker, *Kerameik*, cat. of Museum voor Oudheidkunde en Sierkunst, Kortrijk, Belgium, 1981, no. 624.
3. Victoria and Albert Museum, London, C. 261–1951; Nancy, Musée historique lorrain, inv. K 528; although impressed *TDL*, this group both looks and feels like hard-paste. It is also incised [?] *pa* ... or possibly *ja* ... for Jacques (Saly), see cat. 203.
4. Exh. *Vincennes*, 1977–8, no. 492.

Marseilles, Joseph Gaspard Robert's factory[1]

Joseph Gaspard Robert (d.1799, aged 77)[2] was the son of Jean-Baptiste and Anne-Françoise Goujon. A native of Marseilles, he was involved in making tin-glazed earthenware with his step-father André Estieu.[3] A saucer inscribed *Robert et Estieu à Marseille*[4] survives to document this phase of his career. He seems to have spent some time away from Marseilles, (whether before or after working with Estieu is not clear) and may have learned to make porcelain elsewhere. In 1749 he apparently returned to Marseilles with the idea of establishing his own concern 'mais en ayant été detourné par les difficultés qu'on luy fit craindre alors de la part des entrepreneurs privilegiés de Vincennes, il abandonna ce projet pour former celuy d'une manufacture de fayance . . .'.[5] In 1753 he purchased a former tileworks from Estieu for the sum of 6,500 *livres*.[6] Ten years later on 23 June 1759 he petitioned the *échevins* and *députés* of the Marseilles *Chambre de Commerce*[7] to act on his behalf and request permission from the *contrôleur général* to establish a porcelain factory. In his petition he mentioned that his faïence works had suffered from the economic situation resulting from war. He argued that he would be able to export from Marseilles to the Levant, Italy and Spain, so stimulating the local and national economy, and that the Vincennes/Sèvres factory had enjoyed exclusive privileges long enough and was clearly unable to fulfil domestic demand. His request was to 'fabriquer . . . de la porcelaine de toute qualité peinte et dorée, avec pouvoir de la vendre et débiter dans la ville et son terroir, tant pour l'étranger, que pour en permettre l'entrée dans le royaume . . .'. The Ministre de la Marine, Berryer, wrote to the Marseilles *Chambre de Commerce* from Versailles on 16 July 1759[8] acknowledging their letter of 2 July to the *contrôleur général* and expressing his support for the project. However, he wrote, it was up to the latter to make a decision based on how far the privilege granted to the royal factory was to be extended. Evidently Robert was given the necessary permission to make porcelain, although no document is known authorising the factory. There is no clear evidence to show that Robert began manufacturing porcelain at this point, and the registration of the factory mark in early 1769 suggests that he did not go into production until the mid-1760s.

Although a total of forty new apprentices were taken on in the years between 1754 and 1768,[9] it seems that they were trained in faïence-making rather than porcelain manufacture. More apprentices were employed in the years between 1768 and 1778, one being Jean-Antoine Constantin (1756–1844) who stayed there six years from 26 November 1767. New buildings and land were acquired on 14 April 1762.[10] Five years later Robert was still expanding, purchasing a wall in order to demolish it and add windows to his factory, improving the illumination of the building. In 1771 and 1772 he spent a surprisingly large total of 15,325 *livres* on further acquisitions of land and property. It is probable that the funds may have been provided by his wife Marguerite de Fléchy (or Defléchis), who in May 1768 was given full powers to administer his business affairs in his absence.[11]

On 1 July 1773 Robert signed a contract with Jacob Dortu[12] 'fabriquant de porcelaine de Berlin en Prusse, résidant en cette ville', establishing a partnership for an initial period of twelve years, with the option of extending it at the end of that time. Dortu was to 'composer les pâtes de porcelaine, les couleurs et les dorures, de diriger luy-même toutes les parties de cette fabrication, d'y employer tous ses secrets et ses talents, le tout sous les yeux du dit sieur Robert'. Dortu, therefore, brought technical expertise to the factory. Robert was to furnish all the raw materials and the tools, Dortu contributing 5 per cent of his half share in the company towards their cost. Dortu was to pay half the rent of the premises, and was to receive a half share of the profits. He was forbidden to communicate the secrets of porcelain-making to anyone else, and to work on his own account during the partnership. This agreement apparently lasted no longer than three years, as Dortu went to Marieberg in 1777 and Nyon in 1781.

In July 1777 Robert was honoured by a visit from Monsieur, the King's brother, also known as the comte de Provence.[13] Robert in his own account of the visit,[14] wrote that Monsieur was surprised by the size and design of the large vase displayed in the 'salon attenant le magazin de porcelaine'. The phrase implies that pieces were sold direct from the factory, as seems to have been the normal practice. He also saw a table service consisting of plates and terrines which were larger than usual and large oval dishes for roasts of uncommon size. The service, which was painted and gilt, was to be sent to England. Porcelain flowers were in production, and another service, decorated in blue and white, had been made for M. Borrelly Telmon. The visitors commented on the reasonable prices Robert charged for his porcelain.

Robert made the point to his eminent visitor that he wanted to make porcelain cheap enough to compete with foreign products, but had difficulty in obtaining local raw materials. He hoped that the government would be able to assist by providing funds for research, presumably into the location of clay to make hard-paste porcelain. Kaolin from Alençon was apparently used.[15]

Monsieur visited the porcelain workshops, rather deserted on account of public celebrations, where he watched plates being thrown and commented on the speed of the process. He then went to the glazing shop where the members of his retinue asked about the composition, a secret Robert told only to the prince. He was touched by the sight of the thirty or so boxes of porcelain and faïence which had been ordered and paid for by Monseigneur Padosky, Primate of Poland, before his death.[16] When Robert offered to show Monsieur the painting shop and kilns, he asked whether these were the same as at Paris, and was told that they were. It is likely that he was familiar with the decorating process since he was the protector of a factory at Clignancourt at the very moment of his visit to Provence.

According to Béranger,[17] in 1786 there were ten faïence and two porcelain factories in Marseilles. Like Veuve Perrin and Honoré Savy, Robert was located 'hors la porte de Rome'. The Revolution reduced the number of enterprises, but Robert was still operating in 1793, according to the *Guide Marseillais*.[18] Robert probably closed down the concern voluntarily in 1794. His will shows that he left 50,000 *livres*, which included the factory buildings and a further nine properties.[19]

On the evidence of surviving pieces, the production of the Marseilles factory seems to have been confined to tablewares, especially teawares, and some toilet-articles.[20] The forms do not appear to owe a debt to any other factory in particular, and are not invariably well conceived. A wide range of faïence pieces was made by Robert[21] and it is probable that a detailed study of the tin-glazed wares would shed light on the source of the porcelain shapes and decoration. The latter consists of landscape and figure scenes painted in colours and gilt.[22] Flower painting in at least one quality has been noted.[23] In some cases the flowers are naturalistic and may well be based on engravings, perhaps the same ones as were used by the faïence painters.[24] A toilet pot and cover painted with arms is recorded.[25] Gilding, which was sometimes of a fairly elaborate design, was apparently used freely.[26] Vases and figures are not known to this writer.

A terracotta bust of Gaspard dated *7bre 1790* is in the Sèvres Museum.[27]

1. This account is based on that of Abbé G. Arnaud d'Agnel, *La faïence et la porcelaine de Marseille*, Paris, 1911, which has not been superseded, and quotes documents which the author has been unable to consult herself.
2. On 3 Floréal, l'an VII, Archives départementales, Registre des actes de décès des citoyens de la Municipalité du Midi, Canton de Marseille 201 E 2.773,f. 128. The author is grateful to Danielle Maternati-Baldouy for this reference and for help in supplying details about Robert and his career.
3. Estieu married Jean-Baptiste Robert's widow before 1734 and had been the owner of a faïence factory since 1727.
4. Musée national de Céramique, Sèvres, inv. 7002.
5. See note 7.
6. Archives départementales, Fonds Malauzat, 381 E 364, f. 773.
7. Archives de la Chambre de Commerce de Marseille, HH art. 76, *pièce papier*, quoted d'Agnel, *op. cit.*, pp. 499–500. This

petition gives the only known details of his early life, but it is difficult at this point to know whether they are entirely correct.

8. Archives de la Chambre de Commerce de Marseille, *série* AA, 75, quoted d'Agnel, *op. cit.*, p. 501.
9. Archives départementales, legal section, Fonds Malauzat 381 E, Fonds Laugier 364 E, the lawyers being Maîtres Caillol and Jourdan. The author is grateful to Danielle Maternati-Baldouy for this reference.
10. D'Agnel, *op. cit.*, p. 151, f.n. 3, Etude de Me Cartier, minutes de Me Bègue, *notaire à Marseille*, acte du 14 Avril 1762, f. 232. Robert spent 6,600 *livres*.
11. D'Agnel, *op. cit.*, pp. 151–2, and f.n. 5.
12. *Ibid.*, pp. 497–9.
13. An extract from the *Journal des fêtes données au comte de Provence* is quoted by J.C. Davillier, *Histoire des faïences et porcelaines de Moustiers, Marseille et autres fabriques méridionales*, Paris, 1863, pp. 112–3. It differs little in essence from the longer account signed by Robert himself published by d'Agnel, except that it states that the visit was not arranged in advance.
14. D'Agnel, *op. cit.*, pp. 495–7.
15. Chavagnac and Grollier, 1906, p. 545.
16. The contents of the boxes, of which there were in fact 34, are described in detail in d'Agnel, *op. cit.*, pp. 408–9 and f.n. 1; unfortunately the account, although it shows the range of pieces used in a table service, does not specify which services were faïence and which porcelain.
17. Laurent Pierre Bérenger, *Les Soirées Provençales*, Paris, 1786, Vol. III, p. 203, quoted J.-C. Davillier, *op. cit.*, p. 104, wrongly stating that there were ten 'fabriques de faïence et de porcelaine'. Bérenger, Vol. I, p. 96, classed the faïence and porcelain factories as the third of the principal industries in Marseille, but did not clearly state that the list represented any order of importance. See also *La Faïence de Marseille au XVIIIe siècle, la Manufacture de la Veuve Perrin*, exh. cat., Musées de Marseille, 1990.
18. J.-J. Mazet, *Guide Marseillais*, 1793, p. 111, quoted d'Agnel, p. 153.
19. Archives départementales, Registre des déclarations de succession ADXII Q.9.7/25, 11 Floréal, l'an VII.
20. A large dish illustrated by d'Agnel, *op. cit.*, pl. LVII,4 is probably a basin for a water jug for use in the boudoir. For illustrations of further pieces, see M. Desuelle, 'Robert ou le raffinement des porcelaines de Marseille', *l'Estampille*, 15 June 1988, pp. 44–53.
21. D'Agnel, pl. XXXVI–XLV.
22. A milk jug and cover painted with figures is illus. by Ballu, n.d., pl. 33B.
23. See note 21.
24. *Ibid.*
25. D'Agnel, *op. cit.*, pl. LVII,2
26. *Ibid.*, pl. LVII, 6
27. Illus. d'Agnel, *op. cit.*, unnumbered page before Preface.

214 Two-handled Cup (*écuelle*), *c.*1775–80

D. *without handles*:	8.2 cm
H.	7.1 cm
Marks:	*DR* in monogram painted in underglaze-blue
Reg. No.	Franks 409

Hard-paste porcelain, straight-sided cup on low foot, glazed except around the inside of the rim, showing that it once had a cover, handles of elaborate scroll shape. The decoration consists of pendent flower sprays in pink, iron-red, blue, green and yellow intertwined with a yellow ribbon with an iron-red stripe looped around another of bands of yellow, pale pink and dark pink; rim, foot gilt, handles partly gilt.

Provenance: Bequeathed by Sir A.W. Franks, 1897

Literature: Franks, 1896, no. 409

Comparable Examples: Sèvres, Musée national de Céramique, cup and saucer, painted with flowers and ribbons, inv. 4737,[1] acquired 1854
Switzerland, Geneva, Musée Ariana, chocolate pot and cover painted with scattered flowers and a ribbon, inv. AR 1430, Revilliod coll. and sugar bowl on stand with cover, inv. AR 11472

This cup was acquired without its matching cover and stand. It was intended to hold broth. The decorative scheme and the scroll-form handles suggest a date in the late 1770s. The glaze is characteristically uneven. Chavagnac and Grollier believed that it did not cover the pieces properly because it was applied with a brush, but it is much more likely that the glaze composition was unsuited to the porcelain body.

1. Chavagnac and Grollier, 1906, p. 545.

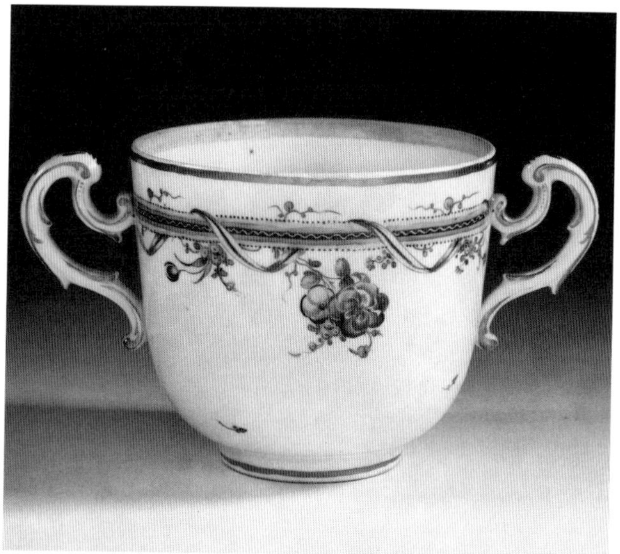

214

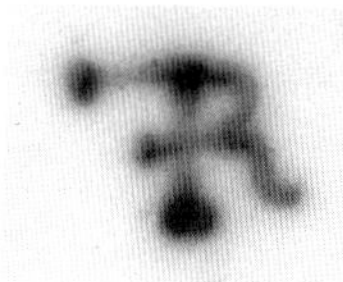

214 *mark*

Niderviller[1]

The porcelain factory at Niderviller in the Sarrebourg region (Moselle) was established by Jean-Louis Beyerlé (1709–86),[2] *conseiller du Roi*, director and treasurer of the Strasbourg Mint in 1749. It grew up alongside the faïence-making concern which had been in existence there since 1735. Workers from Saxony, Frankenthal and Vienna were attracted to Niderviller, and initially kaolin from Passau, Bavaria, was used to make hard-paste porcelain.

In early 1768 Beyerlé ran foul of the decree of 1766 prohibiting the manufacture of anything except ordinary domestic porcelain, undecorated, decorated in blue and white or in a single colour, except by the royal factory. Failing to obtain protection for his factory through an appeal to Bertin, the Controller of Finance, and fearing competition from other enterprises in the region, Beyerlé sold up in December 1770 to Adam-Philippe, comte de Custine (1740–93).[3] François-Antoine Anstett (1732–83) continued to run the factory from day to day, as he had done since 1759, although several painters and modellers left in 1771. They were replaced by others from Ludwigsburg, Höchst and Pfalz-Zweibrücken.

In August 1778 Custine went into partnership with François-Henry Lanfrey (1749–1827), originally of Strasbourg, who contributed extra capital amounting to a maximum of 400,000 *livres* towards building works, the construction of a new kiln, the acquisition of a kaolin source at Saint-Yrieix, near Limoges, and the transfer of the mill for the preparation of raw materials from Niderviller to Schneckenbusch.

Lanfrey, who had no previous experience, stayed at the factory for fifty years. After the departure of Anstett in 1778, Joseph Seeger, a painter, took the title of 'factory chemist'. The sculptor Charles Gabriel Sauvage known as Lemire (1741–1827) was head of the modelling shop and artistic director. Another painter, Pierre Dapremont, took the title of 'commis', or salesman. Lemire had worked for Cyfflé at Lunéville (see p. 256) and was instrumental in obtaining the moulds and other equipment from that factory.

The factory expanded in the early 1780s, and a school of design and modelling was established by Lemire, leading to increased emphasis on the production of figures, especially of biscuit porcelain. Despite the constant loss of workers to the Paris factories from 1784 onwards, the Niderviller concern employed between 150 and 200 workers. However, by the time of the execution of Custine's son in January 1794, only twelve remained.

Throughout the Revolutionary period Lanfrey experienced grave difficulties in continuing production, but kept the factory going even after the execution of Count Custine himself in August 1793. After 1798 conditions began to improve. The factory was sold to Lanfrey on 25 Germinal l'an x (14 April 1802) for the 'profit of the nation and the debtors of the General'. He also purchased the mills and the quarry for 50,100 francs. An inventory drawn up in l'an iv (September 1795–September 1796) shows that there were two porcelain kilns measuring 153 by 36 feet and valued at 7,000 francs. Although production continued in the early nineteenth century, and Lanfrey brought his two sons into the business, the number of workers declined from ninety-seven in 1802 to forty-four in 1826. After François Lanfrey's death in July 1827, his heirs sold the factory.

The later history of the Niderviller factory under Louis-Guillaume Dryander (1792–1865) does not concern us here, especially since the porcelain kilns were demolished around 1830. Reproductions of

Niderviller figures using the old moulds were made in 1886 for the Munich Exhibition and in 1908–9 for the Metz Museum.

Although renowned for its figures, which were made in both earthenware and porcelain, the factory produced a considerable quantity of tableware, usually painted with flowers. Cornflowers painted in overglaze-blue and green on a white ground[4] or coloured flower sprays[5] are found on coffee and tea services and on dinner services which might contain as many as eighty or more pieces. Landscape scenes, often painted in one colour and probably inspired by those found on German porcelain, and *trompe l'oeil* of pieces of painted paper fixed to wood,[6] are also characteristic of Niderviller. Some carefully-executed scenes of birds are known on teawares.[7] Elaborate garnitures of vases with painstakingly-modelled biscuit floral swags and rudimentary handles in the form of female heads, the central element formed as a pendulum clock,[8] show that the factory produced high-quality ornamental pieces.

A considerable number of figures and groups from the factory survive.[9] They fall into the following categories: gallant and peasant subjects, musicians and 'Cries of Paris', children and allegorical subjects,[10] as well as portraits,[11] saints and other miscellaneous types. Some, such as the enamelled *Virgin and Child* attributed to Lemire, presented in September 1784 to the church of Saint-Croix in Niderviller and now in the Musée national de Céramique, Sèvres,[12] are of considerable size. Others, such as a group of the *Rape of Helen* consisting of four figures on a boat at sea,[13] are of some complexity. The range of sculptural pieces produced is perhaps broader than at any other concern on French soil, with the exception of the royal factory.

Little is known about the prices charged by the factory during the eighteenth century, although a *Tarif* dating from the early part of the nineteenth century[14] shows that some biscuit figures, such as a kneeling Venus at 400 francs, were expensive.

Several different factory marks were used, none of which seems to have been formally registered with the authorities. Under Beyerlé's directorship, these marks were the monogram *JLB* or *BN*, for Beyerlé, Niderviller, painted in manganese, and occasionally *HI* incised. Later marks include *CN* for Custine, *Nider V*, *F L NIDERVILLE* (for François Lanfrey), the monogram *FLC*, *LEMIRE PERE/NIDERVILLER*, and interlaced *CC*, often below a crown, the most common mark.

An extensive list of workers at Niderviller published in 1984 includes both faïence and porcelain makers between 1735 and 1793.[15] Many, like François-Antoine Anstett (1732–83), painter and chemist between 1751 and 1759 and factory director from 1759 to 1778, were of Strasbourg origin. In 1759[16] Anstett's salary was 500 *livres* per annum. The Anstett clan, of whom no fewer than thirteen were associated with the Niderviller factory, included the director's brother François-Michel (1740–before 1811), a painter who had been apprenticed to Paul Hannong between about 1755 and 1759 and whilst with him had signed a plaque painted in the style of Berchem *Anstet Michael 1757 16 August*.[17] In 1759, now at Niderviller, he earned 24 *sols* a day as a *garçon-peintre*. He maintained his connections with Strasbourg, becoming a *bourgeois* of the town and a member of the *Tribu de l'Echasse* in 1771. Another painter, Joseph Seeger (*c*.1730–1800), who was at the factory between 1759 and 1770, originated in Vienna. He too enrolled his children in the Niderviller factory's workforce. Philippe Arnold (*c*.1740–*c*.1785) was probably born in Strasbourg, was apprenticed at Frankenthal in the Rhine-Palatinate, and became the factory's leading modeller before his departure for Haguenau in 1780. In 1759 Arnold earned 20 *sols* a day as a *garçon-sculpteur*. The sculptor Jean Stephan (dates unknown, originally from Stuttgart) is recorded at Niderviller between 1768 and 1770.[18] The painter Louis-Victor Gerverot (1747–1829), who was born in Lunéville, apprenticed at Sèvres 'chez son cousin Marmet', worked at Niderviller *c*.1765–6, was in London in 1786,[19] and moved on to other German concerns later. Another famous inhabitant of Lunéville, Charles-Gabriel Sauvage, called Lemire (1741–1827), arrived at Niderviller in 1781 and became the factory's chief modeller. Frédéric-Adolphe Thiebauld, originally of Saxony, a *garçon-peintre* earning 24 *sols* a day in 1759, was married in Sceaux, where he was presumably working, in 1767.[20]

1. This account is based on exh. Sarrebourg, 1986 (which commemorated 250 years of the Niderviller factory) and on C. Soudée-Lacombe, 'Faïenciers et porcelainiers de Niderviller au XVIIIe siècle', *Le Pays Lorrain*, 65e année-1984, pp. 1–76. Research is presently (1990) under way on tablewares and vases made at Niderviller.
2. For a portrait of Beyerlé by Lardouin de Bertainville, 1747, in the Bibliothèque nationale et universitaire de Strasbourg, see Soudée-Lacombe, 1984, p. 6; another, dating from after 1770, by J.J. Sorg showing him in a straw hat, in a private collection, is on p. 7.
3. A portrait of Custine *député de l'Assemblée Constituante et*

Générale de l'Armée du Rhin 1792 l'An 1er de la Rép. Franc. by De la Place, engraved by Coqueret is illustrated by Soudée-Lacombe, 1984, p. 10. For interesting details of his role during the Revolution, and documents listing the charges made against him after his failure to win the battle of Mayence, together with information about his properties, etc., see A. Schrub *et al.*, *Chroniques de la Révolution au pays de Sarrebourg, Sarrebourg, 1989, Vol.* 1, *passim*. This publication also includes information about Custine's son and grandson. Custine's early military career included a period spent in America in the 1780s. In July 1782 he presented General Washington with a porcelain tea service from the factory, decorated with the General's arms and monogram under a crown of laurels. Some pieces survive from this service, see S.G. Detweiler, 'French Porcelain on Federal Tables', *American Ceramic Circle Bulletin/Number 3*, New York, 1982, pp. 87–110, figs. 1–3, and S.G. Detweiler, *George Washington's Chinaware*, New York, 1982, figs. 48–56.

4. For a part coffee and tea service of the Custine period painted with cornflowers consisting of twenty-three items, see Christie's, Amsterdam, 15 November 1989, Lot 101. A similarly decorated part dinner service of 82 items was sold at the same sale, Lot 102. For another part dinner service of 131 pieces, some of which are illus., see Christie's, Amsterdam, 6 June 1990, Lot 322, a 'miniature *tête-à-tête*' Lot 322, and a mixed Niderviller, Amstel and Loosdrecht service, Lot 325.
5. A part dinner service of 90 pieces, including 40 dinner plates, described as 'pattern no. 356', was sold at Christie's, 6 October 1980, Lot 7. A tureen on three feet, cover and stand with two bull-mask handles with pendent rings, decorated with coloured bouquets, was sold at Christie's, 3 December 1984, Lot 54.
6. Dupont, 1987, p. 103, fig. 2; a service painted with coloured landscape scenes in reserve was sold at Christie's, Amsterdam, 6 November 1990, Lot 179.
7. Metz Museum, *tasse litron et soucoupe*, inv. 1112 and jug and cover on three feet, inv. 1111.
8. Musée Nissim de Camondo, Paris, Union Centrale des arts décoratifs, *Guide*, 1973, no. 100, H. of clock vase 36 cm; another *pendule* in the Musée historique lorrain, Nancy, inv. 52.1.1, is illus. in exh. Nancy and Atlanta, 1990, no. 89; a further example was sold by Ader, Picard, Tajan, Paris, 8 November 1990, Lot 669 (Le Tallec Collection).
9. A selection of figures is illustrated by J. Nicolier, 'Les Figurines de Niderviller', *Connaissance des Arts*, no. 71, January 1958, pp. 54–9.
10. An allegorical biscuit group on a blue painted pedestal of *Emile's Progress Watched* by *J.-J. Rousseau* is in the Musée Ariana, Geneva, inv. AR 1443, exh. 'La Famille Constant à Genève', 1968.
11. One of the most impressive, identified as perhaps the marquise de Dreux-Brézé (Custine's daughter), or the comtesse de Sabran (his daughter-in-law), signed *H.S. 1791 Nieder* from the Smith Remington Collection is illus. by Soudée-Lacombe, *op. cit.*, p. 40.
12. Inv. 10 357, H. 65 cm, illus. in colour exh. Sarrebourg, 1986, p. 60.
13. Illus. Nicolier, *op. cit*, p. 54 (Bernheim Collection); exh. Sarrebourg, 1986, p. 81 (private collection).
14. See A. Tainturier, *Recherches sur les anciennes manufactures de porcelaine et de faïence (Alsace et Lorraine)*, Strasbourg, 1868, pp. 90–5.
15. Soudée-Lacombe, 1984, pp. 55–76; a list of the personnel from 1759–70 is given pp. 37–9.
16. A list of 'faïence makers exempt from tax' dated 2 November 1759 first published by A. Jacquemart, *Les Merveilles de la Céramique*, Paris, 1869, giving valuable details about wages, is reproduced by Soudée-Lacombe, *op. cit.*, p. 34.
17. Illus. H. Haug, 'Nouvelles recherches sur la céramique alsacienne du XVIIIe siècle', *Archives alsaciennes d'histoire de l'art*, 1925, opp. p. 186.
18. See exh. Sarrebourg, 1986, p. 26. Gaye Blake Roberts refers in 'Wirksworth – the Elusive Manufactory', *Derby Porcelain International Society Journal*, 2, 1991, pp. 67–9, to the marriage of John Stephan to Catherine Yates on 3 August 1773 in St Alkmund's Church, Derby. Their son, John Charles, was baptised on 19 November 1774 and their daughter, Frances Stephan, baptised on 24 October 1773, was buried on 21 April 1776. John Stephan was the son of Pierre Stephan.
19. A beaker bearing his signature with the Antique Porcelain Company is illustrated by B. Hillier, *Master Potters of the Industrial Revolution, The Turners of Lane End*, London, 1965, frontispiece, fig. 34b. A detailed biography of Gerverot is given in Chapter 6. See also S. Ducret, 'Das Schicksal des grossen Keramikers Louis Victor Gerverot', *Keramos*, April 1965, pp. 29–39; M. Weinert, *Kasseler Porzellan*, Kassel, 1980, p. 106.
20. It has been suggested (exh. Sarrebourg, 1986, p. 36) that he might have originated in Meissen, but his name does not appear in the factory records of painters according to R. Rückert, *Biographische Daten der Meissener Manufakturisten des 18. Jahrhunderts*, Munich, 1990.

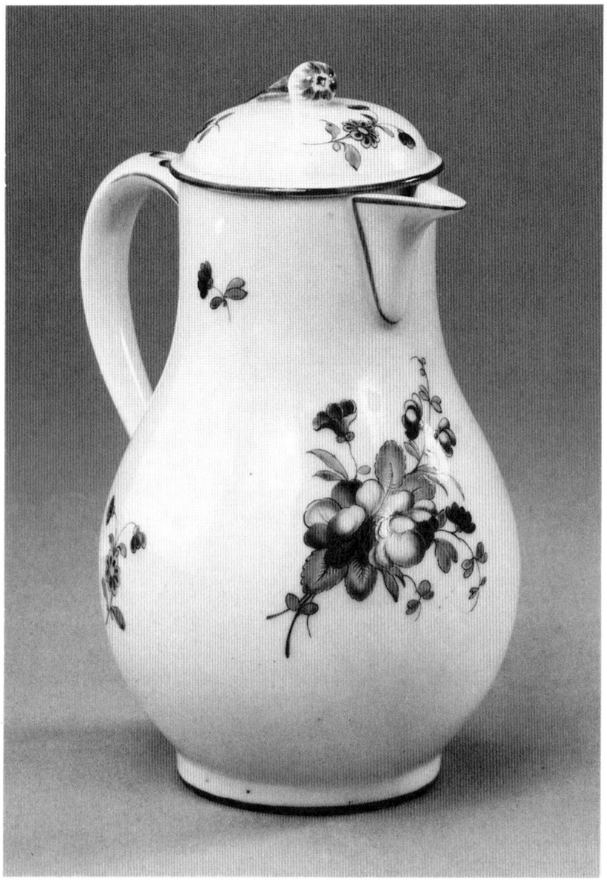

215

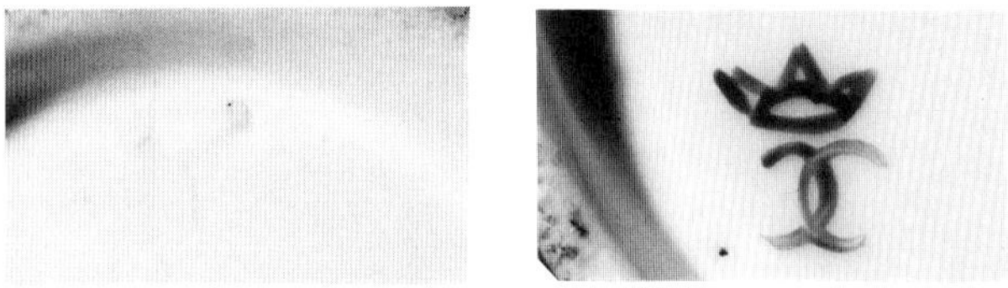

215 *marks*

215 **Jug and Cover,** 1770–93

H. 15.7 cm
Marks: interlaced *CC* crowned painted in blue enamel; incised *K*
Reg. No. Franks 410

Hard-paste porcelain, with loop handle, domed cover, cherry and leaf finial, painted in pink, green, blue, purple, yellow and orange with scattered flower sprays. Rims, foot, handle and spout decorated in pink. Perfect.

Provenance: Bequeathed by Sir A.W. Franks, 1897

Literature: Franks, London 1896, no. 410

W. Chaffers, *The New Keramik Gallery*, London, 1926, Vol. II, p. 349, fig. 309

Comparable Examples: Nancy, Musée historique lorrain, plate with similar decoration, pink rim, same painted mark, inv. 71.2.5

This type of floral decoration is perhaps more typical of that found on tin-glazed earthenware, than on porcelain.

The identity of the workman whose incised initial *K* is found on this jug is unknown. Various members of the Kalt family[1] were employed at Niderviller, but most apparently worked in the faïence factory. Only Pierre Kalt is recorded as a 'mouleur en porcelaine et en terre de pipe' but it seems unlikely that a craftsman responsible for making moulds would mark a jug such as this.

1. A list of workers documented at Niderviller is given in exh. Sarrebourg, 1986, pp. 25–43. It includes Jean Kalt 'tourneur et mouleur' (1732–94, employed in 1786), his sons Joseph Kalt, 'modeleur' (1767–1822, employed in 1787) and Pierre Kalt, 'mouleur en porcelaine et en terre de pipe' (1758–1814, employed 1788–98) and Jean Kalt *le jeune* 'mouleur', whose parents are not recorded, but who was probably also Jean Kalt's son (b.1774[?], employed 1796). Constant Kalt is recorded in 1827 as a 'figuriste en porcelaine'. Marie Françoise Kilber (or Guilbert), a 'modeleuse' (dates unknown, employed 1779–84) is also unlikely to have made this jug.

216 **Plate,** *c.*1780

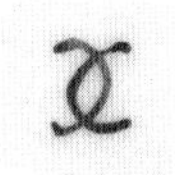

216 *mark*

D. 25.3 cm
Mark: interlaced *CC* painted in sepia
Reg. No. 1938,5–17,1

Hard-paste porcelain, the upper surface moulded with six grooves near the border, lobed rim and large border. Decorated with a design of pendent gilt husks interlaced with a pink husk and flower garland. Each garland springs from an architectural motif painted in sepia near the rim, which is emphasised by bands of sepia, grey and gold. In the centre of the plate is the monogram *KL* in gold and flowers, crowned with a flower wreath and resting on clouds. Rim chipped, and foot rim damaged.

Provenance: Presented by S.G. Davies, 1938

Literature: Unpublished

Comparable Examples: Strasbourg, Musée des arts décoratifs, inv. XXVI.V, illus. H. Jedding, *Europaïsches Porzellan*, Vol. I, Munich, 1971, fig. 802

The porcelain, although white in colour, contains a large number of inclusions which are visible on the underside. The gilding is of high quality.

The monogram has not yet been identified. As another similar plate is known it is possible that this piece is part of a service.

217 **Saucer,** 1770–93

D. 12.8 cm
Marks: *105* below a line and *CC* interlaced, surmounted by a [?] crown motif painted in blue enamel; incised [?] *d*
Reg. No. 1981,1–1,107

Hard-paste porcelain, decorated in blue enamel and gold with a stylised scroll design near the border and in the centre with the initial *A* and crossed branches (gilding partly effaced) surmounted

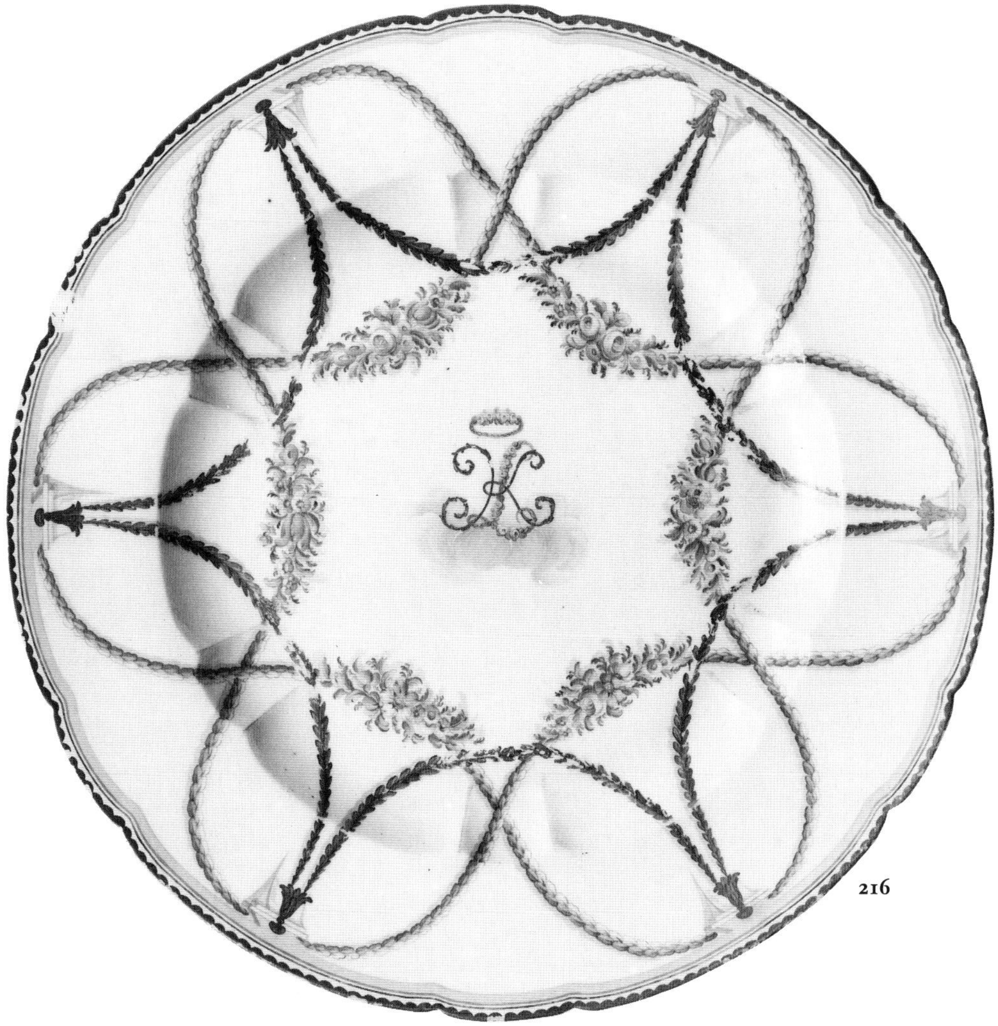

216

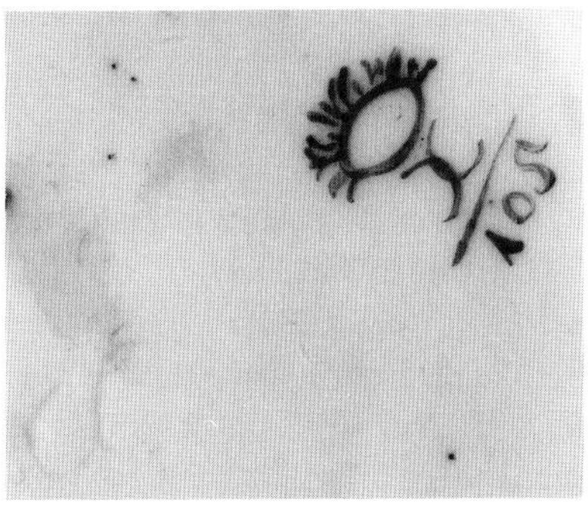

217 *marks*

by a wreath. Gilding on rim rubbed, chip to rim.

Provenance: Bequeathed by Miss C.M. Woodward, 1981

Literature: Unpublished

Comparable Examples: None noted

A cup and saucer in the Grollier Collection with a somewhat similar mark painted in violet and incised *D* is mentioned by Chavagnac and Grollier.[1]

1. Chavagnac and Grollier, 1906, p. 422.

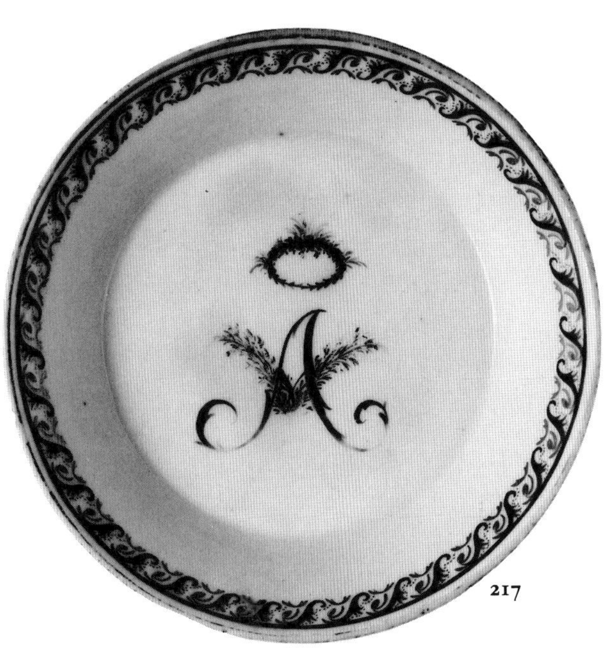

217

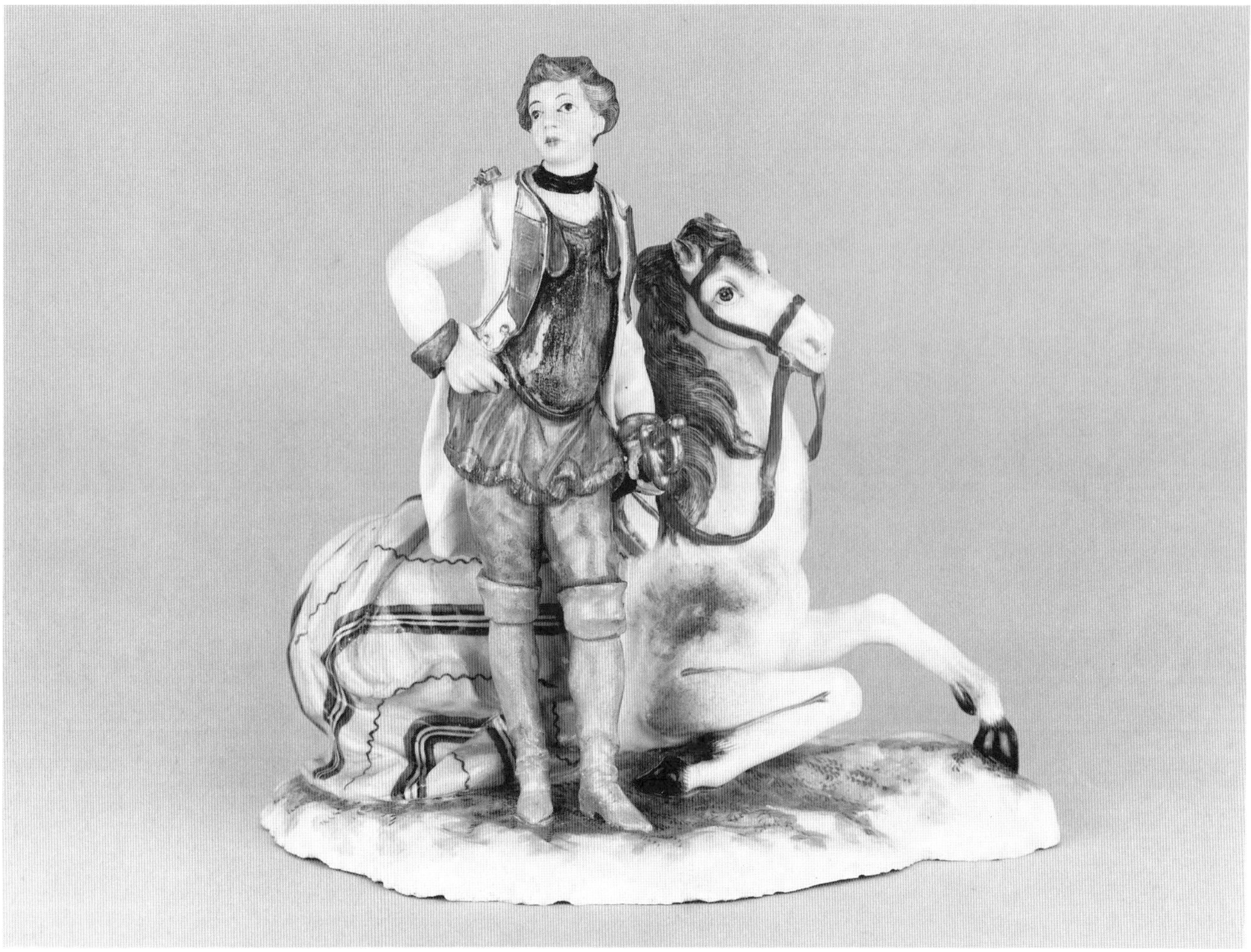

218

218 **Figure of a Warrior Symbolic of Europe**, 1760–80

See colour plate 36
H. 13.9 cm
L. 14.4 cm
Marks: none
Reg. No. 1989,5–6,3

Hard-paste porcelain, hollow, press-moulded, the base made separately. The dappled grey horse, wearing an orange bridle with orange reins and an orange rug striped in darker orange and purple across its back and rump, lies on a grassy mound, its right foreleg bent and left foreleg extended. In front of it stands a warrior holding a sword in his left hand. His right hand is on his hip below his silvery-grey chest armour. His lapels, cuffs, tunic and hose are purplish-pink, trimmed with gold, his knee-boots brownish-orange like the horse's cloth. His brown hair is tied back with an orange ribbon, on his shoulder is a blue bow (broken) and around his neck a black ribbon. Reins, left hand, sword, right hand, lower left of jacket restored. Chips to base. The colour of the chest armour is probably not original.[1]

Provenance: Purchased, 1989; Simon Goldblatt Collection, Sotheby's, 1 May 1956, Lot 148.

Literature: Unpublished

Comparable Examples: Strasbourg, Musée des arts décoratifs, inv. XXI 3, on a different base, illus. exh. Sarrebourg, 1986, no. 31

The iconography of Europe and the Four Parts of the World is discussed in cat. 212.

A mould for this group, the modeller of which has not been identified, apparently survives at the factory.[2] It was also made in tin-glazed earthenware, and an example is in the Musée national de Céramique, Sèvres.[3] A porcelain figure of *Africa* from the same series of the Four Parts of the World is in the Victoria and Albert Museum, London.[4]

1. The author is grateful to the late Mr Nigel Williams of the Department of Conservation, British Museum, for this information. In Mr Williams' opinion the armour was probably originally uncoloured.
2. See exh. Sarrebourg, 1986, no. 31.
3. Illus. Dr Chrompret *et al.*, *Répertoire de la faïence française*, Vol. III, Paris, 1933, pl. 22F.
4. Inv. C.228–1940.

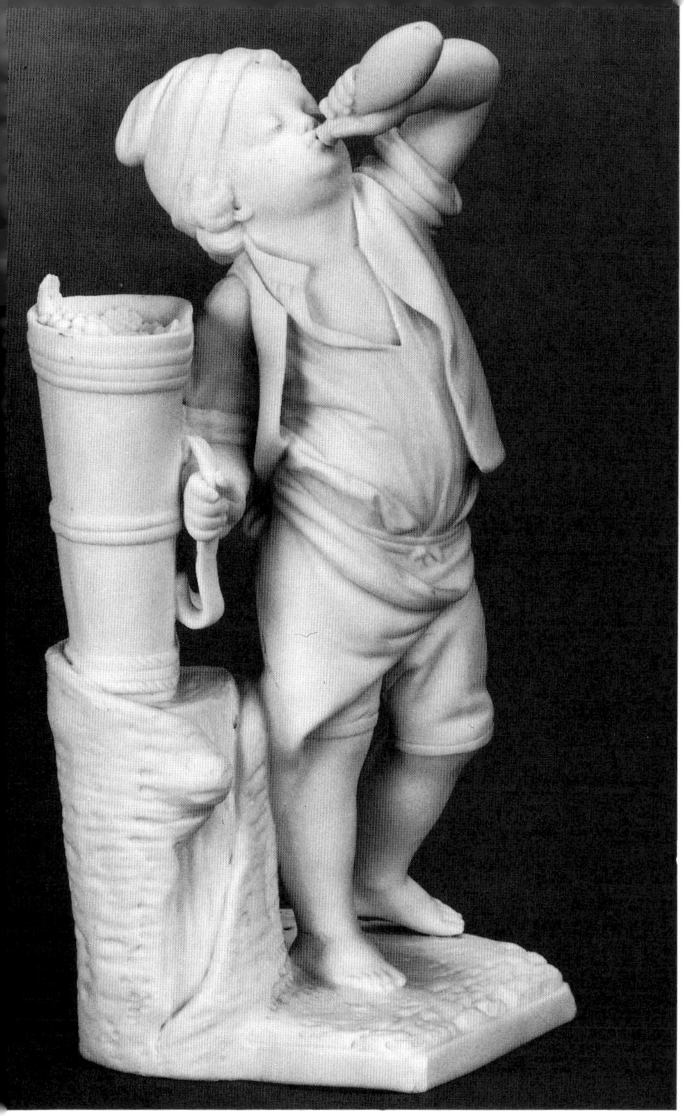

219

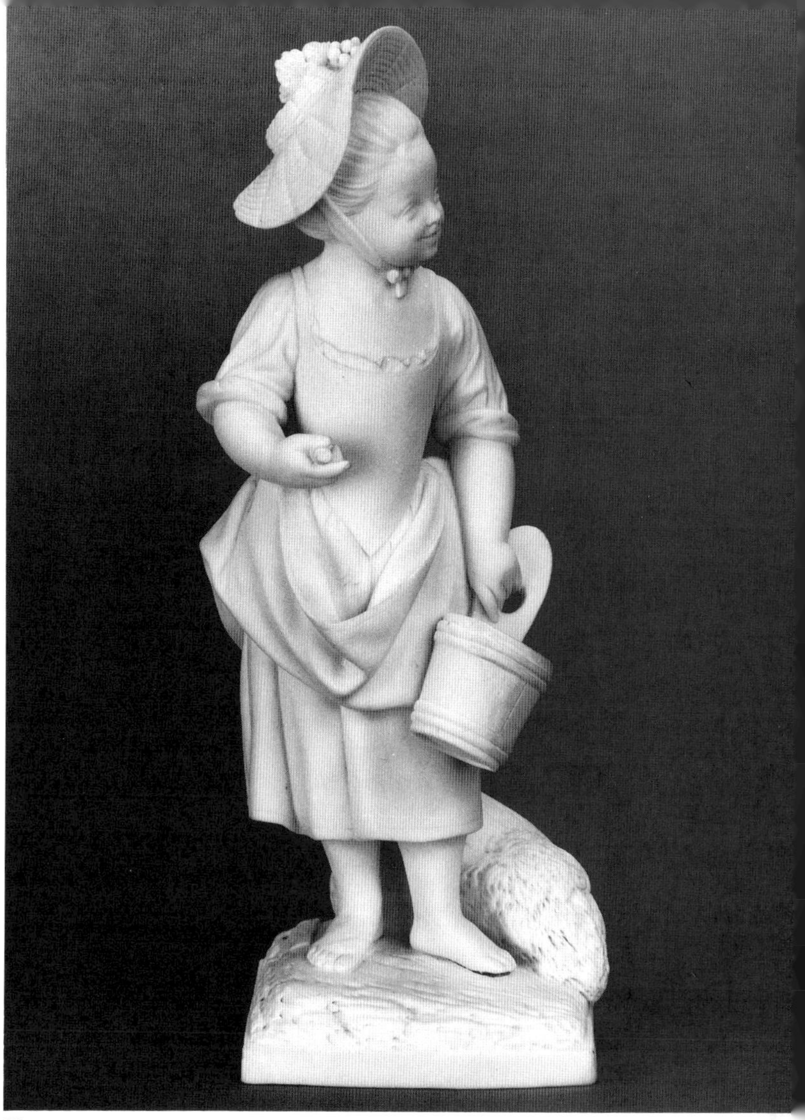

220

219 Figure of a Boy Toper Symbolising the Vintage (*le vendangeur*), *c.*1780

H. 19.9 cm
Marks: *NIDERVILLE* in relief on an applied strip on top of the base behind the boy's left foot (see cat. 220)
Reg. No. FB 37 (AF 3237)

Hard-paste biscuit porcelain, flat, slightly concave base. The boy, who wears a cap over his short curly hair, stands barefoot on a square base at the back of which is a tree-stump. On this rests a container full of grapes topped with three vine leaves, one handle of which the boy holds with his right hand. In his left hand is a bottle which is raised to his lips. His clothing comprises an apron over a pair of knee-length shorts, and a waistcoat under a jacket with sleeves rolled up. Two firecracks on base. Front edges of base chipped.

Provenance: Bequeathed by Sir A.W. Franks, 1897

Literature: Unpublished

Comparable Examples: France, Baron Eugène de Turckheim, exh. *La Porcelaine Française*, 1929, no. 1009, 'Enfant vendangeur. Biscuit'

Sarrebourg, Musée du pays de Sarrebourg, inv. 89.2.1

Nancy, Musée historique lorrain, inv. 68.5.11, unglazed earthenware, H. about 35 cm, modern

A manuscript price list of unknown origin[1] kept in the Department of Medieval and Later Antiquities records a 'vendangeur' in two sizes costing 108 francs. The modeller of this figure has not yet been identified.

Another Niderviller version of this subject is in the Victoria and Albert Museum, London, inv. C.125–1922, illus. Honey, 1950, pl. 91A.

1. It may be a copy of the *Livre des formes* referred to without indication of its present location in exh. Sarrebourg, 1986, pp. 49–50.

220 Figure of Milkmaid (*petite fille au seau*), *c.*1780

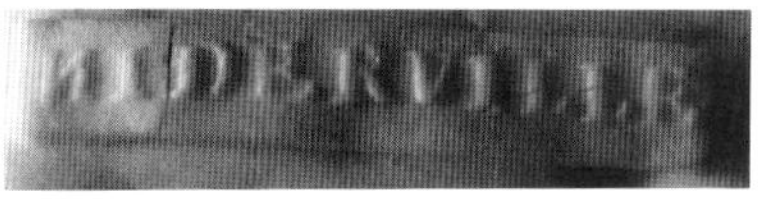

220 *mark*

H. 20.5 cm
Marks: *NIDERVILLE* in relief on an applied strip behind the girl's right foot
Reg. No. FB 37 (AF 3237)

Hard-paste biscuit porcelain with flat, slightly concave base. The girl, who wears a large-brimmed straw bonnet trimmed with a bunch of grapes and leaves, and a full-skirted dress with looped overskirt and jacket laced at the back over a blouse with elbow-length sleeves and low neckline, stands barefoot on a square base at the back of which is a rocky mound which supports her. In her right hand she holds a baton [?], damaged, and in her left a bucket, which is restored.

Provenance: Bequeathed by Sir A.W. Franks, 1897

Literature: Unpublished

Comparable Examples: France, Mulhouse, Musée de l'Impression sur Etoffes, inv. 976.116.1. AD-SIM

No mould survives of this figure which is one of a series of over sixty children produced in faïence, glazed and biscuit porcelain.[1]

1. See exh. Sarrebourg, 1986, pp. 94–7.

Château de Lassay (Orne), Brancas-Lauraguais factory[1]

Louis-Léon-Félicité, duc de Brancas, comte de Lauraguais (1733–1824) was the first to make hard-paste porcelain in France of French raw materials. On the evidence of an oval medallion of a toper in the style of Teniers the Younger,[2] he had succeeded by October 1764. He is likely to have carried out experiments before this date. In 1766 he published *Observations sur le Mémoire de Guettard*,[3] a series of addresses delivered in January of that year to the Académie des Sciences, of which he had been a member from 1758. In this publication he states that he saw M. de Montamy try without success to make porcelain at Bagnolet under the protection of the duc d'Orléans (Louis-Philippe d'Orléans, 1725–85, succeeded his father, who was a recluse, in 1752). D'Arclais de Montamy, author of the *Traité des couleurs de la peinture sur émail*, published in Paris in 1765, was the duc d'Orléans' *premier maître d'hôtel.* He was assisted by a certain Le Guay, who went on to work with Brancas. Although it is now difficult to disentangle the precise sequence of events in the discovery of the raw materials for, and method of making, hard-paste porcelain, it seems likely that it may have been the chemist Jean-Etienne Guettard (1715–86) who discovered the location of the kaolinitic clay in 1751[4] (as he claimed in the controversy which raged between the two men at the Académie des Sciences), and Brancas who succeeded in making porcelain. The clay in question, the first in France to be identified as kaolinitic, is always said to have come from Maupertuis, near Alençon. It was described by Alexandre Brongniart, who inspected the quarries in 1811,[5] as 'grisâtre, jaunâtre, caillouteux' and highly fusible, as it contained quartz and feldspar. Brongniart listed six different quarries in the vicinity of Alençon, one of which yielded clay suitable only for brick- and tile-making.

An interesting sidelight is cast on the discovery of the method of making hard-paste by pages in the *Commonplace Book* kept by Josiah Wedgwood, headed 'From Count Lauraguais to J. Wedgwood'.[6] Most of this undated account is descriptive. It reveals that Lauraguais had made a thorough study of the available literature on porcelain, and considered hard-paste manufacture outside France, as well as Réaumur's experiments. The last two paragraphs tell us the most about Lauraguais:

> In this state, which I have always called an imperfect one, I have for many years carried on a porcelain manufacture, with constant approaches to, and the

strongest hopes of attaining, the desired perfection. For this purpose I have examined all the earths I could meet with, read all I could upon the subject, and conversed & had friendship with some of the most eminent chemists. I have always chose [*sic*] to employ a body, with as little composition of art as I could, that would bear a very considerable degree of fire, and a glaze that required a great heat to flux, – and the body has approached nearer & nearer to a mixture of earths alone of which I have made some of the best ware yet made in England.

This was the state of things when I removed into the country, and by various trials of new earths there and since in London, I have at least acquired a composition of entire English earths, without any admixture of art at all, and which may be made to stand any degree of fire it can receive in a kiln.

In 1766 'the Count de Lauraguais, of London' took out a British patent for fourteen years for 'porcelain made . . . after his new method . . . the same not being fusible by fire, as all other china made there (i.e. in Britain) is'. No specification ever appears to have been enrolled for this patent.[7]

In France, Lauraguais worked at his château at Lassay (Orne). In 1906 one of his experimental kilns there was still standing.[8] The latest dated example of his porcelain is a medallion of Louis XV[9] incised *7bre* (September) *1768*. It is possible that he abandoned the making of porcelain around this time. Few pieces survive, and they are mostly medallions, such as those of the comte de Caylus,[10] Henri IV,[11] Richelieu[12] and one of a head of Minerva.[13] A small number of plates bearing the mark *LB*[14] are known.

It is not known whether Brancas had 'customers' for his pieces, many of which were in tune with the revival of classicism. Horace Walpole may have acquired the figure of Bacchus after Michelangelo listed in his catalogue[15] on one of his visits to Paris. It came from the collection of the comte de Caylus, who died in 1765, a year in which Walpole visited Paris.

Brancas was also a playwright. His affair with the celebrated actress Sophie Arnould was well known to his contemporaries.[16] She introduced him to the architect François-Joseph Belanger, who built a pavilion for him in the garden of his hotel in the rue Taitbout.[17] Imprisoned no less than four times for his controversial views, including a period spent in the fortress of Metz after the condemnation of his writings on inoculation against smallpox, he spent time in exile in England in the 1760s (see above) and in the early 1770s. His published works number at least twenty-seven.[18]

He had a strong interest in English bloodstock, and was the owner of the famous English racehorse Gimcrack, which he took to France and raced $22\frac{1}{2}$ miles within an hour for a large bet.[19] On returning to France from England he wanted to organise horse-racing on English lines, with betting,[20] and influenced the dukes of Chartres and Lauzun to become racing fanatics.

1. This account is based on Chavagnac and Grollier, 1906, pp. 399–405. In his lifetime the count was referred to both as the duc de Brancas and as the duc de Lauraguais. He was born at Versailles, the son of the duc de Villars-Brancas, and married Mademoiselle Gand, princesse d'Isenghien (d.1793), in 1755. In 1814 he was created a *Pair de France*.
2. D'Albis and Romanet, 1980, p. 23, fig. 17.
3. See *Observations sur le Mémoire de M. Guettard Concernant la Porcelaine*, Paris, 1766, p. 63. The British Library copy of this publication is missing. The writer has had access to the Yale University Library example, for which she thanks Lois White and Mark Bromell of the Getty Center Library, Santa Monica, California.
4. Guettard's role is described in *ibid.*, pp. 22–3, but is not related to Brancas' activities. For an outline of Guettard's career, see *Nouvelle Biographie Générale*, Paris, 1858, repr. Copenhagen, 1966, Vol. XXII; he was curator of the duc d'Orléans' (son of the Regent) collection at the Bibliothèque de Sainte-Geneviève, some of which was bequeathed to him, but which he gave to the Duke's son, and received lodging in the Palais Royal.
5. A. Brongniart, *Premier Mémoire des Kaolins ou argiles à Porcelaine, sur la nature, le gisement, l'origine et l'emploi de cette sorte d'argile*, Paris, 1839, p. 258 and pp. 270–2 (also appeared as part of *Mémoires de l'Académie Royale des Sciences*).
6. This book is the property of the Wedgwood Museum, Barlaston, Stoke-on-Trent. The author is grateful to Gaye Blake Roberts for permission to quote the extracts from it.
7. The author is grateful to John Mallet for kindly drawing this patent to her attention, see L. Jewitt, *The Ceramic Art of Great Britain*, London, 1878, Vol. I, p. 114. The patent is referred to in a letter from Wedgwood to Bentley dated 24 October 1767 (deposited by the Wedgwood Museum at the University Library, Keele, Wedgwood Correspondence 18170–25): 'I am very impatient to see a Copy of the Counts Pt. that we may know the worst, but if that does not arrive as soon as this pray let me know what you can about it, whether he does or does not use the SP. [spath fusible] & by what name &c, &c.'
8. Chavagnac and Grollier, 1906, p. 399, f.n. 2, 'Renseignements fournis à M.L. Duval par le marquis de Beauchesne'. The writer is unaware whether it still exists.
9. Chavagnac and Grollier, 1906, p. 404, Musée de Rouen, inv. 1537.
10. Chavagnac and Grollier, 1906, p. 403, dated September 1768, Musée national de Céramique, Sèvres, inv. 6007, illus. Frégnac, 1964, p. 274. The medallion is after Jean-Baptiste Nini.
11. Chavagnac and Grollier, 1906, p. 404, in the possession of Gollier in 1906, dated September 1768; this is probably the

one at the Sèvres Museum, illus. by Landais, 1961, p. 103, fig. 66.

12. Paris, Drouot Richelieu, 6 December 1989, Lot 63, incised monogram, D. 11 cm, believed to be in a French private collection.
13. Chavagnac and Grollier, 1906, p. 403, Musée national de Céramique, Sèvres, inv. 5119. A hitherto unrecorded medallion of Isaac Newton was with Dragesco-Cramoisan, Paris, in autumn 1992, and another of Cardinal Richelieu is in a French private collection.
14. *Ibid.*, p. 404; an example in the Victoria and Albert Museum, London, illus. Frégnac, 1964, p. 274.
15. 'Michael Angelo's Bacchus, made in china of the comte de Lauraguais; from the collection of the comte de Caylus', *A Description of the Villa of Mr. Horace Walpole . . . at Strawberry Hill near Twickenham, Middlesex*, Strawberry Hill, 1784, p. 9.
16. See H. Bonhomme, *La Société Galante et Littéraire au* XVIIIᵉ *Siècle*, Paris, 1880, chapter 'Le comte de Lauraguais et Sophie Arnould', pp. 77–118.
17. See J. Stern, *A l'Ombre de Sophie Arnould, François-Joseph Belanger, architecte du Menus Plaisirs, premier architecte du comte d'Artois*, Paris, 1930, 2 vols.; see Vol. 1, illus. opp. p. 22, opp. p. 24, both drawings in Musée des arts décoratifs, Paris, the first reproduced by M. Gallet, *Paris Domestic Architecture of the 18th Century*, London, 1972, p. 171, dated 1768, building completed 1771. Belanger's 'Projet d'une maison à construire pour le comte de Lauraguais dans la rue Poissonnière' of around 1788 is preserved in the Bibliothèque nationale, Paris, Estampes, HA 58, Stern, *op. cit.*, Vol. 1, p. 218.
18. See *Biographie ancienne et moderne*, Vol. 23, Paris and Leipzig, n.d. (1860).
19. R. Black, in *Horse-Racing in France*, London, 1886, p. 8, quotes Horace Walpole writing to the Reverend W. Cole on 28 February 1766, 'To-day I have been to the Plaine de Sablons, by the Bois de Boulogne, to see a horse rid [*sic*] in person by Count Lauraguais and Lord Forbes'. The Count's horse apparently died. Black also states that Lauraguais was known and disliked at Newmarket.
20. M. Ward, *Forth*, 1982, p. 5.

---

221 **Medallion of Maximilien de Béthune, duc de Sully** (1559–1641), 1764–8

D. 12.8 cm
Marks: *BL* in monogram, *U* and *D* incised
Reg. No. 1990,4–5,1

Hard-paste porcelain[1] circular medallion of greyish shiny appearance, moulded in relief with a portrait to left of the duc de Sully in armour and wearing a ruff. Within the beaded border near the edge is the moulded inscription *MAX. DE BETHUNE, P.S. D'ENRICHEMONT ET DE BOIS-BELLES, D. DE SULLY.*

Provenance: Purchased, 1990; said to be from a private collection, Paris.

Literature: Unpublished

Comparable Examples: USA, private collection. For a similar Sèvres medallion, see cat. 156

For a biography of the duc de Sully, see cat. 156. Although this medallion has probably not been intentionally glazed, its shiny surface reveals that it has picked up a glassy substance during firing, giving it a 'smear-glazed' appearance. Nineteenth-century white stonewares manufactured in England around 1840 are often similar in appearance.

The source of the portrait is unknown. It is slightly larger than cat. 156, and there are variations of detail, such as the leaf decoration on the armour in this example. However, because of the greater shrinkage of soft-paste porcelain, it is possible that both ultimately derive from the same original. A medallion of the comte de Caylus from the Brancas-Lauraguais workshop is known to be based on a terracotta by Jean-Baptiste Nini,[2] but as yet no Nini medallion of Sully has come to light.

The subject enjoyed considerable popularity at French porcelain factories from the 1760s onwards and was often paired with a portrait of Henri IV, as at Mennecy and Sèvres.[3]

For other medallions made at the château de Lassay, see p. 291.

1. According to X-ray diffraction analysis carried out in the British Museum Research Laboratory in April 1990, in which quartz is shown as the major phase, and no mullite is apparently present, ref. BMRL 34594X. The author is grateful to Mavis Bimson for this information. The undamaged condition of the medallion inhibits sampling for further analysis. Monsieur A. d'Albis and Madame F. Treppoz of the Manufacture nationale

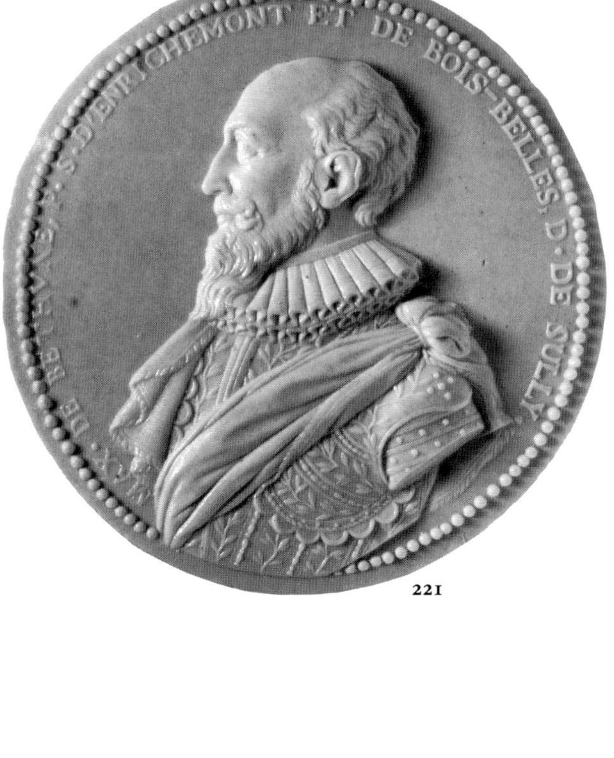

221

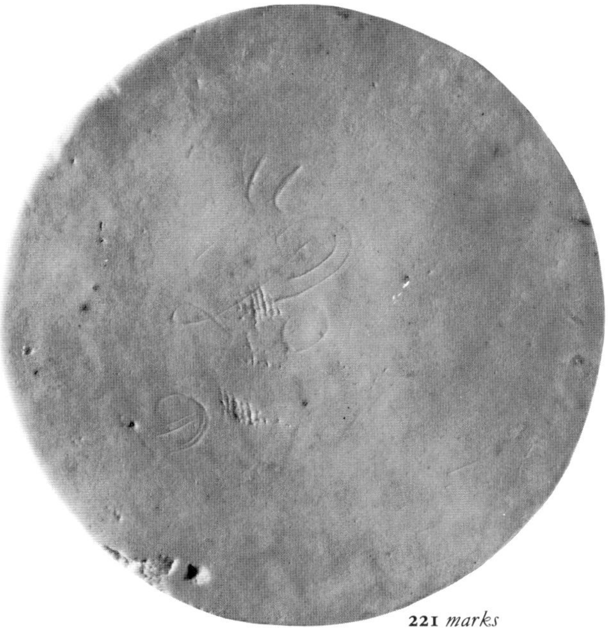

221 *marks*

de Céramique have informed her that their analysis of medallions of Henri IV, Minerva and an unidentified man showed a large amount of quartz in the body, with the addition of mullite. These results are unpublished, and the author is grateful for a personal communication in May 1990.

2. A. Storelli, *Jean-Baptiste Nini, sa vie – son oeuvre 1717–1786*, Tours, 1896, p. 133.
3. Thirty-one medallions of Henri IV and Sully were valued at 9 *livres* in the Sèvres factory inventory dated 20 January 1778. Two of reject quality were sold on 18 June 1773 for 15 *livres* each, MNS, Archives de Sèvres, Vy 5, f.76. A medallion of Henri IV by Brancas-Lauraguais is illustrated by Landais, 1961, p. 103, fig. 66.

Etiolles[1]

Little is known of this porcelain factory, whose exact location has not been discovered. It was situated around the same distance south-east of Paris as Mennecy, that is about 32 km from the city. It was probably established around 1766. Jean-Baptiste Monier declared before M. de Sartine, lieutenant-general of the Paris police, on July 1768[2] that he was continuing the activity of the concern mentioned in an *arrêt* of 15 February 1766. The mark *MP* in monogram for Monier and Pellevé was registered, but may not have been much used, possibly because of a change of ownership. Etienne-Dominique Pellevé (d. 8 February 1776) was a native of Rouen, and was the son of Denis Pierre Pellevé, the first director of the Sinceny (Picardy) faïence factory in the 1740s.[3] He was director of a ceramic factory at Dangu (Eure) from July 1753 for seventeen months.[4] On 29 December 1763[5] he was at the Ottweiler porcelain factory where he undertook to reveal to its owner, Prince Henry William of Nassau-Sarrebrück, the secret of his porcelain body and the improvements he was capable of making to it. He promised to work at the Ottweiler concern for ten years and to give one year's notice of his departure. However, he left suddenly in September 1767 for Hannong's factory at Zweibrücken. Pellevé was instrumental in hiring workers from Ottweiler, such as the modeller Jean Jakob Grässer (b.1752 at Ottweiler).[6] Michel Vanier (1747–90) is known to have gone to Etiolles after his marriage in 1768.[7] A native of Orléans, he had been trained at the factory where his parents worked. Little information has come to light about his activities between 1768 and 1783, when he is recorded as a widower in Paris, having lost his two children, except that he was involved with the Boissettes factory in 1775–6 together with Dominique-Jean-Etienne Pellevé (see p. 301). He is recorded at Etiolles as an *ouvrier* in 1773.[8]

A surviving note in registers kept by a merchant called Dubuisson concerning a factory at Soizy-sous-Etiolles (Soizy is close to Etiolles) may describe pieces made by Monier and Pellevé:[9]

'30 août 1769. Note de l'échantillon de porcelaines confiées à M. Genesty, manufacturier à Soisy-sous-Etioles pour exécuter en sa manufacture.

1 écuelle blanche et son plateau dorés, moyens
1 sucrier blanc sans plateau
2 tasses différentes, 2 de Saxe avec 2 soucoupes
1 théyère bleue garnie
1 moyen sucrier en couleur
1 sallière à 3 pattes de Sèves, 1 dite de table anglaise
2 pots à creme et 1 baignoire à oeil
1 tasse de Saxe de couleur à a corps, dorée'

It is possible that M. Genesty was acting as director, or had perhaps taken over Monier's share of the concern.

The last known reference to the factory occurs in a copy of a report made to Sartine on 19 August 1774 by one of his inspectors, Buhot:[10] 'La Manufacture Etablie à Etioles sous le nom de Monier appartient au Sr, Giros Md tenant le magazin de l'hôtel de Jaback ruë St. Merry, où il vend la porcelaine qu'il fait fabriquer. Elle paroit médiocre en blancheur; mais comme il a du goût, La forme, Les peintures et Dorures la rendent passable.' The identity of the merchant Giros, whose premises were at the hôtel de Jaback (or Jabach) in the rue St. Merry, remains unknown.

As the factory began in 1766 it almost certainly made soft-paste porcelain, and several examples have been noted.[11] All the pieces from this factory so far recorded are domestic wares for the table or boudoir: teapots and coffeepots, sugar bowls, cups and saucers, face cream pots (*pots à pommade*) and a broth bowl and cover. Hard-paste pieces are generally painted in colours with flowers, birds[12] or waterside scenes, occasionally embellished with silver or gold. Some undecorated pieces, such as a moulded teapot with an animal-head spout inspired by the Far East, were sold.[13] A few higher-quality pieces have been traced,[14] but the porcelain body and decoration are usually of indifferent quality and the forms lack elegance. A number of the surviving pieces are incised with their place of origin, Pellevé's name and a date. The earliest is dated 1768 and several are dated 1770, including some incised *Xbre 1770* for December of that year.

The organisation, workforce and distribution of the products of this factory all await further study.[15] The name of one painter, Joseph Albert, has been traced in the Etiolles parish registers in 1774.[16]

1. This account is chiefly based on Chavagnac and Grollier, 1906, pp. 429–31.
2. *Ibid.*, p. 429, quoting Archives nationales, O. 1–2059.
3. Exh. *Faïences françaises*, 1980, p. 265 and Ravel d'Esclapon, 1991, p. 31.
4. Ravel d'Esclapon, 1991, p. 33, f.n. 4, 5.
5. See Noël, 1961, Vol. 1, p. 51, citing Archives d'Etat, Coblenz, 22/280[5], f. 1 *et seq.*
6. *Ibid.*, p. 55.
7. See J. du Pasquier, 'La manufacture des Terres de Bordes en Paludate' in the catalogue of the same title, Musée des arts décoratifs, Bordeaux, 1989, p. 21, which relies on an unpublished thesis of the Ecole du Louvre by P. Venot, 'Michel Vanier à Lille, Valenciennes, Bordeaux'.
8 Ravel d'Esclapon, 1991, p. 34, f.n. 7.
9. Chavagnac and Grollier, 1906, pp. 429–30, quoting Archives de la Seine, registres du commerce 690, f. 58, registre de M. Dubuisson, marchand.
10. MNS, Archives de Sèvres, A2, *liasse* 7.
11. Chavagnac and Grollier, 1906, p. 430.
12. For a jug (*verseuse*) painted with birds, see Ballu, n.d., [1958], pl. 34A.
13. Dupont, 1987, p. 123, fig. 3.
14. Ravel d'Esclapon, 1991, pp. 8, 35, 103, for example (not examined by the writer). Private collection, Paris, an *écuelle* painted with putti in medallions alternating with trophies, a teapot painted with birds in the Sceaux style, a two-handled cup, cover and stand painted with landscape scenes, a coffee-pot with its handle at the side painted with birds, another two-handled cup, cover and stand dated 1771 finely painted with a landscape and flowers and a large tobacco pot and cover painted with a coat-of-arms. The author is grateful to the owner for kindly allowing her to examine these pieces.
15. Alix de Ravel d'Esclapon is preparing a new work on Etiolles porcelain.
16. Ravel d'Esclapon, 1991, p. 40.

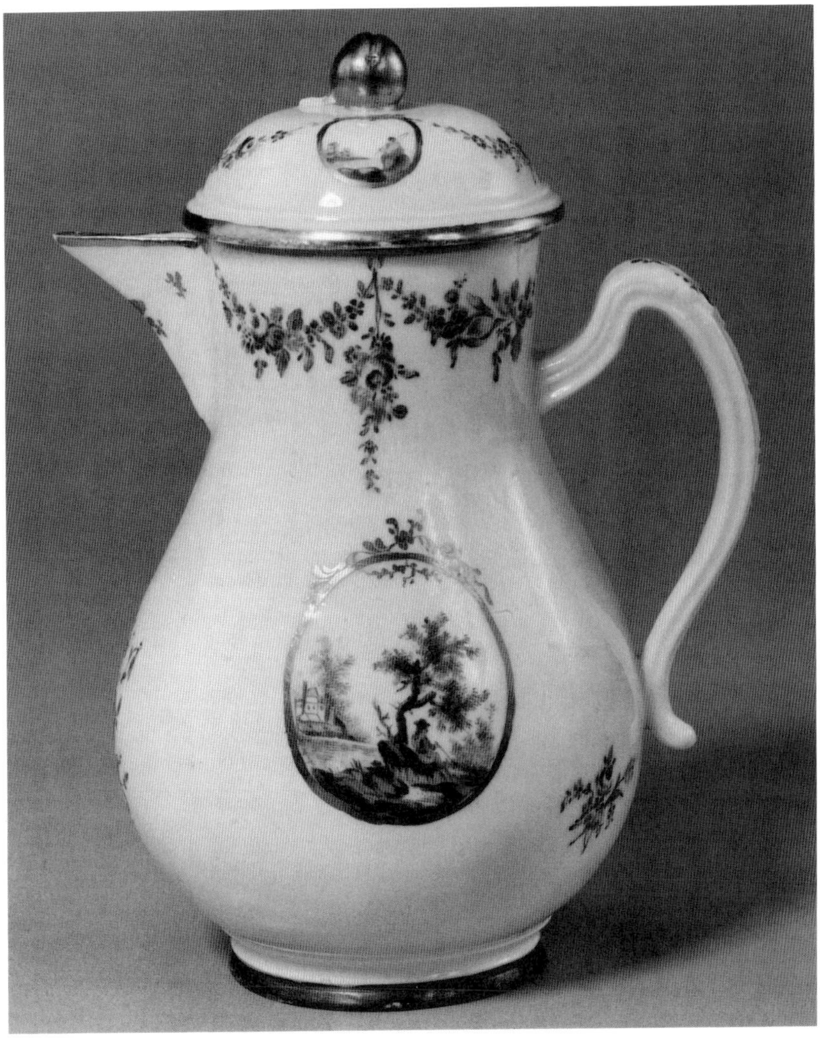

222

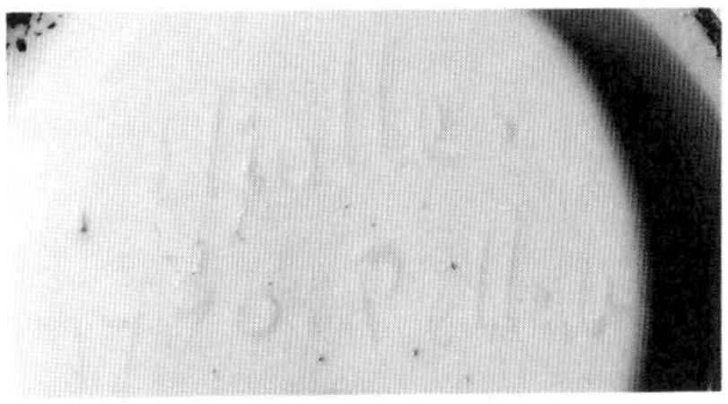

222 *mark*

222 **Jug and Cover,** 1770

H.	16.8 cm	
Marks:	*Etiolles*	incised
	1770 Pellevé	
Reg. No.	F.B.21 (AF 3223)	

Hard-paste porcelain; pear-shaped, with turned foot, moulded grooved handle and domed cover with a circular hole and gilt cherry and leaf knop. The jug is painted with two waterside scenes containing seated figures *en camaïeu pourpre* each within an oval gilt reserve repeated once on the cover, with scattered flower sprays in green, yellow, pink, orange, blue-grey and grey around the lower part and pendent flower garlands near the rim of the jug and on the cover. Rims gilt, gilt flowers around reserve and on handle and spout, foot silvered, repaired, foot chipped.

Provenance: Bequeathed by Sir A.W. Franks, 1897

Literature: E. Hannover, *Pottery and Porcelain, A Handbook for Collectors,* III, *European Porcelain,* London, 1925, p. 328

Comparable Examples: London, Victoria and Albert Museum, teapot dated December 1770 with similar decoration, illus. Honey, 1950, pl. 94A, reg. no. C.330–1919; a large saucer dish dated 1771 is in the same Museum, reg. no. C.112–1972

The porcelain, although highly translucent, exhibits wreathing and the gilding and silvering is inexpertly applied. The decoration of waterside scenes is typical of what was perhaps the second quality production. More elaborately painted pieces with bird subjects were also made.[1]

The jug, which is part of a tea service, may have been intended to hold hot water.

1. Private collection, Paris, see p. 294, f.n. 14. The author is grateful to the owner for allowing her to examine these items in 1989.

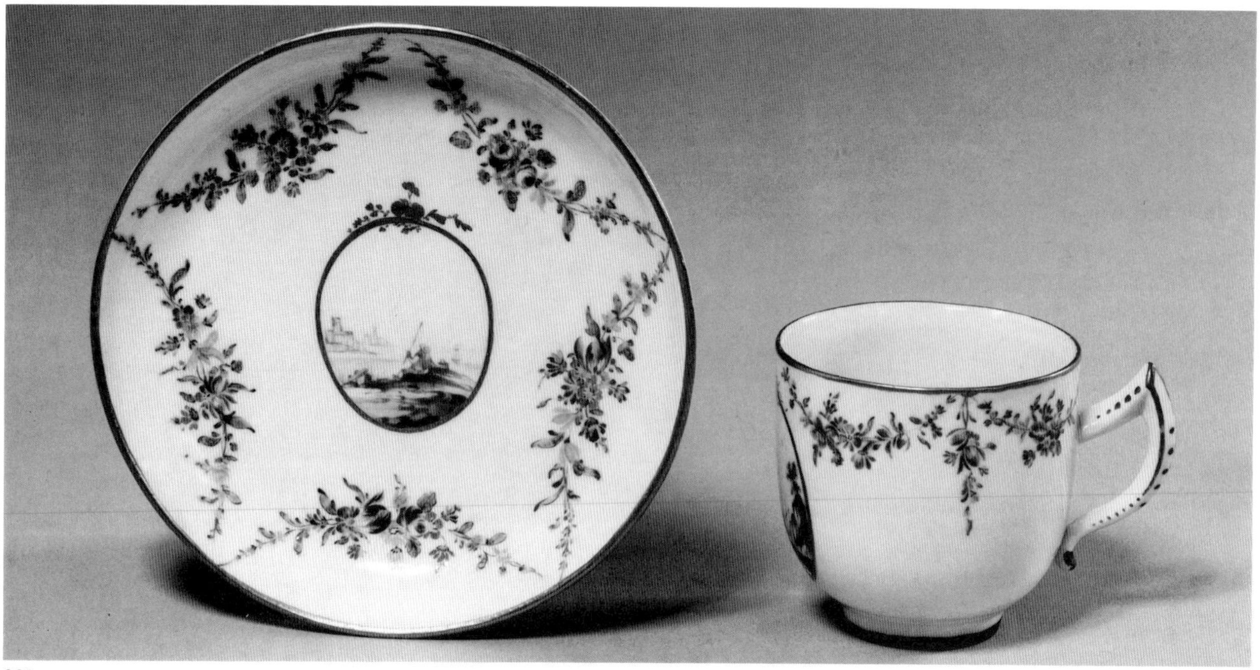

223

223 **Cup and Saucer**, 1770

H. *of cup*	6.2 cm	
D. *of saucer*	13.1 cm	
Marks:	*E* *Pelleve 1770*	incised on saucer; *P* incised on cup
Reg. No.	Franks 411	

Hard-paste porcelain; shallow saucer without well, the grooved handle of the cup pointed at its upper end and with outward 'kick' at the lower end. Painted with waterside scenes *en camaïeu pourpre* within oval gilt reserves, and flower garlands similar to those on jug, cat. 222. Flower spray inside base of cup. Rims gilt, foot and handle of cup decorated in silver.

Provenance: Bequeathed by Sir A.W. Franks, 1897

Literature: Franks, London, 1896, no. 411

Chavagnac and Grollier, 1906, p. 431
Chaffers, 1926, Vol. II, p. 342, fig. 299

Comparable Examples: See cat. 222

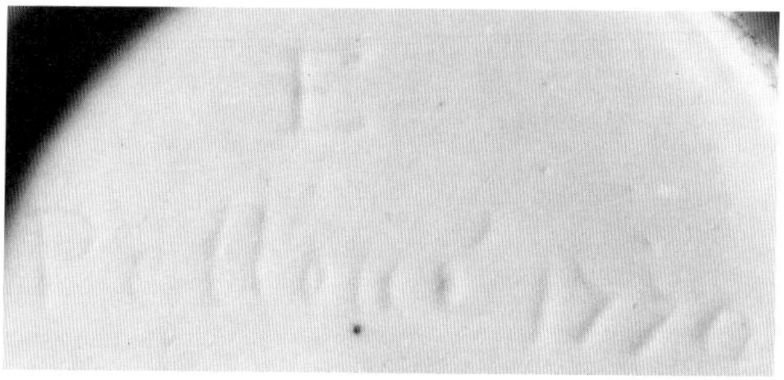

223 *mark (saucer)*

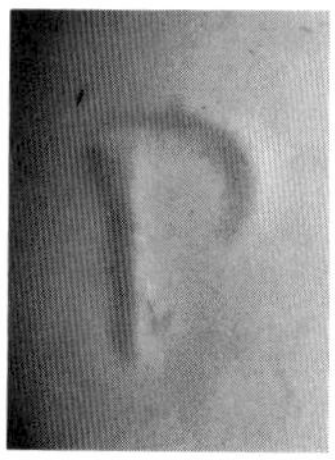

223 *mark (cup*

The saucer has warped in firing, and the foot on both exhibits the same unevenness [?chipping] as on the jug (no. 222). The glaze on the saucer is pitted with pin-holes.

Tamara Préaud has suggested[1] that this may be the *tasse Saxe* referred to Dubuisson's memorandum,[2] on account of the handle form.

1. In correspondence with the author Spring 1991.
2. See p. 294.

Vincennes, Seguin's factory[1]

Little is known about this factory. Sieur Hector Hiacinthe Seguin, treasurer of the duc de Chartres (1747–93) acquired the concern in 1774. The privilege granted on 8 December 1767 to Maurice Desaubiez, which had then passed to J.-B. Laborde, was sold by him to Devisme de Vagay, and then to Seguin.[2] An inventory dated 2 July 1774[3] lists raw materials, moulds and finished porcelain, which were probably passed on to Seguin, together with the 'moules à fayance', which may indicate that tin-glazed wares were also in production. In a letter of 1779[4] Seguin states that he has been owner of the factory for five years at an annual rent of 4,500 *livres* payable to sieur Salette, *homme d'affaires de M. le marquis de Voyer*. A note dated 20 August 1776 and signed by Collet, *contrôleur des bâtiments de Vincennes*[5] describes Seguin as 'chef de la manufacture de porcelaine, logé dans le gouvernement'. He was in the process of moving his shop, located in the 'bâtiment de la grand écurie du roy', to 'la grande salle qu'il occupe à côté de son logement et cela, pour céder cette écurie à Mgr le duc de Chartres'. During this year the factory was referred to as the 'manufacture royale de Vincennes', and its warehouse in Paris bore the duke's emblem, even though no trace has been found of any formal grant of protection to the concern. The mark of a label was registered on 10 February 1777.

Seguin complained of difficulties in covering his costs when he wrote to d'Angiviller on 8 April 1779. He had presumably managed either to increase sales or to find financial support for his factory, since it was still in existence in May 1788 when the original privilege expired. A number of buildings had been put up on the site, which belonged to the King, in the twenty years since it had been first used for a porcelain factory, and Seguin was anxious to recoup his expenses, if the King were to retake possession of the château for his corps of guards. Further research is needed to establish the details of the closure of the factory.

Little is known about the employees of this concern, of which Pierre Lemaire was director. A plan of the buildings casts little light on the organisation of work there.[6]

In his letter to d'Angiviller of 8 April 1779 Seguin makes reference to three services which he was making. One was for the duc de Chartres, another for the comte de Maillebois and the third for Madame la baronne de Neukischen. A number of pieces bearing the label mark and decorated with the duke's monogram and coloured flower sprays have survived.[7]

1. This account is based on Chavagnac and Grollier, 1906, pp. 411–16; some information can be found in Guillebon, 'Les Fourberies de Pierre Antoine Hannong à Sèvres, Vincennes, Vaux et Paris', *Bulletin de la Société de l'histoire de Paris et de l'Ile de France*, 113/114e *année*, 1986/87, pp. 179–222.
2. Guillebon, *op. cit.*, p. 189.
3. *Ibid.*, p. 209, quoting Archives nationales, Minutier central, XCV, 339, 2 July 1774.
4. Chavagnac and Grollier, *op. cit.*, p. 412.
5. *Ibid.*, pp. 411–12, quoting Archives nationales, O[1], 1901–2.
6. Guillebon, *op. cit.*, p. 202, Archives nationales, O[1], 2059.
7. Chavagnac and Grollier, 1906, pp. 415–16.

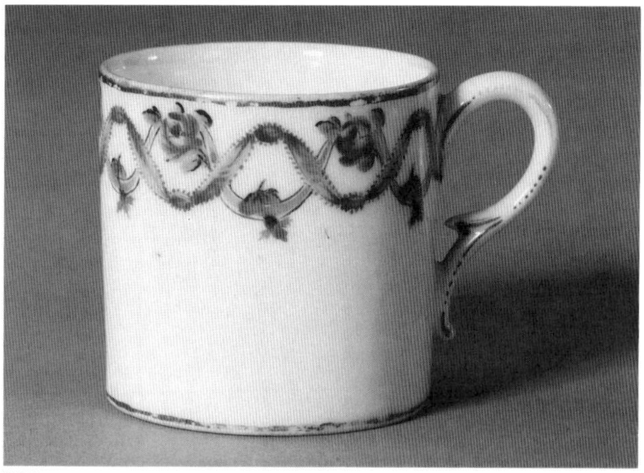
224

224 Cylindrical Cup, *c.*1777–*c.*1788

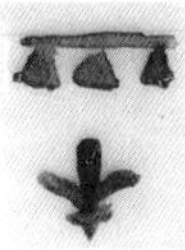
224 *mark*

H. 6 cm
Marks: label above a fleur-de-lys painted overglaze in orange
Reg. No. Franks 407

Hard-paste porcelain, exceptionally white in colour, and highly translucent, shaped handle with out-turned terminal. Decorated in pink, blue, green, black with a rose and forget-me-not garland intertwined with a ribbon; gilt rim and base, handle partly gilt.

Provenance: Bequeathed by Sir A.W. Franks, 1897

Literature: Franks, London, 1896, no. 407

Comparable Examples: None

This piece was attributed to the Orléans factory by Franks. Chavagnac and Grollier[1] listed a *tasse conique* painted with a landscape scene from the Chavagnac Collection and a plate decorated with flowers from the Gasnault Collection as bearing the same mark in red. However, this attribution cannot be upheld (see cat. 226) as there is no evidence that hard-paste was produced commercially at Orléans, despite the presence there in 1777 of kaolin in the 'chambre de composition des pâtes'.[2] The label mark was registered by Seguin on 10 February 1777.[3]

1. Chavagnac and Grollier, 1906, p. 387.
2. *Ibid.*, p. 378.
3. *Ibid.*, p. 411.

225 Cup and Saucer, *c.*1777–*c.*1788

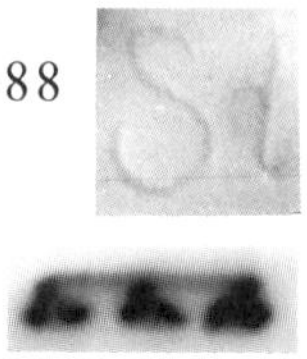
225 *marks*

D. *of saucer:* 12.9 cm
H. *of cup:* 6.4 cm
Marks: label painted in underglaze-blue on saucer; *St* incised on both
Reg. No. Franks 406

Hard-paste porcelain, the saucer decorated in green, blue, pink and black enamels with a rose spray in the centre enclosed by a forget-me-not wreath entwined with a gold ribbon motif between two gilt dentil lines. This pattern is repeated near the border. Scattered stylised leaves and dots between the ornament; gilt rim. The cup is similarly decorated and has a gilt pattern around the reserve containing roses. Foot of cup damaged.

Provenance: Bequeathed by Sir A.W. Franks, 1897

Literature: Franks, 1896, no. 406

Comparable Examples: See Chaffers, 1926, Vol. II, p. 348, fig. 308, sugar bowl and cover

The identity of the 'repairer', whose mark is incised on these pieces, remains unknown.

225

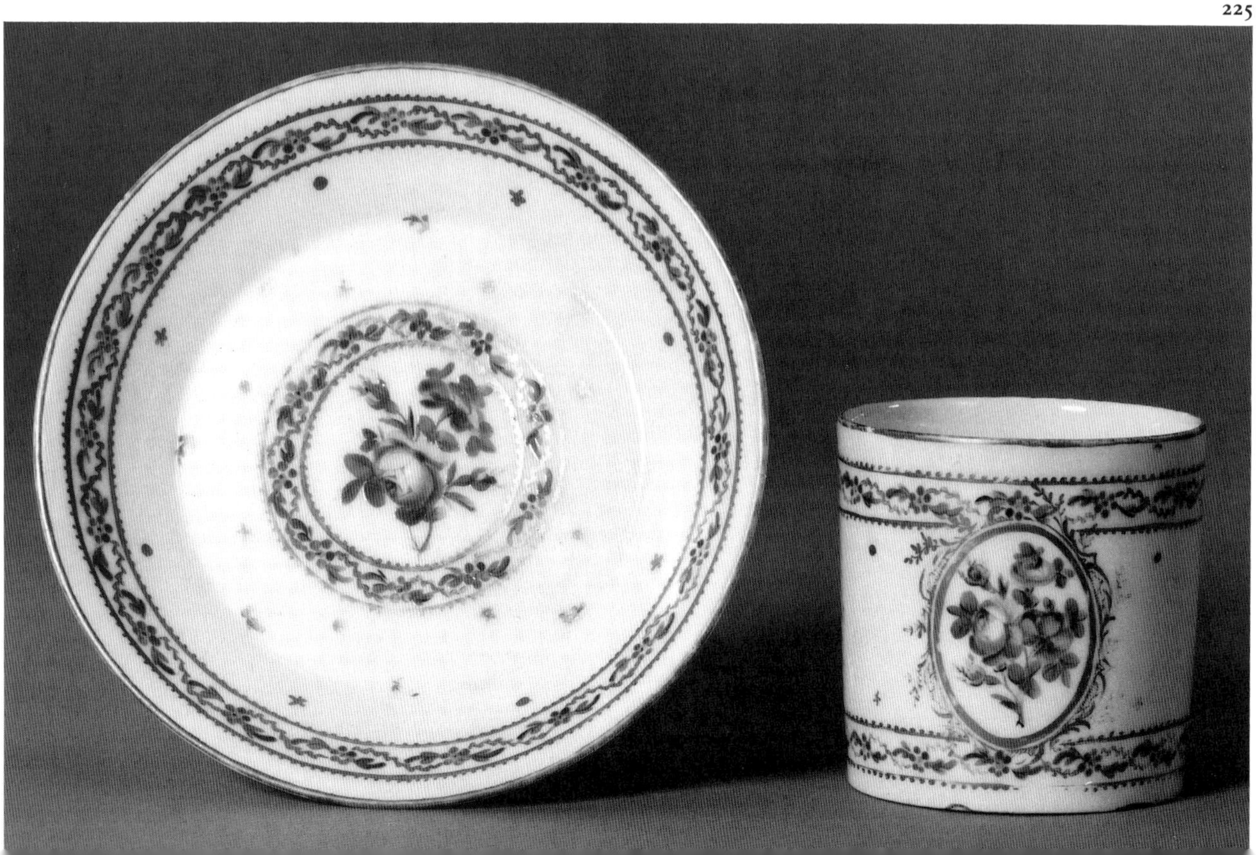

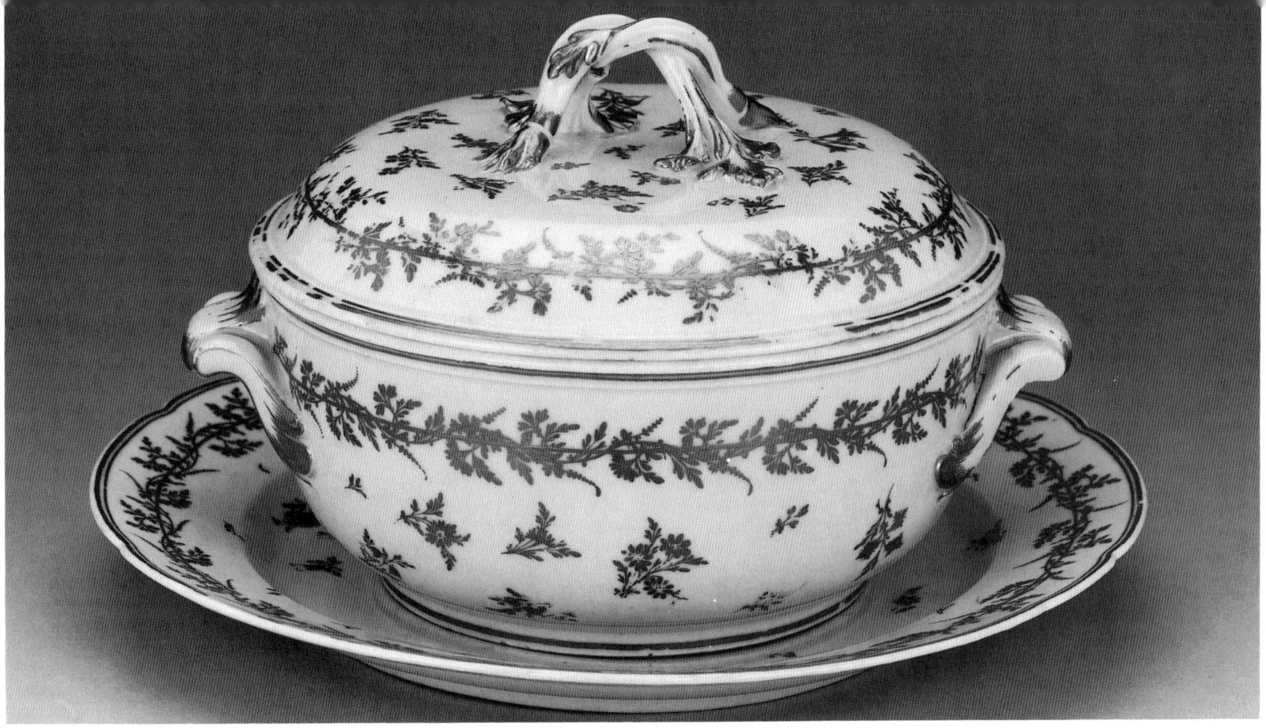

226

226 **Tureen, Cover and Stand,** *c.*1777–*c.*1788

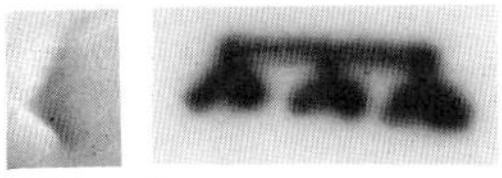

226 *marks*

D. *of stand:*	31.8 cm
H. *of tureen and cover:*	17.4 cm
Marks:	label painted in underglaze-blue on each; *L* incised on tureen
Reg. No.	Franks 404

Hard-paste porcelain, the stand white, the bowl and cover creamier in tone. The shallow stand has a wide shaped rim. There is a glazed-over chip on the foot rim. The tureen has two rococo-style handles, a domed cover and elaborate entwined handles; part of one has cracked in two in firing. The gilt decoration consists of scattered flower sprays, and near the rim of a garland of leaves around a line. Gilt rims, handles partly gilt. The gilding is rubbed, particularly on the stand.

Provenance: Bequeathed by Sir A.W. Franks, 1897

Literature: Franks, 1896, no. 404
Chaffers, 1926, Vol. II, p. 347, fig. 307

Comparable Examples: None

The design of this piece is particularly sophisticated. It was attributed by Franks to Orléans, but the heraldic label mark was registered on 10 February 1777 by Sieur Seguin, who had purchased the factory at the château de Vincennes originally used by Pierre-Antoine Hannong.[1] Additional evidence that it was used at Vincennes is provided by a double salt and a *seau à liqueur* in the Victoria and Albert Museum, London,[2] both bearing the label mark and decorated with flowers and the monogram of Louis-Philippe-Joseph, duc de Chartres (1747–93, became duc d'Orléans in 1785), patron of the factory.

Rather similar handles can be seen on a *tasse à la reine* in the Musée national de Céramique, Sèvres, from the duc d'Orléans factory in rue Amelot, Paris.[3]

1. Chavagnac and Grollier, 1906, pp. 407–15.
2. Reg. nos. C.510A–1909 and C.111–1972.
3. Illus. by Guillebon, 1972, fig. 107.

227 **Soup Plate,** *c.* 1777–88

D.	24.1 cm
Marks:	label painted in underglaze-blue, [?] 1 incised
Reg. No.	1981,1-1,96

Hard-paste porcelain, greyish in tone, moulded, the upturned border with six large and six small lobes at the rim. The decoration consists of a naturalistic flower spray including roses and forget-me-nots painted in pink, orange, yellow, green, bright blue and grey in a rather dry palette in the centre, and three further sprays on the border, as well as four small scattered leaf sprays. There

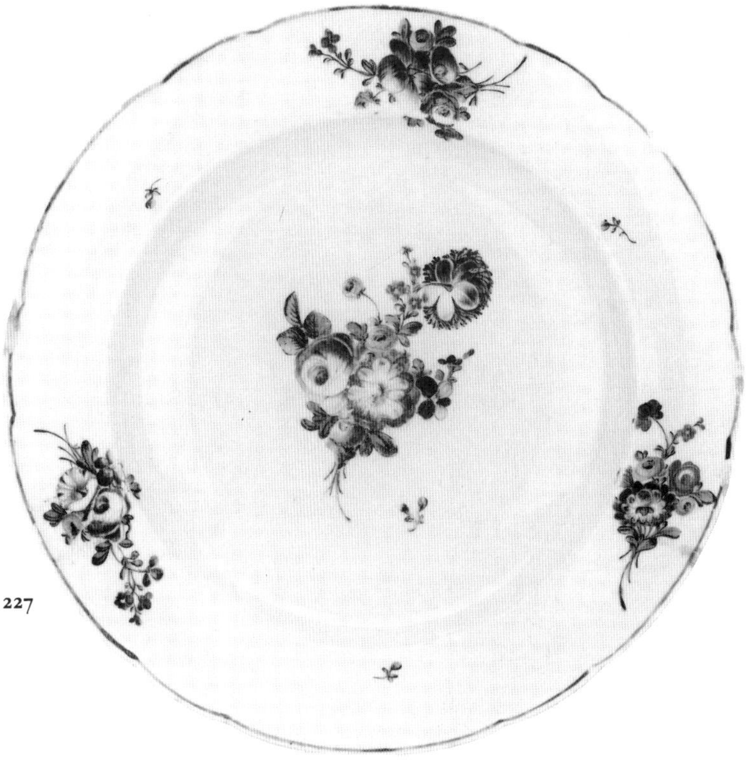

227

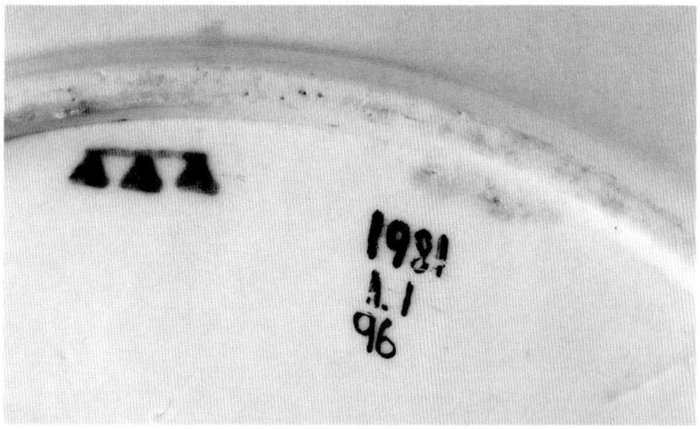

227 *mark*

is a pink line near the rim. Four chips and a crack to rim with some consequent discoloration.

Provenance: Bequeathed by Miss C.M. Woodward, 1981

Literature: Unpublished

Comparable Examples: See Chavagnac and Grollier, 1906, p. 416

The absence of gilding and the comparatively simple decorative scheme suggest that this piece, which forms part of a dinner service, was part of the middle range of the factory's production. The price charged for pieces of this kind has not been discovered.

228 **Jug**, *c.* 1777–88

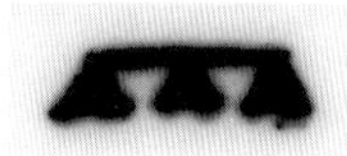

228 *mark*

H.	13.5 cm
Marks:	label painted in underglaze-blue
Reg. No.	Franks 405

Hard-paste porcelain,[1] highly translucent and white in tone, thrown. Pear-shaped, with wavy rim and wide lip, and tapering loop handle. The decoration consists of an oval medallion on each side, one painted in pink, orange, yellow, two shades of green, bright blue and grey with a single bird, the other with two birds, both in a landscape with trees. The medallions are elaborately outlined in gold with a simulated frame and suspended from a pink ribbon depending from a gold hook. The fame is surrounded by flower sprays painted in yellow (below) and blue (above). The medallions are connected by a polychrome flower chain tied with yellow ribbons below the upper handle terminal and below the lip, and there is a polychrome flower spray at the front and back of the jug. Around the neck is a stylised gilt pattern above a pattern of blue dots and below a gilt line. The rim is gilt with a dentil pattern on the inner surface; depending from a gilt line below the rim is a gilt laurel wreath with blue berries. The handle

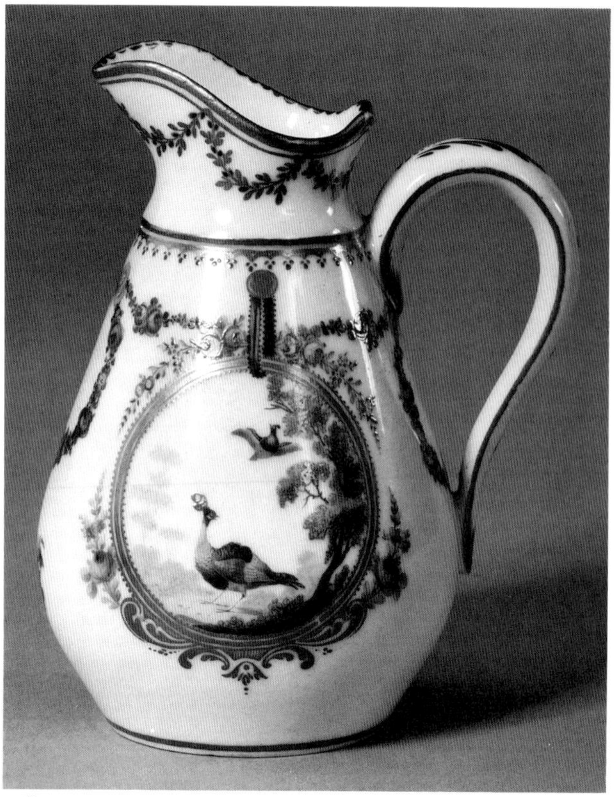

228

is partly gilt, and there is a gilt line near the foot. Inside base of jug uneven with large black inclusions.

Provenance: Bequeathed by Sir A.W. Franks, 1897

Literature: Franks, 1896, no. 405

Comparable Examples: None

Although white in appearance, and markedly different to cat. 227, the paste is marred in several places by numerous tiny black specks. These, together with the appearance of the inside of the jug, indicate production problems. The decoration is nevertheless unexpectedly rich, and is loosely based on Sèvres decorative themes.

1. X-ray diffraction analysis identified quartz, and showed a pattern which probably indicates the presence of mullite, BMRL 6374. The porcelain body may perhaps be considered as a hybrid type.

Boissettes[1]

Little is known about the hard-paste porcelain factory near Melun (Seine-et-Marne), around 32 km (20 miles) from Paris, or indeed about the tin-glazed earthenware factory which preceded it. In 1733 sieur Jacques Thomas Desrues de Boudreville was granted permission to make faïence using local clays.[2] In March 1757 the pottery, which was situated on the banks of the Seine,[3] was let to a certain Jacques Leclerc. In 1766 Louis Quiclet was its director.[4] Recent research suggests that in March 1775 Etienne-Dominique Pellevé, then director of the Etiolles porcelain factory (see pp. 293–296), acted as guarantor for his son Dominique-Jean-Etienne, 'artiste en porcelaine et marchand'[5] and Michel Vanier 'artiste en porcelaine'[6] on the lease of the faïence factory at Boissettes. The lease was to run for nine years from July 1775. The relatively low sums of 400 *livres* for the first three years, succeeded by 600 *livres* and 900 *livres* for the subsequent three-year periods indicate that the description of the kiln and buildings as in a poor state was correct, and that faïence production had ceased some time previously. Jacques Thomas Desrues de Boudreville (d. June 1775) also allowed Vanier and Pellevé to dig clay in the neighbouring terrain which had been used for bricks, and was probably suitable for saggars or other kiln furniture.[7]

Vanier probably left his employment at Etiolles when the factory there closed down in mid-1776. Earlier in the year he had been the subject of legal proceedings as a partner with Barbin's widow Marie-Geneviève Le Bastier in the failed factory at Mennecy, whose workers had been demanding their unpaid wages.[8] D.-J.-E. Pellevé was also in financial trouble, and once again the exact date of his arrival in Boissettes and the length of his stay there is at present unknown. It is probable that he was in Boissettes by March 1776.[9] Although no records have been discovered for workers at the factory before March 1776, and even these are inconclusive,[10] there remains the possibility that it was in production from mid-1775 and ceased some time during the following year, or alternatively in 1777.

On 13 January 1778 an *arrêt de Conseil d'Etat* authorised Jacques-Jean Vermonet (d. 1784) and his son, Jean-Jacques, both *bourgeois de Paris*, to make porcelain. A privilege was granted preventing any other concern operating in the same village, or within two leagues of it, and giving permission for Vermonet's products to be sold from an *entrepôt* in Paris. The factory was probably run by Bernard-Mathieu Aubry on behalf of the owners.[11] No record of the registration of any factory mark has been discovered and doubts have been expressed as to whether the underglaze-blue script *B* mark can be attributed to Boissettes. In the absence of a plausible alternative, however, it is currently considered to be the mark of this concern.

There is some evidence that the duc d'Orléans (1725–85) protected the factory, which infringed the monopoly granted to the royal factory by selling painted and gilded porcelain. On 28 February 1781 the baptism took place in the Boissettes area[12] of a daughter 'du sieur Bernard-Mathieu Aubry, directeur de la manufacture de porcelaine de Mgr le duc d'Orléans, et de demoiselle Jeanne Audibert'. A biscuit group, formerly in the de Courmont collection, of Turenne asleep on a cannon which rests on a chariot inscribed *Manufacture de S.A.S. Mgr le Duc D Orleans A BOISSET*[13] confirms the connection between Louis-Philippe d'Orléans and the factory, which awaits further study. At the time of his death in 1785 the duke was living one league from Boissettes, at Sainte-Assise, with his morganatic wife, Madame de Montesson.

Kaolin from Saint-Yrieix, plastic clay from Montereau-faut-Yonne and sand from Fontainebleau are said to have been used.[14] Few details of the workmen employed, their wages, or of the prices charged, have yet come to light. The names of fewer than ten men employed at Boissettes have been traced in local records. One, named Berger, may have been the Saxon Christian Gottlob Berger who is recorded as a sculptor at Mennecy. Others, too, such as Jacques Curlet, [?] Joseph Boucher, [?] François D'Hebert (or Derbert) and [?] Rémy Demany, also seem to have moved to Boissettes from Mennecy. A painter named Joseph Albert recorded at Boissettes in September 1777 was at Etiolles in 1774.[15]

The sites of the kiln(s) and workshops have been only tentatively identified, although it seems possible that excavation could pinpoint the former.[16]

The factory made a wide range of tablewares decorated with coloured flowers or birds with restrained gilding. Some more elaborately decorated pieces painted with landscapes, and one with a seascape, in cartouches have been traced, as well as monumental vases skilfully painted with flower bouquets.[17] Some pieces, such as a sugar bowl decorated with flowers and a dark blue ribbon motif,[18] consciously imitated Sèvres. The influence of other factories, notably Chantilly for the knops of *écuelles*,[19] is also evident. Biscuit and glazed figures and groups are known, including 'Cries of Paris' (see cat. 231) and groups of three or even four child musicians,[20] which bear some resemblance to Mennecy or even Niderviller groups. A group of fighting boys in the Victoria and Albert Museum, London, has been traced by John Mallet to a Höchst model, suggesting a possible link between the concerns which has not yet been explored.[21]

It is not known when the factory closed down, but it may perhaps have been at the time of the duc d'Orléans' death in 1785.

1 This account is based on G. Leroy, 'La Céramique à Boissettes (Seine-et-Marne) 1732–1781', *Réunion des sociétés des Beaux-Arts*, Vol. XXII, 1898, pp. 197–214; Chavagnac and Grollier, 1906, pp. 554–5, and on the most recent study by A. de Ravel d'Esclapon, *La porcelaine de Boissettes près Melun*, Le Mée-sur-Seine, 1991, which sheds some new light on the history of the factory, its workforce and its products and is based on archival sources. A thesis for the Ecole du Louvre was completed by Elizabeth Cousenon, to which this writer has not had access. The writer has adopted the spelling of the place name with a final 's', which is in current use on maps.

2. Leroy, *op. cit.*, pp. 209–11, reproduces the *arrêt de Conseil d'Etat du Roy* dated 1 December 1733; no examples were included in exh. *Faïences Françaises*, 1980.
3. Ravel d'Esclapon, *op. cit.*, p. 13, plan.
4. Leroy, *op. cit.*, p. 203.
5. Ravel d'Esclapon, *op. cit.*, pp. 18–20, p. 23, f.n. 1, p. 31.
6. *Ibid.*, p. 32.
7. *Ibid.*, p. 18.
8. *Ibid.*, p. 20, Archives de la ville de Paris et de la Seine, D2 B6 1155 (*Jugement du 18 mars 1776*).
9. *Ibid.*, p. 23, f.n. 1.
10. *Ibid.*, pp. 38–40.
11. *Ibid.*, p. 38.
12. Leroy, *op. cit.*, p. 205, no exact source given.
13. Chavagnac and Grollier, 1906, p. 555.
14. Leroy, *op. cit.*, p. 207.
15. Ravel d'Esclapon, *op. cit.*, pp. 38–40.
16. *Ibid.*, p. 21.
17. In a private collection, Paris. In the Ariana Museum, Geneva, are two large dishes inv. AR 1414, 1415 and two large tureens painted with flowers AR 1416, 1417. A plate-warmer (*assiette-réchaud*) painted with bouquets of flowers and with a gilt dentil rim, measuring 24.4 cm in the Musée de Saint-Omer, inv. 84.64, is illus. in exh. Nord-Pas-de-Calais, 1986–7, no. 13. A mustard-pot and stand painted with flowers, inv. D. 11367, and a two-handled sauceboat with a lobed stand, inv. A 13087, are in the Louvre Museum, Paris. Other pieces are illustrated or described in Ravel d'Esclapon, *op. cit.*, *passim*; the teapot with the seascape is in the Musée national de Céramique, Sèvres.
18. N. Ballu, n.d., pl. 34D.
19. Ravel d'Esclapon, *op. cit.*, p. 8, Musée de l'Ile de France, château de Sceaux.
20. Private collection, Paris; a group of four musicians is in the Musée national de Céramique, Sèvres, inv. 13602. These groups are well modelled and painted in green, pink, yellow, mauve, etc.
21. Private communication from John Mallet to the writer; inv. C. 151–1965; the Höchst group is illus. in K. Röder, *Das Höchster Porzellan auf der Jahrtausend-Ausstellung in Mainz 1925*, Mainz, 1930, pl. 39b, no. 213, wheel mark, Bayerisches Nationalmuseum, Munich. Röder draws attention to a similar painted scene on a Frankenthal coffee-pot, suggesting that they may have a common engraved source, which was perhaps also used at Boissettes.

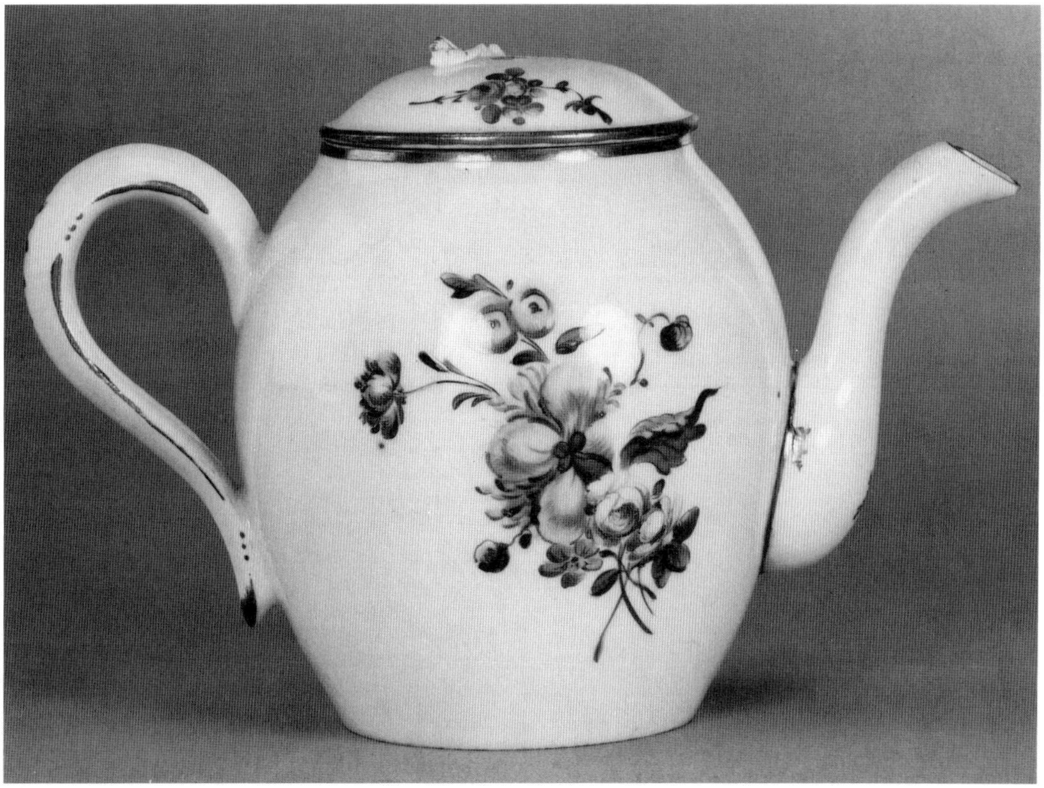

229

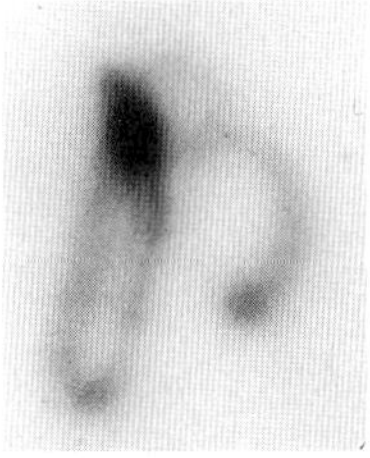

229 *mark*

229 Teapot and Cover, *c.*1778–*c.*1785

H. 10.5 cm
Marks: cursive *B* painted in underglaze-blue
Reg. No. Franks 439

Hard-paste porcelain, with moulded handle ridged down its centre, slightly domed cover with leaf finial and scar where remainder of finial broke away in firing. Painted with flowers in green, brown, orange, yellow, blue and purple. Rims gilt, handle partly gilt, gilt flower sprays on spout. Firecrack at base of spout, and glaze-filled chip at extremity.

Provenance: Bequeathed by Sir A.W. Franks, 1897

Literature: Franks, 1896, no. 439

Comparable Examples: Orléans, Musée Historique[1]

Switzerland, Geneva, Musée Ariana, inv. AR 1423, similarly decorated, shape differs somewhat

London, Victoria and Albert Museum, teapot and cover, reg. no. C.541 and a–1909

The lid is ill-fitting and there are a considerable number of defects of manufacture, such as firecracks, pin-holes, etc., which contradict the initial impression of a well-made and competently decorated pot.

At least two different teapot shapes are known at Boissettes, where flower decoration was commonly used. An ovoid teapot with conical cover and pointed knop[2] seems to be a rarer form than the museum example.

1. Ravel d'Esclapon, 1991, p. 56.
2. *Ibid.*, p. 103, Musée national de Céramique, Sèvres.

230 Tray (*plateau*), *c.*1778–*c.*1785

L. 28.5 cm
Marks: cursive *B* and two dots painted in underglaze-blue; incised *b*
Reg. No. Franks 440

Hard-paste porcelain, thickly potted. Painted in green, blue, yellow, pink, orange, and black enamels with a flower spray on each interior and exterior surface except for the irregularly-shaped end areas. Remains of gilt dentil decoration around inner rim. Chip at one end.

Provenance: Bequeathed by Sir A.W. Franks, 1897

Literature: Franks, 1896, no. 440

Comparable Examples: Paris, private collection, called Paris with no factory specified, illus. Dupont, 1987, p. 32, fig. 1

The shape, referred to for obvious reasons as a *bateau* (or alternatively as a *plateau à raves*), was in production at the Vincennes/Sèvres factory in 1752.[1] It was used

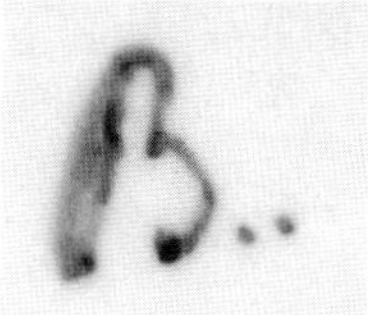

230 *marks*

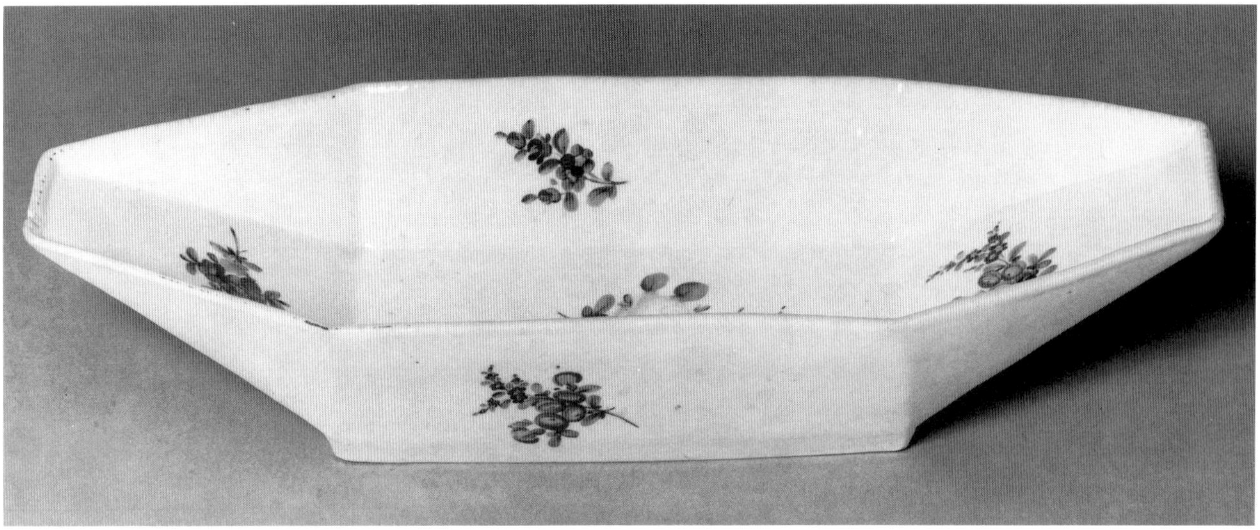

230

there as part of a *déjeuner* also comprising a sugar bowl and cover and a cup and acted as a tray or stand for these pieces. It is not known who designed it, or whether it was based on a metal prototype. It was also in production in England, notably at the Caughley factory, Shropshire.[2] During the nineteenth century the form was manufactured at the Berlin porcelain factory.[3]

1. Brunet and Préaud, 1978, no. 94.
2. An example decorated with an underglaze-blue *chinoiserie* scene is in the collection of Dr Bernard Watney, to whom the author is grateful for this information.
3. Pair of dishes painted with flowers, about 1820, sold Christie's, 30 June 1980, Lot 183.

231 **Pair of Female Figures – Fruit Seller and Vegetable Seller**, *c.*1778–*c.*1785

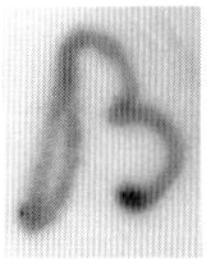

231 *mark*

See colour plate 37

H. 16 cm (vegetable seller); 15.9 cm

Marks: cursive *B* painted in underglaze-blue on both

Reg. No. 1989,5–6,1 and 2

Hard-paste porcelain, moulded. Hollow foot, glazed, except on rim. Each wears a cap (the fruit seller's trimmed with a pink ribbon) and an an orange fichu tucked into the low square neck of her jacket, over which is a long apron edged in blue and with a blue sash (sash omitted on the vegetable seller). The fruit seller, whose jacket is painted with orange dots and has short sleeves, has her left hand on her hip. Around her waist is a tray of fruit (restored) which was probably once supported by her right hand (restored). Her skirt is striped in pink and painted with a narrow green line above a yellow line at the hem. She wears black shoes and buckles and stands on a base imitating rockwork, supported by a tree trunk behind her feet. The vegetable seller wears a pink striped jacket, the sleeves bound in yellow, the hem in orange. Her skirt is similar to that of her companion but striped in pink and blue. Her sabots are orange. On her back is a basket of vegetables (restored), held by painted brown straps in relief (partly missing) over her shoulders.

Provenance: Purchased, 1989; Goldblatt Collection, Sotheby's, 1 May 1956, Lot 79

Literature: Unpublished

Comparable Examples: Sotheby's, 16 June 1987, Lot 79, H. 17 cm

These figures probably formed part of a series of 'Cries of Paris', but they appear to be the only ones known. A note in the Goldblatt sale catalogue (see above) states that it is unusual to find coloured examples, as the known examples are in biscuit. However, this writer is not aware of any biscuit versions of these figures.

The origin of the 'Cries of Paris' or sellers of goods and services in Paris, who announced their wares with shouts or songs, goes back to the early Middle Ages.[1] By the thirteenth century their importance was such that they were the subject of a poem *Crieries de Paris* by G. de la Villeneuve. Today's street vendors in Paris, many of Arab or African origin, and a few remaining trades such as shoeshiners and knife-grinders, are all that remains of a vast army of announcers, or town criers, servers and vendors of all kinds in operation both day and night. They were celebrated by writers and artists,[2] especially in the eighteenth century. Amongst those who represented the Cries are E. Bouchardon, F. Boucher, C. Huet, C.-N. Cochin, G. de Saint-Aubin, A. de Saint-Aubin and A. Watteau. Of these, Bouchardon and Huet had the greatest influence on the European porcelain factories. A *Vendeuse de Pommes* by E. Bouchardon may be the ultimate source for this fruit seller, although

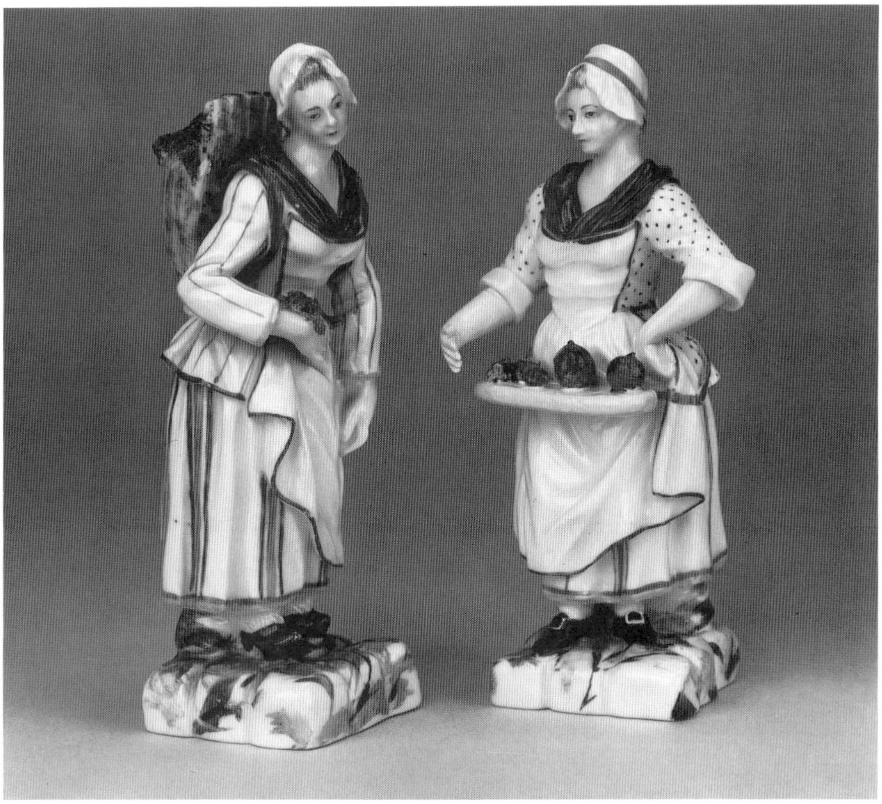

231

the costume is different.[3] A red crayon drawing by C.-N. Cochin *fils* entitled *Le chanteur de cantiques dans les rues de Paris* shows a girl with a similar basket probably carrying fruit,[4] but is unrelated to the porcelain figure.

Figures of the Paris Cries were first manufactured by Meissen, some after E. Bouchardon in 1747, others in 1753 after C. Huet.[5] Although Vincennes issued figures of various occupations,[6] only a few, such as the *Marchande de crème*, the *Petit Marchand de Cochons* and *La Savoyarde tenant un chien*, all attributed to Suzanne after Boucher in 1755, have any serious claim to represent Cries. Sèvres too manufactured only a relatively small number of Cries:[7] various 'marchands', Falconet's *Petit Pâtissier* (1757), Duru's *Amour Remouleur* (1778). A seated figure of a female fruit seller with a pierced basket, probably intended as a flower-holder, is attributed to Chantilly but is apparently unmarked.[8] A Mennecy fish and fruit seller is in the J. Paul Getty Museum, Malibu, California.[9] Cries of various towns were, however, popular at factories in the German-speaking lands.[10] A *Kleine Gemüsehändlerin* was made at Höchst and was apparently based on a Frankenthal model.[11] Fürstenberg even produced Cries of Moscow and Saint-Petersburg after engravings by J.B. Le Prince.[12] It is perhaps not surprising, therefore, that the Niderviller factory made the widest range, embracing more than 60 different models in porcelain and faïence.[13] Examples of a *Marchande de Fruit* and a *Marchande de Légumes* are recorded in faïence: a Strasbourg apple seller marked *PH 653* was on the Zurich market in 1924.[14]

Fruit and vegetable sellers, who bought their wares at the market for resale, were known in the eighteenth century as *poissardes*.[15] The Abbé Jaubert in his *Dictionnaire raisonné universel des arts et métiers*[16] writes: 'Quoique ce nom soit commun à toutes les femmes qui prennent de la Police des lettres regrats, il est cependant plus particulièrement affecté à celles qui dans les marchés publics et sous les pilliers des Halles vendent des fleurs naturelles ou artificielles, des fruits verts ou secs, des légumes de toutes [*sic*] espèce, du beurre, du fromage, du poisson frais, des salines, etc.'. There were so many of these hawkers, forming a potentially powerful group, that the King granted them certain special privileges, including free entry to theatrical performances of a patriotic nature. The *poissardes* had their own colourful slang, used by the playwright Vandé. They were organised in various 'communautés', or guilds, under the jurisdiction of the Paris police.

1. See V. Fournel, *Les Cris de Paris*, Paris, 1887; a recent study

by V. Milliot, *Le Peuple Travesti, les représentations des petits métiers parisiens au* XVIe *et* XVIIIe *siècles*, unpublished doctoral thesis for the University of Paris, I, Centre de Recherche en Histoire Moderne, 1990, 2 vols., explores the subject in depth, giving an extensive bibliography.

2. M. Pitsch, *La Vie Populaire à Paris*, Paris, 1949, 2 vols., gives a list of some of these artists and writers at the end of the text volume; see also M. Pitsch, *Essai de catalogue sur l'iconographie de la vie populaire à Paris* XVIIIe *siècle*, Paris, 1952 for a list of prints by various artists. Prints by a number of artists from all over Europe were shown in exh. *Street criers and itinerant tradesmen in European prints*, Stanford Art Gallery and Achenbach Foundation for Graphic Arts, California Palace of the Legion of Honor, San Francisco, California, 1970, catalogue compiled by D. Miller.
3. An example of this print in the B.M. is illustrated by K.T. Parker, 'Bouchardon's "Cries of Paris"', *Old Master Drawings*, December 1930, pp. 45–8, pl. 25.
4. Photograph in the Getty Photo Archive, whereabouts unknown.
5. A *Fischverkauferin* in a private collection in Munich was exhibited in 1966 in that city, see exh. Rückert, 1966, no. 948, pl. 230, perhaps modelled by Reinicke after 1753 when Jean Charles Huet sent drawings to the Meissen factory, still in production in 1765; a *Bäckerjunge mit Brotkiepe*, no. 953, pl. 231, was modelled in 1747, perhaps by Reinicke, after an engraving by Bouchardon from the series *Etudes prises dans le bas Peuple ou les Cris de Paris*. The watercolour drawings by Christophe Huet used at the Meissen factory are discussed by T.H. Clarke, 'The French Touch at Meissen: Christophe Huet's watercolour drawings for the Cris de Paris, 1753' *1990 International Art Dealers Show Handbook*, Seventh Armory, Park Avenue at 67th Street, New York City, October 1990, pp. 28–33. The author is most grateful to Mr Clarke for his assistance in tracing the source of these figures.
6. See exh. *Vincennes* 1977–8, pp. 149–84 for an almost complete listing of all figures known.
7. See Bourgeois and Lechevallier-Chevignard, n.d. [?1913] for a complete listing of all biscuit figures then known.
8. Sold Parke-Bernet, New York, 8 February 1947, Lot 280, Karrick Riggs Collection.
9. Inv. 86.DE.473, undecorated, incised *DV* on top of base. The author is grateful to the staff of the Getty Museum, especially Charissa Bremer-David, for help in examining this exceptional piece.
10. The fullest work on this subject is K.F. Beall, *Kaufrufe und Strassenhändler, Cries and Itinerant Trades*, Hamburg, 1975, which covers both Europe and the Americas.
11. K. Röder, *Das Höchster Porzellan auf der Jahrtausend-Ausstellung in Mainz 1925*, Mainz, 1930, pl. 201, no. 120, H. 11.3 cm, then in the collection of Frau Dr Otto Gastell, Mainz; refers to F.H. Hofmann, *Frankenthaler Porzellan*, 1911, pl. 91, no. 407.
12. Exh. *Weisses Gold aus Fürstenberg*, Westfälisches Landesmuseum, Münster, Herzog Anton Ulrich-Museum, Brunswick, December 1988–May 1989, no. 216, modelled by A.C. Luplau, 1773. Several other occupations, a girl with fowl, a girl with milk churns, etc., are after Berlin models, nos. 238–42.
13. Exh. Sarrebourg, 1986, pp. 91–4.
14. Sammlung von Antiquitäten und Ölgemälden aus Schweizerischem Privatbesitze, Meisskomer und Helbig, Zurich, 25, 26 February 1924, H. 18 cm.
15. Pitsch, *op. cit.*, p. 62.
16. Abbé Pierre Jaubert, *Dictionnaire raisonné universel des arts et métiers; contenant l'histoire, la description, la police des fabriques et manufactures de France et des pays étrangers*, Paris, 1773, 5 vols.; this passage is quoted by Pitsch, 1949, p. 62.

Lille

A hard-paste porcelain factory was established in the place des Carmes, Lille, by François Leperre shortly before or after it received royal permission and exemption from duties on raw materials in an edict dated 13 January 1784. In April and May 1784 Leperre sought further exemptions on coal together with a loan. The latter was granted to Leperre and his wife Julie Durot. Her father appears to have been associated with Michel Vanier, originally of Orléans (see page 312, f.n. 3) and another man named Paulet in the invention of a firing process using coal. Vanier in fact claimed to be solely responsible for the process.[1] On 31 May 1785 the *intendant* of Flanders, M. Esmangard, wrote to M. de Calonne, his predecessor and now *contrôleur-général des finances*, with a request from the Leperre-Durot enterprise that it take the title 'Manufacture des porcelaines de Monseigneur le Dauphin' and use the Dauphin's arms. Calonne agreed, having received 'un très bel échantillon' or sample of ware, and in July the factory began to use a crowned dolphin as its mark.

However the enterprise seems always to have been prey to financial problems, applying to the municipality for further subventions in May 1785. The two-year absence in Paris of Leperre-Durot and of his leading workmen, summoned by Calonne to demonstrate his coal-firing techniques, was probably responsible for the decline of the factory. In a report of 1789[2] it was described as follows: 'Cette manufacture est très importante. Elle a langui pendant quelques temps par des circonstances particulières et fâcheuses pour les entrepreneurs . . . On y travaille des porcelaines de la plus belle et de la meilleure qualité.'

In 1790 the factory was sold to a shareholding company of which a certain Gaboria became director. Although coal-firing was abandoned, the number of employees doubled to reach 80 in 1791. New public loans were obtained in 1791 and a vigorous export policy instituted, especially towards England. Gaboria was succeeded by Roger, Graindorge (1792) and Renault. In 1801 annual production reached 55,000 cups and service items, 5,000 groups and vases, and 8,000 francs was spent on gold for gilding. The mark *a Lille* belongs to the post-Revolutionary period.[3]

The most impressive pieces ever made at the factory are two versions of a covered vase with dolphin handles, one measuring 57 cm in height. This is painted with scenes of a kiln firing and its lid is pierced for pot-pourri. It was made for Louis, Dauphin of France, in about 1785.[4] The second vase was presented to the *intendant* Calonne in the same year.[5] Two covered vases painted with flower garlands, scrolls and birds are futher proof of the skill of the Lille factory potters.[6] Several marked examples, including salt-cellars, covered saucepans and plates with floral or bird decoration were on the market in Paris in 1990.[7] A water jug measuring 23 cm in height decorated with dead game[8] is a further example of the high-quality production of this factory. The names of the workmen responsible for these exceptional pieces are unknown.

1. Archives départementales, L. 1449, quoted in exh. *Nord-Pas-de- Calais*, 1986–7, p. 53, on which this account of the factory at Lille is based.
2. *Etat des usines et bouches à feu de 1788–89*, Archives départementales, C. 191, quoted *ibid.*, p. 54.
3. A biscuit group, perhaps after Cyfflé, of Belisarius being guided by a child in the Musée des Beaux-Arts de Lille incised *a Lille* is illus. in exh. cat. *Nord-Pas-de-Calais*, 1986–7, no. 31. Another known as 'the Birth of Love' in the Musée de Saint-Omer is no. 33.
4. Amsterdam, Rijksmuseum, inv. R.B.K. 1965–104, unpub-

lished. The author is grateful to Mr J.D. van Dam for supplying information about this piece.
5. Lille, Musée des Beaux-Arts, illus. (when in the Mme. Guy de Wendel Collection) P. Alfassa and J. Guérin, *Porcelaine française du XVIIIe au milieu du XIXe siècle*, Paris, 1932, pl. 87b; see also *La Revue du Louvre*, 1988, no. 2, p. 162.
6. Illus. *La Folie d'Artois*, issued on the occasion of an exhibition at the château de Bagatelle, Paris, 1985, p. 221, with Maurice Segoura.
7. Paris, Ader, Picard, Tajan, 3 October 1990, Lots 6–11.
8. H.-P. Fourest, *Masterpieces of Western and Near Eastern Ceramics, Vol. VI, French Ceramics*, Tokyo, 1979, no. 117, Musée national de Céramique, Sèvres, inv. 3012.

---

232 **Toilet Pot and Cover**, *c.*1790–1800

H. 7.5 cm
Marks: *a. lille* painted in black; incised *h*
Reg. No. Franks 441

Hard-paste porcelain, domed cover and pointed knop. Decorated with a green wreath in a panel surrounded by yellow borders with a stylised purple wreath enclosed by gilt lines; around the rest of the cup, which is similarly painted, is a pattern of blue borders with pendent gold and pink wreaths. The pattern is repeated on the cover. Rims gilt, handle partly gilt. Perfect.

Provenance: Bequeathed by Sir A.W. Franks, 1897

Literature: Franks, 1896, no. 441

Chavagnac and Grollier, 1906, p. 589

Comparable Examples: New York, Sotheby Parke-Bernet, The Harbeson Collection of Porcelain, Continental Porcelain – Part 3, 4 April 1972, Lot 183, called 'covered custard cup', H. $3\frac{3}{8}$ in., not illus.

For pieces with this mark, see Chavagnac and Grollier, *ibid.*

Small pots like these are likely to have been used for face cream.

The wreath may have been intended to enclose a monogram.

A plate in a private collection painted with flowers in colour marked *a LILLE* in blue was exhibited at the Musée des Beaux-Arts, Lille, in 1951[1] and a *trembleuse* cup and saucer with blue flower spray decoration marked *a Lille* is in the Musée de Saint-Omer.[2]

1. Exh. *Céramique régionale ancienne*, Lille, Beaux-Arts, April–May 1951, no. 488.
2. Inv. 84–25, illus. exh. Nord-Pas-de-Calais, 1986–7, no. 26.

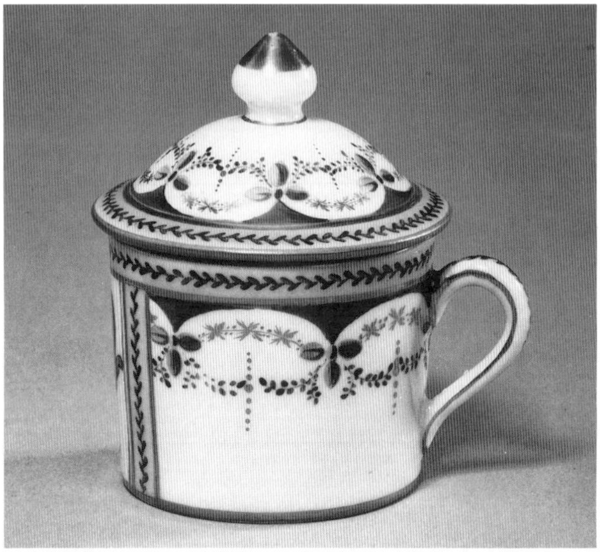

232

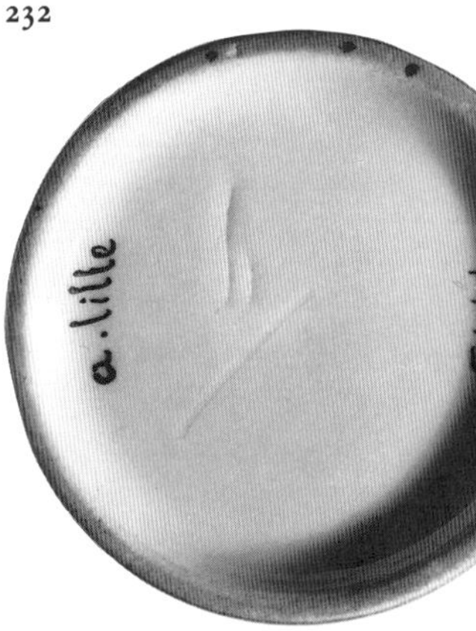

232 *marks*

Valenciennes

Jean-Baptiste Fauquez (b.1742) was authorised by the King to manufacture porcelain for ten years, using a coal-firing process at Valenciennes, on 24 May 1785.[1] On 2 February 1786 Fauquez sold the concern to his brother-in-law Charles-Louis-Joseph-Humbert Lamoninary (1739–1818) and to Michel Vanier[2] for the sum of 24,731 *livres*. Lamoninary is mentioned in a document of 20 October 1787 as the owner of the factory,[3] Vanier having left for Bordeaux in July 1787.[4]

In about 1795 Lamoninary emigrated, but returned to Valenciennes around 1800 and re-opened the factory. In 1803 porcelain was exhibited on the occasion of the Emperor's visit to Douai. Financial difficulties forced the closure and sale of the factory on 30 January 1810.

Clay supplied by Grellet from the Limoges region[5] was used to make hard-paste porcelains, although some soft-paste pieces bearing the factory mark have survived.[6] Teawares, service pieces such as *compotiers* (fruit compote dishes), butter dishes, pierced fruit baskets, water jugs and basins are mostly decorated with flowers (Angoulême sprigs or bouquets) and are based on shapes used at the royal factory, or at the Paris concerns. Sepia-painted landscape scenes are well executed.[7]

Firings were probably frequent and successful. A record made by the inspectors employed by the town magistrates and another from the Department of Hainaut reveals that a large kiln fired on 18 November 1785 was unloaded early on the morning of 25 November. From this kiln were drawn 1,548 items, 668 glazed and the remainder unglazed; the previous biscuit firing of 17 October had been unloaded on 24 October and comprised 940 pieces, 66 of which were defective.

Several names of workers are known. Around 1788 there were about thirty directly concerned with production, and before its closure the factory counted no less than eighty-eight workers including ten throwers, eight modellers, twelve painters and six gold burnishers. Two painters called Barre and Muiten, who had left the factory, were found to be decorating ware outside the factory in 1787; Antoine Gelez, Jean-Philippe Mester and Barthélemy Poinboeuf, as well as Anstett, born in Strasbourg (first name unknown, but see p. 284), were also employed at Valenciennes. Besides Verboeckhoven, two men named Renaud and Gillis, the latter known afterwards at Tournay, are known to have been sculptors at Valenciennes.

1. See A. Lejeal, *Recherches historiques sur les manufactures de faïence et de porcelaine de l'Arrondissement de Valenciennes*, Valenciennes, 1868, p. 65. Dr Lejeal's collection was sold at Valenciennes on 19 January 1880 and contained a considerable number of pieces including biscuit figures after models by Fiquaert as well as 'terres sèches', terracottas and plaster models by B. Verboeckhoven (called Fiquaert 1754–1840) executed for the Valenciennes porcelain factory. A copy of the sale catalogue is in the library of the Sèvres porcelain factory.
2. For Vanier's activities see also Lille, Bordeaux, pp. 307–8, pp. 311–13.
3. Lejeal, *op. cit.*, p. 73, and see pp. 79–94 for an account of Lamoninary's life.
4. Du Pasquier, 1989, p. 22.
5. Chavagnac and Grollier, 1906, p. 600, f.n. 1, quoting Archives de Limoges, Grellet correspondence, 22 July 1785.
6. Exh. Nord-Pas-de-Calais, 1986–7, no. 61, a sugar basin on stand, closely based on the Sèvres form known as *sucrier de Monsieur le Premier*.
7. The most extensive series of illustrations of pieces from this factory is in the above catalogue, nos. 61–77.

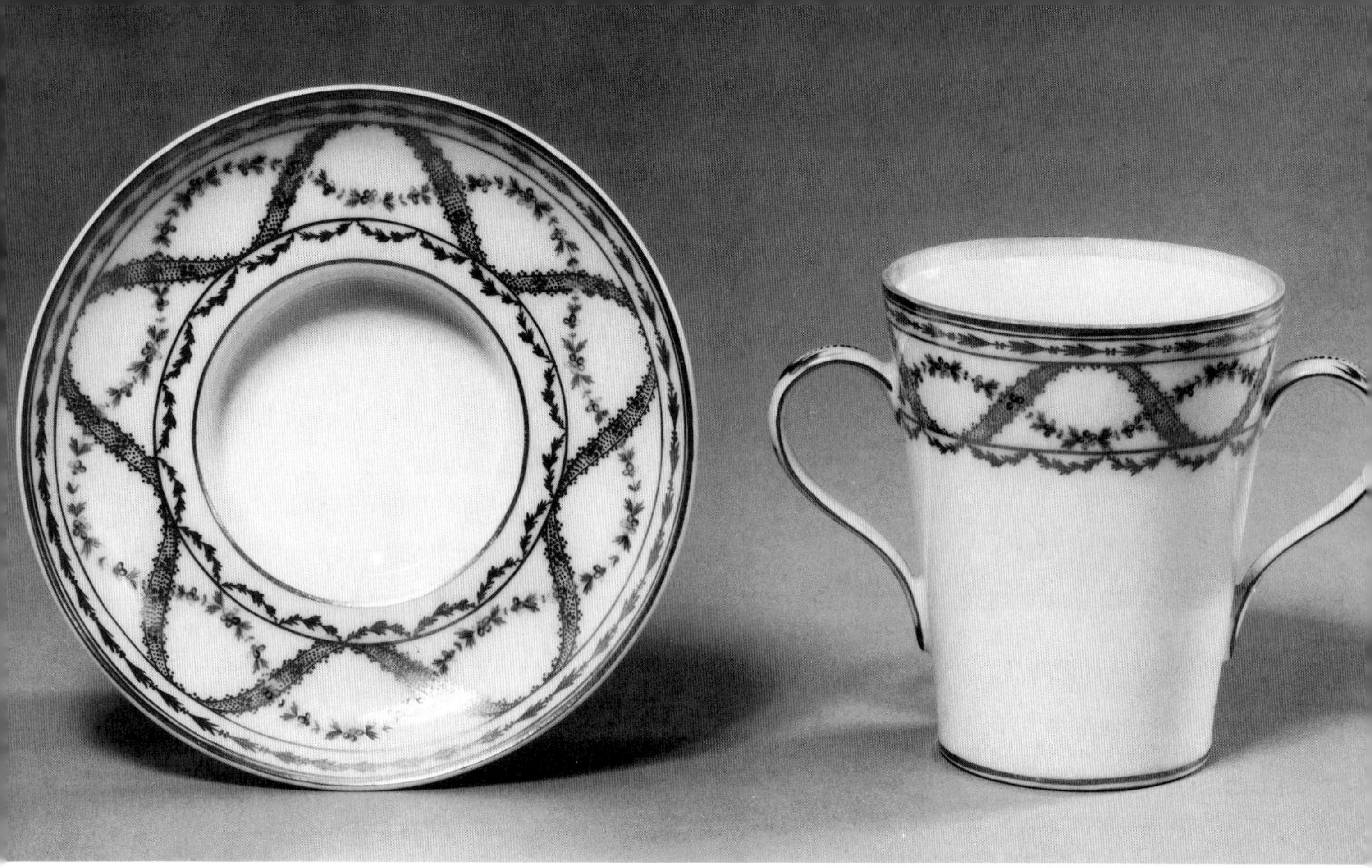

233

233 **Two-handled Cup** (cover missing) **and** ***Trembleuse*** **Saucer**, *c.*1785

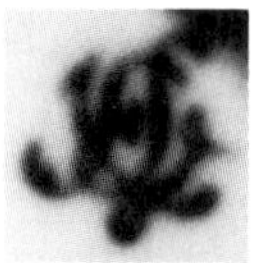

233 *mark*

D. *of saucer:*	15.9 cm
H. *of cup:*	11.2 cm
Marks:	*FLV* in monogram painted in underglaze-blue
Reg. No.	Franks 442

Hard-paste porcelain; flared cup with loop handles and shallow curved saucer with deep well, decorated with gilt ribbon and stylised leaf chains in gold, the ribbon entwined with a flower garland painted in mauve, yellow and green; handles partly gilt, gilt line near foot. One handle repaired.

Provenance: Bequeathed by Sir A.W. Franks, 1897

Literature: Franks, 1896, no. 442
Chaffers, 1926, Vol. II, p. 351, fig. 313

The monogram stands for Fauquez, Lamoninary, Vanier (see *supra*).

Amongst the pieces listed in the report of the November 1785 firing (see *supra*), which were all tablewares, were eighty *Soucoupes de grandes tasses* which might correspond with this saucer.[1]

Around the inside of the rim of the cup the glaze has been carefully wiped away, presumably so that a cover could be fitted.

1. Lejeal, 1868, pp. 69–72.

Bordeaux[1]

The beginnings of porcelain production in Bordeaux remain obscure. In June 1781 Pierre Verneuilh (1708–87), a rich Bordeaux merchant who had sold porcelain from his shop since at least 1774,[2] and his nephew Jean (1750–1832), who had been associated with him since 1779 when the capital of their concern amounted to no less than 120,000 *livres*, became tenants of land close to the Garonne river and of the adjoining château de Bordes. It is considered unlikely that they made much porcelain between 1781 and the arrival of the experienced porcelain-maker Michel Vanier (1747–90)[3] in 1787.

Two pieces of evidence support this view. In his *Journal* François de Paul Latapie, *inspecteur des arts et manufactures*, recorded that in 1785 there were in Bordeaux eight faïence-makers and a porcelain factory supplied with clay from Saint-Yrieix: 'elle est encore bien faible, on n'y travaille qu'en blanc'.[4] Porcelain from Limoges of both first and second quality was still apparently being sent to the Verneuilhs in July 1785, as a surviving invoice from Alluaud of Limoges testifies.[5] Secondly, an inventory dated 3 August 1787[6] contains no mention of any decorating workshop or room where colours were stored or prepared.

The arrival of Vanier in 1787 was crucial. Although the contract he signed with the Verneuilhs on 29 July 1787 has disappeared, a surviving letter from him dated 10 November that same year to François Alluaud (1739–99), maker and seller of a fine porcelain body in Limoges, shows that Vanier rented the factory and in exchange produced for the Verneuilhs white porcelain made with raw materials from Limoges. These pieces are, presumably, those marked with the interlaced *VV*. Vanier, who by November was already negotiating a partnership with Alluaud in order to raise capital, became a salaried employee of the Verneuilhs. He kept some porcelain, marking it with an *A* and *V*, sometimes accompanied by the word *Bordeaux* in capital letters in underglaze-blue. It was not until 1 January 1788 that Alluaud formally became Vanier's partner. Strangely, when Pierre Verneuilh died in September 1787, he left no mention in his will of the porcelain factory.

In December 1787, according to correspondence between Vanier and Alluaud, the former wrote about a coal-fired kiln which he evidently intended to install for the biscuit firing. The enamel kiln was wood- or charcoal-fired and it too was designed by Vanier. Growing financial difficulties forced the closure of the retail outlet at Allées de Tourny in December 1789. An inventory taken before its contents were transferred to another shop in rue Saint-Rémy, Bordeaux, owned by Antoine-Ambrose Omont *jeune* of Paris, who was to act as agent, listed 2,500 items of porcelain. Vanier died not long after on 15 February 1790, apparently in dire financial straits, as his funeral expenses could not be met by his widow.

Although a few firings took place soon after Vanier's death, production ceased. The remaining white porcelain comprising several thousand pieces was decorated in the next few years. Some pieces bear the mark *Omont à Bordeaux*. The factory itself was sold on 13 Floréal, l'an III (2 May 1795). Jean Verneuilh continued selling all kinds of porcelain, including Bordeaux wares, remaining in business until his death in 1832.

A great variety of domestic wares were made at Bordeaux. Teawares of all sorts, large quantities of plates, *compotiers*, soup tureens, terrines, ice-cream coolers, butter dishes on stands, jampots and many other forms are listed in the records of kiln firings.

Snuffboxes, wine-labels, bidets, *veilleuses*, soap dishes, ornamental vases and biscuit figures are known to have been produced, but few have survived.[7] Mostly decorated with floral, bird or occasionally with landscape subjects[8] or trophies, Bordeaux porcelain conforms to the taste of the late eighteenth century, owing a certain debt in some cases to the royal factory for their shapes and to the Paris concerns for their decorative motifs.

The names of forty to fifty workers, both male and female, have been traced, although they have not been published.[9] Many originally worked at Limoges. A moulder named Klein, perhaps of German origin, had been at the Pontenx factory in the Landes region; another, Herbet, had worked at Chantilly. Several other employees also came from Chantilly.

1. This account is based on exh. du Pasquier, 1989, pp. 13–36, which in turn relies on other sources including an unpublished thesis of the Ecole du Louvre by P. Venot, *Michel Vanier à Lille, Valenciennes, Bordeaux*.
2. A bill signed by the Verneuilh brothers and dated October 1774 lists not only faïence but also an expensive 'pot à l'eau et jatte de porcelaine dorée' at 30 *livres* and one 'gobelet doré avec soucoupe', see J. du Pasquier, 'Du nouveau sur la porcelaine de Bordeaux', *Revue historique de Bordeaux et du département de la Gironde*, Vol. XXVI, nouvelle série, 1977, p. 83, f.n. 4; the bill quoted is in Archives départementales de la Gironde, 2 E 1013.
3. Vanier was a native of Orléans, and was apprenticed in the porcelain factory there, where his parents were employed. He left for Etiolles after his marriage in 1768. In 1783 he was a widower in Paris and in 1784 was making porcelain in Lille. In 1785 he went to the Valenciennes factory.
4. Du Pasquier, 1977, *op. cit.*, p. 84.
5. Exh. du Pasquier, 1989, p. 20, f.n. 6; the document is in the Archives départementales de la Haute-Vienne, C. 3004.
6. *Ibid.*, f.n. 5.
7. Several ornamental vases are illus. in exh. du Pasquier, 1989.
8. A water jug and basin in the Louvre Museum, finely painted with waterside scenes is illus. by J. du Pasquier, 'La céramique à Bordeaux et la manufacture des Terres de Bordes (1781–90)', in *Le port des lumières 3. Le décor de la vie, Bordeaux 1781–1790*, Musée des arts décoratifs, Bordeaux, 1989, p. 27. Two flower vases painted with landscape scenes from the Musée des arts décoratifs, Bordeaux, are illustrated in exh. du Pasquier, 1989, no. 97.
9. Exh. du Pasquier, 1989, p. 33, no source given.

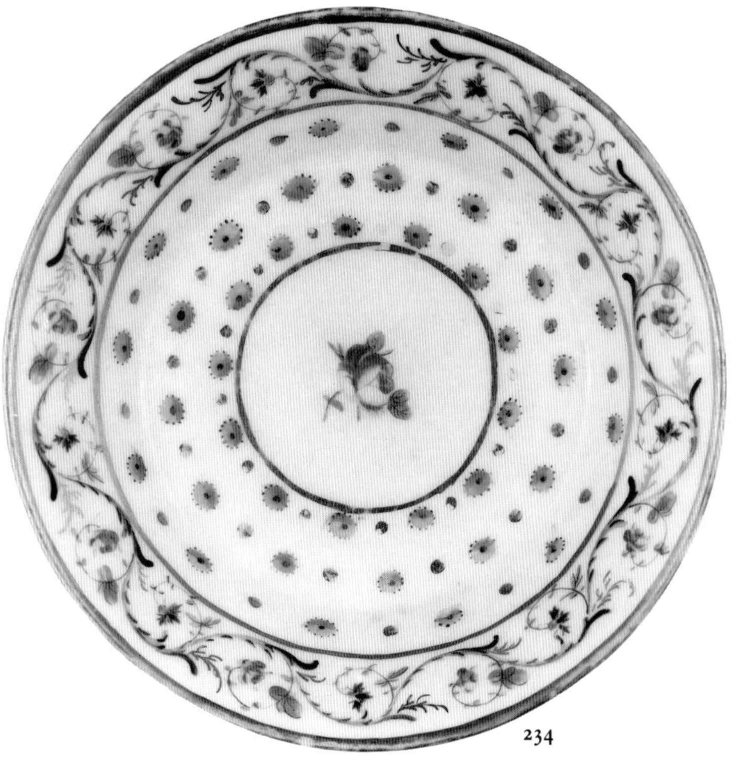

234

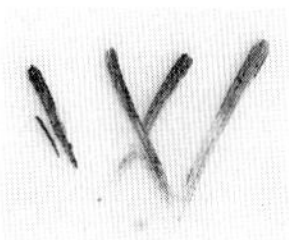

234 *mark*

234 **Saucer,** Verneuilh Factory, 1781–7

D. 12.6 cm
Marks: interlaced *VV* in gold above a dot, almost effaced
Reg. No. FB18 (AF 3220)

Hard-paste porcelain; deep flared sides. Painted in pink, red-brown, mauve, blue, green, and grey with scrolls and stylised flowers and leaves, and with gilt branches on the border which is defined by gilt lines. The rest of the saucer, except for the centre where there is a pink rose, is decorated with yellow and brown *oeil de perdrix* and gilt dots.

Provenance: Bequeathed by Sir A.W. Franks, 1897

Literature: Unpublished

Comparable Examples: None

Although no exact parallel has been discovered, the painted scroll decoration is characteristic of the Verneuilh factory in production at the *château des Terres de Bordes*.[1]

1. The author is most grateful to Jacqueline du Pasquier, *conservateur* at the Musée des arts décoratifs, Bordeaux, for her assistance in the attribution of this piece, and the bowl and cover (cat. 235), and for her generosity in providing information. Seventy-three pieces of which the majority are plates, bearing the mark of the Verneuilhs, from the Musée des arts décoratifs, Bordeaux, the Musée national de Céramique, Sèvres, and the Louvre (a teapot, presently on loan to Bordeaux) are described in exh. du Pasquier, 1989.

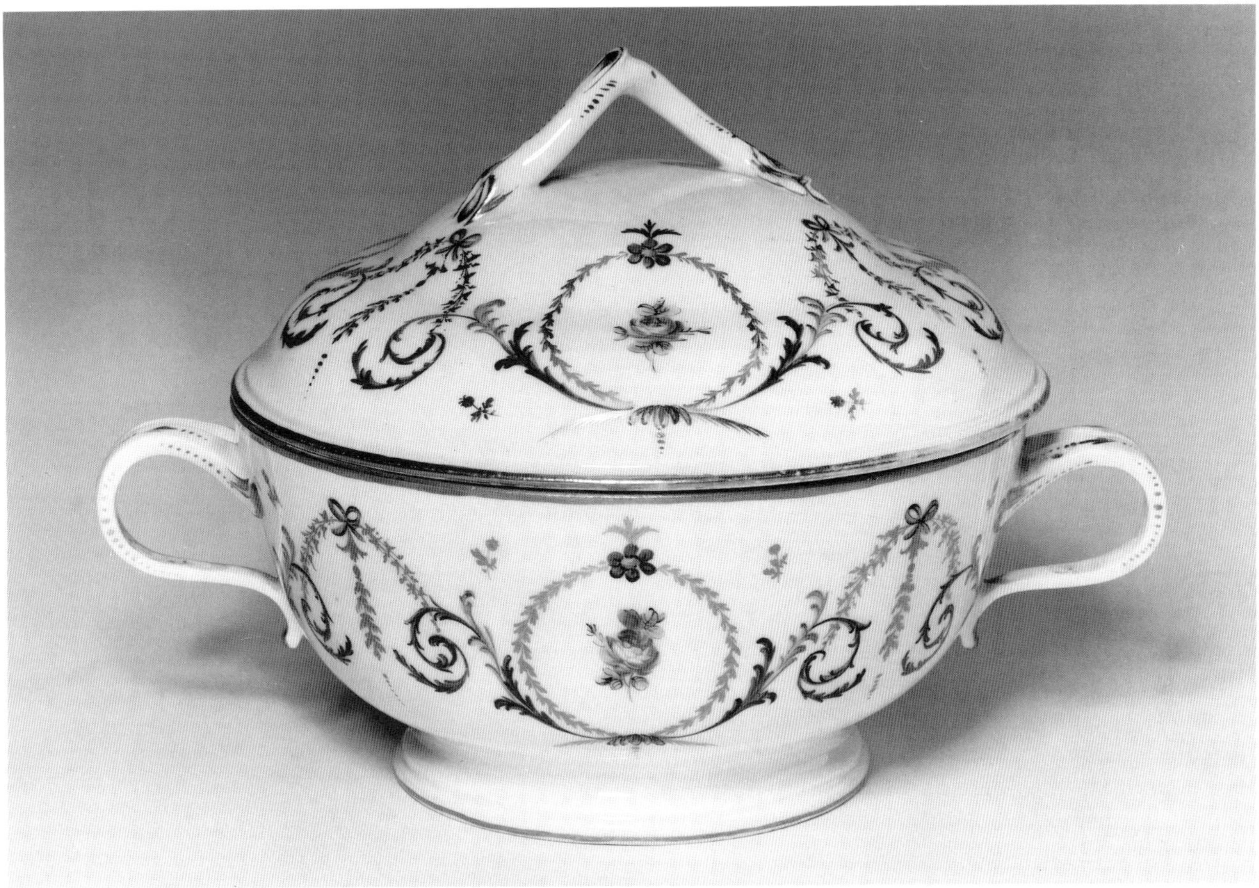

235

235 **Two-handled Bowl and Cover,** Alluaud and Vanier Factory, 1787–90

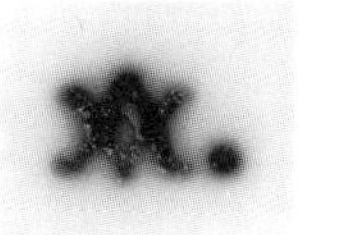

235 *mark*

H. 14 cm
Marks: *VA.* in monogram and a dot painted in underglaze-blue
Reg. No. Franks 412

Hard-paste porcelain, the handles having a double terminal at the upper end and an outward kick at the lower. Domed cover with twig handle. The decoration consists of scrolls painted in orange, purple, yellow, and brown enamels which frame a medallion of gilt leaves enclosing a pink rose. The scrolls are linked by a gilt leaf motif. Rims gilt, handles partly gilt.

Provenance: Bequeathed by Sir A.W. Franks, 1897

Literature: Franks, 1896, no. 412

Comparable Examples: London, Victoria and Albert Museum, teapot and cover (inv. C.25–1922) and cup and cover (inv. C.442&a–1915) decorated with very similar scrolls

The scrolls, like those on the saucer (cat. 234), are typical of Bordeaux-decorated porcelain. A smaller broth bowl measuring 11.6 cm in diameter and 6 cm in height, with slightly different handles is in the Musée national de Céramique, Sèvres. Marked in red with interlaced *VV*, it lacks a cover but does have a slightly lobed stand of circular form, with which the British Museum bowl was probably once provided.[1]

1. Exh. du Pasquier, 1989, no. 9.

Caen

The beginnings of porcelain manufacture at Caen are generally dated to around 1798.[1] Monsieur d'Aigemont-Desmares is known to have been the factory director until late 1802 or early 1803 when he was replaced by Monsieur Ducheval.

In April 1803 the factory showed its wares at the Exposition du produit des arts du Calvados'. The shareholders, who had apparently set up a company six years previously, were awarded a medal. In his report Monsieur Pierre-Aimé Lair commented 'Les objets nombreux exposés à nos regards, nous ont frappé par la blancheur de la pâte, l'élégance des formes, le bon choix des dessins, et le brillant des couleurs'.[2]

The *Annuaire du Calvados* for *l'an* XII (1803–4) records that around forty workers were employed and that '*Citoyen Ducheval, négociant*' was the director.[3] Despite wartime conditions, the concern was expanding. However, this was no longer true by the time of the following year's *Annuaire*, nor had the situation improved by 1805–6. The concern probably closed down in early 1806, and in any case was not represented in the 1806 *Exposition*.

Clay from St Yrieix, near Limoges, was used at first; later, clay from Alençon, Pieux (near Cherbourg) and from a deposit at Beaufray near Laigle, about 50 miles (80 km) or so from Caen, replaced it. A contemporary account of 1803 records the discovery of clay at La Poustière (in the commune of Beaufray) which was initially sent to Paris 'mais depuis peu, on l'envoie à Caen où il est vendu 30 francs le poinçon, mesure d'Orléans, et pesant 483 livres . . .'[4]

1. This account is based on R. de Brébisson, 'La porcelaine de Caen', *Revue normande et percheronne illustrée*, Alençon, 1895, pp. 21–8, who refers to G. Villers, 'Notice sur la manufacture de porcelaine dure de Bayeux', *Annuaire de l'Association Normande*, 1857, as the earliest account. The most recent is J. Le Jeune, *Les anciennes manufactures de porcelaine de Basse-Normandie*, Coutances, 1962, chapter on Caen, pp. 145–73, which refers to examples at the Musée national de Céramique, Sèvres, Musée national Adrien-Dubouché, Limoges, Victoria and Albert Museum, London, Musée Carnavalet, Paris, and in private collections. This author does not cite the sources of his information. For another note on the factory's history see F. Debaisieux, 'Caen. Musée des Beaux-Arts, Orfèvrerie et porcelaine de Caen', in *La Revue du Louvre*, Fév. 1980, no. 1, pp. 54–6, Acquisitions des musées de province. Pieces in the Musée des Beaux-Arts, Caen, are illustrated by Dupont, 1987, pp. 153–4 and p. 156. A *tasse litron et soucoupe* painted with swags of flowers and leaves is in the National Museums on Merseyside, Liverpool Museum, inv. 54.185.114.
2. P.-A. Lair, see '*Mémoires de la Société d'Agriculture et de Commerce de Caen, Mélanges divers*, Vol. II.
3. Quoted Brébisson, *op. cit.*, p. 24.
4. L.-C.-N. Delestang, *Chorographie du IVe arrondissement du département de l'Orne*, Argentan, l'an XI (1803), quoted Brébisson, *op. cit.*, p. 22.

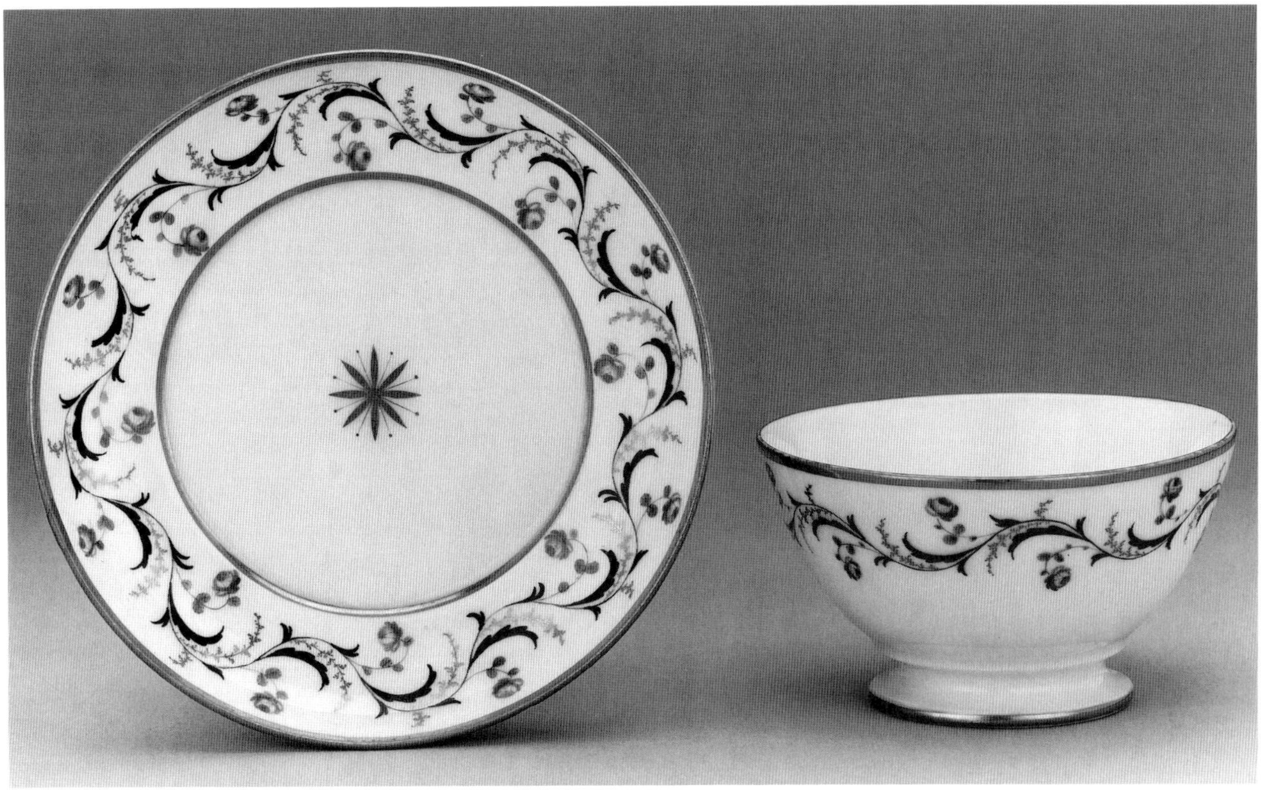

236

236 **Bowl and Stand,** *c.*1798–1806

D. *of stand:*	14.6 cm
H. *of bowl:*	5.8 cm
Marks:	*Caen* stencilled in red on both
Reg. No.	Franks 445

Hard-paste porcelain, the stand with a broad well and shallow curved rim, the bowl on a deep out-turned foot. The decoration consists of a running leaf scroll painted in black enamel from which spring small pink roses on green stems, alternating with sprays of tiny gilt leaves. Rims and edge of well gilt; gilt star motif in centre of stand.

Provenance: Bequeathed by Sir A.W. Franks, 1897

Literature: Franks, 1896, no. 445

Comparable Examples: London, Victoria and Albert Museum, milk jug, coffee can and saucer and sugar bowl, inv. 434 to 7–1899.

Chavagnac believed that the Caen factory principally produced undecorated pieces which were painted in Paris,[1] but this piece, with its rather sparse decoration, was probably painted in Caen.

1. Chavagnac and Grollier, 1906, p. 644.

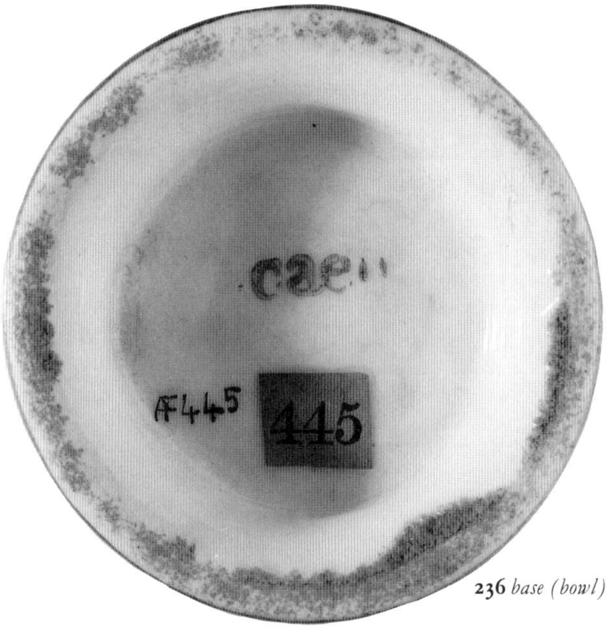

236 *base (bowl)*

Limoges, Tressemanes and Vogt's factory[1]

Gustave Vogt (1849–1937) son of John Vogt, a German merchant who established an import business in New York in the 1840s, went into partnership as an agent in Limoges with Emilien de Tressemanes in 1882.[2] Being unable to keep pace with American demand for porcelain, they set up their own factory in Limoges in 1891. Both dinner services and novelty items were made in the years before the First World War.

1. This factory is one of many operating in Limoges, centre of the French porcelain industry in the nineteenth and twentieth centuries, which remains completely unstudied. Although the author consulted a number of publications held by the Archives de Sèvres issued by the industry in the early years of this century, she was unable to discover information concerning its location, workforce or products.
2. D'Albis and Romanet, 1980, pp. 155–7.

---

237 **Cup with Silver Overlay,** *c.*1891–1900

237 *mark*

H.	3.7 cm
Marks:	*T&V* enclosed within a lozenge above *FRANCE*, printed in green
Reg. No.	OA 10576

Hard-paste eggshell porcelain, highly translucent, almost flat glazed base, curved sides, the surface coloured duck-egg blue, overlaid with a silver scroll pattern alternating with three ogival reserves containing an obelisk incised with hieroglyphs, a tower surmounted by a three-tier ziggurat-like spire, and a banded column with an onion-shaped base. The rim, handle and foot rim are bound in silver.

Provenance: Unknown

Literature: Unpublished

Comparable Examples: None

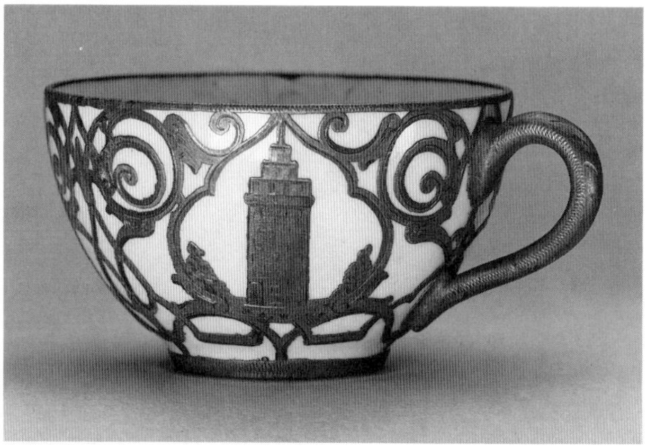

237 *(reproduced slightly larger than lifesize)*

In 1891 the US McKinley Tariff Act obliged manufacturers to add the country of origin to their factory marks; the words 'Made In' and the country of origin generally denote a twentieth-century dating.[1] The date of entry of this cup into the Museum collections is unknown.

The exact method of attaching the silver casing and handle has not been discovered. The cut appearance of some of the edges indicates that the silver was sliced away to produce the pattern. The surface of the casing has also been carefully incised, except on the rim, foot rim and handle where the zigzag pattern has been impressed with a tool. The exotic and eclectic nature of the decorative motifs is perhaps most associated with the decade 1870–80.

A cream jug and stand in the Musée national Adrien-Dubouché, Limoges, is the only other piece (apart from cat. 240) discovered which was decorated in a similar technique.[2] Silver rosettes and scrolls have been applied to the dark blue ground and white, pink and green enamels added as further embellishment. The pieces bear the mark of the Limoges manufacturer Raymond Laporte used between 1883 and 1897 and the saucer is inscribed in red as follows: *Avril 1886 Essai d'application métallique par galvano plastique sur porcelaine Gustave Demartial fils* and *CH. Dumontet sc.* The jug and stand were exhibited in the Exposition de Limoges in 1886 and acquired in November of that year for 125 francs.[3]

1. G. Godden, *Encyclopaedia of British Pottery and Porcelain Marks*, London, 1964, reprinted ed. 1983, p. 11.
2. Inv. ADL 2788, H. of jug to top of handle 12.3 cm; D. of saucer 12.6 cm.
3. The author is grateful to Madame C. Joua for her help in providing information about this piece and for making it available for examination.

Limoges,[1] Gérard, Dufraissex and Abbot's factory

The firm of Gérard, Dufraissex and Abbot was established as Gérard, Dufraissex & Morel in 1881. It belonged to the heirs of François Alluaud and Jean-Baptiste Dufraissex, both porcelain decorators, and Morel who specialised in high-temperature colours. Morel retained links with the firm after 1890 even though the firm was now known as E. Gérard, Dufraissex et Cie between 1890–1900. In 1893 a wide range of table and ornamental wares were exhibited in Chicago, some designed by Albert Dammouse.[2] By 1892 high-temperature colours had already become a hallmark of the firm. Modern machinery and a workforce of 700 made this one of France's foremost porcelain-manufacturing concerns. From 1900 it took the name Gérard, Dufraissex and Abbot. Edgar Abbot, who was from 1886 a partner in the American firm Haviland and Gager, represented Charles Field in the United States, and was responsible for sales in America. The firm is still in production under this name on the same site, first occupied by its predecessor François Alluaud from 1816.

1. In the absence of a detailed study of this firm, the author has based this account on D'Albis and Romanet, 1980, and on Leymarie's article (see note 2).
2. A tea service, a table-centre by Dammouse, a dressing-table set, a dinner service, vases and dishes and an ornamental vase by Dammouse, all in a pre-Art Nouveau style, are illustrated by C. Leymarie in 'L'Industrie de la porcelaine à Limoges, VI, La Maison E. Gérard, Dufraissex et C°', *Revue des Arts Décoratifs*, 13, 1892–3, pp. 387–94.

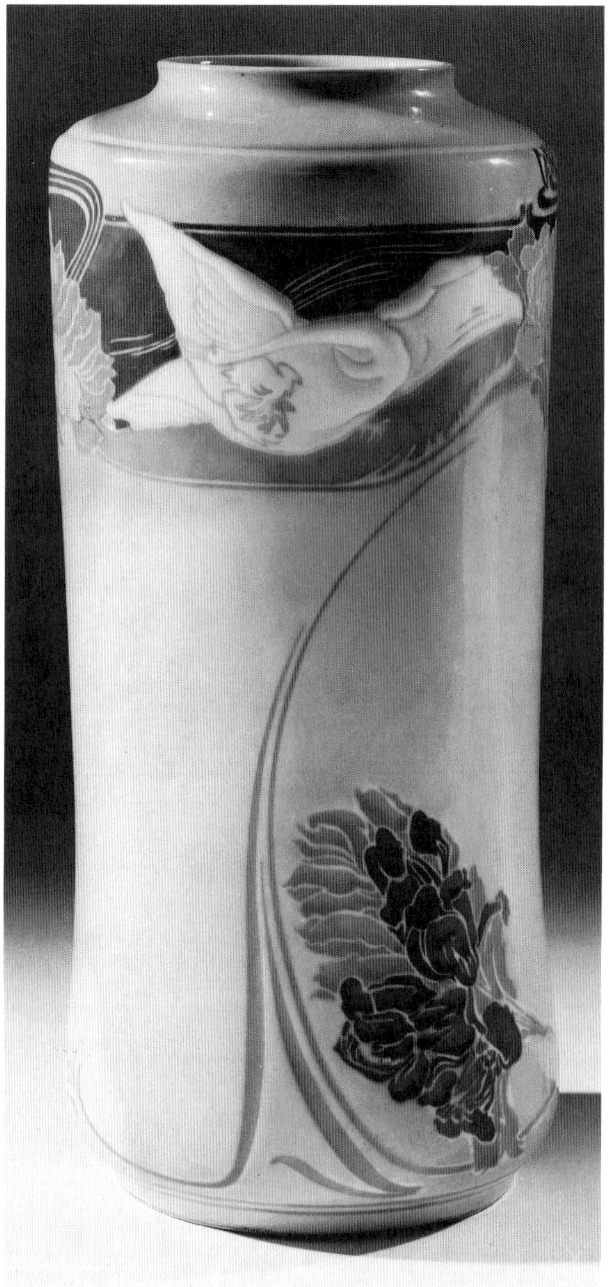

238

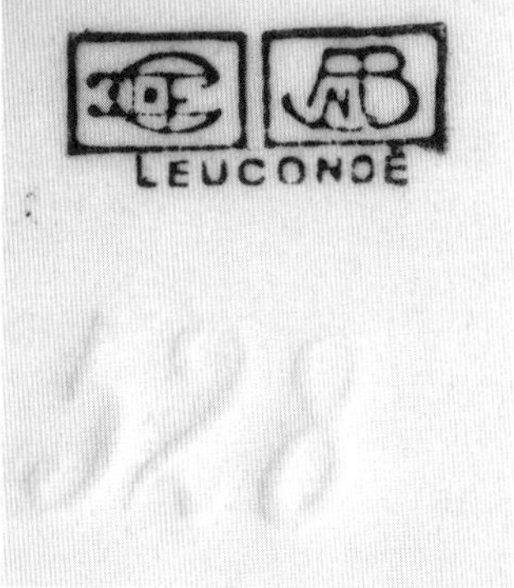

238 *marks*

238 **Vase**, designed 1901–2

H. 30.9 cm
Marks: green printed monogram of Georges de Feure (1868–1943) and of L'Art Nouveau Bing; pattern or range name [?] *LEUCONOE*[1]; incised factory pattern number *528*
Reg. No. 1980,7–11,1

Hard-paste porcelain, of waisted form, cast in two parts. The surface is moulded in low relief with two flying swans and two groups of stylised peonies on the upper register and two stylised peonies springing from the foot of the vase, the motifs connected by swirling stems. The decoration is executed in high-temperature colours: grey for the background and celadon green and a darker green for the plants. The vase is slightly warped and smoke damage sustained in the firing is visible.

Provenance: Purchased 1980

Literature: Rudoe, 1991, no. 58, pp. 35–6

Comparable Examples: Paris, exh. Société des Beaux-Arts, 1902, illus. *Art et Décoration*, 12, 28 July 1902, p. 26

Private collection, France, illus. D'Albis and Romanet, 1980, p. 214 (col. illus.)

USA, New York, Metropolitan Museum, inv. 26.228.9, illus. G. Weisberg, 'Gérard, Dufraissex and Abbot: the 'Manufactory of Art Nouveau Bing Porcelains in Limoges, France'', *Connoisseur*, Vol. 197, no. 792; February 1978, p. 125

USA, Alain Lesieutre Collection, illus. 'Overglaze Imagery, Cone 019–016, November–December 1977, Art Gallery, Visual Arts Center, California State University, Fullerton, no. 34

The vase was designed by Georges de Feure.[2] As it was exhibited by him in Paris at the Société des Beaux-Arts *Salon*, 1902,[3] it was presumably designed shortly before this date. De Feure's works[4] were distributed by Siegfried Bing's retail outlet, the *Maison de l'Art Nouveau* at 22 rue de Provence, Paris, from 1900 until Bing's death in 1905.[5]

The initial contact between Bing and the Limoges porcelain factory dates from 1899.[6] Drawings by de Feure were probably sent through Bing to be translated into models and moulds at the factory itself. Bing had himself been in business in early life as a porcelain manufacturer, purchasing a small factory called Gendarme et Cie in St Genou (Indre) in 1854. It was sold in 1863. In the same year he brought capital to the porcelain factory of Jean Baptiste Ernest Leuillier forming a new company *Leuillier fils et Bing*, in which Bing apparently served as *chef d'atelier*. Their products were sold in the Bing family retail outlet in rue Martel, Paris. By the mid-1860s they had factories in Esternay and Conflans, near Paris. Bing was last listed as associated with this concern in 1881.[7] Bing therefore had the experience to launch this original range of designs and probably used GDA as a result of his contacts with the Haviland family – he was asked to organise the sale of the critic and collector Philippe Burty's collection after his death in 1891 by Burty's wife, and his daughter Madeleine Haviland, who was married to the head of the Haviland factory, Limoges. Bing had known Charles Haviland, a fellow-collector of Japanese art, since at least 1883.[8]

The purchase price of this vase is unknown. A jug from the 1902 *Salon* cost 40 francs,[9] and an ice bucket was purchased by the Musée des arts décoratifs, Paris, for 75 francs after the exhibition.[10]

1. G.P. Weisberg discusses the significance of LEUCONOE as a trademark in 'Gérard, Dufraissex and Abbot: The Manufactory of Art Nouveau Bing Porcelains in Limoges, France', *Connoisseur*, Vol. 197, no. 792, February 1978, p. 129, f.n. 20. Another theory relating to Bing's link with Leuillier is put forward by G.P. Weisberg, *Art Nouveau Bing, Paris Style 1900*, New York, 1986, p. 278, f.n. 19. Two pieces with this mark are in the Musée national Adrien-Dubouché, Limoges: a vase, inv. 4385, and a teapot and cover, inv. 4386. Both were presented by Monsieur E. Gérard in 1911.
2. Georges de Feure (1868–1943) was of Dutch extraction, his real name being Georges Joseph van Sluijters, but lived in Paris from 1890, and was trained as a painter by Jules Chéret (1836–1933). He taught at the Ecole nationale des Beaux-Arts, Paris. A brief biography is given in *Art Nouveau; Belgium, France*, exh., Houston, Institute for the Arts, Rice University, and the Art Institute of Chicago, 1976, Y. Brunhammer *et al.*, pp. 472–3. Further references to his career as a designer are given in Rudoe, 1991, p. 35.
3. *Art et Décoration*, 1, 28 July 1902, p. 26. The vase is also illustrated in an article by W.H., 'Georges de Feure', in the November 1903 issue of *Deutsche Kunst und Dekoration*, p. 316.
4. For other porcelains designed by de Feure, see *The Studio*, Vol. 23, 1901, pp. 64–70, and Weisberg, 1986, pls. 44, 46, fig. 195, pls. 47–9, figs. 198–9, pls. 50–2, pls. 80, 82, figs. 256, 258, 259, pls. 73, 74, figs. 239, 241, pls. 76–7.
5. For Bing, see Weisberg, 1986, *passim*.
6. D'Albis and Romanet, 1980, p. 148.
7. Weisberg, 1986, pp. 12–16.
8. *Ibid.*, p. 20, p. 31.
9. *Ibid.*, p. 245, fig. 241, now in the Musée des arts décoratifs, Paris.
10. *Ibid.*, pl. 73.

239 Milk Jug, Sugar Bowl and Cover, *c.* 1902–3

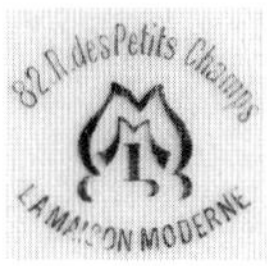

239 *mark*

H. *of jug to top of handle:* 9.1 cm
H. *of bowl to top of handle:* 12.4 cm
Marks: printed in grey *82.R. des Petits Champs LA MAISON MODERNE* and monogram *LMM* of La Maison Moderne on both
Reg. No. 1982,12–3, 5A and 5B

Hard-paste porcelain, each moulded in two parts with integral handle. Decorated in matt orange and olive green with swirling motifs which follow the outline of the form.

Provenance: Purchased, 1982

Literature: Rudoe, 1991, no. 108, p. 48

Comparable Examples: Germany, Berlin, Bröhan Collection, sugar bowl and cup and saucer, Bröhan, 1977, Vol. 2, part 2, pp. 435, 436

Christie's, 30 September 1985, Lot 176, teapot, milk jug, sugar bowl, six cups and saucers

The pieces, which formed part of a teaset,[1] were designed around 1902–3 by Maurice Dufrène (1876–1955) for Julius Meier-Graefe's 'La Maison Moderne' (1898–1903). The set, decorated with a variant of the pattern which includes a rosette motif, was illustrated in *Deutsche Kunst und Dekoration* in 1903,[2] and a version

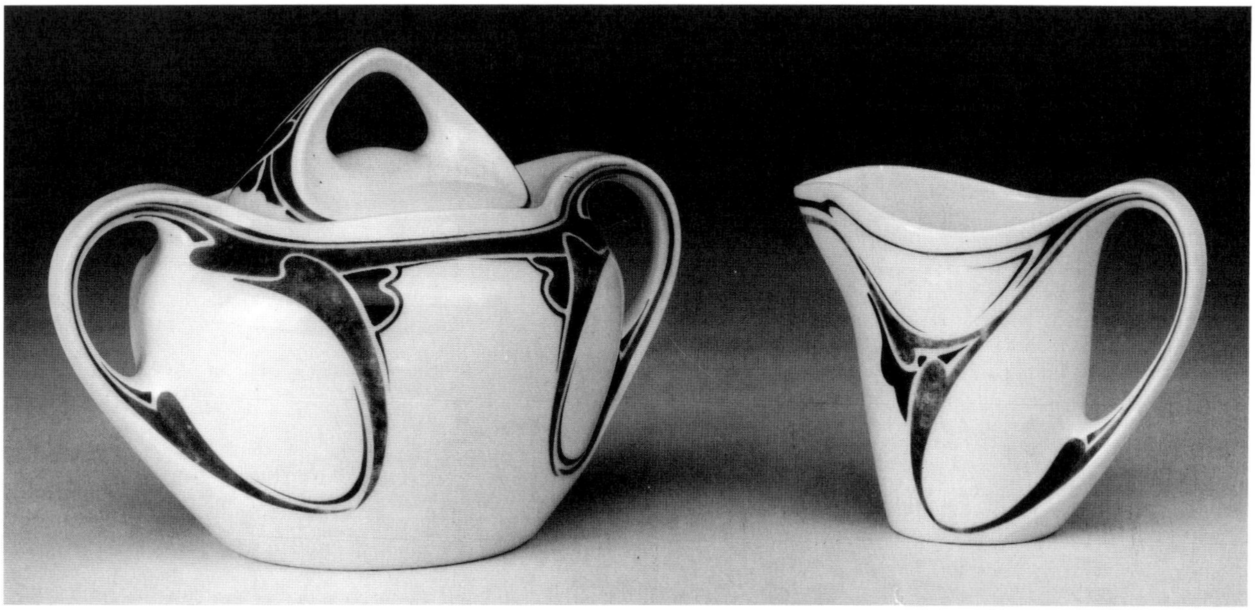

239

including a water jug embellished with roses was illustrated in *The Studio Yearbook of Decorative Art* in 1908.[3] A coffee-pot from a coffee service has been recorded.[4] A variant of the shape with relief decoration was illustrated in *Art et Décoration*, July 1902,[5] but no surviving examples are known.

It has not been possible to discover which factory manufactured these pieces, but it is likely that they were made in Limoges. The decoration, which may have been applied with a stencil, has been overfired; on other examples it is a much deeper green.

The selling price of these pieces has not been discovered.

1. For a matching teapot and cup and saucer in the Professor Hentrich Collection, Düsseldorf, see S. Gauthier and T. Préaud, *Ceramics of the Twentieth Century*, Fribourg, 1982, fig. 12.
2. (Anon) 'Die Welt-Ausstellung in St. Louis', *Deutsche Kunst und Dekoration*, Vol. VI, Heft 7, April 1903, p. 557.
3. *The Studio Yearbook of Decorative Art*, 1908, p. xl, pl. F 31.
4. The Blue Swan, San Francisco, California, exh. 'Overglaze Imagery, Cone 019–016', November–December 1977, Art Gallery, Visual Arts Center, California State University, Fullerton, no. 34.
5. *Art et Décoration*, July 1902, p. 24, tea service of teapot and cover, sugar bowl and cover, milk jug, cup and saucer, see also *Der Moderne Stil*, 5, 1903, p. 10, *Deutsche Kunst und Dekoration*, Vol. VI, Heft 7, 1903, p. 556.

Limoges, factory unknown

240 **Bowl and Cover containing Strainer**, perhaps *c.*1880–90, or later

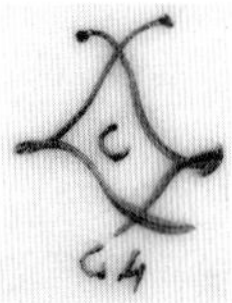

240 *mark*

D. *of bowl:*	20.2 cm
H. *to top of handle:*	18.1 cm
Marks:	interlaced *LL* enclosing *C* above *G4* painted over the glaze in blue (spurious)
Reg. No.	OA 10723

Hard-paste porcelain, pierced domed cover with applied twig handle, strainer with central circular hole and numerous smaller ones. The bowl and cover are each painted with a scene in the style of Watteau: young lovers in a landscape, a girl with a doll in a landscape, in pink, blue, orange, green, brown, yellow and grey-blue on a turquoise ground embellished with silver-coloured metal casing of flower chains, leaves, a trellis design around the painted scenes, and geometric motifs on the bands around the rims and foot. The inner strainer is similarly treated, its rim painted turquoise on upper and lower surfaces. Bowl and cover repaired.

Provenance: Left in the Department by Mrs Hadlow, 1947

Literature: Unpublished

Comparable Examples: Manchester, City Art Galleries, inv. 1932.55–59, five plates painted in a similar style on a turquoise ground, illus. S. Macdonald *Porcelain from Europe*, 1986, no. 99

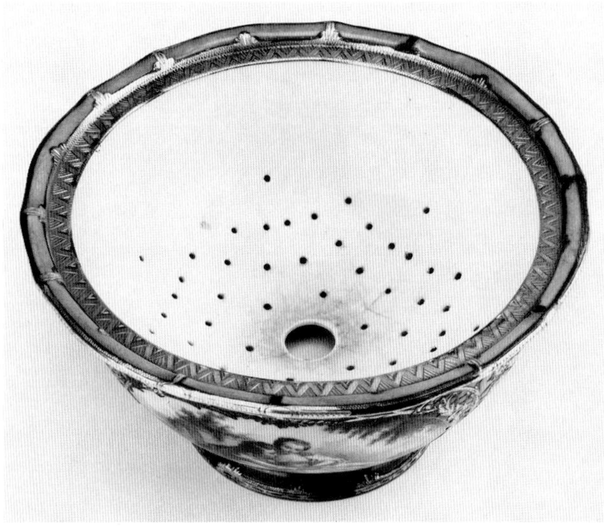

240 *(cover removed, showing strainer)*

This piece, which is doubtless intended to be ornamental rather than functional, was almost certainly made in Limoges, and, as it bears the Sèvres mark, was intended to deceive. The technique used to encase the porcelain is not dissimilar to that found

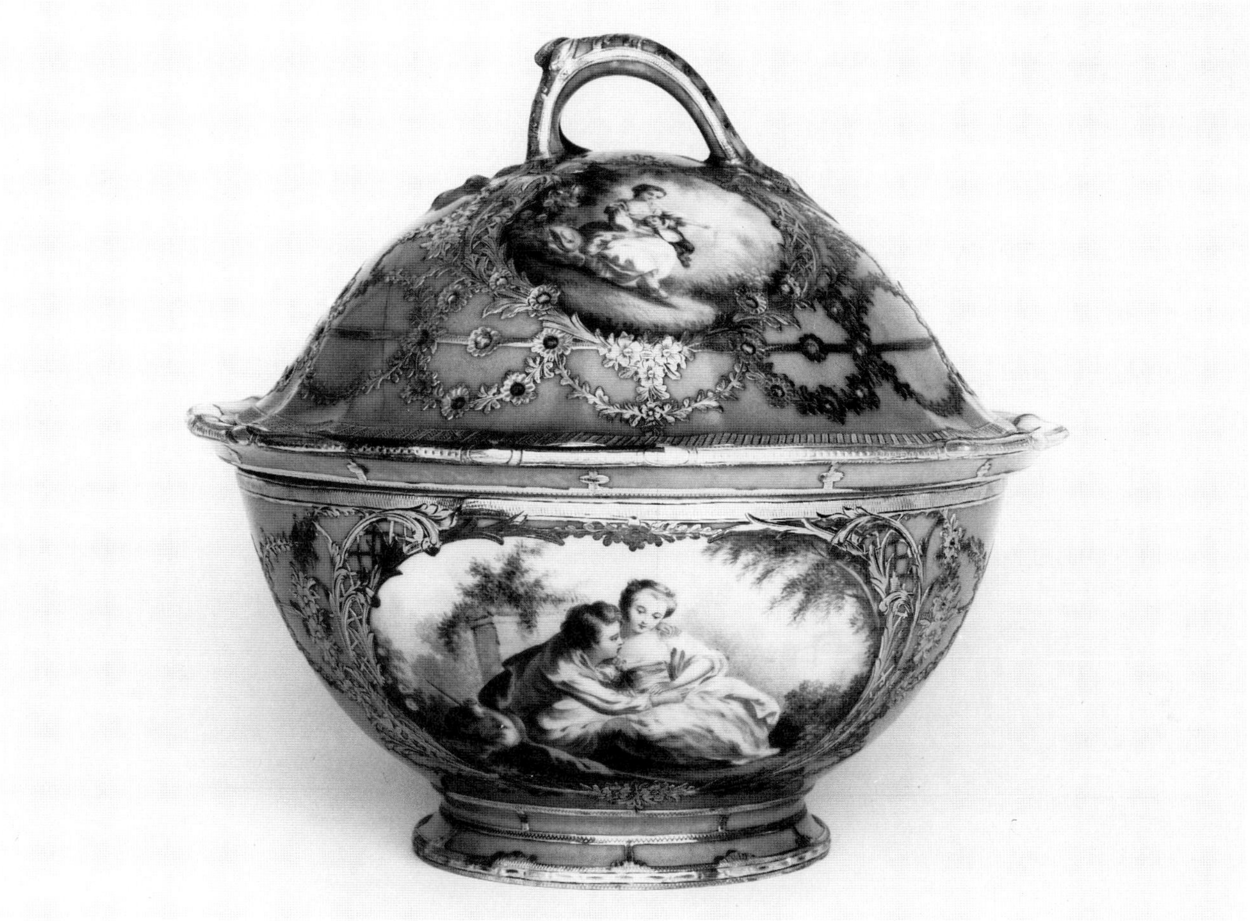

240

on cat. 237, suggesting a date in the late nineteenth century.

It is typical of a large number of pieces still circulating on the market and the ornamentation resembles that on a pair of vases with a blue ground sold in London as Sèvres in 1990.[1] Two vases and a footed bowl painted with Watteau scenes on a dark blue ground bearing fake Sèvres marks were decorated in the twentieth century by a painter named A. Viguier (1880–1969), trained in Limoges and working both there and in Paris.[2]

1. Christie's, South Kensington, 20 February 1990, Lot 162, illus. in colour on cover of catalogue.
2. Donated by Madame Viguier to the Musée national Adrien-Dubouché, Limoges, in 1988, inv. ADL 9435. The author is grateful to Chantal Meslin-Perrier for this information.

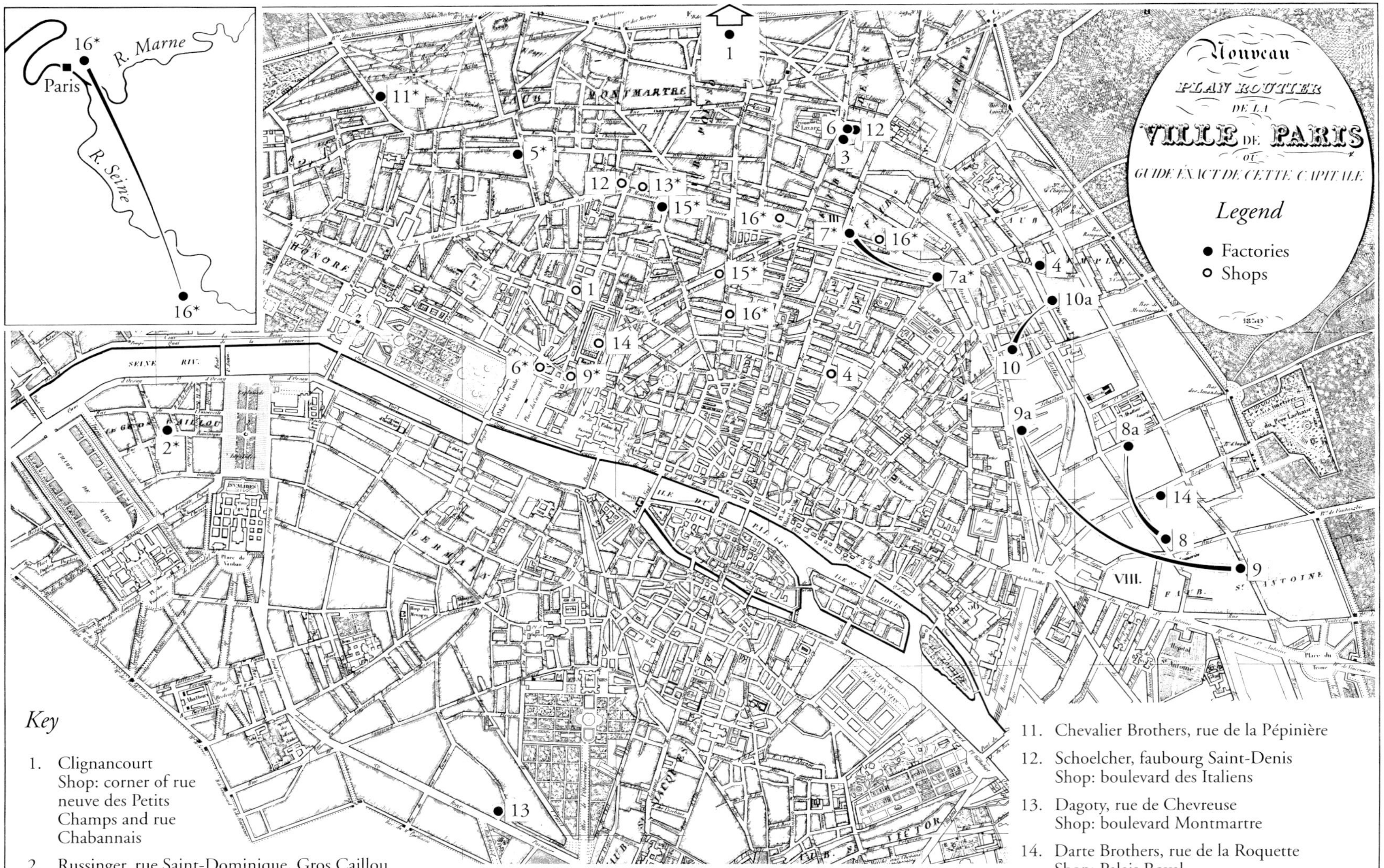

Key

1. Clignancourt
   Shop: corner of rue neuve des Petits Champs and rue Chabannais
2. Russinger, rue Saint-Dominique, Gros Caillou
3. Pierre-Antoine Hannong, rue du faubourg Saint-Denis
4. Locré and Russinger, rue de la Fontaine-au-Roi, La Courtille
   Shop: rue Michel-le-Comte
5. Queen's factory, rue Thiroux
6. Comte d'Artois, rue du faubourg Saint-Denis
   Shop: corner of rue de l'Echelle and rue du Carrousel
7. Duc d'Angoulême, rue de Bondy *later* rue du Temple
8. Nast, rue Popincourt, *later* rue des Amandiers
9. Duc d'Orléans, rue des Boulets, *later* rue Amelot
   Shop: rue du faubourg Saint-Honoré
10. Potter and Blancheron, rue de Crussol, *later* Blancheron, rue des Trois Bornes
11. Chevalier Brothers, rue de la Pépinière
12. Schoelcher, faubourg Saint-Denis
    Shop: boulevard des Italiens
13. Dagoty, rue de Chevreuse
    Shop: boulevard Montmartre
14. Darte Brothers, rue de la Roquette
    Shop: Palais Royal
15. Lebon-Halley, boulevard et rue Montmartre
    Shop: (Lebon) rue neuve Saint-Eustache
16. Jacob Petit, Belleville, *later* Fontainebleau
    Shops: rue de Bondy and rue du Paradis-Poissonnière

*Denotes approximate location

HARD-PASTE FACTORIES IN PARIS

Factories in the Paris area are called by the name most commonly used. In many instances they are known both by their royal protector's, owner's or director's name and by their location. In some instances (eg rue Thiroux) the streets have long since disappeared, or the exact locations of factories (eg Gros Caillou) have not been established. The sites of the factories (and retail outlets, in some instances) are shown as precisely as possible on the map on page 322).

Clignancourt

Established by Pierre Deruelle (b. about 1724), architect and property developer, perhaps as early as 1767, when he purchased buildings from his mother-in-law,[1] it is listed in Thiéry's *Guide des Amateurs* in 1771 and may have been in production some time before this. Located on the corner of the rue Mont-Cenis and the rue Marcadet in Montmartre (the factory buildings were still standing in the first decade of this century),[2] the concern survived the Revolution. From 28 July 1792 it was run by Deruelle's son-in-law, the painter Alexandre Moitte (1750–1828), whose father was *graveur du Roi*, and whose brother was a sculptor.[3] It continued in production until Ventôse l'an VII (1799) when it was sold.

The factory initially used as its mark a windmill, for the area known as the Butte was then covered with several hundred windmills, of which only one now remains. On 24 January 1775 this mark was replaced by the monogram of Louis-Stanislas-Xavier, comte de Provence, later Louis XVIII, then known as Monsieur, who took the factory under his protection. The mark occasionally appears together with an *M* crowned.[4]

In 1780 the director of the Sèvres factory, Antoine Régnier, was authorised by the Lieutenant général de police, Sartine, to inspect the Paris factories to ascertain whether they were contravening the monopoly established in favour of the Sèvres factory by the King in 1766. Sartine's observations include a comment on the excellent administration of the factory and the use of Limoges clays carefully prepared to 'imiter le beau grain de la porcelaine de Saxe.'[5]

Tablewares were the mainstay of the factory. Shapes, such as sugar bowls and covers with stands, wine- and bottle-coolers and *compotiers*, were similar to Sèvres products.[6] Most domestic wares were painted with polychrome flower sprays but figure-painting is sometimes found. Gilding was in common use. Exceptionally, blue, orange and gilt *chinoiseries* were used on a table service which included a fountain.[7] More elaborate decoration was used on vases, which were sometimes painted in sepia in a technique associated with the Viennese Georg Lamprecht, who worked at Clignancourt in 1783 before moving to Sèvres where he was employed between 1784 and 1787. Among several surviving pieces is an *écuelle* painted in bistre inscribed *Georges Lamprecht pint à Paris 1783* and marked with the monogram *LSX*, now in the Musée national de Céramique, Sèvres.[8] The factory's wide range of production is documented in the inventory made on 28 July 1792 at the time of its sale to Moitte.[9]

Moitte paid no less than 72,000 *livres* for the concern, which had about twelve workshops for throwing, modelling, turning, painting, preparing the paste, making the saggars, etc. There were four mills and over 2,000 moulds for all sorts of domestic wares. Moulds of the following figures are also listed in the inventory: children, *vie populaire* (figures and groups), *Four Seasons* and *Silenus*.[10] Some were made in two sizes. A 'bas-relief aux enfants' and a 'Vase Bacchante', as well as a vase 'à cercle d'ornemens' and 'un autre vase cornu' are listed under the heading 'Vases'. Before the execution of the King, the factory was in full production.

Prices for tablewares, which were sold from the shop known as the *Bonnet d'Or* in rue neuve des Petits Champs on the corner with the rue Chabannais, were expensive, but much less than those charged by the royal factory. In February 1779 the marquis de Montesquieu purchased four dozen plates painted with *bouquets détachés* at 48 *livres* the dozen and four wine-glass coolers similarly decorated at 60 *livres* each. With a discount of 10 per cent, the total amounted to 388 *livres* 16 *sols*.[11] The firm also sold through Madame de La Fresnaye at the Palais de Justice. In 1775 Clignancourt porcelain could be purchased at the dealer *Au Petit Dunkerque*, and in 1798 Moitte set up a warehouse at the rue Feydeau, and sold through Guy at the *Petit Dunkerque*.[12] The dealer Descat sold Clignancourt wares from Bordeaux, and there was a not insignificant export trade. On 17 May 1784 the London *Daily Advertiser* included details of a six-day sale at Christie's and Ansell's of 'Table and Dessert Services, Coffee, Tea and Chocolate Equipages . . . of the most delicate approved Patterns and Shapes, finished in a Stile of superior Richness and Elegance, from the choicest specimens of the Seve, Dresden, Berlin, and Monsieur's Manufacture'. On 20 February 1790 the same newspaper advertised Mr Christie's sale of 'French Porcelane' from his 'Room in Pall Mall', consisting of a 'Capital and valuable Assortment of beautiful PORCELANE of Monsieur's Manufactory, consigned from France; Comprehending extensive Table and Dessert Services, Tea and Coffee Equipages, Dejeunes, Vases, Biscuit Figures etc.'[13]

An advertisement in the *Mercure de France* of December 1775 vaunted the high quality of the factory's products:[14]

> La porcelaine de cette manufacture est singulièrement recommandable par sa solidité, la plus grande qu'on connaisse, par le beau blanc du biscuit et pour sa couverte comparable aux ouvrages de l'ancien Japon ainsi que l'élégance des formes et pour le goût des ornements. On y fait toutes pièces propres au service de table, à la décoration des appartements, ainsi que des figures parfaitement modelées, soit seules, soit groupées, petites et grandes. Enfin on peut commander tous les ouvrages qu'on désire de ce genre.
>
> [The porcelain from this factory can be particularly recommended for its strength, as it is the strongest known, for the beautiful white of its biscuit and for its glaze which is comparable with that of old Japanese porcelain, as well as for the elegance of the forms and the taste of the decoration. All sorts of table-service wares are made, as well as decorative pieces for living rooms, and perfectly modelled figures. These are single figures or groups in both small and large sizes. In short, any piece of this kind can be ordered.]

A considerable workforce was employed. In 1780 there were eighty employees, increasing to ninety-four in 1787. Deruelle *fils* and Moitte were responsible for the sculpture workshop, and may perhaps have designed some of the more adventurous forms, such as the 'bouilloire à réchaud à esprit de vin', or kettle on a spirit-lamp, its spouts formed as the necks of swans whose wings fold back on to the body of the kettle.[15]

1. A good account of the factory appears in Guillebon, 1972, pp. 172–80, and Guillebon, *Cahiers*, 1963, pp. 156–70; also see J. Mauzin, 'Les artistes à Montmartre, Pierre Deruelle et Alexandre Moitte, entrepreneurs de la Manufacture de Porcelaine de Clignancourt (1767–1800), *Le Vieux Montmartre*, Société d'Histoire et d'archéologie des XVIIIe et XIXe Arrondissements, nouvelle série, no. 2, 1922, pp. 77–102.
2. Illustrated in Mauzin, *op. cit.*, opp. p. 96. Its demolition was reported in the newspaper *Libre Parole* on 17 June 1908, and according to a note kept amongst the papers of Victor Perrot, who left a collection of Clignancourt porcelain and documents to the Musée de Montmartre, he himself showed the former factory site to the comte de Chavagnac in April 1907. For a further note on the topography of the factory see Guillebon, 1985, pp. 87–9.
3. Moitte's career is outlined in Mauzin, *op. cit.*, pp. 81–102.
4. See Guillebon, *Cahiers*, 1963, pp. 161–2 and exh. *Porcelaines parisiennes*, 1983, pp. 34–5. According to Guillebon, 1972, p. 188 (English edn.), the *Mercure de France* of December 1775 stated that the porcelain bore the mark *M* supporting the fleur-de-lys crown of the Prince of the Blood, that is Monsieur, the King's brother.
5. MNS, Archives de Sèvres, A2, *liasse* 3.
6. Bloit, 1988, p. 37, p. 17, 36.
7. Part of a table-service with this decoration is in a private collection in France, according to Bernard Dragesco, to whom the author is indebted for this information; a shell-shaped fruit dish and a fountain are in the Musée Ariana, Geneva, the fountain is illus. by Guillebon, 1972, p. 79, fig. 63.
8. Guillebon, 1972, p. 71, fig. 56.
9. Archives nationales, Minutier central, *Etude* LVI 392, M^o Préau.
10. Guillebon, *op. cit.*, p. 56, fig. 42, illustrates a biscuit figure of the *Farnese Hercules* measuring 32 cm in height, now in the Musée national de Céramique, Sèvres.
11. Invoice reproduced *ibid.*, p. 70, fig. 55.
12. *Ibid.*, p. 175.
13. References kindly provided by Nancy Valpy.
14. Guillebon, *op. cit.*, p. 178.
15. *Ibid.*, p. 64, fig. 48.

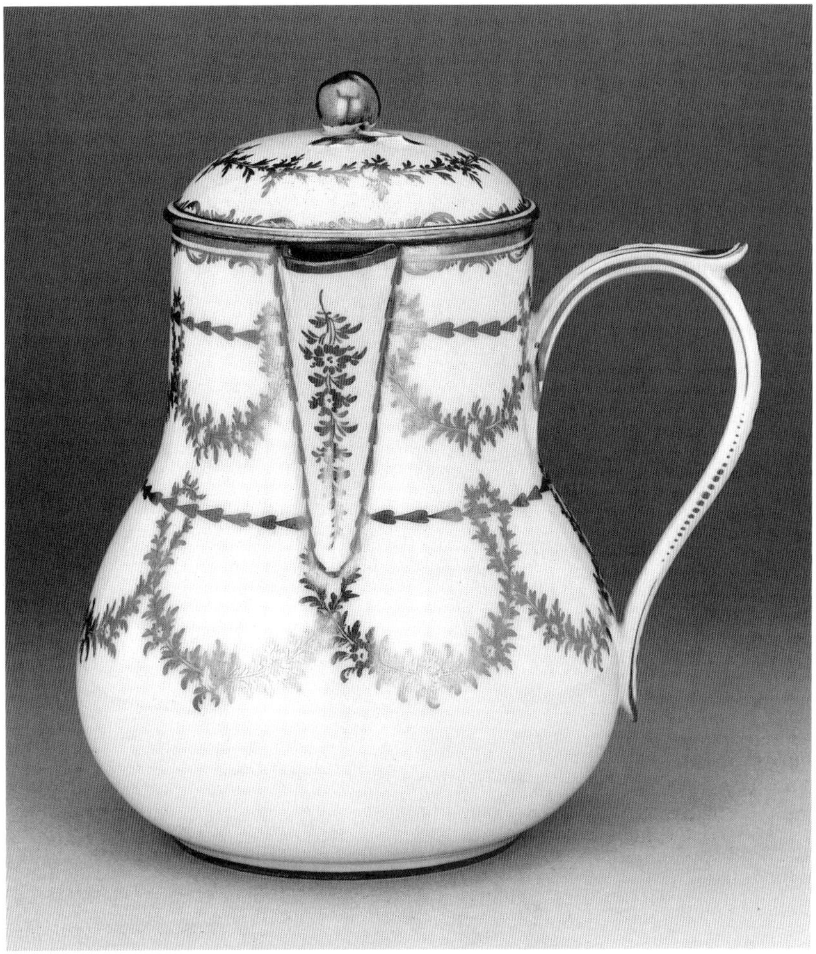

241

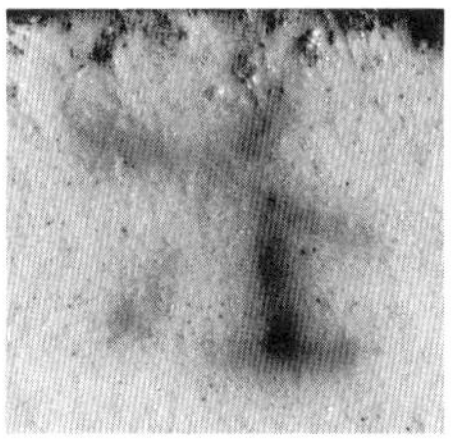

241 *mark*

241 **Chocolate Pot and Cover,** 1767–75

H. *incl. cover:* 17.6 cm
Marks: stylised windmill painted in blue
Reg. No. Franks 422

Hard-paste porcelain, bulbous body and long straight neck with deep lip at side, shaped handle, domed cover with applied cherry and leaf knop. Flat unglazed base on shallow, irregularly-formed foot. Decorated in gold with a stylised leaf and flower design. Knop gilt, gilt husk motif on handle. Gilt line around foot. Chip to rim of pot. Hairline crack on cover.

Provenance: Bequeathed by Sir A.W. Franks, 1897

Literature: Franks, 1896, no. 422

Comparable Examples: None

The presence of small black specks in the glaze, especially on the cover, may indicate that the piece was not decorated immediately after its manufacture, although the gilding is evidently of eighteenth-century date.

Covered pots with handles at the side were in production at the Sèvres factory by 1767, as shown by an example painted with birds by Aloncle.[1] A flower-decorated example from the Boissettes factory is recorded in a French private collection.[2]

1. Baltimore, Walters Art Gallery, inv. 48.664, H. 15 cm.
2. D'Esclapon, 1991, p. 42.

242 **Bowl (*compotier ovale*),** 1775–80

D. 22 cm
Marks: stylised windmill in gold; *LSX* monogram of Monsieur, comte de Provence, stencilled in red, overglaze
Reg. No. Franks 423

Hard-paste porcelain, with six shaped lobes and shallow, irregularly-formed foot. Decorated in green, pink, yellow, orange, blue and grey with scattered flower sprays, each containing a full-blown rose, usually in purple. On the outside of the rim is a stylised gilt design; gilt dentil inside rim, gilt line around foot. Repaired.

Provenance: Bequeathed by Sir A.W. Franks, 1897

Literature: Franks, 1896, no. 423

Chavagnac and Grollier, 1906, p. 504

Comparable Examples: None noted

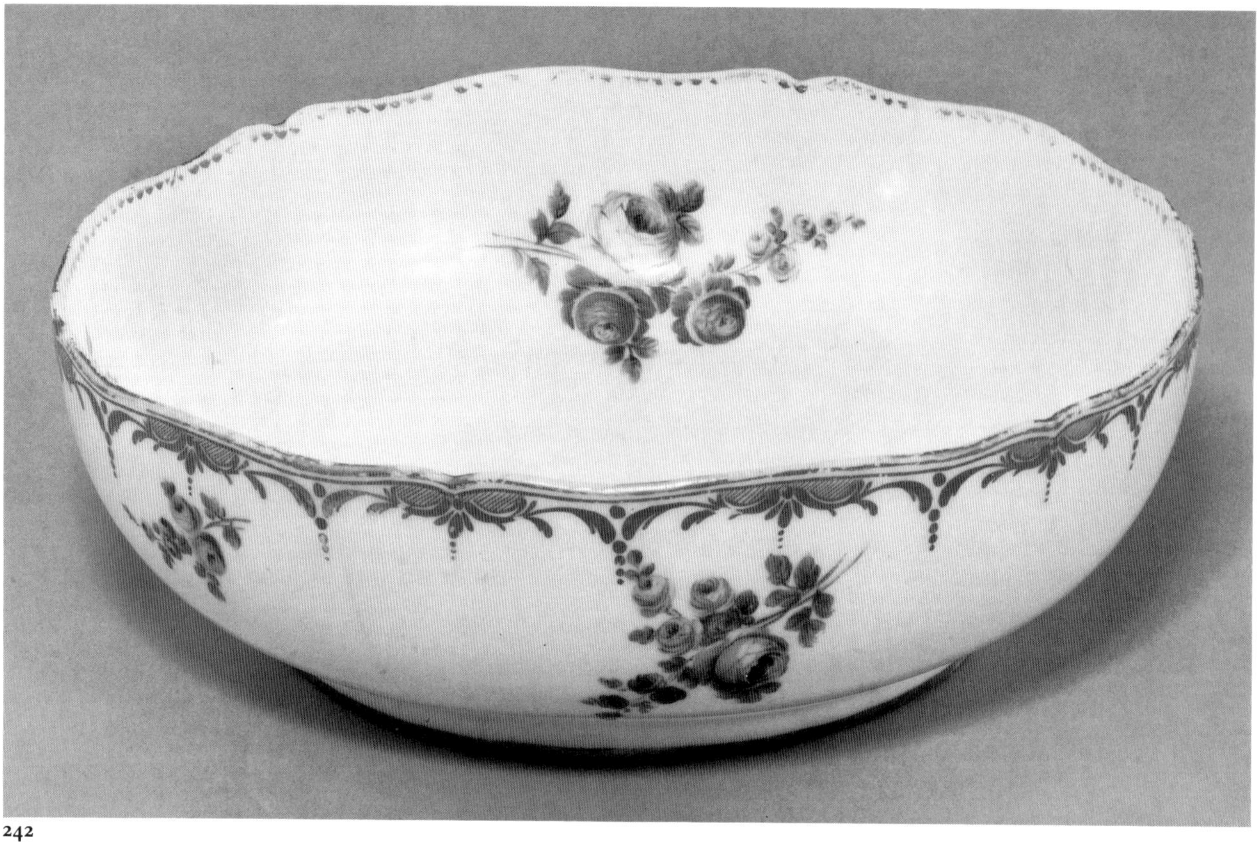

242

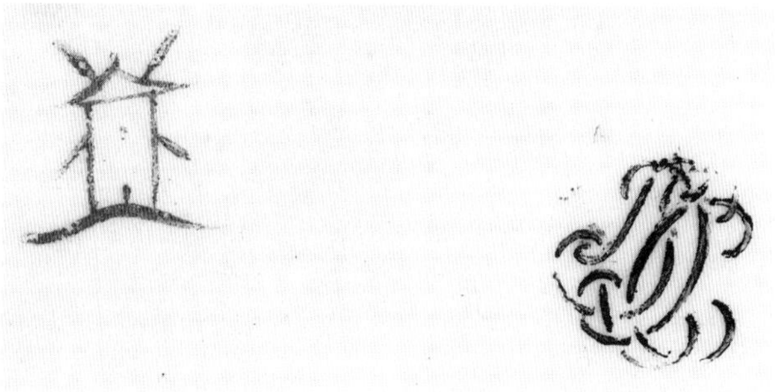

242 *marks*

The bowl formed part of a dessert service and was intended for fruit compote. The monogram of Louis-Stanislas-Xavier, comte de Provence (1755–1824), was introduced as the factory mark on 24 January 1775 when he took under his protection the factory in Montmartre established by Pierre Deruelle between 1767 and 1771. The monogram *LSX* is occasionally found in conjunction with the earliest windmill mark which it was supposed to replace.[1] An undated document surviving in the Musée de Montmartre,[2] Paris, gives the prices for plates, salad bowls in two sizes, wine-coolers, liqueur-coolers, glass-coolers, and *compotiers* of square, oval or shell form, according to their decoration. The five different decors were 'Apoint d'Espagne enor avec guirl. et petits Bouquets dans le fond' at 48 *livres*, with *point d'Espagne* 'à bord bleu celeste et 3. cartels d'oiseaux et au milieu' at the same price, with flowers instead of birds at 39 *livres*, with flower garlands picked out in gold at the same price and 'à roses et feuillage' at 33 *livres*. This piece probably corresponds with the most expensive category.

1. Chavagnac and Grollier, 1906, p. 504, cite the Museum example and a jug and basin with gilt decoration in the Musée national de Céramique, Sèvres, inv. 4959.
2. The author is grateful to Madame Oberthur for kindly allowing her to study this document.

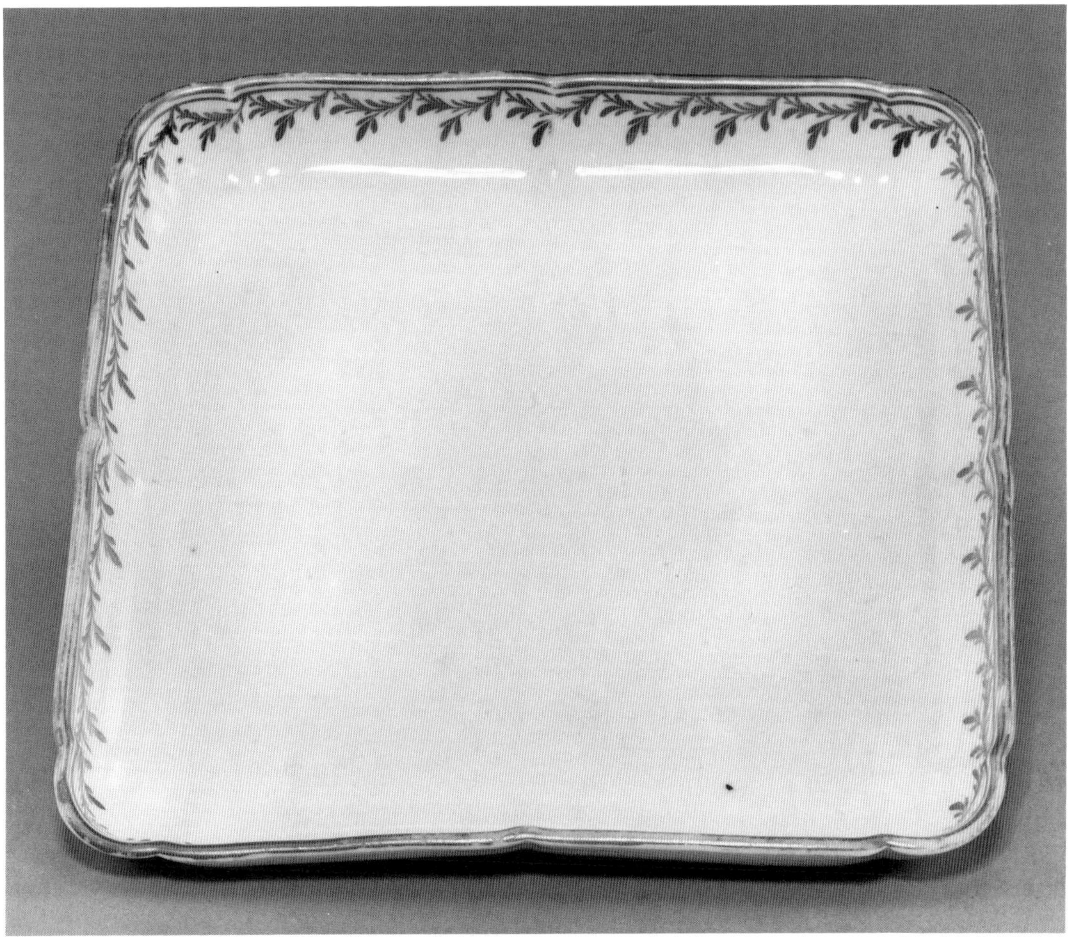

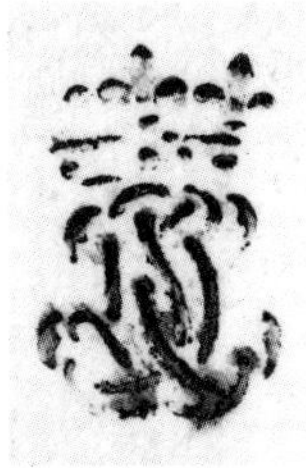

243 *mark*

243

243 **Tray (*plateau*)**, 1775–80

L. 16.3 cm
Marks: *LSX* monogram of Monsieur, comte de Provence, crowned, stencilled in red overglaze
Reg. No. Franks 424

Hard-paste porcelain; moulded with lobed corners and indentation in the centre of each side, decorated in gold with a stylised leaf design depending from a gilt line near the rim, which is gilt. Flat unglazed base. Gilding rubbed.

Provenance: Bequeathed by Sir A.W. Franks, 1897

Literature: Franks, 1896, no. 424

Comparable Examples: Paris, Musée de Montmartre, tray decorated with flowers, illus. Guillebon, 1972, p. 74, fig. 59

Trays like this formed part of a *déjeuner mignonette* or miniature teaset consisting of a teapot, sugar bowl, water jug and cup and saucer.[1] Two rather large pinholes on the base and two more on the upper surface indicate manufacturing difficulties.

1. A Clignancourt *déjeuner* from the Thiers Collection in the Louvre Museum, Paris, is illustrated by J. Mauzin, 'Les artistes à Montmartre, Pierre Deruelle et Alexandre Moitte, entrepreneurs de la manufacture de porcelaine de Clignancourt (1767–1800)', *Le Vieux Montmartre*, Société d'Histoire et d'Archéologie des XVIII et XIXe Arrondissements, Nouvelle Série, no. 2, 1922, p. 87. A photograph between p. 97 and p. 98 shows a *vue intérieure* (i.e. inside the grounds) of the factory in 1908 before the disappearance of the old buildings.

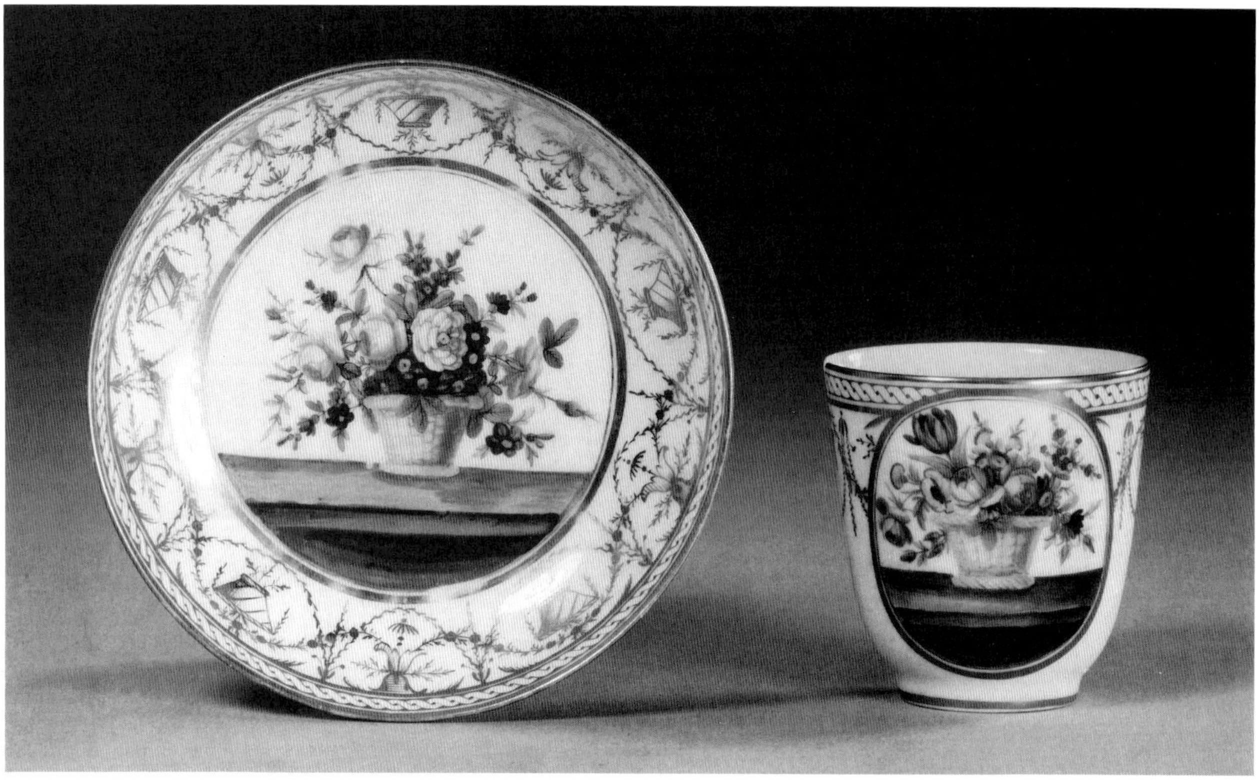

244

244 Cup and Saucer

D. *of saucer:*	12.8 cm
H. *of cup:*	6.6 cm
Marks:	*LSX* monogram of Monsieur, comte de Provence, stencilled in red on both; cursive *L* [?] incised on both
Reg. No.	Franks 425

Hard-paste porcelain, heavily potted. The deep saucer and the cup both have curved sides; the cup handle is of tapering loop form. Painted in green, pink, blue, yellow, orange-red, purple and grey with a basket of stylised flowers on a red-brown 'table' against a white ground. The border decoration consists of gilt baskets of stylised flowers alternating with an acanthus motif and pendent leaf trails. Near the rim is a gilt rope pattern. Rims gilt, foot of cup gilt, handle partly gilt. Rim chipped, several hairline cracks.

Provenance: Bequeathed by Sir A.W. Franks, 1897

Literature: Franks, 1896, no. 425

Comparable Examples: London, Victoria and Albert Museum, inv. C.1333–1919

England, private coll., plate, D. 10 in (note in V&A register).

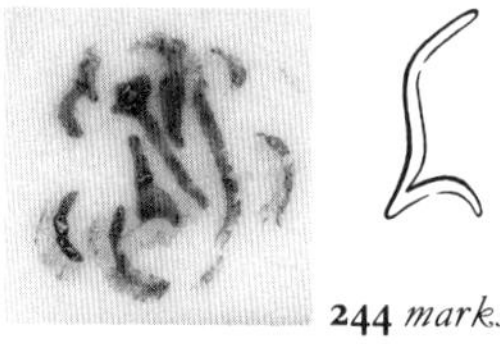

244 *marks*

This type of decoration appears at Sèvres in the 1780s[1] and was popular at the Paris factories.[2] The shape of the cup and saucer and the gilt border pattern are both typical of the Clignancourt factory; the latter is also found on a broth-bowl, cover and stand.[3]

1. See a plate in the Louvre Museum, Paris from the Hope of Craighall service delivered in 1788 illustrated in Dupont, 1987, p. 89, fig. 2.
2. A cream-jug and cover marked *Nast* is similarly decorated, see d'Albis *et. al.*, 1989, no. 166, inv. 25097.
3. Bloit, 1988, p. 44.

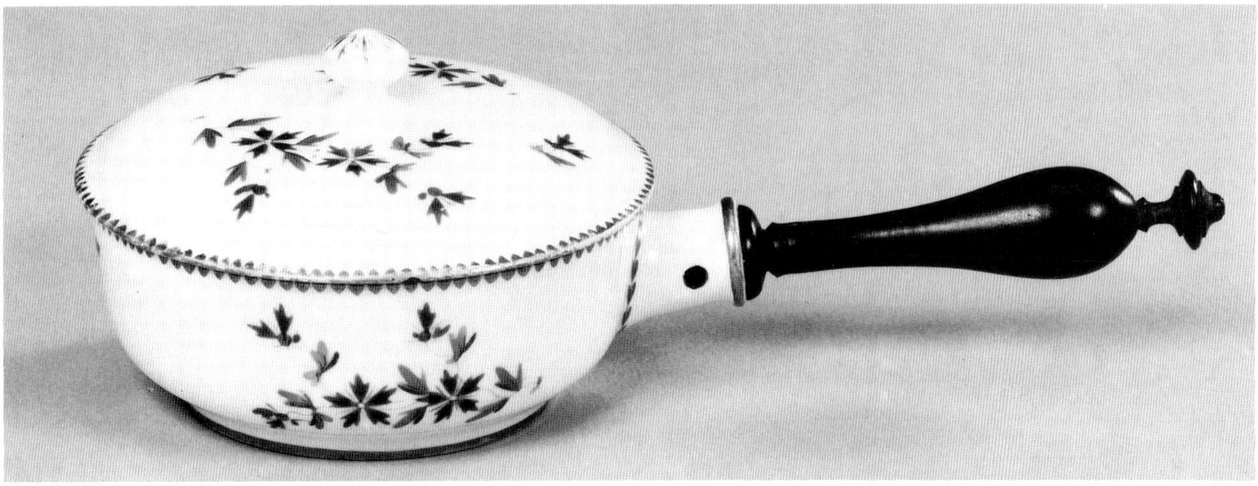

245

245 **Miniature Saucepan and Cover (*poêlon*)**, perhaps *c.* 1792

H. 5.5 cm
Marks: *M* crowned and monogram *LSX* of Monsieur, comte de Provence, stencilled in red overglaze
Reg. No. 1988,6–5,1

Hard-paste porcelain, the lower part bowl-shaped with shallow foot, the handle in the form of a hollow tube pierced by two circular holes and with a turned rim. A wooden handle (probably of nineteenth-century date) is attached to the porcelain by means of two lugs. The cover is slightly domed and has a button knop. The decoration consists of groups of scattered blue star-shaped flowers on pale-purplish stems with green leaves. There is a gilt dentil design around the rims, a gilt leaf design around the base of the handle; the foot and handle terminal are gilt, and the knop gilt with a star-shaped motif. Knop restored, rim of cover chipped. Gilding rubbed.

Provenance: Purchased, 1988

Literature: Unpublished

Comparable Examples: Switzerland, Geneva, Musée Ariana, inv. AR 7462, mark monogram of comte de Provence, D. 8.2 cm

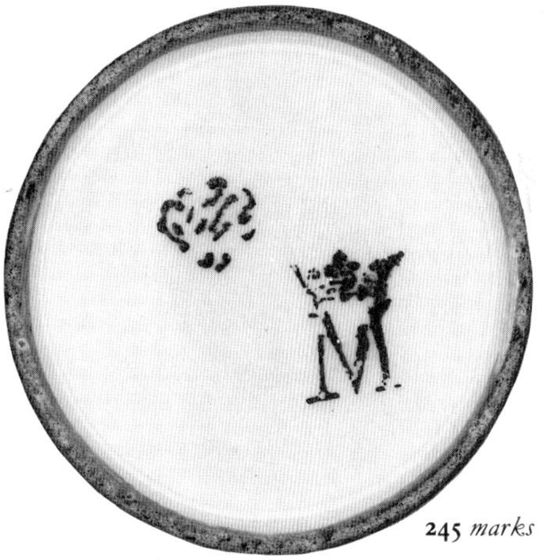

245 *marks*

This small saucepan was probably used on a spirit lamp. *Poêlons*, although not known at the Saint-Cloud, Chantilly or Mennecy factories, were made at Vincennes from 1753,[1] and at Sèvres.[2] Two examples apparently from the Boissettes factory were in the trade in France in 1985.[3] A large example for collective rather than individual use from the duc d'Angoulême's factory,[4] established in the rue de Bondy, Paris, in 1781, and a small one measuring 3.2 cm in height made at the Locré factory,[5] attest to the popularity of the *poêlon* in the later years of the eighteenth century.

There has been some discussion surrounding the significance of the mark *M* crowned, which must surely stand for the comte de Provence, the King's brother, known as Monsieur, protector of the factory from 25 October 1775, and not for Alexandre Moitte. No note of the official registration of the factory marks appears to have been discovered.[6]

1. See exh. *Vincennes*, 1977–8, p. 69. No surviving example has been identified.
2. Verlet, 1953, pl. 7b, date-letter for 1759. Another dated *c.* 1795–7, decorated in gold with a leaf and berry motif is in the Musée des arts décoratifs, Paris, inv. 2640, illus. Brunet and Préaud, 1978, no. 290. An even more simply gilded example with a wooden handle belonged to the comte de Moustier, Minister of France in New York 1787–9 and is preserved in the Mount Vernon Ladies Association of the Union, Virginia, USA, see Detweiler, *French Porcelain*, 1982, p. 93, fig. 8.
3. Orléans, Maître L. Savot, 22 April 1985, Lot unknown, illus. Ravel d'Esclapon, 1991, p. 71, dimensions omitted.
4. Exh. Nord-Pas-de-Calais, 1986–7, no. 51, Musée de Boulogne, inv. C. 334.
5. 'French Porcelain in Palazzo Pitti', compiled by S. Eriksen, Florence, 1973, no. 81, painted with flowers, wooden handle, cover missing.
6. See Guillebon, 1963, no. 31, pp. 161–2 and exh. *Porcelaines parisiennes*, 1983, pp. 34–5.

Russinger's factory,
rue Saint Dominique, Gros Caillou

Little is known about the history and products of this factory. In the *inventaire après décès* of Elizabeth Lauheimerin,[1] wife of Laurent Russinger (1739–1810), dated 27 February 1772, Russinger is described as 'directeur de la manufacture de porcelaine établie à Paris au lieu dit le gros Caillou y demeurant rue S^t^ dominique p.^se^ s.^t^ Sulpice'. The marriage of Russinger and his wife had taken place in Höchst, in the Rhineland Palatinate where he worked at the porcelain factory as a modeller. Before going to Paris, he worked briefly in Pfalz-Zweibrücken.[2] Their son Christopher was a minor in 1772 (i.e. under twenty-five years of age). The deceased's effects were valued at less than 400 *livres* in all. Russinger, according to his own declaration, was in such financial distress that he was obliged to sell her clothes and effects. In addition he was due his salary of 400 *livres* from Mr Provigny 'Entrepreneur delad Manufacture de porcelaine au Gros-Caillou'. Nothing has yet been discovered concerning de Provigny (see cat. 246).

One other source of information concerning this factory has been discovered. It is a copy of a report sent to the chief of the Paris police, M. de Sartine, by one of his inspectors, Sieur Buhot, and is dated 19 August 1774.[3] Under the heading 'Gros Caillou le S Advenier' appears the following:

> Cette manufacture, quoique très ancienne Est encore au Berceau ayant Eté jusqu'à présent Entre de très mauvaises mains. Elle a donné lieu à plus de procédures qu'il ne s'y fait de porcelaines. M De Magnanville Garde de Trésor Royal En a traité en dernier Lieu avec un S. Provigny qui vous Etans Connu, Monsieur, me dispense d'Entrer en détail sur son compte.
>
> Le nouveau Propriétaire trés incertain du succés commence à faire des Essais Et en cas de réussite sur la qualité de sa porcelaine, il n'a intention que de faire des choses ordinaires sans dorure ni différentes couleurs.
>
> [This factory although long established is still in the cradle, having been until now in very bad hands. It has been the subject of more legal proceedings than it has produced porcelain. M. de Magnanville, of the Royal Treasury[4] has lately dealt with a Sieur Provigny in connection with this factory. As he is known to you, Sir, there is no need for me to enter into further detail concerning him.
>
> The new proprietor, very uncertain of success, is beginning experimental work. If he succeeds in making porcelain of a suitable quality, he intends only to produce ordinary wares without gilt decoration or painting in colours.]

It is known that the mark *AD* was registered by Advenier and Lamarre on 26 July 1773, so presumably de Provigny's involvement, which was doubtless purely financial, was fairly short-lived. De Provigny apparently spent more than 100,000 *livres* on the Gros Caillou factory, in two different partnerships.[5] He was also involved with the Swiss, Jacques Louis Broilliet, who established a porcelain factory at Vaugirard on 7 June 1762.[6] The date when the Gros Caillou concern was established, has not yet been discovered.

In 1784 Advenier and Lamarre were notified of the *arrêt* forbidding them to compete with the royal factory. Although a partnership between Lamarre and a certain Despréz is not mentioned in Julien's report of 1798, a cameo medallion of Henri IV, wearing a ruff and shown full-face, is marked *Despréz fils et Lamarre*.[7]

Neither the products of the Gros Caillou factory nor its employees have yet been studied, and the Museum's biscuit portrait plaque of Henri IV (see cat. 246) is the only known signed piece.

1. Paris, Archives nationales, Minutier central, *Etude* LXV, 374.
2. For details of Russinger's earlier career, see E. Kramer, 'Laurentius Russinger, Porzelliner in Hoechst, Gutenbrunn und Paris', *Keramos*, 50 (1970), pp. 83–100.
3. MNS, Archives de Sèvres, A 2, *liasse* 3, *dossier* 7.
4. Jean-Baptiste Tavernier de Boullogne de Magnanville was the nephew of Madame de Pompadour, *Trésorier de l'extraordinaire des guerres en survivance* (1772–9), *fermier-général* 1787–90 and *commissaire du Roi à la nouvelle Compagnie des Indes*; he was also the nephew by marriage of Mesdames de Laborde, d'Harvelay and Lalive de Jully, see Y. Durand, *Les Fermiers Généraux au XVIIIe Siècle*, Paris, 1971, *passim*.
5. Guillebon, 1972, pp. 204–5. This author has not traced the document from which Madame de Guillebon quotes in connection with Jacques Louis Broilliet and M. de Clare, who were also associated in some way with the Gros Caillou venture, perhaps also providing capital. Chavagnac and Grollier, 1906, p. 514 note that Schradre had applied to Régnier, director of the Sèvres factory, for permission to work at the Gros Caillou factory as a painter of 'camaïeu' subjects and that Régnier had forwarded the request to d'Angiviller, the minister responsible, on 11 November 1783.
6. Chavagnac and Grollier, 1906, pp. 417–8.
7. Guillebon, R. de, 'Note sur Despréz, fabricant de camées de Porcelaine. Paris–fin XVIIIe–début XIXe Siècle', *Cahiers*, no. 46–7, 1970, ill. p. 11, in a private collection.

---

246 **Plaque: Henri IV (1553–1610)**, *c.*1772

H. 25.8 cm
W. 18.9 cm
Marks: *A.n°I* and *Deprovigny* incised on reverse
Reg. No. 1989,9–8,1

Hard-paste porcelain, moulded. Oval, and slightly convex, the rim simulating a frame with a ribbon at the upper end. The portrait of Henri IV (1553–1610) to right shows him with a moustache and beard and in armour, with a lace collar at the neck and a sash over his left shoulder. The surface exhibits pin-holes and 'bloats'. On the reverse are two depressions corresponding to the most prominent parts of the relief. At the left of the upper one is a brown splash, probably of iron.

Provenance: Purchased, 1989

Literature: Dawson *et al.*, 1990, p. 674, no. XIIa and b

Comparable Examples: None

The portrait is related to a marble statue of the King by Pierre de Franqueville commissioned in 1605 and in the Salle des Caryatides in the Louvre in 1722.[1]

This plaque is clearly experimental in nature: technically it is of indifferent quality, probably because of poor preparation of the body material. The brown splash on the reverse indicates the presence of iron in the clay which may have been present naturally, or may have come from a metal implement used to manhandle the clay. The design of the ribbon and the low relief of the portrait are both symptomatic of the low quality of the piece.

However, it is one of the few items which can be linked to the short-lived Gros Caillou factory, and the only one documenting the association of de Provigny[2] with the concern. It may perhaps have been made for him, possibly in the first firing (the meaning of the incised code remains unclear).

The earliest porcelain medallion of Henri IV after a medal by Guillaume Dupré dates from 1764–8 when Brancas-Lauraguais (*q.v.*) was making porcelain.[3] It is possible that a Mennecy biscuit portrait plaque of Henri IV was also on sale in the 1760s.[4] A circular hard-paste porcelain medallion incised *Limoges* after Dupré dates from 1771 or shortly afterwards.[5]

Josiah Wedgwood used the same source for a white

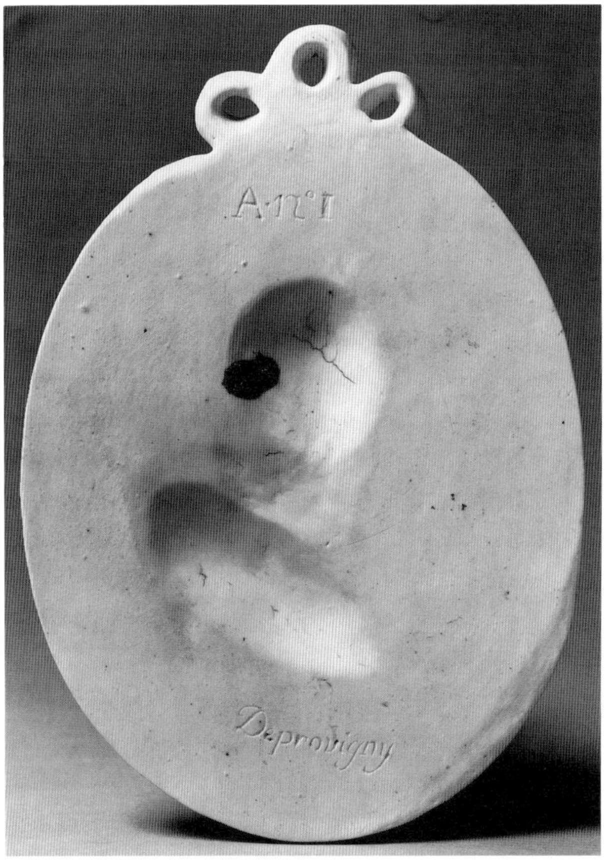

246 *reverse, showing marks*

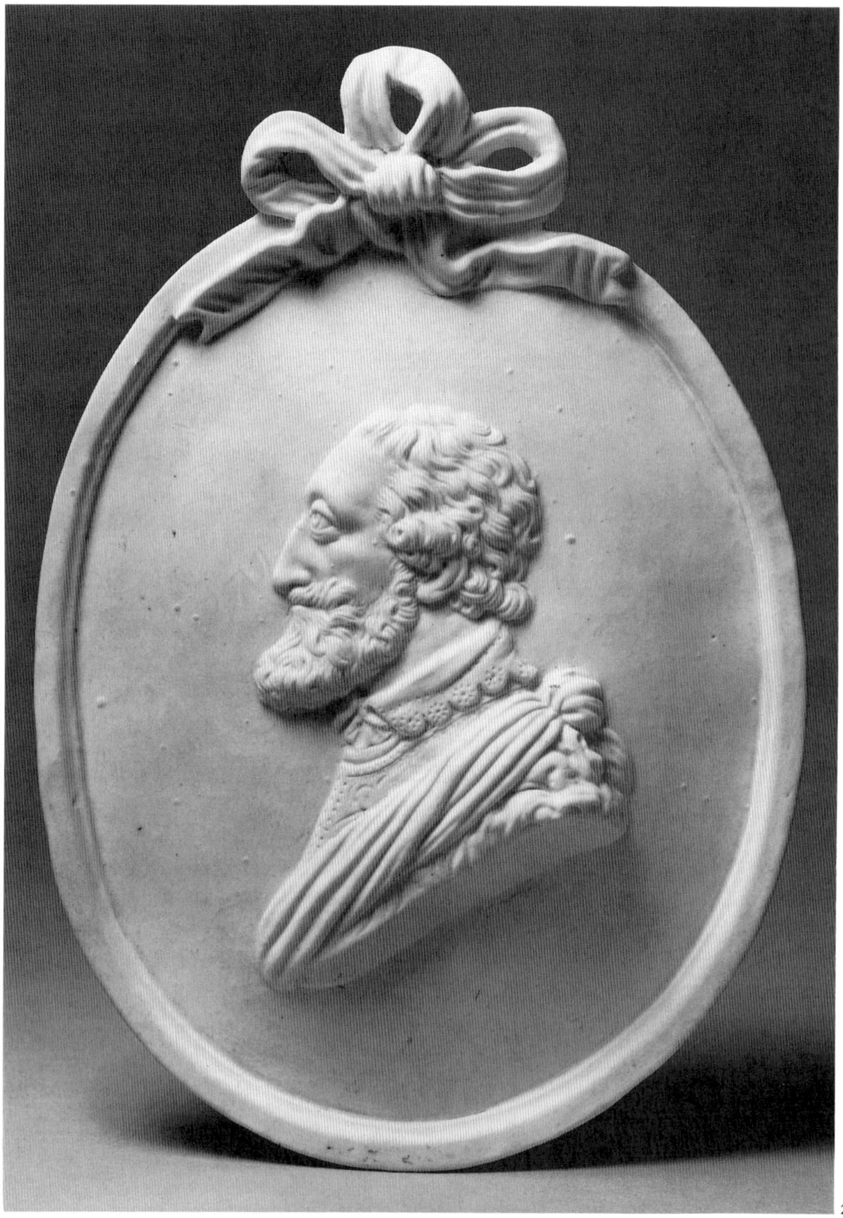

246

terracotta stoneware medallion with a reddish-brown ground. The subject, also made in black basalt and jasper, is listed in the firm's 1773 Catalogue.[6]

There was a veritable cult of King Henri IV in eighteenth-century France, which persisted well into the nineteenth century.[7] He was celebrated by Voltaire in his *La Henriade* (first published unofficially in 1723) as the ideal man of the Enlightenment, adopted by Quesnay and other economists and physiocrats and by the end of the century had become the hero of the mercantilists. From 1766–70 there was a spate of books and plays eulogising him,[8] including a three-act comedy *La Partie de Chasse du roi Henri* of which one edition was illustrated with engravings by Gravelot and Moreau *le Jeune*. His garlanded profile to left can be seen in an allegory of Louis *Le Bien-Aimé* by Boucher dated 1768 and engraved by A. de Saint-Aubin in 1772 for *L'Histoire de la Maison de Bourbon*.[9] A printed cotton made by Dubern et Cie around 1785 entitled *Tombeau de Voltaire* shows Charon taking leave of Voltaire in Elysium where he is being received by Henri IV.[10] The cult seems to have extended to England as a portrait of the King with Maria Augusta is moulded on a majolica dish dating from around 1878.[11] Although Stanislas Poniatowski's will lists no ceramic representation of Henri IV, he owned a marble bust of him, and had devoted himself to the French King.[12]

1. Illus. *IVe Le Centenaire de la Naissance de Henri IV*, June–September 1953, Pau, opp. p. 34, then in the Salle des Etats at the château de Pau. Pau, Musée national du château, inv. P. 44A, exh. *Henri IV et la reconstruction du royaume*, Pau, Musée national du château de Pau, June-October 1989, Paris, Archives nationales, November 1989–February 1990, no. 445.
2. The identity of de Provigny remains obscure.
3. H. Landais, *French Porcelain*, London, 1961, p. 103, fig. 66, Musée national de Céramique, Sèvres. The Sèvres porcelain medallion (see cat. 155) dates from *c.*1766.
4. Sold Parke-Bernet, New York, 7 February 1947, Lot 106, Karrick Riggs Collection, 'Bust-length profile to the left of the bearded monarch with bare head and military attire. Framed. Oval: height 8½ inches'.
5. Sèvres, Musée national de Céramique, d'Albis *et al*, 1989, cat. 154, inv. MNC 25341.
6. R. Reilly, *Wedgwood*, London, 1989, Vol. I, C89; see also M. Newman, 'History in Ceramics', *Antique Dealer and Collectors' Guide*, September 1991, pp. 40–3; fig. 2, shows another portrait of Henri IV in biscuit porcelain on a blue *caillouté* Höchst jug, *c.*1775–80.
7. This subject is most fully treated by M. Reinhard, *La Légende de Henri IV*, Paris, n.d. (1936). A white oval biscuit medallion of Henri IV full-face on a blue ground, with a beaded border and a glazed and gilt rim, said to date from around 1850, in the possession of Madame Léonce Patry, was exh. in *Porcelaine de Limoges des Origines à 1880*, no. 161, pl. XXIX.
8. These include Collé, *La Partie de Chasse du roi Henry*, three-act comedy, Paris, 1766; *Panégyrique d'Henri le Grand*, chez d'Houry, Paris, 1769; Marquis de la Villette, *Eloge historique d'Henri IV*, Amsterdam, 1770; (Prault) *L'Esprit d'Henri IV, ou anecdotes les plus intéressantes . . . et quelques lettres de ce Prince*, Paris, 1770.
9. A. Ananoff, *François Boucher*, Geneva, 1976, Vol. II, no. 650, fig. 1697.
10. USA, Museum of Art, University of Michigan, Ann Arbor, Michigan, exh. *The World of Voltaire*, March–May 1969, cat. 15, lent by Cooper-Hewitt Museum of Design, New York.
11. Sotheby's, Chester, 6 June 1990, Lot 1635.
12. L. Réau, 'Catalogue des oeuvres d'art français de la collection du roi de Pologne Stanislas-Auguste', in 'Archives de l'art français dans les pays du nord et de l'est de l'Europe', *Archives de l'art français*, XVII, 1931–2, reprinted 1969, pp. 247–8.

Pierre-Antoine Hannong's factory,
rue du faubourg Saint-Denis[1]

Pierre-Antoine Hannong (1739–after 1794)[2] acquired the lease of a property at 25, rue du faubourg Saint-Denis in June 1772, having obtained financial support from Louis-Victor de Fusée, comte de Voisenon, and Claude-Martin Dormoy, *ancien conseiller du Roi* and *président de l'éléction de Pithiviers* to the tune of 30,000 *livres*, which they themselves had borrowed. After bailing out Hannong for further substantial sums, they made over their interest in the factory to Mathieu Louis Armand, marquis d'Usson (1749–94)[3] on 18 October 1773. D'Usson contributed the sum of 53,662 *livres* 18 *sols* and wages owing to the employees, hoping to recoup his investment. Another partner, Jacques-Pascal Barrachin, joined the company in February 1774, bringing 6,000 *livres* to it. He soon became involved in a complicated quarrel in which Hannong accused him of removing merchandise to sell in a shop in the rue Platrière, near the Palais Royal, owned by the actor Boutet de Monvel. Towards the end of September 1774, a factory employee named Balthazard Byeller, who had worked at Haguenau and was later manager of the factory in rue Thiroux, and during the Revolution proprietor of a concern in the rue de Rocher, was put forward as director on behalf of d'Usson and Barrachin. Byeller was to receive a salary of 2,000 *livres* per annum, as well as lodging, heating and light, in return for the 'secrets' of porcelain manufacture. On 1 November Hannong departed, leaving the factory 104,887 *livres* in debt.

Although d'Usson lost the remainder of his fortune when he became a partner in the new factory and finally gave up all hope of deriving any benefit from it in October 1774, porcelain continued to be made at rue du faubourg Saint-Denis, first under Hannong's successors up to 1779, and subsequently under the protection of the comte d'Artois (see pp. 350–56). After the Revolution Marc Schoelcher (see pp. 384–5) acquired the premises.

The factory mark of a capital *H* was registered with the authorities on 26 May 1773. However, a lower case *h* painted in underglaze-blue seems to have been in use, sometimes with two crossed pipes, which were also used alone. Since the marquis d'Usson had obtained exemption for the factory from the usual conditions imposed to guarantee the monopoly of the royal factory, coloured decoration and gold was current. Both forms and decoration were rococo in style[4] although a pierced basket in the Musée national Adrien-Dubouché, Limoges, may perhaps owe something to Doccia, or possibly to Saint-Cloud: it is more baroque than rococo. A document dated 1 October 1774 shows that the firm had in stock merchandise totalling 5,000 *livres* described as 'en blanc Pr peindre et doré', and as 'en blanc Pr or et blanc', as well as colours and cobalt to the value of 500 *livres*.[5] Clay was purchased from Grellet of Limoges.[6] A record of one particular firing on 30 August has survived.[7] Of 1,063 pieces in the kiln, four were broken and thirty defective. The firing was evaluated at 1,498 *livres*, and manufacturing costs came to 745 *livres* 9 *sols*: labour costs amounted to 257 *livres* 9 *sols*, wood to 208 *livres*, administration and rents to 200 *livres* and daily expenses to 80 *livres*. An inventory made on the previous day noted 9,332 pieces valued at 22,938 *livres* 15 *sols* 9 *deniers* in stock.

A list of workers dated 28 July 1774 shows that one thrower, Caezar, was a native of Venice and had worked at Nevers, whilst an Austrian named Teitcher had worked at Sceaux. Others came from Berlin, Vienna, Saxony, Würtemberg and Mayence. Three members of the workforce of thirty-eight had worked at La Courtille.[8] In 1774, as the workers had not been paid, one of them named Delymal left to work at the Clignancourt factory.[9]

1. This account is based on Guillebon, 'Les fourberies de Pierre-Antoine Hannong à Sèvres, Vincennes, Vaux et Paris', *Bulletin de la Société de l'histoire de Paris et de l'Ile de France*, 113/114e année, 1986/1987, pp. 179–222.
2. Pierre-Antoine Hannong, who was the eighth child of Paul Hannong and his second wife Catherine Barbe Acker, was born in Strasbourg on 17 January 1739, and was baptised in the parish of Saint-Pierre-le-Vieux. The date of his death is unknown. Guillebon gives the following outline of his later career: on 24 September 1776 he obtained permission of the King of Sardinia to make porcelain in the castle of Vinovo; after losing 300,000 *livres* of the King's money he was dismissed and exiled in January 1780. In January 1781 he tried to obtain money from Sèvres for the secret of hard-paste manufacture which he had sold them twenty years before. In 1783 he tried to set up a new factory at Haguenau, but it lasted no more than a year before he ran into debt. He tried to move it, but by 1786 was in serious financial trouble. He may then have been involved with the factory in the rue Amelot, Paris. In 1793 he tried to claim the directorship of the Sèvres factory, but was unsuccessful. The last we hear of him is at a factory in rue du Mont-Parnasse.
3. The role of the marquis d'Usson is treated by M. Hosotte-Reynaud, 'Le marquis d'Usson et les débuts de la manufacture du faubourg Saint-Denis (1772–1779)', *Cahiers*, 51 (1972), pp. 54–65.
4. For examples see Guillebon, 'Premières porcelaines dures de Paris', *Antologia di Belle Arti*, nuova serie, 29–30, 1986, figs. 1–3, 5–6, 8, 13–15, 17.
5. Guillebon, 1986, p. 40, quoting Archives nationales, Minutier central, *Etude* XV, M° Thiérion, 'Etat général ou sommaire . . .'.
6. Guillebon, *op. cit.*, p. 36.
7. Guillebon, *op. cit.*, pp. 36–7, quoting Archives nationales, T 1042[3], letters from Lecointe to d'Usson, 29, 30 August 1773.
8. *Ibid.*, quoting MNS, Archives de Sèvres, Y 35 *bis*.
9. *Ibid.*, quoting document cited in note 7, 28 July 1774.

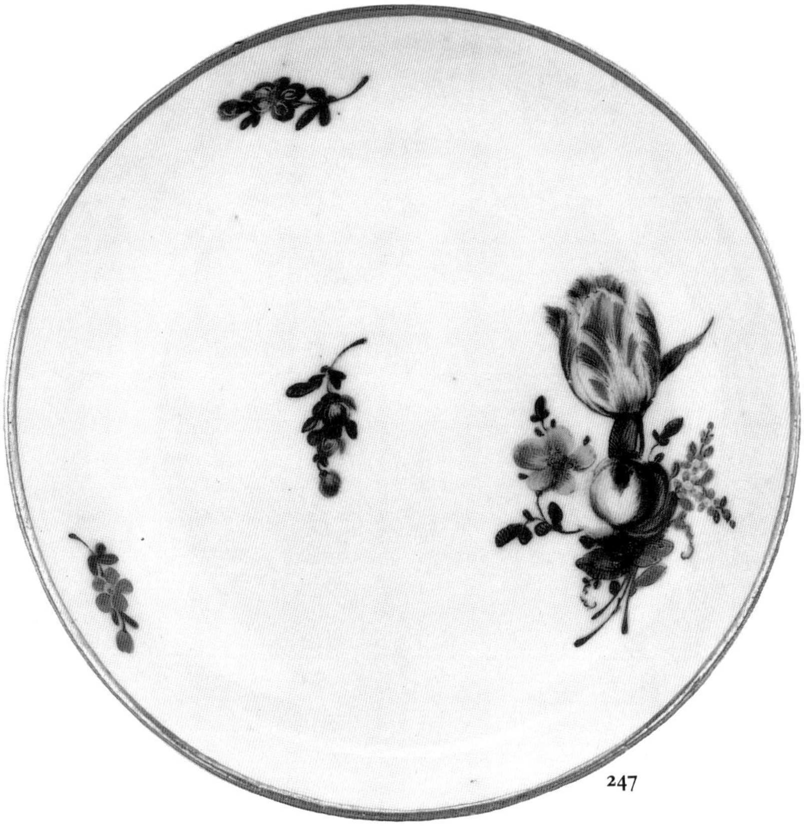

247

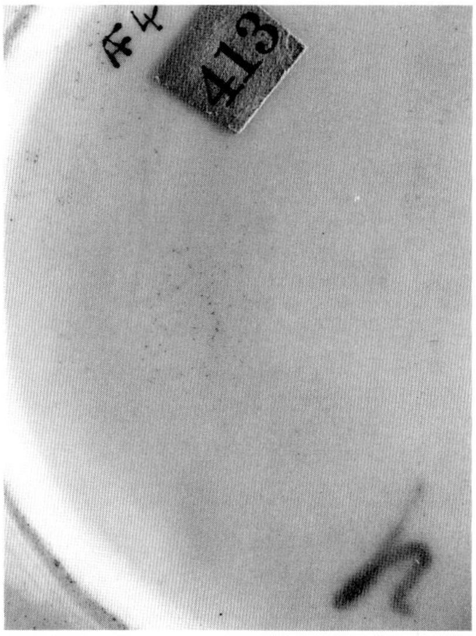

247 *marks*

247 **Saucer**, 1772–4 (or 1779)

D. 12.8 cm
Marks: *h* painted in underglaze-blue; cross incised
Reg. No. Franks 413

Hard-paste porcelain, thickly potted, decorated in green, yellow, orange, purple and brown enamels with scattered flowers; rim gilt. Chip to foot rim.

Provenance: Bequeathed by Sir A.W. Franks, 1897

Literature: Franks, 1896, no. 413

Comparable Examples: None

According to a decree of 15 February 1766 only the Sèvres factory was allowed to produce and sell pieces decorated in colours and gold. Through his wife, Pauline, vicomtesse du Rumain, who was Madame Clothilde's lady-in-waiting, the comte d'Usson requested and was granted exemption from this decree, much to the annoyance of Parent, the director of the Sèvres factory who complained in a letter of 23 August 1778.[1] In theory the gilding on this saucer should not have been applied until after this date, but there is ample evidence that most factories operating in and around Paris disregarded the ruling of 1766. The discoloration and numerous black specks on the reverse suggest that the saucer may have been left in the biscuit state for some time before it was glazed and painted.

1. Quoted by Hosotte-Reynaud, 1972, note 29, A.N., O^1 2059 a–b.

248 **Teapot (*théière*)**, 1772–4 (or 1779)

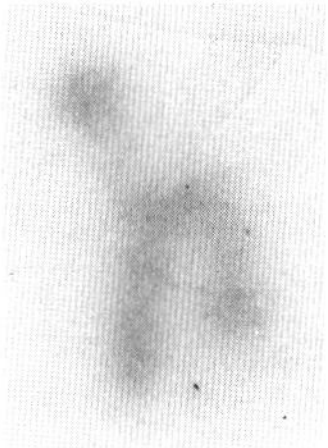

248 *mark*

H. 9.4 cm
Marks: *h* painted in underglaze-blue
Reg. No. 1934,2–13,1

Hard-paste porcelain, finely potted and highly translucent. Of ovoid form with flattened, ear-shaped handle and shallow foot.
Painted in two shades of green, yellow, brown, red-brown, blue and pink with a shepherdess holding a crook in a wooded landscape on one side and with a shepherd holding a crook near a [?] flaming altar on the other. Gilt ornament around the rim, on base and front of spout, on handle and foot. Cover missing. Chips to foot and several hairline cracks to glaze.

Provenance: Presented by Monsieur R. Fenouil, 1934

Literature: Guillebon, 'Premières porcelaines dures de Paris', *Antologia di Belle Arti*, nuova serie, nos. 29–30, 1986, pp. 30–4, fig. 14

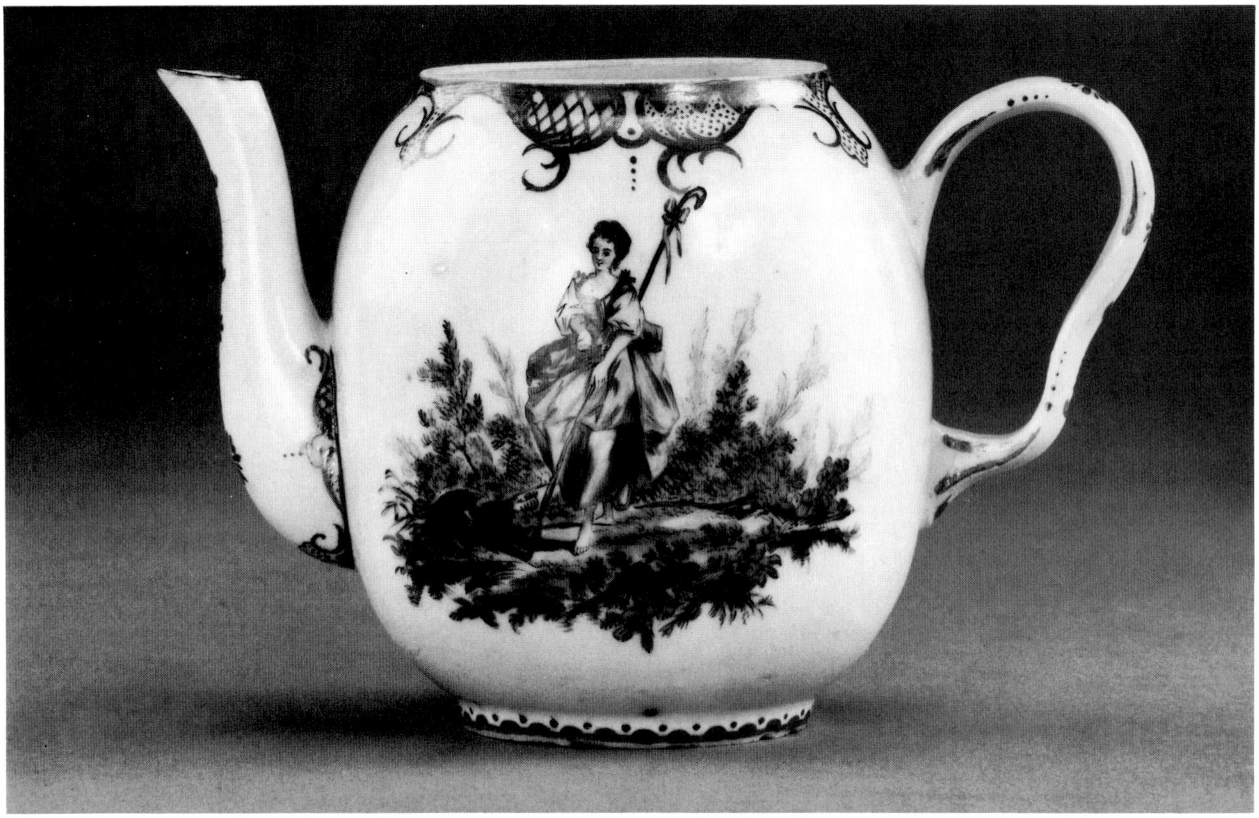

248

Comparable Examples: None

In shape this piece clearly resembles a teapot and cover decorated with polychrome flower chains which bears the mark of Pierre Hannong at Strasbourg.[1] The figure of the shepherdess appears to derive from a print after F. Boucher by Demarteau *l'aîné*.[2]

1. Musée des arts décoratifs, Strasbourg, inv. XXVII.56.
2. Jean-Richard, 1978, nos. 618–19.

Locré and Russinger's factory,
rue de la Fontaine-au-Roi, La Courtille[1]

This was one of the earliest hard-paste porcelain factories in Paris. It was established by Jean-Baptiste Locré (1726–1810) in 1772, in the area known as La Courtille. On 12 August Locré rented a house from the *marchand-horloger* Simon Festau[2] and by December Laurent Russinger (1739–1810) was director of the factory.[3] Locré came from a family of Paris merchant haberdashers and was married at Leipzig at the age of thirty-one to Christiana Caritas Hoffman (1736–1800).[4] Russinger was a native of Höchst in Hesse, Germany, where he worked as a modeller at the porcelain factory.[5] He left Höchst in 1768, arriving in Paris in the same year after a short stay in the porcelain factory at Pfalz-Zweibrücken.

The factory was referred to from the outset as a 'manufacture de porcelaine allemande'. Its mark of two crossed arrows was registered before the lieutenant-general of the Paris police on 14 July 1773.[6] The porcelain body is thought to have been made at the factory itself, initially using clays from the Limoges area, but also, somewhat later, with clays from Cherbourg and Valognes.[7]

After initial financial problems a new company was formed on 2 April 1777 to which Pierre Jean Martin de Bussy, *conseiller du Roi et substitut du Procureur général au Grand Conseil*, brought 36,000 *livres* capital in exchange for 25 per cent of the profits. On 24 July 1777 Russinger's contract was extended for twelve years on highly favourable terms: he was to receive 3,000 *livres* per annum as well as 10 per cent of the factory's profits. The seizure of over two thousand pieces of porcelain worth more than 10,000 *livres* on 12 February 1780, and subsequent condemnation of Locré for contravention of the Sèvres monopoly to a fine of 1,000 *livres* and prohibition on making porcelain, does not seem to have affected the factory's activity. Locré eventually sold out to Russinger on 10 August 1787 for 110,000 *livres*. Three kilns and a horse-powered mill for the preparation of raw materials are mentioned in the contract of sale in which Russinger is called 'co-entrepreneur sans mise de fonds et directeur de la manufacture dans laquelle il demeure'. Russinger purchased a plot of land also in the rue de la Fontaine-au-Roi on 29 March 1792 where he built a new factory, designed by the architect François-Charles-Etienne d'Herbelot. A plan and description of the factory dated 1798[8] shows that two kilns were in use. By 1797 Russinger was deep in debt. Unable to pay for clay from François Pouyat of Limoges, he was forced to accept an advance from him in exchange for allowing him a stake in the factory. In 1800 François Pouyat became sole owner of the concern, which he subsequently sold to his sons Léonard, Jean-Baptiste and Jean for the sum of 8,000 *livres*. Russinger retired in 1808 after teaching the Pouyats how to make porcelain. Léonard Pouyat left Paris for Fours in the Nièvre region to manufacture porcelain which was sent to Paris for decoration. The factory in Paris enjoyed the patronage of the duc de Berry from 1817 until his assassination in 1820, and apparently ceased production in that year. It was sold up in 1823.[9]

The products of the factory were described in *Annonces, affiches et avis divers*, of 16 January 1777. They include table and toilet services as well as ornamental pieces, both glazed and unglazed, *tasses de limonadiers* (cups similar to cat. 48, used by café owners or *limonadiers*), either undecorated, painted in (underglaze) blue or in colours, and with or without gilding.[10] Pieces of considerable size were made, as well as a wide range of allegorical and portrait figures and groups, whose iconography is often close to that of Derby figures.[11] Lifesize portrait busts, such as a notorious bust of Madame du Barry after a plaster by Augustin Pajou (in production at Sèvres from 1771 and sold at 18 *livres*) for which Locré wanted the enormous sum of 12,000 *livres* from the sitter in 1773.[12] A biscuit group signed *LOCRET FECIT ANNO 1774* with the crossed arrows and *Russinger 1773* in a less prominent position commemorates the marriage of the Dauphin and Marie-Antoinette. It is one of the most impressive groups issued by the factory.[13] Another, allegorical of the birth of Marie-Antoinette's son in 1781, is also highly accomplished.[14]

A printed list of prices for Pouyat Frères and Compie shows that the firm produced an extremely wide range of tablewares, teawares and other miscellaneous items, including a restricted number of vases.[15]

Shapes of domestic wares for the table mostly derive from forms developed at Sèvres, although decorative schemes were in general much simpler, often consisting of bouquets of scattered flowers, ribbons entwined with flower garlands or cornflowers painted in colours on a white ground.[16] Some of the earliest pieces are highly feldspathic and have a glassy appearance. These are often painted in underglaze-blue with the simplest of blue sprig designs or stylised trees loosely based on *chinoiserie* motifs.[17] Other recorded examples, such as a pear-shaped jug and cover painted with coloured birds, closely imitate Sèvres.[18]

Animal, landscape, flower and figure painting, as well as coloured grounds, were used for more luxurious pieces, and even *trompe l'oeil* grounds imitating wood are known. One example in a private collection is dated 1778.[19] The factory adapted both its forms and decorative motifs to changes in taste, using heavier gilding, unusual ground colours and classically-influenced forms from the beginning of the nineteenth century.

In the *Almanach Dauphin* of 1777,[20] Russinger is described as a *marchand-mercier*, and is said to have a shop in the rue Michel-Comte. He is also said to be the proprietor of the factory in the rue Fontaine-au-Roi, whose porcelain was considered superior to that of other Paris concerns. In a request made in 1795 to bring wood from Burgundy, Russinger stated that he employed between seventy and eighty workers.[21] By the beginning of the nineteenth century ninety workers were employed; three years later in 1810, there were seventy-eight employees, including twelve painters.[22] A painter, Frédérick, is listed there in 1797, as well as Marx *père*, both probably foreigners. Jean-Léopold Weydinger, who worked at Sèvres as a gilder between 1774 and 1792,[23] and who had trained there, was a painter and gilder at la Fontaine-au-Roi in 1797. He was still working for the Pouyat brothers in January 1819 in the same location. Jean Charles François Leloy (1774–1846) probably also worked there on the composition of decorative schemes before joining Sèvres in 1816. A biscuit group of a hunter incised *Mo* beside the crossed arrows[24] is evidence that one of the Mô brothers recorded at Mennecy in 1767/8, probably Christophe Mô who was a sculptor at Sceaux in 1766, was employed at la Fontaine-au-Roi.

Little is known about the export of porcelain from this factory. However, it has been noted that John Quincy Adams (1767–1848, US Minister to Russia about 1809–14) purchased a large service from the Duke of Mondragone when they were both in Russia, showing that there was a second-hand market in Paris porcelain. George Washington seems to have supplemented a Sèvres service with gilt borders which he had acquired in 1789 from the comte de Moustier, French Minister, with a La Courtille ice-cream cooler.[25]

1. This account is largely based on M. Hosotte-Reynaud, 'Aperçus inédits sur une manufacture de porcelaine de Paris, La Courtille: de Locré à Pouyat (1773–1823)', *Cahiers*, 35 (1964), pp. 156–72 and Guillebon and Lasserre, 1966, pp. 102–19.
2. Hosotte-Reynaud, *op. cit.*, p. 163.
3. Guillebon, 1985, p. 105.
4. Bloit, 1988, pp. 21–3; Jean-Baptiste was the son of Guillaume Locré and his wife Geneviève Vannier, who were married on 16 October 1712, when he described himself as 'marchand tussolier, rubanier, frangier, ouvrier en drap d'or, d'argent et de soie, fils de Sieur Jean Locré, de même vocation' (i.e. a cloth merchant). Miniature portraits of Jean-Baptiste Locré and his wife, formerly in the possession of the last of the Locré line, Baron Louis Jean Napoléon Locré (d.1958) are illus. by Bloit, 1988, p. 26.
5. A biography of Russinger is given by E. Kramer, 'Laurentius Russinger, Porzelliner in Hoechst, Gutenbrunn und Paris', *Keramos*, 50 (1970), pp. 83–100. It has been stated by Guillebon and Lasserre, 1966, p. 102 and by Guillebon, 1985, p. 105, that Russinger came to Paris in 1768 to work for Chapelle at Sceaux, but his name does not appear in the list based on parish registers and *taille* records in the Archives nationales published in exh. Sceaux, 1986, pp. 116–20, and he apparently never actually worked there: Chapelle was only attempting to steal his knowledge.

6. Hosotte-Reynaud, *op. cit.*, p. 162, quoting Archives nationales, O[1] 2060.
7. Guillebon, 1972, p. 252.
8. For a plan of the factory see Guillebon, 1985, pl. LXXXIII, fig. 116, pl. LXXXIV, fig. 117.
9. This date is given by Guillebon, 1985, p. 109, f.n. 476, quoting Archives nationales, Minutier central, *Etude* LX, 656, 16 février 1823 (Me Février et Bertrand).
10. Bloit, *op. cit.*, p. 22.
11. Bloit, *op. cit.*, p. 11, three hunters; p. 14, group for the Marriage of the Dauphin and Marie-Antoinette dated 1774; p. 18, group after Falconet's bather; p. 31, group the Altar of Love; p. 34, groups the Chinese Musicians, the Four Elements; p. 35, groups of lovers and three children; Guillebon and Lasserre, 1966, p. 108, fig. 8, a dancer and two musicians; p. 109, fig. 9, Venus and Cupid; p. 112, fig. 11, allegorical group of the birth of the Dauphin. Three further groups in the State Hermitage Museum, St Petersburg, are illus. and others listed by Birioukova, figs. 86–8.
12. Guillebon, 1972, pp. 144–6. A bust of this subject signed *RUSSINGER FECIT ANNO* [?] was on the market in 1989, Christie's, Monaco, Important Mobilier et Objets d'Art, 18 June 1989, Lot 56, H. 65.5 cm.
13. Bloit, *op. cit.*, p. 14.
14. Victoria and Albert Museum, London, inv. C.234–1915, and d'Albis *et al.*, 1989, cat. 116, inv. MNC 26282.
15. The author is grateful to Tamara Préaud for bringing to her attention three printed sheets dated 1820 in ink kept in the Archives de Sèvres, U 19, *liasse* II, *dossier* I, *Tarif d'autres manufactures.*
16. Hosotte-Reynaud, *op. cit.*, p. 157, p. 160, fig. 1, p. 169. A pair of ice-pails, covers and liners with this type of decoration was sold at Christie's East, New York, 25 September 1985, Lot 125, estate of J. Cummings.
17. Bloit, *op. cit.*, p. 22.
18. Ballu, n.d., pl. 34B.
19. Bloit, *op. cit.*, p. 21, tray, cup and sugar bowl. The inscription occurs on the supposed 'engraving', in reality a hand-painted landscape scene.
20. Guillebon, 1972, p. 252.
21. Chavagnac and Grollier, 1906, p. 492, quoting Archives nationales, F. 12, 1496.
22. Guillebon, 1985, p. 107.
23. Brunet and Préaud, 1978, p. 382.
24. Chavagnac and Grollier, 1906, p. 497.
25. Detweiler, *French Porcelain*, 1982, pp. 94–5.

---

249 **Beaker**, *c.*1773

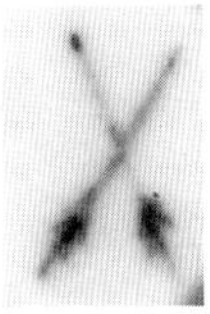

249 *mark*

H.	6.7 cm
D.	7 cm
Marks:	crossed arrows painted in underglaze-blue
Reg. No.	1988,6–4,1

Hard-paste glassy-looking porcelain, highly translucent, the lower part moulded with a ribbed pattern. Painted in underglaze-blue with scroll motifs and pendent dots. The interior has numerous pin-holes and black specks. Crack from rim to middle of ribbed area.

Provenance: Presented by E. Manners, Esq., 1988

Literature: Unpublished

Comparable Examples: None

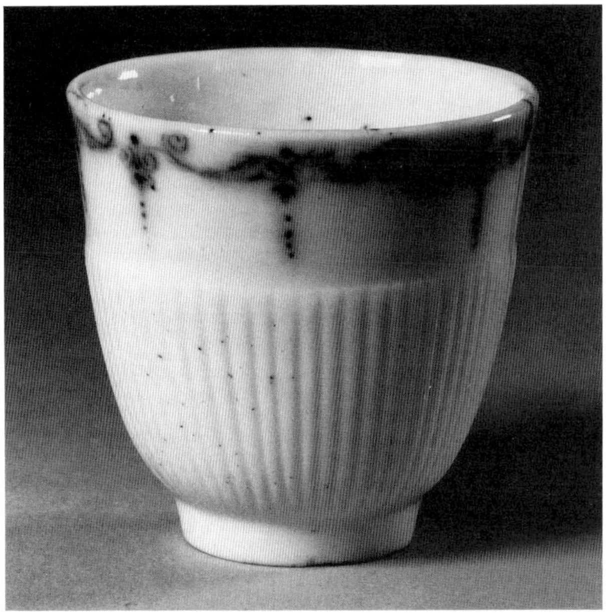

249

The appearance of this piece does not immediately suggest hard-paste porcelain. However, many early Paris porcelains exhibit this glassy quality, despite containing mullite.[1]

A beaker with a similar ribbed moulding decorated with cornflowers is in the Victoria and Albert Museum, London,[2] and another with underglaze-blue painted decoration of scrolls near the rim like this example, but which is incised *D.V*, is in the Cleveland Museum of Art, Cleveland, Ohio, USA.[3]

The function of this beaker is uncertain; it may perhaps have been used as a *tasse de limonadier* by a lemonade seller (see cat. 48).

1. In conversation with Antoine d'Albis, 1988. Madame F. Treppoz of the Manufacture nationale de Sèvres has kindly informed the author in correspondence of July 1990 that in 1984 a 'saladier' (perhaps a *compotier carré*) of Locré porcelain, which was extremely glassy-looking, was found on analysis to contain mullite (the essential component of what we term 'hard-paste') as well as quartz.
2. J. Cushion, *Continental Porcelain*, London, revised edn. 1982, p. 72, pl. 59.
3. Inv. 64.506, H. 7.1 cm, D. 6.6 cm, listed *Bulletin of the Cleveland Museum of Art*, November 1965, p. 153, no. 67.

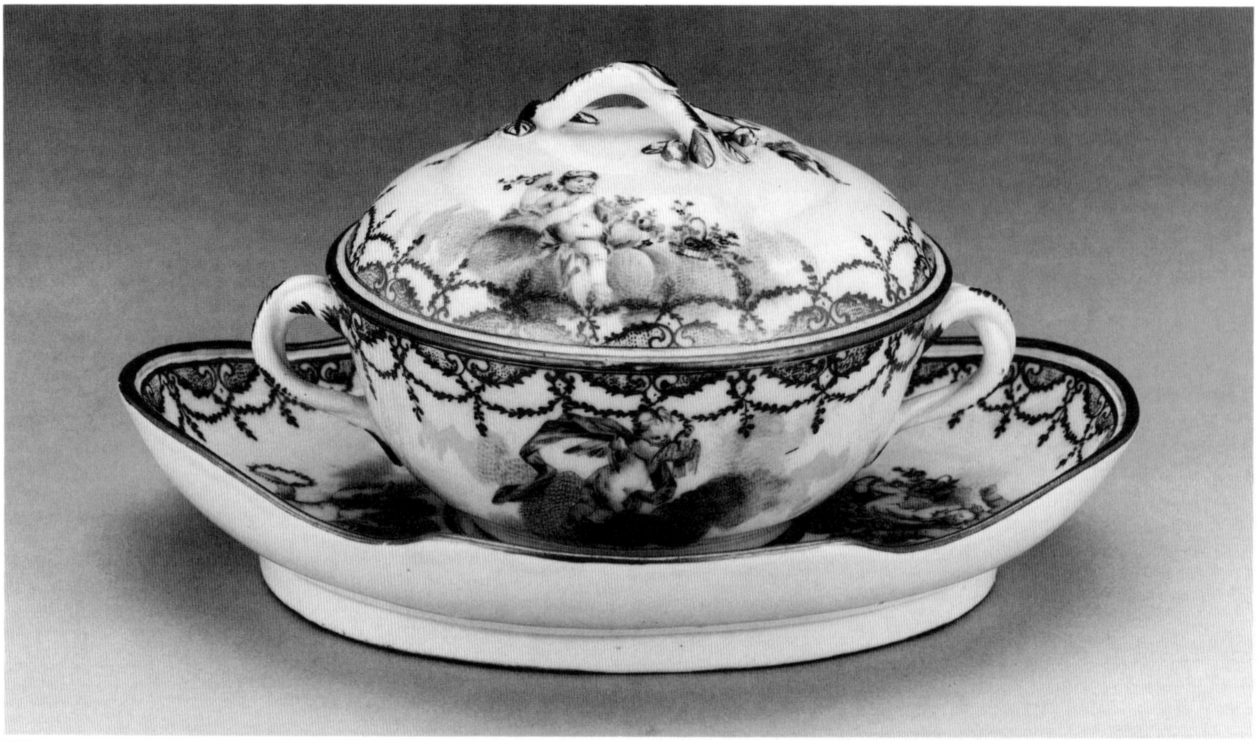

250

250 **Bowl, Cover and Stand (*écuelle couverte et plateau*),** *c.*1775

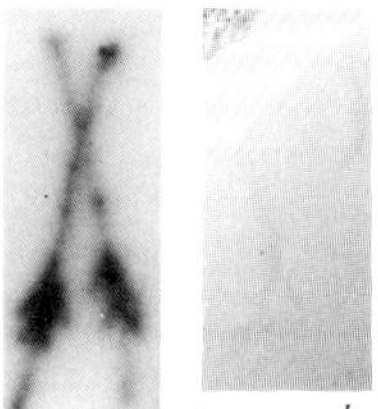

250 *marks*

See colour plate 38

L. *of stand:* 21.1 cm

H. *of bowl and cover:* 9.6 cm

Marks: crossed arrows painted in underglaze-blue on both; cursive *L* incised on stand; two printed labels with descriptions of this piece, one inscribed in ink *From Sale Catalogue*, stuck to base of stand

Reg. No. 1913,12–20,135

Hard-paste porcelain, the stand of moulded lobed form with deep foot, the bowl with double twig handles, the moulded cover domed in two stages with applied laurel leaf and berry finial. The decoration consists of a spray of daisies, roses and other flowers painted in pink, yellow, orange, blue, green and grey matt enamels in the well of the stand, which is defined by a gilt line. At either end in the same palette a putto emblematic of Love on clouds; at one side trophies of music: a horn, a tambourine, a score as well as a scarf and a palm branch, and at the other the heads of two putti playing (?) pipes between a score inscribed *toutes mes passions sont a Venus.* On one side of the bowl are two putti on clouds with a cage from which two doves have escaped. On the other a putto in clouds holds a dove. The cover is painted with a putto in clouds with a basket of flowers and a garland on one side, and on the other with a nude female lying on a white cloth striped brown entangled with a pink one, with a leering satyr attended by a cupid clutching her shoulders. Near each rim is a gilt scroll and dot pattern bounded by a wreath with pendent wreaths below; each rim and parts of handles gilt.

Provenance: Bequeathed by the Reverend A.H.S. Barwell, 1913

Literature: Guillebon, 1972, fig. 198

Comparable Examples: Paris, Michel Bloit Collection, no. 263, together with a similarly decorated cup and saucer, Bloit Collection, no. 161

The form is closely based on the *écuelle ronde, plateau ovale uni* produced at Vincennes around 1750,[1] which enjoyed long-lasting popularity. Other factories, such as Clignancourt, adapted the shape, changing its proportions.[2] Locré seems to have produced an alternative version with an oval stand, and slightly different dimensions.[3] The putti derive from engravings after François Boucher possibly adapted from:

Cover a) *Le Printems* engraved by L. de La Rue;[4]
b) possibly adapted from *Jupiter and Antiope* engraved by Parizeau.[5]

Bowl a) adapted by *L'Amour Oiseleur* engraved by B. Lépicié;[6]
b) unidentified.

Stand a) possibly adapted from *Le Printems* engraved by L. de La Rue;
b) unidentified.

1. See exh. *Vincennes*, 1977–8, p. 50, fig. 85.
2. Guillebon, 1972, fig. 54, Paris, private collection; fig. 56, Musée national de Céramique, Sèvres.
3. French Porcelain in Palazzo Pitti', compiled by S. Eriksen, Florence, 1973, no. 80; the writer has not examined this piece.
4. Jean-Richard, 1978, no. 1267.
5. *Ibid.*, no. 1442.
6. *Ibid.*, no. 1377.

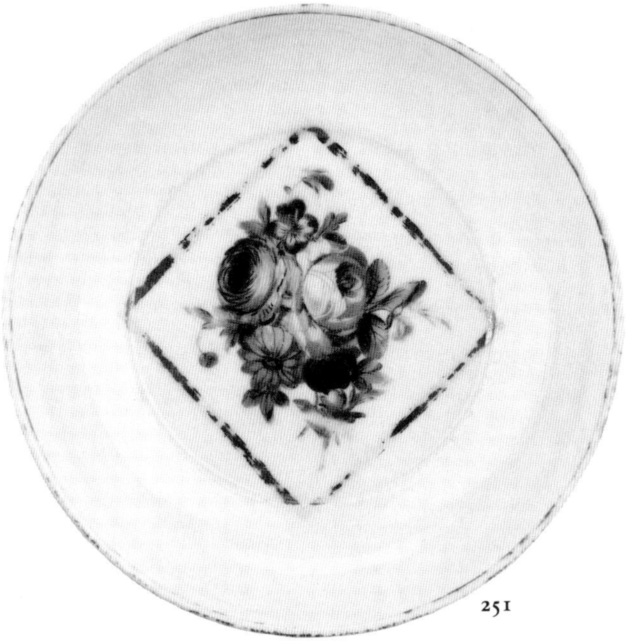

251

251 **Saucer**, *c.*1780

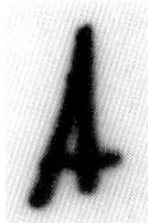

251 *mark*

D. 12.5 cm
Marks: crossed arrows painted in underglaze-blue
Reg. No. Franks 418

Hard-paste porcelain, with deep curved sides. Painted in the centre with a bouquet of roses, a pansy and other flowers in pink, green, yellow, red, blue, violet and brown on a white ground, enclosed by a gilt line. Rim gilt. Gilding rubbed. Two glaze cracks near rim.

Provenance: Bequeathed by Sir A.W. Franks, 1897

Literature: Franks, 1896, no. 418

Comparable Examples: None

This saucer represents the middle range of production of the factory.

252 **Plate (*assiette*)**, 1776–*c.*1793

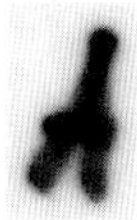

252 *mark*

D. 23.5 cm
Mark: crossed arrows painted in underglaze-blue
Reg. No. Franks 419

Hard-paste porcelain decorated with a scene of a partly-draped angel with a cherub on its shoulders among clouds painted in matt pale blue, grey and white, for the clouds, pink for the

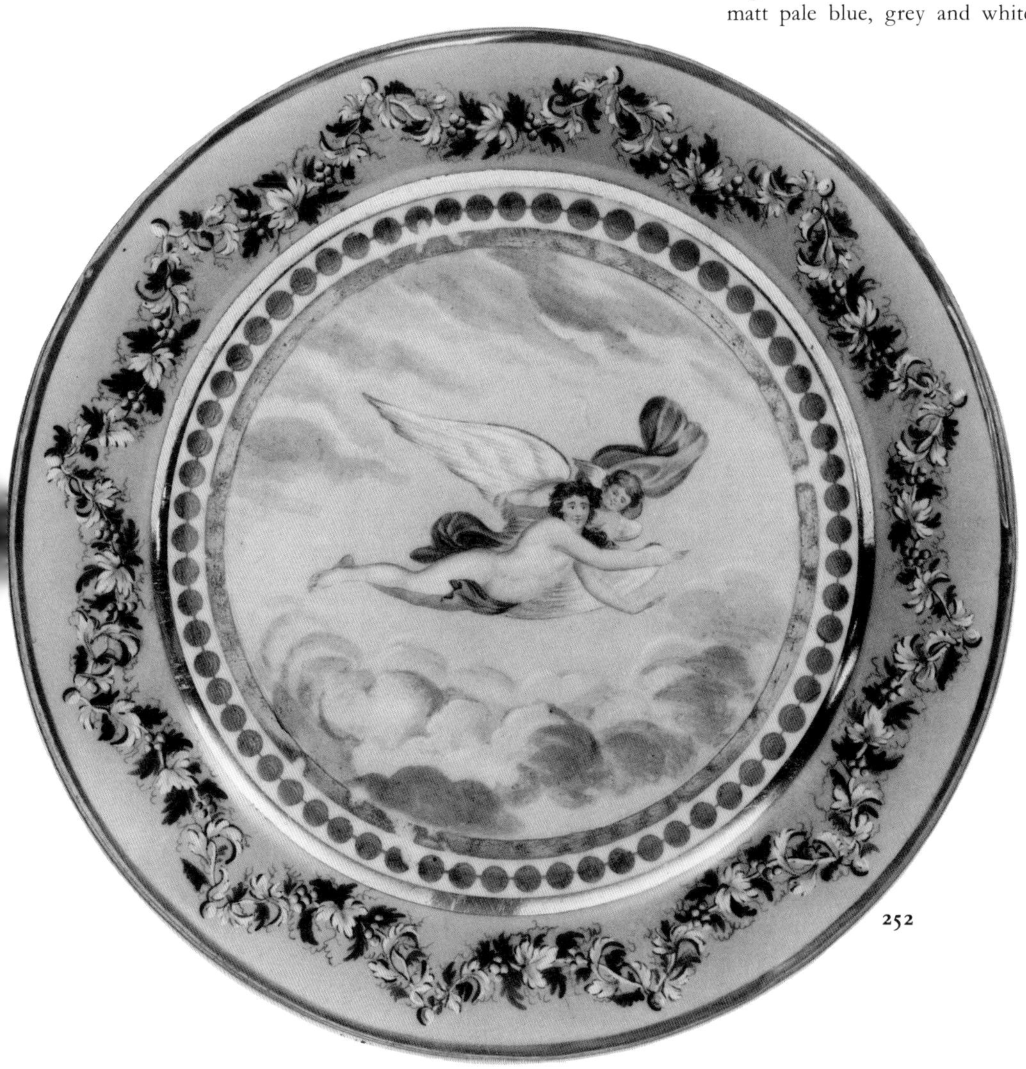

252

drapery, pale yellow and grey for the wings, orange for the angel's wreath, brown for the hair, and vitrified flesh tones. The scene is bordered by two gilt lines enclosing gilt dots. Rim decorated with a vine-leaf trail painted in dark red-brown and grey on a matt salmon-coloured ground. Rim gilt.

Provenance: Bequeathed by Sir A.W. Franks, 1897

Literature: Franks, 1896, no. 419

Comparable Examples: None

The use of matt colours produced without the use of a flux and the salmon-coloured rim show that this factory was in the forefront of fashion, although the decorative subject is in the rococo style. It is hard to imagine that this plate was anything but ornamental.

253 **Cup and Saucer (*tasse litron, soucoupe*)**, late 18th century

H. *of cup:*	6.2 cm
D. *of saucer:*	13 cm
Marks:	crossed arrows painted in underglaze-blue; cursive *N* incised (cup); crossed arrows painted in underglaze-blue (saucer)
Reg. No.	Franks 417

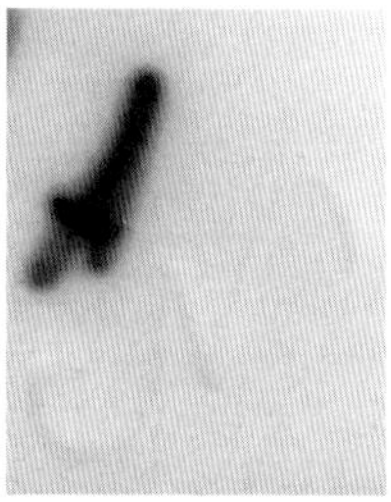

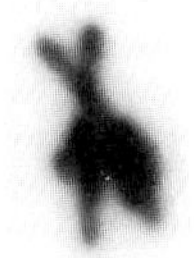

253 *marks*

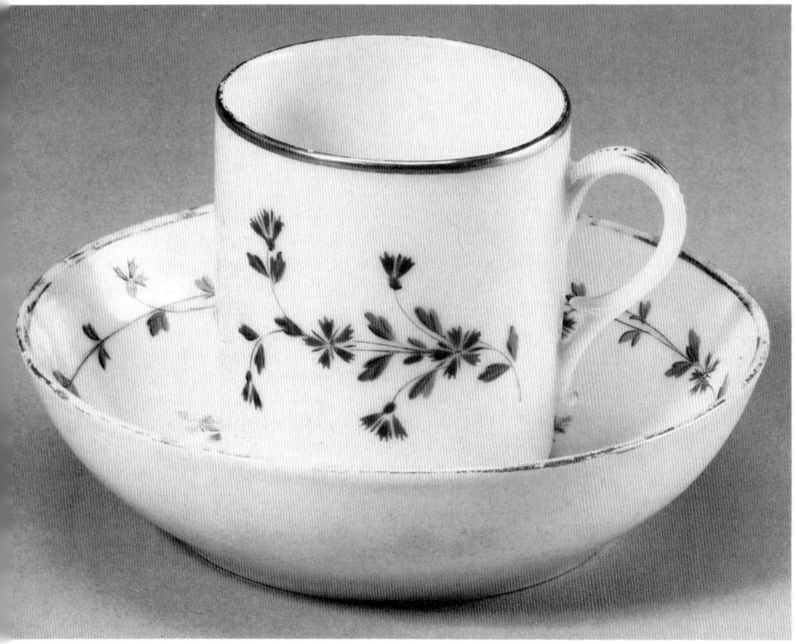

253

Hard-paste porcelain. Straight-sided cup with lower part of handle terminating in a scroll. The saucer, which does not belong, has curved sides and is less white in colour with greyish inclusions in the paste. Both pieces are painted with a cornflower pattern in blue, red, green and grey. The decoration on the cup is brighter in colour, and on the saucer there are in addition three gilt stars, now rubbed. Rims gilt, handle partly gilt. Lower part of handle cracked, saucer repaired and gilding to rim rubbed.

Provenance: Bequeathed by Sir A.W. Franks, 1897

Literature: Franks, 1896, no. 417

Comparable Examples: None

The saucer should be matched with a cup with curved sides.[1] The form of the cup (*gobelet litron*) is influenced by Sèvres, as so often at the Locré factory (see cat. 250).

1. See Guillebon and Lasserre, 1966, p. 105, fig. 1, Lisbon, Museu Nacional de Arte Antiga; col. pl. opp. p. 110, Bordeaux, coll. C. Lasserre.

254 **Jug and Cover**, *c.*1775

H. *to top of knop:*	21.3 cm
Marks:	crossed arrows painted in underglaze-blue
Reg. No.	Franks 416

Hard-paste porcelain, body thrown, handle and cover moulded, moulded applied acorn and leaf finial. Of pear-shaped form with strap handle, gilt metal mount attached to the cover by means of a metal pin. Painted in pink, blue, green, yellow, orange, purple and grey with flowers in a vase, and in a pot on a table, berried leaves, and fruit within a gilt laurel wreath on the body; neck and cover painted with a gilt *oeil-de-perdrix* pattern with purple dots, interrupted by a forget-me-not ribbon pattern. Gilt dentil pattern on rims, gilt line on foot, handle partly gilt. Lip of cover chipped.

Provenance: Bequeathed by Sir A.W. Franks, 1897

Literature: Franks, 1896, no. 416

Comparable Examples: Switzerland, Geneva, Musée Ariana, illus. Guillebon, 1972, p. 250, fig. 192

Lille, Musée des Beaux-Arts, inv. C. 772, illus. exh. Nord-Pas-de-Calais, 1986–7, no. 44

This jug was intended for the toilette, and probably once had a matching basin. Adhesions to the foot rim, firecracks, pin-holes in the paste and 'bloat' disguised by a gilt leaf show that domestic porcelains were not always of the highest quality.

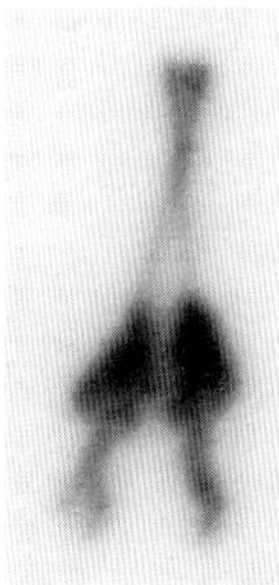

254 *mark*

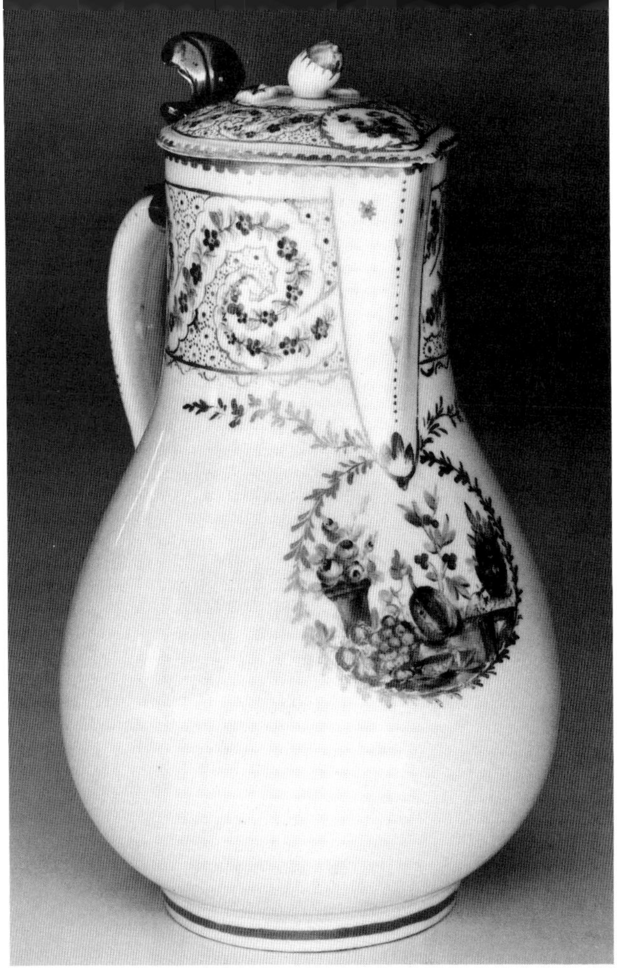

254

255 **Figure of a Young Man**, *c.*1775

H.	24.7 cm
Marks:	crossed arrows and cursive *B* [?] or possibly monogram for J. B. Locré incised
Reg. No.	FB 34 (AF 3234)

Hard-paste porcelain, circular convex base. The youth leans against a tree, his left elbow propped against the stump of a branch, his hand to his cheek. Over his long hair tied *en queue* at the back is a wide-brimmed hat. He wears a long jacket over a tunic tied at the waist, and trousers beneath puttees which button at the side and come over the knee; just below the knee they are tied with a ribbon. His left knee is slightly bent and his head turned to the right. He stands on a rocky base applied with moss. Minor damage to right hand.

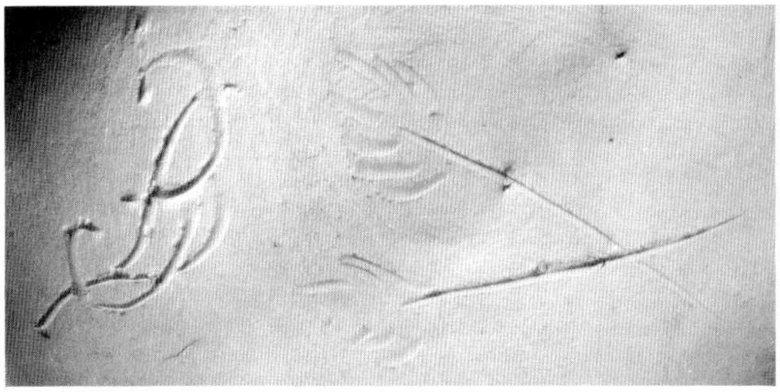

255 *marks*

255 *(right)*, **256** *(left)*

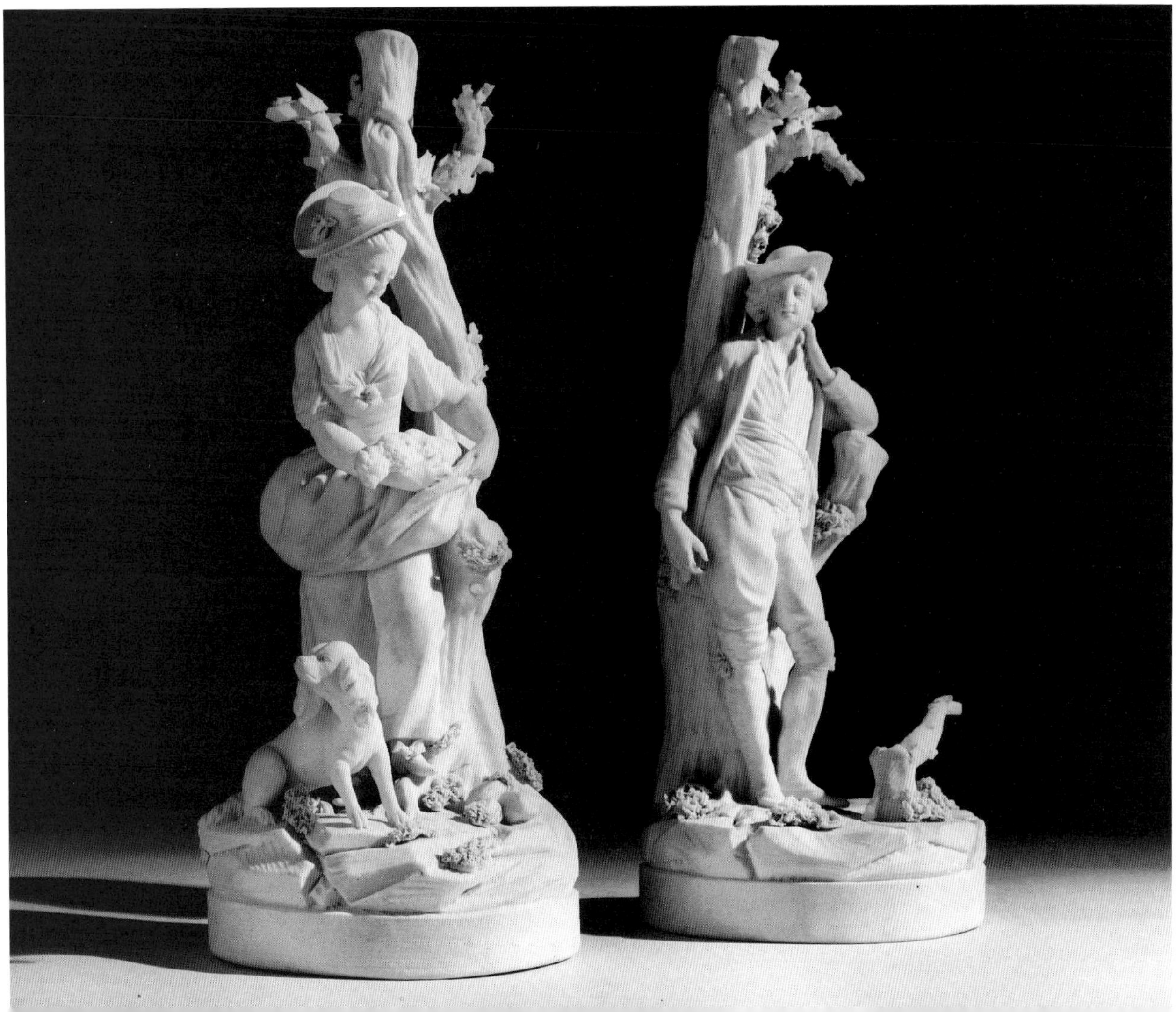

Provenance: Bequeathed by Sir A.W. Franks, 1897

Literature: Unpublished

Comparable Examples: Paris, Dragesco-Cramoisan, 1992, similar figure with a gun and dog, incised with crossed arrows and *MO* (compare Guillebon, 1972, p. 323, no. 148)

The significance of the incised mark is unknown. The model can be compared with a biscuit group of three hunters beneath a tree in the Bloit Collection, Paris.[1]

This figure may be the *Figure avec un arbre* documented in 1780 or perhaps one of the pastoral figures or groups with trees documented in l'an VI.[2]

1. Bloit, 1988, p. 11.
2. Guillebon and Lasserre, 1966, p. 118.

256 **Figure of a Young Woman Holding a Lamb**, *c.*1775

H. 24.4 cm
Marks: crossed arrows and *K* incised
Reg. No. FB 34 (AF 3234)

Hard-paste porcelain, convex base with flattened cone-shaped protuberance in centre. The young woman, who wears a large brimmed hat, a low-cut dress with a bow at the bosom and a billowing drape at the hips, stands with her left foot raised on a tree root. She cradles a lamb in her hands, and wraps part of her dress around it. On the circular rocky base to her right sits a spaniel. Hat restored and front leg of sheep missing.

Provenance: Bequeathed by Sir A.W. Franks, 1897

Literature: Unpublished

Comparable Examples: Paris, Dragesco-Cramoisan, 1992, similar figure incised with crossed arrows and *MO* (compare Guillebon, 1972, p. 323, no. 148)

Although no exactly comparable pieces have been discovered, a shepherdess with flowers in her lap and a shepherd with a gun and barking mastiff in the Bloit Collection, Paris, are the work of the same modeller, who was also responsible for groups of lovers. These pastoral figures are also incised with the crossed torches and *K*. The identity of this modeller or repairer has not yet been discovered, but his signature occurs again on a group after Falconet's *La Femme au Bain*, also in the Bloit Collection.[1]

The mark of the crossed arrows was registered by Jean-Baptiste Locré in 1773. The production of biscuit porcelain figures for the table or for ornamentation seems to have been especially important in the 1770s. In 1777 the factory apparently stole the moulds of six figures by Boizot for the Sèvres factory and put them into production before they had been shown to the King.[2] For a note on the possible documentation of this figure, see cat. 255.

1. Bloit, 1988, p. 18.
2. See Guillebon and Lassere, 1966, pp. 102–18.

257 **Group of Hope and Cupid**, or **Love Nourished by Hope**, probably *c.*1785

H. 28.9 cm
Marks: crossed arrows and another mark incised, perhaps *V*
Reg. No. F.B. 35 (AF 3235)

Hard-paste porcelain of greyish tone. A partly-draped female figure stands on a rocky base with her right knee bent holding Cupid in her arms, who clutches at her drapery, as he aims to suckle at her left breast. His right foot rests on a truncated column ornamented with a floral garland. Behind Hope, whose long hair falls in two tresses on to her shoulders, is an anchor resting on a curled cornucopia from which spill grapes and other fruit. The hollow base is pierced with a small circular hole. One wing and left leg of Cupid, end of anchor and of cornucopia missing, damage to fingers.

Provenance: Bequeathed by Sir A.W. Franks, 1897

Literature: Unpublished

Comparable Examples: USA, Monticello, Thomas Jefferson Memorial Foundation[1]

The Locré factory produced a considerable range of biscuit models, but their iconographical sources and the workmen responsible for modelling and making them have not yet been discovered. One group representing Venus and Cupid has, however, been plausibly related to E.-M. Falconet's *Femme au Bain*.[2] In the list of around sixty figures, groups and clock-cases documented at the factory, this group may correspond with one of two noted in 1826.[3]

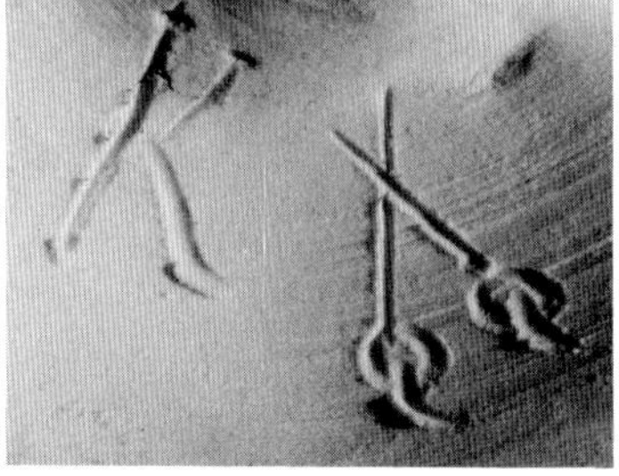

256 *marks*

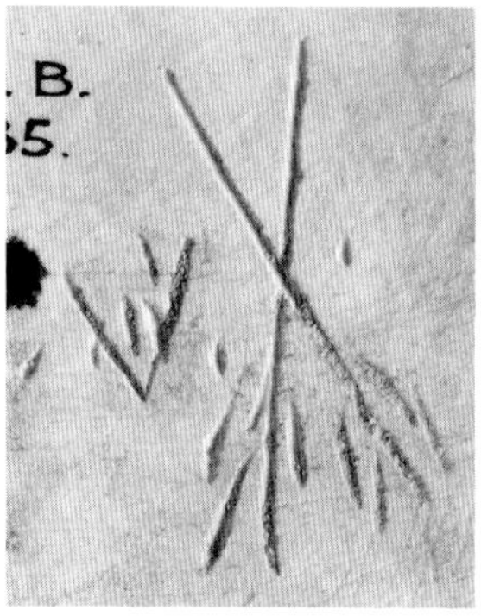

257 *marks*

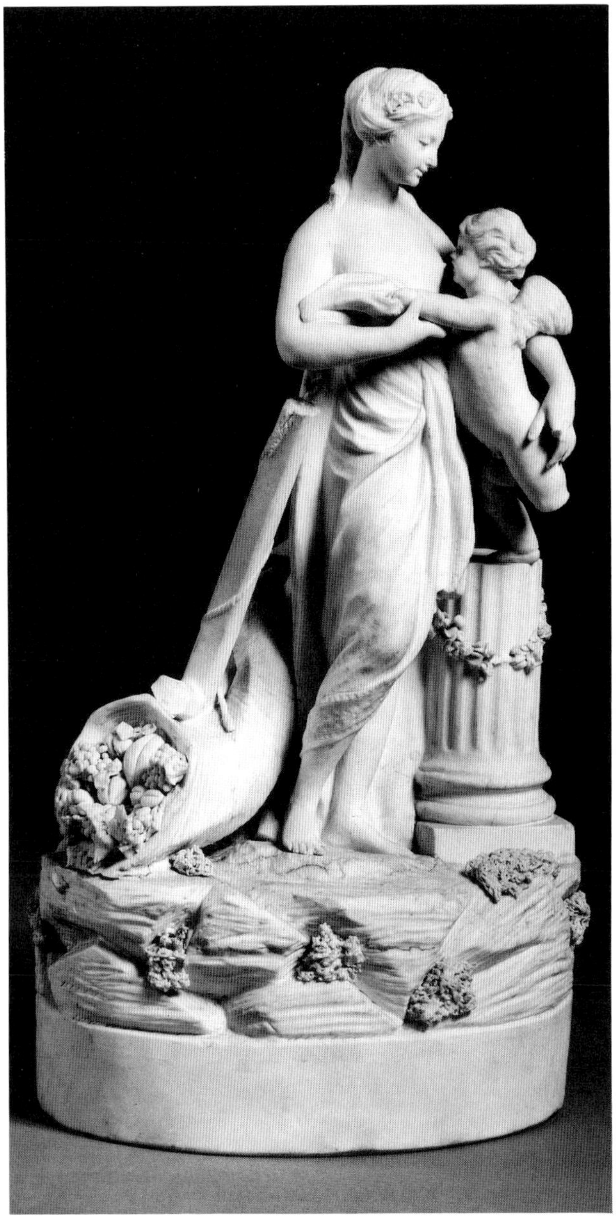

257

The significance of the incised mark is unknown: it is likely to have been used by the 'repairer' of the group.

1. Detweiler, *French Porcelain*, 1982, p. 98, fig. 11, perhaps one of the figures mentioned in the packer's invoice for the eighty-six packing cases probably containing coffee and tea wares, as well as 'figurines', purchased by Thomas Jefferson in Paris on 21 August 1784. The group is unmarked. It is a variant of the BM example: the base, the pedestal and the pose of the figures all differ, although the theme is the same.
2. Bloit, 1988, p. 18.
3. Guillebon and Lasserre, 1966, p. 118, *L'Espérance* and *L'Espérance sur colonne*.

Queen's factory,
rue Thiroux

The factory was established in 1776 by André-Marie Leboeuf (*c*.1755–1810). As he was technically still a minor, being under twenty-five, the contract for the transfer of the land on which the factory stood, in a building recently used for textile manufacture, was signed by his widowed mother and Jacques-Pascal Barrachin.[1] The latter had been a merchant in Lyons, and since 1774 had been associated with the marquis d'Usson at the factory run by Hannong in the faubourg Saint-Denis. Not long before the partnership deeds between Leboeuf and Barrachin were signed, Leboeuf registered his mark[2] of a letter *A* before the lieutenant-general of police. The protection of Marie-Antoinette was given to the factory some two years later, according to a newspaper, *Les Annonces, affiches et avis divers*, published on 16 December 1778, when the mark changed from an *A* in blue to an *A* crowned, in red.

Despite royal protection, a large number of pieces were seized in January 1780 as they infringed the monopoly granted to Sèvres. Tablewares and domestic items such as barbers' bowls, chamber pots and water-jugs and basins, ornamental pieces including candelabra and biscuit figures and groups are recorded in the inventory of the seizure.[3]

Most surviving pieces are of high quality. Clay from the Limoges region was supplied by Grellet, and Baltazard Byeller (*c*.1729–1800) formerly of Haguenau, Alsace, and director at Hannong's concern in the rue du faubourg Saint-Denis from September 1774, acted as production director until around 1791. A certain Vieuse was employed as an administrator 1777–80. Flowers, birds and patterns based on silks were common decorative motifs, and forms were frequently copied from Sèvres.[4] Bird painting is found on a *jardinière* in the Ariana Museum, Geneva.[5] However, the names of only two painters are known. Fribourg was there in 1777, and La Branche, also a gilder, who was a native of Chantilly.[6]

In February 1797 Leboeuf sold the factory to Charles Barthélemy Guy and Marie-Antoine Houzel for 25,500 *livres*, which included porcelain, both finished and unfinished, tools, raw materials, etc.[7] It probably continued in production until around 1806.

1. See Guillebon, 1985, pp. 139–40 for a discussion of the topography of the factory, which stood on ground leased from the Mathurin Order. The contract is in the Archives nationales, Minutier central, *Etude* XV, 904 (Me Thiérion). A map showing the site of the factory in 1786 is fig. 125, pl. XCI in Guillebon, *op. cit.* The factory is the subject of an article by Guillebon, 'La Manufacture de Porcelaine de la rue Thiroux, dite de la Reine'. *Société d'Etudes Historiques du IXème Arrondissement de Paris*, 1988.
2. On 9 September 1776; Archives nationales, O1 2061.
3. MNS, Archives de Sèvres, A4, D5.
4. For example a water-jug and basin decorated with a tulip and scroll pattern, L. of basin, 30 cm, sold Christie's, 3 December 1984, Lot 52, and another in the Musée national de Céramique, painted with flowers, illus. Dupont, 1987, p. 121, fig. 4; shell-shaped dish, Guillebon 1972, p. 91, fig. 72.
5. Guillebon, 1972, p. 93, fig. 73.
6. The names of factory personnel have been extracted from R. Plimval de Guillebon, *Musée du Louvre, département des objets d'art, Catalogue des Porcelaines Françaises I*, Paris, 1992, p. 230, where archival references are given.
7. Guillebon, 1985, p. 137–8, f.n. 858, Archives nationales, CXVII, 982, 30 Pluviôse l'an V (Me Maine), *vente mobiliaire et bail par Leboeuf à Guy et Houzel.*

258 Saucer (*soucoupe*), 1776–*c*.1793

258 *mark*

D.	12.8 cm
Mark:	*A* painted in underglaze-blue
Reg. No.	Franks 428

Hard-paste porcelain, deep saucer with flared sides, painted in green, blue, purple, orange and yellow enamels with scattered flower sprays on a white ground; gilt dentil rim. Gilding rubbed.

Provenance: Bequeathed by Sir A.W. Franks, 1897

Literature: Franks, 1896, no. 428

Comparable Examples: None

The paste is noticeably different from the standard very white hard-paste porcelain made in Paris, which contains a high proportion of kaolin.

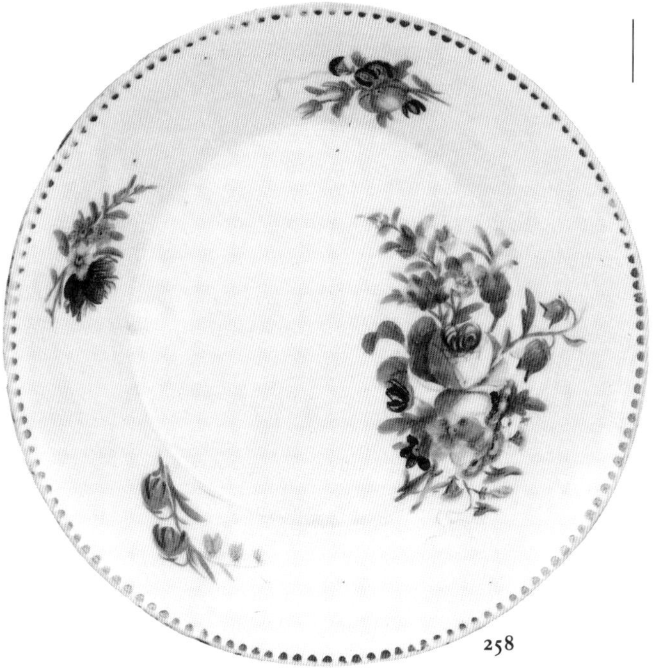

258

259 Cup and Saucer, (*tasse litron et soucoupe*), 1776–*c*.1793

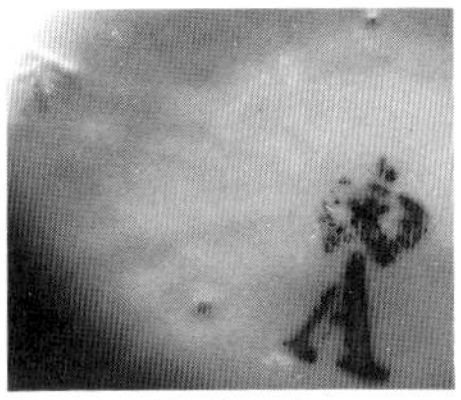

259 *marks (cup)*

D. *of saucer:*	12.6 cm
H. *of cup:*	6.1 cm
Marks:	*A* crowned stencilled in red on both; *K* incised on cup
Reg. No.	Franks 426

Hard-paste porcelain, the cup highly translucent. Deep saucer with flared rim, straight-sided cup with loop handle. Decorated with scattered gilt flower sprays in centre of saucer and around lower part of cup and painted with a band of blue scale ornament enclosing ovals outlined in gold containing flower sprays in blue, orange, yellow, green, pink, dark red and grey, tied with a ribbon bow, each bow linked by a stylised leaf trail. Near the rim is a gilt diaper design. Gilt dentil rims. Handle partly gilt, gilt line near foot of cup. Chip to rim of saucer, foot rim of saucer chipped.

Provenance: Bequeathed by Sir A.W. Franks, 1897

Literature: Franks, 1896, no. 426

Comparable Examples: None

The decoration is typical of the factory. The identity of the repairer using the incised mark *K* is unknown.

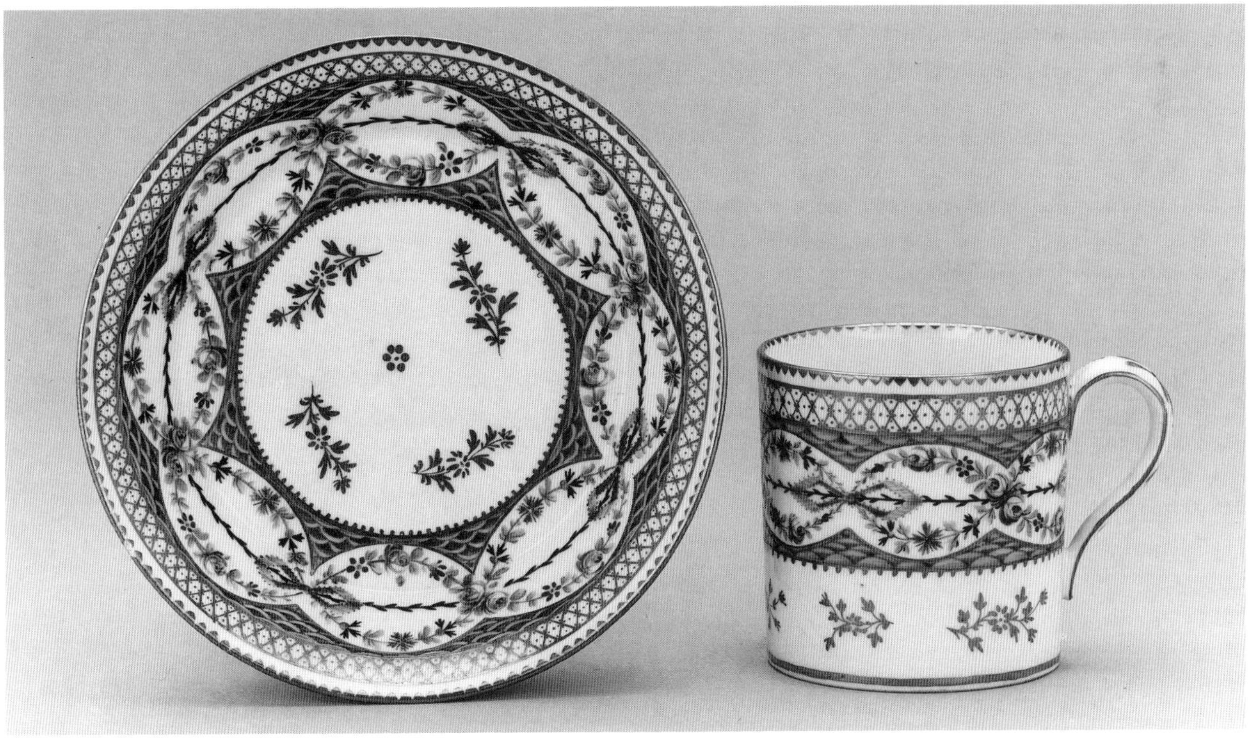

259

Comte d'Artois' factory,
rue du faubourg Saint-Denis[1]

The factory established by Hannong (*q.v.*) came under the patronage of the comte d'Artois on 5 September 1779, when the mark *CP*, for Charles Philippe, comte d'Artois (1757–1836)[2] was registered by Stahn. He had been a painter at the factory since 1772, and had purchased it on 29 October 1779 (probably only on paper, rather than in fact) from Adrien Nicolas, marquis de La Salle, who had been part-owner since 7 October 1774, after the departure of Hannong.[3] The period 1774–9 was marked by considerable financial confusion and by the beginnings of the fight by the Paris factories against the Sèvres monopoly. With the help of the patronage of the comte d'Artois the factory managed to claim special status for itself in January 1787, after a renewed struggle against the power of the royal factory in 1783.[4] Although Stahn is listed in the *arrêt* of 1784, in which the Paris factories were given orders to transfer their activities to 15 leagues outside Paris, the factory was by this time under the ownership of Louis Joseph Bourdon, seigneur des Planches (1723–1800),[5] who had purchased it in 1782. Initially at least he was probably both owner and director. In 1787 a chemist named Antoine Josse is known to have been the *chef des travaux*. By 1793 Bourdon des Planches seems to have been succeeded by Louis Houël, who appears in the rent agreement (*bail*) of 17 Brumaire l'an II, 7 November 1794 as *entrepreneur de la manufacture*. He declared himself familiar with the premises 'au moyen de la jouissance qu'il en a comme étant aux droits du citoyen Bourdon des Planzes'.[6] He remained at the factory until the buildings were sold off by the Huet family in l'an IV (1795–6), and was probably later in partnership with their purchaser, Benjamin. The premises were acquired by Marc Schoelcher (*q.v.*) on 9 Floréal l'an VI (28 April 1798).

To judge from surviving pieces, the products of the factory in the rue du faubourg Saint-Denis while it was under the patronage of the comte d'Artois were of high quality. In a Paris directory of 1789–90[7] the concern was described as making 'tout ce qui est relatif au service et à la décoration: on y traite aussi la partie des figures et autres ouvrages en biscuit'. Plates, broth-bowls and covers,[8] wine-coolers,[9] and wine-glass coolers[10] from table services, sometimes with decoration clearly inspired by Sèvres models, but frequently with original decorative schemes, *cabarets* for the service of tea,[11] water-jugs and basins for the toilet service [?] and biscuit figures and busts are known. Perhaps the most famous of these is the bust of Mirabeau now in the Carnavalet Museum, Paris, for which a terracotta model exists in the Assemblée nationale.[12] Another version of this bust, which must date from around 1792, is in the Musée nationale de Céramique, Sèvres.[13] The factory also manufactured a bust of Necker. The many figures and groups listed in the various inventories[14] include children after both Boucher and Falconet (these may have been in production in the 1770s rather than in the comte d'Artois period), as well as 'Cries of Paris'. In 1785 no less than thirty-five workers were employed in the sculpture workshop.[15] An order placed in 1784 by the factory's patron himself for his residences at the Temple, Paris, Maisons, Saint-Germain and Bagatelle gives a good idea of the range of tablewares, ornamental vases and their prices. Two *vases hollandais* with a blue ground cost 300 *livres* each.[16] Various services with gold decoration on a white ground, or with roses, were also part of this order. A plate painted with *roses et feuillages* cost 18 *livres*.[17]

Despite the precarious financial state of the factory in the 1770s, it was healthy enough during the early 1780s to carry out experiments on coal-firing. In October 1782 work had already begun on the construction of a coal-firing kiln.[18] It was inspected in December that year by Mithouard, the chemist Macquer, Le Roy, Sage (see cat. 287), and d'Arcet, who signed a 'procès-verbal de visitte du four à porcelaine de M. Bourdon Desplanches'. Apparently no changes were made to the interior of a wood-firing kiln, which was made of brick. It consisted of 'une tour flanquée de quatre foyers ou alandiers, en trémie communiquant avec son sol. Quatre galeries d'aspiration fournissait l'air à ces fourneaux dont la grille offrait un plan incliné'. The inside of the kiln was about 2½ metres in diameter and 2½ metres high. The firing carried out on 13 December 1782 lasted twenty-nine hours instead of the usual thirty-eight or forty, and the cost of the raw materials was 310 *livres* 10 *sols* instead of the customary 344 *livres* for wood. The kiln was capable of holding one thousand and forty pieces; 782 were of first quality (this was presumably a biscuit firing), 127 were 'seconds', 131 'thirds', 76 needed refiring, and 24 were broken. Deformation in the kiln was minimal. In 1783 the King was presented with a vase inscribed *cuit au charbon de terre épuré dans la manufacture de Mgr le Comte d'Artois le 8 février 1783*. It 'réunissait la grandeur, le relief, le rond de bosse, l'or incrusté et tous les autres ornements dont la manufacture de Sèvres prétend avoir seule et exclusivement décorer ses fabrications . . .',[19] and was evidence that this factory could equal the royal factory, and deserved to be exempt from the prohibition on competing with it. A pair of blue-ground vases mounted in gilt-bronze and decorated with jewelling, now in the Louvre Museum, are inscribed *cuit au charbon de terre le 11 août 1783*, and bear the mark *CP* and the signature of the enameller Joseph Coteau, who also worked at the royal factory.[20]

Few details are known of the factory employees, except that the factory was of considerable size. A large number of firings were clearly carried out, since the one which took place in July 1786 was the twentieth in that year. The concern operated a shop on the corner of the rue de l'Echelle and the rue du Carrousel[21] which was initially owned by the marquis de La Salle, who rented it out at the beginning of our period to Charles Barthélemy Guy. Guy, the son of a *marchand-mercier*, whose brother-in-law Jean-Baptiste Chaussard was inspector of the factory from 1776 until an unspecified date, took it over entirely on 20 August 1780. He sold porcelain from other factories, as well as millinery and jewellery. In l'an II (1793–4) he went into partnership with his son Charles, and later, in 1797, bought the former Queen's factory together with Houzel. Several outlets were operated by the comte d'Artois' factory in the provinces, at Avignon, Marseille, Caen, Bordeaux and Lyon, and public sales were organised at Orleans.[22] It is not known whether the factory exported direct to other countries, but the comte d'Artois presented to Benjamin Franklin a porcelain barrel painted with flowers which was possibly a product of the factory under his protection.[23] A 'sprig-decorated dessert service with a history of American ownership', which, unlike the barrel, bears the Artois factory mark, is in a museum collection in Boston, Massachusetts, USA.[24]

1. No monograph has been published on this factory. This study is based on Guillebon, 1972, *passim*, particularly pp. 159–62, 264–8. This author does not cite sources of information, except in rare instances.
2. For biographical details of Louis XV's grandson, fifth son of the Dauphin Louis and Marie-Josèphe of Saxony, later King of France, see V.W. Beach, *Charles X of France*, Boulder, Colo., 1971. Further information can be found in *La Folie d'Artois*, issued on the occasion of an exhibition at the château de Bagatelle, Paris, 1985, *passim*, and in particular C. Arnaud, 'Le comte d'Artois et sa coterie', pp. 15–25.
3. Guillebon, *op. cit.*, pp. 158–9, for an outline of the confusing history of the factory after the departure of Hannong.
4. *Ibid.*, pp. 24–7.
5. Bourdon des Planches was a *conseiller du roi* and subsequently *premier commis d'un intendant des finances*.
6. Guillebon, *op. cit.*, p. 160.
7. Gournay, *Tableau général du commerce*, Paris, 1789–90, quoted *ibid.*, p. 167.
8. Dauguet and Guillemé-Brulon, n.d., p. 59, illus.
9. Guillebon, *op. cit.*, p. 21, fig. 13, Musée national de Céramique, Sèvres, decoration of butterflies and coloured stripes similar to cat. 261.
10. *Ibid.*, p. 26, fig. 17, Geneva, Ariana Museum, ribbon and scattered flower decoration.
11. *Ibid.*, p. 28, fig. 20. Nationalmuseum, Stockholm, painted with gallant scenes in the style of Watteau.
12. *Ibid.*, p. 27, figs. 18, 19.
13. Chavagnac and Grollier, p. 487, inv. 7915. Yet another example incised '*manufacture/du fb. Stdenis/No 25*' was acquired by the Musée de la Révolution Française, Vizille, in 1988, inv. 88.44.
14. Guillebon, *op. cit.*, p. 170; the dates of these inventories are not specified by the author.
15. *Ibid.*, p. 41.
16. *Ibid.*, p. 295.

17. *Ibid.*, p. 22.
18. *Ibid.*, p. 50.
19. *Ibid.*, p. 23.
20. *Ibid.*, p. 23, fig. 15.
21. *Ibid.*, pp. 266–7.
22. *Ibid.*, p. 284.
23. Detweiler, *French Porcelain*, 1982, p. 91, fig. 4.
24. *Ibid.*, illus. R. Nylander, 'The First Harrison Gray Otis House', *Antiques.*, Vol. CXVII, June 1975, p. 1131.

260 **Broth Bowl, Cover and Stand (*écuelle couverte et plateau*)**, 1779–89

L. *of stand:*	22 cm
H. *of bowl and cover:*	12.6 cm
Marks:	(remains of) crown in gold, *c.* [?] incised on stand; *CP* crowned in gold on bowl
Reg. No.	Franks 414

Hard-paste porcelain, highly translucent. The stand of oval lobed form with a very shallow well. The bowl, which rests on a circular foot, has flared sides and angular handles. The cover, of flattened domed form, is surmounted by a pomegranate finial. Painted in blue, orange-red, yellow, pink, green, brown and purple with stylised vases of roses, leafy scrolls, garlands and vases. Finial repaired.

Provenance: Bequeathed by Sir A.W. Franks, 1897

Literature: Franks, 1896, no. 414

Comparable Examples: An *écuelle* and stand of the same form made at the duc d'Angoulême's factory and decorated with harbour and ruin scenes on a black ground illus. Guillebon, 1972, p. 121, pl. 90, in the Musée des arts décoratifs, Paris

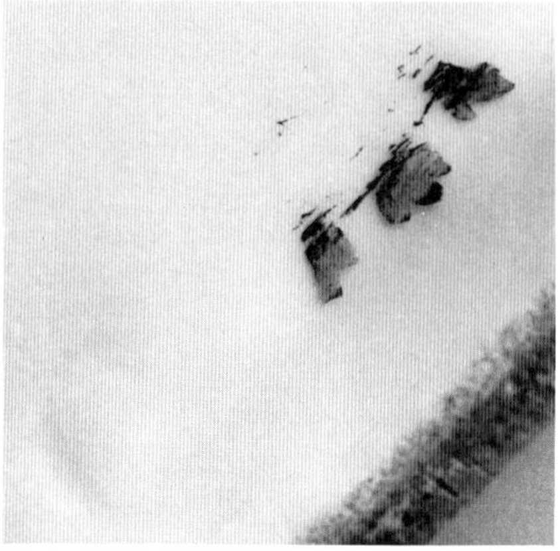

260 *marks (stand)*

260 *mark (bowl)*

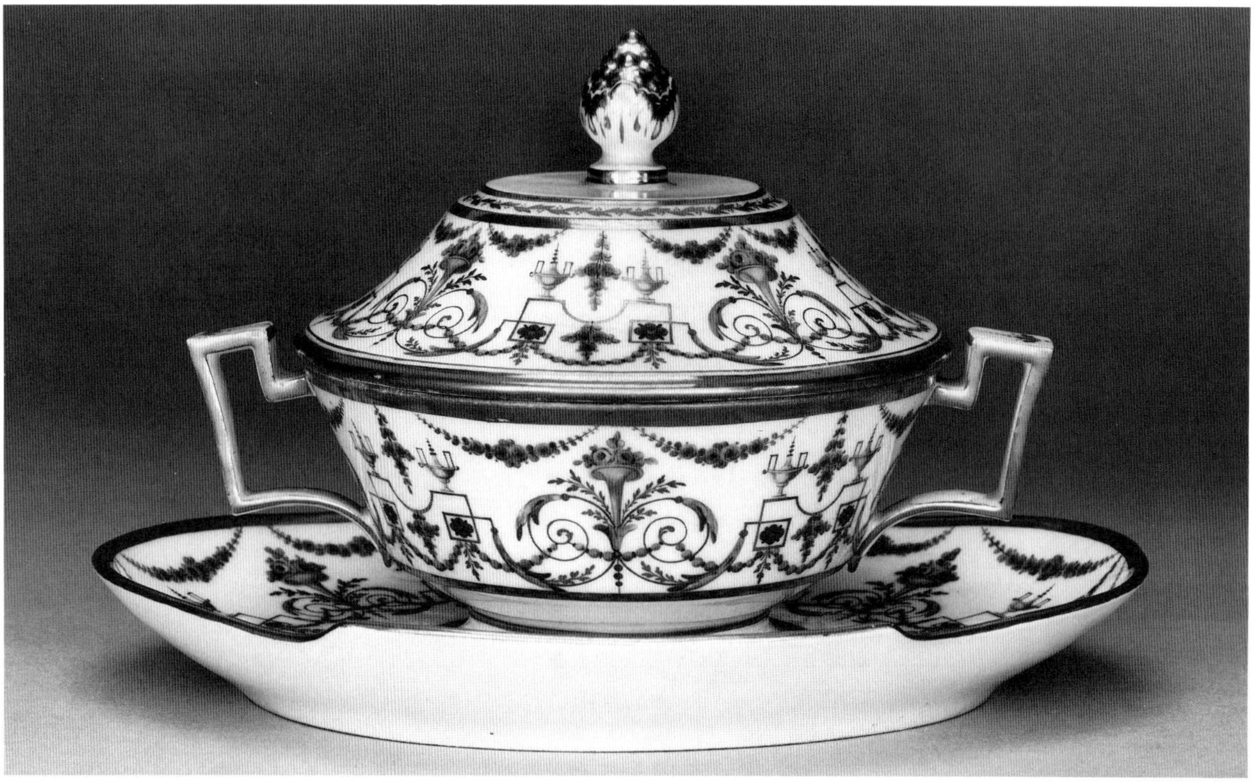

260

There are several defects on the stand, including black specks in the glaze and a firing fault in the well disguised by one of three gilt stylised leaves.

The style of decoration owes something to Henri Salembier (*c.*1753–1820), whose books of ornament were issued from 1777. A wine glass-cooler with rather similar decoration, bearing the mark *CPG* for the Manufacture du Petit Carrousel Paris, is in the Musée national de Céramique, Sèvres.[1]

1. Guillebon, 1972, p. 297, fig. 233.

261 **Cup and Saucer,** 1779–89

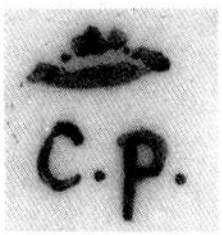

261 *mark*

See colour plate 39
D. *of saucer:* 13.3 cm
H. *of cup:* 6.2 cm
Marks: *c. p.* crowned in gold on both
Reg. No. Franks 415

Hard-paste porcelain. The saucer, which has straight flared sides, is painted in yellow, blue, orange, pink, green and purple with fine stripes alternating with gilt lines and interrupted by gilt dots on the sides and part of the well; in the centre is a landscape with plants and two butterflies, enclosed by a gilt line. The rim has a gold laurel leaf and berry pattern between gilt lines. The straight-sided cup, which has a shaped handle with a 'kick', entirely gilded, has a similar decorative scheme. Hairline crack inside cup.

Provenance: Bequeathed by Sir A.W. Franks, 1897

Literature: Franks, 1986, no. 415

Comparable Examples: Sèvres, Musée national de Céramique, *seau à bouteille* with comparable decoration illus. Guillebon, 1972, p. 21, fig. 13

The butterflies have been identified as follows:[1]

1. on the saucer at the left, a day-flying moth, species unknown;
2. on the saucer at the right, *Pieris rapae*, or small white, probably a female second brood;[2]
3. on the cup, *Lasiommata maera*, or large wall brown, perhaps the southern variety *Adstra*.[3]

Butterfly decors, normally of a stylised kind, were popular at the end of the eighteenth century and beginning of the nineteenth, especially on Paris porcelain.

1. The author is most grateful to Bernard Dragesco for the identification of these butterflies.
2. L.G. Higgins and N.D. Riley, *A Field Guide to the Butterflies of Britain and Europe*, London, 1970, pp. 43–4 and pl. 5, 3b.
3. *Ibid.*, p. 228 and pl. 149, 1c, 1d.

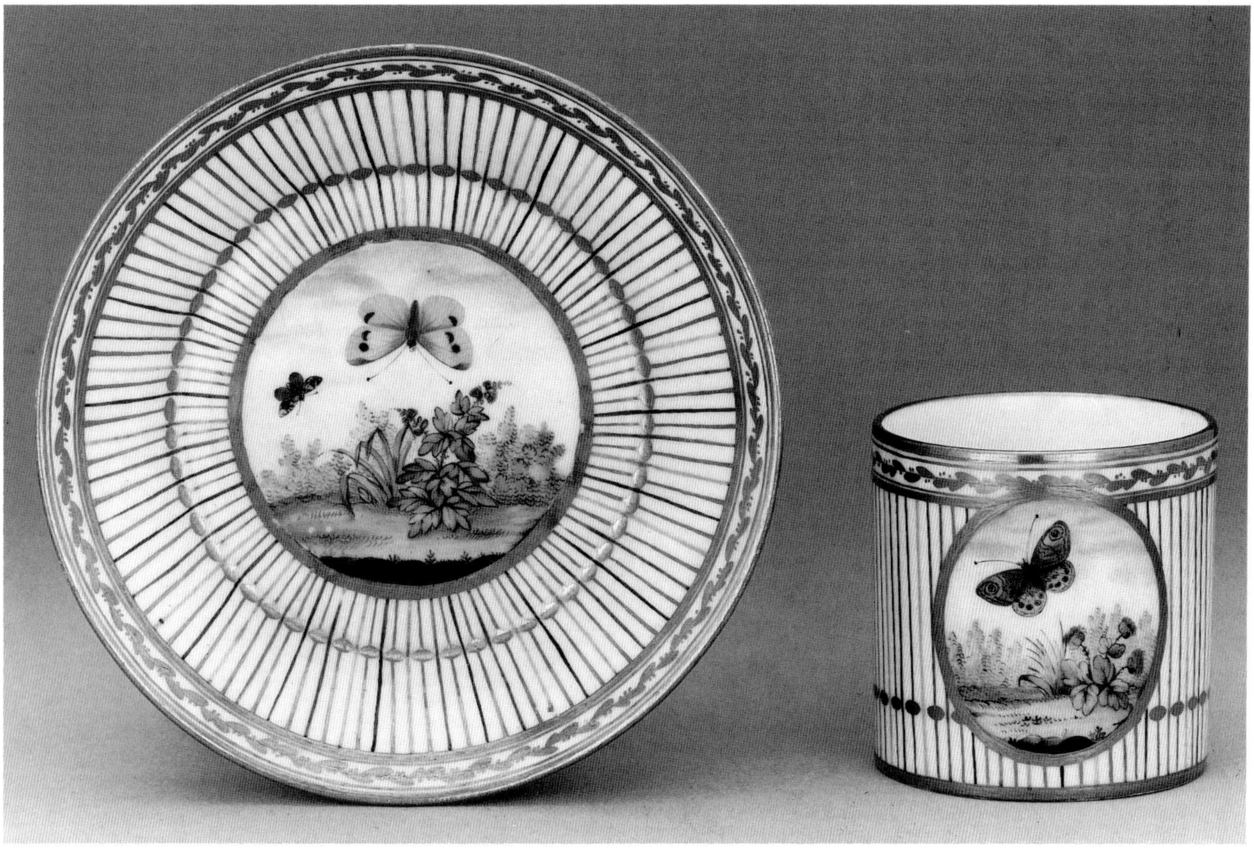

261

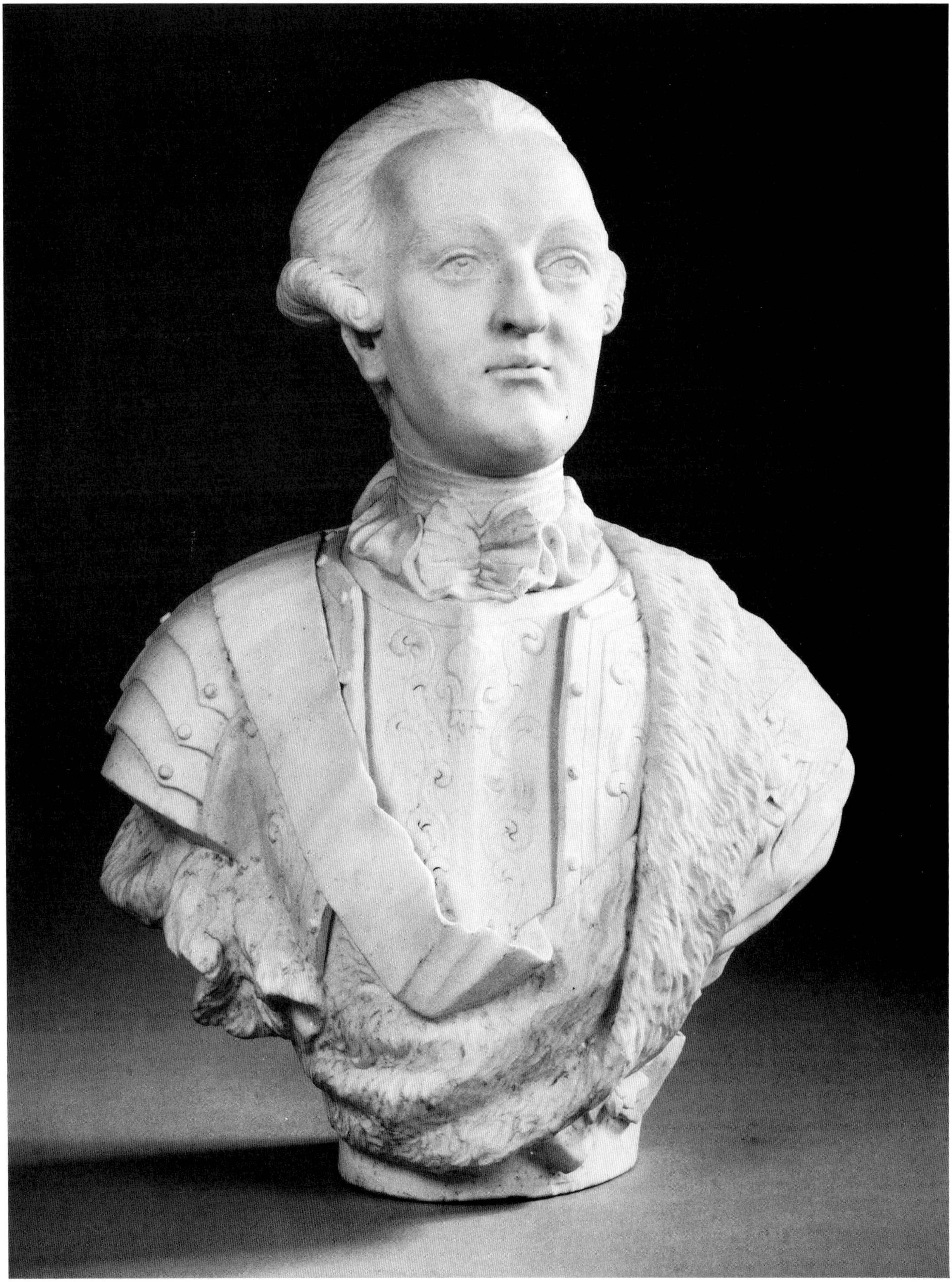

262

262 **Bust of Louis-Philippe-Joseph, duc d'Orléans, known as 'Philippe Egalité'** (1747–93), 1779–89

H. 33.3 cm
Marks: none
Reg. No. F.B.39 (AF 3239)

Hard-paste biscuit porcelain, hollow, moulded in two parts. He wears a cuirass, sash over his right shoulder, fur stole and the star of the Order of the Saint-Esprit on his left breast.[1] His hair is tied behind with a ribbon bow.

Provenance: Bequeathed by Sir A.W. Franks, 1897

Literature: Unpublished

Comparable Examples: None

Louis-Philippe-Joseph d'Orléans was born at Saint-Cloud, son of Louis-Philippe, duc d'Orléans and his wife Louise-Henriette de Bourbon-Conti. He was known as duc de Montausier until the death of his grandfather in 1752, and then as duc de Chartres until 1785 when he became duc d'Orléans on the death of his father.[2] In 1778 he played a leading role in the battle of Ushant which may explain why he is shown here in military costume,[3] despite the fact that his conduct was judged unsatisfactory. The British Library lists a large number of pamphlets concerning his infamous role as a regicide.

The duc de Chartres visited England in May 1783 under the name of the comte de Joinville, staying at 35 Portland Place, London, a house which he had rented the previous year through his friend Nathaniel Parker Forth. He attended the House of Commons, was entertained by various Dukes and received by King George III.[4] In March 1784 Chartres returned to London, and in that year his (English) horse ran in the Epsom Derby. A second visit in 1784 was succeeded by three further visits the following year.

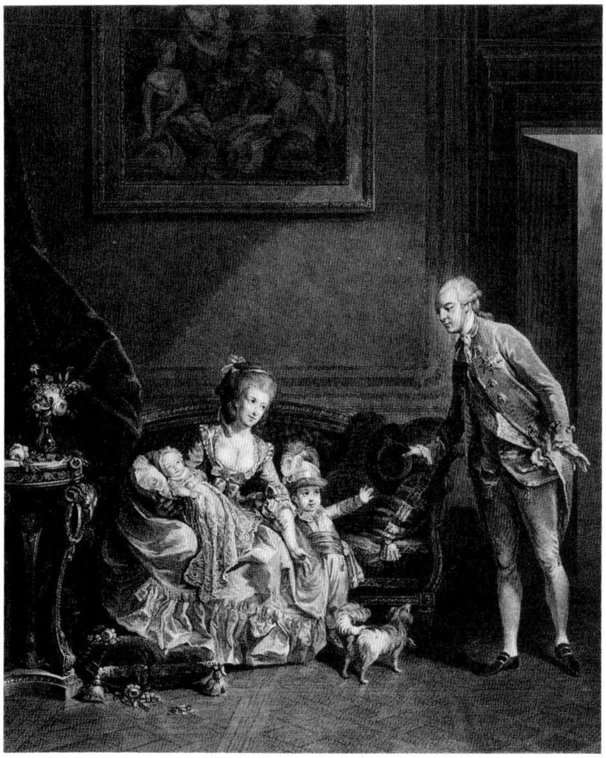

Fig 262a

This bust has long been identified as Philippe Egalité and corresponds with respect to the physiognomy if not the costume with an engraving of 1779 by A. de Saint-Aubin and H. Helman after a painting by C. Le Peintre *peintre de S.A.S. Mgr Le Duc de Chartres* (fig. 262a).[5] A bust of a lady in a private collection in France, which is apparently of similar size and general appearance (the paste is greyish and flawed by numerous iron stains as on the Museum example),[6] corresponds with the duchesse de Chartres shown in the same engraving. It is incised *C*, probably the mark of the modeller or repairer. The place of manufacture of these busts has not been determined, and the long-standing attribution[7] to the factory at the faubourg St Lazare under the protection of the comte d'Artois cannot be confirmed.

It is probable that it was produced between 1779 and 1789. In the latter year the duc d'Orléans enjoyed enormous popularity and several relief portrait busts of him were modelled at the Wedgwood factory, Staffordshire, for use as snuffbox tops and buttons.[8]

The Orléans family gave their protection to porcelain manufacturers from early in the eighteenth century when Monsieur, the King's brother, assisted in establishing a privilege for the Saint-Cloud porcelain factory in 1702. His son, the Regent, is said to have communicated a new secret of porcelain manufacture to the then director of Saint-Cloud, Henri II Trou, in 1722. The succeeding Duke supported Le Guay, Guettard and probably even Brancas-Lauraguais who all carried out or observed experiments to make hard-paste porcelain at Bagnolet (see p. 290). Much later the duc de Chartres extended protection both to a hard-paste porcelain factory in Orléans, and to another at Vincennes. It is just possible that this bust was made at the Vincennes factory, but as yet no documentation has been discovered to substantiate this attribution.

1. The duc de Chartres was received into the Order of the Saint-Esprit on 30 May 1762, and was created chevalier of the Order of Saint-Louis on 6 February 1776, A. Britsch, *La Jeunesse de*

Philippe Egalité, Paris, 1926, pp. 60–1, p. 270.

2. For the genealogy of the Orléans family descending from Louis XIII, and drawings, paintings, engravings, documents, etc., illustrating the life of Philippe Egalité, see exh. *Louis-Philippe, L'Homme et Le Roi 1773–1850*, Paris, Hôtel de Rohan, Archives nationales, October 1974–February 1975. His building works at the Palais Royal are discussed by A. Foray in *Le Palais Royal*, exh., Paris, Musée Carnavalet, May–September 1988, pp. 146–71; see cat. 160 for a portrait of the duc de Chartres. A portrait of him as a child signed *F. Boucher 1749* is illus. by E. Waterhouse, *The James A. de Rothschild Collection at Waddesdon Manor, Paintings*, Fribourg, 1967, no. 94.
3. He was painted in the uniform of a colonel-general of the Hussars by Reynolds for the Prince of Wales in 1785, see O. Millar, *The Later Georgian Pictures in the Collection of Her Majesty the Queen*, London, 1969, no. 1025. The print by J.R. Smith is in the Department of Prints and Drawings, B.M., inv. 1902–10–11–5029.
4. Ward, 1982, pp. 110–11.
5. There are two examples of this print in the Department of Prints and Drawings, B.M., reg. no. 1891,5–11,187 and 1917,12–8,1548. The author is grateful to Frances Dunkels for making these available to her. The engraving is illus. in A. Castelot, *Le Prince Rouge Philippe-Egalité*, Paris, 1962, pl. 6. For a terracotta medallion by Chinard in Musée des Beaux-Arts, Lyon, showing Philippe Egalité in profile to left in a fur hat with a cockade, see M. Beurdeley, *La France à l'encan 1789–1799*, Paris, 1981, p. 52, fig. 49.
6. The author is grateful to Bernard Dragesco for this information.
7. This attribution was made by Monsieur E. Musscher, who may have examined the bust.
8. See D. Bindman, A. Dawson and M. Jones, exh. 'The Shadow of the Guillotine', British Museum, London, May–September 1989, cats. 37d, 38c.

Duc d'Angoulême's factory, *rue de Bondy, (1781–c.1790),* later *Dihl and Guérhard,* *rue du Temple (1789–1828)*[1]

During the 1780s and indeed until *c.*1807 the factory making hard-paste porcelain established on 25 February 1781 in the rue de Bondy by Christophe Dihl (1752–1830), Antoine Guérhard (d.1793) and his wife Louise-Françoise-Madeleine Croizé (1751–1831), enjoyed a leading position and considerable prosperity. The original capital seems to have been only 8,000 *livres*, supplied by Guérhard and his wife. Dihl, a native of Neustadt in the German Palatinate, and a modeller, brought the technical expertise. After his arrival on French soil in 1778, he set up in the rue Vieille-du-Temple, Paris, making vases mounted with porcelain figures, medallions, busts and figures. He brought to the Dihl and Guérhard partnership a number of moulds, some of which were probably the work of Lemire.[2] Madame Guérhard was responsible for the accounts and for sales.

The factory registered its mark, *GA* interlaced, in November 1781, the second letter probably standing for the duc d'Angoulême (1775–1844), who became the factory's protector at an early stage, even though aged only five. Royal protection enabled the factory to make and sell coloured and gilt porcelain, despite the monopoly granted to the Sèvres factory in 1766. In 1784 a second attempt to enforce the privilege (the first was in 1779) forced Dihl to admit that he could not fire his porcelain using coal, or move the factory outside Paris, and obliged him to seek the protection of the King himself. However, widespread opposition from all the Paris factories making hard-paste porcelain prevented their removal. After Madame Guérhard had made representations to d'Angiviller, the factory was given complete exemption from the normal restrictive conditions in January 1787. This was on the grounds that the factory was almost as much a national asset as Sèvres, and should be kept on French soil.

In November 1787 a new deed of partnership was signed for eighteen years. Dihl and Madame Guérhard were each to be paid 2,000 *livres* annually, and extensive premises in the hôtel Bergeret, rue du Temple, were acquired for 330,000 *livres*.[3] Guérhard died on 28 April 1793. Four years later his widow married Christophe Dihl and a new partnership deed was drawn up, although the factory kept its old name. Its prosperity at this time is undoubted: in 1793, as a result of the execution of the marquis de Custine, Dihl took on around fifty workers from the Niderviller factory. Others from Nyon (Switzerland), Bourg-la-Reine, Strasbourg and Sèvres were also on the payroll.[4]

Despite minor difficulties, the factory survived the Revolution and rivalled Sèvres in the quality of its porcelain, overtaking it in sales by l'an v (1796–7). In the early years of the nineteenth century the factory was extremely successful, but by 1807 Madame Dihl was requesting a loan of 150,000 francs from the Ministry of the Interior, since 800,000 francs of merchandise ordered by England and Russia had remained unsold because of the blockade. The loan was granted, but despite the factory's apparent prosperity, another loan, this time for 200,000 francs, was sought in 1809. Although singled out for admiration in April 1810 by Prince Clary and Aldringen, who visited the factory shop while in Paris for the marriage of Marie-Louise and the Emperor Napoleon, the concern was financially unsound. It remained so until 1818, when the first sale of its property took place. Worse followed five years later, then in 1828 it was dissolved. Dihl died, a ruined man, in February 1830 and his wife in July 1831.

The products of this factory were of the highest quality. Under the protection of the duc d'Angoulême, tablewares painted with cornflowers, leaf trails, stars and geometric motifs, which were also commonly found on the products of concerns such as the Queen's factory, were the mainstay of the rue de Bondy works. Forms were also generally similar to those in production elsewhere, with a few daring exceptions in a rather Germanic style, such as a sugar bowl on four feet, cover and stand now in the Louvre Museum.[5] Pastoral, marine and figure subjects painted with exceptional skill are also found on pieces made at the rue de Bondy, which employed a team of gifted painters on porcelain. During the heyday of the factory at the very end of the century and until *c.*1810, unusual grounds imitating hardstones, such as agate or tortoise-shell, in combination with gilt anthemion motifs, on vases and footed cups are characteristic of the factory.[6] Pieces decorated with finely painted naturalistic flowers on a gold ground (see cat. 270) are also known, and may perhaps have been a special commission as they would have been extremely costly. A magnificent tabletop dated 1804 and signed Leguay, decorated with classical scenes, presented by Napoleon to Charles IV of Spain and Queen Marie Louise, was only one of many surviving pieces which were clearly destined for a royal owner.[7] Biscuit figures also formed part of the factory's output. They were initially in a rococo style also popular at Locré's factory, but by 1797 had become heavily classical in feeling. Medallions encased in glass as well as teeth were manufactured.[8] At least some of this porcelain found its way to England as the *Daily Advertiser* of 17 March 1792 records: 'Messrs Turner and Hutchins sold a beautiful cabinet of matchless Seve Porcelane that this country cannot equal; Table and Dessert services of the D'Angouleme Manufactory etc. Property of the MARQUIS de la LUZERNE, Ambassador from the Court of France to his Britannic Majesty, deceased, at this House on the North Side of Portman-Square'.[9]

During his nine-year residence at Passy on the outskirts of Paris, Benjamin Franklin bought a tea service for his daughter, Sarah Franklin Bache. Pieces from this service, decorated with cornflowers, have been presented by descendants to public collections in the United States.[10] Governor Morris, when visiting Paris in 1790, described Dihl as a Swiss or German who boasted much of his work, but with reason: ''Tis a pity that some Vases of most exquisite Workmanship should be of brittle China Ware. In Spite of Reason a Person possessed of Money would I think be obliged to make some Purchases. Am to go again for the Purpose of seeing the Work in its different Stages.' Finding the prices too high and the delivery times too long at Sèvres, he returned to the

Angoulême factory with the comtesse de Flahaut, agreeing that the porcelain there was 'handsomer and cheaper than that of Sèvres'. A table service was then ordered for Washington, which appears in his invoices for the furnishing of his official residences at 2,384 *livres*. Duty amounted to £7. 1*s*. 4*d*.[11] Figures and groups formed part of the service and Morris wrote a note to Washington on 24 January 1790 to explain how the three groups, two vases and twelve figures should be arranged:[12]

> The Vases may be used as they are or when occasion serves, the Tops may be laid aside and the Vases filled with natural flowers. When the whole Surtout is to be used for large Companies the large Group will be in the middle the two smaller ones at the two Ends – the Vases in the Spaces between the three and the figures distributed along the Edges or rather along the Sides . . .

When Morris was acting as Minister Plenipotentiary to the Court of Louis XVI, he made further expeditions to the factory in 1792 and 1793, where he bought 'Dishes and ornamental China to a too large Amount', paying 24 *livres* for a large bowl, 72 *livres* for two dozen plates, and 12 *livres* for a butter-dish, amongst other purchases.[13]

The factory employed no less than twelve sculptors and thirty painters in 1785. In the next decade it may well have had a total of around two hundred or more workers of various kinds on its payroll. By 1807 the number had fallen to around thirty or forty and in 1810 it was no more than fifteen.[14] Its most spectacular painted pieces testify to the skills of painters such as Etienne-Charles Le Guay (1762–1846), his wife Marie-Victoire Jacquotot (1801–42), Piat-Joseph Sauvage (1744–1818), Martin Drölling (1752–1817) and Jacques-François Swebach known as Swebach-Desfontaines (1769–1823). Drölling executed a portrait of Dihl on porcelain dated 1800, and of Bonaparte as First Consul dated 1803.[15] Both these plaques are signed by the painter. Little has been discovered about the wages and working conditions of these painters, or of other employees of the factory, although detailed lists of the prices paid per item to the throwers during the Revolutionary period have survived.[16]

Dihl was proud of his technical abilities, as we can see from his portrait by Leguay in which he is shown with a palette, and pots of colours.[17] The same year (1797) a report on his colours was made to the physical and mathematical section of the Institut national de France by three eminent chemists, Jean Darcet (1725–1801, co-director of the Sèvres factory, 1782–93), Louis Guyton and Antoine Fourcroy, who visited his factory several times, making various experiments. Dihl's coal-fired kiln was reproduced by Brongniart, who considered it typical of Paris hard-paste kilns in 1789, in his *Traité de la Céramique*.[18]

1. This account is based on Guillebon, 'La manufacture de porcelaine de Guérhard et Dihl dite du duc d'Angoulême', privately published by French Porcelain Society, IV, 1988; see also Guillebon, 1982, *passim*.
2. For biographical details of Lemire see exh. Sarrebourg, 1986–7, p. 26.
3. Guillebon, 1982, discusses extensively both the rue de Bondy and the rue du Temple sites of the factory, pp. 195–208; plans of the factory are illustrated in Guillebon, 1985, pl. LXXXIX, XC.
4. Guillebon, 1988, pp. 10–13, gives a summary list of factory employees which contains more names than in her 1982 publication, pp. 209–10.
5. Guillebon, 1972, p. 125, fig. 94.
6. Illus. in colour, Guillebon, 1972, p. 133, fig. 101.
7. *Ibid.*, p. 136–7, figs. 104–5.
8. Guillebon, 1982, p. 191.
9. The author is grateful to Nancy Valpy for this information.
10. Detweiler, *French Porcelain*, 1982, pp. 97–8, fig. 10, a teapot in the collection of the University of Pennsylvania, dated by this writer to around 1784. Other pieces can be found in the Museum of Art, Carnegie Institute, Pittsburgh, USA.
11. Detweiler, *op. cit.*, pp. 100–1, and see Detweiler, *Washington*, 1982, p. 212.
12. Detweiler, *French Porcelain*, 1982, p. 101; an unmarked biscuit group of Venus and two cupids which belonged to a descendant and is now in the collection of the Mount Vernon Ladies' Association is illustrated on p. 102, fig. 15.
13. *Ibid.*, p. 104; f.n. 46 gives further details of Morris's purchases, partly taken from L. Schreider III, 'Gouverneur Morris: Connoisseur of French Art', *Apollo*, Vol. 93, no. 112, June 1971, pp. 470–83, and from the Morris Papers, Library of Congress, Vols. 33, 35.
14. Guillebon, 1985, p. 23, f.ns. 151, 152.
15. Musée national de Céramique, Sèvres, inv. 2976, H. 62 cm; Madame Redondin Collection, H. 57 cm; both illus. 'Les Porcelaines de Paris de 1800 à 1850', Sèvres, Musée national de Céramique, June–October 1970, see *Cahiers*, 46–7 (1970), p. 43, nos. 75b, 75c; portrait of Napoleon illus. Guillebon, 1972, p. 126, fig. 95.
16. The author is grateful to Tamara Préaud for drawing these to her attention. They are preserved in the Archives de Sèvres, U 19, *liasse* II, *dossier* I, *Tarif d'autres manufactures*, and provide a wealth of information on the diversity of production, which awaits analysis. Bowls (*bols*) were apparently made in nine different sizes, and coffee-pots in eight sizes.
17. Illus. in colour in Guillebon, *Cahiers*, 46–7 (1970), p. 41 and Guillebon, 1972, fig. 98.
18. A. Brongniart, 1844, *Atlas*, pl. LVIII, fig. 2.

263 **Teapot and Cover (*théière litron*)**, *c.*1781–93

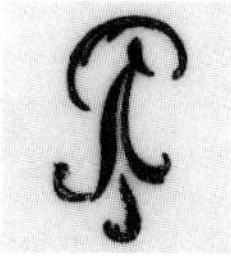

263 *mark*

H. 11.9 cm
Marks: *GA* in gold
Reg. No. Franks 432

Hard-paste porcelain, moulded; straight sides, out-turned rim, the two lugs of the flat cover with its pine-cone knop fitting into two slots in the inner rim so that the cover, pierced by a circular hole, sits below the rim. The spout is moulded on the outer surface with eight facets; the upper surface of the ear-shaped handle has a raised moulding near the top and tapers towards the lower end. Decorated with four rectangular underglaze-blue panels, two of which enclose a spray of full-blown pink roses on a white ground within a gilt medallion; alternating with the panels are four vertically-arranged pink rose garlands on a ground of gilt dots. Gilt scrolls and leaves decorate the upper part of the pot, the edge of the cover, the spout and part of the handle; there is a pattern of stylised gilt leaves around the base of the spout and around the handle terminals. Rims, edges of handle and mouth of spout gilt. Spout repaired.

Provenance: Bequeathed by Sir A.W. Franks, 1897

Literature: Franks, 1896, no. 432

Comparable Examples: Sèvres, Musée national de Céramique, inv. 2471[2], H. 12.3 cm, similar band of flowers on a gilt ground arranged horizontally around top of body[1]

Production faults include a firecrack and a hole on the base, and drips of gilding below each blue panel.

The teapot would have formed part of a teaset, but no matching cups and saucers, milk jug or sugar bowl have been discovered. A *déjeuner* from the same factory, which includes a variant of this teapot (the handle is simpler), richly decorated with animals painted in colours within gilt reserves, is in the Musée des arts décoratifs, Paris.[2]

Despite its rather severe neo-classical form, the decoration is partly rococo in style, a combination often found in Paris porcelains of the 1770s and 1780s.

1. Frégnac, 1964, p. 307.
2. *Ibid.*

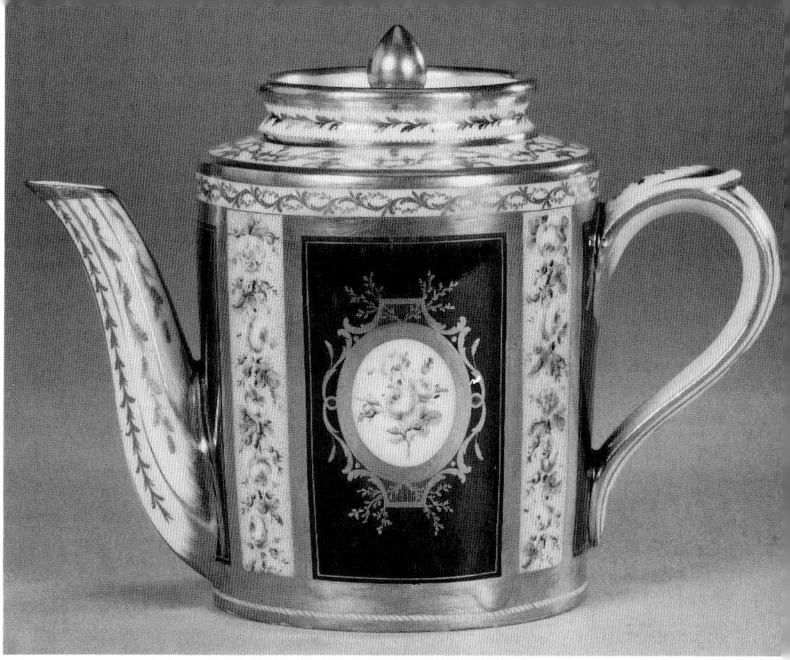

263

264 **Cup (*tasse litron*)**, *c.*1781–93

H. 6.2 cm
Marks: *MANUF*RE*/de M*GR *le Duc/d' angouleme/a Paris* stencilled in red overglaze, partly obliterated; *DE* painted in gold
Reg. No. Franks 429

Hard-paste porcelain, straight-sided with shaped handle. Decorated on a lilac ground with a portrait of a girl in a white headdress, a low-cut purple dress, orange skirt and white apron holding a spindle in her left hand, against a grey ground enclosed by an oval gilt band. Gilt leaf and rosette design near rim between two gilt lines; handle, foot and inner rim of cup gilt. Minute chips to foot rim.

Provenance: Bequeathed by Sir A.W. Franks, 1897

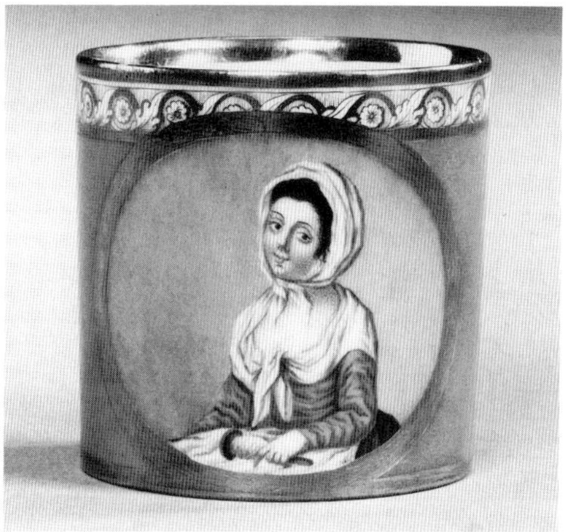

264

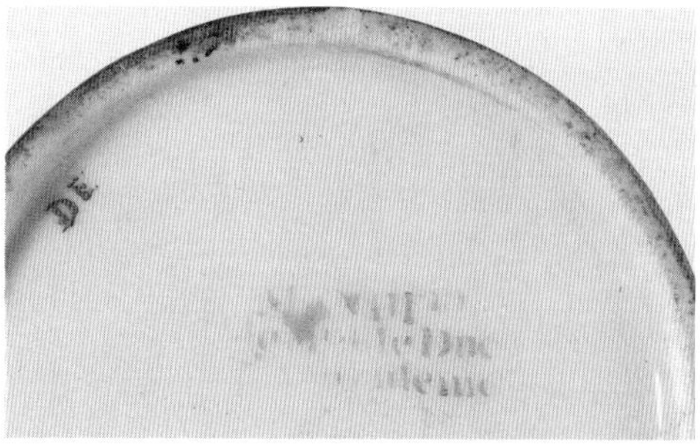

264 *marks*

Literature: Franks, 1896, no. 429

Comparable Examples: None

Unusual ground colours enjoyed an increasing vogue at the end of the eighteenth century. This lilac ground is a low-temperature colour derived from iron oxide fired in the muffle kiln. Dihl was particularly interested in ceramic colours, submitting a report on them to the French Institute in November 1797. His work may very well have been based on notes made by the Viennese, Zwinger, purchased from his widow.[1]

Gilder's marks are rarely found on pieces from this factory, and the mark 'DE' has not been identified.

A somewhat similar scene of a woman in an interior can be found on a *tasse litron* bearing the *M* crowned mark.[2]

1. Guillebon, 1985, pp. 131–2.
2. Guillebon, 1963, p. 170, fig. 17.

265 Cup and Saucer (*tasse litron et soucoupe*), *c.*1781–93

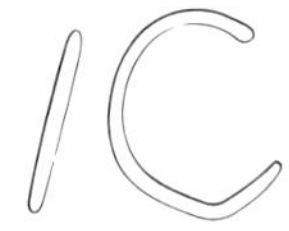

265 *mark*

D. *of saucer:*	12.7 cm
H. *of cup:*	6.2 cm
Marks:	*MANUFRE/de M.GR le Duc/d'Angouleme/à Paris* stencilled in red on saucer; *IC* incised on cup
Reg. No.	1936,7-15,136

Hard-paste porcelain; the deep saucer with flared sides and the straight-sided cup with shaped handle. The cup is painted in *camaïeu bistre* with a winter scene of two peasants beneath a tree collecting bundles of faggots, one setting off with a bundle on his back towards a stone bridge leading to a ruin. In the background is a tower-like building surrounded by a wall, trees and hills, a circular building with a conical roof behind walls and a church, or monastery. Rim, interior of cup, foot and handle richly gilt. The border of the saucer is similarly painted with a shepherd guarding sheep by a tree and a wooded landscape with a running dog. In the centre on a white ground is a gilt star motif. Rim and edge of well of saucer gilt. Two chips and a hairline crack to rim of saucer; rim of cup restored.

Provenance: Presented by F. Howard Paget, 1936 (owner of the Derby Porcelain Factory at King Street from 1917 until 1936)[1]

Literature: Unpublished

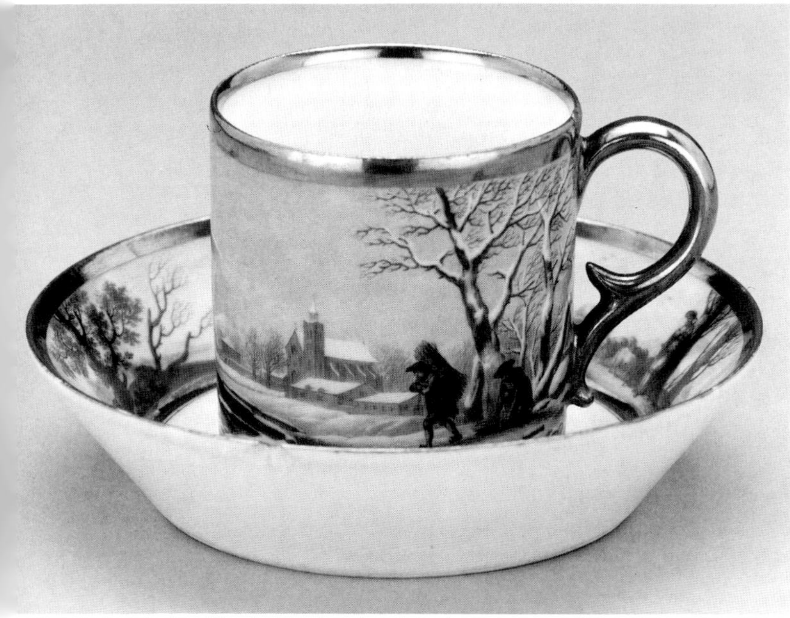

265

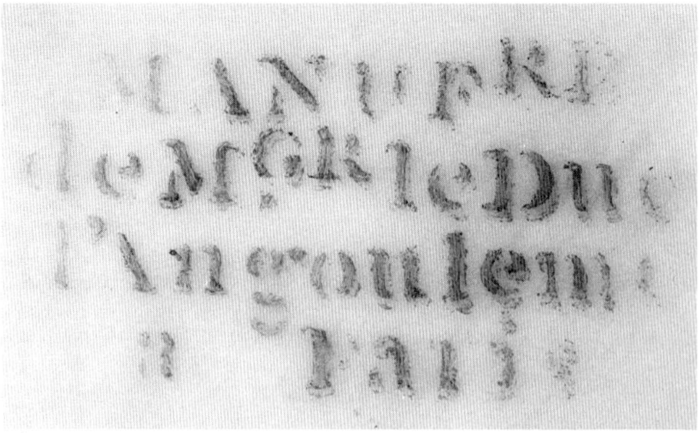

265 *mark*

Comparable Examples: Scotland, private collection, painted with a similar scene

The painting on the cup, which is almost certainly based on unidentified engravings, is accomplished, but cannot be attributed to any particular painter. The identity of the workman using the initials *IC* incised on the cup is unknown.

A snow scene, which includes a building in the Gothic style, is painted on a cup and saucer from the Dagoty factory, which also has rich gilding.[2]

1. For a survey of the Paget Gift in the British Museum which consists principally of Derby biscuit porcelain figures and groups, see A. Dawson, 'The F. Howard Paget Collection in the British Museum', *Derby Porcelain International Society Newsletter*, no. 11, January 1988, pp. 12–15.
2. Illustrated A. Faÿ-Hallé and B. Mundt, *Nineteenth Century European Porcelain*, Fribourg, 1983, p. 40, fig. 44; Rueil-Malmaison, inv. MN 47-2928/2929.

266 Vase, *c.*1781–93

H.	27 cm
W.	23 cm
Marks:	*MANUFAture* [sic] *de Monsr Le duc d'angouleme Rue de Bondy* in gold; *2* in underglaze-blue
Reg. No.	1990,7-8,1

Hard-paste porcelain, moulded. The lower part of the urn-shaped body is moulded with laurel leaves in relief. The neck, which has a moulded out-turned rim, springs from the turned upper shoulder. Flat turned foot fixed to body by means of a screw-and-nut attachment.

The handles are moulded to resemble canework. The lower end terminates below the shoulder, splitting in two about halfway along its length and bending back on itself to its elaborate upper terminal in the form of a leafy branch. The upper part and shoulder are painted with white, green, mauve, red and orange scrolls, vases, swags and wreaths and are embellished with gilding. There are two *grisaille* landscapes on the shoulder. The body of vase is painted yellow; the handles, leaf-moulding, foot and rim are gilt and there is a pattern of stylised leaves, flowers and scrolls on the foot, and of gilt flower sprays in ovals on the rim. Two small chips to body (repainted).

Provenance: Purchased, 1990

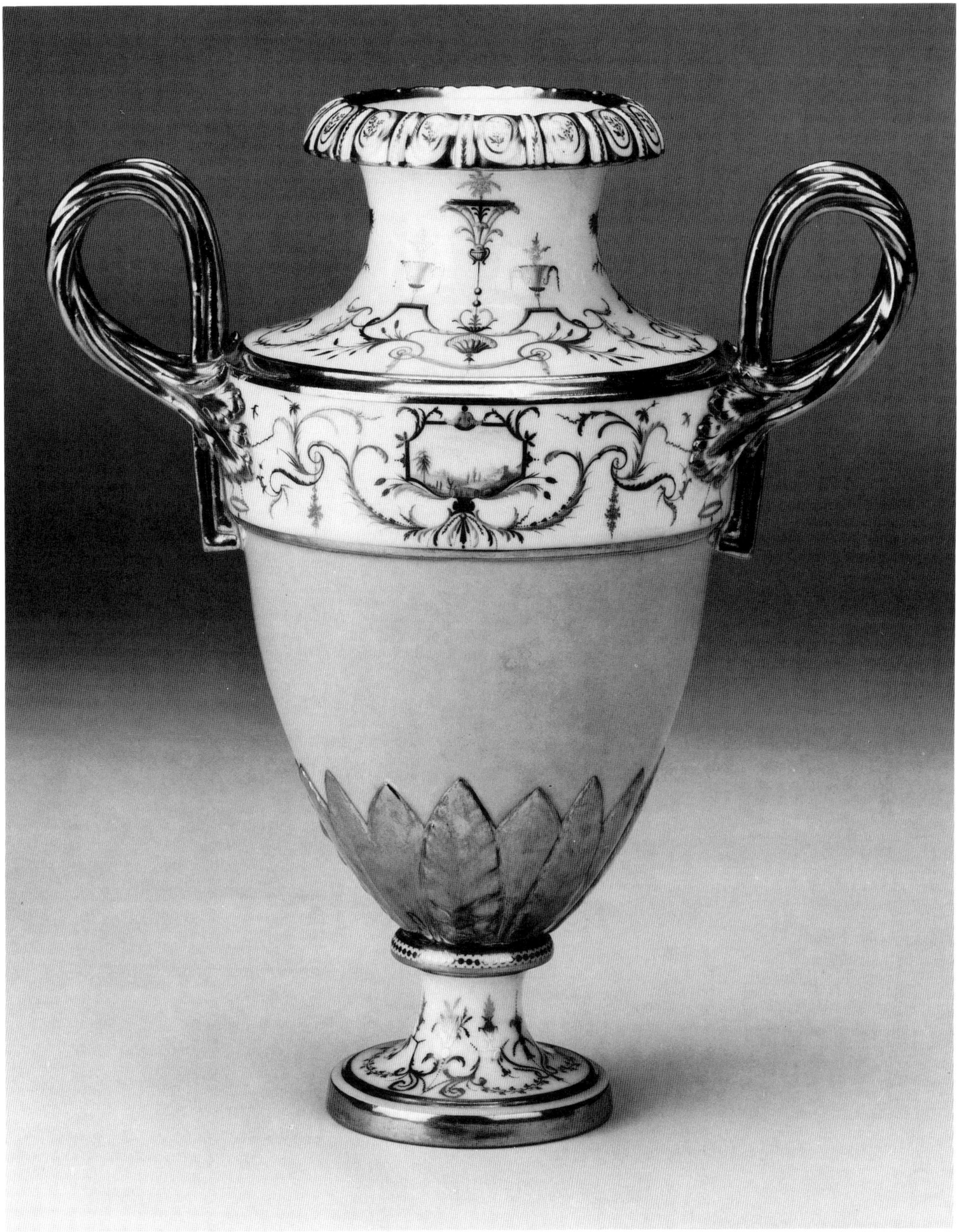

266

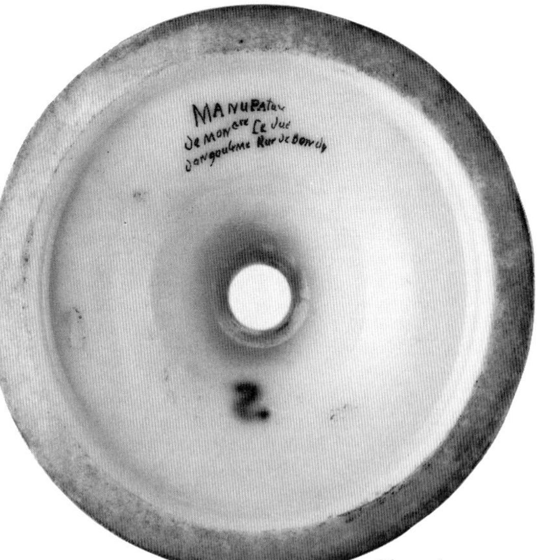

266 *mark*

Literature: Unpublished

Comparable Examples: None

The palette used is similar to that on the broth bowl, cover and stand cat. 260.

A vase of not dissimilar form is shown in an undated painting by Michel-Bruno Bellengé (1726–1793), *Bouquet de fleurs décoratif.*[1] At Sèvres this form was described as *étrusque.*[2]

The design source for this vase has not yet been discovered.

1. M. and F. Faré, *La vie silencieuse en France, la nature morte au* xviiie *siècle*, Fribourg, 1976, p. 247, fig. 393, Pardo Collection, Paris.
2. The author is grateful to Tamara Préaud for this information.

267 Saucer (*soucoupe litron*), *c.*1795–1800

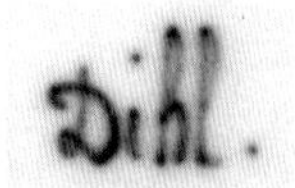

267 *mark*

D. 13 cm
Marks: *Dihl.* painted in script in underglaze-blue
Reg. No. Franks 431

Hard-paste porcelain, deep flared sides. The decoration consists of a gilt stylised flower on a white ground in the well, and gilt S-scrolls and stylised flowers and leaves on a tortoise-shell ground. The rim and the edge of the well are both decorated with a deep gilt band and with another extremely narrow gilt band.

Provenance: Bequeathed by Sir A.W. Franks, 1897

Literature: Franks, 1896, no. 431

Comparable Examples: None

An inclusion and several pin-holes on the base show that this piece, despite its expensive decoration, is not of the highest quality.

Pieces with grounds imitating hardstones or tortoise-shell were one of the specialities of Christopher Erasimus Dihl, who had his portrait painted by Etienne-Charles Le Guay in 1797 with one of his tortoise-shell ground vases.[1]

In his *Traité des Arts Céramiques*,[2] Alexandre Brongniart gives the following technical information concerning this high-temperature (*grand feu*)[3] ground-colour (*écaille*), which he describes as one of the easiest to achieve: it is based on 15 per cent manganese oxide (metalloide), 20 per cent *terre d'ombre* (a brown colour) and 65 per cent glaze material. The *terre d'ombre* is calcined and the ingredients mixed, ground and put through lawn sieves. The next stage involves melting the mixture at a high temperature in a crucible and grinding up the result, which is then sprinkled over the surface of the pot, to which the mordant has already been applied. The colour is fired in the coolest part of the kiln.

The mark found on this saucer, together with the characteristic gilded decoration, can be paralleled on other surviving examples with the same decoration.[4]

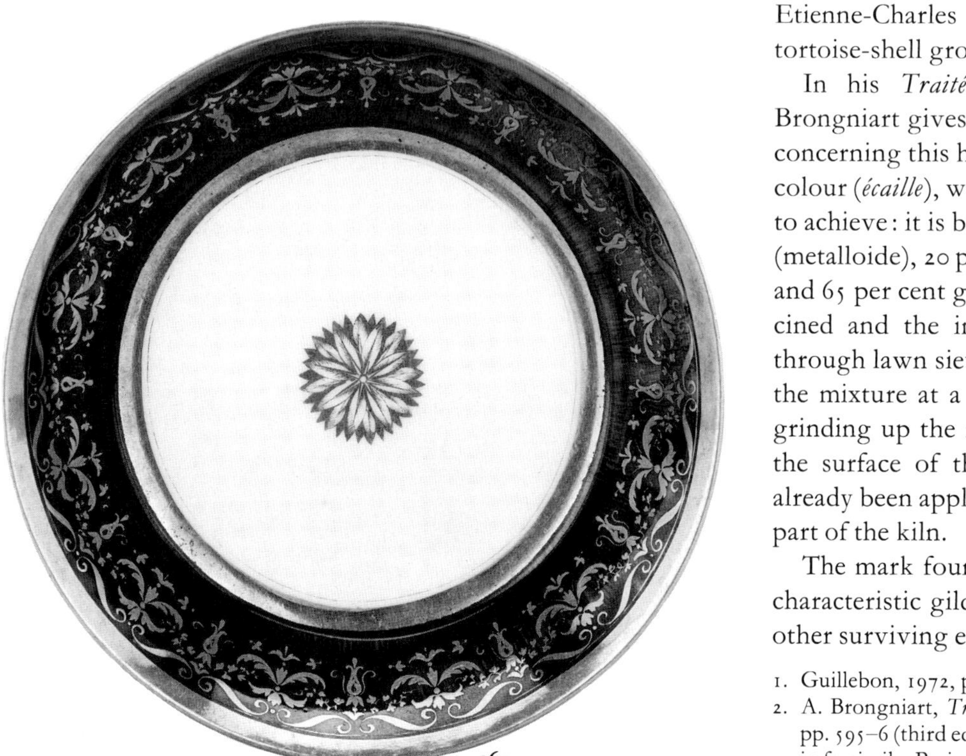

267

1. Guillebon, 1972, pl. 98 (colour)
2. A. Brongniart, *Traité des Arts Céramiques*, Paris, 1844, Vol. II pp. 595–6 (third edition, with notes by A. Salvetat, 1877, issued in facsimile, Paris 1977).

3. Brongniart, *op. cit.*, p. 585, explains that he uses the term in a special sense, to mean colours which can be fired at the same time as the glaze (*glaçure*) even though they may only be fired in a muffle kiln. In fact Brongniart's earliest published account of tortoise-shell grounds dates from 1802 and appeared in the *Journal des Mines*, Vol. XII, 1802 (an x), no. 67, pp. 58–80, 'Essai sur les couleurs obtenues des oxydes métalliques, et fixées par la fusion sur les différents corps vitreux'. The colours come under the heading 'bistres et roussâtres' (p. 77) and are obtained from a mixture of manganese, copper oxide and iron oxide 'oxide de fer de terre d'ombre'. On hard-paste porcelain feldspar is used as a flux.
4. See, for example, a footed bowl in the Musée national de Céramique, Sèvres, inv. 26278, illus. d'Albis *et al.*, 1989, no. 162.

268 **Plate**, *c.* 1815–20

D. 24.1 cm
Marks: *M.r de Dihl et Guerhard à Paris* stencilled in grey (see cat. 269)
Reg. No. 1926,10–16,1

Hard-paste porcelain, with flared sides. The decoration consists of two red roses on a marble table against a brown ground, enclosed by gilt bands; on the border is a gilt design of lotus and fern motifs and scrolls. Both sides of rim gilt, exterior of foot rim gilt.

Provenance: Presented by Mrs M.A. Francis, 1926; 'said to have been purchased by the grandfather of Mr E.J. Francis, husband of the donor, at the Beckford Sale at Fonthill in 1822' (note in B.M. Register)[1]

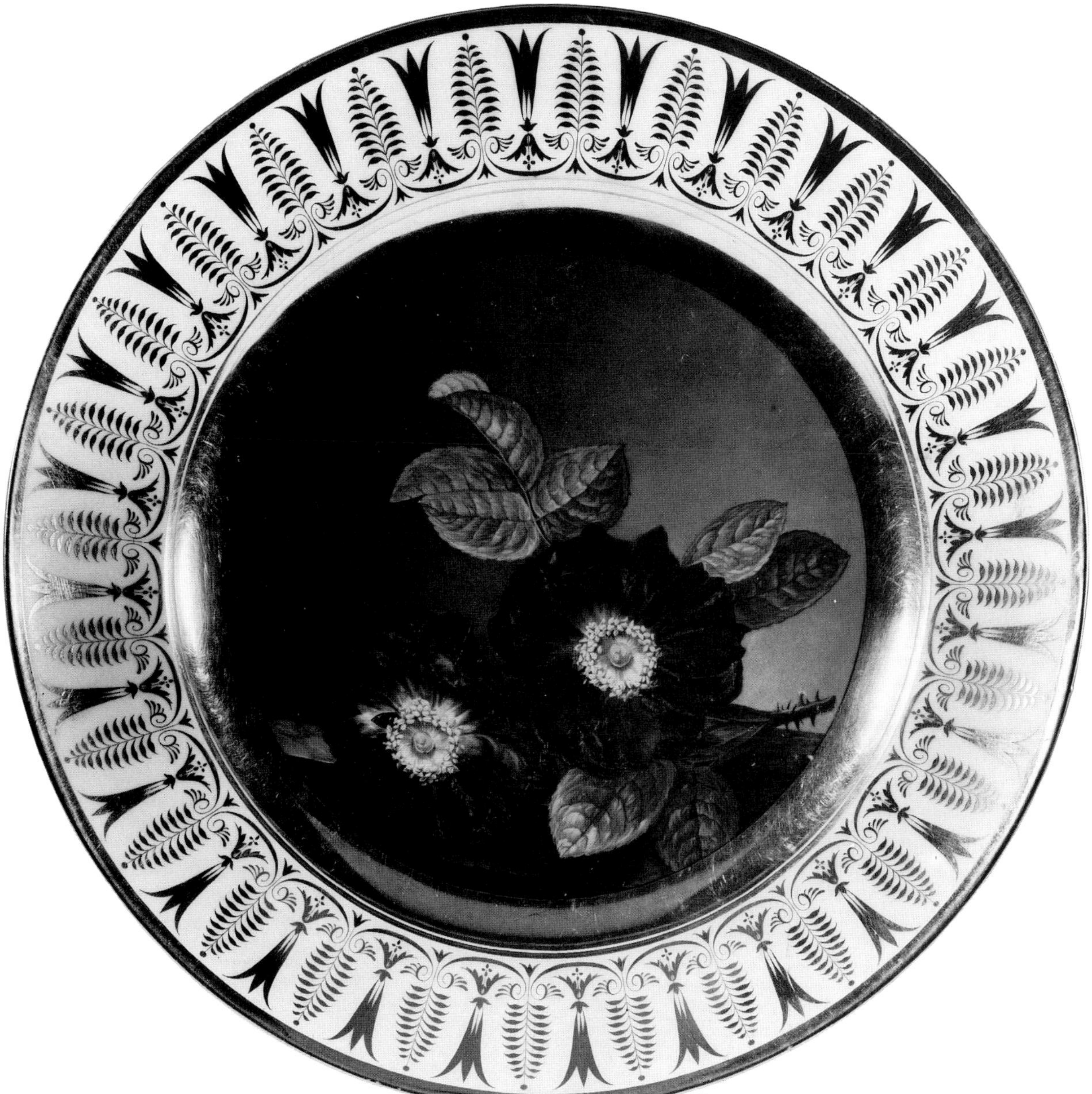

268

Literature: Unpublished

Comparable Examples: None

This plate was intended as a cabinet piece rather than for domestic use. Botanical decoration enjoyed a great vogue all over Europe (including Britain) in the first two decades of the nineteenth century and many porcelain factories, such as Berlin,[2] Vienna,[3] and Derby[4] produced botanical services accurately painted with flowers from contemporary botanical publications.

In France the most successful flower-painters were Gerardus (1746–1822) and Cornelis (1756–1840) van Spaendonck, whose works were adapted by the porcelain factories. Cornelis van Spaendonck was employed as artistic director at the Sèvres factory from 1795–1800, 1802–3 and 1808–9. However, no direct source for the painting on this plate has yet been discovered amongst his works.

Other Paris concerns such as Darte and Sèvres also sold plates decorated with botanically accurate flower decoration.[5]

1. There were several pieces in Beckford's possession which may be related to this plate and its companion piece (see cat. 269): In the China Closet in a passage leading from the lobby were 'Two French cabinet CUPS and SAUCERS, gold ground, antique borders, painted with flowers by *Van Spandonck*, in a style of peculiar excellence'; in the Lancaster Gallery was 'A set of very fine FRENCH PLATES, painted in flowers', see J. Rutter, *A Description of Fonthill Abbey and Demesne Wilts; The Seat of William Beckford, Esq., including a list of its numerous and valuable Paintings, Cabinets, and other Curiosities*, Shaftesbury, 1822, p. 54, p. 56. The catalogue of the *Magnificent Effects at Fonthill Abbey, Wilts.* for the sale by Christie's on the premises on 18 September 1822 (Second Day's Sale), Lot 46 seems to refer to another pair: 'Two gold-ground cabinet coffee cups and saucers, 1 *painted in roses*, 1 *with tulips*, by Van Spandonck', whilst the ones in the *Description* are probably Lot 29 on 19 September 1822 (Third Day's Sale): 'Two French cabinet cups and saucers, gold ground, antique borders, painted with flowers by Van Spandonck in a style of peculiar excellence'. Lot 9 on the same day was 'Two *very fine French plates*, painted in flowers'. On the Sixth Day's Sale, 23 September 1822, is a further group, Lot 84 'Four very fine French plates with flowers of Dihl's manufacture'. The situation is somewhat complicated by the fact that the sale did not in the event take place in September, but was rescheduled for October, and a new catalogue printed. The entries seem to correspond, however, except for two additional lots in the Fourth Day's Sale on 4 October 1822: Lot 23 'Two gold ground French cups and saucers, exquisitely painted in roses and hearts-eases, by Van Spandonck' and Lot 24 'Two ditto, wild poppies and anemonies [*sic*]'. The two Museum plates can probably be identified as part of Lot 84, 23 September 1822 (Sixth Day's Sale), corresponding with Lot 84, 7 October 1822, 'Four very fine French plates with flowers of Dihl's manufacture'.
2. E. Köllmann and M. Jarchow, *Berliner Porzellan*, Munich, 1987, Textband, p. 197, fig. 116; Bildband, p. 463, fig. 315a, b.
3. K. Tasnàdi-Marik illustrates a bowl, cover and stand and a soup plate (it is hard to imagine this plate painted with a white rabbit amongst meticulously painted flowers and leaves in use) in the Budapest Museum of Applied Arts in *Viennese Porcelain*, Corvina, 1971, pls. 21, 24.
4. For example, a plate illus. by J. Twitchett, *Derby Porcelain*, London, 1980, pl. 233.
5. Nine matching plates sold Paris, Ader, Picard, Tajan (Hôtel Drouot), 4 March 1981, Lot 39; Guillebon, 1972, pp. 196–7, figs. 151–2. For a Sèvres plate of 1822 painted by Philippine in the Musée national de Céramique, Sèvres, see Verlet, 1953, pl. 120. The lasting fashion for this type of décor is shown by two plates dating from a decade later. M.L. Casanova, *Le Porcellane Francesi nei Musei di Napoli*, Naples, 1974, cat. 220, two plates dated 1832 and 1834 in the Museo di Capodimonte, Naples, inv. 6991, 6992.

269 **Plate**, *c*.1815–20

D. 23.9 cm

Marks: *Mr de Dihl et Guerhard à Paris* stencilled in grey; cursive *L* incised

Reg. No. 1926,10–16,2

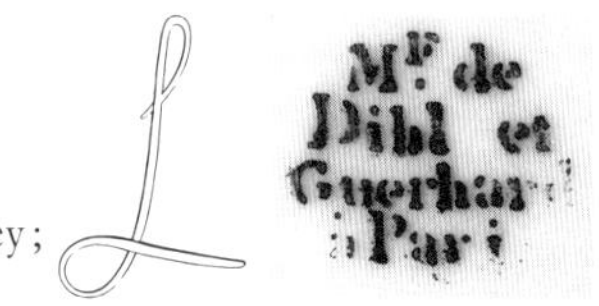

269 *marks*

Hard-paste porcelain, with flared sides. The decoration consists of two pink full-blown roses in front of a dark brown vase of [?] classical form on a table against a yellowish-brown ground, enclosed by a gilt band; running around the border is a gilt design of stylised flowers alternating with paterae and leaves. Rim gilt.

Provenance: Presented by Mrs M.A. Francis, 1926; 'said to have been purchased by the grandfather of Mr E.J. Francis, husband of the donor, at the Beckford Sale at Fonthill in 1822' (note in BM register)[1]

Literature: A. Scott-James, R. Desmond, F. Wood, *The British Museum Book of Flowers*, London, 1989, pl. 87

Comparable Examples: None

For a discussion of this type of decoration, see cat. 268.

1. See cat. 268, f.n. 1.

270 **Cup and Saucer (*tasse litron*)**, *c*.1815–20

See colour plate 40

D. *of saucer:* 13.1 cm

H. *of cup:* 6.1 cm

Marks: Beckford and Hamilton crests of a heron (left) and an oak within an oval reserve and *Manufre de MMrs. Dihl. & Guerhard . a Paris* all in gold

Reg. No. 1936,7–15,135

Hard-paste porcelain, the cup heavily potted. Deep saucer with flared sides, straight-sided cup with scroll handle out-turned at its lower end. The sides of the saucer and the exterior of the cup are painted in pink, yellow, purple, white, green and black with marguerites on a gold ground. On the well and exterior of saucer is a gilt pattern of stylised leaves alternating with paterae and leaves. Interior of cup gilt (*doublé d'or*).

Provenance: Presented by F. Howard Paget, Esq., 1936[1]

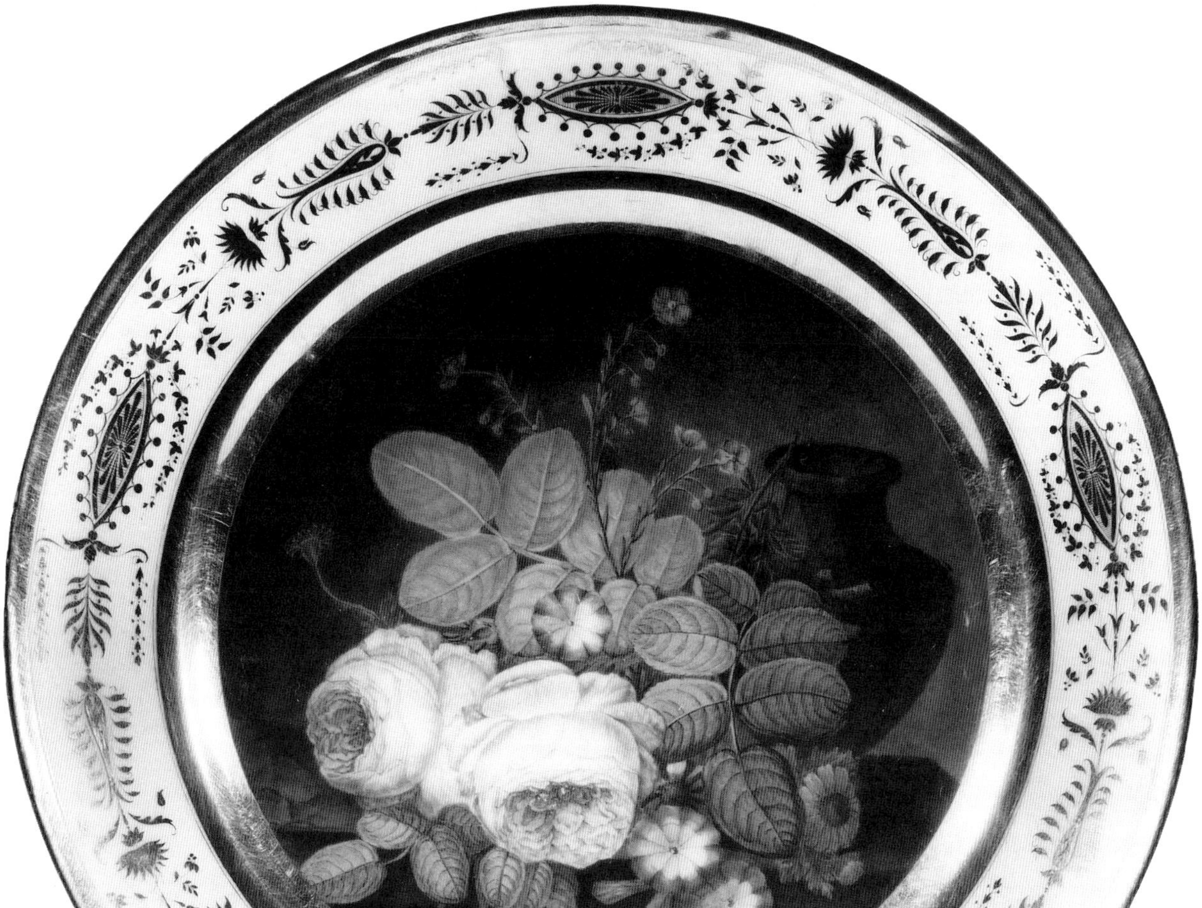

269

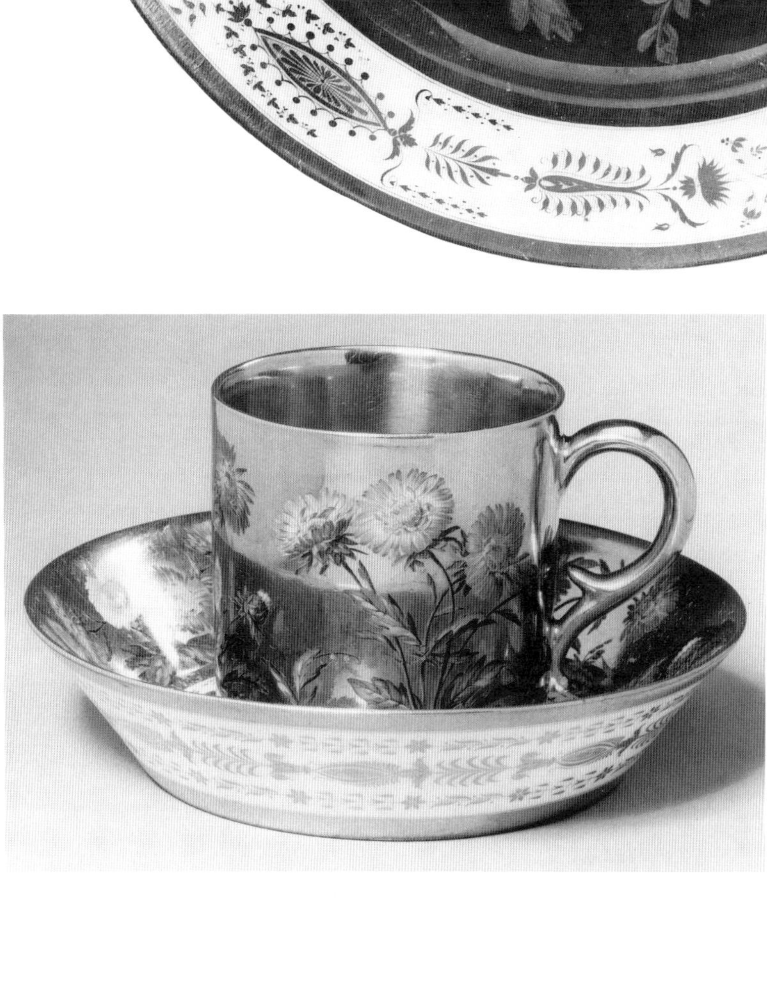

270

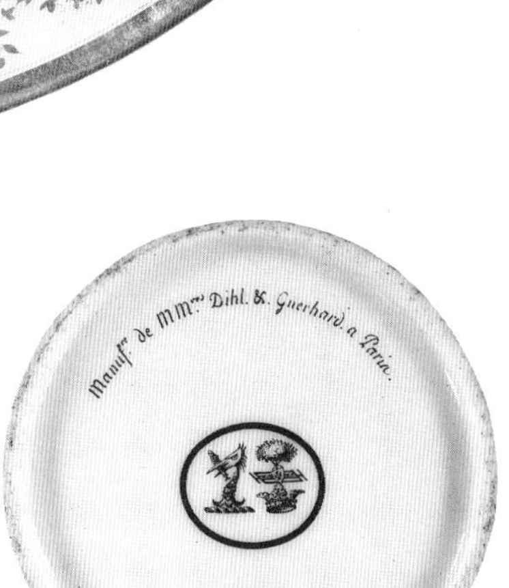

270 *marks*

Literature: Unpublished

Comparable Examples: Paris, Musée des arts décoratifs, illus. Guillebon, 1972, p. 134, fig. 102, painted with tulips

Private Collection: four cups and saucers painted with flowers, marked with Beckford and Hamilton crests.

This cup is a most luxurious production, and was certainly not intended for use. The devices on the bases indicate that the pieces were made for William Beckford (1760–1844) perhaps as a special order around 1810 when his daughter Susan married Alexander, later 10th Duke of Hamilton (1767–1853). Beckford owned gold ground cups and saucers painted with flowers, but none of the six in his sale in 1822 can be identified with the Museum example.[2] The later history of the Museum cup and saucer has not been established.

A slightly less opulent version of this decor occurs on a cup and saucer painted with poppies, harebells, daisies, cornflowers, grasses, etc., on a pale grey ground. The interior of the cup is not gilt.[3]

Flowers on a gold ground occur on two cups from the Derby factory during the Duesbury and Kean period (about 1795–6).[4]

1. See W. King, 'The F. Howard Paget Collection of Porcelain', *British Museum Quarterly*, Vol. XI, 1936–7, p. 15; A. Dawson 'The F. Howard Paget Collection in the British Museum', *Derby Porcelain International Society Newsletter*, no. 11, January 1988, pp. 12–15.
2. See cat. 268, f.n. 1.
3. Frégnac (ed.), 1964, p. 306, Musée national Adrien-Dubouché, Limoges, inv. ADL 1424.
4. J. Twitchett, *Derby Porcelain*, London, 1980, p. 151, fig. 34.

271 Cup and Saucer (*tasse litron*), *c.*1815–20

H. *of cup:*	5.2 cm
D. *of saucer:*	10 cm
Marks:	*Manufre de MM. Guerhard et Dihl, à Paris* printed in red on both; *D* in red on cup, cursive *D* incised on saucer
Reg. No.	Franks 430

Hard-paste porcelain, highly translucent; straight-sided cup with ear-shaped scroll handle, saucer with flared sides. The decoration consists of sprays of cornflowers painted in blue, red, green and brownish-black. Rims gilt, handle partly gilt. Perfect.

Provenance: Bequeathed by Sir A.W. Franks, 1897

Literature: Franks, 1896, no. 430

Comparable Examples: Paris, Louvre Museum, pair of cups and saucers; D. of saucer 8.8 cm, H. of cup, 3.6 cm[1]

There are a surprising number of production faults on this cup and saucer from one of the leading fac-

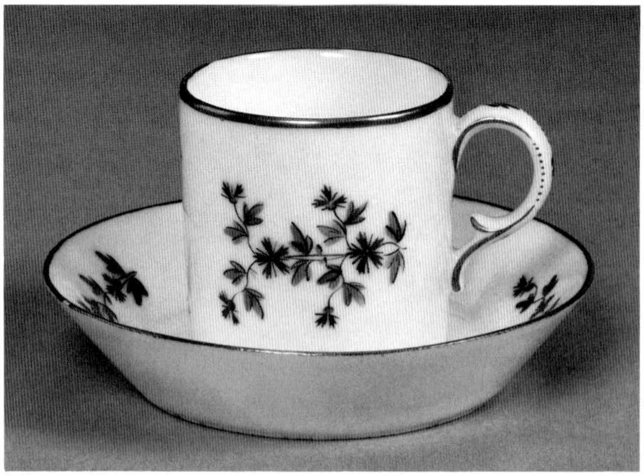

271

271 marks (cup)

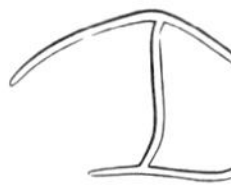

271 *incised mark (saucer)*

tories in Paris: the glaze has 'shrunk' on the base of the saucer, both foot rims have traces of bedding material used to stop the glaze from sticking to the saggar during firing, and the saucer is badly warped, with some small inclusions and poorly applied gilding on the rim. As domestic items of indifferent quality they offer great contrast to items such as cat. 270.

The *gobelet litron* shape appears at Sèvres in 1752; by 1757 five sizes were in production.[2] The examples in the Louvre (see above) show that the factory in the rue de Bondy also made more than one size.

The pattern commonly known as the Angoulême sprig, or in France as *barbeaux*, was used in the late eighteenth and early nineteenth centuries on all sorts of domestic wares. Pieces from table-services made at the rue de Bondy have been recorded.[3] Most Paris factories, including Locré's factory[4] as well as Valenciennes[5] and Niderviller[6] also used the pattern. It became popular outside France, particularly in England as at the Coalport factory, Shropshire, and at John Turner's factory, Lane End, Staffordshire.[7]

1. *Musée du Louvre, Nouvelles Acquisitions* . . . 1984, no. 95.
2. Savill, 1988, II, pp. 501–2.
3. Macdonald, 1986, no. 103, four square *compotiers* and ten shell-shaped *compotiers*, inv. 1985. 30/4.31/10; Eriksen, 1973, no. 94,

two footed trays each with seven dessert cups.

4. For a sugar bowl, cover and stand similar in shape to the Sèvres *sucrier de Monsieur le Premier*, see exh. Nord-Pas-de-Calais, 1986–7, no. 47.
5. *Ibid.*, nos. 67–8, water jug and basin, Lille, Musée des Beaux-Arts, inv. C 708; butter dish, cover and stand, Saint-Omer, Musée Sandelin, inv. 84.84.
6. Macdonald, 1986, no. 101, coffee can and saucer, inv. 1917.394/2.
7. G. Godden, *Coalport and Coalbrookdale Porcelains*, London, 1970, pl. 34 and D. Holgate and G. Godden, 'The Turner porcelains *c.*1786–*c.*1805', in G. Godden, *Staffordshire Porcelain*, London, 1983, pl. 143. Both these illustrations show pieces made around 1800.

Nast's factory,
rue Popincourt (1783–c.1787), rue des Amandiers (c.1789–1835)[1]

Népomucène-Jean-Hermann Nast (1754–1817), a native of Radesburg, Styria, Austria, who came to France in 1779, was one of the most successful of all the Paris porcelain manufacturers. In 1783 he took over the factory in rue Popincourt[2] originally started by Pierre Lemaire, for whom Nast had worked at the Vincennes hard-paste factory. Nast is said to have started from nothing, yet his father was a *maître bourrelier* (master saddler) and his grandfather, who was an earthenware manufacturer, a burgher of Radesburg. On arriving in France he had first worked as a saddler at Versailles. However, at the time of his marriage in 1789 he was estimated to be worth no less than 84,000 *livres*. His source of capital at the original factory in rue Popincourt remains unknown. He succeeded in keeping the factory going throughout the Revolutionary period, despite being obliged to borrow 55,000 francs between 1792 and 1794. By 1812 he was immensely prosperous. From 1813 his two sons worked with him, continuing to run the factory after their father's death in 1817. In March 1831 the elder, Henri, became sole owner of the factory, but worsening economic conditions forced its closure in 1835. It apparently still enjoyed a considerable reputation long after its closure and a 'grande coupe avec ornements en relief' was awarded an honourable mention by the jury of the 1851 Exhibition.[3]

Nast senior, of whom several portraits survive,[4] produced some original and splendid forms and decorative schemes. Most date from after the Revolution. Until then the decoration on his porcelain differed little from those of his competitors.[5] In the early years of the nineteenth century he was manufacturing such extraordinary pieces as the 'Arabian coffee-pot', a type of filter coffeemaker consisting of a two-handled lidded upper part resting on a teapot-like lower part, based on a design by the chemist, politician and philanthropist Antoine Alexis Cadet de Vaux (1734–1828) who was his inseparable friend.[6] The inventory taken after his death of his wife Edmée Lecoutre[7] shows that he manufactured such domestic articles as chamber pots, pharmacy jars and lamps. He also manufactured barometers, one of which is still in the possession of a descendant.[8] Louis Prudhomme mentions in his *Miroir historique* ...[9] Nast's three immense *magasins* and the range of products at all prices. Undecorated porcelain was of course the cheapest, followed by gilded porcelain. Most expensive of all was painted and gilt porcelain, sometimes enriched by sculptural additions. A plate might cost anything from 200–500 francs. Thirty-six different decors can be seen on a surviving sample plaque dating from the beginning of the nineteenth century.[10] A bill dated 8 Floréal l'an x (28 April 1802) for porcelain to the value of 4,314 francs, 90 sous supplied to the dealer Flandin gives a good idea of the range and cost of Nast's products.[11] Fulwar Skipwith, American Consul in Paris, commented in a letter of September 1806 to James Madison '. . . Mr Nast, the China Manufacturer has at last executed the order which I gave him on my arrival here for your Table and Dessert sets of china . . . This china in whiteness is not much inferior to the china of the celebrated Manufactury of Sêve, & is just 40% cheaper . . .' The service of 96 dinner plates, 24 soup plates, 36 dessert plates, 18 covered cups, 2 ice-cream coolers and 2 tureens cost $595.37. An ice-cream cooler from the service, which has striking black-and-white decoration on a matt orange ground, is in the White House Collection, Washington, DC.[12]

The success of Nast's coloured grounds, many of them matt, owed a great deal to the chemist Nicolas Vauquelin (1763–1829).[13] He perfected chrome green in 1802 and directed Nast's laboratories up to 1828. Gifted painters, such as Louis Pierre Schilt (1790–1859), who later worked at Sèvres from 1818 to 1855,[14] were responsible for top-quality painted scenes. Luxurious productions frequently depended on lavish gilding and the relief border decoration perfected by Nast himself and patented by him in 1810. This kind of ornamentation was effectively used on cups and saucers, sometimes gilded on their interior surface,[15] plates[16] and even barometers,[17] as well as on a highly elaborate teapot from a service for King Ferdinand VII and Queen Isabella of Braganza. The service was made between their marriage in 1816 and her death in 1818.[18] Two other landscape painters, Camille Flers (1802–68) and his pupil Louis Nicolas Cabat (1812–93), and modellers named Pajou and J.B.P. Klagmann (1810–67), are known to have worked for Nast.[19]

A wide range of biscuit figures was also in production. Most are neo-classical in style. A bust of Hoche bears the unusual incised mark *C^en^ Nast* indicating that it was produced during the Revolution.[20] A blue and white biscuit Vase Medicis ornamented with bacchanalian figures in relief measuring 35 cm in height presented to the Musée national de Céramique, Sèvres, by a descendant of Nast is incised inside *Manufre de porcelaine du Cn Nast à Paris*.[21] Even larger pieces are known, such as a basket supported by four biscuit porcelain Antique female figures resting on a porcelain base with four feet, which is no less than 48 cm in height.[22] A clock case of blue and white biscuit porcelain in imitation of Wedgwood measuring 44 cm in height is in a private collection.[23] A bust of Napoleon after Chaudet is 45 cm in height.[24] Two monumental vases each 71 cm in height painted with scenes in the classical taste after Jean-Victor Bertin were once in the Nast family collections.[25] A small portrait medallion of Nast himself on a blue ground is dated on the reverse *Anné 1815 xbre*.[26]

The organisation of the workshops and store areas (*magasins*) has been described[27] as follows: the main building housed three stores on the ground floor. These were for reject-quality porcelain, for undecorated porcelain (this room was on the street) and for second-quality undecorated porcelain, together with the muffle-kilns. On the first floor were three stores for decorated porcelain. On the second floor was a workshop for *pâte crue* (clay), a store for rouletted pieces, and the enamelling workshop. Below the roof on the third floor were several well-lit workshops for the designers, painters and burnishers, as well as storerooms for first-quality porcelain awaiting decoration. Wood for firing the kilns was kept in the courtyard, whilst additional stocks were located over the road from the factory itself. In a building in the courtyard were the mould-chamber, the lathe shop, a store for prepared clay, another for 'raw' clay (*terre brute*) and an area housing the colours.

1. This account is based on Guillebon, 1972, pp. 258–62 and 1985, pp. 69–72. In these publications Nast's full name is given in varying forms. A good range of the factory's productions is illustrated in D. Guillemé-Brulon, 'La porcelaine de Nast', *L'Estampille*, no. 149, September 1982, pp. 32–44.
2. For a discussion of the factory site, now 70 rue du Chemin-Vert, see the text of a lecture given by Guillebon, 'De quelques immeubles parisiens encore existant ayant abrité des manufactures de porcelaine entre 1785 et 1835', Ville de Paris, Commission du Vieux Paris, procès-verbal du séance du ler décembre 1981, publ. *Supplément au Bulletin municipal officiel de la Ville de Paris*, 6 janvier 1983, no. 2 (1981, no. 10), pp. 13–16.
3. Chavagnac and Grollier, 1906, p. 573.
4. Guillebon, 1972, p. 271, fig. 211.
5. A teapot of *litron* form painted in sepia with a cow is illus. by Guillebon, 1985, pl. XXI, fig. 34, private collection.
6. Guillebon, 1985, pl. XXVIII, figs. 45, 46, and see pp. 70–1, f.n. 19 for a 'Dissertation sur le café'.
7. Archives nationales, Minutier central, *Etude* XXXVIII, *liasse*

943, 8 février 1811 (Me Passez), *inventaire après décès*, quoted extensively in Guillebon, 1985, *passim*.
8. See Bloit, 1988, p. 71, thermometer set in a porcelain plaque of around 50 cm in length.
9. Louis Prudhomme, *Miroir historique, politique et critique de l'ancien et du nouveau Paris et du département de la Seine*, Paris, 1807, 3rd edn., Vol. 1, p. 32, quoted Guillebon, 1985, p. 71.
10. Guillebon, 1972, figs. 210, 217.
11. Published in full, Guillebon, 1985, pp. 197–9; kept at the MNS, Archives de Sèvres.
12. See Detweiler, *French Porcelain*, 1982, p. 107, fig. 19. The shipping invoice, dated 3 September 1806, survives amongst the Madison Papers at the New York Public Library.
13. A biography of Vauquelin, citing his published work, is given in P. Larousse, *Grand Dictionnaire Universel du XIXe siècle*, Geneva and Paris, 1982, deuxième partie, pp. 814–15.
14. Brunet and Préaud, 1978, p. 380.
15. Bloit, 1988, p. 70; Guillebon, 1985, pl. LIII, fig. 75.
16. Bloit, 1988, p. 71.
17. *Ibid.*
18. Guillebon, 1972, p. 283, fig. 220, Madrid, Museo Arqueològico Nacional.
19. Guillebon, 1972, p. 261.
20. Chavagnac and Grollier, 1906, p. 575; now in the Musée national de Céramique, Sèvres, inv. 11025 exh. 'Porcelaines de Paris de 1800 à 1850' June–October 1970, *Cahiers*, 1970, nos. 46–47, no. 188.
21. Musée national de Céramique, Sèvres, inv. 12598, Nast gift, illus. Guillebon, 1985, pl. LII, fig. 74.
22. Boulogne-sur-Seine, Bibliothèque Marmottan, illus. Guillebon, 1985, pl. LI, fig. 73.
23. Boulogne-sur-Seine, private collection, Guillebon, 1972, p. 273, fig. 213 and Guillebon, 1985, pl. LV, fig. 77.
24. Boulogne-sur-Seine, Bibliothèque Marmottan, illus. Guillebon, 1985, pl. LVI, fig. 78.
25. Now in the Louvre Museum, Paris, inv. OA 11267, 11268, see P. Ennès, 'Deux vases de la manufacture parisienne de Nast, illustrant l'origine de l'architecture et l'origine du chapiteau corinthien', *Revue du Louvre*, 1990, 3, Chronique des Amis du Louvre, I–II.
26. Roger Imbert Collection, exh. Porcelaines de Paris de 1800 à 1850, *Cahiers*, 1970, nos. 46–7, no. 129 *bis*.
27. See Guillebon, 1985, p. 13, quoting *inventaire après décès* of Madame Nast, 8 février 1811, Archives nationales, Minutier central, *Etude*, XXXVIII, *liasse* 943 (*notaire* Passez). See Chavagnac and Grollier, 1906, p. 571 for a description of the factory premises in 1827.

272 **Bowl on Circular Foot and Stand (*jatte et son présentoir*)**, *c.*1810

H. *of bowl on foot:*	12.2 cm
D. *of stand:*	19.4 cm
Marks:	*nast à paris par brevet d'inv, on* painted in gold on both
Reg. No.	Franks 433

Hard-paste porcelain, the stand circular with out-turned rim decorated with milled palmette motifs, the edge of the well milled in a rope-pattern, wide turned foot. Exterior rim of breast-shaped bowl milled with a leaf and bead design. At the upper and lower end of the cylindrical support flanked by three grotesque one-legged animal terms, is a band of milled leaf decoration, repeated on the rim of the circular foot. The underside of the foot has a central circular hole surrounded by an inner foot rim. The interior of the bowl is gilt. All the milled areas and the grotesque animals are decorated with matt gilding. The remaining decoration consists of burnished gilt bands on the rims and next to the matt areas.

Provenance: Bequeathed by Sir A.W. Franks, 1897

Literature: Franks, 1986, no. 433

Comparable Examples: None

Florence, Pitti Palace, cup and saucer of less elaborate form marked *nast ../a/paris*, inv. A.c.e. 1911, n.803, illus. Eriksen, 1973, no. 105, formerly belonged to Grand Duke of Tuscany

Paris, Musée des arts décoratifs, circular dish or stand, inv. 3659, gift of F. Nast, 1867

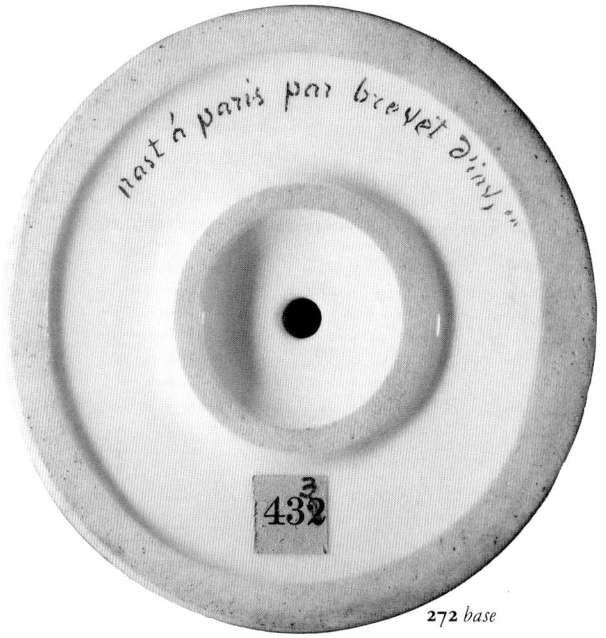

272 *base*

This type of milled decoration is known as *à la molette*.

On 13 May 1810 Jean-Népomucène-Hermann Nast was granted a patent[1] for ten years for his method of producing relief borders and ornaments on glazed and unglazed porcelain both before and after firing.[2] In order to avoid deforming the shape of the piece, it was moulded more thickly than normal. When dry enough to be turned, it was placed on the lathe, with the aid of a support, and moistened with slip brushed on to the surface. The milling tool (*molette*) was first soaked in turpentine or other greasy liquid so that the

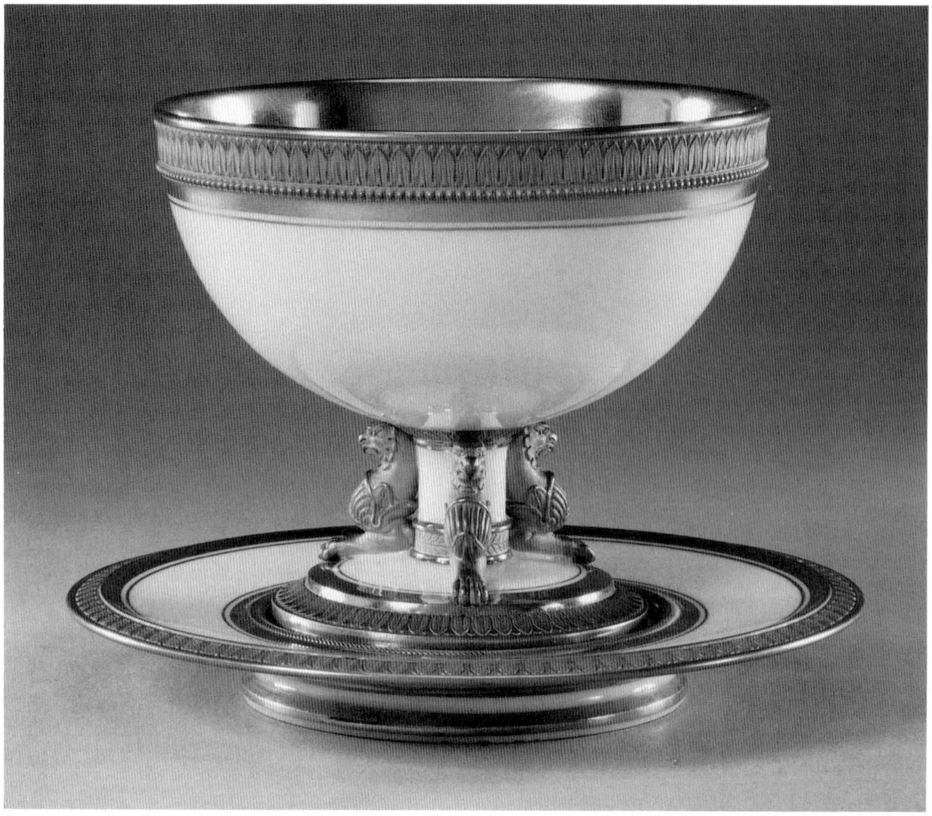

272

leather-hard porcelain would not stick to it, then rotated on the piece. As this example was easy to manipulate, the decoration would have been done directly on to it rather than on to a mould, the method used for irregularly formed pieces.

Pieces such as this were probably intended as ornaments rather than for use.

A cup and saucer with an elaborate handle bearing the mark *Deroche* in gold is decorated with bands of similar relief ornament *à la molette*.[3]

1. *Description des Machines et Procédés spécifiés dans les brevets d'invention de perfectionnement et d'importation dont la durée est expirée*, Paris, 1827, p. 213, no. 1312, 13 mai 1810, together with 'Brevet de Perfectionnements et d'Additions', 26 October 1810, p. 216. There is a copy of this book in the British Library, pressmark PP 1645a.
2. This would seem most unlikely, but the last sentence of the introductory paragraph reads 'A l'aide du procédé que nous allons décrire, toutes les difficultés sont surmontées, et l'on embellit, au moyen de la *molette*, toutes les pièces de porcelaine émaillées et non émaillées, avant et après la cuisson'.
3. Musée du Louvre, *Nouvelles acquisitions*, 1985, no. 97, p. 168. Other pieces by Nast are illustrated by Guillebon, 1972, p. 275, fig. 214, cup on three eagle feet and saucer, Musée national de Céramique, Sèvres, p. 283, fig. 220, teapot and cover, Museo Arqueòlogico Nacional, Madrid; plate illustrated by Dauguet and Guillemé-Brulon, n.d., p. 67; cups and saucers, barometer, plate, private collection, illus. by Bloit, 1988, pp. 70–1; a *surtout* of four elements, inv. MNC 25621, illustrated in d'Albis *et al.*, 1989, no. 171.

273 Plate (*assiette*), *c.*1810

See colour plate 34

D. 23.8 cm
Marks: *nast* painted in red; [?] *19* incised; Drury Fortnum collection number *C.255* and *CDF* in monogram painted in red
Reg. No. 1899,10–6,5

Hard-paste porcelain, heavily potted with three prominent stilt marks on base. Painted with a young woman with long red hair in a blue bandeau seated on a box, wearing a classical-style robe

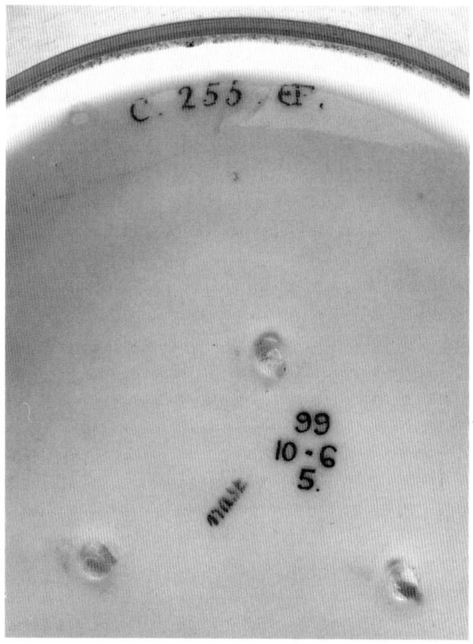

273 *marks. Traces of the supports used in the kiln are visible.*

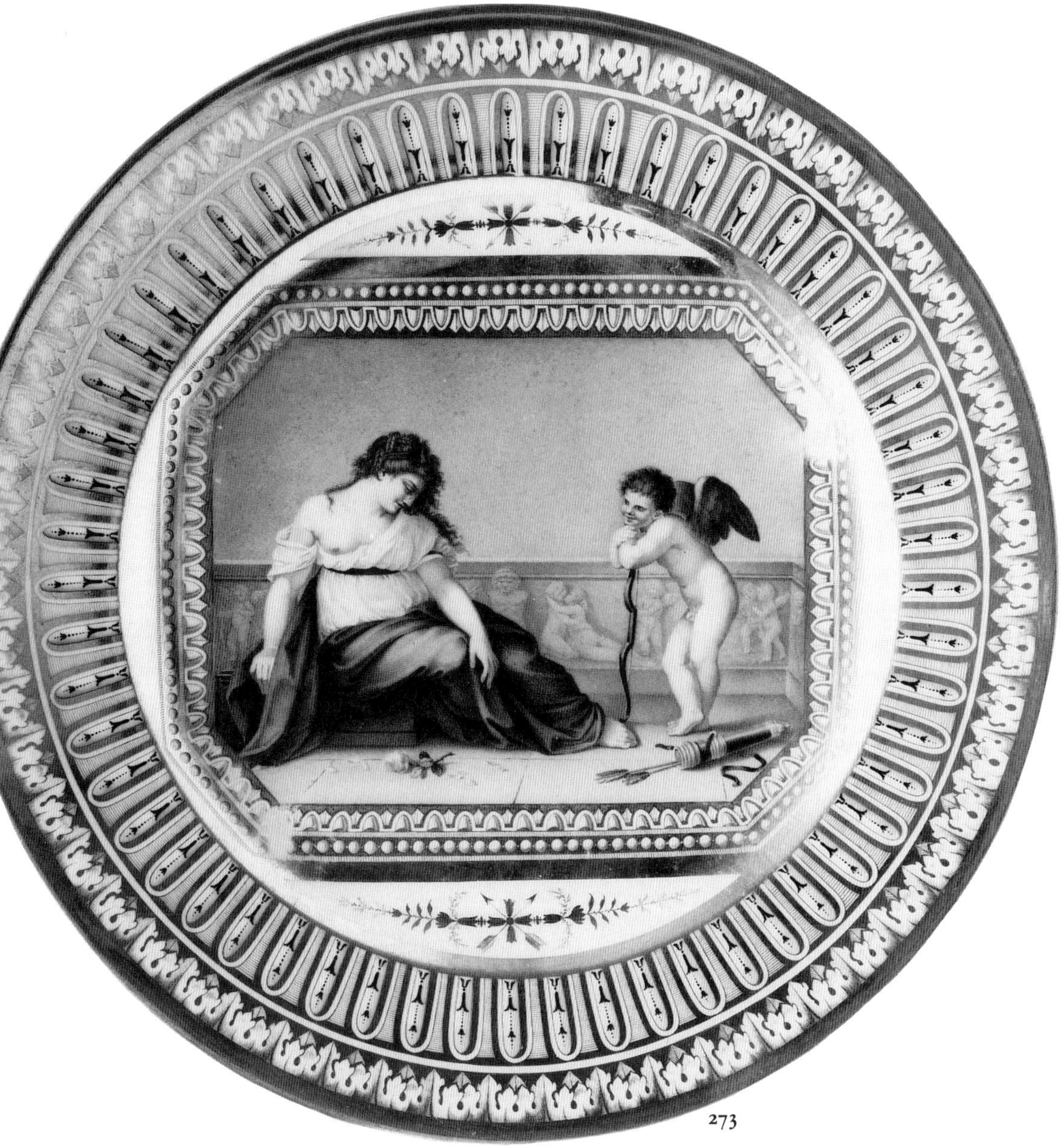

273

in white which leaves the right breast exposed and a long brown overgarment. On the floor beside her is a pink rose, some of its petals scattered beside it. In front of her stands a cupid, naked and leaning on his orange-red bow, his wings painted yellow and grey. To his left lies his red-brown and yellow quiver containing two arrows. The dado in the background depicts putti and a male term in pale brown; the rest of the background is an even paler brown. The scene is enclosed within an octagonal gilt frame. Near the edge of the plate is a gilt acanthus leaf pattern; another pattern of gilt paterae heightened in black with a lotus motif also decorates the rim. Underside of plate border gilt. Perfect.

Provenance: Bequeathed by C.D.E. Fortnum, Esq., DCL, FSA, 1899[1]

Literature: Unpublished

Comparable Examples: Sèvres, Musée national de Céramique, plate painted with a mother and child in classical dress in an interior, illus. Guillebon, 1972, p. 10, fig. 2

This plate was clearly intended as a cabinet piece. Its painting is of the highest quality generally associated with the Nast factory, but cannot be attributed in the present state of knowledge to any particular factory painter, and the dating of the plate remains problematical. The subject is based on one of three drawings commissioned from P.-P. Prud'hon (1758–1823) and exhibited in the *Salon* of 1793, entitled *Le Cruel rit des pleurs qu'il fait verser*. It was engraved by J.-L. Copia (1764–99), and may never have been executed as a painting by Prud'hon himself.[2] There is no evidence that Prud'hon worked directly for Nast, but another of his compositions, *L'Amour caressant sa mère*, was intended for the tops of bonbon boxes sold by the *confiseur* Berthelemot.[3]

1. For a note on C.D.E. Fortnum (1820–99), a Trustee of the British Museum, see cat. 93.
2. E. Dacier, *La Gravure de Genre et de Moeurs*, Paris, 1925, pl. LXXXVI, no. 132 and p. 103; for the companion drawing *L'Amour réduit à la raison*, see pl. LXXXVI, no. 133; J. Guiffrey, 'L'Oeuvre de Pierre-Paul Prud'hon', *Archives de l'Art Français*, nouvelle période, Vol. XIII, 1924, no. 19, pp. 9–11, discusses *Le Cruel rit des pleurs qu'il fait verser*; Anita Brookner has evaluated Prud'hon's work in 'Prud'hon: Master Decorator of the Empire', *Apollo*, Vol. LXXX, no. 31, September 1964, pp. 192–8.
3. Guiffrey, *op. cit.*, pp. 22–3.

274 Plate (*assiette*), *c.*1810

D. 23.7 cm
Marks: *NAST* stencilled in red; Drury Fortnum collection number *C. 256* and *CDF* in monogram painted in red
Reg. No. 1899,10–6, 6

Hard-paste porcelain, heavily potted with three prominent stilt marks on base. Painted with a seated female shown in profile to right, her brown hair held in a narrow white bandeau. She wears a blue and white robe in the classical style, partly shot with yellow and brown, with a gilt brooch at the right shoulder and a gilt bracelet on the right forearm. It leaves her left breast bare. In her arms she holds a naked child which rests its head on her left shoulder. Behind her sits a child partly clothed by a green drapery and at her left knee is a reclining naked child who is taking grapes from her left hand. In the background is a grey-green fringed curtain. The rim is decorated in gold with circles, enclosed by beads and separated by a stylised lily motif, containing alternately

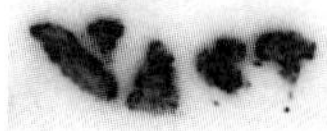

274 *mark*

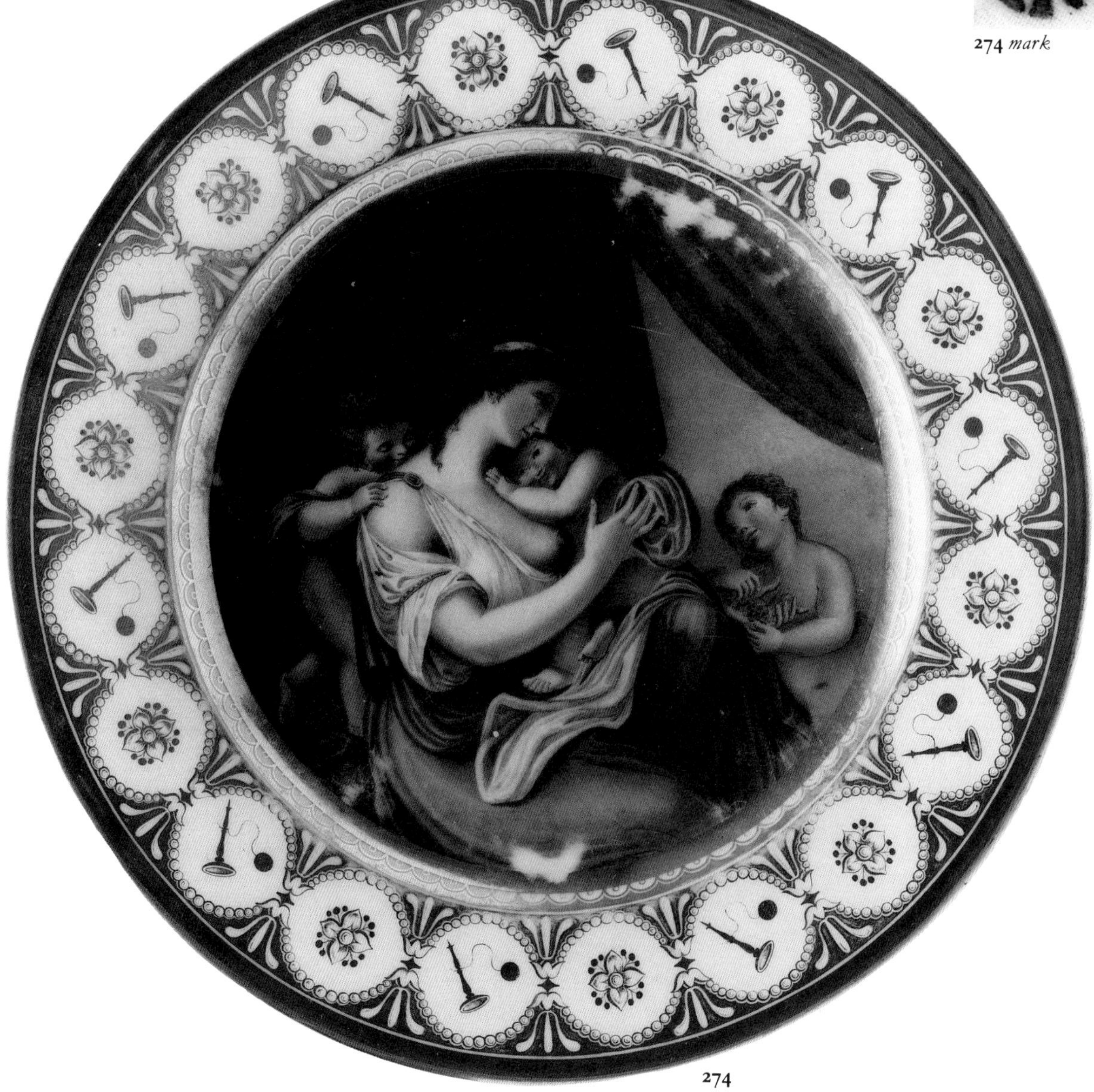

274

a rosette and a cup and ball toy. At the inner edge of the rim is a semicircle and dot motif between two gilt bands. Inner and outer edge of rim gilt, gilt band around foot.

Provenance: Bequeathed by C.D.E. Fortnum, Esq., DCL, FSA, 1899[1]

Literature: Unpublished

Comparable Examples: See cat. 277

Like the previous example this plate is of high quality and was intended as a cabinet piece. It cannot be attributed to any particular factory painter and the source of the decoration remains unknown. Its date of manufacture is conjectural.

1. For a note on C.D.E. Fortnum (1820–99), see cat. 93.

275 **Plate (*assiette*)**, *c.*1815–20

D. 24 cm
Marks: *nast* . . painted in grey [?] *79* incised; Drury Fortnum collection number *C.257* painted in red (*CDF* monogram almost effaced)
Reg. No. 1899,10–6,7

Hard-paste porcelain, heavily potted with three prominent stilt marks on base. Decorated on the rim with panels of butterflies painted in yellow, orange-red, black and brown on a ground of gilt dots, alternating with larger compartments of gilt lines and leaf trails on a grey-blue ground. The well is painted with pink full-blown roses alternating with other flowers, a band of gilt rose and leaf ornament on a grey-blue ground, and in the centre a gilt leaf and concentric pattern. Both sides of rim gilt, outer edge of foot rim gilt. Gilding rubbed and scratched.

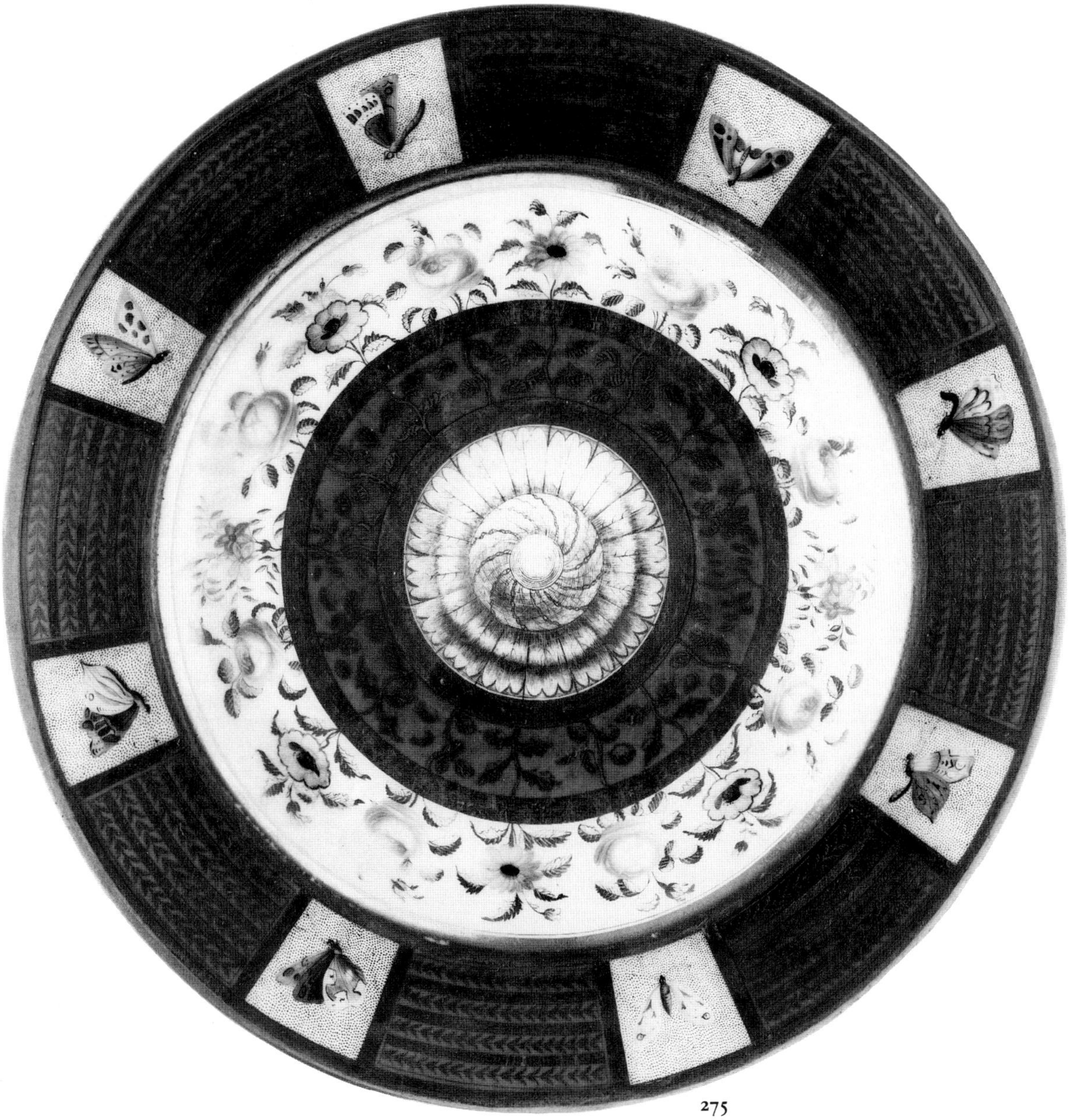

275

275 *marks*

Provenance: Bequeathed by C.D.E. Fortnum, Esq., DCL, FSA, 1899[1]

Literature: Unpublished

Comparable Examples: None

The profile of this plate is flatter than cats. 273–4. Despite the rich decoration, several firing faults are visible and there is a residue of foreign material at one place inside the foot rim.

Butterflies were enormously popular as a decorative motif from the end of the eighteenth century (see cat. 261), occurring on a most spectacular water jug and basin from the Petit Carousel factory, Paris, now in the Musée national de Céramique, Sèvres,[2] as well as on a cup and saucer from the same factory.[3]

1. For a note on C.D.E. Fortnum (1820–99), see cat. 93.
2. Guillebon, 1972, p. 299, fig. 235.
3. Also in the Musée national de Céramique, Sèvres, illus. exh. *Porcelaines parisiennes* 1983, p. 8.

276 **Plate**, attributed to Nast, probably *c*.1815–20

D. 23.5 cm
Marks: [?] *c* incised; collector's mark *C.254.* and monogram *CDF* painted in red; inscribed *Lucrèce* in gold
Reg. No. 1899,10–6,4

Hard-paste porcelain, heavily potted; three stilt marks on reverse. The painted decoration consists of a female bust portrait to right on a matt grey ground, depicting a young woman with a bandeau and arrow through her coiled hair wearing a purple garment in classical style pinned at the left shoulder by a sunburst brooch. Around the well is a gilt pattern of palmettes and scrolls; on the border are four male heads *en grisaille* within gilt 'frames' alternating with gilt flying birds, their plumage picked out in black, within oval gilt laurel leaf wreaths, and butterflies *en grisaille* in lozenge-shaped frames, on a ground of tiny gilt dots. Each motif is enclosed by gilt scrolls. Gilt rim. Reverse of border gilt.

Provenance: Bequeathed by C.D.E. Fortnum, Esq., DCL, FSA, 1899[1]

Literature: Unpublished

Comparable Examples: None

This plate conforms in shape, weight, dimensions and type of painted subject and border decoration to the marked Nast examples, cats. 273–5. These plates also share the characteristic three stilt marks on the reverse left by the kiln support.

The source of the portrait of Lucretia is unknown; it is in the style of P.-P. Prud'hon.[2]

The plate was evidently intended as a cabinet piece. Classical subjects were popular at the Nast factory,[3] as well as at Chamberlain's factory, Worcester, England[4] and in many other places, even as far as St Petersburg.[5] The story of the spread of this essentially Parisian style throughout Europe awaits further study.

1. For a note on C.D.E. Fortnum, see cat. 93.
2. A drawing of a female head by Prud'hon, without the bandeau and arrow, was sold at Christie's, 7 April 1981, Lot 172; photograph in Getty Center Photo Archive, Santa Monica, California; see also another entitled *La Mère Heureuse* in the Chevrier-Marcille collection.
3. See Guillebon, 1972, p. 10, fig. 2.
4. See G. Godden, *Chamberlain-Worcester Porcelain 1788–1852*, London, 1982, illustrations *passim.*, list of subjects p. 175.
5. See exh. 'An Imperial Fascination: Porcelain. Dining with the Czars. Peterhof', 'A la Vieille Russie', New York City, 15 March–20 April 1991, nos. 100, 101.

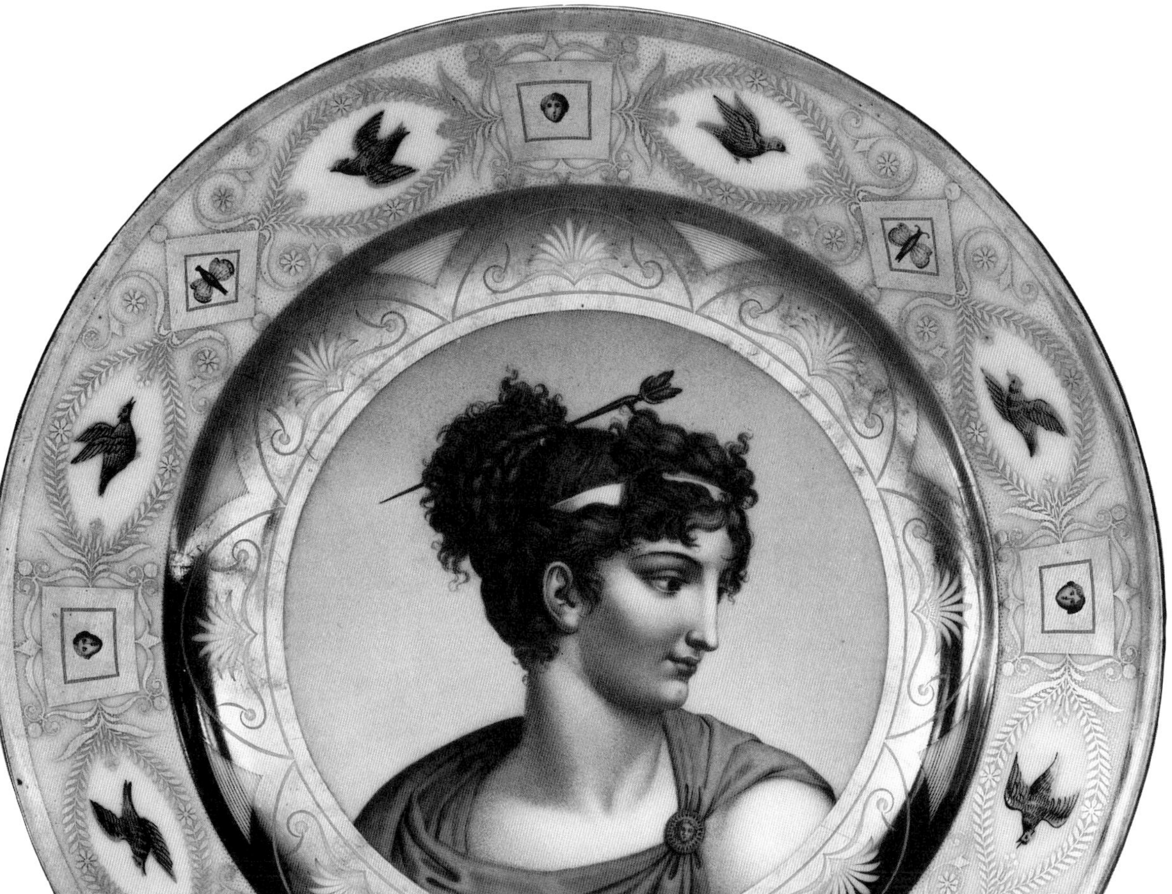

276

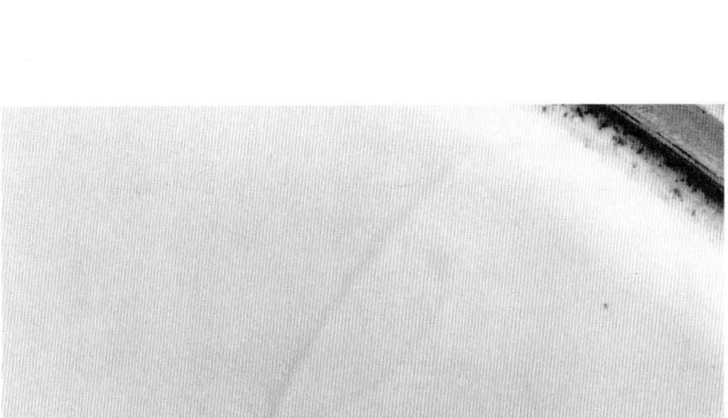

276 *mark*

277 **Plate**, attributed to Nast, *c.*1825

D. 23.7 cm
Marks: [?] p incised; collection number *C.253.* and monogram *CDF* painted in red; inscribed *phillis* in gold
Reg. No. 1899,10–6,3

Hard-paste porcelain, heavily potted; three stilt marks on reverse. The painted decoration consists of a three-quarters full-face to left portrait of a young girl in an interior, holding a lamb. She wears a low-cut green dress trimmed with lace and a jewel at the front, with full pale yellow sleeves, and a blue wrap. Her blonde hair falls in long ringlets. She leans on a table on which the lamb is placed, its forelegs in the air. Behind her at the right is a purple curtain; to the left in the background is a classical moulding in matt pale brown. Around the well is a gilt pattern forming an oval 'frame' to the 'picture'. On the border is gilt pattern of six panels of cornucopiae alternating with larger panels of palmettes. Footrim and both sides of rim gilt.

Provenance: Bequeathed by C.D.E. Fortnum, Esq., DCL, FSA, 1899[1]
Literature: Unpublished
Comparable Examples: None

For comments on the attribution, see cat. 276.

1. For a note on C.D.E. Fortnum, see cat. 93.

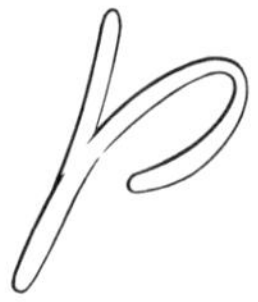
277 *mark*

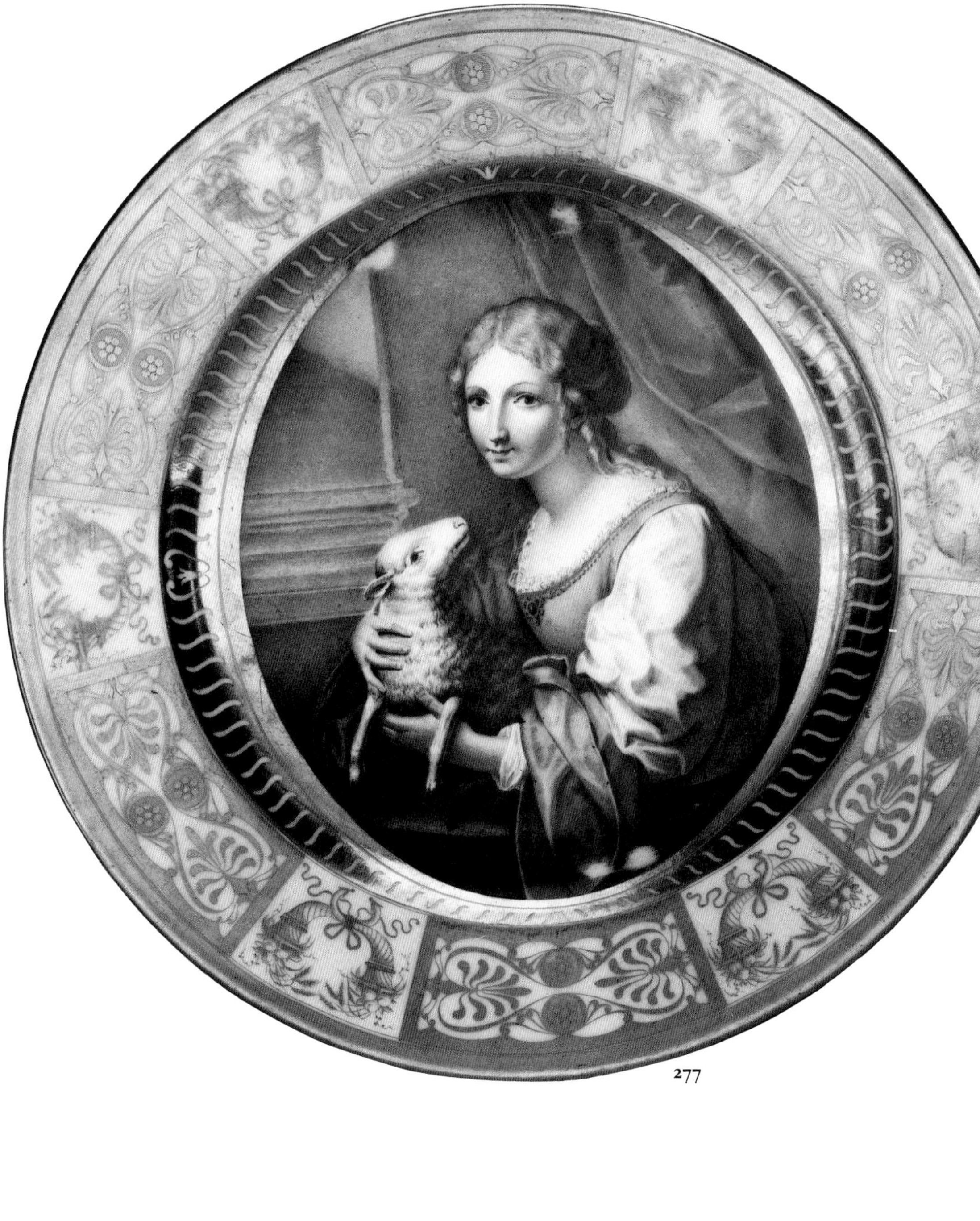
277

Duc d'Orléans' factory,
rue des Boulets (c.1784–6) and rue Amelot (1786–9)[1]

The first trace of this factory occurs on 22 April 1784[2] when Louis Honoré Delamarre de Villiers appeared before the lieutenant of the Paris police to register the mark[3] of the porcelain factory he had set up on a site purchased specially for this purpose. On 1 May 1785 he is recorded in partnership with Jean-Baptiste-Augustin Outrequin de Montarcy 'pour l'exploitation du privilège ou permission accordé par Sa Majesté d'une manufacture de porcelaine établie à Paris, rue de Boulets, faubourg Saint-Antoine'.[4] Delamarre sold out to Outrequin on 26 June 1786 in return for the sum of 2,400 *livres* to be paid annually. Outrequin obtained sole ownership of all the raw materials, tools, kilns and furniture, including the contents of the shop in the faubourg Saint-Honoré.[5] Three days previously Edmé Alexis Toulouse, the fifth son of a master cartwright of the rue de Charonne, Paris, who in 1779 had worked in a porcelain factory in the rue Fontaine-au-Roi, is recorded as director of the factory with a half share in it. However the partnership lasted only until 11 July 1789 when Toulouse went bankrupt. In the documents drawn up at this time, Outrequin de Montarcy, listed under the heading 'chirographaires' (creditors), is described as follows: 'ancien propriétaire, ensuite associé, postérieurement vendeur et en dernier lieu cessionnaire toujours sans inventaires, et aujourd'hui créancier suivant les livres du commerce déposés au consuls'. He is also listed as 'créancier pour marchandises d'ancienne fabrication, données en confiance à l'effet d'en faire la vente pour son compte'.[6] It is clear that Outrequin de Montarcy still had a close connection with the concern even after he had sold it, and its affairs were not on a businesslike footing. The ownership of the factory, which had occupied premises in the rue Amelot from 6 August 1786,[7] was transferred to Toulouse's creditors on 7 September 1789. It was sold on 14 September 1790 and resold a few days later to an English businessman named Baverstock. On 24 January 1796 Pierre Lemaire (see p. 297) and Antoine Josse (see p. 350) formed a partnership to carry on the concern.[8]

The duc d'Orléans (Louis-Philippe-Joseph, later known as 'Egalité', inherited the title in 1785) granted his personal protection to the factory on 6 August 1786, or at least on this date gave Montarcy permission to erect a sign over the factory entrance 'Manufacture du duc d'Orléans'. On 9 November 1786 Toulouse registered the mark *LP*. There is no reason to think that the duc d'Orléans invested any of his vast fortune in this factory.[9]

In July 1789 there were at least three painters working at the factory, according to the document drawn up when Toulouse filed for bankruptcy.[10] They were 'Birwiche, ouvrier peintre pour ouvrages' who was owed 366 *livres*, 'Queth' and 'Wagner', owed 665 *livres* and 415 *livres* respectively. Rent of the factory, including the porter's wages amounted to 4,100 *livres*. A 'marchand de terres à Alençon' named Royer was owed 160 *livres*, and two 'négociants', Petit *frères* on the quai des Miramionnes, and Pouyat of Limoges, were owed 77 *livres* 6 *sols* and 5,299 *livres* 16 *sols* respectively. The factory, its site, machinery, raw materials and kilns were valued at 23,398 *livres*, a relatively modest sum, whilst the stock came to 52,380 *livres* 9 *sols* and 3 *deniers*. Unfired porcelain in stock was valued at 11,854 *livres*. A number of 'faïenciers' are given as good debtors of the factory, most of them in Paris, but Goubert of Rouen, and Jacquier of Lyon are included in the list. Amongst the bad debtors were Berger 'commissionnaire' of Belleville, owing 1,775 *livres*, Bochet 'négociant' of Poitiers, owing 189 *livres* 16 *sols*, Barré, described as a sculptor of Sceaux, owing 79 *livres*, 'Eckard garnisseur', owing 297 *livres*, a moulder called Kouglemann, owing 354 *livres*, and 'Vivien, tourneur à Vincennes', owing 17 *livres*.

Surviving examples of porcelain from this factory are relatively uncommon. Both shapes and decoration, which frequently consisted of flowers, were strongly influenced by Sèvres.[11]

1. This account is based on Guillebon, 1972, pp. 195–8, and Chavagnac and Grollier, 1906, pp. 577–86.
2. Guillebon, 1972, p. 195.
3. Illus. Guillebon, 1972, p. 326, fig. 182.
4. *Op. cit.*, p. 196.
5. *Ibid.*
6. Published in full by Chavagnac and Grollier, 1906, pp. 579–81, quoting Archives de la Seine, *registre du commerce*, Toulouse, 126.
7. For a detailed study of the complex changes of ownership of the factory site and adjoining properties in the rue Amelot, see the text of a lecture given by Guillebon, 1983, pp. 10–13.
8. Guillebon, 1985, pp. 72–7; this account includes a detailed description of the factory site.
9. For a study of the power and wealth of the Orléans estate, see B.F. Hyslop, *L'Apanage de Philippe-Egalité, duc d'Orléans (1785–1791)*, Paris, 1965.
10. Chavagnac and Grollier, 1906, *op. cit.*, pp. 579–81.
11. *Ibid.*, pp. 584, 586, lists pieces in the Grollier Collection and the Sèvres Museum (all now in the Musée national de Céramique, Sèvres). For two covered *trembleuse* cups and saucers, see Frégnac, 1964, pp. 310–11.

278 **Cup and Saucer**, 1784–89

D. *of saucer:*	12.1 cm
H. *of cup:*	6.2 cm
Marks:	.*LP*. crowned painted in underglaze-blue on both; *j* [?] incised on cup
Reg. No.	FB 11 (AF 3214)

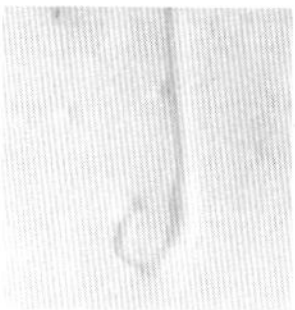

278 *mark (cup)*

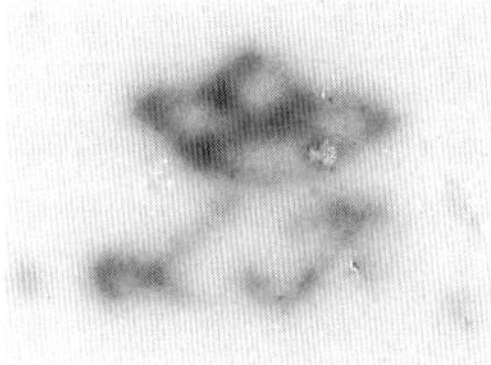

278 *mark (saucer)*

Hard-paste porcelain, thinly potted and highly translucent. Deep saucer with flared sides, straight-sided cup with ear-shaped

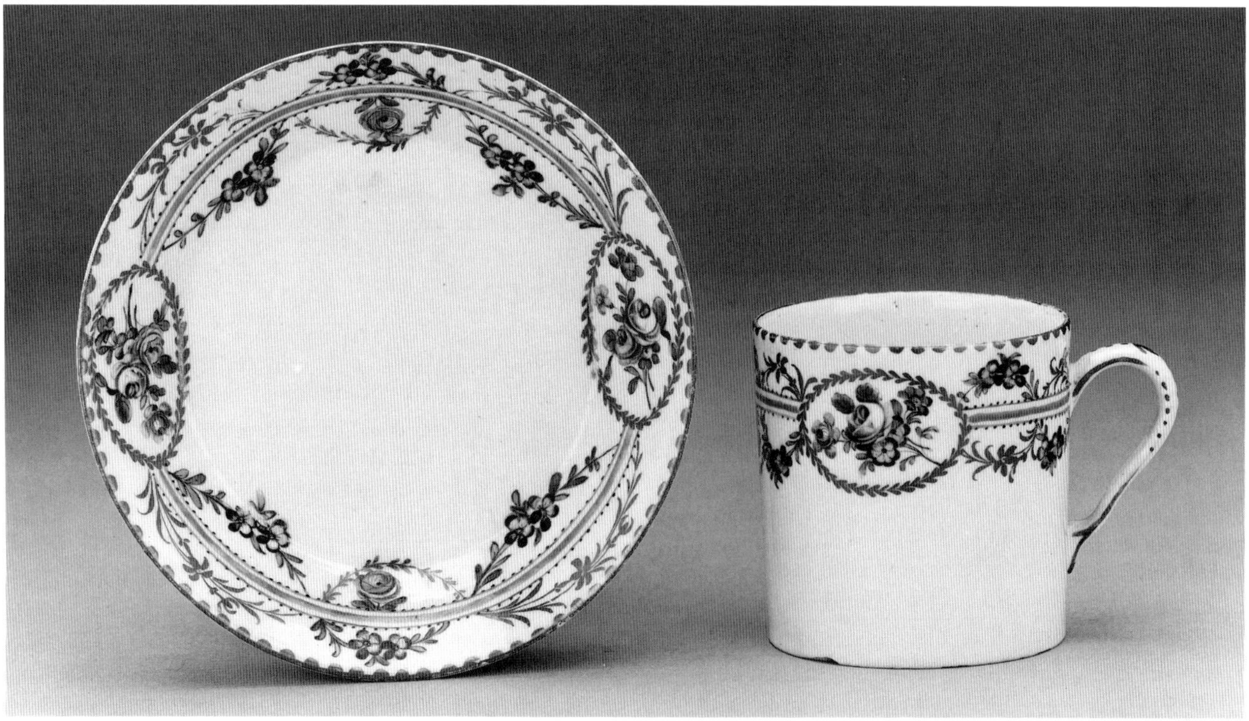

278

handle. Painted in pink, orange-red, yellow, purple, blue, green and grey around the border with two flower sprays within a gilt leaf chain and with violas alternating with a rose entwined around a pink and blue ribbon; gilt stylised leaves near rim, gilt, dentil design around rim. Rim of saucer repaired.

Provenance: Bequeathed by Sir A.W. Franks, 1897

Literature: Unpublished

Comparable Examples: None

The quality of the porcelain is poor, despite its whiteness: there are numerous inclusions, the glaze is unevenly applied in places and the foot rim of the saucer is gritty and has apparently been damaged during the manufacturing process. The decoration is rather crudely painted.

Potter and Blancheron's factory, later *Blancheron,*

rue de Crussol (1790–8), rue des Trois Bornes (1798–1802)[1]

In 1789 Christopher Potter, an Englishman,[2] requested a privilege for seven years to set up a concern to paint and print on glass, porcelain and faïence. Despite the support of the Académie des Sciences and the personal intervention of Jean-Sylvain Bailly, President of the Assemblée Nationale, the privilege was refused. In 1790 Potter was nevertheless in business at premises in the rue de Crussol,[3] apparently under the patronage of the Prince of Wales.[4] He ordered clay from Alluaud of Limoges on 12 September 1790[5] and so must have been in production by this time. In February 1792 he enlarged his premises, which originally consisted only of two workshops and a shed in one building, to include a second structure containing a coach house (*remise*) with nine rooms above it and a loft, as well as another shed.[6] On 28 January 1793 he ceded the lease of the buildings in rue de Crussol to Jacques Bernard Balan, and on 8 February sold up entirely. Balan was the intermediary of Etienne Jean Louis Blancheron, who had been the director of the factory since its establishment, and who purchased it on 2 March 1794. He in turn sold up on 5 November 1797.[7]

A list of the items sold by Potter to Blancheron on 8 February 1793[8] shows that three grades of porcelain were made. Table-services, toilet articles, candelabra, tobacco boxes, buttons and clocks were amongst the products. Flower, landscape, butterfly, animal, bird and figure decoration were in use.

In 1798 Blancheron moved to the rue des Trois Bornes, where he remained until 1802. Despite making heavy losses, Blancheron operated until his bankruptcy in 1802 with one kiln and three muffle-kilns for enamelling. He made tablewares and even, possibly, a clock 'designée sous le nom de l'amour', for which eleven moulds were inventoried in May 1802 by Christophe Russinger.[9] In a letter to Alluaud at Limoges (who presumably supplied Blancheron with clay), he referred to his five throwers 'who did the work of eight'.[10] The few details known about

Blancheron indicate production on a considerable scale. His wares were known even in America: a cup and saucer in the White House Collection, Washington, DC, seems to have been purchased by James Monroe during his period as American Minister to France from 1794 to 1796. It was sold to the Madisons in 1803.[11]

1. This account is based on Guillebon, 1972, p. 202, and pp. 272–3; see also Guillebon, 1985, pp. 89–93, 141–3.
2. Potter (d. 1817) who probably came from the same family as his namesake (1591–1646), Vice-Chancellor of the University of Oxford and a leading Arminian, became owner of a Cambridgeshire estate in 1777 where he cultivated woad and made dyes. After acting as a leading victualling contractor in the American War of Independence, he tried in 1780, 1781 and 1784 to gain a seat in Parliament. In 1781 he was returned for Colchester but was unseated on petition for corrupt practices. In 1784 he was unseated on the grounds of having been declared bankrupt and having no property qualification, and although he appealed successfully was subsequently defeated. In 1789 he settled in Paris. In 1792 he bought the Chantilly factory from Antheaume de Surval, and established other factories at Forges and Montereau. In January 1793 he was in England on the evidence of a letter to William Duesbury, owner of the Derby porcelain factory, from R. Roe, mentioning a meeting between Potter and 'Dr Johnson' (not Samuel Johnson), published by J.V.G. Mallet, 'Johnson and Porcelain Manufacture', *Journal of the Royal Society of Arts*, August 1985, pp. 626–7. In 1793 he was imprisoned in Beauvais and Chantilly and in 1796 offered a bribe from Barras to Lord Malmesbury to conclude peace. In 1798 and 1802 he was oustandingly successful at Industrial Exhibitions held in Paris. These details are taken from the *Dictionary of National Biography*, entry by J.G. Alger.
3. The topography of rue de Crussol, built in 1782, is discussed by Guillebon, 1983, pp. 16–19, and that of the rue des Trois Bornes in Guillebon, 1985, p. 143.
4. Guillebon, 1972, p. 272; Guillebon, 1983, p. 17, f.n. 103 quotes Archives départementales de la Haute-Vienne, C 2994, f. 132 *et. seq.*, but the question of how this patronage operated on foreign soil has not been explored.
5. Guillebon, 1985, p. 89, f.n. 238, quoting *ibid.*
6. Guillebon, 1983, p. 17.
7. Guillebon, 1985, pp. 89–90.
8. Guillebon, 1985, p. 91, f.n. 268, quoting Archives nationales, Minutier central, *Etude* CXVII, *liasse* 965, 8 février 1793 (M° Delamotte).
9. Guillebon, 1985, p. 142, f.n. 907, quoting Archives nationales, Minutier central, *Etude* XXII, *liasse* 163, 23 Germinal l'an X (13 April 1802), M° Camusat.
10. *Ibid.*, f.n. 905, quoting Archives départementales de la Haute-Vienne, Z 18, letter from Blancheron to Alluaud, 11 Pluviôse l'an X (31 January 1802).
11. See Detweiler, *French Porcelain*, 1982, p. 95, cup and saucer marked *EB* in gold/iron-red; gilt monogram *M* apparently applied later after a drawing by Dolley Madison, illus. p. 96, fig. 9.

---

279 Teabowl and Saucer, *c.*1794

D. *of saucer:* 13.7 cm
H. *of cup:* 6 cm
Marks: *PB* painted in underglaze-blue on saucer; *Potter* above *42* surmounted by *B* painted in underglaze-blue on cup
Reg. No. Franks 435

Hard-paste porcelain; deep saucer with curved rim, thickly potted; trumpet-shaped cup with flared foot, highly translucent. The decoration consists of a gilt border pattern of stylised leaves and flowers depending from a zigzag line enclosing a leaf motif; gilt rims, foot of cup gilt, gilt line around edge of border of saucer and one enclosing the central scene of a putto painted *en grisaille* on a mauve ground. On the saucer the putto symbolises Music and plays a lute; on the cup he holds a palette and brushes in his left hand and paints a picture with his right, to symbolise Painting.

Provenance: Bequeathed by Sir A.W. Franks, 1897

Literature: Franks, 1896, no. 435

Guillebon, 1972, fig. 238

Comparable Examples: London, Victoria and Albert Museum, teabowl and saucer, butterfly decoration, same mark, inv. C.79–1909

The decoration on this cup and saucer, which is of high quality, has much in common with allegorical cartouches after Boucher in fashion at the Sèvres fac-

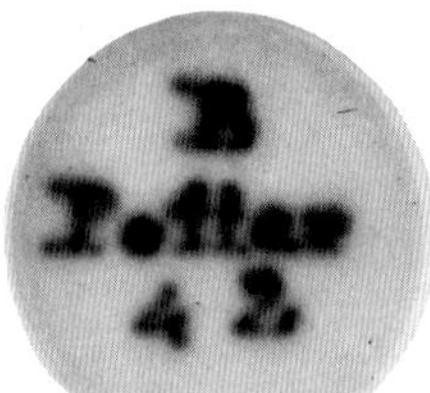

279 *mark (teabowl)*

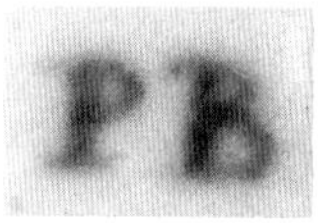

279 *mark (saucer)*

tory at least two decades earlier. The colour scheme, however, is typical of the end of the century.

The significance of the number *42* beneath the mark has not been discovered. It may be a painter's mark, or an internal factory mark.

280 Cup and Saucer (*tasse litron et soucoupe*), late 18th century

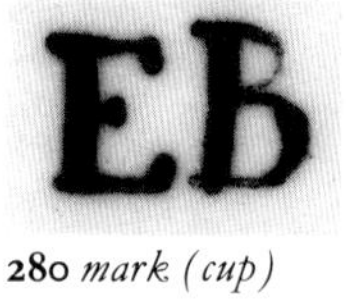

280 *mark (cup)*

D. *of saucer:* 14.6 cm
H. *of cup:* 7.4 cm
Marks: *EB* painted in underglaze-blue on both
Reg. No. Franks 436

Hard-paste porcelain, highly translucent, deep saucer with flared sides, straight-sided cup, ear-shaped handle terminating in out-

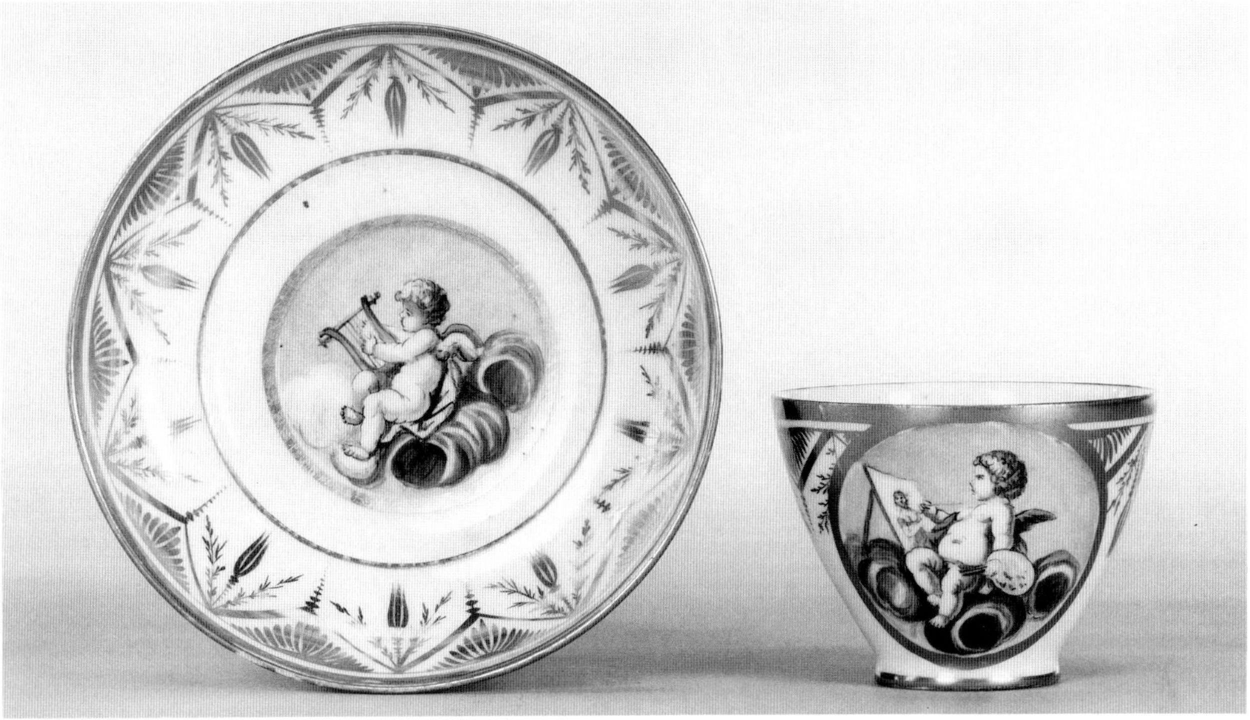

279

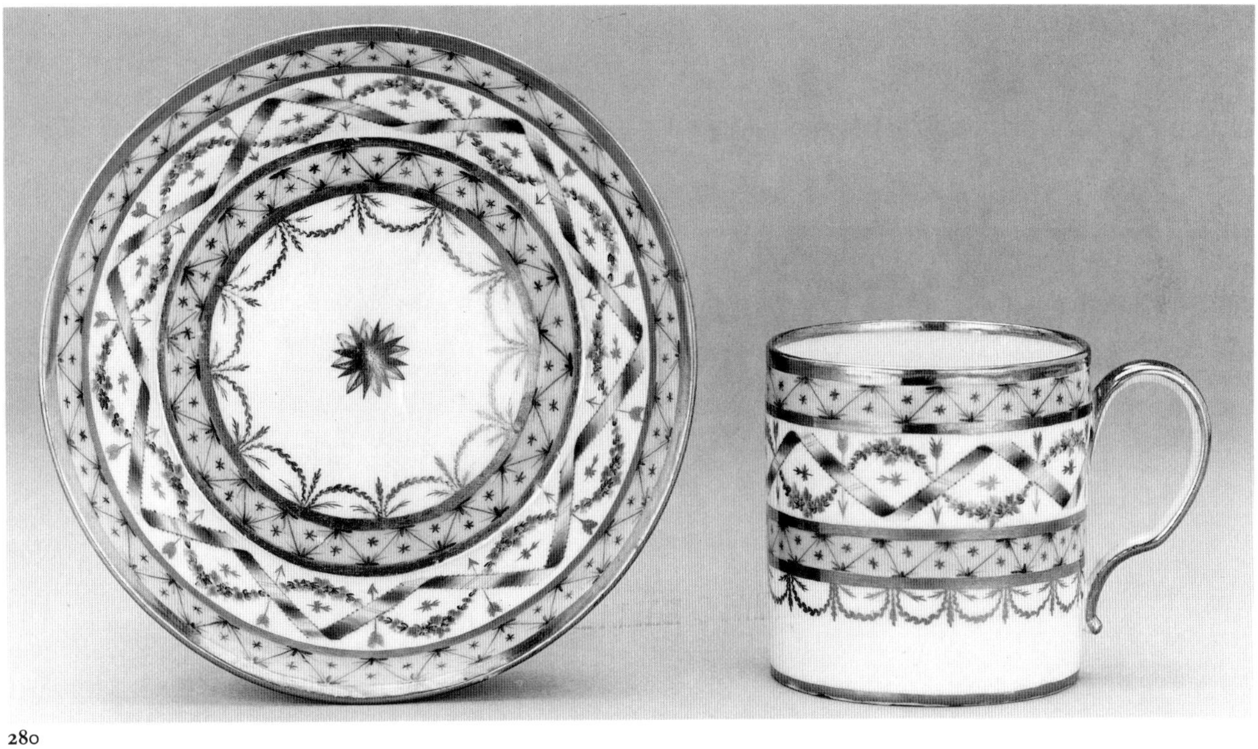

280

turned 'kick'. The decoration consists of pendent gilt stylised leaves, two bands of a purple star and diaper pattern on a yellow ground, enclosing a wider band with a pink zigzag ribbon and orange flower garland design. Rims and handle gilt; gilt star in centre of saucer. Handle repaired. Chip to foot of cup. Saucer cracked.

Provenance: Bequeathed by Sir A.W. Franks, 1897

Literature: Franks, 1896, no. 436

Comparable Examples: None

The porcelain is of poor quality, despite its translucency. The pattern is perhaps based on a textile design.

Chevalier Brothers' factory,
rue de la Pépinière[1]

On 18 February 1793 the following advertisement appeared in *Annonces Particulières*, no. 49:[2] 'La manufacture de porcelaines établie rue de la Pépinière, Faubourg Saint-Honoré, no. 560. sera ouverte le 20 février 1793. La beauté de cette manufacture ne laisse rien à désirer, tant pour l'élégance et la partie des formes, que pour la peinture et la dorure'. The concern was established by Pierre César Chevalier, who had been 'entrepreneur des peintures du ci-devant Monsieur', and his brother Jacques Léopold, also a painter. It has been suggested[3] that both these men may have been house-painters, as they have not been traced as artists, but this seems unlikely. Records of orders of clay from Alluaud of Limoges dating back to 20 August 1792[4] indicate that the factory may have been in existence some time before its opening was publicly announced. In a denunciation made on 10 February 1794, Pierre César was accused of having trade contacts with the English as well as with St Petersburg during 1792.

On 30 April 1793 the brothers were referred to as 'manufacturiers de porcelaine demeurant rue de la Pépinière' in the lease on a building they rented as a boutique 'd'une maison établie sur les terrains du ci-devant hôpital des Quinze-Vingt'. Between August 1793 and 22 June 1794 orders of clay from Alluaud were sent to 'Chevalier et Hubert', but the identity of the latter remains unknown. In l'an II (1793–4) a certain Daudin, or Dodin, is mentioned in the journal of the porcelain-maker Guy[5] as being the director of the concern.

The Chevalier brothers were also involved in trafficking in specie through Alluaud of Limoges, who was the director of the Mint in that town. On 3 July 1795 they put in a bid to acquire the royal porcelain factory at Limoges, which was considered by Benezech, Minister of the Interior. However, they were unsuccessful and the concern was sold to natives of Limoges. Despite this they continued to obtain clay from Alluaud until at least as late as 26 June 1798.[6] In 1799 Alluaud sent a debt collector to various Paris porcelain factories, including Chevalier. On 3 September the Chevalier brothers were found to be insolvent, even though some of their consignments of clay had cost as much as 30,000 *livres* in the preceding period.[7] In the following year, on 26 August, the building occupied by the Chevalier brothers was taken over by Jacques Fourmy.[8]

The factory never seems to have registered a mark. The Museum tray (cat. 281) is the only piece known to bear the mark in gold *chevalier a paris*, and matches the cup and saucer (cat. 281) which bear only the letters *CH* in gold. A few pieces with this mark have been traced,[9] most with similar decoration of scenes based on paintings or engravings by David Teniers the Younger. Nothing is known about the factory's workforce, or about the prices charged for the products.

1. This account is based on Guillebon, 1985, pp. 112–6.
2. *Op. cit.*, pp. 112–13, quoting A. Lesur and Tardy, *La Porcelaine Française*, Paris, 1967, p. 346.
3. *Op. cit.*, p. 112.
4. *Ibid.*, quoting Archives départementales de la Haute-Vienne, Limoges, C 2994, f. 157v.
5. *Op. cit.*, p. 113, quoting Archives de la ville de Paris, D. 5 B6 2566.
6. *Ibid.*, quoting Archives départementales de la Haute-Vienne, Limoges, L 1205.
7. *Ibid.*, quoting L 1199.
8. *Ibid.*

9. Macdonald, 1986, no. 105, teapot and cover, inv. 1980.237; teapot in a private collection, Great Britain, also decorated with Teniers scenes; Guillebon, 1972, p. 147, fig. 113, ice-cream cooler decorated to simulate marble, Musée national de Céramique, Sèvres.

281 Tea Set: Tray, Sugar Bowl and Cover, Teapot and Cover, Milk Jug, Cup and Saucer, 1793–*c.*1799

See colour plate 41

L. *of tray:*	24.9 cm
H. *of sugar-bowl (to top of finial):*	12.1 cm
H. *of teapot (to top of finial):*	13.1 cm
H. *of milk jug (to top of handle):*	14.2 cm
H. *of cup:*	6.3 cm
D. *of saucer:*	12.7 cm
Marks:	*CH* in gold on cup, sugar bowl, teapot, jug; *chevalier a paris* in gold on unglazed base of tray
Reg. No.	Franks 434 (cup and saucer); 1985,1–3,1 (tray), 2 (sugar bowl), 3 (teapot), 4 (jug)

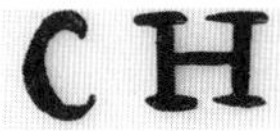

281 *mark (cup)*

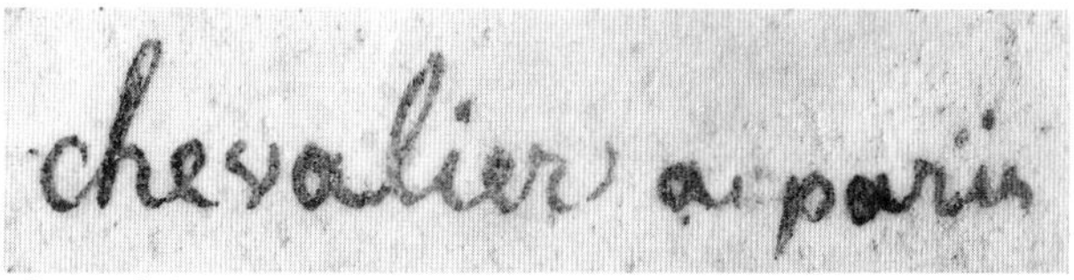

281 *mark (tray)*

Hard-paste porcelain, moulded. The tray is square with flared sides and shaped corners; the sugar bowl conical with two rudimentary ring handles, a domed cover and onion-shaped knop; the teapot straight-sided with inverted shoulder, scroll handle, curved spout, domed cover with two lugs and onion-shaped knop; the jug with a pear-shaped body and high strap handle, cup and saucer of *litron* form. The decoration of peasants making merry in a landscape is painted in brown, blue, mauve, yellow, green and black on an orange ground between black bands interrupted by gilt stars. Gilt foliate motif in centre of tray (repeated on saucer), which is also embellished with gilt stars. Tray restored, handle and lip of jug restored, knop of sugar bowl restuck, spout

281

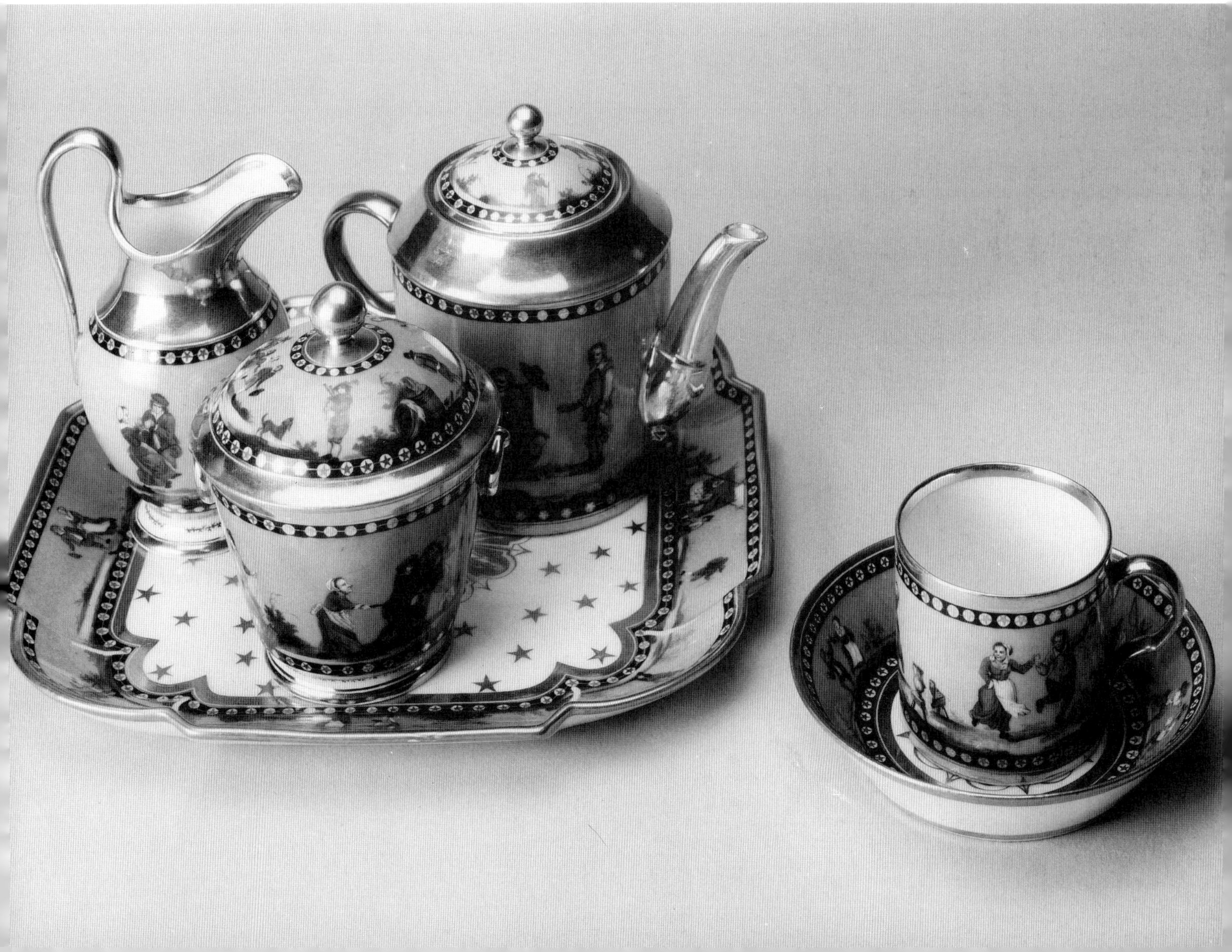

of teapot restored. Gilt rims, knops, handles, upper part of jug and teapot gilt.

Provenance: Bequeathed by Sir A.W. Franks, 1897 (cup and saucer); purchased, 1985

Literature: Franks, 1896, no. 434

Guillebon, 1972, p. 150, fig. 115

Macdonald, 1986, p. 61

Comparable Examples: Manchester City Art Galleries, inv. 1980.237, teapot and cover of similar but not identical form, marked *CH* in gold (see above)

England, private collection, cup and saucer, marked *CH* in gold (with matching tray, whereabouts unknown)

London, Anton Kristensen (1985), tray, teapot and cover, milk jug, sugar bowl and cover, water jug and cover on three feet, two cups and saucers, painted with *grisaille* figures scenes on a gold striped ground, *CH* mark

The Manchester teapot has a gallery above the shoulder and is slightly smaller, but its decoration is related to that on the tea set. The gilt pattern on the rim of the cup and saucer in a private English collection is the same as on the Manchester teapot and the painted decoration is in a similar style and palette. The dancing couple on this saucer reappear on the Museum cup, in a slightly different colouring.

The scenes on the Museum pieces are based on a painting by David Teniers the Younger called *Feste de Village*, engraved by J.-P. Le Bas.[1] Parts of this scene were used by at least three different Sèvres painters from as early as 1760, and it appears on the famous gold box commissioned by the duc de Choiseul in 1770.[2]

The shapes of the pieces do not conform exactly to those manufactured at other Paris concerns, such as Nast.

The tray is not large enough to hold each piece, and was presumably intended for the teapot, sugar bowl and jug only, whilst the cup and saucer were in use.

1. Engraving in Department of Prints and Drawings, BM, 1850–7–13–55.
2. Sassoon, 1991, p. 72; engraving reproduced p. 77.

Marc Schoelcher's factory, faubourg Saint-Denis[1]

Marc Schoelcher (1766–1832), a native of Fessenheim (Haut-Rhin) in Alsace, came to Paris in about 1789. He probably initially worked for Laurent Russinger at the porcelain factory in the rue de la Fontaine-au-Roi.[2] Before establishing his own factory he was in business as a porcelain merchant in the rue de la Monnaie. On 29 March 1798 (9 Floréal l'an VI) he purchased the existing porcelain factory in the faubourg Saint-Denis (see comte d'Artois' factory, page 350), paying the Benjamin family 35,000 francs 'en espèces sonnantes d'or ou d'argent' for various buildings and land on a site now adjacent to the Gare de l'Est.[3]

Schoelcher was in production for around a decade. A billhead of May 1803 shows that he made table- and dessert-services, *cabarets*, vases, biscuit figures and groups, and clocks, 'et tout qui concerne la chimie et le limonadier à l'instar de Chantilly . . .'.[4] Coloured grounds, such as tortoise-shell, agate, blue, brown and even green grounds, were made. Several interesting cup shapes have been traced.[5] The work of painters such as Isabey, Vernet and Devéria, and of engravers such as Janinet and Louis and Garneray, was copied to decorate some of the more luxurious productions.[6]

In 1806 Schoelcher rented a retail outlet on the boulevard des Italiens,[7] where he also sold porcelain from other concerns, especially from Fleury's factory, also situated in the faubourg Saint-Denis. In about 1810 Marc Schoelcher ceased to make porcelain. From this time the firm merely decorated blanks. However, in the *Annales de l'industrie*, 1820, an account of the Louvre Exhibition in the previous year mentions him as a 'fabricant de porcelaine à Paris, boulevard des Italiens au coin de la rue Grange-Batelière'. His products were praised for the beauty of their forms, the vivacity of their colours and the elegance of their ornaments. The factory, described as one of the largest in Paris, was given a silver medal. In 1820 it went under the name 'Manufacture de Monsieur [i.e the King's brother, whose title was duc d'Artois] et Madame la Duchesse de Berry'.[8] On 21 August 1823 Madame Schoelcher, who had owned the buildings in the faubourg Saint-Denis since her separation from her husband in 1806, sold up. Her son Victor, best known as a politician, ceased to trade entirely in 1834.

Little is known about the employees of this factory. A Monsieur Roger, whose forename remains unknown, is recorded as its director in May 1798.[9] A scene on a stand forming part of an *écuelle et plateau* now in the Palacio Nacional de Quéluz near Lisbon is signed *Freund*,[10] but this painter may have worked outside the factory.

1. This account is based on R. de Plinval-Salgues, 'Les Schoelcher et la porcelaine Paris 1798–1834', *Cahiers*, no. 6, (1957), pp. 52–67 and Guillebon, 1985, p. 93–8.
2. Marc Schoelcher was born on 26 April 1766, the son of Jean-Baptiste Schoelcher, a *cultivateur*, and his wife Jeanne Hoffmann, see Guillebon, 1985, p. 94, f.n. 313,314. His mother was related to Christiana Caritas Hoffmann. Laurent Russinger (*qv*) and his son Christophe were witnesses at the marriage of Schoelcher and Victoire Jacob on 20 June 1796.
3. The topography of the factory is discussed by Guillebon, 1985, pp. 97–8. A plan of the factory is shown on pl. LXXXI, fig. 114 and another on pl. LXXXII, fig. 115.
4. Chavagnac and Grollier, 1906, p. 485.
5. Plinval-Salgues, 1957, p. 57, figs. 9–14.
6. *Ibid.*, p. 59, fig. 17; col. pl. opp. p. 52; p. 53, fig. 4; p. 60, fig. 19.
7. The shop is shown in *La promenade parisienne*, illus. by Guillebon, 1972, p. 35, fig. 25. A plan of the shop in a dossier dated 19 March 1816, Archives nationales, Minutier central, *Etude* LXIX, is illus. by Guillebon, 1985, pl. XCII, fig. 126.
8. Two bill-heads showing the names of Monsieur and the duchesse de Berry in the Bibliothèque de l'Institut d'art et d'archéologie, Paris, are illustrated by Guillebon, 1972, p. 162, fig. 125, p. 163, fig. 126. Chavagnac, 1906, p. 485, states that the factory enjoyed royal patronage in 1820, but gives no source for this; it is presumably the *Annales de l'industrie*, 1820, which the author has not seen.
9. Guillebon, 1985, p. 82.
10. Illus. by Guillebon, 1972, pp. 38–40, figs. 27–9.

282 Gravy Pot and Cover (*pot à jus et son couvercle*), *c.*1810

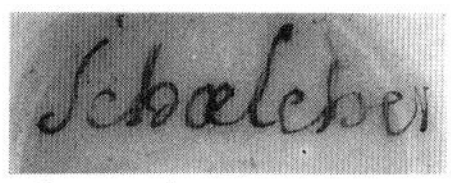

282 *mark*

H. incl. cover: 9.8 cm
Mark: *Schoelcher* painted in script in orange-red overglaze
Reg. No. FB 19 (AF 3221)

Hard-paste porcelain, highly translucent; of conical form with stepped turned base and circular hollow foot; angular handle. The rim is unglazed and discoloured. The domed cover is surmounted by a pine-cone shaped knop (replacement). Painted with stylised roses and leaves in matt green and black, and in matt and tooled gold. The foot, lower part of cup, handle and rims are gilt. There is a manufacturing fault on the exterior of the foot, disguised by gilding.

Provenance: Bequeathed by Sir A.W. Franks, 1897

Literature: Unpublished

Comparable Examples: Sèvres, Musée national de Céramique, inv. MNCS 14602, illus. Guillebon, 1985, pl. XXVI, fig. 41

Pots such as this were probably sold in sets with a matching tray, for meat juices.

The rather severe decorative scheme is typical of the early nineteenth century.

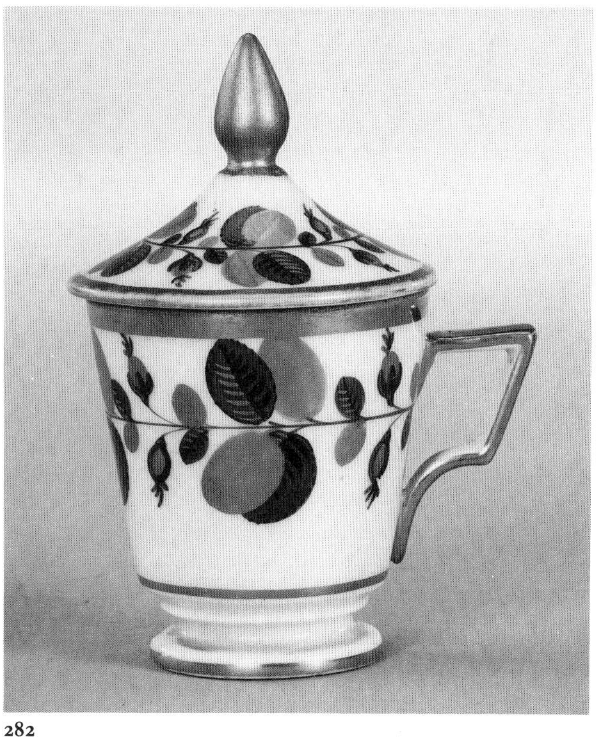

282

Dagoty's factory,
rue de Chevreuse[1]

In April 1800 Pierre-Louis (1771–1840) and Etienne-Jean-Baptiste Dagoty (1772–1800) acquired a nine-year lease on the porcelain factory which had been in operation between 1795 and 1797 under the ownership of Roger and Bougon.[2] The premises at 1586 rue de Chevreuse, faubourg Montparnasse, were extensive,[3] consisting of two large buildings of several storeys with cellars and attics, a courtyard, and gardens. The three Dagoty brothers (the third, Isidore, died in 1800 and played no part in the factory) had worked for Guérhard and Dihl after the early death of their father,[4] and then set up as decorators in the boulevard des Italiens. Papers among Etienne's effects include a sales register started in December 1797 and a list of outgoings from September/October 1799, indicating that the Dagotys were manufacturing porcelain shortly before the deeds to their property were signed. This seems likely, as a service was supplied to Maximilian Joseph of Bavaria in 1800.[5]

From 1804 Pierre-Louis Dagoty was the sole owner of the concern, as his brother's son disposed of his interest in August of that year. In May 1807 the lease was renewed for a further nine years, despite the uncertain nature of trade. In March Dagoty had been granted a loan of no less than 80,000 francs to sustain the factory, which had suffered the loss of its export trade to Northern Europe, especially St Petersburg and Moscow, as a consequence of war. The factory was already under the protection of the Empress Josephine, and had supplied porcelain for the palaces of Versailles and Compiègne.[6] Although Dagoty only took up 30,000 francs of the loan he was unable to pay off the interest until 1811.

On 1 January 1816 Dagoty went into partnership with François-Maurice Honoré's son, Edouard. The rue de Chevreuse factory was united with Honoré's factory in the petite rue neuve Saint-Gilles, another concern at Saint-Yrieix (Limoges) and a retail outlet in the boulevard Poissonnière.[7] This partnership was dissolved in 1820. Dagoty kept the Saint-Yrieix factory, selling it three years later to Dominique Deruelle.

Dagoty's own shop in the boulevard Montmartre was stocked with a wide range of porcelains designed to appeal to the fashionable world. It is described in some detail in Tristant l'Hermitte's account of Paris in 1811: fine table-services 'qui unissent à l'élégance des formes la beauté des couleurs et le fini des peintures', vases costing 100 *louis*, elegant and complex coffee-making equipment, and chimney-ornaments in questionable taste.[8] Some pieces were less expensive, such as plates decorated with the initial *N* surmounted by the Imperial crown sold to the Sèvres Museum for 50 francs a dozen in 1804.[9]

The products of the factory were invariably of high quality, although the extravagance of the forms and the combination of lavish gilding and biscuit porcelain, especially when used for cups and saucers, was not always artistically successful. A pattern-book or *Recueil de modèles de porcelaine peinte et dorée de la manufacture de Dagoty et Honoré*[10] illustrates handles of cups and spouts of teapots formed of bird or winged serpent heads, designs which were certainly put into production as several surviving examples show.[11] They appear to be characteristic of this factory. So also are some particularly attractive ground colours, including a matt pale blue[12] and a red lacquer ground colour used to great effect with gold *chinoiseries*.[13] Landscape scenes in the Flemish style,[14] classical figures based on those discovered at Herculaneum and Pompeii,[15] La Fontaine fables[16] and sepia scenes of Prince Czartoryski's Polish residences after Jean-Pierre Norblin de la Gourdaine[17] are amongst the wide repertoire of decoration found on Dagoty's wares. Biscuit busts of the duc de Berry and of Louis XVIII (H. 20 cm) marked *Dagoty et Honoré à Paris* on gilt drum-shaped pedestals are recorded.[18]

Rich decoration required a large staff. When Dagoty requested a loan in 1807 he stated that he employed one hundred workers. A police report of 1807 stated that there were ninety workers, and that the annual output was worth 300,000 francs, making it the second most productive of eight factories for which figures were available.[19] Economic problems had reduced the workforce to fifty-six by 1810.[20]

The inventory taken in 1804[21] shows the extent of the factory buildings, which included a large number of workshops. Three large sheds housed kiln furniture (*cazettes* or saggars), a muffle-kiln, the laboratory and the stables. One *atelier* may have stored finished items as it was fitted with shelves and mirrors; throwers occupied two further workshops; a casting shop also contained 'un four de six pieds . . . garni de ses rondins de fer'. Further workshops were provided for the painters, for the preparation of the porcelain body, for making *cazettes*, for six muffle-kilns of differing sizes and for a *cabinet de chimie*. A report of 1810[22] mentions that Dagoty employed five throwers, eighteen painters and gilders, four burnishers (usually women) and in addition had several workers who prepared the clays: a *marcheur de terre*, a *batteur de pâte* ('wedger') and a *chef des pâtes*, who was responsible for the raw materials (apart from colours and gold). In August 1804 Robert Lévy is recorded as the technical director of the factory, but no other names of personnel are known.

1. This account is based on Guillebon, 1985, *passim* and especially pp. 82–5.
2. Guillebon, 1989, p. 82.
3. For the topography of the factory, see *ibid.*, pp. 84–5. In 1821 the total surface occupied by the factory was 2,428 square metres. A plan by Vasserot of the quartier du Luxembourg shows the position of the factory, illus. pl. LXXIX, fig. 112, Archives nationales, F[31] 93. The building still exists as it was in 1821. Further information is given in Guillebon, 1983, pp. 19–24.
4. Jean-Baptiste-André Dagoty (1740–86) was an engraver and was the son of the painter, engraver and naturalist, Jean-Fabien Gautier Dagoty (or d'Agoty) (1710–81). His *Histoire naturelle ou Exposition générale de toutes ses parties gravées et imprimées en couleurs naturelles; avec des notes historiques*, published at Paris, 1781, is in the British Library.
5. The service survives in the Royal Palace, Munich, Guillebon, 1985, p. 60.
6. Guillebon, 1985, p. 22 and f.n. 140; Dagoty supplied porcelain to the value of 20,716 francs for the palaces, according to a list dated 9 July 1807, Archives nationales F[12] 1559.
7. For a bill-head [?] issued by the Manufacture de Porcelaine de S.M. L'Impératrice from the Boutique de Mr Dagoty, Boulevard Poissonnière, no. 4, see Guillebon, 1972, p. 175, fig. 137.
8. Guillebon, 1985, p. 84, quoting Jouy, *L'Hermite de la Chaussée d'Antin ou observations sur les moeurs et les usages parisiens au commencement du XIXème siècle*, Paris, 1814, Vol. I, p. 25, 31 août 1811.
9. *Ibid.*, p. 53, quoting Musée national de Céramique, *Registre d'entrée*, inv. 317–3.
10. Illus. Guillebon, 1972, p. 154, fig. 117; further cups are shown in colour, p. 157, fig. 120; pattern-book in the Library, Musée des arts décoratifs, Paris, partly published by S. Messinger, *Les carnets des tasses, aquarelles*, Paris, 1991.
11. Eriksen, 1973, no. 85, coffee-service from the collections of the Grand Duchy of Tuscany.
12. Guillebon, 1972, p. 161, fig. 124, col. illus. showing this colour used for Herculaneum figure decoration on a *cabaret* in the Musée Ariana, Geneva.
13. *Ibid.*, p. 165, fig. 130, cup and saucer form Musée national de Malmaison.
14. Eriksen, 1973, no. 92.
15. *Ibid.*, no. 89; a tea service on a tray with four paw feet painted with Pompeian subjects on a black ground from the Jacques Kugel Collection, Paris, is illus. by Bloit, 1988, p. 73.
16. Eriksen, 1973, no. 83, coffee service, col. ill. opp. p. 18.
17. Guillebon, 1985, pl. XLV, figs. 65 (drawing dated 1802), 66, one of twelve plates dated 1802 and 1804. Krakow, National Museum, Czartoryski Collection.
18. Christie's, 3 July 1989, Lot 49; another of Eugène de Beauharnais was sold in the same rooms, 13 March 1989, Lot 25.
19. Guillebon, 1985, p. 14.
20. *Ibid.*, p. 23.
21. *Ibid.*, p. 85, quoting Archives nationales, Minutier central, *Etude* V, *liasse* 878, 13 Frimaire l'an IX (4 December 1804), Me Vingtain.
22. *Ibid.*, p. 25, quoting MNS, Archives de Sèvres, U 19, *liasse* 3.

283 **Plate**, *c.*1810–15

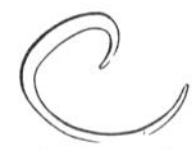

283 *mark*

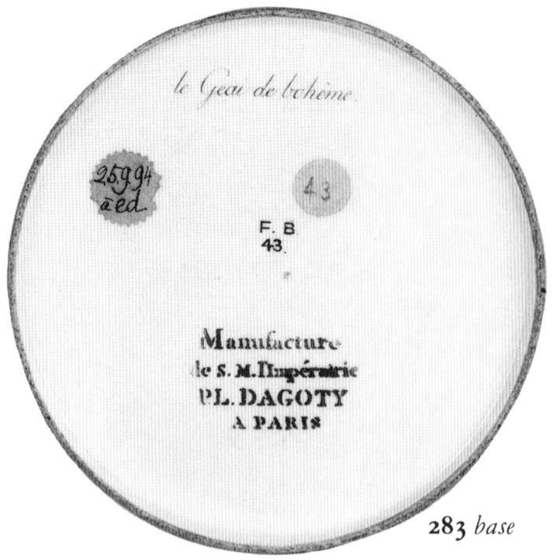

283 *base*

D. 22 cm
Marks: *Manufacture/de S.M. Impériale/P.L. DAGOTY/A PARIS* stencilled in red; *C* or *D* incised; paper label inscribed in ink *25.9.94/à ed*
Reg. No. FB 43 (AF 3242)

Hard-paste porcelain. Painted in the centre on a white ground with *le Geai de bohême* (title inscribed in red on reverse of plate) on a mound facing left with a butterfly at the right in yellow, orange-red, black, three different colours of brown, pink, and green. The border is painted matt powder blue. Gilt decoration of palmettes and scrolls between gilt bands on rim, well bordered by a fine gilt line next to a broader band. Single stilt mark in centre of base.

Provenance: Bequeathed by Sir A.W. Franks, 1897

Literature: Unpublished

Comparable Examples: Italy, Florence, Pitti Palace, matt green border, painted with *Faisan de la Chine*, see A. d'Agliano *et al.*, *Porcellane dell'Ottocento a Palazzo Pitti, Nineteenth Century Porcelain in Palazzo Pitti*, Florence, 1983, cat. 3

This plate was probably part of a set. The source of the decoration has not yet been discovered: it does not appear to be based on any illustration in Buffon's *Histoire Naturelle des Oiseaux*.

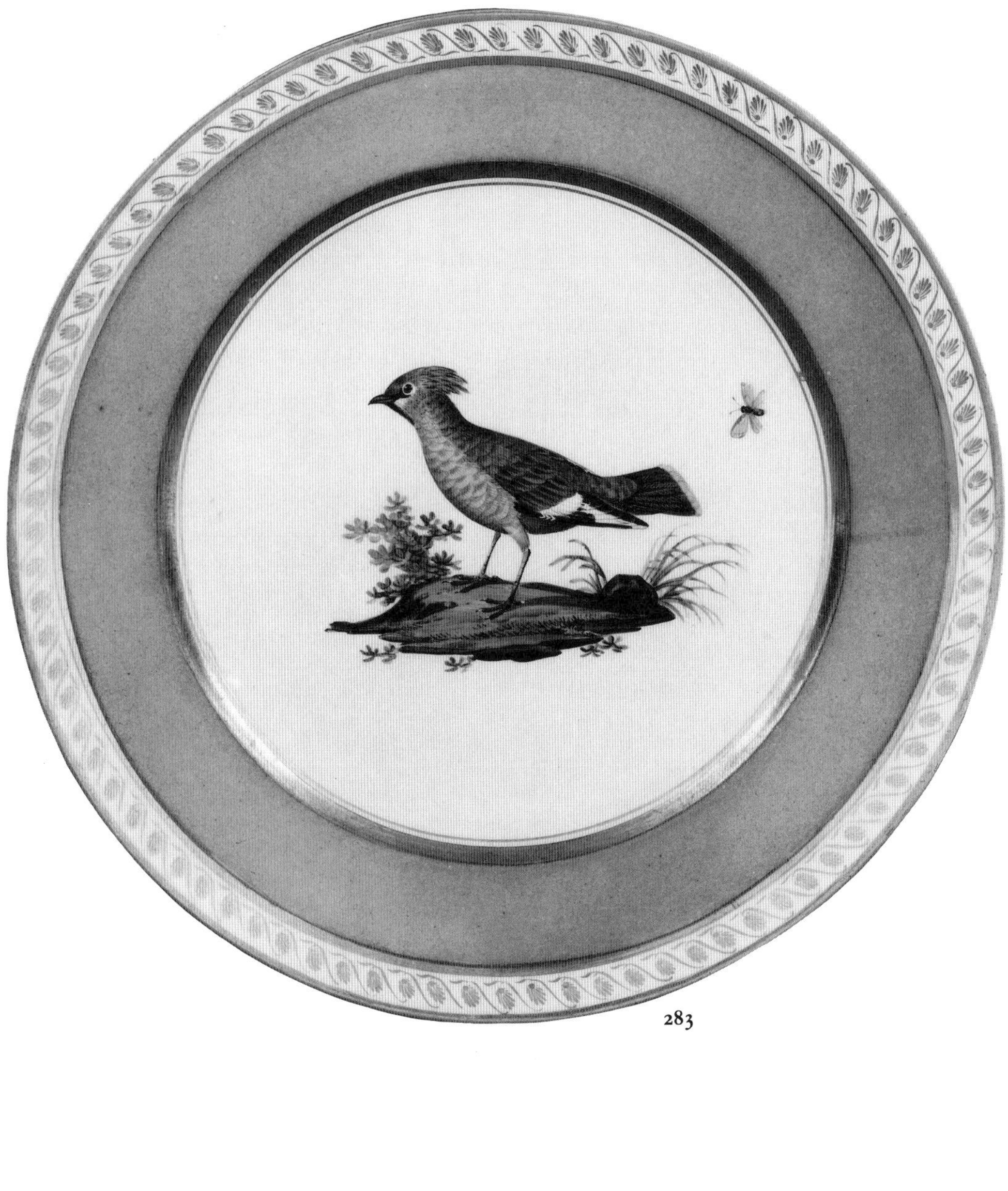

283

Darte Brothers' factory,
rue de la Roquette and Palais Royal[1]

Louis-Joseph (1765–1843) and Jean-François Darte (*c.*1768–1834) were initially in partnership with their brother Joseph (dates unknown) at a porcelain factory at 3 rue de Charonne which they established on 3 Floréal l'an III (22 April 1795). By 13 Thermidor l'an XI (1 August 1803) they had begun the process of separation. After 12 Messidor l'an XII (1 July 1804) there were two porcelain manufacturing businesses under the name of Darte. On 12 June 1808 Louis-Joseph and Jean-François set up a partnership called *Darte frères*. Production took place at 90 rue de la Roquette, faubourg Saint-Antoine, in a building known as the hôtel Montalembert, which the brothers had acquired as a *bien national* on 26 May 1804. Several views of the building can be seen on a tripod bowl now in the Musée national de Céramique, Sèvres.[2] The firm's retail outlet was in the so-called Galerie de Pierre in the Palais du Tribunal, from 1809 known under its pre-Revolutionary name of Palais Royal.[3] In the same year the factory obtained the protection of the Emperor's mother, adopting the title of 'Manufacture de porcelaine de S.A.I. Madame Mère de S.M.I. l'Empereur et Roi'. In July 1824 Louis-Joseph Darte took into partnership his son Auguste Rémi, but this was dissolved a year later. On 26 September 1828 Louis-Joseph was declared bankrupt, although he was trading between April 1829 and around 1833.

Surviving pieces from the Darte brothers' factory are of high quality. The firm gained a silver medal at the 1806 Industrial Exhibition for its domestic wares as well as for its unusually large pieces decorated by Dagoty or Caron. A second silver medal was awarded to the firm at the 1819 exhibition, for pieces of exceptional size and for the beauty of their colours. Plates painted with copies of Old Masters[4] or with fruit, flowers or birds, with richly gilt border patterns on a dark blue ground, are characteristic of the factory.[5]

Some idea of prices charged can be gained from two bills which have been published, which are unfortunately undated. The first is to Monsieur Flandin and was made out before the abandonment of the Revolutionary calendar (ie before 1805), as it is headed '12 Fructidor' (no year given). Twelve pairs of tea cups *nouvelle forme* were 2 *livres* 5 *sols* the pair, two coffee-pots of the third size cost 6 *livres*, one *thaier* [sic] *Ronde forme annulaire* was 5 *livres*, oval cups of the second size were 5 *livres*, oval cups of the new shape were 4 *livres*, cream-pots of the new shape were 3 *livres* 10 *sols* each, 'ordinary' ones cost 10 *sols* less, and in a smaller size were 2 *livres* 10 *sols* and sugar bowls of the first size were 3 *livres*. After a reduction of 5 per cent, the total due was 81 *livres* 14 *sols*. The billhead gives the address of their *entrepôts* as Palais-Egalité nos. 34 et 35, Galerie de pierre, côte du café de Foi, and mentions amongst their products 'beaux Vases forme de Médicis, et nouvelle forme, Vases à fleurs pour garniture de cheminée, Tasses antiques et modernes, Services de Table, de Dessert, à Thé et à Café, etc.'.[6] A later bill amounts to the large sum of 1,778 francs for a dessert service with a blue ground and matt gold border 'et vermicelli en or Pale'. The service included forty-eight plates at 15 francs each, two circular sugar bowls on feet ('sur griffes') which cost 54 francs each, a (fruit) basket 'à palmette sur griffes' costing 120 francs and a tea service of twelve cups and saucers, a teapot, a sugar bowl and a cream jug amounting to 390 francs, as well as other items.[7] The factory evidently manufactured a large range of domestic and ornamental wares, and was introducing many new forms in the first decade of the nineteenth century. A handsome ice-cream cooler decorated in black and gold may have been purchased by the American Chancellor Robert Livingston during his stay as American Minister in Paris between 1801–4, or possibly later.[8]

However, like most of the other Paris concerns it suffered from adverse economic conditions during the Napoleonic wars. In 1807 the firm sought a loan of 30,000 francs from the Ministry of the Interior. It was renewed in 1808 and 1809, when it stood at 22,000 francs. Six thousand francs was still outstanding in 1810. The number of employees was given in a report of 1807 by the prefect Frochot to the Ministry as between 80 and 100 in peacetime and the annual turnover as 250,000 to 280,000 francs.[9] He commented on the good management of the factory, its fine workshops and the richness of its products. In another report drawn up by the Prefecture of Police dated February 1807, the annual production was given as only 70,000 francs and the workforce 150.[10]

Few names of employees have been discovered. Pierre Tharaud (1783–1843) of Limoges was director of the factory before 1830.[11] Some details of the workforce are given in a document dating from 1810:[12] there were twelve throwers, one pupil, six *garnisseurs et mouleurs*, one figure-maker, one *batteur de pâte* (who prepared the clay by manipulating it), nineteen moulders, one saggar thrower (*tourneur de cazettes*, responsible for making the fireclay containers in which pieces were protected from the flames in the kiln, and from each other), four kiln-loaders (*enfourneurs*), two *émailleurs* (presumably to prepare colours), two woodmen (to chop wood into suitable lengths for the kiln), one workman to oversee the enamel kiln, one overseer (*chef*), one salesman (*commis*), twelve painters and six burnishers.

1. This account is based on Guillebon, 1972, pp. 221–2 and Guillebon, 1985, pp. 124–6. The author is grateful to Régine de Guillebon for providing information about the Darte brothers' dates of birth and death.
2. Inv. MNCS 22331, illus. in colour in Guillebon, 1972, p. 189, fig. 146. For a history of the building in rue de la Roquette, see Guillebon, 'L'ancien hôtel Dunoyer, puis Montalembert, manufacture de porcelaine des frères Darte, rue de la Roquette (11e)', commission du Vieux Paris, *Cahiers de la Rotonde*, 7, previously published as a supplement to *Bulletin municipal officiel, 13 janvier 1981, no. 4*.
3. Commercial premises in the Palais Royal became more and more sought after. In 1823 the rental of an arcade there was 8,000 francs, according to the *Almanach historique et commercial du Palais Royal ou le Conducteur de l'étranger dans cet edifice pour l'année 1827*, 'mais aujourd'hui leurs locations doivent être plus considérables pour la raison que les marchands ont imaginé qu'une boutique au Palais Royal était un piédestal pour arriver à la Fortune. Dans les boutiques brillantes qui occupent le fond des galeries, se trouve réuni avec goût tout ce que l'homme a pu inventer de plus riche et de plus élégant pour satisfaire son luxe et ses plaisirs . . . La mode y a établi son empire . . . ses prêtres et ses prêtresses y règnent en souverain; de là elle se répand dans tous les départemens . . .'. Further details can be found in exh. *Le Palais Royal*, Paris, Musée Carnavalet, May–September 1988.
4. Guillebon, 1972, p. 183, fig. 142.
5. *Ibid.*, pp. 193–7, figs. 148–52.
6. Guillebon, 1985, pl. LXIII, fig. 85.
7. *Ibid.*, pl. LXVIII, fig. 94.
8. It survives in Clermont State Historic Park, New York State Office of Parks and Recreation, see Detweiler, *French Porcelain*, 1982, p. 106, fig. 18.
9. Guillebon, 1985, p. 124, quoting Archives nationales, F12 2391, 24, 28 July 1807, 29 August 1809.
10. *Ibid.*, p. 14, quoting Archives nationales, F12 1569.
11. D'Albis and Romanet, 1980, p. 78.
12. Guillebon, 1985, p. 124, quoting MNS, Archives de Sèvres, U 19, *liasse* 3, *état* B 1.

284 **Saucer,** *c.*1815–20

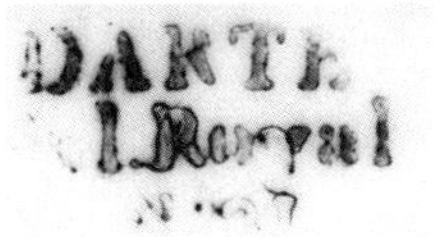

284 *marks*

L.	14.4 cm
Marks:	*DARTE (Pa) 1 Royal* No *21* printed in red (partly effaced)
Reg. No.	FB14 (AF 3217)

Hard-paste porcelain moulded in the form of a scallop shell, the centre with a gilt flower motif, each groove of the shell gilt, edge, 'handle' and exterior of heart-shaped foot rim gilt. Gilding slightly rubbed.

Provenance: Bequeathed by Sir A.W. Franks, 1897

Literature: Unpublished

Comparable Examples: None

Saucers of this form which matched shell-moulded cups were manufactured at several factories such as Schoelcher,[1] Locré,[2] and Dagoty and other anonymous concerns (cat. 285).[3]

For other ceramics inspired by shell forms, see the Colin Harper Collection sale catalogue.[4]

For the history of the Palais Royal, part of which was developed as shops by the duc de Chartres after it was made over to him on 30 December 1780 by his father, the duc d'Orléans, see d'Espezel.[5] The arcades and wooden galleries described as early as 1786 in *Mémoires Secrètes* as a *camp des Tartares* continued in business throughout the Revolutionary period. They became even more insalubrious in the first two decades of the nineteenth century and were used as a setting for Balzac's *Illusions Perdues*, *Peau de Chagrin* and *Splendeurs et misères des courtisanes.*

1. R. de Plinval-Salgues, 'Les Schoelcher et la porcelaine, Paris 1798–1834, *Cahiers*, no. 6 (1957), p. 57, fig. 9.
2. Guillebon and Lasserre, 1966, p. 105, fig. 5, example in Museu Nacional de Arte Antiga, Lisbon.
3. D'Albis *et al.*, 1989, no. 163, cup and saucer, inv. MNC 25080.
4. Phillips, London, 24 and 25 January 1990.
5. P. d'Espezel, *Le Palais Royal*, Paris, 1936. For a description of the Palais Royal in 1836 see F. Trollope, *Paris and the Parisians*, Gloucester, 1985 edition, Letter XLVII, pp. 299–306. A fuller study is that of recent exh. *Le Palais Royal*, Paris, Musée Carnavalet, May–September 1988, which deals in detail with the building and its occupants from the 17th century to the present day, and includes a bibliography.

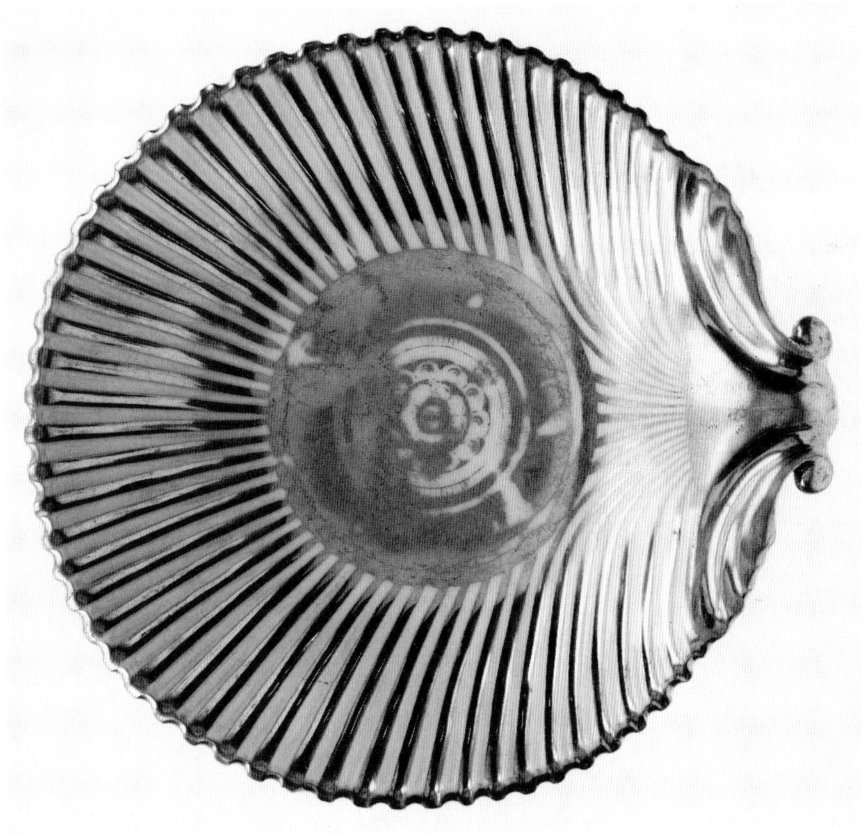

284

Lebon-Halley
boulevard et rue Montmartre[1]

This firm was a decorating and retailing operation only. Little is known of its history, except that it came into being as a result of the marriage of Lebon (forename unknown) to the daughter of Charles Halley, which probably took place *c.*1811.

Charles Halley was in business as a *faïencier* at 6 rue Montmartre from 1793. He is listed in the Paris *Almanach de commerce* between 1805 and 1812. In 1803 he is recorded as a porcelain retailer (*marchand*), residing in the rue Montmartre at the corner of the boulevard. A bill formerly in the Chavagnac Collection dated 8 Nivôse l'an XII (30 December 1803) announces that HALLEY 'tient magasin de porcelain du plus nouveau goût, fait exécuter toutes commandes en peintures, dorures et chiffres etc.'.[2] In 1801 he was buying porcelain from the firm of Deuster in the rue de la Folie Méricourt; later he switched to Nast. He also seems to have bought from the factory in the rue Thiroux.[3]

Lebon kept a shop called 'Au bon père de famille' in the rue neuve Saint-Eustache from at least l'an x, (1801–2), having moved from other premises. In the Almanach of 1806 he is described as selling glass, porcelain, faïence, liqueurs and candles. After the restoration of the monarchy Lebon-Halley obtained the patronage of Monsieur, the King's brother. A card titled *Lebon-Halley/Gendre et successeur de Mr Halley* claimed that the firm in Paris had 'un grand assortiment de porcelaines/Blanches e décorées, les cristaux unis et/taillés riches et les bronzes dorés en/Pendules, Flambeaux, Surtouts de table, etc. . .'. The concern appears for the last time in the *Almanach* of 1822.

No names of personnel have been discovered.

1. This account is based on Guillebon, 1985, pp. 154–5.
2. Chavagnac and Grollier, 1906, p. 657.
3. Among the twenty or so pieces with the Halley mark in the Musée Ariana, Geneva, is a trumpet-shaped vase in two parts, inv. AR 2160, painted with *grisaille* female medallion heads on a dark brown ground bearing the mark *A* in underglaze-blue. It was probably decorated in the Halley workshops. Three pieces from this collection are illus. by Guillebon, 1972, pp. 217–19, figs. 166–8.

285 **Saucer**, *c.*1815–20

L. 14.9 cm
Marks: *Le Bon. halley* inscribed in gold; *g* incised
Reg. No. FB 15 (AF 3218)

Hard-paste porcelain, moulded with raised ribs to resemble a scallop shell. Decorated in gold on the upper surface, around underside of rim and outer side of circular foot. Rubbed gilding. Cracks to base.

Provenance: Bequeathed by Sir A.W. Franks, 1897
Literature: Unpublished
Comparable Examples: None

This piece is similar but not identical in form to cat. no. 284. The handle terminal is more elaborate, and the ribs and foot quite different.

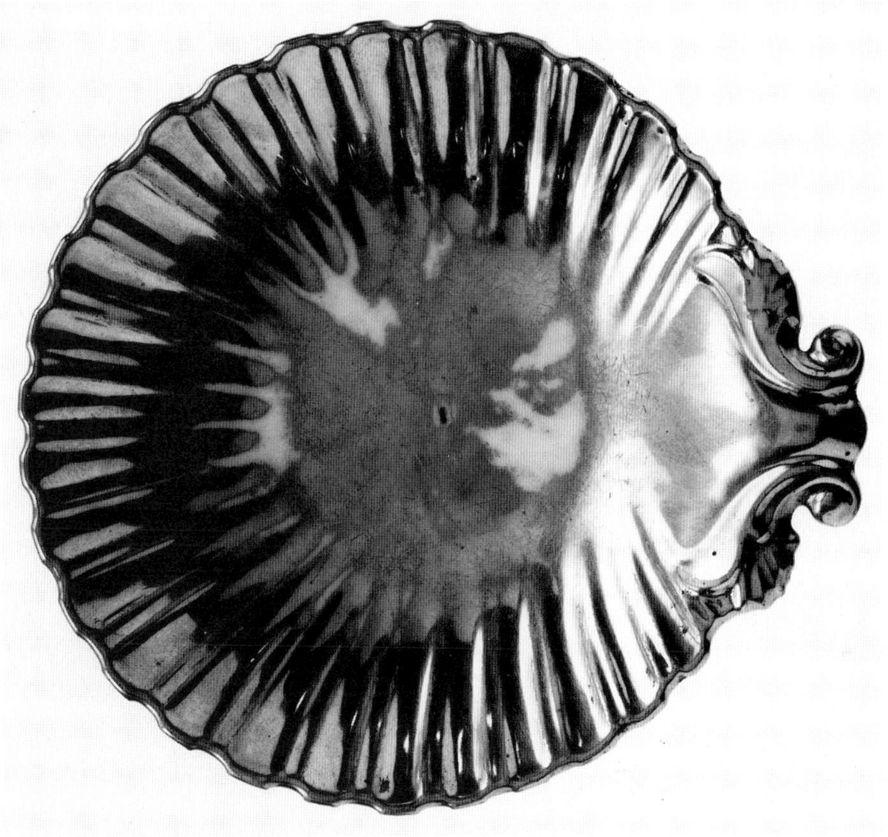

285

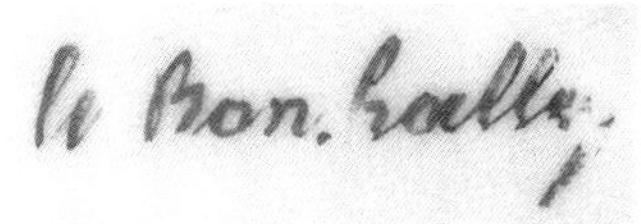

285 *mark*

Jacob Petit's factory,
Belleville (1830–?) and Fontainebleau (c.1834–48)

Jacob Petit (b. 1796 as Jacob Mardochée, d. 1868) studied painting in the *atelier* of Gros, subsequently travelling around Europe designing opera sets. In 1830, on his return to France, he published his *Receuil de décorations intérieures*, and established a porcelain factory at Belleville, Paris, which by June 1834 he had moved to Fontainebleau.[1] Not long afterwards his pieces were favourably received at the Industrial Exhibition of 1834. There are two mentions of him in the Catalogue: 'L'exhibition [*sic*] de M. Jacob Petit est . . . extrêmement remarquable; quelques-unes des pièces qu'il produit . . . sa pendule (pl. VI–2 [this shows a larger and slightly different piece to this watch-case, but one which is comparable in style]) . . . attestent à la fois un grand goût de dessin, en même temps qu'une grande superiorité de fabrication'.[2] Later in the discussion on porcelain[3] the author remarks on the novelty, boldness and originality of Petit's products, which must arouse either admiration or strong criticism, and goes on to comment on them at length. He notes that they achieve a ready sale both at home and abroad, that they are sold by Petit in the white to the *marchands de porcelaine* (the *pendule* was sold from this factory for 250 francs), that their elaborate moulded forms represent a great technical advance, and that only one firing was used to achieve a glazed piece, cutting out the biscuit stage.

By 1839 Petit seems to have been based purely at Fontainebleau, although he had a warehouse at 26 rue de Bondy, Paris. On 24 March 1848 he was registered as a bankrupt. An attempt to set up a factory at Sèvres was prevented by the police in 1850. His Fontainebleau concern was sold in 1862 to one of his workers, Jacquemein, who resold it to Raingo and Vialatte, and his mark is reputed to have been used by all of these. Petit is recorded in rue du Paradis-Poissonière, Paris, up to 1866.

Pieces with the marks of a Paris porcelain retailer, and of two Brussels decorators, Paneel and Chappel, are known.[4] Two fine vases painted in orange on a black ground with classical subjects[5] show that Petit's porcelains are not restricted to the neo-rococo pieces with which he is most strongly identified.

1. Jacob Petit is discussed most fully by Guillebon, 1972, pp. 238–44, and see R. de Plinval-Salgues, 'L'exotisme de Jacob Petit', *Art de France*, Paris, Vol. III, 1962, pp. 195–200, and Guillebon, 'Les porcelaines de Jacob Petit', *Plaisir de France*, no. 365, March 1969, pp. 2–8. Pieces from the collection of the Comte de B. are reproduced by A. Jacob, 'La côte des porcelaines de Jacob Petit', *ABC Décor*, July–August 1976, nos. 41–2, pp. 9–14. Some interesting examples are reproduced in A. d'Agliano *et al.*, *Porcellane dell'Ottocento a Palazzo Pitti*, Florence, 1983, nos. 11–14. For a series of *veilleuses* in the collection of Monsieur and Madame Broulard see M.-C. Delacroix, 'Les tisanières de Jacob Petit', *L'Estampille*, no. 102, October 1978, pp. 12–25.
2. S. Flachat, *L'Industrie. Exposition de 1834*, Paris, n.d. (1834), pp. 48–9.
3. *Ibid.*, pp. 62–4.
4. Delacroix, *op. cit.*, p. 14, no examples are cited. The retailer's name is given as Shoelder, but this may be an error for Schoelcher.
5. Musée national de Céramique, Sèvres, inv. 25633 12, see d'Albis *et al*, 1989, no. 185.

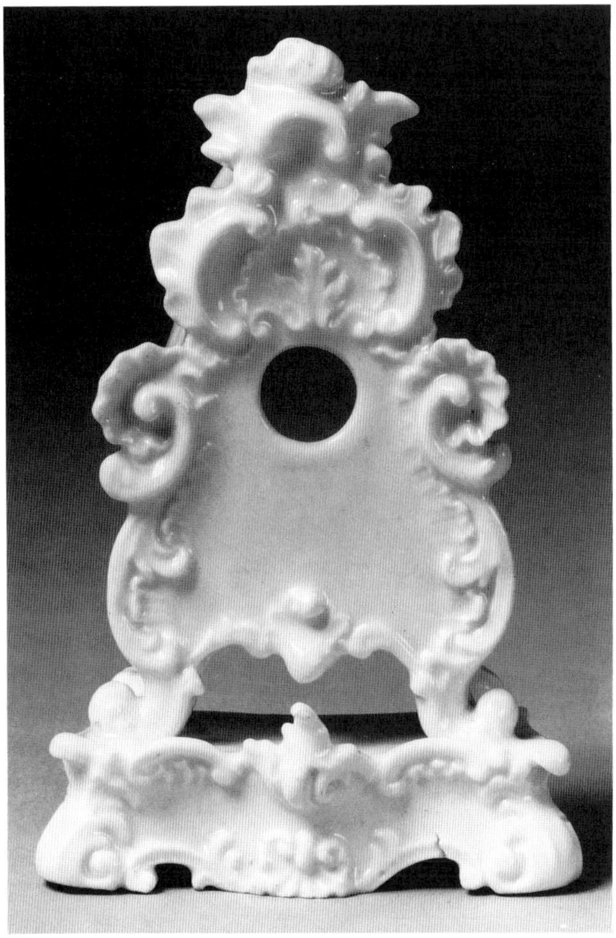

286

286 **Clock Case**, Jacob Petit, *c.*1835–40

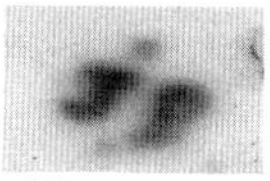

286 *mark*

H.	12.7 cm
Marks:	*JP* painted in underglaze-blue
Reg. No.	Franks 437

Hard-paste porcelain, glazed except inside the sides of the upper part, moulded in the form of a clock of triangular form on four scroll feet, the front decorated with numerous scrolls, leaves, shells, etc. in the rococo style, standing on a hollow rectangular pedestal similarly ornamented on the front and sides. The reverse of the clock case has a groove into which the metal door of the mechanism would have fitted (see below). Small chip at the back.

Provenance: Bequeathed by Sir A.W. Franks, 1897

Literature: Franks, 1896, no. 437

Chaffers, 1926, Vol. II, p. 357, fig. 325

Comparable Examples: Limoges, Musée national Adrien-Dubouché, inv. 23612[3] (on loan from Musée national de Céramique, Sèvres), decorated with applied coloured flowers on a turquoise ground, and gilt.

It is likely that this piece was intended to be decorated and fitted with a watch like the one in Limoges. On the Limoges example the movement slots into the ledge at the back and is kept in place by a screw at either side.

This clock case is typical of the exaggerated second rococo style for which Petit is famous.

Unidentified Factories

PARIS

287 **Portrait Medallion of B.G. Sage** (1740–1824), perhaps *c.*1779

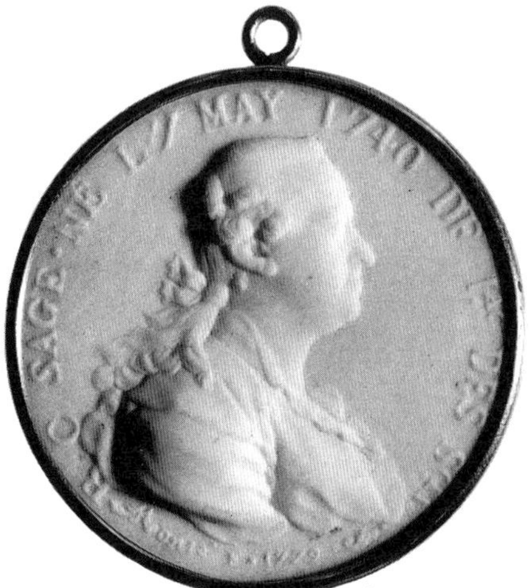

287

D. 5.1 cm
Marks: signed *Monie F. 1779* on truncation
Reg. No. Franks 399

Hard-paste porcelain, granular, with an unglazed moulded portrait of Balthasar-Georges Sage to right wearing a wig *en queue* and a loose jacket. The inscription reads *B.C* [sic] *SAGE. NE L 7 MAY 1740 DE L.AC DES S.CES*. The reverse is flat and has a hemispherical hole near the top intended for a metal loop. In gilt-metal frame with suspension loop.

Provenance: Bequeathed by Sir A.W. Franks, 1897

Literature: Franks, 1896, no. 399

A. Dawson, 'Medals as Models for Ceramic Medallions, a mystery story', *The Medal*, Summer 1987, p. 30

Comparable Examples: None

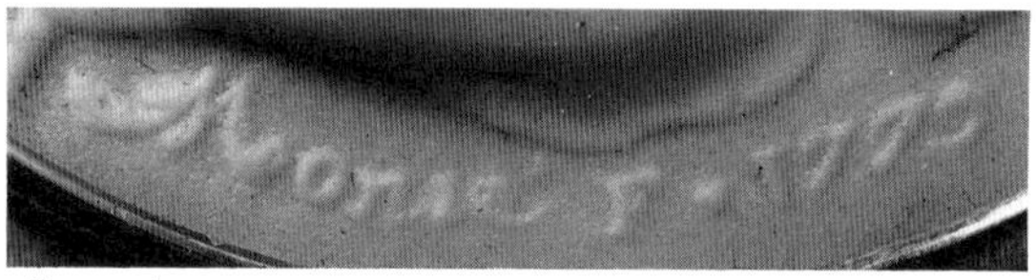

287 *mark*

Although this medallion was attributed by Franks to the Sèvres factory, there is no evidence that it was made there, and it does not correspond to other medallions made at Sèvres. It is likely to be of Paris origin and to date from the late eighteenth century or early nineteenth century. It is worth noting that on 13 December 1782 Sage, together with Mithouard, Macquer, Le Roy and d'Ariet, signed 'procés verbal de visitte du four à porcelaine de Bourdon-Desplanches'.[1]

The medallion is based on a medal by an unknown medallist Monié of which only one example, in private hands in the United States, is known (see fig. 287a).[2] Both Forrer and Bénézit give vague and contradictory information about Monié.[3]

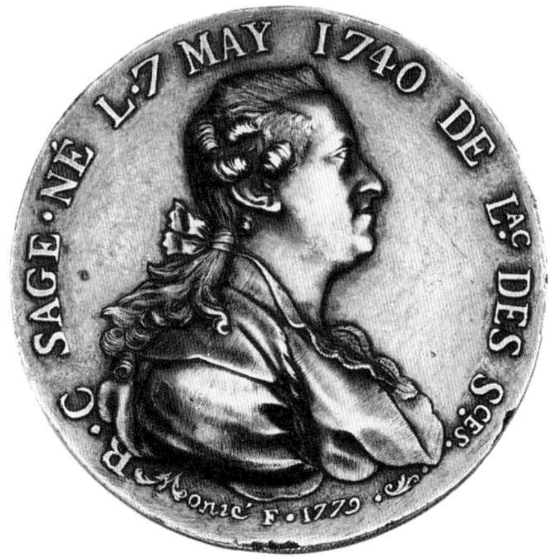

Fig 287a Bronze medal of B.G. Sage, D. *6 cm*

Sage was born in Paris, the son of a *marchand-apothicaire-épicier*, and studied physics under the Abbé Nollet.[4] His first communication to the Académie des Sciences in 1766 concerned *terre noire* from the Noyon area. In 1770 he became an *adjoint-chimiste* of the Académie, and in 1778 was given a chair of *Minéralogie docimastique* which entitled him to apartments in the Hôtel des Monnaies, together with a large room for his laboratory, library and mineral specimens. This room, sumptuously decorated by Antoine, the King's architect, is shown in an engraving by Née after Meunier,[5] and remains virtually unaltered to this day.

In the late 1770s his experiments purporting to show that he had found gold in ordinary earth aroused the opposition of his fellow scientists, which intensified when he contested Lavoisier's ideas and the new system of chemical classification. Narrowly escaping in 1793 under the *loi des suspects*, he managed to regain favour under Napoleon, and was even awarded the Ordre de Saint-Michel by Louis XVIII. He was blind for many years at the end of his life, and died on 9 September 1824 in the Hôtel des Monnaies. His collection of over two hundred objects made of various hardstones, pictures, drawings, miniatures and sculptures was sold in Paris in February 1827.[6]

1. Guillebon, 1972, p. 50.
2. A note in the Archives of the Académie des Sciences de l'Institut de France records that there was one in the trade in Paris in 1936 but the price of 700 francs was considered too high for the Académie to purchase it. None exists in the Hôtel des Monnaies, nor in the British Museum Department of Coins and Medals. In the same American private collection there is also a medallion, probably made of gelatin, of I.C.P. Le Noir, lieutenant-général de police, 1777, signed *Monié F.*, analysed by Michael Cowell of the BM Research Laboratory, to whom the author is indebted, BMRL 6233. The *procureur au Parlement*, Pierre de Ravisy (b. 1741), was also the subject of a medal by Monié in 1778, see *Bulletin de la Société française de Numismatique*, Janvier 1959, p. 264. A medallion of Christian VII of Denmark by Monié is recorded by G. Galster, *Danske og Norske Medailler og Jetons ca. 1533–ca. 1788*, Copenhagen, 1936. The writer is grateful to Richard Margolis for this reference.
3. L. Forrer, *Biographical Dictionary of Medallists*, Vol. IV, 1909, p. 135; E. Bénézit, *Dictionnaire critique et documentaire des peintres, sculpteurs, dessinateurs et graveurs*, Paris, 1976, Vol. 6, p. 178, and p. 198.
4. Biographical information extracted from P. Dorveaux, 'Apothicaires membres de l'Académie Royale des Sciences XI Balthazar-Georges Sage', *Revue de l'Histoire de la Pharmacie*, 1936, pp. 1–31.
5. Reprod. F. Mazerolle, *Hôtel des Monnaies*, Paris, 1907, p. 82. Also illus. by P. Dehaye in 'L'Ecole des Mines à la Monnaie', *Le Club français de la médaille*, 82/83, premier trimestre 1984, p. 3.
6. An annotated catalogue of the sale at 3, quai Voltaire, Paris, held by Messrs Bonnefons de la Vialle, Léman and Bon on 8 February 1827 and following days is in the British Library, pressmark 562. e. 64. (6).

288 **Cup and Saucer**, probably *c.* 1810–15

D. *of saucer:*	12.8 cm
H. *of cup:*	5.9 cm
Marks:	V^e M/& C stencilled in red on saucer
Reg. No.	Franks 438

Hard-paste porcelain, thrown. Deep saucer with flared sides, straight-sided cup with ear-shaped handle terminating in a 'kick'.

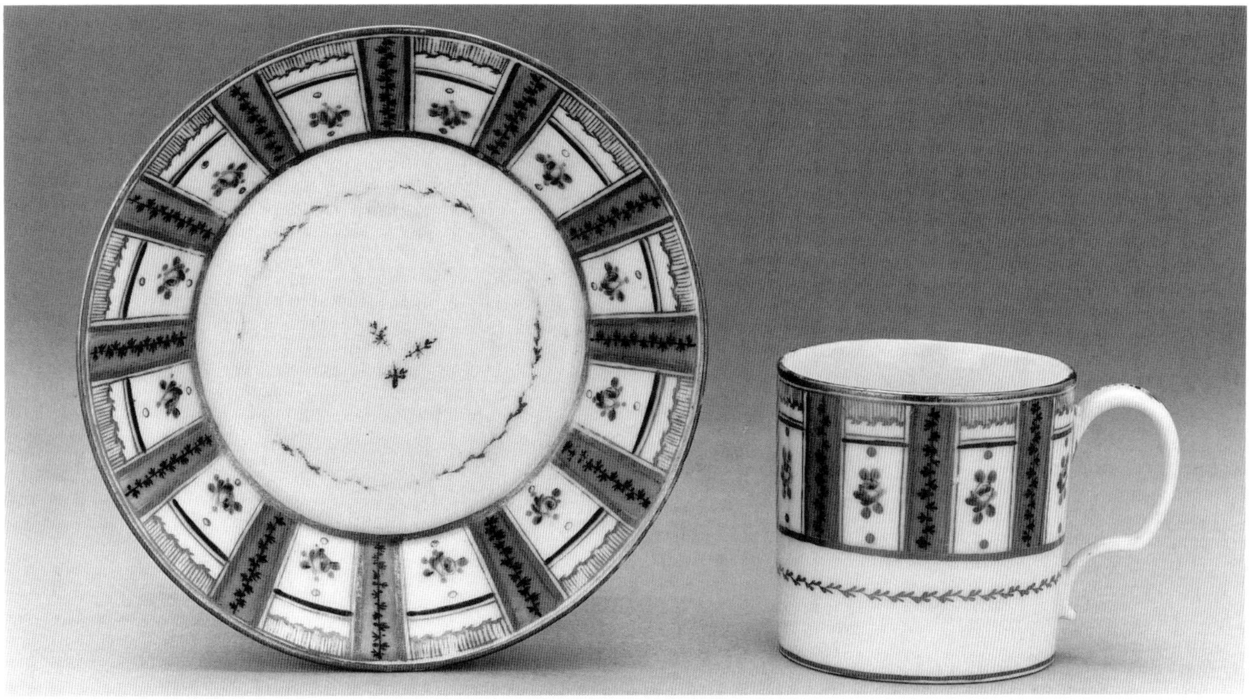

288

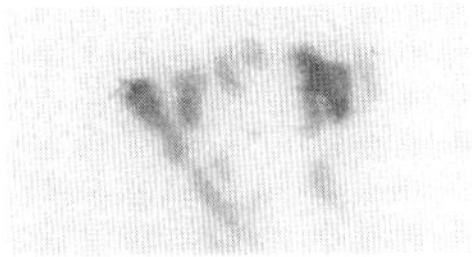

288 *mark (saucer)*

The decoration on the cup consists of a gilt leaf trail below a pattern of rose on a white ground between two gilt dots, which is enclosed by a gilt line below and a blue line above, alternating with a vertical panel of a black leaf trail on a salmon-pink ground. Near the rim is a pattern of vertical gilt lines above a gilt leaf trail. Rim gilt, handle partly gilt, gilt line near foot. The pattern is repeated on the saucer with the addition of a gilt flower trail and gilt flower spray.

Provenance: Bequeathed by Sir A.W. Franks, 1897

Literature: Franks, 1896, no. 438

Comparable Examples: W. Chaffers, *Marks and Monograms on European and Oriental Pottery and Porcelain with historical notices of each Manufactory*, London, 1886, mark as above 'stencilled in red on a cup and saucer with deep border of gold, painted festoons and scrolls' (possibly this piece)

The mark on this piece appears to be otherwise unrecorded. The style of the decoration suggests a date in the early nineteenth century and the pieces were probably made in Paris.

289 **Plate**, porcelain probably made in Paris, decorated in Naples by Sebastiano Cipolla, *c.*1826–40

D. 23.2 cm
Marks: *Cipolla/in Napoli* painted in blue enamel; *P* incised; *Il Tavernaro Fuori Grotta* inscribed in gold
Reg. No. FB42 (AF 3241)

Hard-paste porcelain; deep curved border, unevenly glazed on inside of foot rim. Painted in red, blue, yellow, pink, green, orange, purple, brown, black, grey and salmon-colour with a scene of a barefoot woman holding a young child in her arms and with a boy standing up at her right beside a street vendor serving hot spaghetti cooking over a barrel. Behind him are buildings, from which are suspended sausages and a ham. A boy in a red cap in the entrance to the shop behind leans on a basket. In front of him is a table bearing dishes of food beside which stand two children. The gilt border is decorated with a resist design of morning glories interrupted by a shield of arms.

The shield is divided per pale: Dexter: Quarterly: 1 and 4 per pale indented sable and or, on a chief azure two unidentified charges argent, 2 and 3 gules on a shield argent a cross couped gules, a chief argent. Sinister per saltire gules and azure, a cockatrice argent, on a chief or three unidentified charges. The shield is surmounted by a silver helm affronte, the visor closed and a viscount's coronet. Crest: a demi lion gules holding in the right gant a shield as in the first and fourth quarters of the dexter impalement.

Provenance: Bequeathed by Sir A.W. Franks, 1897

Literature: Unpublished

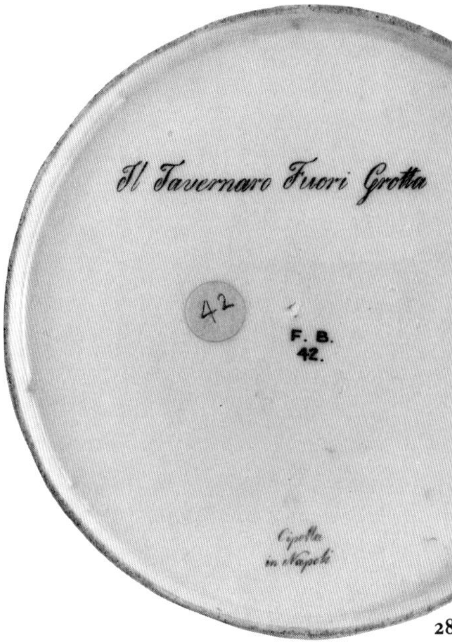

289 *base*

Comparable Examples: Italy, Naples, Museo di Capodimonte, same scene, with additions, on shaped porcelain plaque mounted on a table forming part of the 'grande fioriera'[1]

Italy, Christie's, Rome, Mobili, Oggetti d'Arte, Porcellane, etc., 30 November 1988, Lot 399, same scene with additions on a tray, part of tea service presented by Carlo Alberto di Sardegna to Marshal Delle Torre, now in a private collection, Naples (1989)

USA, Sotheby's, New York, 27 October 1992, Lot 171, same armorials and border pattern, scene of a couple and child in Abruzzi costume, signed *Cipolla in Napoli*[2]

There was a considerable export trade in undecorated hard-paste porcelains from Paris to many European countries, which has not yet been studied in detail. Although it is not possible at this stage to attribute this plate with certainty to any Paris factory, it is likely that it was made in France rather than Italy where it was painted by Sebastiano Cipolla (dates unknown) who was awarded a silver medal 'per le miniature su porcellana'[3] in the Esposizione delle Industrie Napoletane, 1840. The arms are unidentified.

The decoration on this and similar pieces of porcelain reflects contemporary Italian interest in regional and national identity.

1. See A. Caròla Perrotti, 'Porcellane e terraglie napoletane dell' Ottocento', *Estratto dalla Storia di Napoli*, Vol. IX, col. pl. (undated); said to be signed *Giovine 1828* like the other five plaques, but signature not visible. The 'grande fioriera' was awarded a silver medal at the Espozione delle Industrie Napoletane, 1836, see *op. cit.*, p. 847.
2. Further Lots (173–5) in this sale are signed *Giovine in Napoli* and *Acietto Napoli* 1836.
3. Caròla-Perrotti, *op. cit.*, pp. 850, 856.

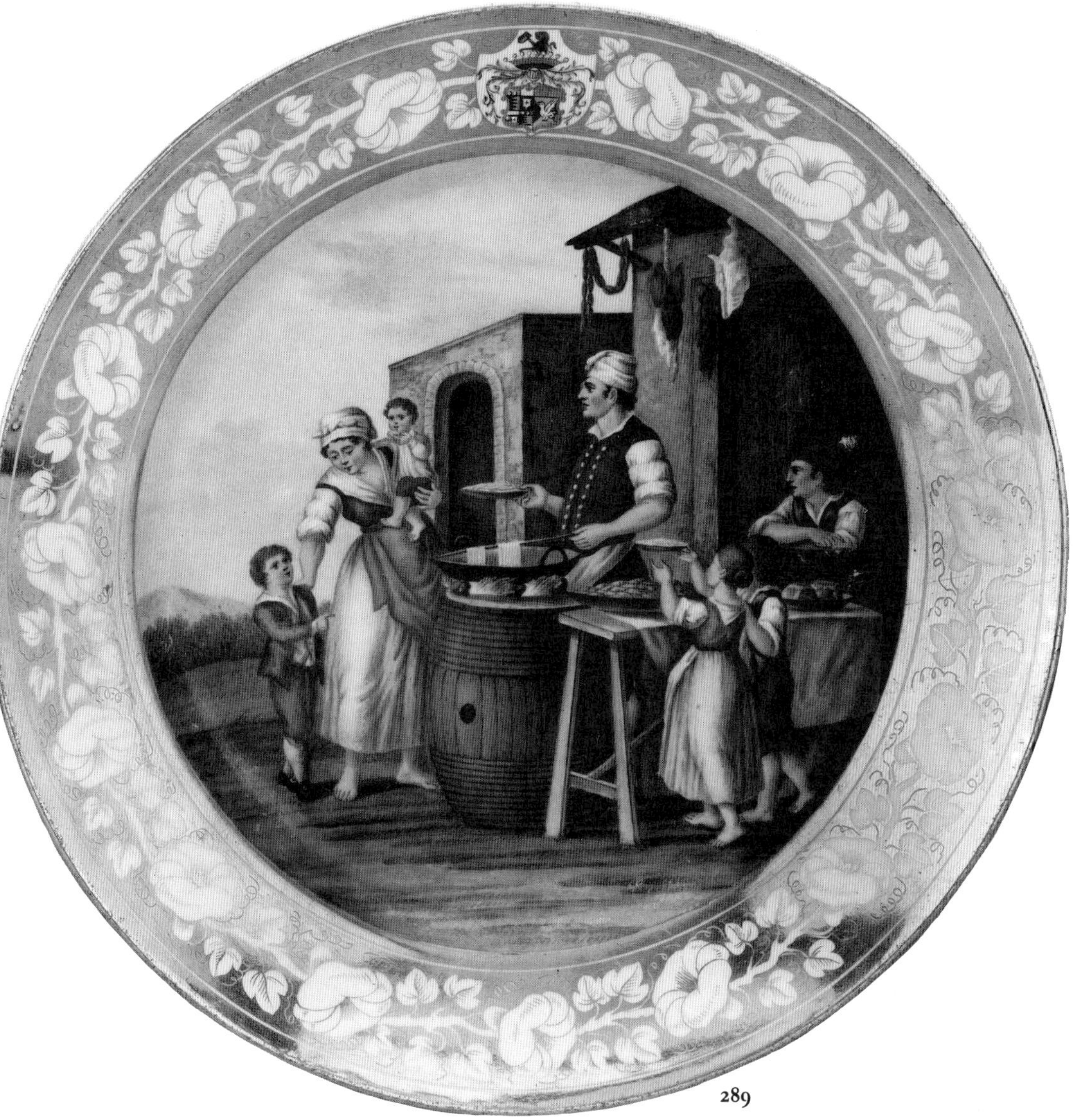

289

290 **Figure of an Elephant with Three Riders on an Ormolu Base**, probably *c.* 1860

See colour plate 42

Max. H. *with stand:*	34 cm
Marks:	none
Reg. No.	Franks 119

Hard-paste porcelain, moulded, the white body coloured green and covered with a thick whitish glaze. Balanced between the elephant's ears, which each have a tassel hanging over them, is a bulbous vase with integral cover, pierced with five circular holes around the upper part, 'held' by a female oriental figure in a long robe seated sideways to right. Behind her on a howdah is a sage seated on a cushion forming a detachable cover, and resting on the elephant's rump is a female oriental mandolin player seated cross-legged sideways to right. Underneath near the elephant's front legs are two circular holes. Inside the hollow body is a column with a circular hole through its flat top. The figure is fixed to the ormolu stand by means of metal screw-and-nut fitments and metal prongs through the feet. Glaze poorly applied, particularly on the left hindquarter, and mould line visible on rump, trunk, and cover which is hollow, its underside pierced by a circular hole. The mount consists of a cast ormolu 'frame' in the rococo style within which is a thin sheet of tooled ormolu. Neck of front and centre figures repaired, tail repaired.

Provenance: Bequeathed by Sir A.W. Franks, 1897

Literature: Franks, 1896, no. 119

E.W. Mew, *Dresden China*, New York, 1909, pl. 12

Honey, 1934, p. 69; revised edn. 1954, p. 57

C. Albiker, *Die Meissner Porzellantiere im 18. Jahrhundert*, Berlin, 1959, p. 27, no. 254

Tait, 1962, p. 16, pl. xxii; revised edn. 1972, pp. 35–6, pl. 22

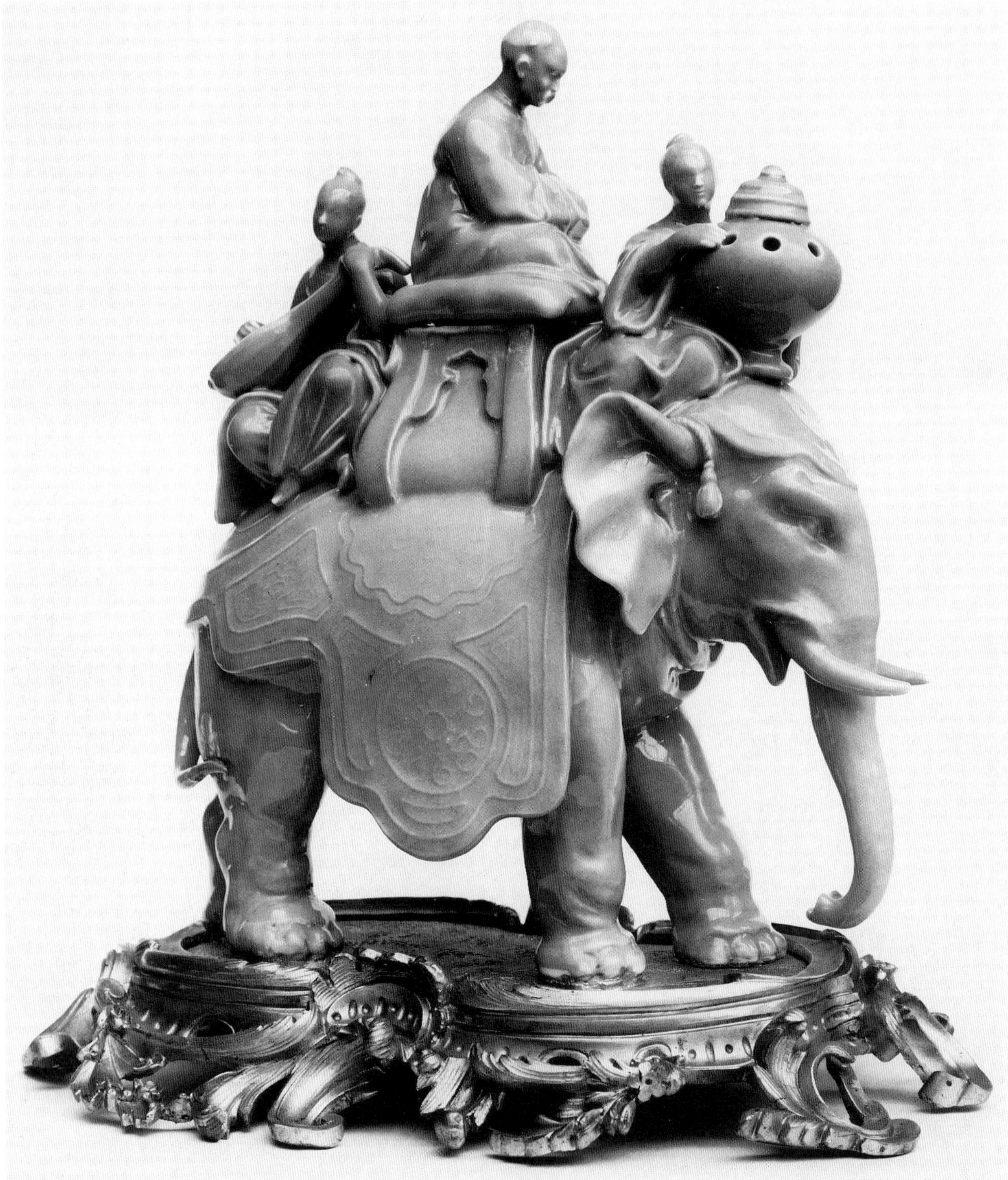

290

H. Tait, 'Ormolu-Mounted 'Celadon' Elephants of Early Meissen Porcelain', *Ars Ceramica*, no. 6, 1989, pp. 50–3

Comparable Examples: Paris, Sir John Abdy Collection, formerly in the collection of Sir B. Eckstein, Bt., sold Sotheby's, 31 May 1949, Lot 163, pl. XXVII.

Paris, with André Mavon, illus. *Apollo*, Vol. LXXXIX, no. 86, April 1969, p. cix and Tait, 1989, p. 52, fig. 5

Sotheby's, Belgravia, 3 February 1972, Lot 122, coloured version on integral porcelain plinth fixed to wooden stand, illus. Tait, 1989, p. 52, fig. 6

Christie's, 21 May 1992, Lot 251, coloured version, H. 28.5 cm including rectangular base

USA, Boston, Museum of Fine Arts, illus. Rathbone, 1968, col. pl. p. 36, and Munger *et al.*, 1992, no. 191.

Exhibited: London, British Museum, March–September 1990, 'Fake? The Art of Deception', no. 227

The age and origin of this piece, once thought to have been made at Meissen in the mid-eighteenth century, have been the subject of discussion since 1934.[1]

The appearance on the market of a coloured version of the group, plausibly attributed to a Paris factory around 1860, together with the poor workmanship of the 'celadon' example and the lack of any known comparable elephant made at Meissen in the eighteenth century have all contributed to the re-assessment of this group. However, the question of whether it was made to deceive remains open, as does the place of its manufacture. It is still considered likely that it was made in Paris, but in the absence of any marked example or documentation, such as a catalogue or contemporary advertisement, its origin remains unresolved.

In 1969 the ormolu base was declared by the foremost specialist of the time to be of eighteenth-century date, although this opinion was no longer unanimously held.[2]

1. Honey, 1934, p. 182, f.n. 60.
2. Letter from W.W. Winkworth and reply from F.J.B. Watson, *Burlington Magazine*, Vol. CXI, no. 796, July 1969, pp. 452–3.

PARIS OR LIMOGES

291 **Cup on Three Feet and Saucer,** Paris or Limoges, factory unknown, *c.*1830

D. *of saucer:* 17.5 cm
H. *of cup (to top of handle):* 13.2 cm
Marks: (?) *h.* and *P* incised on unglazed base of cup, *11* on saucer
Reg. No. 1924,11–15,1

Hard-paste porcelain, moulded, heavily potted. Saucer with out-turned rim and deep, turned foot, straight-sided cup with turned band below flared rim, elaborate scroll handle, its lower terminal in the form of a female mask, and three paw feet. Decorated with a gilt pattern of scrolls and stylised leaves and a painted pattern running around the upper part of the cup of orange 'jewels' within star-shaped 'mounts' each enclosed by a circular reserve. Inside of cup partly gilt, feet gilt, handle partly gilt, with the exception of the lower terminal. Chip to underside of rim and foot rim of saucer.

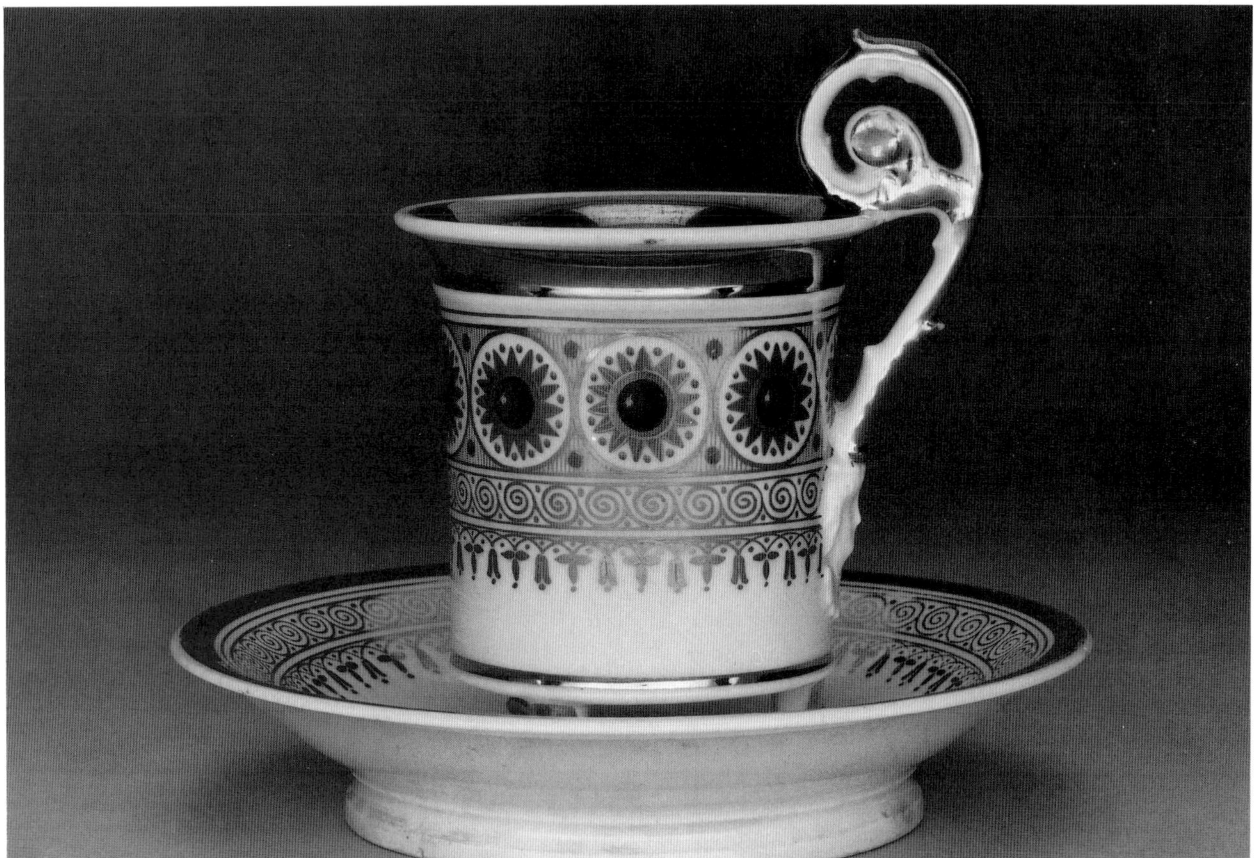

291

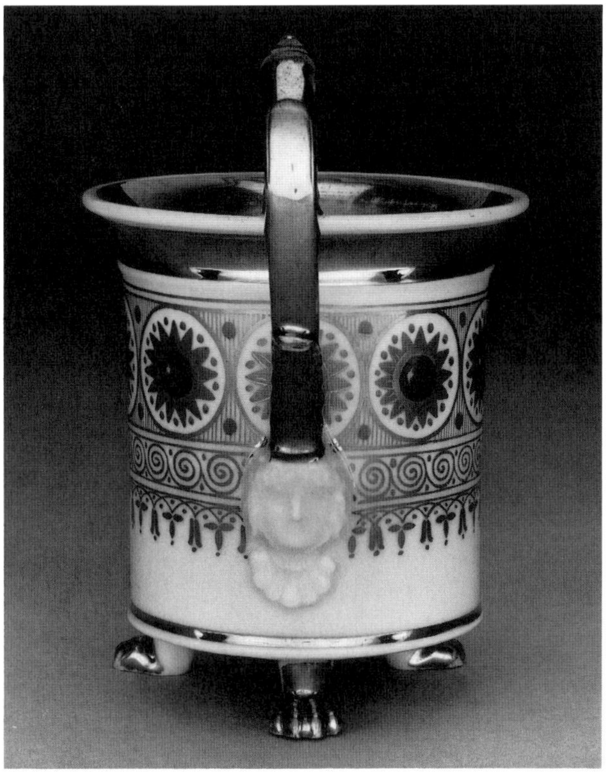

291

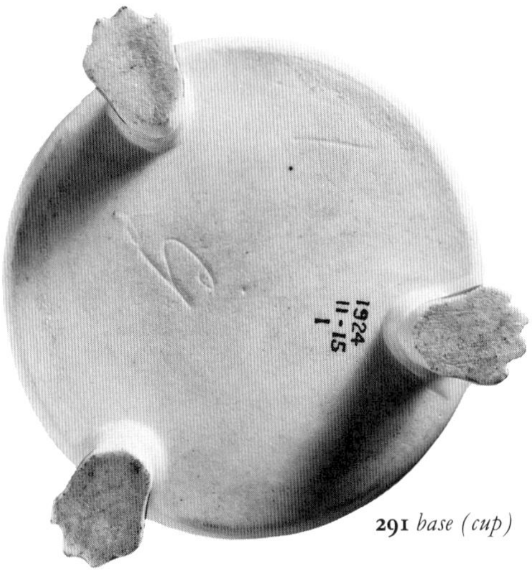

291 *base (cup)*

291 *mark (saucer)*

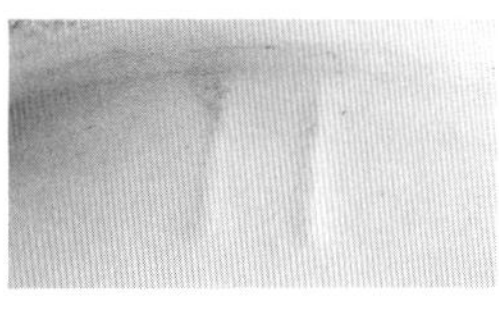

Provenance: Presented by Major H.M. Gallatly, 1924 (said to be Gardner, Russia)

Literature: Unpublished

Comparable Examples: Dupont, 1987, p. 147, Musée national Adrien-Dubouché, Limoges, with the addition of a band of beaded ornament near foot and rim of cup.[1]

A cup apparently of similar form but without the turned band, which has not been examined by the author and may have a different handle terminal, is decorated with a printed 'banknote' and signed by the decorator *Gonord, rue Moreau*, but its place of manufacture is unknown.[2] Other cups without the three feet and with somewhat different handles made at the Tharaud factory, Limoges, are in the Musée national Adrien-Dubouché, Limoges.[3] A further cup and saucer of a rather similar type lavishly decorated and with a monogram within a crowned shield is in the same Museum.[4] Chantal Meslin-Perrier has kindly drawn to the author's attention a sheet of designs from the Bonneval, Limoges, factory catalogue kept at the Musée national Adrien-Dubouché, in which no. 16 is a straight-sided cup with everted rim on three feet with a similar scroll handle above the rim. The deep saucer has flared sides.

A printed list issued by Pouyat brothers of rue fontaine au Roy, faubourg du Temple, Paris, and Fours, département of Nièvre[5] includes a *tasse nouv. forme sur griffes* available undecorated in three qualities (*choix*), the most expensive at 4 francs. With cornflowers (*barbeaux*, abbreviated to *barbx*) and a gilt line it sold for 5 francs, the largest of three sizes with a gilt line selling for 6 francs 50 centimes.

In our present state of knowledge, it is clearly not possible to say whether this cup and saucer were made in Paris or Limoges.

A cabinet cup of related form on three paw feet was manufactured at the Swansea, Wales, porcelain factory.[6]

1. Inv. ADL 2542, unmarked except for ɔc incised on saucer, attributed to 'Limoges' in Museum documentation, presented by Haviland on the occasion of the 1867 International Exhibition.
2. Musée national de Céramique, Sèvres, inv. 14620, exh. *Les porcelaines de Paris*, *Cahiers*, 46–47, 1970, cat. 279.
3. Illustrated D. Dauguet, 'La porcelaine de Limoges', *L'Estampille*, no. 147, July 1982, pp. 30–1, printed decoration.
4. Inv. ADL 3153, presented in 1866 by Monsieur Gabriel Thomas as Nast, but unmarked except for incised *C* and *11*; D. of saucer 16.7 cm. The author is grateful to Chantal Meslin-Perrier for providing information about this piece and the one in note 1.
5. MNS, Archives de Sèvres, U 19, *liasse* II, *dossier* I, dated 1820 in ink. The author is grateful to Tamara Préaud for bringing these sheets to her attention.
6. A.E. Jones and Sir Leslie Joseph, *Swansea Porcelain Shapes and Decoration*, Cowbridge, 1988, p. 139, no. 1, no date given, presumably contemporary with French cups of this shape, H. 6.8 cm excl. feet.

UNIDENTIFIED FACTORY

292 **Figure of a Lawyer**, factory unknown, perhaps Eastern France, probably 19th century

H. 23 cm
Marks: *M.G.* incised
Reg. No. Franks 393

Unglazed porcelain of soft-paste type, hollow, with circular hole in the concave base. The grotesque figure, who has a large wart on his left forehead, a pendulous jaw and rotund paunch, is shown with his head turned slightly to the right. He wears a wig and lawyer's bands over his jacket, which is pleated at the back and has deep cuffs and large pockets. In the left-hand pocket is a scroll. He wears breeches and buckled shoes with a heel. In his right hand he holds a [?] money bag, and in his left a scroll.

Provenance: Bequeathed by Sir A.W. Franks, 1897

Literature: Franks, 1896, no. 393

Comparable Examples: None

This figure was attributed to the Sèvres factory by Franks, but has not been traced in the factory records. The rather coarse yellowish paste is unlike Sèvres biscuit porcelain, and the subject is untypical of the royal/state factory. It has not proved possible to ascertain the origin of the piece. It is however suggested that it may have been made in one of the many factories in Eastern France in the first half of the nineteenth century. It is just possible that it has a theatrical connotation.

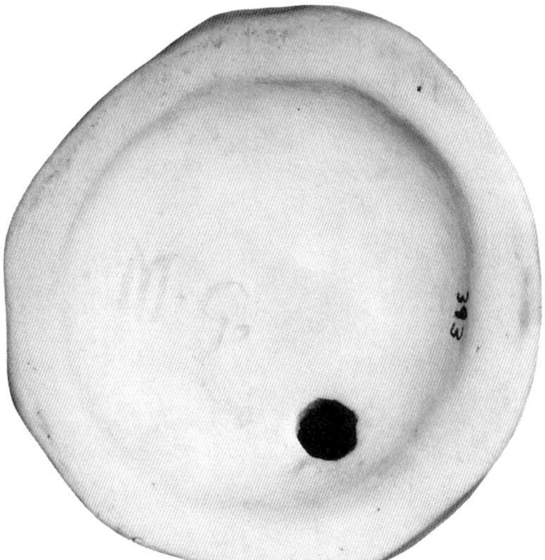

292 *base*

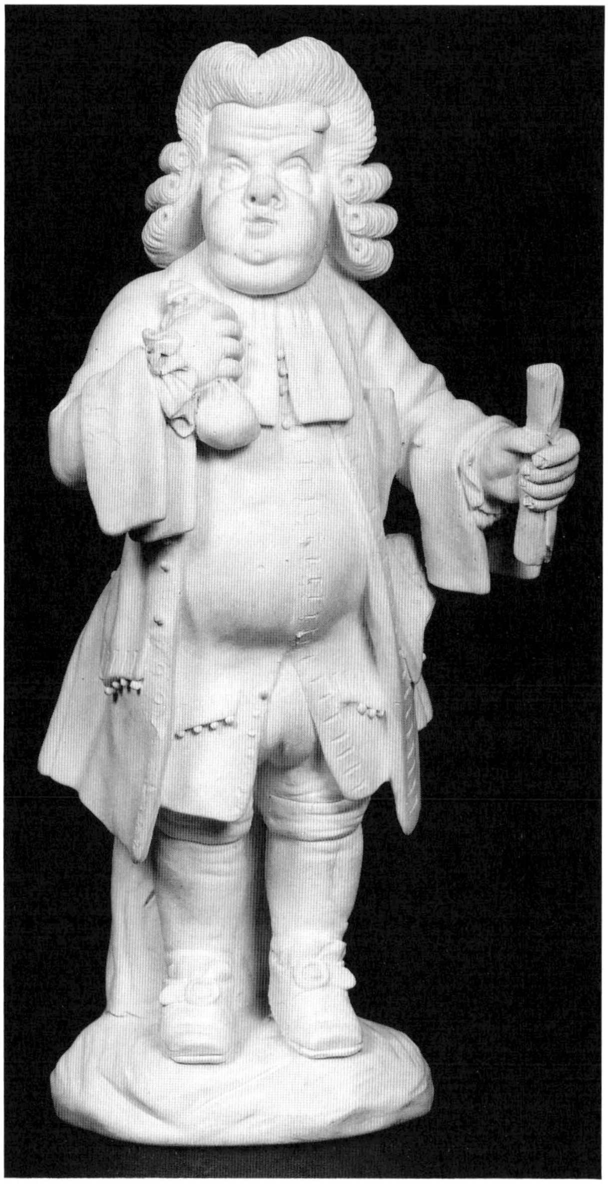

292

Addendum

These pieces, catalogued in 1896 by Augustus Wollaston Franks as French, have been reattributed to factories outside France.

Catalogue numbers 293–5 are here fully described and illustrated as research for this catalogue has recently led to their correct identification. Catalogue numbers 296–300 are listed briefly since they are recognised types of non-French porcelain.

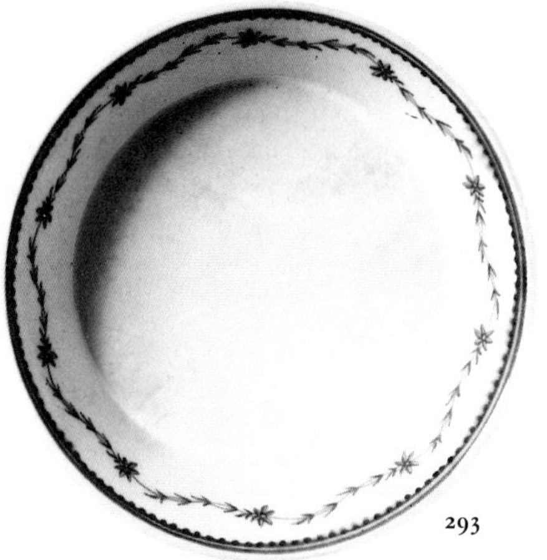

293

293 **Saucer**, Probably Tournai (present-day Belgium), late 18th or early 19th century

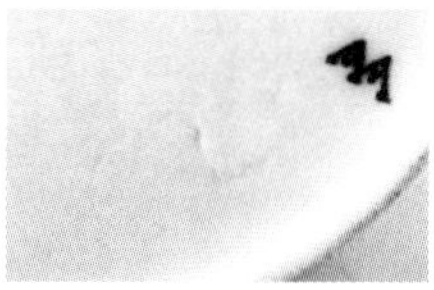

293 *marks*

D. 13 cm
Marks: *AA* painted in underglaze-blue; *C 2* [?] incised
Reg. No. Franks 371

Soft-paste porcelain, thrown, with deep flared sides. Painted in bright underglaze-blue with a stylised garland pattern. Slightly warped in firing.

Provenance: Bequeathed by Sir A.W. Franks, 1897

Literature: Franks, 1896, no. 371

Comparable Examples: None

The paste is marked by discolourations.

The pattern, although similar to the *ronce* pattern in common use at Arras (see cats. 208–9), is known on a series of pieces made at the Tournai factory.[1] The painted mark does not conform to the *AR* of Arras, nor does it closely resemble any of the marks known to have been used at Tournai.[2] However, both these factories still await further systematic research.

The incised marks have not been traced

1. *Porcelaine de Tournai, collection du Musée d'Arras*, Musée des Beaux-Arts d'Arras, June 1991, cat. compiled by A. Notter, nos. 298–306. For an extensive dinner service painted with this pattern, see Christie's, Amsterdam, 18 November 1992, Lot 129.
2. A table of 167 painted and incised marks on 87 Arras pieces in museums in the Nord-Pas-de-Calais is published in *Porcelaine d'Arras, collection du Musée d'Arras*, Musée des Beaux-Arts d'Arras, Feb. 1992. pp. 111–15; 186 Tournai marks are shown in the catalogue cited in f.n. 1 and 36 in exh. *La porcelaine de Tournai dans les collections publiques et privées du nord de la France*, Saint-Omer. Oct.–Dec. 1987, cat. compiled by G. Blazy.

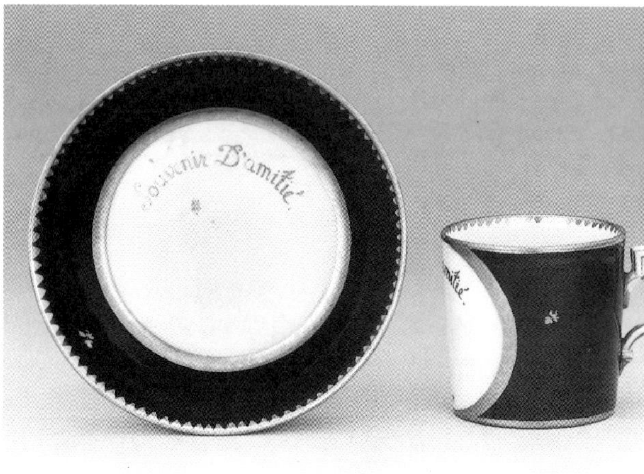

294

294 **Cup and Saucer,** Ansbach (Germany), *c.* 1790

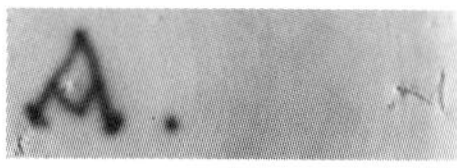

294 *marks*

D. *of saucer:* 13 cm
H. *of cup:* 6.2 cm
Marks: *A.* painted in underglaze-blue on both; *7* incised on saucer
Reg. No. Franks 427

Hard-paste porcelain, deep saucer with flared sides, cup with angular handle. Both are decorated in underglaze-blue with gilt rims and dentil pattern on inside of rim of cup and at its foot; within a white oval reserve on the cup is inscribed in gold *Souvenir D'amitié*. The reserve is outlined by a gold line lightly tooled with a fish-scale pattern. The same inscription on the well of the saucer is enclosed by a similarly tooled gold band. Two small gilt flowers on each conceal firing faults. Firing crack in base of cup.

Provenance: Bequeathed by Sir A.W. Franks, 1897

Literature: Franks, 1896, no. 427

Comparable Examples: Germany, Residenz Ansbach, Beyer Collection; inv. K485 Ans, saucer has monogram *E* for Elisabeth Craven, second wife of Markgraf Alexander (r. 1757–91, d. 1806, England)

This cup and saucer were attributed by Franks to the factory in rue Thiroux, Paris (see p. 348 ff.), operating under the protection of Marie-Antoinette between 1776 and 1792.

Although the factory mark is rather similar to that found on cat. 258, this cup is typical in shape and style of decoration to the products of the Ansbach-Bruckberger factory which used this mark in several different versions, some including an eagle or the arms of Ansbach.[1]

1. The author is grateful to Dr Martin Krieger for the positive identification of this cup and saucer.

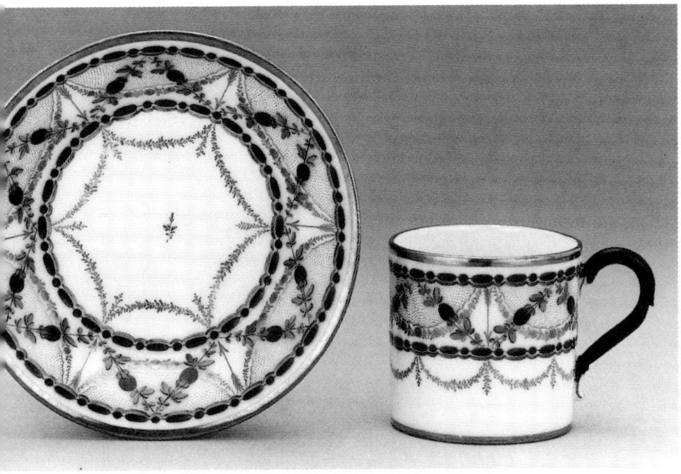

295

295 **Cup and Saucer,** *c.* 1770–1800, place of manufacture unknown

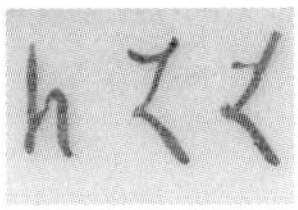

295 *mark*

D. *of saucer:* 12.9 cm
H. *of cup:* 6 cm
Marks: *hzz* or *hll* in gold on both
Reg. No. Franks 444

Hard-paste porcelain painted in blue with an egg-and-dart motif enclosing border decoration of stylised leaves and berries and gilt swags, arrows and dots. Below the border hang stylised gilt swags. Replacement metal handle riveted to cup.

Provenance: Bequeathed by Sir A.W. Franks, 1897

Literature: Franks, 1896, no. 444

Chaffers, 1926, vol. II, p. 359, fig. 327

Chavagnac and Grollier, 1906, p. 415

Comparable Examples: None

These pieces were attributed in 1896 to the Vincennes hard-paste porcelain factory by Franks. In 1906 the letters *H et L* were presumed by Chavagnac and Grollier[1] to stand for Hannong and La Borde associated at Vincennes between about 1769 and 1770. The same authors also mention that Messieurs de Laborde and Hocquart were owners of a concern at Vaux in 1769.[2] However, factory marks in gold are rarely found on porcelain, and it is likely that this is a gilder's mark. Therefore it has not been possible to attribute this cup and saucer to any particular factory in France or elsewhere.

1. Chavagnac and Grollier, 1906, p. 414.
2. *Ibid.*, p. 446.

296 **Plate**, now attributed to the Tournai factory, Belgium, probably *c.* 1763–75, formerly thought to be perhaps Lille

D. 20.9 cm
Marks: *L* in blue, indecipherable incised mark
Reg. No. Franks 346

Soft-paste porcelain with shaped rim and moulded basketwork border, painted with four flower sprays on border and a flowering plant in centre in underglaze-blue.

For a plate with similar decoration, see *Porcelaine de Tournai, Collection du Musée d' Arras*, catalogue compiled by A. Notter, Arras, 1992, no. 136. A Caughley example is illustrated in G. Godden, *Caughley and Worcester Porcelains, 1775–1800*, Woodbridge, 1981, p. xxv, fig. c.

297 **Cream pot and Cover** (as 296)

H. 8.1 cm (inc. cover)
Marks: *J, p* incised
Reg. No. Franks 346A

Soft-paste porcelain, of bulbous form, with angular handle and domed cover with cherry knop, decorated with blue and gold with a medallion suspended from a ribbon, with gilt enrichments, gilt border pattern, gilt line near foot.

The form of the cream pot is illustrated in Notter, *op. cit.*, p. 23; for an example see no. 188.

298 **Figure of a Bagpiper,** now attributed to the Bow porcelain factory, England, *c.* 1755, formerly thought to be Mennecy porcelain

H. 24 cm
Marks: None
Reg. No. Franks 360

Glazed soft-paste porcelain. The figure wears a wide-brimmed hat and a loose cloak.

Literature: Bow Porcelain 1744–1776, exhibition, British Museum, London, October 1959–April 1960, no. 47.

299 **Cup and Saucer,** now attributed to the Pfalz-Zweibrücken factory, Germany, formerly thought to be Strasbourg porcelain

H. *of cup:* 6.5 cm
D. *of saucer:* 13.2 cm
Marks: *PZ* in monogram, *R.* painted in blue, *I F* above a cross incised on saucer, *PZ* painted in blue, *I* (?) *K* incised on cup
Reg. No. Franks 403

Hard-paste porcelain, straight-sided cup and flared saucer painted with bouquets of flowers in colours. Gilt rims, gilt decoration on handle of cup.

300 **Sugar-bowl and Cover,** now attributed to the Caughley factory, England, *c.* 1780, formerly thought to be 'rue de la Roquette factory,' Paris

H. 12.4 cm (inc. cover)
Marks: *S* in blue
Reg. No. Franks 420

Steatitic porcelain, with straight sides, domed cover and large flattened knop. Painted with stylised flowers in dark underglaze-blue, gilt geometric pattern on cover and inside rim of bowl, gilt rims and knop, gilt line near foot.

301 **Saucer** (as 300)

D. 13.8 cm
Marks: *S* in blue, *32* in gold inside foot rim
Reg. No. Franks 421

Steatitic porcelain, painted with stylised flowers in dark underglaze-blue, geometric border decoration in gold, rim gilt.

The painted pattern is similar to that on a dinner service illustrated by G. Godden, *Caughley and Worcester Porcelains, 1775–1800*, London, 1969, pl. 116. The form of the sugar bowl (cat. 300) is not illustrated in this work.

Recent Acquisitions

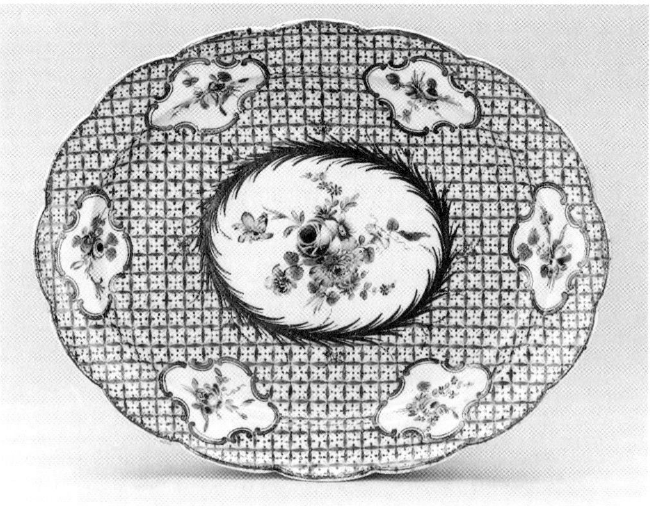

302

302 **Oval Dish**, Chantilly, 1753

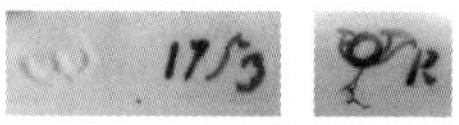

302 *marks*

L.	30 cm
W.	23 cm
Marks:	hunting horn beside *R* in blue above ?cursive *L* in puce, all overglaze; *1753* in blue; *B* incised near footrim
Reg. No.	1994, 4–6, 1

Soft-paste porcelain with a lead glaze, moulded with sixteen lobes. The decoration consists of six shaped reserves near the rim painted overglaze with flowers in pink, blue, green, yellow and black on a white ground enclosed by gilt scrolls and a central panel of flowers outlined with gilt fronds suggestive of bulrush plants from which spring delicate gilt flower stems alternating with a single sprig on an overglaze blue diaper-pattern ground enriched with blue and gilt dots. Gilt dentil pattern on rim. Brownish discoloration in places on underside of dish.

Provenance: Purchased, 1994

Literature: Le Duc, 1996, pp. 238–9

Comparable Examples: Paris, Musée des arts décoratifs, illus. Frégnac, 1964, p. 110 (painted with flowers)

The shape of this dish suggests that it once had a matching covered tureen, although none has been traced. It is one of the only pieces of French soft-paste porcelain to bear a date, and may possibly have been part of a specially-commissioned service. Le Duc has tentatively linked it to the marriage of Louis-Joseph de Bourbon-Condé and Charlotte de Rohan-Soubise which took place in 1753, but no evidence has yet been found to support the theory that any such service was ordered by the Prince or anyone else for the occasion, nor that any was made to celebrate or commemorate the marriage.

The *R* painted in blue next to the hunting horn on the reverse of the dish is likely to be the mark of the painter of the diaper-pattern ground. Amongst the workers listed by Préaud and Le Duc,[1] Jean-Baptiste Robin called Nemon or Nemont, listed at the factory as a painter in 1745, 1748, 1750, 1752 and 1754 is perhaps the most likely to have used this mark. The mark in puce is more difficult to attribute to any of the workers so far traced at Chantilly, particularly as it is not easily decipherable. The incised *B*, which differs from the one found on cat. 45, remains unattributed to any individual.

Le Duc's suggestion[2] that the gilding enclosing the reserves might not be contemporaneous with the rest of the decoration seems untenable in view of the thick and lustrous appearance of the gold. It compares in quality with gilding on Vincennes and early Sèvres porcelains.

1. Le Duc, 1996, pp. 426–43. (Full reference on p. vii.)
2. *Op cit.*, p. 238

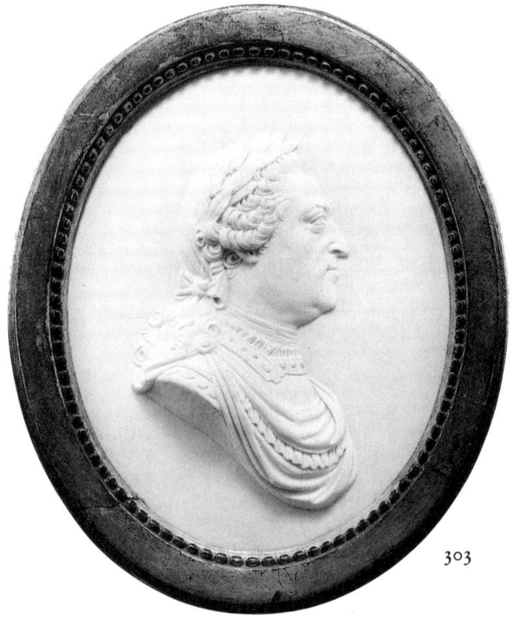

303

303 **Plaque: Louis XV (reigned 1715–74),** Mennecy, about 1765–73

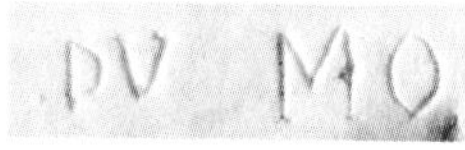

303 *marks*

H.	19.8 cm (*excl. frame*), 25 cm (*incl. frame*)
W.	16 cm (*excl. frame*), 21.1 cm (*incl. frame*)
Marks:	*DV MO* incised on reverse
Reg. No.	1999, 9–3, 1

Oval soft-paste biscuit porcelain portrait plaque in high relief to right of King Louis XV wearing a laurel-leaf-and-berry wreath in a gilt wooden frame. Two depressions on reverse where clay has been pushed forward into the mould. Broken and repaired just above the portrait.

Provenance: Purchased with the generous assistance of the Anthony du Boulay Charitable Trust, 1999

Literature: Unpublished

Comparable Examples: Sèvres, Musée national de Céramique, inv. 13434, incised *DV* and *ch* (Grollier Bequest, 1908)

USA, New York, sold from the Karrick Riggs Collection, 1947[1]

Little is known about the scope of biscuit porcelain production at Mennecy, although the evidence of surviving figures and groups suggests that the factory had some claim to rival Vincennes/Sèvres. At least one other plaque of this type is known; there are three examples of a comparable plaque of

King Henri IV of France: in the Musée national de Céramique, Sèvres;[2] the Musée des arts décoratifs, Strasbourg[3] and in the Karrick Riggs Collection.[4] The second is incised *DV* on the reverse. A standing figure of Louis XV crowned with a laurel wreath incised *DV* was recorded in the Darblay Collection by Chavagnac and Grollier.[5] Nicole Duchon has published extracts from various inventories of the Mennecy factory, but only the one taken on 14 November 1765 of the Mennecy porcelain in Charles Hennique's establishment in the rue Saint-Honoré, Paris, lists busts of Louis XV in biscuit.[6] No plaques or medallions are recorded in the extracts. Nevertheless, evidence suggests that the Mennecy factory played a role in reinforcing the image of the French monarchy.

Two brothers by the name Mô, Christophe and Jean-Baptiste, are listed at the Mennecy factory,[7] although only the elder seems to have been recorded as a sculptor. Christophe was baptised on 5 November 1739 at Saint-Firmin (Senlis), the son of an employee at the menagerie at Chantilly. He was a modeller at the Saint-Cloud factory from 1765–7.[8] Between 1767 and 1770 he is known first as a worker then as a sculptor at Mennecy, where he was married in January 1768. By 1770 he had left for Paris and the Faubourg Montmartre, where he was listed as a sculptor. From 1776–80 he worked at Sceaux and later modelled creamwares at Montereau-fault-Yonne from 1780-4. He died there on 24 February 1784. His younger brother Jean-Baptiste was baptised on 3 August 1746 also at Saint-Firmin. Between 1768 and 1771 he is recorded as a worker at Mennecy, and was married there in October 1769. He was at Bourg-la Reine in 1772[9] and Sceaux in 1773, and may have been in Montereau-fault-Yonne in 1781. Jean-Baptiste Mô signed at least one work which he evidently either modelled or repaired, or both.[10] Until a fully signed example of a portrait plaque comes to light, it is unwise to speculate on which one of the brothers might have been the author of this example. Unlike many porcelain portrait medallions, it does not appear to be closely related to any medallic or sculptural image of the monarch.

1. For details, see p. 52, fn. 14 in this catalogue.
2. Inv. 13435, Grollier Bequest, 1908
3. Inv. XX.19, in wooden frame, see H. Haug and A. Riff, *Musées de la Ville de Strasbourg, Compte-Rendu 1919–1921*, Strasbourg, 1922, p. 24.
4. For details, see p. 52, fn. 14 in this catalogue.
5. Chavagnac and Grollier, 1906, p. 107; for a biscuit bust on pedestal in the Musée des arts décoratifs, Paris, see p. 52, fn. 14 in this catalogue.
6. Duchon, 1988, p. 149. Six busts are listed.
7. Details of the careers of the Mô brothers have been taken from Duchon, 1988, pp. 113–4.
8. See C. Soudée-Lacombe, 'Les porcelainiers de Saint-Cloud d'après les archives', in S. de Jouvigny *et al.*, *La Porcelaine de Saint-Cloud, une entreprise pionnière sur les bords de la Seine*, exh. Musée de Saint-Cloud, Sept.–Nov. 1997, p. 22. Only one bust (on a baroque pedestal) is known from Saint-Cloud, an unidentified man, see T. Rodrigues (ed.), *Treasures from the North*, Christie's, London, 13 January–13 February 2000 and Whitworth Art Gallery, Manchester, February–April 2000, no. 147.
9. A biscuit porcelain group of Perseus and Andromeda incised *MO BR* is likely to be by Jean-Baptiste Mô, see Mentmore sale catalogue, Sotheby Parke Bernet, London, 24 May 1977, Lot 2088.
10. See p. 52, fn. 17 in this catalogue.

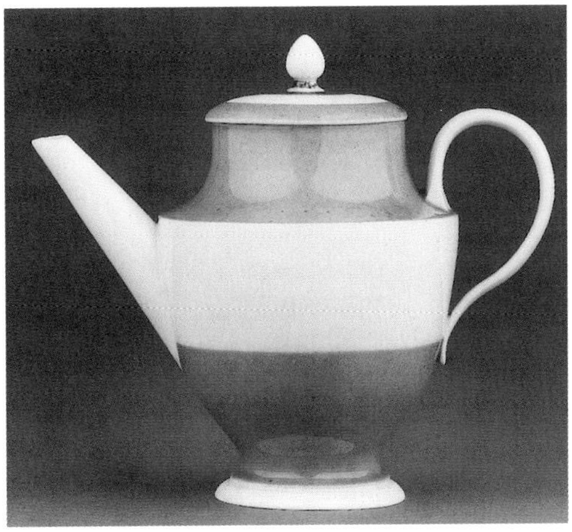

304

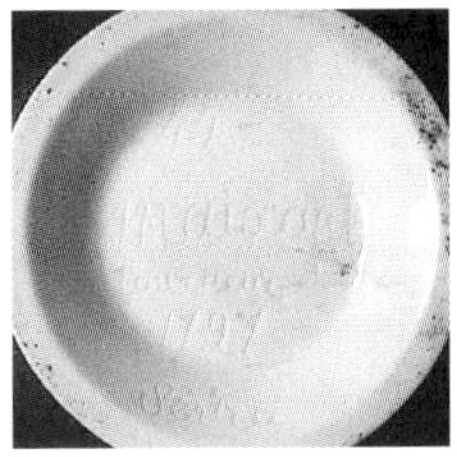

304 *mark*

304 **Teapot and cover (théière à bandeau),** Sèvres, 1797

H. *incl. cover:*	14.4 cm
Max. w:	16.9 cm
Marks:	*44-/Maixant/tourneur/1797/Sévre (sic)* incised for the thrower Michel-Etienne Maixant (who also used the signature Méxant) recorded at Sèvres 1787–98.
Reg. No.	1998, 3-3, 1

Soft-paste porcelain, thrown, ovoid body, high shoulder, wide neck, flared stepped foot, straight spout and tapering loop handle; slightly domed cover with pine-cone knop. Decorated with a band of turquoise on the neck and one on the lower part of the body, except for the edge of the foot. Crack from neck to foot on one side of spout; black ?overfired colour on lower part of knop and around its base; brownish discoloration on edge of cover.

Provenance: Purchased, 1998

Literature: Unpublished

Comparable Examples: London, Victoria and Albert Museum, inv. Circ. 796&a–1956 decorated with a band of foliage and turquoise *oeil-de-perdrix*, gilt rims[1]

This teapot is exceptional in two respects. It is unfinished and is incised with the signature of a thrower and a date. Various imperfections in the glaze, such as tears, black specks and a small unglazed area below the neck on one side, as well as a small splash of turquoise on the base of the inside of the teapot probably explain why no further decoration, whether painted or gilt, was added to the piece.

Nine hard-paste examples of the *theyere nouvelle forme bandeau* are recorded in the kiln firing of 13 June 1789.[2] Soft-paste teapots of this shape were fired on 28 October and 10 and 30 November that year.[3] By 20 Thermidor an IV (8 August 1796) the shape had been altered (*rectifié*).[4] The Museum example may have been the one fired on 3 January 1797 (15 Nivôse an V) or on 26 February 1797 (7 Ventôse an V). No others under this name appear in the record of firings of soft-paste during 1797.

A plaster model of the teapot and of its handle survive in the factory archive.

1. There is an atypical gilt pattern at the base of spout. The teapot is marked with interlaced *LLs* in purplish enamel and *Sevre/Cm* in blue enamel for the painter Michel-Gabriel Commelin (1768–1802). A matching tray inv. Circ. 795–1956 and a cup and saucer, inv. Circ. 797&a–1956 exhibit various firing defects. The sugar bowl is marked as the tray, the cup bears *LLs* and *m* in purple perhaps for the painter Madame Morin (1774–90) on the cup and in blue on the saucer.
2. MNS, Archives de Sèvres, H Vc'3.
3. *Ibid.*, Vc'2, unpaginated.
4. *Ibid.*, Va'14(2).

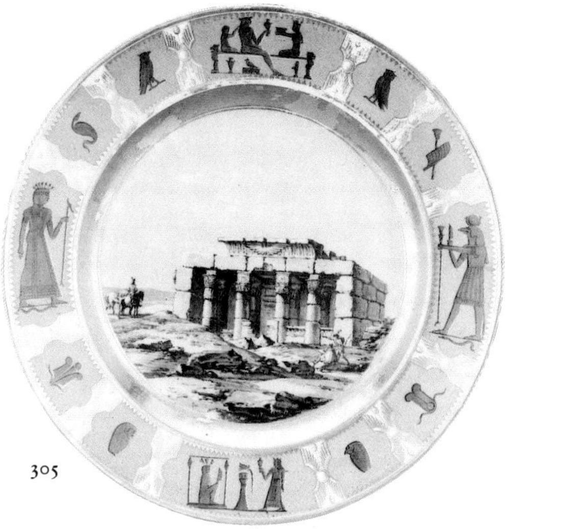

305

305 **Plate,** Sèvres, 1804–5

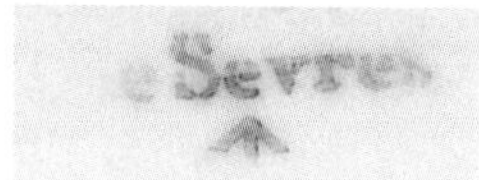

305 *mark*

D. 23.8 cm

Marks: [*Manufacture/d*]*e Sevres* above date code for 1804–5 painted in red; signed *SW* in dark brown at lower left foreground of painted scene; *-11-1 aut 1* for 1 August 1803 and *?cc* incised; *ruines d'un temple vis a vis/LATOPOLIS pres de THEBE* inscribed in purple; label inscribed in black ink *Manufactured . . . /This plate is one of 3 Sevres plates which were thrown out of the windows of the Tuileries during the Revolution of 1848 J E Davies F Woodvale*; areas of rubbed gilding on well of plate restored.

Reg. No. 1993, 6–10,1

305 *marks*

Hard-paste porcelain plate painted in yellowish-brown on a pale yellowish-brown ground with a scene of two figures at the left, one sketching an Egyptian temple in a desert landscape strewn with stones, the other watching him, and at the right a man in military attire mounted on a horse and holding another horse. On the border are dark green Egyptian hieroglyphs on a pale green ground interrupted by gilt motifs. Rim and underside of rim gilt, gilt line around outer edge of footrim.

Provenance: Purchased, 1993; sold Christie's, 1 March 1993, lot 279

Literature: Unpublished

The scene on this plate, showing the temple now known as Esna, is based on a drawing by Baron Dominique Vivant Denon (1747–1825)[1] in the Department of Prints and Drawings, although it differs in detail. In the drawing there are three seated figures at the right beside the temple, one in front of it and an indistinct group of three horsemen at the left. The drawing was engraved by Jean-Baptiste Reville and appears as plate 53 of the plates volume of Denon's *Voyage dans la Basse et la Haute Egypte, pendant les campagnes de Général Bonaparte.*[2] A pencil and watercolour drawing for the border[3] signed on the reverse in pencil by Brongniart *père* and dated 20 Vend 13 (12 September 1804)[4] is related to this plate. The temple in the centre is shown in a very summary fashion in pencil. The border is a pale blue-green with darker blue-green hieroglyphs corresponding with those on the Museum plate, interrupted by motifs in yellow and brown to suggest the gilt border design. Yellow and brown are also used to indicate the gilding. Only one feature is absent: the dentil gilding on the border. Théodore Brongniart, the father of Alexandre Brongniart, the factory director from 1800, designed the plate borders.[5] The painter who signed the central scene, Jacques-François-Joseph Swebach-Desfontaines (1769–1823), was the son of a painter, sculptor and self-taught engraver. Trained in Paris, he began exhibiting at the age of fourteen and took part in the *Salon* between 1791 and 1824. He was a prolific painter of landscapes and military and historical subjects. It was perhaps as a consequence of obtaining a commission in 1800 for an equestrian portrait of the Empress Josephine for Malmaison that he was taken on at Sèvres in 1802, remaining until 1813. He was one of the factory's leading landscape artists.

The hieroglyphs are indecipherable. They were copied at random from various plates in Denon's work, as their meaning was not understood until Champollion's ground-breaking work in 1822.

The plate, which cost 105 francs to manufacture and had a selling price of 120 francs,[6] is apparently unique and is probably a trial piece. It is related to an example in the Wellington Museum, Apsley House, London,[7] which forms part of the second of two renowned 'Egyptian services'. The plates and other elements of this service, one of the most impressive ever produced, have a dark blue (*beau bleu*) ground. They are ornamented with scenes similar to the one on this plate, painted in sepia and with gilt hieroglyphs on the border. Amongst the components of the dessert-service were not only plates, but jam-pots, and sugar bowls of extraordinary form, fruit-dishes and baskets, as well as a centrepiece of temples, obelisks, pylons, colonnades and colossi. Its conception was the result of an idea put forward by Denon to Alexandre Brongniart, the newly appointed director of the Sèvres factory. Denon had accompanied Bonaparte on his Egyptian Campaign in 1798, describing his journey and the campaign in a two-volume work (see above). The (first) service was made to order, and was delivered to the saleroom (*magasin de vente*) on 31 December 1806. It was promised to Tsar Alexander I of Russia as a present at Tilsit in 1807 and was delivered in October the following year.[8] Now in the Ceramic Museum at Kuskovo, near Moscow (a few pieces are in the Hermitage Museum, St Petersburg), it also includes a plate painted with the temple of Latopolis.[9] Like all the painted scenes, this was the work of Jacques-François-Joseph Swebach-Desfontaines. Whilst the service was in production, the Empress Josephine visited the factory and expressed her pleasure at seeing it. When Napoleon offered her a gift of 30,000 francs of Sèvres porcelain after their divorce on 16 December 1809, she showed little hesitation in ordering a similar service. This second service, which included 66 plates, also painted by Swebach, was delivered to Malmaison on 1 December 1812. It did not, however, meet with Josephine's approval and was eventually returned to the factory. In March 1818 it was offered by King Louis XVIII to the Duke of Wellington and remained in his possession until June 1979 when it was purchased for the British nation.

The Egyptian Service has remained a subject of fascination. Certain elements of it were reproduced in 1993 to coincide with the 'Tables Royales'[10] and 'Egyptomania'[11] exhibitions held in Paris in 1994 before travelling to Ottawa and Vienna.[12] Each of these exhibitions included pieces from the service. In addition, two of the seven *cabarets*, or tea or coffee services with similar decoration were included, making the point that the decor found favour with both the Emperor and Empress in the years 1808–10. Both owned a set. Three members of Josephine's household were presented by the Emperor with similar *cabarets*.[13] There is, therefore, the possibility that this plate was made for the Emperor or his circle.

The past history of this plate has not been established. The identity of J.E. Davies and E. Woodvale, whose names appear on the inscribed label stuck to the back of the plate, is unknown. The inscription itself, which is undatable, no doubt represents nothing more than a tradition.

1. For Denon, see M.-A. Dupuy (ed.), *Dominique-Vivant Denon, L'Oeil de Napoléon*, Paris, Louvre Museum, exh. 20 Oct 1999–17 Jan 2000.
2. The voyage and the publication are discussed by C. Orgogozo in Dupuy (ed.), 1999, pp. 108–27.
3. Exhibited in *Egypte-France*, Oct.–Nov. 1949, probably no. 333, one of four border designs, in a Sèvres porcelain exhibition in Moscow, Yerevan and Leningrad, no catalogue, 1974 and Autun, Bibliothèque Municipale, *L'Egypte redécouverte*, May–Oct. 1988, cat. by M.-J. Perrat, extract from *Les Collections égyptiennes des Musées de Saône-et-Loire*, Autun, 1988, no. 56, illus on a panel (details from Archives de Sèvres).
4. MNS, Archives de Sèvres, R. VI, f. 23, S §5, 1805, no. 4.
5. Another drawing for the Egyptian Service (see below) for a plate with gilt hieroglyphs on a dark blue border and a temple with the caption CONTRA LATOPOLIS inscribed *Brongniart architecte* was illustrated by C. Truman, *The Sèvres Egyptian Service 1810–12*, London, 1982, p. 36. pl. 16. It was exhibited in Scandinavia in 1982, H. Dahlbäck-Lutteman and A. Hallé, *Porslin från Sèvres*, Nationalmuseum, Stockholm, February–April 1982, Kunstindustrimuseet, Oslo, June–September 1982, Veslandske Kunstindustrimuseum, September–October 1982, no. 154, illus. and in New York City, Osterberg (ed.), 1997, no. 13, illus.
6. MNS, Archives de Sèvres, Carton Pb 1, Appréciations de pièces terminées Peinture et Dorure, 28 Brumaire an XIII, Assiette Egyptienne ailes rehaussé en brun par Drois (Gilbert Drouet, painter 1785–1825). The painted scene by Swebach was costed at 50 francs.
7. Illus. C. Truman, *The Sèvres Egyptian Service 1810–12*, London 1982, p. 36, pl. 16.
8. It is discussed by T. Preáud, exh. cat *Versailles et les tables royales en Europe*, 1993 (for full reference see p. viii), pp. 360–1, and P. Arizzoli-Clementel, *ibid.*, pp. 362–4.
9. *Ibid.*, p. 361, one of forty-four exhibited; see also N. Kazakiévitch, 'Porcelaine de Sèvres. Le service égyptien en Russie', *Sèvres. Revue de la Société des Amis du Musée national de Céramique*, no. 4, 1995, pp. 24–9.
10. See n. 2.
11. J.-M. Humbert, M. Pantazzi, C. Ziegler, *Egyptomania, L'Egypte dans l'art occidental 1730–1930*, Musée du Louvre, Paris, January–April 1994, Ottawa, Musée des beaux-arts de Canada, June–September 1994, Vienna, Kunsthistorisches Museum, Oct 1994–Jan 1995, nos 116–35.
12. A record of the reproductions can be found in *Réminiscences d'Egypte . . .*, booklet produced by the Sèvres factory as promotional literature, with a foreword by G. Touzenis.
13. *Egyptomania*, 1994, nos. 136–7; for a list of Sèvres decorated with Egyptian subjects, see Chevallier, 2000.

306 **Plate**, Sèvres, 1820–7

D. 23.6 cm

Marks: signed *CD 1827* in pale brown in foreground of painted scene for the painter Charles Develly; interlaced *LL* enclosing a fleur de lys above *Sevres/21* printed over the glaze in blue; *30 nov.20 P=* painted in green; *17.a.il. delle B.* painted in gold for the gilder Demoiselle Virginie Boullemier; *lv* and *20-2* for February 1820 incised; remains of printed collection label [probably of Prince Metternich, see below]

Reg. No. 1993, 7–20, 1

Hard-paste porcelain plate decorated in the central well with a scene of a distillery with five workers engaged in various tasks. At the right a man in grey trousers, overshirt, apron and hat is stirring a brown liquid in a shallow

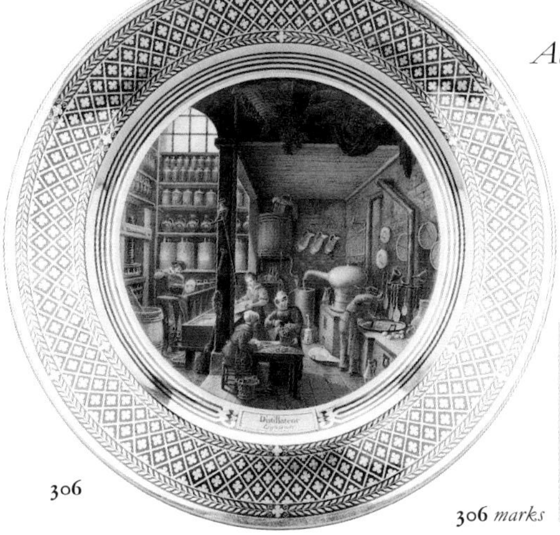

306

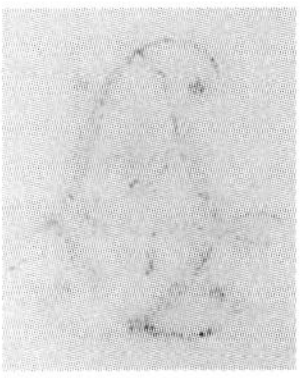

306 *marks*

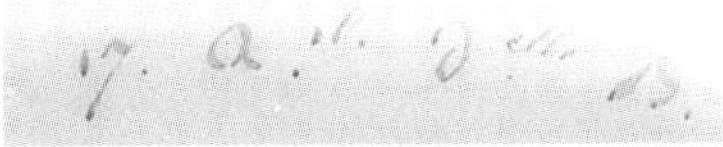

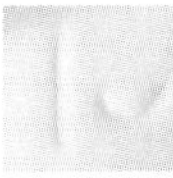

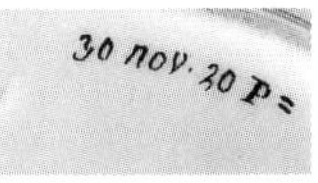

metal pan. There are six white eggs beside the pan, probably for clarifying the liquid it contains. In the foreground are two women, one seated at a table wearing a red skirt and jacket with a grey and black checked apron and a white bonnet, preparing almonds, stored in a basket at her side. At the other side of the table is a woman in a yellowish-green dress and a white bonnet with a basket of green grapes. Behind the women is a young man in a grey tunic over a white shirt pouring white liquid from a copper utensil into a wooden trough. To the left in the background can be seen another young man in a grey-blue shirt and blue cap with a wooden shovel raised over a conical copper-lidded vessel, which is one of several fitted into a bench, their pointed ends terminating in a tap near the floor. On the walls at the right are ladles hung from a metal bar, funnels, sieves and covers hung on the brick wall, and two pipes, one going down behind a still from which a colourless liquid flows down a curved pipe into a vat. Jugs and a barrel with a pipe at its base controlled by a tap are both fixed to the back wall. At the left are shelves of containers of different shapes and colours. In the left foreground are a press and a barrel. Stored in the loft above the wooden ceiling of the workshop are sacks and bundles of leaves. One sack is inscribed *ANIS* (aniseed). The scene is enclosed by a band of five gilt lines and is inscribed *Distillateur/liquoriste.* The richly gilt border design of a trellis enclosing a quatrefoil motif is enclosed by a laurel leaf and quatrefoil band. Rim gilt on inner and outer edge; gilt line around outer edge of foot.

Provenance: Purchased, 1993; sold Christie's, 28 June 1993, lot 34

Literature: Unpublished

The marks reveal the manufacturing process: the plate was thrown in Feburary 1820 as the incised marks show; the workman is unidentified. The ground colour was laid on on 30 November 1820. The gilding was finished on 7 April 1821, when the factory mark used between 1814–24 with the date 1821 was applied even though the painted scene was not completed until 1827.

This plate was one of 108 forming part of a service known as the *Service des arts industriels* made at Sèvres between 1820–35,[1] which was presented on 16 May 1836 by King Louis Philippe to Clemens Wenzel Nepomuk Lothar, Prinz von Metternich, the Chancellor of the Austrian Empire.[2] The plate is believed to come from a descendant. Not many plates from the service have left family possession. There are four in the Forsyth Wickes collection in the Museum of Fine Arts, Boston, USA,[3] one in the Nelson-Atkins Museum of Art, Kansas City, USA,[4] one in the Cooper-Hewitt, National Design Museum, Smithsonian Institution/Art Resource, New York,[5] one in the Rhode Island School of Design[6] and one in the National Museum of Wales.[7] A further nineteen plates (five of which depict the making and decorating of porcelain at Sèvres, which

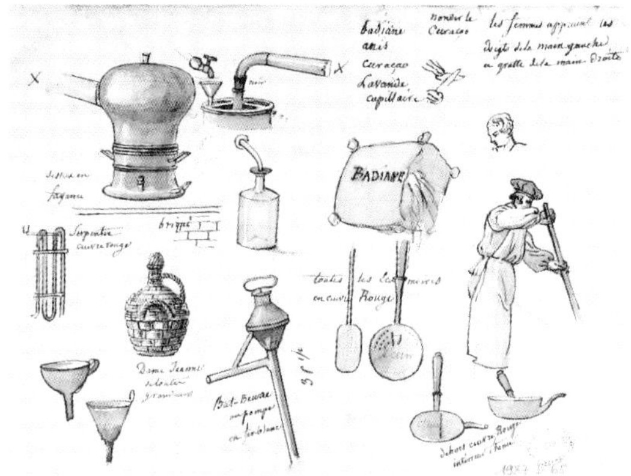

Fig. 306a

evidence suggests were not part of the gift to Metternich), two sugar bowls and two ice-cream coolers are in the Musée national de Céramique, Sèvres.[8] Two fruit dishes are in a Paris private collection.

Like numerous other magnificent services made in the early years of the nineteenth century, this was not a special order. It was probably conceived by Brongniart himself to illustrate the progress of industry in France,[9] a subject of enormous contemporary interest. Some pieces of the service were shown at the Expositions des manufactures Royales held at the Louvre on 1 January 1828 and 1829, but this plate was not exhibited. Jean-Charles Develly (1785–1849, employed at Sèvres between 1813 and 1847) a gifted artist and one of the most prolific there in the first half of the nineteenth century,[10] was chosen to paint the service. He devised original compositions, many based on sketches he took in various workshops in and around Paris. Amongst his papers preserved in the factory archive is a final list of 158 crafts to be painted on 180 plates with some names and addresses of establishments he visited, unfortunately not including the distillery shown on the Museum plate. However, two sheets of sketches in pencil and ink and ink and wash over pencil relating to this plate have survived in the factory archive (see fig. 306a).[11] These depict equipment such as slotted ladles (*écumoires*) for removing froth on the surface of a boiling liquid, funnels and a pump used in the process of distillation. Precise notes on the materials used to make these reveal Develly's quest for authenticity. At the top right of one of the sheets[12] are notes on the preparation of curaçao, suggesting at the least that he visited a distillery where liqueur was made from this plant. There is only one Paris concern listed in the *Almanach de Commerce* of 1820 in which curaçao is mentioned, 'Cognac, gendre et successeur de M. Hernu, fab. de caraçao et d'esprit de vin rectifié' of 12, rue Neuve-St. Roch. The sketches also show a figure of a man stirring similar to that in the right foreground, as well as a head of a young man resembling the one in the middle ground and a half-lenth in pencil of a woman seated at a table. As Ennès has pointed out,[13] Develley's attention to detail and his skill in depicting figures in an interior are extraordinary. This is remarked on in a sheet recording the sum of 100 francs paid to Develly for 'Peinture des sujets L'un dans L'autre très soignés à tous égards'.[14] Ennès also explains the painter's method: the reverse of pieces of paper on which his compositions were drawn was covered with graphite and applied to the porcelain. Using a pointed tool or pencil the design, for which he received 15 francs,[15] was transferred to the porcelain. The piece was then painted in at least two stages: a rough sketch *ébauche ou première peinture* followed by retouching (*retouche*), each stage necessitating a separate firing. Extra firings might be necessary to add additional details, and the gold circle framing the composition was also fired separately.[16]

Demoiselle Virginie Boullemier (1799–1842, employed at Sèvres between 1815–42) was a member of a family of gilders, several of whom were concerned with the decoration of this service.[17] It has been suggested that the gold pattern may have been printed on, although no related copper-plate has survived.[18] In 1821 the 'dorure mosaïque' was costed at 7 francs 25 centimes, the gold at 5 francs and the burnishing at 1 franc 25 centimes. The inscription was costed at 1 franc 50 centimes. These costs were revised at a slightly higher total for the final costing of 4 December 1829. The final manufacturing cost came to 167 francs 45 centimes on a selling price of 200 francs.[19] The records reveal that second quality plates were used for this splendid service. At this period only a small quantity of plates was successfully fired, and Brongniart was obliged to use those with small black specks in the glaze or other imperfections. For this reason the plan for the service specifies that the mosaic-pattern gilding must cover the border completely.

1. Other plates with the same border decoration are known, but were decorated later outside the factory. For examples see de Guillebon, 1992, nos 104–7, Louvre Museum, Paris. Nos 104–6 actually received their ground colour on the same date as the British Museum plate. To allow for the risk of failure in the kiln, it was general practice to prepare more plates than were needed, and these surplus plates must have been sold in an unfinished state.
2. This service has been studied in detail by Pierre Ennès, 'Four plates from the Sèvres *Service des arts industriels* (1820–1835)', *Journal of the Museum of Fine Arts, Boston*, vol. 2, 1990, pp. 89–106. Although only 108 plates are recorded in the gift to Metternich, there were in fact 119 in all. Some were evidently retained in France, in particular those depicting porcelain manufacture at Sèvres, now at the Musée national de Sèvres. The plates, their subjects and the date they were decorated are listed on pp. 102–3. This plate, listed as no. 40, was painted between 19 March–10 April 1827. See also D.A. Long, 'Sèvres Service des Arts Industriels', *Tools and Trades*, vol. 9, 1996, pp. 28–52.
3. See Ennès, 1990: Munger *et al.*, 1992, no. 159; Ostergard (ed.), 1997, nos. 148a–d.
4. *Ibid.*, no. 148e.
5. *Ibid.*, no. 148f.
6. Inv. 84.021, noted by Ennès, 1990, p. 106, fn. 24.
7. O. Fairclough, 'A Sèvres Plate and Lithography', *Print Quarterly*, XI, 1994, pp. 410–19. Three plates were sold at Christie's, 3 June 1996, Lots 340–2, and two at Christie's, 24 February 1997, Lots 256–7.
8. See Ennès, 1990, p. 105, fn. 11 and Long, 1996, p. 32.
9. See Ennès, 1990, p. 92 and fn. 7.
10. His career was studied by Marcelle Brunet in *L'Oeuvre de Jean-Charles Develly à la Manufacture de Sèvres, 1813–1848*, unpublished thesis for the Ecole du Louvre, 1947, and in 'Jean-Charles Develly et la manufacture de Sèvres' in *Carnet de la Sabretache*, 5th series, vol. 6, pp. 444–51.
11. MNS, Archives de Sèvres, 1987 D 65, 66.
12. MNS, Archives de Sèvres, 1987 D 65.
13. Ennès, 1990, p. 95, 97.
14. MNS, Archives de Sèvres, Pb 7, *liasse* 1, *dossier* 6, Services de table, no 5, service des arts industriels.
15. *Ibid.*
16. See Ennès, 1990, p. 102.
17. The plate in the Cooper-Hewitt, National Design Museum, New York, for instance, was gilded by Boullemier *fils*, that is Hilaire-François Boullemier (b. 1798), see Ostergard (ed.), 1997, no. 147.
18. Ostergard (ed.), 1997, p. 367. A printed frieze is found on the border of a plate from the service 'des Petites Chasses' of 1819, see *ibid.*, 1997, p. 232. Tamara Préaud in discussion with the writer in February 2000 drew attention to the regularity of the six border zones on the Museum plate which suggests transfers could have been fitted together around its circumference. Nevertheless, it is strange that this method was not noted in the production records.
19. MNS, Archives de Sèvres, Pb 7, *liasse* 7, *dossier* 6.

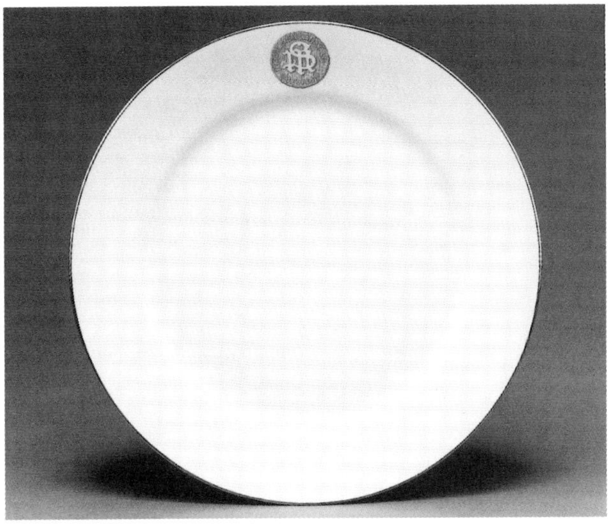

307–1, 2, 4

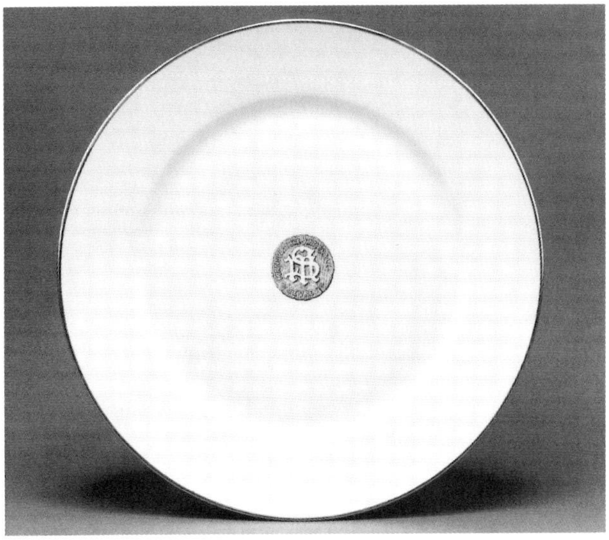

307–3

307 **Four plates (assiettes unies),** Sèvres, 1886–1918

1. D. 22.8 cm
Marks: *S. 86* within an oval printed in green; *DORE A SEVRES 88* and monogram *RF* within a double circle printed in red; *IV* and *al 86 5* incised
Reg. No. 1999, 7–2,3

Hard-paste porcelain, glazed, printed in gold on rim *MANUFACTURE NATIONALE SEVRES* and *MS* in monogram, the device imitating a seal; rim gilt on inner and outer edge, gilt line around outer edge of footrim. The plate was made on 5 April 1886, glazed in 1886 and gilt in 1888.

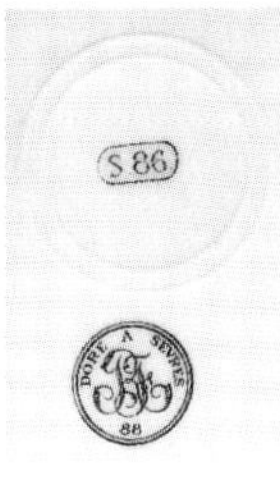

307–1 *mark*

2. D. 22.9 cm
Marks: *S. 87.* within an oval, printed in green; *DORE A SEVRES 88* and monogram *RF* within a double circle printed in red; *A* and *al 87 4* incised
Reg. No. 1999, 7–2,1

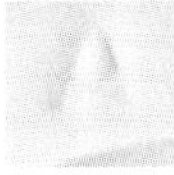

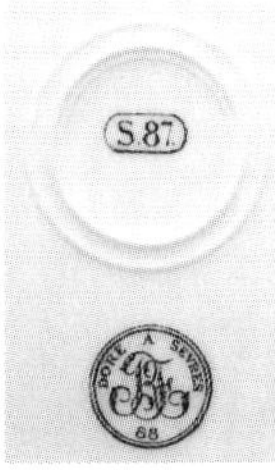

For the description, see above.

Made on 4 April 1887, glazed in 1887 and gilt in 1888.

307–2 *marks*

3. D. 23.1 cm
Marks: *S. 91* within an oval printed in green and *DORE A SEVRES 92* and the monogram *RF* within a double circle printed in red; *III* and *?E 90 7*
Reg. No. 1999, 7–2,4

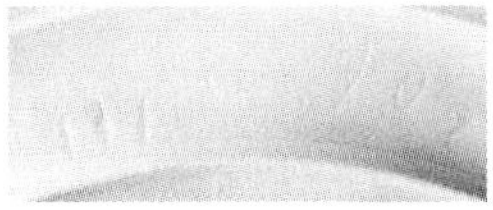

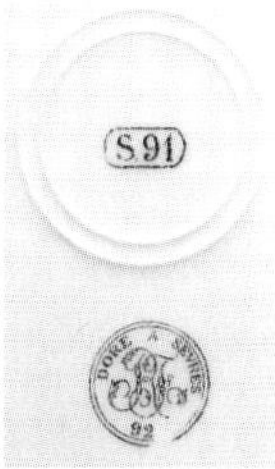

Made on 7 (?) 1890, glazed in 1891 and gilded in 1892. The device is in the centre on this plate.

307–3 *marks*

4. D. 23 cm
Marks: *S. 1905* within a triangle printed in green and *MANUFACTURE DE L'ETAT DORÉ A SÈVRES 1918* and monogram *RF* printed in red; *IV* and A.*05.7*
Reg. No. 1999, 7–2,2

Made on 7 August 1905, glazed in 1905 and gilded in 1918. The device is on the rim on this plate.

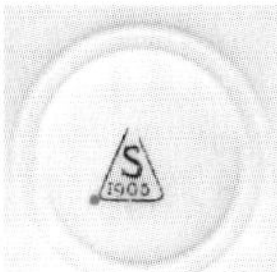

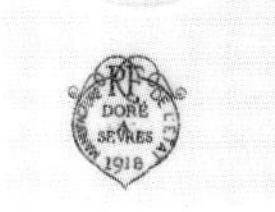

307–4 *marks*

Provenance: All presented by M. George Touzenis, Director of the Manufacture nationale de Sèvres, 1999, accompanied by a presentation box tied with blue tape printed in white with *Manufacture nationale de Sèvres* and the company device of interlaced *LL*s

Literature: Unpublished

These plates were all decorated between 1886 and 1918 as part of an extensive dinner and dessert-service for use in the Director's residence. The service no doubt suffered breakages, necessitating replacement pieces. Still occasionally in use, the service now comprises 305 pieces. There are 189 plates, 74 dessert dishes, 10 fruit bowls and several serving dishes. A matching tea and coffee service consists of 60 cups and saucers. It is poorly recorded in the factory archives, although the proof sheet of the monogram survives in a bundle of others, indicating a large production of such commissioned services; the copper plate is untraceable. It was engraved by Mademoiselle Emilie Péronard who was paid 40 francs in July 1888 and 20 francs in September 1888.[1] Other women workers would have cut up the transfers, applied them to the plates and burnished them, together with the gilt line on the rim, probably applied by a workman, but the archives do not reveal who carried out these operations on this service. Although the gilt device is in the style of the later part of the nineteenth century, the service has never been replaced with an updated version.

1. MNS, Archives de Sèvres, HVj 93 Registre des travaux, Peinture, dorure, brunissage et montage, 1888, f. 477 and f. 477v.

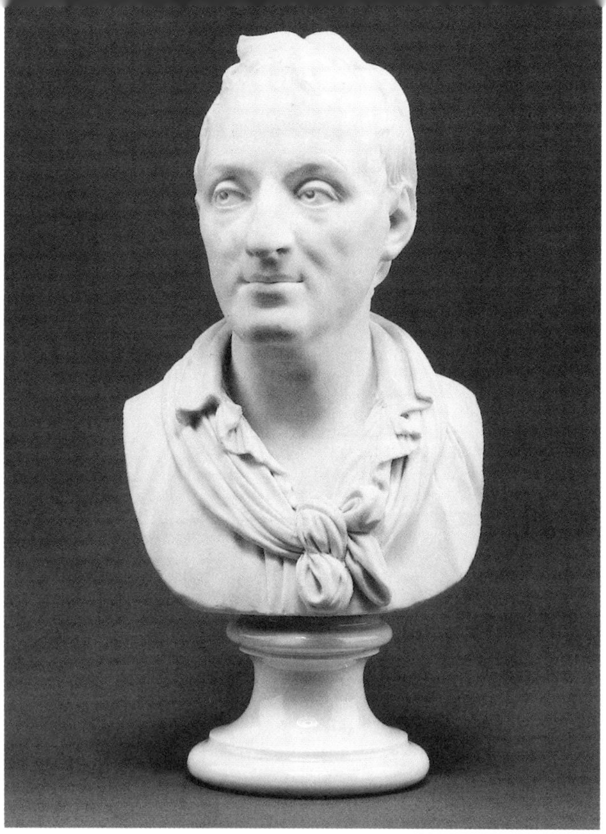

308

308 **Bust of Denis Diderot (1713–84),** Sèvres, perhaps about 1768

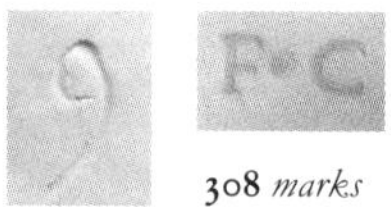

308 *marks*

H. (*including pedestal*):	21.1 cm
H. of bust:	16.3 cm
max. W.	10.6 cm
Marks:	cursive *9* incised in centre on reverse for an unidentified repairer; *F.C* incised on underside of pedestal for an unidentified thrower
Reg. No.	1993, 10–9, 1

Hard-paste porcelain bust of Diderot, his head turned slightly to his right, wearing a ruffled shirt under a scarf tied in front, stuck on a glazed hard-paste porcelain circular turned pedestal.

Provenance: Purchased, 1993

Literature: Unpublished

The bust of the *philosophe* and author of the *Encyclopédie* was attributed by Bourgeois and Lechevallier-Chevignard[1] to J.B. Lemoyne and the model dated to 1768. The first mention of it in the factory sales records is on 20 October 1768 when two examples were sold for cash at 60 *livres* each,[2] but the model is likely to be slightly earlier. Its recent attribution to the sculptor Marie-Anne Collot (1748–1821), Falconet's pupil and eventual daughter-in-law,[3] who was known for her lifelike portraits,[4] seems plausible, despite the fact that no supporting documentary evidence has yet been found in the factory archive. Falconet was in charge of the sculpture workshop at the factory from 1757–66 and was in a position to arrange for Mademoiselle Collot to use its kilns to fire her terracottas. Diderot, in a letter of 6/7 November 1766 to Falconet soon after his departure for Russia, writes 'Nos deux bustes sont revenus de la manufacture ... Mademoiselle, j'ai le front et le nez rouges, mais cela n'empêche pas que ce ne soit très-beau, très-ressemblant, très-fin, plus que je ne suis, et tout aussi vivant'.[5] In his *Salon* of 1767 Diderot referred to his portrait bust by Collot, an example of which belonged to Grimm, which was so good that it caused Falconet to destroy his own portrait of Diderot. Collot did a second undraped portrait of Diderot for Catherine the Great of Russia.[6]

A terracotta related to the British Museum biscuit portrait survives in the Musée national de Céramique, Sèvres.[7] Plaster models are kept in the factory archives, as well as moulds for two sizes.[8]

Little is known of the mounting of small busts like these (see cat. nos 150, 151); it is possible that the pedestal may be of nineteenth-century date.

There are at least two other Sèvres biscuit porcelain busts said to represent Diderot, but which have not yet been securely identified.[9] Ten examples were fired in *an II* (1794)[10] and the record of the firings reveals that there were two sizes in production. Sales were made on 20 Floréal an III to Citoyen Monbreton for 120 *livres*[11] and on 5 Vendémiaire an IV to Citoyen Longchamp for 600 *livres*.[12] These rather expensive pieces are likely to have been a larger version. On the other hand, the high price could be the effect of hyper-inflation during the Revolutionary period.

The factory records show that a bust of Diderot was still in production in the last third of the nineteenth century.

1. Bourgeois and Lechevallier-Chevignard, n.d. (1913), no. 192, pl. 40.
2. MNS Archives de Sèvres, Vy 4, f. 157. Four busts of Diderot are listed in the inventory of the sculptors' workshop taken on 1 January 1774 when they were valued at 48 *livres*.
3. M.-L. Becker, 'Marie-Anne Collot, l'art de la terre cuite au féminin', *L'Objet d'Art*, June 1998, no. 325, pp. 73–82.
4. For Collot, see L. Réau, 'L'Oeuvre de Marie-Anne Collot' in Réau, 1922, pp. 429–48, 517–9; L. Réau, 'Une femme-sculpteur française au XVIIIe siècle, Marie-Anne Collot (Madame Falconet)', *L'art et les artistes*, 1923, pp. 165–71; L. Réau, 'Les bustes de Marie-Anne Collot', *La Renaissance*, November 1931, pp. 306–12; L. Réau, 'Une femme-sculpteur française au XVIIIe siècle, Marie-Anne Collot (1748–1821)', *Bulletin de la Société d'Art Français*, pp. 219–29; A.G. Raymond, 'Le buste d'Etienne-Noël Damilaville par Marie-Anne Collot', *Revue du Louvre*, pp. 255–60. I am grateful to Guilhem Scherf for assistance in obtaining copies of the above.
5. Denis Diderot, *Correspondance*, ed. G. Roth and J. Varloot, Paris, 1961, vol. VI, p. 349. The other bust was of Prince Galizine.
6. The marble, signed and dated 1772, is in the Hermitage Museum, St. Petersburg, illus. Becker, 1998, p. 79, fig. 11.
7. Inv. MNC 8881, acquired 1890, source unknown, H. (including pedestal) 34.5 cm; H. (without pedestal) 28 cm.
8. These have not been examined by the writer, and may be of a different model. A biscuit bust corresponding to the present example on a blue and gilt pedestal is in the Réserve des Modèles, no. 576, and is impressed *1959*.
9. A photograph of one is on file in the Sèvres archive; another, dated 1905, is in the Musée national de Sèvres, inv. 15185.
10. MNS Archives de Sèvres, Vc' 4.
11. MNS Archives de Sèvres, Vy 12, f. 42.
12. MNS Archives de Sèvres, Vy 12, f. 63.

309 **Medallion of Jean-Jacques Hettlinger (1734–1803),** Sèvres, 1790

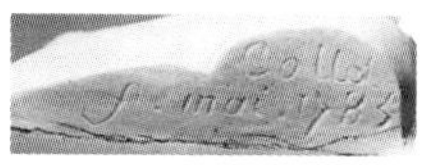

309 *mark*

H.	14.5 cm
W.	12.2 cm
D. *of plaque:*	7 mm
Marks:	*Collet/f.mai 1785* incised on truncation
Reg. No.	1993, 1–1,1

Hard-paste unglazed porcelain, coloured pale blue, oval medallion with applied moulded portrait of Jean-Jacques Hettlinger to left in very high relief on a washed blue ground. He wears a wig with queue tied with a ribbon, and a fur-trimmed jacket over a lace-trimmed shirt. Edge of

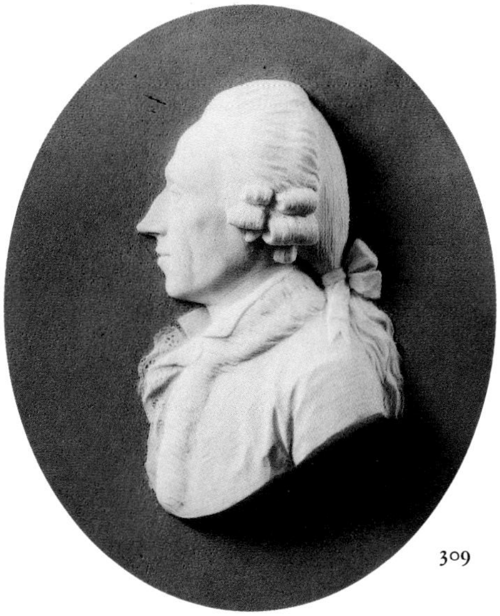

309

medallion damaged, neck crack, firecrack on lower right running under truncation.

Provenance: Presented by the British Museum Society, 1993

Literature: Dawson, 1994, no. 168, fn. 4

Comparable Examples: Sèvres, Musée national de la Céramique, plaster ground coloured blue, signed and dated as above[1]

USA, New York, Metropolitan Museum of Art, signed and dated as above[2]

Switzerland, Château de Penthes, Pregny, Geneva, Musée des Suisses à l'étranger, inv. A 711, see *Grandes Heures de l'Amitié Franco-Suisse*, Château de Coppet, Musée des Suisses au Service Etranger, July–October 1967, no. 814 (modern cast in uncoloured biscuit porcelain)

Christie's, South Kensington, London, 5 November 1998, Lot 204 (illus.), now in a French private collection

Paris, private collection[3]

A further example acquired in the USA was recorded in the trade in January 1996 by the Archive of the Sèvres factory

The medallion was modelled in May 1785 by Jacques Auguste Collet[4] who was taken on at the Sèvres factory soon after 7 October 1783 when d'Angivillier approved his nomination by Boizot, on condition that he won second prize at the Académie de Saint-Luc.[5] A list of modellers and sculptors at the factory drawn up in the Revolutionary years and dated 21 March 1795 gives his starting date as October 1783 and his age as forty-four.[6] His salary was 84 *livres* initially, increasing by 3 *livres* in 1786, and reaching 90 *livres* in 1788. He continued to work for the factory throughout the Revolution, until an VIII when he was no longer required. However, in an XIII he was again employed, this time in a supernumerary capacity.

Neither the model nor the mould for the medallion, which is carefully finished, have survived in the factory archive; for a blue-ground plaster, see above. Twelve examples are recorded as having been successfully fired on 1 February 1790 and delivered to 'M. Hettling', presumably for his family or friends.[6] No other medallions of Hettlinger are known.

The medallion, like the one of Alexandre Brachard (cat. no. 168) is an unusual example of a portrait of a member of the Sèvres factory workforce. Hettlinger,[7] a native of Wintherthur, Switzerland, was apprenticed as a barber-surgeon in Zurich between 1750–3. In 1756, through his connection with a certain Beugnère de la Tour, or Bongier, he obtained a post as doctor at the latter's copper mine in Baïgorry, Navarre, where he remained until 1784. During this period he undertook administrative tasks and made some technical advances, eventually becoming director of the mines and 'Inspecteur général des mines de Navarre'. His study of natural history, and in particular of entomology, resulted in several publications as well as in his election to the Academy of Sciences of Lisbon and the Physical Society of Zurich. The exact circumstances surrounding his appointment in 1784 as the Sèvres factory's inspector and co-director are unknown. In July 1793, as disorder due to Revolutionary events increased, he was briefly imprisoned at Sainte-Pélagie. However on 13 pluviôse an III (1 January 1795) he was appointed one of three directors by the Comité de l'Agriculture et des Arts, and effectively ran the factory during one of its most difficult periods until the appointment of Alexandre Brongniart. He kept his title even after this, but died soon after.[8] Hettlinger, described in a letter of 8 May 1793,[9] as '5 pieds 2p. Cheveux chatains et coupés, presque pas de sourcils, yeux gris-bleu, visage maigre et pâle', had a remarkable sideline in feather pictures, which he sold before, during and after the Revolution.[10]

A portrait of Hettlinger in profile to right preserved in the archives of the factory dated 1785 by Pithou *le jeune*[11] engraved by N. Thomas may be the source for this medallion. It shows him in an oval frame with a ribbon and laurel wreath emphasising his status and accompanied by what might loosely be called tools of his trade. At the right are: a retort, a ?brazier, an inkwell and feather pen, a scroll, a pair of dividers and a scroll with the rubric *MINERALOGIE*. At the right are three volumes, one open to show the title *[HISTOIRE] NATURELLE DE PLINE*, signalling both that he was a man of learning and that he was versed in science. Another portrait preserved at the factory,[12] which is anonymous and undated, is a pencil half-length black chalk study of him in gentleman's attire, his head turned slightly to left, probably done from the life. A terracotta bust of Hettlinger attributed to Henry Victor Roguier, sculptor and modeller at Sèvres 1783–94, is thought to date from 1790, the same year in which the production of the medallions is recorded.[13]

1. H. 14.3 cm, w. 12.1 cm (without frame). Illus. W. Ganz, 'Jean-Jacques Hettlinger, un Suisse, directeur de la Manufacture de Porcelaine de Sèvres', *Versailles, Revue de la Société suisse des amis de Versailles*, Coppet, no. 7, January 1961, p. 38. I am grateful to M. J.-R. Bory for this reference and for information on the status of the medallion in the Musée des Suisses à l'étranger (see below).
2. Inv. 45.174.4.
3. Bernard Dragesco kindly provided information on this and the other comparable examples.
4. MNS Archives de Sèvres, H 3. I owe this reference and others on Collet's career to Tamara Préaud.
5. MNS Archives de Sèvres, D 3, *liasse* 2, Citoyens composant le Departement des Modeleurs et Sculpteurs, An 1 Germinal ?? Le Cit Le Riche en est chef. I am grateful to Bernard Dragesco for this reference.
6. MNS Archives de Sèvres, HVc'4, Enfournements de Sculptures. Hettlinger himself was collector of medallions which he purchased from the factory. Many are recorded in the papers kept in a box of documents referring to Hettlinger in the factory archive, *carton* Y38.
7. Biographical details extracted from Ganz, 1961.
8. See G. Lechevallier-Chevignard, *La Manufacture de Porcelaine de Sèvres*, Paris, 1908, p. 98, pp. 118–21.
9. Actually a *laissez passer* to the Garde Nationale at Sèvres, copy kept in the factory archive, see n. 6.
10. For an example on a table of *c.*1790 purchased by Paul I of Russia, see *Treasures of the Czars*, exh. at J. Kugel, Paris, 1998, cat. compiled by A. Chouvalov and A. Kugel, no. 182.
11. For Nicolas-Pierre Pithou, *jeune*, see Savill, 1988, III, pp. 1060–63.
12. MNS Archives de Sèvres, R 183.
13. Musée national de Céramique, inv. 2822, acquired 1839, illustrated by Lechevallier-Chevignard, 1908 (see n. 8 above), p. 117.

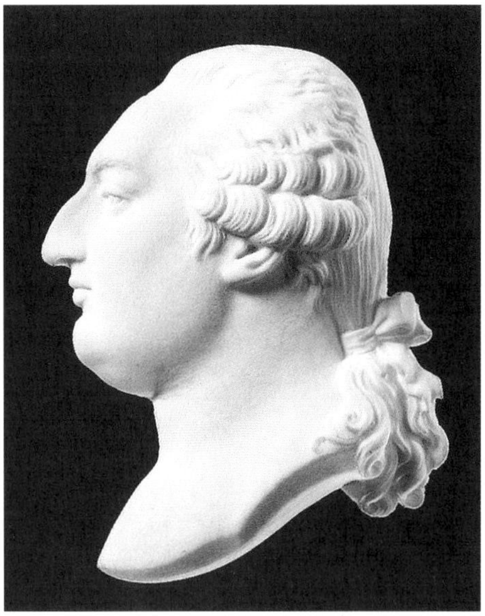

310

310 **Relief bust of King Louis XVI (1754–93)**, probably Sèvres, mid-19th century or later

H. 6.5 cm
Marks: unmarked
Reg. No. 1988, 10–11,3

Hard-paste porcelain, moulded. The King is shown to left wearing a wig en queue. Remains of brown adhesive on reverse

Provenance: Purchased, 1988

Literature: Unpublished

Medallions with this portrait in relief were made at Sèvres from 1774 and were still in demand up to 1792. Although recorded between 1789–90 in *découpé* form,[1] far more reliefs were sold around 1814 at the time of the restoration of the monarchy when they seem to have been particularly popular for mounting either singly (as on cat. no. 172) or in a panel[2] and were available in various sizes. The lack of a modeller's or repairer's mark and the rather coarse relief probably indicate a date after Brongniart's death for this and cat. nos 311 and 312. It is also possible that the reliefs were made elsewhere than at Sèvres.

1. MNS, Archives de Sèvres, Vc'4.
2. For a mounted series see Paris, Hôtel Drouot, Couturier and Nicolay, Succession du Prince J. L. de Faucigny-Lucinge, 23 October 1992, Lot 116. The practice of mounting portrait medallions in series behind glass is thought to date from the second half of the nineteenth century.

311 **Relief bust of Queen Marie-Antoinette (1755–93)**, probably Sèvres, mid-19th century or later

H. 7.2 cm
Marks: unmarked
Reg. No. 1988, 10–11,2

Hard-paste porcelain, moulded. The Queen is shown to right wearing a coronet.

Provenance: Purchased, 1988

Literature: Unpublished

Comparable examples: Paris, Hôtel Drouot, Couturier and Nicolay, Succession du Prince J.-L. de Faucigny-Lucinge, lot 116

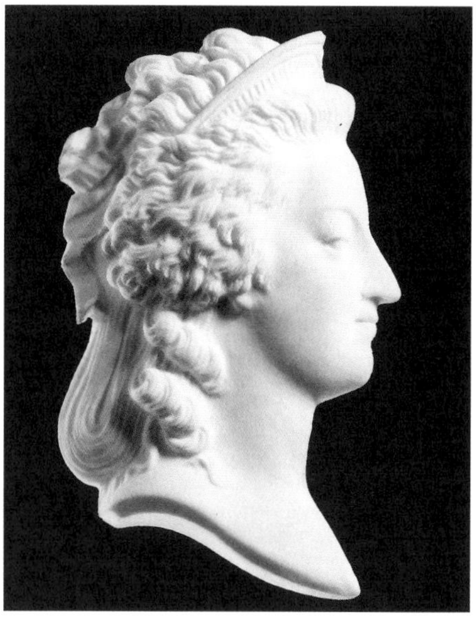

311

This medallion is a rather coarser verion, reversed, of the portrait medallion cat. no. 157, probably first modelled in 1773. For the dating of this example, see cat. no. 310. Produced in thousands at Sèvres in *découpé* form in 1791, the relief was revived from 1814.

312 **Relief bust of King Louis XVIII (1755–1824, reigned 1814/15)**, probably Sèvres, mid-19th century or later

H. 5.5 cm
Marks: unmarked
Reg. No. 1988, 10–11,1

Hard-paste porcelain, moulded. The King is shown to left wearing three decorations just distinguishable on his left breast, and a sash. There is a crown in relief on his epaulette.

Provenance: Purchased, 1988

Literature: Unpublished

Comparable examples: see above

The relief is similar to cat. no. 169.

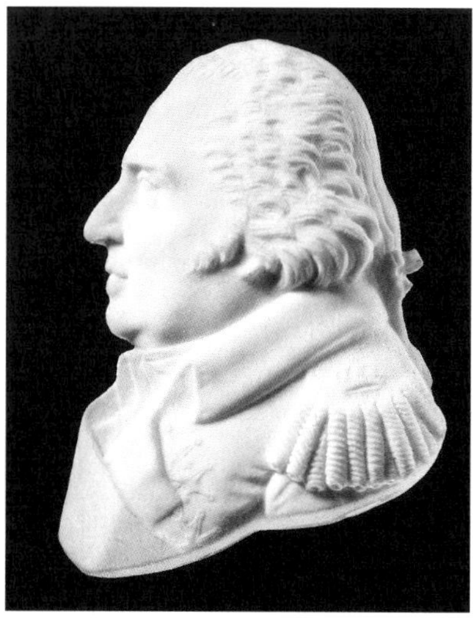

312

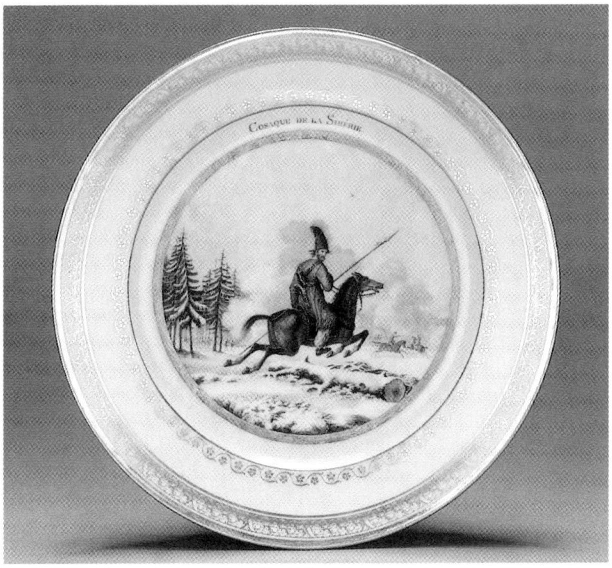

313

313 **Plate**, Dagoty factory, Paris, *c.* 1810–12

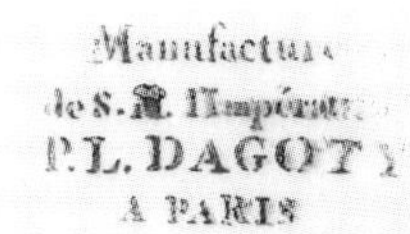

313 *mark*

D. 23.6 cm
Marks: *Manufacture/ de S. M. l'Impératrice/ P.L. DAGOTY/ A PARIS* stencilled in red
Reg. No. 1993, 6–11,1

Hard-paste porcelain, thrown. Painted in the well of the plate with a horseman wearing a green conical hat and a red coat and holding a lance, jumping across a log in a snowy battlefield with soldiers fighting in the far distance, inscribed above in gold *COSAQUE DE LA SIBÉRIE* (Siberian Cossack). Gilt motifs on a very pale yellow ground include a band of acanthus near the rim, which is gilt.

Provenance: Purchased, 1993

Comparable Examples: see cat. nos 314, 315

Literature: Unpublished

For discussion see cat. no. 315.

314 **Plate**, Dagoty factory, Paris, *c.* 1810–12

D. 23.6 cm
Marks: as above, incised (?) *21*
Reg. No. 1993, 6–11,2

Hard-paste porcelain, thrown. Painted in the well of the plate with a soldier in a green uniform and hat, a sword at his side and carrying a bayonet in a snowy wooded landscape with troops fighting in the distance, inscribed above in gold *CHASSEUR DE LA LIGNE RUSSE* (Light Infantryman of the Russian Line).

For discussion see cat. no. 315.

315 **Plate**, Dagoty factory, Paris, *c.* 1810–12

D. 23.6 cm
Marks: as on cat. no. 313
Reg. No. 1993, 6–11,3

Hard-paste porcelain, thrown. Painted in the well of the plate with a horseman crossing a frozen stream into a wood. He wears a yellow coat with purple stripes tied with a grey sash, orange trousers and a fur hat with an orange crown. He carries two sheaves of arrows and turns to aim an arrow from his bow behind him. Two soldiers on a bridge are shooting in the same direction. Inscribed above in gold *CALMOUK TORGAUTE ENTRE LE WOLGA ET LE JAÏK* (Torgut Kalmuck between the Volga and the Yaik).[1]

The painter responsible for the detailed scenes on cat. nos 313, 314 and 315 remains unknown. A rather similar horseman (probably a Polish member of the light horse in the service of the Imperial Army) in a snowy landscape with a battle scene in the background is painted on one of six glass panels, at least one of which is signed *Dagoty* and dated 1809.[2] The subjects, which may represent officers of the Napoleonic army in Russia, are in the style of Jacques François-Joseph Swebach-Desfontaines (1769–1823), but do not appear in any of the four hundred plates in the four volumes of *Encyclopédie Pittoresque ou suite de Compositions, Caprices, et Etudes Gravée au trait par Swebach dit Fontaine*.[3] It is likely that the plates were produced during Napoleon's Russian campaign before his defeat in 1812.

1. The Torguts are a West Mongolian Kalmuck tribe. The Yaik River is now more usually known as the Ural River. It rises in the Urals and flows into the Caspian Sea. I am grateful to Barry Ager and to Chris Thomas of the British Library for their assistance in translating this inscription.
2. In the Musée national de Céramique, Sèvres, inv. 26639, illus. C. Bouchon, 'Les porcelainiers et la peinture sur verre (1800–1850)', *Sèvres, Revue de la Société des Amis du Musée national de Céramique*, no. 3, 1994, p. 16, fig. 2, and p. 19.
3. Published at Paris, n.d. I am grateful to Amy Clarke for searching these volumes.

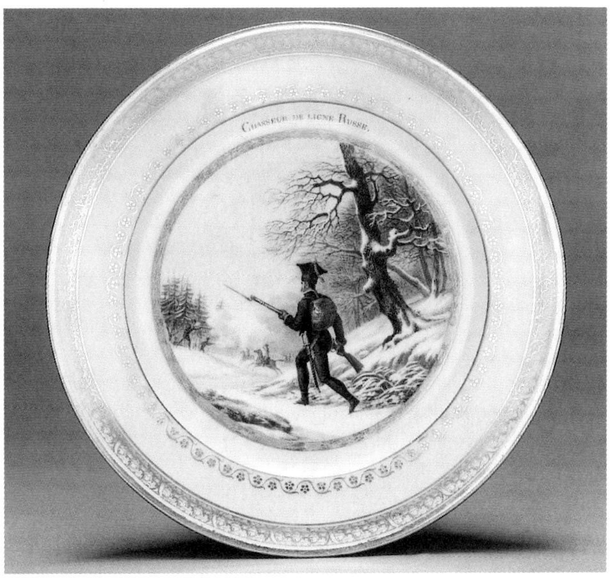

314

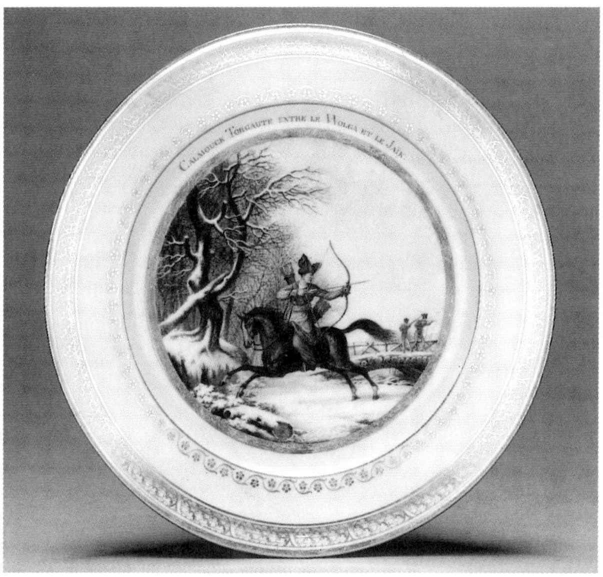

315

Concordance of Catalogue and Register Numbers

OA stands for Old Acquisition, for which acquisition details are uncertain.

In 1897 Augustus Franks bequeathed his collection exhibited at Bethnal Green Museum the previous year; collection numbers prefixed "Franks" were catalogued by him in 1896. Further items bequeathed by him are prefixed "FB" together with the Franks Bequest register numbers.

Several objects have the same register number, but have been catalogued separately.

OA 10450	25
OA 10454	36
OA 10576	237
OA 10719	28
OA 10720	196
OA 10721	107
OA 10723	240
FB 11 (AF 3214)	278
FB 14 (AF 3217)	284
FB 15 (AF 3218)	285
FB 16 (AF 3219)	130
FB 18 (AF 3220)	234
FB 19 (AF 3221)	282
FB 21 (AF 3223)	222
FB 26 (AF 3193)	2
FB 28 (AF 3228)	20
FB 30 (AF 3230)	10
FB 34 (AF 3234)	255
FB 34 (AF 3234)	256
FB 35 (AF 3235)	257
FB 36 (AF 3236)	144
FB 37 (AF 3237)	219
FB 37 (AF 3237)	220
FB 39 (AF 3239)	262
FB 42 (AF 3241)	289
FB 43 (AF 3242)	283
FB 7 (AF 3192)	38
FB 8 (AF 3211)	18
FB 9 (AF 3212)	29
Franks 119	290
Franks 329	3
Franks 330	4
Franks 331	5
Franks 332	6
Franks 333	8
Franks 334	9
Franks 335	27
Franks 336	24
Franks 337	30
Franks 338	19
Franks 339	31
Franks 340	12
Franks 341	21
Franks 342	11
Franks 343	13
Franks 344, 344A	14
Franks 345	15
Franks 346	296
Franks 347	37
Franks 348	47
Franks 349	42
Franks 350	50
Franks 351	41
Franks 352	53
Franks 353	54
Franks 354	51
Franks 355	57
Franks 356	59
Franks 357	58
Franks 358	55
Franks 359	201
Franks 360	298
Franks 361	61
Franks 361	62
Franks 362	198
Franks 363	199
Franks 364	200
Franks 365	206
Franks 366	207
Franks 367	204
Franks 368	205
Franks 369	208
Franks 370	209
Franks 371	293
Franks 372	64
Franks 373	67
Franks 374	68
Franks 375	74
Franks 376	66
Franks 377	71
Franks 378	78
Franks 379	79
Franks 380	94
Franks 381	116
Franks 382	118
Franks 383	127
Franks 384	129
Franks 385	122
Franks 386	131
Franks 387	132
Franks 388	133
Franks 388	133
Franks 389	193
Franks 390	178
Franks 391	181
Franks 392	145
Franks 393	292
Franks 394	158
Franks 395	161
Franks 395	164
Franks 395	165
Franks 395	166
Franks 396	173
Franks 397	169
Franks 398	172
Franks 399	287
Franks 400	211
Franks 401	210
Franks 403	299
Franks 404	226
Franks 405	228
Franks 406	225
Franks 407	224
Franks 409	214
Franks 410	215
Franks 411	223
Franks 412	235
Franks 413	247
Franks 414	260
Franks 415	261
Franks 416	254
Franks 417	253
Franks 418	251
Franks 419	252
Franks 420	300
Franks 421	301
Franks 422	241
Franks 423	242
Franks 424	243
Franks 425	244
Franks 426	259
Franks 427	294
Franks 428	258
Franks 429	264
Franks 430	271
Franks 431	267
Franks 432	263
Franks 433	272
Franks 434	281
Franks 435	279
Franks 436	280
Franks 436A	297
Franks 437	286
Franks 438	288
Franks 439	229
Franks 440	230
Franks 441	232
Franks 442	233
Franks 444	295
Franks 445	236
Franks 506	65
Franks 73	123
1899,10-6,3	277
1899,10-6,4	276
1899,10-6,5	273
1899,10-6,6	274

1899,10–6,7	275
1899,10–6,8	93
1899,10–6,9	111
1899,10–6,10	128
1899,10–6,11	187
1899,10–6,12	190
1899,10–6,42	202
1901,4–25,1	191
1901,12–16,1	43
1906,11–3,1757	176
1909,12–1,8	153
1909,12–1,161	174
1909,12–1,162	175
1909,12–1,218	154
1909,12–1,367	162
1913,12–20,133	194
1913,12–20,134	33
1913,12–20,135	250
1923,3–14,135	16
1923,3–14,162	70
1923,3–14,168	86
1924,2–11,1	46
1924,11–15,1	291
1926,10–16,1	268
1926,10–16,2	269
1926,12–22,1	69
1927,10–13,1	188
1928,5–19,1	73
1928,7–18,9	203
1929,10–17,1	75
1930,5–14,1	76
1931,10–19,7	22
1931,10–19,8	23
1931,10–19,9	32
1931,10–19,10	60
1931,10–19,11	49
1931,10–19,12	45
1931,10–19,13	39
1931,10–19,14	95
1931,10–19,15	88
1931,10–19,16	92
1931,10–19,17	170
1931,10–19,18	171
1931,10–19,19	163
1931,10–19,20	160
1931,10–19,21	167
1934,2–13,1	248
1934,7–22,12	17
1935,12–18,1 and 2	125
1936,7–15,135	270
1936,7–15,136	265
1937,6–14,1	48
1937,11–17,1	80
1937,12–16,1	213
1938,2–16,1	72
1938,2–17,1	81
1938,4–14,1	140
1938,5–17,1	216
1938,7–13,1	35
1939,3–4,1	126
1939,5–4,1	82
1940,10–2,1	212
1940,4–1,7	1
1940,4–1,21	197
1941,4–7,1	177
1942,4–8,2	52
1948,12–3,1	112
1948,12–3,2 and 3	109
1948,12–3,4	108
1948,12–3,5	106
1948,12–3,6	141
1948,12–3,7	120
1948,12–3,8	113
1948,12–3,9	83
1948,12–3,10	84
1948,12–3,11	124
1948,12–3,12	114
1948,12–3,13	121
1948,12–3,14 and 15	102
1948,12–3,16 and 17	103
1948,12–3,18	97
1948,12–3,19 and 20	85
1948,12–3,21	134
1948,12–3,22	87
1948,12–3,23	147
1948,12–3,24	148
1948,12–3,25	149
1948,12–3,26 and 27	105
1948,12–3,28 and 29	119
1948,12–3,30 and 31	115
1948,12–3,32 and 33	139
1948,12–3,34 and 35	96
1948,12–3,36	143
1948,12–3,37	142
1948,12–3,38	146
1948,12–3,39	91
1948,12–3,40	90
1948,12–3,41	137
1948,12–3,42	99
1948,12–3,43	100
1948,12–3,44	101
1948,12–3,45	136
1948,12–3,46	89
1948,12–3,47	104
1948,12–3,48	138
1948,12–3,49	117
1948,12–3,50	110
1948,12–3,51	98
1948,12–3,52	135
1957,12–1,52	56
1977,11–2,1	44
1980,7–11,1	238
1981,1–1,96	227
1981,1–1,102	195
1981,1–1,106	26
1981,1–1,107	217
1981,6–2,1	185
1981,6–2,2	184
1982,12–3,5A and 5B	239
1985, 1–3, 1 to 4	281
1985,12–3,1 and 2	180
1986,10–15,1	157
1986,10–18,1	183
1987,1–6,1	63
1987,1–7,1	40
1987,7–6,1	179
1987,11–2,1	192
1987,12–1,1	182
1987,12–6,1	7
1988,6–4,1	249
1988,6–5,1	245
1988,7–1,1	151
1988,7–1,2	150
1988,7–2,1	159
1988,10–10, 1 to 3	34
1988,10–11,1	312
1988,10–11,2	311
1988,10–11,3	310
1989,5–6,1 and 2	231
1989,5–6,3	218
1989,5–6,4	77
1989,7–7,1	156
1989,9–8,1	246
1990,4–5,1	221
1990,7–8,1	266
1991,10–10,1 and 2	186
1992,1–6,1	152
1992,2–2,1	168
1992,4–2,1	155
1992,7–9,1	189
1993,1–1,1	309
1993,6–10,1	305
1993,6–11,1	313
1993,6–11,2	314
1993,6–11,3	315
1993,7–210,1	306
1993,10–9,1	308
1994,4–6,1	302
1998,3–3,1	304
1999,7–2,1 to 4	307
1999,9–3,1	303

Selected Bibliography

Further references will be found in the catalogue entries and the historical essays preceding each factory or, in the case of Vincennes/Sèvres, preceding each section.

Throughout the text and Bibliography the following abbreviations are used: *Cahiers* for *Cahiers de la Céramique et des Arts du feu*; *ECC Trans.* for *Transactions of the English Ceramic Circle*

Adams, Elizabeth and Redstone, David, *Bow Porcelain*, London, 1981.

Albiker, Carl, *Die Meissner Porzellantiere im 18. Jahrhundert*, Berlin, 1959.

Alfassa, Paul and Guérin, Jacques, *Porcelaine française du XVIIe au milieu du XIXe siècle*, Paris, 1932.

Ananoff, Alexandre, *L'Oeuvre dessiné de François Boucher (1703–1770)*, Paris, 1976, 2 vols.

Anon ('D.C.'), 'Thomas Goode's and the Czar', *The Antique Collector*, October 1987, p. 105.

Anon ('G.M.'), 'Paris Studio Talk', *The Studio, an illustrated magazine of fine and applied art*, Vol. XXIII, 1901, pp. 64–9.

Anon ('W.H.'), 'Kunstlerische Farben-Drucke', *Deutsche Kunst und Dekoration*, VI Jahrg., Heft 7, April 1903, pp. 317–48.

Arminjon, Cathérine and Blondel, Nicole, *Objets civils domestiques, vocabulaire typologique*, Paris, 1984.

Arnason, H. Harvard, *Jean-Antoine Houdon, le plus grand sculpteur français du XVIIIe siècle*, Lausanne, 1976.

Austin, John C., *Chelsea Porcelain at Williamsburg*, Williamsburg, Virginia, 1977.

Ballu, Nicole, 'La carrière des Dubois', *Cahiers*, no. 10, 1958, pp. 92–3.

Ballu, Nicole, 'Influence de l'Extrême-Orient sur le style de Chantilly au XVIIIe siècle, *Cahiers*, no. 11, 1958, pp. 100–12.

Ballu, Nicole, *La porcelaine française*, Paris, n.d. (1958).

Baltard, Louis Pierre, *Paris et ses Monuments Mesurés Dessinés et Gravés par Baltard, Architecte*, Paris, An XIII (1805).

Barbe, Gérard, *Le service du Roi Louis-Philippe au Château de Fontainebleau*, privately published, Paris, 1989.

Barbe, Gérard, 'Déjeuners en porcelaine de Sèvres de 1830 à 1848', *L'Estampille*, no. 235, avril 1990, pp. 58–69.

Baulez, Christian, 'Notes sur quelques meubles et objets d'art des appartements intérieurs de Louis XVI et de Marie-Antoinette', *La Revue du Louvre*, 5/6, 1978, pp. 359–73.

Beach, Vincent W., *Charles X of France – His Life and Times*, Boulder, Colorado, 1971.

Beall, Karen F., *Kaufrufe und Strassenhändler, Cries and Itinerant Trades*, Hamburg, 1975.

Beaucamp-Markowsky, Barbara, *Boîtes en Porcelaine des manufactures européennes au 18e siècle*, Fribourg, 1985.

Bellaigue, Geoffrey de, 'Sèvres Artists and their sources I: Paintings and Drawings', *Burlington Magazine*, Vol. CXXII, no. 931, October 1980, pp. 667–76.

Bellaigue, Geoffrey de, *Sèvres Porcelain in the Collection of Her Majesty the Queen: The Louis XVI Service*, Cambridge, 1986.

Bellaigue, Sir Geoffrey de, 'Sèvres', in *J. Pierpont Morgan, Collector, European Decorative Arts from the Wadsworth Atheneum*, ed. L.H. Roth, 1987.

Belleudy, Jules, 'Joseph Le Riche', *Bulletin de la société de l'histoire de l'art français*, 1924, 1er fascicule, pp. 31–7.

Bénézit, Emmanuel, *Dictionnaire critique et documentaire des peintres, sculpteurs, dessinateurs et graveurs*, Paris, 1976.

Benker, Gertrud S., *Alte Bestecke: ein Beitrag zur Geschichte der Tischkultur*, Munich, 1978.

Berges, Ruth, *Collectors' Choice of Porcelain and Faïence*, South Brunswick and New York, 1967.

Berges, Ruth, 'Mennecy Porcelains from the Elizabeth Parke Firestone Collection', *Connoisseur*, Vol. 170, no. 686, April 1969, pp. 247–54.

Berges, Ruth, 'Falconet at Sèvres', *Antique Collector*, Vol. 59, no. 4, April 1988, pp. 74–9.

Berthier, Paul, *Réflexions sur l'art et la vie de Jean-Philippe Rameau (1683–1764)*, Paris, 1957.

Besterman, Theodore, *Voltaire*, Oxford, 2nd ed., 1976.

Bimson, Mavis, 'The examination of ceramics by X-ray powder diffraction', *Studies in Conservation*, 14, 1969, pp. 83–9.

Birioukova, Nina, *Figurines et Groupes en Porcelaine des Manufactures Françaises du XVIIIe siècle*, Leningrad, 1962.

Birioukova, Nina, 'A propos des marques sur les biscuits de Vincennes et de Sèvres', *Cahiers*, no. 40, 1968, pp. 257–61.

Bloit, Michel, *Trois siècles de Porcelaine de Paris*, Paris, 1988.

Bodelsen, Merete, 'Sèvres-Copenhagen, Crystal Glazes and Stoneware at the turn of the Century', *The Royal Copenhagen Manufactory 1775–1975*, Copenhagen, 1975, pp. 59–84.

Bodin, Chevalier Soulange, 'Notice nécrologique sur Madame la marquise de Grollier', *Annales d'Horticulture*, December 1828, pp. 348–54.

Boinet, Amedée C.L., 'Les bustes de Caffiéri de la Bibliothèque Sainte-Geneviève', *Gazette des Beaux-Arts*, 5e période, III, 1921, pp. 133–46.

Bourgeois, Emile, 'L'état civil des bustes et médaillons de Marie-Antoinette et de Louis XVI', *La revue de l'art ancien et moderne*, Vol. XXII, no. 129, 10 December 1907, pp. 401–12; Vol. XXIII, no. 130, 10 January 1908, pp. 31–44.

Bourgeois, Emile, *Le Biscuit de Sèvres au XVIIIe Siècle*, Paris, 1909, 2 vols.

Bourgeois, Emile and Lechevallier-Chevignard, Georges, *Le Biscuit de Sèvres – receuil des modèles de la manufacture de Sèvres au XVIII (18) siècle*, Paris, n.d. (1913).

Bowes Museum, Barnard Castle, County Durham, *French Art, the Bowes Museum*, County Museum Service Durham County Council, n.d.

Bradley, H. Gilbert, *Ceramics of Derbyshire 1750–1975*, privately published, London, 1978.

Brancas, Louis-Léon-Félicité, duc de, *Observations sur le Mémoire de M. Guettard Concernant la Porcelaine*, Paris, 1766.

Brébisson, R. de, 'La porcelaine de Caen', *Revue Normande et Percheronne*, Alençon, 1895, pp. 21–8.

Bresc-Bautier, Geneviève and Pinget, Anne, *Sculptures des jardins du Louvre, du Carrousel et des Tuileries*, Paris, 1986.

Britsch, Amedée, *La Jeunesse de Philippe-Egalité*, Paris, 1926.

Bröhan, Karl H., *Kunst der Jahrhundertwende und der zwanziger Jahre, Sammlung Karl H. Bröhan, Berlin*, Berlin 1977, Vol. 2, part 2.

Brongniart, Alexandre, 'Essai sur les couleurs obtenues des oxydes métalliques, et fixées par la fusion sur les différents corps vitreux', *Journal des Mines*, Vol. XII, an 10 (1802), no. 67, pp. 58–80.

Brongniart, Alexandre, *Première Mémoire des Kaolins ou argiles à Porcelaine, sur la nature, le gisement, l'origine et l'emploi de cette sorte d'argile*, Paris, 1839.

Brongniart, Alexandre, *Traité des arts céramiques ou des poteries*, Paris, 1844, 3 vols.

Brookner, Anita, 'Prud'hon: Master Decorator of the Empire', *Apollo*, Vol. LXXX, no. 31, September 1964, pp. 192–8.

Brown, Laurence, *A Catalogue of British Historical Medals 1760–1960*, London, 1980.

Brunet, Marcelle, *The Frick Collection, An Illustrated Catalogue, Vol. VII, Porcelains, Oriental and French*, New York, 1974.

Brunet, Marcelle and Préaud, Tamara, *Sèvres, des origines à nos jours*, Fribourg, 1978.

Bryant, G.E., *The Chelsea Porcelain Toys: Scent-Bottles, Bonbonnières, Etuis, Seals and Statuettes, made at the Chelsea Factory, 1745–1769, and Derby-Chelsea, 1770–1784*, London, 1925.

Burollet, Thérèse, *Musée Cognacq-Jay, II, Porcelaines*, Paris, 1983.

Buten, David, *18th-Century Wedgwood, A Guide for Collectors and Connoisseurs*, London, 1980.

Butler, Kira, 'Sèvres for the Imperial Court,' *Apollo*, Vol. CI, no. 160, June 1975, pp. 452–7.

Casanova, Maria Letizia, *Le Porcellane Francesi nei Musei di Napoli*, Naples, 1974.

Cavrois, Baron L., *Le refuge d'Etrun et la manufacture de porcelaines d'Arras*, Arras, 1877.

Chabanon, Michel-Paul-Gui, *Eloge sur M. Rameau*, Paris, 1764.

Chaffers, William, *The New Keramik Gallery*, London, 1926.

Charles, Rollo, *Continental Porcelain of the Eighteenth Century*, London, 1964.

Charleston, Robert J.C., 'Sèvres and other French porcelain in Earl Spencer's collection at Althorp', *Connoisseur*, Vol. CLXXIII, no. 696, February 1970, pp. 77–86.

Chavagnac, Xavier de, 'Porcelaines de Sèvres, collection E.M. Hodgkins', *Les Arts*, no. 89, May 1909, pp. 1–32.

Chavagnac, Xavier de, *Catalogue des porcelaines françaises de M.J. Pierpont Morgan*, Paris, 1910.

Chavagnac, comte Xavier de and Grollier, marquis de, *Histoire des manufactures françaises de porcelaine*, Paris, 1906.

Chevallier, Bernard, 'Sèvres sous le Second Empire', *L'Estampille*, no. 112, August 1979, pp. 28–39.

Chevallier, Bernard, 'Les marques en creux de la porcelaine de Sèvres (1801–1871)', *Keramik-Freunde der Schweiz*, 94, December 1980, pp. 5–23.

Choiseul-Gouffier, comtesse de, née comtesse de Tiesenhausen, *Mémoires historiques sur l'Empereur Alexandre et la Cour de Russie*, Paris, 1829.

Chompret, J., Bloch, J., Guérin, Jacques and Alfassa, Paul, *et al.*, *Répertoire de la faïence française publié à l'occasion de "l'Exposition rétrospective de la Faïence Française" au Musée des arts décoratifs*, Paris, 1933, 8 vols.

Clarke, T.H., 'French Influences at Chelsea', *ECC Trans.*, Vol. 4, Part 5 (1959), pp. 45–57.

Clarke, T.H., 'The French Touch at Meissen: Christophe Huet's watercolour drawings for the Cris de Paris, 1753', *1990 International Art Dealers' Show Handbook*, Seventh Regiment Armory, Park Avenue at 67th Street, New York City, October 1990, pp. 28–33.

Clifford, Timothy, 'Wedgwood at the National Portrait Gallery', review, *Burlington Magazine*, Vol. CXV, no. 849, December 1973, pp. 832–5.

Clifford, Timothy, 'Nicolas Gauron – A Virtuoso Modeller at Tournai and Chelsea', *The Rococo in England, a Symposium*, ed. C. Hind, Victoria and Albert Museum, London, 1986, pp. 161–74.

Cordey, Jean, *Inventaire des biens de Madame de Pompadour rédigé après son décès*, Paris, 1939.

Courajod, Louis, *Livre-journal de Lazare-Duvaux, marchand-bijoutier ordinaire du roy 1748–1758, précédé d'une étude sur le goût et le commerce des objets d'art au milieu du XVIIIe siècle*, Paris, 1878, 2 vols.

Craven, Babette, 'French Soft Paste Porcelain in the Collection of Mr and Mrs William Brown Meloney', *Connoisseur*, Vol. CXLIII, no. 577, April 1959, pp. 135–42.

Cushion, John P., *Continental Porcelain*, London, revised ed. 1982.

D'Agnel, Abbé G. Arnaud, *La faïence et la porcelaine de Marseille*, Paris, 1911.

D'Albis, Antoine, 'Procédés de fabrication de la porcelaine tendre de Vincennes, d'après les livres de Hellot', *Faenza*, LXIX (1983), no. 3–4, pp. 202–15.

D'Albis, Antoine, 'Les premières années de la manufacture des porcelaines de Vincennes', *Faenza*, LXX (1984), no. 5–6, pp. 479–93.

D'Albis, Antoine, 'The early years of the porcelain manufactory of Vincennes', *The International Ceramics Fair and Seminar, London, Handbook*, June 1986, pp. 10–23.

D'Albis, Antoine and Préaud, Tamara, *Les éléments de datation des porcelaines de Vincennes avant 1753*, privately published in typescript by the French Porcelain Society, London, II, 1986.

D'Albis, Antoine, 'Gravant's secret or the first royal privilege of Vincennes', *The International Ceramics Fair and Seminar, London, Handbook*, June 1987, pp. 10–19.

D'Albis, Antoine, 'A documentary Vincennes *inventaire*', *Sotheby's Art at Auction 1987–1988*, London, 1988, pp. 366–71.

D'Albis *et al.*, *Sèvres, Musée national de Céramique, nouvelles acquisitions (1979–1989)*, Paris, 1989.

D'Albis, Jean and Romanet, Céleste, *La Porcelaine de Limoges*, Paris, 1980.

D'Espezel, Pierre, *Le Palais Royal*, Paris, 1936.

Dacier, Emile, 'L'Antiquaire de Saint-Louis', *La Revue de l'Art Ancien et Moderne*, Vol. XIII, no. 73, April 1903, pp. 241–54.

Dacier, Emile, *La Gravure en France au XVIIIe siècle, La Gravure de Genre et de Moeurs*, Paris and Brussels, 1925.

Dacier, Baron Bon Joseph, 'Notice sur la vie et les ouvrages de M. le comte de Choiseul-Gouffier', *Mémoire de l'Académie des inscriptions et belles-lettres*, 23 July 1819, pp. 1–24.

Dallot-Naudin, Yvonne, 'Mennecy, porcelaine tendre, une grace féminine', *ABC Décor*, May 1983, no. 220, pp. 17–28, 37–48 and in Malgras, Gilbert-Jean, *Porcelaines tendres françaises*, Paris, 1983, pp. 113–52.

Dallot-Naudin, Yvonne and Jacob, Alain, 'Porcelaines de Vincennes: sur les traces de Buffon', *ABC Décor*, October 1983, no. 225, pp. 17–24, 37–44 and in Malgras, Gilbert-Jean, *Porcelaines tendres françaises*, Paris, 1983, pp. 217–30.

Dallot-Naudin, Yvonne, 'Porcelaine de Saint-Cloud à l'heure nippone', *ABC Décor*, June 1983, no. 221, pp. 29–36 and in Malgras, Gilbert-Jean, *Porcelaines tendres françaises*, Paris, 1983, pp. 105–12.

Dallot-Naudin, Yvonne and Jacquemart, Albert, 'Saint-Cloud, une porcelaine royale', *ABC Décor*, April 1983, no. 219, pp. 13–24, 41–52 and in Malgras, Gilbert-Jean, *Porcelaines tendres françaises*, Paris, 1983, pp. 69–104.

Dallot-Naudin, Yvonne, 'Chantilly 1ere partie, triomphe de la porcelaine française', *ABC Décor*, September 1982, no. 212, pp. 18–48 and in Malgras, Gilbert-Jean, *Porcelaines tendres françaises*, Paris, 1983, pp. 9–68.

Dallot-Naudin, Yvonne and Jacob, Alain, 'Une soeur de Mennecy, Bourg-la-Reine', in Malgras, Gilbert-Jean, *Porcelaines tendres françaises*, Paris, 1983, pp. 153–60.

Darblay, Aymé, *Villeroy, son passé, sa fabrique de porcelaine, son état actuel*, Corbeil, 1901.

Dardenne, E.J., *Essai sur Paul-Louis Cyfflé*, Brussels, 1912.

Dauguet, Claire and Guillemé-Brulon, Dorothée, *La porcelaine française*, Paris, n.d.

Dauterman, Carl C., 'Chinoiserie Motifs and Sèvres: some fresh evidence', *Apollo*, Vol. LXXXIV, no. 58, December 1966, pp. 476–81.

Dauterman, Carl C., *The Wrightsman Collection, Vol. IV, Porcelain*, New York, 1970.

Dauterman, Carl C., *Sèvres Porcelain, Makers and Marks of the Eighteenth Century*, New York, 1986.

Davillier, J.C., *Histoire des faïences et porcelaines de Moustiers, Marseille et autres fabriques méridionales*, Paris, 1863.

Davis, I.M., *The Harlot and the Statesman, the story of Elizabeth Armistead and Charles James Fox*, London, 1986.

Davis, Stewart G., 'Some English pottery and porcelain figures connected with Alsace and Lorraine', *Burlington Magazine*, Vol. LI, no. CCVI, November 1927, pp. 221–8.

Dawson, Aileen, 'French Biscuit Porcelain in the style of Wedgwood's Jasperware', *Apollo*, Vol. CXVI, no. 246, August 1982, pp. 94–102.

Dawson, Aileen, 'Copiers or Competitors? Wedgwood and the French Porcelain Factories', *Grosvenor House Antiques Fair 1983 Handbook*, pp. 37–9.

Dawson, Aileen, 'Europaïsche Keramik im British Museum', *Weltkunst*, 1 July 1985, pp. 1878–82.

Dawson, Aileen, 'Pieces for Presentation', *Ceramics*, February/March 1986, pp. 71–6.

Dawson, Aileen, 'Two Napoleonic Sèvres Ice-Pails: A Present for an Emperor', *Apollo*, Vol. CXXIV, no. 296, October 1986, pp. 328–33.

Dawson, Aileen, 'Sèvres porcelain in the V & A, new light on some eighteenth-century hard-paste rarities', *V & A Album 5*, London, 1986, pp. 343–52.

Dawson, Aileen, 'Medals as Models for Ceramic Medallions, a mystery story', *The Medal*, Summer 1987, p. 30.

Dawson, Aileen, 'The F. Howard Paget Collection in the British Museum', *Derby Porcelain International Society Newsletter*, no. 11, January 1988, pp. 12–15.

Dawson, Aileen *et al.*, 'Recent acquisitions of post-medieval ceramics and glass in the British Museum's Department of Medieval and Later Antiquities 1982–88', *Burlington Magazine*, May 1988, Vol. CXXX, no. 1022, p. 399–404.

Dawson, Aileen, 'Gold Foil Decoration on enamel, glass and porcelain: a new look', *Burlington Magazine*, Vol. CXXXII, no. 1046, May 1990, pp. 336–42.

Dawson, Aileen *et al.*, 'Recent acquisitions of post-medieval ceramics and metalwork in the British Museum's Department of Medieval and Later Antiquities (1988–1990), *Burlington Magazine*, Vol. CXXXII, no. 1050, September 1990, pp. 671–6.

Daydi, M. Olivar, *La Porcelana en Europa*, Barcelona, 1953, 2 vols.

Dazincourt, Joseph-Jean-Baptiste Albouy called, *Notice historique sur Préville*, Paris, 1800.

De Plas, Solange, *Les faïences de Strasbourg et l'Est de la France*, Paris, n.d.

Debaisieux, Françoise, 'Caen. Musée des Beaux-Arts, orfèvrerie et porcelaine de Caen', *La Revue du Louvre*, 1980, no. 1–80, pp. 54–6.

Dehaye, Pierre, 'L'Ecole des Mines à la Monnaie', *Le Club français de la médaille*, 82/83, premier trimestre 1984, pp. 2–5.

Demmin, Auguste, *Guide de l'Amateur de Faïences et Porcelaines*, Paris, Vol. II, 1873, 4th ed.

Dennis, Faith, *The Metropolitan Museum, Three centuries of French domestic silver: its makers and its marks*, New York, 1960, 2 vols.

Deroubaix, Christine, *Les porcelaines de Tournai du Musée de Mariemont*, Mariemont, 1958.

Description des Machines et Procédés specifiés dans les brevets d'invention de perfectionnement et d'importation dont la durée est expirée, Paris, 1827.

Detweiler, Susan G., 'French Porcelain on Federal Tables', *American Ceramic Circle Bulletin/Number 3*, New York, 1982, pp. 87–110.

Detweiler, Susan G., *George Washington's Chinaware*, New York, 1982.

Diderot, Denis, *Le Neveu de Rameau*, Livre de Poche ed., Paris, 1984.

Dorveaux, Paul, 'Apothicaires membres de l'Académie Royale des Sciences XI Balthazar-Georges Sage', *Revue de l'histoire de la pharmacie*, 1936, pp. 1–31.

Draper, James, 'New Terracottas by Boizot and Julien', *Metropolitan Museum Journal*, 12/1977, pp. 141–9.

Drey, Rudolf, E.A., 'Une série de vases de pharmacie en porcelaine tendre de Chantilly', *Revue d'Histoire de la Pharmacie*, Vol. XX, no. 210, September 1971, pp. 475–8.

Drey, Rudolf, E.A., *Apothecary Jars*, London, 1978.

Drey, Rudolf, E.A., *Les Pots de pharmacie du monde entier*, Paris, 1978.

Du Pasquier, Jacqueline, 'Du nouveau sur la porcelaine de Bordeaux', *Revue historique de Bordeaux et du Département de la Gironde*, Tome XXVI, nouvelle série, 1977, pp. 79–89.

Du Pasquier, Jacqueline, 'La céramique à Bordeaux et la manufacture des Terres de Bordes (1781–1790)', *Le port des lumières 3. Le décor de la vie, Bordeaux 1781–1790*, Musée des arts décoratifs, Bordeaux, 1989.

Duchon, Nicole, *La Manufacture de porcelaine de Mennecy Villeroy*, Le Mée-sur-Seine, 1988.

Dupont, Patrick, *Porcelaines françaises aux XVIIIe et XIXe siècles*, Paris, 1987.

Durand, Yves, *Les Fermiers Généraux au XVIIIe siècle*, Paris, 1971.

Easum, Chester V., *Prince Henry of Prussia, brother of Frederick the Great*, Madison, Wisconsin, 1942.

Emerson, J., *Selections of French Porcelain from the Eighteenth Century European Porcelain Collection of the Seattle Art Museum*, privately published in typescript by the French Porcelain Society, VI, London, 1990.

Ennès, Pierre, 'Le surtout de mariage en porcelaine de Sèvres, du Dauphin, 1769–1770', *La Revue de l'Art*, no. 76, June 1987, pp. 63–73.

Eriksen, Svend, *Sèvres Porcelain, the James A. de Rothschild Collection at Waddesdon Manor*, Fribourg, 1968.

Eriksen, Svend, *French Porcelain in Palazzo Pitti*, Florence, 1973.

Eriksen, Svend, *Early Neo-Classicism in France*, London, 1974.

Eriksen, Svend, *The David Collection, French Porcelain*, Copenhagen, 1980.

Eriksen, Svend and de Bellaigue, Geoffrey, *Sèvres Porcelain: Vincennes and Sèvres 1740–1800*, London 1987.

Esperandieu, Emile, 'Renseignements inédits sur la collection du comte de Choiseul-Gouffier', *Mémoires de la société national des antiquaires de France*, Vol. 158, sixième série, VII, 1899, pp. 161–211.

Espinay de Saint Luc, Michel de, *Contribution à l'iconologie du XVIIIe siècle: le biscuit de Sèvres et le théâtre italien de 1752 à 1781* . . ., unpublished thesis for the Ecole du Louvre.

Fairclough, Oliver, 'Two Pieces from the Sèvres *Service Iconographique Grec*', *National Art Collections Fund Review 1990*, pp. 149–52.

Faré, Michel and Fabrice, *La vie silencieuse en France, la nature morte au XVIIIe siècle*, Fribourg, 1976.

Faÿ-Hallé, Antoinette and Mundt, Barbara, *Porcelain of the Nineteenth Century*, New York, 1983.

Flammeront, J., 'Les portraits de Marie-Antoinette', *Gazette des Beaux-Arts*, Part 1, Vol. XVIII, July 1897, pp. 5–21; Part 2, Vol. XVIII, October 1897, pp. 283–303; Part 3, Vol. XIX, March 1898, pp. 183–95, May 1898, pp. 379–92.

Forrer, Leonard S., *Biographical Dictionary of Medallists, Coin-, Gem- and Seal-Engravers, Mint-Masters, &c. ancient and modern, with references to their works, 500 BC–AD 1900*, London, 1907.

Foster, Kate, 'Chelsea Scent-Bottles: "Girl-in-a-Swing" and another Group', *ECC Trans.*, Vol. 6, Part 3, 1967, pp. 284–91.

Fourest, Henry-Pierre, 'Origines de la porcelaine tendre en France au XVIIIe siècle', *Cahiers*, no. 16, 1959, pp. 226–43.

Fourest, Henry-Pierre, 'Sur l'apparition de la polychromie dans la porcelaine française', *Cahiers*, no. 19, 1960, pp. 172–83.

Fourest, Henry-Pierre and Giacomotti, Jeanne, *L'Oeuvre des faïenciers français du XVIe à la fin du XVIIIe siècle*, Paris, 1966.

Fourest, Henry-Pierre, *Masterpieces of Western and Near Eastern Ceramics*, Tokyo, 1979.

Fournel, Victor, *Les Cris de Paris*, Paris, 1887.

Franks, Sir Augustus Wollaston, *Catalogue of a Collection of Continental Porcelain*, London, 1896.

Frégnac, Claude (ed.), *Les porcelainiers du XVIIIe siècle français*, Paris, 1964.

Frégnac, Claude, *La faïence européenne, le guide du connaisseur*, Fribourg, 1976.

Freyburger, Ronald, '"Chinese" genre painting at Sèvres', *American Ceramic Circle Bulletin*, 1, 1970–1, pp.29–44.

Frick Collection, *The Frick Collection, an Illustrated Catalogue, Volume II, Paintings, French, Italian and Spanish*, New York, 1968.

Gabszewicz, Anton, and Freeman, Geoffrey, *Bow Porcelain, The Collection formed by Geoffrey Freeman*, London, 1982.

Gage, Deborah and Marsh, Madeleine, *Tobacco Containers & Accessories, Their Place in 18th Century European Social History*, London, 1988.

Garnier, Edouard, 'La manufacture de Sèvres pendant la Révolution', *La Nouvelle Revue*, 1891. (Extracts bound together and kept at the Sèvres factory archive.)

Garnier, Edouard, *La manufacture de Sèvres en l'an VIII*, Paris, 1888.

Garsonnin, Dr., 'Manufactures de porcelaine', *Mémoires de la société archéologique et historique de l'Orléanais*, Vol. 35, 1920, pp. 305–51.

Gauthier, Serge and Préaud, Tamara, *Ceramics of the Twentieth Century*, Fribourg, 1982.

Gerspach, Edouard, *Documents sur les anciennes faïenceries françaises et la manufacture de Sèvres*, Paris, 1891.

Girdlestone, Cuthbert M., *Jean-Philippe Rameau: His Life and Work*, London, 1957, revised ed., Bruges, 1962.

Godden, Geoffrey, *Encyclopaedia of British Pottery and Porcelain Marks*, London, 1964, repr. 1983.

González-Palacios, Alvar, *Il Tempio del Gusto*, Milan, 1984, 2 vols.

Gower, Lord Ronald C.S.L., *Iconographie de la Reine Marie-Antoinette*, Paris, 1883.

Grüber, Alain, *L'Argenterie de Maison du XVIe au XIXe siècle*, Fribourg, 1982.

Guiffrey, Jean, 'L'Oeuvre de Pierre-Paul Prud'hon', *Archives de l'Art Français*, nouvelle période, Vol. XIII, 1924.

Guillebon, see also Plinval-Salgues.

Guillebon, Régine de Plinval de, 'La manufacture de porcelaine de Clignancourt dite du comte de Provence', *Cahiers*, no. 31, 1963, pp. 156–70.

Guillebon, Régine de Plinval de and Lasserre, Charles, 'La production de la manufacture de La Courtille XVIIIe et XIXe siècle', *Cahiers*, no. 38, 1966, pp. 102–18.

Guillebon, Régine de Plinval de, 'Note sur Despréz, fabricant de camées de porcelaine, Paris – fin XVIIIe – début XIXe siècle', *Cahiers*, nos 46–7, 1970, pp. 10–12.

Guillebon, Régine de Plinval de, *Porcelaine de Paris 1770–1850*, Fribourg, 1972.

Guillebon, Régine de Plinval de, 'L'ancien hôtel Dunoyer, puis Montalembert, manufacture de porcelaine des frères Darte, rue de la Roquette (11e)', *Cahiers de la Rotonde*, 7, previously published as a supplement to *Bulletin municipal officiel*, 13 January 1981, no. 4.

Guillebon, Régine de Plinval de, 'La manufacture de porcelaine de Dihl et Guérhard rue de Bondy, et rue du Temple', *Bulletin de la Société de l'histoire de Paris et de l'Ile de France*, 109e année, 1982, pp. 177–212.

Guillebon, Régine de, 'Une note sur quelques immeubles parisiens encore existants ayant abrité des manufactures de porcelaine entre 1785 et 1835', *Supplément du Bulletin municipal officiel de la Ville de Paris*, 6 January 1983, no. 2, pp. 4–35.

Guillebon, Régine de Plinval de, *La Porcelaine à Paris sous le Consulat et l'Empire*, Geneva, 1985.

Guillebon, Régine de Plinval de, 'Premières porcelaines dures de Paris', *Antologia di Belle Arti*, Nuova serie, nos. 29–30, 1986, pp. 29–44.

Guillebon, Régine de Plinval de, 'Les fourberies de Pierre Antoine Hannong à Sèvres, Vincennes, Vaux et Paris, *Bulletin de la Société de l'histoire de Paris et de l'Ile de France*, 113/114e année, 1986/87, pp. 179–222.

Guillebon, Régine de Plinval de, *La manufacture de porcelaine de Guérhard et Dihl dite du duc d'Angoulême*, privately published in typescript by the French Porcelain Society, IV, London, 1988.

Guillebon, Régine de Plinval de, 'La manufacture de porcelaine de la rue Thiroux, dite de la Reine', *Societé d'études historiques du IXe arrondissement de Paris*, Paris, 1988, pp. 1–17.

Guillebon, Régine de Plinval de, *Musée du Louvre, département des Objets d'art, Catalogue des Porcelaines françaises I*, Paris, 1992.

Guillemé-Brulon, Dorothée, 'Rare biscuit de Sèvres façon Wedgwood au Palais Royal de Madrid', *Cahiers*, no. 40, 1968, pp. 252–6.

Guillemé-Brulon, Dorothée, 'Porcelaine de Sèvres: le service de l'Impératrice Catherine II, *L'Estampille*, no. 167, March 1984, pp. 45–56.

Hallé, see also Faÿ-Hallé.

Hamilton-Dalrymple, Hew, *Genealogical Account of the Dalrymples of Stair*, privately printed, 1909.

Hannover, Emil and Rackham, Bernard, *Pottery and Porcelain, A Handbook for Collectors, III European Porcelain*, London, 1925.

Haskell, Francis and Penny, Nicholas, *Taste and the Antique: the lure of classical sculpture 1500–1900*, New Haven and London, 1981.

Haug, Hans, *Les faïences et porcelaines de Strasbourg*, Strasbourg, 1922.

Haug, Hans, *La collection céramique du Musée des arts décoratifs de Strasbourg*, Strasbourg, 1924.

Haug, Hans, 'Nouvelles recherches sur la céramique alsacienne du XVIIIe siècle', *Archives alsaciennes d'histoire de l'art*, 1925, pp. 178–207.

Haug, Hans, 'Strasbourg entre Chantilly et Meissen 1744-1749', *Cahiers*, no. 1, December 1955, pp. 24–37.

Haug, Hans, 'Les grandes statuettes de Strasbourg 1749–1754', *Cahiers*, no. 9, 1958.

Hawes, Vivian S. and Corsiglia, Christina S., *The Rita and Frits Markus Collection of European Ceramics & Enamels*, Boston (Mass.), 1984.

Heal, Ambrose, *London Tradesmen's Cards of the XVIII Century*, London, 1925.

Herbert, Robert L., *David, Voltaire, Brutus and the French Revolution: an essay in art and politics*, London, 1972.

Hernmarck, Carl, *The Art of the European Silversmith 1430–1830*, London, 1977.

Heuser, Emil, *Porzellan von Strassburg und Frankenthal*, Neustadt an der Haardt, 1922.

Hobson, Robert L., *Catalogue of the collection of English porcelain in the Department of British and Medieval Antiquities and Ethnography of the British Museum*, London, 1905.

Hofmann, Friedrich H., *Frankenthaler Porzellan*, Munich, 1911, 2 vols.

Hofmann, Friedrich H., *Das Porzellan der Europaïschen Manufakturen im XVIII Jahrhundert*, Berlin, 1932.

Honey, William B., *Dresden China*, London, 1934.

Honey, William B., *European Ceramic Art from the end of the Middle Ages to about 1815. An illustrated Historical Survey*, London, 1949.

Honey, William B., *French Porcelain of the 18th Century*, London, 1950.

Hood, Graham, 'French Porcelain from the J.P. Morgan Collection at the Wadsworth Atheneum', *Connoisseur*, Vol. CLVIII, no. 636, February 1965, pp. 131–7.

Hosotte-Reynaud, Marie-Antoinette, 'La manufacture de Pont-aux-Choux (1743–1788)', *Mémoire de la Fédération des sociétés historiques et archéologiques de Paris et de l'Ile-de-France*, XVI-XVII, 1967, pp. 274–92.

Hosotte-Reynaud, Marie-Antoinette, 'Le marquis d'Usson et les débuts de la manufacture du faubourg-Saint-Denis (1772–1779)', *Cahiers*, no. 51, 1972, pp. 54–65.

Hunt, Leslie B., 'Gold in the Pottery Industry. The History and Technology of Gilding Processes', *Gold Bulletin*, Vol. 12, no. 3, July 1979, pp. 116–27.

Hunt, Leslie B., 'The Gilding of European Porcelain', *Connoisseur*, Vol. 204, no. 820, June 1980, pp. 106–13.

Huntington Collection, *The Huntington Art Collections: A Handbook*, San Marino (Calif.), 1986.

Imbert, H., 'Un portrait de Rameau', *Jean Philippe Rameau (1683–1764) Oeuvres Complètes*, Paris, 1896, 2 vols, reprinted New York, 1968.

Ingamells, John, *The Wallace Collection, Catalogue of Pictures III*, London, 1989.

Jacob, Monique, *The Castle of Saumur and the Museum of Applied Arts*, Saumur, 1980.

Jarry, Madeleine, *Chinoiserie: Chinese influence on European decorative art, 17th and 18th centuries*, Fribourg and London, 1981

Jean-Richard, Pierrette, *L'œuvre gravé de François Boucher dans la collection Edmond Rothschild*, Paris, 1978.

Jewitt, Llewellyn, *The Ceramic Art of Great Britain, from pre-historic times down to the present day*, London, 1878, 2 vols.

Joicey, J.G., 'Mr. J.G. Joicey's collection of Sèvres porcelain', *Connoisseur*, Vol. XI, 1905, pp. 139–47.

Jokelson, Paul, *Sulphides, the Art of Cameo Incrustation*, New York, 1968.

Jonas, Édouard, *Collections léguées à la ville de Paris par Ernest Cocnacq, Catalogue*, Paris, 1930.

Jones, Mark, *Medals of the French Revolution*, London, 1977.

Kahn, Gustave, 'Les objets d'art aux Salons', *Art et Décoration*, Vol. XII, July 1902, pp. 24–32.

King, William, *Catalogue of the Jones Collection, II, Ceramics, ormolu, goldsmiths' work, enamels, sculpture, tapestry, books, and prints*, London, 1924.

King, William, 'Vincennes Porcelain in the British Museum – I', *Apollo*, Vol. XII, no. 70, October 1930, pp. 280–4.

King, William, 'Vincennes Porcelain in the British Museum – II', *Apollo*, Vol. XIII, no. 78, June 1931, pp. 367–70.

King, William, 'Two Sèvres Porcelain Vases, *British Museum Quarterly*, no. 3, 3 March 1936, p. 130.

King, William, 'The F. Howard Paget Collection of Porcelain', *British Museum Quarterly*, Vol. XI, 1936–1937, pp. 15–16.

King, William, 'Etude anglaise sur les porcelaines de Vincennes', *Bulletin de la Société des Amis de Vincennes*, March 1939, no. 15, pp. 194–6.

King, William, 'The Eckstein Bequest of European Ceramics', *British Museum Quarterly*, XVI, no. 3, 1951, pp. 80–1.

Kingery, W. David and Vandiver, Pamela, *Ceramic Masterpieces, Art, Structure and Technology*, New York and London, 1986.

Klaber, Pamela, 'The Enid Goldblatt Collection', *Antique Collector*, July 1984, pp. 69–73, August 1984, pp. 30–5.

Klein, Adalbert, *Kataloge des Kunstmuseums Düsseldorf-Keramik, Band 1 Europaïsches Porzellan im Hetjens Museum*, Düsseldorf, 1966.

Köllmann, Erich and Jarchow, Margarete, *Berliner Porzellan*, Munich, 1987, 2 vols.

Kosareva, Nina, 'Masterpieces of Eighteenth-Century French Sculpture', *Apollo*, Vol. CI, no. 160, June 1975, pp. 443–51.

Kramer, Ernst, 'Laurentius Russinger, Porzelliner in Hoechst, Gutenbrunn und Paris, *Keramos*, no. 50, 1970, pp. 83–100.

Krauel, R., *Prinz Heinrich von Preussen in Paris während der Jahre 1784 und 1788 bis 1789*, Berlin, 1901.

La Laurencie, Lionel de, 'Quelques documents sur Jean-Philippe Rameau et sa famille', *Mercure Musical et S.I.M.*, 15 June 1907, pp. 541–614.

La Laurencie, Lionel de, *Rameau*, Paris, n.d. (1908).

Labayle, Françoise, *La porcelaine de Saint-Cloud*, Rennes, 1982.

Lacoudre, Noël, *Electricité et Archéologie*, Paris, 1988.

Laking, Guy F., *Sèvres Porcelain of Buckingham Palace and Windsor Castle*, London, 1907.

Landais, Hubert, *French Porcelain*, London, 1961.

Landon, Charles P., *Galerie historique des hommes les plus célèbres de tous les siècles et de toutes les nations*, Paris, 1805–11,

12 vols and supplement.

Lane, Arthur, 'Sèvres and other porcelain in the collection of Viscount and Viscountess Gage at Firle Place, Sussex', *Connoisseur*, Vol. CXXXV, no. 545, April 1955, pp. 158–63.

Larivière, C. de, 'Le Prince Henri de Prusse à Paris en 1784 et 1788', *Revue politique et littéraire*, nos. 11, 13, 4th series, Vol. XVI, 1901, pp. 334–40 and 393–8.

Larpent, Sir George, *The Private Journal of F.S. Larpent, Esq. . . ., attached to the head-quarters of Lord Wellington during the Peninsular War, from 1812 to its close*, London, 1853, 3 vols.

Lauth, Charles, *La manufacture nationale de Sèvres et la porcelaine nouvelle*, lecture given 28 October 1884, Palais de l'Industrie, printed version in the Library of the Musée des arts décoratifs, Paris.

Lauth, Charles and Vogt, Georges, *Notes techniques sur la fabrication de la porcelaine nouvelle*, Paris, 1885.

Lauth, Charles, *La manufacture nationale de Sèvres 1879–1887*, Paris, 1889.

Le Clerc, Georges L., comte de Buffon, *Histoire Naturelle des Oiseaux*, Paris, 1770–86, 10 vols.

Le Duc, Geneviève, 'La manufacture de Bourg-la-Reine, faïences et porcelaines tendres (1772–1804)', *Cahiers*, no. 39, 1967, pp. 162–75.

Le Duc, Geneviève, *La porcelaine de Villeroy*, privately published in typescript by the French Porcelain Society, III, London, 1987.

Le Duc, Geneviève and Plinval de Guillebon, Régine de, 'Contribution à l'étude de la manufacture de faïence et de porcelaine de Saint-Cloud pendant ses cinquante premières années', *Keramik-Freunde der Schweiz Mitteilungsblatt*, no. 105, March 1991, pp. 3–53.

Le Jeune, Jean, *Les anciennes manufactures de porcelaine de Basse-Normandie*, Coutances, 1962.

Lechevallier-Chevignard, Georges, 'Jean-Jacques Caffieri (1766–1767)', *Archives de l'art français*, nouvelle période, Vol. II, IIe fascicule, 1908, pp. 129–33.

Lechevallier-Chevignard, Georges, *La manufacture de porcelaine de Sèvres*, Paris, 1908.

Lechevallier-Chevignard, Georges and Sandier, Alexandre, *Formes et décors modernes de la manufacture nationale de Sèvres*, Paris, n.d. (?1914).

Lechevallier-Chevignard, Georges and Savreux, Maurice, *Le Biscuit de Sèvres. Directoire, Consulat, et Premier Empire*, Paris, 1923.

Lechevallier-Chevignard, Georges, *La décoration moderne à la manufacture nationale de Sèvres*, Paris, n.d. (?1929).

Lejéal, Dr Alfred, *Recherches historiques sur les manufactures de faïence et de porcelaine de l'Arrondissement de Valenciennes*, Valenciennes, 1868.

Leroy, G., 'La céramique à Boissettes (Seine-et-Marne) 1732–1781', *Réunion des Sociétés des Beaux-Arts*, Vol. XXII, 1898, pp. 197–214.

Levitine, George, *The Sculpture of Falconet*, Greenwich (Conn.), 1972.

Leymarie, Camille, 'L'industrie de la porcelaine à Limoges, VI, la maison E. Gérard, Dufraisseix et Co, *La Revue des Arts Décoratifs*, no. 13, 1892–3, pp. 387–94.

Linsky Collection, *The Jack and Belle Linsky Collection in the Metropolitan Museum of Art*, New York, 1984.

Litchfield, Frederick, 'Imitations and Reproductions, Part I – Sèvres Porcelain', *Connoisseur*, Vol. XLIX, no. 193, September 1917, pp. 3–14.

Lohmeyer, Karl, *Die Fürstlich Nassau-Saarbrückische Porzellanmanufaktur Ottweiler*, Leipzig, 1934.

Ludmann, Jean-Daniel, 'Strasbourg à la recherche d'un style 1709–1750', *ABC Décor*, November 1973, pp. 35–54, 83–94.

Macdonald, Sally, *Porcelain from Europe*, Manchester City Art Galleries, 1986.

Mackenna, F. Severne, *Chelsea Porcelain, The Triangle and Raised Anchor Wares*, Leigh-on-Sea, 1948.

Malgras, Gilbert-Jean, (ed.), *Porcelaines tendres françaises*, Paris, 1983.

Mallet, John V.G., 'A Chelsea Talk', *ECC Trans.*, Vol. 6, Part 1, 1965, pp. 15–29.

Mathieu, Jean in association with Préaud, Tamara, *La porcelaine de Sèvres*, Paris, 1982.

Mauzin, J., 'Les artistes à Montmartre, Pierre Deruelle et Alexandre Moitte, entrepreneurs de la manufacture de porcelaine de Clignancourt (1767–1800)', *Le Vieux Montmartre, société d'histoire et d'archéologie des XVIIIe et XIXe Arrondissements*, nouvelle série, no. 2, 1922, pp. 77–102.

Mazerolle, Fernand, *L'Hôtel des Monnaies, les bâtiments, le musée, les ateliers*, Paris, 1907.

Menager, D., *Catalogue raisonné des biscuits de porcelaine de Vincennes et de Sèvres au XVIIIe siècle dans les collections du Musée national de Céramique, Sèvres*, unpublished *mémoire* for the Ecole du Louvre, April 1985, 2 vols.

Mew, Egan, W., *Dresden China*, London, 1934.

Millar, Oliver, *The later Georgian Pictures in the Collection of Her Majesty the Queen*, London, 1969, 2 vols.

Montagu, Jennifer, 'Some lesser-known busts of Voltaire', *Connoisseur*, Vol. CLXVII, no. 674, April 1968, pp. 225–9.

Moriamé, Chevalier Eugène Soil de and Formanoir, Lucien Delplace de, *La manufacture impériale et royale de porcelaine de Tournay*, Tournai, 1937.

Mossé, Claude, *L'Antiquité dans la Révolution française*, Paris, 1989.

Munger, Jeffrey *et al.*, *The Forsyth Wickes Collection in the Museum of Fine Arts, Boston*, Boston (Mass.), 1992.

Munhall, Edgar, 'Savoyards in French eighteenth-century art', *Apollo*, Vol. LXXXVII, no. 72, February 1968, pp. 86–94.

Munhall, Edgar, 'A Sèvres Biscuit Bust of Louis XV acquired by the Frick Collection in Memory of Guy Bauman, *Metropolitan Museum Journal*, 27, 1992, pp. 121–8.

Musée du Louvre, *Nouvelles acquisitions du département des Objets d'Art 1980–1984*, Paris, 1985.

Musée du Louvre, *Nouvelles acquisitions du département des Objets d'Art 1985–1989*, Paris, 1990.

Nisbet, Anne-Marie, Masséna, Victor André and Blondel, Nicole, *L'Empire à Table*, Paris, 1988.

Nocq, Henry, *Le poinçon de Paris, répertoire des maîtres-orfèvres de la juridiction de Paris depuis le Moyen-age jusqu'à la fin du XVIIIe siècle*, Paris, 1926–31, 4 vols.

Noël, Maurice, *Recherches sur la céramique lorraine au XVIIIe siècle*, unpublished thesis, IIIe cycle, Faculté des Lettres, University of Nancy, 1961, 2 vols.

Noël, Maurice, 'Les biscuits de Cyfflé: étude de thèmes', *Annales de l'Est, Mémoire 34, La Lorraine dans L'Europe des Lumières*, Nancy, 1968, pp. 237–52.

Noël, M. 'La faïencerie de Toul et les Terres de Lorraine', *Etudes Touloises*, no. 11, 1978, fascicule 1, pp. 13–27.

Nordenfalk, Carl, *Sèvres et les Cinq Sens*, Stockholm, 1984.

Ortengren, K., *Klassiska porslinsdekorer*, Åarhus, 1973.

Ourry, E.T. Maurice, *Mémoires de Préville et de Dazincourt*, Paris, 1822.

Parker, K.T., 'Bouchardon's "Cries of Paris"', *Old Master Drawings*, December 1930, pp. 45–8.

Pauwels, A.G. and van Hoonacker, J., *Keramiek*, catalogue of Museum Voor Oudheidkunde en Sierkunst, Kortrijk, Belgium, 1981.

Peyret, Nicolas, 'Les Bourdaloues, des vases de nuit au grand jour', *L'Estampille*, Mars 1970, no. 8, pp. 46–53.

Piot, Eugène, 'Etudes céramiques, la manufacture royale de faïence fine et de porcelaine établie à Orléans en 1753', *Le Cabinet de l'Amateur*, Paris, 1863.

Pitsch, Marguerite, *La vie populaire à Paris au XVIIIe siècle*, Paris, 1949, 2 vols.

Pitsch, Marguerite, *Essai de catalogue sur l'iconographie de la vie populaire à Paris au XVIIIe siècle*, Paris 1952.

Plinval-Salgues, Régine de, 'Les Schoelcher et la porcelaine', *Cahiers*, no. 6, 1957, pp. 52–67.

Plinval-Salgues, Régine, 'L'exotisme de Jacob Petit', *Art de France*, Vol. III, 1963, pp. 195–200.

Poisson, Georges, Aries, Maddy, Henry, Corinne and Flot, Françoise, *Catalogue raisonné des collections, Hauts-de-Seine*, Musée de l'Ile de France, Château de Sceaux, 1985.

Ponert, Dieter J., *Berlin Museum, Kunstgewerbe I, Keramik, Hafnerkeramik und Terracotta, Fayence, Porzellan*, Berlin, 1985.

Porcelain from the Frances Oliver Collection, Birmingham, Alabama, 1980.

Préaud, Tamara, 'Sèvres enamelled porcelain: eight dies (and a quarrel) rediscovered', *Burlington Magazine*, Vol. CXXVIII, no. 999, June 1986, pp. 391–7.

Préaud, Tamara, 'Un fonds méconnu, la série des paysages conservés à la Bibliothèque de la Manufacture de Sèvres', *Cahiers*, no. 58, 1976, pp. 36–55.

Préaud, Tamara, 'Le "style Renaissance" à Sèvres au XIXe siècle', *Revue d'art canadienne*, VI/I, 1979, pp. 28–35.

Préaud, Tamara, 'Sèvres, la Chine et les "chinoiseries" au XVIIIe siècle', *Journal of the Walters Art Gallery*, 47, 1989, pp. 39–52.

Préaud, Tamara and d'Albis, Antoine, *La porcelaine de Vincennes*, Paris, 1991.

Pressouyre, Sylvia, 'Les Fontes de Primatice à Fontainebleau', *Bulletin Monumental*, Vol. 127, III, 1969, pp. 223–39.

Puaux, René, 'George de Feure', *Deutsche Kunst und Dekoration*, VI Jahrg., Heft 7, April 1903, pp. 313–16.

Rathbone, Perry T., *The Forsyth Wickes Collection*, Museum of Fine Arts, Boston, dist. by New York Graphic Society, Greenwich (Conn.), 1968.

Ravel d'Esclapon, Alix de, *La porcelaine de Boissettes près Melun*, Le Mée-sur-Seine, 1991.

Réau, Louis, *Etienne-Maurice Falconet*, Paris, 1922.

Réau, Louis, 'Le "Faune au Chevreau" de Saly', *Bulletin de la société de l'histoire de l'art français*, 1924, 1er fascicule, pp. 6–15.

Réau, Louis, 'L'Hébé de Saly', *Bulletin de la société de l'histoire de l'art français*, 1927, 1er fascicule, pp. 8–11.

Réau, Louis, 'Catalogue des œuvres d'art français de la collection du roi de Pologne Stanislas-Auguste', in 'L'art français dans les pays du nord et de l'est de l'Europe (XVIIIe–XIXe siècles)', *Archives de l'art français*, XVII, 1931–2, reprinted 1969, pp. 227–48.

Reid, Loren, *Charles James Fox, a Man for the People*, London and Harlow, 1969.

Reilly, Robin, *Wedgwood*, London, 1989, 2 vols.

Reilly, Robin and Savage, George, *Wedgwood, the Portrait Medallions*, London, 1973.

Reinhard, Marcel, *La Légende de Henri IV*, Paris, n.d. (1936).

RLH (Hobson, R.L.), 'Gifts from the Bloxam Collection', *British Museum Quarterly*, Vol. III, no. 2 (1928), pp. 35–8.

Röder, Kurt, *Das Höchster Porzellan auf der Jahrtausend-Ausstellung in Mainz 1925*, Mainz, 1930.

Roth, Linda Horvitz (ed.), *J. Pierpont Morgan, Collector, European Decorative Arts from the Wadsworth Atheneum*, Wadsworth Atheneum, Hartford (Conn.), 1987.

Rudoe, Judy, *Decorative Arts 1850–1950: A Catalogue of the British Museum Collection*, London, 1991.

Rutter, John, *A Description of Fonthill Abbey and Demesne in the County of Wilts; including a list of its Paintings, Cabinets, &c*, Shaftesbury, 1822.

Sainsbury, Wilfred J., 'Sèvres Soft-Paste Biscuit Figures Part I, *Apollo*, Vol. LI, no. 303, May 1950, pp. 133–6; Part II, Vol. LI, no. 304, June 1950, pp. 168–71.

Sainsbury, Wilfred J., 'A Rogue's Gallery of Continental Soft-Paste Porcelain', *Apollo*, Vol. LIII, no. 311, January 1951, pp. 11–12.

Sainsbury, Wilfred J., 'More about Sèvres Soft-Paste Biscuit, *Apollo Miscellany*, 1951, p. 37.

Sainsbury, Wilfred J., 'Vincennes Porcelain', *Connoisseur*, Vol. CXXXIII, no. 535, February 1954, pp. 3–8.

Sainsbury, Wilfred J., 'Large groups and figures in the soft-paste biscuit of Vincennes-Sèvres', *Antiques*, Vol. LXXXVII, no. 4, April 1965, pp. 430–3.

Sainsbury, Wilfred J., 'Small figures and groups in the soft-paste biscuit of Vincennes-Sèvres', *Antiques*, Vol. LXXXVIII, no. 6, December 1965, pp. 824–8.

Sainsbury, Wilfred J., 'Les marques sur les biscuits en pâte tendre de Vincennes et de Sèvres', *Cahiers*, no. 37, 1966, pp. 14–29.

Sandoz, Marc, 'Jean-Jacques Lagrenée, peintre d'histoire (1739–1821)', *Bulletin de la société de l'histoire de l'art français*, 1962, pp. 121–33.

Sandoz, Marc, *Les Lagrenée II, Jean Jacques Lagrenée (le jeune)*, Paris, 1988.

Sassoon, Adrian, *Vincennes and Sèvres Porcelain, Catalogue of the Collections, The J. Paul Getty Museum, Malibu, California, 1991*, Malibu (Calif.), 1991.

Savage, George, *18th-Century German Porcelain*, London, 1958.

Savage, George, *Porcelain through the Ages*, London, 1961.

Savage, George, *Seventeenth and Eighteenth-Century French Porcelain*, London, 1960; new ed. 1969.

Savill, Rosalind, 'François Boucher and the Porcelains of Vincennes and Sèvres', *Apollo*, Vol. CXV, no. 241, March 1982, pp. 162–69.

Savill, Rosalind, '"Cameo Fever": six pieces from the Sèvres porcelain dinner service made for Catherine II of Russia', *Apollo*, Vol. CXVI, no. 249, November 1982, pp. 304–11.

Savill, Rosalind, 'A neglected Sèvres porcelain vase in the Wallace Collection', *Antologia di Belle Arti*, no. 27–8, 1985, pp. 69–72.

Savill, Rosalind, 'A pair of Sèvres vases: from the collection of Sir Richard Wallace to the J. Paul Getty Museum', *J. Paul Getty Museum Journal*, Vol. 14, 1986, pp. 135–42.

Savill, Rosalind, *The Wallace Collection, Catalogue of Sèvres Porcelain, London*, London, 1988, 3 vols.

Scott, C.M. and G.R., *Antique Porcelain Digest*, Newport, (Mon.) 1961.

Scott, Barbara, 'The Duchess of Berry as a patron of the Arts', *Apollo*, Vol. CXXIV, no. 296, October 1986, pp. 345–53.

Scott-James, Anne, Desmond, Ray and Wood, Frances, *The British Museum Book of Flowers*, London, 1987.

Sellers, Charles C., *Benjamin Franklin in Portraiture*, New Haven and London, 1962.

Shifman, Barry, 'Eighteenth-Century Sèvres porcelain: two rare *Cuvettes Mahon*', *Apollo*, Vol. CXXI, no. 275, January 1985, pp. 24–9.

Shono, Masako, *Japanisches Aritaporzellan im sogenannten "Kakiemonstil" als Vorbild für die Meissener Porzellanmanufaktur*, Munich, 1973.

Soudée-Lacombe, Chantal, 'Faïenciers et porcelainiers de Niderviller au XVIIIe siècle', *Le Pays Lorrain*, 65e année, 1984, no. 1, pp. 1–76.

Soulié, Eudoxe, *Notice des peintures et sculptures composant le Musée impériale de Versailles*, Versailles, 1854.

Steiskal-Paur, R., 'Kostbarkeiten aus Porzellan', *Weltkunst*, 15 October 1982, pp. 2897–901.

Storelli, A., *Jean-Baptiste Nini, sa vie – son œuvre 1717–1786*, Tours, 1896.

Tait, Hugh, *Porcelain*, London, 1962, revised ed. 1972.

Tait, Hugh, 'Exciting Pâte-sur-Pâte Find in the British Museum', *Ars Ceramica*, no. 2, 1985, pp. 16–17.

Tait, Hugh (ed.), *Seven Thousand Years of Jewellery*, London, 1986.

Tait, Hugh, 'Ormolu-Mounted "Celadon" Elephants of

Early Meissen Porcelain', *Ars Ceramica*, no. 6, 1989, pp. 50–3.

Tasnádi-Marik, Klara, *Viennese Porcelain*, Budapest, 1971.

Taylor, Samuel, 'Artists and *Philosophes* as mirrored by Sèvres and Wedgwood', *The Artist and the Writer in France, Essays in Honour of Jean Seznec*, ed. F. Haskell, A. Levi, R. Shackleton, Oxford, 1974, pp. 21–39.

Terrasson, Jeanine, *Madame de Pompadour et la création de la "Porcelaine de France"*, Paris, 1969.

Terrasson, Jeanine, *Les Hannong et leurs manufactures, Strasbourg, Frankenthal*, Paris, n.d. (1971).

Thore, Dr., *Les anciennes fabriques de faïence et de porcelaine de l'arrondissement de Sceaux*, Paris, 1868.

Tidswell, T. Harrison, 'The influence of Oriental Porcelain on Western Ceramics', *Apollo*, Vol. CX, no. 211, September 1979, p. 210–23.

Tilmans, Emile, *Porcelaines de France*, Paris, 1953.

Toulgoët-Tréanna, Pierre de, 'Verres et cristaux incrustés dits sulfures', *Cahiers*, no. 40, 1968, pp. 238–51.

Treppoz, Françoise, and d'Albis, Antoine, 'Identification de différents types de porcelaines anciennes à l'aide de l'analyse par diffraction X', *Faenza*, Vol. LXXIII, no. 1–3, 1987, pp. 40–63.

Trollope, Frances M., *Paris and the Parisians in 1835*, originally published in New York, 1836, Gloucester, 1985 edition.

Truman, Charles, 'A Saint-Cloud *Nécessaire de Voyage* circa 1750', *Connoisseur*, Vol. 203, no. 818, April 1980, pp. 253–5.

Truman, Charles, *The Sèvres Egyptian Service 1810–12*, London, 1982.

Troude, Albert, *Choix de modèles de la Manufacture Nationale des porcelaines de Sèvres appartenant au Musée céramique*, n.d. (1897).

Turner, W., 'Madeley Porcelain, Part I', *Connoisseur*, Vol. XXII (1908), no. 11, pp. 153–60; Part II, pp. 248–54.

Ujfalvy-Bourdon, Charles E. de, *Les Biscuits de Porcelaine*, Paris, 1893.

Verlet, Pierre, Grandjean, Serge and Brunet, Marcelle, *Sèvres, I, le XVIIIe siècle; les XIXe et XXe siècles. II, les Marques de Sèvres*, Paris, 1953.

Verlet, Pierre, *La Maison du XVIIIe siècle en France, Société, Décoration, Mobilier*, Paris, 1966.

Vivanti, Corrado, 'Henry IV, the Gallic Hercules', *Journal of the Warburg and Courtauld Institutes*, Vol. 30, 1967, pp. 176–97.

Vuaflart, Albert and Bourin, Henri, *Les portraits de Marie-Antoinette, étude d'iconographie critique*, Paris, 1909–10, 2 vols.

Walpole, Horace, *A Description of the Villa of Mr Horace Walpole Youngest son of Sir Robert Walpole Earl of Orford at Strawberry Hill near Twickenham Middlesex with an inventory of Furniture, Pictures Curiosities &c*, Strawberry Hill, 1784.

Ward, Marion, *Forth*, London, 1982.

Wark, Robert R., French Decorative Art in the Huntingdon Collection, San Marino (Calif.), 1979.

Watney, Bernard, *English Blue and White Porcelain of the 18th Century*, London, 1979, repr. 2nd ed.

Watson, Francis, J.B., 'Walpole and the taste for French in Porcelain in Eighteenth Century England', *Horace Walpole, Writer, Politician and Connoisseur, Essays on the 250th Anniversary of Walpole's Birth*, ed. Smith, Warren H., New Haven and London, 1967.

Weisberg, Gabriel T., 'Gérard, Dufraissex and Abbot: the Manufactory of Art Nouveau Bing Porcelains in Limoges, France', *Connoisseur*, Vol. 197, no. 792, February 1978, pp. 125–9.

Weisberg, Gabriel T., *Art Nouveau Bing, Paris Style 1900*, New York, 1986.

Wibiral, Friedrich, *L'Iconographie d'Antoine van Dyck d'après les recherches de H. Weber*, Leipzig, 1877.

Wills, Geoffrey, 'Some French and English Porcelain at Woburn Abbey', *Apollo*, Vol. LXIII, no. 371, January 1956, pp. 14–17.

Wills, Geoffrey, 'Dr Martin Lister and Early French Porcelain', *Connoisseur*, Vol. CXLI, no. 568, April 1958, pp. 74–6.

Winter, Carl, 'Louis Clarke as a Collector', *Apollo*, Vol. LXXVII, no. 5, July 1962, pp. 377–83.

Zelleke, Ghenete, *From Chantilly to Sèvres: French Porcelain and the Dukes of Richmond*, privately published by the French Porcelain Society, London, VII, 1991.

Zick, Gisela, 'Parva Sed Apta: Eine Terrakottagruppe von Louis-Simon Boizot in suddeutschem Privatbesitz', *Keramos*, 123, January 1989, pp. 45–9.

Exhibition Catalogues

Catalogues which are referred to in the text in abbreviated form are listed alphabetically by abbreviation

Alexandre-Théodore Brongniart 1739–1813, Musée Carnavalet, Paris, April–July 1986.

Allen, 1987: Allen, Armin, B., *European Pottery and Porcelain*, London, June 1987 (catalogue of a selling exhibition).

Allen, 1989: Allen, Armin, B., *The Henry C. and Martha L. Isaacson Collection*, London, June 1987 (catalogue of a selling exhibition).

Arnaud, C., 'Le comte d'Artois et sa coterie', *La Folie d'Artois*, Château de Bagatelle, Paris, 1985, pp. 15–25.

Arras, 1992: Notter, Annick, *et al.*, *Porcelaine d'Arras, collection du musée d'Arras*, Musée des Beaux-Arts, Arras, February 1992.

British Museum, 1990: Ayers, John, Impey, Oliver and Mallet, John, *Porcelain for Palaces: the fashion for Japan in Europe 1650–1750*, British Museum, London, July–November 1990.

Brunhammer, Yvonne *et al.*, *Art Nouveau: Belgium, France*, Institute for the Arts, Rice University, Houston, Texas and the Art Institute of Chicago, 1976.

Céramique régionale, 1951: *Céramique régionale ancienne*, Palais des Beaux-Arts, Lille, April–May 1951.

Christie's, *Art Treasures Exhibition 1932*, London, 1932.

Dawson, Aileen, *Documentary Continental Ceramics from the British Museum*, International Ceramics Fair and Seminar, London, June 1985.

Diderot et l'Art de Boucher à David, Hôtel de la Monnaie, Paris, October 1984–January 1985.

Die Verführung der Europa, Staatliche Museen Preussische Kulturbesitz Kunstgewerbemuseum, Berlin, August–October 1988.

Du Pasquier, 1989: Du Pasquier, Jacqueline, *La manufacture des Terres de Bordes en Paludate*, Musée des arts décoratifs, Bordeaux, 5 May–14 September 1989.

Düsseldorf, 1975: Klein, Adalbert, Faÿ-Hallé, Antoinette and Préaud, Tamara, *Sèvres Porzellan vom 18. Jahrhundert bis zur Gegenwart*, Hetjens-Museum, Düsseldorf, October–November 1975.

European Porcelain Special Exhibition, Metropolitan Museum, New York, March–May 1949.

Faïences Françaises, 1980: Faÿ-Hallé, Antoinette, Fontan, Elisabeth, Le Duc, Geneviève, *Faïences Françaises XVIe–XVIIIe siècles*, Paris, Grand Palais, June–August 1980.

Grands Services, 1951: Grandjean, Serge and Brunet, Marcelle, *Les Grands Services de Sèvres*, Musée national de Céramique, Sèvres, May–July 1951.

Henri IV et la reconstruction du royaume, Musée national du château de Pau, Pau, June–October 1989, Archives nationales, Paris, November 1989–February 1990.

La France et la Russie au siècle des lumières, Grand Palais, Paris, November 1986–February 1987.

La porcelaine française, 1929: *La porcelaine française de 1673 à 1914, la porcelaine contemporaine de Limoges*, Pavillon de Marsan, Paris, November–December 1929.

La Révolution Française, 1989: *La Révolution Française et l'Europe 1789–1799*, March–June 1989, Grand Palais, Paris, 20th exhibition of the Council of Europe.

Le Centenaire de la Naissance de Henri IV, Pau, 1953.

Le Palais Royal, Musée Carnavalet, Paris, May–September 1988.

Les porcelaines de Paris, 1970: *Les porcelaines de Paris de 1800 à 1850*, Musée national de Céramique, Sèvres, June–October 1970, catalogue in *Cahiers*, nos. 46–7, 1970, pp. 21–108.

Ludmann, Jean-Daniel, *Les œuvres de Hannong: Faïences de Strasbourg et Haguenau*, Musée des arts décoratifs, Palais-Rohan, Strasbourg, January–March 1975.

Madame, Duchesse de Berry, Palais Dobrée, Nantes, December 1963–February 1964.

Mallett & Son, *Exhibition of Art Treasures*, Grafton Galleries, London, 1928.

Marie-Antoinette, archiduchesse, dauphine et reine, château de Versailles, May–November 1955.

Mosel, Christel, *Kunsthandwerk in Umbruch, Jugenstil und Zwanziger Jahre*, Kestner-Museum, Hanover, 1971.

Nancy and Atlanta, 1991: *French Ceramics, 18th and 19th Century Masterpieces, from Lorraine*, Musée Historique Lorrain, Nancy, March–June 1991.

Nagatake, Y., Yabe, Y. and Minamoto, H., *The World of Kakiemon*, eight venues in Japan, March–July 1982 (catalogue published by Asahi News Department).

Nord-Pas-de-Calais, 1986–7: Becquart, Geneviève, Blazy, Guy, Davy, Annick and Scottez-De Wambrechies, Annie, *La porcelaine française du XVIIIe siècle dans les musées du Nord-Pas-de-Calais*, Musée de l'hôtel Sandelin, Saint-Omer, Musée des Beaux-Arts, Lille, Musée des Beaux-Arts, Arras, 1986–7.

Overglaze Imagery, Cone 019-016, Art Gallery, Visual Arts Center, California State University, Fullerton, November–December 1977.

Porcelaines Parisiennes, 1983: *Porcelaines Parisiennes 1770–1870*, Mairie Annexe des 10e et 16e arrondissements, Paris, Musée municipal, Saint-Dié, Musée Sandelin, Saint-Omer, 1983.

Queen's Gallery 1979–80: Bellaigue, Geoffrey de, *Sèvres Porcelain from the Royal Collection*, The Queen's Gallery, Buckingham Palace, London, 1979–80.

Rückert, 1966: Rückert, Rainer, *Meissener Porzellan 1710–1810*, Bayerisches Nationalmuseum, Munich, 1966.

Saint-Cloud, 1980: Fourest, Henri-Pierre and Le Duc, Geneviève, *La porcelaine de Saint-Cloud*, Musée historique du Parc de Saint-Cloud, May–June 1980.

Sarrebourg, 1986: Fresquet, J.C., Heckenbenner, Danielle, Soudée-Lacombe, Chantal, *Figurines de faïence et de porcelaine (XVIIIe siècle)*, Musée du Pays de Sarrebourg, Sarrebourg, June–September 1986.

Sceaux, 1986: Aries, M., and Gautier, C., *Sceaux, Bourg-la-Reine, 150 ans de céramique des collections privées aux collections publiques*, Orangerie du château de Sceaux, Sceaux, April–June 1986.

Sèvres de 1850 à nos jours, Louvre des Antiquaires, Paris, February–April 1973.

Sèvres XIXe siècle, 1975: Faÿ-Hallé, Antoinette and Préaud, Tamara, *Porcelaines de Sèvres au XIXe siècle*, Musée national de Céramique, Sèvres, May–November 1975.

Sèvres XXe siècle, 1987: Hallé, Antoinette and Guillaume, Valérie, *Porcelaines de Sèvres au XXe siècle*, Musée national de Céramique, Sèvres, April–August 1987.

Street Criers and Itinerant Tradesmen in European Prints, Stanford Art Gallery and Achenbach Foundation for Graphic Arts, California Palace of the Legion of Honor, San Francisco, California, 1970.

Tentoonstelling van Oude Kunst (Exhibition of Art belonging to the International Trade), Rijksmuseum, Amsterdam, 1936.

Vincennes, 1977–8: Hallé, Antoinette and Préaud, Tamara, *Porcelaines de Vincennes, les Origines de Sèvres*, Grand Palais, Paris, October 1977–January 1978.

Vindry, G., *Les peintres de la famille de Jean-Honoré Fragonard*, Villa-Musée Fragonard, Grasse, April–May 1988.

Weisses Gold aus Fürstenberg, Kulturgeschichte im Spiegel des Porzellans 1747–1830, Westfälisches Landesmuseum, Münster, Herzog Anton Ulrich-Museum, Brunswick, December 1988–May 1989.

Williams 1975: Williams, Winifred, *Exhibition of Eighteenth Century European White Porcelain*, London, June 1975 (catalogue of a selling exhibition).

Williams, 1978: Williams, Winifred, *Eighteenth Century French Porcelain*, London, July 1978 (catalogue of a selling exhibition).

The World of Voltaire, Museum of Art, University of Michigan, Ann Arbor, Michigan, March–May 1969.

Photographic Acknowledgements

Photography by the British Museum Photographic Service (Peter Stringer; Saul Peckham for the Recent Acquisitions).

The author would also like to thank the following for supplying additional photographs:

Bath Preservation Trust, Beckford Tower, Bath: fig. 123b

Bibiothèque Nationale, Paris, Département des Estampes: fig. 41b

Christies, London: fig. 99d

Manufacture Nationale de Sèvres Archives: figs 68a, 72a, 87a, 123a, 123b, 131a, 133a, 179a, 182b, 203a, 306a

Réunion des musées nationaux: fig. 21a (Musée du Louvre, inv. RF 326)

Richard Margolis Collection: fig 287a

Musée National de céramique, Sèvres: figs 174a, 175a.

Index

Page numbers in bold refer to the main catalogue entries with illustrations